W9-BKU-070

WEST ACADEMIC PUBLISHING'S LAW SCHOOL ADVISORY BOARD

INTERNATIONAL LAW

CASES AND COMMENTARY

Fifth Edition

■ ■ ■

by

Mark Weston Janis
William F. Starr Professor of Law
University of Connecticut
Visiting Fellow & Formerly Reader in Law
University of Oxford

John E. Noyes
Roger J. Traynor Professor of Law
California Western School of Law
Past President
American Branch of the International Law Association

AMERICAN CASEBOOK SERIES®

Mat #41250251

444 Cedar Street, Suite 700
St. Paul, MN 55101
1-877-888-1330

Printed in the United States of America

ISBN: 978-0-314-28041-1

To Janet, Matthew, Robert & Abigail, Philip & Angela, and Edward & Christine

—MWJ

To Barbara, Sarah & Jacob, and Ellen

—JEN

PREFACE TO THE FIFTH EDITION

> A comprehensive and scientific knowledge of international law is highly necessary, not only to lawyers practicing in our commercial ports, but to every [one] who is animated by liberal views, and a generous ambition to assume stations of high public trust. It would be exceedingly to the discredit of any person who should be called to take a share in the councils of the nation, if [that person] should be found deficient in the great leading principles of this law; and I think I cannot be mistaken in considering the elementary learning of the law of nations, as not only an essential part of the education of an American lawyer, but as proper to be academically taught.—James Kent, 1 *Commentaries on American Law* 20 (2d ed. 1832).

The teaching of international law in the American law school goes back at least as far as the Columbia lectures of Chancellor James Kent (1763–1847) and the four volumes of his *Commentaries on American Law* (1826–1830), the first great U.S. legal treatise. Kent's *Commentaries* begin with 200 pages devoted to the law of nations. The tradition of an American casebook on international law also dates to the 19th century. In 1893, Freeman Snow's *Cases and Opinions on International Law* made its appearance, followed in 1906 by a greatly developed and very influential revision, *Cases on International Law* by James Brown Scott.

Our casebook builds on this by now long-standing tradition, but departs from some of its immediate predecessors by providing an intellectual consolidation of what may have become a too-great proliferation of topics, issues, and cases. Our ambition is simply to teach: to give law professors and law students the cases and commentary necessary to achieve a first-class professional education in the fundamentals of international law. No matter what international law specialty a student may go on to study or to practice—international corporate law, international environmental law, international litigation, international human rights, etc.—we mean to lay the foundation for that study and practice in the pages that follow.

We believe that the order of our chapters constitutes a sensible organization for most courses in international law. Chapter 1 introduces international law, looking briefly at the subject's history and presenting and discussing two sample, albeit well-known, cases to illuminate the nature of international legal rules and international legal process. Chapters 2 and 3 examine the sources of international law in greater depth, showing the student how lawyers, judges, and jurists draw international legal rules from a variety of sources, *e.g.*, treaties, custom, general principles, natural law, *jus cogens*, and equity. Chapters 4 and 5 return to international legal process, exploring the ways in which international law is applied first in municipal courts and second in international tribunals. We then turn to the relationship between international law and the actors in international relations: individuals and international human rights law in Chapter 6, states in Chapter 7, and regimes and international organizations, governmental and non-governmental, in Chapter 8. Finally, we address four topics of great practical importance in modern international law: the use of force in Chapter 9, the law of the sea in Chapter 10, international conflict of laws in Chapter 11, and foreign law and governments in Chapter 12.

Many chapters deserve six hours of class, *i.e.*, about two weeks. So, even though this casebook is briefer than most, there is still about twenty weeks of material between the covers; in most courses some pruning will need be done. Ordinarily, we expect that teachers will choose to teach Chapters 1 through 5 in about seven or eight weeks and then choose from among Chapters 6 to 12 for an additional six or seven weeks. We have tried to make the later seven chapters free-standing so that any of them can be taught in any order after the first five chapters are completed.

For students who wish to go beyond the casebook, quite a number of textbooks are available, including James Crawford, *Brownlie's Principles of Public International Law* (Oxford 8th ed. 2012), Mark Weston Janis, *International Law* (Aspen 6th ed. 2012), and *Oppenheim's International Law* (Longman 9th ed. by Robert Jennings & Arthur Watts 1992). There are thousands of other books, articles, cases, and treaties cited below. However, footnotes and string citations from excerpted materials have ordinarily been omitted; when footnotes have been retained in the materials, the original's number has been used; brackets or three asterisks mark other omissions.

Chapters 1, 3, 4, 6, 11, and 12 have been the principal responsibility of Mark Janis, Chapters 2, 7, 8, and 10 the principal responsibility of John Noyes, and Chapters 5 and 9 shared between us. The two of us have used these materials over quite a number of years and, by now, have traded many ideas and much wording on most pages. We have also been fortunate in the assistance of others, and at the risk of inadvertently leaving out some names, let us mention those who have helped along the way: William Aceves, Dapo Akande, William Alford, Craig Allen, Nicholas Bamforth, Robert Barker, David Bederman, Howard Berman, Rudolf Bernhardt, Phillip Blumberg, Anthony Bradley, John Bridge, Ian Brownlie, Thomas Buergenthal, Elizabeth Burleson, Cindy Buys, David Caron, John Chung, James Cooper, Michael Dessent, Laura Dickinson, Richard Edwards, Richard Finkmoore, Tim Fisher, Peter Fitzgerald, Maria Frankowska, James Friedberg, Edward Gordon, Ruth Gordon,

Richard Graving, Christine Gray, Anita Halvorssen, Joseph Isanga, Richard Kay, Jeffrey Kelleher, David Kennedy, Chin Kim, Harold Koh, Vaughan Lowe, Robert Lutz, William Lynch, Hugh Macgill, Phyllis Marion, James Maxeiner, Diane May, Samuel Menefee, John Murphy, James Nafziger, Ved Nanda, Michael Newton, Nell Newton, Jeremy Paul, John Quigley, Jeremy Rabkin, James Ranney, Michael Reisman, Leila Sadat, Dan Sarooshi, Niels Schaumann, Henry Schermers, Stephen Schwebel, Ronald Sievert, Steven Smith, Louis Sohn, Barbara Stark, Henry Steiner, Kenneth Vandevelde, Carol Weisbrod, and David Wirth. Many students and librarians at California Western School of Law, the University of Connecticut School of Law, the University of Oxford, and the Roger Williams University School of Law also provided able research support: Daniel Bender, Elizabeth Bonner, William Bookheim, Alexander Cogbill, Kristin Collins, Cavan Cox, Sarah Cox, Sanja Djajic, Todd Dressel, Stephanie Edwards, Jordan Furrow, Derek Ghan, Darlene Glenn, Barbara Glennan, Betsy Golden, Alecia Gordon, Anne Gregory, Douglas Heim, Eric Hisey, Brent Houston, Edward Johnson, Kathleen Kim, Regina Knoll, Esra Krause, Ownie Lee, Meridee López, William de la Mare, Alexa Millinger, Kenneth Naide, Omar Nassar, Loretta Nelms-Reyes, Jane Petitmermet, William Powers, Lara Prodanovich, Rachel Smith, Joanna Taatjes, Risto Vahimets, Liam Vavasour, Tara Velez, Linda Weathers, Bobbi Ann Weaver, David Woods, Katherine Young, and Teodora Ziamous. The technical assistance of Ana Contreras, Mark Doner, Carol Dulawan, Heddy Fujikawa, Elizabeth Johnson, Margaret Kent, Linda Kirk, Cheryl Meegan, Sandra Michalik, Sandra Moreau, Mary Ellen Norvell, Marian Roosa, Delia Roy, Jacqueline Sewell, Anita Simons, Sonia Smith, Joyce Stallworth, Donna Vella, and Joan Wood was indispensable. We thank Coalter Lathrop of Sovereign Geographic, Inc. and David Swanson of David Swanson Cartography for preparing the maps and diagrams.

MARK WESTON JANIS
Hartford & Oxford

JOHN E. NOYES
San Diego

January 2014

ACKNOWLEDGMENTS

Excerpts from the following books, articles, cases, and treaties appear with the kind permission of the copyright holders. Every reasonable effort was made to locate and contact the holders of copyrights.

Alford, Roger P., "Foreign Relations as a Matter of Interpretation: The Use and Abuse of Charming Betsy," 67 OHIO ST. L.J. 1339 (2006). Reprinted with permission of Professor Roger P. Alford.

American Law Institute, Foreign Relations Law of the United States §§ 1, 301 Comment a. © 1987 by the American Law Institute. Reprinted with permission.

—, *AM & S Europe Limited v. Commission of the European Communities*, [1982] ECR 1575.

Anand, R.P., "Transit Passage and Overflight in International Straits," 26 Indian Journal of International Law 81 (1986). © 1986 by Indian Journal of International Law.

—, Antarctic Treaty Consultative Meeting (34th : 2011 : Buenos Aires) Final Report of the Thirty-fourth Antarctic Treaty Consultative Meeting, General Guidelines for Visitors to the Antarctic, Resolution 3 (2011). Buenos Aires, Argentina, 20 June–1 July 2011. Reprinted with permission of the Secretariat of the Antarctic Treaty.

Beddard, Ralph, Human Rights and Europe 4 (1980). © Professor R. Beddard.

Bederman, David J., "Revivalist Canons and Treaty Interpretation," 41 UCLA L. REV. 953 (1994). © 1994 by UCLA Law Review. Reprinted with permission of UCLA Law Review, William S. Hein & Co., Inc. and Professor D. Bederman.

Bederman, David J., "The Souls of International Organizations: Legal Personality and the Lighthouse at Cape Spartel," 36 VA. J. INT'L L. 275, 367 (1996). © 1996 by Virginia Journal of International Law. Reprinted with permission of the Virginia Journal of International Law.

Benedick, Richard Elliot, "The Improbable Montreal Protocol: Science, Diplomacy, and Defending the Ozone Layer," Am. Meteorological Soc. (2004). Reprinted with permission of the American Meteorological Society.

Bingham, Tom, "The Alabama Claims Arbitration," 54 INT'L & COMP. L.Q. 1 (2005). © 2005 British Institute of International and Comparative Law. Reprinted with permission of Cambridge University Press.

Buergenthal, Thomas, The Normative and Institutional Evolution of International Human Rights. Human Rights Quarterly 19:4 (1997), 702–723. © The Johns Hopkins University Press. Reprinted with permission of The Johns Hopkins University Press.

—, The Caroline Dispute, 29 British and Foreign State Papers 1129; 30 British and Foreign State Papers 195. Crown copyright is reproduced with the permission of the Controller of Her Majesty's Stationery Office, Core Licence No. C2010002357.

Caron, David D., "Protection of the Stratospheric Ozone Layer and the Structure of International Environmental Lawmaking," 14 Hastings Int'l & Comp. L. Rev. 755, 774 (1991). © 1991 Hastings College of Law. Reprinted with permission of the Hastings International and Comparative Law Review.

—, Cession of Alaska (1867), 134 Consolidated Treaty Series 331 (1969). © 1969 by Oceana Publications, Inc.

Chesterman, Simon, "Leading From Behind," Ethics and International Affairs (2011). © 2011 Council for Ethics in International Affairs. Reprinted with permission of Cambridge University Press.

Christie, Donna R., " It Don't Come EEZ: The Failure and Future of Coastal State Fisheries Management," 14 J. of Transnational L. & Pol. 1, 34 (2004). © 2004 Florida State University College of Law. Reprinted with permission of the Florida State University College of Law.

Christopher, Warren and Mosk, Richard M., "The Iranian Hostage Crisis and the Iran–U.S. Claims Tribunal: Implications for International Dispute Resolution and Diplomacy." Reprinted from Pepperdine Dispute Resolution Law Journal, Volume 7, Number 2, 2007. Copyright 2007 by the Pepperdine University School of Law.

—, *CMS Gas Transmission v. Argentina*, ICSID Case No. ARB/01/8 (Sept. 25 2007). Reprinted with permission of the International Centre for Settlement for Investment Disputes (ICSID).

Committee on the Formation of Customary (General) International Law, "3rd Interim Report," International Law Association, Report of the 67th Conference 623 (1996). © 1996 by the International Law Association. Reprinted with the permission of the International Law Association.

—, Committee of Inquiry into Shipping, Report 551 (London: HMSO, Comnd. 4338, 1970). Crown copyright is reproduced with the permission of the Controller of Her Majesty's Stationery Office, Core Licence No. C2010002357.

—, Damian Thomas v. Jamaica, U.N. Human Rights Committee Communication No. 800/1998, U.N. Doc. CCPR/65/D/800/1998, 7 International Human Rights Report, No. 2, 326 (2000). Reprinted with permission of the Human Rights Law Centre.

—, The Declaration of Principles Governing the Sea–Bed and the Ocean Floor, and the Subsoil Thereof, Beyond the Limits of National Jurisdiction, G.A. Res. 2749 (XXV), 25 U.N. GAOR Supp. (No. 28), 24, U.N. Doc. A/8028 (1970). © 1970 by the United Nations.

—, Deputy Legal Adviser Elizabeth Wilmhurst (Resignation Letter), Mar. 18, 2003. Crown copyright is reproduced with the permission of the Controller of Her Majesty's Stationery Office, Core Licence No. C2010002357.

—, The Dogger Bank Case (*Great Britain v. Russia*), Report of February 26, 1905, The Hague Court Rep. © 1916 by the Carnegie Endowment for International Peace.

—, Duchy of Sealand Case, (1978) 80 International Law Reports 683. Reprinted with permission of Cambridge University Press.

—, The Eastern Greenland Case, P.C.I.J., Series A/B, No. 53 (1933), 3 World Court Reports. Reprinted with permission of Oceana Publications, Inc.

Edis, Richard, "A Job Well Done: The Founding of the United Nations Revisited," Cambridge Review of International Affairs, Vol. 6, No. 1, at 29 (1992). Reprinted with permission from Taylor & Francis Ltd, http://www.tandf.co.uk/journals.

Fletcher, William A., "International Human Rights in American Courts," 93 VA. L. REV. 652 (2007). Reprinted with permission of Virginia Law Review.

Ford, Richard T., "Law's Territory (A History of Jurisdiction)," 97 MICH. L. REV. 843 (1999). © 1999 by Michigan Law Review. Reproduced with permission from The Michigan Law Review Association and Professor R. Ford.

Franck, Thomas M., "Criminals, Combatants, or What? An Examination of the Role of Law in Responding to the Threat of Terror." Reproduced with permission from 98 AJIL 686 (2002). © The American Society of International Law.

Franck, Thomas M., "Nation Against Nation: What Happened to the U.N. Dream and What the U.S. Can Do About It." © 1985 by Thomas B. Franck. Used with permission of Oxford University Press, Inc.

Franck, Thomas M., and Faiza Patel, "UN Police Action in Lieu of War: 'The Old Order Changeth.'" Reproduced with permission from 85 AJIL 63 (1991). © The American Society of International Law.

—, "Friends of the Earth Case," Bund für Umwelt und Naturschutz Deutschland, Landesverband Nordrhein-Westfalen eV v. Bezirksregierung Arnsberg, [2011] EUECJ C-115/09 (European Court of Justice, Fourth Chamber).

—, Furundžija, Prosecutor v., Case No. IT–95–17/1 (Appeals Chamber, International Criminal Tribunal for the former Yugoslavia, 2002). Reprinted courtesy of the International Criminal Tribunal for the former Yugoslavia (ICTY).

Goodman, Ryan and Jinks, Derek, "Measuring the Effects of Human Rights Treaties," 14 EUR. J. INT'L L. 171 (2003). © 2003 European Journal of International Law. Reprinted with permission of European Journal of International Law.

Grotius, Hugo, The Freedom of the Seas. Reprinted by permission of the publisher from The Freedom of the Sea, Hugo Grotius (Washington, DC; Carnegie Endowment for International Peace, 1916). www.ceip.org.

—, Guidelines on the Recognition of New States in Eastern Europe and in the Soviet Union, 31 ILM 1486 (1992). © The American Society of International Law. Reprinted with permission.

Henkin, Louis, "The Use of Force: Law and U.S. Policy," Right v. Might: International Law and the Use of Force 37. © 1989. Council on Foreign Relations Press. Reprinted with permission of the Council on Foreign Relations.

Henkin, Louis, "Will the U.S. Supreme Court Fail International Law?," Newsletter of the American Society of International Law, Aug.-Sept. 1992, at 1–2. © The American Society of International Law.

International Human Rights Law and Practice Committee, "Final Report on the Impact of International Human Rights Law on General International Law," International Law Association, Report of the 73rd Conference 663 (2008). © 2008 International Law Association. Reprinted with permission of the International Law Association.

Janis, Mark W., "Individuals as Subjects of International Law," 17 CORNELL INT'L L.J. 61 (1984). © by Cornell International Law Journal.

Janis, Mark W., "The Doctrine of Forum Non Conveniens and the Bhopal Case," 34 Netherlands International Law Review 192 (1987). Reprinted with the kind permission of Brill N.V.

Janis, Mark Weston, America and the Law of Nations 1776–1939 (2010). © M.W. Janis.

Janis, Mark Weston, International Law (6th ed. 2012). © Mark Janis.

—, Kadi & Al Barakaat International Foundation v. Council of the European Union & European Commission, 2008 E.C.R. I–06351.

—, Key Achievements of the Montreal Protocol to Date United Nations Environment Programme (UNEP) Ozone Secretariat (Sept. 2010). © 2010 United Nations. Reprinted with permission of the United Nations.

Koskenniemi, Martti, "The Future of Statehood," 32 HARV. INT'L L.J. 397, 408 (1991). © (1991) by the President and Fellows of Harvard College and the Harvard International Law Journal.

Krasner, Stephen D., "Structural Causes and Regime Consequences: Regimes as Intervening Variables," in *International Regimes* 1 (Stephen D. Krasner ed. 1983). Reprinted with permission by Professor Stephen D. Krasner.

Lebow, Richard Ned, "Accidents and Crises: The Dogger Bank Affair," 31 Naval War College Review, No. 1, at 66 (Summer 1978). Reprinted with permission of the Naval War College Press.

—, I Maccabees 8. Scripture quotation found on pp. 167–168 from I Maccabees 8 is taken from Today's English Version Deutero canonicals/Apocrypha. Copyright © 1979, 1992 American Bible Society. Used by permission.

Mann, F.A., "Contempt of Court in the House of Lords and the European Court of Human Rights," 95 Law Quarterly Review 348 (1979). Reprinted with permission of Sweet & Maxwell.

Matheson, Michael J., "The Fifty-Eighth Session of the International Law Commission," 101 AM. J. INT'L L. 407 (2007). Reprinted with permission of American Journal of International Law.

—, Memorandum from British Attorney-General Lord Goldsmith to Prime Minister Tony Blair, Mar. 7, 2003. Crown copyright is reproduced with the permission of the Controller of Her Majesty's Stationery Office, Core Licence No. C2010002357.

Meron, Theodor, "The Humanization of Humanitarian Law." Reproduced with permission from 94 AJIL 239 (2000). © The American Society of International Law.

Meron, Theodor, "Revival of Customary Humanitarian Law," 99 AM. J. INT'L L. 816 (2005). Reprinted with permission of American Society of International Law.

—, The Michael Domingues Case, Digest of United States Practice in International Law (Sally J. Cummins & David P. Stewart eds. 2002). Reprinted by permission of International Law Institute.

Milanović, Marko and Papić, Tatjana, "As Bad as it Gets: The European Court Of Human Rights's *Behrami and Saramati* Decision and General International Law," 58 INT'L & COMP. L.Q. 267 (2009). © 2009 British Institute of International and Comparative Law. Reprinted with permission of Cambridge University Press.

Miner, Roger, J, "The Reception of Foreign Law in the U.S. Federal Courts," 43 American Journal of Comparative Law, 581, 588-89 (1995). Reprinted with permission of the American Journal of Comparative Law.

Morison, Samuel Eliot, Commager, Henry Steele and Leuchtenberg, William E., 1 The Growth of the American Republic 204 (7th ed. 1980). Reprinted with permission of Oxford University Press, Inc.

—, The Naulilaa Case, *Portugal v. Germany*, Special Arbitral Tribunal, Judgment of 31 July 1928, 2 United Nations Report of International Arbitral Awards 1012 (2006). © 2006 by the United Nations.

Newton, Mike, "The Military Lawyer: Nuisance or Necessity?" (2004). Reprinted with the permission of Mike Newton and the Institute of International Humanitarian Law.

O'Connell, D.P., 1 State Succession in Municipal Law and International Law 7 (1967). Reprinted with the permission of Cambridge University Press.

O'Connell, Mary Ellen, "Lawful Self–Defense to Terrorism," 63 U. PITT. L. REV. 889 (2002). Reprinted with the permission of Mary Ellen O'Connell.

Oppenheim, L., International Law: Volume I—Peace 108 (H. Lauterpacht ed., 8th ed. 1955). © 1930 by Pearson Education Reprinted by permission of Pearson Education, Inc., Upper Saddle River, NJ.

—, *Our Common Future* (The Brundtland Report), Report of the World Commission on Environment and Development, U.N. Doc. A/42/427, Annex (1987). © 1987 United Nations. Reprinted with the permission of the United Nations.

Oxman, Bernard H., "The Regime of Warships Under the United Nations Convention on the Law of the Sea," 24 VA. J. INT'L L. 809, 861–62 (1984). © 1984 by Virginia Journal of International Law.

—, Peace of Westphalia (1648), 1 Consolidated Treaty Series 198 (1969). © 1969 by Oceana Publications, Inc.

—, Rainbow Warrior (*New Zealand v. France*), 82 Int'l L. Rep. 559 (1990). Reprinted with the kind permission of Mr. Michael F. Hoellering and Cambridge University Press.

—, Rainbow Warrior Case, Ruling [of July 6, 1986, by the U.N. Secretary-General] Pertaining to the Differences Between France and New Zealand Arising from the Rainbow Warrior Affair, 19 *Reports of International Arbitral Awards* 199 (2006). Reprinted with permission of the United Nations.

—, Reference Re Secession of Quebec (1998). Reproduced with permission from 37 ILM 1340 (1998). © The American Society of International Law.

—, Regina v. Keyn, Great Britain, Court for Crown Cases Reserved, 2 Law Reports (Exchequer Division) 63 (1876). Reprinted with permission of the Council of Law Reporting for England & Wales.

Reisman, W. Michael, "Criteria for the Lawful Use of Force in International Law," 10 YALE J. INT'L L. 279 (1985). © 1985 by Yale Journal of International Law.

—, Report of the International Law Commission on its Work of its Fifty-Eighth Session, U.N. GAOR, 61st Sess., Supp. No. 10, draft art. 18, U.N. Doc. A/61/10 (2006). © 2006 United Nations. Reprinted with the permission of the United Nations.

—, Report of the International Law Commission on the Work of its Fifty-Third Session, U.N. Doc. A/56/10 (2001), in 2 *Yearbook of the International Law Commission*, U.N. Doc. A/CN.4/SER.A/ 2001/Add.1 (Part 2) (2001). © 2001 United Nations.

—, Report of the International Law Commission on the Work of its Sixty-Third Session, U.N. Doc. A/66/10 Add. 1 (2011). © 2011 United Nations. Reprinted with permission of the United Nations.

—, Republic of Croatia et al. v. Girocredit Bank A.G. der Sparkassen (1996). Reproduced with permission from 36 ILM 1520 (1998). © The American Society of International Law.

Responsibilities and Obligations of States Sponsoring Persons and Entities with Respect to Activities in the Area, Seabed Disputes Chamber of the International Tribunal for the Law of the Sea (ITLOS), Advisory Opinion, ITLOS Case No. 17 (2011). Reproduced courtesy of the International Tribunal for the Law of the Sea.

Rona, Gabor, "The ICRC's Status: In a Class of Its Own" (Feb. 2004), www.icrc.org. Reprinted with the permission of the International Committee of the Red Cross.

Rostow, Eugene V., "Until What? Enforcement Action or Collective Self-defense?" Reproduced with permission from 85 AJIL 506 (1999). © The American Society of International Law.

Rusk, Dean, "The Role and Problem of Arbitration with Respect to Political Disputes," in Carbonneau, Thomas E., ed. Resolving Transnational Disputes Through International Arbitration (1984). © 1984 by the Rector and Visitors of the University of Virginia. Reprinted with permission of University of Virginia Press.

Sadat, Leila Nadya, "Shattering the Nuremberg Consensus: U.S. Rendition Policy and International Criminal Law," 2008 YALE J. INT'L AFF. 65. Reprinted with permission of Yale Journal of International Affairs.

Sadat, Leila Nadya & Carden, Richard, "The New International Criminal Court: An Uneasy Revolution," 88 GEO. L.J. 381 (2000). Reprinted with permission of the publisher, Georgetown Law Journal © 2000.

—, Safer Ships, Cleaner Seas, Report of Lord Donaldson's Inquiry Into the Prevention of Pollution from Merchant Shipping, Cm. 2560 (1994). Crown copyright is reproduced with the permission of the Controller of Her Majesty's Stationery Office, Core Licence No. C2010002357.

—, "SAIGA" M/V, (No. 2), Saint Vincent and the Grenadines v. Guinea, International Tribunal for the Law of the Sea (1999). Reproduced courtesy of the International Tribunal for the Law of the Sea.

Scharf, Michael P. and Williams, Paul R., Shaping Foreign Policy in Times of Crisis: The Role of International Law and the State Department Legal Adviser (2010). © 2010 Michael P. Scharf and Paul R. Williams. Reprinted with permission of Cambridge University Press.

Schiffrin, Natalia, "Jamaica Withdraws the Right of Individual Petition under the International Covenant on Civil and Political Rights." Reproduced with permission from 92 AJIL 563 (1998). © The American Society of International Law.

—, The Shrimp–Turtle Case, United States–Import Prohibition of Certain Shrimp and Shrimp Products, World Trade Organization, Report of the Appellate Body, AB–1998–4 (1998). Reproduced with permission from 38 ILM 121 (1999). © The American Society of International Law.

—, Situation in the Democratic Republic of the Congo in the Case of the Prosecutor v. Thomas Lubanga Dyilo, Decision on the Confirmation of Charges, International Criminal Court, Pre-trial Chamber I, ICC-

01/04-01/06, Jan. 29 2007. © 2003-2012 International Criminal Court.

—, Situation in the Democratic Republic of the Congo in the Case of the Prosecutor v. Thomas Lubanga Dyilo, Judgment Pursuant to Article 74 of the Statute, International Criminal Courts Trial Chamber I, ICC-01/04-01/06, Mar. 14, 2012. © 2003-2012 International Criminal Court.

Sloane, Robert D., "Breaking the Genuine Link: The Contemporary International Legal Regulation of Nationality," 50 Harvard Int'l L.J. 1, 60 (2009). Reprinted with permission.

—, Supplement to An Agenda for Peace, Position Paper of the Secretary–General on the Occasion of the Fiftieth Anniversary of the United Nations A/50/60–S/1995/1, 3 January 1995, at 5 (2d ed. 1995). © 1995 by the United Nations.

Szasz, Paul C., "The Security Council Starts Legislating. Reproduced with permission from 96 AJIL 901 (2002). © The American Society of International Law.

—, Tadić, Prosecutor v., Case No. IT–94–1 (Appeals Chamber, International Criminal Tribunal for the former Yugoslavia, 1995). Reprinted courtesy of the International Criminal Tribunal for the former Yugoslavia (ICTY).

—, Tadić, Prosecutor v., Case No. IT–94–1–A (Appeals Chamber, International Criminal Tribunal for the former Yugoslavia, 1999). Reprinted courtesy of the International Criminal Tribunal for the former Yugoslavia (ICTY).

Taft IV, William H., "A View from the Top: American Perspectives on International Law After the Cold War," 31 YALE J. INT'L L. 503 (2006). Reprinted with permission of Yale Journal of International Law.

—, "The Texaco/Libya Arbitration, Award of 19 January 1977." Reproduced with permission from 17 ILM 1–37 (1978). © The American Society of International Law.

—, "The Tinoco Arbitration." Reproduced with permission from 18 AJIL 147–74 (1924). © The American Society of International Law.

—, Treaty of Paris (1783), 48 Consolidated Treaty Series 487 (1969). © 1969 by Oceana Publications, Inc.

Vagts, Detlev V., "An Introduction to International Civil Practice," 17 VAND. J. TRANSNAT'L L. 1 (1984). Permission granted to reprint from the Vanderbilt Journal of Transnational Law, which is the copyright holder.

Vázquez, Carlos Manuel, "Treaties as the Law of the Land: The Supremacy Clause and the Judicial Enforcement of Treaties," 122 HARV. L. REV. 621 (2008). Reprinted with permission of Harvard Law School.

Verdross, Alfred von, "Forbidden Treaties in International Law." Reproduced with permission from 31 AJIL 571 (1937). © The American Society of International Law.

Vriens, Lauren, "Troubles Plague UN Human Rights Council," Council on Foreign Relations, *Backgrounder*, May 13, 2009. From CFR.org. Reprinted with permission.

Wilson, Julian, "US Exports In Anti-Trust: The Primacy of Economic Muscle Over International Law," International Litigation News, July 1995, at 3, 4. Published by the International Bar Association. Reprinted with permission of the International Bar Association Publications.

Wright, Quincy, "National Courts and Human Rights—The Fujii Case." Reproduced with permission from 45 AJIL 62 (1951). © The American Society of International Law.

SUMMARY OF CONTENTS

TABLE OF CONTENTS

TABLE OF MAPS AND FIGURES

TABLE OF CASES

The principal cases are in bold type.

TABLE OF TREATIES AND OTHER INSTRUMENTS

INTERNATIONAL LAW

CASES AND COMMENTARY

Fifth Edition

CHAPTER 1

THE NATURE OF INTERNATIONAL LAW

■ ■ ■

International law is sometimes compared unfavorably with other kinds of law, especially the law of nation states. At first glance, international law seems to lack an effective legislature, a generally competent judiciary, and a powerful executive. Yet, whatever its theoretical ambiguities, international law has been practiced by lawyers for centuries. This chapter explains the nature of international law by introducing the history of the discipline and by exploring two sample international law cases. These two cases, *McCann* and *Filartiga*, begin to show how international law is in fact, in the real world, legislated, adjudicated, and enforced.

A. THE HISTORY OF INTERNATIONAL LAW

MARK WESTON JANIS, INTERNATIONAL LAW

1–4 (6th ed. 2012)

The roots of international law run deep in history. In early religious and secular writings, there are many evidences of what we now know as international law; there are, for example, the detailed peace treaties and alliances concluded between the Jews and the Romans, Syrians, and Spartans. The Romans knew of a *jus gentium*, a law of nations, which Gaius, in the second century, saw as a law "common to all men," a universal law that could be applied by Roman courts to foreigners when the specific law of their own nation was unknown and when Roman law was inapposite. In the seventeenth century, the Dutch jurist Hugo Grotius argued that the law of nations also established legal rules that bound the sovereign states of Europe, then just emerging from medieval society, in their relations with one another. Grotius' classic of 1625, *The Law of War and Peace*, is widely acknowledged, more than any other work, as founding the modern discipline of the law of nations, a subject that, in 1789, the English philosopher Jeremy Bentham renamed and refashioned as "international law." Nowadays, the terms *the law of nations* and *international law* are often used interchangeably.

At least since the end of the Thirty Years War in 1648, world politics has principally involved the relations of more or less independent sovereign states. An important part of international law has consequently had to do with the establishment of a set of mutually agreed-upon rules respecting the nature of these states and their fundamental rights and obligations *inter se*. If there is a single international legal principle underlying the modern state system, it probably is the one neatly framed by Montesquieu in 1748 and offered to Napoleon in 1806 by Talleyrand: "that nations ought to do to one another in peace, the most good, and in war, the least evil possible."

International law is sometimes conceived to be divided into public and private parts, the first concerning the legal relations of states, the second involving the law governing the foreign transactions of individuals and corporations. However, the public-private division of international law can be misleading. Many of the laws and processes traditionally within the ambit of public international law actually concern private, not public, parties, while much of the domain of private international law covers the transactions of public entities. Nonetheless, the terms *public* and *private* international law are highly popular and, in a rough kind of way, do compartmentalize legal rules addressing two problem areas: Public international law mostly concerns the political interactions of states; private international law relates to legal aspects of the international economy and conflicts and cooperation among national legal systems.

Few deny that the rules of international law actually influence state behavior. Even international law's most famous jurisprudential critic, John Austin, acknowledged in 1832 that international legal rules were effective. At the same time, however, he argued that, because there was no international sovereign to enforce it, international law could not be the same sort of positive law as that enacted by sovereign states for internal application:

> [T]he law obtaining between nations is not positive law: for every positive law is set by a given sovereign to a person or persons in a state of subjection to its author. As I have already intimated, the law obtaining between nations is law (improperly so called) set by general opinion. The duties which it imposes are enforced by moral sanctions: by fear on the part of nations, or by fear on the part of sovereigns, of provoking general hostility, and incurring its probable evils, in case they shall violate maxims generally received and respected.

Just a few years later, in 1836, the United States diplomat Henry Wheaton, in the first great English-language treatise on international law, was already grappling with Austin's characterization of the rules governing international politics as being a form of mere "morality." Wheaton accepted Austin's view that international law's principal sanction was "the hazard of provoking the hostility of other communities," but contended that "[e]xperience shows that these motives, even in the worst times, do really afford a considerable security for the observance of justice between States, if they do not furnish the perfect sanction annexed by the lawgiver to the observance of the municipal code of any particular State." Unlike Austin, Wheaton found international law sufficiently law-like to justify calling it "law," a definitional outcome reached by generations of subsequent international lawyers.

Whether the international rules regulating interstate behavior are to be properly termed "legal" or "moral" is in truth a question that can only be answered after one has made more or less arbitrary definitions of what really constitutes "law" and "morality," a sometimes sterile exercise.[12] Suffice it to say at this early stage of our own discussion that there are a great many rules regulating international politics commonly referred to as "international law" and that these rules are usually, for one reason or another, observed in international practice. Moreover, there is no doubt that the norms of international law are frequently applied as rules of decision by law courts, domestic as well as international.

B. AN INTERNATIONAL LAW SAMPLER

The two cases that follow explore some of the different ways in which international law is actually made, applied, and enforced. The *McCann Case* illustrates an international legal rule made by a treaty, adjudicated by an international court, and enforced by a regional international legal system. The *Filartiga Case* shows a customary or perhaps fundamental international legal norm adjudicated by a municipal—*i.e.*, a domestic—court and enforced (or not) by the ordinary mechanisms of that domestic legal system. The Notes and Questions that follow introduce several of the central issues about the rules, processes, actors, and domains of international law, topics that occupy us throughout the book.

MCCANN V. UNITED KINGDOM

European Court of Human Rights,
Judgment of 5 September 1995

1. The case * * * originated in an application (no. 18984/91) against the United Kingdom of Great Britain and Northern Ireland lodged * * * by Ms. Margaret McCann, Mr. Daniel Farrell and Mr. John Savage, who are all Irish and United Kingdom citizens. They are representatives of the estates of Mr. Daniel McCann, Ms. Mairead Farrell and Mr. Sean Savage. * * *

13. Before 4 March 1988, and probably from at least the beginning of the year, the United Kingdom, Spanish and Gibraltar authorities were aware that the Provisional IRA (Irish Republican Army—"IRA") were

[12] "The only intelligent way to deal with a verbal question like that concerning the definition of the word 'law' is to give up thinking and arguing about it." Williams, "International Law and the Controversy Concerning the Word 'Law,' " 22 *British Yearbook of International Law* 146, 163 (1945).

planning a terrorist attack on Gibraltar. It appeared from the intelligence received and from observations made by the Gibraltar police that the target was to be the assembly area south of Ince's Hall where the Royal Anglican Regiment usually assembled to carry out the changing of the guard every Tuesday at 11.00 hours. * * *

23. [On March 5, 1988, a] briefing by the representative of the Security Services included inter alia the following assessments:

(a) the IRA intended to attack the changing of the guard ceremony in the assembly area outside Ince's Hall on the morning of Tuesday 8 March 1988;

(b) [a group] of three would be sent to carry out the attack, consisting of Daniel McCann, Sean Savage and a third member, later positively identified as Mairead Farrell. McCann had been previously convicted and sentenced to two years' imprisonment for possession of explosives. Farrell had previously been convicted and sentenced to fourteen years' imprisonment for causing explosions. She was known during her time in prison to have been the acknowledged leader of the IRA wing of prisoners. Savage was described as an expert bomb-maker. Photographs were shown of the three suspects;

(c) the three individuals were believed to be dangerous terrorists who would almost certainly be armed and who, if confronted by security forces, would be likely to use their weapons;

(d) the attack would be by way of a car bomb. It was believed that the bomb would be brought across the border in a vehicle and that it would remain hidden inside the vehicle;

(e) the possibility that a "blocking" car—i.e. a car not containing a bomb but parked in the assembly area in order to reserve a space for the car containing the bomb—would be used had been considered, but was thought unlikely. * * *

24. Various methods of detonation of the bomb were mentioned at the briefing[.] Use of a remote-control device was considered to be far more likely since it was safer from the point of view of the terrorist who could get away from the bomb before it exploded and was more controllable than a timer which once activated was virtually impossible to stop. * * *

45. At about 14.50 hours [on March 6] it was reported to the operations room that the suspects McCann and Farrell had met with a second man identified as the suspect Savage and the three were looking at a white Renault car in the car-park of the assembly area.

Witness H stated that the three suspects spent some considerable time staring across to where a car had been parked, as if, in his assessment, they were studying it to make sure it was absolutely right for the effect of the bomb. [Detective Constable] Viagas also witnessed the three suspects meeting in the area of the car-park, stating that all three turned and stared towards where the car was parked. He gave the time as about 14.55 hours. He stated that the Security Services made identification of all three at this moment.

At this moment, the possibility of effecting an arrest was considered. There were different recollections. [Deputy Commissioner] Colombo stated that he was asked whether he would hand over control to the military for the arrest but that he asked whether the suspects had been positively identified; he was told that there was 80% identification. Almost immediately the three suspects moved away from the car through the Southport Gate. He recalled that the movement of the three suspects towards the south gave rise to some discussion as to whether this indicated that the three suspects were on reconnaissance and might return for the car. It was for this reason that the decision was taken not to arrest at this point. * * *

55. The evidence at the inquest given by the soldiers and Police Officer R and DC Ullger was that the soldiers had practised arrest procedures on several occasions with the police before 6 March 1988. According to these rehearsals, the soldiers were to approach the suspects to within a close distance, cover the suspects with their pistols and shout "Stop. Police. Hands up." or words to that effect. They would then make the suspects lie on the ground with their arms away from their bodies until the police moved in to carry out a formal arrest. Further, DC Ullger stated that special efforts had been made to identify a suitable place in Gibraltar for the terrorists to be held in custody following their arrest.

56. On reaching the junction of Smith Dorrien Avenue with Winston Churchill Avenue, the three suspects crossed the road and stopped on the other side talking. Officer R, observing, saw them appear to exchange newspapers. At this point, Soldiers C and D were approaching the junction from Smith Dorrien Avenue. Soldiers A and B emerging from Landport tunnel also saw the three suspects at the junction from their position where the pathway to the tunnel joined Corral Road.

57. As the soldiers converged on the junction, however, Savage split away from suspects McCann and Farrell turning south towards the Landport tunnel. McCann and Farrell continued north up the right-hand pavement of Winston Churchill Avenue.

58. Savage passed Soldiers A and B, brushing against the shoulder of B. Soldier B was about to turn to effect the arrest but A told him that they should continue towards suspects McCann and Farrell, knowing that C and D were in the area and that they would arrest Savage. Soldiers C

and D, aware that A and B were following suspects McCann and Farrell, crossed over from Smith Dorrien Avenue and followed Savage. * * *

60. Soldiers A and B continued north up Winston Churchill Avenue after McCann and Farrell, walking at a brisk pace to close the distance. McCann was walking on the right of Farrell on the inside of the pavement. He was wearing white trousers and a white shirt, without any jacket. Farrell was dressed in a skirt and jacket and was carrying a large handbag.

61. When Soldier A was approximately ten metres (though maybe closer) behind McCann on the inside of the pavement, McCann looked back over his left shoulder. McCann appeared to look directly at A and the smile left his face, as if he had a realisation of who A was and that he was a threat.

Soldier A drew his pistol, intending to shout a warning to stop at the same time, though he was uncertain if words actually came out. McCann's hand moved suddenly and aggressively across the front of his body. A thought that he was going for the button to detonate the bomb and opened fire. He shot one round into McCann's back from a distance of three metres (though maybe it might have been closer). Out of the corner of his eye, A saw a movement by Farrell. Farrell had been walking on the left of McCann on the side of the pavement next to the road. A saw her make a half turn to the right towards McCann, grabbing for her handbag which was under her left arm. A thought that she was also going for a button and shot one round into her back. He did not disagree when it was put to him that the forensic evidence suggested that he may have shot from a distance of three feet. Then A turned back to McCann and shot him once more in the body and twice in the head. A was not aware of B opening fire as this was happening. He fired a total of five shots.

62. Soldier B was approaching directly behind Farrell on the road side of the pavement. He was watching her. When they were three to four metres away and closing, he saw in his peripheral vision that McCann turned his head to look over his shoulder. He heard what he presumed was a shout from A which he thought was the start of the arrest process. At almost the same instant, there was a firing to his right. Simultaneously, Farrell made a sharp movement to her right, drawing the bag which she had under her left arm across her body. He could not see her hands or the bag and feared that she was going for the button. He opened fire on Farrell. He deemed that McCann was in a threatening position and was unable to see his hands and switched fire to McCann. Then he turned back to Farrell and continued firing until he was certain that she was no longer a threat, namely, her hands away from her body. He fired a total of seven shots.

63. Both soldiers denied that Farrell or McCann made any attempt to surrender with their hands up in the air or that they fired at the two

suspects when they were lying on the ground. At the inquest, Soldier A stated expressly that his intention had been to kill McCann "to stop him becoming a threat and detonating that bomb."

64. The shooting took place on the pavement in front of a Shell petrol station in Winston Churchill Avenue. * * *

68. The shooting took place on a fine Sunday afternoon, when there were many people out on the streets and the roads were busy with traffic. The Shell garage was also overlooked by a number of apartment buildings. The shooting consequently was witnessed by a considerable number of people, including police officers involved in the operation, police officers who happened to pass the area on other duties, members of the surveillance team and a number of civilians and off-duty policemen.

69. Almost all the witnesses who gave evidence at the inquest recalled that Farrell had carried her bag under her right arm, not as stated by Soldiers A and B under her left arm. The Coroner commented in his summing-up to the jury that this might have had significance with regard to the alleged justification of the soldiers for opening fire, namely, the alleged movement of the bag across the front of her body.

70. More significantly, three witnesses, two of whom gave an interview on the controversial television documentary concerning the events "Death on the Rock," gave evidence which suggested that McCann and Farrell had been shot while lying on the ground. They stated that they had witnessed the shooting from apartment buildings overlooking the Shell petrol station.

Witness Testimony ←

71. Mrs. Celecia saw a man lying on a pavement with another nearby with his hands outstretched: while she did not see a gun she heard shots which she thought came from that direction. After the noise, the man who she had thought was shooting appeared to put something inside his jacket. When shown a photograph of the aftermath of the scene, Mrs. Celecia failed to identify either Soldier A or B as the man whom she thought that she had seen shooting.

72. Mr. Proetta saw a girl put her hands up though he thought it was more in shock than in surrender. After she had been shot and fallen to the ground, he heard another fusillade of shots. He assumed that the men nearby were continuing to fire but agreed that there was an echo in the area and that the sound could have come from the Landport tunnel area.

Mrs. Proetta saw a man and a woman raise their hands over their shoulders with open palms. They were shot, according to her recollection by men who jumped the barrier. When the bodies were on the ground, she heard further shots and saw a gun in the hand of a man crouching nearby, though she did not see any smoke or cartridges ejecting from the gun. She assumed since she saw a gun that shots came from it. It also appears that once the bodies fell they were obscured from her view by a low wall and all she saw was a man pointing in their direction.

73. Mr. Bullock recalled seeing a man reeling backwards under fire with his hands thrown back.

None of the other witnesses saw McCann or Farrell put their hands up or the soldiers shoot at the bodies on the ground.

74. Witness I, a member of the surveillance team, stated that he saw McCann and Farrell shot when they were almost on the ground, but not on the ground.

75. While the soldiers were not sure that any words of warning were uttered by Soldier A, four witnesses (Officers P and Q, Witness K and Police Constable Parody) had a clear recollection of hearing words "Police, Stop" or words to that effect.

76. Officer P, who was approaching from the north and had reached the perimeter wall of the Shell garage, states that he saw McCann make a move as if going for a gun and that Farrell made a move towards her handbag which made him think that she was going for a detonator. Officer Q, who was watching from the other side of the road, also saw Farrell make a move towards her handbag, as did Police Constable Parody, an off-duty policeman watching from an overlooking apartment.

[The Court gives various accounts of the facts of the fatal shooting of Savage.]

96. * * * The bomb-disposal team opened the suspect white Renault car but found no explosive device or bomb. The area was declared safe between 19.00 and 20.00 hours. * * *

98. Inside Farrell's handbag was found a key ring with two keys and a tag bearing a registration number MA9317AF. This information was passed at about 17.00 hours to the Spanish police who commenced a search for the car on the suspicion that it might contain explosives. During the night of 6 to 7 March, the Spanish police found a red Ford Fiesta with that registration number in La Linea. Inside the car were found keys for another car, registration number MA2732AJ, with a rental agreement indicating that the car had been rented at 10.00 hours on 6 March by Katharine Smith, the name on the passport carried in Farrell's handbag.

99. At about 18.00 hours on 8 March, a Ford Fiesta car with registration number MA2732AJ was discovered in a basement car-park in Marbella. It was opened by the Malaga bomb-disposal squad and found to contain an explosive device in the boot concealed in the spare-wheel compartment. The device consisted of five packages of Semtex explosive (altogether 64 kg) to which were attached four detonators and around which were packed 200 rounds of ammunition. There were two timers

marked 10 hrs 45 mins and 11 hrs 15 mins respectively. The device was not primed or connected.

100. In the report compiled by the Spanish police on the device dated Madrid 27 March 1988, it was concluded that there was a double activating system to ensure explosion even if one of the timers failed; the explosive was hidden in the spare-wheel space to avoid detection on passing the Spanish/Gibraltarian customs; the quantity of explosive and use of cartridges as shrapnel indicated the terrorists were aiming for greatest effect; and that it was believed that the device was set to explode at the time of the military parade on 8 March 1988. * * *

103. An inquest by the Gibraltar Coroner into the killings was opened on 6 September 1988. The families of the deceased (which included the applicants) were represented, as were the SAS [Special Air Service] soldiers and the United Kingdom Government. The inquest was presided over by the Coroner, who sat with a jury chosen from the local population. * * *

121. The jury returned verdicts of lawful killing by a majority of nine to two.

122. The applicants were dissatisfied with these verdicts and commenced actions in the High Court of Justice in Northern Ireland against the Ministry of Defence for the loss and damage suffered by the estate of each deceased as a result of their death. The statements of claim were served on 1 March 1990.

123. On 15 March 1990 the Secretary of State for Foreign and Commonwealth Affairs issued certificates under section 40(3)a of the Crown Proceedings Act 1947, as amended by the Crown Proceedings (Northern Ireland) Order 1981. Section 40(2)b of the same Act excludes proceedings in Northern Ireland against the Crown in respect of liability arising otherwise than "in respect of Her Majesty's Government in the United Kingdom." A similar exemption applies to the Crown in Northern Ireland pursuant to the 1981 Order. A certificate by the Secretary of State to that effect is conclusive. The certificates stated in this case that any alleged liability of the Crown arose neither in respect of Her Majesty's Government in the United Kingdom, nor in respect of Her Majesty's Government in Northern Ireland.

124. The Ministry of Defence then moved to have the actions struck out. The applicants challenged the legality of the certificates in judicial review proceedings. Leave to apply for judicial review was granted ex parte on 6 July 1990, but withdrawn on 31 May 1991, after a full hearing, on the basis that the application had no reasonable prospects of success. Senior Counsel advised that an appeal against this decision would be futile.

The applicants' High Court actions were struck off on 4 October 1991.

125. On 28 April 1988 Thames Television broadcast its documentary entitled "Death on the Rock," during which a reconstruction was made of the alleged surveillance of the terrorists' car by the Spanish police and witnesses to the shootings described what they had seen, including allegations that McCann and Farrell had been shot while on the ground. A statement by an anonymous witness was read out to the effect that Savage had been shot by a man who had his foot on his chest. The Independent Broadcasting Authority had rejected a request made by the Foreign and Commonwealth Secretary to postpone the programme until after the holding of the inquest into the deaths. * * *

141. The applicants lodged their application (no. 18984/91) with the [European Human Rights] Commission on 14 August 1991. They complained that the killings of Daniel McCann, Mairead Farrell and Sean Savage by members of the SAS (Special Air Service) constituted a violation of Article 2 of the [European Human Rights] Convention.

142. On 3 September 1993 the Commission declared the applicants' complaint admissible.

In its report of 4 March 1994 (Article 31), it expressed the opinion that there had been no violation of Article 2 (eleven votes to six). * * *

143. The Government submitted that the deprivations of life to which the applications related were justified under Article 2 para. 2(a) as resulting from the use of force which was no more than absolutely necessary in defence of the people of Gibraltar from unlawful violence and the Court was invited to find that the facts disclosed no breach of Article 2 of the Convention in respect of any of the three deceased.

144. The applicants submitted that the Government have not shown beyond reasonable doubt that the planning and execution of the operation was in accordance with Article 2 para. 2 of the Convention. Accordingly, the killings were not absolutely necessary within the meaning of this provision.

145. The applicants alleged that the killing of Mr. McCann, Ms. Farrell and Mr. Savage by members of the security forces constituted a violation of Article 2 of the Convention which reads:

> 1. Everyone's right to life shall be protected by law. No one shall be deprived of his life intentionally save in the execution of a sentence of a court following his conviction of a crime for which this penalty is provided by law.
>
> 2. Deprivation of life shall not be regarded as inflicted in contravention of this Article when it results from the use of force which is no more than absolutely necessary:
>
> (a) in defence of any person from unlawful violence;

(b) in order to effect a lawful arrest or to prevent the escape of a person lawfully detained;

(c) in action lawfully taken for the purpose of quelling a riot or insurrection.

146. The Court's approach to the interpretation of Article 2 must be guided by the fact that the object and purpose of the Convention as an instrument for the protection of individual human beings requires that its provisions be interpreted and applied so as to make its safeguards practical and effective.

147. It must also be borne in mind that, as a provision which not only safeguards the right to life but sets out the circumstances when the deprivation of life may be justified, Article 2 ranks as one of the most fundamental provisions in the Convention—indeed one which, in peacetime, admits of no derogation under Article 15. Together with Article 3 of the Convention, it also enshrines one of the basic values of the democratic societies making up the Council of Europe (see the above-mentioned Soering judgment, p. 34, para. 88). As such, its provisions must be strictly construed. * * *

165. While accepting that the Convention institutions are not in any formal sense bound by the decisions of the inquest jury, the Government submitted that the verdicts were of central importance to any subsequent examination of the deaths of the deceased. Accordingly, the Court should give substantial weight to the verdicts of the jury in the absence of any indication that those verdicts were perverse or ones which no reasonable tribunal of fact could have reached. In this connection, the jury was uniquely well-placed to assess the circumstances surrounding the shootings. The members of the jury heard and saw each of the seventy-nine witnesses giving evidence, including extensive cross-examination. With that benefit they were able to assess the credibility and probative value of the witnesses' testimony. The Government pointed out that the jury also heard the submissions of the various parties, including those of the lawyers representing the deceased. * * *

170. As regards the appreciation of these facts from the standpoint of Article 2, the Court observes that the jury had the benefit of listening to the witnesses first hand, observing their demeanor and assessing the probative value of their testimony.

Nevertheless, it must be borne in mind that the jury's finding was limited to a decision of lawful killing and, as is normally the case, did not provide reasons for the conclusion that it reached. In addition, the focus of concern of the inquest proceedings and the standard applied by the jury was whether the killings by the soldiers were reasonably justified in the circumstances as opposed to whether they were "absolutely necessary" under Article 2 para. 2 in the sense developed above.

171. Against this background, the Court must make its own assessment whether the facts as established by the Commission disclose a violation of Article 2 of the Convention. * * *

174. The applicants alleged that there had been a premeditated plan to kill the deceased. While conceding that there was no evidence of a direct order from the highest authorities in the Ministry of Defence, they claimed that there was strong circumstantial evidence in support of their allegation. They suggested that a plot to kill could be achieved by other means such as hints and innuendoes, coupled with the choice of a military unit like the SAS which, as indicated by the evidence given by their members at the inquest, was trained to neutralize a target by shooting to kill. Supplying false information of the sort that was actually given to the soldiers in this case would render a fatal shooting likely. The use of the SAS was, in itself, evidence that the killing was intended. * * *

178. The Commission concluded that there was no evidence to support the applicant's claim of a premeditated plot to kill the suspects.

179. The Court observes that it would need to have convincing evidence before it could conclude that there was a premeditated plan, in the sense developed by the applicants.

180. In the light of its own examination of the material before it, the Court does not find it established that there was an execution plot at the highest level of command in the Ministry of Defence or in the Government, or that Soldiers A, B, C and D had been so encouraged or instructed by the superior officers who had briefed them prior to the operation, or indeed that they had decided on their own initiative to kill the suspects irrespective of the existence of any justification for the use of lethal force and in disobedience to the arrest instructions they had received. Nor is there evidence that there was an implicit encouragement by the authorities or hints and innuendoes to execute the three suspects. * * *

184. The Court therefore rejects as unsubstantiated the applicants' allegations that the killing of the three suspects was premeditated or the product of a tacit agreement amongst those involved in the operation.

185. The applicants [also] submitted that it would be wrong for the Court, as the Commission had done, to limit its assessment to the question of the possible justification of the soldiers who actually killed the suspects. It must examine the liability of the Government for all aspects of the operation. Indeed, the soldiers may well have been acquitted at a criminal trial if they could have shown that they honestly believed the ungrounded and false information they were given. * * *

186. * * * In sum, they submitted that the killings came about as a result of incompetence and negligence in the planning and conduct of the anti-terrorist operation to arrest the suspects as well as a failure to

maintain a proper balance between the need to meet the threat posed and the right to life of the suspect. * * *

191. The Commission considered that, given the soldiers' perception of the risk to the lives of the people of Gibraltar, the shooting of the three suspects could be regarded as absolutely necessary for the legitimate aim of the defence of others from unlawful violence. It also concluded that, having regard to the possibility that the suspects had brought in a car bomb which, if detonated, would have occasioned the loss of many lives and the possibility that the suspects could have been able to detonate it when confronted by the soldiers, the planning and execution of the operation by the authorities did not disclose any deliberate design or lack of proper care which might have rendered the use of lethal force disproportionate to the aim of saving lives. * * *

[The Court concludes that "the actions of the soldiers do not, in themselves, give rise to a violation of" Article 2, and then turns to the question "whether the anti-terrorist operation as a whole was controlled and organised in a manner which respected the requirements of Article 2."]

203. It may be questioned why the three suspects were not arrested at the border immediately on their arrival in Gibraltar and why, as emerged from the evidence given by Inspector Ullger, the decision was taken not to prevent them from entering Gibraltar if they were believed to be on a bombing mission. Having had advance warning of the terrorists' intentions it would certainly have been possible for the authorities to have mounted an arrest operation. Although surprised at the early arrival of the three suspects, they had a surveillance team at the border and an arrest group nearby. In addition, the Security Services and the Spanish authorities had photographs of the three suspects, knew their names as well as their aliases and would have known what passports to look for.

204. On this issue, the Government submitted that at that moment there might not have been sufficient evidence to warrant the detention and trial of the suspects. Moreover, to release them, having alerted them to the authorities' state of awareness but leaving them or others free to try again, would obviously increase the risks. Nor could the authorities be sure that those three were the only terrorists they had to deal with or of the manner in which it was proposed to carry out the bombing.

205. The Court confines itself to observing in this respect that the danger to the population of Gibraltar—which is at the heart of the Government's submissions in this case—in not preventing their entry must be considered to outweigh the possible consequences of having insufficient evidence to warrant their detention and trial. In its view, either the authorities knew that there was no bomb in the car—which the Court has already discounted—or there was a serious miscalculation by

those responsible for controlling the operation. As a result, the scene was set in which the fatal shooting, given the intelligence assessments which had been made, was a foreseeable possibility if not a likelihood. The decision not to stop the three terrorists from entering Gibraltar is thus a relevant factor to take into account under this head. * * *

212. Although detailed investigation at the inquest into the training received by the soldiers was prevented by the public interest certificates which had been issued, it is not clear whether they had been trained or instructed to assess whether the use of firearms to wound their targets may have been warranted by the specific circumstances that confronted them at the moment of arrest.

Their reflex action in this vital respect lacks the degree of caution in the use of firearms to be expected from law enforcement personnel in a democratic society, even when dealing with dangerous terrorist suspects, and stands in marked contrast to the standard of care reflected in the instructions in the use of firearms by the police which had been drawn to their attention and which emphasised the legal responsibilities of the individual officer in the light of conditions prevailing at the moment of engagement.

This failure by the authorities also suggests a lack of appropriate care in the control and organisation of the arrest operation.

213. In sum, having regard to the decision not to prevent the suspects from travelling into Gibraltar, to the failure of the authorities to make sufficient allowances for the possibility that their intelligence assessments might, in some respects at least, be erroneous and to the automatic recourse to lethal force when the soldiers opened fire, the Court is not persuaded that the killing of the three terrorists constituted the use of force which was no more than absolutely necessary in defence of persons from unlawful violence within the meaning of Article 2 para. 2(a) of the Convention.

214. Accordingly, the Court finds that there has been a breach of Article 2 of the Convention. * * *

FOR THESE REASONS, THE COURT

1. Holds by ten votes to nine that there has been a violation of Article 2 of the Convention;

2. Holds unanimously that the United Kingdom is to pay to the applicants, within three months, £38,700 for costs and expenses incurred in the Strasbourg proceedings, less 37,731 French francs to be converted into pounds sterling at the rate of exchange applicable on the date of delivery of the present judgment;

3. Dismisses unanimously the applicants' claim for damages;

4. Dismisses unanimously the applicants' claim for costs and expenses incurred in the Gibraltar inquest;

5. Dismisses unanimously the remainder of the claims for just satisfaction.

JOINT DISSENTING OPINION OF JUDGES RYSSDAL, BERNHARDT, THOR VILHJALSSON, GÖLCÜKLÜ, PALM PEKKANEN, SIR JOHN FREELAND, BAKA AND JAMBREK

1. We are unable to subscribe to the opinion of a majority of our colleagues that there has been a violation of Article 2 of the Convention in this case. * * *

4. As to the section dealing with the application of Article 2 to the facts of the case, we fully concur in rejecting as unsubstantiated the applicants' allegations that the killing of the three suspects was premeditated or the product of a tacit agreement among those involved in the operation (paragraph 184).

5. We also agree with the conclusion * * * that the actions of the four soldiers who carried out the shootings do not, in themselves, give rise to a violation of Article 2. It is rightly accepted that those soldiers honestly believed, in the light of the information which they had been given, that it was necessary to act as they did in order to prevent the suspects from detonating a bomb and causing serious loss of life: the actions which they took were thus perceived by them as absolutely necessary in order to safeguard innocent lives.

6. We disagree, however, with the evaluation made by the majority (paragraphs 202–14) of the way in which the control and organisation of the operation were carried out by the authorities. It is that evaluation which, crucially, leads to the finding of violation.

7. We recall at the outset that the events in this case were examined at the domestic level by an inquest held in Gibraltar over a period of nineteen days between 6 and 30 September 1988. The jury, after hearing the evidence of seventy-nine witnesses (including the soldiers, police officers and surveillance personnel involved in the operation and also pathologists, forensic scientists and experts on the detonation of explosive devices), and after being addressed by the Coroner in respect of the applicable domestic law, reached by a majority of nine to two a verdict of lawful killing. The circumstances were subsequently investigated in depth and evaluated by the Commission, which found in its report, by a majority of eleven to six, that there had been no violation of the Convention.

The finding of the inquest, as a domestic tribunal operating under the relevant domestic law, is not of itself determinative of the Convention issues before the Court. But, having regard to the crucial importance in this case of a proper appreciation of the facts and to the advantage undeniably enjoyed by the jury in having observed the demeanour of the witnesses when giving their evidence under examination and cross-examination, its significance should certainly not be underestimated. Similarly, the Commission's establishment and evaluation of the facts is not conclusive for the Court; but it would be mistaken for the Court, at yet one further remove from the evidence as given by the witnesses, to fail to give due weight to the report of the Commission, the body which is primarily charged under the Convention with the finding of facts and which has, of course, great experience in the discharge of that task.

[The dissenting judges disagree with the legal evaluations of the Court about the alleged failures of the United Kingdom and conclude:]

25. The accusation of a breach by a state of its obligation under Article 2 of the Convention to protect the right to life is of the utmost seriousness. For the reasons given above, the evaluation in paragraphs 203 to 213 of the judgment seems to us to fall well short of substantiating the finding that there has been a breach of the Article in this case. We ourselves follow the reasoning and conclusion of the Commission in its comprehensive, painstaking and notably realistic report. Like the Commission, we are satisfied that no failings have been shown in the organisation and control of the operation by the authorities which could justify a conclusion that force was used against the suspects disproportionately to the purpose of defending innocent persons from unlawful violence. We consider that the use of lethal force in this case, however regrettable the need to resort to such force may be, did not exceed what was, in the circumstances as known at the time, "absolutely necessary" for that purpose and did not amount to a breach by the United Kingdom of its obligations under the Convention.

NOTES AND QUESTIONS

1. *European Human Rights Law*. The European Court of Human Rights in Strasbourg, France, can be described as an "international court" in at least two ways. Constitutionally, the Court is established by a treaty: the 1950 European Convention for the Protection of Human Rights and Fundamental Freedoms, 213 U.N.T.S. 221 (signed at Rome November 4, 1950; entered into force September 3, 1953). More about treaties is found in Chapter 2. We consider international adjudication in Chapter 5. Substantively, the rules the Court applies are international law: human rights norms made and protected by the same European Human Rights Convention. As of 2013, some 47 European countries were parties to the European Human Rights Convention and subject to Strasbourg's jurisdiction. The structure and substance of European human rights law are more fully explored in Chapter 6. Also see Mark W. Janis, Richard S. Kay & Anthony W. Bradley, *European Human Rights Law* (3d ed. 2008); Robin C.A. White &

Clare Ovey, *Jacobs, White & Ovey, The European Convention on Human Rights* (5th ed. 2010). For more on *McCann* and other cases relating to terrorism from the European Court of Human Rights, see John Hedigan, "The European Convention on Human Rights and Counter-Terrorism," 28 *Fordham International Law Journal* 392 (2005).

2. *The Nature of Treaties.* In *McCann*, the European Court of Human Rights applied a substantive rule drawn from the 1950 European Human Rights Convention: Article 2 protecting the right to life. The ordinary theory explaining the legally binding effect of an international agreement is that a sovereign state may exercise its sovereignty not only by making domestic law but also by making international law. Hence, Article 2 obliges the United Kingdom in international law because of the U.K.'s own consent.

In this way, the European Convention on Human Rights resembles an international contract among states, but the Convention may also be said to resemble an international statute in that it provides a generally applicable set of rules for all its member states. This helps explain why states are considered to be not only the legislators of international law but also subjects of international law. Of course, since states are sovereign, multilateral treaties, unlike municipal statutes, do not bind non-parties. We consider the nature of the sovereign state in Chapter 7.

3. McCann *and the Court of Public Opinion.* When the British government, then the Conservative government of John Major, complied with the *McCann* judgment and paid the sums ordered by the European Court of Human Rights, it was condemned in the British media. The *Daily Mail*, for example, gave the payment its main headline: "£40,000 PRESENT FOR IRA FAMILIES." *Daily Mail* (London), Dec. 27, 1995, at 1. The front-page story began as follows: "The Government handed a Christmas gift of nearly £40,000 to relatives of three IRA terrorists." *Id.* The article said that members of the House of Commons "branded the decision 'appalling' and 'unthinkable' " and that the "[f]amilies of IRA victims were also horrified." *Id.* The *Times* took a more nuanced position, noting that "[o]nly certain aspects of the [Gibraltar] operation have been condemned in this judgment," but still remarking that the "cost of denying the IRA the status of an army is to swallow hard when a continental court wags its finger." *The Times* (London), Sept. 28, 1995, at 21.

4. *The Efficacy of International Law.* The British government was originally reluctant to pay the *McCann* judgment. The Prime Minister "had hinted that the Gibraltar case and other setbacks suffered by the United Kingdom before the European Court might cause it to withdraw from the convention." John Cary Sims, "Compliance Without Remands: The Experience under the European Convention on Human Rights," 36 *Arizona State Law Journal* 639, 650 (2004). Why in the end did the U.K. government satisfy the Strasbourg Court's judgment? What "sanction" could have been applied against the U.K. if the government had failed to comply with the ruling? Why should a sovereign state like the United Kingdom voluntarily comply with an international court judgment like *McCann*? What would the

United Kingdom lose if it were to be expelled from other European institutions for failure to comply with decisions of the European Court of Human Rights? Could the United Kingdom expect other states to comply with the Convention if it repudiated the Court's judgment? Would repudiation spoil the U.K.'s reputation and make it more difficult for the government to conclude treaties in the future?

The many European countries that are parties to the European Convention on Human Rights have their own domestic legal rules and processes protecting human rights. Why should they also enter into an international legal system establishing European rules about human rights and setting up European institutions to enforce those rules? How close are the European Court of Human Rights and European human rights law in form and substance to the U.S. Supreme Court and U.S. constitutional law, especially the Bill of Rights?

FILARTIGA V. PENA-IRALA

630 F.2d 876 (2d Cir. 1980)

IRVING R. KAUFMAN, CIRCUIT JUDGE:

Upon ratification of the Constitution, the thirteen former colonies were fused into a single nation, one which, in its relations with foreign states, is bound both to observe and construe the accepted norms of international law, formerly known as the law of nations. Under the Articles of Confederation, the several states had interpreted and applied this body of doctrine as a part of their common law, but with the founding of the "more perfect Union" of 1789, the law of nations became preeminently a federal concern.

Implementing the constitutional mandate for national control over foreign relations, the First Congress established original district court jurisdiction over "all causes where an alien sues for a tort only [committed] in violation of the law of nations." Judiciary Act of 1789, ch. 20, § 9(b), 1 Stat. 73, 77 (1789), *codified at* 28 U.S.C. § 1350. Construing this rarely-invoked provision, we hold that deliberate torture perpetrated under color of official authority violates universally accepted norms of the international law of human rights, regardless of the nationality of the parties. Thus, whenever an alleged torturer is found and served with process by an alien within our borders, § 1350 provides federal jurisdiction. Accordingly, we reverse the judgment of the district court dismissing the complaint for want of federal jurisdiction.

I

The appellants, plaintiffs below, are citizens of the Republic of Paraguay. Dr. Joel Filartiga, a physician, describes himself as a longstanding opponent of the government of President Alfredo Stroessner, which has held power in Paraguay since 1954. His daughter, Dolly

Filartiga, arrived in the United States in 1978 under a visitor's visa, and has since applied for permanent political asylum. The Filartigas brought this action in the Eastern District of New York against Americo Norberto Pena-Irala (Pena), also a citizen of Paraguay, for wrongfully causing the death of Dr. Filartiga's seventeen-year old son, Joelito. Because the district court dismissed the action for want of subject matter jurisdiction, we must accept as true the allegations contained in the Filartigas' complaint and affidavits for purposes of this appeal.

The appellants contend that on March 29, 1976, Joelito Filartiga was kidnapped and tortured to death by Pena, who was then Inspector General of Police in Asuncion, Paraguay. Later that day, the police brought Dolly Filartiga to Pena's home where she was confronted with the body of her brother, which evidenced marks of severe torture. As she fled, horrified, from the house, Pena followed after her shouting, "Here you have what you have been looking for so long and what you deserve. Now shut up." The Filartigas claim that Joelito was tortured and killed in retaliation for his father's political activities and beliefs.

Shortly thereafter, Dr. Filartiga commenced a criminal action in the Paraguayan courts against Pena and the police for the murder of his son. As a result, Dr. Filartiga's attorney was arrested and brought to police headquarters where, shackled to a wall, Pena threatened him with death. This attorney, it is alleged, has since been disbarred without just cause.

During the course of the Paraguayan criminal proceeding, which is apparently still pending after four years, another man, Hugo Duarte, confessed to the murder. Duarte, who was a member of the Pena household, claimed that he had discovered his wife and Joelito *in flagrante delicto*, and that the crime was one of passion. The Filartigas have submitted a photograph of Joelito's corpse showing injuries they believe refute this claim. Dolly Filartiga, moreover, has stated that she will offer evidence of three independent autopsies demonstrating that her brother's death "was the result of professional methods of torture." Despite his confession, Duarte, we are told, has never been convicted or sentenced in connection with the crime.

In July of 1978, Pena sold his house in Paraguay and entered the United States under a visitor's visa. He was accompanied by Juana Bautista Fernandez Villalba, who had lived with him in Paraguay. The couple remained in the United States beyond the term of their visas, and were living in Brooklyn, New York, when Dolly Filartiga, who was then living in Washington, D.C., learned of their presence. Acting on information provided by Dolly the Immigration and Naturalization Service arrested Pena and his companion, both of whom were subsequently ordered deported on April 5, 1979 following a hearing. They had then resided in the United States for more than nine months.

Almost immediately, Dolly caused Pena to be served with a summons and civil complaint at the Brooklyn Navy Yard, where he was being held pending deportation. The complaint alleged that Pena had wrongfully caused Joelito's death by torture and sought compensatory and punitive damages of $10,000,000. The Filartigas also sought to enjoin Pena's deportation to ensure his availability for testimony at trial. The cause of action is stated as arising under "wrongful death statutes; the U.N. Charter, the Universal Declaration on Human Rights; the U.N. Declaration Against Torture; the American Declaration of the Rights and Duties of Man; and other pertinent declarations, documents and practices constituting the customary international law of human rights and the law of nations," as well as 28 U.S.C. § 1350, Article II, sec. 2 and the Supremacy Clause of the U.S. Constitution. Jurisdiction is claimed under the general federal question provision, 28 U.S.C. § 1331 and, principally on this appeal, under the Alien Tort Statute, 28 U.S.C. § 1350.

* * * The Filartigas submitted the affidavits of a number of distinguished international legal scholars, who stated unanimously that the law of nations prohibits absolutely the use of torture as alleged in the complaint.[4] Pena, in support of his motion to dismiss on the ground of *forum non conveniens*, submitted the affidavit of his Paraguayan counsel, Jose Emilio Gorostiaga, who averred that Paraguayan law provides a full and adequate civil remedy for the wrong alleged. Dr. Filartiga has not commenced such an action, however, believing that further resort to the courts of his own country would be futile. * * *

The district court continued the stay of deportation for forty-eight hours while appellants applied for further stays. These applications were denied by a panel of this Court on May 22, 1979, and by the Supreme Court two days later. Shortly thereafter, Pena and his companion returned to Paraguay.

II

Appellants rest their principal argument in support of federal jurisdiction upon the Alien Tort Statute, 28 U.S.C. § 1350, which provides: "The district courts shall have original jurisdiction of any civil

[4] Richard Falk, the Albert G. Milbank Professor of International Law and Practice at Princeton University, and a former Vice President of the American Society of International Law, avers that, in his judgment, "it is now beyond reasonable doubt that torture of a person held in detention that results in severe harm or death is a violation of the law of nations." Thomas Franck, professor of international law at New York University and Director of the New York University Center for International Studies offers his opinion that torture has now been rejected by virtually all nations, although it was once commonly used to extract confessions. Richard Lillich, the Howard W. Smith Professor of Law at the University of Virginia School of Law, concludes, after a lengthy review of the authorities, that officially perpetrated torture is "a violation of international law (formerly called the law of nations)." Finally, Myres McDougal, a former Sterling Professor of Law at the Yale Law School, and a past President of the American Society of International Law, states that torture is an offense against the law of nations, and that "it has long been recognized that such offenses vitally affect relations between states."

action by an alien for a tort only, committed in violation of the law of nations or a treaty of the United States." Since appellants do not contend that their action arises directly under a treaty of the United States, a threshold question on the jurisdictional issue is whether the conduct alleged violates the law of nations. In light of the universal condemnation of torture in numerous international agreements, and the renunciation of torture as an instrument of official policy by virtually all of the nations of the world (in principle if not in practice), we find that an act of torture committed by a state official against one held in detention violates established norms of the international law of human rights, and hence the law of nations.

The Supreme Court has enumerated the appropriate sources of international law. The law of nations "may be ascertained by consulting the works of jurists, writing professedly on public law; or by the general usage and practice of nations; or by judicial decisions recognizing and enforcing that law." *United States v. Smith*, 18 U.S. (5 Wheat.) 153, 160–61 (1820); *Lopes v. Reederei Richard Schroder*, 225 F.Supp. 292, 295 (E.D.Pa.1963). In *Smith*, a statute proscribing "the crime of piracy [on the high seas] as defined by the law of nations," 3 Stat. 510(a) (1819), was held sufficiently determinate in meaning to afford the basis for a death sentence. The *Smith* Court discovered among the works of Lord Bacon, Grotius, Bochard and other commentators a genuine consensus that rendered the crime "sufficiently and constitutionally defined." *Smith*, *supra*, 18 U.S. (5 Wheat.) at 162.

The Paquete Habana, 175 U.S. 677 (1900), reaffirmed that

> where there is no treaty, and no controlling executive or legislative act or judicial decision, resort must be had to the customs and usages of civilized nations; and, as evidence of these, to the works of jurists and commentators, who by years of labor, research and experience, have made themselves peculiarly well acquainted with the subjects of which they treat. Such works are resorted to by judicial tribunals, not for the speculations of their authors concerning what the law ought to be, but for trustworthy evidence of what the law really is.

Id. at 700. Modern international sources confirm the propriety of this approach. * * *

The United Nations Charter (a treaty of the United States, *see* 59 Stat. 1033 (1945)) makes it clear that in this modern age a state's treatment of its own citizens is a matter of international concern. It provides:

> With a view to the creation of conditions of stability and well-being which are necessary for peaceful and friendly relations among nations ... the United Nations shall promote ...

> universal respect for, and observance of, human rights and fundamental freedoms for all without distinctions as to race, sex, language or religion.

Id. Art. 55. And further:

> All members pledge themselves to take joint and separate action in cooperation with the Organization for the achievement of the purposes set forth in Article 55.

Id. Art. 56.

While this broad mandate has been held not to be wholly self-executing, *Hitai v. Immigration and Naturalization Service*, 343 F.2d 466, 468 (2d Cir. 1965), this observation alone does not end our inquiry. For although there is no universal agreement as to the precise extent of the "human rights and fundamental freedoms" guaranteed to all by the Charter, there is at present no dissent from the view that the guaranties include, at a bare minimum, the right to be free from torture. This prohibition has become part of customary international law, as evidenced and defined by the Universal Declaration of Human Rights, General Assembly Resolution 217(III)(A) (Dec. 10, 1948) which states, in the plainest of terms, "no one shall be subjected to torture."[10] The General Assembly has declared that the Charter precepts embodied in this Universal Declaration "constitute basic principles of international law." G.A.Res. 2625 (XXV) (Oct. 24, 1970).

Particularly relevant is the Declaration on the Protection of All Persons from Being Subjected to Torture, General Assembly Resolution 3452, 30 U.N. GAOR Supp. (No. 34) 91, U.N.Doc. A/1034 (1975)[.] The Declaration expressly prohibits any state from permitting the dastardly and totally inhuman act of torture. Torture, in turn, is defined as "any act by which severe pain and suffering, whether physical or mental, is intentionally inflicted by or at the instigation of a public official on a person for such purposes as . . . intimidating him or other persons." The Declaration goes on to provide that "[w]here it is proved that an act of torture or other cruel, inhuman or degrading treatment or punishment has been committed by or at the instigation of a public official, the victim shall be afforded redress and compensation, in accordance with national law." This Declaration, like the Declaration of Human Rights before it, was adopted without dissent by the General Assembly. Nayar, "Human Rights: The United Nations and United States Foreign Policy," 19 *Harv. Int'l L.J.* 813, 816 n.18 (1978).

These U.N. declarations are significant because they specify with great precision the obligations of member nations under the Charter. Since their adoption, "[m]embers can no longer contend that they do not

---

[10] Eighteen nations have incorporated the Universal Declaration into their own constitutions. 48 *Revue Internationale de Droit Penal* Nos. 3 & 4, at 211 (1977).

know what human rights they promised in the Charter to promote." Sohn, "A Short History of United Nations Documents on Human Rights," in *"The United Nations and Human Rights," 18th Report of the Commission* (Commission to Study the Organization of Peace ed. 1968). Moreover, a U.N. Declaration is, according to one authoritative definition, "a formal and solemn instrument, suitable for rare occasions when principles of great and lasting importance are being enunciated." 34 U.N. ESCOR, Supp. (No. 8) 15, U.N. Doc. E/cn.4/1/610 (1962) (memorandum of Office of Legal Affairs, U.N. Secretariat). Accordingly, it has been observed that the Universal Declaration of Human Rights "no longer fits into the dichotomy of 'binding treaty' against 'nonbinding pronouncement,' but is rather an authoritative statement of the international community." *E. Schwelb, Human Rights and the International Community* 70 (1964). Thus, a Declaration creates an expectation of adherence, and "insofar as the expectation is gradually justified by State practice, a declaration may by custom become recognized as laying down rules binding upon the States." 34 U.N. ESCOR, *supra.* Indeed, several commentators have concluded that the Universal Declaration has become, *in toto*, a part of binding, customary international law. Nayar, *supra*, at 816–17; Waldock, "Human Rights in Contemporary International Law and the Significance of the European Convention," *Int'l & Comp. L.Q.*, Supp. Publ. No. 11 at 15 (1965).

Turning to the act of torture, we have little difficulty discerning its universal renunciation in the modern usage and practice of nations. *Smith*, *supra*, 18 U.S. (5 Wheat.) at 160–61. The international consensus surrounding torture has found expression in numerous international treaties and accords. *E.g.*, *American Convention on Human Rights*, Art. 5, OAS Treaty Series No. 36 at 1, OAS Off. Rec. OEA/Ser 4 v/II 23, doc. 21, rev. 2 (English ed., 1975) ("No one shall be subjected to torture or to cruel, inhuman or degrading punishment or treatment"); International Covenant on Civil and Political Rights, U.N. General Assembly Res. 2200 (XXI)A, U.N. Doc. A/6316 (Dec. 16, 1966) (identical language); European Convention for the Protection of Human Rights and Fundamental Freedoms, Art. 3, Council of Europe, European Treaty Series No. 5 (1968), 213 U.N.T.S. 211 (*semble*). The substance of these international agreements is reflected in modern municipal—*i.e.* national—law as well. Although torture was once a routine concomitant of criminal interrogations in many nations, during the modern and hopefully more enlightened era it has been universally renounced. According to one survey, torture is prohibited, expressly or implicitly, by the constitutions of over fifty-five nations, including both the United States and Paraguay. Our State Department reports a general recognition of this principle:

> There now exists an international consensus that recognizes basic human rights and obligations owed by all governments to their citizens. . . . There is no doubt that these rights are often

> violated; but virtually all governments acknowledge their validity.

Department of State, *Country Reports on Human Rights for 1979*, published as Joint Comm. Print, House Comm. on Foreign Affairs, and Senate Comm. on Foreign Relations, 96th Cong. 2d Sess. (Feb. 4, 1980), Introduction at 1. We have been directed to no assertion by any contemporary state of a right to torture its own or another nation's citizens. Indeed, United States diplomatic contacts confirm the universal abhorrence with which torture is viewed:

> In exchanges between United States embassies and all foreign states with which the United States maintains relations, it has been the Department of State's general experience that no government has asserted a right to torture its own nationals. Where reports of torture elicit some credence, a state usually responds by denial or, less frequently, by asserting that the conduct was unauthorized or constituted rough treatment short of torture.[15]

Memorandum of the United States as *Amicus Curiae* at 16 n.34.

Having examined the sources from which customary international law is derived—the usage of nations, judicial opinions and the works of jurists[16]—we conclude that official torture is now prohibited by the law of nations. The prohibition is clear and unambiguous, and admits of no distinction between treatment of aliens and citizens. Accordingly, we must conclude that the dictum in *Dreyfus v. Von Finck*, [534 F.2d 24, 31 (2d Cir.), *cert. denied,* 429 U.S. 835 (1976)], to the effect that "violations of international law do not occur when the aggrieved parties are nationals of the acting state," is clearly out of tune with the current usage and practice of international law. The treaties and accords cited above, as well as the express foreign policy of our own government, all make it clear that international law confers fundamental rights upon all people vis-á-vis their own governments. While the ultimate scope of those rights will be a subject for continuing refinement and elaboration, we hold that the right to be free from torture is now among them. * * *

[15] The fact that the prohibition of torture is often honored in the breach does not diminish its binding effect as a norm of international law. As one commentator has put it, "The best evidence for the existence of international law is that every actual State recognizes that it does exist and that it is itself under an obligation to observe it. States often violate international law, just as individuals often violate municipal law; but no more than individuals do States defend their violations by claiming that they are above the law." J. Brierly, *The Outlook for International Law* 4–5 (Oxford 1944).

[16] *See also Ireland v. United Kingdom*, Judgment of Jan. 18, 1978 (European Court of Human Rights), *summarized in* [1978] Yearbook, European Convention on Human Rights 602 (Council of Europe) (holding that Britain's subjection of prisoners to sleep deprivation, hooding, exposure to hissing noise, reduced diet and standing against a wall for hours was "inhuman and degrading," but not "torture" within meaning of European Convention on Human Rights).

IV * * *

In the twentieth century the international community has come to recognize the common danger posed by the flagrant disregard of basic human rights and particularly the right to be free of torture. Spurred first by the Great War, and then the Second, civilized nations have banded together to prescribe acceptable norms of international behavior. From the ashes of the Second World War arose the United Nations Organization, amid hopes that an era of peace and cooperation had at last begun. Though many of these aspirations have remained elusive goals, that circumstance cannot diminish the true progress that has been made. In the modern age, humanitarian and practical considerations have combined to lead the nations of the world to recognize that respect for fundamental human rights is in their individual and collective interest. Among the rights universally proclaimed by all nations, as we have noted, is the right to be free of physical torture. Indeed, for purposes of civil liability, the torturer has become—like the pirate and slave trader before him—*hostis humani generis*, an enemy of all mankind. Our holding today, giving effect to a jurisdictional provision enacted by our First Congress, is a small but important step in the fulfillment of the ageless dream to free all people from brutal violence.

NOTES AND QUESTIONS

1. *Individuals as Subjects of International Law. Filartiga* involved international human rights claims of Paraguayan citizens against an official of the government of Paraguay. *McCann* concerned individuals' international human rights claims against the U.K. government. Why in principle and practice should either the Paraguayan or U.K. government be subject to international law rules or process with respect to complaints by their own or foreign nationals?

J.L. Brierly in his classic British introduction to international law defined the discipline "as the body of rules and principles of action which are binding upon civilized states in their relations with one another." J.L. Brierly, *The Law of Nations* 1 (4th ed. 1949). How well does Brierly's definition describe the law the rules of which were actually applied in *Filartiga* and *McCann*? How might this definition be reformulated in the light of these two cases where individual rights in international law are in issue? More about individual rights under international law is in Chapter 6.

2. *States as Subjects of International Legal Process.* In *McCann*, the United Kingdom was subject to the jurisdiction of the European Court of Human Rights because it had signed and ratified an international convention formally and explicitly accepting the jurisdiction of the Court. Furthermore, in accordance with the terms of the treaty the U.K. government had itself submitted the dispute to the Court for judgment. In *Filartiga* why should Paraguayan government officials be subject to the jurisdiction of United States federal courts in New York? If it appeared unlikely that the

government of Paraguay would permit the Filartigas to sue in Paraguayan courts, would it be likely that the Paraguayan courts would respect or enforce a U.S. judgment in favor of the Filartigas? More on conflict and cooperation among national legal systems is found in Chapters 11 and 12.

3. *Perspectives on Litigating International Human Rights Law.* Each of the participants in *Filartiga* had a particular perspective on the case. Why did the Filartigas bring the case in a U.S. court? In some cases it was possible for litigants like the Filartigas to win significant monetary damages to redress violations of international law. Professor Murphy pointed out that at one point in time in Alien Tort Claims Act litigation "the chances for a successful civil suit were substantially greater than those for a successful criminal prosecution." John F. Murphy, "Civil Liability for the Commission of International Crimes as an Alternative to Criminal Prosecution," 12 *Harvard Human Rights Journal* 1, 47 (1999). So too for claims against "perpetrators of international terrorism." John F. Murphy, "Civil Lawsuits as a Legal Response to International Terrorism," in *Civil Litigation Against Terrorism* 37, 44 (John Norton Moore ed. 2004). Probably, the Filartigas' battle was more about political goals and public recognition of their cause than actually to win monetary damages. Roberts B. Owen, the Legal Adviser to the U.S. Department of State at the time of the case, viewed Dr. Filartiga as "one of the leading political opponents of the present [Paraguayan] regime." Roberts B. Owen, "Address at the Annual Dinner of the American Branch of the International Law Association, the Princeton Club, New York City, November 14, 1980," *Proceedings and Committee Reports of the American Branch of the International Law Association 1981–1982*, at 14.

Owen also described how lawyers for the U.S. government were divided about what side to take in *Filartiga*, some feeling that there was "a consensus that customary international law now imposes upon every government an obligation to refrain from torture" and others concerned that "our courts and our government would gradually become self-appointed policemen for the world." *Id.* at 16. Finally, "after much soul-searching and debate," the U.S. government chose to file its *amicus* brief for the plaintiff's position, Owen agreeing "that it is a good thing for the U.S. courts to be available to provide remedies for persons aggrieved by violations of internationally protected rights." *Id.* When the U.S. government fails to take foreign opinion into account, the United States can lose some of its ability to influence world politics. See Joseph S. Nye, Jr., "The Decline of America's Soft Power: Why Washington Should Worry," 83 *Foreign Affairs*, May/June 2004, at 16.

Over and above his judgment, Judge Kaufman had strong views about the case. He authored an article on *Filartiga* in which he wrote that "the decision breaks new ground in the body of law governing torture." Irving R. Kaufman, "A Legal Remedy for International Torture?," *New York Times Magazine*, Nov. 9, 1980, at 44. Several years later he chose *Filartiga* to conclude an article about his judicial career. Irving R. Kaufman, "The Anatomy of Decisionmaking," 53 *Fordham Law Review* 1, 20–22 (1984). Others, too, soon underlined the importance of *Filartiga*. See, for example,

Gabriel M. Wilner, "*Filartiga v. Peña-Irala*: Comments on Sources of Human Rights Law and Means of Redress for Violations of Human Rights," 11 *Georgia Journal of International and Comparative Law* 317 (1981). *Filartiga* was recognized as a "landmark legal precedent." Beth Stephens, "*Filartiga v. Peña-Irala*: From Family Tragedy to Human Rights Accountability," 37 *Rutgers Law Journal* 623 (2006). The case "triggered a sea change in international human rights litigation." Harold Hongju Koh, "*Filartiga v. Peña-Irala*: Judicial Internationalization into Domestic Law of the Customary International Law Norm Against Torture," in *International Law Stories* 45, 46 (John E. Noyes, Laura A. Dickinson & Mark W. Janis eds. 2007).

The lawyers who brought the *Filartiga* case hoped for just this. They explained that they turned to the Alien Tort Claims Act, "a little-used 200–year old statute," in their search for a way to give lawyers "the opportunity to establish that officials who violate the rights of their own citizens could be brought to justice in U.S. courts." After *Filartiga,* their goal "was to bring more cases, obtain more circuit court opinions in our favor and make the *Filartiga* principle unassailable." They plainly acknowledged that they were "political lawyers, [wanting] to use the *Filartiga* precedent to fight those who were violating human rights." Michael Ratner & Beth Stephens, "The Center for Constitutional Rights: Using Law and the *Filartiga* Principle in the Fight for Human Rights," in American Civil Liberties Union, *International Civil Liberties Report*, Dec. 1993, at 29. For an excellent account of the efforts made by the attorneys in *Filartiga*, see William J. Aceves, *The Anatomy of Torture: A Documentary History of Filartiga v. Pena-Irala* (2007). In general, for the relation between municipal courts and international law, see Chapter 4.

4. *The Fate of* Filartiga. On its facts, would *Filartiga* be decided the same way today? The first significant holding of the Supreme Court on the Alien Tort Claims Act, Sosa v. Alvarez-Machain, 542 U.S. 692 (2004), seemed to preserve a *Filartiga*-like cause of action. However, a second Supreme Court ATCA judgment, Kiobel v. Royal Dutch Petroleum Co., 133 S.Ct. 1659 (2013), raised doubts about whether the territorial linkages of a case like *Filartiga* would nowadays satisfy the Court's presumption against the extraterritorial application of a U.S. statute. We consider both *Sosa* and *Kiobel* and their implications in Chapter 4.

5. *The Nature of Customary International Law*. Whatever the eventual outcome of the Supreme Court's test about the extraterritorial reach of the Alien Tort Claims Act, *Filartiga* remains an excellent introduction to the nature of customary international law. In theory, at least, customary international law is developed as a result of the actual practice of states. If the Paraguayan government and other governments do actually torture their own citizens, how can there be a rule of customary international law proscribing such practice? Is the court in *Filartiga* truly applying customary international law, or is it perhaps finding and applying rules drawn from

some sort of fundamental international law, an international human rights law analogous to municipal constitutional guarantees of human rights?

Note the diverse evidences of international law employed by the *Filartiga* court in deciding that international law prohibits torture. Did the court give any one kind of evidence primacy over the others? Did some evidences seem more or less persuasive? Did the judgment demonstrate that Paraguay has consented to the rule prohibiting torture or only that the community of nations generally supports such a rule? Chapter 3 further explores customary international law and the various non-consensual sources of international law, such as *jus cogens*.

6. *The Efficacy of International Law*. Although one might assume that national courts, like the United States federal courts, are usually more efficacious than international courts, here the expectation was reversed in practice. Though the decision of the international court in *McCann* was respected, the decisions of the national courts in *Filartiga* were not. On remand, the district court imposed a judgment for $10,385,364 against Pena-Irala in order "to reflect adherence to the world community's proscription of torture and to attempt to deter its practice," 577 F.Supp. 860, 867 (E.D.N.Y.1984), but these damages were never paid.

Nonetheless, *Filartiga* had considerable effect as a judicial precedent, spawning many subsequent cases in U.S. courts. The jurisdiction of the Alien Tort Claims Act grew to reach not only individual actors, but also governments and private corporations. Plaintiffs included non-governmental organizations as well as individuals. Moreover, courts in other countries, including Spain, the Netherlands, and the United Kingdom, followed in *Filartiga*'s wake. Association of the Bar of the City of New York, Panel, "The Making of *Filartiga v. Peña*: The Alien Tort Claims Act After Twenty-Five Years," 9 *New York City Law Review* 249, 267–73 (2006).

7. *The Organization of the Book*. The international rules, processes, and actors introduced in the international law sampler cases, *McCann* and *Filartiga,* are explored in more depth below. Chapter 2 examines treaties. Chapter 3 turns to customary international law and other sources of international law such as general principles of law, natural law, *jus cogens*, and equity. Chapter 4 considers the role of national courts in applying international law. Chapter 5 discusses public international arbitration and the International Court of Justice. The later chapters in the book deal with various actors involved with and some of the substantive issues addressed by international law: Chapter 6 the protection of individuals (including European human rights law); Chapter 7 the rights, duties, and relations of sovereign states; Chapter 8 international organizations, and especially the United Nations; Chapter 9 the use of force; Chapter 10 the law of the sea; Chapter 11 international conflict of laws; and Chapter 12 foreign law and foreign governments.

CHAPTER 2

TREATIES

■ ■ ■

The primary focus of this chapter is on treaties, very important for international lawyers. Treaties are one of the major sources of international law. The notion of sources is introduced in Part A. Treaties number in the tens of thousands and address virtually every area of human endeavor. Part B of this chapter reproduces several treaties, indicating something of their variety and raising questions about how and why they are made. Part C then addresses aspects of the law of treaties, a body of rules about the making, interpretation, and termination of treaties. The Vienna Convention on the Law of Treaties, which is often consulted on such rules, is reproduced in the Appendix of this book.

A. THE SOURCES OF INTERNATIONAL LAW

The term "sources" can be used in at least two ways when referring to the sources of international law. One way is to think of a *material source* of an international rule: the place one looks to actually read a rule of international law. So, for example, any given treaty may prescribe a specific legal obligation, *e.g.*, the United Nations Charter provides in Article 2(4) that "All Members shall refrain in their international relations from the threat or use of force against the territorial integrity or political independence of any State, or in any other manner inconsistent with the Purposes of the United Nations."

A second way to think about a source of international law is as a *formal source*, that is, a fashion in which international lawyers, judges, and jurists agree that international law may be made. The notion of a formal source of international law is related to ideas in the philosophy of law about rules of recognition and validating norms. For any legal system to function effectively in practice, the participants in that system must agree on what counts as a legal rule and what does not. An ordinary starting point for international lawyers from most any part of the globe when thinking about the formal sources of international law is Article 38 of the Statute of the International Court of Justice.

STATUTE OF THE INTERNATIONAL COURT OF JUSTICE, ARTICLE 38

June 26, 1945, 59 Stat. 1031, T.S. No. 993

1. The Court, whose function is to decide in accordance with international law such disputes as are submitted to it, shall apply:

(a) international conventions, whether general or particular, establishing rules expressly recognized by the contesting States;

(b) international custom, as evidence of a general practice accepted as law;

(c) the general principles of law recognized by civilized nations;

(d) subject to the provisions of Article 59, judicial decisions and the teachings of the most highly qualified publicists of the various nations, as subsidiary means for the determination of rules of law.

2. This provision shall not prejudice the power of the Court to decide a case *ex aequo et bono*, if the parties agree thereto.

NOTES AND QUESTIONS

1. *Sources Not Listed in Article 38.* Article 38 of the ICJ Statute is often taken to be a listing of the sources of international law, but note the following reservations. First, Article 38 nowhere mentions "sources." Strictly speaking, Article 38 is an instruction only to the judges of the International Court; it does not by its terms apply to other international courts or lawyers. Second, in practice, judges on other tribunals (and even sometimes those on the ICJ itself) and other practicing international lawyers do use other sources of international law than those listed in Article 38, *e.g.*, natural law, equitable principles, *jus cogens*, and the resolutions of international organizations. These other sources of international law are considered alongside customary international law and the general principles of law in Chapter 3.

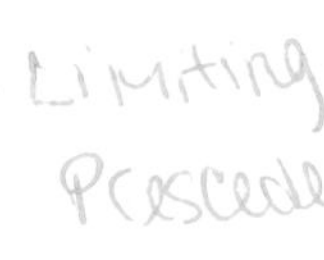

2. *Judicial Decisions as Sources of International Law.* Article 38(1)(d) refers to Article 59, which reads: "The decision of the Court has no binding force except between the parties and in respect of that particular case." This language seems to be meant to limit any inference that the reference to "judicial decisions" allows judicial precedent itself to be a source of international law. Although judicial precedent is quite an ordinary source of law in common law legal systems like those in the United States and England, many civil law legal systems formally restrict the judicial role to merely applying the law. As we shall see in Chapter 3 and throughout the book, Article 59 has, however, not prevented the International Court from relying heavily on its own past decisions as a guide in finding customary international law.

3. Ex Aequo et Bono. Article 38(2) allows the Court to decide *ex aequo et bono*, by what is equal and good, if the parties agree, but there has never been such agreement. Neither the International Court of Justice nor its predecessor, the Permanent Court of International Justice, has ever played an *ex aequo et bono* role in over 90 years. Article 38(2) has, however, caused problems for the Court's use of equity, a topic also explored in Chapter 3.

4. *The Hierarchy of the Sources of International Law*. Are treaties the primary source of international law? Partly because "international conventions" are listed first in Article 38(1), the judges of the ICJ and other international lawyers have often given treaties pride of place among the sources of international law. There are other reasons too for thinking of treaties as primary among the rules of international law. Treaties ordinarily clearly show the legal rule because they are in written form. Moreover, treaties are subject to the explicit acceptance of states. Treaties therefore can often be clearer in their terms and more certain in their acceptance than other sorts of international law sources. Furthermore, since the 19th century treaties have been widely used by states. Many areas that used to be the province of customary international law, *e.g.*, the law of the sea and the law of treaties, have now been put into conventions. However, as we shall see here and in Chapter 3, treaties do not cover all topics in international law, nor do they include all states as parties. Sometimes treaties may even be trumped by other forms of international law, especially natural law or *jus cogens*, and they always need to be interpreted in practice by judges or commentators who will use other sources of international law in their interpretations.

B. A TREATY SAMPLER

The conclusion of treaties between nations is a natural feature of human society. For as long as there have been written records, there have been international compacts. The six sample agreements excerpted below span more than two thousand years. Among other things, they demonstrate the permanence of treaties as part of the human experience. They also introduce treaties as vehicles for: (1) forming military and political alliances; (2) peace-making; (3) creating new states; (4) exchanging territory; and (5) controlling international violence. Today, as before, treaties constitute the most frequent sort of international law made in practice. The treaties below provide an idea of the actual "feel" and nature of international agreements.

THE TREATY BETWEEN THE JEWS AND THE ROMANS (CIRCA 160 B.C.)

1 Maccabees 8:1–29 (*Good News Bible with Deuterocanonicals/Apocrypha*)

Judas had heard about the Romans and their reputation as a military power. He knew that they welcomed all those who joined them as allies and that those who came to them could be sure of the friendship of

Rome. People had told him about the wars the Romans had fought and their heroic acts among the Gauls, whom they had conquered and forced to pay taxes. He had been told what they had done in Spain when they captured the silver mines and the gold mines there. By careful planning and persistence, they had conquered the whole country, even though it was far from Rome. They had overcome the kings from distant lands who had fought against them; they had defeated them so badly that the survivors had to pay annual taxes. They had fought and conquered Philip and Perseus, kings of Macedonia, and all who had joined them against Rome. They had even defeated Antiochus the Great, king of Syria, who had attacked them with 120 elephants, cavalry, chariots, and a powerful army. They took him alive and forced him and his successors to pay heavy taxes, to give hostages, and to surrender India, Media, Lydia, and some of their best lands. They took these and gave them to King Eumenes.

When the Greeks made plans to attack and destroy them, the Romans learned of the plans and sent a general to fight against them. The Romans killed many of the Greeks, took their wives and children captive, plundered their possessions, occupied their land, tore down their fortresses, and made them slaves, as they are today. They also destroyed or made slaves of other kingdoms, the islands, and everyone who had ever fought against them. But they maintained their friendship with their allies and those who relied on them for protection. They conquered kings near and far, and everyone who heard of their reputation was afraid of them. They helped some men to become kings, while they deposed others; they had become a world power. In spite of all this, no Roman ever tried to advance his own position by wearing a crown or putting on royal robes. They created a senate, and each day 320 senators came together to deliberate about the affairs of the people and their well-being. Each year they entrusted to one man the responsibility of governing them and controlling their whole territory. Everyone obeyed this one man, and there was no envy or jealousy among them.

Judas chose Eupolemus, the son of John and grandson of Accos, and Jason son of Eleazar and sent them to Rome to make a treaty of friendship and alliance with the Romans. He did this to eliminate Syrian oppression, since the Jews clearly saw that they were being reduced to slavery. After a long and difficult journey, Eupolemus and Jason reached Rome and entered the Senate. They addressed the assembly in these terms: "Judas Maccabeus, his brothers, and the Jewish people have sent us here to make a mutual defense treaty with you, so that we may be officially recorded as your friends and allies."

The Romans accepted the proposal, and what follows is a copy of the letter which was engraved on bronze tablets and sent to Jerusalem to remain there as a record of the treaty:

May things go well forever for the Romans and for the Jewish nation on land and sea! May they never have enemies, and may they never go to war! But if war is declared first against Rome or any of her allies anywhere, the Jewish nation will come to her aid with whole-hearted support, as the situation may require. And to those at war with her, the Jews shall not give or supply food, arms, money, or ships, as was agreed in Rome. The Jews must carry out their obligations without receiving anything in return.

In the same way, if war is declared first against the Jewish nation, the Romans will come to their aid with hearty support, as the situation may require. And to their enemies there shall not be given or supplied food, arms, money, or ships, as was agreed in Rome. The Romans must carry out their obligations without deception.

These are the terms of the treaty that the Romans have made with the Jewish people.

NOTES AND QUESTIONS

1. *The Historical Permanence of Treaties.* The Treaty Between the Jews and the Romans we have from the Bible, affirmed in historical sources. See Dov Gera, *Judaea and Mediterranean Politics 219 to 161 B.C.E.* 303–17 (1998). Despite its antiquity, this treaty of peace and alliance has quite a modern ring to it. Compare, for example, the North Atlantic Treaty, Apr. 4, 1949, T.I.A.S. No. 1964, 34 U.N.T.S. 243, which created the North Atlantic Treaty Organization to provide for the collective self-defense of its members.

2. *Reciprocity, Good Faith, and the Willingness to Conclude Treaties.* The first part of the extract is more or less its legislative history. What does it tell us about the reasons why the Jews sought a treaty? A modern author believes that the Jews may have wanted Rome's direct assistance, but they also likely "sought acceptance and respectability, and wanted to use their recognition by the most powerful country of the time to establish friendships with states closer to home, who would take their cue from the Roman attitude." Gera, *supra* Note 1, at 314. Why did the Romans consent?

How was the Treaty Between the Jews and the Romans to be enforced? If the Romans had not had a good record of respecting their treaty commitments, would the Jews have been as eager to enter into an alliance with them? Reciprocal good faith always seems to have been one of the key components in ensuring the obligatory force of treaties.

3. *In Written Form.* Why was it important that the Jewish-Roman treaty be in writing? Was it to make sure the terms were clear? Would it help ensure the continuing efficacy of the treaty after those who negotiated the agreement had passed from the scene? What could have been the disadvantages of an unwritten agreement?

4. *Religion and International Law.* The highly influential Dutch jurist Hugo de Groot (or Grotius) relied heavily on the Bible for his evidences of the law of nations in his seminal treatise of 1625, *De Jure Belli Ac Pacis, The Law of War and Peace.* Grotius cited a great number of treaties that were made between the Jews and their neighbors as proof for the proposition that treaties with those not believing in God were permitted. His other principal evidences were drawn from the great Greek and Roman classical authors. See Mark W. Janis, "Religion and the Literature of International Law: Some Standard Texts," in *Religion and International Law* 121, 124 (Mark W. Janis & Carolyn Evans eds. 1999).

5. *The Intertemporal Problem.* On the face of it, does the Treaty between the Jews and the Romans look to be part of "international law" as we now understand the concept? Would the Jews and the Romans have thought of the Treaty as creating "legal" obligations? How possible is it for people in one time or place to use terms and concepts common to peoples from other times and places? Questions like this are sometimes thought of as part of the intertemporal problem of international law. Questions of intertemporal law arise today in a variety of contexts, including cases concerning the acquisition of territory. See the *Minquiers and Ecrehos Case* in Chapter 5.

THE PEACE OF WESTPHALIA (1648)

1 Consolidated Treaty Series 198

A Treaty of Peace between the Empire *and* Sweden, *concluded and sign'd at* Osnabrug *the 24th of* October, 1648. *The King of* France *was comprehended in this Treaty as an Ally of* Sweden.

Be it known to all and singular whom it does concern, or whom it may in any manner concern, That after the Differences and Troubles which began several years ago in the *Roman* Empire, had come to such a height, that not only all *Germany*, but likewise some neighbouring Kingdoms, especially *Sweden* and *France*, found themselves so involv'd in them, that from thence there arose a long and cruel War[.] At last it fell out by an Effect of the Divine Bounty, that both sides turn'd their Thoughts towards the means of making Peace, and that by a mutual Agreement made at *Hamburg* the 25th of *December* N.S. [New Style, or Gregorian calendar] or the 15th O.S. [Old Style, or Julian calendar] 1641. between the Parties, the 11th N.S. or the 1st O.S. 1643. was by common Consent appointed for beginning the Assembly or Congress of Plenipotentiaries at *Osnabrug*, and at *Munster* in *Westphalia*.

* * * After having invok'd the Assistance of God, and reciprocally exchang'd the Originals of their respective full Powers, they transacted and agreed among themselves, to the Glory of God, and Safety of the Christian World (the Electors, Princes and States of the Sacred *Roman* Empire being present, approving and consenting) the Articles of Peace and Amity, whereof the Tenour follows.

THE RE-ESTABLISHMENT OF PEACE AND AMITY.

I. That there be a Christian, universal and perpetual Peace, and a true and sincere Friendship and Amity between his Sacred Imperial Majesty, the House of *Austria*, and all his Allies and Adherents, and the Heirs and Successors of each of them, chiefly the King of *Spain*, and the Electors, Princes and States of the Empire, of the one side; and her Sacred Royal Majesty, and the Kingdom of *Sweden*, her Allies and Adherents, and the Heirs and Successors of each of them, especially the most Christian King, the respective Electors, Princes and States of the Empire, of the other side; and that this Peace be observ'd and cultivated sincerely and seriously, so that each Party may procure the Benefit, Honour and Advantage of one another, and thereby the Fruits of this Peace and Amity may be seen to grow up and flourish anew, by a sure and reciprocal maintaining of a good and faithful Neighbourhood between the *Roman* Empire and the Kingdom of *Sweden* reciprocally.

AN AMNESTY FROM ALL HOSTILITY.

II. That there be on both sides a perpetual Oblivion and Amnesty of all that has been done since the beginning of these Troubles, in what Place or in what Manner soever Hostilities may have been exercis'd by the one or the other Party; so that neither for any of those things, nor upon any other Account or Pretext whatsoever, any Act of Hostility or Enmity, Vexation or Hindrance shall be exercis'd or suffer'd, or caus'd to be exercis'd, either as to Persons, Conditions, Goods or Security, either by one's self or by others, in private, or openly, directly or indirectly, under form of Right or Law, or by open Deed, either within, or in any Place whatsoever without the Empire, notwithstanding all former Compacts to the contrary; but that all Injuries, Violences, Hostilities and Damages, and all Expences that either side has been oblig'd to be at, as well before as during the War, and all Libels by Words or Writing shall be entirely forgotten, without any regard to Persons or Things; so that whatever might be demanded or pretended by one against the other upon this account, shall be bury'd in perpetual Oblivion. * * *

POINT OF ECCLESIASTICAL GRIEVANCES, OR OF RELIGION.

V. Now whereas the Grievances of the one and the other Religion, which were debated amongst the Electors, Princes and States of the Empire, have been partly the Cause and Occasion of the present War, it has been agreed and transacted in the following manner.

1. * * * That there be an exact and reciprocal Equality amongst all the Electors, Princes and States of both Religions[.]

LIBERTY OF CONSCIENCE.

28. It has moreover been found good, that those of the Confession of *Augsburg* [Protestants], who are Subjects of the Catholicks, and the Catholick Subjects of the States of the Confession of *Augsburg*, who had not the public or private Exercise of their religion in any time of the year 1624 and who after the Publication of the Peace shall possess and embrace a Religion different from that of the Lord of the Territory, shall in consequence of the said Peace be patiently suffer'd and tolerated, without any Hindrance or Impediment to attend their Devotions in their Houses and in private, with all Liberty of Conscience, and without any Inquisition or Trouble, and even to assist in their Neighbourhood, as often as they have a mind, at the publick Exercise of their Religion, or send their children to foreign Schools of their Religion, or have them instructed in their Families by private Masters; provided the said Vassals and Subjects do their Duty in all other things, and hold themselves in due Obedience and Subjection, without giving occasion to any Disturbance or Commotion. In like manner Subjects, whether they be Catholicks, or of the Confession of *Augsburg*, shall not be despis'd any where upon account of their Religion, nor excluded from the Community of Merchants, Artizans or Companies, nor depriv'd of Successions, Legacies, Hospitals, Lazar-Houses, or Alms-Houses, and other Privileges or Rights, and far less of Church-yards, and the Honour of Burial; nor shall any more be exacted of them for the Expence of their Funerals, than the Dues usually paid for Burying–Places in Parish-Churches: so that in these and all other the like things they shall be treated in the same manner as Brethren and Sisters, with equal Justice and Protection. * * *

THE RE-ESTABLISHMENT OF THE ESTATES OF THE EMPIRE TO THEIR ANCIENT RIGHTS.

VIII. And in order to prevent for the future all Differences in the Political State, all and every the Electors, Princes, and States of the *Roman* Empire shall be so establish'd and confirm'd in their ancient Rights, Prerogatives, Liberties, Privileges, free Exercise of their Territorial Right, as well in Spirituals and Temporals, Seigneuries, Regalian Rights, and in the possession of all these things, by virtue of the present Transaction, that they may not be molested at any time in any manner, under any pretext whatsoever.

1. That they enjoy without contradiction the Right of Suffrage in all Deliberations touching the Affairs of the Empire, especially in the manner of interpreting Laws, resolving upon a War, imposing Taxes, ordering Levies and quartering of Soldiers, building for the publick Use new Fortresses in the Lands of the States, and reinforcing old Garisons,

Figure 2.A

Europe in 1648

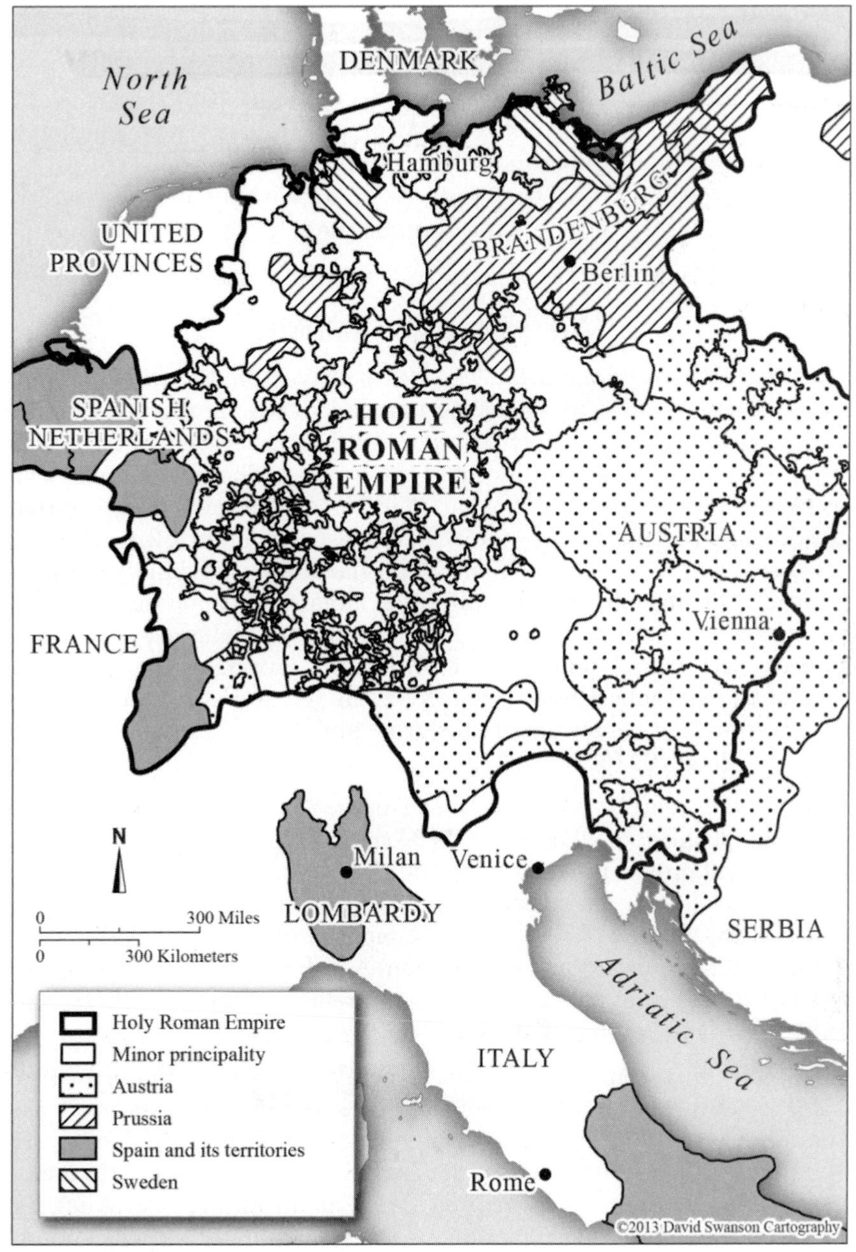

making of Peace and Alliances, and treating of other such-like Affairs; so that none of those or the like things shall be done or receiv'd afterwards, without the Advice and Consent of a free Assembly of all the States of the Empire: That, above all, each of the Estates of the Empire shall freely and for ever enjoy the Right of making Alliances among themselves, or with Foreigners, for the Preservation and Security of every one of them: provided nevertheless that these Alliances be neither against the Emperor nor the Empire, nor the publick Peace, nor against this Transaction especially; and that they be made without prejudice in every respect to the Oath whereby every one of them is bound to the Emperor and the Empire.

NOTES AND QUESTIONS

1. *The Peace of Westphalia.* The Peace of Westphalia, which brought to a close the savage Thirty Year War, included the Treaty of Osnabrück between Sweden and the Holy Roman Empire, excerpted above, and the Treaty of Münster, between France and the Empire. The Holy Roman Empire was a loose political entity in the heart of Europe composed of a variety of principalities, free cities, and other territories. See Figure 2.A. During the medieval era, which the Thirty Years War shattered, individuals did not owe allegiance only to one territorial ruler. Instead, that era "had been characterized by criss-crossing political, legal, religious, and moral allegiances. The ties of feudalism, of King and baron, of the Holy Roman Empire, of the Catholic Church, indeed of all the settled order of medieval Europe, bound men and women this way and that." Mark Weston Janis, *International Law* 169 (6th ed. 2012).

One of the central issues of the Thirty Years War was the right of princes and peoples to choose to be Catholic or Protestant. Besides the Treaty's general provisions respecting amity and amnesty, some of its clauses about religious liberty have been reproduced above. For discussion of the relevance of the Peace of Westphalia for modern conceptions of free exercise of religion and public order, see Gordon A. Christenson, " 'Liberty of the Exercise of Religion' in the Peace of Westphalia," 21 *Transnational Law & Contemporary Problems* 721 (2012).

For many historians and lawyers, the Peace of Westphalia marks the beginning of the era of "modern international relations" and hence of "modern international law." Yet, the Peace itself was drafted by Europeans already well familiar with international compacts, who probably had little idea that others would view their newly crafted Peace as an innovation. What makes the Peace of Westphalia so compelling as a starting point? Besides ending the Thirty Years War, the Peace of Westphalia in Article VIII "re-established" the "electors, princes, and states of the Roman Empire" to "their ancient Rights." Were these "ancient Rights," described as protecting the German states from any "molestation," a kind of state sovereignty that became the fundamental building block for modern international politics? The Peace of Westphalia did not formally dissolve the Holy Roman Empire, with which the various "Electors, Princes, and States" remained affiliated. But did the Treaty signal a move away from a hierarchical political order in which one Empire, linked to the Roman Catholic Church, played a prominent role, and a corresponding move toward a multi-polar world? See Leo Gross, "The Peace of Westphalia, 1648–1948," 42 *American Journal of International Law* 20 (1948).

2. *Sovereignty and International Law.* Note how ironic it is that states chose to agree in a treaty to limit their freedom of action in order to assure their sovereignty. The success of international law as a political and intellectual discipline over the past five centuries has had much to do with international law's utility in regulating and cementing a world political system based on more or less sovereign states.

It should be no surprise that the modern intellectual constructs of both state sovereignty and international law emerged at the same time as the Thirty Years War. A principal craftsman of the notion of the sovereign state was the English philosopher, Thomas Hobbes, who published his celebration of the sovereign state, *Leviathan*, in 1651. Hobbes argued that all humankind required "a Common Power, to keep them in awe, and to direct their actions to the Common Benefit." Meantime, Hugo Grotius fashioned a legal system in his *De Jure Belli Ac Pacis* (1625) that explained that no sovereign state was so powerful as not to need the advantages of laws based on both natural law and positive consent. For Grotius, the exercise of positive consent was not to be taken lightly; treaties bound a nation's entire people and had to be interpreted and carried out in good faith. The powerful combination of Hobbes's sovereign state and Grotius's international law has defined much of international relations ever since. See Mark W. Janis, "Sovereignty and International Law: Hobbes and Grotius," in *Essays in Honour of Wang Tieya* 391 (Ronald St. John Macdonald ed. 1994). For more on the sovereign state, see Chapter 7.

THE TREATY OF PARIS (1783)

United States and Great Britain, 12 Bevans 8, 48 Consolidated Treaty Series 487

Concluded at Paris September 3, 1783; ratified by Congress January 14, 1784; proclaimed January 14, 1784.

In the name of the Most Holy and Undivided Trinity.

It having pleased the Divine Providence to dispose the hearts of the Most Serene and Most Potent Prince George the Third, by the grace of God King of Great Britain, France, and Ireland, Defender of the Faith, Duke of Brunswick and Lunenburg, Arch-Treasurer and Prince Elector of the Holy Roman Empire, & c. and of the United States of America, to forget all past misunderstandings and differences that have unhappily interrupted the good correspondence and friendship which they mutually wish to restore; and to establish such a beneficial and satisfactory intercourse between the two countries, upon the ground of reciprocal advantages and mutual convenience, as may promote and secure to both perpetual peace and harmony; and having for this desirable end already laid the foundation of peace and reconciliation, by the provisional articles signed at Paris, on the 30th of November, 1782, by the Commissioners empowered on each part; which articles were agreed to be inserted in, and to constitute the treaty of peace proposed to be concluded between the Crown of Great Britain and the said United States, but which treaty was not to be concluded until terms of peace should be agreed upon between Great Britain and France, and His Britannick Majesty should be ready to conclude such treaty accordingly; and the treaty between Great Britain and France having since been concluded, His Britannick Majesty and the United States of America, in order to carry into effect the provisional articles above mentioned, according to the tenor thereof, have constituted and appointed, that is to say, his Britannick Majesty, on his part, David Hartley, Esq., Member of the Parliament of Great Britain: and the said United States, on their part, John Adams, Esq., late a Commissioner of the United States of America at the Court of Versailles, late Delegate in Congress from the State of Massachusets, and Chief Justice of the said State, and Minister Plenipotentiary of the said United States to their High Mightinesses the States General of the United Netherlands; Benjamin Franklin, Esq., late Delegate in Congress from the State of Pennsylvania, President of the Convention of the said State, and Minister Plenipotentiary from the United States of America at the Court of Versailles; John Jay, Esq., late President of Congress, and Chief Justice of the State of New York, and Minister Plenipotentiary from the said United States at the Court of Madrid; to be the Plenipotentiaries for the concluding and signing the present definitive treaty: who, after having reciprocally communicated their respective full powers, have agreed upon and confirmed the following articles:

Article I. His Britannick Majesty acknowledges the said United States, viz. New Hampshire, Massachusets Bay, Rhode Island and Providence Plantations, Connecticut, New York, New Jersey, Pennsylvania, Delaware, Maryland, Virginia, North Carolina, South Carolina, and Georgia, to be Free, Sovereign and Independent States; that he treats with them as such; and for himself, his heirs and successors, relinquishes all claims to the government, propriety, and territorial rights of the same, and every part thereof.

II. And that all disputes which might arise in future on the subject of the boundaries of the said United States may be prevented, it is hereby agreed and declared, that the following are, and shall be, their boundaries, viz. From the north-west angle of Nova Scotia, viz. that angle which is formed by a line drawn due north from the source of Saint Croix river to the Highlands, along the said Highlands which divide those rivers that empty themselves into the river St. Lawrence, from those which fall into the Atlantic ocean, to the north-westernmost head of Connecticut river;

thence down along the middle of that river to the forty-fifth degree of north latitude; from thence, by a line due west on said latitude until it strikes the river Iroquois or Cataraquy; thence along the middle of said river into Lake Ontario; through the middle of said lake, until it strikes the communication by water between that lake and lake Erie; thence along the middle of said communication into lake Erie; through the middle of said lake until it arrives at the water communication between that lake and lake Huron; thence along the middle of said water communication into the lake Huron; thence through the middle of said lake to the water communication between that lake and lake Superior; thence through lake Superior, northward of the Isles Royal and Phelipeaux, to the Long Lake; thence through the middle of said Long Lake, and the water communication between it and the Lake of the Woods, to the said Lake of the Woods; thence through the said lake to the most north-western point thereof, and from thence on a due west course to the river Mississippi; thence by a line to be drawn along the middle of the said river Mississippi, until it shall intersect the northernmost part of the thirty-first degree of north latitude:—South, by a line to be drawn due east from the determination of the line last mentioned, in the latitude of thirty-one degrees north of the equator, to the middle of the river Apalachicola or Catahouche; thence along the middle thereof to its junction with the Flint river; thence strait to the head of St. Mary's river, and thence down along the middle of St. Mary's River to the Atlantic ocean:—East, by a line to be drawn along the middle of the river St. Croix, from its mouth in the bay of Fundy, to its source; and from its source directly north to the aforesaid Highlands, which divide the rivers that fall into the Atlantic ocean from those which fall into the river St. Lawrence: comprehending all islands within twenty leagues of any part of the shores of the United States, and lying between lines to be drawn due east from the points where the aforesaid boundaries between Nova Scotia on the one part, and East Florida on the other, shall respectively touch the bay of Fundy, and the Atlantic ocean; excepting such islands as now are, or heretofore have been, within the limits of the said province of Nova Scotia.

III. It is agreed, that the people of the United States shall continue to enjoy, unmolested, the right to take fish of every kind of the grand bank and on all the other banks of Newfoundland: also in the gulph of Saint Lawrence, and at all other places in the sea where the inhabitants of both countries used at any time heretofore to fish. And also that the inhabitants of the United States shall have liberty to take fish of every kind on such part of the coast of Newfoundland as British fishermen shall use, (but not to dry or cure the same on that island) and also on the coasts, bays, and creeks of all other of His Britannick Majesty's dominions in America; and that the American fishermen shall have liberty to dry

Figure 2.B

The United States in 1783

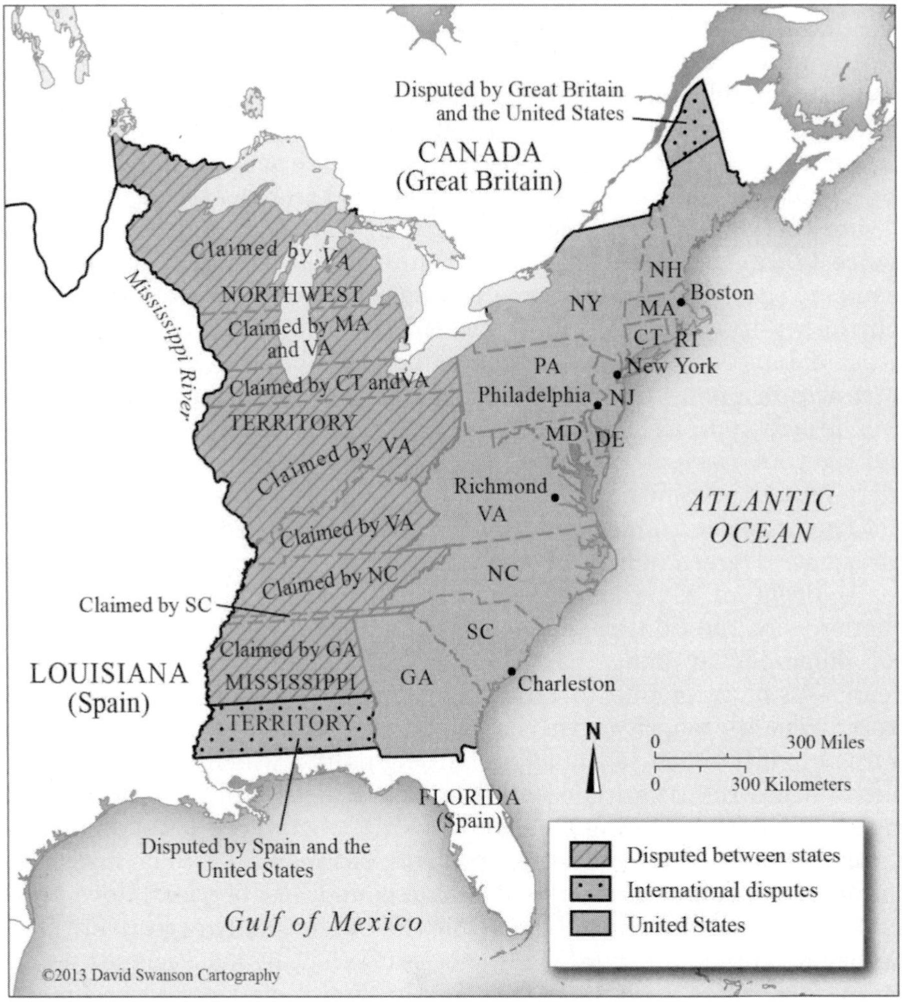

and cure fish in any of the unsettled bays, harbours, and creeks of Nova Scotia, Magdalen Islands, and Labrador, so long as the same shall remain unsettled; but so soon as the same, or either of them, shall be settled, it shall not be lawful for the said fishermen to dry or cure fish at such settlement without a previous agreement for that purpose with the inhabitants, proprietors, or possessors of the ground.

IV. It is agreed, that creditors on either side shall meet with no lawful impediment to the recovery of the full value, in sterling money, of all *bona fide* debts heretofore contracted.

V. It is agreed, that the Congress shall earnestly recommend it to the legislatures of the respective states, to provide for the restitution of all estates, rights, and properties, which have been confiscated, belonging to real British subjects: and also of the estates, rights, and properties, of persons resident in districts in the possession of his Majesty's arms, and who have not borne arms against the said United States: and that persons of any other description shall have free liberty to go to any part or parts of any of the Thirteen United States, and therein to remain twelve months unmolested in their endeavours to obtain the restitution of such of their estates, rights, and properties, as may have been confiscated: and that Congress shall also earnestly recommend to the several states, a reconsideration and revision of all acts or laws regarding the premises, so as to render the said laws or acts perfectly consistent not only with justice and equity, but with that spirit of conciliation which, on the return of the blessings of peace, should universally prevail. And that Congress shall also earnestly recommend to the several states, that the estates, rights, and properties, of such last-mentioned persons shall be restored to them, they refunding to any persons who may be now in possession the *bona fide* price (where any has been given) which such persons may have paid on purchasing any of the said lands, rights, or properties, since the confiscation.

And it is agreed, that all persons who have any interest in confiscated lands, either by debts, marriage settlements or otherwise, shall meet with no lawful impediment in the prosecution of their just rights.

VI. That there shall be no future confiscations made, nor any prosecutions commenced against any person or persons, for or by reason of the part which he or they may have taken in the present war; and that no person shall, on that account, suffer any future loss or damage either in his person, liberty, or property; and that those who may be in confinement on such charges at the time of the ratification of the treaty in America, shall be immediately set at liberty, and the prosecutions so commenced be discontinued.

VII. There shall be a firm and perpetual peace between His Britannick Majesty and the said States, and between the subjects of the one and the citizens of the other, wherefore, all hostilities, both by sea and land, shall from henceforth cease: all prisoners on both sides shall be set at liberty, and his Britannick Majesty shall, with all convenient speed, and without causing any destruction, or carrying away any negroes, or other property of the American inhabitants, withdraw all his armies, garrisons, and fleets, from the said United States, and from every port, place, and harbour within the same; leaving in all fortifications the American artillery that may be therein: and shall also order and cause all archives, records, deeds, and papers, belonging to any of the said States, or their citizens, which in the course of the war may have fallen into the hands of his officers, to be forthwith restored and delivered to the proper states and persons to whom they belong.

VIII. The navigation of the river Mississippi, from its source to the ocean, shall for ever remain free and open to the subjects of Great Britain, and the citizens of the United States.

IX. In case it should so happen, that any place or territory belonging to Great Britain, or to the United States, should have been conquered by the arms of either from the other, before the arrival of the said provisional articles in America, it is agreed, that the same shall be restored without difficulty, and without requiring any compensation.

X. The solemn ratifications of the present treaty, expedited in good and due form, shall be exchanged between the contracting parties in the space of six months, or sooner if possible, to be computed from the day of the signature of the present treaty.

In witness whereof, we the under-signed, their Ministers Plenipotentiary, have, in their name, and in virtue of our full powers, signed with our hands the present definitive treaty, and caused the seals of our arms to be affixed thereto.

Done at Paris, this third day of September, in the year of our Lord one thousand seven hundred and eighty-three.

D. HARTLEY.

JOHN ADAMS.
B. FRANKLIN.
JOHN JAY.

NOTES AND QUESTIONS

1. *Recognition of the United States*. Did Article I of the 1783 Peace of Paris merely declare Britain's formal recognition of the sovereignty of the United States as it had been already objectively established in 1776 by the United States itself in the Declaration of Independence? U.S. Supreme Court Justice Chase wrote in 1796:

> I have ever considered it as the established doctrine of the United States, that their independence originated from, and commenced with, the declaration of congress, on the 4th of July, 1776; and that no other period can be fixed on for its commencement; and that all laws made by the legislatures of the several states, after the declaration of independence, were the laws of sovereign and independent governments.

Ware v. Hylton, 3 U.S. (3 Dall.) 199, 224 (1796). We return to *Ware v. Hylton* in Chapter 4.

Is Justice Chase's view persuasive? Or did the Peace of Paris itself constitute the sovereignty of the United States as of January 14, 1784, when the Treaty came into force? When preparing to negotiate the Treaty of Paris with the Americans, the British government debated these alternatives, which reflect the theoretical distinction in international law between the "declaratory" and "constitutive" theories of recognition, a topic to which we return in Chapter 7. Some in the British Cabinet thought the Foreign Office should orchestrate the negotiations, on the grounds that the United States was already independent, while others argued that responsibility should rest instead with the Colonial and Home Offices. Britain initially instructed its negotiator to pursue a peace treaty with the representatives of the "Colonies or plantations," but John Jay and Benjamin Franklin refused to proceed until those instructions were changed. See Andrew Cunningham McLaughlin, *The Confederation and the Constitution 1783–1789*, at 6, 12–14 (1905).

2. *Effect of Treaties on Third Parties*. Does Article II delimiting the boundaries of the United States in 1783 legally bind any country except the United States and the United Kingdom? When, if ever, can treaties create obligations for nonparties? See Articles 34–38 of the Vienna Convention on the Law of Treaties, reproduced in the Appendix, and the discussion of customary international law in Chapter 3.

3. *Maritime Issues*. Article III concerns fishing off the shores of the United States and Canada. Fishing disputes between the two countries have continued to the present day. In 1984, the International Court of Justice decided the *Gulf of Maine Case* and again divided fishing rights between the United States and Canada in that area. Definition of the Maritime Boundary in the Gulf of Maine Area, 1984 I.C.J. 246. The allocation of salmon fishing rights among the United States, Canada, and Native Americans has been the subject of difficult treaty negotiations. See, *e.g.*, Treaty Concerning Pacific Salmon, Jan. 28, 1985, T.I.A.S. No. 11,091, 1469 U.N.T.S. 357, and Pacific Salmon Agreement, June 30, 1999, *available as subsequently amended at* http://www.psc.org/pubs/treaty/treaty.pdf (last visited Dec. 8, 2013). In Chapter 3, Part E we read the *North Sea Cases*, an example of the International Court's maritime boundary delimitation work, and in Chapter 10 we explore fishing rights and other maritime issues.

4. *The Peace of Paris and the U.S. Constitution*. On balance, the Peace of Paris was a diplomatic triumph for the new United States:

> This Peace of Paris certainly gives the lie to the epigram that "America never lost a war, or won a peace conference." Considering that the British still held New York, Charleston, Savannah, Detroit, and several other posts in the Northwest, that Washington's army was almost incapable of further effort, and that the British navy had recovered command of the sea, it is surprising what wide boundaries and favorable terms the United States obtained.

Samuel Eliot Morison, Henry Steele Commager & William E. Leuchtenberg, 1 *The Growth of the American Republic* 204 (7th ed. 1980).

Following the Peace of Paris, U.S. state courts proved unable or unwilling to protect the rights of British subjects detailed in Articles IV, V, and VI. As a result, Britain remained in occupation of much of what was then the Northwest Territory (later the states of Illinois, Indiana, Michigan, Ohio, and Wisconsin). This in turn was one impetus to the calling of the Constitutional Convention in 1787, to the establishment of U.S. federal courts in 1789 under the new U.S. Constitution, and to the mention of treaties in the Constitution's Supremacy Clause, Article VI(2). See Chapter 4.

5. *Who Makes Treaties?* Unsurprisingly, the Permanent Court of International Justice concluded in The S.S. "Wimbledon," 1923 P.C.I.J., Ser. A, No. 1, at 15, 25, that "the right of entering into international engagements is an attribute of State sovereignty." It may be more unexpected that sub-state actors, such as the component parts of federal states, also make some sorts of international agreements. Moreover, international organizations may sometimes possess treaty-making authority. See Chapter 8. Paralleling the Vienna Convention on the Law of Treaties is the Vienna Convention on the Law of Treaties between States and International Organizations or between International Organizations, Mar. 21, 1986, 25 *International Legal Materials* 543 (1986). The European Community is a party to hundreds of treaties. See http://ec.europa.eu/world/agreements/default.home.do (last visited Dec. 8, 2013). Why are international agreements made by non-state actors legally binding? See Duncan B. Hollis, "Why State Consent Still Matters—Non-State Actors, Treaties, and the Changing Sources of International Law," 23 *Berkeley Journal of International Law* 137 (2005).

THE CESSION OF ALASKA (1867)

11 Bevans 1216, 15 Stat. 539, Treaty Series 301, 134 Consolidated Treaty Series 331

Convention signed at Washington March 30, 1867

Senate advice and consent to ratification April 9, 1867

Ratified by Russia May 3, 1867

Ratified by the President of the United States May 28, 1867

Ratifications exchanged at Washington June 20, 1867

Entered into force June 20, 1867

Proclaimed by the President of the United States June 20, 1867

The United States of America and His Majesty the Emperor of all the Russias, being desirous of strengthening, if possible, the good understanding which exists between them, have, for that purpose, appointed as their Plenipotentiaries: the President of the United States, William H. Seward, Secretary of State; and His Majesty the Emperor of all the Russias, the Privy Counsellor Edward de Stoeckl, his Envoy Extraordinary and Minister Plenipotentiary to the United States.

And the said Plenipotentiaries, having exchanged their full powers, which were found to be in due form, have agreed upon and signed the following articles:

ARTICLE I.

His Majesty the Emperor of all the Russias agrees to cede to the United States, by this convention, immediately upon the exchange of the ratifications thereof, all the territory and dominion now possessed by his said Majesty on the continent of America and in the adjacent islands, the same being contained within the geographical limits herein set forth, to wit: The eastern limit is the line of demarcation between the Russian and the British possessions in North America, as established by the convention between Russia and Great Britain, of February 28–16, 1825, and described in Articles III and IV of said convention, in the following terms:

"Commencing from the southernmost point of the island called Prince of Wales Island, which point lies in the parallel of 54 degrees 40 minutes north latitude, and between the 131st and the 133d degree of west longitude, (meridian of Greenwich,) the said line shall ascend to the north along the channel called Portland channel, as far as the point of the continent where it strikes the 56th degree of north latitude; from this last mentioned point, the line of demarcation shall follow the summit of the mountains situated parallel to the coast as far as the point of intersection of the 141st degree of west longitude, (the same meridian); and finally, from the said point of intersection, the said meridian line of the 141st degree, in its prolongation as far as the Frozen ocean.

"IV. With reference to the line of demarcation laid down in the preceding article, it is understood—

"1st. That the island called Prince of Wales Island shall belong wholly to Russia," (now, by this cession, to the United States.)

"2d. That whenever the summit of the mountains which extend in a direction parallel to the coast from the 56th degree of north latitude to the point of intersection of the 141st degree of west longitude shall prove to be at the distance of more than ten marine leagues from the ocean, the limit between the British possessions and the line of coast which is to belong to Russia as above mentioned (that is to say, the limit to the possessions ceded by this convention) shall be formed by a line parallel to the winding of the coast, and which shall never exceed the distance of ten marine leagues therefrom."

The western limit within which the territories and dominion conveyed, are contained, passes through a point in Behring's straits on the parallel of 65 degrees 30 minutes north latitude, at its intersection by the meridian which passes midway between the islands of Krusenstern, or Ignalook, and the island of Ratmanoff, or Noonarbook, and proceeds due north, without limitation, into the same Frozen ocean. The same western limit, beginning at the same initial point, proceeds thence in a course nearly southwest, through Behring's straits and Behring's sea, so as to pass midway between the northwest point of the island of St. Lawrence and the southeast point of Cape Choukotski, to the meridian of 172 west longitude; thence, from the intersection of that meridian, in a southwesterly direction, so as to pass midway between the island of Attou and the Copper island of the Kormandorski couplet or group, in the North Pacific ocean, to the meridian of 193 degrees west longitude, so as to include in the territory conveyed the whole of the Aleutian islands east of that meridian.

ARTICLE II.

In the cession of territory and dominion made by the preceding article, are included the right of property in all public lots and squares, vacant lands, and all public buildings, fortifications, barracks, and other edifices which are not private individual property. It is, however, understood and agreed, that the churches which have been built in the ceded territory by the Russian government, shall remain the property of such members of the Greek Oriental Church resident in the territory, as may choose to worship therein. Any government archives, papers, and documents relative to the territory and dominion aforesaid, which may be now existing there, will be left in the possession of the agent of the United States; but an authenticated copy of such of them as may be required, will be, at all times, given by the United States to the Russian government or to such Russian officers or subjects, as they may apply for.

ARTICLE III.

The inhabitants of the ceded territory, according to their choice, reserving their natural allegiance, may return to Russia within three years; but if they should prefer to remain in the ceded territory, they, with the exception of uncivilized native tribes, shall be admitted to the enjoyment of all the rights, advantages and immunities of citizens of the United States, and shall be maintained and protected in the free enjoyment of their liberty, property and religion. The uncivilized tribes will be subject to such laws and regulations as the United States may, from time to time, adopt in regard to aboriginal tribes of that country.

ARTICLE IV.

His Majesty the Emperor of all the Russias shall appoint, with convenient despatch, an agent or agents for the purpose of formally delivering to a similar agent or agents appointed on behalf of the United States, the territory, dominion, property, dependencies and appurtenances which are ceded as above, and for doing any other act which may be necessary in regard thereto. But the cession, with the right of immediate possession, is nevertheless to be deemed complete and absolute on the exchange of ratifications, without waiting for such formal delivery.

ARTICLE V.

Immediately after the exchange of the ratifications of this convention, any fortifications or military posts which may be in the ceded territory, shall be delivered to the agent of the United States, and any Russian troops which may be in the Territory shall be withdrawn as soon as may be reasonably and conveniently practicable.

ARTICLE VI.

In consideration of the cession aforesaid, the United States agree to pay at the Treasury in Washington, within ten months after the exchange of the ratifications of this convention, to the diplomatic representative or other agent of his Majesty the Emperor of all the Russias, duly authorized to receive the same, seven million two hundred thousand dollars in gold. The cession of territory and dominion herein made is hereby declared to be free and unincumbered by any reservations, privileges, franchises, grants, or possessions, by any associated companies, whether corporate or incorporate, Russian or any other, or by any parties, except merely private individual property holders; and the cession hereby made, conveys all the rights, franchises, and privileges now belonging to Russia in the said territory or dominion, and appurtenances thereto.

ARTICLE VII.

When this Convention shall have been duly ratified by the President of the United States, by and with the advice and consent of the Senate, on the one part, and on the other by His Majesty the Emperor of all the Russias, the ratifications shall be exchanged at Washington within three months from the date hereof, or sooner, if possible.

In faith whereof, the respective plenipotentiaries have signed this convention, and thereto affixed the seals of their arms.

Done at Washington, the thirtieth day of March in the year of our Lord one thousand eight hundred and sixty-seven.

WILLIAM H. SEWARD
EDOUARD DE STOECKL

THE KELLOGG-BRIAND PACT (1928)

Renunciation of War as an Instrument of National Policy,
2 Bevans 732, 46 Stat. 2343, Treaty Series 796, 94 L.N.T.S. 57

Treaty signed at Paris August 27, 1928

Senate advice and consent to ratification January 15, 1929

Ratified by the President of the United States January 17, 1929

Ratifications deposited at Washington March 2–July 24, 1929

Entered into force July 24, 1929

Proclaimed by the President of the United States July 24, 1929

The President of the German Reich, the President of the United States of America, His Majesty the King of the Belgians, the President of the French Republic, His Majesty the King of Great Britain, Ireland and the British Dominions Beyond the Seas, Emperor of India, His Majesty the King of Italy, His Majesty the Emperor of Japan, the President of the Republic of Poland, the President of the Czechoslovak Republic,

Deeply sensible of their solemn duty to promote the welfare of mankind;

Persuaded that the time has come when a frank renunciation of war as an instrument of national policy should be made to the end that the peaceful and friendly relations now existing between their peoples may be perpetuated;

Convinced that all changes in their relations with one another should be sought only by pacific means and be the result of a peaceful and orderly process, and that any signatory Power which shall hereafter seek to promote its national interests by resort to war should be denied the benefits furnished by this Treaty;

Hopeful that, encouraged by their example, all the other nations of the world will join in this humane endeavor and by adhering to the present Treaty as soon as it comes into force bring their peoples within the scope of its beneficent provisions, thus uniting the civilized nations of the world in a common renunciation of war as an instrument of their national policy;

Have decided to conclude a Treaty and for that purpose have appointed * * * Plenipotentiaries * * * who, having communicated to one another their full powers found in good and due form have agreed upon the following articles:

ARTICLE I

The High Contracting Parties solemnly declare in the names of their respective peoples that they condemn recourse to war for the solution of international controversies, and renounce it as an instrument of national policy in their relations with one another.

ARTICLE II

The High Contracting Parties agree that the settlement or solution of all disputes or conflicts of whatever nature or of whatever origin they may be, which may arise among them, shall never be sought except by pacific means.

ARTICLE III

The present Treaty shall be ratified by the High Contracting Parties named in the Preamble in accordance with their respective constitutional requirements, and shall take effect as between them as soon as all their several instruments of ratification shall have been deposited at Washington.

This Treaty shall, when it has come into effect as prescribed in the preceding paragraph, remain open as long as may be necessary for adherence by all the other Powers of the world. Every instrument evidencing the adherence of a Power shall be deposited at Washington and the Treaty shall immediately upon such deposit become effective as between the Power thus adhering and the other Powers parties hereto.

It shall be the duty of the Government of the United States to furnish each Government named in the Preamble and every Government subsequently adhering to this Treaty with a certified copy of the Treaty and of every instrument of ratification or adherence. It shall also be the duty of the Government of the United States telegraphically to notify such Governments immediately upon the deposit with it of each instrument of ratification or adherence.

IN FAITH WHEREOF the respective Plenipotentiaries have signed this Treaty in the French and English languages both texts having equal force, and hereunto affix their seals.

DONE at Paris, the twenty-seventh day of August in the year one thousand nine hundred and twenty-eight.

[For Germany:]
Gustav Stresemann

[For the United States:]
Frank B. Kellogg

[For the United Kingdom:]
Cushendun

[For the Dominion of Canada:]
W.L. Mackenzie King

[For the Commonwealth of Australia:]
A.J. McLachlan

[For the Dominion of New Zealand:]
C.J. Parr

[For Belgium:]
Paul Hymans

[For France:]
Ari Briand

[For India:]
Cushendun

[For Italy:]
G. Manzoni

[For Japan:]
Uchida

[For Poland:]
August Zaleski

[For the Union of South Africa:]
J.S. Smit

[For Czechoslovakia:]
Dr. Eduard Benes

[For the Irish Free State:]
Liam T. MacCosgair

NOTES AND QUESTIONS

1. *The Efficacy of International Law.* The Cession of Alaska and the Kellogg-Briand Pact make a nice contrast when discussing the efficacy of international law. It is easy to see how the 1867 Cession of Alaska "worked"—Russia ceded the Alaska Territory to the United States and the United States paid the Tsar $7,200,000 in gold. After the conclusion of the treaty, Russian officials left Alaska, U.S. officials arrived, and money changed hands. It is much more difficult to see how the 1928 Kellogg-Briand Pact "worked." What good were "solemn" renunciations of war, especially in light of the developments in world politics in the 1930s and 1940s: the participation of Germany and the Soviet Union in the Spanish Civil War, the invasion of Ethiopia by Italy, the invasion of Manchuria by Japan, the invasion of Czechoslovakia by Germany, the invasion of Poland by Germany and the Soviet Union, the invasion of the Baltic States and Finland by the Soviet Union, the invasion of France, the Netherlands, Belgium, Denmark, Norway, and the Soviet Union by Germany, the German attack on the United Kingdom, the Japanese invasion of China, Malaya, Indonesia, and the Philippines, and the Japanese attack on the United States? If the Treaty of Cession of Alaska shows treaties at their most efficacious, does the Kellogg-Briand Pact show them at their least efficacious?

2. *"Hard" and "Soft" International Law.* Are both the Cession of Alaska and the Kellogg-Briand Pact the same sort of international law? Some international lawyers distinguish between "hard" and "soft" international law, a distinction with at least two meanings. First, the distinction may refer to the difference between rules of law meant to be followed and norms meant merely to set out preferred outcomes. Are these two treaties examples of this distinction? Eighty years ago, Manley Hudson, a Harvard Law School professor and American judge on the World Court, argued that the Kellogg-Briand Pact should be viewed as a "fundamental law" and "approached in a state of mind wholly different from that in which we approach the ordinary international treaty." International Law Association, *Report of the Thirty-Eighth Conference (Budapest)* 12 (1934). Hudson argued that "[w]e are holding ahead of us great ideals. We may not succeed in realizing all of them, but I feel, as a member of this generation, that it will have been a great thing for us who are engaged in such an enterprise." *Id.* at 66.

Second, the distinction between hard and soft law may refer to the difference between formal sources of law (such as treaties) and instruments that are not formally legal sources (such as mutual declarations of government leaders issued at the end of a diplomatic conference). Such declarations may contain non-binding statements of principle. In Chapter 3, Part D we examine soft law of this second type and ask whether it can have any legal significance.

Is it fair to conclude that the Kellogg-Briand Pact was meant to be only aspirational? If so, was it wrong then to try and execute individuals for the violation of its principles as was done at the Nuremberg trial of Nazi war criminals? See Chapter 6.

3. *Bilateral and Multilateral Treaties*. It is conceptually possible for issues addressed in a multilateral treaty such as the Kellogg-Briand Pact to be addressed in a series of bilateral agreements. The Kellogg-Briand Pact was initiated when the French Foreign Minister, Aristide Briand, encouraged by some influential U.S. citizens, proposed that the United States and France conclude a bilateral treaty banning war as an instrument of national policy. The United States responded by suggesting a multilateral treaty, and negotiations leading to the Kellogg-Briand Pact resulted. See E.H. Carr, *International Relations Between the Two World Wars 1919–1939*, at 117–20 (1947); David Hunter Miller, *The Peace Pact of Paris* (1928). Why was the Kellogg-Briand Pact drawn up as a multilateral treaty? Would the conclusion of a series of bilateral agreements have been too cumbersome? Was the subject matter of the Kellogg-Briand Pact particularly appropriate for multilateral treatment? Is it more likely that the rules established in a multilateral treaty will pass into customary international law? Use of multilateral treaties increased significantly in the 20th century.

4. *Signing Treaties*. Note the various steps involved in formal treaty making reflected in the headnotes to the Cession of Alaska and the Kellogg-Briand Pact. Signing a treaty may, but often does not, signify a country's formal acceptance of it. See Articles 11–12 of the Vienna Convention on the Law of Treaties, reproduced in the Appendix. Is there any legal significance to signing a treaty when that act does not express a state's consent to be bound by the treaty? On December 31, 2000, President Clinton signed the Rome Statute establishing the International Criminal Court, which we will consider in Chapter 6. After President George W. Bush took office, his administration wrote the Secretary-General of the United Nations to inform him "that the United States does not intend to become a party" to the Rome Statute and that "[a]ccordingly, the United States has no legal obligations arising from its signature." *Quoted in* Sean D. Murphy, "Contemporary Practice of the United States Relating to International Law," 96 *American Journal of International Law* 706, 724 (2002). What were those "legal obligations"? See Article 18 of the Vienna Convention.

5. *Entry Into Force*. Article III of the Kellogg-Briand Pact provides that the treaty enters into force when all the negotiating states have accepted it and deposited their instruments of ratification with the "depositary" (in this case, the U.S. government). A multilateral treaty may contain provisions making the treaty's entry into force subject to a variety of conditions. For example, the 1982 Convention on the Law of the Sea entered into force in November 1994 in accordance with its Article 308, which provides for the

Convention's entry into force "12 months after the date of deposit of the sixtieth instrument of ratification or accession." Twenty-five states with merchant fleets comprising not less than 50 per cent of the world's gross tonnage had to accept the 1974 International Convention for the Safety of Life at Sea before it could enter into force. What factors influence decisions concerning the number or characteristics of accepting states necessary for a treaty's entry into force? Why do treaty negotiators sometimes seek a delay between the final necessary acceptance of a treaty and the date on which it formally enters into force? If a treaty is silent about its entry into force, the general rule, as reflected in Article 24 of the Vienna Convention on the Law of Treaties, is that the treaty "enters into force as soon as consent to be bound by the treaty has been established for all the negotiating States."

CORDELL HULL, THE MEMOIRS OF CORDELL HULL

Vol. 1, at 831–37, 839–42 (1948)

New decisions confronted us in the summer of 1940 as Great Britain's plight on the high seas grew acute. Contrasted with the period before we entered the First World War, it was perilous. A quarter of a century before, Britain had the assistance of the French and Italian fleets in the Atlantic and Mediterranean, and of the Japanese fleet in the Pacific. Now the French fleet lay immobile, German submarines operated out of French ports, the Italian Navy was an enemy and the Japanese Navy a potential enemy. Britain's shipping losses were rising dangerously. If she were to survive, it was necessary for her not only to purchase huge quantities of war supplies in this country, but also to get them safely to the United Kingdom.

British Ambassador Lord Lothian came in to see me on August 4, the day before my departure for White Sulphur Springs, and expressed his Government's "urgent desire" to purchase from us a number of older type destroyers. Britain, he said, needed them to bridge over what he described as her "present emergency situation." * * *

When Lothian came to my office on August 4 I could appreciate Britain's dangers as fully as he could depict them. He said Britain had lost five destroyers during the previous week alone. Destroyers, he pointed out, were vitally important in combating submarine activities and other enemy action in the English Channel where large warships could not be used to advantage.

He said he had already discussed the question with the President [Franklin D. Roosevelt] while I was at Havana, and now desired to lay the situation before me in the hope that something might be done within the next few weeks. He added that Britain would be willing to make available to us facilities for naval and air bases in certain British islands adjacent to Central and South America and in Bermuda, as well as for aircraft bases in Newfoundland. He said he would give us later in the day a memorandum indicating the bases and facilities Britain had in mind. * * *

I * * * pointed out the legal difficulties in the way of our selling the destroyers. The United States Code forbade the departure of vessels from American waters outfitted for cruising against a foreign nation with which we were at peace. Also, the National Defense Act, approved June 28, 1940, forbade the sale of naval equipment without the approval of the Chief of Naval Operations, and military equipment without the approval of the Chief of Staff of the Army. * * *

During my three weeks rest at White Sulphur Springs I had a private telephone line into my apartment there and received daily pouches from the State Department, hence closely followed and participated in the destroyers-bases negotiations in the hands of the President and [Undersecretary of State Sumner] Welles. A few hours after I returned to Washington on August 23, I went to the White House to attend a Cabinet meeting. * * *

In talking over the bases with the President, I found he had an amazing personal knowledge of almost all of them. He had either cruised, swum, or fished in those harbors. He knew how many feet deep and wide they were and how many ships they would take.

He also knew the penurious condition of the native populations of most of the islands, and consequently did not want to assume the burden of administering those populations. Therefore he had changed, during my absence from Washington, from his original idea of outright purchase of the bases to that of 99–year leases. I had originally favored outright cession, but was willing to agree to leases instead. * * *

That evening [August 24] I met Lothian at the White House[.]

Lothian argued * * * that, if the transaction were treated as a bargain, Mr. Churchill did not feel that he could give us, in return for fifty "oldish destroyers," the right to get whatever air and naval bases in Newfoundland, Bermuda, the Bahamas, Jamaica, St. Lucia, Trinidad, and British Guiana we might choose to ask for, "because the British Government might incur the charge of defaulting on its share of the bargain if it created difficulties about any particular thing the United States Government wanted."

"I think," he said, "Mr. Churchill feels that British public opinion would not support a bargain of this kind if it was presented as a contract and that it would in practice lead to the most dangerous controversies between the United States and Great Britain.["]

In general, Lothian argued to the President and me that there should not be cold commercial bargaining but a friendly interest between the two Governments. This would afford a basis for gifts back and forth which would be voluntary and apparently without definite understanding in advance.

After Lothian had finished his arguments, I said for the third time to the Ambassador, and for the first time to the President, that the latter had no authority whatever to make a gift of public property to any Government or individual. Mr. Roosevelt at once agreed with me. I said, and he agreed, that a different arrangement would be necessary to achieve our objectives.

The President thereupon left it to me to work out a solution with Lothian.

The following morning I called to my office Green H. Hackworth, Legal Adviser of the State Department, whose advice was always invaluable to me, and Judge Townsend of the Department of Justice, to try to find a way out. After some discussion, Hackworth suddenly suggested that there might be a compromise after all between Churchill's desire for reciprocal gifts and our own legal position that the President could not give away the destroyers but had to get something in return.

Since the British had not stated precisely what bases they intended to lease to us, why not divide them into two parcels? The first would comprise the bases in Newfoundland and Bermuda. These Britain could lease us as an outright gift. The second would comprise the bases around the Caribbean, strategically more valuable to us because of their nearness to the Panama Canal. These could be leased to us in consideration of the cession of the 50 destroyers.

I saw at once that here was the formula for which we had been looking.

We thereupon set to work to redraft the proposals. Leaving Hackworth and Townsend to complete the drafting, I telephoned the President, told him Hackworth had offered a solution, and asked if I could send Hackworth to outline it to him. That afternoon Hackworth and Townsend saw the President, who agreed to the compromise. * * *

Lothian having cabled to London the location of the bases the President had in mind, Churchill agreed and himself added the island of Antigua, in the Caribbean, which he said might be useful as a base for flying boats.

That steaming night of August 27, Lothian, [Secretary of the Navy Frank] Knox, and [the Chief of Naval Operations, Admiral Harold R.] Stark all appeared at my apartment at about ten-thirty. For more than an hour we four went over the draft I had given Stark. Lothian at first had a few suggestions for revision, but eventually seemed quite satisfied and said he would send the note to his Government.

The negotiations now remained in abeyance for two days, until Lothian could hear from his Government. On August 29 I handed the Ambassador an informal memorandum from myself to argue further our idea that the destroyers and bases should not be dealt with as outright gifts. * * *

That night at seven o'clock Lord Lothian called at my apartment and left with me his Government's counterproposal. I called Admirals Stark and Woodson and also Green Hackworth to my apartment, and we went over it carefully. We found that Lothian's draft differed in only a few details from my proposal, and added the island of Antigua, which was quite agreeable to us. We made a few changes in the text, and I then telephoned Lothian, who came back to my apartment at ten-thirty. He agreed to our changes.

The following day, August 30, I telephoned the changes to the President at Hyde Park and received his approval.

We drafted at the State Department a message for the President to send to Congress along with the exchange of notes between Lothian and myself. I sent all three documents to the President at Hyde Park on August 31. It was understood that the notes should be signed and exchanged on Monday September 2. The President gave his approval to the three documents, making only a slight change in the message, and handed them to me when I met him at the Union Station in Washington Sunday afternoon September 1.

The President also handed me a letter from himself, which said: "I have carefully read the note from the British Ambassador and your reply thereto as Secretary of State of the United States.

"I give my full and cordial approval to both of these notes." He signed his full name.

Lord Lothian, who had spent the week end in Boston, returned to Washington Monday afternoon, and came to my apartment at seven o'clock that evening. There we signed and exchanged the notes confirming the destroyers-bases transactions.

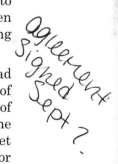

Lothian also handed me his reply to an *aide-mémoire* I had previously given him requesting assurances concerning the disposition of the British fleet. My *aide-mémoire* had referred to the June 4 speech of the Prime Minister in which he said that if the waters surrounding the British Isles became untenable for British warships, the British fleet would in no event be surrendered or sunk but would be sent overseas for the defense of other parts of the Empire. It then asked "whether the foregoing statement represents the settled policy of the British Government."

Lothian stated in his reply: "His Majesty's Ambassador is instructed by the Prime Minister to inform Mr. Secretary Hull that this statement certainly does represent the settled policy of His Majesty's Government. Mr. Churchill must however observe that these hypothetical contingencies seem more likely to concern the German fleet or what is left of it than the British fleet."

The last sentence was Churchill's own addition. The Prime Minister now agreed to having the exchange of *aides-mémoire* published on condition that the main notes regarding the bases and destroyers should be made public first.

The following morning, September 3, I sent to the White House the President's message to Congress, which he had signed and handed to me; the destroyers-bases notes, and an opinion of Attorney General Robert H. Jackson declaring the transaction legal. All these were for communication to Congress. * * *

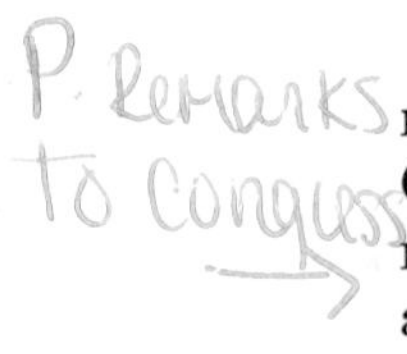

Thus were concluded within a week negotiations among the most momentous in our history. As the President said in his message to Congress: "This is the most important action in the reinforcement of our national defense that has been taken since the Louisiana Purchase. Then as now, considerations of safety from overseas attack were fundamental."

Mention of the Louisiana Purchase was not without significance because it, too, had been made without authorization from Congress and, though the reaction to the destroyers-bases exchange throughout the nation was, in general, wholeheartedly favorable, some opponents objected that Congress should have given its approval.

We based our stand, however, on the necessity for defense. "Preparation for defense," said the President's message, "is an inalienable prerogative of a sovereign state. Under present circumstances this exercise of sovereign right is essential to the maintenance of our peace and safety."

The President pointed out that the exchange was not inconsistent in any sense with our status of peace. He put the value of the new bases to the Western Hemisphere as "beyond calculation." They were essential, he said, to the protection of the Panama Canal, Central America, the northern portion of South America, the Antilles, Canada, Mexico, and our Eastern and Gulf seaboards. * * *

A few international lawyers might have argued that we had violated the Hague Convention of 1907 in that we, a neutral, had sold warships to a belligerent. However, that convention started off with the proposition that "belligerents are bound to respect the sovereign rights of neutral Powers." Neutrals like Poland, Norway, Denmark, The Netherlands, Luxemburg, and Belgium, could testify that the principles of the Hague Convention had not protected them. The convention laid down rights and duties of neutrals and belligerents alike, and the Axis dictators, who had wrecked the convention and alone would have a motive for questioning our transaction, were estopped, by every rule of reason and law, from raising the question. It would be absurd to contend that the convention, which represented a compromise between rights and duties of belligerents on the one hand and neutrals on the other, should bind only the neutrals.

The destroyers-bases transaction went into effect with great speed. The destroyers, reconditioned and stocked with food and munitions, were turned over to Britain at once. Experts of both Governments met and agreed on the exact sites of the eight bases we had acquired, extending along four thousand miles of Atlantic seaboard.

To judge from the many cables I received from our diplomatic missions abroad in the days that followed, the effect of the destroyers-bases deal went far beyond the physical fact that Britain now had 50 more destroyers and we had eight more bases. It was a demonstration to the world that this Government believed that Britain had a real chance to hold fast against all Hitler's might. It showed that we were willing to go beyond ordinary methods and to find new means to aid the major democracy fighting Nazism.

THE HULL-LOTHIAN AGREEMENT (1940)

54 Stat. 2405, 12 Bevans 551

The British Ambassador (Lothian) to the U.S. Secretary of State (Hull):

BRITISH EMBASSY
WASHINGTON, D.C.,
September 2nd, 1940

SIR,

I have the honour under instructions from His Majesty's Principal Secretary of State for Foreign Affairs to inform you that in view of the friendly and sympathetic interest of His Majesty's Government in the United Kingdom in the national security of the United States and their desire to strengthen the ability of the United States to cooperate effectively with the other nations of the Americas in the defence of the Western Hemisphere, His Majesty's Government will secure the grant to the Government of the United States, freely and without consideration, of the lease for immediate establishment and use of naval and air bases and facilities for entrance thereto and the operation and protection thereof, on the Avalon Peninsula and on the southern coast of Newfoundland, and on the east coast and on the Great Bay of Bermuda.

Furthermore, in view of the above and in view of the desire of the United States to acquire additional air and naval bases in the Caribbean and in British Guiana, and without endeavouring to place a monetary or commercial value upon the many tangible and intangible rights and properties involved, His Majesty's Government will make available to the United States for immediate establishment and use naval and air bases and facilities for entrance thereto and the operation and protection thereof, on the eastern side of the Bahamas, the southern coast of Jamaica, the western coast of St. Lucia, the west coast of Trinidad in the Gulf of Paria, in the island of Antigua and in British Guiana within fifty miles of Georgetown, in exchange for naval and military equipment and material which the United States Government will transfer to His Majesty's Government.

All the bases and facilities referred to in the preceding paragraphs will be leased to the United States for a period of ninety-nine years, free from all rent and charges other than such compensation to be mutually agreed on to be paid by the United States in order to compensate the owners of private property for loss by expropriation or damage arising out of the establishment of the bases and facilities in question.

His Majesty's Government, in the leases to be agreed upon, will grant to the United States for the period of the leases all the rights, power, and authority within the bases leased, and within the limits of the territorial waters and air spaces adjacent to or in the vicinity of such bases, necessary to provide access to and defence of such bases, and appropriate provisions for their control.

Without prejudice to the above-mentioned rights of the United States authorities and their jurisdiction within the leased areas, the adjustment and reconciliation between the jurisdiction of the authorities of the United States within these areas and the jurisdiction of the authorities of the territories in which these areas are situated, shall be determined by common agreement.

The exact location and bounds of the aforesaid bases, the necessary seaward, coast and anti-aircraft defences, the location of sufficient military garrisons, stores and other necessary auxiliary facilities shall be determined by common agreement.

His Majesty's Government are prepared to designate immediately experts to meet with experts of the United States for these purposes. Should these experts be unable to agree in any particular situation, except in the case of Newfoundland and Bermuda, the matter shall be settled by the Secretary of State of the United States and His Majesty's Secretary of State for Foreign Affairs.

I have the honour to be, with the highest consideration, Sir,

Your most obedient, humble servant,

LOTHIAN

The U.S. Secretary of State (Hull) to the British Ambassador (Lothian):

DEPARTMENT OF STATE
WASHINGTON
September 2, 1940

EXCELLENCY:

I have received your note of September 2, 1940, of which the text is as follows:

[Here the text of the preceding letter is quoted verbatim.]

I am directed by the President to reply to your note as follows:

The Government of the United States appreciates the declarations and the generous action of His Majesty's Government as contained in your communication which are destined to enhance the national security of the United States and greatly to strengthen its ability to cooperate effectively with the other nations of the Americas in the defense of the Western Hemisphere. It therefore gladly accepts the proposals.

The Government of the United States will immediately designate experts to meet with experts designated by His Majesty's Government to determine upon the exact location of the naval and air bases mentioned in your communication under acknowledgment.

In consideration of the declarations above quoted, the Government of the United States will immediately transfer to His Majesty's Government fifty United States Navy destroyers generally referred to as the twelve hundred-ton type.

Accept, Excellency, the renewed assurances of my highest consideration.

CORDELL HULL

NOTES AND QUESTIONS

1. *Background to the Negotiations.* In 1940, when Germany quickly overran France, President Roosevelt was concerned that Britain might fall too and Germany simply capture any requested U.S. destroyers. Did the United Kingdom have the will to carry on the fight? A British attack on the French fleet may have helped convince Roosevelt to conclude the Hull-Lothian Agreement. French warships were confined to port, but Churchill, fearing Germany would seize and employ them, demanded that the French warships docked in Algeria surrender to the United Kingdom, sail to Allied

ports, or face a British attack. When the French failed to surrender or sail, the Royal Navy "attacked with devastating force, destroying a number of French ships and killing 1,300 French sailors." France condemned this "act of mass murder." Germany used the incident in its anti-British propaganda. Roosevelt, however, "saw the attack as a confirmation of British resolve, and soon supplied Britain with the 50 destroyers." "Churchill's Deadly Decision," http://www.pbs.org/wnet/secrets (Apr. 16, 2010 episode of *Secrets of the Dead*) (last visited Dec. 8, 2013). For more background on the bases-for-destroyers deal, see William H. Langenberg, "Destroyers for Naval Bases: Highlights of an Unprecedented Trade," in *The Use of Force, Human Rights, and General International Legal Issues* 519 (62 *International Law Studies*, Richard B. Lillich & John Norton Moore eds. 1980).

2. *Bilateral v. Multilateral Treaty Negotiations*. Contrast the intimate bilateral negotiations leading up to the Hull-Lothian Agreement with the enormous multilateral context of some modern treaty-drafting conferences. The 1982 Convention on the Law of the Sea, for example, was the result of more than 15 years of multilateral negotiation, first during 1968–1973 in the Sea-Bed Committee established by the U.N. General Assembly and then during 1973–1982 in the Third United Nations Conference on the Law of the Sea (UNCLOS III). Altogether, thousands of diplomats from more than 150 states met hundreds of times. The negotiating agenda was complex, encompassing virtually every issue relating to use of and control over the oceans and ocean resources. States with common initial negotiating positions on one issue often found themselves at odds concerning other issues. Excellent studies of the UNCLOS III negotiations include Edward L. Miles, *Global Ocean Politics: The Decision Process at the Third United Nations Conference on the Law of the Sea, 1973–1982* (1998), Clyde Sanger, *Ordering the Oceans: The Making of the Law of the Sea* (1987), and William Wertenbaker, "The Law of the Sea," *The New Yorker,* Aug. 1, 1983, at 38 (Part I), Aug. 8, 1983, at 56 (Part II). More on the law of the sea is found in Chapter 10.

Can it be said that the domestic legal analogy to the Hull-Lothian negotiations is the drafting of a contract while the municipal analogy to the U.N. Law of the Sea Conference is the meeting of a legislative assembly? Does that make some treaties rather like contracts and others more like statutes?

3. *Terminology*. The Hull-Lothian Agreement took the form of an exchange of notes between the British and U.S. governments. Treaties have various designations:

> Among the terms used are: treaty, convention, agreement, protocol, covenant, charter, statute, act, declaration, *concordat*, exchange of notes, agreed minute, memorandum of agreement, memorandum of understanding, and *modus vivendi*. Whatever their designation, all agreements have the same legal status, except as their provisions or the circumstances of their conclusion indicate otherwise.

Restatement (Third) of the Foreign Relations Law of the United States § 301, Comment a (1987).

4. *Domestic Interests in Treaty Negotiations*. Note that the drafting of the Hull-Lothian Agreement involved the U.S. State Department, including Secretary of State Hull and Legal Adviser Hackworth, the Justice Department, and President Roosevelt. At the U.N. Law of the Sea Conference, the U.S. delegation often numbered more than a hundred persons. This permitted various U.S. "interests" to be represented, including the Departments of State, Defense, Interior, Commerce, and Justice. Altogether some 20 U.S. government agencies participated in the U.S. Inter-agency Task Force that "coordinated" U.S. law of the sea negotiations. As Ann Hollick, a long-time commentator on U.S. law of the sea politics, has written, the U.S. delegation "was usually the scene of more intense negotiations than was UNCLOS itself," leading to important problems in making and executing U.S. policy, to "discontent and suspicion" among delegates from other countries, and to impatience in Congress. Ann L. Hollick, *U.S. Foreign Policy and the Law of the Sea* 35 (1981). Ultimately, the Reagan administration repudiated some of the positions of the Nixon, Ford, and Carter administrations and refused to sign, much less to promote the ratification of, the 1982 Law of the Sea Convention. See Chapter 10.

5. *The Legality of Executive Agreements in U.S. Law*. The Hull-Lothian Agreement was an "international executive agreement" (of which more in Chapter 4), but was it legal at U.S. law? Did the Hull-Lothian Agreement violate federal law prohibiting the departure, much less the sale, of warships to a combatant when the U.S. was a neutral in a war? Did it violate the 1907 Hague Convention on Rights and Duties of Neutral Powers in Naval War, 36 Stat. 2415, 1 Bevans 723, a multilateral treaty accepted by the United States following a two-thirds vote of the Senate expressing its advice and consent in accordance with Article II(2) of the U.S. Constitution? The Hague Convention prohibited the supply of warships by a neutral country to a belligerent. Secretary of State Hull thought that the United States was not in breach, writing that the Nazis had "wrecked the convention." Might he also have argued the U.S. actions did not violate the Hague Convention because the United Kingdom was not a party and, according to Article 28, the Convention applied only when "all the belligerents are parties"? If the United States had been prohibited from supplying warships under the Hague Convention, could an executive agreement have "undone" it? After all, the Hague Convention was a treaty to which the U.S. Senate had given its advice and consent. Could an executive agreement have overridden a federal statute specifying requirements for disposing of U.S. naval ships?

Could the President legally make the Hull-Lothian Agreement without the Senate giving its advice and consent? On that point, Attorney General Jackson opined to President Roosevelt on August 27, 1940:

> The President's power over foreign relations while "delicate, plenary and exclusive" is not unlimited. Some negotiations involve commitments as to the future which would carry an obligation to

P. Power over foreign affairs.

> exercise powers vested in the Congress. Such Presidential arrangements are customarily submitted for ratification by a two-thirds vote of the Senate before the future legislative power of the country is committed. However, the acquisitions which you are proposing to accept are without express or implied promises on the part of the United States to be performed in the future. * * * The Executive Agreement obtains an opportunity to establish naval and air bases for the protection of our coastline but it imposes no obligation upon the Congress to appropriate money to improve the opportunity. It is not necessary for the Senate to ratify an opportunity that entails no obligation.

5 G.H. Hackworth, *Digest of International Law* 405–06 (1943).

Note the variety of possible U.S. legal issues: How "legal" was the Hull-Lothian Agreement given U.S. statutes, previous U.S. treaties ratified following the advice and consent of the Senate, and U.S. constitutional requirements for concluding international agreements? By what procedures, legal or political, might questions concerning the legality of the Hull-Lothian Agreement have been addressed? Critical views of the Hull-Lothian Agreement are to be found in Robert Shogan, *Hard Bargain* (1995), and in Aaron Xavier Fellmeth, "A Divorce Waiting to Happen: Franklin Roosevelt and the Law of Neutrality, 1935–1941," 3 *Buffalo Journal of International Law* 413 (1996–1997).

6. *Dualism.* How do the problems of the "legality" of the Hull-Lothian Agreement differ at U.S. and international law? Even if the Hull-Lothian Agreement were illegal in U.S. law because it violated a preexisting statute, that illegality would not prevent the United States from still being bound in international law to honor its treaty obligation to the United Kingdom. The International Court has ruled: "It is a generally accepted principle of international law that in the relations between powers who are contracting parties to a treaty, the provisions of municipal law cannot prevail over those in a treaty." Greco-Bulgarian Communities Case, 1930 P.C.I.J., Ser. B, No. 17, at 32. The principle is reaffirmed in Article 27 of the Vienna Convention on the Law of Treaties. Should the same principle apply when an action purporting to enter into a treaty violates a state's municipal *procedures* for approving treaties? See Article 46 of the Vienna Convention and the *Eastern Greenland Case* at the end of this chapter. That there are separate spheres of municipal and international law is sometimes referred to as "dualism." See Chapter 4.

7. *Lawyering.* Is Attorney General Jackson's statement, quoted in Note 5 above, persuasive? What should be the role of government lawyers when they advise political leaders about the legality of a proposed international action? Should the lawyers simply provide "objective" legal advice? Should they try to fashion a legal rationale to justify a President's action? Do you think Cordell Hull was effectively kept out of some of the negotiations of the Hull-Lothian Agreement because it was feared he had a legalistic attitude? The advice of government lawyers apparently made a difference in how the

bases-for-destroyers deal was structured. President Roosevelt at one point, reflecting Jackson's view that federal statutes precluded the President from simply giving destroyers to the British, told Prime Minister Churchill that "[t]he trouble is I have an Attorney General and he says I have got to bargain." Perhaps, Churchill grumbled, "you ought to trade these destroyers for a new Attorney General." *Quoted in* Shogan, *supra* Note 5, at 222.

How do government officials obtain advice about international law? In the United States, international lawyers working for the State Department's Office of the Legal Adviser (known as "L") participate in treaty negotiations, process international claims, respond to questions from foreign governments and private lawyers, and advise U.S. officials on a wide range of international legal questions. In earlier times, such distinguished lawyers as Thomas Jefferson, James Madison, and James Monroe personally handled the legal work of the State Department when they served as Secretaries of State. In 1891 the Office of the Solicitor of the Department of State was created, though the Solicitor was officially employed by the Department of Justice. Congress established the Office of the Legal Adviser in 1931. See Richard B. Bilder, "The Office of the Legal Adviser: The State Department Lawyer and Foreign Affairs," 56 *American Journal of International Law* 633, 634–36 (1962). For an excellent inside account of the work of L and the efficacy of the Legal Adviser's advice, see Michael P. Scharf & Paul R. Williams, *Shaping Foreign Policy in Times of Crisis: The Role of International Law and the State Department Legal Adviser* (2010). See also Stephen Bouwhuis, "The Role of an International Legal Adviser to Government," 61 *International and Comparative Law Quarterly* 939 (2012) (comparing roles of legal advisers in several developed countries). In the United States, the Department of Defense and other government agencies also employ lawyers to advise about international legal matters.

C. THE LAW OF TREATIES

This part introduces a detailed and complex area of international law, the law of treaties. The law of treaties plays roughly the same role in international law as the law of contracts plays in municipal law: it establishes rules about the making and interpretation of agreements, their observation, modification, and termination. Throughout this part, we see that courts, both international and municipal, may grapple with law of treaty issues.

THE RESERVATIONS TO THE GENOCIDE CONVENTION CASE

1951 I.C.J. 15, 31

[When states began to sign, ratify, or accede to the 1948 Convention for the Prevention and Punishment of Genocide, some made reservations, *i.e.*, unilateral statements purporting to exclude or modify the legal effect of particular treaty articles for a reserving country. Other states objected to some of the Genocide Convention reservations. The General Assembly of the United Nations debated the validity of the reservations, expressing particular concern about whether reserving states' ratifications or accessions would count towards the 20 acceptances needed for the Genocide Convention to enter into force. The Secretary-General of the United Nations also needed to know the legal effect of reservations, since the United Nations was the depositary for many treaties.]

On November 16th, 1950, the General Assembly of the United Nations adopted the following resolution:

> The General Assembly, * * *
>
> 1. Requests the International Court of Justice to give an Advisory Opinion on the following questions:
>
> In so far as concerns the Convention on the Prevention and Punishment of the Crime of Genocide in the event of a State ratifying or acceding to the Convention subject to a reservation made either on ratification or on accession, or on signature followed by ratification:
>
> I. Can the reserving State be regarded as being a party to the Convention while still maintaining its reservation if the reservation is objected to by one or more of the parties to the Convention but not by others?
>
> II. If the answer to Question I is in the affirmative, what is the effect of the reservation as between the reserving State and:
>
> (*a*) The parties which object to the reservation?
>
> (*b*) Those which accept it?

[The Court first addresses Question I.]

It is well established that in its treaty relations a State cannot be bound without its consent, and that consequently, no reservation can be effective against any State, without its agreement thereto. It is also a generally recognized principle that a multilateral convention is the result of an agreement freely concluded upon its clauses and that consequently none of the contracting parties is entitled to frustrate or impair, by means of unilateral decisions or particular agreements, the purpose and *raison d'être* of the convention. To this principle was linked the notion of the integrity of the convention as adopted, a notion which in its traditional concept involved the proposition that no reservation was valid unless it was accepted by all the contracting parties without exception, as would have been the case if it had been stated during the negotiations.

The concept, which is directly inspired by the notion of contract, is of undisputed value as a principle. However, as regards the Genocide Convention, it is proper to refer to a variety of circumstances which would lead to a more flexible application of this principle. Among these circumstances may be noted the clearly universal character of the United Nations under whose auspices the Convention was concluded, and the very wide degree of participation envisaged by Article XI of the Convention.

[A]lthough the Genocide Convention was finally approved unanimously, it is nevertheless the result of a series of majority votes. The majority principle, while facilitating the conclusion of multilateral conventions, may also make it necessary for certain States to make reservations. This observation is confirmed by the great number of reservations which have been made of recent years to multilateral conventions.

In this state of international practice, it could certainly not be inferred from the absence of an article providing for reservations in a multilateral convention that the contracting States are prohibited from making certain reservations. * * *

The Court * * * must now determine what kind of reservations may be made and what kind of objections may be taken to them.

The solution of these problems must be found in the special characteristics of the Genocide Convention. The origins and character of that Convention, the objects pursued by the General Assembly and the contracting parties, the relations which exist between the provisions of the Convention, *inter se*, and between those provisions and these objects, furnish elements of interpretation of the will of the General Assembly and the parties. The origins of the Convention show that it was the intention of the United Nations to condemn and punish genocide as "a crime under international law" involving a denial of the right of existence of entire human groups, a denial which shocks the conscience of mankind and results in great losses to humanity, and which is contrary to moral law and to the spirit and aims of the United Nations. The first consequence arising from this conception is that the principles underlying the Convention are principles which are recognized by civilized nations as binding on States, even without any conventional obligation. A second consequence is the universal character both of the condemnation of genocide and of the co-operation required "in order to liberate mankind from such an odious scourge" (Preamble to the Convention). The Genocide Convention was therefore intended by the General Assembly and by the contracting parties to be definitely universal in scope. It was in fact approved on December 9th, 1948, by a resolution which was unanimously adopted by 56 States.

The objects of such a convention must also be considered. The Convention was manifestly adopted for a purely humanitarian and civilizing purpose. It is indeed difficult to imagine a convention that might have this character to a greater degree, since its object on the one hand is to safeguard the very existence of certain human groups and on the other to confirm and endorse the most elementary principles of morality. In such a convention the contracting States do not have any interests of their own; they merely have, one and all, a common interest, namely, the accomplishment of those high purposes which are the *raison d'être* of the convention. Consequently, in a convention of this type one cannot speak of individual advantages or disadvantages to States, or of the maintenance of a perfect contractual balance between rights and duties. The high ideals which inspired the Convention provide, by virtue of the common will of the parties, the foundation and measure of all its provisions.

The foregoing considerations, when applied to the question of reservations, and more particularly to the effects of objections to reservations, lead to the following conclusions.

The object and purpose of the Genocide Convention imply that it was the intention of the General Assembly and of the States which adopted it that as many States as possible should participate. The complete exclusion from the Convention of one or more States would not only restrict the scope of its application, but would detract from the authority of the moral and humanitarian principles which are its basis. It is inconceivable that the contracting parties readily contemplated that an objection to a minor reservation should produce such a result. But even less could the contracting parties have intended to sacrifice the very object of the Convention in favor of a vain desire to secure as many participants as possible. The object and purpose of the Convention thus limit both the freedom of making reservations and that of objecting to them. It follows that it is the compatibility of a reservation with the object and purpose of the Convention that must furnish the criterion for the attitude of a State in making the reservation on accession as well as for the appraisal by a State in objecting to the reservation. Such is the rule of conduct which must guide every State in the appraisal which it must make, individually and from its own standpoint, of the admissibility of any reservation. * * *

It results from the foregoing consideration that Question I, on account of its abstract character, cannot be given an absolute answer. The appraisal of a reservation and the effect of objections that might be made to it depend upon the particular circumstances of each individual case.

Having replied to Question I, the Court will now examine Question II, which is framed as follows:

> If the answer to Question I is in the affirmative, what is the effect of the reservation as between the reserving State and:
>
> (*a*) the parties which object to the reservation?
>
> (*b*) those which accept it?

[E]ach State which is a party to the Convention is entitled to appraise the validity of the reservation, and it exercises this right individually and from its own standpoint. As no State can be bound by a reservation to which it has not consented, it necessarily follows that each State objecting to it will or will not, on the basis of its individual appraisal within the limits of the criterion of the object and purpose stated above, consider the reserving States to be a party to the Convention. In the ordinary course of events, such a decision will only affect the relationship between the State making the reservation and the objecting State[.]

For these reasons,

THE COURT IS OF OPINION,

In so far as concerns the Convention on the Prevention and Punishment of the Crime of Genocide, in the event of a State ratifying or acceding to the Convention subject to a reservation made either on ratification or on accession, or on signature followed by ratification,

On Question I:

by seven votes to five,

that a State which has made and maintained a reservation which has been objected to by one or more of the parties to the Convention but not by others, can be regarded as being a party to the Convention if the reservation is compatible with the object and purpose of the Convention; otherwise, that State cannot be regarded as being a party to the Convention.

On Question II:

by seven votes to five,

(*a*) that if a party to the Convention objects to a reservation which it considers to be incompatible with the object and purpose of the Convention, it can in fact consider that the reserving State is not a party to the Convention;

(*b*) that if, on the other hand, a party accepts the reservation as being compatible with the object and purpose of the Contention, it can in fact consider that the reserving State is a party to the Convention[.]

DISSENTING OPINION OF JUDGES GUERRERO,
SIR ARNOLD MCNAIR, READ, HSU MO

We regret that we are unable to concur in the Opinion of the Court[.]

[I]t will make our examination of the problem more realistic if we state that before the end of 1950 the Secretary-General had received notice of eighteen reservations, proposed, some by one State, some by another, the total number of States being eight, and that those reservations relate to Article IV (removal of any jurisdictional immunities of "constitutionally responsible rulers, public officials or private individuals"), Article VI (jurisdiction of municipal tribunals), Article VII (extradition), Article IX (the compulsory jurisdiction of the International Court of Justice), and Article XII (the "colonial clause"). Every one of the eight reserving States has made a reservation against, or in regard to, Article IX. * * *

We believe that the integrity of the terms of the Convention is of greater importance than mere universality in its acceptance. While it is undoubtedly true that the representatives of the governments, in drafting and adopting the Genocide Convention, wished to see as many States become parties to it as possible, it was certainly not their intention to achieve universality at any price. There is no evidence to show that they desired to secure wide acceptance of the Convention even at the expense of the integrity or uniformity of its terms, irrespective of the wishes of those States which have accepted all the obligations under it.

It is an undeniable fact that the tendency of all international activities in recent times has been towards the promotion of the common welfare of the international community with a corresponding restriction of the sovereign power of individual States. So, when a common effort is made to promote a great humanitarian object, as in the case of the Genocide Convention, every interested State naturally expects every other interested State not to seek any individual advantage or convenience, but to carry out the measures resolved upon by common accord. Hence, each party must be given the right to judge the acceptability of a reservation and to decide whether or not to exclude the reserving State from the Convention, and we are not aware of any case in which this right has been abused. It is therefore not universality at any price that forms the first consideration. It is rather the acceptance of common obligations—keeping step with like-minded States—in order to attain a high objective for all humanity, that is of paramount importance. Such being the case, the conclusion is irresistible that it is necessary to apply to the Genocide Convention with even greater exactitude than ever the existing rule which requires the consent of all parties to any reservation to a multilateral convention. In the interests of the international community, it would be better to lose as a party to the Convention a State which insists in face of objections on a modification of the terms of the Convention, than to permit it to become a party against the wish of a State or States which have irrevocably and unconditionally accepted all the obligations of the Convention.

The Opinion of the Court seeks to limit the operation of the new rule to the Genocide Convention. We foresee difficulty in finding a criterion which will establish the uniqueness of this Convention and will differentiate it from the other humanitarian conventions which have been, or will be, negotiated under the auspices of the United Nations or its Specialized Agencies and adopted by them. But if the Genocide Convention is in any way unique, its uniqueness consists in the importance of regarding it as a whole and maintaining the integrity and indivisibility of its text, whereas it seems to us that the new rule propounded by the majority will encourage the making of reservations.

NOTES AND QUESTIONS

1. *The Genocide Convention.* The United Nations, formed in 1945 at the end of World War II, has as one of its purposes "promoting and encouraging respect for human rights." U.N. Charter, art. 1(3). See Chapter 8 for background on the United Nations and Chapter 6 for more on U.N. human rights instruments and institutions. In 1948 the U.N. General Assembly adopted both the Universal Declaration on Human Rights, reproduced in the Appendix, and the Genocide Convention, the first of several multilateral human rights treaties the Assembly was to adopt. The Convention defines genocide in terms of specific acts (*e.g.*, killing group members) "committed with intent to destroy, in whole or in part, a national, ethnical, racial or religious group," and it deems "genocide, whether committed in time of peace or in time of war, * * * a crime under international law." Convention on the Prevention and Punishment of the Crime of Genocide, arts. I-II, Dec. 9, 1948, 102 Stat. 3045, 78 U.N.T.S. 277. The Convention entered into force in 1951 and as of December 2013 numbers 144 parties.

2. *The International Court of Justice.* The *Reservations to the Genocide Convention Case* is our first principal excerpt from a decision of the International Court of Justice. The ICJ, the successor to the Permanent International Court of Justice, was created as a part of the United Nations at the end of World War II. In the *Genocide Case* the General Assembly of the United Nations requested the Court to issue an advisory opinion, which is not legally binding but may have persuasive power. The Court also hears interstate cases where the states involved mutually consent to the Court's jurisdiction and where the Court's judgment is legally binding. More on the ICJ and its advisory and contentious jurisdiction appears in Chapter 5.

3. *The Sources of the Law of Treaties.* What are the sources of legal rules governing reservations, treaty interpretation, treaty termination, and other matters related to treaties? Modern international lawyers often consult the Vienna Convention on the Law of Treaties (see Appendix). This Convention was drafted by the International Law Commission (ILC), a body of legal experts created by the U.N. General Assembly pursuant to Article 13 of the U.N. Charter to encourage "the progressive development of international law and its codification." The Vienna Convention was adopted and opened for signature in 1969 by a diplomatic conference. Prior to the Vienna Convention, no treaty codified the law of treaties. After the Vienna Convention entered into force in 1980, it became binding as treaty law for those states that accepted it—113 as of July 2013. Many Vienna Convention

rules are regarded as customary international law, a subject we explore in Chapter 3. The ILC began to study the specific topic of treaty reservations in 1993, and in 2011 adopted a "Guide to Practice on Reservations to Treaties." *Report of the International Law Commission on the Work of its Sixty-third Session*, U.N. Doc. A/66/10 (2011), at 19.

4. *Treaty Provisions Expressly Permitting or Prohibiting Reservations.* The *Genocide Convention Case* concerns a treaty that is silent about the permissibility of reservations. Treaty negotiators sometimes specify whether reservations are permissible. Some multilateral treaties expressly permit reservations, at least for certain treaty articles. Others—for example, the 1982 Convention on the Law of the Sea, which addresses a wide range of oceans issues—expressly prohibit them. See Vienna Convention on the Law of Treaties, arts. 19–20(1). According to a study of some 276 multilateral treaties that were finalized after 1951 and for which the U.N. Secretary-General is the depositary, 20 percent (55) strictly prohibit any reservations, while 48 percent (133) contain no language about reservations; others either expressly permit reservations or, while generally precluding reservations, allow parties to opt out of specific treaty provisions. See Jean Galbraith, "Treaty Options: Towards a Behavioral Understanding of Treaty Design," 53 *Virginia Journal of International Law* 309, 324–28 (2013).

5. *Object and Purpose.* The object and purpose of a treaty is of central importance for several law of treaties issues, including treaty interpretation (see Vienna Convention on the Law of Treaties, arts. 31, 33), treaty modification (art. 41), suspension of treaty obligations (art. 58), material breach (art. 60), and, as we saw in the *Reservations to the Genocide Convention Case*, reservations. How can we determine the object and purpose of a treaty? According to the ICJ, where should we look to find the Genocide Convention's object and purpose? Does it seem to you that "[p]roperly used the notion of object and purpose creates an overarching normative element," adding to our understanding of treaties? Jan Klabbers, "Treaties, Object and Purpose" ¶ 23, in 9 *Max Planck Encyclopedia of Public International Law* 1135 (Rüdiger Wolfrum ed. 2012).

Might a reservation to a dispute settlement provision, such as Article IX of the Genocide Convention, violate a treaty's object and purpose? That Article provides that disputes "relating to the interpretation, application or fulfilment of the present Convention, including those relating to the responsibility of a State for genocide * * * shall be submitted to the International Court of Justice at the request of any of the parties to the dispute." Some countries, including the United States, entered reservations to Article IX when they ratified the Genocide Convention. Others, *e.g.*, the Netherlands, have objected that those reservations are incompatible with the object and purpose of the Convention. There is some judicial opinion on the issue. In Armed Activities on the Territory of the Congo (Democratic Republic of the Congo v. Rwanda), 2006 I.C.J. 6, 32 (Jurisdiction and Admissibility), the ICJ found that Article IX "does not affect substantive obligations relating to acts of genocide," and concluded that Rwanda's Article IX reservation was not "incompatible with the object and purpose of the Convention." Do you agree? Five judges in the case, noting that Article IX applied *inter alia* to disputes concerning "fulfilment" of the Genocide Convention, thought that an Article IX reservation might "be regarded as incompatible" with the Convention's object and purpose and suggested that "the Court should revisit" the matter. Joint Separate Opinion of Judges Higgins, Kooijmans, Elaraby, Owada, and Simma, *id.* at 66, 72. With respect to the compatibility of dispute settlement provisions with treaty object and purpose, could there be different answers for different treaties? Does much depend on the particular features of a dispute settlement or review arrangement and how integrally it links to substantive obligations? Who determines whether reservations concerning substantive obligations of a human rights treaty are compatible with the treaty's object and purpose if no international tribunal has jurisdiction to rule on the matter?

6. *Comparing Approaches to the Validity of Reservations.* The majority and dissenting opinions in the *Reservations to the Genocide Convention Case* reflected differing views about the contractual nature of treaties. The majority decision presumed that states have a great deal of discretion to bind themselves or not to the provisions of international agreements. Articles 2(1)(d) and 19–21 of the Vienna Convention on the Law of Treaties follow the ICJ's majority opinion in the *Genocide Case*, allowing reservations that are compatible with a treaty's object and purpose when the treaty itself does not preclude or limit the types of reservations that are permissible. This approach can lead to a complicated web of different obligations with respect to the same treaty. For example, suppose three states accept a convention. Only the first makes a reservation to a particular article when it accepts the convention; the second state accepts the reservation; and the third state objects to the reservation and expressly indicates that it does not regard the convention as in force between itself and the reserving state. What treaty obligations bind each pair of these three states? Now picture the complications when a convention features dozens of parties, many different reservations, and various reactions by different states to each of those reservations. Can we even be certain about all the resulting relationships? For example, is a reservation that violates a treaty's object and purpose void *ab initio*? Or will it be ineffective only with respect to treaty parties that object to it in a timely manner? See Vienna Convention on the Law of Treaties, art. 19(c); Edward T. Swaine, "Treaty Reservations," in *The Oxford Guide to Treaties* 276, 285–88 (Duncan B. Hollis ed. 2012). A simpler approach would have been to adopt the "extreme 'sovereignty' theory," once favored by the Soviet Union, under which a state could enter any reservation it liked. See I.M. Sinclair, "Vienna Conference on the Law of Treaties," 19 *International and Comparative Law Quarterly* 47, 55–57 (1970). Neither the International Court in the *Reservations to the Genocide Convention Case* nor the ILC in drafting the Vienna Convention followed that "extreme 'sovereignty' " approach. Why has it not found favor?

The dissenting opinion in the *Reservations to the Genocide Convention Case* took, if you will, a more statutory approach toward treaties, paying rather more attention to the will of the international community. In a multilateral treaty with a significant moral mission like the Genocide Convention, should community sentiment play a larger role than in a more transactional bilateral agreement, say the Cession of Alaska? According to the Inter-American Court of Human Rights, a human rights treaty is "in reality [a] framework enabling states to make binding unilateral commitments not to violate the human rights of individuals within their jurisdiction." Advisory Opinion on Reservations, Inter-Am. Ct. H.R. (ser. A) No. 2, ¶ 33 (1982). If one regards a human rights treaty as a "framework" allowing unilateral commitments, rather than as "legislation," does it follow that states should be free to make reservations?

7. *The Consequences of an Invalid Reservation*. If a reservation to a human rights treaty is found to be invalid, what should be the consequences? Should the reserving state remain bound by the treaty except for the provision to which the reservation related? Or should the invalidity of a reservation mean that the reserving state is not a party to the treaty at all? Or should the invalid reservation be severed from the reserving state's acceptance of the treaty, leaving that state bound by the entire treaty? Should severability depend on the intent of the reserving state? See Ryan Goodman, "Human Rights Treaties, Invalid Reservations, and State Consent," 96 *American Journal of International Law* 531 (2002); Swaine, *supra* Note 6, at 293–97.

In the Belilos Case, 10 E.H.R.R. 466 (1988), the European Court of Human Rights in Strasbourg considered a claim that Switzerland violated the right "to a fair and public hearing within a reasonable time by an independent and impartial tribunal established by law" provided by Article 6(1) of the European Convention on Human Rights. Marlène Belilos had been convicted by the Lausanne Police Board for participating in an illegal demonstration. She invoked the procedures of the European human rights system, claiming a breach of Article 6(1) on the grounds that the Police Board was not impartial and that Swiss law did not provide for independent appellate review of factual Police Board findings. Switzerland in fact allowed only limited appellate judicial review of Police Board decisions. Switzerland had entered a reservation to Article 6(1) when it accepted the European Convention on Human Rights, a reservation that, according to Switzerland, shielded it from liability. The European Court of Human Rights found the Swiss reservation invalid because it was too vague and did not comply with the Convention's rules concerning when reservations were permissible. Should Switzerland still be bound by the European Human Rights Convention despite the invalidity of its reservation? The Strasbourg Court concluded that Switzerland was bound and simply severed the invalid reservation. The Court ultimately concluded that Switzerland's treatment of Marlène Belilos violated Article 6(1). For further discussion, see Susan Marks, "Reservations Unhinged: The *Belilos* Case Before the European Court of Human Rights," 39 *International and Comparative Law Quarterly* 300 (1990).

8. *Reservations, Understandings, and Declarations.* States sometimes attach unilateral understandings and declarations, as well as reservations, when they accept treaties. Only reservations have the potential formally to limit the scope of a state's acceptance of a treaty. Nevertheless, declarations and understandings suggest how a state, in its diplomatic practice, is likely to interpret articles or words in a treaty. Should a state's declarations and understandings also dictate how its municipal courts interpret a treaty? In Chapter 4, we explore how authority concerning treaties is allocated among various branches of the U.S. federal government, and between the federal and state governments.

EASTERN AIRLINES, INC. V. FLOYD

499 U.S. 530 (1991)

JUSTICE MARSHALL delivered the opinion of the Court.

Article 17 of the Warsaw Convention[1] sets forth conditions under which an international air carrier can be held liable for injuries to passengers. This case presents the question whether Article 17 allows recovery for mental or psychic injuries unaccompanied by physical injury or physical manifestation of injury.

I

On May 5, 1983, an Eastern Airlines flight departed from Miami, bound for the Bahamas. Shortly after takeoff, one of the plane's three jet engines lost oil pressure. The flight crew shut down the failing engine and turned the plane around to return to Miami. Soon thereafter, the second and third engines failed due to loss of oil pressure. The plane began losing altitude rapidly, and the passengers were informed that the plane would be ditched in the Atlantic Ocean. Fortunately, after a period of descending flight without power, the crew managed to restart an engine and land the plane safely at Miami International Airport.

Respondents, a group of passengers on the flight, brought separate complaints against petitioner, Eastern Airlines, Inc. (Eastern), each claiming damages solely for mental distress arising out of the incident. The District Court entertained each complaint in a consolidated proceeding. Eastern conceded that the engine failure and subsequent preparations for ditching the plane amounted to an "accident" under Article 17 of the Convention but argued that Article 17 also makes physical injury a condition of liability. * * * The District Court concluded that mental anguish alone is not compensable under Article 17.

The Court of Appeals for the Eleventh Circuit reversed, holding that the phrase "lésion corporelle" in the authentic French text of Article 17

[1] Convention for the Unification of Certain Rules Relating to International Transportation by Air, Oct. 12, 1929, 49 Stat. 3000, T.S. No. 876 (1934), note following 49 U.S.C. App. § 1502 (hereinafter Warsaw Convention or Convention).

encompasses purely emotional distress. To support its conclusion, the court examined the French legal meaning of the term "lésion corporelle," the concurrent and subsequent history of the Convention, and cases interpreting Article 17. We granted certiorari [and] now hold that Article 17 does not allow recovery for purely mental injuries.

II

"When interpreting a treaty, we 'begin "with the text of the treaty and the context in which the written words are used." ' " *Volkswagenwerk Aktiengesellschaft v. Schlunk*, 486 U.S. 694, 699 (1988), quoting *Société Nationale Industrielle Aérospatiale v. United States District Court*, 482 U.S. 522, 534 (1987), quoting *Air France v. Saks*, 470 U.S. 392, 397 (1985). "Other general rules of construction may be brought to bear on difficult or ambiguous passages." *Volkswagenwerk, supra,* at 700. Moreover, " 'treaties are construed more liberally than private agreements, and to ascertain their meaning we may look beyond the written words to the history of the treaty, the negotiations, and the practical construction adopted by the parties.' " *Saks, supra,* at 396, quoting *Choctaw Nation of Indians v. United States*, 318 U.S. 423, 431–432 (1943). We proceed to apply these methods in turn.

A

Because the only authentic text of the Warsaw Convention is in French, the French text must guide our analysis. See *Saks, supra*, at 397–399. The text reads as follows:

> Le transporteur est responsable du dommage survenu *en cas de mort, de blessure ou de toute autre lésion corporelle* subie par un voyageur lorsque l'accident qui a causé le dommage s'est produit à bord de l'aéronef ou au cours de toutes opérations d'embarquement et de débarquement. [49 Stat. 3005 (emphasis added).]

The American translation of this text, employed by the Senate when it ratified the Convention in 1934, reads:

> The carrier shall be liable for damage sustained *in the event of the death or wounding of a passenger or any other bodily injury* suffered by a passenger, if the accident which caused the damage so sustained took place on board the aircraft or in the course of any of the operations of embarking or disembarking. [49 Stat. 3018 (emphasis added).]

Thus, under Article 17, an air carrier is liable for passenger injury only when three conditions are satisfied: (1) there has been an accident, in which (2) the passenger suffered "mort," "blessure," "ou . . . toute autre lésion corporelle," and (3) the accident took place on board the aircraft or in the course of operations of embarking or disembarking. As petitioner concedes, the incident here took place on board the aircraft and was an "accident" for purposes of Article 17. Moreover, respondents concede that they suffered neither "mort" nor "blessure" from the mishap. Therefore, the narrow issue presented here is whether, under the proper interpretation of "lésion corporelle," condition (2) is satisfied when a passenger has suffered only a mental or psychic injury.

We must consider the "French legal meaning" of "lésion corporelle" for guidance as to the shared expectations of the parties to the Convention because the Convention was drafted in French by continental jurists. Perhaps the simplest method of determining the meaning of a phrase appearing in a foreign legal text would be to consult a bilingual dictionary. Such dictionaries suggest that a proper translation of "lésion corporelle" is "bodily injury." See, *e.g.*, J. Jéraute, Vocabulaire Français-Anglais et Anglais-Français de Termes et Locutions Juridiques 205 (1953) (translating "bodily harm" or "bodily injury" as "lésion ou blessure corporelle"); see also *id.*, at 95 (translating the term "lésion" as "injury, damage, prejudice, wrong"), *id.* at 41 (giving as one sense of "corporel" the English word "bodily"), 3 Grand Larousse de la Langue Française 1833 (1987) (defining "lésion" as a "[m]odification de la structure d'un tissu vivant sous l'influence d'une cause morbide"). These translations, if correct, clearly suggest that Article 17 does *not* permit recovery for purely psychic injuries. [However,] we recognize that dictionary definitions may be too general for purposes of treaty interpretation. Our concerns are partly allayed when, as here, the dictionary translation accords with the wording used in the "two main translations of the 1929 Convention in English" [*i.e.*, the U.S. and British translations]. We turn, then, to French legal materials to determine whether French jurists' contemporary understanding of the term "lésion corporelle" differed from its translated meaning.

In 1929, as in the present day, lawyers trained in French civil law would rely on the following principal sources of French law: (1) legislation, (2) judicial decisions, and (3) scholarly writing. See generally 1 M. Planiol & G. Ripert, Traité élémentaire de droit civil, pt. 1, Nos. 10, 122, 127 (12th ed. 1939) (Louisiana State Law Inst. trans. 1959); F. Gény, Méthode d'Interprétation et Sources en Droit Privé Positif Nos. 45–50 (2d ed. 1954) (Louisiana State Law Inst. trans. 1963); R. David, French Law: Its Structure, Sources, and Methodology 154 (M. Kindred trans. 1972). Our review of these materials indicates neither that "lésion corporelle" was a widely used legal term in French law nor that the term specifically encompassed psychic injuries.

Turning first to legislation, we find no French legislative provisions in force in 1929 that contained the phrase "lésion corporelle." * * *

Turning next to cases, we likewise discover no French court decisions in or before 1929 that explain the phrase "lésion corporelle," nor do the parties direct us to any. * * *

Turning finally to French treatises and scholarly writing covering the period leading up to the Warsaw Convention, we find no materials (and the parties have brought none to our attention) indicating that "lésion corporelle" embraced psychic injury. Subsequent to the adoption of the Warsaw Convention, some scholars have argued that "lésion corporelle" as used in Article 17 should be interpreted to encompass such injury. See, *e.g.*, Mankiewicz[, The Liability Regime of the International Air Carrier] 146 [(1981) (hereinafter Mankiewicz)] (arguing that "in French law the expression *lésion corporelle* covers any 'personal' injury whatsoever"); G. Miller, Liability in International Air Transport 128 (1977) (hereinafter Miller) (arguing that "a liberal interpretation of [Article 17] would be more in line with the spirit of the Convention"). These scholars draw on the fact that, by 1929, France—unlike many other countries—permitted tort recovery for mental distress. However, this *general* proposition of French tort law does not demonstrate that the *specific* phrase chosen by the contracting parties—"lésion corporelle"—covers purely psychic injury.

We find it noteworthy, moreover, that scholars who read "lésion corporelle" as encompassing psychic injury do not base their argument on explanations of this term in French cases or French treatises or even in the French Civil Code; rather, they chiefly rely on the principle of French tort law that any damage can "give rise to reparation when it is real and has been verified." 2 Planiol & Ripert, *supra*, at pt. 1, No. 868. We do not dispute this principle of French law. However, * * * since our task is to "give the specific words of the treaty a meaning consistent with the shared expectations of the contracting parties," *Saks, supra*, at 399, we find it unlikely that those parties' apparent understanding of the term "lésion corporelle" as "bodily injury" would have been displaced by a meaning abstracted from the French law of damages. Particularly is this so when the cause of action for psychic injury that evidently was possible under French law in 1929 would not have been recognized in many other countries represented at the Warsaw Convention.

[The Court considers in detail the structure of Article 17 and continues:] In sum, neither the Warsaw Convention itself nor any of the applicable French legal sources demonstrates that "lésion corporelle" should be translated other than as "bodily injury"—a narrow meaning excluding purely mental injuries. However, because a broader interpretation of "lésion corporelle" reaching purely mental injuries is plausible, and the term is both ambiguous and difficult, we turn to additional aids to construction.

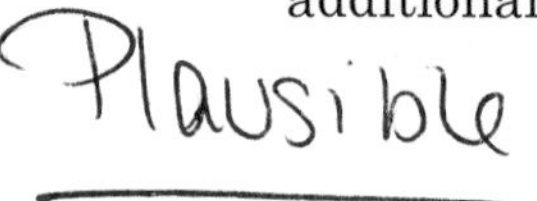

B

Translating "lésion corporelle" as "bodily injury" is consistent, we think, with the negotiating history of the Convention. "The treaty that became the Warsaw Convention was first drafted at an international conference in Paris in 1925." *Air France v. Saks*, 470 U.S. at 401. See generally [1925 Paris] Conférence Internationale de Droit Privé Aérien (1936) (hereinafter Paris Conference). The final protocol of the Paris Conference contained an article specifying that: " 'The carrier is liable for accidents, losses, breakdowns, and delays. It is not liable if it can prove that it has taken reasonable measures designed to pre-empt damage. . . . ' " It appears that "this expansive provision, broadly holding carriers liable in the event of an accident, would almost certainly have permitted recovery for all types of injuries, including emotional distress." Sisk, Recovery for Emotional Distress Under the Warsaw Convention: The Elusive Search for the French Legal Meaning of *Lésion Corporelle*, 25 Texas Int'l L.J. 127, 142 (1990), citing Miller 124.

The Paris Conference appointed a committee of experts, the Comité International Technique d'Experts Juridiques Aeriens (CITEJA), to revise its final protocol for presentation to the Warsaw Conference. The CITEJA draft split the liability article of the Paris Conference's protocol into three provisions with one addressing damages for injury to passengers, the second addressing injury to goods, and the third addressing losses caused by delay. The CITEJA subsection on injury to passengers introduced the phrase "en cas de mort, de blessure ou de toute autre lésion corporelle." This language was retained in Article 17 ultimately adopted by the Warsaw Conference. Although there is no definitive evidence explaining why the CITEJA drafters chose this narrower language, we believe it is reasonable to infer that the Conference adopted the narrower language to limit the types of recoverable injuries.[9]

Our review of the documentary record for the Warsaw Conference confirms—and courts and commentators appear universally to agree—that there is no evidence that the drafters or signatories of the Warsaw Convention specifically considered liability for psychic injury or the meaning of "lésion corporelle." Two explanations commonly are offered for

---

[9] Courts and commentators, including the Court of Appeals, have cited the doctoral thesis of a French scholar, Yvonne Blanc–Dannery, as extrinsic evidence of the Warsaw parties' intent. According to Mankiewicz, the Blanc–Dannery thesis was written under the supervision of Georges Ripert. Georges Ripert was a leading French delegate at the Warsaw Convention and an expert of the French Government at the CITEJA proceedings. Mankiewicz translates a passage from the Blanc–Dannery thesis as follows: " 'The use of the expression *lésion* after the words "death" and "wounding" encompasses and contemplates cases of traumatism and nervous troubles, the consequences of which do not immediately become manifest in the organism but which can be related to the accident.' " * * * Even if Mankiewicz's translation is accurate, * * * Blanc–Dannery's asserted definition is not supported by evidence from the CITEJA or Warsaw proceedings. In the absence of such support we find the Blanc–Dannery thesis to have little or no value as evidence of the drafters' intent.

why the subject of mental injuries never arose during the Convention proceedings: (1) many jurisdictions did not recognize recovery for mental injury at that time, or (2) the drafters simply could not contemplate a psychic injury unaccompanied by a physical injury. Indeed, the unavailability of compensation for purely psychic injury in many common and civil law countries at the time of the Warsaw Conference persuades us that the signatories had no specific intent to include such a remedy in the Convention. [The Court surveys the status of recovery for mental distress in France, the United Kingdom, U.S. jurisdictions, the Netherlands, Germany, Switzerland, and the Soviet Union.] Because such a remedy was unknown in many, if not most, jurisdictions in 1929, the drafters most likely would have felt compelled to make an unequivocal reference to purely mental injury if they had specifically intended to allow such recovery.

In this sense, we find it significant that, when the parties to a different international transport treaty wanted to make it clear that rail passengers could recover for purely psychic harms, the drafters made a specific modification to this effect. The liability provision of the Berne Convention on International Rail, drafted in 1952, originally conditioned liability on "la mort, les blessures et toute autre atteinte, à l'intégrité corporelle." International Convention Concerning the Carriage of Passengers and Luggage By Rail, Berne, Oct. 25, 1952, 242 U.N.T.S. 355, Article 28, p. 390. The drafters subsequently modified this provision to read "l'intégrité physique *ou mentale*." See Additional Convention to the International Convention Concerning the Carriage of Passengers and Luggage by Rail (CIV) of Feb. 25, 1961, Relating to the Liability of the Railway for Death of and Personal Injury to Passengers, done Feb. 26, 1966, Art. 2 (emphasis added).

The narrower reading of "lésion corporelle" also is consistent with the primary purpose of the contracting parties to the Convention: limiting the liability of air carriers in order to foster the growth of the fledgling commercial aviation industry. Indeed, it was for this reason that the Warsaw delegates imposed a maximum recovery of $8,300 for an accident—a low amount even by 1929 standards. Whatever may be the current view among Convention signatories, in 1929 the parties were more concerned with protecting air carriers and fostering a new industry than providing full recovery to injured passengers, and we read "lésion corporelle" in a way that respects that legislative choice.

C

We also conclude that, on balance, the evidence of the post-1929 "conduct" and "interpretations of the signatories" supports the narrow translation of "lésion corporelle."

In the years following adoption of the Convention, some scholars questioned whether Article 17 extended to mental or emotional injury. See, *e.g.*, Beaumont, Need for Revision and Amplification of the Warsaw Convention, 16 J. Air L. & Com. 395, 402 (1949); R. Coquoz, Le Droit Privé International Aérien 122 (1938); Sullivan, The Codification of Air Carrier Liability by International Convention, 7 J. Air. L. 1, 19 (1936). In 1951, a committee composed of 20 Warsaw Convention signatories met in Madrid and adopted a proposal to substitute "affection corporelle" for "lésion corporelle" in Article 17. The French delegate to the committee proposed this substitution because, in his view, the word "lésion" was too narrow, in that it "presupposed a rupture in the tissue, or a dissolution of continuity" which might not cover an injury such as mental illness or lung congestion caused by a breakdown in the heating apparatus of the aircraft. The United States delegate opposed this change if it "implied the inclusion of mental injury or emotional disturbances or upsets which were not connected with or the result of bodily injury," but the committee adopted it nonetheless. Although the committee's proposed amendment was never subsequently implemented, its discussion and vote in Madrid suggest that, in the view of the 20 signatories on the committee, "lésion corporelle" in Article 17 had a distinctly physical scope.

In finding that the signatories' post-1929 conduct supports the broader interpretation of "lésion corporelle," the Court of Appeals relied on three international agreements: The Hague Protocol of 1955, The Montreal Agreement of 1966, and the Guatemala City Protocol of 1971. For each of these agreements, the Court of Appeals emphasized that English translations rendered "lésion corporelle" as "personal injury," instead of "bodily injury." In our view, none of these agreements support the broad interpretation of "lésion corporelle" reached by the Court of Appeals. * * *

We must also consult the opinions of our sister signatories in searching for the meaning of a "lésion corporelle." *See Saks*, 470 U.S., at 404. The only apparent judicial decision from a sister signatory addressing recovery for purely mental injuries under Article 17 is that of the Supreme Court of Israel. That court held that Article 17 does allow recovery for purely psychic injuries. See *Cie Air France v. Teichner*, 39 Revue Française de Droit Aérien, at 243, 23 Eur. Tr. L., at 102.

Teichner arose from the hijacking in 1976 of an Air France flight to Entebbe, Uganda. Passengers sought compensation for psychic injuries caused by the ordeal of the hijacking and detention at the Entebbe Airport. While acknowledging that the negotiating history of the Warsaw Convention was silent as to the availability of such compensation, the court determined that "desirable jurisprudential policy" ("la politique jurisprudentielle souhaitable") favored an expansive reading of Article 17 to reach purely psychic injuries. In reaching this conclusion, the court emphasized the post-1929 development of the aviation industry and the evolution of Anglo-American and Israeli law to allow recovery for psychic injury in certain circumstances. In addition, the court followed the view of Miller that this expansive construction was desirable to avoid an apparent conflict between the French and English versions of the Guatemala City Protocol.

Although we recognize the deference owed to the Israeli court's interpretation of Article 17, we are not persuaded by that court's reasoning. Even if we were to agree that allowing recovery for purely psychic injury is desirable as a policy goal, we cannot give effect to such policy without convincing evidence that the signatories' intent with respect to Article 17 would allow such recovery. As discussed, neither the language, negotiating history, nor postenactment interpretations of Article 17 clearly evidences such intent. Nor does the Guatemala City Protocol support the Israeli court's conclusion because nothing in the Protocol purports to amend Article 17 to reach mental injuries. Moreover, although the Protocol reflects a liberalization of attitudes toward passenger recovery in that it provides for strict liability, see Article IV, the fact that the Guatemala City Protocol is still not in effect after almost 20 years since it was drafted should caution *against* attaching significance to it.

Moreover, we believe our construction of Article 17 better accords with the Warsaw Convention's stated purpose of achieving uniformity of rules governing claims arising from international air transportation. [T]he Montreal Agreement subjects international carriers to strict liability for Article 17 injuries sustained on flights connected with the United States. Recovery for mental distress traditionally has been subject to a high degree of proof, both in this country and others. We have no doubt that subjecting international air carriers to *strict* liability for purely mental distress would be controversial for most signatory countries. Our construction avoids this potential source of divergence.

III

We conclude that an air carrier cannot be held liable under Article 17 when an accident has not caused a passenger to suffer death, physical injury, or physical manifestation of injury. * * *

Eastern urges us to hold that the Warsaw Convention provides the exclusive cause of action for injuries sustained during international air transportation. The Court of Appeals did not address this question, and we did not grant certiorari to consider it. We therefore decline to reach it here.

The judgment of the Court of Appeals is reversed.

NOTES AND QUESTIONS

1. *The Warsaw Convention.* Issues arising under the 1929 Warsaw Convention and subsequent protocols have frequently been litigated in

municipal courts. One general goal of the Convention was, as the *Eastern Airlines* Court stated, to "achiev[e] uniformity of rules governing claims arising from international air transportation," especially with respect to claims for personal injuries arising out of accidents, for damaged or lost baggage, and for damages caused by flight delays. Another aim was to balance the interests of passengers seeking recovery with airlines' interests in limiting their liability, resulting in caps on damages. For background, see Andreas F. Lowenfeld & Allan I. Mendelsohn, "The United States and the Warsaw Convention," 80 *Harvard Law Review* 497 (1967).

The 1999 Montreal Convention for the Unification of Certain Rules for International Carriage by Air, Senate Treaty Doc. No. 106–45 (2000), which, *inter alia*, removes limits on air carrier liability for accident victims unless the airline proves it is not negligent or that a third party was alone responsible for damages, was intended to replace the Warsaw Convention and several subsequent protocols. See Bin Cheng, "A New Era in the Law of International Carriage by Air: From Warsaw (1929) to Montreal (1999)," 53 *International and Comparative Law Quarterly* 833 (2004); Sean D. Murphy, "Contemporary Practice of the United States Relating to International Law," 98 *American Journal of International Law* 169, 177–79 (2004). The Montreal Convention entered into force in November 2003; as of December 2013, there were 104 parties, including the United States.

2. *The Law of Treaty Interpretation.* How much attention should be paid to the text of a treaty? In 1844, the British judge Stephen Lushington, construing a treaty of commerce between Britain and Turkey, said that in such treaties "we cannot expect to find the same nicety of strict definition as in modern documents, such as deeds, or Acts of Parliament[;] it has never been the habit of those engaged in diplomacy to use legal accuracy, but rather to adopt more liberal terms." An interpreter therefore "ought to look at all the historical circumstances attending" the treaties, "in order to ascertain what was the true intention of the contracting parties, and to give the widest scope to the language of the treaties in order to embrace within it all the objects intended to be included." Maltass v. Maltass, 1 Rob. Ecc. 67, 76 (Prerogative Ct. 1844).

The U.S. Supreme Court has not always followed the approach to treaty interpretation set out in *Eastern Airlines*, where the Court turned first to the treaty text. During the first half of the 20th century, for example, the Court "expressly adopted a purposive approach to treaty interpretation designed, fundamentally, to advance amicable relations between the United States and its treaty partners." Michael P. Van Alstine, "Treaties in the Supreme Court, 1901–1945," in *International Law in the U.S. Supreme Court: Continuity and Change* 191, 193–94 (David L. Sloss, Michael D. Ramsey & William S. Dodge eds. 2011). In addition, the Court at that time "firmly endorsed, and repeatedly applied, a presumption in favor of a liberal recognition of individual rights secured by treaties." *Id.* at 194.

Negotiation of the treaty interpretation articles of the 1969 Vienna Convention on the Law of Treaties occasioned lively debate about the importance of a treaty's text. Professor Myres McDougal, a member of the U.S. delegation to the conference negotiating the Vienna Convention, condemned placing primary emphasis on treaty text as "an exercise in primitive and potentially destructive formalism." Myres S. McDougal, "The International Law Commission's Draft Articles upon Interpretation: Textuality *Redidivus*," 61 *American Journal of International Law* 992, 997 (1967). The U.S. delegation proposed that treaties be interpreted "in good faith in order to determine the meaning to be given to its terms in the light of all relevant factors," attaching to its proposal a non-exhaustive list of nine factors, including the treaty's "objects and purposes," "the preparatory work of the treaty," "the circumstances of its conclusion," and "any rules of international law applicable in the relations between the parties." U.N. Doc. A/CONF.39/C.1/L.156 (1968). See "Vienna Conference on the Law of Treaties: Statement of Professor Myres S. McDougal, United States Delegation, to Committee of the Whole, April 19, 1968," 62 *American Journal of International Law* 1021 (1968). However, some delegates from other countries stressed the importance of treaty text. Dr. Eduardo Jimenez de Arechega of Uruguay, a member of the International Law Commission soon to be elected to the International Court of Justice, thought that "if respect for the wording of a treaty that had been signed and ratified was not something sacred, * * * an essential advantage of written and conventional law would be lost." *Quoted in* I.M. Sinclair, "Vienna Conference on the Law of Treaties," 19 *International and Comparative Law Quarterly* 47, 63 (1970). Why might recourse to the *travaux préparatoires* be controversial? What was the final outcome of the negotiations concerning treaty interpretation? Does the Vienna Convention give primacy to the treaty text, or does it represent a "grab bag" approach? See Articles 31–33 of the Vienna Convention, reproduced in the Appendix.

Although the United States is not a party to the Vienna Convention and the *Eastern Airlines* Court did not cite it, did or should the Court nonetheless follow it? Other U.S. courts and the U.S. State Department have invoked the Vienna Convention with respect to various law of treaties issues. In Chubb & Son, Inc. v. Asiana Airlines, 214 F.3d 301, 308–09 (2d Cir. 2000), *cert. denied*, 533 U.S. 928 (2001), the judgment accepted the Vienna Convention "as an authoritative guide to the customary international law of treaties" and noted that "[t]he United States Department of State considers the Vienna Convention in dealing with day-to-day treaty problems and recognizes the Vienna Convention as in large part the authoritative guide to current treaty law and practice." See Maria Frankowska, "The Vienna Convention on the Law of Treaties Before United States Courts," 28 *Virginia Journal of International Law* 287, 299, 326–52 (1988).

Should the same treaty interpretation approach be used for all types of treaties? Should a human rights treaty, such as the Genocide Convention or the European Convention on Human Rights, which we considered in the *McCann Case* in Chapter 1 and which we revisit in Chapter 6, be liberally interpreted to further its objectives? What about a treaty creating an international organization, such as the U.N. Charter? We consider the latter question in connection with the *Reparation Case* in Chapter 8. See Catherine Brölmann, "Specialized Rules of Treaty Interpretation: International Organizations," in *The Oxford Guide to Treaties* 507 (Duncan B. Hollis ed. 2012); Başak Çalí, "Specialized Rules of Treaty Interpretation: Human Rights," in *id.* at 525.

3. *Uniformity of Treaty Interpretation and the Decisions of Foreign Courts.* In interpreting a treaty, what use should a municipal court make of foreign judicial interpretations? In his opinion in a case interpreting the meaning of the word "accident" in Article 17 of the Warsaw Convention, Justice Scalia cited the Supreme Court's unanimous opinion in *Eastern Airlines* favorably for having "carefully considered foreign case law." Justice Scalia noted the value of looking to other states' interpretations of the same treaty provision:

> We can, and should, look to decisions of other signatories when we interpret treaty provisions. Foreign constructions are evidence of the original shared understanding of the contracting parties. Moreover, it is reasonable to impute to the parties an intent that their respective courts strive to interpret the treaty consistently. (The Warsaw Convention's preamble specifically acknowledges "the advantage of regulating *in a uniform manner* the conditions of . . . the liability of the carrier." (emphasis added).) Finally, even if we disagree, we surely owe the conclusions reached by appellate courts of other signatories the courtesy of respectful consideration.

Olympic Airways v. Husain, 540 U.S. 644, 660–61 (2004) (Scalia, J., dissenting). (The majority in *Olympic Airlines* thought that the foreign case law relied on by Justice Scalia—intermediate appellate court decisions from Britain and Australia—was "not inconsistent" with the majority's interpretation of Article 17; and, in any event, the majority cautioned against following the foreign appellate opinions, both because of "substantial factual distinctions between these cases" and because "the respective courts of last resort—the House of Lords and High Court of Australia—have yet to speak." *Id.* at 655 n.9.)

Is it possible to reduce the risk of different municipal court interpretations of the same treaty provision? Should a municipal court more or less automatically defer to an interpretation of a treaty provision made by a foreign court? Should a foreign court's decision interpreting a treaty be accorded weight if the foreign court's approach to treaty interpretation differs from the approach of the domestic court? Compare the approaches to treaty interpretation used by the U.S. Supreme Court in *Eastern Airlines* and by the Israeli Supreme Court in *Teichner*, discussed in *Eastern Airlines*. Could we significantly reduce uncertainty by agreeing on a standard method of treaty interpretation, such as that of the Vienna Convention on the Law of Treaties? If not, what does a standard method of treaty interpretation accomplish? See Alex Glashauser, "Difference and Deference in Treaty Interpretation," 50 *Villanova Law Review* 25 (2005); John E. Noyes, "Memorializing UNCLOS III, Interpreting the Law of the Sea Convention, and the *Virginia*

Commentary," in *Peaceful Order in the World's Oceans* 218 (Myron Nordquist & Michael Lodge eds. 2014). Could treaty negotiators themselves promote more uniform interpretations by municipal courts? How? When the drafters of the Warsaw Convention provided that only the French text was "authentic," did they eliminate one possible source of ambiguity?

4. *Treaties and the Intersection of Municipal and International Law.* The intersection of international and municipal law may also challenge the uniform application of treaties. For example, a municipal court might find that a treaty provision implicitly refers to its own municipal law. See Zicherman v. Korean Air Lines Co., Ltd., 516 U.S. 217 (1996) (concluding that the term "*dommage*" in the French text of Article 17 of the Warsaw Convention means "legally cognizable harm," but that "Article 17 leaves it to adjudicating courts to specify what harm is cognizable"). A municipal court also might not view the treaty rule as controlling in light of competing rules of municipal law. In El Al Israel Airlines, Ltd. v. Tseng, 525 U.S. 155 (1999), the plaintiff argued that she had a cause of action under New York state law for assault and false imprisonment when she was searched for explosives at Kennedy Airport before boarding an international flight. The Supreme Court, answering the question left open at the end of *Eastern Airlines*, concluded that Article 17 of the Warsaw Convention provided the exclusive basis for liability, preempting state law claims. More on the relationship between treaties and U.S. state law appears in Chapter 4.

5. *Comparing Statutory Interpretation and Treaty Interpretation.* Does the methodology of treaty interpretation differ from that of statutory interpretation? How do a treaty's *travaux préparatoires* differ from a statute's legislative history? What are the implications of those differences for how a treaty should be interpreted and how it may change? Professor Bederman explored how to cure ambiguities in U.S. statutes and in treaties:

> Despite all the debate regarding the allocation of interpretative power between Congress and the courts over statutes, all agree that, provided a statute is at least constitutional, Congress always has the last word in construction. Congress can and does fix its drafting mistakes after being prompted by the courts. * * *
>
> With treaties, however, there is no convenient way to cure defects in construction. Treaties have dual status in both international and domestic law. An American court could adopt an interpretation at variance with our treaty partners, but that new construction would have no force on the international plane. In such a situation, the United States could well be in default of its international obligations. To reconcile the internal and international meanings of a treaty, the United States government would be forced to renegotiate the agreement. Because any process of negotiation is consensual, there is no guarantee that a reconciliation could occur.

David J. Bederman, "Revivalist Canons and Treaty Interpretation," 41 *UCLA Law Review* 953, 1023–24 (1994).

6. *Modifying Treaties.* May a court or tribunal in effect modify a treaty via interpretation? How can such behavior be reconciled with the premise that consent between or among states creates legal rules in treaties? What features of Articles 31–32 of the Vienna Convention on the Law of Treaties might authorize an interpreter to "change" the meaning of a treaty? Are particular types of treaties particularly amenable to "evolutive interpretation"? See Malgosia Fitzmaurice, "Dynamic (Evolutive) Interpretation of Treaties, Part I," 21 *Hague Yearbook of International Law* 101 (2008); Jean-Marc Sorel & Valérie Boré Eveno, "1969 Vienna Convention Article 31: General Rule of Interpretation," in 1 *The Vienna Conventions on the Law of Treaties: A Commentary* 804, ¶¶ 51–56 (Olivier Corten & Pierre Klein eds. 2011).

How else may treaties be modified? Certainly, parties to a treaty may explicitly change it. Parties to a multilateral treaty may formally modify or amend it. See Articles 39–41 of the Vienna Convention. An amendment is typically regarded as a new treaty, binding only on states that affirmatively accept it. Because multilateral treaty negotiations are often time-consuming and cumbersome, states sometimes provide mechanisms for amending treaty provisions that vary the normal rules for amendments. For example, widely accepted treaties prepared by the International Maritime Organization, which often contain detailed requirements concerning matters of vessel safety and vessel operation, contain a "tacit amendment procedure" for technical amendments. Under this procedure, a supermajority of states voting in an IMO committee may propose an amendment, which is "deemed accepted" unless, within a certain time frame, a specified number of states affirmatively object to the amendment; even if an amendment is "accepted," no state objecting within the time frame is bound by it. See, *e.g.*, the International Convention on Standards of Training, Certification and Watchkeeping of Seafarers, July 7, 1978, art. XII(1)(a), 1361 U.N.T.S. 2, 195 (accepted by 158 parties, representing 98.8% of the world shipping tonnage, as of December 2013.)

7. *Excusing Treaty Violations and Terminating Treaties.* Given the core principle of *pacta sunt servanda*—the obligation to comply with treaties in good faith—should it ever be legally permissible to excuse treaty violations or to unilaterally terminate treaties? Why? Consider these questions as you read the next case and its Notes.

CMS GAS TRANSMISSION CO. V. ARGENTINA

ICSID Case No.ARB/01/8, Decision on Annulment, Sept. 25, 2007, available at https://icsid.worldbank.org/ICSID/ (last visited Dec. 8, 2013)

A. Introduction

1. On 8 September 2005, the Argentine Republic (Argentina) filed with the Secretary-General of the International Centre for Settlement of

Investment Disputes (ICSID) an application in writing, requesting the annulment of an Award dated 12 May 2005 rendered by the Tribunal in the arbitration between CMS Gas Transmission Company (CMS) and the Argentine Republic. * * *

B. The Dispute

30. In order to put an end to the economic crisis of the late 1980s, Argentina adopted in 1989 an economic recovery plan which included a privatization program of government-owned industries and public utilities. For that purpose, it enacted [various laws] pegging the Argentine currency to the United States dollar.

31. Within this framework, Gas Law N° 24.076 of May 1992, implemented by various decrees, established the legal framework for the privatization of the gas industry and regulated the transport and distribution of natural gas. The Law established a new regulatory regime [that] determin[ed] the tariffs charged by the transporters to the distributors.

32. Gas del Estado, a national State-owned monopoly, was thus divided into two transportation companies and eight distributor companies to be privatized. Transportadora de Gas del Norte [TGN] was one of the companies established as a result of this restructuring. In December 1992, TGN was granted a license to transport gas in Argentina through the operation of the North and Central West pipelines in conformity with Decree 2.255/92.

[CMS Gas Argentina, a wholly owned subsidiary of CMS, a U.S. corporation, bought a total of 29.42% of TGN.]

34. [I]n CMS's view, under the regime established by those laws and decrees and by the license granted to TGN, tariffs were to be calculated in dollars, conversion to pesos to be effected at the time of billing and tariffs adjusted every six months in accordance with the United States Producer Price Index (US-PPI). * * *

35. Towards the end of the 1990s a serious economic crisis began to unfold in Argentina. The representatives of the gas companies agreed twice, subject to certain conditions, in January 2000 and July 2000, to defer the US-PPI adjustment of the gas tariffs. [O]n several occasions [Argentine authorities] confirmed the continuing freeze of the US-PPI adjustment.

36. In late 2001, the crisis deepened and, on 6 January 2002, Law N° 25.561 declared a public emergency. Under that Law the right of licensees of public utilities to adjust tariffs according to the US-PPI was

terminated, as well as the calculation of tariffs in dollars. The tariffs were redenominated in pesos at the rate of one peso to one dollar.[2]

[An ICSID arbitral tribunal was constituted at the request of CMS, challenging the measures taken by Argentina.]

38. [I]n an Award of 12 May 2005, the Tribunal rejected CMS' claims of expropriation under Article IV and of discriminatory and arbitrary treatment under Article II(2)(b) of the [1991] Argentina-US Bilateral Investment Treaty (the BIT). On the other hand it ruled that Argentina had "breached its obligations to accord the investor the fair and equitable treatment guaranteed in Article II(2)(a) of the Treaty and to observe the obligations entered into with regard to the investment guaranteed in Article II(2)(c) of the Treaty." It did not accept Argentina's "defenses" based on necessity and article XI of the BIT. It awarded CMS compensation of US$133.2 million. * * *

E. Fair and Equitable Treatment * * *

77. CMS asserted before the Tribunal that Argentina had breached the provisions of Article II(2)(a) of the BIT according fair and equitable treatment to investments covered by the Treaty. The Tribunal stated that "a stable legal and business environment is an essential element of fair and equitable treatment" and observed that "[t]he measures that are complained of did in fact entirely transform and alter the legal and business environment under which the investment was decided and made." It concluded that those measures "resulted in the objective breach of the standard laid down in Article II(2)(a) of the Treaty."

[The Annulment Committee found no reason to annul the Tribunal's finding a violation of Article II(2)(a).]

G. State of Necessity under Customary International Law and Article XI of the BIT

(a) The Award

101. The Tribunal recorded that "Argentina has contended in the alternative that in the event the Tribunal should come to the conclusion that there was a breach of the Treaty the Respondent should be exempted from liability in light of the existence of a state of necessity or state of emergency." Argentina invoked the existence of such a state under both customary international law and Article XI of the BIT. * * *

102. The Tribunal considered that Article 25 of the Articles of the International Law Commission (ILC) on State Responsibility "adequately reflects the state of customary international law on the question of necessity." Under that article:

---

[2] From March 2002 onwards the official exchange rate for the peso was in the region of 3–3.85 per US$1, a devaluation of more than 60%.

1. Necessity may not be invoked by a State as a ground for precluding the wrongfulness of an act not in conformity with an international obligation of that State unless the act:

(a) is the only way for the State to safeguard an essential interest against a grave and imminent peril; and

(b) does not seriously impair an essential interest of the State or States towards which the obligation exists, or of the international community as a whole.

2. In any case, necessity may not be invoked by a State as a ground for precluding wrongfulness if:

(a) the international obligation in question excludes the possibility of invoking necessity; or

(b) the State has contributed to the situation of necessity.

103. The Tribunal then undertook the task of finding whether the Argentine crisis met the various requirements of Article 25. It expressed doubts as to whether "an essential interest" of the State was involved in the matter and whether there was in this case a "grave and imminent peril." It added that the measures taken by Argentina "were not the only steps available" to safeguard its interest and concluded that the conditions set out under paragraph 1(a) of Article 25 were not met. * * *

105. Passing to paragraph 2 of that Article, the Tribunal examined whether the object and purpose of the BIT excluded necessity. It arrived to the conclusion that "the Argentine crisis was severe but did not result in total economic and social collapse" and that in such a situation the "Treaty will prevail over any plea of necessity."

106. The Tribunal further observed that Argentina's "government policies and their shortcomings significantly contributed to the crisis" and that consequently state of necessity was precluded by paragraph 2(b) of Article 25.

107. Finally the Tribunal observed that all the conditions governing necessity under Article 25 must be cumulatively satisfied. It concluded that "the requirements of necessity under customary international law have not been fully met so as to preclude the wrongfulness of the acts."

108. Then the Tribunal noted that "[t]he discussion on necessity and emergency is not confined to customary international law as there are also specific provisions of the Treaty dealing with this matter." In this respect it first recalled that Article XI of the BIT provides:

This treaty shall not preclude the application by either Party of measures necessary for the maintenance of public order, the fulfillment of its obligations with respect to the maintenance or restoration of international peace or security, or the protection of its own essential security interests.

109. In this respect the Tribunal first determined that "there is nothing in the context of customary international law or the object and purpose of the Treaty that could on its own exclude major economic crises from the scope of Article XI." It added that "[a]gain, the issue is then to establish how grave an economic crisis must be so as to qualify as an essential security interest, a matter discussed above."

110. Then the Tribunal, in the light of a lengthy discussion of the question by the Parties and their experts, expressed the view that "the clause of Article XI of the Treaty is not a self-judging clause." Accordingly it decided that the judicial review it had to perform under that clause was a "substantive review." * * *

(d) The Committee's view * * *

128. [T]he Tribunal * * * assimilated the conditions necessary for the implementation of Article XI of the BIT to those concerning the existence of the state of necessity under customary international law. Moreover, * * * the Tribunal dealt with the defense based on customary law before dealing with the defense drawn from Article XI. * * *

129. [T]here is some analogy in the language used in Article XI of the BIT and in Article 25 of the ILC's Articles on State Responsibility. The first text mentions "necessary" measures and the second relates to the "state of necessity." However Article XI specifies the conditions under which the Treaty may be applied, whereas Article 25 is drafted in a negative way: it excludes the application of the state of necessity on the merits, unless certain stringent conditions are met. Moreover, Article XI is a threshold requirement: if it applies, the substantive obligations under the Treaty do not apply. By contrast, Article 25 is an excuse which is only relevant once it has been decided that there has otherwise been a breach of those substantive obligations.

130. Furthermore Article XI and Article 25 are substantively different. The first covers measures necessary for the maintenance of public order or the protection of each Party's own essential security interests, without qualifying such measures. The second subordinates the state of necessity to four conditions. It requires for instance that the action taken "does not seriously impair an essential interest of the State or States towards which the obligation exists, or of the international community as a whole," a condition which is foreign to Article XI. * * *

131. Those two texts having a different operation and content, it was necessary for the Tribunal to take a position on their relationship and to decide whether they were both applicable in the present case. The Tribunal did not enter into such an analysis, [incorrectly] assuming that Article XI and Article 25 are on the same footing.

132. [T]he excuse based on customary international law could only be subsidiary to the exclusion based on Article XI.

133. [I]f the Tribunal was satisfied by the arguments based on Article XI, it should have held that there had been "no breach" of the BIT. * * *

134. [According to the ILC,] necessity in customary international law [as found in Article 25] goes to the issue of [state] responsibility[.] Only if [the Tribunal] concluded that there was conduct not in conformity with the Treaty would it have had to consider whether Argentina's responsibility could be precluded * * * under customary international law. * * *

136. The Committee recalls * * * that it has only a limited jurisdiction under Article 52 of the ICSID Convention. In the circumstances, the Committee cannot simply substitute its own view of the law and its own appreciation of the facts for those of the Tribunal. Notwithstanding the identified errors and lacunas in the Award, it is the case in the end that the Tribunal applied Article XI of the Treaty. Although applying it cryptically and defectively, it applied it. There is accordingly no manifest excess of powers.

[After rejecting Argentina's necessity defense, the Tribunal turned to compensation. The Tribunal again relied on the ILC's Articles on State Responsibility, this time invoking Article 27, which provides that "a circumstance precluding wrongfulness," such as necessity, "is without prejudice to * * * the question of compensation for any material loss caused by the act in question." According to the Tribunal, any necessity could only temporarily suspend the right to compensation during a period of emergency, which had passed. The Tribunal based compensation on the damages suffered by CMS from 2000 to 2007. The Annulment Committee once more concludes that there was no basis for annulling the Tribunal's award.]

NOTES AND QUESTIONS

1. *ICSID Arbitration.* Note the variety of forums in which international law is interpreted and applied. Government officials regularly invoke treaties in negotiations and diplomatic interactions, and treaties may be interpreted and applied by municipal courts (*e.g.*, the U.S. Supreme Court in *Eastern Airlines*) and various international courts (*e.g.*, the International Court of Justice in the *Reservations to the Genocide Convention Case* above and the European Court of Human Rights in *McCann* in Chapter 1). The *CMS Case* was brought initially in an International Centre for Settlement of Investment Disputes (ICSID) arbitral tribunal. We will see some additional examples of different arbitral and judicial forums in Chapter 3 before we study international legal process in more depth in Chapters 4, 5, and 6.

The ICSID Convention—formally, the Convention on the Settlement of Investment Disputes between States and Nationals of Other States, Mar. 18,

1965, 575 U.N.T.S. 159—provides standard clauses and procedures for the arbitration of international investment disputes. The Convention also created an international institution to help administer arbitrations. As of November 2013, 150 states were parties to the ICSID Convention, including the United States and Argentina. The Executive Directors of the International Bank for Reconstruction and Development (the World Bank) formulated this framework Convention in light of the perceived "need for international cooperation for economic development, and the role of private international investment therein." *Id.* preamble.

The number of arbitrations instituted by investors against host countries has grown dramatically since the end of the 20th century, with ICSID handling most of those cases. See United Nations Conference on Trade and Development, *Recent Developments in Investor-State Dispute Settlement* 2–4 (2013), *available at* http://unctad.org/en/PublicationsLibrary/webdiaepcb 2013d3_en.pdf (last visited Dec. 8, 2013). Argentina has been the defendant in over 50 cases, the most of any country. *Id.* at 29. As of November 2013, some 276 ICSID arbitrations had been concluded. See the list of cases at https://icsid.worldbank.org/ICSID (last visited Dec. 8, 2013). What are the advantages of ICSID arbitration for an investor? For the host state? For more background about the ICSID Convention, see Christoph H. Schreuer *et al.*, *The ICSID Convention: A Commentary* (2d ed. 2009).

Becoming a state party to the ICSID Convention does not automatically constitute consent to arbitration; there must be separate written consent. Consent to an ICSID arbitration generally precludes other remedies. See ICSID Convention, arts. 25–27. In the *CMS Case*, the jurisdiction of the ICSID arbitral tribunal was authorized in the U.S.-Argentina Treaty Concerning the Reciprocal Encouragement and Protection of Investment, Nov. 14, 1991, 31 *International Legal Materials* 124 (1992) (the U.S.-Argentina BIT).

2. *Bilateral Investment Treaties (BITs).* International lawyers advising clients who invest in foreign countries work with a wide variety of laws and legal instruments. In the CMS-Argentina transaction, public/private contracts, U.S. law, Argentinian law, and international law were all in play. As the case reports, when Argentina changed its laws in response to economic difficulties, it required that CMS assess gas tariffs in devalued pesos rather than in dollars. Argentina also limited CMS's ability to adjust its tariffs in line with U.S. inflation indices. The company sought protection, invoking the 1991 U.S.-Argentina BIT. This treaty is one of over 2,500 BITs in existence; there are as well several multilateral investment protection treaties, including the North American Free Trade Agreement, Dec. 17, 1992, 32 *International Legal Materials* 289 (1993), and the European Energy Charter Treaty, Dec. 17, 1994, 2080 U.N.T.S. 95.

What protection does the U.S.-Argentina BIT provide investors? One expert termed investment treaty provisions ensuring "fair and equitable treatment," such as Article II(2)(a) of the U.S.-Argentina BIT highlighted in paragraph 77 of the *CMS Case*, as being at "the heart of the investment regime." José Enrique Alvarez, "The Public International Law Regime Governing International Investment," 344 *Recueil des Cours* 195, 319 (2011). In addition to setting out substantive protections, the U.S.-Argentina BIT authorizes arbitration of investment disputes directly with host states. Such treaty-based procedural protections for investors constituted a particularly dramatic development in Latin America, where host countries had long insisted on inserting a "Calvo clause" in investment contracts, requiring investors to seek remedies only by litigating before host country courts. BITs such as the one between the United States and Argentina link investment contracts to treaty provisions setting out standards of treatment for investors and providing options for international dispute settlement. See Francisco Orrego Vicuña, "Of Contracts and Treaties in the Global Market," 8 *Max Planck Yearbook of United Nations Law* 341 (2004). For more background on U.S. BITs, see Kenneth J. Vandevelde, *U.S. International Investment Agreements* (2009).

3. *Annulment v. Appeal.* It was an ICSID Annulment Committee that decided the *CMS Case* excerpted above. The ICSID Convention provides for an annulment system as the exclusive mechanism for reviewing ICSID awards. See ICSID Convention, art. 53(1). The drafters of the Convention allowed arbitral tribunal awards to be annulled only if an arbitral tribunal violated basic due process guidelines, such as operating in manifest excess of its powers. See *id.* art. 52. Even significant errors in interpreting the law may not justify annulment of an award. Why? Should ICSID instead allow appeals, to review the substantive correctness of arbitral awards and to promote consistency in the decisions of arbitral tribunals? See Asif H. Qureshi, "An Appellate System in International Investment Arbitration?," in *The Oxford Handbook of International Investment Law* 1154 (Peter Muchlinski, Federico Ortino & Christoph Schreuer eds. 2008); Claire Stockford, "Appeal versus Annulment: Is the ICSID Annulment Process Working or Is It Now Time for an Appellate Mechanism?," in *Investment Treaty Arbitration and International Law* 307 (Ian A. Laird & Todd J. Weiler eds. 2012).

4. *Enforcement of ICSID Awards.* According to Article 54(1) of the ICSID Convention, "[e]ach Contracting State shall recognize an award rendered pursuant to this Convention as binding and enforce the pecuniary obligations imposed by that award within its territories as if it were a final judgment of a court in that State." Apart from that formal provision, what reasons might prompt a host country that has lost an ICSID case to comply with the award? Does Article 54(1) provide any grounds for a host state to resist enforcement? Argentina has in general refused to enforce ICSID awards. See Eric David Kasenetz, Note, "Desperate Times Call for Desperate Measures: The Aftermath of Argentina's State of Necessity and the Current Fight in the ICSID," 41 *George Washington International Law Review* 714, 739–43 (2010); and see generally Chapter 4 concerning the reception of international law in national legal systems. If Argentina does not enforce an ICSID award against it, what options are open to a disappointed investor?

Enforcement questions also have been prominent in the aftermath of Argentina's default on its government bonds, another response to its economic crisis. Bond holders that did not renegotiate repayment terms have sued Argentina in national courts, but principles of sovereign immunity, which we consider in Chapter 12, have complicated many efforts to recover on the original terms of the bonds. See J.F. Hornbeck, "Argentina's Defaulted Sovereign Debt: Dealing with the 'Holdouts,'" *CRS Report for Congress* No. R41029, Feb. 6, 2013.

5. *Treaty Interpretation and the Excuse of Necessity*. Should the concept of necessity in Article XI of the U.S.-Argentina BIT, quoted in paragraph 108 of the *CMS* opinion, be conflated with the meaning of necessity in Article 25 of the International Law Commission's 2001 Draft Articles on State Responsibility? How should Article XI be interpreted? What materials should be consulted? If necessity exists under Article XI of the U.S.-Argentina BIT, what consequences follow? If no necessity is found under Article XI, should a tribunal turn to Article 25 of the ILC's Draft Articles? If an investment treaty does not contain an article similar to Article XI, would Article 25 then apply? See Andrea K. Bjorklund, "Emergency Exceptions: State of Necessity and *Force Majeure*," in *The Oxford Handbook of International Investment Law* 459 (Peter Muchlinski, Federico Ortino & Christoph Schreuer eds. 2008); Anthea Roberts, "Power and Persuasion in Investment Treaty Interpretation: The Dual Role of States," 104 *American Journal of International Law* 179 (2010).

6. *Circumstances Precluding Wrongfulness and the Law of State Responsibility*. Did the *CMS* Annulment Committee suggest that there are two sorts of international law concerning treaty issues? Do issues such as reservations, treaty interpretation, amendments, and treaty termination fall within the "law of treaties"? Are matters such as remedies for breach and excuses for non-performance part of a separate "law of state responsibility"? Or are both the law of treaties and state responsibility just part of international law? Whatever the answer, the law of state responsibility applies both to treaties and to obligations arising from other sources of international law, *e.g.*, customary international law. Within the law of state responsibility, necessity, along with, for example, self-defense and *force majeure*, constitute valid excuses or, to use the terminology of the International Law Commission, "circumstances precluding wrongfulness" justifying at least temporary suspension of a state's international law obligations. We more fully discuss the rather difficult and ambiguous law of state responsibility in a Note on State Responsibility in Chapter 6.

7. *Treaty Termination and the Law of Treaties*. A state may also avoid its obligations under a treaty if there are grounds for terminating it, a matter governed by the law of treaties. Relatively uncontroversial is termination of a treaty by agreement of the parties or in accordance with the treaty's terms. See Article 54 of the Vienna Convention on the Law of Treaties, reproduced in the Appendix. What other law of treaties grounds justify suspending or terminating a treaty, and what are the consequences of suspension or

termination? See Vienna Convention, arts. 55–68. Are treaties like or unlike contracts between private parties? See Marco Bronckers & Freya Baetens, "Reconsidering Financial Remedies in WTO Dispute Settlement," 16 *Journal of International Economic Law* 281, 291–95 (2013).

What are reasons for narrowly construing the grounds for treaty termination? In the Case Concerning the Gabčíkovo-Nagymaros Project (Hungary-Slovakia), 1997 I.C.J. 3, Hungary unsuccessfully argued termination of a bilateral treaty, concluded between Hungary and Czechoslovakia in 1977, which obligated Hungary to help develop a hydroelectric project on the Danube River. One of Hungary's arguments was that the 1977 treaty was terminated due to a "fundamental change of circumstances" (also known as *rebus sic stantibus*): (1) the fall of Communism in Eastern Europe and the end of efforts to integrate socialist economies; (2) changed estimates of the economic profitability of the agreed works; (3) the emergence of Slovakia and the Czech Republic as entirely new states, successors to Czechoslovakia (more on state succession appears in Chapter 7); (4) increased knowledge about environmental hazards and risks; and (5) the emergence of environmentally active segments of the populations in the former Soviet bloc countries. The International Court of Justice held that these changes did not constitute a fundamental change of circumstances. What changes *would* be fundamental enough to justify suspending or terminating a treaty? How do you reconcile the principle of *pacta sunt servanda, i.e.*, the rule that treaties are binding on the parties and must be carried out in good faith, with the doctrine of fundamental change of circumstances? See Vienna Convention on the Law of Treaties, art. 62; Detlev F. Vagts, "*Rebus* Revisited: Changed Circumstances in Treaty Law," 43 *Columbia Journal of Transnational Law* 459 (2005).

THE EASTERN GREENLAND CASE

Denmark/Norway, 1933 P.C.I.J., Ser. A/B, No. 53, 3 *World Court Reports* 151
(Manley O. Hudson ed., reprinted 1969)

By an Application instituting proceedings, filed with the Registry of the Court on July 12th, 1931, * * * the Royal Danish Government, relying on the optional clause of Article 36, paragraph 2, of the Statute, brought before the Permanent Court of International Justice a suit against the Royal Norwegian Government on the ground that the latter Government had, on July 10th, 1931, published a proclamation declaring that it had proceeded to occupy certain territories in Eastern Greenland, which, in the contention of the Danish Government, were subject to the sovereignty of the Crown of Denmark. The Application, after thus indicating the subject of the dispute, proceeds * * * to formulate the claim by asking the Court for judgment to the effect that "the promulgation of the above-mentioned declaration of occupation and any steps taken in this respect by the Norwegian Government constitute a violation of the existing legal situation and are accordingly unlawful and invalid." * * *

At the beginning of the present century, opinion again began to be manifested in favour of the more effective occupation of the uncolonized areas in Greenland, in order that the risk of foreign settlement might be obviated.

During the Great War of 1914 to 1918, Denmark by treaty ceded to the United States of America her West Indian Islands—the Danish Antilles—and, during the negotiations for the conclusion of the treaty, broached to the American Secretary of State—at first in conversation and subsequently, on December 27th, 1915, by a written communication—the question of the extension of Danish activities throughout all Greenland. As the result, the United States signed on August 4th, 1916, the same day as the treaty for cession of the Antilles, a declaration to the effect that the United States would not object to the Danish Government extending their political and economic interests to the whole of Greenland.

On July 12th, 1919, the Danish Minister of Foreign Affairs instructed the Danish Minister at Christiania that a Committee had just been constituted at the Peace Conference "for the purpose of considering the claims that may be put forward by different countries to Spitzbergen," and that the Danish Government would be prepared to renew before this Committee the unofficial assurance already given (on April 2nd, 1919) to the Norwegian Government, according to which Denmark, having no special interests at stake in Spitzbergen, would raise no objection to Norway's claims upon that archipelago. In making this statement to the Norwegian Minister for Foreign Affairs, the Danish Minister was to point out "that the Danish Government had been anxious for some years past to obtain the recognition by all the interested Powers of Denmark's sovereignty over the whole of Greenland, and that she intended to place that question before the above-mentioned Committee;" and, further, that the Danish Government felt confident that the extension of its political and economic interests to the whole of Greenland "would not encounter any difficulties on the part of the Norwegian Government."

On July 14th, 1919, the Danish Minister saw M. Ihlen, the Norwegian Minister of Foreign Affairs, who merely replied on this occasion "that the question would be considered." The Norwegian Minister recorded his conversation with the Danish representative in a minute, the accuracy of which has not been disputed by the Danish Government. On July 22nd following, M. Ihlen made a statement to the Danish Minister to the effect "that the Norwegian Government would not make any difficulties in the settlement of this question" (i.e., the question raised on July 14th by the Danish Government). These are the words recorded in the minute by M. Ihlen himself. According to the report made by the Danish Minister to his own Government, M. Ihlen's words were that "the plans of the Royal [Danish] Government respecting Danish sovereignty over the whole of Greenland . . . would meet with no difficulties on the part of Norway." It is this statement by the Norwegian Minister for Foreign Affairs which is described in this judgment as the "Ihlen declaration." * * *

This declaration by M. Ihlen has been relied on by Counsel for Denmark as a recognition of an existing Danish sovereignty in Greenland. The Court is unable to accept this point of view. A careful examination of the words used and of the circumstances in which they were used, as well as of the subsequent developments, shows that M. Ihlen cannot have meant to be giving then and there a definitive recognition of Danish sovereignty over Greenland, and shows also that he cannot have been understood by the Danish Government at the time as having done so. In the text of M. Ihlen's minute, submitted by the Norwegian Government, which has not been disputed by the Danish Government, the phrase used by M. Ihlen is couched in the future tense: "*ne fera pas de difficultés*;" he had been informed that it was at the Peace Conference that the Danish Government intended to bring up the question: and two years later—when assurances had been received from the Principal Allied Powers—the Danish Government made a further application to the Norwegian Government to obtain the recognition which they desired of Danish sovereignty over all Greenland.

Nevertheless, the point which must now be considered is whether the Ihlen declaration—even if not constituting a definitive recognition of Danish sovereignty—did not constitute an engagement obliging Norway to refrain from occupying any part of Greenland.

The Danish request and M. Ihlen's reply were recorded by him in a minute, worded as follows:

> I. The Danish Minister informed me to-day that his Government has heard from Paris that the question of Spitzbergen will be examined by a Commission of four members (American, British, French, Italian). If the Danish Government is questioned by this Commission, it is prepared to reply that Denmark has no interests in Spitzbergen, and that it has no reason to oppose the wishes of Norway in regard to the settlement of this question.
>
> Furthermore, the Danish Minister made the following statement:
>
> The Danish Government has for some years past been anxious to obtain the recognition of all the interested Powers of Denmark's sovereignty over the whole of Greenland, and it proposes to place this question before the above-mentioned Committee at the same time. During the negotiations with the

Figure 2.C

Greenland, Spitzbergen, Norway, Denmark, and the Arctic Region

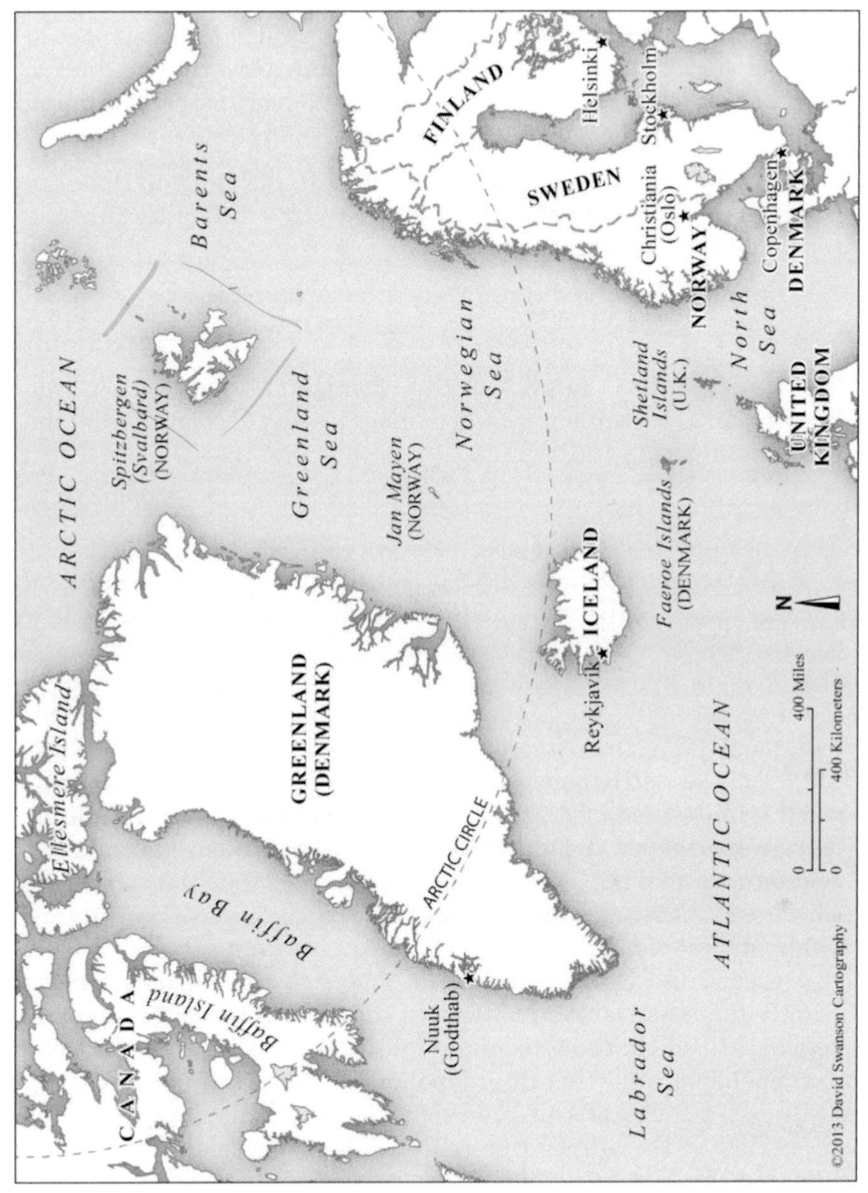

U.S.A. over the cession of the Danish West Indies, the Danish Government raised this question in so far as concernsrecognition by the Government of the U.S.A., and it succeeded in inducing the latter to agree that, concurrently with the conclusion of a convention regarding the cession of the said islands, it would make a declaration to the effect that the Government of the U.S.A. would not object to the Danish Government extending their political and economic interests to the whole of Greenland.

The Danish Government is confident (he added) that the Norwegian Government will not make any difficulties in the settlement of this question.

I replied that the question would be examined.

14/7–19 Ih.

II. To-day I informed the Danish Minister that the Norwegian Government would not make any difficulties in the settlement of this question.

22/7–19 Ih.

The incident has, therefore, reference, first to the attitude to be observed by Denmark before the Committee of the Peace Conference at Paris in regard to Spitzbergen, this attitude being that Denmark would not "oppose the wishes of Norway in regard to the settlement of this question;" as is known, these wishes related to the sovereignty over Spitzbergen. Secondly, the request showed that "the Danish Government was confident that the Norwegian Government would not make any difficulty" in the settlement of the Greenland question; the aims that Denmark had in view in regard to the last-named island were to secure the "recognition by all the Powers concerned of Danish sovereignty over the whole of Greenland," and that there should be no opposition "to the Danish Government extending their political and economic interests to the whole of Greenland." It is clear from the relevant Danish documents which preceded the Danish Minister's *démarche* at Christiania on July 14th, 1919, that the Danish attitude in the Spitzbergen question and the Norwegian attitude in the Greenland question were regarded in Denmark as interdependent, and this interdependence appears to be reflected also in M. Ihlen's minute of the interview. Even if this interdependence—which, in view of the affirmative reply of the Norwegian Government, in whose name the Minister for Foreign Affairs was speaking, would have created a bilateral engagement—is not held to have been established, it can hardly be denied that what Denmark was asking of Norway ("not to make any difficulties in the settlement of the [Greenland] question") was equivalent to what she was indicating her readiness to concede in the Spitzbergen question (to refrain from opposing "the wishes of Norway in regard to the settlement of this question"). What Denmark desired to obtain from Norway was that the latter should do nothing to obstruct the Danish plans in regard to Greenland. The declaration which the Minister for Foreign Affairs gave on July 22nd, 1919, on behalf of the Norwegian Government, was definitely affirmative: "I told the Danish Minister to-day that the Norwegian Government would not make any difficulty in the settlement of this question."

The Court considers it beyond all dispute that a reply of this nature given by the Minister for Foreign Affairs on behalf of his Government in response to a request by the diplomatic representative of a foreign Power, in regard to a question falling within his province, is binding upon the country to which the Minister belongs. * * *

The Court readily understands that Norway should feel concern for the interests of the Norwegian hunters and fishermen on the East coast of Greenland; but it cannot forget, in this connection, that as early as December 1921, Denmark announced her willingness to do everything in her power to make arrangements to safeguard Norwegian subjects against any loss they might incur as a result of the Decree of May 10th, 1921 (letter from the Danish Minister at Christiania dated December 19th, 1921, to the Norwegian Minister for Foreign Affairs). The Convention of July 9th, 1924, was a confirmation of Denmark's friendly disposition in respect of these Norwegian hunting and fishing interests.

What the Court cannot regard as being in accordance with the undertaking of July 22nd, 1919, is the endeavour to replace an unconditional and definitive undertaking by one which was subject to reservations: and what it is even more difficult for the Court to admit is that, notwithstanding the undertaking of July 22nd, 1919, by which she promised to refrain from making difficulties in the settlement of the Greenland question, Norway should have stipulated that "Eastern Greenland must be Norwegian." This pretension was already apparent at the end of a letter of January 12th, 1923, from the Norwegian Minister at Copenhagen to the Danish Minister for Foreign Affairs; and it was enunciated very definitely on September 28th, 1923, in the minutes of the sixth meeting of the Conference which drew up the Convention of July 9th, 1924, and again in the Protocol signed on January 28th, 1924, referred to above.

The Court is unable to read into the words of the Ihlen declaration "in the settlement of this question" (i.e., the Greenland question) a condition which would render the promise to refrain from making any difficulties inoperative should a settlement not be reached. The promise was unconditional and definitive. It was so understood by the Norwegian Minister for Foreign Affairs when he told the Danish Minister at Christiania on November 7th, 1919, that "it was a pleasure to Norway to recognize Danish sovereignty over Greenland" (dispatch from the Danish Minister at Christiania to the Danish Minister for Foreign Affairs of

November 8th, 1919). It was also in the same sense that the Danish Minister at Christiania had understood the Ihlen declaration, when he informed the Danish Minister for Foreign Affairs on July 22nd, 1919, that M. Ihlen had told him "that the plans of the Royal Government in regard to the sovereignty of Denmark over the whole of Greenland would not encounter any difficulties on the part of Norway."

It follows that, as a result of the undertaking involved in the Ihlen declaration of July 22nd, 1919, Norway is under an obligation to refrain from contesting Danish sovereignty over Greenland as a whole, and *a fortiori* to refrain from occupying a part of Greenland.

NOTES AND QUESTIONS

1. The Status of Greenland. When it determined rights to sovereignty over Greenland in 1933, the Permanent Court of International Justice did not consider the views of the indigenous Inuit population. In Chapter 7, Part C we contrast current international law concerning the right of "peoples" to self-determination. For background on Denmark's and Norway's claims to and activities in Greenland prior to the *Eastern Greenland Case*, see Oscar Svarlien, *The Eastern Greenland Case in Historical Perspective* (1964).

Denmark granted a measure of home rule to Greenland (population 58,000) in 1979. Following a 2008 referendum, Greenland implemented a self-government agreement giving it more local authority, including over natural resources. The Danish prime minister pledged that Greenland may gain full independence whenever it wishes. See Sara Lyall, "Fondly, Greenland Loosens Danish Rule," *New York Times*, June 22, 2009, at A4; "The Right of Arctic Peoples," *The Economist*, July 18, 2009, at 49.

2. *Unwritten Treaties.* Did the Court decide that there was a treaty between Norway and Denmark trading Norwegian claims to Greenland for Danish claims to Spitzbergen? May a treaty be unwritten? How was the Ihlen Declaration enough to commit Norway in international law? Would a like assurance be binding in the domestic law of contract?

What does the case say to states and diplomats about the possible legal effects of their negotiating behavior? Here are some observations of Dean Rusk, U.S. Secretary of State in the Kennedy and Johnson administrations between 1961 and 1969, that show that the lesson of *Eastern Greenland* has not been entirely forgotten.

> One evening, after a highball or two, I suggested to [the Foreign Minister of Honduras] that we toss a coin for [the Swan Islands in the Caribbean, claimed by both Honduras and the United States]. Fortunately, he refused because the International Court of Justice seemed to say in the *Greenland* case that a government has a right to rely upon the statement of a Foreign Minister with respect to a territorial matter. If there is anything clear about our Constitution,

it is that the Secretary of State cannot go around the world tossing coins for American territory.

Dean Rusk, "The Role and Problems of Arbitration with Respect to Political Disputes," in *Resolving Transnational Disputes Through International Arbitration* 15, 18 (Thomas E. Carbonneau ed. 1984).

3. *The Validity of Treaties Made in Violation of Municipal Constitutional Procedures.* Should it make any difference that Norwegian constitutional law required parliamentary assent to the making of treaties? Should Denmark have been on notice about this Norwegian municipal rule? Should Denmark have reasonably expected that the Norwegian Foreign Minister (or the Danish Foreign Minister) would be able legally to bind the state with simply an oral statement? Read Article 46 of the Vienna Convention on the Law of Treaties in the Appendix. Does Article 46 satisfactorily treat the issue of compliance with municipal procedures for treaty-making? Why does Article 46 not simply say that, at international law, municipal law can never trump a treaty—a notion we discussed in connection with the Hull-Lothian Agreement earlier in this chapter?

In Land and Maritime Boundary between Cameroon and Nigeria (Cameroon v. Nigeria: Equatorial Guinea intervening), 2002 I.C.J. 303, Cameroon invoked a 1975 Cameroon-Nigeria treaty known as the Maroua Declaration. Nigeria argued that Cameroon knew or should have known that Nigeria's head of state, who had signed the Declaration, lacked authority to unilaterally bind Nigeria to a treaty. Under Nigerian law, Nigeria's Supreme Military Council had to approve treaties. The International Court of Justice noted that Article 46 of the Vienna Convention on the Law of Treaties required Nigeria to meet two requirements to prove invalidity: (1) municipal rules about who has authority to accept treaties on behalf of a state must be of fundamental importance; and (2) the violation of municipal law regarding competence to enter into treaties must be "manifest." Nigeria satisfied the first prong (would this condition ever not be met?), but not the second. *Id.* at 430. According to the ICJ, "there is no general legal obligation for States to keep themselves informed of legislative and constitutional developments in other States which are or may become important for the international relations of these States." *Id.* See also Article 7(2) of the Vienna Convention. Is this situation comparable to *Eastern Greenland*, where Norway's rules were both familiar to Denmark and similar to those in the Danish Constitution?

Suppose the head of a democratic state formally accepts a treaty without obtaining legislative approval required by its municipal law. Should we ever conclude that the state has not given its consent to be bound by the treaty under international law? Suppose the treaty affects the disposition of territory, as in the Cession of Alaska. Should it be easier at international law to invalidate that treaty if it is not approved in accordance with municipal procedures, than to invalidate other types of treaties? See Malgosia Fitzmaurice & Olufemi Elias, *Contemporary Issues in the Law of Treaties* 372–87 (2005).

4. *Other Possible Bases for Norway's Legal Commitment in* Eastern Greenland. Is the legal basis for the result in the *Eastern Greenland Case* altogether clear? Could Norway's legal commitment in the *Eastern Greenland Case* have been due to something quite different from a treaty? Could it, for example, be seen as the result of a consummated transaction, a bargain made by the two states—Denmark trading its claims to Spitzbergen for Norway's claims to Greenland—with the Court simply enforcing good faith respect for the status quo? Was there also a bargain for Greenland made in 1916 between Denmark and the United States when Denmark ceded the Danish Antilles in the West Indies to the U.S. in exchange for $25,000,000 in gold? In a written statement accompanying the treaty of cession, U.S. Secretary of State Robert Lansing declared that the United States would "not object to the Danish Government extending their political and economic interests to the whole of Greenland." Convention between the United States and Denmark for Cession of the Danish West Indies, Aug. 4, 1916, 39 Stat. 1706, 1715. Compared to Norway, would the United States be just as or more committed to respect Danish sovereignty over all of Greenland? After all, the U.S. declaration was made in writing, and Denmark legally ceded territories to which it had undisputed title.

Or could the basis of obligation in *Eastern Greenland* be explained on yet other grounds? For example, was the Ihlen Declaration simply a unilateral promise enforceable at international law? In the 1974 *Nuclear Tests Cases*, involving challenges to French atmospheric nuclear testing in the Pacific, the International Court of Justice decided that statements by French officials constituted binding promises not to conduct further testing, and that the Court was "therefore not called upon to give a decision" in the *Cases*. (Australia v. France), 1974 I.C.J. 253, 272; (New Zealand v. France), 1974 I.C.J. 457, 478.

> 46. [D]eclarations made by way of unilateral acts, concerning legal or factual situations, may have the effect of creating legal obligations. Declarations of this kind may be, and often are, very specific. When it is the intention of the State making the declaration that it should become bound according to its terms, that intention confers on the declaration the character of a legal undertaking, the State being thenceforth legally required to follow a course of conduct consistent with the declaration. An undertaking of this kind, if given publicly, and with an intent to be bound, even though not made within the context of international negotiations, is binding. In these circumstances, nothing in the nature of a *quid pro quo* nor any subsequent acceptance of the declaration, nor even any reply or reaction from other States, is required for the declaration to take effect, since such a requirement would be inconsistent with the strictly unilateral nature of the juridical act by which the pronouncement by the State was made. * * *

> 48. * * * Whether a statement is made orally or in writing makes no essential difference[.] [T]he question of form is not decisive. * * *
>
> 49. One of the basic principles governing the creation and performance of legal obligations, whatever their source, is the principle of good faith. * * * Just as the very rule of *pacta sunt servanda* in the law of treaties is based on good faith, so also is the binding character of an international obligation assumed by unilateral declaration.

Id. at 472–73.

Alternatively, might the Ihlen Declaration be looked on as an international form of estoppel that was binding on Norway because of the reasonable expectations of Denmark?

CHAPTER 3

CUSTOM AND THE NON-CONSENSUAL SOURCES OF INTERNATIONAL LAW

■ ■ ■

At first glance, one might think that treaties provide all that international law needs by way of rules. Nowadays, there are tens of thousands of international agreements, most all of which offer the distinct advantages of explicitly expressing international norms and the consent of sovereign states. However, other sorts of international law remain just as important as before. This is so for at least two reasons. First, treaty provisions need to be interpreted and, if treaty interpretation is not to be pure discretion, some guidance from other forms of law is called for. Second, treaties never bind all states, and there need to be some rules of more general application. In the pages of this chapter, we explore first customary international law, often conceived as constituting an implicit sort of international agreement, and then the non-consensual sources of international law, where the pretense that international law is always based on the consent of states is finally abandoned.

A. CUSTOMARY INTERNATIONAL LAW

Next to treaties, international lawyers work most often with customary international law. As you read through the materials in this part, evaluate the role of decision makers in determining rules of custom and consider whether custom is best viewed as a consensual source of international law.

THE PAQUETE HABANA

175 U.S. 677 (1900)

MR. JUSTICE GRAY delivered the opinion of the court.

These are two appeals from decrees of the District Court of the United States for the Southern District of Florida, condemning two fishing vessels and their cargoes as prize of war.

Each vessel was a fishing smack, running in and out of Havana, and regularly engaged in fishing on the coast of Cuba; sailed under the Spanish flag; was owned by a Spanish subject of Cuban birth, living in the city of Havana; was commanded by a subject of Spain, also residing in

Havana; and her master and crew had no interest in the vessel, but were entitled to shares, amounting in all to two thirds, of her catch, the other third belonging to her owner. Her cargo consisted of fresh fish, caught by her crew from the sea, put on board as they were caught, and kept and sold alive. Until stopped by the blockading squadron, she had no knowledge of the existence of the war, or of any blockade. She had no arms or ammunition on board, and made no attempt to run the blockade after she knew of its existence, nor any resistance at the time of the capture. * * *

Both the fishing vessels were brought by their captors into Key West. A libel for the condemnation of each vessel and her cargo as prize of war was there filed on April 27, 1898; a claim was interposed by her master, on behalf of himself and the other members of the crew, and of her owner; evidence was taken, showing the facts above stated; and on May 30, 1898, a final decree of condemnation and sale was entered, "the court not being satisfied that as a matter of law, without ordinance, treaty or proclamation, fishing vessels of this class are exempt from seizure."

Each vessel was thereupon sold by auction; the Paquete Habana for the sum of $490; and the Lola for the sum of $800. There was no other evidence in the record of the value of either vessel or of her cargo. * * *

We are then brought to the consideration of the question whether, upon the facts appearing in these records, the fishing smacks were subject to capture by the armed vessels of the United States during the recent war with Spain.

By an ancient usage among civilized nations, beginning centuries ago, and gradually ripening into a rule of international law, coast fishing vessels, pursuing their vocation of catching and bringing in fresh fish, have been recognized as exempt, with their cargoes and crews, from capture as prize of war.

This doctrine, however, has been earnestly contested at the bar; and no complete collection of the instances illustrating it is to be found, so far as we are aware, in a single published work, although many are referred to and discussed by the writers on international law, notably in 2 Ortolan, Règles Internationales et Diplomatie de la Mer, (4th ed.) lib. 3, c. 2, pp. 51–56; in 4 Calvo, Droit International, (5th ed.) §§ 2367–2373; in De Boeck, Propriété Privée Ennemie sous Pavillon Ennemi, §§ 191–196; and in Hall, International Law, (4th ed.) § 148. It is therefore worth the while to trace the history of the rule, from the earliest accessible sources, through the increasing recognition of it, with occasional setbacks, to what we may now justly consider as its final establishment in our own country and generally throughout the civilized world.

The earliest acts of any government on the subject, mentioned in the books, either emanated from, or were approved by, a King of England.

In 1403 and 1406, Henry IV issued orders to his admirals and other officers, entitled "Concerning Safety for Fisherman—*De Securitate pro Piscatoribus*." By an order of October 26, 1403, reciting that it was made pursuant to a treaty between himself and the King of France; and for the greater safety of the fishermen of either country, and so that they could be, and carry on their industry, the more safely on the sea, and deal with each other in peace; and that the French King had consented that English fishermen should be treated likewise; it was ordained that French fishermen might, during the then pending season for the herring fishery, safely fish for herrings and all other fish, from the harbor of Gravelines and the island of Thanet to the mouth of the Seine and the harbor of Hautoune. And by an order of October 5, 1406, he took into his safe conduct, and under his special protection, guardianship and defense, all and singular the fishermen of France, Flanders and Brittany, with their fishing vessels and boats, everywhere on the sea, through and within his dominions, jurisdictions and territories, in regard to their fishery, while sailing, coming and going, and, at their pleasure, freely and lawfully fishing, delaying or proceeding, and returning homeward with their catch of fish, without any molestation or hindrance whatever; and also their fish, nets, and other property and goods soever; and it was therefore ordered that such fishermen should not be interfered with, provided they should comport themselves well and properly, and should not, by color of these presents, do or attempt, or presume to do or attempt, anything that could prejudice the King, or his kingdom of England, or his subjects. 8 Rymer's Foedera, 336, 451.

The treaty made October 2, 1521, between the Emperor Charles V and Francis I of France, through their ambassadors, recited that a great and fierce war had arisen between them, because of which there had been, both by land and by sea, frequent depredations and incursions on either side, to the grave detriment and intolerable injury of the innocent subjects of each; and that a suitable time for the herring fishery was at hand, and, by reason of the sea being beset by the enemy, the fishermen did not dare to go out, whereby the subject of their industry, bestowed by heaven to allay the hunger of the poor, would wholly fail for the year, unless it were otherwise provided—*quo fit, ut piscaturae commoditas, ad pauperum levandam famem a coelesti numine concessa, cessare hoc anno omnino debeat, nisi aliter provideatur*. And it was therefore agreed that the subjects of each sovereign, fishing in the sea, or exercising the calling of fishermen, could and might, until the end of the next January, without incurring any attack, depredation, molestation, trouble or hindrance soever, safely and freely, everywhere in the sea, take herrings and every other kind of fish, the existing war by land and sea notwithstanding; and further that, during the time aforesaid, no subject of either sovereign should commit, or attempt or presume to commit, any depredation, force, violence, molestation or vexation, to or upon such fishermen, or their vessels, supplies, equipments, nets and fish, or other goods soever truly appertaining to fishing. * * *

The herring fishery was permitted, in time of war, by French and Dutch edicts in 1536. Bynkershoek Quæstiones Juris Publicæ, lib. 1, c. 3; 1 Emerigon des Assurances, c. 4, sect. 9; c. 12, sect. 19, § 8.

France, from remote times, set the example of alleviating the evils of war in favor of all coast fishermen. In the compilation entitled Us et Coutumes de la Mer, published by Cleirac in 1661, and in the third part thereof, containing "Maritime or Admiralty Jurisdiction—*la Jurisdiction de la Marine ou d'Admirauté*—as well in time of peace as in time of war," article 80 is as follows: "The admiral may in time of war accord fishing truces—*tresves pescheresses*—to the enemy and to his subjects; provided that the enemy will likewise accord them to Frenchmen." Cleirac, 544. Under this article, reference is made to articles 49 and 79 respectively of the French ordinances concerning the Admiralty in 1543 and 1584, of which it is but a reproduction. 4 Pardessus, Collection de Lois Maritimes, 319; 2 Ortolan, 51. And Cleirac adds, in a note, this quotation from Froissart's Chronicles: "Fishermen on the sea, whatever war there were in France and England, never did harm to one another; so they are friends, and help one another at need—*Pescheurs sur mer, quelque guerre qui soit en France et Angleterre, jamais ne se firent mal l'un à l'autre; ainçois sont amis, et s'aydent l'un à l'autre au besoin.*"

The same custom would seem to have prevailed in France until towards the end of the seventeenth century. For example, in 1675, Louis XIV and the States General of Holland, by mutual agreement, granted to Dutch and French fishermen the liberty, undisturbed by their vessels of war, of fishing along the coasts of France, Holland and England. D'Hauterive et De Cussy, Traités de Commerce, pt. 1, vol. 2, p. 278. But by the ordinances of 1681 and 1692 the practice was discontinued, because, Valin says, of the faithless conduct of the enemies of France, who, abusing the good faith with which she had always observed the treaties, habitually carried off her fishermen, while their own fished in safety. 2 Valin sur l'Ordonnance de la Marine, (1776) 689, 690; 2 Ortolan, 52; De Boeck, § 192.

The doctrine which exempts coast fishermen with their vessels and cargoes from capture as prize of war has been familiar to the United States from the time of the War of Independence.

On June 5, 1779, Louis XVI, our ally in that war, addressed a letter to his admiral, informing him that the wish he had always had of alleviating, as far as he could, the hardships of war, had directed his attention to that class of his subjects which devoted itself to the trade of fishing, and had no other means of livelihood; that he had thought that the example which he should give to his enemies, and which could have no other source than the sentiments of humanity which inspired him, would determine them to allow to fishermen the same facilities which he should consent to grant; and that he had therefore given orders to the commanders of all his ships not to disturb English fishermen, nor to arrest their vessels laden with fresh fish, even if not caught by those vessels; provided they had no offensive arms, and were not proved to have made any signals creating a suspicion of intelligence with the enemy; and the admiral was directed to communicate the King's intentions to all officers under his control. By a royal order in council of November 6, 1780, the former orders were confirmed; and the capture and ransom, by a French cruiser, of *The John and Sarah*, an English vessel, coming from Holland, laden with fresh fish, were pronounced to be illegal. 2 Code des Prises, (ed. 1784) 721, 901, 903.

Among the standing orders made by Sir James Marriott, Judge of the English High Court of Admiralty, was one of April 11, 1780, by which it was "ordered, that all causes of prize of fishing boats or vessels taken from the enemy may be consolidated in one monition, and one sentence or interlocutory, if under 50 tons burden, and not more than six in number." Marriott's Formulary, 4. But by the statements of his successor, and of both French and English writers, it appears that England, as well as France, during the American Revolutionary War, abstained from interfering with the coast fisheries. *The Young Jacob and Johanna*, 1 C. Rob. 20; 2 Ortolan, 53; Hall, § 148.

In the treaty of 1785 between the United States and Prussia, article 23, (which was proposed by the American Commissioners, John Adams, Benjamin Franklin and Thomas Jefferson, and is said to have been drawn up by Franklin,) provided that, if war should arise between the contracting parties, "all women and children, scholars of every faculty, cultivators of the earth, artisans, manufacturers and fishermen, unarmed and inhabiting unfortified towns, villages or places, and in general all others whose occupations are for the common subsistence and benefit of mankind, shall be allowed to continue their respective employments, and shall not be molested in their persons; nor shall their houses or goods be burnt or otherwise destroyed, nor their fields wasted, by the armed force of the enemy, into whose power, by the events of war, they may happen to fall; but if anything is necessary to be taken from them for the use of such armed force, the same shall be paid for at a reasonable price." 8 Stat. 96; 1 Kent Com. 91 note; Wheaton's History of the Law of Nations, 306, 308. Here was the clearest exemption from hostile molestation or seizure of the persons, occupations, houses and goods of unarmed fishermen inhabiting unfortified places. The article was repeated in the later treaties between the United States and Prussia of 1799 and 1828. 8 Stat. 174, 384. And Dana, in a note to his edition of Wheaton's International Law, says: "In many treaties and decrees, fishermen catching fish as an article of food are added to the class of persons whose occupation is not to be disturbed in war." Wheaton's International Law, (8th ed.) § 345, note 168. * * *

In the war with Mexico in 1846, the United States recognized the exemption of coast fishing boats from capture. In proof of this, counsel have referred to records of the Navy Department, which this court is clearly authorized to consult upon such a question. *Jones v. United States*, 137 U.S. 202; *Underhill v. Hernandez*, 168 U.S. 250, 253.

By those records it appears that Commodore Conner, commanding the Home Squadron blockading the east coast of Mexico, on May 14, 1846, wrote a letter from the ship Cumberland, off Brazos Santiago, near the southern point of Texas, to Mr. Bancroft, the Secretary of the Navy, enclosing a copy of the commodore's "instructions to the commanders of the vessels of the Home Squadron, showing the principles to be observed in the blockade of the Mexican ports," one of which was that "Mexican boats engaged in fishing on any part of the coast will be allowed to pursue their labors unmolested;" and that on June 10, 1846, those instructions were approved by the Navy Department[.]

International law is part of our law, and must be ascertained and administered by the courts of justice of appropriate jurisdiction, as often as questions of right depending upon it are duly presented for their determination. For this purpose, where there is no treaty, and no controlling executive or legislative act or judicial decision, resort must be had to the customs and usages of civilized nations; and, as evidence of these, to the works of jurists and commentators, who by years of labor, research and experience, have made themselves peculiarly well acquainted with the subjects of which they treat. Such works are resorted to by judicial tribunals, not for the speculations of their authors concerning what the law ought to be, but for trustworthy evidence of what the law really is. *Hilton v. Guyot*, 159 U.S. 113, 163, 164, 214, 215.

Wheaton places, among the principal sources of international law, "Text-writers of authority, showing what is the approved usage of nations, or the general opinion respecting their mutual conduct, with the definitions and modifications introduced by general consent." As to these he forcibly observes: "Without wishing to exaggerate the importance of these writers, or to substitute, in any case, their authority for the principles of reason, it may be affirmed that they are generally impartial in their judgment. They are witnesses of the sentiments and usages of civilized nations, and the weight of their testimony increases every time that their authority is invoked by statesmen, and every year that passes without the rules laid down in their works being impugned by the avowal of contrary principles." Wheaton's International Law, (8th ed.) § 15.

Chancellor Kent says: "In the absence of higher and more authoritative sanctions, the ordinances of foreign States, the opinions of eminent statesmen, and the writings of distinguished jurists, are regarded as of great consideration on questions not settled by conventional law. In cases where the principal jurists agree, the presumption will be very great in favor of the solidity of their maxims; and no civilized nation, that does not arrogantly set all ordinary law and justice at defiance, will venture to disregard the uniform sense of the established writers on international law." 1 Kent Com. 18.

It will be convenient, in the first place, to refer to some leading French treatises on international law, which deal with the question now before us, not as one of the law of France only, but as one determined by the general consent of civilized nations.

"Enemy ships," say Pistoye and Duverdy, in their Treatise on Maritime Prizes, published in 1855, "are good prize. Not all, however; for it results from the unanimous accord of the maritime powers that an exception should be made in favor of coast fishermen. Such fishermen are respected by the enemy, so long as they devote themselves exclusively to fishing." 1 Pistoye et Duverdy, tit. 6, c. 1, p. 314.

[The Court cites numerous other French, English, Argentinian, German, Dutch, Austrian, Spanish, Portuguese, and Italian jurists.]

This review of the precedents and authorities on the subject appears to us abundantly to demonstrate that at the present day, by the general consent of the civilized nations of the world, and independently of any express treaty or other public act, it is an established rule of international law, founded on considerations of humanity to a poor and industrious order of men, and of the mutual convenience of belligerent States, that coast fishing vessels, with their implements and supplies, cargoes and crews, unarmed, and honestly pursuing their peaceful calling of catching and bringing in fresh fish, are exempt from capture as prize of war.

The exemption, of course, does not apply to coast fishermen or their vessels, if employed for a warlike purpose, or in such a way as to give aid or information to the enemy; nor when military or naval operations create a necessity to which all private interests must give way.

Nor has the exemption been extended to ships or vessels employed on the high sea in taking whales or seals, or cod or other fish which are not brought fresh to market, but are salted or otherwise cured and made a regular article of commerce.

This rule of international law is one which prize courts, administering the law of nations, are bound to take judicial notice of, and to give effect to, in the absence of any treaty or other public act of their own government in relation to the matter. * * *

To this subject, in more than one aspect, are singularly applicable the words uttered by Mr. Justice Strong, speaking for this court: "Undoubtedly, no single nation can change the law of the sea. That law is of universal obligation, and no statute of one or two nations can create obligations for the world. Like all the laws of nations, it rests upon the common consent of civilized communities. It is of force, not because it was prescribed by any superior power, but because it has been generally accepted as a rule of conduct. Whatever may have been its origin, whether in the usages of navigation, or in the ordinances of maritime States, or in both, it has become the law of the sea only by the concurrent sanction of those nations who may be said to constitute the commercial world. Many of the usages which prevail, and which have the force of law, doubtless originated in the positive prescriptions of some single State, which were at first of limited effect, but which, when generally accepted, became of universal obligation." "This is not giving to the statutes of any nation extra-territorial effect. It is not treating them as general maritime laws; but it is recognition of the historical fact that by common consent of mankind these rules have been acquiesced in as of general obligation. Of that fact, we think, we may take judicial note. Foreign municipal laws must indeed be proved as facts, but it is not so with the law of nations." *The Scotia*, 14 Wall. 170, 187, 188.

The position taken by the United States during the recent war with Spain was quite in accord with the rule of international law, now generally recognized by civilized nations, in regard to coast fishing vessels.

On April 21, 1898, the Secretary of the Navy gave instructions to Admiral Sampson, commanding the North Atlantic Squadron, to "immediately institute a blockade of the north coast of Cuba, extending from Cardenas on the east to Bahia Honda on the west." Bureau of Navigation Report of 1898, appx. 175. The blockade was immediately instituted accordingly. On April 22, the President issued a proclamation, declaring that the United States had instituted and would maintain that blockade, "in pursuance of the laws of the United States, and the law of nations applicable to such cases." 30 Stat. 1769. And by the act of Congress of April 25, 1898, c. 189, it was declared that the war between the United States and Spain existed on that day, and had existed since and including April 21.

On April 26, 1898, the President issued another proclamation, which, after reciting the existence of the war, as declared by Congress, contained this further recital: "It being desirable that such war should be conducted upon principles in harmony with the present views of nations and sanctioned by their recent practice." This recital was followed by specific declarations of certain rules for the conduct of the war by sea, making no mention of fishing vessels. 30 Stat. 1770. But the proclamation clearly manifests the general policy of the Government to conduct the war in accordance with the principles of international law sanctioned by the recent practice of nations.

On April 28, 1898, (after the capture of the two fishing vessels now in question,) Admiral Sampson telegraphed to the Secretary of the Navy as follows: "I find that a large number of fishing schooners are attempting to get into Havana from their fishing grounds near the Florida reefs and coasts. They are generally manned by excellent seamen, belonging to the maritime inscription of Spain, who have already served in the Spanish navy, and who are liable to further service. As these trained men are naval reserves, have a semi-military character, and would be most valuable to the Spaniards as artillerymen, either afloat or ashore, I recommend that they should be detained prisoners of war, and that I should be authorized to deliver them to the commanding officer of the army at Key West." To that communication the Secretary of the Navy, on April 30, 1898, guardedly answered: "Spanish fishing vessels attempting to violate blockade are subject, with crew, to capture, and any such vessel or crew considered likely to aid enemy may be detained." Bureau of Navigation Report of 1898, appx. 178. The Admiral's despatch assumed that he was not authorized, without express order, to arrest coast fishermen peaceably pursuing their calling; and the necessary implication and evident intent of the response of the Navy Department were that Spanish coast fishing vessels and their crews should not be interfered with, so long as they neither attempted to violate the blockade, nor were considered likely to aid the enemy.

The Paquete Habana, as the record shows, was a fishing sloop of 25 tons burden, sailing under the Spanish flag, running in and out of Havana, and regularly engaged in fishing on the coast of Cuba. Her crew consisted of but three men, including the master, and, according to a common usage in coast fisheries, had no interest in the vessel, but were entitled to two thirds of her catch; the other third belonging to her Spanish owner who, as well as the crew, resided in Havana. On her last voyage, she sailed from Havana along the coast of Cuba about 200 miles and fished for 25 days off the cape at the west end of the island within the territorial waters of Spain and was going back to Havana with her cargo of live fish, when she was captured by one of the blockading squadron on April 25, 1898. She had no arms or ammunition on board; she had no knowledge of the blockade or even of the war until she was stopped by a blockading vessel; she made no attempt to run the blockade and no resistance at the time of the capture; nor was there any evidence whatever of likelihood that she or her crew would aid the enemy.

In the case of the Lola, the only differences in the facts were that she was a schooner of 35 tons burden and had a crew of six men, including the master; that after leaving Havana and proceeding some 200 miles along the coast of Cuba, she went on about 100 miles farther to the coast of Yucatan, and there fished for eight days; and that, on her return, when near Bahia Honda on the coast of Cuba, she was captured with her cargo of live fish on April 27, 1898. These differences afford no ground for distinguishing the two cases.

Each vessel was of a moderate size, such as is not unusual in coast fishing smacks, and was regularly engaged in fishing on the coast of Cuba. The crew of each were few in number, had no interest in the vessel, and received, in return for their toil and enterprise, two thirds of her catch; the other third going to her owner by way of compensation for her use. Each vessel went out from Havana to her fishing ground and was captured when returning along the coast of Cuba. The cargo of each consisted of fresh fish caught by her crew from the sea and kept alive on board. Although one of the vessels extended her fishing trip across the Yucatan Channel and fished on the coast of Yucatan, we cannot doubt that each was engaged in the coast fishery and not in a commercial adventure within the rule of international law.

The two vessels and their cargoes were condemned by the District Court as prize of war; the vessels were sold under its decrees; and it does not appear what became of the fresh fish of which their cargoes consisted.

Upon the facts proved in either case, it is the duty of this court, sitting as the highest prize court of the United States, and administering the law of nations, to declare and adjudge that the capture was unlawful, and without probable cause; and it is therefore, in each case,

Ordered, that the decree of the District Court be reversed, and the proceeds of the sale of the vessel, together with the proceeds of any sale of her cargo, be restored to the claimant, with damages and costs.

NOTES AND QUESTIONS

1. *The Spanish-American War. Paquete Habana* emerged from the 1898 Spanish-American War, here described by Professor Dodge:

> Cuba was then a colony of Spain. For three years Spanish authorities had struggled to put down a Cuban insurgency, most notoriously with a policy of "reconcentration" that forced people from the countryside into fortified areas where thousands died from unsanitary conditions. Reports of atrocities in the American "yellow press," reaching a public already hostile to European involvement in the Western hemisphere and sympathetic to U.S. expansion, produced strong anti-Spanish feelings. Then, on February 15, 1898, an enormous explosion ripped through the battleship *Maine*, sending her to the bottom of Havana harbor, with a loss of 266 lives. From then on, "Cuban issues consumed the body politic, displacing all other concerns."
>
> After negotiations failed to convince Spain to grant Cuba independence, President McKinley sent a message to Congress on April 11 asking for authority to intervene. Congress responded on

> April 20, 1898, with a joint resolution declaring "[t]hat the people of the Island of Cuba are, and of right ought to be, free and independent;" demanding "that the Government of Spain at once relinquish its authority and government in the Island of Cuba and withdraw its land and naval forces from Cuba and Cuban waters;" and directing the President "to use the entire land and naval forces of the United States, and to call into the actual service of the United States the militia of the several States, to such an extent as may be necessary to carry these resolutions into effect."

William S. Dodge, "*The Paquete Habana*: Customary International Law as Part of Our Law," in *International Law Stories* 175, 176–77 (John E. Noyes, Laura A. Dickinson & Mark W. Janis eds. 2007).

2. *Usages as Law*. The 1900 judgment of the U.S. Supreme Court in *Paquete Habana* is probably the best-known decision of a U.S. court finding and applying customary international law. The case is frequently cited with respect to at least three issues: (1) the manner of determining rules of customary international law; (2) the way in which customary international law is incorporated into the municipal law of the United States; and (3) the proper relationship between the U.S. courts and the executive branch in legal matters touching on international relations. At this point, we are especially interested in the first issue.

Justice Gray opined that the rule providing for the exemption of coastal fishing vessels from capture as prizes of war began as "an ancient usage among civilized nations" and then "gradually ripened into a rule of international law." Regardless of what proof of the rule might be offered, why should such a transformative proposition be valid? Why should or how can the "usages" of states "ripen" into legal rules? Why should states or municipal courts give such "ripened usages" the force of law and apply them as rules of decision in cases before them? Are there any analogies in municipal law to the notion of usages ripening into obligatory rules of law?

3. *Evidences of Law*. Turning to his proof, what did Justice Gray employ as factual evidences "to trace the history of the rule"? Beginning with the first recitations, the orders of Henry IV in 1403 and 1406, in what sense are these evidences "international" usages? Is the next bit of proof, the 1521 treaty between Emperor Charles V and Francis I of France, any more "international"? Of all the evidences and usages shown, are some more persuasive as forms of proof than others?

4. *Contradictory Practice*. When can it be said that a usage "ripens" into a rule of customary international law? What about contradictory practice? For example, the 1675 agreement between Louis XIV and the States General of Holland had to be discontinued in 1681 and 1692 because the enemies of the French monarch "habitually carried off his fishermen, while their own fished in safety." Does such contradictory practice prevent the rule from ripening? Does one know if the rule has ripened by merely weighing the

cited bits of practice? Or must the record of practice be overwhelmingly conclusive before the rule ripens?

5. Opinio Juris. Ordinarily in positivist theory, it is said that customary international law is based on consistent state practice plus *opinio juris*, the belief that states act in a certain way because required to do so by law or necessity. Some equate *opinio juris* with "acceptance as law." See Article 38(1)(b) of the ICJ Statute. Is there any proof of *opinio juris* in *Paquete Habana*? *Opinio juris* is vital if custom is to be deemed the implicit agreement of states. If *opinio juris* is often a legal fiction, what is the real nature of customary international law? Does state practice without clear *opinio juris* still constitute a consensual source of international law?

A study by the International Committee of the Red Cross argued that "[w]hen there is sufficiently dense practice, an *opinio juris* is generally contained within that practice and, as a result, it is not usually necessary to demonstrate separately the existence of an *opinio juris*." Jean-Marie Henckaerts, "Study on Customary International Humanitarian Law: A Contribution to the Understanding and Respect for the Rule of Law in Armed Conflict," 87 *International Review of the Red Cross* 175, 182 (2005). Do you agree? Would the evidence reviewed in *Paquete Habana* demonstrate such dense practice?

6. *Custom and Municipal Law*. Note briefly here the other two "lessons" of *Paquete Habana* mentioned in Note 2. First, the Supreme Court held that "international law is part of our law," an important proposition about the incorporation of customary international law into U.S. municipal law, a proposition reaffirmed by the Supreme Court in 2004, with a citation to *Paquete Habana*. Sosa v. Alvarez-Machain, 542 U.S. 692, 729–30 (2004).

Second, in *Paquete Habana* the Supreme Court noted that it was "the general policy of the Government to conduct the war in accordance with the principles of international law." Did this satisfactorily establish why the Supreme Court had the constitutional authority to trump an executive decision with customary international law? Had both the President and the Court agreed that the actions of the Executive ought in any case be subject to customary international law? See Jordan Paust, "*Paquete* and the President: Rediscovering the Brief for the United States," 34 *Virginia Journal of International Law* 981 (1994). We return to the incorporation of customary international law and to the balance of powers in foreign relations among the President, the Congress, and U.S. courts in Chapter 4.

State courts too look at evidences of international practice to find or not find customary international law. In Commissioner of Correction v. Coleman, 303 Conn. 800 (2012), the Connecticut Supreme Court considered a claim by an inmate that force-feeding violated international law. *Id.* at 838. The Connecticut court identified the rule that customary international law was binding on it if the alleged norm "reflects a wide acceptance among the states and it appears the states follow the practice from a sense of legal obligation." *Id.* However, after considering evidence of state practice including international declarations, domestic judicial decisions, foreign statutes, and the practice of the European Court of Human Rights, the court concluded "there is no international consensus regarding whether states may force-feed inmates." *Id.* at 839–844.

THE ASYLUM CASE

Colombia v. Peru, 1950 I.C.J. 266

[Victor Raúl Haya de la Torre, the unsuccessful leader of a military revolt in Peru in 1948, sought political asylum in the Colombian embassy in Lima. Peru, however, rejected Colombia's assertion of diplomatic asylum for Haya de la Torre and refused to give him safe-conduct to leave the country, insisting that he, instead, be given over to Peru for trial for military rebellion. The dispute was referred to the International Court of Justice, which first decided that Colombia had no treaty right to unilaterally declare Haya de la Torre entitled to the status of a political offender eligible for diplomatic asylum. The ICJ then turned to customary international law:]

The Colombian Government has finally invoked "American international law in general." In addition to the rules arising from agreements which have already been considered, it has relied on an alleged regional or local custom peculiar to Latin-American states.

The Party which relies on a custom of this kind must prove that this custom is established in such a manner that it has become binding on the other Party. The Colombian Government must prove that the rule invoked by it is in accordance with a constant and uniform usage practised by the States in question, and that this usage is the expression of a right appertaining to the State granting asylum and a duty incumbent on the territorial State. This follows from Article 38 of the Statute of the Court which refers to international custom as "evidence of a general practice accepted as law."

In support of its contention concerning the existence of such a custom, the Colombian government has referred to a large number of extradition treaties which, as already explained, can have no bearing on the question now under consideration. It has cited conventions and agreements which do not contain any provision concerning the alleged rule of unilateral and definitive qualification such as the Montevideo Convention of 1889 on international penal law, the Bolivarian Agreement of 1911 and the Havana Convention of 1928. It has invoked conventions which have not been ratified by Peru, such as the Montevideo Conventions of 1933 and 1939. The Convention of 1933, has, in fact, been ratified by not more than eleven States and the Convention of 1939 by two States only.

It is particularly the Montevideo Convention of 1933 which Counsel for the Colombian Government has also relied on in this connexion. It is contended that this Convention has merely codified principles which were already recognized by Latin-American custom, and that it is valid against Peru as a proof of customary law. The limited number of States which have ratified this Convention reveals the weakness of this argument, and furthermore, it is invalidated by the preamble which states that this Convention modifies the Havana Convention.

Finally, the Colombian Government has referred to a large number of particular cases in which diplomatic asylum was in fact granted and respected. But it has not shown that the alleged rule of unilateral and definitive qualification was invoked or—if in some cases it was in fact invoked—that it was, apart from conventional stipulations, exercised by the States granting asylum as a right appertaining to them and respected by the territorial States as a duty incumbent on them and not merely for reasons of political expediency. The facts brought to the knowledge of the Court disclose so much uncertainty and contradiction, so much fluctuation and discrepancy in the exercise of diplomatic asylum and in the official views expressed on various occasions, there has been so much inconsistency in the rapid succession of conventions on asylum, ratified by some States and rejected by others, and the practice has been so much influenced by considerations of political expediency in the various cases, that it is not possible to discern in all this any constant and uniform usage, accepted as law, with regard to the alleged rule of unilateral and definitive qualification of the offense.

The Court cannot therefore find that the Colombian Government has proved the existence of such a custom. But even it could be supposed that such a custom existed between certain Latin-American States only, it could not be invoked against Peru which, far from having by its attitude adhered to it, has, on the contrary, repudiated it by refraining from ratifying the Montevideo Conventions of 1933 and 1939, which were the first to include a rule concerning the qualification of the offence in matters of diplomatic asylum. * * *

For these reasons, the Court has arrived at the conclusion that Colombia, as the State granting asylum, is not competent to qualify the offence by a unilateral and definitive decision, binding on Peru.

NOTES AND QUESTIONS

1. *The* Asylum Case. At the time, the ICJ's judgment in the *Asylum Case* was attacked because it "unmistakably pronounced a death sentence upon the institution of asylum." Manuel R. Garcia-Mora, "The Colombian-Peruvian Asylum Case and the Doctrine of Human Rights," 37 *Virginia Law Review* 927, 965 (1951). This was too great an alarm; the doctrine of asylum for political offenders has remained alive and well. See L.C. Green, "The

Right of Asylum in International Law," 3 *University of Malaya Law Review* 223 (1961). Indeed, many Latin American countries, albeit not Peru, responded to the *Asylum Case* by drafting the Caracas Convention on Diplomatic Asylum, specifically providing that "[i]t shall rest with the state granting asylum to determine the nature of the offense or the motive for the nature of the offense or the motive for the prosecution." *Id.* at 238–39.

More recently, Ecuador granted diplomatic asylum in London to WikiLeaks founder, Julian Assange, sought by the United Kingdom for extradition to Sweden on allegations of sexual molestation and rape. British authorities have refused to let Assange leave the country under Ecuadorian protection. The United Kingdom is not a party to the Convention on Diplomatic Asylum, and there is no provison for diplomatic asylum in the Vienna Convention on Diplomatic Relations. What guidance does the *Asylum Case* give Ecuador and Britain in resolving the Assange dispute? See Alison Duxbury, "Assange and the Law of Diplomatic Relations," 16 *ASIL Insights*, Issue 32 (2012).

2. *Regional and Particular Custom*. The more lasting contribution of the *Asylum Case* has been its proposition, though not proved by the practice in this case, that there can be a regional or particular rule of customary international law. A more successful argument based on a non-universal customary rule was accepted by the Court in the Anglo-Norwegian Fisheries Case, 1951 I.C.J. 116, 139, respecting Norway's assertion of a wider than ordinary exclusive fishing zone: "The notoriety of the facts, the general toleration of the international community, Great Britain's position in the North Sea, her own interest in the question, and her prolonged abstention would in any case warrant Norway's enforcement of her system against the United Kingdom." Might it have been sounder for the PCIJ in the *Eastern Greenland Case* in Chapter 2 to view the Ihlen Declaration as evidence of a particular custom rather than as a tacit treaty binding Norway and Denmark? What is the force, if any, of a regional custom against parties outside the region?

3. *General and Specific International Law*. Is a regional custom as suggested in the *Asylum Case* also an example of a specific international law? Would the rules in *Paquete Habana* be examples of general international law?

> General international law is a concept that is often used but rarely defined. It is the opposite of special international law (*lex specialis*) which governs particular topics (international trade law, law of the sea, etc.). Examples of general international law are the law of treaties as codified in the Vienna Convention on the Law of Treaties and the law of state responsibility as codified in the Articles on the Responsibility of States for Internationally Wrongful Acts.

International Human Rights Law and Practice Committee, "Final Report on the Impact of International Human Rights Law on General International

Law," in International Law Association, *Report of the Seventy-Third Conference (Rio de Janiero)* 663, 664 (2008).

Is general international law, whether set out in treaties or custom, those principles and rules applicable to all the various sorts of specific international law—not only international trade law and the law of the sea, but also, *e.g.*, the law of armed conflict, international environmental law, international human rights law, international commercial law, diplomatic immunity, as well as specific law made in bilateral and multilateral conventions? What if there is conflict between a general international law and a specific international law? International lawyers often invoke the Latin maxim *lex specialis derogat legi generali* (specific law trumps general law).

Are there some rules of customary international law so important that opting out is not possible? Are such non-derogable rules what is meant by *jus cogens* or "fundamental norms"? See the materials and discussion in Part C below. Professors Bradley and Gulati seemed to conflate ordinary customary international law and *jus cogens* norms, arguing that all international legal rules that are not derived from treaties are customary international law. Curtis A. Bradley & Mitu Gulati, "Withdrawing From International Custom," 120 *Yale Law Journal* 202, 204 (2010). In rebuttal, Professor Dodge reasserted a more traditional doctrine. William S. Dodge, "Withdrawing from Customary International Law: Some Lessons from History," 120 *Yale Law Journal Online* 169 (2010), http://yalelawjournal.org/the-yale-law-journal-pocket-part/international-law/withdrawing-from-customary-international-law:-some-lessons-from-history/ (last visited Dec. 8, 2013).

4. *The Persistent Objector.* Is a state bound by a rule of customary international law if it has persistently objected to the rule from the time it was first asserted? See Jonathan I. Charney, "The Persistent Objector Rule and the Development of Customary International Law," 56 *British Yearbook of International Law* 1 (1986). Should *silence*—merely refraining from ratifying conventions—suffice to demonstrate a state's persistent objection? Should the International Court insist on more concrete forms of persistent objection if a state is to escape being bound by a universal, rather than a regional, rule of customary international law? See David J. Bederman, *The Spirit of International Law* 73–74 (2002).

THE LOTUS CASE

France v. Turkey,
1927 P.C.I.J., Ser. A, No. 10

By a special agreement signed at Geneva on October 12th, 1926, between the Governments of the French and Turkish Republics * * * the Court has to decide the following questions:

> (1) Has Turkey, contrary to Article 15 of the Convention of Lausanne of July 24th, 1923, respecting conditions of residence and business and jurisdiction, acted in conflict with the principles of international law—and if so, what principles—by

instituting, following the collision which occurred on August 2nd, 1926, on the high seas between the French steamer *Lotus* and the Turkish steamer *Boz-Kourt* and upon the arrival of the French steamer at Constantinople—as well as against the captain of the Turkish steamship—joint criminal proceedings in pursuance of Turkish law against M. Demons, officer of the watch on board the *Lotus* at the time of the collision, in consequence of the loss of the *Boz-Kourt* having involved the death of eight Turkish sailors and passengers? * * *

THE FACTS. * * *

On August 2nd, 1926, just before midnight, a collision occurred between the French mail steamer *Lotus*, proceeding to Constantinople, and the Turkish collier *Boz-Kourt*, between five and six nautical miles to the north of Cape Sigri (Mitylene). The *Boz-Kourt*, which was cut in two, sank and eight Turkish nationals who were on board perished. After having done everything possible to succour the shipwrecked persons, of whom ten were able to be saved, the *Lotus* continued on its course to Constantinople, where it arrived on August 3rd.

At the time of the collision, the officer of the watch on board the *Lotus* was Monsieur Demons, a French citizen, lieutenant in the merchant service and first officer of the ship, whilst the movements of the *Boz-Kourt* were directed by its captain, Hassan Bey, who was one of those saved from the wreck.

As early as August 3rd the Turkish police proceeded to hold an enquiry into the collision on board the *Lotus*; and on the following day, August 4th, the captain of the *Lotus* handed in his master's report at the French Consulate-General, transmitting a copy to the harbour master.

On August 5th, Lieutenant Demons was requested by the Turkish authorities to go ashore to give evidence. The examination, the length of which incidentally resulted in delaying the departure of the *Lotus*, led to the placing under arrest of Lieutenant Demons—without previous notice being given to the French Consul-General—and Hassan Bey, amongst others. This arrest, which has been characterized by the Turkish Agent as arrest pending trial (*arrestation préventive*), was effected in order to ensure that the criminal prosecution instituted against the two officers, on a charge of manslaughter, by the Public Prosecutor of Stamboul, on the complaint of the families of the victims of the collision, should follow its normal course.

The case was first heard by the Criminal Court of Stamboul on August 28th. On that occasion, Lieutenant Demons submitted that the Turkish Courts had no jurisdiction; the Court, however, overruled his objection. When the proceedings were resumed on September 11th, Lieutenant Demons demanded his release on bail: this request was complied with on September 13th, the bail being fixed at 6,000 Turkish pounds.

On September 15th, the Criminal Court delivered its judgment, the terms of which have not been communicated to the Court by the Parties. It is, however, common ground, that it sentenced Lieutenant Demons to 80 days' imprisonment and a fine of 22 pounds, Hassan Bey being sentenced to a slightly more severe penalty. * * *

The action of the Turkish judicial authorities with regard to Lieutenant Demons at once gave rise to many diplomatic representations and other steps on the part of the French Government or its representatives in Turkey, either protesting against the arrest of Lieutenant Demons or demanding his release, or with a view to obtaining the transfer of the case from the Turkish Courts to the French Courts.

As a result of these representations, the Government of the Turkish Republic declared on September 2nd, 1926, that "it would have no objection to the reference of the conflict of jurisdiction to the Court at The Hague."

The French Government having, on the 6th of the same month, given "its full consent to the proposed solution," the two Governments appointed their plenipotentiaries with a view to the drawing up of the special agreement to be submitted to the Court; this special agreement was signed at Geneva on October 12th, 1926, as stated above, and the ratifications were deposited on December 27th, 1926.

THE LAW.

I.

Before approaching the consideration of the principles of international law contrary to which Turkey is alleged to have acted—thereby infringing the terms of Article 15 of the Convention of Lausanne of July 24th, 1923, respecting conditions of residence and business and jurisdiction—, it is necessary to define, in the light of the written and oral proceedings, the position resulting from the special agreement. For, the Court having obtained cognizance of the present case by notification of a special agreement concluded between the Parties in the case, it is rather to the terms of this agreement than to the submissions of the Parties that the Court must have recourse in establishing the precise points which it has to decide. In this respect the following observations should be made:

1.—The collision which occurred on August 2nd, 1926, between the S.S. *Lotus*, flying the French flag, and the S.S. *Boz-Kourt*, flying the Turkish flag, took place on the high seas: the territorial jurisdiction of any State other than France and Turkey therefore does not enter into account.

2.—The violation, if any, of the principles of international law would have consisted in the taking of criminal proceedings against Lieutenant Demons. It is not therefore a question relating to any particular step in these proceedings—such as his being put to trial, his arrest, his detention pending trial or the judgment given by the Criminal Court of Stamboul—but of the very fact of the Turkish Courts exercising criminal jurisdiction. That is why the arguments put forward by the Parties in both phases of the proceedings relate exclusively to the question whether Turkey has or has not, according to the principles of international law, jurisdiction to prosecute in this case. * * *

Article 6 of the Turkish Penal Code, Law No. 765 of March 1st, 1926 (Official Gazette No. 320 of March 13th, 1926), runs as follows:

[*Translation.*]

> Any foreigner who, apart from the cases contemplated by Article 4, commits an offence abroad to the prejudice of Turkey or of a Turkish subject, for which offence Turkish law prescribes a penalty involving loss of freedom for a minimum period of not less than one year, shall be punished in accordance with the Turkish Penal Code provided that he is arrested in Turkey. The penalty shall however be reduced by one third and instead of the death penalty, 20 years of penal servitude shall be awarded.
>
> Nevertheless, in such cases, the prosecution will only be instituted at the request of the Minister of Justice or on the complaint of the injured Party.
>
> If the offence committed injures another foreigner, the guilty person shall be punished at the request of the Minister of Justice, in accordance with the provisions set out in the first paragraph of this article, provided however that:
>
> (1) the article in question is one for which Turkish law prescribes a penalty involving loss of freedom for a minimum period of three years;
>
> (2) there is no extradition treaty or that extradition has not been accepted either by the government of the locality where the guilty person has committed the offence or by the government of his own country.

Even if the Court must hold that the Turkish authorities had seen fit to base the prosecution of Lieutenant Demons upon the above-mentioned Article 6, the question submitted to the Court is not whether that article is compatible with the principles of international law; it is more general. The Court is asked to state whether or not the principles of international law prevent Turkey from instituting criminal proceedings against Lieutenant Demons under Turkish law. Neither the conformity of Article

6 in itself with the principles of international law nor the application of that article by the Turkish authorities constitutes the point at issue; it is the very fact of the institution of proceedings which is held by France to be contrary to those principles. * * *

II.

Having determined the position resulting from the terms of the special agreement, the Court must now ascertain which were the principles of international law that the prosecution of Lieutenant Demons could conceivably be said to contravene.

It is Article 15 of the Convention of Lausanne of July 24th, 1923, respecting conditions of residence and business and jurisdiction, which refers the contracting Parties to the principles of international law as regards the delimitation of their respective jurisdiction.

This clause is as follows:

> Subject to the provisions of Article 16, all questions of jurisdiction shall, as between Turkey and the other contracting Powers, be decided in accordance with the principles of international law.

The French Government maintains that the meaning of the expression "principles of international law" in this article should be sought in the light of the evolution of the Convention. Thus it states that during the preparatory work, the Turkish Government, by means of an amendment to the relevant article of a draft for the Convention, sought to extend its jurisdiction to crimes committed in the territory of a third State, provided that, under Turkish law, such crimes were within the jurisdiction of Turkish Courts. This amendment, in regard to which the representatives of France and Italy made reservations, was definitely rejected by the British representative; and the question having been subsequently referred to the Drafting Committee, the latter confined itself in its version of the draft to a declaration to the effect that questions of jurisdiction should be decided in accordance with the principles of international law. The French Government deduces from these facts that the prosecution of Demons is contrary to the intention which guided the preparation of the Convention of Lausanne.

The Court must recall in this connection what it has said in some of its preceding judgments and opinions, namely, that there is no occasion to have regard to preparatory work if the text of a convention is sufficiently clear in itself. Now the Court considers that the words "principles of international law," as ordinarily used, can only mean international law as it is applied between all nations belonging to the community of States. * * *

III.

The Court, having to consider whether there are any rules of international law which may have been violated by the prosecution in pursuance of Turkish law of Lieutenant Demons, is confronted in the first place by a question of principle which, in the written and oral arguments of the two Parties, has proved to be a fundamental one. The French Government contends that the Turkish Courts, in order to have jurisdiction, should be able to point to some title to jurisdiction recognized by international law in favour of Turkey. On the other hand, the Turkish Government takes the view that Article 15 allows Turkey jurisdiction whenever such jurisdiction does not come into conflict with a principle of international law.

The latter view seems to be in conformity with the special agreement itself, No. 1 of which asks the Court to say whether Turkey has acted contrary to the principles of international law and, if so, what principles. According to the special agreement, therefore, it is not a question of stating principles which would permit Turkey to take criminal proceedings, but of formulating the principles, if any, which might have been violated by such proceedings.

This way of stating the question is also dictated by the very nature and existing conditions of international law.

International law governs relations between independent States. The rules of law binding upon States therefore emanate from their own free will as expressed in conventions or by usages generally accepted as expressing principles of law and established in order to regulate the relations between these co-existing independent communities or with a view to the achievement of common aims. Restrictions upon the independence of States cannot therefore be presumed.

Now the first and foremost restriction imposed by international law upon a State is that—failing the existence of a permissive rule to the contrary—it may not exercise its power in any form in the territory of another State. In this sense jurisdiction is certainly territorial; it cannot be exercised by a State outside its territory except by virtue of a permissive rule derived from international custom or from a convention.

It does not, however, follow that international law prohibits a State from exercising jurisdiction in its own territory, in respect of any case which relates to acts which have taken place abroad, and in which it cannot rely on some permissive rule of international law. Such a view would only be tenable if international law contained a general prohibition to States to extend the application of their laws and the jurisdiction of their courts to persons, property and acts outside their territory, and if, as an exception to this general prohibition, it allowed States to do so in certain specific cases. But this is certainly not the case under international law as it stands at present. Far from laying down a general prohibition to the effect that States may not extend the application of their laws and the jurisdiction of their courts to persons, property and acts outside their territory, it leaves them in this respect a wide measure of discretion which is only limited in certain cases by prohibitive rules; as regards other cases, every State remains free to adopt the principles which it regards as best and most suitable. * * *

In these circumstances, all that can be required of a State is that it should not overstep the limits which international law places upon its jurisdiction; within these limits, its title to exercise jurisdiction rests in its sovereignty.

It follows from the foregoing that the contention of the French Government to the effect that Turkey must in each case be able to cite a rule of international law authorizing her to exercise jurisdiction, is opposed to the generally accepted international law to which Article 15 of the Convention of Lausanne refers. * * *

IV.

The Court will now proceed to ascertain whether general international law, to which Article 15 of the Convention of Lausanne refers, contains a rule prohibiting Turkey from prosecuting Lieutenant Demons.

For this purpose, it will in the first place examine the value of the arguments advanced by the French Government, without however omitting to take into account other possible aspects of the problem, which might show the existence of a restrictive rule applicable in this case.

The arguments advanced by the French Government, other than those considered above, are, in substance, the three following:

(1) International law does not allow a State to take proceedings with regard to offenses committed by foreigners abroad, simply by reason of the nationality of the victim; and such is the situation in the present case because the offence must be regarded as having been committed on board the French vessel.

(2) International law recognizes the exclusive jurisdiction of the State whose flag is flown as regards everything which occurs on board a ship on the high seas.

(3) Lastly, this principle is especially applicable in a collision case.

As regards the first argument, the Court feels obliged in the first place to recall that its examination is strictly confined to the specific situation in the present case, for it is only in regard to this situation that its decision is asked for.

As has already been observed, the characteristic features of the situation of fact are as follows: there has been a collision on the high seas between two vessels flying different flags, on one of which was one of the persons alleged to be guilty of the offence, whilst the victims were on board the other.

This being so, the Court does not think it necessary to consider the contention that a State cannot punish offences committed abroad by a foreigner simply by reason of the nationality of the victim. For this contention only relates to the case where the nationality of the victim is the only criterion on which the criminal jurisdiction of the State is based. Even if that argument were correct generally speaking—and in regard to this the Court reserves its opinion—it could only be used in the present case if international law forbade Turkey to take into consideration the fact that the offence produced its effects on the Turkish vessel and consequently in a place assimilated to Turkish territory in which the application of Turkish criminal law cannot be challenged, even in regard to offenses committed there by foreigners. But no such rule of international law exists. No argument has come to the knowledge of the Court from which it could be deduced that States recognize themselves to be under an obligation towards each other only to have regard to the place where the author of the offence happens to be at the time of the offence. On the contrary, it is certain that the courts of many countries, even of countries which have given their criminal legislation a strictly territorial character, interpret criminal law in the sense that offences, the authors of which at the moment of commission are in the territory of another State, are nevertheless to be regarded as having been committed in the national territory, if one of the constituent elements of the offence, and more especially its effects, have taken place there. French courts have, in regard to a variety of situations, given decisions sanctioning this way of interpreting the territorial principle. Again, the Court does not know of any cases in which governments have protested against the fact that the criminal law of some country contained a rule to this effect or that the courts of a country construed their criminal law in this sense. Consequently, once it is admitted that the effects of the offence were produced on the Turkish vessel, it becomes impossible to hold that there is a rule of international law which prohibits Turkey from prosecuting Lieutenant Demons because of the fact that the author of the offence was on board the French ship. * * *

The second argument put forward by the French Government is the principle that the State whose flag is flown has exclusive jurisdiction over everything which occurs on board a merchant ship on the high seas.

It is certainly true that—apart from certain special cases which are defined by international law—vessels on the high seas are subject to no authority except that of the State whose flag they fly. In virtue of the principle of the freedom of the seas, that is to say, the absence of any territorial sovereignty upon the high seas, no State may exercise any kind of jurisdiction over foreign vessels upon them. Thus, if a war vessel, happening to be at the spot where a collision occurs between a vessel flying its flag and a foreign vessel, were to send on board the latter an officer to make investigations or to take evidence, such an act would undoubtedly be contrary to international law.

But it by no means follows that a State can never in its own territory exercise jurisdiction over acts which have occurred on board a foreign ship on the high seas. A corollary of the principle of the freedom of the seas is that a ship on the high seas is assimilated to the territory of the State the flag of which it flies, for, just as in its own territory, that State exercises its authority upon it, and no other State may do so. All that can be said is that by virtue of the principle of the freedom of the seas, a ship is placed in the same position as national territory; but there is nothing to support the claim according to which the rights of the State under whose flag the vessel sails may go farther than the rights which it exercises within its territory properly so called. It follows that what occurs on board a vessel on the high seas must be regarded as if it occurred on the territory of the State whose flag the ship flies. If, therefore, a guilty act committed on the high seas produces its effects on a vessel flying another flag or in foreign territory, the same principles must be applied as if the territories of two different States were concerned, and the conclusion must therefore be drawn that there is no rule of international law prohibiting the State to which the ship on which the effects of the offence have taken place belongs, from regarding the offence as having been committed in its territory and prosecuting, accordingly, the delinquent.

This conclusion could only be overcome if it were shown that there was a rule of customary international law which, going further than the principle stated above, established the exclusive jurisdiction of the State whose flag was flown. The French Government has endeavoured to prove the existence of such a rule, having recourse for this purpose to the teachings of publicists, to decisions of municipal and international tribunals, and especially to conventions which, whilst creating exceptions to the principle of the freedom of the seas by permitting the war and police vessels of a State to exercise a more or less extensive control over the merchant vessels of another State, reserve jurisdiction to the courts of the country whose flag is flown by the vessel proceeded against.

In the Court's opinion, the existence of such a rule has not been conclusively proved.

In the first place, as regards teachings of publicists, and apart from the question as to what their value may be from the point of view of establishing the existence of a rule of customary law, it is no doubt true that all or nearly all writers teach that ships on the high seas are subject exclusively to the jurisdiction of the State whose flag they fly. But the important point is the significance attached by them to this principle; now it does not appear that in general, writers bestow upon this principle a scope differing from or wider than that explained above and which is equivalent to saying that the jurisdiction of a State over vessels on the high seas is the same in extent as its jurisdiction in its own territory. On the other hand, there is no lack of writers who, upon a close study of the special question whether a State can prosecute for offences committed on board a foreign ship on the high seas, definitely come to the conclusion that such offences must be regarded as if they had been committed in the territory of the State whose flag the ship flies, and that consequently the general rules of each legal system in regard to offences committed abroad are applicable.

In regard to precedents, it should first be observed that, leaving aside the collision cases which will be alluded to later, none of them relates to offences affecting two ships flying the flags of two different countries, and that consequently they are not of much importance in the case before the Court. * * *

On the other hand, there is no lack of cases in which a State has claimed a right to prosecute for an offence, committed on board a foreign ship, which it regarded as punishable under its legislation. Thus Great Britain refused the request of the United States for the extradition of John Anderson, a British seaman who had committed homicide on board an American vessel, stating that she did not dispute the jurisdiction of the United States but that she was entitled to exercise hers concurrently. This case, to which others might be added, is relevant in spite of Anderson's British nationality, in order to show that the principle of the exclusive jurisdiction of the country whose flag the vessel flies is not universally accepted. * * *

Finally, as regards conventions expressly reserving jurisdiction exclusively to the State whose flag is flown, it is not absolutely certain that this stipulation is to be regarded as expressing a general principle of law rather than as corresponding to the extraordinary jurisdiction which these conventions confer on the state-owned ships of a particular country in respect of ships of another country on the high seas. Apart from that, it should be observed that these conventions relate to matters of a particular kind, closely connected with the policing of the seas, such as the slave trade, damage to submarine cables, fisheries, etc., and not to common-law offences. Above all it should be pointed out that the offences contemplated by the conventions in question only concern a single ship; it is impossible therefore to make any deduction from them in regard to matters which concern two ships and consequently the jurisdiction of two different States.

The Court therefore has arrived at the conclusion that the second argument put forward by the French Government does not, any more than the first, establish the existence of a rule of international law prohibiting Turkey from prosecuting Lieutenant Demons.

It only remains to examine the third argument advanced by the French Government and to ascertain whether a rule specially applying to collision cases has grown up, according to which criminal proceedings regarding such cases come exclusively within the jurisdiction of the State whose flag is flown.

In this connection, the Agent for the French Government has drawn the Court's attention to the fact that questions of jurisdiction in collision cases, which frequently arise before civil courts, are but rarely encountered in the practice of criminal courts. He deduces from this that, in practice, prosecutions only occur before the courts of the State whose flag is flown and that circumstance is proof of a tacit consent on the part of States and, consequently, shows what positive international law is in collision cases.

In the Court's opinion, this conclusion is not warranted. Even if the rarity of the judicial decisions to be found among the reported cases were sufficient to prove in point of fact the circumstance alleged by the Agent for the French Government, it would merely show that States had often, in practice, abstained from instituting criminal proceedings, and not that they recognized themselves as being obliged to do so; for only if such abstention were based on their being conscious of having a duty to abstain would it be possible to speak of an international custom. The alleged fact does not allow one to infer that States have been conscious of having such a duty; on the other hand, as will presently be seen, there are other circumstances calculated to show that the contrary is true.

So far as the Court is aware there are no decisions of international tribunals in this matter; but some decisions of municipal courts have been cited. Without pausing to consider the value to be attributed to the judgments of municipal courts in connection with the establishment of the existence of a rule of international law, it will suffice to observe that the decisions quoted sometimes support one view and sometimes the other. Whilst the French Government have been able to cite the *Ortigia-Oncle-Joseph* case before the Court of Aix and the *Franconia-Strathclyde* case before the British Court for Crown Cases Reserved, as being in favour of the exclusive jurisdiction of the state whose flag is flown, on the other hand the *Ortigia-Oncle-Joseph* case before the Italian Courts and the *Ekbatana-West-Hinder* case before the Belgian Courts have been cited in support of the opposing contention.

Lengthy discussions have taken place between the Parties as to the importance of each of these decisions as regards the details of which the Court confines itself to a reference to the Cases and Counter-Cases of the

Parties. The Court does not think it necessary to stop to consider them. It will suffice to observe that, as municipal jurisprudence is thus divided, it is hardly possible to see in it an indication of the existence of the restrictive rule of international law which alone could serve as a basis for the contention of the French Government. * * *

The Court, having arrived at the conclusion that the arguments advanced by the French Government either are irrelevant to the issue or do not establish the existence of a principle of international law precluding Turkey from instituting the prosecution which was in fact brought against Lieutenant Demons, observes that in the fulfilment of its task of itself ascertaining what the international law is, it has not confined itself to a consideration of the arguments put forward, but has included in its researches all precedents, teachings and facts to which it had access and which might possibly have revealed the existence of one of the principles of international law contemplated in the special argument. The result of these researches has not been to establish the existence of any such principle. It must therefore be held that there is no principle of international law, within the meaning of Article 15 of the Convention of Lausanne of July 24th, 1923, which precludes the institution of the criminal proceedings under consideration. Consequently, Turkey, by instituting, in virtue of the discretion which international law leaves to every sovereign State, the criminal proceedings in question, has not, in the absence of such principles, acted in a manner contrary to the principles of international law within the meaning of the special agreement. * * *

FOR THESE REASONS,

The Court,

having heard both Parties,

gives by the President's casting vote—the votes being equally divided—, judgment to the effect

(1) that, following the collision which occurred on August 2nd, 1926, on the high seas between the French steamship *Lotus* and the Turkish steamship *Boz-Kourt*, and upon the arrival of the French ship at Stamboul, and in consequence of the loss of the *Boz-Kourt* having involved the death of eight Turkish nationals, Turkey, by instituting criminal proceedings in pursuance of Turkish law against Lieutenant Demons, officer of the watch on board the *Lotus* at the time of the collision, has not acted in conflict with the principles of international law, contrary to Article 15 of the Convention of Lausanne of July 24th, 1923, respecting conditions of residence and business and jurisdiction.

NOTES AND QUESTIONS

1. *Positivism and International Law. Lotus* "attracted more attention among international lawyers than any other decision of the 1920s, at the time and ever since." Ole Spiermann, *International Legal Argument in the Permanent Court of International Justice: The Rise of the International Judiciary* 247 (2005). It involved a narrow, albeit interesting, jurisdictional issue in international conflict of laws, but the PCIJ sought to teach a far broader lesson. The judgment became one of the most usually cited positivist opinions about the nature of international law, because it argued in part III that the "rules of law binding upon States therefore emanate from their own free will as expressed in conventions or by usages generally accepted as expressing principles of law." The ruling half of an evenly divided Court in *Lotus* maintained that all international legal rules are based on state consent: "Restrictions upon the independence of States cannot therefore be presumed." No room was given to general principles, fundamental norms, natural law, or equity as sources of international law; state sovereignty was seen as the fundamental principle of international law from which all other international legal principles and rules are derived. Looking at other cases above, *e.g.*, *Filartiga* and *Paquete Habana*, and below, *e.g.*, *Texaco/Libya*, *AM & S*, *Smith*, and *North Sea Continental Shelf*, is the strict positivism of the *Lotus* judgment too restrictive?

2. *The Burden of Proof.* In the context of the case, the positivist presumption meant that the Court put the burden of proof on France rather than on Turkey. The Court ruled that France had to prove that there was a rule of customary international law restricting Turkish independence rather than making Turkey prove that its prosecution of Lieutenant Demons was sanctioned by international law. Given the uncertainty of the evidence of customary international law, was not this allocation of the burden of proof crucial to the outcome of the case? Would a less positivist position have enabled the Court to rely less heavily on the burden of proof as a way of deciding the case?

3. *Tacit Agreement and the Formation of Rules of Customary International Law.* In order to satisfy its burden of proof in *Lotus*, would France have had to establish that Turkey itself, in its international relations, affirmatively consented to a rule of international law that prohibited the prosecution of Lieutenant Demons in Turkish court? Or would it suffice, under a positivist conception of universal custom, to establish expressions of consent by some states, followed by the silence of other states? Is it possible to establish tacit consent?

The *Lotus* Court was formally bound by Article 38(1)(b) of the 1920 Statute of the Permanent Court of International Justice, a provision identical to Article 38(1)(b) of the ICJ Statute. Does Article 38(1)(b) take a positivist view of international custom? If so, does it answer the question whether each affected state must accept a customary rule in order to be bound by it, or whether instead some general acceptance by states suffices? Does a positivist account of customary international law accurately reflect how it develops? Consider the following view:

> * * * When one examines the emergence of such universally applicable customary rules and principles as those relating to diplomatic immunities, the prohibition of piracy and privateering, and sovereign rights over the continental shelf, it is impossible to show that every State positively consented to the emergence of the rule in question. Yet it is virtually unanimously accepted by the authorities that these rules have come to bind all States.
>
> The nature of the process by which these customary rules emerged seems to be more along the following lines. Some States actively created the practice, some by initiating it, some by imitating it, and others still, who were directly affected by the claims in question, by acquiescing in it. This initiation, imitation and acquiescence may plausibly be described in terms of consent. But others still, who were not directly affected, sat by and did nothing, and in due course found themselves bound by the emerging rule.

Committee on the Formation of Customary (General) International Law, "3rd Interim Report," in International Law Association, *Report of the Sixty-Seventh Conference (Helsinki)* 623, 630 (1996). Does "sitting by and doing nothing" signify tacit consent?

4. *Jurisdiction.* In international law, "jurisdiction" refers to the authority of states to determine or affect legal relationships of private parties. One important distinction is between enforcement jurisdiction (the authority of a state to investigate, collect evidence, or arrest) and legislative jurisdiction (the authority of a state to apply its laws). As to enforcement jurisdiction, the *Lotus* Court gave the example of a "a war vessel, happening to be at [a] spot [on the high seas] where a collision occurs between a vessel flying its flag and a foreign vessel." Were the war vessel to send "on board the latter an officer to make investigations or take evidence," that action, the Court concluded, "would undoubtedly be contrary to international law." At issue in *Lotus* itself, however, was the validity at international law of an exercise of legislative jurisdiction—Turkey's authority to apply its own criminal laws to Lt. Demons's conduct with respect to the collision on the high seas.

The most traditional international law bases of legislative jurisdiction are territoriality, where proscribed conduct and its consequences occur within a state's territory, and nationality, where a state's citizen has violated its laws. What other possible bases of jurisdiction are discussed in the *Lotus Case*? When the Court concluded that international law did not prohibit Turkey's prosecution of Lt. Demons under Turkish law, did that mean that France lost its jurisdiction with respect to Lt. Demons's conduct? More on jurisdiction and conflicts of jurisdiction appears in Chapter 11, and more on a state's jurisdiction over its own and foreign flag vessels comes in Chapter 10.

5. *Reversal of the Rule in* Lotus. As a matter of maritime law, many observers strongly disagreed with the *Lotus* decision, feeling that it exposed shipboard officers to double prosecution and could lead to unnecessary delays in maritime traffic. In the 1958 Geneva Convention on the High Seas, Article 11(1) provides that in cases involving collisions on the high seas, only the flag state or the national state of the accused may prosecute the officer in a case of a collision on the high seas. The same anti-*Lotus* rule resurfaced in Article 97(1) of the 1982 Convention on the Law of the Sea. These treaty articles illustrate how a treaty may sometimes reverse a rule of customary international law. Should custom be able to reverse a treaty rule?

6. *Treaty Interpretation.* Note that in *Lotus* two treaties were involved as well as customary international law. The first treaty, the special agreement of October 12, 1926, provided authority for the Permanent Court of International Justice to hear the case and set the questions that the Court was to address. The second treaty was the 1923 Convention of Lausanne, Article 15 of which referred to "principles of international law." The PCIJ took that phrase to refer to what it termed "general international law." Do either "principles of international law" or "general international law" encompass more than just customary international law? Was the Court's reluctance to examine the *travaux préparatoires* of Article 15 appropriate? Compare the approach toward treaty interpretation taken in the *Eastern Airlines Case* in Chapter 2, and see Articles 31–32 of the Vienna Convention on the Law of Treaties in the Appendix.

THE TEXACO/LIBYA ARBITRATION

Award of 19 January 1977, 17 *International Legal Materials* 1 (1978)

Acting in his capacity as Sole Arbitrator [Professor René-Jean Dupuy], pursuant to the appointment made on 18 December 1974 by the President of the International Court of Justice, of an arbitration between, on the one hand, the Government of the Libyan Arab Republic and, on the other, California Asiatic Oil Company and Texaco Overseas Petroleum Company,

The undersigned Sole Arbitrator has rendered the following award on the merits:

I. THE FACTS

1. The present arbitration arises out of 14 Deeds of Concession concluded between the competent Libyan Authorities (Petroleum Commission or Petroleum Ministry, depending on the date of the contracts [which were concluded during 1955–1957, 1959, and 1966]) and the above-mentioned companies[.]

3. Among the provisions which are contained in the model contract annexed to the Petroleum Law of 1955 and reproduced in the contracts

concluded by the concessionaire companies, Clause 16 is worth, at this time, special mention. * * *

The final version of Clause 16 * * * reads as follows:

> The Government of Libya will take all steps necessary to ensure that the Company enjoys all the rights conferred by this Concession. The contractual rights expressly created by this concession shall not be altered except by mutual consent of the parties.
>
> This Concession shall throughout the period of its validity be construed in accordance with the Petroleum Law and the Regulations in force on the date of execution of the agreement of amendment by which this paragraph (2) was incorporated into this concession agreement. Any amendment to or repeal of such Regulations shall not affect the contractual rights of the Company without its consent. * * *

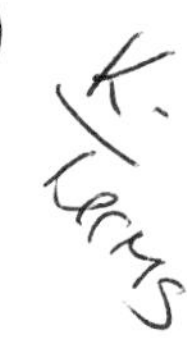

7. Law No. 11 of 1974 (the Decree of Nationalization of 11 February 1974) nationalized the totality of the properties, rights, assets and interests of California Asiatic Oil Company and Texaco Overseas Petroleum Company arising out of the 14 Deeds of Concession held by those companies. The more important aspects of this second text may be summarized as follows:

—it was directed against only the plaintiff companies, to the exclusion of any other company or enterprise;

—the text provided for the nationalization of all the properties and interests, rights and assets of California Asiatic Oil Company and Texaco Overseas Petroleum Company;

—the provisions relating to possible compensation (Article 2) were nothing more than a repetition of those which were already contained in Law No. 66 of 1973 (Article 2);

—the transfer of all the properties, rights and assets to N.O.C. [the Libyan National Oil Company] was confirmed (Article 6);

—finally, Article 7 effected a fundamental change in Amoseas, a company governed by foreign law; it was changed into a non-profit company, the assets of which were completely owned by N.O.C. Amoseas lost its name and was renamed the "Om el Jawabi Company."

II. THE PROCEDURE

8. The Tribunal should now, on the one hand, recall and complete the indications already given in its Preliminary Award of 27 November 1975 relating to the arbitration procedure and, on the other, pronounce on the law applicable to the arbitration of which it has been seized.

A. The Development of the Procedure:

9.—by two separate letters, dated 2 September 1973, California Asiatic Oil Company and Texaco Overseas Petroleum Company notified the Government of the Libyan Arab Republic that, pursuant to Article 20(1) of the Law on Petroleum of 1955 and to Clause 28 of the Deeds of Concession, they intended to submit to arbitration the dispute between them and the Government and advised the Government that they had appointed as arbitrator a member of the New York Bar, Mr. Fowler Hamilton.

—during the time which was allowed it by Clause 28 of the Deeds of Concession (and which expired on 1 December 1973), the Government of the Libyan Arab Republic did not appoint its arbitrator and, by a circular letter of 8 December 1973, it declared that it rejected the request for arbitration;

—the Libyan Government's failure and refusal to appoint an arbitrator led the companies to use the provision of Clause 28 of the Deeds of Concession which allows the concessionaires to request that the President of the International Court of Justice appoint a Sole Arbitrator: this was the purpose of the joint letter which the two companies sent on 3 April 1974 to the President of the International Court of Justice[.]

III. THE MERITS

17. In their final submissions, those which were stated both at the close of their Memorial on the Merits and at the close of the oral hearings, the plaintiffs requested that the Arbitral Tribunal rule:

A. Finding in favor of the Companies as follows:

(1) that the Deeds of Concession are binding on the Parties;

(2) that Libya, in adopting the Decrees of 1973 and 1974 and by its subsequent action pursuant thereto, breached its obligations under the Deeds of Concession;

(3) that Libya be held to perform the Deeds of Concession and fulfill their terms; and

(4) that Libya have 90 days after the award, being from the time of the declaration of the award or from the date fixed by the Sole Arbitrator, to inform the Arbitral Tribunal of the measures which it has taken in order to comply with and to execute the award. * * *

SECTION I: Concerning the Binding Nature of the Deeds of Concession
* * *

B. How did the parties to these Deeds of Concession deal with the question of the applicable law? * * *

23. What was the law applicable to these contracts? It is this particular question that the parties intended to resolve in adopting Clause 28 of the Deeds of Concession in a form which must be recalled here:

> This concession shall be governed by and interpreted in accordance with the principles of the law of Libya common to the principles of international law and in the absence of such common principles then by and in accordance with the general principles of law, including such of those principles as may have been applied by international tribunals.

Thus, a complex system to determine the law applicable or the "choice of law" has been provided by the contracting parties involving a two-tier system:

—the principles of Libyan law were applicable to the extent that such principles were common to principles of international law;

—alternatively, in the absence of such conformity, reference was made to general principles of law. * * *

1. First question: Did the parties have the right to choose the law or the system of law which was to govern their contract? * * *

32. For the time being, it will suffice to note that the evolution which has occurred in the old case law of the Permanent Court of International Justice is due to the fact that, while the old case law viewed the contract as something which could not come under international law because it could not be regarded as a treaty between States, under the new concept treaties are not the only type of agreements governed by such law. And it should be added that, although they are not to be confused with treaties, contracts between States and private persons can, under certain conditions, come within the ambit of a particular and new branch of international law: the international law of contracts. * * *

SECTION II: Did the Libyan Government, in adopting the nationalization measures of 1973 and 1974, breach its obligations under the contracts?

53. The Tribunal must now rule on the point whether, in adopting nationalization measures in 1973 and 1974, the defendant Government has, or has not, breached its obligations arising from the contracts it executed. For this purpose, this Tribunal should examine the various reasons which could be envisaged in order to justify the defendant Government's behavior and which, if established, would constitute

reasons for freeing or exonerating it from the obligation which it had assumed and from its related responsibilities.

Three types of reasons could be put forward in order to justify, or attempt to justify, the behavior of the defendant government:

—the first reason could be based on the nature of the contracts under dispute: if they were administrative contracts, they could give rise, under certain conditions, to amendments or even to abrogation on the part of the contracting State; in relation to concession contracts, the nationalization measures would then be analyzed as being decisions bringing about, at least implicitly, abrogation;

—the second reason could be based on the concept of sovereignty and on the very nature of measures of nationalization;

—the third reason, lastly, could be deduced from the present status of international law, and in particular from certain resolutions concerning natural resources and wealth as adopted, in the last few years, by the United Nations. * * *

C. The present state of international law and the resolutions concerning natural resources and wealth adopted by the United Nations

80. This Tribunal has stated that it intends to rule on the basis of positive law, but now it is necessary to determine precisely the content of positive law and to ascertain the place which resolutions by the General Assembly of the United Nations could occupy therein.

In its Preliminary Award of 27 November 1975, this Tribunal postponed the examination of the objection raised by the Libyan Government in its Memorandum of 26 July 1974 according to which:

> Nationalization is an act related to the sovereignty of the State. This fact has been recognized by the consecutive Resolutions of the United Nations on the sovereignty of States over their natural resources, the last being Resolution No. 3171 of the United Nations General Assembly adopted on December 13, 1973, as well as paragraph (4/E) of Resolution No. 3201 (S–VI) adopted on 1 May, 1974. The said Resolutions confirm that every State maintains complete right to exercise full sovereignty over its natural resources and recognize Nationalization as being a legitimate and internationally recognized method to ensure the sovereignty of the State upon such resources. Nationalization, being related to the sovereignty of the State, is not subject to foreign jurisdiction. Provisions of the International Law do not permit a dispute with a State to be referred to any Jurisdiction other than its national Jurisdiction. In affirmance of this principle, Resolutions of the General Assembly provide that any dispute related to Nationalization or its consequences should be

settled in accordance with provisions of domestic law of the State.

81. * * * The practice of the United Nations, referred to in the Libyan Government's Memorandum, does not contradict in any way the status of international law as indicated above. This Tribunal wishes first to recall the relevant passages for this case of Resolution 1803 (XVII) entitled "Permanent Sovereignty over Natural Resources," as adopted by the General Assembly on 14 December 1962:

> 3. In cases where authorization is granted, the capital imported and the earnings on that capital shall be governed by the terms thereof, by the national legislation in force, and by international law. . . .
>
> 4. Nationalization, expropriation or requisitioning shall be based on grounds or reasons of public utility, security or the national interest which are recognized as overriding purely individual or private interests, both domestic and foreign. In such cases the owner shall be paid appropriate compensation, in accordance with the rules in force in the State taking such measures in the exercise of its sovereignty and in accordance with international law. . . .

82. The Memorandum of the Libyan Government which has just been quoted relies, however, on more recent Resolutions of the General Assembly (3171 and 3201 (S–VI), in particular) which, according to this Government would as a practical matter rule out any recourse to international law and would confer an exclusive and unlimited competence upon the legislation and courts of the host country.

Although not quoted in the Libyan Memorandum, since subsequent to the date of 26 July 1974, Resolution 3281 (XXIX), proclaimed under the title "Charter of Economic Rights and Duties of the States" and adopted by the General Assembly on 12 December 1974, should also be mentioned with the two Resolutions in support of the contention made by the Libyan Government. Two portions of such Resolutions are of particular interest in the present case:

—Resolution 3201 (S–VI) adopted by the General Assembly on 1 May 1974 under the title "Declaration on the Establishment of a New International Economic Order," Article 4, paragraph (e):

> Full permanent sovereignty of every State over its natural resources and all economic activities. In order to safeguard these resources, each State is entitled to exercise effective control over them and their exploitation with means suitable to its own situation, including the right to nationalization or transfer of ownership to its nationals, this right being an expression of the full permanent sovereignty of the State. No State may be

subjected to economic, political or any other type of coercion to prevent the free and full exercise of this inalienable right.

—Article 2 of Resolution 3281 (XXIX):

> 1. Every State has and shall freely exercise full permanent sovereignty, including possession, use and disposal, over all its wealth, natural resources and economic activities.
>
> 2. Each State has the right . . .
>
> c) To nationalize, expropriate or transfer ownership of foreign property, in which case appropriate compensation should be paid by the State adopting such measures, taking into account its relevant laws and regulations and all circumstances that the State considers pertinent. In any case where the question of compensation gives rise to a controversy, it shall be settled under the domestic law of the nationalizing State and by its tribunals, unless it is freely and mutually agreed by all States concerned that other peaceful means be sought on the basis of the sovereign equality of States and in accordance with the principal [*sic*] of free choice of means.

Substantial differences thus exist between Resolution 1803 (XVII) and the subsequent Resolutions as regards the role of international law in the exercise of permanent sovereignty over natural resources. This aspect of the matter is directly related to the instant case under consideration; this Tribunal is obligated to consider the legal validity of the above-mentioned Resolutions and the possible existence of a custom resulting therefrom.

83. The general question of the legal validity of the Resolutions of the United Nations has been widely discussed by the writers. This Tribunal will recall first that, under Article 10 of the U.N. Charter, the General Assembly only issues "recommendations," which have long appeared to be texts having no binding force and carrying no obligations for the Member States.

Refusal to recognize any legal validity of United Nations Resolutions must, however, be qualified according to the various texts enacted by the United Nations. These are very different and have varying legal value, but it is impossible to deny that the United Nations' activities have had a significant influence on the content of contemporary international law. In appraising the legal validity of the above-mentioned Resolutions, this Tribunal will take account of the criteria usually taken into consideration, *i.e.*, the examination of voting conditions and the analysis of the provisions concerned.

84. (1) With respect to the first point, Resolution 1803 (XVII) of 14 December 1962 was passed by the General Assembly by 87 votes to 2, with 12 abstentions. It is particularly important to note that the majority voted for this text, including many States of the Third World, but also several Western developed countries with market economies, including the most important one, the United States. The principles stated in this Resolution were therefore assented to by a great many States representing not only all geographical areas but also all economic systems.

From this point of view, this Tribunal notes that the affirmative vote of several developed countries with a market economy was made possible in particular by the inclusion in the Resolution of two references to international law, and one passage relating to the importance of international cooperation for economic development. According to the representative of Tunisia:

> . . . the result of the debate on this question was that the balance of the original draft resolution was improved—a balance between, on the one hand, the unequivocal affirmation of the inalienable right of States to exercise sovereignty over their natural resources and, on the other hand, the reconciliation or adaptation of this sovereignty to international law, equity and the principles of international cooperation. (17 U.N. GAOR 1122, U.N. Doc. A/PV.1193 (1962).)

The reference to international law, in particular in the field of nationalization, was therefore an essential factor in the support given by several Western countries to Resolution 1803 (XVII).

85. On the contrary, it appears to this Tribunal that the conditions under which Resolutions 3171 (XVIII), 3201 (S–VI) and 3281 (XXIX) (Charter of the Economic Rights and Duties of States) were notably different:

—Resolution 3171 (XVIII) was adopted by a recorded vote of 108 votes to 1, with 16 abstentions, but this Tribunal notes that a separate vote was requested with respect to the paragraph in the operative part mentioned in the Libyan Government's Memorandum whereby the General Assembly stated that the application of the principle according to which nationalizations effected by States as the expression of their sovereignty implied that it is within the right of each State to determine the amount of possible compensation and the means of their payment, and that any dispute which might arise should be settled in conformity with the national law of each State instituting measures of this kind. As a consequence of a roll-call, this paragraph was adopted by 86 votes to 11 (Federal Republic of Germany, Belgium, Spain, United States, France, Israel, Italy, Japan, The Netherlands, Portugal, United Kingdom), with 28 abstentions (South Africa, Australia, Austria, Barbados, Canada, Ivory

Coast, Denmark, Finland, Ghana, Greece, Haiti, India, Indonesia, Ireland, Luxembourg, Malawi, Malaysia, Nepal, Nicaragua, Norway, New Zealand, Philippines, Rwanda, Singapore, Sri Lanka, Sweden, Thailand, Turkey).

This specific paragraph concerning nationalizations, disregarding the role of international law, not only was not consented to by the most important Western countries, but caused a number of the developing countries to abstain.

—Resolution 3201 (S–VI) was adopted without a vote by the General Assembly, but the statements made by 38 delegates showed clearly and explicitly what was the position of each main group of countries. The Tribunal should therefore note that the most important Western countries were opposed to abandoning the compromise solution contained in Resolution 1803 (XVII).

—The conditions under which Resolution 3281 (XXIX), proclaiming the Charter of Economic Rights and Duties of States, was adopted also show unambiguously that there was no general consensus of the States with respect to the most important provisions and in particular those concerning nationalization. Having been the subject matter of a roll-call vote, the Charter was adopted by 118 votes to 6, with 10 abstentions. The analysis of votes on specific sections of the Charter is most significant insofar as the present case is concerned. From this point of view, paragraph 2(c) of Article 2 of the Charter, which limits consideration of the characteristics of compensation to the State and does not refer to international law, was voted by 104 to 16, with 6 abstentions, all of the industrialized countries with market economies having abstained or having voted against it.

86. * * * As this Tribunal has already indicated, the legal value of the resolutions which are relevant to the present case can be determined on the basis of circumstances under which they were adopted and by analysis of the principles which they state:

—With respect to the first point, the absence of any binding force of the resolutions of the General Assembly of the United Nations implies that such resolutions must be accepted by the members of the United Nations in order to be legally binding. In this respect, the Tribunal notes that only Resolution 1803 (XVII) of 14 December 1962 was supported by a majority of Member States representing all of the various groups. By contrast, the other Resolutions mentioned above, and in particular those referred to in the Libyan Memorandum, were supported by a majority of States but not by any of the developed countries with market economies which carry on the largest part of international trade.

87. (2) With respect to the second point, to wit the appraisal of the legal value on the basis of the principles stated, it appears essential to

this Tribunal to distinguish between those provisions stating the existence of a right on which the generality of the States has expressed agreement and those provisions introducing new principles which were rejected by certain representative groups of States and having nothing more than a *de lege ferenda* value only in the eyes of the States which have adopted them; as far as the others are concerned, the rejection of these same principles implies that they consider them as being *contra legem*. With respect to the former, which proclaim rules recognized by the community of nations, they do not create a custom but confirm one by formulating it and specifying its scope, thereby making it possible to determine whether or not one is confronted with a legal rule. As has been noted by Ambassador Castañeda, "[such resolutions] do not create the law; they have a declaratory nature of noting what does exist" (129 R.C.A.D.I. 204 (1970), at 315).

On the basis of the circumstances of adoption mentioned above and by expressing an *opinio juris communis*, Resolution 1803 (XVII) seems to this Tribunal to reflect the state of customary law existing in this field. Indeed, on the occasion of the vote on a resolution finding the existence of a customary rule, the States concerned clearly express their views. The consensus by a majority of States belonging to the various representative groups indicates without the slightest doubt universal recognition of the rules therein incorporated, *i.e.*, with respect to nationalization and compensation of the use of the rules in force in the nationalizing State, but all this in conformity with international law.

88. While Resolution 1803 (XVII) appears to a large extent as the expression of a real general will, this is not at all the case with respect to the other Resolutions mentioned above, which has been demonstrated previously by analysis of the circumstances of adoption. In particular, as regards the Charter of Economic Rights and Duties of States, several factors contribute to denying legal value to those provisions of the document which are of interest in the instant case.

—In the first place, Article 2 of this Charter must be analyzed as a political rather than as a legal declaration concerned with the ideological strategy of development and, as such, supported only by non-industrialized States.

—In the second place, this Tribunal notes that in the draft submitted by the Group of 77 to the Second Commission, the General Assembly was invited to adopt the Charter "as a first measure of codification and progressive development" within the field of the international law of development. However, because of the opposition of several States, this description was deleted from the text submitted to the vote of the Assembly. * * *

89. Such an attitude is further reinforced by an examination of the general practice of relations between States with respect to investments.

This practice is in conformity, not with the provisions of Article 2(c) of the above-mentioned Charter conferring exclusive jurisdiction on domestic legislation and courts, but with the exception stated at the end of this paragraph. Thus a great many investment agreements entered into between industrial States or their nationals, on the one hand, and developing countries, on the other, state, in an objective way, the standards of compensation and further provide, in case of dispute regarding the level of such compensation, the possibility of resorting to an international tribunal. In this respect, it is particularly significant in the eyes of this Tribunal that no fewer than 65 States, as of 31 October 1974, had ratified the Convention on the Settlement of Investment Disputes between States and Nationals of other States, dated March 18, 1965. * * *

SECTION V. Operative part:

FOR THESE REASONS,

The undersigned Sole Arbitrator

1. pronounces and decides that the Deeds of Concession in dispute are binding upon the parties;

2. pronounces and decides that the Libyan Government, the defendant, in adopting measures of nationalization in 1973 and 1974, breached its obligations arising from the said Deeds of Concession;

3. pronounces and decides that the Libyan Government, the defendant, is legally bound to perform these contracts and to give them full effect[.]

NOTES AND QUESTIONS

1. *Historical Context.* Why did Libya nationalize the property of foreign oil companies? What had changed between the signing of the oil concession contracts, primarily in the 1950's, and Libya's 1974 nationalization decree? Note the following: First, the oil companies had discovered and were producing oil. Second, scores of former European colonies had gained their independence. Third, the government of Libya changed. Itself a former colony, Libya became independent in 1951 under the rule of King Idris, a pro-Western monarch. In 1969, Colonel Muammar Qaddafi seized power in a coup; his dictatorship stressed themes of Arab nationalism, opposition to neo-colonialism, and socialism. Qaddafi remained in power until 2011, when he was killed in Libya by a rebel militia.

2. *"Mixed" International Arbitrations.* One of the advantages of international arbitration is that it can be tailor-made to fit specific cases. Here the Deeds of Concession between the U.S. oil companies and the Libyan government provided that an aggrieved party could request the President of the International Court of Justice to appoint a sole arbitrator if the other party refused to make an appointment to a three-judge panel. Appointment by the President of the International Court did not, of course, make this an

ICJ proceeding. Here, because both private and public parties were involved, the procedure was a "mixed" form of international arbitration. Why would the parties drafting the Deeds of Concession have chosen international arbitration to settle their disputes? Why would Libya renege on its promise to arbitrate?

3. *Individuals and International Law*. The excerpts from the case focus on the question of the legal effect of United Nations General Assembly resolutions and only touch on a variety of other interesting issues in international law raised by the opinion. Paragraph 23 recited the choice-of-law provision in Clause 28 of the Deeds of Concession, which referred to Libyan law, international law, and the general principles of law. In his opinion, the Arbitrator, Professor Dupuy, reviewed and rejected the positivist doctrine of the 19th and early 20th centuries that held that international law could only bind states. Neither the classical law of nations of the 17th and 18th centuries nor the modern international law of the later 20th century held such a restrictive view. Both permit individuals, including private corporations, as well as states to be subjects of international law. The Arbitrator found that under modern international law, contracts may be "delocalized" from municipal law and "internationalized." Paragraph 32 summed up this analysis. More on individuals as subjects of international law is to be found in Chapter 6. For more on the *Texaco/Libya Case*, see Robert B. von Mehren & P. Nicholas Kourides, "International Arbitrations Between States and Private Parties: The Libyan Nationalization Cases," 75 *American Journal of International Law* 476 (1981).

4. *The Role of U.N. General Assembly Resolutions in Making Customary International Law*. The large part of the *Texaco/Libya Case* excerpted above concerns Libya's contention that international law permitted the Government to nationalize foreign investments without reference to any standards of foreign or international law. The Libyan argument rested on the foundations of the 1973 and 1974 U.N. General Assembly resolutions proclaiming a New International Economic Order (NIEO). The legal question for the Arbitrator was whether these NIEO resolutions had any legal force, especially in the light of U.N. General Assembly Resolution 1803 (XVII) of 1962, which recited that in the case of nationalization "the owner shall be paid appropriate compensation, in accordance with the rules in force in the State taking such measures in the exercise of its sovereignty, and in accordance with international law." The NIEO resolutions seemed to leave such compensation questions simply to the law of the nationalizing state. As the Arbitrator wrote, there were "substantial differences" between the rules in the 1962 and NIEO resolutions. The Arbitrator felt obliged "to consider the legal validity of the above-mentioned Resolutions and the possible existence of a custom resulting therefrom."

Though U.N. General Assembly resolutions are formally only "recommendations," the Arbitrator needed to explore whether they could nonetheless pass into customary international law. What theory justifies treating some General Assembly resolutions as customary international law?

What is the state practice? The *opinio juris*? As a matter of law-finding, what are the advantages and disadvantages of resolutions *vis-à-vis* other possible forms of customary international law? Since Article 10 of the U.N. Charter deems General Assembly resolutions "recommendations," did it violate the spirit as well as the letter of the Charter to give resolutions, by any logic, the force of law? Noting that the General Assembly "is not a law-making body," Judge Cabranes of the U.S. Second Circuit has opined that its resolutions are therefore "not proper sources of customary international law because they are merely aspirational and were never intended to be binding on member States of the United Nations." Flores v. Southern Peru Copper Corp., 414 F.3d 233, 259 (2d Cir. 2003). Non-binding resolutions of international organizations are often categorized as soft law, a concept we explore in Part D below. Is the absence of any general international legislative organ a sufficient reason to try to "elevate" the status of General Assembly resolutions?

5. *Evaluating General Assembly Resolutions*. In looking at General Assembly voting, was the Arbitrator right in disregarding majority voting and relying instead on consensus? Was the Arbitrator right in putting great weight on the fact that the 1962 Resolution was "assented to by a great many states representing not only all geographical areas but also all economic systems"? Even if only such a consensus could elevate a resolution from a recommendation to a custom, did not the voting for the NIEO resolutions at least demonstrate that most states no longer supported the 1962 rule? Was it possible that the General Assembly actions in 1973–1974 destroyed the old customary rule but failed to establish a new rule? Would this have left a *Lotus*-like gap in international law?

In looking to the votes of states on General Assembly resolutions, should the votes of some states be given proportionately greater weight? This could be based on population, economic or political power, or their contributions to the U.N. budget.

The International Law Commission has adopted "the formation and evidence of customary international law" as a new topic for its investigation. Their work is not to look at the substantive rules of custom, "but, rather, at the secondary rules regarding how such law is formed and the types of evidence relevant in determining whether the requirements set forth in those secondary rules have been met." Sean D. Murphy, "The Expulsion of Aliens and Other Topics: The Sixty-Fourth Session of the International Law Commission," 107 *American Journal of International Law* 164 (2013). The Commission is likely to look, *inter alia*, at the status of resolutions of international organizations. *Id*. Reflecting on Professor Dupuy's holding in *Texaco/Libya*, what suggestions would you make to the Commission?

6. *The Efficacy of the Arbitral Award*. On September 25, 1977, Libya agreed to pay Texaco and Standard Oil of California $76 million in crude oil to compensate them for the nationalization of their subsidiaries. The agreement effectively terminated the international arbitral proceedings. "Libya to Compensate Two U.S. Companies," *New York Times*, Sept. 26, 1977, at 55. What were the inducements for Libya finally to compensate the

American oil companies? What difference might the arbitral award have made? Would Libya be looking to reassure potential new foreign investors? Was there fear of diplomatic pressure? Was Libya afraid of recognition and enforcement actions brought on the basis of the arbitral judgment in third countries? The New York Convention on the Recognition and Enforcement of Foreign Arbitral Awards, June 10, 1958, 330 U.N.T.S. 38 (in force for 149 states as of December 2013), in fact does provide for the recognition and enforcement of many foreign arbitral awards, and is widely used in commercial cases. See http://www.newyorkconvention.org (last visited Dec. 8, 2013); Emmanuel Gaillard & Domenico Di Pietro, *Enforcement of Arbitration Agreements and International Arbitral Awards: The New York Convention in Practice* (2008). More on the New York Convention appears in Chapter 11. Compare the enforcement of arbitral awards in favor of investors under the ICSID Convention, discussed in connection with the *CMS Case* in Chapter 2.

7. *Claims and Counterclaims.* Countries frequently do not litigate their differences over customary international law; no third-party decision maker may have jurisdiction to rule on competing contentions. When a rule of customary international law is clear—few if any international lawyers will contest, for example, that a country's territorial sea may extend no farther than 12 nautical miles from its coastal baselines—there may be debate about how the law applies in particular circumstances. But is it any surprise, given the cases we have read, that countries sometimes disagree about what rules of customary international law govern a dispute? How are competing claims asserted when there is no third-party decision maker? One traditional method is a formal diplomatic protest followed by a diplomatic response. Even though such competing claims may not be definitively resolved, does the fact that countries use legal language suggest one way in which international law is efficacious? Does international law sometimes provide the language for framing disputes in international relations? Could the claim/counterclaim process help clarify the content of international law?

B. GENERAL PRINCIPLES OF LAW

Sometimes neither treaties nor custom provide a rule to decide a case involving international law. Then the judge or other seeker may look outside the theoretically consensual sources to non-consensual sources. The first such source we examine is general principles of law.

THE AM & S CASE

AM & S Europe Limited v. Commission of the European Communities, European Court of Justice, [1982] E.C.R. 1575

Opinion of Advocate General Sir Gordon Slynn
Delivered on 26 January 1982

In February 1979, officials of the [European Community's] Commission required the applicants to make available documents which they wished to see in connection with an investigation being conducted pursuant to Article 14(1) of Council Regulation 17 of 6 February 1962. This was said to be an investigation of competitive conditions concerning the production and distribution of zinc metal and its alloys and zinc concentrates in order to verify that there is no infringement of Articles 85 and 86 of the EEC Treaty [relating to the European Community's competition law]. The applicants produced copies of most of the documents. Some, however, were not produced; so far as relevant, on the basis that they were covered by legal confidentiality, which entitled the applicants to withhold them. * * *

The parties were invited to state at the re-opened oral hearing their views on the law as to, and legal opinions relating to, the existence and extent of the protection granted in investigative proceedings instituted by public authorities for the purpose of detecting offenses of an economic nature, especially in the field of competition, to correspondence passing between

(a) two lawyers,

(b) an independent lawyer and his client,

(c) an undertaking and a lawyer in a permanent contractual relationship, or who is an employee of the undertaking,

(d) a legal adviser to, and an employee of, an undertaking or an employee of an associated undertaking,

(e) employees of an undertaking, or different but associated undertakings, where the correspondence mentions legal advice given by an independent lawyer or legal adviser serving one of the undertakings or other undertakings in the same group. * * *

The Commission's investigative powers for the purpose of carrying out the duties assigned to it by Article 89 of the EEC Treaty, and provisions adopted under Article 87 of the Treaty, are so far as relevant conferred by Article 14 of Regulation 17. It may "undertake all necessary investigations into undertakings and associations of undertakings" and, to that end, its authorised officials are empowered to examine books and business records, to take copies of them, and to ask for oral explanations. There is no reference to any exemption or protection which may be claimed on the basis of legal confidence. Is that silence conclusive that no such protection is capable of applying in any form and in any situation? In my view it is not. The essential enquiry is, first, whether there is a principle of Community law existing independently of the regulation, and, secondly, whether the regulation does on a proper construction restrict the application of that principle. The question is not whether a principle of Community law derogates from Article 14, but whether Article 14 excludes the application of a principle of Community law. * * *

That general principles which have not been expressly stated in the Treaty or in subordinate legislation may exist as part of Community law, the observance of which the Court is required to ensure, needs no emphasis. This was made clear in an article by Judge Pescatore to be found in *Les Cahiers de Droit Européen* in 1968 at p. 629. It does not seem to me that the principle is limited to "fundamental rights" which are more particularly dealt with in the article. It has a broader base. Such indeed appears to be accepted by both parties to this application. The Commission argue that there has to be a consensus among the laws of all the Member States, and that the Court cannot establish a principle which goes beyond that accepted by any one of the Member States. It cited no specific authority for that proposition, nor indicated what is the necessary level or degree of consensus required to establish the existence of a general principle. The CCBE [Consultative Committee of the Bars and Law Societies of the European Community], whose views broadly on the point were adopted by the applicants, submits that the aim of Community law is to find the best solution in qualitative terms, having regard to the spirit, orientation and general tendency of the national laws. * * *

That national law may be looked at on a comparative basis as an aid to consideration of what is Community law is shown in many cases[.] Such a course is followed not to import national laws as such into Community law, but to use it as a means of discovering an *unwritten* principle of Community law. The suggestions made at times in this case, implicitly if not explicitly, that the applicants were trying to force into an unreceptive mould a purely local rule of the common law seems to me unfair to the argument of the applicants, who were seeking, like the CCBE and the United Kingdom Government, to distil a principle which is part of Community law by reference to national laws and which, in its detailed application, required adaptation to Community procedures.

In looking at national laws it does not seem to me that it can be a pre-condition of the existence of a rule of Community law that the principle should be expressed identically, or should be applied in identical form, in all of the Member States. Unanimity, as to a subject which is relevant to a Community law problem, may well be a strong indication of the existence of a rule of Community law. Total unanimity of expression and application is not, however, necessary. It is at best unlikely, not least as the Community grows in size. It seems to me highly probable that there are differences in the various Member States in the application of the principles of "la bonne administration de la justice," rejection of "un deni de justice" and in the "principe de proportionalité." Yet such differences do not prevent such principles from being part of Community law. * * *

The Court has been provided with extracts from legislation, case decisions and the opinions of academic authors and a welter of case references. Rather than set those out *in extenso* I propose to summarise what seems to me to be the relevant features for present purposes, fully conscious of the risks that a summary may oversimplify and is incomplete. I deal first with the general position as to the protection of legal confidence and then consider the position in relation to competition law.

In Belgium, it seems that confidential communications between lawyer and client are protected and cannot be seized or used as evidence. Although the basis of the rule may have been that information confided to the lawyer must be protected, it seems from the opinion of Monsieur l'Auditeur Huberlant and the decision of the Counseil d'Etat of 8 June 1961, that it also covers confidential advice given to the client. There exists also a more general principle which protects the privacy of correspondence—see Articles 10 and 22 of the Constitution.

In Denmark, the rule of the professional secret prevents lawyers from giving evidence of confidential information confided to them in their professional capacity and a lawyer can refuse to produce documents covered by professional secrecy. Communications between an accused person and his lawyer are protected in the hands of the accused under section 786 of the Code of Procedure. This rule seems to apply also in civil proceedings.

In Germany, confidential communications to a lawyer are protected in his hands, and breach of the professional confidentiality by a lawyer is a criminal offence. Thus such documents in the hands of the lawyer cannot be seized (section 97 of the Code of Criminal Procedure). Documents in the hands of the client can, it appears, be seized unless they come into existence after the commencement of criminal proceedings.

In France, breach of the rule of professional secrecy is a criminal offence, and although it seems that documents may be seized in some circumstances even in the hands of the lawyer, the importance of the rule is stressed in Lemaire *Les règles de la profession de l'avocat* which has been provided for the Court. This rule appears to be closely linked with the right to a fair trial (les droits de la défense).

The principle of the "droits de la défense" appears to cover confidential documents passing in both directions between lawyer and client and includes protection from seizure of legal advice given to the client before commencement of proceedings and found in his possession or in the possession of a person associated with him. There is also it seems a wider protection for confidential letters than exists under the common law systems. * * *

In Greece it seems that confidential communications in the hands of lawyers are protected in investigative proceedings instituted by judicial or administrative authorities. Documents in the hands of the client are covered by the general principle of privacy defined in Article 9 of the Constitution. The power to search the client's premises is circumscribed by sections 253 *et seq.* of the Code of Criminal Procedure.

In Ireland and the United Kingdom, although there may be differences in detail, broadly the law of the two Member States is the same and it is set out more fully in the opinion of Warner A.G. It should be repeated, however, that it covers both (a) communications between a person and his lawyer for the purpose of obtaining or giving legal advice whether or not in connexion with pending or contemplated legal proceedings and (b) communications between a person and his lawyer and other persons for the dominant purpose of preparing for pending or contemplated legal proceedings.

In Italy, as in most of the Member States, the law forbids lawyers from giving evidence of the information confided in them by their clients and entitles them to withhold documents covered by the doctrine of professional secrecy. On the other hand, it seems that, in the case of criminal investigations, documents held by a lawyer may be seized unless they have been entrusted to him for the preparation of his client's defence. Protection is wider in civil proceedings but it does not, in any case, appear to extend to documents in the hands of the client. It seems that, in the case of lawyers, professional secrecy is a reflection of the right to a fair trial guaranteed by Article 24 of the Constitution.

In Luxembourg, rules of professional secrecy and "les droits de la défense," it would seem, protect legal confidences in the hands of the lawyer, and of the client after proceedings have begun, but little case law has been produced showing the application of these rules in practice.

Dutch law forbids the revelation of confidences by persons exercising a profession, such as lawyers. Coupled with this there is a right to refuse to give evidence on matters covered by professional secrecy. These matters include not only the information revealed by the client but also, in the case of lawyers, the legal advice they have given. Article 98 of the Code of Criminal Procedure provides that, when the premises of someone bound by professional secrecy are searched, the doctrine of professional secrecy must be observed and documents covered by it cannot be seized. There appears to be no authority holding or denying that legal correspondence found in the hands of the client is protected.

This summary is substantially, if not entirely, accepted by the Commission, the applicants and the body representing the Bars of all the Member States as being a fair and acceptable statement of the laws of the Member States.

It seems to me significant that they were able to reach agreement as to the existence of the principles which are set out in the document which they prepared to read to the Court.

From this it is plain, as indeed seems inevitable, that the position in all the Member States is not identical. It is to my mind equally plain that there exists in all the Member States a recognition that the public interest and the proper administration of justice demand as a general rule that a client should be able to speak freely, frankly and fully to his lawyer. * * * Whether it is described as the right of the client or the duty of the lawyer, this principle has nothing to do with the protection or privilege of the lawyer. It springs essentially from the basic need of a man in a civilized society to be able to turn to his lawyer for advice and help, and if proceedings begin, for representation; it springs no less from the advantages to a society which evolves complex law reaching into all the business affairs of persons, real and legal, that they should be able to know what they can do under the law, what is forbidden, where they must tread circumspectly, where they run risks.

[The Advocate General also addresses the position of in-house counsel in various states, concluding that "in some Member States full-time employment is incompatible with the full professional states of a lawyer (apparently in Belgium, France, Italy, and Luxembourg)," whereas "in others the employed lawyer remains subject to professional discipline and ethics."]

Decision * * *

2. The application is based on the submission that in all the Member States written communications between lawyer and client are protected by virtue of a principle common to all those States, although the scope of that protection and the means of securing it vary from one country to another. According to the applicant, it follows from that principle which, in its view, also applies "within possible limits" in Community law, that the Commission may not when undertaking an investigation pursuant to Article 14(3) of Council Regulation No. 17 of 6 February 1962, claim production, at least in their entirety, of written communications between lawyer and client if the undertaking claims protection and takes "reasonable steps to satisfy the Commission that the protection is properly claimed" on the ground that the documents in question are in fact covered by legal privilege. * * *

5. The contested decision, based on the principle that it is for the Commission to determine whether a given document should be used or not, requires AM & S Europe to allow the Commission's authorized inspectors to examine the documents in question in their entirety. Claiming that those documents satisfy the conditions for legal protection as described above, the applicant has requested the Court to declare Article 1(b) of the above-mentioned decision void, or, alternatively, to

declare it void in so far as it requires the disclosures to the Commission's inspector of the whole of each of the documents for which the applicant claims protection on the grounds of legal confidence. * * *

(a) The interpretation of Article 14 of Regulation No. 17

15. The purpose of Council Regulation No. 17 which was adopted pursuant to the first subparagraph of Article 87(1) of the Treaty, is, according to paragraph (2)(a) and (b) of that article, "to ensure compliance with the prohibitions laid down in Article 85(1) and in Article 86" of the Treaty and "to lay down detailed rules for the application of Article 85(3)." The regulation is thus intended to ensure that the aim stated in Article 3(f) of the Treaty is achieved. To that end it confers on the Commission wide powers of investigation and of obtaining information by providing in the eighth recital in its preamble that the Commission must be empowered, throughout the Common Market, to require such information to be supplied and to undertake such investigations "as are necessary" to bring to light infringements of Articles 85 and 86 of the Treaty.

16. In Articles 11 and 14 of the regulation, therefore, it is provided that the Commission may obtain "information" and undertake the "necessary" investigations, for the purpose of proceedings in respect of infringements of the rules governing competition. Article 14(1) in particular empowers the Commission to require production of business records, that is to say, documents concerning the market activities of the undertaking, in particular as regards compliance with those rules. Written communications between lawyer and client fall, in so far as they have a bearing on such activities, within the category of documents referred to in Articles 11 and 14.

17. Furthermore, since the documents which the Commission may demand are, as Article 14(1) confirms, those whose disclosure it considers "necessary" in order that it may bring to light an infringement of the Treaty rules on competition, it is in principle for the Commission itself, and not the undertaking concerned or a third party, whether an expert or an arbitrator, to decide whether or not a document must be produced to it.

(b) Applicability of the protection of confidentiality in Community law

18. However, the above rules do not exclude the possibility of recognizing, subject to certain conditions, that certain business records are of a confidential nature. Community law, which derives from not only the economic but also the legal interpenetration of the Member States, must take into account the principles and concepts common to the laws of those States concerning the observance of confidentiality, in particular, as regards certain communications between lawyer and client. That confidentiality serves the requirement, the importance of which is recognized in all of the Member States, that any person must be able,

without constraint, to consult a lawyer whose profession entails the giving of independent legal advice to all those in need of it.

19. As far as the protection of written communications between lawyer and client is concerned, it is apparent from the legal systems of the Member States that, although the principle of such protection is generally recognized, its scope and the criteria for applying it vary, as has, indeed, been conceded both by the applicant and by the parties who have intervened in support of its conclusions.

20. Whilst in some of the Member States the protection against disclosure afforded to written communications between lawyer and client is based principally on a recognition of the very nature of the legal profession, inasmuch as it contributes towards the maintenance of the rule of law, in other Member States the same protection is justified by the more specific requirement (which, moreover, is also recognized in the first-mentioned States) that the rights of the defence must be respected.

21. Apart from these differences, however, there are to be found in the national laws of the Member States common criteria inasmuch as those laws protect, in similar circumstances, the confidentiality of written communications between lawyer and client provided that, on the one hand, such communications are made for the purposes and in the interests of the client's rights of defence and, on the other hand, they emanate from independent lawyers, that is to say, lawyers who are not bound to the client by relationship of employment. * * *

27. In view of all these factors it must therefore be concluded that although Regulation No. 17, and in particular Article 14 thereof, interpreted in the light of its wording, structure and aims, and having regard to the laws of the Member States, empowers the Commission to require, in course of an investigation within the meaning of that Article, production of the business documents the disclosure of which it considers necessary, including written communications between lawyer and client, for proceedings in respect of any infringements of Articles 85 and 86 of the Treaty, that power is, however, subject to a restriction imposed by the need to protect confidentiality, on the conditions defined above, and provided that the communications in question are exchanged between an independent lawyer, that is to say one who is not bound to his client by a relationship of employment, and his client. * * *

(d) The confidential nature of the documents at issue

33. It is apparent from the documents which the applicant lodged at the Court on 9 March 1981 that almost all the communications which they include were made or are connected with legal opinions which were given towards the end of 1972 and during the first half of 1973.

34. It appears that the communications in question were drawn up during the period preceding, and immediately following, the accession of

the United Kingdom to the Community, and that they are principally concerned with how far it might be possible to avoid conflict between the applicant and the Community authorities on the applicant's position, in particular with regard to the Community provisions on competition. In spite of the time which elapsed between the said communications and the initiation of a procedure, those circumstances are sufficient to justify considering the communications as falling within the context of the rights of the defence and the lawyer's specific duties in that connection. They must therefore be protected from disclosure.

35. In view of that relationship and in the light of the foregoing considerations the written communications at issue must accordingly be considered, in so far as they emanate from an independent lawyer entitled to practise his profession in a Member State, as confidential and on that ground beyond the Commission's power of investigation under Article 14 of Regulation No. 17.

NOTES AND QUESTIONS

1. *EC Competition Law.* The European Community (now the European Union) has a comprehensive system of competition (antitrust) law and procedure. The EC Commission has the power to investigate and to prosecute possible monopolistic and anti-competitive economic activities. In *AM & S*, since the United Kingdom had just joined the Common Market, what kinds of questions about its on-going activities and EC competition law would a company like AM & S probably have asked its lawyers? How would the answers to these questions have helped the investigations of the Commission?

2. *The Advocate General.* The reading begins with the opinion of Sir Gordon Slynn, one of the EC's Advocates General. The Advocate General is a position unknown to the United States but is somewhat akin to an official *amicus* or friend of the court in U.S. practice. In European Court of Justice (ECJ) cases the opinions of the Advocates General ordinarily are published both because they amplify ECJ opinions and because they have some persuasive value of their own.

3. *Gaps in the Law.* EC competition law is, of course, a form of international law. It is constituted fundamentally by treaty rules like Articles 85–89 of the Treaty of Rome and partly by rules like Council Regulation 17 generated by delegated powers given to the institutions making up the EC, a regional international organization. The legal question in this case was what to do when there was a gap (a *lacuna*) in international law. Here neither the Rome Treaty nor the rules made by the EC institutions determined whether there was a right to lawyer-client confidentiality in EC law, and if there was such a right how it was defined. Should international courts like the ECJ be more or less reluctant than municipal courts to fill gaps when formal sources are silent? Should it make a difference that some municipal legal systems

(often in the common law tradition) profess to be more willing than others (often in the civil law tradition) to let courts fill gaps in law?

4. *The EC and General Principles of Law.* In *AM & S,* the European Court of Justice turned to general principles of law to fill a gap. Did the fact that municipal legal systems used certain similar rules make it plain that states had consented to establishing a rule in international law? What are other consensual arguments justifying the use of general principles to find or develop rules of international law? Non-consensual arguments? Was the Advocate General seeking to avoid the gap problem when he presumed that looking at national laws meant "not to import national laws as such into Community law," but to use the search "as a means of discovering an *unwritten* principle of Community law"? Was this "discovery" really just a justification for a form of judicial discretion and law-making?

The ECJ has been ready to recognize quite a number of general principles of law to close gaps and create a new and coherent legal order for Europe. Other ECJ-recognized general principles include the principle of equal treatment, the principle of proportionality, the principle of legal certainty, and the principle of the protection of fundamental rights. Takis Tridimas, *The General Principles of EC Law* 4 (2007).

5. *The ECJ Judgment.* The ECJ masked any judicial dissent with a single judgment that never disclosed the individual votes or opinions of the panel. Did the judgment in *AM & S* show signs of being a compromise? Was it more or less well reasoned than the opinion of the Advocate General? Was it more or less formal, *i.e.*, apparently based on the words of the Treaty of Rome and Council Regulation No. 17? Did the judges adequately explain why communications with independent (out-of-house) counsel were to be protected by privilege but not those with in-house counsel?

6. *"Civilized Nations."* General principles of law are included among the sources of international that the International Court of Justice is permitted to apply. Article 38(1)(c) of the ICJ Statute authorizes the Court to use "the general principles of law recognized by civilized nations." When the clause was originally drafted for the Permanent Court of International Justice in 1920, the term "civilized nations" was meant to exclude most non-European nations; nowadays the term has been rejected by commentators and judges alike. See Gerrit W. Gong, *The Standard of "Civilization" in International Society* (1984).

7. *The Comparative Law Search.* Of course, *AM & S* was a case before the European Court of Justice, not the ICJ, and accordingly the ECJ needed only compare the domestic practices of the nine states then members of the European Community. The basic theory behind general principles of law is that some legal principles are so general or fundamental that they are to be found in all or nearly all legal systems. In *AM & S* the presumption was that if rules protecting lawyer-client communication could be found in every municipal legal system within the European Community, then such rules were to be presumed to be included within the body of EC law.

In a case before the ICJ or another tribunal, to how many municipal legal systems should that tribunal be obliged to turn in order to discern a general principle? The Appeals Chamber of the International Criminal Tribunal for the former Yugoslavia (ICTY) faced this question in Prosecutor v. Erdemović, Case No. IT–96–22–A (Oct. 7, 1997), asking whether duress was a complete defense for a soldier charged with a war crime or a crime against humanity involving the killing of innocent individuals. The Tribunal's Statute is silent on the issue. In their Joint Separate Opinion, Judges McDonald and Vohrah found that no customary international law rule could be derived. They then turned to a general principles search. Noting the "practical impossibility" of conducting a "comprehensive survey of all legal systems of the world," they surveyed only "those jurisdictions whose jurisprudence is, as a practical matter, accessible to us in an effort to discern a general trend, policy or principle underlying the concrete rules of that jurisdiction which comports with the object and purpose of the establishment of the International Tribunal." They asked whether duress was a complete defense in civil law systems (Belgium, Chile, Finland, France, Germany, Italy, Mexico, the Netherlands, Nicaragua, Norway, Panama, Poland, Spain, Sweden, Venezuela, and the former Yugoslavia); in common law systems (Australia, Canada, England, India, Malaysia, Nigeria, South Africa, the United Kingdom, and the United States); and in the law of "other states" (China, Ethiopia, Japan, Morocco, and Somalia). Judges McDonald and Vohrah concluded that the "positions of the principal legal systems of the world" differ, and that "no consistent rule" applies. Did this mean there was a gap in international law? Prompted by their view that "the law * * * must serve broader normative purposes in light of its social, political and economic role," and that the issue before the Tribunal concerned "the most heinous crimes known to humankind," they joined a 3–2 majority, holding that "duress cannot afford a complete defence to a soldier charged with crimes against humanity or war crimes in international law involving the taking of innocent lives." *Id.* ¶¶ 57, 72, 75, 88. Two other ICTY opinions are excerpted below, one in this chapter, the second in Chapter 9.

8. *The Problem of In-house and Foreign Lawyers.* Notice that the search for common legal rules in *AM & S* was conducted on the assumption that only the minimum content of rules found in all relevant European municipal legal systems would be presumed to exist in EC law. This "lowest common denominator" approach thus excluded communications with certain kinds of lawyers. Most notably, some European countries do not allow in-house counsel to be members of the bar, and the *AM & S* decision refused to protect the communications both of in-house counsel and of foreign lawyers not accredited by an EC member nation. For early hostile reactions, see Joseph P. Griffin, Book Review, 79 *American Journal of International Law* 834 (1985) (reviewing C.S. Kerse, *EEC Antitrust Procedure, Supplement 1984*). Nonetheless, the discriminatory distinction persists, not only in EC law, but in the municipal practice of at least seven of the EU member states: Austria, Belgium, France, Italy, Luxembourg, the Netherlands, and Sweden. See Mary Daly, "Cultural, Ethical, and Legal Challenges," 46 *Emory Law*

Journal 1057, 1102–08 (1997). The on-going plight of in-house counsel under the *AM & S* rule is described in Sue Bentch, "Confidentiality, Corporate Counsel, and Competition Law: Representing Multi-National Corporations in the European Union," 35 *St. Mary's Law Journal* 1003, 1005–13 (2004), and John Gergacz, "In-House Counsel and Corporate Communications: Can EU Law after *Akzo Nobel* and U.S. Law after *Gucci* be Harmonized? Critiques and a Proposal," 45 *International Lawyer* 817 (2011).

9. *Domestic Courts and International Law.* Note that decisions of municipal courts play two distinct roles as sources of international law. First, as we saw in Part A, domestic judgments are sometimes employed to demonstrate state practice; *i.e.*, they are evidences to be weighed in determining customary international law. Second, as we see in this part, the holdings of municipal judges are crucial to the comparative law search to fill gaps using general principles of law. Moreover, as we explore in the next chapter, municipal judgments play an important third role in international law: enforcing international legal norms of any sort at the domestic level. What problems are posed by this increasingly complex relationship between the domestic judge and the determination and application of international law? See Anthea Roberts, "Comparative International Law? The Role of National Courts in Creating and Enforcing International Law," 60 *International and Comparative Law Quarterly* 57 (2011).

C. NATURAL LAW AND *JUS COGENS*

We have now explored the three principal formal sources of international law set forth in Article 38(1) of the Statute of the International Court of Justice; these are the rules that the Court "shall apply" as it decides "in accordance with international law such disputes as submitted to it": "(a) international conventions, whether general or particular, establishing rules expressly recognized by the contesting states [Treaties, Chapter 2]; (b) international custom, as evidence of a general practice accepted as law [Customary International Law, Chapter 3.A]; (c) the general principles of law recognized by civilized nations [General Principles of Law, Chapter 3.B]." Although the first two sources—treaty and custom—may be said by positivists to be more or less consensual among states, the third source—general principles of law—clearly involves, as we have seen, some judicial or doctrinal initiative beyond a search for inter-state agreement on rules. Indeed, the same may well be true even for most rules of customary international law.

Historically, one of the most important sources of the law of nations was natural law, but nowadays the function of this avowedly non-consensual source has been largely replaced by the notion of *jus cogens* or compelling norm. *Jus cogens* is sometimes dated from the work in the 1930's of the Austrian law professor, Alfred von Verdross. An excerpt from his work follows an example of earlier use of a natural law concept in the 1820 U.S. Supreme Court piracy judgment, *Smith*. The Notes hark back to Chapter 1's *Filartiga Case* where natural law, *jus cogens*, customary international law, and general principles of law all seemed to be blended. We then use a 2000 decision by an Appeals Chamber of the International Tribunal for the former Yugoslavia and a 2002 report from the Inter-American Commission on Human Rights to explore *jus cogens* and the related concept of obligations *erga omnes*. A good question to keep in mind throughout this part is what role should non-consensual norms play in modern international law?

UNITED STATES V. SMITH

18 U.S. (5 Wheat.) 153 (1820)

This was an indictment for piracy against the prisoner Thomas Smith, before the Circuit Court of Virginia, on the act of Congress, of the 3d of March, 1819, c.76.

The jury found a special verdict as follows: "We, of the jury, find, that the prisoner, Thomas Smith, in the month of March, 1819, and others, were part of the crew of a private armed vessel, called the Creollo, (commissioned by the government of Buenos Ayres, a colony then at war with Spain,) and lying in the port of Margaritta; that in the month of March, 1819, the said prisoner and others of the crew mutinied, confined their officer, left the vessel, and in the said port of Margaritta, seized by violence a vessel called the Irresistible, a private armed vessel, lying in that port, commissioned by the government of Artigas, who was also at war with Spain; that the said prisoner and others, having so possessed themselves of the said vessel, the Irresistible, appointed their officers, proceeded to sea on a cruize, without any documents or commission whatever; and while on that cruize, in the month of April, 1819, on the high seas, committed the offence charged in the indictment, by the plunder and robbery of the Spanish vessel therein mentioned. If the plunder and robbery aforesaid be piracy under the act of the Congress of the United States, entitled, 'An act to protect the commerce of the United States, and punish the crime of piracy,' then we find the said prisoner guilty; if the plunder and robbery, above stated, be not piracy under the said act of Congress, then we find him, not guilty."

The Circuit Court divided on the question, whether this be piracy as defined by the law of nations, so as to be punishable under the act of Congress, of the 3d of March, 1819, and thereupon the question was certified to this Court for its decision. * * *

MR. JUSTICE STORY delivered the opinion of the court. The act of Congress upon which this indictment is founded provides, "that if any person or persons whatsoever, shall, upon the high seas, commit the crime of piracy, as defined by the law of nations, and such offender or offenders shall be brought into, or found in the United States, every such offender or offenders shall, upon conviction thereof, &c. be punished with death."

The first point made at the bar is, whether this enactment be a constitutional exercise of the authority delegated to Congress upon the subject of piracies. The constitution declares, that Congress shall have power "to define and punish piracies and felonies committed on the high seas, and offences against the law of nations." The argument which has been urged in behalf of the prisoner is, that Congress is bound to define, in terms, the offence of piracy, and is not at liberty to leave it to be ascertained by judicial interpretation. * * *

But supposing Congress were bound in all the cases included in the clause under consideration to define the offence, still there is nothing which restricts it to a mere logical enumeration in detail of all the facts constituting the offence. Congress may as well define by using a term of a known and determinate meaning, as by an express enumeration of all the particulars included in that term. That is certain which is by necessary reference made certain. When the act of 1790 declares, that any person who shall commit the crime of robbery, or murder, on the high seas, shall be deemed a pirate, the crime is not less clearly ascertained than it would be by using the definitions of these terms as they are found in our treatises of the common law. In fact, by such a reference, the definitions are necessarily included, as much as if they stood in the text of the act. In respect to murder, where "malice aforethought" is of the essence of the offence, even if the common law definition were quoted in express terms, we should still be driven to deny that the definition was perfect, since the meaning of "malice aforethought" would remain to be gathered from the common law. There would then be no end to our difficulties, or our definitions, for each would involve some terms which might still require some new explanation. Such a construction of the constitution is, therefore, wholly inadmissible. To define piracies, in the sense of the constitution, is merely to enumerate the crimes which shall constitute piracy; and this may be done either by a reference to crimes having a technical name, and determinate extent, or by enumerating the acts in detail, upon which the punishment is inflicted.

It is next to be considered, whether the crime of piracy is defined by the law of nations with reasonable certainty. What the law of nations on this subject is, may be ascertained by consulting the works of jurists, writing professedly on public law; or by the general usage and practice of nations; or by judicial decisions recognising and enforcing that law. There is scarcely a writer on the law of nations, who does not allude to piracy as a crime of a settled and determinate nature; and whatever may be the diversity of definitions, in other respects, all writers concur, in holding, that robbery, or forcible depredations upon the sea, *animo furandi*, is piracy. The same doctrine is held by all the great writers on maritime law, in terms that admit of no reasonable doubt. The common law, too, recognises and punishes piracy as an offence, not against its own municipal code, but as an offence against the law of nations, (which is part of the common law,) as an offence against the universal law of society, a pirate being deemed an enemy of the human race. Indeed, until the statute of 28th of Henry VIII, ch. 15, piracy was punishable in England only in the admiralty as a civil law offence; and that statute, in changing the jurisdiction, has been universally admitted not to have changed the nature of the offence. Sir Charles Hedges, in his charge at the Admiralty sessions, in the case of Rex v. Dawson, (5 *State Trials*,) declared in emphatic terms, that "piracy is only a sea term for robbery, piracy being a robbery committed within the jurisdiction of the admiralty." Sir Leoline Jenkins, too, on a like occasion, declared that "a robbery, when committed upon the sea, is what we call a 'piracy;' " and he cited the civil law writers, in proof. And it is manifest from the language of Sir William Blackstone,[a] in his comments on piracy, that he considered the common law definition as distinguishable in no essential respect from that of the law of nations. So that, whether we advert to writers on the common law, or the maritime law, or the law of nations, we shall find that they universally treat of piracy as an offence against the law of nations, and that its true definition by that law is robbery upon the sea. And the general practice of all nations in punishing all persons, whether natives or foreigners, who have committed this offence against any persons whatsoever, with whom they are in amity, is a conclusive proof that the offence is supposed to depend, not upon the particular provisions of any municipal code, but upon the law of nations, both for its definition and punishment. We have, therefore, no hesitation in declaring, that piracy, by the law of nations, is robbery upon the sea, and that it is sufficiently and constitutionally defined by the fifth section of the act of 1819. * * *

It is to be certified to the Circuit Court, that upon the facts stated, the case is piracy, as defined by the law of nations, so as to be punishable under the act of Congress of the 3d of March, 1819.

NOTES AND QUESTIONS

1. *An Enemy of All Mankind*. Remember the next-to-last line of the *Filartiga* judgment in Chapter 1: "Indeed, for purposes of civil liability, the torturer has become—like the pirate and the slave trader before him—*hostis*

[a] To show that piracy is defined by the law of nations, the following citations are believed to be sufficient: [Story fills almost eighteen subsequent pages with citations at length from, *inter alia*, Grotius, Bynkershoek, Azuni, Bacon, Martens, Rutherforth, Woodeson, Bulamaqui, Calvinus, Bouchard, Bonnemant, Valin, Straccha, Casaregis, Brown, Beames, Molloy, Marshall, Viner, Cowell, Comyn, Coke, Jenkins, Targa, Hawkins, Blackstone, Hedges, Holt, Ward, and Erskine. Pp. 163–180. He concludes:] The foregoing collection of doctrines, extracted from writers on the civil law, the law of nations, the maritime law, and the common law, in the most ample manner confirms the opinion of the Court in the case in the text; and it is with great diffidence submitted to the learned reader to aid his future researches in a path, which, fortunately for us, it has not been hitherto necessary to explore with minute accuracy.

humani generis, an enemy of all mankind." *Smith* was one of the two principal cases relied on by the *Filartiga* court to demonstrate that rules of the law of nations "may be ascertained by consulting the works of the jurists, writing professedly on public law; or by the general usage and practice of nations; or by judicial decisions recognizing and enforcing that law." The other was *Paquete Habana*. The similarities between *Filartiga* and *Smith* are great, even greater than between *Filartiga* and *Paquete Habana*. Most important, both *Smith* and *Filartiga* held that an individual could be found guilty of violating the law of nations. In *Paquete Habana* the guilty party was a state. Pirate, slave trader, torturer—all were viewed as acting so contrary to fundamental norms that their actions were seen to be universally proscribed and their persons subject to punishment by all courts.

2. *Custom? General Principle? Natural Law?* Jus Cogens? Another similarity between *Filartiga* and *Smith* is their mutual confusion about what the source of the rule is. In contrast, *Paquete Habana* and *AM & S* are clearer: *Paquete Habana* weighed evidences of state practice to find custom, and *AM & S* examined comparative municipal law rules to find a general principle. However, do there not seem to be traces of custom, general principles, natural law, and *jus cogens* in both *Filartiga* and *Smith*? *Smith* and *Filartiga* were both cited in Beanal v. Freeport-McMoran, Inc., 197 F.3d 161 (5th Cir. 1999), where the court rejected an Indonesian citizen's claims that environmental degradation amounted to cultural genocide because it destroyed a tribe's cultural and social framework. The legal evidence presented described only an "amorphous right * * * devoid of discernable means to define or identify conduct that constitutes a violation of international law." *Id.* at 168. The *Beanal* court, like the courts in *Smith* and *Filartiga*, did not make it clear whether it was looking for a rule of customary international law, general principles of law, natural law, or *jus cogens*, but its language, like that of *Smith* and *Filartiga*, looked for some sort of universality: "it would be imprudent for a United States tribunal to declare an amorphous cause of action under international law that has failed to garner universal acceptance." *Id.* Can it be said that *Smith*, *Filartiga*, and *Beanal* all looked to find some non-treaty international law rule general or universal enough to bind apparently non-consenting states? How well does this kind of search fit into the positivist insistence in *Lotus* that all rules of international law must be based on state consent?

3. *Defining International Criminal Law*. Some positivists rejected the notion that international law provided a substantive definition of the crime of piracy. In 1932, a Harvard research project proposed a treaty premised on the view "that piracy is not a crime by the law of nations." Instead, piracy "is the basis of an extraordinary jurisdiction in every state to seize and to prosecute and punish persons, and to seize and dispose of property, for factual offenses which are committed outside the * * * ordinary jurisdiction of the prosecuting state and which do not involve attacks on its peculiar interests." Harvard Research Project, 26 *American Journal of International Law Supplement* 739, 760 (1932).

However, modern international criminal law has followed the logic behind *Smith*, recognizing that customary and other non-consensual international legal rules can in some instances serve as the foundation for criminal prosecutions. In the words of Judge Meron, it is

> realistic to expect a would-be offender to be aware of well-established principles of the law of nations. After all, customary humanitarian law for the most part prohibits acts that everyone would assume to be criminal anyway: rape, murder, torture, deportations, pillage, attacking civilians, and so forth. Thus, in my view, customary law can provide a safe basis for a conviction, but only if genuine care is taken to determine that the legal principle was firmly established at the time of the offense so that the offender could have identified the rule he was expected to obey. This, in a nutshell, has been the approach of the ICTY.

Theodor Meron, "Revival of Customary Humanitarian Law," 99 American Journal of International Law 816 (2005). We look at the ICTY, the International Criminal Tribunal for the former Yugoslavia, when we consider the *Furundžija Case* later in this chapter.

4. *Piracy in U.S. Law.* The statute used to convict Thomas Smith remains in the U.S. Code at 18 U.S.C. § 1651, and other U.S. statutes also address piracy. See 18 U.S.C. §§ 1652–1661. Would section 1651, which today carries a mandatory life sentence rather than the death penalty, now support a U.S. criminal conviction? The issue is not hypothetical. An upsurge in pirate attacks in recent years, especially off Somalia in northeast Africa, has led to the capture of some pirates with trials in different national courts. We see one such case, *Dire*, in Chapter 10, where we place piracy in the context of the law of the sea. For a discussion of modern-day piracy, see "Agora: Piracy Prosecutions," 104 *American Journal of International Law* 397 (2010); Max Boot, "Piracy, Then and Now: How Piracy was Defeated in the Past and Can Be Again," 88 *Foreign Affairs*, July–Aug. 2009, at 94; James Kraska & Brian Wilson, "The Pirates of the Gulf of Aden: The Coalition is the Strategy," 45 *Stanford Journal of International Law* 243 (2009).

ALFRED VON VERDROSS, "FORBIDDEN TREATIES IN INTERNATIONAL LAW"

31 *American Journal of International Law* 571 (1937)

I. THE PRINCIPLE * * *

Our starting-point is the uncontested rule that, as a matter of principle, states are free to conclude treaties on any subject whatsoever. All we have to investigate, therefore, is whether this rule does or does not admit certain exceptions. The answer to this question depends on the preliminary question, whether general international law contains rules which have the character of *jus cogens*. For it is obvious that if general international law consists *exclusively* of noncompulsory norms, states are always free to agree on treaty norms which deviate from general international law, without by doing so, violating general international law. If, on the other hand, general international law does contain also norms which have the character of *jus cogens*, things are very different. For it is the quintessence of norms of this character that they prescribe a certain, positive or negative behavior unconditionally; norms of this character, therefore, cannot be derogated from by the will of the contracting parties.

The existence of such norms in general international law is particularly contested by those authors who base the whole international law on the agreement of the *wills* of the states; consequently, they know no other international law but treaty law. But they overlook the fact that each treaty presupposes a number of norms necessary for the very coming into existence of an international treaty. These are the norms determining which persons are endowed with the capacity to act in international law, what intrinsic and extrinsic conditions must be fulfilled that an international treaty may come into existence, what juridical consequences are attached to the conclusion of an international treaty. These principles concerning the conditions of the validity of treaties cannot be regarded as having been agreed upon by treaty; they must be regarded as valid independently of the will of the contracting parties. That is the reason why the *possibility* of norms of general international law, norms determining the limits of the freedom of the parties to conclude treaties, cannot be denied *a priori*.

But this reasoning does not decide the problem whether such compulsory norms concerning the contents of international treaties do exist in fact. A careful investigation, however, reveals the existence of such norms. Two groups of these norms can be distinguished. The first group consists of different, single, compulsory norms of customary international law. General international law requires states, for instance, not to disturb each other in the use of the high seas. An international treaty between two or among more states tending to exclude other states from the use of the high seas, would be in contradiction to a compulsory principle of general international law. International law authorizes states to occupy and to annex *terra nullius*. In consequence, an international treaty by which two states would bind themselves to prevent other states from making such acquisitions of territory would be violative of general international law. In the same way, a treaty binding the contracting parties to prevent third states from the exercise of other rights of sovereignty acknowledged by general international law, such as passage through the territorial waters of other states, would be in contradiction to international law.

But apart from these and other positive norms of general international law, there is a second group which constitutes *jus cogens*.

This second group consists of the general principle prohibiting states from concluding treaties *contra bonos mores*. This prohibition, common to the juridical orders of all civilized states, is the consequence of the fact that every juridical order regulates the rational and moral coexistence of the members of a community. No juridical order can, therefore, admit treaties between juridical subjects, which are obviously in contradiction to the ethics of a certain community. * * *

II. THE DIFFERENT KINDS OF INTERNATIONAL TREATIES *CONTRA BONOS MORES*

The application in international law of the general principle, according to which treaties *contra bonos mores* are void, is not free from difficulties. These difficulties are the consequence of the fact that the ethics of the international community are much less developed than the ethics of national communities; further, the international community embraces different juridical systems, built upon different moral conceptions. But, on the other hand, these difficulties must not be overestimated. For, as we shall show, there are between the subjects of international law far-reaching agreements concerning many single values notwithstanding different basic conceptions.

In order to advance the solution of our problem, it is necessary to see what treaties are regarded as being *contra bonos mores* by the law of civilized nations. To this problem the decisions of the courts of civilized nations give an unequivocal answer. The analysis of these decisions shows that everywhere such treaties are regarded as being *contra bonos mores* which *restrict the liberty of one contracting party in an excessive or unworthy manner or which endanger its most important rights.*

This and similar formulas prove that the law of civilized states starts with the idea which demands the establishment of a juridical order guaranteeing the rational and moral coexistence of the members. It follows that all those norms of treaties which are incompatible with this goal of all positive law—a goal which is implicitly presupposed—must be regarded as void.

This general principle is not disproved by the fact that different states have different conceptions as to the position of the members of the community. There is, *e.g.*, a different conception as to the position of men toward the community under a democratic, fascist or socialistic régime. But everywhere treaties are regarded as immoral which force one contracting party into a situation which is in contradiction to the ethics of the community.

In order to know what international treaties are immoral, we must ask what are the moral tasks states have to accomplish in the international community. In doing so, we must restrict ourselves to find those principles which correspond to the universal ethics of the international community. We must, so to speak, try to find the *ethical minimum* recognized by all the states of the international community, and must leave aside those particular tasks of the state represented only by particular régimes.

Using the utmost prudence, we can say that the following tasks most certainly devolve upon a state recognized by the modern international community: *maintenance of law and order within the state, defense against external attacks, care for the bodily and spiritual welfare of citizens at home, protection of citizens abroad.* A treaty norm, therefore, which prevents a state from fulfilling one of these essential tasks must be regarded as immoral.

On this basis the following international treaties are immoral and, consequently, void:

1. An international treaty binding a state to reduce its police or its organization of courts in such a way that it is no longer able to protect at all or in an adequate manner, the life, the liberty, the honor or the property of men on its territory. Such a treaty would, however, also be violative of positive international law, if the state were prevented from protecting the above-named rights of *aliens*, because international law obliges states to protect aliens in ways common to civilized nations (principle of the international minimum standard).

2. An international treaty binding a state to reduce its army in such a way as to render it defenseless against external attacks. It is immoral to keep a state as a sovereign community and to forbid it at the same time to defend its existence.

The situation is different if a state is placed under the protectorate of another state, because in this case the defense of the protected state against external attacks is the duty of the protecting state. The same is true if the existence of a state is effectively guaranteed by one or more Powers, because in this case the defense is the duty of the guarantor. But it would be immoral to oblige a state to remain defenseless.

3. An international treaty binding a state to close its hospitals or schools, to extradite or sterilize its women, to kill its children, to close its factories, to leave its fields unploughed, or in other ways to expose its population to distress. * * *

IV. PROPOSALS

In consequence of the above deductions, this writer ventures to propose[:]

A treaty norm is void if it is either in violation of a compulsory norm of general international law or *contra bonos mores.*

A treaty norm is *contra bonos mores* if a state is prevented by an international treaty from fulfilling the universally recognized tasks of a civilized state. * * *

If the immorality of a treaty norm is contested, the dispute has to be submitted to the decision of an arbitration tribunal or of the Permanent Court of International Justice.

NOTES AND QUESTIONS

1. *The Challenge to Legal Positivism*. This 1937 article by Vienna's Professor Alfred von Verdross has been singled out as an important step in the development of Article 53 of the Vienna Convention on the Law of the Treaties concerning peremptory norms of international law. E. Jimenez de Arechaga, *El Derecho Internacional Contemporaneo* 79 (1980). Verdross's article was an affirmative answer to the question of whether there may ever be rules of international law not made by state consent. It challenged the notions of legal positivists who read moral and natural law out of municipal and international law, a formalistic position that became increasingly uncomfortable as totalitarian parties captured the machineries of state power in 20th-century Europe.

After 1937, the horrors of Nazi-occupied Europe catapulted natural law in the guise of fundamental norms to the forefront of legal thought. As one leading textbook put it not long after World War II:

> In so far as the revival of the authority of natural law, in its modern connotation, has tended to undermine the rigid positivism of the nineteenth century, that development received an accession of strength[.] The rise of the German and the other totalitarian dictatorships, trampling upon the rights of man and universally accepted notions of law, once more tended to bring into prominence the importance and the vitality of legal standards which, though they may not be enforceable before municipal courts, are of an enduring validity transcending the positive law of any one sovereign State.

L. Oppenheim, *International Law: A Treatise: Volume I—Peace* 108 (H. Lauterpacht ed., 8th ed. 1955). To what extent do beliefs in legal positivism and that states alone are legitimate sources of legal rules depend on an unrealistic expectation that governments will always act responsibly?

2. *Kinds of* Jus Cogens. Verdross's first category of compulsory norms contains rules drawn from "general international law" that constrain treaty-making. How certain must a rule of general international law be before it can trump a contrary treaty rule? How many states must agree in a treaty before a first category compulsory norm can be upset? Compare the formulation in Articles 53 and 64 of the Vienna Convention on the Law of Treaties, which are in the Appendix. Two of Verdross's three examples of the first category concern the purported illegality of treaty restraints on uses of the oceans.

How true are such assertions today, after recent developments in the law of the sea? See Chapter 10.

Verdross's second category of compulsory norms contains *jus cogens* rules prohibiting treaties *contra bonos mores*, a category he justified as stemming from the general principles of law recognized by civilized nations. Such norms trump both conventional and customary law. Does it make sense to treat such norms as general principles *à la* 38(1)(c) of the ICJ Statute? Why not simply accept them as a form of natural or fundamental law? If they are not viewed as natural or fundamental law, how are they different from natural law? See "Colloquy: *Jus Cogens*," between Mark W. Janis and Mary Ellen Turpel & Philippe Sands, 3 *Connecticut Journal of International Law* 359 (1988).

3. *An "Ethical Minimum" to the Law.* Verdross granted that the ethics of democratic, fascist, and socialist regimes are different, but he argued that there is at least an "ethical minimum" to them all. Given the record of World War II, should a *jus cogens* norm need meet even such an "ethical minimum"?

4. *Individuals and* Jus Cogens. Are Verdross's examples of immoral treaties too oriented to the protection of weak states and too little directed to the protection of even weaker individuals? Should there be (are there) such fundamental norms of international law protecting individuals? What should they be? How can they be justified as "real" international law?

5. Jus Cogens *and International Dispute Settlement.* Should we look to cure any uncertainties regarding the content of *jus cogens* norms by authorizing an international tribunal to hear a contested claim, as Professor Verdross suggested at the close of the excerpt above? Compare Article 66 of the Vienna Convention on the Law of Treaties, which provides that questions about *jus cogens* are subject to obligatory dispute settlement before the International Court of Justice—the only questions that the Vienna Convention so links to the ICJ.

6. *The* Southwest Africa Cases. In the *Southwest Africa Cases* (Ethiopia v. South Africa; Liberia v. South Africa), 1966 I.C.J. 6, 235, the International Court of Justice rejected the right of Ethiopia and Liberia, as former members of the League of Nations, to bring suit on behalf of the peoples of Southwest Africa. Ethiopia and Liberia had claimed that South Africa had violated its Mandate under the League of Nations to "promote to the utmost the material and moral well-being and the social progress of the inhabitants of the territory." In holding that Ethiopia and Liberia did not have standing to protect the peoples of Southwest Africa, the ICJ ruled in part:

> 49. * * * Throughout this case it has been suggested, directly or indirectly, that humanitarian considerations are sufficient in themselves to generate legal rights and obligations, and that the Court can and should proceed accordingly. The Court does not think so. It is a court of law, and can take account of moral principles only in so far as these are given a sufficient expression in legal form.

Law exists, it is said, to serve a social need; but precisely for that reason it can do so only through and within the limits of its own discipline. Otherwise, it is not a legal service that would be rendered. * * *

51. [T]he Court must examine what is perhaps the most important contention of a general character that has been advanced in connection with this aspect of the case, namely the contention by which it is sought to derive a legal right or interest in the conduct of the mandate from the simple existence, or principle, of the "sacred trust." The sacred trust, it is said, is a "sacred trust of civilization." Hence all civilized nations have an interest in seeing that it is carried out. An interest, no doubt;—but in order that this interest may take on a specifically legal character, the sacred trust itself must be or become something more than a moral or humanitarian ideal. In order to generate legal rights and obligations, it must be given juridical expression and be clothed in legal form. One such form might be the United Nations trusteeship system,—another, as contained in Chapter XI of the Charter concerning non-self-governing territories, which makes express reference to "a sacred trust." In each case the legal rights and obligations are those, and only those, provided for by the relevant texts, whatever these may be.

Judge Philip Jessup, whom the United States had nominated to the ICJ, argued that the Court had refused to decide the merits of Ethiopia's and Liberia's claim on grounds—lack of standing—that had already been decided in their favor in 1962. Professor Perez has suggested that "[i]t might have been disastrous for the Court to reach the merits yet see its decision ignored by the major powers who alone were capable of compelling South Africa's compliance through Security Council action." Antonio F. Perez, "The Passive Virtues and the World Court: Pro-Dialogic Abstention by the International Court of Justice," 18 *Michigan Journal of International Law* 399, 413 (1997). Does the ICJ gain or lose legitimacy when it fails to decide a case because of fears its decision will not be enforced? On concerns about the efficacy of the ICJ, see Chapter 5.

7. Jus Cogens *and Obligations* Erga Omnes. Compare the reluctance of the ICJ to permit Ethiopia and Liberia to protect a "sacred trust" in Southwest Africa with Professor Verdross's insistence on the role of *jus cogens* in international law. The ICJ has moved closer to the position advanced by Professor Verdross. In 1970, in paragraphs 33 and 34 of the *Barcelona Traction Case*, reproduced in Chapter 6, the Court recognized the concept of "obligations *erga omnes*"—"the obligations of a State toward the international community as a whole." The Court cited, as examples, the international legal proscriptions against interstate aggression, genocide, slavery, and racial discrimination. Does this mean that the ICJ would now allow a state to pursue a judicial action in the common interest with regard to such issues? Following are two cases where, unlike the ICJ in *Southwest*

Africa, other international fora have recognized claims as being both obligations *erga omnes* and governed by *jus cogens* norms.

PROSECUTOR V. FURUNDŽIJA

Case No. IT–95–17/1 (Appeals Chamber, International Criminal Tribunal for the former Yugoslavia, 2002), 121 *International Law Reports* 213 (2002)

[In upholding the conviction of the commander of a unit of the Croatian Defence Council for the torture and rape of a Bosnian Muslim woman during the conflict in Bosnia-Herzegovina, the Appeals Chamber of the International Criminal Tribunal for the former Yugoslavia found that torture was a violation of customary international law. The Chamber cited, *inter alia*, the *Filartiga Case* featured in Chapter 1 above: "the torturer has become, like the pirate and the slave trader before him, *hostis humani generis*, an enemy of all mankind." The Chamber went on to explore obligations *erga omnes* and *jus cogens* norms:]

Furthermore, the prohibition of torture imposes upon States obligations *erga omnes*, that is, obligations owed towards all the other members of the international community, each of which then has a correlative right. In addition, the violation of such an obligation simultaneously constitutes a breach of the correlative right of all members of the international community and gives rise to a claim for compliance accruing to each and every member, which then has the right to insist on fulfilment of the obligations or in any case to call for the breach to be discontinued. * * *

While the *erga omnes* nature just mentioned appertains to the area of international enforcement (*latu sensu*), the other major feature of the principle proscribing torture relates to the hierarchy of rules in the international normative order. Because of the importance of the values it protects, this principle has evolved into a peremptory norm or *jus cogens*, that is, a norm that enjoys a higher rank in the international hierarchy than treaty law and even "ordinary" customary rules. The most conspicuous consequence of this higher rank is that the principle at issue cannot be derogated from by States through international treaties or local or special customs or even general customary rules not endowed with the same normative force.

Clearly, the *jus cogens* nature of the prohibition against torture articulates the notion that the prohibition has now become one of the most fundamental standards of the international community. Furthermore, this prohibition is designed to produce a deterrent effect, in that it signals to all members of the international community and the individuals over whom they wield authority that the prohibition of torture is an absolute value from which nobody must deviate.

The fact that torture is prohibited by a peremptory norm of international law has other effects at the inter-state and individual levels. At the inter-state level, it serves to internationally de-legitimize any legislative, administrative or judicial act authorizing torture. It would be senseless to argue, on the one hand, that on account of the *jus cogens* value of the prohibition against torture, treaties or customary rules providing for torture would be null and void *ab initio*, and then be unmindful of a State say, taking national measures authorizing or condoning torture or absolving its perpetrators through an amnesty law. If such a situation were to arise, the national measures, violating the general principle and any relevant treaty provision, would produce the legal effects discussed above and in addition would not be accorded international legal recognition. Proceedings could be initiated by potential victims if they had *locus standi* before a competent international or national judicial body with a view to asking it to hold the national measure to be internationally unlawful; or the victim could bring a civil suit for damage in a foreign court, which would therefore be asked *inter alia* to disregard the legal value of the national authorizing act. What is even more important is that perpetrators of torture acting upon or benefiting from those national measures may nevertheless be held criminally responsible for torture, whether in a foreign State, or in their own State under a subsequent regime. In short, in spite of possible national authorization by legislative or judicial bodies to violate the principle banning torture, individuals remain bound to comply with that principle. As the International Military Tribunal at Nuremberg put it: "individuals have international duties which transcend the national obligations of obedience imposed by the individual State."

Furthermore, at the individual level, that is, that of criminal liability, it would seem that one of the consequences of the *jus cogens* character bestowed by the international community upon the prohibition of torture is that every State is entitled to investigate, prosecute and punish or extradite individuals accused of torture, who are present in a territory under its jurisdiction. Indeed, it would be inconsistent on the one hand to prohibit torture to such an extent as to restrict the normally unfettered treaty-making power of sovereign States, and on the other hand bar States from prosecuting and punishing those torturers who have engaged in this odious practice abroad. This legal basis for States' universal jurisdiction over torture bears out and strengthens the legal foundation for such jurisdiction found by other courts in the inherently universal character of the crime. It has been held that international crimes being universally condemned wherever they occur, every State has the right to prosecute and punish the authors of such crimes. As stated in general terms by the Supreme Court of Israel in *Eichmann*, and echoed by a USA court in *Demjanjuk*, "it is the universal character of [international crimes] which vests in every State the authority to try and punish those who participated in their commission."

THE MICHAEL DOMINGUES CASE: ARGUMENT OF THE UNITED STATES

Office of the Legal Adviser, United States Department of State, *Digest of United States Practice in International Law 2001*, at 303 (Sally J. Cummins & David P. Stewart eds. 2002)

[Michael Domingues was convicted in Nevada state court of two murders committed when he was sixteen years old. He was sentenced to death, a sentence affirmed by the Supreme Court of Nevada, despite Dominigues's claim that the death penalty for juveniles sixteen years old violated the International Covenant on Civil and Political Rights [ICCPR] and customary international law. After the United States Supreme Court refused to review the case, Domingues petitioned the Inter-American Commission on Human Rights, an international body authorized only to deliver a non-legally-binding Report. Following are excerpts from the Argument of the United States in 2001 and from the Report of the Inter-American Commission on Human Rights in 2002 about whether a persistent objector may still be bound in customary international law and whether there is a *jus cogens* norm prohibiting the execution of juvenile offenders.

The United States first argued that Nevada's imposition of the death penalty on juvenile offenders violated neither any treaty obligation of the United States nor any rule of customary international law. The United States then turned to the legal status of the United States as a persistent objector and to *jus cogens*.]

The United States has Persistently Objected to the Development of a Customary International Legal Principle Prohibiting the Execution of Juvenile Offenders

Even if the execution of sixteen and seventeen-year-old offenders were prohibited by customary international law—which it is not—the United States has consistently and persistently objected to the application of such a principle to the United States. It is generally accepted that a state may contract out of a custom in the process of formation by persistent objection. *See* Restatement (Third) Foreign Relations Law of the United States 102 cmt. d ("In principle a dissenting state which indicates its dissent from a practice while the law is still in the process of development is not bound by that rule of law even after it matures.") On this basis, therefore, the United States would not be bound by such principle if it existed.

As a matter of domestic law, the laws of many states within the United States provide for the prosecution of juveniles as adults for the most serious crimes, either automatically or after a transfer review process. Half of the states in the United States permit juveniles to be prosecuted as adults in certain capital cases: five states have chosen age seventeen as the minimum age and, in eighteen states, sixteen is the minimum age. Persons under sixteen years of age at the time of the crime may not be subject to capital punishment in the United States, as the U.S. Supreme Court held that such executions would violate the U.S. Constitution.

[T]he United States has persistently asserted its right to execute juvenile offenders in multiple international fora, such as the United Nations General Assembly, the United Nations Commission on Human Rights, responses to the U.N. Special Rapporteurs, the Council of Europe, the Organization for Security and Cooperation in Europe, the Organization of American States, and the Inter-American Commission on Human Rights. * * *

There Exists No Jus Cogens *Prohibition o*
the Execution of Juvenile Offenders

A *jus cogens* norm holds the highest hierarchical position among all other international norms and principles. As a consequence, *jus cogens* norms are deemed to be non-derogable. Shaw, Malcolm N., *International Law* (4th) 1997, at 544. For a norm to be *jus cogens*, the international community of States as a whole must accept and recognize not only the norm but also its peremptory character. Vienna Convention on the Law of Treaties, art 53; *see also* Restatement of Foreign Relations Law of the United States (Third) § 102(3). * * *

There is no *jus cogens* norm that establishes eighteen years as the minimum age at which an offender can receive a sentence of death. In order to so hold, the Commission would have to decide that this alleged prohibition has similar force to prohibitions such as those against piracy and genocide. There is simply no support for this proposition.

THE MICHAEL DOMINGUES CASE: REPORT OF THE INTER-AMERICAN COMMISSION ON HUMAN RIGHTS

Report No. 62/02, Merits, Case 12.285,
Michael Domingues/United States, Oct. 22, 2002

[The Commission reviewed the facts and the proceedings in the case.]

84. In the Commission's view, * * * by persisting in the practice of executing offenders under age 18, the U.S. stands alone amongst the traditional developed world nations and those of the inter-American system, and has also become increasingly isolated within the entire global community. [T]he world community considers the execution of offenders aged below 18 years at the time of their offence to be inconsistent with prevailing standards of decency. The Commission is therefore of the view

that a norm of international customary law has emerged prohibiting the execution of offenders under the age of 18 years at the time of their crime.

85. Moreover, the Commission is satisfied, based upon the information before it, that this rule has been recognized as being of a sufficiently indelible nature to now constitute a norm of *jus cogens*[.] [N]early every nation state has rejected the imposition of capital punishment to individuals under the age of 18. They have done so through ratification of the ICCPR, U.N. Convention on the Rights of the Child, and the American Convention on Human Rights, treaties in which this proscription is recognized as non-derogable, as well as through corresponding amendments to their domestic laws. The acceptance of this norm crosses political and ideological boundaries and efforts to detract from this standard have been vigorously condemned by members of the international community as impermissible under contemporary human rights standards. Indeed, it may be said that the United States itself, rather than persistently objecting to the standard, has in several significant respects recognized the propriety of this norm by, for example, prescribing the age of 18 as the federal standard for the application of capital punishment and by ratifying the Fourth Geneva Convention without reservation to this standard. On this basis, the Commission considers that the United States is bound by a norm of *jus cogens* not to impose capital punishment on individuals who committed their crimes when they had not yet reached 18 years of age. As a *jus cogens* norm, this proscription binds the community of States, including the United States. The norm cannot be validly derogated from, whether by treaty or by the objection of a state, persistent or otherwise.

86. Interpreting the terms of the American Declaration in light of this norm of *jus cogens*, the Commission therefore concludes in the present case that the United States has failed to respect the life, liberty and security of the person of Michael Domingues by sentencing him to death for crimes that he committed when he was 16 years of age, contrary to Article I of the American Declaration.

NOTES AND QUESTIONS

1. *Human Rights Tribunals*. An Appeals Chamber of the International Tribunal for the former Yugoslavia decided the *Furundžija Case*. This Tribunal was established by the United Nations Security Council to prosecute individuals under international criminal law for crimes committed in the former Yugoslavia. See http://www.icty.org (last visited Dec. 8, 2013). For more on international criminal law, see the discussion of the Nuremberg Tribunal and the International Criminal Court in Chapter 6. Another decision by the International Tribunal for the former Yugoslavia appears in Chapter 9, Part A, and we also examine the U.N. Security Council in Chapter 9.

The Inter-American Commission on Human Rights, which decided the *Domingues Case*, may hear individual petitions concerning the 1948 American Declaration of the Rights and Duties of Man pursuant to the Charter of the Organization of American States, Apr. 30, 1948, 2 U.S.T. 2394, 119 U.N.T.S. 3, *as amended*, Feb. 27, 1967, 21 U.S.T. 607, 721 U.N.T.S. 324, a treaty to which the United States is a party. The Commission also has jurisdiction pursuant to the American Convention on Human Rights, Nov. 22, 1969, 1144 U.N.T.S. 123, which the United States has not accepted. See http://www.oas,org/en/iachr (last visited July 10, 2013). There is also an Inter-American Court of Human Rights, which has a more limited jurisdiction than the European Court of Human Rights; for example, the Inter-American Court cannot hear individual petitions. We met the European Court in the *McCann Case* in Chapter 1 and explore that Court further in Chapter 6. For more on the Inter-American Commission and the Inter-American Court, see Christina M. Cerna, "International Law and the Protection of Human Rights in the Inter-American System," 19 *Houston Journal of International Law* 731 (1997).

2. *Defining Obligations* Erga Omnes. The nature of obligations *erga omnes* has been widely debated. The International Law Commission, for example, endorsed both the concept and the list in *Barcelona Traction, i.e.*, that obligations *erga omnes* include proscriptions against interstate aggression, genocide, slavery, and racial discrimination. U.N. Doc. A/31/10 (1976), art. 19(3), *reprinted in* 2 *Yearbook of the International Law Commission* 73, U.N. Doc. A/CN.4/Ser.A/1976/Add.1 (1976). The Commission added obligations based on the prohibition of colonial domination by force and obligations essential to preserve the human environment, such as those prohibiting massive pollution of the seas or the atmosphere. One definition is that *erga omnes* norms "articulate basic interests and needs as well as fundamental values of the international community as a whole." Jost Delbrück, " 'Laws in the Public Interest'—Some Observations on the Foundations and Identification of *erga omnes* Norms in International Law," in *Liber Amicorum Günther Jaenicke-Zum 85. Geburstag* 17, 18 (Volkmar Götz *et al.* eds. 1998).

Are the obligations in *Furundžija* and *Domingues jus cogens* norms or norms *erga omnes*? How close are the concepts of *jus cogens* and obligations *erga omnes*? Are they both forms of natural law? An independent study group led by Professor Koskenniemi, considering the general topic of the fragmentation of international law, evaluated the hierarchy of norms in international law:

> As between *jus cogens* and *erga omnes* norms, the study group rejected the suggestion that the two categories were coterminous. Rather, according to the conclusions, "while all obligations established by *jus cogens* norms . . . also have the character of *erga omnes* obligations, the reverse is not necessarily true" in that "[n]ot all *erga omnes* norms are established by peremptory norms of general international law." For example, some obligations

concerning the global commons may be thought to have *erga omnes* status but are clearly not *jus cogens*.

Michael J. Matheson, "The Fifty-Eighth Session of the International Law Commission," 101 *American Journal of International Law* 407, 425 (2007). Do you agree? Is every *jus cogens* norm an obligation *erga omnes*? Is the reverse true? Even if the substance of obligations *erga omnes* and *jus cogens* norms is identical, the focus of the concepts may be different. As noted in the *Furundžija Case*, the concept of obligations *erga omnes* relates to whom obligations are owed and who correspondingly may raise a claim for compliance; the concept of *jus cogens* is often used when describing the peremptory effect and higher rank of certain rules of international law.

Does the *erga omnes* concept necessarily refer only to obligations owed to the entire world? In 2012 the International Court of Justice ruled that Senegal had breached its obligations under the Convention Against Torture and Other Cruel, Inhuman or Degrading Treatment or Punishment, Dec. 10, 1984, 1465 U.N.T.S. 85, by failing either to prosecute or extradite Hissène Habré, the former president of Chad. Questions Relating to the Obligation to Prosecute or Extradite (Belgium v. Spain), 2012 I.C.J. ___. Habré, who was accused of torture, war crimes, and crimes against humanity, had been residing in Senegal. When Belgium brought the claim, Senegal challenged Belgium's standing because "none of the alleged victims was of Belgian nationality at the time of the alleged offenses." *Id.* ¶ 65. The ICJ found that Belgium did have standing:

> The States parties to the Convention have a common interest to ensure, in view of their shared values, that acts of torture are prevented and that, if they occur, their authors do not enjoy impunity. [O]bligations [under the Convention] are owed by any State party to all the other States parties to the Convention. All the States parties "have a legal interest" in the protection of the rights involved (*Barcelona Traction, Light and Power Company, Limited, Judgment, I.C.J. Reports 1970*, p. 32, para. 33). These obligations may be defined as "obligations *erga omnes parties*" * * *.

Id. ¶ 68. As of December 2013, 154 states were parties to the Torture Convention.

3. *Defining* Jus Cogens. How do we know what is and is not a *jus cogens* norm? The ICJ has held that the principles underlying the Genocide Convention are peremptory (*i.e., jus cogens*) norms. See the *Reservations to the Genocide Convention Case*, excerpted in Chapter 2. In the *Military and Paramilitary Activities In and Against Nicaragua Case*, the Court cited authorities indicating that Article 2(4) of the U.N. Charter condemning the use of force had moved from treaty rule to a norm of *jus cogens*. 1986 I.C.J. 14, especially paragraph 190. We explore Article 2(4) in Chapter 9.

A recent careful study concluded that "without a procedure for ascertaining its content and applying it to concrete cases, *jus cogens* will continue to be more of a mission statement than a practicable legal instrument." Andreas L. Paulus, "*Jus Cogens* in a Time of Hegemony and Fragmentation," 74 *Nordic Journal of International Law* 297, 330 (2005). What would be an appropriate procedure for deciding what should or should not be a *jus cogens* rule? Are human rights norms like those in *Furundžija* and *Domingues* more likely to be *jus cogens* than other kinds of international rules?

4. *The Persistent Objector and Diplomatic Practice.* We saw in the *Asylum Case* above that the ICJ recognized the right of Peru to be free of a regional rule of customary international law on the grounds that Peru "repudiated it by refraining from ratifying the Montevideo Conventions of 1933 and 1939, which were the first to include" the alleged customary rule in treaty form. In the *Domingues Case* the United States argued that it had "persistently asserted its right to execute juvenile offenders in multiple international fora, such as the United Nations General Assembly, the United Nations Commission on Human Rights, responses to the U.N. Special Rapporteurs, the Council of Europe, the Organization for Security and Cooperation in Europe, the Organization of American States, and the Inter-American Commission on Human Rights." Evidences of state diplomatic practice are, of course, plentiful in proofs of customary international law, as we have seen in cases such as *Paquete Habana* and *Filartiga*. Is it possible for a state to opt out of customary international law through persistent objection in its diplomatic practice? Professor Charney sees persistent objections as contributing to the development (or not) of a new customary rule, but concludes that once a "rule settle[s]," if only a few states carry on objecting, "they will not be able to block a finding that the new rule represents international law." Jonathan I. Charney, "The Persistent Objector Rule and the Development of Customary International Law," 56 *British Yearbook of International Law* 1, 24 (1986).

How persuasive were the arguments of the United States and the Inter-American Commission on Human Rights in *Domingues*? Did the conclusion by the Commission that the norm against juvenile execution is now *jus cogens* put the question outside the realm of an *Asylum*-like argument about the status of the persistent objector *vis-à-vis* customary international law? Professor Shelton submitted that "although the idea of *jus cogens* originated solely as a limitation on the treaty-making power of states, today an assertion that a norm is *jus cogens* seems more often intended to over-ride the will of persistent objectors to the emergence of the norm as customary international law." Dinah Shelton, "Normative Hierarchy in International Law," 100 *American Journal of International Law* 291, 304 (2006).

What role should international and foreign law play in U.S. constitutional law? This controversial topic is more closely considered in Chapter 4. For now, note that international and foreign law played a part in the analysis of the majority of the Supreme Court when it ultimately overturned the juvenile death penalty in Roper v. Simmons, 543 U.S. 551 (2005).

D. SOFT LAW

The Rio Declaration, excerpted in this part, is one example of "soft law." Consider whether such an instrument should count as international law, how it compares to the sources you have studied, and how it could influence the development of treaties and customary international law.

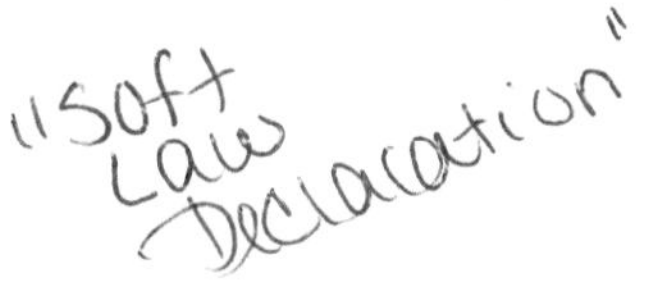

RIO DECLARATION ON ENVIRONMENT AND DEVELOPMENT

June 14, 1992, UNCED Doc. A/CONF.151/5/Rev.1,
U.N. Doc. A/CONF.151/26 (Vol. I), Annex I,
31 *International Legal Materials* 874 (1992)

The United Nations Conference on Environment and Development,

Having met at Rio de Janeiro from 3 to 14 June 1992,

Reaffirming the Declaration of the United Nations Conference on the Human Environment, adopted at Stockholm on 16 June 1972, and seeking to build upon it,

With the goal of establishing a new and equitable global partnership through the creation of new levels of cooperation among States, key sectors of societies and people,

Working towards international agreements which respect the interests of all and protect the integrity of the global environmental and developmental system,

Recognizing the integral and interdependent nature of the Earth, our home,

Proclaims that: * * *

Principle 2

States have, in accordance with the Charter of the United Nations and the principles of international law, the sovereign right to exploit their own resources pursuant to their own environmental and developmental policies, and the responsibility to ensure that activities within their jurisdiction or control do not cause damage to the environment of other States or of areas beyond the limits of national jurisdiction.

Principle 3

The right to development must be fulfilled so as to equitably meet developmental and environmental needs of present and future generations. * * *

Principle 17

Environmental impact assessment, as a national instrument, shall be undertaken for proposed activities that are likely to have a significant adverse impact on the environment and are subject to a decision of a competent national authority. * * *

Principle 26

States shall resolve all their environmental disputes peacefully and by appropriate means in accordance with the Charter of the United Nations.

NOTES AND QUESTIONS

1. *The Stockholm and Rio Conferences.* The 1972 Stockholm Conference on the Human Environment and the 1992 U.N. Conference on Environment and Development—the "Earth Summit" that produced the Rio Declaration—were major events in the history of international environmental law. In addition to contributing soft law declarations, they generated new institutions and legal instruments. The United Nations Environment Programme (UNEP) was established at the Stockholm Conference. UNEP has initiated multilateral treaty negotiations leading, for example, to the 1985 Convention for the Protection of the Ozone Layer, considered in Chapter 8. The Rio Earth Summit also produced environmental treaties and approved Agenda 21, which sets priorities and details steps for addressing a wide range of environmental challenges. Other major environmental conferences have followed the Rio Earth Summit at ten-year intervals.

2. *The Nature of Soft Law.* We have already seen one example of soft law in the Kellogg-Briand Treaty in Chapter 2. The term "soft law" aptly describes Kellogg-Briand: its norms, while aspirational and indeterminate ("soft"), are embodied in a legal instrument, a treaty ("law").

With the Rio Declaration we see a different type of soft law, a written instrument that is not a treaty. The authors of the Rio Declaration did not regard it as legally binding. Is the Declaration nonetheless "law" because it consolidates international opinion, may help shape international expectations, and produces some reliance? Does international law encompass norms of whatever nature that somehow influence the behavior of states and other international actors? Should a court charged with applying international law rely on the Rio Principles? How is a court—or any other decision maker—to determine which international norms are legally binding except by reference to accepted categories such as treaties, customary international law, and general principles? In any society, non-legal norms may affect behavior, sometimes giving rise to strong community expectations, but is not law by definition legally binding and non-law not legally binding? See Michael Bothe, "Legal and Non-legal Norms—A Meaningful Distinction in International Relations?," 11 *Netherlands Yearbook of International Law* 65 (1980); Jan Klabbers, "The Redundancy of Soft Law," 65 *Nordic Journal of International Law* 167 (1996).

Soft law may take a variety of forms in addition to declarations emanating from international conferences such as the Earth Summit. Other examples include memoranda of understanding, most resolutions of international organizations, *e.g.*, those considered in the *Texaco/Libya Case* above, and codes of conduct, *e.g.*, the Food and Agriculture Organization's 1995 Code of Conduct for Responsible Fisheries, which we consider in Chapter 10. Who authors soft law? Is it always states or international organizations? How should we characterize the Guidelines of the Global Reporting Initiative, an effort initiated by non-governmental organizations to encourage sustainability monitoring and reporting by companies and organizations? See https://www.globalreporting.org (last visited Dec. 8, 2013). Is that Initiative also an example of soft law? For introductions to soft law and its various roles, see Dinah Shelton, "Soft Law," in *Routledge Handbook of International Law* 68 (David Armstrong ed. 2009); Daniel Thürer, "Soft Law," in 9 *Max Planck Encyclopedia of Public International Law* 269 (Rüdiger Wolfrum ed. 2012).

3. *Soft Law and Treaties*. How exactly should we distinguish the Rio Principles from a treaty, such as the Cession of Alaska or the Genocide Convention (see Chapter 2)? Why might international actors prefer one or the other vehicle? For states, what are the advantages and disadvantages of soft law? Could soft law help pave the way for treaties? May soft law also usefully supplement treaties, providing later glosses or understandings concerning treaty provisions? Is soft law relevant in interpreting treaties? Some treaties explicitly provide that states parties or a treaty-compliance body may issue non-binding recommendations; an example is Article IX of the 1959 Antarctic Treaty, which we study in Chapter 8.

4. *Soft Law and Customary International Law*. What is the relationship between soft law and customary international law? Does soft law count as state practice or *opinio juris*? May soft law instruments such as the Rio Declaration influence future state practice?

May and should soft law instruments influence judicial or arbitral pronouncements? Was it wrong of the arbitrator in the *Texaco/Libya Case* above to rely on a General Assembly resolution when the Assembly, according to Article 10 of the U.N. Charter, is authorized only to make "recommendations"? What persuaded the arbitrator that a General Assembly resolution had evidentiary value for customary international law? Should the Rio Principles be given similar weight? In Legality of the Threat or Use of Nuclear Weapons, Advisory Opinion, 1996 I.C.J. 226, 241, the International Court of Justice noted that countries, in their statements to the Court, had cited Rio Principle 2, but the Court did not explicitly pronounce on its legal relevance. However, the Court, echoing phrases in Principle 2, found that "the general obligation of States to ensure that activities within their jurisdiction and control respect the environment of other States or of areas beyond national control is now part of the corpus of international law relating to the environment." *Id.* at 242. And consider Principle 17 on environmental impact assessments. The ICJ, in Case Concerning Pulp Mills on the River Uruguay (Argentina v. Uruguay), 2010 I.C.J. 14, 83, referred both to environmental treaties and to soft law instruments (though not Principle 17) in concluding that there was now "a requirement under general international law to undertake an environmental impact assessment where there is a risk that [a] proposed industrial activity may have a significant adverse impact in a transboundary context[.]"

5. *Soft Law and Nonconsensual International Law*. Should the Rio Principles fill gaps in international law if there is no applicable treaty or customary international law rule? Do any of the Rio Principles reproduced above state fundamental, *jus cogens* norms? If so, how, if at all, does their (re)statement in a soft law declaration contribute to creating nonconsensual obligations?

E. EQUITY

Although equity is not explicitly mentioned as a source of law in Article 38(1) of the Statute of the International Court of Justice, international lawyers and tribunals—including the ICJ itself—sometimes apply equity. With respect to the materials in this part, consider what authority there is for the use of equity, its content, and the relationship between equity and other sources of international law.

THE CAYUGA INDIANS CASE

American and British Claims Arbitration, *Nielsen Reports* 203, 307 (1926)

This is a claim of Great Britain, on behalf of the Cayuga Indians in Canada, against the United States by virtue of certain treaties between the State of New York and the Cayuga Nation in 1789, 1790, and 1795, and the Treaty of 1814 between the United States and Great Britain, known as the Treaty of Ghent.

At the time of the American Revolution, the Cayugas, a tribe of the Six Nations or Iroquois, occupied that part of Central New York lying about Cayuga Lake. During the Revolution, the Cayugas took the side of Great Britain, and as a result their territory was invaded and laid waste by Continental troops. Thereupon the greater part of the tribe removed to Buffalo Creek, and after 1784 a considerable portion removed thence to the Grand River in Canada. By 1790 the majority of the tribe were probably in Canada. In 1789 the State of New York entered into a treaty with the Cayugas who remained at Cayuga Lake, recognized as the Cayuga Nation, whereby the latter ceded the lands formerly occupied by the Tribe to New York and the latter covenanted to pay an annuity of $500 to the nation. In this treaty a reservation at Cayuga Lake was provided for. As there was much dissatisfaction with this treaty on the part of the Indians, who asserted that they were not properly represented, it was confirmed by a subsequent treaty in 1790 and finally by one in 1795, executed by the principal chiefs and warriors both from Buffalo Creek and from the Grand River. By the terms of the latter treaty, in which, as we hold, the covenants of the prior treaties were merged, the State covenanted, among other things, with the "Cayuga Nation" to pay to the said "Cayuga Nation" 1800 dollars a year forever thereafter, at Canandaigua, in Ontario County, the money to be paid to "the Agent of Indian Affairs under the United States for the time being, residing within this State" and, if there was no such agent, then to a person to be appointed by the Governor. Such agent or person appointed by the Governor was to pay the money to the "Cayuga Nation," taking the receipt of the nation and also a receipt on the counterpart of the treaty, left in the possession of the Indians, according to a prescribed form. By this treaty the reservation provided for in the Treaty of 1789 was sold to the State.

There are receipts upon the counterpart of the Treaty of 1795 down to and including 1809, and these receipts and the receipt for 1810, retained by New York, show that the only persons who can be identified among those to whom the money was paid, and the only persons who can be shown to have held prominent positions in the tribe, were then living in Canada. In 1811 an entire change appears. From that time a new set of names, of quite different character, appear on the receipts retained by New York. From that time there are no receipts upon the counterpart. Since that time, it is conceded, no part of the moneys paid under the treaty has come in any way to the Cayugas in Canada, but the whole has been paid to Cayugas in the United States, and since 1829 in accordance with treaties in which the Canadian Cayugas had no part or in accordance with legislation of New York. The claim is: (1) That the Cayugas in Canada, who assert that they have kept up their tribal organization and undoubtedly have included in their number the principal personages of the tribe according to its original organization, are the "Cayuga Nation," covenantees in the Treaty of 1795, and that as such they, or Great Britain on their behalf, should receive the whole amount of the annuity from 1810 to the present. In this connection it is argued that the covenant could only be discharged by payment to those in possession of the counterpart of the treaty and indorsement of a receipt thereon, as in the treaty prescribed. (2) In the alternative, that the Canadian Cayugas, as a part of the posterity of the original nation, and numerically the greater part, have a proportion of the annuity for the future and a proportion of the payments since 1810, to be ascertained by reference to the relative numbers in the United States and in Canada for the time being.

As the occasion of the change that took place in and after 1811 was the division of the tribe at the time of the War of 1812, those in the United States and those in Canada taking the part of the United States and of Great Britain, respectively, Great Britain invokes Article IX of the Treaty of Ghent, by which the United States agreed to restore to the Indians with whom that Government had been at war "all the

possessions, rights, and privileges which they may have enjoyed or been entitled to" in 1811 before the war. * * *

It can not be doubted that until the Cayugas permanently divided, all the sachems and warriors, wherever they lived, whether at Cayuga Lake, Buffalo Creek, or the Grand River in Canada, were regarded as entitled to and did share in the money paid on the annuity. Indeed it is reasonably certain that the larger number and the more important of those who signed the Treaty of 1795 were then, or were soon thereafter, permanently established in Canada. It is clear that the greater number and more important of those who signed the annuity receipts from the date of the treaty until 1810 were Canadian Cayugas. We find the person through whom, by the terms of the treaty, the money was to be paid, writing to the Governor of New York in 1797 that the Canadian Cayugas had not received their fair proportion in a previous payment and proposing to make the sum up to them at the next payment. Everything indicates that down to the division the money was regarded as payable to and was paid to and divided among the Cayugas as a people. The claim of the Canadian Cayugas, who are in fact the greater part of that people, is founded in the elementary principle of justice that requires us to look at the substance and not stick in the bark of the legal form.

But there are special circumstances making the equitable claim of the Canadian Cayugas especially strong.

In the first place, the Cayuga Nation had no international status. As has been said, it existed as a legal unit only by New York law. It was a *de facto* unit, but *de jure* was only what Great Britain chose to recognize as to the Cayugas who moved to Canada and what New York recognized as to the Cayugas in New York or in their relations with New York. As to the annuities, therefore, the Cayugas were a unit of New York law, so far as New York law chose to make them one. When the tribe divided, this anomalous and hard situation gave rise to obvious claims according to universally recognized principles of justice.

In the second place, we must bear in mind the dependent legal position of the individual Cayugas. Legally they could do nothing except under the guardianship of some sovereign. They could not determine what should be the nation, nor even whether there should be a nation legally. New York continued to deal with the New York Cayugas as a "nation." Great Britain dealt with the Canadian Cayugas as individuals. The very language of the treaty was in this sense imposed on them. What to them was a covenant with the people of the tribe and its posterity had to be put into legal terms of a covenant with a legal unit that might and did come to be but a fraction of the whole. American Courts have agreed from the beginning in pronouncing the position of the Indians an anomalous one. When a situation legally so anomalous is presented, recourse must be had to generally recognized principles of justice and fair dealing in order to determine the rights of the individuals involved. The same considerations of equity that have repeatedly been invoked by the courts where strict regard to the legal personality of a corporation would lead to inequitable results or to results contrary to legal policy, may be invoked here. In such cases courts have not hesitated to look behind the legal person and consider the human individuals who were the real beneficiaries. Those considerations are even more cogent where we are dealing with Indians in a state of pupilage toward the sovereign with whom they were treating.

There is the more warrant for so doing under the terms of the treaty by virtue of which we are sitting. It provides that decision shall be made in accordance with principles of international law and of equity. Merignhac considers that an arbitral tribunal is justified in reaching a decision on universally recognized principles of justice where the terms of submission are silent as to the grounds of decision and even where the grounds of decision are expressed to be the "principles of international law." He considers, however, that the appropriate formula is that "international law is to be applied with equity." *Traité théorique et pratique de l'arbitrage international*, § 303. It is significant that the present treaty uses the phrase "principles of international law and equity." When used in a general arbitration treaty, this can only mean to provide for the possibility of anomalous cases such as the present.

An examination of the provisions of arbitration treaties shows a recognition that something more than the strict law must be used in the grounds of decision of arbitral tribunals in certain cases; that there are cases in which—like the courts of the land—these tribunals must find the grounds of decision, must find the right and the law, in general considerations of justice, equity, and right dealing guided by legal analogies and by the spirit and received principles of international law.

* * * Our conclusion on this branch of the cause is that, according to general and universally recognized principles of justice and the analogy of the way in which English and American courts, on proper occasions, look behind what in such cases they call "the corporate fiction" in the interests of justice or of the policy of the law (Daimler Company, Ltd. *v.* Continental Tyre and Rubber Company, Ltd. [1916] 2 A.C. 307, 315–316, 338 ff.; 1 Cook (Corporations, 8 ed. § 2)), on the division of the Cayuga Nation the Cayuga Indians permanently settled in Canada became entitled to their proportionate share of the annuity and that such share ought to have been paid to them from 1810 to the present time.

NOTES AND QUESTIONS

1. *The Definition of the "Cayuga Nation."* In the *Cayuga Indians Case* how was the "Cayuga Nation" defined? Were there different definitions of it made in U.S. law, in British law, and in international law? Were the

agreements of 1789, 1790, and 1795 between the United States and the Cayuga Nation governed by U.S. or international law? What about the 1814 Treaty of Ghent between the United States and Great Britain?

2. *Individual and Group Rights in International Law.* Notice how the arbitral panel looked behind the "legal person" of the Cayuga Nation so it could protect "human individuals who were the real beneficiaries" of the treaties. How much deference should international law show to other "legal persons"? Was the peculiarity here that the Cayuga Nation was a "nation" but not a "state," and thus unable to vindicate its own international legal rights? In 2010, a committee of the International Law Association characterized the *Cayuga Indians* decision as a "down" because it "denied indigenous peoples the status of a 'legal unit of international law.' " ILA Committee on the Rights of Indigenous Peoples, "Interim Report," in International Law Association, *Report of the Seventy-Fourth Conference (The Hague)* 834, 835 (2010). Questions about the relationship of individuals to international law and their international legal rights and obligations *vis-à-vis* their own and other states are raised in Chapter 6, and questions about the group rights of "peoples" are addressed in Chapter 7.

Should the Cayuga Nation now bring a case to another international forum? For an argument that the Cayuga Nation should make a claim against the United States at the Inter-American Commission of Human Rights, see Carrie Garrow, "Following Deskaheh's Legacy: Reclaiming the Cayuga Indian Nation's Land Rights at the Inter-American Commission on Human Rights," 35 *Syracuse Journal of International Law & Commerce* 341 (2008). The Inter-American Commission on Human Rights was the process employed in the *Michael Domingues Case* above. More about the Inter-American system is to be found in the Notes following that case.

3. *The Varieties of Equity.* The treaty providing for the resolution of the *Cayuga Indians* dispute explicitly called for the application of "the principles of international law and of equity." Therefore, the arbitral tribunal was not concerned that its use of equity necessarily be within the rules of international law, *i.e.*, that it be equity *intra legem*. The tribunal had a warrant to apply equity at least to fill gaps in the law, *i.e.*, equity *praeter legem,* and perhaps even against the law, *i.e.*, equity *contra legem*. Did the *Cayuga Indians* tribunal really venture beyond equity *intra legem*? Can it really be said that the tribunal moved to fill gaps in international law or to reverse international law?

The arbitral tribunal was persuaded that "as a matter of justice" the Canadian Cayugas had a good claim against the United States: "The claim of the Canadian Cayugas, who are in fact the greater part of that people, is founded in the elementary principle of justice that requires us to look at the substance and not stick in the bark of the legal form." Should international law be more or less able than municipal law "to look at the substance" of disputes and "not stick in the bark of the legal form"? On the one hand, formal agreements among sovereign states may deserve special respect. On the other hand, without municipal-type legislative organs, international law may become especially rigid.

THE MEUSE CASE

Judge Hudson's Opinion,
1937 P.C.I.J., Ser. A/B, No. 70, at 73

The Netherlands Government has asked the Court to say that the alimentation of certain canals by the Neerhaeren Lock with water taken from the Meuse elsewhere than at Maestricht is contrary to the Treaty of 1863, and to order that Belgium should discontinue that alimentation.

[I]s this a case in which affirmative relief should be given by the Court? Or should it be said, in the terms of the alternative Belgian submission, that the Netherlands has in some measure *perdu le droit d'invoquer* the Treaty against Belgium? [The Netherlands had taken water from the River Meuse by operating a lock at Bosscheveld.]

What are widely known as principles of equity have long been considered to constitute a part of international law, and as such they have often been applied by international tribunals. Mérignhac, *Traité théorique et pratique de l'Arbitrage international* (1895), p. 295; Ralston, *Law and Procedure of International Tribunals* (new ed., 1926), pp. 53–57. A sharp division between law and equity, such as prevails in the administration of justice in some States, should find no place in international jurisprudence; even in some national legal systems, there has been a strong tendency towards the fusion of law and equity. Some international tribunals are expressly directed by the *compromis* which control them to apply "law and equity." See the Cayuga Indians Case, Nielsen's Report of the United States-British Claims Arbitration (1926), p. 307. Of such a provision, a special tribunal of the Permanent Court of Arbitration said in 1922 that "the majority of international lawyers seem to agree that these words are to be understood to mean general principles of justice as distinguished from any particular systems of jurisprudence." Proceedings of the United States-Norwegian Tribunal (1922), p. 141. Numerous arbitration treaties have been concluded in recent years which apply to differences "which are justiciable in their nature by reason of being susceptible of decision by the application of the principles of law or equity." Whether the reference in an arbitration treaty is to the application of "law and equity" or to justiciability dependent on the possibility of applying "law or equity," it would seem to envisage equity as a part of law.

The Court has not been expressly authorized by its Statute to apply equity as distinguished from law. Nor, indeed, does the Statute expressly direct its application of international law, though as has been said on several occasions the Court is "a tribunal of international law." Series A, No. 7, p. 19; Series A, Nos. 20/21, p. 124. Article 38 of the Statute expressly directs the application of "general principles of law recognized by civilized nations," and in more than one nation principles of equity have an established place in the legal system. The Court's recognition of equity as a part of international law is in no way restricted by the special power conferred upon it "to decide a case *ex aequo et bono*, if the parties agree thereto." It must be concluded, therefore, that under Article 38 of the Statute, if not independently of that Article, the Court has some freedom to consider principles of equity as part of the international law which it must apply.

It would seem to be an important principle of equity that where two parties have assumed an identical or a reciprocal obligation, one party which is engaged in a continuing non-performance of that obligation should not be permitted to take advantage of a similar non-performance of that obligation by the other party. The principle finds expression in the so-called maxims of equity which exercised great influence in the creative period of the development of the Anglo-American law. Some of these maxims are, "Equality is equity"; "He who seeks equity must do equity." It is in line with such maxims that "a court of equity refuses relief to a plaintiff whose conduct in regard to the subject-matter of the litigation has been improper." 13 Halsbury's *Laws of England* (2nd ed., 1934), p. 87. A very similar principle was received into Roman Law. The obligations of a vendor and a vendee being concurrent, "neither could compel the other to perform unless he had done, or tendered, his own part." Buckland, *Text Book of Roman Law* (2nd ed., 1932), p. 493. The *exceptio non adimpleti contractus* required a claimant to prove that he had performed or offered to perform his obligation. Girard, *Droit romain* (8th ed., 1929), p. 567; Saleilles, in 6 *Annales de Droit commercial*, (1892), p. 287, and 7 *id.* (1893), pp. 24, 97 and 175. This conception was the basis of Articles 320 and 322 of the German Civil Code, and even where a code is silent on the point Planiol states the general principle that "dans tout rapport synallagmatique, chacune des deux parties ne peut exiger la prestation qui lui est due que si elle-offre elle-même d'exécuter son obligation." Planiol, *Droit civil*, Vol. 2 (6th ed., 1912), p. 320. * * *

One result of applying the principle will be that even if the Court should be of the opinion that the Belgian action with regard to the functioning of the Neerhaeren Lock is contrary to the Treaty of 1863, it should nevertheless refuse in this case to order Belgium to discontinue that action. In equity, the Netherlands is not in a position to have such relief decreed to her. Belgium cannot be ordered to discontinue the operation of the Neerhaeren Lock when the Netherlands is left free to continue the operation of the Bosscheveld Lock.

NOTES AND QUESTIONS

1. *Justifying a Recourse to Equity*. Unlike the arbitrators in the *Cayuga Indians Case*, Judge Hudson in the *Meuse Case* had no explicit charge from the states involved to apply equity as well as law to the dispute. How then did Hudson justify his use of equity? If the principles of equity are part of international law, does any kind of equity exist outside international law? Given Hudson's reasoning, would an "international law and equity" authorization *à la Cayuga Indians* have been simply redundant?

The European Court of Human Rights turned to equity without an explicit agreement in a recent determination of damages: "[Our] guiding principle is equity which above all involves flexibility and an objective consideration of what is just, fair and reasonable in all the circumstances of the case." Al-Jedda v. United Kingdom, European Court of Human Rights, Judgment of 7 July 2011, ¶ 14.

2. *Searching for General Principles*. Hudson noted that equity could be a type of "general principle," which the Court is authorized to apply under Article 38(1)(c) of its Statute. How thorough a search of municipal law did Judge Hudson make in search of his general principle? How did it compare to Advocate General Slynn's search of municipal law in the *AM & S Case*? Was Hudson's search meant to be universal? If so, did it succeed?

3. *The Effect of Applying Equity*. What was the effect of Judge Hudson's application of equity to the facts of the *Meuse Case*? What were the parties supposed to do if they accepted Hudson's decision?

4. Ex Aequo et Bono. By Article 38(2) of its Statute, the International Court of Justice may decide a case *ex aequo et bono,* but only if the states party to the dispute specifically authorize it to do so. The Court has never been so authorized. What in practice would be the difference between applying equitable principles pursuant to Article 38(1)(c) and deciding *ex aequo et bono* pursuant to Article 38(2)?

THE NORTH SEA CONTINENTAL SHELF CASES

Federal Republic of Germany v. Denmark; Federal Republic of Germany v. Netherlands, 1969 I.C.J. 3

Articles 1 to 3 of the Special Agreement between the Governments of Denmark and the Federal Republic of Germany [and another between the Governments of the Netherlands and the Federal Republic of Germany, both dated February 2, 1967, provide] as follows:

ARTICLE 1

(1) The International Court of Justice is requested to decide the following question:

What principles and rules of international law are applicable to the delimitation as between the Parties of the areas of the continental shelf in the North Sea which appertain to each of them beyond the partial boundary determined by the above-mentioned Convention of 9 June 1965?

(2) The Governments of the Kingdom of Denmark and of the Federal Republic of Germany [and of the Netherlands] shall delimit the continental shelf in the North Sea as between their countries by agreement in pursuance of the decision requested from the International Court of Justice. * * *

3. [T]he North Sea, which lies between continental Europe and Great Britain in the east-west direction, is roughly oval in shape and stretches from the straits of Dover northwards to a parallel drawn between a point immediately north of the Shetland Islands and the mouth of the Sogne Fiord in Norway, about 75 kilometres above Bergen, beyond which is the North Atlantic Ocean. In the extreme northwest, it is bounded by a line connecting the Orkney and Shetland island groups; while on its north-eastern side, the line separating it from the entrances to the Baltic Sea lies between Hanstholm at the north-west point of Denmark, and Lindesnes at the southern tip of Norway. Eastward of this line the Skagerrak begins. Thus, the North Sea has to some extent the general look of an enclosed sea without actually being one. Round its shores are situated, on its eastern side and starting from the north, Norway, Denmark, the Federal Republic of Germany, the Netherlands, Belgium and France; while the whole western side is taken up by Great Britain, together with the island groups of the Orkneys and Shetlands. From this it will be seen that the continental shelf of the Federal Republic is situated between those of Denmark and the Netherlands.

4. The waters of the North Sea are shallow, and the whole seabed consists of continental shelf at a depth of less than 200 metres, except for the formation known as the Norwegian Trough, a belt of water 200–650 metres deep, fringing the southern and south-western coasts of Norway to a width averaging about 80–100 kilometres. Much the greater part of this continental shelf has already been the subject of delimitation by a series of agreements concluded between the United Kingdom (which, as stated, lies along the whole western side of it) and certain of the States on the eastern side, namely Norway, Denmark and the Netherlands. These three delimitations were carried out by the drawing of what are known as "median lines" which, for immediate present purposes, may be described as boundaries drawn between the continental shelf areas of "opposite" States, dividing the intervening spaces equally between them. * * *

5. In addition to the partial boundary lines Federal Republic/ Denmark and Federal Republic/Netherlands, which * * * were respectively established by the agreements of 9 June 1965 and 1 December 1964, and which are shown as lines A–B and C–D on Map 3

[Figure 3.A,] another line has been drawn in this area, namely that represented by the line E–F on that map. This line, which divides areas respectively claimed (to the north of it) by Denmark, and (to the south of it) by the Netherlands, is the outcome of an agreement between those two countries dated 31 March 1966, reflecting the view taken by them as to what are the correct boundary lines between their respective continental shelf areas and that of the Federal Republic, beyond the partial boundaries A–B and C–D already drawn. These further and unagreed boundaries to seaward, are shown on Map 3 by means of the dotted lines B–E and D–E. They are the lines, the correctness of which in law the Court is in effect, though indirectly, called upon to determine. Also shown on Map 3 are the two pecked lines B–F and D–F, representing approximately the boundaries which the Federal Republic would have wished to obtain in the course of the negotiations that took place between the Federal Republic and the other two Parties prior to the submission of the matter to the Court. The nature of these negotiations must now be described.

6. Under the agreements of December 1964 and June 1965, already mentioned, the partial boundaries represented by the map lines A–B and C–D had, according to the information furnished to the Court by the Parties, been drawn mainly by application of the principle of equidistance, using that term as denoting the abstract concept of equidistance. A line so drawn, known as an "equidistance line," may be described as one which leaves to each of the parties concerned all those portions of the continental shelf that are nearer to a point on its own coast than they are to any point on the coast of the other party. An equidistance line may consist either of a "median" line between "opposite" States, or of a "lateral" line between "adjacent" States. In certain geographical configurations of which the Parties furnished examples, a given equidistance line may partake in varying degree of the nature both of a median and of a lateral line. There exists nevertheless a distinction to be drawn between the two, which will be mentioned in its place.

7. The further negotiations between the Parties for the prolongation of the partial boundaries broke down mainly because Denmark and the Netherlands respectively wished this prolongation also to be effected on the basis of the equidistance principle,—and this would have resulted in the dotted lines B–E and D–E, shown on Map 3; whereas the Federal Republic considered that such an outcome would be inequitable because it would unduly curtail what the Republic believed should be its proper share of continental shelf area, on the basis of proportionality to the length of its North Sea coastline. It will be observed that neither of the lines in question, taken by itself, would produce this effect, but only both of them together—an element regarded by Denmark and the Netherlands as irrelevant to what they viewed as being two separate and self-contained delimitations, each of which should be carried out without reference to the other.

Figure 3.A

Based on Map 3 from the *North Sea Continental Shelf Cases*

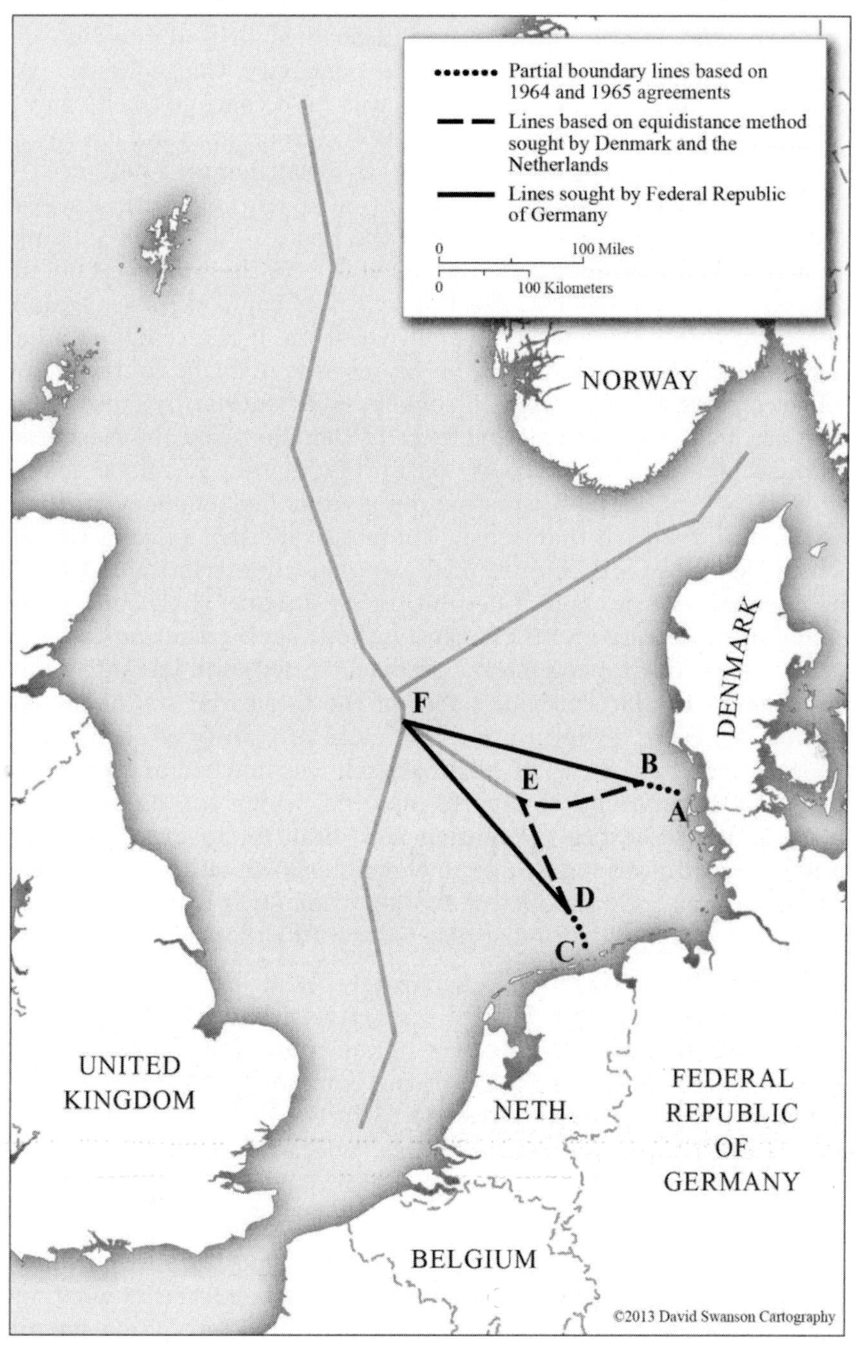

8. The reason for the result that would be produced by the two lines B–E and D–E, taken conjointly, is that in the case of a concave or recessing coast such as that of the Federal Republic on the North Sea, the effect of the use of the equidistance method is to pull the line of the boundary inwards, in the direction of the concavity. Consequently, where two such lines are drawn at different points on a concave coast, they will, if the curvature is pronounced, inevitably meet at a relatively short distance from the coast, thus causing the continental shelf area they enclose, to take the form approximately of a triangle with its apex to seaward and, as it was put on behalf of the Federal Republic, "cutting off" the coastal State from the further areas of the continental shelf outside of and beyond this triangle. The effect of concavity could of course equally be produced for a country with a straight coastline if the coasts of adjacent countries protruded immediately on either side of it. In contrast to this, the effect of coastal projections, or of convex or outwardly curving coasts such as are, to a moderate extent, those of Denmark and the Netherlands, is to cause boundary lines drawn on an equidistance basis to leave the coast on divergent courses, thus having a widening tendency on the area of continental shelf off that coast. These two distinct effects, which are shown in sketches I–III [Figure 3.B], are directly attributable to the use of the equidistance method of delimiting continental shelf boundaries off recessing or projecting coasts. It goes without saying that on these types of coasts the equidistance method produces exactly similar effects in the delimitation of the lateral boundaries of the territorial sea of the States concerned. However, owing to the very close proximity of such waters to the coasts concerned, these effects are much less marked and may be very slight,—and there are other aspects involved, which will be considered in their place. It will suffice to mention here that, for instance, a deviation from a line drawn perpendicular to the general direction of the coast, of only 5 kilometres, at a distance of about 5 kilometres from that coast, will grow into one of over 30 at a distance of over 100 kilometres.

9. After the negotiations, separately held between the Federal Republic and the other two Parties respectively, had in each case, for the reasons given in the two preceding paragraphs, failed to result in any agreement about the delimitation of the boundary extending beyond the partial one already agreed, tripartite talks between all the Parties took place in The Hague in February–March 1966, in Bonn in May and again in Copenhagen in August. These also proving fruitless, it was then decided to submit the matter to the Court. * * *

25. The Court now turns to the legal position regarding the equidistance method. The first question to be considered is whether the 1958 Geneva Convention on the Continental Shelf is binding for all the Parties in this case—that is to say whether, as contended by Denmark and the Netherlands, the use of this method is rendered obligatory for the

Figure 3.B

Sketches Illustrating the Geographical Situations Described in Paragraph 8 of the Judgment in the *North Sea Continental Shelf Cases*

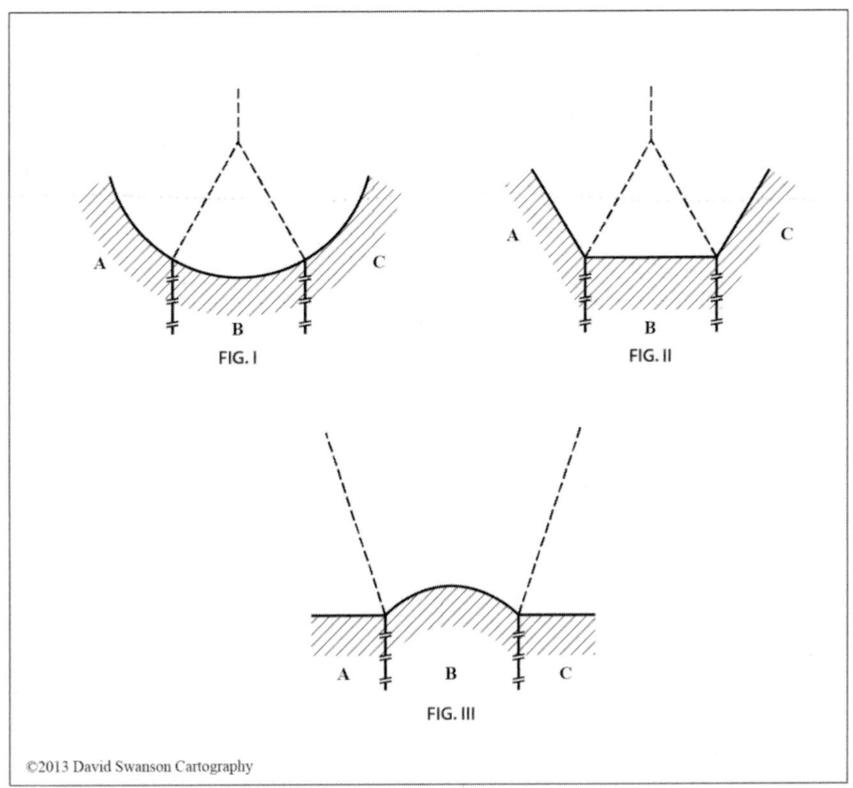

present delimitations by virtue of the delimitations provision (Article 6) of that instrument, according to the conditions laid down in it. Clearly, if this is so, then the provisions of the Convention will prevail in the relations between the Parties, and would take precedence of any rules having a more general character, or derived from another source. On that basis the Court's reply to the question put to it in the Special Agreements would necessarily be to the effect that as between the Parties the relevant provisions of the Convention represented the applicable rules of law—that is to say constituted the law for the Parties—and its sole remaining task would be to interpret those provisions, in so far as their meaning was disputed or appeared to be uncertain, and to apply them to the particular circumstances involved.

26. The relevant provisions of Article 6 of the Geneva Convention, paragraph 2 of which Denmark and the Netherlands contend not only to be applicable as a conventional rule, but also to represent the accepted

rule of general international law on the subject of continental shelf delimitation, as it exists independently of the Convention, read as follows:

> 1. Where the same continental shelf is adjacent to the territories of two or more States whose coasts are opposite each other, the boundary of the continental shelf appertaining to such States shall be determined by agreement between them. In the absence of agreement, and unless another boundary line is justified by special circumstances, the boundary is the median line, every point of which is equidistant from the nearest point of the baselines from which the breadth of the territorial sea of each State is measured.
>
> 2. Where the same continental shelf is adjacent to the territories of two adjacent States, the boundary of the continental shelf shall be determined by agreement between them. In the absence of agreement, and unless another boundary line is justified by special circumstances, the boundary shall be determined by application of the principle of equidistance from the nearest points of the baselines from which the breadth of the territorial sea of each State is measured.

The Convention received 46 signatures and, up-to-date, there have been 39 ratifications or accessions. It came into force on 10 June 1964, having received the 22 ratifications or accessions required for that purpose (Article 11), and was therefore in force at the time when the various delimitations of continental shelf boundaries described earlier (paragraphs 1 and 5) took place between the Parties. But, under the formal provisions of the Convention, it is in force for any individual State only in so far as, having signed it within the time-limit provided for that purpose, that State has also subsequently ratified it; or, not having signed within that time-limit, has subsequently acceded to the Convention. Denmark and the Netherlands have both signed and ratified the Convention, and are parties to it, the former since 10 June 1964, the latter since 20 March 1966. The Federal Republic was one of the signatories of the Convention, but has never ratified it, and is consequently not a party.

27. It is admitted on behalf of Denmark and the Netherlands that in these circumstances the Convention cannot, as such, be binding on the Federal Republic, in the sense of the Republic being contractually bound by it. But it is contended that the Convention, or the régime of the Convention, and in particular of Article 6, has become binding on the Federal Republic in another way,—namely because, by conduct, by public statements and proclamations, and in other ways, the Republic has unilaterally assumed the obligations of the Convention; or has manifested its acceptance of the conventional régime; or has recognized it as being generally applicable to the delimitation of continental shelf areas. * * *

28. As regards these contentions, it is clear that only a very definite, very consistent course of conduct on the part of a State in the situation of the Federal Republic could justify the Court in upholding them; and, if this had existed—that is to say if there had been a real intention to manifest acceptance or recognition of the applicability of the conventional régime—then it must be asked why it was that the Federal Republic did not take the obvious step of giving expression to this readiness by simply ratifying the Convention. In principle, when a number of States, including the one whose conduct is invoked, and those invoking it, have drawn up a convention specifically providing for a particular method by which the intention to become bound by the régime of the convention is to be manifested—namely by the carrying out of certain prescribed formalities (ratification, accession), it is not lightly to be presumed that a State which has not carried out these formalities, though at all times fully able and entitled to do so, has nevertheless somehow become bound in another way. Indeed if it were a question not of obligation but of rights,—if, that is to say, a State which, though entitled to do so, had not ratified or acceded, attempted to claim rights under the convention, on the basis of a declared willingness to be bound by it, or of conduct evincing acceptance of the conventional régime, it would simply be told that, not having become a party to the convention it could not claim any rights under it until the professed willingness and acceptance had been manifested in the prescribed form. * * *

30. Having regard to these considerations of principle, it appears to the Court that only the existence of a situation of estoppel could suffice to lend substance to this contention,—that is to say if the Federal Republic were now precluded from denying the applicability of the conventional régime, by reason of past conduct, declarations, etc., which not only clearly and consistently evinced acceptance of that régime, but also had caused Denmark or the Netherlands, in reliance on such conduct, detrimentally to change position or suffer some prejudice. Of this there is no evidence whatever in the present case. * * *

37. It is maintained by Denmark and the Netherlands that the Federal Republic, whatever its position may be in relation to the Geneva Convention, considered as such, is in any event bound to accept delimitation on an equidistance-special circumstances basis, because the use of this method is not in the nature of a merely conventional obligation, but is, or must now be regarded as involving, a rule that is part of the *corpus* of general international law;—and, like other rules of general or customary international law, is binding on the Federal Republic automatically and independently of any specific assent, direct or indirect, given by the latter. This contention has both a positive law and a more fundamentalist aspect. As a matter of positive law, it is based on the work done in this field by international legal bodies, on State practice and on the influence attributed to the Geneva Convention itself,—the claim

being that these various factors have cumulatively evidenced or been creative of the *opinio juris sive necessitatis*, requisite for the formation of new rules of customary international law. In its fundamentalist aspect, the view put forward derives from what might be called the natural law of the continental shelf, in the sense that the equidistance principle is seen as a necessary expression in the field of delimitation of the accepted doctrine of the exclusive appurtenance of the continental shelf to the nearby coastal State, and therefore as having an *a priori* character of so to speak juristic inevitability.

[The Court first analyzes and rejects the *a priori* argument, concluding:]

55. In the light of this history, and of the record generally, it is clear that at no time was the notion of equidistance as an inherent necessity of continental shelf doctrine entertained. Quite a different outlook was indeed manifested from the start in current legal thinking. It was, and it really remained to the end, governed by two beliefs;—namely, first, that no one single method of delimitation was likely to prove satisfactory in all circumstances, and that delimitation should, therefore, be carried out by agreement (or by reference to arbitration); and secondly, that it should be effected on equitable principles. It was in pursuance of the first of these beliefs that in the draft that emerged as Article 6 of the Geneva Convention, the Commission gave priority to delimitation by agreement,—and in pursuance of the second that it introduced the exception in favour of "special circumstances." Yet the record shows that, even with these mitigations, doubts persisted, particularly as to whether the equidistance principle would in all cases prove equitable.

56. [T]he inherency contention as now put forward by Denmark and the Netherlands inverts the true order of things in point of time and that, so far from an equidistance rule having been generated by an antecedent principle of proximity inherent in the whole concept of continental shelf appurtenance, the latter is rather a rationalization of the former—an *ex post facto* construct directed to providing a logical juristic basis for a method of delimitation propounded largely for different reasons, cartographical and other. Given also that * * * the theory cannot be said to be endowed with any quality of logical necessity either, the Court is unable to accept it. * * *

60. The conclusions so far reached leave open, and still to be considered, the question whether on some basis other than that of an *a priori* logical necessity, i.e., through positive law processes, the equidistance principle has come to be regarded as a rule of customary international law, so that it would be obligatory for the Federal Republic in that way, even though Article 6 of the Geneva Convention is not, as such, opposable to it. For this purpose it is necessary to examine the status of the principle as it stood when the Convention was drawn up, as

it resulted from the effect of the Convention, and in the light of State practice subsequent to the Convention; but it should be clearly understood that in the pronouncements the Court makes on these matters it has in view solely the delimitation provisions (Article 6) of the Convention, not other parts of it, nor the Convention as such.

61. The first of these questions can conveniently be considered in the form suggested on behalf of Denmark and the Netherlands themselves in the course of the oral hearing, when it was stated that they had not in fact contended that the delimitation article (Article 6) of the Convention "embodied already received rules of customary law in the sense that the Convention was merely declaratory of existing rules." Their contention was, rather, that although prior to the Conference, continental shelf law was only in the formative stage, and State practice lacked uniformity, yet "the process of the definition and consolidation of the emerging customary law took place through the work of the International Law Commission, the reaction of governments to that work and the proceedings of the Geneva Conference"; and this emerging customary law became "crystallized in the adoption of the Continental Shelf Convention by the Conference."

62. Whatever validity this contention may have in respect of at least certain parts of the Convention, the Court cannot accept it as regards the delimitation provision (Article 6), the relevant parts of which were adopted almost unchanged from the draft of the International Law Commission that formed the basis of discussion at the Conference. The status of the rule in the Convention therefore depends mainly on the processes that led the Commission to propose it. These processes have already been reviewed in connection with the Danish-Netherlands contention of an *a priori* necessity for equidistance, and the Court considers this review sufficient for present purposes also, in order to show that the principle of equidistance, as it now figures in Article 6 of the Convention, was proposed by the Commission with considerable hesitation, somewhat on an experimental basis, at most *de lege ferenda*, and not at all *de lege lata* or as an emerging rule of customary international law. This is clearly not the sort of foundation on which Article 6 of the Convention could be said to have reflected or crystallized such a rule.

63. The foregoing conclusion receives significant confirmation from the fact that Article 6 is one of those in respect of which, under the reservations article of the Convention (Article 12) reservations may be made by any State on signing, ratifying or acceding,—for, speaking generally, it is a characteristic of purely conventional rules and obligations that, in regard to them, some faculty of making unilateral reservations may, within certain limits, be admitted;—whereas this cannot be so in the case of general or customary law rules and obligations

which, by their very nature, must have equal force for all members of the international community, and cannot therefore be the subject of any right of unilateral exclusion exercisable at will by any one of them in its own favour. Consequently, it is to be expected that when, for whatever reason, rules or obligations of this order are embodied, or are intended to be reflected in certain provisions of a convention, such provisions will figure amongst those in respect of which a right of unilateral reservation is not conferred, or is excluded. This expectation is, in principle, fulfilled by Article 12 of the Geneva Continental Shelf Convention, which permits reservations to be made to all the articles of the Convention "other than to Articles 1 to 3 inclusive"—these three Articles being the ones which, it is clear, were then regarded as reflecting, or as crystallizing, received or at least emergent rules of customary international law relative to the continental shelf, amongst them the question of the seaward extent of the shelf; the juridical character of the coastal State's entitlement; the nature of the rights exercisable; the kind of natural resources to which these relate; and the preservation intact of the legal status as high seas of the waters over the shelf, and the legal status of the superjacent air-space.

64. The normal inference would therefore be that any articles that do not figure among those excluded from the faculty of reservation under Article 12, were not regarded as declaratory of previously existing or emergent rules of law; and this is the inference the Court in fact draws in respect of Article 6 (delimitation)[.]

69. [T]he Geneva Convention did not embody or crystallize any pre-existing or emergent rule of customary law, according to which the delimitation of continental shelf areas between adjacent States must, unless the Parties otherwise agree, be carried out on a equidistance-special circumstances basis. A rule was of course embodied in Article 6 of the Convention, but as a purely conventional rule. Whether it has since acquired a broader basis remains to be seen: *qua* conventional rule however, as has already been concluded, it is not opposable to the Federal Republic.

70. The Court must now proceed to the last stage in the argument put forward on behalf of Denmark and the Netherlands. This is to the effect that even if there was at the date of the Geneva Convention no rule of customary international law in favour of the equidistance principle, and no such rule was crystallized in Article 6 of the Convention, nevertheless such a rule has come into being since the Convention, partly because of its own impact, partly on the basis of subsequent State practice,—and that this rule, being now a rule of customary international law binding on all States, including therefore the Federal Republic, should be declared applicable to the delimitation of the boundaries between the Parties' respective continental shelf areas in the North Sea.

71. In so far as this contention is based on the view that Article 6 of the Convention has had the influence, and has produced the effect, described, it clearly involves treating that Article as a norm-creating provision which has constituted the foundation of, or has generated a rule which, while only conventional or contractual in its origin, has since passed into the general *corpus* of international law, and is now accepted as such by the *opinio juris*, so as to have become binding even for countries which have never, and do not, become parties to the Convention. There is no doubt that this process is a perfectly possible one and does from time to time occur: it constitutes indeed one of the recognized methods by which new rules of customary international law may be formed. At the same time this result is not lightly to be regarded as having been attained. * * *

75. The Court must now consider whether State practice in the matter of continental shelf delimitation has, subsequent to the Geneva Convention, been of such a kind as to satisfy this requirement. [S]ome 15 cases have been cited in the course of the present proceedings, occurring mostly since the signature of the 1958 Geneva Convention, in which continental shelf boundaries have been delimited according to the equidistance principle—in the majority of the cases by agreement, in a few others unilaterally—or else the delimitation was foreshadowed but has not yet been carried out. Amongst these 15 are the four North Sea delimitations United Kingdom/Norway-Denmark-Netherlands, and Norway/Denmark already mentioned in paragraph 4 of this Judgment. But even if these various cases constituted more than a very small proportion of those potentially calling for delimitation in the world as a whole, the Court would not think it necessary to enumerate or evaluate them separately, since there are, *a priori*, several grounds which deprive them of weight as precedents in the present context.

76. To begin with, over half the States concerned, whether acting unilaterally or conjointly, were or shortly became parties to the Geneva Convention, and were therefore presumably, so far as they were concerned, acting actually or potentially in the application of the Convention. From their action no inference could legitimately be drawn as to the existence of a rule of customary international law in favour of the equidistance principle. As regards those States, on the other hand, which were not, and have not become parties to the Convention, the basis of their action can only be problematical and must remain entirely speculative. Clearly, they were not applying the Convention. But from that no inference could justifiably be drawn that they believed themselves to be applying a mandatory rule of customary international law. There is not a shred of evidence that they did and * * * there is no lack of other reasons for using the equidistance method, so that acting, or agreeing to act in a certain way, does not of itself demonstrate anything of a juridical nature. * * *

81. The Court accordingly concludes that if the Geneva Convention was not in its origins or inception declaratory of a mandatory rule of customary international law enjoining the use of the equidistance principle for the delimitation of continental shelf areas between adjacent States, neither has its subsequent effect been constitutive of such a rule; and that State practice up-to-date has equally been insufficient for the purpose. * * *

83. The legal situation therefore is that the Parties are under no obligation to apply either the 1958 Convention, which is not opposable to the Federal Republic, or the equidistance method as a mandatory rule of customary law, which it is not. But as between States faced with an issue concerning the lateral delimitation of adjacent continental shelves, there are still rules and principles of law to be applied; and in the present case it is not the fact either that rules are lacking, or that the situation is one for the unfettered appreciation of the Parties. Equally, it is not the case that if the equidistance principle is not a rule of law, there has to be as an alternative some other single equivalent rule.

84. As already indicated, the Court * * * has to indicate to the Parties the principles and rules of law in the light of which the methods for eventually effecting the delimitation will have to be chosen. The Court will discharge this task in such a way as to provide the Parties with the requisite directions, without substituting itself for them by means of a detailed indication of the methods to be followed and the factors to be taken into account for the purposes of a delimitation the carrying out of which the Parties have expressly reserved to themselves.

85. It emerges from the history of the development of the legal régime of the continental shelf, which has been reviewed earlier, that the essential reason why the equidistance method is not to be regarded as a rule of law is that, if it were to be compulsorily applied in all situations, this would not be consonant with certain basic legal notions which, as has been observed in paragraphs 48 and 55, have from the beginning reflected the *opinio juris* in the matter of delimitation; those principles being that delimitation must be the object of agreement between the States concerned, and that such agreement must be arrived at in accordance with equitable principles. On a foundation of very general precepts of justice and good faith, actual rules of law are here involved which govern the delimitation of adjacent continental shelves—that is to say, rules binding upon State for all delimitations;—in short, it is not a question of applying equity simply as a matter of abstract justice, but of applying a rule of law which itself requires the application of equitable principles, in accordance with the ideas which have always underlain the development of the legal régime of the continental shelf in this field, namely:

(*a*) the parties are under an obligation to enter into negotiations with a view to arriving at an agreement, and not merely to go through a formal process of negotiation as a sort of prior condition for the automatic application of a certain method of delimitation in the absence of agreement; they are under an obligation so to conduct themselves that the negotiations are meaningful, which will not be the case when either of them insists upon its own position without contemplating any modification of it;

(*b*) the parties are under an obligation to act in such a way that, in the particular case, and taking all the circumstances into account, equitable principles are applied,—for this purpose the equidistance method can be used, but other methods exist and may be employed, alone or in combination, according to the areas involved;

(*c*) * * * the continental shelf of any State must be the natural prolongation of its land territory and must not encroach upon what is the natural prolongation of the territory of another State. * * *

88. The Court comes next to the rule of equity. The legal basis of that rule in the particular case of the delimitation of the continental shelf as between adjoining States has already been stated. It must however be noted that the rule rests also on a broader basis. Whatever the legal reasoning of a court of justice, its decisions must by definition be just, and therefore in that sense equitable. Nevertheless, when mention is made of a court dispensing justice or declaring the law, what is meant is that the decision finds its objective justification in considerations lying not outside but within the rules, and in this field it is precisely a rule of law that calls for the application of equitable principles. There is consequently no question in this case of any decision *ex aequo et bono*, such as would only be possible under the conditions prescribed by Article 38, paragraph 2, of the Court's Statute. * * *

89. It must next be observed that, in certain geographical circumstances which are quite frequently met with, the equidistance method, despite its known advantages, leads unquestionably to inequity, in the following sense:

(*a*) The slightest irregularity in a coastline is automatically magnified by the equidistance line as regards the consequences for the delimitation of the continental shelf. Thus it has been seen in the case of concave or convex coastlines that if the equidistance method is employed, then the greater the irregularity and the further from the coastline the area to be delimited, the more unreasonable are the results produced. So great an exaggeration of the consequences of a natural geographical feature must be remedied or compensated for as far as possible, being of itself creative of inequity.

(*b*) In the case of the North Sea in particular, where there is no outer boundary to the continental shelf, it happens that the claims of several States converge, meet and intercross in localities where, despite their distance from the coast, the bed of the sea still unquestionably consists of continental shelf. A study of these convergences, as revealed by the maps, shows how inequitable would be the apparent simplification brought about by a delimitation which, ignoring such geographical circumstances, was based solely on the equidistance method. * * *

91. Equity does not necessarily imply equality. There can never be any question of completely refashioning nature, and equity does not require that a State without access to the sea should be allotted an area of continental shelf, any more than there could be a question of rendering the situation of a State with an extensive coastline similar to that of a State with a restricted coastline. Equality is to be reckoned within the same plane, and it is not such natural inequalities as these that equity could remedy. But in the present case there are three States whose North Sea coastlines are in fact comparable in length and which, therefore, have been given broadly equal treatment by nature except that the configuration of one of the coastlines would, if the equidistance method is used, deny to one of these States treatment equal or comparable to that given the other two. Here indeed is a case where, in a theoretical situation of equality within the same order, an inequity is created. What is unacceptable in this instance is that a State should enjoy continental shelf rights considerably different from those of its neighbours merely because in the one case the coastline is roughly convex in form and in the other it is markedly concave, although those coastlines are comparable in length. It is therefore not a question of totally refashioning geography whatever the facts of the situation but, given a geographical situation of quasi-equality as between a number of States, of abating the effects of an incidental special feature from which an unjustifiable difference of treatment could result. * * *

101. For these reasons,

THE COURT,

by eleven votes to six,

finds that, in each case,

(A) the use of the equidistance method of delimitation not being obligatory as between the Parties; and

(B) there being no other single method of delimitation the use of which is in all circumstances obligatory;

(C) the principles and rules of international law applicable to the delimitation as between the Parties of the areas of the continental shelf in the North Sea which appertain to each of them beyond the partial boundary determined by the agreements of 1 December 1964 and 9 June 1965, respectively, are as follows:

(1) delimitation is to be effected by agreement in accordance with equitable principles, and taking account of all the relevant circumstances, in such a way as to leave as much as possible to each Party all those parts of the continental shelf that constitute a natural prolongation of its land territory into and under the sea, without encroachment on the natural prolongation of the land territory of the other;

(2) if, in the application of the preceding sub-paragraph, the delimitation leaves to the Parties areas that overlap, these are to be divided between them in agreed proportions or, failing agreement, equally, unless they decide on a régime of joint jurisdiction, user, or exploitation for the zones of overlap or any part of them;

(D) in the course of the negotiations, the factors to be taken into account are to include:

(1) the general configuration of the coasts of the Parties, as well as the presence of any special or unusual features;

(2) so far as known or readily ascertainable, the physical and geological structure, and natural resources, of the continental shelf areas involved;

(3) the element of a reasonable degree of proportionality, which a delimitation carried out in accordance with equitable principles ought to bring about between the extent of the continental shelf areas appertaining to the coastal State and the length of its coast measured in the general direction of the coastline, account being taken for this purpose of the effects, actual or prospective, of any other continental shelf delimitations between adjacent States in the same region.

NOTES AND QUESTIONS

1. *A Hierarchy of Sources?* The *North Sea* judgment provides an excellent resume of the sources of international law, beginning with treaties, moving to custom, and finishing with equity. Did the ICJ's ordering of the sources reflect a necessary hierarchy of the sources of international law, *i.e.*, do treaties necessarily "trump" custom, which in turn "trumps" equity? Did the Court also implicitly invoke general principles of law when it addressed estoppel (paragraph 30) or "very general precepts of justice and good faith" (paragraph 85)? If so, would treaties and custom necessarily trump such general principles? Note too the Court's willingness to consider, in paragraphs 37 and 55, arguments based not on positive law, but on the "more fundamentalist" view that principles of general international law governing delimitation might be derived, as a matter of "juristic inevitability," from "the natural law of the continental shelf." Where would such general international law fit in a hierarchy of sources?

Pay special attention to the Court's detailed analysis of the ways in which customary international law might relate to Article 6(2) of the 1958

Continental Shelf Convention. The three-step process went: the Convention might (1) "embody" or codify the custom, (2) "crystallize" the custom, or (3) contribute to the subsequent development of the custom. Was the Court's rejection of possibility (3) as persuasive as its rejection of (1) and (2)? Looking at *North Sea*, Professor Schachter pointed out that a new treaty might not only itself contribute to the development of custom but might also generate complying practice that contributed to custom. Oscar Schachter, "Entangled Treaty and Custom," in *International Law at a Time of Perplexity* 717, 723–29 (Yoram Dinstein ed. 1989).

2. *The Gap Problem and Judicial Law-making.* What were the perils if the ICJ simply came up empty handed in its search for an applicable rule? Was the Court willing to rule that international law provides no guidance for Germany, Denmark, and the Netherlands? Would such a finding of a *lacuna* or gap have fulfilled the expectations of the three countries when they entrusted the dispute to the Court? Did the parties expect that the ICJ would help in ways that diplomatic negotiations had not?

Was it the expectation of the parties that the ICJ would make new international law? Professor Cassese wrote: "Whenever an international court or tribunal applies equity, it creates law between the parties in dispute." Antonio Cassese, *International Law* 155 (2001). Looking at the judicial reasoning in *Cayuga Indians*, *Meuse*, and *North Sea*, do you agree?

3. *The Recourse to Equity in* North Sea. Compare the source of equitable principles to the source of such principles in *Meuse*. *North Sea* showed no borrowing from municipal legal systems. Where then did the equitable rule come from? Did it really emerge from customary international law, as the Court seemed to suggest by its reference to *opinio juris* in paragraph 85? Did the Court cite sufficient evidence of state practice?

Note that the ICJ was asked to decide what "principles and rules of international law" were applicable to the delimitation of continental shelf between West Germany and Denmark, and between West Germany and the Netherlands. Could the parties have asked the Court to decide the case *ex aequo et bono* pursuant to Article 38(2) of the ICJ Statute? What extra power would the Court have had in *North Sea* if it had an *ex aequo et bono* authorization?

4. *Article 38(1)(d) of the ICJ Statute.* Once rendered, the *North Sea* judgment became part of the corpus of evidence of international law. Could other courts deciding continental shelf cases rely on *North Sea* as a subsidiary source of international law per Article 38(1)(d)? How would a subsequent delimitation case differ then from *North Sea*, especially if the countries affected by the judgment were to adopt it without protest? Can the ICJ's exercise of discretion be a doubtful exercise yet still provide a sound foundation for subsequent practice?

The work of respected scholars may, like judicial opinions, be used "as subsidiary means for the determination of rules of law" under Article 38(1)(d). Recall Justice Gray's reference in *Paquete Habana*, the first case in this chapter, to evidence of "the customs and usages of civilized nations" found by consulting "the works of jurists and commentators, who by years of labor, research and experience, have made themselves peculiarly well acquainted with the subjects of which they treat." Is collaborative work by groups of international legal experts particularly influential? In Chapter 2 and Chapter 6 we consider the International Law Commission's contributions to the law of treaties and the law of state responsibility; the ILC has studied and drafted reports on many other topics as well. Reports prepared by committees of the non-governmental International Law Association typically contain extensive information about state practice supporting analyses of international law rules. The two-volume *Customary International Humanitarian Law* (Jean-Marie Henckaerts & Louise Doswald-Beck eds. 2005), prepared by the International Committee on the Red Cross, and the *San Remo Manual on International Law Applicable to Armed Conflicts at Sea* (Louise Doswald-Beck ed. 1995), the work product of experts convened by the International Institute of Humanitarian Law, are examples of thorough collaborative studies.

5. *The Content of Equitable Principles.* What principles of equity did the Court use in *North Sea*? If it would be inequitable to give comparable coastlines different allotments of continental shelf, why was it equitable to deprive land-locked countries of all continental shelf belonging to their continent? Why was this a better kind of equity than one based on equidistance or on population, economic need, or use?

In a subsequent maritime delimitation case, the ICJ observed: "Equity as a legal concept is a direct emanation of the idea of justice." Tunisia/Libya Continental Shelf Case, 1982 I.C.J. 18, 60. Does this simply beg the question about how one determines the content of an equitable rule? Does the substance of the equitable principle in *North Sea* ultimately depend solely on judicial discretion? As it was said of English equity, does an equitable result depend only on the length of the Chancellor's shoe?

6. *The Need to Delimit the Continental Shelf.* Note the geographical elements of the problem as sketched in Map 3. Because of the indentation of the German shore, delimitation by the equidistance method bent the line along the route D–E–B. Germany preferred D–F–B. Why had it not been important to delimit the shelf prior to the 1960's? See Chapter 10 for further discussion of the continental shelf.

7. *Different Meanings of Equity.* Note the use of equity in the Charter of Economic Rights and Duties of States considered by Professor Dupuy in the *Texaco/Libya Arbitration.* There are at least 12 references to equity in the Charter: "the development of international economic relations on a just and equitable basis," "a new system of international economic relations based on equity, sovereign equality, and interdependence of the interests of developed and developing countries," a "new international economic order, based on equity," "equitable benefits for all peace-loving states," "a just and equitable economic and social order," "more rational and equitable international economic relations," "mutual and equitable benefit" (twice),

"remunerative and equitable prices," "equitable development of the world economy," "share equitably," and "stable, equitable and remunerative prices for primary products." What did these references to equity mean? Were the meanings all the same? Compare the use of "equity" in promoting the New International Economic Order with its use in international arbitral and judicial decisions like *Cayuga Indians*, *Meuse*, and *North Sea*.

8. *The Parties' Delimitation of the North Sea Continental Shelf*. The *North Sea* judgment left Germany, Denmark, and the Netherlands to agree on the delimitation of the continental shelf taking into account the Court's statement of applicable equitable principles; the Court itself was not asked to draw maritime boundaries for the parties, as was true in some later cases. See, *e.g.*, Maritime Delimitation in the Area between Greenland and Jan Mayen, 1993 I.C.J. 38. The parties eventually negotiated a division of the continental shelf that gave Germany more area than it would have had using just the equidistance method. See Figure 3.C; Agreements Delimiting the Continental Shelf in the North Sea, Jan. 28, 1971, 10 *International Legal Materials* 600 (1971).

Figure 3.C

Negotiated Boundaries Following the Decision in the *North Sea Continental Shelf Cases*

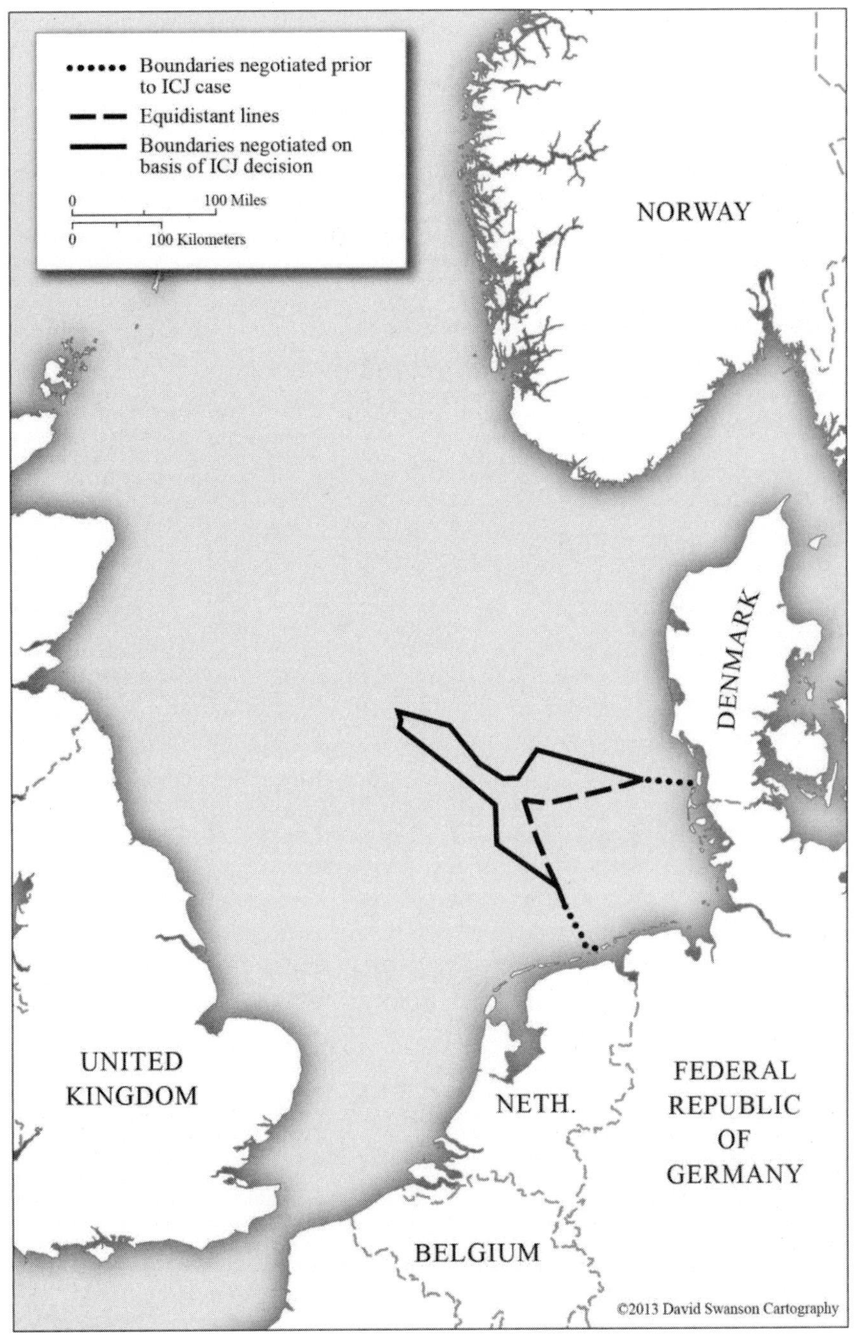

CHAPTER 4

INTERNATIONAL LAW AND MUNICIPAL LAW

■ ■ ■

In most instances, when international legal rules are applied in practice, they are applied by municipal courts. Decisions about whether international legal rules are available as domestic rules of decision, *i.e.*, about the "incorporation" of international law into domestic legal process, are ordinarily made by municipal legal systems. Those decisions are generally governed by the municipal legal system's own constitutional law.

In this chapter, we look only at the constitutional rules governing the incorporation of international law into U.S. law. Such rules about incorporation are easily grouped into those involving treaties and those concerning all other forms of international law, a category traditionally called, in England and America, "the law of nations."

A. TREATIES AND THE CONSTITUTION

As we noted in our discussion of the 1783 Peace of Paris in Chapter 2, one of the principal reasons why the United States abandoned the Articles of Confederation for the Constitution of 1787 was the failure of the several states to honor their treaty obligations to the United Kingdom. Accordingly, the new Constitution made explicit provision for the national enforcement of treaty obligations, notably including U.S. treaties within the Constitution's Article VI's Supremacy Clause. Our first case below, *Ware v. Hylton* from 1796, saw the Supreme Court enforcing the Supremacy Clause against a recalcitrant Virginia.

WARE V. HYLTON

3 U.S. (3 Dall.) 199 (1796)

Chase, Justice—The Defendants in error [Hylton and Eppes], on the [7th] day of July, 1774, passed their penal bond to Farrell & Jones [now their administrator, Ware], for the payment of £2,976 11s 6d, of good British money. * * *

On the 20th of October, 1777, the legislature of the commonwealth of Virginia, passed a law to sequester British property. In the 3d section of the law, it was enacted, "that it should be lawful for any citizen of

Virginia, owing money to a subject of Great Britain, to pay the same, or any part thereof, from time to time, as he should think fit, into the loan office, taking thereout a certificate for the same, in the name of the creditor, with an endorsement, under the hand of the commissioner of the said office, expressing the name of the payer; and shall deliver such certificate to the governor and the council, whose receipt shall discharge him from so much of the debt. And the governor and the council shall, in like manner, lay before the General Assembly, once in every year, an account of these certificates, specifying the names of the persons by, and for whom they were paid; and shall see to the safe keeping of the same; subject to the future directions of the legislature; provided, that the governor and the council may make such allowance, as they shall think reasonable, out of the interest of the money so paid into the loan office, to the wives and children, residing in the state, of such creditor."

On the 26th of April, 1780, the Defendants in error, paid into the loan office of Virginia, part of their debt, to wit, 3,111 1/9 dollars, equal to £933 14s 0d Virginia currency; and obtained a certificate from the commissioners of the loan office, and a receipt from the governor [Thomas Jefferson] and the council of Virginia, agreeably to the above, in part recited law.

The Defendants in error being sued, on the above bond, in the Circuit Court of Virginia, pleaded the above law, and the payment above stated, in bar of so much of the Plaintiff's debt. The plaintiff, to avoid this bar, replied the fourth article of the Definitive Treaty of Peace, between Great Britain and the United States, of the 3rd September, 1783. To this replication there was a general demurrer and joinder. The circuit court allowed the demurrer, and the plaintiff brought the present writ of error.

The case is of very great importance, not only from the property that depends on the decision, but because the effect and operation of the treaty are necessarily involved. * * *

It appears to me that the plea, by the Defendant, of the act of Assembly, and the payment agreeably to its provisions, which is admitted, is a bar to the plaintiff's action, for so much of his debt as he paid into the loan office; unless the plea is avoided, or destroyed, by the Plaintiff's replication of the fourth article of the Definitive Treaty of Peace, between Great Britain and the United States on the 3rd September, 1783.

The question then may be stated thus: Whether the 4th article of the said treaty nullifies the law of Virginia, passed on the 20th of October, 1777; destroys the payment made under it; and revives the debt, and gives a right of recovery thereof, against the original debtor?

It was doubted by one of the counsel for the Defendants in error (Mr. [John] Marshall) whether Congress had a power to make a treaty, that could operate to annul a legislative act of any of the states, and to destroy rights acquired by, or vested in individuals, in virtue of such acts. Another of the Defendant's counsel (Mr. Campbell) expressly, and with great zeal, denied that Congress possessed such power.

But a few remarks will be necessary to show the inadmissibility of this objection to the power of Congress.

1st. The legislatures of all the states, have often exercised the power of taking the property of its citizens for the use of the public, but they uniformly compensated the proprietors. The principle to maintain this right is for the public good, and to that the interest of individuals must yield. The instances are many, and among them are lands taken for forts, magazines, or arsenals; or for public roads, or canals; or to erect towns.

2nd. The legislatures of all the states have often exercised the power of divesting rights vested; and even of impairing, and, in some instances, of almost annihilating the obligation of contracts, as by tender laws, which made an offer to pay, and a refusal to receive, paper money, for a specie debt, an extinguishment, to the amount tendered.

3rd. If the Legislature of Virginia could, by a law, annul any former law; I apprehend that the effect would be to destroy all rights acquired under the law so nullified.

4th. If the Legislature of Virginia could not by ordinary acts of legislation, do these things, yet possessing the supreme sovereign power of the state, she certainly could do them, by a treaty of peace; if she had not parted with the power or making such treaty. If Virginia had such power before she delegated it to Congress, it follows, that afterwards, that body possessed it. Whether Virginia parted with the power of making treaties of peace, will be seen by a perusal of the ninth article of the Confederation (ratified by all the states on the 1st of March, 1781), in which it was declared, That "the United States in Congress assembled, shall have the sole and exclusive right and power of determining on peace, or war, except in the two cases mentioned in the 6th article; and of entering into treaties and alliances, with a proviso, when made, respecting commerce." This grant has no restriction, nor is there any limitation on the power in any part of the confederation. A right to make peace, necessarily includes the power of determining on what terms peace shall be made. A power to make treaties must of necessity imply a power, to decide the terms on which they shall be made. A war between two nations can only be concluded by treaty.

Surely, the sacrificing public, or private, property, to obtain peace cannot be the cases in which a treaty would be void. Vatt. lib.2 c. 12.s.160. 161. p. 173. lib. 6. c.2.s. 2. It seems to me that treaties made by Congress, according to the Confederation, were superior to the laws of the states, because the Confederation made them obligatory on all the states. They were so declared by Congress on the 13th of April, 1787; were so admitted by the legislatures and executives of most of the states; and were so decided by the judiciary of the general government, and by the judiciaries of some of the state governments.

If doubts could exist before the establishment of the present national government, they must be entirely removed by the 6th article of the Constitution, which provides "That all treaties made, or which shall be made under the authority of the United States, shall be the supreme law of the land; and the Judges in every State shall be bound thereby, anything in the Constitution or laws, of any state to the contrary notwithstanding." There can be no limitation on the power of the people of the United States. By their authority, the state constitutions were made, and by their authority the Constitution of the United States was established: and they had the power to change or abolish the State Constitutions, or to make them yield to the general government, and to treaties made by their authority. A treaty cannot be the Supreme law of the land, that is of all the United States, if any act of a State Legislature can stand in its way. If the Constitution of a State (which is the fundamental law of the State, and paramount to its Legislature) must give way to a treaty, and fall before it; can it be questioned, whether the less power, an act of the State Legislature, must not be prostrate? It is the declared will of the people of the United States that every treaty made, by the authority of the United States, shall be superior to the Constitution and laws of any individual State; and their will alone is to decide. If a law of a State, contrary to a treaty, is not void, but voidable only by a repeal, or nullification by a State Legislature, this certain consequence follows, that the will of a small part of the United States may control or defeat the will of the whole. * * *

On the best investigation I have been able to give the fourth article of the treaty, I cannot conceive, that the wisdom of men could express their meaning in more accurate and intelligible words, or in words more proper and effectual to carry their intention into execution. I am satisfied, that the words, in their natural import, and common use, give a recovery to the British creditor from his original debtor of the debt contracted before the treaty, notwithstanding the payment thereof into the public treasuries, or loan offices, under the authority of any state law; and, therefore, I am of opinion, that the judgment of the circuit court ought to be reversed, and that judgment ought to be given, on the demurrer, for the Plaintiff in error; with the costs in the circuit court, and the costs of the appeal.

NOTES AND QUESTIONS

1. *The Political Importance of* Ware v. Hylton. Remember how difficult it would have been for the New Republic if the Court had found for Virginia:

> [T]he Court had to face the practical situation then existing. * * * The Court knew that the United States must somehow satisfy Great Britain on the subject and the very national existence of the United States might depend upon it. The realism of this becomes apparent when it is recalled that the British had stated that they would not evacuate their troops from the western forts until Article 4 [of the Peace treaty] was actually being carried out.

Willard Bruce Cowles, *Treaties and Constitutional Law: Property Interferences and Due Process of Law* 84 (1941). A judgment unfavorable to the United Kingdom might have even led to war. Michael D. Ramsey, "The Power of the States in Foreign Affairs: The Original Understanding of Foreign Policy Federalism," 75 *Notre Dame Law Review* 341, 422 (1999).

Moreover, "the Justices were surely also aware that Congress had debated this issue in 1794 (after the trial in *Ware* but before the Court's opinion) and had defeated bills to renounce pre-war debts." William N. Eskridge, Jr., "All About Words: Early Understandings of the 'Judicial Power' in Statutory Interpretation, 1776–1806," 101 *Columbia Law Review* 990, 1098 (2001). In deciding *Ware*, the "Court would perhaps never perceive itself to be on firmer ground in enforcing treaties than when enforcing the very treaty whose violation had led to the Constitutional Convention." Tim Wu, "Treaties' Domains," 93 *Virginia Law Review* 571, 606 (2007).

2. *John Marshall and Nationalism. Ware v. Hylton* was the only case where the future Chief Justice, John Marshall, argued before the Supreme Court. It was ironic that he "had to argue a cause [Virginia's] that ran counter to his deeply felt nationalist sentiments." "Editorial Note to Ware, Administrator of Jones, v. Hylton, 1790–1796," in 5 *The Papers of John Marshall* 295, 298–99 (Charles F. Hobson *et al.* eds. 1987). Marshall's legal strategy allowed "him to fulfill his duty to his client without sacrificing his personal view," *i.e.*, by attempting to avoid the Supremacy Clause and instead strive to reconcile the national 1783 treaty and the Virginia state law. *Id.* at 298. Marshall persuaded the circuit court to take this path but not the Supreme Court. Marshall was, of course, a strong nationalist once on the Court, as we see in *Foster & Elam* below.

3. *The Role of Congress in Executing Treaties.* On its face, Article VI's Supremacy Clause addresses issues of American federalism, limiting the powers of the several states, *e.g.*, respecting treaties. But does Article VI also limit the powers of Congress in "executing" treaties? Must Congress always pass implementing legislation for treaties to have authority in domestic law? This was and is the rule in English law. In *Foster v. Neilson* below, Chief Justice John Marshall charted a new course for U.S. constitutional law, with what became the doctrine of "self-executing treaties."

Did *Ware* provide a foundation for the self-executing treaty doctrine? Even Professor Yoo, a critic, admitted that *Ware* "stands as the most authoritative declaration of self-executing treaties from the Framing Period." John C. Yoo, "Globalism and the Constitution: Treaties, Non-Self-Execution, and the Original Understanding," 99 Columbia Law Review 1955, 2079 (1999). Yoo, however, maintained that *Ware* only rejected the powers of Virginia and other states *vis-à-vis* treaties; it did not concern the role of Congress. *Id.* at 2080. Professor Vázquez remarked that Yoo's view—"that treaties can be self-executing [only] if they regulate matters outside Article I['s legislative powers]" is based on "no discernible textual or structured reason" and is unsupported by "subsequent judicial doctrine." Carlos Manuel Vázquez, "Laughing at Treaties," 99 *Columbia Law Review* 2154, 2213–14 (1999). Keep this debate in mind as you read *Foster & Elam* and the other following cases. Is it Yoo or Vázquez who has a better understanding of the importance of *Ware*?

4. *Self-executing Treaties.* Perhaps the most important U.S. constitutional law decision concerning the relationship of international law and U.S. municipal law is *Foster & Elam*, where Chief Justice Marshall introduced the concept, though not the exact term, of "self-executing treaties." Besides noting how and why Chief Justice Marshall employed the concept of self-executing treaties, pay particular attention to why the litigants and the U.S. Supreme Court in *Foster & Elam* needed to know whether the treaty provision in question could serve as a rule of decision. This part also considers cases addressing additional complications to treaty reception introduced in the United States by the doctrines of federalism and separation of powers.

FOSTER & ELAM V. NEILSON

27 U.S. (2 Pet.) 253 (1829)

MR. CHIEF JUSTICE MARSHALL delivered the opinion of the Court.

This suit was brought by the plaintiffs in error [Foster & Elam], in the court of the United States for the eastern district of Louisiana, to recover a tract of land lying in that district, about 30 miles east of the Mississippi, and in the possession of the defendant [Neilson]. The plaintiffs claimed under a grant for 40,000 arpents of land, made by the Spanish governor, on the 2d of January 1804, to Jayme Joydra, and ratified by the king of Spain on the 29th of May 1804. * * * The defendant excepted to the petition of the plaintiffs, alleging that it does not show a title on which they can recover; that the territory within which the land claimed is situated, had been ceded, before the grant, to France, and by France to the United States; and that the grant is void, being made by persons who had no authority to make it. * * *

The case presents this very intricate, and, at one time, very interesting question: To whom did the country between the Iberville and the Perdido rightfully belong, when the title now asserted by the plaintiffs was acquired? This question has been repeatedly discussed, with great talent and research, by the government of the United States and that of Spain. The United States have perseveringly and earnestly insisted, that by the treaty of St. Ildefonso, made on the 1st of October, in the year 1800, Spain ceded the disputed territory, as part of Louisiana, to France; and that France, by the treaty of Paris, signed on the 30th of April 1803, and ratified on the 21st of October, in the same year, ceded it to the United States. Spain has, with equal perseverance and earnestness, maintained, that her cession to France comprehended that territory only which was, at that time, denominated Louisiana, consisting of the island of New Orleans, and the country she received from France, west of the Mississippi.

[Marshall introduces and discusses the complicated negotiations among France, Spain, Great Britain, and the United States over the territory and then suggests that perhaps the Court need not actually answer the question about ownership.]

A "treaty of amity, settlement and limits, between the United States of America and the king of Spain," was signed at Washington, on the 22d day of February 1819. By the second article, "his Catholic majesty cedes to the United States, in full property and sovereignty, all the territories which belong to him, situated to the eastward of the Mississippi, known by the name of East and West Florida." The eighth article stipulates, "that all the grants of land made before the 24th of January 1818, by his Catholic majesty, or by his lawful authorities, in the said territories ceded by his majesty to the United States, shall be ratified and confirmed to the persons in possession of the lands, to the same extent that the same grants would be valid, if the territories had remained under the dominion of his Catholic majesty."

[W]e think, the sound construction of the eighth article will not enable this court to apply its provisions to the present case. The words of the article are, that "all the grants of land, made before the 24 of January 1818, by his Catholic majesty, & c., shall be ratified and confirmed to the persons in possession of the lands, to the same extent that the same grants would be valid, if the territories had remained under the dominion of his Catholic majesty." Do these words act directly on the grants, so as to give validity to those not otherwise valid? Or do they pledge the faith of the United States to pass acts which shall ratify and confirm them?

A treaty is, in its nature, a contract between two nations, not a legislative act. It does not generally effect, of itself, the object to be accomplished; especially, so far as its operation is infra-territorial; but is carried into execution by the sovereign power of the respective parties to the instrument.

Figure 4.A

Southeast United States

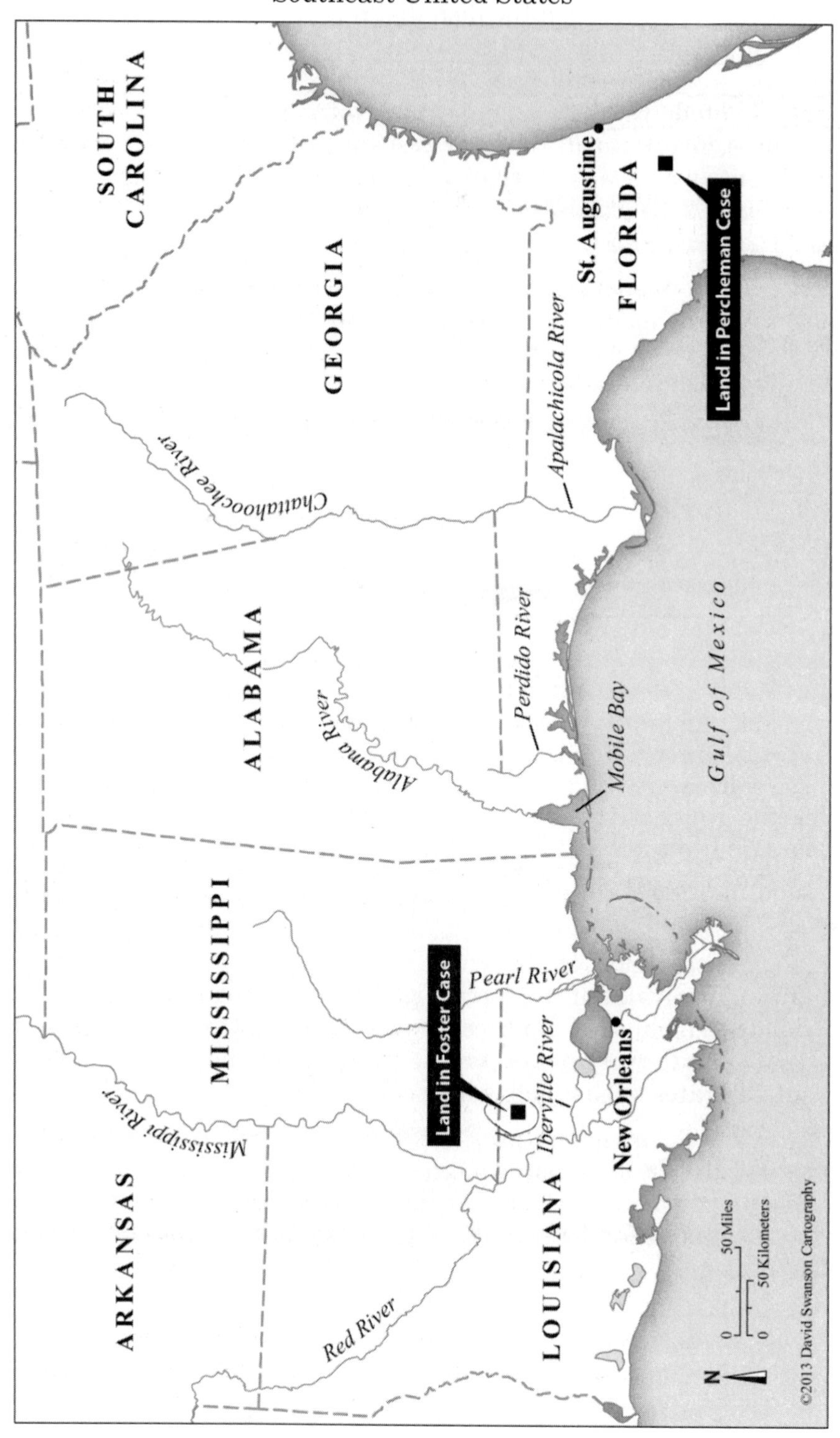

In the United States, a different principle is established. Our constitution declares a treaty to be the law of the land. It is, consequently, to be regarded in courts of justice as equivalent to an act of the legislature, whenever it operates of itself, without the aid of any legislative provision. But when the terms of the stipulation import a contract—when either of the parties engages to perform a particular act, the treaty addresses itself to the political, not the judicial department; and the legislature must execute the contract before it can become a rule for the court.

The article under consideration does not declare that all the grants made by his Catholic majesty, before the 24th of January 1818, shall be valid, to the same extent as if the ceded territories had remained under his dominion. It does not say, that those grants are hereby confirmed. Had such been its language, it would have acted directly on the subject, and would have repealed those acts of congress which were repugnant to it; but its language is, that those grants shall be ratified and confirmed to the persons in possession, &c. By whom shall they be ratified and confirmed? This seems to be the language of contract; and if it is, the ratification and confirmation which are promised must be the act of the legislature. Until such act shall be passed, the court is not at liberty to disregard the existing laws on the subject.

NOTES AND QUESTIONS

1. *The Application of International Law by Municipal Courts*. We have moved from the legislative process of international law—how international legal rules are made—to the discipline's judicial and executive process—who applies the rules of international law and how such decisions are made effective. We begin with municipal courts. The great majority of international law cases that are settled by formal judicial process are decided by domestic not by international courts. For most lawyers practicing international law, domestic law courts are the usual fora foreseen in negotiations and employed in litigation. Here for reasons of space and audience we look only at the municipal practice of the United States. *American International Law Cases* publishes cases in which U.S. state and federal courts have used international law; there are over 7,000 such cases, just from the years 1990–2011.

The overwhelming majority of U.S. court cases involving international law concern treaties; the most important case is *Foster & Elam v. Neilson*. Not only did the case establish the proposition of the "self-executing" treaty in U.S. law, but it introduced the notion into international law generally, making *Foster & Elam* one of the most significant U.S. contributions to the discipline world-wide.

2. *Dualism and Monism*. Note that in *Foster & Elam* Marshall's approach to the nature of international law was fundamentally "dualistic," *i.e.*, he saw international law and municipal law not as parts of an integrated

"monistic" legal system but each as a separate and discrete legal system. Accordingly, rules from one system must be specially incorporated into the other in order that they be applied there. Did Marshall justify this presumption? Did his justification depend either on the idea that treaties are contracts between nations or on the deference that Marshall accorded the sovereign power of states within their own territory?

3. *The Self-executing Nature of the 1819 Treaty of Amity.* That Marshall's approach in *Foster & Elam* was formal, looking at the literal language of the 1819 Treaty of Amity, was confirmed in United States v. Percheman, 32 U.S. (7 Pet.) 51 (1833). In *Percheman*, when Marshall examined the Spanish-language version of the Treaty, he held that the selfsame Article 8 of the 1819 Treaty was in truth self-executing. However, unlike the land at issue in *Foster & Elam*, which was located "between the Iberville and the Perdido" rivers, the land that Percheman claimed under an 1815 Spanish grant was located east of the Perdido, in present-day Florida, territory unambiguously outside the area of the Louisiana Purchase. Other means of determining self-execution or not are explored in many of the cases below.

4. *Treaties and the Supremacy Clause.* Although Chief Justice Marshall did not find the 1819 Treaty of Amity to be self-executing in *Foster & Elam*, he laid the foundations for the doctrine of self-executing treaties in U.S. law by relying on Article VI(2) of the Constitution, the Supremacy Clause:

> This Constitution, and the laws of the United States which shall be made in Pursuance thereof; and all Treaties made, or which shall be made, under the Authority of the United States, shall be the supreme law of the land; and the Judges in every State shall be bound thereby, any thing in the Constitution or Laws of any State to the contrary notwithstanding.

Note that the wording of the Supremacy Clause hints that the Founders' central concern was to bind the judges of the states to uphold the U.S. Constitution, federal laws, and U.S. treaties *vis-à-vis* state laws and constitutions, just the issue in *Ware v. Hylton* above. *Foster & Elam* involved, but avoided, a potential clash between a U.S. treaty and federal law; the U.S. Congress in 1804 had nullified Spanish land grants in the location of the land at issue in *Foster*, and in 1812 had admitted the state of Louisiana into the Union. We examine both kinds of conflicts below: first, clashes involving state law—*Asakura, Sei Fujii, Missouri v. Holland,* and *Medellín*—and, second, conflicts involving national law and institutions—*Whitney, Belmont, Curtiss-Wright,* and *Dames & Moore*. As you read these cases, reflect on how U.S. constitutional law, particularly its complex principles of self-execution, federalism, and separation of powers, often makes it difficult to predict the outcome of treaty-related controversies.

ASAKURA V. CITY OF SEATTLE

265 U.S. 332 (1924)

MR. JUSTICE BUTLER delivered the opinion of the Court.

Plaintiff in error is a subject of the Emperor of Japan, and, since 1904, has resided in Seattle, Washington. Since July, 1915, he has been engaged in business there as a pawnbroker. The city passed an ordinance, which took effect July 2, 1921, regulating the business of pawnbroker and repealing former ordinances on the same subject. It makes it unlawful for any person to engage in the business unless he shall have a license, and the ordinance provides "that no such license shall be granted unless the applicant be a citizen of the United States." Violations of the ordinance are punishable by fine or imprisonment or both. Plaintiff in error brought this suit in the Superior Court of King County, Washington, against the city, its Comptroller and its Chief of Police to restrain them from enforcing the ordinance against him. He attacked the ordinance on the ground that it violates the treaty between the United States and the Empire of Japan, proclaimed April 5, 1911, 37 Stat. 1504; violates the constitution of the State of Washington, and also the due process and equal protection clauses of the Fourteenth Amendment of the Constitution of the United States. He declared his willingness to comply with any valid ordinance related to the business of pawnbroker. It was shown that he had about $5,000 invested in his business, which would be broken up and destroyed by the enforcement of the ordinance. The Superior Court granted the relief prayed. On appeal, the Supreme Court of the State held the ordinance valid and reversed the decree. The case is here on writ of error[.]

Does the ordinance violate the treaty? Plaintiff in error invokes and relies upon the following provisions: "The citizens or subjects of each of the High Contracting Parties shall have liberty to enter, travel and reside in the territories of the other to carry on trade, wholesale and retail, to own or lease and occupy houses, manufactories, warehouses and shops, to employ agents of their choice, to lease land for residential and commercial purposes, and generally to do anything incident to or necessary for trade upon the same terms as native citizens or subjects, submitting themselves to the laws and regulations there established. . . . The citizens or subjects of each . . . shall receive, in the territories of the other, the most constant protection and security for their persons and property. . . ."

A treaty made under the authority of the United States "shall be the supreme law of the land; and the judges in every State shall be bound thereby, any thing in the constitution or laws of any State to the contrary notwithstanding." Constitution, Art. VI, § 2.

The treaty-making power of the United States is not limited by any express provision of the Constitution, and, though it does not extend "so far as to authorize what the Constitution forbids," it does extend to all proper subjects of negotiation between our government and other nations. The treaty was made to strengthen friendly relations between the two nations. As to the things covered by it, the provision quoted establishes the rule of equality between Japanese subjects while in this country and native citizens. Treaties for the protection of citizens of one country residing in the territory of another are numerous, and make for good understanding between nations. The treaty is binding within the State of Washington. The rule of equality established by it cannot be rendered nugatory in any part of the United States by municipal ordinances or state laws. It stands on the same footing of supremacy as do the provisions of the Constitution and laws of the United States. It operates of itself without the aid of any legislation, state or national; and it will be applied and given authoritative effect by the courts.

The purpose of the ordinance complained of is to regulate, not to prohibit, the business of pawnbroker. But it makes it impossible for aliens to carry on the business. It need not be considered whether the State, if it sees fit, may forbid and destroy the business generally. Such a law would apply equally to aliens and citizens, and no question of conflict with the treaty would arise. The grievance here alleged is that plaintiff in error, in violation of the treaty, is denied equal opportunity. * * *

By definition contained in the ordinance, pawnbrokers are regarded as carrying on a "business." A feature of it is the lending of money upon the pledge or pawn of personal property which, in case of default, may be sold to pay the debt. While the amounts of the loans made in that business are relatively small and the character of property pledged as security is different, the transactions are similar to loans made by banks on collateral security. * * * We have found no state legislation abolishing or forbidding the business. Most, if not all, of the States provide for licensing pawnbrokers and authorize regulation by municipalities. While regulation has been found necessary in the public interest, the business is not on that account to be excluded from the trade and commerce referred to in the treaty. Many worthy occupations and lines of legitimate business are regulated by state and federal laws for the protection of the public against fraudulent and dishonest practices. There is nothing in the character of the business of pawnbroker which requires it to be excluded from the field covered by the above quoted provision, and it must be held that such business is "trade" within the meaning of the treaty. The ordinance violates the treaty. The question in the present case relates solely to Japanese subjects who have been admitted to this country. We do not pass upon the right of admission or the construction of the treaty in this respect, as that question is not before us and would require consideration of other matters with which it is not now necessary to deal. We need not consider other grounds upon which the ordinance is attacked.

Decree reversed.

NOTES AND QUESTIONS

1. *Treaties and State Law. Asakura* is an example of a state law being "trumped" by a U.S. treaty rule. The case cited *Foster & Elam* for the proposition that a treaty "operates of itself without the aid of any legislation, state or national; and it will be applied and given authoritative effect by the Courts." But did the *Asakura* Court analyze the problem of self-execution? Was it plain that the treaty norm applied in *Asakura* was self-executing by the test set out in *Foster & Elam*? What arguments might be made for and against it being self-executing?

2. *The* Asakura Case *and U.S.-Japanese Relations. Asakura* was decided at a time when U.S. politics were increasingly hostile to Japanese immigration to the United States. Despite opposition from Japan and from the U.S. State Department, the House and Senate overwhelmingly passed legislation in 1924 that barred Japanese nationals from settling in the United States. The anti-Japanese bill passed the House 326–71 and the Senate 62–6. The Japanese Ambassador warned that the bill "would seriously wound the proper susceptibilities of the Japanese nation" and could endanger "the otherwise happy and mutually advantageous relations existing between our two countries." "Immigration Bill Is Passed Intact, Barring Japanese," *New York Times*, Apr. 13, 1924, at 1; "Immigration Bill Passes the Senate by Vote of 62 to 6," *New York Times*, Apr. 19, 1924, at 1.

U.S.-Japanese relations only worsened. In July 1937, Japan invaded China. As one measure of protest, the United States served notice on July 26, 1939, that the U.S.-Japanese Treaty of Commerce and Navigation, at issue in *Asakura*, would be terminated in six months, permitting the United States, *inter alia*, to restrict U.S. exports to and imports from Japan. Herbert Feis, *The Road to Pearl Harbor* 8, 21–23 (1965). On December 7, 1941, the Japanese Navy launched a devastating surprise attack on the U.S. naval base at Pearl Harbor, an act of aggression that united the formerly neutrality-prone U.S. House and Senate with President Roosevelt, and the United States declared war on Japan. Anti-Japanese sentiment remained strong in the United States after the end of the Second World War in 1945, as witnessed by the next case, *Sei Fujii*. The California Supreme Court was no longer bound, of course, by the now-repudiated 1911 friendship, commerce, and navigation treaty applied by the U.S. Supreme Court in *Asakura*.

SEI FUJII V. CALIFORNIA

38 Cal.2d 718, 242 P.2d 617 (1952)

GIBSON, CHIEF JUSTICE.

Plaintiff, an alien Japanese who is ineligible to citizenship under our naturalization laws, appeals from a judgment declaring that certain land purchased by him in 1948 had escheated to the state. There is no treaty between this country and Japan which confers upon plaintiff the right to own land, and the sole question presented on this appeal is the validity of the California alien land law.

UNITED NATIONS CHARTER

It is first contended that the land law has been invalidated and superseded by the provisions of the United Nations Charter pledging the member nations to promote the observance of human rights and fundamental freedoms without distinction as to race. Plaintiff relies on statements in the preamble and in articles 1, 55 and 56 of the Charter.

It is not disputed that the charter is a treaty, and our federal Constitution provides that treaties made under the authority of the United States are part of the supreme law of the land and that the judges in every state are bound thereby. U.S. Const., art. VI. A treaty, however, does not automatically supersede local laws which are inconsistent with it unless the treaty provisions are self-executing. In the words of Chief Justice Marshall: A treaty is "to be regarded in courts of justice as equivalent to an act of the Legislature, whenever it operates of itself, without the aid of any legislative provision. But when the terms of the stipulation import a contract—when either of the parties engages to perform a particular act, the treaty addresses itself to the political, not the judicial department; and the Legislature must execute the contract, before it can become a rule for the court." Foster v. Neilson, 1829, 2 Pet. (U.S.) 253.

In determining whether a treaty is self-executing courts look to the intent of the signatory parties as manifested by the language of the instrument, and, if the instrument is uncertain, recourse may be had to the circumstances surrounding its execution. * * *

In order for a treaty provision to be operative without the aid of implementing legislation and to have the force and effect of a statute, it must appear that the framers of the treaty intended to prescribe a rule that, standing alone, would be enforceable in the courts. * * *

It is clear that the provisions of the preamble and of Article 1 of the charter which are claimed to be in conflict with the alien land law are not self-executing. They state general purposes and objectives of the United Nations Organization and do not purport to impose legal obligations on the individual member nations or to create rights in private persons. It is equally clear that none of the other provisions relied on by plaintiff is self-executing. Article 55 declares that the United Nations "shall promote: * * * universal respect for, and observance of, human rights and fundamental freedoms for all without distinction as to race, sex, language, or religion," and in Article 56, the member nations "pledge themselves to take joint and separate action in cooperation with the

Organization for the achievement of the purposes set forth in Article 55." Although the member nations have obligated themselves to cooperate with the international organization in promoting respect for, and observance of, human rights, it is plain that it was contemplated that future legislative action by the several nations would be required to accomplish the declared objectives, and there is nothing to indicate that these provisions were intended to become rules of law for the courts of this country upon the ratification of the charter.

The language used in articles 55 and 56 is not the type customarily employed in treaties which have been held to be self-executing and to create rights and duties in individuals. For example, the treaty involved in Clark v. Allen, 331 U.S. 503, 507–508, relating to the rights of a national of one country to inherit real property located in another country, specifically provided that "such national shall be allowed a term of three years in which to sell the [property] . . . and withdraw the proceeds . . ." free from any discriminatory taxation. In Nielsen v. Johnson, 279 U.S. 47, 50, the provision treated as being self-executing was equally definite. There each of the signatory parties agreed that "no higher or other duties, charges, or taxes of any kind, shall be levied" by one country on removal of property therefrom by citizens of the other country "than are or shall be payable in each state, upon the same, when removed by a citizen or subject of such state respectively." In other instances treaty provisions were enforced without implementing legislation where they prescribed in detail the rules governing rights and obligations of individuals or specifically provided that citizens of one nation shall have the same rights while in the other country as are enjoyed by that country's own citizens. * * * Asakura v. Seattle, 265 U.S. 332, 340[.]

It is significant to note that when the framers of the charter intended to make certain provisions effective without the aid of implementing legislation they employed language which is clear and definite and manifests that intention. For example, Article 104 provides: "The Organization shall enjoy in the territory of each of its Members such legal capacity as may be necessary for the exercise of its functions and the fulfillment of its purposes." Article 105 provides: "1. The Organization shall enjoy in the territory of each of its Members such privileges and immunities as are necessary for the fulfillment of its purposes. 2. Representatives of the Members of the United Nations and officials of the Organization shall similarly enjoy such privileges and immunities as are necessary for the independent exercise of their functions in connection with the Organization." In Curran v. City of New York, 77 N.Y.S.2d 206, 212, these articles were treated as being self-executory.

The provisions in the charter pledging cooperation in promoting observance of fundamental freedoms lack the mandatory quality and definiteness which would indicate an intent to create justiciable rights in private persons immediately upon ratification. Instead, they are framed as a promise of future action by the member nations. Secretary of State Stettinius, Chairman of the United States delegation at the San Francisco Conference where the charter was drafted, stated in his report to President Truman that Article 56 "pledges the various countries to cooperate with the organization by joint and separate action in the achievement of the economic and social objectives of the organization without infringing upon their right to order their national affairs according to their own best ability, in their own way, and in accordance with their own political and economic institutions and processes." * * *

The humane and enlightened objectives of the United Nations Charter are, of course, entitled to respectful consideration by the courts and legislatures of every member nation, since that document expresses the universal desire of thinking men for peace and for equality of rights and opportunities. The charter represents a moral commitment of foremost importance, and we must not permit the spirit of our pledge to be compromised or disparaged in either our domestic or foreign affairs. We are satisfied, however, that the charter provisions relied on by plaintiff were not intended to supersede existing domestic legislation, and we cannot hold that they operate to invalidate the alien land law.

[The court concludes, however, that the California Alien Land Law is invalid, because it violates the 14th Amendment to the U.S. Constitution.]

NOTES AND QUESTIONS

1. *The California Alien Land Law*. The 1920 California Alien Land Law had originally aimed at preventing the ownership of land by Asian nationals. By 1952, however, it affected principally Japanese aliens, since by then nationals of the Philippines, China, and India could effectively seek U.S. naturalization. See Lawrence E. Davies, "California's Law on Land is Upset," *New York Times*, Apr. 18, 1952, at 7.

2. *The Self-executing Treaty Doctrine and the U.N. Charter*. Is it self-evident that the *Sei Fujii* court was correct in holding the U.N. Charter provisions at issue not to be self-executing? The District Court of Appeal of California had found the Charter provisions self-executing. See Sei Fujii v. State, 217 P.2d 481 (Cal.App.1950), *rehearing denied,* 218 P.2d 595 (Cal.App.1950). When treaty provisions concerning individual rights conflict with state legislation, does a better case exist for finding the treaty to be self-executing than when a treaty conflicts with congressional action? Quincy Wright noted that Article 56 of the U.N. Charter imposes obligations on the United States as a party, and that Charter provisions do not prevent U.S. courts from interpreting and enforcing the obligations. Quincy Wright, "National Courts and Human Rights—The Fujii Case," 45 *American Journal of International Law* 62 (1951). The critical question then became, in Wright's

view, whether U.S. obligations under Article 56 were of a character that U.S. courts "can apply." "[C]ommon sense suggests that 'separate action in cooperation with the organization' implies, as a minimum, abstention from separate action, such as enforcement of racially discriminating land laws, which would oppose the purposes of the organization." *Id.* at 72. Wright concluded:

> National courts may not always give a sound interpretation to treaty obligations in respect to human rights, but they are more likely to be guided by general principles than are local legislatures. * * * There is no fundamental reason why the function of incorporating international law into municipal law should be regarded as a legislative rather than a judicial function.

Id. at 80–81. See also Richard Lillich, "Invoking International Human Rights Law in Domestic Courts," 54 *University of Cincinnati Law Review* 367 (1985).

Professor Lockwood surveyed the use of the United Nations Charter in state and federal courts from 1946 to 1955 and found that "the Charter played a significant role in helping American courts find the United States Constitution—to redefine the due process and equal protection clauses of the 14th Amendment and the due process clause of the Fifth Amendment to reflect antiracial discrimination norms central to the Charter." Bert B. Lockwood, Jr., "The United Nations Charter and United States Civil Rights Litigation: 1946–1955," 69 *Iowa Law Review* 901, 902 (1984). Lockwood examined *Sei Fujii* and the seminal U.S. Supreme Court civil rights cases, in which human rights provisions of the Charter were raised but not addressed by the Court, and concluded that the Charter was "an important influence on the judiciary, *sub silentio.*" *Id.* at 949.

How well do U.S. courts do nowadays? Professor Buergenthal argued that the United States lags behind other Western democracies in implementing international treaties protecting human rights. Thomas Buergenthal, "Modern Constitutions and Human Rights Treaties," 36 *Columbia Journal of Transnational Law* 211 (1997). Professor Waters submitted that international human rights treaties play a greater role in U.S. law than one might suspect. Melissa A. Waters, "Creeping Monism: The Judicial Trend Toward Interpretive Incorporation of Human Rights Treaties," 107 *Columbia Law Review* 628 (2007).

3. *Applying the Self-executing Treaty Rule.* If the 1911 treaty analyzed in *Asakura* had been still in force in 1948, would it have conferred upon Sei Fujii the right to own land? Why was the *Sei Fujii* court more concerned than the *Asakura* court to analyze whether a treaty rule, in this case the U.N. Charter, was self-executing?

If the U.S. Senate, in the course of giving its advice and consent to a treaty, expresses an opinion as to whether a treaty is self-executing, should a U.S. court defer to that opinion? Should it defer to a Senate declaration that a treaty is not self-executing if the language of the treaty would otherwise suggest that it is? Should the positions of other countries, expressed during the negotiation of a treaty, be taken into account in determining the incorporation of a treaty into U.S. municipal law?

What position should a U.S. court take if the evidence concerning whether a treaty is self-executing is ambiguous? Should a U.S. court presume that a treaty provision is or is not self-executing? Is the court under an obligation to try to give effect to treaty purposes if the language of the treaty can be read both ways? See the judicial debate in *Medellín* below.

4. *Treaties and State Law.* A treaty "trumps" state law only when the treaty provision is incorporated in U.S. law either because it is self-executing or because it has been implemented by congressional legislation. In *Missouri v. Holland*, which follows, the Supreme Court did not need to address the self-executing treaty doctrine because Congress had passed a statute implementing the treaty at issue.

MISSOURI V. HOLLAND

252 U.S. 416 (1920)

MR. JUSTICE HOLMES delivered the opinion of the court.

This is a bill in equity brought by the State of Missouri to prevent a game warden of the United States from attempting to enforce the Migratory Bird Treaty Act of July 3, 1918, c. 128, 40 Stat. 755, and the regulations made by the Secretary of Agriculture in pursuance of the same. The ground of the bill is that the statute is an unconstitutional interference with the rights reserved to the States by the Tenth Amendment, and that the acts of the defendant done and threatened under that authority invade the sovereign right of the State and contravene its will manifested in statutes. * * *

On December 8, 1916, a treaty between the United States and Great Britain was proclaimed by the President. It recited that many species of birds in their annual migrations traversed certain parts of the United States and of Canada, that they were of great value as a source of food and in destroying insects injurious to vegetation, but were in danger of extermination through lack of adequate protection. It therefore provided for specified close seasons and protection in other forms, and agreed that the two powers would take or propose to their law-making bodies the necessary measures for carrying the treaty out. The above mentioned Act of July 3, 1918, entitled an act to give effect to the convention, prohibited the killing, capturing or selling any of the migratory birds included in the terms of the treaty except as permitted by regulations compatible with those terms, to be made by the Secretary of Agriculture. Regulations were proclaimed on July 31, and October 25, 1918. It is unnecessary to go into any details, because, as we have said, the question raised is the general one whether the treaty and statute are void as an interference with the rights reserved to the States.

To answer this question it is not enough to refer to the Tenth Amendment, reserving the powers not delegated to the United States, because by Article II, § 2, the power to make treaties is delegated expressly, and by Article VI treaties made under the authority of the United States, along with the Constitution and laws of the United States made in pursuance thereof, are declared the supreme law of the land. If the treaty is valid there can be no dispute about the validity of the statute under Article I, § 8, as a necessary and proper means to execute the powers of the Government. The language of the Constitution as to the supremacy of treaties being general, the question before us is narrowed to an inquiry into the ground upon which the present supposed exception is placed.

It is said that a treaty cannot be valid if it infringes the Constitution, that there are limits, therefore, to the treaty-making power, and that one such limit is that what an act of Congress could not do unaided, in derogation of the powers reserved to the States, a treaty cannot do. An earlier act of Congress [of March 4, 1913] that attempted by itself and not in pursuance of a treaty to regulate the killing of migratory birds within the States had been held bad in the District Court. *United States v. Shauver*, 214 Fed. Rep. 154. *United States v. McCullagh*, 221 Fed. Rep. 288. Those decisions were supported by arguments that migratory birds were owned by the States in their sovereign capacity for the benefit of their people, and that under cases like *Geer v. Connecticut*, 161 U.S. 519, this control was one that Congress had no power to displace. The same argument is supposed to apply now with equal force.

Whether the two cases cited were decided rightly or not they cannot be accepted as a test of the treaty power. Acts of Congress are the supreme law of the land only when made in pursuance of the Constitution, while treaties are declared to be so when made under the authority of the United States. It is open to question whether the authority of the United States means more than the formal acts prescribed to make the convention. We do not mean to imply that there are no qualifications to the treaty-making power; but they must be ascertained in a different way. It is obvious that there may be matters of the sharpest exigency for the national well being that an act of Congress could not deal with but that a treaty followed by such an act could, and it is not lightly to be assumed that, in matters requiring national action, "a power which must belong to and somewhere reside in every civilized government" is not to be found. What was said in that case with regard to the powers of the States applies with equal force to the powers of the nation in cases where the States individually are incompetent to act. We are not yet discussing the particular case before us but only are considering the validity of the test proposed. With regard to that we may add that when we are dealing with words that also are a constituent act, like the Constitution of the United States, we must realize that they have called into life a being the development of which could not have been foreseen completely by the most gifted of its begetters. It was enough for them to realize or to hope that they had created an organism; it has taken a century and has cost their successors much sweat and blood to prove that they created a nation. The case before us must be considered in the light of our whole experience and not merely in that of what was said 100 years ago. The treaty in question does not contravene any prohibitory words to be found in the Constitution. The only question is whether it is forbidden by some invisible radiation from the general terms of the Tenth Amendment. We must consider what this country has become in deciding what that Amendment has reserved.

The State as we have intimated founds its claim of exclusive authority upon an assertion of title to migratory birds, an assertion that is embodied in statute. No doubt it is true that as between a State and its inhabitants the State may regulate the killing and sale of such birds, but it does not follow that its authority is exclusive of paramount powers. To put the claim of the State upon title is to lean upon a slender reed. Wild birds are not in the possession of anyone; and possession is the beginning of ownership. The whole foundation of the State's rights is the presence within their jurisdiction of birds that yesterday had not arrived, tomorrow may be in another State and in a week a thousand miles away. If we are to be accurate we cannot put the case of the State upon higher ground than that the treaty deals with creatures that for the moment are within the state borders, that it must be carried out by officers of the United States within the same territory, and that but for the treaty the State would be free to regulate this subject itself.

As most of the laws of the United States are carried out within the States and as many of them deal with matters which in the silence of such laws the State might regulate, such general grounds are not enough to support Missouri's claim. Valid treaties of course "are as binding within the territorial limits of the States as they are elsewhere throughout the dominion of the United States." No doubt the great body of private relations usually fall within the control of the State, but a treaty may override its power. We do not have to invoke the later developments of constitutional law for this proposition; it was recognized as early as *Hopkirk v. Bell*, 3 Cranch, 454, with regard to statutes of limitation, and even earlier, as to confiscation, in *Ware v. Hylton*, 3 Dall. 199. It was assumed by Chief Justice Marshall with regard to the escheat of land to the State in *Chirac v. Chirac*, 2 Wheat. 259, 275. So as to a limited jurisdiction of foreign consuls within a State. *Wildenhus's Case*, 120 U.S. 1. Further illustration seems unnecessary, and it only remains to consider the application of established rules to the present case.

Here a national interest of very nearly the first magnitude is involved. It can be protected only by national action in concert with that of another power. The subject matter is only transitorily within the State and has no permanent habitat therein. But for the treaty and the statute there soon might be no birds for any powers to deal with. We see nothing in the Constitution that compels the Government to sit by while a food supply is cut off and the protectors of our forests and our crops are destroyed. It is not sufficient to rely upon the States. The reliance is vain, and were it otherwise, the question is whether the United States is forbidden to act. We are of opinion that the treaty and statute must be upheld.

Decree affirmed.

NOTES AND QUESTIONS

1. *Constitution-based Limitations to the Treaty-making Power.* Justice Holmes wrote that "we do not mean to imply that there are no qualifications to the treaty-making power; but they must be ascertained in a different way." How well did he explicate that way? Is the problem here that Missouri's alleged constitutional prohibition was via "some invisible radiation from the general terms of the Tenth Amendment"? Would a specific constitutional prohibition, *e.g.*, respecting rights to a jury trial in criminal cases, suffice as a qualification on or a limitation to the treaty-making power? In Reid v. Covert, 354 U.S. 1 (1957), which concerned rights to a jury trial under Article III and the Fifth and Sixth Amendments, the Supreme Court held that "no agreement with a foreign nation can confer power on the Congress, or on any other branch of Government, which is free from the restraints of the Constitution." *Id.* at 16.

Justice Holmes in *Missouri v. Holland* justified the Supreme Court's decision in part because "a national interest of very nearly the first magnitude is involved." The Treaty was commended in the press as "probably the most important movement for the protection of birds ever instituted in this country or the Dominion." "Safety for the Birds," *New York Times*, Dec. 5, 1916, at 10. Would Missouri's authority to regulate migratory birds have been greater if the national need had been less?

In *Missouri v. Holland*, questions about the scope of the treaty-making power were posed starkly because a federal statute regulating migratory birds, passed before the 1916 treaty was concluded, had been struck down. Did Holmes mean to say that the federal government could achieve ends by way of treaty-making when it cannot do so by simple legislation?

2. *The Historical Context.* Note Holmes's language about Americans' cost in "sweat and blood to prove that they created a nation." Holmes had fought in the Civil War as a Union Army officer in the 20th Massachusetts Volunteer Regiment. He was shot twice, at Ball's Bluff in 1861 and at Antietam in 1862. Both times Holmes was near death. Many of his friends served alongside him and were killed or injured. When his close friend, Henry Abbott, was killed in the 1864 Wilderness Campaign, Holmes wrote, "nearly every Regimental [officer] I know or cared for is dead or wounded."

Altogether, about 360,000 died for the Union; about 200,000 more died for the Confederacy. Is it hard to understand why Holmes was committed to the national union of the United States? See Mark W. Janis, "*Missouri v. Holland*: Birds, Wars, and Rights," in *International Law Stories* 207, 216–17 (John E. Noyes, Laura A. Dickinson & Mark W. Janis eds. 2007).

3. *The Politics and Law of Federalism*. There have always been political and legal tensions between the several states and the United States. The Civil War was, in large measure, about whether the federal government, increasingly dominated by the North and West, would be permitted to interfere with and perhaps even prohibit the South's "peculiar institution," slavery. The controversy over state or federal regulation of migratory birds detailed in *Missouri v. Holland* took place within the context of this larger issue. Holmes's nationalistic judgment was immediately controversial, and so it has remained. *Missouri v. Holland* was at the center of legal and political debates about whether the federal government and its treaties should limit state laws providing for "separate-but-equal" treatment of minorities and prohibiting inter-racial marriages. Advocating the states-rights point of view, the President of the American Bar Association complained in 1949 that *Missouri v. Holland* promoted what he disparagingly termed "so-called human rights." Frank E. Holman, "International Proposals affecting So-Called Human Rights," 14 *Law and Contemporary Problems* 479 (1949).

Nowadays, the debate over Holmes's judgment in *Missouri v. Holland* focuses on such states-rights issues as women's rights, affirmative action, and the death penalty. See Curtis A. Bradley, "The Treaty Power and American Federalism," 120 *Yale Law Journal* 202, 204 (2010); David M. Golove, "Treaty-Making and the Nation: The Historical Foundations of the Nationalist Conception of the Treaty Power," 98 *Michigan Law Review* 1075 (2000); Oona A. Hathaway *et al.*, "The Treaty Power: Its History, Scope, and Limits," 98 *Cornell Law Review* 239 (2013). For the Supreme Court's contrasting views on the power of the states in foreign affairs, compare its judgment in *Missouri v. Holland* with *Medellín* below.

4. *State Law and Foreign Affairs*. Federalism limits states in their attempts to legislate respecting foreign affairs. In Crosby v. National Foreign Trade Council, 530 U.S. 363 (2000), the U.S. Supreme Court struck down a statute of Massachusetts prohibiting state agencies from purchasing goods or services from companies doing business with Burma. In 2012 the Supreme Court held that an Arizona statute aimed at curbing illegal aliens was preempted by national powers to regulate immigration. Arizona v. United States, 132 S. Ct. 2492 (2012).

Some commentators have argued that it would be appropriate for states to take a larger role in international politics. See Joel P. Trachtman, "Nonactor States in U.S. Foreign Relations," 92 *American Society of International Law Proceedings* 350 (1998); Curtis A. Bradley, "The Treaty Power and American Federalism," 97 *Michigan Law Review* 390 (1998). Most, however, have supported the long-standing position that the United States should speak with one voice in foreign affairs. See Brannon P. Denning &

Jack H. McCall, Jr., "The Constitutionality of State and Local 'Sanctions' Against Foreign Countries: Affairs of State, States' Affairs, or a Sorry State of Affairs?," 26 *Hastings Constitutional Law Quarterly* 307 (1999); Martin S. Flaherty, "Are We to be a Nation? Federal Power vs. 'States' Rights' in Foreign Affairs," 70 *University of Colorado Law Review* 1277 (1999).

WHITNEY V. ROBERTSON

124 U.S. 190 (1888)

MR. JUSTICE FIELD delivered the opinion of the court.

The plaintiffs are merchants, doing business in the city of New York, and in August, 1882, they imported a large quantity of "centrifugal and molasses sugars," the produce and manufacture of the island of San Domingo. These goods were similar in kind to sugars produced in the Hawaiian Islands, which are admitted free of duty under the treaty with the king of those islands, and the act of Congress, passed to carry the treaty into effect. They were duly entered at the custom house at the port of New York, the plaintiffs claiming that by the treaty with the Republic of San Domingo the goods should be admitted on the same terms, that is, free of duty, as similar articles, the produce and manufacture of the Hawaiian Islands. The defendant, who was at the time collector of the port, refused to allow this claim, treated the goods as dutiable articles under the acts of Congress, and exacted duties on them to the amount of $21,936. The plaintiffs appealed from the collector's decision to the Secretary of the Treasury, by whom the appeal was denied. They then paid under protest the duties exacted, and brought the present action to recover the amount. * * *

The treaty with the king of the Hawaiian Islands [of January 30, 1875] provides for the importation into the United States, free of duty, of various articles, the produce and manufacture of those islands, in consideration, among other things, of like exemption from duty, on the importation into that country, of sundry specified articles which are the produce and manufacture of the United States. 19 Stat. 625. The language of the first two articles of the treaty, which recite the reciprocal engagements of the two countries, declares that they are made in consideration "of the rights and privileges" and "as an equivalent therefor," which one concedes to the other.

The plaintiffs rely for a like exemption of the sugars imported by them from San Domingo upon the 9th article of the treaty with the Dominican Republic [of February 8, 1867], which is as follows: "No higher or other duty shall be imposed on the importation into the United States of any article the growth, produce, or manufacture of the Dominican Republic, or of her fisheries; and no higher or other duty shall be imposed on the importation into the Dominican Republic of any article the growth, produce, or manufacture of the United States, or their fisheries, than are or shall be payable on the like articles the growth, produce, or manufacture of any other foreign country, or its fisheries." 15 Stat. 473, 478. * * *

But * * * there is [a] complete answer to the pretensions of the plaintiffs. The [1870] Act of Congress under which the duties were collected authorized their exaction. It is of general application, making no exceptions in favor of goods of any country. It was passed after the Treaty with the Dominican Republic; and if there be any conflict between the stipulations of the Treaty and the requirements of the law the latter must control. * * * By the Constitution a treaty is placed on the same footing, and made of like obligation, with an act of legislation. Both are declared by that instrument to be the supreme law of the land, and no superior efficacy is given to either over the other. When the two relate to the same subject, the courts will always endeavor to construe them so as to give effect to both, if that can be done without violating the language of either; but if the two are inconsistent, the one last in date will control the other, provided always the stipulation of the treaty on the subject is self-executing. If the country with which the treaty is made is dissatisfied with the action of the legislative department, it may present its complaint to the executive head of the government, and take such other measures as it may deem essential for the protection of its interests. The courts can afford no redress. Whether the complaining nation has just cause of complaint, or our country was justified in its legislation, are not matters for judicial cognizance.

Judgment affirmed.

NOTES AND QUESTIONS

1. *The Last-in-time Rule*. With *Whitney* we move to the second sort of conflicts between treaties and U.S. domestic law—clashes with national law and institutions. Though the Court in *Whitney* refused to enforce a U.S. treaty promising to provide most favored nation treatment to imports from San Domingo (present-day Dominican Republic), it made the general proposition that in case of a conflict between a federal statute and a treaty, "the one last in date will control," a proposition favorable to the status of international agreements. Does Article VI(2) of the Constitution, the Supremacy Clause, itself prescribe any rule as to the relationship between federal law and treaties? Is any other solution preferable to the last-in-time rule? How far should the courts go as they "always endeavor to construe" treaties and federal statutes "so as to give effect to both"?

2. *Self-executing Treaties*. Would the Supreme Court in *Whitney* have needed to apply the last-in-time rule if the 1867 treaty with the Dominican Republic were not self-executing? Should the 1875 treaty with Hawaii, which entered into effect in 1876, have allowed the plaintiffs to import sugar duty-free, overriding the 1870 statute that the Court used as its rule of decision? Why was the treaty with Hawaii not self-executing? See David Sloss, "Non-

Self-Executing Treaties: Exposing a Constitutional Fallacy," 36 *U.C. Davis Law Review* 1, 32–35 (2002).

3. *Dualism, Treaties, and the Role of Courts.* Note that the Supreme Court took a dualistic view of the relationship between international law and municipal law: "If the country with which the treaty is made is dissatisfied with the action of the legislative department, it may present its complaint to the executive head of the government, and take such other measures as it may deem essential for the protection of its interests." Dualism remains popular in the United States as a way to protect the U.S. democratic decision-making process, especially the domestic legislative process. See Jonathan Turley, "Dualistic Values in the Age of International Legisprudence," 44 *Hastings Law Journal* 185 (1993).

In the United Kingdom, where no treaty is considered self-executing, the courts have taken a comparable stand about the dualistic nature of international law and municipal law. For example, in *The Parlement Belge*, a British court refused to incorporate a treaty provision that gave immunity to a Belgian packet-boat conveying mails because the immunity had not been enacted into statutory form by the British Parliament. 4 P.D. 129 (1879). Responding to an objection that this broke faith with Belgium, the judge wrote: "I acknowledge the hardship, but the remedy, in my opinion, is not to be found in depriving the British subject without his consent, direct or implied, or his right of action against a wrong-doer, but by the agency of diplomacy, and proper measures of compensation arrangement, between the Governments of Great Britain and Belgium." *Id.* at 155. Where, then, in the *Whitney Case* should the government of San Domingo have gone to complain about the actions of the United States?

Many civil law jurisdictions take an opposite tack from the tradition in the United Kingdom and provide that treaties, and indeed international law in general, are supreme over municipal law in municipal courts, even if not incorporated by legislation. See Mark Weston Janis, *International Law* 103–05 (6th ed. 2012).

UNITED STATES V. BELMONT

301 U.S. 324 (1937)

MR. JUSTICE SUTHERLAND delivered the opinion of the Court.

This is an action at law brought by petitioner against respondents in a federal district court to recover a sum of money deposited by a Russian corporation (Petrograd Metal Works) with August Belmont, a private banker doing business in New York City under the name of August Belmont & Co. August Belmont died in 1924; and respondents are the duly-appointed executors of his will. A motion to dismiss the complaint for failure to state facts sufficient to constitute a cause of action was sustained by the district court, and its judgment was affirmed by the court below. The facts alleged, so far as necessary to be stated, follow.

The corporation had deposited with Belmont, prior to 1918, the sum of money which petitioner seeks to recover. In 1918, the Soviet Government duly enacted a decree by which it dissolved, terminated and liquidated the corporation (together with others), and nationalized and appropriated all of its property and assets of every kind and wherever situated, including the deposit account with Belmont. As a result, the deposit became the property of the Soviet Government, and so remained until November 16, 1933, at which time the Soviet Government released and assigned to petitioner all amounts due to that government from American nationals, including the deposit account of the corporation with Belmont. Respondents failed and refused to pay the amount upon demand duly made by petitioner.

The assignment was effected by an exchange of diplomatic correspondence between the Soviet Government and the United States. The purpose was to bring about a final settlement of the claims and counterclaims between the Soviet Government and the United States; and it was agreed that the Soviet Government would take no steps to enforce claims against American nationals; but all such claims were released and assigned to the United States, with the understanding that the Soviet Government was to be duly notified of all amounts realized by the United States from such release and assignment. The assignment and requirement for notice are parts of the larger plan to bring about a settlement of the rival claims of the high contracting parties. The continuing and definite interest of the Soviet Government in the collection of assigned claims is evident; and the case, therefore, presents a question of public concern, the determination of which well might involve the good faith of the United States in the eyes of a foreign government. The court below held that the assignment thus effected embraced the claim here in question; and with that we agree.

That court, however, took the view that the situs of the bank deposit was within the State of New York; that in no sense could it be regarded as an intangible property right within Soviet territory; and that the nationalization decree, if enforced, would put into effect an act of confiscation. And it held that a judgment for the United States could not be had, because, in view of that result, it would be contrary to the controlling public policy of the State of New York. The further contention is made by respondents that the public policy of the United States would likewise be infringed by such a judgment. * * *

We do not pause to inquire whether in fact there was any policy of the State of New York to be infringed, since we are of opinion that no state policy can prevail against the international compact here involved. * * *

We take judicial notice of the fact that coincident with the assignment set forth in the complaint, the President recognized the Soviet

Government, and normal diplomatic relations were established between that government and the Government of the United States, followed by an exchange of ambassadors. The effect of this was to validate, so far as this country is concerned, all acts of the Soviet Government here involved from the commencement of its existence. The recognition, establishment of diplomatic relations, the assignment, and agreements with respect thereto, were all parts of one transaction, resulting in an international compact between the two governments. That the negotiations, acceptance of the assignment and agreements and understandings in respect thereof were within the competence of the President may not be doubted. Governmental power over internal affairs is distributed between the national government and the several states. Governmental power over external affairs is not distributed, but is vested exclusively in the national government. And in respect of what was done here, the Executive had authority to speak as the sole organ of that government. The assignment and the agreements in connection therewith did not, as in the case of treaties, as that term is used in the treaty making clause of the Constitution (Art. II, § 2), require the advice and consent of the Senate.

A treaty signifies "a compact made between two or more independent nations with a view to the public welfare." *Altman & Co. v. United States*, 224 U.S. 583, 600. But an international compact, as this was, is not always a treaty which requires the participation of the Senate. There are many such compacts, of which a protocol, a modus vivendi, a postal convention, and agreements like that now under consideration are illustrations. [A]lthough this might not be a treaty requiring ratification by the Senate, it was a compact negotiated and proclaimed under the authority of the President, and as such was a "treaty" within the meaning of the Circuit Court of Appeals Act, the construction of which might be reviewed upon direct appeal to this court.

Plainly, the external powers of the United States are to be exercised without regard to state laws or policies. The supremacy of a treaty in this respect has been recognized from the beginning. Mr. Madison, in the Virginia Convention, said that if a treaty does not supersede existing state laws, as far as they contravene its operation, the treaty would be ineffective. "To counteract it by the supremacy of the state laws, would bring on the Union the just charge of national perfidy, and involve us in war." 3 Elliot's Debates 515. And see *Ware v. Hylton*, 3 Dall. 199, 236–237. And while this rule in respect of treaties is established by the express language of cl. 2, Art. VI, of the Constitution, the same rule would result in the case of all international compacts and agreements from the very fact that complete power over international affairs is in the national government and is not and cannot be subject to any curtailment of interference on the part of the several states. Compare *United States v. Curtiss-Wright Export Corp.*, 299 U.S. 304, 316, et seq. In respect of all international negotiations and compacts, and in respect of our foreign relations generally, state lines disappear. As to such purposes the State of New York does not exist. Within the field of its powers, whatever the United States rightfully undertakes, it necessarily has warrant to consummate. And when judicial authority is invoked in aid of such consummation, state constitutions, state laws, and state policies are irrelevant to the inquiry and decision. It is inconceivable that any of them can be interposed as an obstacle to the effective operation of a federal constitutional power. Cf. *Missouri v. Holland*, 252 U.S. 416; *Asakura v. Seattle*, 265 U.S. 332, 341.

NOTES AND QUESTIONS

1. *The Roosevelt-Litvinov Agreement*. The *Belmont Case* validated the Roosevelt-Litvinov Agreement, a matter of some importance in U.S.-U.S.S.R. relations. At the time of the Supreme Court's decision there were 15 similar law suits in the U.S. courts involving more than $8,000,000. The Petrograd/Metal Works deposit with August Belmont & Co. was itself only $25,438. "Pact with Soviet on Claims Upheld," *New York Times*, May 4, 1937, at 14. To gain U.S. recognition of the Soviet Union, Maxim Litvinov, the Soviet Foreign Minister, not only assigned assets, like those in this case, to the United States, but pledged that the U.S.S.R. would not propagandize in the United States and that it would give religious freedom to U.S. citizens resident in the Soviet Union. The Soviet Union also gave up its claims against the United States for damage caused by U.S. troops during a 1918 intervention in Siberia. The exchange of letters comprising the Roosevelt-Litvinov Agreement appears at 28 *American Journal of International Law* 1 (Supp. 1934). For more on *Belmont*, see Stephen Millett, *The Constitutionality of Executive Agreements: An Analysis of United States v. Belmont* (1990).

2. *Executive Agreements and the Constitution*. Is it plain that the Constitution meant to give all international agreements supremacy over state laws or only those that had been favorably reviewed by the Senate? As a result of cases like *Belmont*, the term "treaty" really has two meanings in the U.S. Constitution. First, there is the "treaty" in Article II(2) that requires the "advice and consent" of the Senate. Second, there is the "treaty" in Article VI(2) that, along with the Constitution and U.S. law, is given supremacy. Should executive agreements benefit from *Foster*'s doctrine of self-execution or *Whitney*'s last-in-time rule? Although scholars have exhaustively explored the original intent of the drafters of the Constitution, it is far from agreed whether it was originally intended that executive agreements have much the same force in domestic law as treaties approved by the Senate. See Bruce Ackerman & David Golove, "Is NAFTA Constitutional?," 108 *Harvard Law Review* 799 (1995); Michael D. Ramsey, "Executive Agreements and the (Non)Treaty Power," 77 *North Carolina Law Review* 134 (1998); Peter J. Spiro, "Treaties, Executive Agreements, and Constitutional Method," 79 *Texas Law Review* 961 (2001).

In practice, executive agreements have proven to be enormously important. Between 1980 and 1992, some 4,510 new executive agreements were made against only 218 treaties that received the advice and consent of the Senate. Detlev F. Vagts, "International Agreements, the Senate and the Constitution," 36 *Columbia Journal of Transnational Law* 143, 145 (1997). It is hard to see how the U.S. could honor its international obligations in practice if every international agreement required Senate approval. As Professor Vagts has observed, "[r]unning the likes of 6,500 agreements through the Senate for its advice and consent would be enormously disruptive and would likely prevent the conduct of almost all other business, unless some massive unanimous consent operation could be mounted." *Id.*

UNITED STATES V. CURTISS-WRIGHT

299 U.S. 304 (1936)

MR. JUSTICE SUTHERLAND delivered the opinion of the Court.

On January 27, 1936, an indictment was returned in the court below, the first count of which charges that appellees, beginning with the 29th day of May, 1934, conspired to sell in the United States certain arms of war, namely 15 machine guns, to Bolivia, a country then engaged in armed conflict in the Chaco, in violation of the Joint Resolution of Congress approved May 28, 1934, and the provisions of a proclamation issued on the same day by the President of the United States pursuant to authority conferred by § 1 of the resolution. In pursuance of the conspiracy, the commission of certain overt acts was alleged, details of which need not be stated. The Joint Resolution (c. 365, 48 Stat. 811) follows:

> *Resolved by the Senate and House of Representatives of the United States of America in Congress assembled*, That if the President finds that the prohibition of the sale of arms and munitions of war in the United States to those countries now engaged in armed conflict in the Chaco may contribute to the reestablishment of peace between those countries, and if after consultation with the governments of other American Republics and with their cooperation, as well as that of such other governments as he may deem necessary, he makes proclamation to that effect, it shall be unlawful to sell, except under such limitations and exceptions as the President prescribes, any arms or munitions of war in any place in the United States to the countries now engaged in that armed conflict, or to any person, company, or association acting in the interest of either country, until otherwise ordered by the President or by Congress.

* * * It is contended that by the Joint Resolution, the going into effect and continued operation of the resolution was conditioned (a) upon the President's judgment as to its beneficial effect upon the reestablishment

of peace between the countries engaged in armed conflict in the Chaco; (b) upon the making of a proclamation, which was left to his unfettered discretion, thus constituting an attempted substitution of the President's will for that of Congress; (c) upon the making of a proclamation putting an end to the operation of the resolution, which again was left to the President's unfettered discretion; and (d) further, that the extent of its operation in particular cases was subject to limitation and exception by the President, controlled by no standard. In each of these particulars, appellees urge that Congress abdicated its essential functions and delegated them to the Executive.

Whether, if the Joint Resolution had related solely to internal affairs it would be open to the challenge that it constituted an unlawful delegation of legislative power to the Executive, we find it unnecessary to determine. The whole aim of the resolution is to affect a situation entirely external to the United States, and falling within the category of foreign affairs. The determination which we are called to make, therefore, is whether the Joint Resolution, as applied to that situation, is vulnerable to attack under the rule that forbids a delegation of the law-making power. In other words, assuming (but not deciding) that the challenged delegation, if it were confined to internal affairs, would be invalid, may it nevertheless be sustained on the ground that its exclusive aim is to afford a remedy for a hurtful condition within foreign territory?

It will contribute to the elucidation of the question if we first consider the differences between the powers of the federal government in respect of foreign or external affairs and those in respect of domestic or internal affairs. That there are differences between them, and that these differences are fundamental, may not be doubted.

The two classes of powers are different, both in respect of their origin and their nature. The broad statement that the federal government can exercise no powers except those specifically enumerated in the Constitution, and such implied powers as are necessary and proper to carry into effect the enumerated powers, is categorically true only in respect of our internal affairs. In that field, the primary purpose of the Constitution was to carve from the general mass of legislative powers *then possessed by the states* such portions as it was thought desirable to vest in the federal government, leaving those not included in the enumeration still in the states. That this doctrine applies only to powers which the states had, is self evident. And since the states severally never possessed international powers, such powers could not have been carved from the mass of state powers but obviously were transmitted to the United States from some other source. During the colonial period, those powers were possessed exclusively by and were entirely under the control of the Crown. By the Declaration of Independence, "the Representatives of the United States of America" declared the United [not the several]

Colonies to be free and independent states, and as such to have "full Power to levy War, conclude Peace, contract Alliances, establish Commerce and to do all other Acts and Things which Independent States may of right do."

As a result of the separation from Great Britain by the colonies acting as a unit, the powers of external sovereignty passed from the Crown not to the colonies severally, but to the colonies in their collective and corporate capacity as the United States of America. Even before the Declaration, the colonies were a unit in foreign affairs, acting through a common agency—namely the Continental Congress, composed of delegates from the 13 colonies. That agency exercised the powers of war and peace, raised an army, created a navy, and finally adopted the Declaration of Independence. Rulers come and go; governments end and forms of government change; but sovereignty survives. A political society cannot endure without a supreme will somewhere. Sovereignty is never held in suspense. When, therefore, the external sovereignty of Great Britain in respect of the colonies ceased, it immediately passed to the Union. That fact was given practical application almost at once. The treaty of peace, made on September 23, 1783, was concluded between his Brittanic Majesty and the "United States of America."

The Union existed before the Constitution, which was ordained and established among other things to form "a more perfect Union." Prior to that event, it is clear that the Union, declared by the Articles of Confederation to be "perpetual," was the sole possessor of external sovereignty and in the Union it remained without change save in so far as the Constitution in express terms qualified its exercise. The Framers' Convention was called and exerted its powers upon the irrefutable postulate that though the states were several their people in respect of foreign affairs were one. In that convention, the entire absence of state power to deal with those affairs was thus forcefully stated by Rufus King:

> The states were not "sovereigns" in the sense contended for by some. They did not possess the peculiar features of sovereignty,—they could not make war, nor peace, nor alliances, nor treaties. Considering them as political beings, they were dumb, for they could not speak to any foreign sovereign whatever. They were deaf, for they could not hear any propositions from such sovereign. They had not even the organs or facilities of defence or offence, for they could not of themselves raise troops, or equip vessels, for war.

It results that the investment of the federal government with the powers of external sovereignty did not depend upon the affirmative grants of the Constitution. The powers to declare and wage war, to conclude peace, to make treaties, to maintain diplomatic relations with other sovereignties, if they had never been mentioned in the Constitution, would have vested in the federal government as necessary concomitants of nationality. Neither the Constitution nor the laws passed in pursuance of it have any force in foreign territory unless in respect of our own citizens; and operations of the nation in such territory must be governed by treaties, international understandings and compacts, and the principles of international law. As a member of the family of nations, the right and power of the United States in that field are equal to the right and power of the other members of the international family. Otherwise, the United States is not completely sovereign. The power to acquire territory by discovery and occupation, the power to expel undesirable aliens, the power to make such international agreements as do not constitute treaties in the constitutional sense, none of which is expressly affirmed by the Constitution, nevertheless exist as inherently inseparable from the conception of nationality. This the court recognized, and in each of the cases cited found the warrant for its conclusions not in the provisions of the Constitution, but in the law of nations.

In *Burnet v. Brooks*, 288 U.S. 378, 396, we said, "As a nation with all the attributes of sovereignty, the United States is vested with all the powers of government necessary to maintain an effective control of international relations."

Not only, as we have shown, is the federal power over external affairs in origin and essential character different from that over internal affairs, but participation in the exercise of the power is significantly limited. In this vast external realm, with its important, complicated, delicate and manifold problems, the President alone has the power to speak or listen as a representative of the nation. He *makes* treaties with the advice and consent of the Senate; but he alone negotiates. Into the field of negotiation the Senate cannot intrude; and Congress itself is powerless to invade it. As Marshall said in his great argument of March 7, 1800, in the House of Representatives: "The President is the sole organ of the nation in its external relations, and its sole representative with foreign nations." The Senate Committee on Foreign Relations at a very early day in our history (February 15, 1816), reported to the Senate, among other things, as follows:

> The President is the constitutional representative of the United States with regard to foreign nations. He manages our concerns with foreign nations and must necessarily be most competent to determine when, how, and upon what subjects negotiation may be urged with the greatest prospect of success. For his conduct he is responsible to the Constitution. The committee consider this responsibility the surest pledge for the faithful discharge of his duty. They think the interference of the Senate in the direction of foreign negotiations calculated to diminish that responsibility and thereby to impair the best

> security for the national safety. The nature of transactions with foreign nations, moreover, requires caution and unity of design, and their success frequently depends on secrecy and dispatch.

It is important to bear in mind that we are here dealing not alone with an authority vested in the President by an exertion of legislative power, but with such an authority plus the very delicate, plenary and exclusive power of the President as the sole organ of the federal government in the field of international relations—a power which does not require as a basis for its exercise an act of Congress, but which, of course, like every other governmental power, must be exercised in subordination to the applicable provisions of the Constitution. It is quite apparent that if, in the maintenance of our international relations, embarrassment—perhaps serious embarrassment—is to be avoided and success for our aims achieved, congressional legislation which is to be made effective through negotiation and inquiry within the international field must often accord to the President a degree of discretion and freedom from statutory restriction which would not be admissible were domestic affairs alone involved. Moreover, he, not Congress, has the better opportunity of knowing the conditions which prevail in foreign countries, and especially is this true in time of war. He has his confidential sources of information. He has his agents in the form of diplomatic, consular and other officials. Secrecy in respect of information gathered by them may be highly necessary, and the premature disclosure of it productive of harmful results. Indeed, so clearly is this true that the first President refused to accede to a request to lay before the House of Representatives the instructions, correspondence and documents relating to the negotiation of the Jay Treaty—a refusal the wisdom of which was recognized by the House itself and has never since been doubted. In his reply to the request, President Washington said:

> The nature of foreign negotiations requires caution, and their success must often depend on secrecy; and even when brought to a conclusion a full disclosure of all the measures, demands, or eventual concessions which may have been proposed or contemplated would be extremely impolitic; for this might have a pernicious influence on future negotiations, or produce immediate inconveniences, perhaps danger and mischief, in relation to other powers. The necessity of such caution and secrecy was one cogent reason for vesting the power of making treaties in the President, with the advice and consent of the Senate, the principle on which that body was formed confining it to a small number of members. To admit, then, a right in the House of Representatives to demand and to have as a matter of course all the papers respecting a negotiation with a foreign power would be to establish a dangerous precedent. * * *

In the light of the foregoing observations, it is evident that this court should not be in haste to apply a general rule which will have the effect of condemning legislation like that under review as constituting an unlawful delegation of legislative power. The principles which justify such legislation find overwhelming support in the unbroken legislative practice which has prevailed almost from the inception of the national government to the present day.

[W]e conclude there is sufficient warrant for the broad discretion vested in the President to determine whether the enforcement of the statute will have a beneficial effect upon the reestablishment of peace in the affected countries; whether he shall make proclamation to bring the resolution into operation; whether and when the resolution shall cease to operate and to make proclamation accordingly; and to prescribe limitations and exceptions to which the enforcement of the resolution shall be subject.

NOTES AND QUESTIONS

1. *The Historical Context.* The Chaco War between Bolivia and Paraguay (1932–1935) was a godsend for Curtiss-Wright. One author, referring to the "sordid circumstances" of the affair, noted that exports of the bombers to Bolivia provided Curtiss-Wright with nearly two-thirds of its total foreign sales in 1933. Robert A. Divine, "The Case of the Smuggled Bombers," in *Quarrels That Have Shaped the Constitution* 210, 213–14 (John A. Garraty ed. 1964). The Chaco War, costing more than 100,000 lives, was finally settled by the mediation of six neutral American nations organized by Argentina's foreign minister, Carlos Saavedra Lamas, a diplomatic achievement leading to the award of the 1936 Nobel Peace Prize. See http://nobelprize.org/peace/laureates/1936/lamas-bio.html (last visited Dec. 10, 2013).

The indictment of the company and some of its officers was politically significant in the United States, making the front page. "Gun-Running Laid to Aircraft Heads," *New York Times*, Jan. 28, 1936, at 1. After a federal district judge held that the President had no power to outlaw shipments of arms to belligerent nations, the case went to the U.S. Supreme Court where in oral argument there was sharp questioning by judges well-experienced in foreign affairs, *e.g.*, by Chief Justice Hughes, who had been Secretary of State, and Justice Sutherland, who had been a member of the Senate Foreign Relations Committee. "Presidential Ban on Arms Held Void," *New York Times*, Mar. 26, 1936, at 15; "Embargo Argued in Supreme Court," *New York Times*, Nov. 20, 1936, at 10. The 7–1 opinion in *Curtiss-Wright* in favor of the President was again first-page news. "High Court Backs Neutrality Power Held by President," *New York Times*, Dec. 22, 1936, at 1. *Curtiss-Wright* was considered a significant contribution to U.S. neutrality policy in general and to President Roosevelt's attempts to keep all of the Americas out of the impending war in Europe in particular. Delbert Clark, "Monroe Doctrine

'Expanded': American Republics' Joint Policy on Peace Removes Old 'Unilateral' Stigma," *New York Times*, Dec. 27, 1936, at E5.

2. *Executive Lawmaking*. Albeit *Curtiss-Wright* does not concern a treaty, its analysis of the foreign affairs power of the federal government serves as a foundation for subsequent case law like *Dames & Moore* below that measures the President's authority to make and apply international agreements. In *Curtiss-Wright,* Justice Sutherland was at pains to distinguish executive lawmaking in the international realm from that sort of executive lawmaking that the Supreme Court had struck down in a series of judgments limiting the President's domestic power. See, for example, the Court's judgments in A.L.A. Schechter Poultry Corp. v. United States, 295 U.S. 495 (1935), and Carter v. Carter Coal Co., 298 U.S. 238 (1936). In a few months the Court would retreat even on the domestic front. See NLRB v. Jones & Laughlin Steel Corp., 301 U.S. 1 (1937). Formerly a senator, Justice Sutherland "was greatly influenced both by the emergence of the United States as a world power and the constitutional vision of [President Theodore] Roosevelt," and was a "strong supporter" of an "ambitious [U.S.] foreign policy." David Gartner, "Foreign Relations, Strategic Doctrine, and Presidential Politics," 63 *Alabama Law Review* 499, 529 (2012).

3. *The Source of Foreign Affairs Powers*. Did the judgment in *Curtiss-Wright* mean that some federal powers in international affairs are extra-constitutional? What was the view of Justice Chase in *Ware v. Hylton*? He acknowledged that Congress had some necessary powers even before the ratification of the Articles of Confederation in 1781:

> The powers of congress [between 1774 and 1781] originated from necessity, and arose out of, and were only limited by events; or, in other words, they were revolutionary in their very nature. Their extenst depended on the exigencies and necessities of public affairs. It was absolutely and indispensably necessary that congress should possess the power of conducting the war against Great Britain, and therefore, if not expressly given by all (as it was by some of the states), I do not hesitate to say, that congress did rightfully possess such power. The authority to make war, of necessity, implies the power to make peace; or the war must be perpetual. I entertain this general idea, that the several states retained all internal sovereignty, and that congress properly possessed the great rights of external sovereignty[.]

3 U.S. (3 Dall.) 199, 232 (1796).

In *Missouri v. Holland*, Justice Holmes looked at the wording of Article VI(2) of the Constitution and noted that "Acts of Congress are the supreme law of the land only when made in pursuance of the Constitution, while treaties are declared to be so when made under the authority of the United States." Does the wording of the Supremacy Clause advance the notion that the federal government possesses powers in foreign affairs that go beyond the Constitution? Justice Sutherland wrote in *Curtiss-Wright*: "A political society cannot endure without a supreme will somewhere. Sovereignty is never held in suspense."

Note that, "[a]lthough the concept of executive plenary power over foreign relations found its fullest expression in *Curtiss-Wright*, Justice Sutherland's method of finding extra-constitutional authority for federal action over foreign affairs was entirely familiar to Supreme Court jurisprudence." Sarah H. Cleveland, "The Plenary Power Background of *Curtiss-Wright*," 70 *University of Colorado Law Review* 1127, 1135 (1999). Throughout the 19th century the Court had expanded the federal executive branch's extra-constitutional powers at the expense of both Congress and the states in a number of fields, including Indian affairs, immigration, and territories. *Id.* at 1136–54.

4. *The Balance of Foreign Relations Powers Among the Different Branches*. Note that even if one concludes that the federal government has special powers in the field of foreign relations, it is still unclear as to what the balance of foreign relations powers is among the Congress, the President, and the federal courts. Although Justice Sutherland's opinion in *Curtiss-Wright* was a strong endorsement of presidential powers, the executive acts in question were based on a congressional resolution. The next case, *Dames & Moore*, explains more about setting a proper balance among the three branches of the federal government in matters concerning foreign affairs.

DAMES & MOORE V. REGAN

453 U.S. 654 (1981)

JUSTICE REHNQUIST delivered the opinion of the Court.

The questions presented by this case touch fundamentally upon the manner in which our Republic is to be governed. Throughout the nearly two centuries of our Nation's existence under the Constitution, this subject has generated considerable debate. We have had the benefit of commentators such as John Jay, Alexander Hamilton, and James Madison writing in The Federalist Papers at the Nation's very inception, the benefit of astute foreign observers of our system such as Alexis de Tocqueville and James Bryce writing during the first century of the Nation's existence, and the benefit of many other treatises as well as more than 400 volumes of reports of decisions of this Court. As these writings reveal it is doubtless both futile and perhaps dangerous to find any epigrammatical explanation of how this country has been governed.

* * * We are confined to a resolution of the dispute presented to us. That dispute involves various Executive Orders and regulations by which the President nullified attachments and liens on Iranian assets in the United States, directed that these assets be transferred to Iran, and suspended claims against Iran that may be presented to an International Claims Tribunal. This action was taken in an effort to comply with an Executive Agreement between the United States and Iran. We granted

certiorari before judgment in this case, and set an expedited briefing and argument schedule, because lower courts had reached conflicting conclusions on the validity of the President's actions and, as the Solicitor General informed us, unless the Government acted by July 19, 1981, Iran could consider the United States to be in breach of the Executive Agreement.

[T]he decisions of the Court in this area have been rare, episodic, and afford little precedential value for subsequent cases. The tensions present in any exercise of executive power under the tripartite system of Federal Government established by the Constitution have been reflected in opinions by Members of this Court more than once. The Court stated in *United States* v. *Curtiss-Wright Export Corp.*, 299 U.S. 304, 319–320 (1936):

> [W]e are here dealing not alone with an authority vested in the President by an exertion of legislative power, but with such an authority plus the very delicate, plenary and exclusive power of the President as the sole organ of the federal government in the field of international relations—a power which does not require as a basis for its exercise an act of Congress, but which, of course, like every other governmental power, must be exercised in subordination to the applicable provisions of the Constitution.

And yet 16 years later, Justice Jackson in his concurring opinion in *Youngstown* [*Sheet & Tube Co.* v. *Sawyer*, 343 U.S. 579 (1952)], which both parties agree brings together as much combination of analysis and common sense as there is in this area, focused not on the "plenary and exclusive power of the President" but rather responded to a claim of virtually unlimited powers for the Executive by noting:

> The example of such unlimited executive power that must have most impressed the forefathers was the prerogative exercised by George III, and the description of its evils in the Declaration of Independence leads me to doubt that they were creating their new Executive in his image.

As we now turn to the factual and legal issues in this case, we freely confess that we are obviously deciding only one more episode in the never-ending tension between the President exercising the executive authority in a world that presents each day some new challenge with which he must deal and the Constitution under which we all live and which no one disputes embodies some sort of system of checks and balances.

I

On November 4, 1979, the American Embassy in Tehran was seized and our diplomatic personnel were captured and held hostage. In response to that crisis, President Carter, acting pursuant to the

International Emergency Economic Powers Act, 91 Stat. 1626, 50 U.S.C. §§ 1701–1706 (1976 ed., Supp. III) (hereinafter IEEPA), declared a national emergency on November 14, 1979, and blocked the removal or transfer of "all property and interests in property of the Government of Iran, its instrumentalities and controlled entities and the Central Bank of Iran which are or become subject to the jurisdiction of the United States. . . ." Exec. Order No. 12170, 3 CFR 457 (1980), note following 50 U.S.C. § 1701 (1976 ed., Supp. III). President Carter authorized the Secretary of the Treasury to promulgate regulations carrying out the blocking order. On November 15, 1979, the Treasury Department's Office of Foreign Assets Control issued a regulation providing that "[u]nless licensed or authorized . . . any attachment, judgment, decree, lien, execution, garnishment, or other judicial process is null and void with respect to any property in which on or since [November 14, 1979,] there existed an interest of Iran." 31 CFR § 535.203(e) (1980). The regulations also made clear that any licenses or authorizations granted could be "amended, modified, or revoked at any time." § 535.805.

On November 26, 1979, the President granted a general license authorizing certain judicial proceedings against Iran but which did not allow the "entry of any judgment or of any decree or order of similar or analogous effect. . . ." § 535.504(a). On December 19, 1979, a clarifying regulation was issued stating that "the general authorization for judicial proceedings contained in § 535.504(a) includes pre-judgment attachment." § 535.418.

On December 19, 1979, petitioner Dames & Moore filed suit in the United States District Court for the Central District of California against the Government of Iran, the Atomic Energy Organization of Iran, and a number of Iranian banks. In its complaint, petitioner alleged that its wholly owned subsidiary, Dames & Moore International, S. R. L., was a party to a written contract with the Atomic Energy Organization, and that the subsidiary's entire interest in the contract had been assigned to petitioner. Under the contract, the subsidiary was to conduct site studies for a proposed nuclear power plant in Iran. As provided in the terms of the contract, the Atomic Energy Organization terminated the agreement for its own convenience on June 30, 1979. Petitioner contended, however, that it was owed $3,436,694.30 plus interest for services performed under the contract prior to the date of termination. The District Court issued orders of attachment directed against property of the defendants, and the property of certain Iranian banks was then attached to secure any judgment that might be entered against them.

On January 20, 1981, the Americans held hostage were released by Iran pursuant to an Agreement entered into the day before and embodied in two Declarations of the Democratic and Popular Republic of Algeria. The Agreement stated that "[i]t is the purpose of [the United States and

Iran] . . . to terminate all litigation as between the Government of each party and the nationals of the other, and to bring about the settlement and termination of all such claims through binding arbitration." In furtherance of this goal, the Agreement called for the establishment of an Iran-United States Claims Tribunal which would arbitrate any claims not settled within six months. Awards of the Claims Tribunal are to be "final and binding" and "enforceable . . . in the courts of any nation in accordance with its laws." Under the Agreement, the United States is obligated

> to terminate all legal proceedings in United States courts involving claims of United States persons and institutions against Iran and its state enterprises, to nullify all attachments and judgments obtained therein, to prohibit all further litigation based on such claims, and to bring about the termination of such claims through binding arbitration.

In addition, the United States must "act to bring about the transfer" by July 19, 1981, of all Iranian assets held in this country by American banks. One billion dollars of these assets will be deposited in a security account in the Bank of England, to the account of the Algerian Central Bank, and used to satisfy awards rendered against Iran by the Claims Tribunal.

On January 19, 1981, President Carter issued a series of Executive Orders implementing the terms of the agreement. These Orders revoked all licenses permitting the exercise of "any right, power, or privilege" with regard to Iranian funds, securities, or deposits; "nullified" all non-Iranian interests in such assets acquired subsequent to the blocking order of November 14, 1979; and required those banks holding Iranian assets to transfer them "to the Federal Reserve Bank of New York, to be held or transferred as directed by the Secretary of the Treasury." Exec. Order No. 12279, 46 Fed. Reg. 7919.

On February 24, 1981, President Reagan issued an Executive Order in which he "ratified" the January 19th Executive Orders. Exec. Order No. 12294, 46 Fed. Reg. 14111. Moreover, he "suspended" all "claims which may be presented to the . . . Tribunal" and provided that such claims "shall have no legal effect in any action now pending in any court of the United States." The suspension of any particular claim terminates if the Claims Tribunal determines that it has no jurisdiction over that claim; claims are discharged for all purposes when the Claims Tribunal either awards some recovery and that amount is paid, or determines that no recovery is due.

Meanwhile, on January 27, 1981, petitioner moved for summary judgment in the District Court against the Government of Iran and the Atomic Energy Organization, but not against the Iranian banks. The District Court granted petitioner's motion and awarded petitioner the amount claimed under the contract plus interest. Thereafter, petitioner attempted to execute the judgment by obtaining writs of garnishment and execution in state court in the State of Washington, and a sheriff's sale of Iranian property in Washington was noticed to satisfy the judgment. However, by order of May 28, 1981, as amended by order of June 8, the District Court stayed execution of its judgment pending appeal by the Government of Iran and the Atomic Energy Organization. The District Court also ordered that all prejudgment attachments obtained against the Iranian defendants be vacated and that further proceedings against the bank defendants be stayed in light of the Executive Orders discussed above.

On April 28, 1981, petitioner filed this action in the District Court for declaratory and injunctive relief against the United States and the Secretary of the Treasury, seeking to prevent enforcement of the Executive Orders and Treasury Department regulations implementing the Agreement with Iran. * * *

II

The parties and the lower courts, confronted with the instant questions, have all agreed that much relevant analysis is contained in *Youngstown Sheet & Tube Co. v. Sawyer*, 343 U.S. 579 (1952). Justice Black's opinion for the Court in that case, involving the validity of President Truman's effort to seize the country's steel mills in the wake of a nationwide strike, recognized that "[t]he President's power, if any, to issue the order must stem either from an act of Congress or from the Constitution itself." Justice Jackson's concurring opinion elaborated in a general way the consequences of different types of interaction between the two democratic branches in assessing Presidential authority to act in any given case. When the President acts pursuant to an express or implied authorization from Congress, he exercises not only his powers but also those delegated by Congress. In such a case the executive action "would be supported by the strongest of presumptions and the widest latitude of judicial interpretation, and the burden of persuasion would rest heavily upon any who might attack it." When the President acts in the absence of congressional authorization he may enter "a zone of twilight in which he and Congress may have concurrent authority, or in which its distribution is uncertain." In such a case the analysis becomes more complicated, and the validity of the President's action, at least so far as separation-of-powers principles are concerned, hinges on a consideration of all the circumstances which might shed light on the views of the Legislative Branch toward such action, including "congressional inertia, indifference or quiescence." Finally, when the President acts in contravention of the will of Congress, "his power is at its lowest ebb," and the Court can sustain his actions "only by disabling the Congress from acting upon the subject." * * *

III

In nullifying post-November 14, 1979, attachments and directing those persons holding blocked Iranian funds and securities to transfer them to the Federal Reserve Bank of New York for ultimate transfer to Iran, President Carter cited five sources of express or inherent power. The Government, however, has principally relied on § 1702(a)(1) [of the IEEPA], as authorization for these actions. Section 1702(a)(1) provides in part:

> At the times and to the extent specified in section 1701 of this title, the President may, under such regulations as he may prescribe, by means of instructions, licenses, or otherwise—
>
> (A) investigate, regulate, or prohibit—
>
> (i) any transactions in foreign exchange,
>
> (ii) transfers of credit or payments between, by, through, or to any banking institution, to the extent that such transfers or payments involve any interest of any foreign country or a national thereof,
>
> (iii) the importing or exporting of currency or securities, and
>
> (B) investigate, regulate, direct and compel, nullify, void, prevent or prohibit, any acquisition, holding, withholding, use, transfer, withdrawal, transportation, importation or exportation of, or dealing in, or exercising any right, power, or privilege with respect to, or transactions involving, any property in which any foreign country or a national thereof has any interest;
>
> by any person, or with respect to any property, subject to the jurisdiction of the United States.

[Justice Rehnquist concludes that these provisions of the IEEPA explicitly authorized the President to nullify the attachments and transfer the assets.]

Because the President's action in nullifying the attachments and ordering the transfer of the assets was taken pursuant to specific congressional authorization, it is "supported by the strongest of presumptions and the widest latitude of judicial interpretation, and the burden of persuasion would rest heavily upon any who might attack it." *Youngstown,* 343 U.S., at 637 (Jackson, J., concurring). Under the circumstances of this case, we cannot say that petitioner has sustained that heavy burden. A contrary ruling would mean that the Federal Government as a whole lacked the power exercised by the President, and that we are not prepared to say.

IV

Although we have concluded that the IEEPA constitutes specific congressional authorization to the President to nullify the attachments and order the transfer of Iranian assets, there remains the question of the President's authority to suspend claims pending in American courts. Such claims have, of course, an existence apart from the attachments which accompanied them. In terminating these claims through Executive Order No. 12294, the President purported to act under authority of both the IEEPA and 22 U.S.C. § 1732, the so-called "Hostage Act." 48 Fed. Reg. 14111 (1981).

We conclude that although the IEEPA authorized the nullification of the attachments, it cannot be read to authorize the suspension of the claims. The claims of American citizens against Iran are not in themselves transactions involving Iranian property or efforts to exercise any rights with respect to such property. An *in personam* lawsuit, although it might eventually be reduced to judgment and that judgment might be executed upon, is an effort to establish liability and fix damages and does not focus on any particular property within the jurisdiction. The terms of the IEEPA therefore do not authorize the President to suspend claims in American courts.

[Similarly, the Hostage Act does not authorize the President to suspend the claims.]

Although we have declined to conclude that the IEEPA or the Hostage Act directly authorizes the President's suspension of claims for the reasons noted, we cannot ignore the general tenor of Congress' legislation in this area in trying to determine whether the President is acting alone or at least with the acceptance of Congress. As we have noted, Congress cannot anticipate and legislate with regard to every possible action the President may find it necessary to take or every possible situation in which he might act. * * *

Not infrequently in affairs between nations, outstanding claims by nationals of one country against the government of another country are "sources of friction" between the two sovereigns. *United States v. Pink,* 315 U.S. 203, 225 (1942). To resolve these difficulties, nations have often entered into agreements settling the claims of their respective nationals. As one treatise writer puts it, international agreements settling claims by nationals of one state against the government of another "are established international practice reflecting traditional international theory." L. Henkin, Foreign Affairs and the Constitution 262 (1972). Consistent with that principle, the United States has repeatedly exercised its sovereign authority to settle the claims of its nationals against foreign countries. Though those settlements have sometimes been made by treaty, there has also been a longstanding practice of settling such claims by executive agreement without the advice and consent of the Senate. Under such agreements, the President has agreed to renounce or extinguish claims of United States nationals against foreign governments in return for lump-sum payments or the establishment of arbitration procedures. * * * It is clear that the practice of settling claims continues today. Since 1952, the President has entered into at least 10 binding settlements with foreign nations, including an $80 million settlement with the Peoples Republic of China.

Crucial to our decision today is the conclusion that Congress has implicitly approved the practice of claim settlement by executive agreement. This is best demonstrated by Congress' enactment of the International Claims Settlement Act of 1949, 64 Stat. 13, as amended, 22 U.S.C. § 1621 *et seq.* * * * By creating a procedure to implement future settlement agreements, Congress placed its stamp of approval on such agreements. * * *

In addition to congressional acquiescence in the President's power to settle claims, prior cases of this Court have also recognized that the President does have some measure of power to enter into executive agreements without obtaining the advice and consent of the Senate. In *United States v. Pink*, 315 U.S. 203 (1942), for example, the Court upheld the validity of the Litvinov Assignment, which was part of an Executive Agreement whereby the Soviet Union assigned to the United States amounts owed to it by American nationals so that outstanding claims of other American nationals could be paid. The Court explained that the resolution of such claims was integrally connected with normalizing United States relations with a foreign state:

> Power to remove such obstacles to full recognition as settlement of claims of our nationals . . . certainly is a modest implied power of the President. . . . No such obstacle can be placed in the way of rehabilitation of relations between this country and another nation, unless the historic conception of the powers and responsibilities . . . is to be drastically revised.

Similarly, Judge Learned Hand recognized:

> The constitutional power of the President extends to the settlement of mutual claims between a foreign government and the United States, at least when it is an incident to the recognition of that government; and it would be unreasonable to circumscribe it to such controversies. The continued mutual amity between the nation and other powers again and again depends upon a satisfactory compromise of mutual claims; the necessary power to make such compromises has existed from the earliest times and been exercised by the foreign offices of all civilized nations. [*Ozanic v. United States*, 188 F.2d 228, 231 (2d Cir. 1951).]

In light of all of the foregoing—the inferences to be drawn from the character of the legislation Congress has enacted in the area, such as the IEEPA and the Hostage Act, and from the history of acquiescence in executive claims settlement—we conclude that the President was authorized to suspend pending claims pursuant to Executive Order No. 12294. As Justice Frankfurter pointed out in *Youngstown*, 343 U.S., at 610–611, "a systematic, unbroken, executive practice, long pursued to the knowledge of the Congress and never before questioned . . . may be treated as a gloss on 'Executive Power' vested in the President by § 1 of Art. II." Past practice does not, by itself, create power, but "long-continued practice, known to and acquiesced in by Congress, would raise a presumption that the [action] had been [taken] in pursuance of its consent. . . . " *United States v. Midwest Oil Co.*, 236 U.S. 459, 474 (1915). Such practice is present here and such a presumption is also appropriate. In light of the fact that Congress may be considered to have consented to the President's action in suspending claims, we cannot say that action exceeded the President's powers.

NOTES AND QUESTIONS

1. *The Hostages Crisis. Dames & Moore* grew out of the 1979–1981 hostages crisis. We look again at the U.S.-Iran conflict when we read the *Diplomatic and Consular Staff Case* in Chapter 5. Why did President Carter block all Iranian assets in the United States? Why did he initially permit private suits against Iran like that brought by Dames & Moore? Did the executive branch "use" private litigants to further the goals of American foreign policy? On President Carter's attempt to end the hostages crisis before he left office, see Jimmy Carter, *Keeping Faith: Memoirs of a President* 580–95 (1982). President Carter wrote that the "release of the American hostages had almost become an obsession with me." *Id.* at 594. For an account of the role of U.S. law firms in negotiating the assets-for-hostages agreement, see James B. Stewart, *The Partners: Inside America's Most Powerful Law Firms* 19–52 (1983).

2. *The* Youngstown *Test.* The test articulated by Justice Jackson in Youngstown Sheet & Tube Co. v. Sawyer, 343 U.S. 579 (1952), was used quite effectively by Justice Rehnquist in *Dames & Moore*. In *Youngstown*, the test was employed to invalidate President Truman's seizure of steel mills during the Korean War because the presidential act conflicted with congressional intent. However, in *Dames & Moore*, the test was used to validate the acts of Presidents Carter and Reagan to end the Iranian hostage crisis. The presidential acts easier to validate were those nullifying attachments of Iranian property and transferring the assets to the Federal Reserve Bank. Here it seems that the President acted well within the specific authorization of Congress in the International Emergency Economic Powers Act. More difficult for the Court were the presidential acts suspending U.S. litigation in favor of claims arbitration before an international tribunal in The Hague. How persuasive need evidence be that suspension of claims was an ordinary

feature of U.S. international practice? The "10 binding settlements with foreign nations" noted by the Court can be distinguished from the suspension of claims in *Dames & Moore*, *e.g.,* because those ten settlements were made pursuant to powers specifically delegated to the President in peace treaties or because they involved lump sum payments to the United States for distribution to claimants. See "Supreme Court, 1980 Term," 95 *Harvard Law Review* 91, 192–98 (1981). But even if there was sufficient relevant evidence that suspension of claims was customary, how did that custom make the suspension constitutional?

3. *The Constitution and U.S. International Legal Obligations.* If the Supreme Court had found that the executive branch could not lawfully terminate the legal suits against Iran in United States courts, would this have affected the international legal obligations of the United States? What would have been the practical effect? The possibility that the United States might not be able to honor its international legal commitment to Iran persuaded the Supreme Court to hold a rare special session to decide the case. Linda Greenhouse, "High Court Hears Iran Assets Case," *New York Times*, June 25, 1981, at D3. *Dames & Moore* is a satisfying case for an international lawyer, demonstrating the Supreme Court's commitment to upholding the international legal obligations of the United States. Much more disquieting is the case that follows, *Medellín*, where the Supreme Court seemed all too ready to disregard the nation's international legal responsibilities.

MEDELLÍN V. TEXAS

552 U.S. 491 (2008)

ROBERTS, C.J., delivered the opinion of the Court, in which SCALIA, KENNEDY, THOMAS, and ALITO, JJ., joined. STEVENS, J., filed an opinion concurring in the judgment. BREYER, J., filed a dissenting opinion, in which SOUTER and GINSBURG, JJ., joined.

CHIEF JUSTICE ROBERTS delivered the opinion of the Court.

The International Court of Justice (ICJ), located in the Hague, is a tribunal established pursuant to the United Nations Charter to adjudicate disputes between member states. In the *Case Concerning Avena and Other Mexican Nationals (Mex. v. U.S.)*, 2004 I.C.J. 12 (Judgment of Mar. 31) (*Avena*), that tribunal considered a claim brought by Mexico against the United States. The ICJ held that, based on violations of the Vienna Convention, 51 named Mexican nationals were entitled to review and reconsideration of their state-court convictions and sentences in the United States. This was so regardless of any forfeiture of the right to raise Vienna Convention claims because of a failure to comply with generally applicable state rules governing challenges to criminal convictions.

In *Sanchez-Llamas v. Oregon*, 548 U.S. 331 (2006)—issued after *Avena* but involving individuals who were not named in the *Avena* judgment—we held that, contrary to the ICJ's determination, the Vienna Convention did not preclude the application of state default rules. After the *Avena* decision, President George W. Bush determined, through a Memorandum to the Attorney General (Feb. 28, 2005), that the United States would "discharge its international obligations" under *Avena* "by having the State courts give effect to the decision."

Petitioner José Ernesto Medellín, who had been convicted and sentenced in Texas state court for murder, is one of the 51 Mexican nationals named in the *Avena* decision. Relying on the ICJ's decision and the President's Memorandum, Medellín filed an application for a writ of habeas corpus in state court. The Texas Court of Criminal Appeals dismissed Medellín's application as an abuse of the writ under state law, given Medellín's failure to raise his Vienna Convention claim in a timely manner under state law. We granted certiorari to decide two questions. *First*, is the ICJ's judgment in *Avena* directly enforceable as domestic law in a state court in the United States? *Second*, does the President's Memorandum independently require the States to provide review and reconsideration of the claims of the 51 Mexican nationals named in *Avena* without regard to the state procedural default rules? We conclude that neither *Avena* nor the President's Memorandum constitutes directly enforceable federal law that pre-empts state limitations on the filing of successive habeas petitions. We therefore affirm the decision below.

I

A

In 1969, the United States, upon the advice and consent of the Senate, ratified the Vienna Convention on Consular Relations (Vienna Convention or Convention), Apr. 24, 1963, [1970] 21 U.S.T. 77, T.I.A.S. No. 6820, and the Optional Protocol Concerning the Compulsory Settlement of Disputes to the Vienna Convention (Optional Protocol or Protocol), Apr. 24, 1963, [1970] 21 U.S.T. 325, T.I.A.S. No. 6820. The preamble to the Convention provides that its purpose is to "contribute to the development of friendly relations among nations." Toward that end, Article 36 of the Convention was drafted to "facilitat[e] the exercise of consular functions." It provides that if a person detained by a foreign country "so requests, the competent authorities of the receiving State shall, without delay, inform the consular post of the sending State" of such detention, and "inform the [detainee] of his righ[t]" to request assistance from the consul of his own state.

The Optional Protocol provides a venue for the resolution of disputes arising out of the interpretation or application of the Vienna Convention. Under the Protocol, such disputes "shall lie within the compulsory jurisdiction of the International Court of Justice" and "may accordingly be brought before the [ICJ] . . . by any party to the dispute being a Party to the present Protocol."

The ICJ is "the principal judicial organ of the United Nations." United Nations Charter, Art. 92, 59 Stat. 1051, T.S. No. 993 (1945). It was established in 1945 pursuant to the United Nations Charter. The ICJ Statute—annexed to the U.N. Charter—provides the organizational framework and governing procedures for cases brought before the ICJ.

Under Article 94(1) of the U.N. Charter, "[e]ach Member of the United Nations undertakes to comply with the decision of the [ICJ] in any case to which it is a party." The ICJ's jurisdiction in any particular case, however, is dependent upon the consent of the parties. See Art. 36, 59 Stat. 1060. The ICJ Statute delineates two ways in which a nation may consent to ICJ jurisdiction: It may consent generally to jurisdiction on any question arising under a treaty or general international law, Art. 36(2), or it may consent specifically to jurisdiction over a particular category of cases or disputes pursuant to a separate treaty. Art. 36(1). The United States originally consented to the general jurisdiction of the ICJ when it filed a declaration recognizing compulsory jurisdiction under Art. 36(2) in 1946. The United States withdrew from general ICJ jurisdiction in 1985. By ratifying the Optional Protocol to the Vienna Convention, the United States consented to the specific jurisdiction of the ICJ with respect to claims arising out of the Vienna Convention. On March 7, 2005, subsequent to the ICJ's judgment in *Avena*, the United States gave notice of withdrawal from the Optional Protocol to the Vienna Convention. Letter from Condoleezza Rice, Secretary of State, to Kofi A. Annan, Secretary-General of the United Nations.

B

Petitioner José Ernesto Medellín, a Mexican national, has lived in the United States since preschool. A member of the "Black and Whites" gang, Medellín was convicted of capital murder and sentenced to death in Texas for the gang rape and brutal murders of two Houston teenagers.

On June 24, 1993, 14-year-old Jennifer Ertman and 16-year-old Elizabeth Pena were walking home when they encountered Medellín and several fellow gang members. Medellín attempted to engage Elizabeth in conversation. When she tried to run, petitioner threw her to the ground. Jennifer was grabbed by other gang members when she, in response to her friend's cries, ran back to help. The gang members raped both girls for over an hour. Then, to prevent their victims from identifying them, Medellín and his fellow gang members murdered the girls and discarded their bodies in a wooded area. Medellín was personally responsible for strangling at least one of the girls with her own shoelace.

Medellín was arrested at approximately 4 a.m. on June 29, 1993. A few hours later, between 5:54 and 7:23 a.m., Medellín was given *Miranda* warnings; he then signed a written waiver and gave a detailed written confession. Local law enforcement officers did not, however, inform Medellín of his Vienna Convention right to notify the Mexican consulate of his detention. Medellín was convicted of capital murder and sentenced to death; his conviction and sentence were affirmed on appeal.

Medellín first raised his Vienna Convention claim in his first application for state postconviction relief. The state trial court held that the claim was procedurally defaulted because Medellín had failed to raise it at trial or on direct review. The trial court also rejected the Vienna Convention claim on the merits, finding that Medellín had "fail[ed] to show that any non-notification of the Mexican authorities impacted on the validity of his conviction or punishment." The Texas Court of Criminal Appeals affirmed.

Medellín then filed a habeas petition in Federal District Court. The District Court denied relief, holding that Medellín's Vienna Convention claim was procedurally defaulted and that Medellín had failed to show prejudice arising from the Vienna Convention violation.

While Medellín's application for a certificate of appealability was pending in the Fifth Circuit, the ICJ issued its decision in *Avena*. The ICJ held that the United States had violated Article 36(1)(b) of the Vienna Convention by failing to inform the 51 named Mexican nationals, including Medellín, of their Vienna Convention rights. In the ICJ's determination, the United States was obligated "to provide, by means of its own choosing, review and reconsideration of the convictions and sentences of the [affected] Mexican nationals." The ICJ indicated that such review was required without regard to state procedural default rules.

The Fifth Circuit denied a certificate of appealability. The court concluded that the Vienna Convention did not confer individually enforceable rights. The court further ruled that it was in any event bound by this Court's decision in *Breard v. Greene*, 523 U.S. 371, 375 (1998) (*per curiam*), which held that Vienna Convention claims are subject to procedural default rules, rather than by the ICJ's contrary decision in *Avena*.

This Court granted certiorari. Before we heard oral argument, however, President George W. Bush issued his Memorandum to the United States Attorney General, providing:

> I have determined, pursuant to the authority vested in me as President by the Constitution and the laws of the United States of America, that the United States will discharge its international obligations under the decision of the International Court of Justice in [*Avena*], by having State courts give effect to the decision in accordance with general principles of comity in

cases filed by the 51 Mexican nationals addressed in that decision.

Medellín, relying on the President's Memorandum and the ICJ's decision in *Avena*, filed a second application for habeas relief in state court. Because the state-court proceedings might have provided Medellín with the review and reconsideration he requested, and because his claim for federal relief might otherwise have been barred, we dismissed his petition for certiorari as improvidently granted.

The Texas Court of Criminal Appeals subsequently dismissed Medellín's second state habeas application as an abuse of the writ. In the court's view, neither the *Avena* decision nor the President's Memorandum was "binding federal law" that could displace the State's limitations on the filing of successive habeas applications. We again granted certiorari.

II * * *

No one disputes that the *Avena* decision—a decision that flows from the treaties through which the United States submitted to ICJ jurisdiction with respect to Vienna Convention disputes—constitutes an *international* law obligation on the part of the United States. But not all international law obligations automatically constitute binding federal law enforceable in United States courts. The question we confront here is whether the *Avena* judgment has automatic *domestic* legal effect such that the judgment of its own force applies in state and federal courts.

This court has long recognized the distinction between treaties that automatically have effect as domestic law, and those that—while they constitute international law commitments—do not by themselves function as binding federal law. The distinction was well explained by Chief Justice Marshall's opinion in *Foster v. Neilson*, 2 Pet. 253, 315 (1829), overruled on other grounds *United States v. Percheman*, 7 Pet. 51 (1833), which held that a treaty is "equivalent to an act of the legislature," and hence self-executing, when it "operates of itself without the aid of any legislative provision." When, in contrast, "[treaty] stipulations are not self-executing they can only be enforced pursuant to legislation to carry them into effect." *Whitney v. Robertson*, 124 U.S. 190, 194 (1888). In sum, while treaties "may comprise international commitments . . . they are not domestic law unless Congress has either enacted implementing statutes or the treaty itself conveys an intention that it be 'self-executing' and is ratified on those terms." *Igartúa-De La Rosa* v. *United States*, 417 F.3d 145, 150 (CA1 2005) (en banc) (Boudin, C.J.).[2]

[2] The label "self-executing" has on occasion been used to convey different meanings. What we mean by "self-executing" is that the treaty has automatic domestic effect as federal law upon ratification. Conversely, a "non-self-executing" treaty does not by itself give rise to domestically enforceable federal law. Whether such a treaty has domestic effect depends upon implementing legislation passed by Congress.

A treaty is, of course, "primarily a compact between independent nations." *Head Money Cases*, 112 U.S. 580, 598 (1884). It ordinarily "depends for the enforcement of its provisions on the interest and the honor of the governments which are parties to it." *Ibid.*; see also The Federalist No. 33, p. 207 (J. Cooke ed. 1961) (A. Hamilton) (comparing laws that individuals are "bound to observe" as "the supreme law of the land" with "a mere treaty, dependent on the good faith of the parties"). "If these [interests] fail, its infraction becomes the subject of international negotiations and reclamations. . . . It is obvious that with all this the judicial courts have nothing to do and can give no redress." *Head Money Cases, supra*, at 598. Only "[i]f the treaty contains stipulations which are self-executing, that is, require no legislation to make them operative, [will] they have the force and effect of a legislative enactment." *Whitney, supra*, at 194.

Medellín and his *amici* nonetheless contend that the Optional Protocol, United Nations Charter, and ICJ Statute supply the "relevant obligation" to give the *Avena* judgment binding effect in the domestic courts of the United States. Because none of these treaty sources creates binding federal law in the absence of implementing legislation, and because it is uncontested that no such legislation exists, we conclude that the *Avena* judgment is not automatically binding domestic law.

A

The interpretation of a treaty, like the interpretation of a statute, begins with its text. Because a treaty ratified by the United States is "an agreement among sovereign powers," we have also considered as "aids to its interpretation" the negotiation and drafting history of the treaty as well as "the postratification understanding" of signatory nations.

As a signatory to the Optional Protocol, the United States agreed to submit disputes arising out of the Vienna Convention to the ICJ. The Protocol provides: "Disputes arising out of the interpretation or application of the [Vienna] Convention shall lie within the compulsory jurisdiction of the International Court of Justice." Of course, submitting to jurisdiction and agreeing to be bound are two different things. A party could, for example, agree to compulsory nonbinding arbitration. Such an agreement would require the party to appear before the arbitral tribunal without obligating the party to treat the tribunal's decision as binding. * * *

The most natural reading of the Optional Protocol is as a bare grant of jurisdiction. * * * The Protocol says nothing about the effect of an ICJ decision and does not itself commit signatories to comply with an ICJ judgment. The Protocol is similarly silent as to any enforcement mechanism.

The obligation on the part of signatory nations to comply with ICJ judgments derives not from the Optional Protocol, but rather from Article 94 of the United Nations Charter—the provision that specifically addresses the effect of ICJ decisions. Article 94(1) provides that "[e]ach Member of the United Nations *undertakes to comply* with the decision of the [ICJ] in any case to which it is a party." The Executive Branch contends that the phrase "undertakes to comply" is not "an acknowledgment that an ICJ decision will have immediate legal effect in the courts of U.N. members," but rather "a *commitment* on the part of U.N. Members to take *future* action through their political branches to comply with an ICJ decision."

We agree with this construction of Article 94. The Article is not a directive to domestic courts. It does not provide that the United States "shall" or "must" comply with an ICJ decision, nor indicate that the Senate that ratified the U.N. Charter intended to vest ICJ decisions with immediate legal effect in domestic courts. Instead, "[t]he words of Article 94 . . . call upon governments to take certain action." * * *

The remainder of Article 94 confirms that the U.N. Charter does not contemplate the automatic enforceability of ICJ decisions in domestic courts.[6] Article 94(2)—the enforcement provision—provides the sole remedy for noncompliance: referral to the United Nations Security Council by an aggrieved state.

The U.N. Charter's provision of an express diplomatic—that is, nonjudicial—remedy is itself evidence that ICJ judgments were not meant to be enforceable in domestic courts. And even this "quintessentially *international* remed[y]" is not absolute. First, the Security Council must "dee[m] necessary" the issuance of a recommendation or measure to effectuate the judgment. Second, as the President and Senate were undoubtedly aware in subscribing to the U.N. Charter and Optional Protocol, the United States retained the unqualified right to exercise its veto of any Security Council resolution. * * *

If ICJ judgments were instead regarded as automatically enforceable domestic law, they would be immediately and directly binding on state and federal courts pursuant to the Supremacy Clause. Mexico or the ICJ would have no need to proceed to the Security Council to enforce the judgment in this case. Noncompliance with an ICJ judgment through exercise of the Security Council veto—always regarded as an option by the Executive and ratifying Senate during and after consideration of the U.N. Charter, Optional Protocol, and ICJ Statute—would no longer be a

[6] Article 94(2) provides in full: "If any party to a case fails to perform the obligations incumbent upon it under a judgment rendered by the Court, the other party may have recourse to the Security Council, which may, if it deems necessary, make recommendations or decide upon measures to be taken to give effect to the judgment."

viable alternative. There would be nothing to veto. In light of the U.N. Charter's remedial scheme, there is no reason to believe that the President and Senate signed up for such a result. * * *

In this case, the dissent—for a grab bag of no less than seven reasons—would tell us that this *particular* ICJ judgment is federal law. That is no sort of guidance. Nor is it any answer to say that the federal courts will diligently police international agreements and enforce the decisions of international tribunals only when they *should* be enforced. The point of a non-self-executing treaty is that it "addresses itself to the political, *not* the judicial department; and the legislature must execute the contract before it can become a rule for the Court." The dissent's contrary approach would assign to the courts—not the political branches—the primary role in deciding when and how international agreements will be enforced. To read a treaty so that it sometimes has the effect of domestic law and sometimes does not is tantamount to vesting with the judiciary the power not only to interpret but also to create the law. * * *

D

Our holding does not call into question the ordinary enforcement of foreign judgments or international arbitral agreements. Indeed, we agree with Medellín that, as a general matter, "an agreement to abide by the result" of an international adjudication—or what he really means, an agreement to give the result of such adjudication domestic legal effect—can be a treaty obligation like any other, so long as the agreement is consistent with the Constitution. The point is that the particular treaty obligations on which Medellín relies do not of their own force create domestic law.

III

Medellín next argues that the ICJ's judgment in *Avena* is binding on state courts by virtue of the President's February 28, 2005 Memorandum. The United States contends that while the *Avena* judgment does not of its own force require domestic courts to set aside ordinary rules of procedural default, that judgment became the law of the land with precisely that effect pursuant to the President's Memorandum and his power "to establish binding rules of decision that preempt contrary state law." Accordingly, we must decide whether the President's declaration alters our conclusion that the *Avena* judgment is not a rule of domestic law binding in state and federal courts.

A

The United States maintains that the President's constitutional role "uniquely qualifies" him to resolve the sensitive foreign policy decisions that bear on compliance with an ICJ decision and "to do so expeditiously." We do not question these propositions. In this case, the President seeks to vindicate the United States interests in ensuring the reciprocal observance of the Vienna Convention, protecting relations with foreign governments, and demonstrating commitment to the role of international law. These interests are plainly compelling.

Such considerations, however, do not allow us to set aside first principles. The President's authority to act, as with the exercise of any governmental power, "must stem either from an act of Congress or from the Constitution itself." *Youngstown* [*Sheet & Tube Co. v. Sawyer*, 343 U.S. 579, 585 (1952)]; *Dames & Moore v. Regan*, 453 U.S. 654, 668 (1981).

Justice Jackson's familiar tripartite scheme provides the accepted framework for evaluating executive action in this area. First, "[w]hen the President acts pursuant to an express or implied authorization of Congress, his authority is at its maximum, for it includes all that he possesses in his own right plus all that Congress can delegate." *Youngstown*, 343 U.S., at 635 (Jackson, J., concurring). Second, "[w]hen the President acts in absence of either a congressional grant or denial of authority, he can only rely upon his own independent powers, but there is a zone of twilight in which he and Congress may have concurrent authority, or in which its distribution is uncertain." *Id.* at 637. In this circumstance, Presidential authority can derive support from "congressional inertia, indifference or quiescence." *Ibid.* Finally, "[w]hen the President takes measures incompatible with the expressed or implied will of Congress, his power is at its lowest ebb," and the Court can sustain his actions "only by disabling the Congress from acting upon the subject." *Id.* at 637–638.

B

The United States marshals two principal arguments in favor of the President's authority "to establish binding rules of decision that preempt contrary state law." The Solicitor General first argues that the relevant treaties give the President the authority to implement the *Avena* judgment and that Congress has acquiesced in the exercise of such authority. The United States also relies upon an "independent" international dispute-resolution power wholly apart from the asserted authority based on the pertinent treaties. Medellín adds the additional argument that the President's Memorandum is a valid exercise of his power to take care that the laws be faithfully executed.

1

The United States maintains that the President's Memorandum is authorized by the Optional Protocol and the U.N. Charter. That is, because the relevant treaties "create an obligation to comply with *Avena*," they "*implicitly* give the President authority to implement that treaty-based obligation." As a result, the President's Memorandum is well grounded in the first category of the *Youngstown* framework.

We disagree. The President now has an array of political and diplomatic means available to enforce international obligations, but unilaterally converting a non-self-executing treaty into a self-executing one is not among them. The responsibility for transforming an international obligation rising from a non-self-executing treaty into domestic law falls to Congress. As this Court has explained, when treaty stipulations are "not self-executing they can only be enforced pursuant to legislation to carry them into effect." *Whitney, supra,* at 194. Moreover, "[u]ntil such act shall be passed, the Court is not at liberty to disregard the existing laws on the subject." *Foster, supra,* at 315.

The requirement that Congress, rather than the President, implement a non-self-executing treaty derives from the text of the Constitution, which divides the treaty-making power between the President and the Senate. The Constitution vests the President with the authority to "make" a treaty. Art. II, § 2. If the Executive determines that a treaty should have domestic effect of its own force, that determination may be implemented "in mak[ing]" the treaty, by ensuring that it contains language plainly providing for domestic enforceability. If the treaty is to be self-executing in this respect, the Senate must consent to the treaty by the requisite two-thirds vote, consistent with all other constitutional restraints. * * *

A non-self-executing treaty, by definition, is one that was ratified with the understanding that it is not to have domestic effect of its own force. That understanding precludes the assertion that Congress has implicitly authorized the President—acting on his own—to achieve precisely the same result. We therefore conclude, given the absence of congressional legislation, that the non-self-executing treaties at issue here did not "express[ly] or implicit[ly]" vest the President with the unilateral authority to make them self-executing. Accordingly, the President's Memorandum does not fall within the first category of the *Youngstown* framework.

Indeed, the preceding discussion should make clear that the non-self-executing character of the relevant treaties not only refutes the notion that the ratifying parties vested the President with the authority to unilaterally make treaty obligations binding on domestic courts, but also implicitly prohibits him from doing so. When the President asserts the power to "enforce" a non-self-executing treaty by unilaterally creating domestic law, he acts in conflict with the implicit understanding of the ratifying Senate. His assertion of authority, insofar as it is based on the pertinent non-self-executing treaties, is therefore within Justice Jackson's third category, not the first or even the second.

Each of the two means described above for giving domestic effect to an international treaty obligation under the Constitution—for making law—requires joint action by the Executive and Legislative Branches:

The Senate can ratify a self-executing treaty "ma[de]" by the Executive, or, if the ratified treaty is not self-executing, Congress can enact implementing legislation approved by the President. It should not be surprising that our Constitution does not contemplate vesting such power in the Executive alone. As Madison explained in the Federalist No. 47, under our constitutional system of checks and balances, "[t]he magistrate in whom the whole executive power resides cannot of himself make a law." That would, however, seem an apt description of the asserted executive authority unilaterally to give the effect of domestic law to obligations under a non-self-executing treaty. * * *

In any event, even if we were persuaded that congressional acquiescence could support the President's asserted authority to create domestic law pursuant to a non-self-executing treaty, such acquiescence does not exist here. The United States first locates congressional acquiescence in Congress's failure to act following the President's resolution of prior ICJ controversies. A review of the Executive's actions in those prior cases, however, cannot support the claim that Congress acquiesced in this particular exercise of Presidential authority, for none of them remotely involved transforming an international obligation into domestic law and thereby displacing state law.

The United States also directs us to the President's "related" statutory responsibilities and to his "established role" in litigating foreign policy concerns as support for the President's asserted authority to give the ICJ's decision in *Avena* the force of domestic law. Congress has indeed authorized the President to represent the United States before the United Nations, the ICJ, and the Security Council, but the authority of the President to represent the United States before such bodies speaks to the President's *international* responsibilities, not any unilateral authority to create domestic law. The authority expressly conferred by Congress in the international realm cannot be said to "invite" the Presidential action at issue here. At bottom, none of the sources of authority identified by the United States supports the President's claim that Congress has acquiesced in his asserted power to establish on his own federal law or to override state law.

None of this is to say, however, that the combination of a non-self-executing treaty and the lack of implementing legislation precludes the President from acting to comply with an international treaty obligation. It is only to say that the Executive cannot unilaterally execute a non-self-executing treaty by giving it domestic effect. That is, the non-self-executing character of a treaty constrains the President's ability to comply with treaty commitments by unilaterally making the treating binding on domestic courts. The President may comply with the treaty's obligations by some other means, so long as they are consistent with the

Constitution. But he may not rely upon a non-self-executing treaty to "establish binding rules of decision that preempt contrary state law."

2

We thus turn to the United States claim that—independent of the United States' treaty obligations—the Memorandum is a valid exercise of the President's foreign affairs authority to resolve claims disputes with foreign nations. The United States relies on a series of cases in which this Court has upheld the authority of the President to settle foreign claims pursuant to an executive agreement. See [*Am. Ins. Ass'n. v.*] *Garamendi*, 539 U.S. [396, 415 (2003)]; *Dames & Moore*, 453 U.S., at 679–680; *United States v. Pink*, 315 U.S. 203, 229 (1942); *United States v. Belmont*, 301 U.S. 324, 330 (1937). In these cases this Court has explained that, if pervasive enough, a history of congressional acquiescence can be treated as a "gloss on 'Executive Power' vested in the President by § 1 of Art. II." *Dames & Moore, supra*, at 686.

This argument is of a different nature than the one rejected above. Rather than relying on the United States' treaty obligations, the President relies on an independent source of authority in ordering Texas to put aside its procedural bar to successive habeas petitions. Nevertheless, we find that our claims-settlement cases do not support the authority that the President asserts in this case.

The claims-settlement cases involve a narrow set of circumstances: the making of executive agreements to settle civil claims between American citizens and foreign governments or foreign nationals. See, *e.g., Belmont, supra*, at 327. They are based on the view that "a systematic, unbroken, executive practice, long pursued to the knowledge of the Congress and never before questioned," can "raise a presumption that the [action] had been [taken] in pursuance of its consent." *Dames & Moore, supra*, at 686. As this Court explained in *Garamendi*,

> Making executive agreements to settle claims of American nationals against foreign governments is a particularly longstanding practice. . . . Given the fact that the practice goes back over 200 years, and has received congressional acquiescence throughout its history, the conclusion that the President's control of foreign relations includes the settlement of claims is indisputable. 529 U.S., at 415.

Even still, the limitations on this source of executive power are clearly set forth and the Court has been careful to note that "[p]ast practice does not, by itself, create power." *Dames & Moore, supra*, at 686.

The President's Memorandum is not supported by a "particularly longstanding practice" of congressional acquiescence, but rather is what the United States itself has described as "unprecedented action." Indeed, the Government has not identified a single instance in which the

President has attempted (or Congress has acquiesced in) a Presidential directive issued to state courts, much less one that reaches deep into the heart of the State's police powers and compels state courts to reopen final criminal judgments and set aside neutrally applicable state laws. The Executive's narrow and strictly limited authority to settle international claims disputes pursuant to an executive agreement cannot stretch so far as to support the current Presidential Memorandum.

3

Medellín argues that the President's Memorandum is a valid exercise of his "Take Care" power. The United States, however, does not rely upon the President's responsibility to "take Care that the Laws be faithfully executed." U.S. Const., Art. II, § 3. We think this is a wise concession. This authority allows the President to execute the laws, not make them. For the reasons we have stated, the *Avena* judgment is not domestic law; accordingly, the President cannot rely on his Take Care powers here.

The judgment of the Texas Court of Criminal Appeals is affirmed.

JUSTICE STEVENS, concurring in the judgment.

There is a great deal of wisdom in Justice Breyer's dissent. I agree that the text and history of the Supremacy Clause, as well as this Court's treaty-related cases, do not support a presumption against self-execution. I also endorse the proposition that the Vienna Convention on Consular Relations "is itself self-executing and judicially enforceable." Moreover, I think this case presents a closer question than the Court's opinion allows. In the end, however, I am persuaded that the relevant treaties do not authorize this Court to enforce the judgment of the International Court of Justice (ICJ) in *Case Concerning Avena and Other Mexican Nationals.* * * *

Absent a presumption one way or the other, the best reading of the words "undertakes to comply" is, in my judgment, one that contemplates future action by the political branches. I agree with the dissenters that "Congress is unlikely to authorize automatic judicial enforceability of *all* ICJ judgments, for that could include some politically sensitive judgments and others better suited for enforcement by other branches." But this concern counsels in favor of reading any ambiguity in Article 94(1) as leaving the choice of whether to comply with ICJ judgments, and in what manner, "to the political, not the judicial department." *Foster v. Neilson*, 2 Pet. 253, 314 (1829).

[T]he costs of refusing to respect the ICJ's judgment are significant. The entire Court and the President agree that breach will jeopardize the United States' "plainly compelling" interests in "ensuring the reciprocal observance of the Vienna Convention, protecting relations with foreign governments, and demonstrating commitment to the role of international law." When the honor of the Nation is balanced against the modest cost of compliance, Texas would do well to recognize that more is at stake than whether judgments of the ICJ, and the principled admonitions of the President of the United States, trump state procedural rules in the absence of implementing legislation.

The Court's judgment, which I join, does not foreclose further appropriate action by the State of Texas.

JUSTICE BREYER, with whom JUSTICE SOUTER and JUSTICE GINSBURG join, dissenting.

The Constitution's Supremacy Clause provides that "all Treaties . . . which shall be made . . . under the Authority of the United States, shall be the supreme Law of the Land; and the Judges in every State shall be bound thereby." Art. VI, cl. 2. The Clause means that the "courts" must regard "a treaty . . . as equivalent to an act of the legislature, whenever it operates of itself without the aid of any legislative provision." *Foster v. Neilson*, 2 Pet. 253, 314 (1829) (majority opinion of Marshall, C.J.). * * *

I believe the treaty obligations, and hence the judgment, resting as it does upon the consent of the United States to the ICJ's jurisdiction, bind the courts no less than would "an act of the [federal] legislature." [*Ibid.*]

I * * *

The critical question here is whether the Supremacy Clause requires Texas to follow, *i.e.*, to enforce, this ICJ judgment. The Court says "no." And it reaches its negative answer by interpreting the labyrinth of treaty provisions as creating a legal obligation that binds the United States internationally, but which, for Supremacy Clause purposes, is not automatically enforceable as domestic law. * * *

In my view, the President has correctly determined that Congress need not enact additional legislation. The majority places too much weight upon treaty language that says little about the matter. The words "undertak[e] to comply," for example, do not tell us whether an ICJ judgment rendered pursuant to the parties' consent to compulsory ICJ jurisdiction does, or does not, automatically become part of our domestic law. To answer that question we must look instead to our own domestic law, in particular, to the many treaty-related cases interpreting the Supremacy Clause. Those cases, including some written by Justices well aware of the Founders' original intent, lead to the conclusion that the ICJ judgment before us is enforceable as a matter of domestic law without further legislation.

A

Supreme Court case law stretching back more than 200 years helps explain what, for present purposes, the Founders meant when they wrote that "all Treaties . . . shall be the supreme Law of the Land." Art. VI, cl. 2. In 1796, for example, the Court decided the case of *Ware v. Hylton*, 3 Dall.

199. A British creditor sought payment of an American's Revolutionary War debt. The debtor argued that he had, under Virginia law, repaid the debt by complying with a state statute enacted during the Revolutionary War that required debtors to repay money owed to British creditors into a Virginia state fund. The creditor, however, claimed that this state-sanctioned repayment did not count because a provision of the 1783 Paris Peace Treaty between Britain and the United States said that " 'the creditors of either side should meet with no lawful impediment to the recovery of the full value . . . of all *bona fide* debts, theretofore contracted' "; and that provision, the creditor argued, effectively nullified the state law. The Court, with each Justice writing separately, agreed with the British creditor, held the Virginia statute invalid, and found that the American debtor remained liable for the debt.

The key fact relevant here is that Congress had not enacted a specific statute enforcing the treaty provision at issue. Hence the Court had to decide whether the provision was (to put the matter in present terms) "self-executing." Justice Iredell, a member of North Carolina's Ratifying Convention, addressed the matter specifically, setting forth views on which Justice Story later relied to explain the Founders' reasons for drafting the Supremacy Clause. 3 J. Story, Commentaries on the Constitution of the United States 696–697 (1833). * * *

Justice Iredell pointed out that some Treaty provisions, those, for example, declaring the United States an independent Nation or acknowledging its right to navigate the Mississippi River, were "*executed*," taking effect automatically upon ratification. Other provisions were "executory," in the sense that they were "to be carried into execution" by each signatory nation "in the manner which the Constitution of that nation prescribes." *Before* adoption of the U.S. Constitution, all such provisions would have taken effect as domestic law *only if* Congress on the American side, or Parliament on the British side, had written them into domestic law.

But, Justice Iredell adds, *after* the Constitution's adoption, while further parliamentary action remained necessary in Britain (where the "practice" of the need for an "act of parliament" in respect to "any thing of a legislative nature" had "been constantly observed"), further legislative action in respect to the treaty's debt-collection provision *was no longer necessary* in the United States. The ratification of the Constitution with its Supremacy Clause means that treaty provisions that bind the United States may (and in this instance did) also enter domestic law without further congressional action and automatically bind the States and courts as well.

"Under this Constitution," Justice Iredell concluded, "so far as a treaty constitutionally is binding, upon principles of *moral obligation*, it is also by the vigour of its own authority to be executed in fact. It would not otherwise be the *Supreme law* in the new sense provided for." * * *

Some 30 years later, the Court returned to the "self-execution" problem. In *Foster*, 2 Pet. 253, the Court examined a provision in an 1819 treaty with Spain ceding Florida to the United States; the provision said that " 'grants of land made' " by Spain before January 24, 1818, " 'shall be ratified and confirmed' " to the grantee. Chief Justice Marshall, writing for the Court, noted that, as a general matter, one might expect a signatory nation to execute a treaty through a formal exercise of its domestic sovereign authority (*e.g.*, through an act of the legislature). But in the United States "*a different principle*" applies. (emphasis added). The Supremacy Clause means that, here, a treaty is "the law of the land . . . to be regarded in Courts of justice as equivalent to an act of the legislature" and "operates of itself without the aid of any legislative provision" unless it specifically contemplates execution by the legislature and thereby "*addresses itself to the political, not the judicial department.*" (emphasis added). The Court decided that the treaty provision in question was *not* self-executing; in its view, the words "shall be ratified" demonstrated that the provision foresaw further legislative action.

The Court, however, changed its mind about the result in *Foster* four years later, after being shown a less legislatively oriented, less tentative, but equally authentic Spanish-language version of the treaty. See *United States v. Percheman*, 7 Pet. 51, 88–89 (1833). And by 1840, instances in which treaty provisions automatically became part of domestic law were common enough for one Justice to write that "it would be a bold proposition" to assert "that an act of Congress must be first passed" in order to give a treaty effect as "a supreme law of the land." *Lessee of Pollard's Heirs v. Kibbe*, 14 Pet. 353, 388 (1840) (Baldwin, J., concurring).

Since *Foster* and *Pollard*, this Court has frequently held or assumed that particular treaty provisions are self-executing, automatically binding the States without more. * * *

Of particular relevance to the present case, the Court has held that the United States may be obligated by treaty to comply with the judgment of an international tribunal interpreting that treaty, despite the absence of any congressional enactment specifically requiring such compliance. See *Comegys v. Vasse*, 1 Pet. 193, 211–212 (1828) (holding that decision of tribunal rendered pursuant to a United States-Spain treaty, which obliged the parties to "undertake to make satisfaction" of treaty-based rights, was "conclusive and final" and "not re-examinable" in American courts); see also *Meade v. United States*, 9 Wall. 691, 725 (1870) (holding that decision of tribunal adjudicating claims arising under United States-Spain treaty "was final and conclusive, and bar[red] a recovery upon the merits" in American court).

All of these cases make clear that self-executing treaty provisions are not uncommon or peculiar creatures of our domestic law; that they cover a wide range of subjects; that the Supremacy Clause itself answers the self-execution question by applying many, but not all, treaty provisions directly to the States; and that the Clause answers the self-execution question differently than does the law in many other nations. The cases also provide criteria that help determine *which* provisions automatically so apply—a matter to which I now turn.

B

1

The case law provides no simple magic answer to the question whether a particular treaty provision is self-executing. But the case law does make clear that, insofar as today's majority looks for language about "self-execution" in the treaty itself and insofar as it erects "clear statement" presumptions designed to help find an answer, it is misguided. * * *

The many treaty provisions that this Court has found self-executing contain no textual language on the point. Few, if any, of these provisions are clear. Those that displace state law in respect to such quintessential state matters as, say, property, inheritance, or debt repayment, lack the "clea[r] state[ment]" that the Court today apparently requires. This is also true of those cases that deal with state rules roughly comparable to the sort that the majority suggests require special accommodation. These many Supreme Court cases finding treaty provisions to be self-executing cannot be reconciled with the majority's demand for textual clarity.

Indeed, the majority does not point to a single ratified United States treaty that contains the kind of "clea[r]" or "plai[n]" textual indication for which the majority searches. [T]he issue whether further legislative action is required before a treaty provision takes domestic effect in a signatory nation is often a matter of how that Nation's domestic law regards the provision's legal status. And that domestic status-determining law differs markedly from one nation to another. As Justice Iredell pointed out 200 years ago, Britain, for example, taking the view that the British Crown makes treaties but Parliament makes domestic law, virtually always requires parliamentary legislation. And the law of other nations, the Netherlands for example, directly incorporates many treaties concluded by the executive into its domestic law even without explicit parliamentary approval of the treaty.

The majority correctly notes that the treaties do not explicitly state that the relevant obligations are self-executing. But given the differences among nations, why would drafters write treaty language stating that a provision about, say, alien property inheritance, is self-executing? How could those drafters achieve agreement when one signatory nation follows one tradition and a second follows another? Why would such a difference matter sufficiently for drafters to try to secure language that would prevent, for example, Britain's following treaty ratification with a further law while (perhaps unnecessarily) insisting that the United States apply a treaty provision without further domestic legislation? Above all, what does the absence of specific language about "self-execution" prove? It may reflect the drafters' awareness of national differences. It may reflect the practical fact that drafters, favoring speedy, effective implementation, conclude they should best leave national legal practices alone. It may reflect the fact that achieving international agreement on *this* point is simply a game not worth the candle.

In a word, for present purposes, the absence or presence of language in a treaty about a provision's self-execution proves nothing at all. At best the Court is hunting the snark. At worst it erects legalistic hurdles that can threaten the application of provisions in many existing commercial and other treaties and make it more difficult to negotiate new ones.

2

The case law also suggests practical, context-specific criteria that this Court has previously used to help determine whether, for Supremacy Clause purposes, a treaty provision is self-executing. The provision's text matters very much. But that is not because it contains language that explicitly refers to self-execution. For reasons I have already explained, one should not expect *that* kind of textual statement. Drafting history is also relevant. But, again, that is not because it will explicitly address the relevant question. Instead text and history, along with subject matter and related characteristics will help our courts determine whether, as Chief Justice Marshall put it, the treaty provision "addresses itself to the political . . . department[s]" for further action or to "the judicial department" for direct enforcement. *Foster*, 2 Pet., at 314; see also *Ware*, 3 Dall., at 244 (opinion of Chase, J.) ("No one can doubt that a treaty may stipulate, that certain acts shall be done by the Legislature; that other acts shall be done by the Executive; and others by the Judiciary").

In making this determination, this Court has found the provision's subject matter of particular importance. Does the treaty provision declare peace? Does it promise not to engage in hostilities? If so, it addresses itself to the political branches. Alternatively, does it concern the adjudication of traditional private legal rights such as rights to own property, to conduct a business, or to obtain civil tort recovery? If so, it may well address itself to the Judiciary. Enforcing such rights and setting their boundaries is the bread-and-butter work of the courts.

One might also ask whether the treaty provision confers specific, detailed individual legal rights. Does it set forth definite standards that judges can readily enforce? Other things being equal, where rights are specific and readily enforceable, the treaty provision more likely "addresses" the judiciary.

Alternatively, would direct enforcement require the courts to create a new cause of action? Would such enforcement engender constitutional controversy? Would it create constitutionally undesirable conflict with the other branches? In such circumstances, it is not likely that the provision contemplates direct judicial enforcement.

Such questions, drawn from case law stretching back 200 years, do not create a simple test, let alone a magic formula. But they do help to constitute a practical, context-specific judicial approach, seeking to separate run-of-the-mill judicial matters from other matters, sometimes more politically charged, sometimes more clearly the responsibility of other branches, sometimes lacking those attributes that would permit courts to act on their own without more ado. And such an approach is all that we need to find an answer to the legal question now before us.

C

Applying the approach just described, I would find the relevant treaty provisions self-executing as applied to the ICJ judgment before us (giving that judgment domestic legal effect) for the following reasons, taken together.

First, the language of the relevant treaties strongly supports direct judicial enforceability, at least of judgments of the kind at issue here. The Optional Protocol bears the title "Compulsory Settlement of Disputes," thereby emphasizing the mandatory and binding nature of the procedures it sets forth. 21 U.S.T., at 326. The body of the Protocol says specifically that "any party" that has consented to the ICJ's "compulsory jurisdiction" may bring a "dispute" before the court against any other such party. Art. I. And the Protocol contrasts proceedings of the compulsory kind with an alternative "conciliation procedure," the recommendations of which a party may decide "not" to "accep[t]." Art. III. Thus, the Optional Protocol's basic objective is not just to provide a forum for *settlement* but to provide a forum for *compulsory* settlement.

Moreover, in accepting Article 94(1) of the Charter, "[e]ach Member . . . undertakes to comply with the decision" of the ICJ "in any case to which it is a party." 59 Stat. 1051. And the ICJ Statute (part of the U.N. Charter) makes clear that, a decision of the ICJ between parties that have consented to the ICJ's compulsory jurisdiction has "*binding force* . . . between the parties and in respect of that particular case." Art. 59 (emphasis added). Enforcement of a court's judgment that has "binding force" involves quintessential judicial activity. * * *

I recognize, as the majority emphasizes, that the U.N. Charter uses the words "undertakes to comply," rather than, say, "shall comply" or "must comply." But what is inadequate about the word "undertak[e]"? A leading contemporary dictionary defined it in terms of "lay[ing] oneself under obligation . . . to perform or to execute." Webster's New International Dictionary 2770 (2d ed. 1939). And that definition is just what the equally authoritative Spanish version of the provision (familiar to Mexico) says directly: The words "comprومete a cumplir" indicate a present obligation to execute, without any tentativeness of the sort the majority finds in the English word "undertakes." See Carta de las Naciones Unidas, Articulo 94, 59 Stat. 1175 (1945); Spanish and English Legal and Commercial Dictionary 44 (1945) (defining "comprometer" as "become liable"); *id.*, at 59 (defining "cumplir" as "to perform, discharge, carry out, execute"); see also Art. 111, 59 Stat. 1054 (Spanish-language version equally valid); *Percheman*, 7 Pet., at 88–89 (looking to Spanish version of a treaty to clear up ambiguity in English version). * * *

I also recognize, as the majority emphasizes, that the U.N. Charter says that "[i]f any party to a case fails to perform the obligations incumbent upon it under a judgment rendered by the [ICJ], the other party may have recourse to the Security Council." Art. 94(2). And when the Senate ratified the charter, it took comfort in the fact that the United States has a veto in the Security Council.

But what has that to do with the matter? To begin with, the Senate would have been contemplating politically significant ICJ decisions, not, *e.g.*, the bread-and-butter commercial and other matters that are the typical subjects of self-executing treaty provisions. And in any event, both the Senate debate and U.N. Charter provision discuss and describe what happens (or does not happen) when a nation decides *not* to carry out an ICJ decision. The debates refer to remedies for a breach of our promise to carry out an ICJ decision. The Senate understood, for example, that Congress (unlike legislatures in other nations that do not permit domestic legislation to trump treaty obligations) can block through legislation self-executing, as well as non-self-executing determinations. The debates nowhere refer to the method we use for affirmatively carrying out an ICJ obligation that no political branch has decided to dishonor, still less to a decision that the President (without congressional dissent) seeks to enforce. For that reason, these aspects of the ratification debates are here beside the point.

The upshot is that treaty language says that an ICJ decision is legally binding, but it leaves the implementation of that binding legal obligation to the domestic law of each signatory nation. In this Nation, the Supremacy Clause, as long and consistently interpreted, indicates that ICJ decisions rendered pursuant to provisions for binding adjudication must be domestically legally binding and enforceable in domestic courts *at least sometimes*. And for purposes of this argument, that conclusion is all that I need. The remainder of the discussion will explain why, if ICJ judgments *sometimes* bind domestic courts, then they have that effect here.

Second, the Optional Protocol here applies to a dispute about the meaning of a Vienna Convention provision that is itself self-executing and judicially enforceable. The Convention provision is about an individual's "rights," namely, his right upon being arrested to be informed of his separate right to contact his nation's consul. See Art. 36(1)(b). The provision language is precise. The dispute arises at the intersection of an individual right with ordinary rules of criminal procedure; it consequently concerns the kind of matter with which judges are familiar. The provisions contain judicially enforceable standards. * * *

Third, logic suggests that a treaty provision providing for "final" and "binding" judgments that "settl[e]" treaty-based disputes is self-executing insofar as the judgment in question concerns the meaning of an underlying treaty provision that is itself self-executing. Imagine that two parties to a contract agree to binding arbitration about whether a contract provision's word "grain" includes rye. They would expect that, if the arbitrator decides that the word "grain" does include rye, the arbitrator will then simply read the relevant provision as if it said "grain including rye." They would also expect the arbitrator to issue a binding award that embodies whatever relief would be appropriate under that circumstance. * * *

Fourth, the majority's very different approach has seriously negative practical implications. The United States has entered into at least 70 treaties that contain provisions for ICJ dispute settlement similar to the Protocol before us. Many of these treaties contain provisions similar to those this Court has previously found self-executing—provisions that involve, for example, property rights, contract and commercial rights, trademarks, civil liability for personal injury, rights of foreign diplomats, taxation, domestic-court jurisdiction, and so forth. If the Optional Protocol here, taken together with the U.N. Charter and its annexed ICJ Statute, is insufficient to warrant enforcement of the ICJ judgment before us, it is difficult to see how one could reach a different conclusion in any of these other instances. And the consequence is to undermine longstanding efforts in those treaties to create an effective international system for interpreting and applying many, often commercial, self-executing treaty provisions. I thus doubt that the majority is right when it says, "We do not suggest that treaties can never afford binding domestic effect to international tribunal judgments." In respect to the 70 treaties that currently refer disputes to the ICJ's binding adjudicatory authority, some multilateral, some bilateral, that is just what the majority has done.

Nor can the majority look to congressional legislation for a quick fix. Congress is unlikely to authorize automatic judicial enforceability of *all* ICJ judgments, for that could include some politically sensitive judgments and others better suited for enforcement by other branches: for example, those touching upon military hostilities, naval activity, handling of nuclear material, and so forth. Nor is Congress likely to have the time available, let alone the will, to legislate judgment-by-judgment enforcement of, say, the ICJ's (or other international tribunals') resolution of non-politically-sensitive commercial disputes. And as this Court's prior case law has avoided laying down bright-line rules but instead has adopted a more complex approach, it seems unlikely that Congress will find it easy to develop legislative bright lines that pick out those provisions (addressed to the Judicial Branch) where self-execution seems warranted. But, of course, it is not necessary for Congress to do so—at least not if one believes that this Court's Supremacy Clause cases *already* embody criteria likely to work reasonably well. It is those criteria that I would apply here.

Fifth, other factors, related to the particular judgment here at issue, make that judgment well suited to direct judicial enforcement. The specific issue before the ICJ concerned " 'review and reconsideration' " of the "possible prejudice" caused in each of the 51 affected cases by an arresting State's failure to provide the defendant with rights guaranteed by the Vienna Convention. This review will call for an understanding of how criminal procedure works, including whether, and how, a notification failure may work prejudice. As the ICJ itself recognized, "it is the judicial process that is suited to this task." Courts frequently work with criminal procedure and related prejudice. Legislatures do not. Judicial standards are readily available for working in this technical area. Legislative standards are not readily available. Judges typically determine such matters, deciding, for example, whether further hearings are necessary, after reviewing a record in an individual case. Congress does not normally legislate in respect to individual cases. Indeed, to repeat what I said above, what kind of special legislation does the majority believe Congress ought to consider?

Sixth, to find the United States' treaty obligations self-executing as applied to the ICJ judgment (and consequently to find that judgment enforceable) does not threaten constitutional conflict with other branches; it does not require us to engage in nonjudicial activity; and it does not require us to create a new cause of action. The only question before us concerns the application of the ICJ judgment as binding law applicable to the parties in a particular criminal proceeding that Texas law creates independently of the treaty. I repeat that the question before us does not involve the creation of a private right of action (and the majority's reliance on authority regarding such a circumstance is misplaced).

Seventh, neither the President nor Congress has expressed concern about direct judicial enforcement of the ICJ decision. To the contrary, the President favors enforcement of this judgment. Thus, insofar as foreign policy impact, the interrelation of treaty provisions, or any other matter within the President's special treaty, military, and foreign affairs responsibilities might prove relevant, such factors *favor*, rather than militate against, enforcement of the judgment before us.

For these seven reasons, I would find that the United States' treaty obligation to comply with the ICJ judgment in *Avena* is enforceable in court in this case without further congressional action beyond Senate ratification of the relevant treaties. The majority reaches a different conclusion because it looks for the wrong thing (explicit textual expression about self-execution) using the wrong standard (clarity) in the wrong place (the treaty language). Hunting for what the text cannot contain, it takes a wrong turn. It threatens to deprive individuals, including businesses, property owners, testamentary beneficiaries, consular officials, and others, of the workable dispute resolution procedures that many treaties, including commercially oriented treaties, provide. In a world where commerce, trade, and travel have become ever more international, that is a step in the wrong direction.

Were the Court for a moment to shift the direction of its legal gaze, looking instead to the Supremacy Clause and to the extensive case law interpreting that Clause as applied to treaties, I believe it would reach a better supported, more felicitous conclusion. That approach, well embedded in Court case law, leads to the conclusion that the ICJ judgment before us is judicially enforceable without further legislative action. * * *

III

Because the majority concludes that the Nation's international legal obligation to enforce the ICJ's decision is not automatically a domestic legal obligation, it must then determine whether the President has the constitutional authority to enforce it. And the majority finds that he does not.

In my view, that second conclusion has broader implications than the majority suggests. The President here seeks to implement treaty provisions in which the United States agrees that the ICJ judgment is binding with respect to the *Avena* parties. Consequently, his actions draw upon his constitutional authority in the area of foreign affairs. In this case, his exercise of that power falls within that middle range of Presidential authority where Congress has neither specifically authorized nor specifically forbidden the Presidential action in question. See *Youngstown Sheet & Tube Co. v. Sawyer*, 343 U.S. 579, 637 (1952) (Jackson, J., concurring). At the same time, if the President were to have the authority he asserts here, it would require setting aside a state procedural law.

It is difficult to believe that in the exercise of his Article II powers pursuant to a ratified treaty, the President can *never* take action that would result in setting aside state law. Suppose that the President believes it necessary that he implement a treaty provision requiring a prisoner exchange involving someone in state custody in order to avoid a proven military threat. Or suppose he believes it necessary to secure a foreign consul's treaty-based rights to move freely or to contact an arrested foreign national. Does the Constitution require the President in each and every such instance to obtain a special statute authorizing his action? On the other hand, the Constitution must impose significant restrictions upon the President's ability, by invoking Article II treaty-implementation authority, to circumvent ordinary legislative processes and to pre-empt state law as he does so.

Previously this Court has said little about this question. It has held that the President has a fair amount of authority to make and to implement executive agreements, at least in respect to international claims settlement, and that this authority can require contrary state law to be set aside. See, *e.g.*, [*United States v.*] *Pink,* [315 U.S. 203,] 223, 230–231, 233–234 [(1942)]; *United States v. Belmont*, 301 U.S. 324, 326–327 (1937). It has made clear that principles of foreign sovereign immunity trump state law and that the Executive, operating without explicit legislative authority, can assert those principles in state court. See *Ex parte Peru*, 318 U.S. 578, 588 (1943). It has also made clear that the Executive has inherent power to bring a lawsuit "to carry out treaty obligations." *Sanitary Dist. of Chicago v. United States*, 266 U.S. 405, 425, 426 (1925). But it has reserved judgment as to "the scope of the President's power to preempt state law pursuant to authority delegated by . . . a ratified treaty"—a fact that helps to explain the majority's inability to find support in precedent for its own conclusions. *Barclays Bank PLC v. Franchise Tax Bd. of Cal.*, 512 U.S. 298, 329 (1994).

Given the Court's comparative lack of expertise in foreign affairs; given the importance of the Nation's foreign relations; given the difficulty of finding the proper constitutional balance among state and federal, executive and legislative, powers in such matters; and given the likely future importance of this Court's efforts to do so, I would very much hesitate before concluding that the Constitution implicitly sets forth broad prohibitions (or permissions) in this area.

I would thus be content to leave the matter in the constitutional shade from which it has emerged. Given my view of this case, I need not answer the question. And I shall not try to do so. That silence, however, cannot be taken as agreement with the majority's Part III conclusion.

IV

The majority's two holdings taken together produce practical anomalies. They unnecessarily complicate the President's foreign affairs task insofar as, for example, they increase the likelihood of Security Council *Avena* enforcement proceedings, of worsening relations with our neighbor Mexico, of precipitating actions by other nations putting at risk American citizens who have the misfortune to be arrested while traveling abroad, or of diminishing our Nation's reputation abroad as a result of our failure to follow the "rule of law" principles that we preach. The holdings also encumber Congress with a task (postratification legislation) that, in respect to many decisions of international tribunals, it may not want and which it may find difficult to execute. At the same time, insofar as today's holdings make it more difficult to enforce the judgments of international tribunals, including technical non-politically-controversial judgments, those holdings weaken that rule of law for which our Constitution stands.

These institutional considerations make it difficult to reconcile the majority's holdings with the workable Constitution that the Founders envisaged. They reinforce the importance, in practice and in principle, of asking Chief Justice Marshall's question: Does a treaty provision address the "Judicial" Branch rather than the "Political Branches" of Government. And they show the wisdom of the well-established precedent that indicates that the answer to the question here is "yes."

V

In sum, a strong line of precedent, likely reflecting the views of the Founders, indicates that the treaty provisions before us and the judgment of the International Court of Justice address themselves to the Judicial Branch and consequently are self-executing. In reaching a contrary conclusion, the Court has failed to take proper account of that precedent and, as a result, the Nation may well break its word even though the President seeks to live up to that word and Congress has done nothing to suggest the contrary.

For the reasons set forth, I respectfully dissent.

NOTES AND QUESTIONS

1. *The Supreme Court and the Vienna Convention on Consular Relations.* The Supreme Court has long been troubled by problems with U.S. states failing to comply with the Vienna Convention. In Breard v. Greene, 523 U.S. 371 (1998), a 6–3 majority of the Court refused to stay Virginia's execution of a Paraguayan citizen who had not been informed of his right to contact the Paraguayan consulate. Moreover, a Paraguayan complaint against the United States was pending before the International Court of Justice. The Supreme Court majority held that "[e]ven were Breard's Vienna Convention claim properly raised and proved, it is extremely doubtful that the violation should result in the overturning of a final judgment of conviction without some showing that the violation had an effect on the trial."

Id. at 377. The three dissenting judges were ready to hear the international legal issues raised by the case.

Despite an order of the ICJ to delay, Virginia executed Breard. Virginia's Governor noted both the U.S. Supreme Court opinion and the conflicting advice of President Clinton's Secretary of State and Attorney General (Madeline Albright urged a stay; but Janet Reno argued that Virginia was not bound to listen to the International Court). "Statement by Governor Jim Gilmore concerning the Execution of Angel Breard," Commonwealth of Virginia Office of the Governor Press Release, Apr. 14, 1998. However, "[u]nder the international law of state responsibility, compliance with the internal laws of the Commonwealth of Virginia and of the federal laws of the United States cannot relieve the U.S. from international responsibility for an admitted violation of the Vienna Convention and a potential violation of the UN Charter." Peter H.F. Bekker & Keith Highet, "International Court of Justice Orders U.S. to Stay Execution of Paraguayan National in Virginia," *ASIL Insights*, Apr. 1998. Why would the Supreme Court be more concerned with honoring its international legal obligations to Iran in *Dames & Moore* than with honoring those to Paraguay in *Breard* or to Mexico in *Medellín*?

2. *Deference to International Law and International Tribunals.* After choosing to disregard the International Court of Justice proceedings in *Breard*, U.S. courts responded similarly to the International Court proceedings and judgments in LaGrand (Germany v. United States), 2001 I.C.J. 466, and Avena (Mexico v. United States), 2004 I.C.J. 12. When should a U.S. court give effect to the rulings of an international court or tribunal? Some commentators believe it is a mistake to take U.S. violations of international law too seriously. "All states violate international law some of the time." Ann Bradford & Eric A. Posner, "Universal Exceptionalism in International Law," 52 *Harvard International Law Journal* 3, 53 (2011). Do you agree? What are the bad, as well as the good, outcomes for a state when it fails to comply with international law or the judgments of an international court?

3. *Texas and* Medellín. Notwithstanding the Supreme Court's adverse judgment in *Medellín*, the United States still tried to persuade Texas to comply with the ICJ decision. U.S. Secretary of State Rice and U.S. Attorney General Mukasey wrote to Governor Perry of Texas asking "that Texas take the steps necessary to give full effect to the *Avena* decision." *Quoted in* John R. Crook, "Contemporary Practice of the United States Relating to International Law," 102 *American Journal of International Law* 860, 862 (2008). However, Texas was adamant in its refusal to comply. The Texas Governor's office maintained that the "world court has no standing in Texas and Texas is not bound by a ruling or edict from a foreign court." *Quoted in id.* Texas executed Medellín in early August 2008. James C. McKinley, Jr., "Texas Executes Mexican Despite Objections from Bush and International Court," *New York Times*, Aug. 6, 2008, at A6.

4. Medellín *and Self-execution.* Does *Medellín* contribute to our understanding about when a treaty provision is self-executing? Chief Justice

Roberts conceded that "[n]o one disputes that the *Avena* decision—a decision that flows from the treaties through which the United States submitted to ICJ jurisdiction with respect to Vienna Convention disputes—constitutes an *international* law obligation on the part of the United States," but argued that because the United States could block Security Council enforcement of *Avena*, the U.S. international obligation was not intended to be self-executing and a part of domestic law. Justice Breyer's dissent gave seven reasons why he felt the treaty terms at issue in the case were self-executing: i) mandatory and binding language; ii) relation to a specific individual right; iii) logic; iv) diplomatic imperatives; v) judicial nature of the task; vi) no non-judicial activity required; and vii) no presidential or congressional concern with judicial enforcement of the treaty.

Chief Justice Roberts dismissed Justice Breyer's seven reasons for self-execution as "a grab bag" that give "no sort of guidance." Chief Justice Roberts quoted the 1884 *Head Money Cases*: "a treaty is, of course, 'primarily a contract between nations,'" which "ordinarily 'depends for the enforcement of its provisions on the interest and the honor of the governments which are party to it.'" Does that passage suggest it is rare for U.S. treaties to be self-executing? Note that the *Head Money* Court, immediately following the passage quoted by Roberts, went on to find that "a treaty may also contain provisions which confer certain rights upon the citizens or subjects of one of the nations residing in the territorial limits of the other":

> The constitution of the United States places such provisions * * * in the same category as other laws of congress by its declaration that "this constitution and the laws made in pursuance thereof, and all treaties made or which shall be made under authority of the United States, shall be the supreme law of the land." A treaty, then, is a law of the land as an act of congress is, whenever its provisions prescribe a rule by which the rights of the private citizen or subject may be determined. And when such rights are of a nature to be enforced in a court of justice, that court resorts to the treaty for a rule of decision for the case before it as it would to a statute.

112 U.S. 580, 598–99 (1812). Why did Chief Justice Roberts not analyze the Supremacy Clause and its history? What was his alternative to Justice Breyer's "grab bag"? Do you agree with Professor McGuinness's critique: "Given the Court's mode of determining when a treaty is self-executing, there is no clear guidance for predicting the likely outcomes of future cases"? Margaret E. McGuinness, "International Decision: *Medellín v. Texas*," 102 *American Journal of International Law* 622, 627 (2008). See also John Quigley, "A Tragi-Comedy of Errors Erodes Self-Execution of Treaties: *Medellín v. Texas* and Beyond," 45 *Case Western Reserve Journal of International Law* 403 (2012). Did Roberts or Breyer better reflect U.S. precedent about the incorporation of treaties in U.S. law?

Professor Sloss suggested that much of the usual analysis of self-execution fails to distinguish between "two very different questions": (1) "what does the treaty obligate the United States to do?," and (2) "which government actors within the United States have the power and duty to implement the treaty domestically?" David L. Sloss, "Executing *Foster v. Neilson*: The Two-Step Approach to Analyzing Self-Executing Treaties," 53 *Harvard International Law Journal* 136, 187 (2012). If you employ this two-part analysis on some of the treaties above from *Ware* to *Medellín*, does it help make sense of the jurisprudence?

5. Medellín *and Treaty Interpretation*. Did Chief Justice Roberts or Justice Breyer do a better job of interpreting the text of Article 94 of the U.N. Charter—a focus of Chief Justice Roberts's approach, and one of Justice Breyer's seven factors? How should a U.S. court interpret a treaty? See the *Eastern Airlines Case* in Chapter 2. Was it proper for Justice Breyer to look at the Spanish language version of Article 94(1) to construe the meaning of the phrase "undertakes to comply"? Note also the ICJ's own interpretation of "undertake" in Application of the Convention on the Prevention and Punishment of the Crime of Genocide (Bosnia and Herzegovina v. Serbia and Montenegro), 2007 I.C.J. 43, 111: "The ordinary meaning of the word 'undertake' is to give a formal promise, to bind or engage oneself, to give a pledge or promise, to agree, to accept an obligation. It is a word regularly used in treaties setting out the obligations of the Contracting Parties. It is not merely hortatory or purposive. The undertaking is unqualified[.]" Professor Carlos Vázquez has written:

> In international law usage, an "undertaking" is well recognized to be a hard, immediate obligation. That Article 94 uses the term in this sense is confirmed by the Spanish version of this Article, which uses in place of this term a phrase that translates most closely as "agrees to comply." To the majority, the term suggested that future acts were contemplated. Of course, compliance with an ICJ judgment will necessarily require action subsequent to the ICJ's decision (unless the judgment is purely prohibitory, in which case compliance would require future inaction). But it is not obvious why any contemplated future action would have to come from the legislature rather than the courts (that is, through future judicial rulings enforcing the ICJ judgments).
>
> The key to this puzzle appears to lie in the fact that, in colloquial English usage, the term "undertakes" has acquired a secondary meaning denoting a "soft" obligation, a meaning along the lines of the verbs to "attempt" or to "endeavor" or to "give it a shot." If the Court understood the term "undertakes" to mean "endeavor" or "try," then it read Article 94 to leave the United States with the discretion not to comply or, in its own words, with "the option of noncompliance."

Carlos Manuel Vázquez, "Treaties as the Law of the Land: The Supremacy Clause and the Judicial Enforcement of Treaties," 122 *Harvard Law Review* 599, 621–22 (2008).

6. Medellín *and Presidential Powers.* Chief Justice Roberts did "not question" the proposition "that the President's constitutional role 'uniquely qualifies' him to resolve the sensitive foreign policy decisions that bear on compliance with an ICJ decision and 'to do so expeditiously.' " However, he held that the "responsibility for transforming an international obligation rising from a non-self-executing treaty into domestic law falls to Congress." Does this logic show traditional or proper judicial deference to the determinations of the President in foreign affairs? Why should a judge's opinion trump that of the President? Did the Supreme Court give less deference in *Medellín* to presidential efforts to carry out an obligation arising under an Article II treaty approved with the advice and consent of the U.S. Senate—the U.N. Charter—than it did in *Dames & Moore* to presidential implementation of an executive agreement? See Lori F. Damrosch, "*Medellín* and *Sanchez-Llamas*: Treaties from John Jay to John Roberts," in *International Law in the U.S. Supreme Court: Continuity and Change* 451, 461–64 (David L. Sloss, Michael D. Ramsey & William S. Dodge eds. 2011). Would Chief Justice Roberts have ordered Texas to comply with a U.S. executive agreement with Mexico, in which the President pledged to carry out the ICJ's *Avena* order?

7. *The Supreme Court and the International Reputation of the United States.* Has *Medellín* sullied the reputation of the United States? Is the U.S. Supreme Court an institution that can be trusted to comply with America's international legal obligations? The majority opinion admitted that the United States was legally bound to comply both with the Vienna Convention and with the ICJ judgment in *Avena*, but found that, in the circumstances of this case, a U.S. federal state, Texas, was permitted to reject both international law and a presidential order. The Court's admission of national weakness and disunity might well have dismayed Benjamin Franklin, who once famously said: "We must all hang together, or assuredly we will all hang separately." Benjamin Franklin, "At the Signing of the Declaration of Independence (July 4, 1776)," in *Bartlett's Familiar Quotations* 348 (Emily Morison Beck et al. eds., 15th ed. 1980). Compare Chief Justice Roberts's states-rights stance in *Medellín* with Justice Holmes's nationalistic posture in *Missouri v. Holland*. Is *Medellín* simply yet another instance in the centuries-long battle between American nationalists and states-rights advocates?

The emotive force of *Medellín* divided the *Wall Street Journal*. Its news article on the case was generally hostile to the majority opinion. Jess Bravin, "Court Deals Blow to International Treaties," *Wall Street Journal*, Mar. 28, 2008, at A3. Its editorial lauded Chief Justice Roberts: "the *Medellín* majority has delivered a victory for legal modesty and the U.S. Constitution." Editorial, "International Law and Domestic Order," *Wall Street Journal*, Mar. 28, 2008, at A14.

The Supreme Court's recent willingness to disregard the international legal commitments of the United States has, in the view of some, contributed to the Court being taken less seriously abroad. See Adam Liptak, "U.S. Court, a Longtime Beacon, Is Now Guiding Fewer Nations," *New York Times*, Sept. 18, 2008, at A1. As long ago as 1994, Justice Blackmun lamented: "At best, I would say that the present Supreme Court enforced *some* principles of international law and *some* of its obligations *some* of the time." Harry A. Blackmun, "The Supreme Court and the Law of Nations," 104 *Yale Law Journal* 39, 49 (1994) (emphasis in original). Looking at recent cases, how would you now characterize the record of the Court?

B. THE LAW OF NATIONS IN AMERICAN LAW

Long before 1789, when the English philosopher Jeremy Bentham coined the word *international* to distinguish *internal* from *international* jurisprudence, English law recognized two ancestors of what we now call *international law*: the law of treaties and the law of nations. M.W. Janis, "Jeremy Bentham and the Fashioning of 'International Law,'" 78 *American Journal of International Law* 405 (1984). More than two hundred years after Bentham's linguistic invention, Anglo-American law still solves problems about incorporating rules of international law into municipal law with doctrinal answers set in these two traditional categories. We have already studied the American approach to incorporation of treaties (a path directed by the U.S. Constitution and much at odds with the English approach). Now we ask how the U.S. legal system incorporates the law of nations (a route in this case similar to that of other common law countries). In the United States, the *law of nations* has come to include more or less all of the modern sorts of non-treaty rules we examined in Chapter 3, most notably customary international law, general principles of law, and *jus cogens*. We begin our story in 1784 with the classic pre-Constitutional American case, *Respublica v. De Longchamps*. Pay special attention to how American judges since the 18th century have used precedent and principle to give body to the concept of the *law of nations*.

RESPUBLICA V. DE LONGCHAMPS

Court of Oyer and Terminer at Philadelphia,
1 U.S. (1 Dall.) 111 (1784)

CHARLES JULIAN DE LONGCHAMPS, commonly called the *Chevalier de Longchamps*, was indicted, that "he, on the 17th of May 1784, in the dwelling-house of his excellency the French minister plenipotentiary, in the presence of Francis Barbe Marbois, unlawfully and insolently did threaten and menace bodily harm and violence to the person of the said Francis Barbe Marbois, he being consul-general of France to the United States, consul for the state of Pennsylvania, Secretary of the French legation &c. resident in the house aforesaid, and under the protection of the law of nations and this commonwealth." And that "afterwards, to wit on the 19th of May, in the public street, &c., he, said Charles Julian de Longchamps, unlawfully, premeditatedly and violently, in and upon the person of the said Francis Barbe Marbois, under the protection of the laws of the nations, and in the peace of this commonwealth, then and there being, an assault did make, and him, the said Francis Barbe Marbois unlawfully and violently did strike and otherwise, &c., in violation of the laws of nations, against the peace and dignity of the United States and of the commonwealth of Pennsylvania."—To these charges, the defendant pleaded not guilty.

The evidence in support of the first count, was, that on the 17th of May, de Longchamps went to the house of the minister of France, and after some conversation with Monsieur Marbois, was heard to exclaim in a loud and menacing tone, "*Je vous deshonnerera, Policon, Coquin,*" addressing himself to that gentleman. That the noise being heard by the minister, he repaired to the room from which it issued, and that, in his presence, the defendant repeated the insult offered to Monsieur Marbois, in nearly the same terms.

In support of the second count, it appeared, that de Longchamps and Monsieur Marbois, having met in Market street, near the coffee-house, entered into a long conversation, in the course of which, the latter said, that he would complain to the civil authority, and the former replied, "you are a blackguard." The witnesses generally deposed, that de Longchamps struck the cane of Monsieur Marbois, before that gentleman used any violent gestures, or even appeared incensed; but that as soon as the stroke was given, Monsieur Marbois employed his stick with great severity, until the spectators interfered and separated the parties. One of the witnesses, indeed, said, that previously to engaging with their canes, he observed the two gentlemen, at the same instant, lay their hands on each others shoulders, in a manner so gentle, that he, who had heard it was customary among the French to part with mutual salutations, imagined a ceremony of that kind was about to take place, and was surprised to see de Longchamps step back, and strike the cane of Monsieur Marbois.

On the part of the defendant, evidence was produced of his having served with honour in the French armies, and his commission of sub-brigadier in the dragoons of Noailles, was read. It appeared, that the occasion of his calling on Monsieur Marbois, was to obtain authentications of these, and some other papers relative to his family, his rank in France, and his military promotions, in order to refute several publications, which had been made in the newspapers, injurious to his character and pretensions. The refusal of Monsieur Marbois to grant the authentications required, was the ground of de Longchamps' resentment, and the immediate cause of his menaces at the minister's house. * * *

MCKEAN, CHIEF JUSTICE.—This is a case of the first impression in the United States. It must be determined on the principles of the laws of nations, which form a part of the municipal law of Pennsylvania; and, if the offenses charged in the indictment have been committed, there can be no doubt, that those laws have been violated. The words used in the minister's house (which is to be considered as a foreign domicil, where the minister resides in full representation of his sovereign, and where the laws of the state do not extend), may be compared to the same words applied to the Judges in a court of justice, where they sit in representation of the majesty of the people of Pennsylvania. In that case, the offender would be immediately committed to jail, without the preliminary process of an indictment by a grand jury; and, in the case before us, if the offender is convicted, he may certainly be punished by fine and imprisonment.

In actions of slander, words were formerly construed in the mildest sense they would admit; but reason has superceded such forced interpretations, and words are now to be taken according to their ordinary import and meaning. Those expressed by the defendant are evidently of a tendency so opprobrious and violent, that they cannot fail to aggravate the outrage which has been committed.

As to the assault, this is, perhaps, one of that kind, in which the insult is more to be considered, than the actual damage; for, though no great bodily pain is suffered by a blow on the palm of the hand, or the skirt of the coat, yet these are clearly within the legal definition of assault and battery, and among gentlemen, too often, induce duelling, and terminate in murder. As, therefore, anything attached to the person, partakes of its inviolability; de Longchamps' striking Monsieur Marbois' cane, is a sufficient justification of that gentleman's subsequent conduct. * * *

Charles Julian de Longchamps: You have been indicted for unlawfully and violently threatening and menacing bodily harm and violence to the person of the Honorable Francis Barbe de Marbois, secretary to the legation from France, and consul-general of France to the United States of America, in the mansion-house of the minister plenipotentiary of France; and for an assault and battery committed upon the said secretary and consul, in a public street in the City of Philadelphia. To this Indictment you have pleaded, that you were not guilty, and for trial put yourself upon the country; an unbiased jury, upon a fair trial, and clear evidence, have found you guilty.

These offenses having been thus legally ascertained and fixed upon you, his Excellency the President, and the Honorable the Supreme Executive Council, attentive to the honor and interest of this state, were pleased to inform the judges of this court, as they had frequently done before, that the minister of France had earnestly repeated a demand, that you, having appeared in his house in the uniform of a French regiment, and having called yourself an officer in the troops of his Majesty, should be delivered up to him for these outrages, as a Frenchman to be sent to

France; and wished us in this stage of your prosecution, to take into mature consideration, and in the most solemn manner to determine:—

> 1. Whether you could be legally delivered up by council, according to the claim made by the late minister of France?
>
> 2. If you could not be thus legally delivered up, whether your offenses in violation of the law of nations, being now ascertained and verified according to the laws of this commonwealth, you ought not to be imprisoned, until his most Christian Majesty shall declare, that the reparation is satisfactory? * * *

To these questions we have given the following answers in writing:— * * *

> 1. And as to the first question, we answer, That it is our opinion, that, in this case, Charles Julian de Longchamps cannot be legally delivered up by council, according to the claim made by the minister of France. Though, we think, cases may occur, where council could, *pro bono publico*, and to prevent atrocious offenders evading punishment, deliver them up to the justice of the country to which they belong, or where the offenses were committed.
>
> 2. Punishments must be inflicted in the same county where the criminals were tried and convicted, unless the record of the attainder be removed into the supreme court, which may award execution in the county where it sits; they must be such as the laws expressly prescribe; or where no stated or fixed judgment is directed, according to the legal discretion of the court; but judgments must be certain and definite in all respects. Therefore, we conclude, that the defendant cannot be imprisoned, until his most Christian Majesty shall declare that the reparation is satisfactory. * * *

The foregoing answers having been given, it only remains for the court to pronounce sentence upon you. This sentence must be governed by a due consideration of the enormity and dangerous tendency of the offenses you have committed, of the willfulness, deliberation, and malice, wherewith they were done, of the quality and degree of the offended and offender, the provocation given, and all other circumstances which may any way aggravate or extenuate the guilt.

The first crime in the indictment is an infraction of the law of nations. This law, in its full extent, is part of the law of this state, and is to be collected from the practice of different nations, and the authority of writers. The person of a public minister is sacred and inviolable. Whoever offers any violence to him, not only affronts the sovereign he represents, but also hurts the common safety and well-being of nations—he is guilty of a crime against the whole world.

All the reasons, which establish the independency and inviolability of the person of a minister, apply likewise to secure the immunities of his house. It is to be defended from all outrage; it is under a peculiar protection of the laws; to invade its freedom, is a crime against the state and all other nations.

The *comites* of a minister, or those of his train, partake also of his inviolability. The independency of a minister extends to all his household; these are so connected with him, that they enjoy his privileges and follow his fate. The secretary to the embassy has his commission from the sovereign himself; he is the most distinguished character in the suite of a public minister, and is in some instances considered as a kind of public minister himself. Is it not, then, an extraordinary insult, to use threats of bodily harm to his person, in the domicil of the minister plenipotentiary? If this is tolerated, his freedom of conduct is taken away, the business of his sovereign cannot be transacted, and his dignity and grandeur will be tarnished.

You then have been guilty of an atrocious violation of the law of nations; you have grossly insulted gentlemen, the peculiar objects of this law (gentlemen of amiable characters, and highly esteemed by the government of this state), in a most wanton and unprovoked manner: and it is now the interest as well as duty of the government, to animadvert upon your conduct with a becoming severity—such a severity as may tend to reform yourself, to deter others from the commission of the like crime, preserve the honor of the state, and maintain peace with our great and good ally, and the whole world. * * *

Upon the whole THE COURT, after a most attentive consideration of every circumstance in this case, do award, and direct me to pronounce the following sentence:—

That you pay a fine of 100 French crowns to the commonwealth; that you be imprisoned until the 4th day of July 1786, which will make a little more than two years imprisonment in the whole; that you then give good security to keep the peace, and be of good behaviour to all public ministers, secretaries to embassies, and consuls, as well as to all the liege people of Pennsylvania, for the space of seven years, by entering into a recognisance, yourself in a thousand pounds, and two securities in 500 pounds each: that you pay the costs of this prosecution, and remain committed until this sentence be complied with.

NOTES AND QUESTIONS

1. *The Law of Nations in the Common Law.* The *De Longchamps Case* preceded the establishment of the federal judiciary. McKean, Chief Justice of

Pennsylvania, recited Blackstone's familiar 18th-century formula of the English common law: "the law of nations * * * forms a part of the municipal law." This doctrine about the incorporation of the law of nations into the common law predates the Constitution and the Supremacy Clause of Article VI. What are we to make of the fact that the Supremacy Clause mentions treaties but not the law of nations? Was or is the law of nations the same as customary international law?

2. *The Political Context.* Would American sovereignty have been imperilled if the new United States had delivered up De Longchamps to be shipped off to France as was sought by the French Minister? Or if the United States had imprisoned De Longchamps for so long as the French King should dictate? Was it politically useful to rely on the law of nations in refusing the French requests? The Marbois-De Longchamps affair was a cause of concern among leading Americans, including Benjamin Franklin, George Washington, Thomas Jefferson, James Madison, John Adams, James Monroe, John Jay, Benjamin Harrison, and Charles Pinckney. See William R. Casto, "The Federal Courts' Protective Jurisdiction Over Torts Committed in Violation of the Law of Nations," 18 *Connecticut Law Review* 467, 492 n.143 (1986). A little over a week after De Longchamps assaulted Marbois, Thomas Jefferson wrote to James Madison to complain that Pennsylvania was "so indecisive" in taking steps with respect to the case: "They have not yet declared what they can or will do. . . . The affair is represented to Congress who will have the will but not the power to interpose. It will probably go next to France and bring on serious consequences." Letter of May 25, 1784, *quoted in id.* at 493 n.146. The *De Longchamps Case* provided ammunition for those favoring the creation of a federal judiciary under the U.S. Constitution with jurisdiction to hear cases involving foreign citizens. See Article III(2) of the Constitution.

3. *Crimes in Violation of the Law of Nations.* Was it fair to De Longchamps that he should be subjected to a fine of 100 French crowns and more than two years' imprisonment for an infraction of the law of nations, a law "collected from the practice of different nations, and the authority of writers"? How certain was that law? Should the law have been found in some specific statute of the United States or Pennsylvania? After United States v. Hudson & Goodwin, 11 U.S. (7 Cranch) 32 (1812), and United States v. Coolidge, 14 U.S. (1 Wheat.) 415 (1816), the doctrine of "common law crimes" lost favor. Defendants today are prosecuted in the United States only for violations of criminal statutes.

A criminal statute, however, may define a crime by explicitly incorporating the law of nations. For example, 18 U.S.C. § 1651 applies to anyone who, "on the high seas, commits the crime of piracy as defined by the law of nations, and is afterwards brought into or found in the United States." In United States v. Smith, 18 U.S. (5 Wheat.) 153 (1820), Justice Story found this statute sufficiently determinate to support the conviction and execution of several men for the crime of piracy. See *Smith* in Chapter 3.

4. *An Evolving Doctrine.* The very antiquity of the doctrine that the law of nations is part of the common law raises important questions. How has

the practice evolved over time? How should a domestic legal system reconcile the traditional doctrine with modern principles of constitutional and statutory law?

In the United States, looking, *inter alia*, at *De Longchamps* and *Smith*, the Supreme Court has held that Congress intended the 1789 Alien Tort Statute, refreshed in 1980 by *Filartiga*, one of the cases we read in Chapter 1, to provide another avenue, without further act of Congress, of redress for international law violations committed by individuals. Such wrongs must be at least as definite as the traditional international offences involving ambassadors and piracy. See *Sosa v. Alvarez-Machain* and *Kiobel v. Royal Dutch Petroleum Co.* below. The incorporation doctrine has also evolved in other common law countries. For the United Kingdom, see Philip Sales & Joanne Clement, "International Law in Domestic Courts: The Developing Framework," 124 *Law Quarterly Review* 388, 413–20 (2008).

MURRAY V. SCHOONER CHARMING BETSY

6 U.S. (2 Cranch) 64 (1804)

MARSHALL, *Ch. J.*, delivered the opinion of the court:

The Charming Betsy was an American built vessel, belonging to citizens of the United States, and sailed from Baltimore, under the name of the Jane, on the 10th of April 1800, with a cargo of flour for St. Bartholomew; she was sent out for the purpose of being sold. The cargo was disposed of at St. Bartholomew; but finding it impossible to sell the vessel at that place, the master proceeded with her to the island of St. Thomas, where she was disposed of to Jared Shattuck, who changed her name to that of the Charming Betsy, and having put on board her a cargo consisting of American produce, cleared her out, as a Danish vessel, for the island of Guadaloupe.

On her voyage, she was captured by a French privateer, and eight hands were put on board her for the purpose of taking her into Guadaloupe as a prize. She was afterwards recaptured by Captain Murray, commander of the Constellation frigate, and carried into Martinique. It appears, that the master of the Charming Betsy was willing to be taken into that island; but when there, he claimed to have his vessel and cargo restored, as being the property of Jared Shattuck, a Danish burgher.

Jared Shattuck was born in the United States, but had removed to the island of St. Thomas, while an infant, and was proved to have resided there ever since the year 1789 or 1790. He had been accustomed to carry on trade as a Danish subject; had married a wife and acquired real property in the island, and also taken the oath of allegiance to the crown of Denmark in 1797.

Considering him as an American citizen, who was violating the law prohibiting all intercourse between the United States and France, or its dependencies, or the sale of the vessel as a mere cover to evade that law, Captain Murray sold the cargo of the Charming Betsy, which consisted of American produce, in Martinique, and brought the vessel into the port of Philadelphia, where she was libelled under what is termed the non-intercourse law. The vessel and cargo were claimed by the consul of Denmark as being the *bona fide* property of a Danish subject.

This cause came on to be heard before the judge for the district of Pennsylvania, who declared the seizure to be illegal, and that the vessel ought to be restored, and the proceeds of the cargo paid to the claimant, or his lawful agent, together with costs and such damages as should be assessed by the clerk of the court, who was directed to inquire into and report the amount thereof; for which purpose, he was also directed to associate with himself two intelligent merchants of the district, and duly inquire what damage Jared Shattuck had sustained by reason of the premises. If they should be of opinion that the officers and crew of the Constellation had conferred any benefit on the owner of the Charming Betsy, by rescuing her out of the hands of the French captors, they were, in the adjustment, to allow reasonable compensation for the service.

In pursuance of this order, the clerk associated with himself two merchants, and reported, that having examined the proofs and vouchers exhibited in the cause, they were of opinion that the owner of the vessel and cargo had sustained damage to the amount of $20,594.16, from which is to be deducted the sum of $4,363.86, the amount of money paid into court arising from the sales of the cargo, and the further sum of $1300, being the residue of the proceeds of the said sales remaining, to be brought into court, $5,663.86. This estimate is exclusive of the value of the vessel, which was fixed at $3000. To this report, an account is annexed, in which the damages, without particularizing the items on which the estimate was formed, were stated at $14,930.30.

No exceptions having been taken to this report, it was confirmed, and, by the final sentence of the court, Captain Murray was ordered to pay the amount thereof. From this decree, an appeal was prayed to the circuit court, where the decree was affirmed so far as it directed restitution of the vessel, and payment to the claimant of the net proceeds of the sale of the cargo in Martinique, and reversed for the residue. From this decree, each party has appealed to this court.

It is contended on the part of the captors, in substance, 1st. That the vessel Charming Betsy and cargo are confiscable under the laws of the United States. If not so, 2d. That the captors are entitled to salvage. If this is against them, 3d. That they ought to be excused from damages, because there was probable cause for seizing the vessel and bringing her into port.

1. Is the Charming Betsy subject to seizure and condemnation for having violated a law of the United States? The libel claims this forfeiture under the act passed in February 1800, further to suspend the commercial intercourse between the United States and France and the dependencies thereof. That act declares "that all commercial intercourse," & c. It has been very properly observed, in argument, that the building of vessels in the United States for sale to neutrals, in the islands, is, during war, a profitable business, which congress cannot be intended to have prohibited, unless that intent be manifested by express words or a very plain and necessary implication. It has also been observed, that an act of congress ought never to be construed to violate the law of nations, if any other possible construction remains, and consequently, can never be construed to violate neutral rights, or to affect neutral commerce, further than is warranted by the law of nations as understood in this country. These principles are believed to be correct, and they ought to be kept in view, in construing the act now under consideration.

The first sentence of the act which describes the persons whose commercial intercourse with France or her dependencies is to be prohibited, names any person or persons, resident within the United States, or under their protection. Commerce carried on by persons within this description is declared to be illicit. From persons the act proceeds to things, and declares explicitly the cases in which the vessels employed in this illicit commerce shall be forfeited. Any vessel owned, hired or employed, wholly or in part, by any person residing within the United States, or by any citizen thereof, residing elsewhere, which shall perform certain acts recited in the law, becomes liable to forfeiture. It seems to the court, to be a correct construction of these words, to say, that the vessel must be of this description, not at the time of the passage of the law, but at the time when the act of forfeiture shall be committed.

The cases of forfeiture are, 1st. A vessel of the description mentioned, which shall be voluntarily carried, or shall be destined, or permitted to proceed to any port within the French republic. She must, when carried, or destined, or permitted, to proceed to such port, be a vessel within the description of the act. The second class of cases are those where vessels shall be sold, bartered, intrusted or transferred, for the purpose that they may proceed to such port or place. This part of the section makes the crime of the sale dependent on the purpose for which it was made. If it was intended, that any American vessel, sold to a neutral, should, in the possession of that neutral, be liable to the commercial disabilities imposed on her while she belonged to citizens of the United States, such extraordinary intent ought to have been plainly expressed; and if it was designed to prohibit the sale of American vessels to neutrals, the words placing the forfeiture on the intent with which the sale was made ought not to have been inserted. The third class of cases are those vessels which shall be employed in any traffic by or for any person resident within the territories of the French republic, or any of its dependencies. In these cases, too, the vessels must be within the description of the act, at the time the fact producing the forfeiture was committed.

The Jane having been completely transferred, in the island of St. Thomas, by a *bona fide* sale, to Jared Shattuck, and the forfeiture alleged to have accrued on a fact subsequent to that transfer, the liability of the vessel to forfeiture must depend on the inquiry, whether the purchaser was within the description of the act.

Jared Shattuck having been born within the United States, and not being proved to have expatriated himself, according to any form prescribed by law, is said to remain a citizen, entitled to the benefit, and subject to the disabilities, imposed upon American citizens; and therefore, to come expressly within the description of the act which comprehends American citizens residing elsewhere.

Whether a person born within the United States, or becoming a citizen according to the established laws of the country, can divest himself absolutely of that character, otherwise than in such manner as may be prescribed by law, is a question which it is not necessary at present to decide. The cases cited at bar, and the arguments drawn from the general conduct of the United States on this interesting subject, seem completely to establish the principle, that an American citizen may acquire, in a foreign country, the commercial privileges attached to his domicil, and be exempted from the operation of an act expressed in such general terms as that now under consideration. Indeed, the very expressions of the act would seem to exclude a person under the circumstances of Jared Shattuck. He is not a person under the protection of the United States. The American citizen who goes into a foreign country, although he owes local and temporary allegiance to that country, is yet, if he performs no other act changing his condition, entitled to the protection of his own government; and if, without the violation of any municipal law, he should be oppressed unjustly, he would have a right to claim that protection, and the interposition of the American government in his favor, would be considered a justifiable interposition. But his situation is completely changed, where, by his own act, he has made himself the subject of a foreign power. Although this act may not be sufficient to rescue him from punishment for any crime committed against the United States, a point not intended to be decided, yet it certainly places him out of the protection of the United States, while within the territory of the sovereign to whom he has sworn allegiance, and consequently, takes him out of the description of the act.

It is, therefore, the opinion of the court, that the Charming Betsy, with her cargo, being at the time of her re-capture the *bona fide* property of a Danish burgher, is not forfeitable, in consequence of her being employed in carrying on trade and commerce with a French island.

2. The vessel not being liable to confiscation, the court is brought to the second question, which is:

Are the recaptors entitled to salvage?

[The Court decides that there was no good cause to seize and sell the *Charming Betsy*:]

Neither is it proved * * * that the Charming Betsy was in such imminent hazard of being condemned [by the French admiralty courts] as to entitle the re-captors to salvage.

[The Court affirms the portion of the circuit court's order directing restitution of the vessel and payment of the net proceeds of the sale of cargo, but reverses the circuit court's rejection of additional damages. Dissatisfied with the trial court's estimate of damages, the Supreme Court remands the case for determination of additional damages. A footnote at the end of the case reads:] Captain Murray was reimbursed his damages, interest and charges, out of the treasury of the United States, by an act of congress, January 31st, 1805.

NOTES AND QUESTIONS

1. *The Roles of the Law of Nations in U.S. Municipal Law.* The relationship between the law of nations and U.S. municipal law was also explored in two cases already considered, Filartiga v. Pena-Irala, 630 F.2d 876 (2d Cir. 1980) (in Chapter 1), and The Paquete Habana, 175 U.S. 677 (1900) (in Chapter 3). In *Filartiga* the court looked to the law of nations because it was construing a U.S. statute that expressly referred to it.

In *The Paquete Habana*, the Supreme Court derived a common law rule of decision directly from the law of nations, even without a statutory reference. It is *The Paquete Habana* where the famous quote, "International law is part of our law," appears. How should U.S. courts today use the law of nations when no statute expressly requires its application? The doctrine that the law of nations is part of the common law of the United States is discussed in Mark Weston Janis, *International Law* 105–11 (6th ed. 2012), Louis Henkin, "International Law as Law in the United States," 82 *Michigan Law Review* 1555 (1984), and Harold G. Maier, "The Authoritative Sources of Customary International Law in the United States," 10 *Michigan Journal of International Law* 450 (1989).

Yet another function of the law of nations is illustrated by *The Charming Betsy*. Here in holding that the vessel was to be treated as belonging to a Danish citizen and hence not subject to forfeit, Chief Justice John Marshall famously ruled: "[A]n act of congress ought never to be construed to violate the law of nations, if any other possible construction remains, and consequently, can never be construed to violate neutral rights, or to affect neutral commerce, further than is warranted by the law of nations as understood in this country."

2. *American Neutrality.* Like *De Longchamps, Charming Betsy* shows an early American court treading carefully to avoid a possible conflict between the United States and a stronger and potentially dangerous European state. Here in 1800 the scenario was set deep in the quarter-century struggle, 1789–1815, after the French Revolution between France and Great Britain. Not until 1812 would the United States officially become involved, going to war with the United Kingdom in what Americans call the "War of 1812" (1812–1815). However, there was considerable violence before then. Most pertinent to *Charming Betsy* was the "Quasi-War" with France between 1798 and 1800 when "French privateers captur[ed] hundreds of American ships * * * and infect[ed] American coastal waters, crippling foreign commerce." Roger P. Alford, "Foreign Relations as a Matter of Interpretation: The Use and Abuse of *Charming Betsy*," 67 *Ohio State Law Journal* 1339, 1345 (2006).

In the 19th century and before, states often authorized private vessels to attack pirates or enemies; vessels so authorized were known as privateers. When U.S. naval vessels captured foreign privateers, pirates, or American vessels that violated U.S. law, *e.g.*, by illegally trading with belligerents, Navy captains like Murray and their crews brought captured vessels to port as "prizes" and shared in the proceeds from the sale of the vessels and their cargoes. In this case lower courts found Captain Murray's seizure of the *Charming Betsy* illegal because she was deemed a neutral vessel. Moreover:

> Captain Murray's timing could not have been worse. Two days [after the Acting Secretary of the Navy considered whether or not to pay a bond to appeal the trial court's judgment,] on May 14, 1801, the Pasha of Tripoli declared war against the United States after Jefferson refused to pay the annual tribute to stave off state-sponsored pirates in the Mediterranean. Thus, at the same time the Jefferson Administration was deciding whether to defend Captain Murray's mistreatment of the neutral vessel *Charming Betsy*, it was fighting a war in North Africa to defend the principle of safe passage of neutral vessels from Barbary pirates. In justifying the first overseas war for the young nation, it could hardly afford the perception that its own naval officers were insensitive to the principle of freedom for neutral commerce on the high seas.

Id. at 1349.

Central to Marshall's concern was French maritime practice. Thanks to Napoleon's personal intervention, French admiralty courts had begun to respect neutral shipping even when carrying goods originating in or destined for a hostile nation. On May 29, 1800, a week after Murray and his vessel, the *Constellation*, had set out to sea, the French courts adopted this new, more neutral-friendly rule. "Hard luck or not [for Captain Murray], the [Supreme Court] accepted the invitation * * * to presume that, had the schooner [*Charming Betsy*] been brought into French court, she would have been recognized as Danish and released with damages and costs." Frederick C. Leiner, "The Charming Betsy and the Marshall Court," 45 *American*

Journal of Legal History 1, 14 (2001). If the *Charming Betsy* would not have been condemned by a French court, no salvage would have been due its recaptors in a U.S. court. At the time, the United States boasted the "second largest merchant marine in the world, and much of the nation's prosperity was linked to trade with the belligerents." *Id.* at 17. In *Charming Betsy*, Marshall's key interest was "the reinforcement of international law norms at a time when a militarily weak neutral nation with extensive mercantile interests at stake desperately wanted the law [of neutrality] respected." *Id.* at 18.

3. *The* PLO Case. A judgment that may have overly "stretched" the interpretation of a treaty so as to avoid conflict with U.S. domestic law was United States v. Palestine Liberation Organization, 695 F.Supp. 1456 (S.D.N.Y. 1988), where a U.S. district court judge ruled that the 1987 Anti-Terrorism Act would not be applied to close down the New York office of the Palestine Liberation Organization (PLO) because, as a Permanent Observer to the 1947 United Nations, the PLO was protected by the U.S.-U.N. Headquarters Agreement, June 26, 1947, 61 Stat. 3416, 11 U.N.T.S. 11. Rejecting the U.S. government's argument that the Anti-Terrorism Act trumped the Headquarters Agreement because of the later-in-time rule expressed in *Whitney*, the judge held there was insufficient proof that Congress meant to override the treaty obligations of the United States.

The Reagan administration was split in the aftermath of the *PLO Case*. A high Justice Department official told the *New York Times* that "[t]here is a unanimous belief in this department that the decision should be appealed," but the State Department's Legal Adviser, Abraham Sofaer, countered: "It was a grave mistake for Congress to attempt to close the P.L.O. office. It would violate the United Nations Headquarters Agreement." Clovis Maksoud, the representative of the Arab League in the United States, stated that an appeal "would erode the credibility of the United States in the Middle East." Robert Pear, "U.S. Officials Split Over Whether to Appeal Ruling on P.L.O.," *New York Times*, Aug. 28, 1988, § 1, at 5.

Finally, President Reagan himself resolved the dispute between Justice and State, deciding not to appeal the district court's judgment. On August 29, 1988, the Justice Department issued the following statement: "It is the Administration's normal policy to appeal adverse district court decisions of this kind. But it was decided, in light of foreign policy considerations, including the U.S. role as host to the United Nations organization, not to appeal in this instance." Robert Pear, "U.S. Will Allow P.L.O. to Maintain Its Office at U.N.," *New York Times*, Aug. 30, 1988 at A1. Professor Rosalyn Higgins, later a judge on the International Court of Justice, called the *PLO Case* "a remarkable piece of judicial reasoning, at once admirably purpose-oriented but unpersuasive." Rosalyn Higgins, *Problems and Process: International Law and How We Use It* 215 (1994). Did the *PLO Case* go too far in attempting to reconcile U.S. law and international law?

4. *The Political Question Doctrine.* U.S. courts sometimes invoke the "political question doctrine" to abstain from deciding sensitive foreign policy

questions. According to Justice Powell, the doctrine involves a three-part inquiry: "(i) Does the issue involve resolution of questions committed by the text of the Constitution to a coordinate branch of Government? (ii) Would resolution of the question demand that a court move beyond areas of judicial expertise? (iii) Do prudential considerations counsel against judicial intervention?" Goldwater v. Carter, 444 U.S. 996, 998 (1979) (Powell, J., concurring). See also Baker v. Carr, 369 U.S. 186 (1962). In the *PLO Case* discussed in the preceding Note, the court, although acknowledging that "not all questions touching upon international relations are automatically political questions," nevertheless relied on the political question doctrine to conclude that it would not order the executive branch to arbitrate its dispute concerning the PLO mission. 695 F.Supp. at 1463. The International Court of Justice had ruled, in an advisory opinion, that arbitration of the dispute concerning the PLO mission was required under the U.S.-U.N. Headquarters Agreement. Applicability of the Obligation to Arbitrate Under Section 21 of the United Nations Headquarters Agreement of 26 June 1947, 1988 I.C.J. 12.

SOSA V. ALVAREZ-MACHAIN

542 U.S. 692 (2004)

SOUTER, J., delivered the opinion of the Court, Parts I and III of which were unanimous, Part II of which was joined by REHNQUIST, C.J., and STEVENS, O'CONNOR, SCALIA, KENNEDY and THOMAS, JJ., and Part IV of which was joined by STEVENS, O'CONNOR, KENNEDY, GINSBURG, and BREYER, JJ. SCALIA, J., filed an opinion concurring in part and concurring in the judgment, in which REHNQUIST, C.J., and THOMAS, J., joined. GINSBURG, J., filed an opinion concurring in part and concurring in the judgment, in which BREYER, J., joined. BREYER, J., filed an opinion concurring in part and concurring in the judgment.

JUSTICE SOUTER delivered the opinion of the Court.

The two issues are whether respondent Alvarez-Machain's allegation that the Drug Enforcement Administration instigated his abduction from Mexico for criminal trial in the United States supports a claim against the Government under the Federal Tort Claims Act (FTCA or Act), 28 U.S.C. § 1346(b)(1), §§ 2671–2680, and whether he may recover under the Alien Tort Statute (ATS), 28 U.S.C. § 1350. We hold that he is not entitled to a remedy under either statute.

I

We have considered the underlying facts before, *United States v. Alvarez-Machain*, 504 U.S. 655 (1992). In 1985, an agent of the Drug Enforcement Administration (DEA), Enrique Camarena-Salazar, was captured on assignment in Mexico and taken to a house in Guadalajara, where he was tortured over the course of a 2-day interrogation, then murdered. Based in part on eyewitness testimony, DEA officials in the

United States came to believe that respondent Humberto Alvarez-Machain (Alvarez), a Mexican physician, was present at the house and acted to prolong the agent's life in order to extend the interrogation and torture.

In 1990, a federal grand jury indicted Alvarez for the torture and murder of Camarena-Salazar, and the United States District Court for the Central District of California issued a warrant for his arrest. The DEA asked the Mexican Government for help in getting Alvarez into the United States, but when the requests and negotiations proved fruitless, the DEA approved a plan to hire Mexican nationals to seize Alvarez and bring him to the United States for trial. As so planned, a group of Mexicans, including petitioner Jose Francisco Sosa, abducted Alvarez from his house, held him overnight in a motel, and brought him by private plane to El Paso, Texas, where he was arrested by federal officers.

Once in American custody, Alvarez moved to dismiss the indictment on the ground that his seizure was "outrageous governmental conduct," and violated the extradition treaty between the United States and Mexico. The District Court agreed, the Ninth Circuit affirmed, and we reversed, holding the fact of Alvarez's forcible seizure did not affect the jurisdiction of a federal court. The case was tried in 1992, and ended at the close of the Government's case, when the District Court granted Alvarez's motion for a judgment of acquittal.

In 1993, after returning to Mexico, Alvarez began the civil action before us here. He sued Sosa, Mexican citizen and DEA operative Antonio Garate-Bustamante, five unnamed Mexican civilians, the United States, and four DEA agents. So far as it matters here, Alvarez sought damages from the United States under the FTCA, alleging false arrest, and from Sosa under the ATS, for a violation of the law of nations. The former statute authorizes suit "for . . . personal injury . . . caused by the negligent or wrongful act or omission of any employee of the Government while acting within the scope of his office or employment." 28 U.S.C. § 1346(b)(1). The latter provides in its entirety that "[t]he district courts shall have original jurisdiction of any civil action by an alien for a tort only, committed in violation of the law of nations or a treaty of the United States." § 1350.

The District Court granted the Government's motion to dismiss the FTCA claim but awarded summary judgment and $25,000 in damages to Alvarez on the ATS claim. A three-judge panel of the Ninth Circuit then affirmed the ATS judgment, but reversed the dismissal of the FTCA claim. 266 F.3d 1045 (2001).

A divided en banc court came to the same conclusion. 331 F.3d, at 641. As for the ATS claim, the court called on its own precedent, "that [the ATS] not only provides federal courts with subject matter jurisdiction, but also creates a cause of action for an alleged violation of the law of nations." The Circuit then relied upon what it called the "clear and universally recognized norm prohibiting arbitrary arrest and detention," to support the conclusion that Alvarez's arrest amounted to a tort in violation of international law. On the FTCA claim, the Ninth Circuit held that, because "the DEA had no authority to effect Alvarez's arrest and detention in Mexico," the United States was liable to him under California law for the tort of false arrest.

We granted certiorari in these companion cases to clarify the scope of both the FTCA and the ATS. We now reverse in each.

II

[The Court finds that "the liability asserted here falls within the FTCA exception to waiver of sovereign immunity for claims 'arising in a foreign country,'" and holds that "the exception bars all claims based on any injury suffered in a foreign country, regardless of where the tortious act or omission occurred."]

III

Alvarez has also brought an action under the ATS against petitioner, Sosa, who argues (as does the United States supporting him) that there is no relief under the ATS because the statute does no more than vest federal courts with jurisdiction, neither creating nor authorizing the courts to recognize any particular right of action without further congressional action. Although we agree the statute is in terms only jurisdictional, we think that at the time of enactment the jurisdiction enabled federal courts to hear claims in a very limited category defined by the law of nations and recognized at common law. We do not believe, however, that the limited, implicit sanction to entertain the handful of international law *cum* common law claims understood in 1789 should be taken as authority to recognize the right of action asserted by Alvarez here.

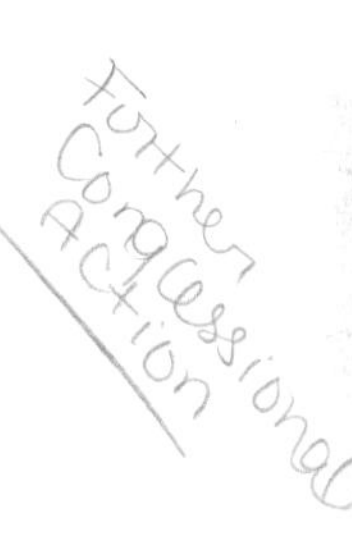

A

Judge Friendly called the ATS a "legal Lohengrin," *IIT v. Vencap, Ltd.*, 519 F.2d 1001, 1015 (C.A.2 1975); "no one seems to know whence it came," and for over 170 years after its enactment it provided jurisdiction in only one case. The first Congress passed it as part of the Judiciary Act of 1789, in providing that the new federal district courts "shall also have cognizance, concurrent with the courts of the several States, or the circuit courts, as the case may be, of all causes where an alien sues for a tort only in violation of the law of nations or a treaty of the United States." Act of Sept. 24, 1789, ch. 20, § 9*(b)*, 1 Stat. 79.

The parties and *amici* here advance radically different historical interpretations of this terse provision. Alvarez says that the ATS was intended not simply as a jurisdictional grant, but as authority for the creation of a new cause of action for torts in violation of international law. We think that reading is implausible. As enacted in 1789, the ATS gave the district courts "cognizance" of certain causes of action, and the term bespoke a grant of jurisdiction, not power to mold substantive law. See *e.g.*, The Federalist No. 81, pp. 447, 451 (J. Cooke ed. 1961) (A. Hamilton) (using "jurisdiction" interchangeably with "cognizance"). The fact that the ATS was placed in § 9 of the Judiciary Act, a statute otherwise exclusively concerned with federal-court jurisdiction, is itself support for its strictly jurisdictional nature. Nor would the distinction between jurisdiction and cause of action have been elided by the drafters of the Act or those who voted on it. As Fisher Ames put it, "there is a substantial difference between the jurisdiction of courts and rules of decision." 1 Annals of Cong. 807 (Gales ed. 1834). It is unsurprising, then, that an authority on the historical origins of the ATS has written that "section 1350 clearly does not create a statutory cause of action," and that the contrary suggestion is "simply frivolous." Casto, The Federal Courts' Protective Jurisdiction Over Torts Committed in Violation of the Law of Nations, 18 Conn. L.Rev. 467, 479, 480 (1986) (hereinafter Casto, Law of Nations); Cf. Dodge, The Constitutionality of the Alien Tort Statute: Some Observations on Text and Context, 42 Va. J. Int'l L. 687, 689 (2002). In sum, we think the statute was intended as jurisdictional in the sense of addressing the power of the courts to entertain cases concerned with a certain subject.

But holding the ATS jurisdictional raises a new question, this one about the interaction between the ATS at the time of its enactment and the ambient law of the era. Sosa would have it that the ATS was stillborn because there could be no claim for relief without a further statute expressly authorizing adoption of causes of action. *Amici* professors of federal jurisdiction and legal history take a different tack, that federal courts could entertain claims once the jurisdictional grant was on the books, because torts in violation of the law of nations would have been recognized within the common law of the time. We think history and practice give the edge to this latter position.

1

"When the *United States* declared their independence, they were bound to receive the law of nations, in its modern state of purity and refinement." *Ware v. Hylton*, 3 Dall. 199, 281 (1796) (Wilson, J.). In the years of the early Republic, this law of nations comprised two principal elements, the first covering the general norms governing the behavior of national states with each other: "*the science which teaches the rights subsisting between nations or states, and the obligations correspondent to those rights,*" E. de Vattel, The Law of Nations, Preliminaries § 3 (J. Chitty et al. transl. and ed 1883) (hereinafter Vattel), or "that code of public instruction which defines the right and prescribes the duties of nations, in their intercourse with each other," 1 James Kent Commentaries 1. This aspect of the law of nations thus occupied the executive and legislative domains, not the judicial. See 4 W. Blackstone, Commentaries on the Laws of England 68 (1769) (hereinafter Commentaries) ("[O]ffenses against" the law of nations are "principally incident to whole states or nations").

The law of nations included a second, more pedestrian element, however, that did fall within the judicial sphere, as a body of judge-made law regulating the conduct of individuals situated outside domestic boundaries and consequently carrying an international savor. To Blackstone, the law of nations in this sense was implicated "in mercantile questions, such as bills of exchange and the like; in all marine causes, related to freight, average, demurrage, insurances, bottomry . . . ; [and] in all disputes relating to prizes, to shipwrecks, to hostages, and ransom bills." *Id.*, at 67. The law merchant emerged from the customary practices of international traders and admiralty required its own transnational regulation. And it was the law of nations in this sense that our precursors spoke about when the Court explained the status of coast fishing vessels in wartime grew from "ancient usage among civilized nations, beginning centuries age, and gradually ripening into a rule of international law . . . " *The Paquete Habana*, 175 U.S. 677, 686 (1900).

There was, finally a sphere in which these rules binding individuals for the benefit of other individuals overlapped with the norms of state relationships. Blackstone referred to it when he mentioned three specific offenses against the law of nations addressed by the criminal law of England: violation of safe conducts, infringements of the rights of ambassadors, and piracy. 4 Commentaries 68. An assault against an ambassador, for example, impinged upon the sovereignty of the foreign nation and if not adequately redressed could rise to an issue of war. See Vattel 463–464. It was this narrow set of violations of the law of nations, admitting of a judicial remedy and at the same time threatening serious consequences in international affairs, that was probably on the minds of the men who drafted the ATS with the reference to tort.

2

Before there was any ATS, a distinctly American preoccupation with these hybrid international norms had taken shape owing to the distribution of political power from independence through the period of confederation. The Continental Congress was hamstrung by its inability to "cause infractions of treaties, or of the law of nations to be punished," J. Madison, Journal of the Constitutional Convention 60 (E. Scott ed. 1893), and in 1781 the Congress implored the States to vindicate rights under the law of nations. In words that echo Blackstone, the congressional resolution called upon state legislatures to "provide expeditious, exemplary, and adequate punishment" for "the violation of safe conducts or passports, . . . of hostility against such as are in amity, . . . with the United States, . . . infractions of the immunities of ambassadors and other public ministers . . . [and] infractions of treaties and conventions to which the United States are a party." 21 Journals of the Continental Congress 1136–1137 (G. Hunt ed. 1912) (hereinafter Journals of the Continental Congress). The resolution recommended that the States "authorise suits . . . for damages by the party injured, and for compensation to the United States for damage sustained by them from an injury done to a foreign power by a citizen." *Id.*, at 1137[.] Apparently only one State acted upon the recommendation, see First Laws of the State of Connecticut 82, 83 (J. Cushing ed. 1982) (1784 compilation; exact date of Act unknown), but Congress had done what it could to signal a commitment to enforce the law of nations.

Appreciation of the Continental Congress's incapacity to deal with this class of cases was intensified by the so-called Marbois incident of May 1784, in which a French adventurer, Longchamps, verbally and physically assaulted the Secretary of the French Legion in Philadelphia. See *Respublica v. De Longchamps*, 1 Dall. 111 (O.T. Phila. 1784).[11] Congress called again for state legislation addressing such matters, and concern over the inadequate vindication of the law of nations persisted through the time of the constitutional convention. During the Convention itself, in fact, a New York City constable produced a reprise of the Marbois affair and Secretary Jay reported to Congress on the Dutch Ambassador's protest, with the explanation that "the federal government does not appear . . . to be vested with any Judicial Powers competent to the Cognizance and Judgment of such Cases." Casto, Law of Nations 494, and n. 152.

The Framers responded by vesting the Supreme Court with original jurisdiction over "all Cases affecting Ambassadors, other public ministers and Consuls." U.S. Const., Art. III, § 2, and the First Congress followed through. The Judiciary Act reinforced this Court's original jurisdiction over suits brought by diplomats, see 1 Stat. 80, ch. 20, § 13, created alienage jurisdiction, § 11 and, of course, included the ATS, § 9.

---

[11] The French minister plenipotentiary lodged a formal protest with the Continental Congress, 27 Journals of the Continental Congress 478, and threatened to leave Pennsylvania "unless the decision on Longchamps Case should give them full satisfaction." Letter from Samuel Hardy to Gov. Benjamin Harrison of Virginia, June 24, 1784, in 7 Letters of Members of the Continental Congress 558, 559 (E. Burnett ed. 1934). Longchamps was prosecuted for a criminal violation of the law of nations in state court.

The Congress could only pass resolutions, one approving the state-court proceedings, 27 Journals of the Continental Congress 503, another directing the Secretary of Foreign Affairs to apologize and to "explain to Mr. De Marbois the difficulties that may arise . . . from the nature of a federal union," 28 Journals of the Continental Congress 314, and to explain to the representative of Louis XVI that "many allowances are to be made for" the young Nation. *Ibid.*

3

[D]espite considerable scholarly attention, it is fair to say that a consensus understanding of what Congress intended has proven elusive.

Still, the history does tend to support two propositions. First, there is every reason to suppose that the First Congress did not pass the ATS as a jurisdictional convenience to be placed on the shelf for use by a future Congress or state legislature that might, some day, authorize the creation of causes of action or itself decide to make some element of the law of nations actionable for the benefit of foreigners. The anxieties of the preconstitutional period cannot be ignored easily enough to think that the statute was not meant to have a practical effect. Consider that the principal draftsman of the ATS was apparently Oliver Ellsworth,[13] previously a member of the Continental Congress that had passed the 1781 resolution and a member of the Connecticut Legislature that made good on that congressional request. See generally W. Brown, The Life of Oliver Ellsworth (1905). Consider, too, that the First Congress was attentive enough to the law of nations to recognize certain offenses expressly as criminal, including the three mentioned by Blackstone. See An Act for the Punishment of Certain Crimes Against the United States, § 8, 1 Stat. 113–114 (murder or robbery, or other capital crimes, punishable as piracy if committed on the high seas), and § 28, *id.*, at 118 (violation of safe conducts and assaults against ambassadors punished by imprisonment and fines described as "infract[ions of] the law of nations"). It would have been passing strange for Ellsworth and this very Congress to vest federal courts expressly with jurisdiction to entertain civil causes brought by aliens alleging violations of the law of nations, but to no effect whatever until the Congress should take further action. There is too much in the historical record to believe that Congress would have enacted the ATS only to leave it lying fallow indefinitely.

The second inference to be drawn from the history is that Congress intended the ATS to furnish jurisdiction for a relatively modest set of actions alleging violations of the law of nations. Uppermost in the legislative mind appears to have been offenses against ambassadors; violations of safe conduct were probably understood to be actionable, and individual actions arising out of prize captures and piracy may well have also been contemplated. But the common law appears to have understood only those three of the hybrid variety as definite or actionable, or at any rate, to have assumed only a very limited set of claims. As Blackstone had put it, "offenses against this law [of nations] are principally incident to whole states or nations," and not individuals seeking relief in court. 4 Commentaries 68.

---

13 The ATS appears in Ellsworth's handwriting in the original version of the bill in the National Archives. Casto, Law of Nations 498, n. 169.

4

The sparse contemporaneous cases and legal materials referring to the ATS tend to confirm both inferences, that some, but few, torts in violation of the law of nations were understood to be within the common law. * * *

Then there was the 1795 opinion of Attorney General William Bradford, who was asked whether criminal prosecution was available against Americans who had taken part in the French plunder of a British slave colony in Sierra Leone. 1 Op. Atty. Gen. 57. Bradford was uncertain, but he made it clear that a federal court was open for the prosecution of a tort action growing out of the episode:

> But there can be no doubt that the company or individuals who have been injured by these acts of hostility have a remedy by a *civil* suit in the courts of the United States; jurisdiction being expressly given to these courts in all cases where an alien sues for a tort only, in violation of the laws of nations, or a treaty of the United States. . . . [*Id.*, at 59.]

Although it is conceivable that Bradford (who had prosecuted in the Marbois incident) assumed that there had been a violation of a treaty, that is certainly not obvious, and it appears likely that Bradford understood the ATS to provide jurisdiction over what must have amounted to common law causes of action.

B

Against these indications that the ATS was meant to underwrite litigation of a narrow set of common law actions derived from the law of nations, Sosa raises two main objections. First, he claims that this conclusion makes no sense in view of the Continental Congress's 1781 recommendation to state legislatures to pass laws authorizing such suits. Sosa thinks state legislation would have been "absurd," if common law remedies had been available. Second, Sosa juxtaposes Blackstone's treatise mentioning violations of the law of nations as occasions for criminal remedies, against the statute's innovative reference to "tort," as evidence that there was no familiar set of legal actions for exercise of jurisdiction under the ATS. Neither argument is convincing.

The notion that it would have been absurd for the Continental Congress to recommend that States pass positive law to duplicate remedies already available at common law rests on a misunderstanding of the relationship between common law and positive law in the late 18th century, when positive law was frequently relied upon to reinforce and give standard expression to the "brooding omnipresence" of the common law then thought discoverable by reason. As Blackstone clarified the relation between positive law and the law of nations, "those acts of parliament, which have from time to time been made to enforce this universal law, or to facilitate the execution of [its] decisions, are not to be considered as introductive of any new rule, but merely as declaratory of the old fundamental constitutions of the kingdom; without which it must cease to be a part of the civilized world." 4 Commentaries 67. Indeed, Sosa's argument is undermined by the 1781 resolution on which he principally relies. Notwithstanding the undisputed fact (per Blackstone) that the common law afforded criminal law remedies for violations of the law of nations, the Continental Congress encouraged state legislatures to pass criminal statutes to the same effect, and the first Congress did the same.

Nor are we convinced by Sosa's argument that legislation conferring a right of action is needed because Blackstone treated international law offenses under the rubric of "public wrongs," whereas the ATS uses a word, "tort," that was relatively uncommon in the legal vernacular of the day. It is true that Blackstone did refer to what he deemed the three principal offenses against the law of nations in the course of discussing criminal sanctions, observing that it was in the interest of sovereigns "to animadvert upon them with a becoming severity, that the peace of the world may be maintained," 4 Commentaries 68. But Vattel explicitly linked the criminal sanction for offenses against ambassadors with the requirement that the state, "at the expense of the delinquent, give full satisfaction to the sovereign who has been offended in the person of his minister." Vattel 463–464. Cf. Stephens, Individuals Enforcing International Law: The Comparative and Historical Context, 52 DePaul L.Rev. 433, 444 (2002) (observing that a "mixed approach to international law violations, encompassing both criminal prosecution ... and compensation to those injured through a civil suit, would have been familiar to the founding generation"). The 1781 resolution goes a step further in showing that a private remedy was thought necessary for diplomatic offenses under the law of nations. And the Attorney General's Letter of 1795, as well as the two early federal precedents discussing the ATS, point to a prevalent assumption that Congress did not intend the ATS to sit on the shelf until some future time when it might enact further legislation.

In sum, although the ATS is a jurisdictional statute creating no new causes of action, the reasonable inference from the historical materials is that the statute was intended to have practical effect the moment it became law. The jurisdictional grant is best read as having been enacted on the understanding that the common law would provide a cause of action for the modest number of international law violations with a potential for personal liability at the time.

IV

We think it is correct, then, to assume that the First Congress understood that the district courts would recognize private causes of action for certain torts in violation of the law of nations, though we have found no basis to suspect Congress had any examples in mind beyond those torts corresponding to Blackstone's three primary offenses: violation of safe conducts, infringement of the rights of ambassadors, and piracy. We assume, too, that no development in the two centuries from the enactment of § 1350 to the birth of the modern line of cases beginning with *Filartiga v. Pena-Irala*, 630 F.2d 876 (C.A.2 1980), has categorically precluded federal courts from recognizing a claim under the law of nations as an element of common law; Congress has not in any relevant way amended § 1350 or limited civil common law power by another statute. Still, there are good reasons for a restrained conception of the discretion a federal court should exercise in considering a new cause of action of this kind. Accordingly, we think courts should require any claim based on the present-day law of nations to rest on a norm of international character accepted by the civilized world and defined with a specificity comparable to the features of the 18th century paradigms we have recognized. This requirement is fatal to Alvarez's claim.

A

A series of reasons argue for judicial caution when considering the kinds of individual claims that might implement the jurisdiction conferred by the early statute. First, the prevailing conception of the common law has changed since 1789 in a way that counsels restraint in judicially applying internationally generated norms. When § 1350 was enacted, the accepted conception was of the common law as "a transcendental body of law outside of any particular State but obligatory within it unless and until changed by statute." *Black and White Taxicab & Transfer Co. v. Brown and Yellow Taxicab & Transfer Co.,* 276 U.S. 518, 533 (1928) (Holmes J., dissenting). Now, however, in most cases where a court is asked to state or formulate a common law principle in a new context, there is a general understanding that the law is not so much found or discovered as it is either made or created. Holmes explained famously in 1881 that

> in substance the growth of the law is legislative . . . [because t]he very considerations which judges most rarely mention, and always with an apology, are the secret root from which the law draws all the juices of life. I mean, of course, considerations of what is expedient for the community concerned. [The Common Law 31–32 (Howe ed. 1963).]

One need not accept the Holmesian view as far as its ultimate implications to acknowledge that a judge deciding reliance on an international norm will find a substantial element of discretionary judgment in the decision.

Second, along with, and in part driven by, that conceptual development in understanding common law has come an equally significant rethinking of the role of the federal courts in making it. *Erie R. Co. v. Tompkins*, 304 U.S. 64 (1938), was the watershed in which we denied the existence of any federal "general" common law, *id.*, at 78, which largely withdrew to havens of specialty, some of them defined by express congressional authorization to devise a body of law directly. Elsewhere, this Court has thought it was in order to create federal common law rules in interstitial areas of particular federal interest. [W]e have even assumed competence to make judicial rules of decision of particular importance to foreign relations, such as the act of state doctrine, see *Banco Nacional de Cuba v. Sabbatino*, 376 U.S. 398, 427 (1964)[;] the general practice has been to look for legislative guidance before exercising innovative authority over substantive law. It would be remarkable to take a more aggressive role in exercising a jurisdiction that remained largely in shadow for much of the prior two centuries.

Third, this Court has recently and repeatedly said that a decision to create a private right of action is one better left to legislative judgment in the great majority of cases. * * *

Fourth, the subject of those collateral consequences is itself a reason for a high bar to new private causes of action for violating international law, for the potential implications for the foreign relations of the United States of recognizing such causes should make courts particularly wary of impinging on the discretion of the Legislative and Executive Branches in managing foreign affairs. It is one thing for American courts to enforce constitutional limits on our own State and Federal Governments' power, but quite another to consider suits under rules that would go so far as to claim a limit on the power of foreign governments over their own citizens, and to hold that a foreign government or its agent has transgressed those limits. Yet modern international law is very concerned with just such questions, and apt to stimulate calls for vindicating private interests in § 1350 cases. Since many attempts by federal courts to craft remedies for the violation of new norms of international law would raise risks of adverse foreign policy consequences, they should be undertaken, if at all, with great caution. Cf. *Tel-Oren v. Libyan Arab Republic*, 726 F.2d 774, 813 (C.A.D.C. 1984) (Bork, J., concurring) (expressing doubt that § 1350 should be read to require "our courts [to] sit in judgment of the conduct of foreign officials in their own countries with respect to their own citizens").

The fifth reason is particularly important in light of the first four. We have no congressional mandate to seek out and define new and debatable violations of the law of nations, and modern indications of congressional understanding of the judicial role in the field have not affirmatively encouraged greater judicial creativity. It is true that a clear mandate appears in the Torture Victim Protection Act of 1991, 106 Stat. 73, providing authority that "establish[es] an unambiguous and modern basis for" federal claims of torture and extrajudicial killing. But that affirmative authority is confined to specific subject matter, and although the legislative history includes the remark that § 1350 should "remain intact to permit suits based on other norms that already exist or may ripen in the future into rules of customary international law," Congress as a body has done nothing to promote such suits. Several times, indeed, the Senate has expressly declined to give the federal courts the task of interpreting and applying international human rights law, as when its ratification of the International Covenant on Civil and Political Rights declared that the substantive provisions of the document were not self-executing. 138 Cong. Rec. 8071 (1992).

These reasons argue for great caution in adapting the law of nations to private rights. Justice Scalia (opinion concurring in part and concurring in judgment) concludes that caution is too hospitable, and a word is in order to summarize where we have come so far and to focus our difference with him on whether some norms of today's law of nations may ever be recognized legitimately by federal courts in the absence of congressional action beyond § 1350. All Members of the Court agree that § 1350 is only jurisdictional. We also agree, or at least Justice Scalia does not dispute, that the jurisdiction was originally understood to be available to enforce a small number of international norms that a federal court could properly recognize as within the common law enforceable without further statutory authority. Justice Scalia concludes, however, that two subsequent developments should be understood to preclude federal courts from recognizing any further international norms as judicially enforceable today, absent further congressional action. As described before, we now tend to understand common law not as a discoverable reflection of universal reason but, in a positivistic way, as a product of human choice. And we now adhere to a conception of limited judicial power first expressed in reorienting federal diversity jurisdiction, see *Erie R. Co. v. Tompkins*, 304 U.S. 64 (1938), that federal courts have no authority to derive "general" common law.

Whereas Justice Scalia sees these developments as sufficient to close the door to further independent judicial recognition of actionable international norms, other considerations persuade us that the judicial power should be exercised on the understanding that the door is still ajar subject to vigilant doorkeeping, and thus open to a narrow class of international norms today. *Erie* did not in terms bar any judicial recognition of new substantive rules, no matter what the circumstances, and post-*Erie* understanding has identified limited enclaves in which federal courts may derive some substantive law in a common law way. For two centuries we have affirmed that the domestic law of the United

States recognizes the law of nations. See, *e.g. Sabbatino*, 376 U.S., at 423 ("[I]t is, of course, true that United States courts apply international law as a part of our own in appropriate circumstances"); *Paquete Habana*, 175 U.S., at 700 ("International law is part of our law, and must be ascertained and administered by the courts of justice of appropriate jurisdiction, as often as questions of right depending upon it are duly presented for their determination"); *The Nereide*, 9 Cranch 388, 423 (1815) (Marshall, C.J.) ("[T]he Court is bound by the law of nations which is a part of the law of the land"); see also *Texas Industries, Inc. v. Radcliff Materials, Inc.*, 451 U.S. 630, 641 (1981) (recognizing that "international disputes implicating . . . our relations with foreign nations" are one of the "narrow areas" in which "federal common law" continues to exist). It would take some explaining to say now that federal courts must avert their gaze entirely from any international norm intended to protect individuals.

We think an attempt to justify such a position would be particularly unconvincing in light of what we know about congressional understanding bearing on this issue lying at the intersection of the judicial and legislative powers. The First Congress, which reflected the understanding of the framing generation and included some of the Framers, assumed that federal courts could properly identify some international norms as enforceable in the exercise of § 1350 jurisdiction. We think it would be unreasonable to assume that the First Congress would have expected federal courts to lose all capacity to recognize enforceable international norms simply because the common law might lose some metaphysical cachet on the road to modern realism. Later Congresses seem to have shared our view. The position we take today has been assumed by some federal courts for 24 years, ever since the Second Circuit decided *Filartiga v. Pena-Irala*, 630 F.2d 876 (C.A.2 1980), and for practical purposes the point of today's disagreement has been focused since the exchange between Judge Edwards and Judge Bork in *Tel-Oren v. Libyan Arab Republic*, 726 F.2d 774 (C.A.D.C.1984). Congress, however, has not only expressed no disagreement with our view of the proper exercise of the judicial power, but has responded to its most notable instance by enacting legislation supplementing the judicial determination in some detail. See *supra* (discussing the Torture Victim Protection Act).

While we agree with Justice Scalia to the point that we would welcome any congressional guidance in exercising jurisdiction with such obvious potential to affect foreign relations, nothing Congress has done is a reason for us to shut the door to the law of nations entirely. It is enough to say that Congress may do that at any time (explicitly, or implicitly by treaties or statutes that occupy the field) just as it may modify or cancel any judicial decision so far as it rests on recognizing an international norm as such.

C

We must still, however, derive a standard or set of standards for assessing the particular claim Alvarez raises, and for this case it suffices to look to the historical antecedents. Whatever the ultimate criteria for accepting a cause of action subject to jurisdiction under § 1350, we are persuaded that federal courts should not recognize private claims under federal common law for violations of any international law norm with less definite content and acceptance among civilized nations than the historical paradigms familiar when § 1350 was enacted. See, *e.g. United States v. Smith*, 5 Wheat. 153, 163–180, n. a. (1820) (illustrating the specificity with which the law of nations defined piracy). This limit upon judicial recognition is generally consistent with the reasoning of many of the courts and judges who faced the issue before it reached this Court. See *Filartiga, supra*, at 890 ("[F]or purposes of civil liability, the torturer has become—like the pirate and slave trader before him—*hostis humani generis*, an enemy of all mankind"): *Tel-Oren, supra*, at 781 (Edwards, J., concurring) (suggesting that the "limits of section 1350's reach" be defined by "a handful of heinous actions—each of which violates definable, universal and obligatory norms"); see also *In re Estate of Marcos Human Rights Litigation*, 25 F.3d 1467, 1475 (C.A.9 1994) ("Actionable violations of international law must be of a norm that is specific, universal, and obligatory"). And the determination whether a norm is sufficiently definite to support a cause of action[20] should (and, indeed, inevitably must) involve an element of judgment about the practical consequences of making that cause available to litigants in the federal courts.

Thus, Alvarez's detention claim must be gauged against the current state of international law, looking to those sources we have long, albeit cautiously, recognized.

> [W]here there is no treaty, and no controlling executive or legislative act or judicial decision, resort must be had to the customs and usages of civilized nations; and, as evidence of these, to the works of jurists and commentators, who by years of labor, research and experience, have made themselves peculiarly well acquainted with the subjects of which they treat. Such works are resorted to by judicial tribunals, not for the speculations of their authors concerning what the law ought to be, but for trustworthy evidence of what the law really is. [*The Paquete Habana*, 175 U.S. at 700.]

[20] A related consideration is whether international law extends the scope of liability for a violation of a given norm to the perpetrator being sued, if the defendant is a private actor such as a corporation or an individual. Compare *Tel–Oren v. Libyan Arab Republic*, 726 F.2d 774, 791–795 (C.A.D.C.1984) (Edwards, J., concurring) (insufficient consensus in 1984 that torture by private actors violates international law), with *Kadic v. Karadžić*, 70 F.3d 232, 239–241 (C.A.2 1995) (sufficient consensus in 1995 that genocide by private actors violates international law).

To begin with, Alvarez cites two well-known international agreements that, despite their moral authority, have little utility under the standard set out in this opinion. He says that his abduction by Sosa was an "arbitrary arrest" within the meaning of the Universal Declaration of Human Rights (Declaration), G.A. Res. 217A (III), U.N. Doc. A/810 (1948). And he traces the rule against arbitrary arrest not only to the Declaration, but also to article nine of the International Covenant on Civil and Political Rights (Covenant), Dec. 19, 1996, 999 U.N.T.S. 171, to which the United States is a party, and to various other conventions to which it is not. But the Declaration does not of its own force impose obligations as a matter of international law. See Humphrey, The UN Charter and the Universal Declaration of Human Rights, in The International Protection of Human Rights 39, 50 (E. Luard ed. 1967) (quoting Eleanor Roosevelt calling the Declaration " 'a statement of principles . . . setting up a common standard of achievement for all peoples and all nations' " and " 'not a treaty or international agreement . . . impos[ing] legal obligations' "). And, although the Covenant does bind the United States as a matter of international law, the United States ratified the Covenant on the express understanding that it was not self-executing and so did not itself create obligations enforceable in the federal courts. Accordingly, Alvarez cannot say that the Declaration and Covenant themselves establish the relevant and applicable rule of international law. He instead attempts to show that prohibition of arbitrary arrest has attained the status of binding customary international law.

Here, it is useful to examine Alvarez's complaint in greater detail. As he presently argues it, the claim does not rest on the cross-border feature of his abduction. Although the District Court granted relief in part on finding a violation of international law in taking Alvarez across the border from Mexico to the United States, the Court of Appeals rejected that ground of liability for failure to identify a norm of requisite force prohibiting a forcible abduction across a border. Instead, it relied on the conclusion that the law of the United States did not authorize Alvarez's arrest, because the DEA lacked extraterritorial authority under 21 U.S.C. § 878, and because Federal Rule of Criminal Procedure 4(d)(2) limited the warrant for Alvarez's arrest to "the jurisdiction of the United States." It is this position that Alvarez takes now: that his arrest was arbitrary and as such forbidden by international law not because it infringed the prerogatives of Mexico, but because no applicable law authorized it.

Alvarez thus invokes a general prohibition of "arbitrary" detention defined as officially sanctioned action exceeding positive authorization to detain under the domestic law of some government, regardless of the circumstances. Whether or not this is an accurate reading of the Covenant, Alvarez cites little authority that a rule so broad has the status of a binding customary norm today.[27] He certainly cites nothing to justify the federal courts in taking his broad rule as the predicate for a federal lawsuit, for its implications would be breathtaking. His rule would support a cause of action in federal court for any arrest, anywhere in the world, unauthorized by the law of the jurisdiction in which it took place, and would create a cause of action for any seizure of an alien in violation of the Fourth Amendment, supplanting the actions under Rev. Stat. § 1979, 42 U.S.C. § 1983 and *Bivens v. Six Unknown Fed. Narcotics Agents*, 403 U.S. 388 (1971), that now provide damages remedies for such violations. It would create an action in federal court for arrests by state officers who simply exceed their authority; and for the violation of any limit that the law of any country might place on the authority of its own officers to arrest. And all of this assumes that Alvarez could establish that Sosa was acting on behalf of a government when he made the arrest, for otherwise he would need a rule broader still.

Alvarez's failure to marshal support for his proposed rule is underscored by the Restatement (Third) of Foreign Relations Law of the United States (1987), which says in its discussion of customary international human rights law that a "state violates international law if, as a matter of state policy, it practices, encourages, or condones . . . prolonged arbitrary detention." *Id.*, § 702. Although the Restatement does not explain its requirements of a "state policy" and of "prolonged" detention, the implication is clear. Any credible invocation of a principle against arbitrary detention that the civilized world accepts as binding customary international law requires a factual basis beyond relatively brief detention in excess of positive authority. Even the Restatement's limits are only the beginning of the enquiry, because although it is easy to say that some policies of prolonged arbitrary detentions are so bad that those who enforce them become enemies of the human race, it may be harder to say which policies cross that line with the certainty afforded by Blackstone's three common law offenses. In any event, the label would never fit the reckless policeman who botches his warrant, even though that same officer might pay damages under municipal law.

---

27 Specifically, he relies on a survey of national constitutions, Bassiouni, Human Rights in the Context of Criminal Justice: Identifying International Procedural Protections and Equivalent Protections in National Constitutions, 3 Duke J. Comp. & Int'l L. 235, 260–261 (1993); a case from the International Court of Justice, *United States v. Iran*, 1980 I.C.J. 3, 42; and some authority drawn from the federal courts. None of these suffice. The Bassiouni survey does show that many nations recognize a norm against arbitrary detention, but that consensus is at a high level of generality. The *Iran* case, in which the United States sought relief for the taking of its diplomatic and consular staff as hostages, involved a different set of international norms and mentioned the problem of arbitrary detention only in passing; the detention in that case was, moreover, far longer and harsher the Alvarez's. See 1980 I.C.J., at 42, ¶ 91 ("detention of [United States] staff by a group of armed militants" lasted "many months"). And the authority from the federal courts, to the extent it supports Alvarez's position, reflects a more assertive view of federal judicial discretion over claims based on customary international law than the position we take today.

Whatever may be said for the broad principle Alvarez advances, in the present, imperfect world, it expresses an aspiration that exceeds any binding customary rule having the specificity we require. Creating a private cause of action to further that aspiration would go beyond any residual common law discretion we think is appropriate to exercise. It is enough to hold that a single illegal detention of less than a day, followed by the transfer of custody to lawful authorities and a prompt arraignment, violates no norm of customary international law so well defined as to support the creation of a federal remedy. * * *

The judgment of the Court of Appeals is

Reversed.

NOTES AND QUESTIONS

1. *The Aftermath of* Alvarez-Machain. The opinions in *Sosa* briefly recounted the facts and judgment in United States v. Alvarez-Machain, 504 U.S. 655 (1992), where the Supreme Court ruled that a U.S.-government kidnapping in Mexico did not violate the terms of the U.S.-Mexican extradition treaty. What *Sosa* could only hint at was the overwhelming outrage with which *Alvarez-Machain* was greeted. Mexico especially was deeply upset with the decision. Tim Golden, "After Court Ruling, Mexico Tells U.S. Drug Agents to Halt Activity," *New York Times*, June 16, 1992, at 19. Political leaders in the Caribbean, Latin America, Canada, Australia, and Europe also objected. See Jonathan A. Bush, "How Did We Get Here? Foreign Abduction After *Alvarez-Machain*," 45 *Stanford Law Review* 939, 941–42 & nn.11–15 (1993). The Supreme Court's judgment in *Alvarez-Machain* appeared all the more preposterous when the trial judge ultimately acquitted the Mexican doctor on the grounds that the U.S. government's evidence against him "had been based on 'hunches' and the 'wildest speculation' and had failed to support the charges that he had participated in the torture of the drug agent." Seth Mydans, "Judge Clears Mexican in Agent's Killing," *New York Times*, Dec. 15, 1992, at A20. President-elect Bill Clinton condemned *Alvarez-Machain*: "I think that in the absence of some evidence the [Mexican] government was actually taking a dive or trying to thwart us that the principle the Supreme Court articulated was way too broad." Frank J. Murray, "Clinton Hits Court's Kidnapping Decision," *The Washington Times*, Dec. 16, 1992, at A4. The *Washington Post* opined that "the U.S. government's performance was both embarrassing and badly misguided." "The Collapse of the Alvarez Case," *Washington Post*, Dec. 17, 1992, at A22. As President, Mr. Clinton promised Mexico that the United States government would not conduct any cross-border kidnapping. Steven A. Holmes, "U.S. Gives Mexico Abduction Pledge," *New York Times*, June 22, 1993, at A11.

2. Alvarez-Machain *and International Law*. Professor Louis Henkin, then President of the American Society of International Law, wrote:

> During its past term, the U.S. Supreme Court had one of its infrequent opportunities to take international law seriously and to assure that the Executive Branch takes international law seriously. The Supreme Court failed. The Attorney General was "gratified."
>
> [T]he "victory" for the Department of Justice may prove to be pyrrhic. The judicial-executive distortion of standard extradition treaties is remediable, and our treaty partners will no doubt find their remedies. In reaction to general outrage, the United States will—at the least—have to disown that interpretation if it is to maintain its network of extradition treaties, as important to the United States as to any state in the world.
>
> The larger, longer question is whether the Government of the United States—all branches—is prepared to commit itself to taking international law seriously. * * *
>
> If the Attorney General continues to refuse to take international law seriously, if the Supreme Court refuses to compel the Department of Justice to take international law seriously, it is up to the President of the United States. * * *
>
> If the President will not act, it will be up to Congress. The Constitution put international law in the special care of Congress when it gave to that branch the power to define offenses against the Law of Nations.

Louis Henkin, "Will the U.S. Supreme Court Fail International Law?," *Newsletter of the American Society of International Law*, Aug.–Sept. 1992, at 1, 1–2. Should Congress have responded to *Alvarez-Machain* by making it a federal crime for any U.S. official to kidnap any person in violation of international law? Under Article I(8) of the U.S. Constitution (see Appendix), Congress has the power to "define and punish * * * Offences against the Law of Nations."

3. *Dr. Alvarez-Machain Revisited.* Twelve years after its controversial judgment in *United States v. Alvarez-Machain*, the Supreme Court revisited Dr. Alvarez-Machain. Released and returned to Mexico, Alvarez-Machain sued both the U.S. government and the individuals involved in his kidnapping. As we saw in *Sosa*, the Supreme Court decided in 2004 that Alvarez-Machain could not recover damages, either against the United States under the Federal Tort Claims Act or against the individual kidnappers under the Alien Tort Statute. Though Alvarez-Machain was again disappointed by the Supreme Court, international law was much better served in the second judgment.

4. Filartiga v. Pena-Irala *Revisited.* The Court's judgment in *Sosa* was authored by Justice Souter, who conducted a masterful analysis of the Alien Tort Statute, writing an opinion that is careful and sophisticated with respect to international law. Justice Souter reaffirmed much of Judge Kaufman's 1980 opinion in *Filartiga* that ushered in so much human rights litigation in the next three decades. *Sosa* is based on an elegant and nuanced reading of

the cases and commentary that have appeared since *Filartiga.* For the purposes of the Alien Tort Statute, it is the judgment's Part III, which dealt with the Alien Tort Statute as it was in 1789, and Part IV, which dealt with a reading of the Alien Tort Statute in today's law, that are most important. Justice Souter's interpretation of the Statute in 1789 represented the unanimous(!) opinion of the Court, while his interpretation of the modern Statute marshaled the support of six of the nine Justices. The judgment preserved the Alien Tort Statute as a living, albeit limited, part of U.S. federal law relating to the law of nations.

5. *"Definite" Violations of the Law of Nations.* The *Sosa* Court unanimously agreed that three violations of the law of nations were definite enough in 1789 (and presumably today?) to be prosecuted under the Alien Tort Statute: offenses against ambassadors (the subject matter of *De Longchamps*), violations against safe conducts, and piracy (the subject matter of *Smith*). Justice Souter (for six members of the Court) also accepted that new violations may become definite enough in modern international law to qualify for Alien Tort Statute protection, but, he said, "we think courts should require any claim based on the present-day law of nations to rest on a norm of international character accepted by the civilized world and defined with a specificity comparable to the features of the 18th-century paradigms we have recognized." Evaluate the Court's rejection of Alvarez-Machain's claim to such a violation. What now is the status of other kinds of violations accepted as definite enough by earlier lower courts, *e.g., Filartiga* in Chapter 1?

6. *Proving the Law of Nations in U.S. Law. Sosa* is an excellent example of proving the law of nations in the common law, specifically in the federal law of the United States. Locate the different evidences employed to show what a "tort" committed in violation of the "law of nations" meant in 1789 and what it means today. Justice Souter used evidences drawn at least from the following categories: the legislative histories of the Congress before the Constitution, the founding fathers drafting the Constitution, and the First Congress; writers on the law of nations from Blackstone to modern law review articles; judicial decisions from the Supreme Court and other courts; U.S. executive branch and legislative branch practice; and international conventions and declarations. Compare the proof of the law of nations in *Sosa* with some of the other judicial decisions proving international, but non-treaty, rules: *Filartiga, Paquete Habana, Lotus, AM & S, Smith,* and *De Longchamps.*

KIOBEL V. ROYAL DUTCH PETROLEUM CO.

133 S.Ct. 1659 (2013)

Chief Justice ROBERTS delivered the opinion of the Court.

Petitioners, a group of Nigerian nationals residing in the United States, filed suit in federal court against certain Dutch, British, and Nigerian corporations. Petitioners sued under the Alien Tort Statute, 28 U.S.C. § 1350, alleging that the corporations aided and abetted the

Nigerian Government in committing violations of the law of nations in Nigeria. The question presented is whether and under what circumstances courts may recognize a cause of action under the Alien Tort Statute, for violations of the law of nations occurring within the territory of a sovereign other than the United States.

I

Petitioners were residents of Ogoniland, an area of 250 square miles located in the Niger delta area of Nigeria and populated by roughly half a million people. When the complaint was filed, respondents Royal Dutch Petroleum Company and Shell Transport and Trading Company, p.l.c., were holding companies incorporated in the Netherlands and England, respectively. Their joint subsidiary, respondent Shell Petroleum Development Company of Nigeria, Ltd. (SPDC), was incorporated in Nigeria, and engaged in oil exploration and production in Ogoniland. According to the complaint, after concerned residents of Ogoniland began protesting the environmental effects of SPDC's practices, respondents enlisted the Nigerian Government to violently suppress the burgeoning demonstrations. Throughout the early 1990's, the complaint alleges, Nigerian military and police forces attacked Ogoni villages, beating, raping, killing, and arresting residents and destroying or looting property. Petitioners further allege that respondents aided and abetted these atrocities by, among other things, providing the Nigerian forces with food, transportation, and compensation, as well as by allowing the Nigerian military to use respondents' property as a staging ground for attacks.

Following the alleged atrocities, petitioners moved to the United States where they have been granted political asylum and now reside as legal residents. They filed suit in the United States District Court for the Southern District of New York, alleging jurisdiction under the Alien Tort Statute and requesting relief under customary international law. The ATS provides, in full, that "[t]he district courts shall have original jurisdiction of any civil action by an alien for a tort only, committed in violation of the law of nations or a treaty of the United States." According to petitioners, respondents violated the law of nations by aiding and abetting the Nigerian Government in committing (1) extrajudicial killings; (2) crimes against humanity; (3) torture and cruel treatment; (4) arbitrary arrest and detention; (5) violations of the rights to life, liberty, security, and association; (6) forced exile; and (7) property destruction. The District Court dismissed the first, fifth, sixth, and seventh claims, reasoning that the facts alleged to support those claims did not give rise to a violation of the law of nations. The court denied respondents' motion to dismiss with respect to the remaining claims, but certified its order for interlocutory appeal pursuant to § 1292(b).

The Second Circuit dismissed the entire complaint, reasoning that the law of nations does not recognize corporate liability. We granted certiorari to consider that question. After oral argument, we directed the parties to file supplemental briefs addressing an additional question: "Whether and under what circumstances the [ATS] allows courts to recognize a cause of action for violations of the law of nations occurring within the territory of a sovereign other than the United States." 132 S.Ct. 1738 (2012). We heard oral argument again and now affirm the judgment below, based on our answer to the second question.

II

Passed as part of the Judiciary Act of 1789, the ATS was invoked twice in the late 18th century, but then only once more over the next 167 years. The statute provides district courts with jurisdiction to hear certain claims, but does not expressly provide any causes of action. We held in *Sosa v. Alvarez-Machain,* 542 U.S. 692 (2004), however, that the First Congress did not intend the provision to be "stillborn." The grant of jurisdiction is instead "best read as having been enacted on the understanding that the common law would provide a cause of action for [a] modest number of international law violations." *Id.,* at 724. We thus held that federal courts may "recognize private claims [for such violations] under federal common law." *Id.,* at 732. The Court in *Sosa* rejected the plaintiff's claim in that case for "arbitrary arrest and detention," on the ground that it failed to state a violation of the law of nations with the requisite "definite content and acceptance among civilized nations." *Id.,* at 699, 732.

The question here is not whether petitioners have stated a proper claim under the ATS, but whether a claim may reach conduct occurring in the territory of a foreign sovereign. Respondents contend that claims under the ATS do not, relying primarily on a canon of statutory interpretation known as the presumption against extraterritorial application. That canon provides that "[w]hen a statute gives no clear indication of an extraterritorial application, it has none," *Morrison v. National Australia Bank Ltd.,* 130 S.Ct. 2869, 2878 (2010), and reflects the "presumption that United States law governs domestically but does not rule the world," .

This presumption "serves to protect against unintended clashes between our laws and those of other nations which could result in international discord." *EEOC v. Arabian American Oil Co.,* 499 U.S. 244 (1991) (*Aramco*). As this Court has explained:

> "For us to run interference in . . . a delicate field of international relations there must be present the affirmative intention of the Congress clearly expressed. It alone has the facilities necessary to make fairly such an important policy decision where the possibilities of international discord are so

> evident and retaliative action so certain." *Benz v. Compania Naviera Hidalgo, S.A.*, 353 U.S. 138 (1957). The presumption against extraterritorial application helps ensure that the Judiciary does not erroneously adopt an interpretation of U.S. law that carries foreign policy consequences not clearly intended by the political branches.

We typically apply the presumption to discern whether an Act of Congress regulating conduct applies abroad. See, *e.g., Aramco, supra,* at 246 ("These cases present the issue whether Title VII applies extraterritorially to regulate the employment practices of United States employers who employ United States citizens abroad"); *Morrison, supra* (noting that the question of extraterritorial application was a "merits question," not a question of jurisdiction). The ATS, on the other hand, is "strictly jurisdictional." *Sosa*, 542 U.S., at 713. It does not directly regulate conduct or afford relief. It instead allows federal courts to recognize certain causes of action based on sufficiently definite norms of international law. But we think the principles underlying the canon of interpretation similarly constrain courts considering causes of action that may be brought under the ATS.

Indeed, the danger of unwarranted judicial interference in the conduct of foreign policy is magnified in the context of the ATS, because the question is not what Congress has done but instead what courts may do. This Court in *Sosa* repeatedly stressed the need for judicial caution in considering which claims could be brought under the ATS, in light of foreign policy concerns. As the Court explained, "the potential [foreign policy] implications . . . of recognizing . . . . causes [under the ATS] should make courts particularly wary of impinging on the discretion of the Legislative and Executive Branches in managing foreign affairs." *Id.*, at 727 ("Since many attempts by federal courts to craft remedies for the violation of new norms of international law would raise risks of adverse foreign policy consequences, they should be undertaken, if at all, with great caution"); ("[T]he possible collateral consequences of making international rules privately actionable argue for judicial caution"). These concerns, which are implicated in any case arising under the ATS, are all the more pressing when the question is whether a cause of action under the ATS reaches conduct within the territory of another sovereign.

These concerns are not diminished by the fact that *Sosa* limited federal courts to recognizing causes of action only for alleged violations of international law norms that are " 'specific, universal, and obligatory.' " *Id.*, at 732. As demonstrated by Congress's enactment of the Torture Victim Protection Act of 1991, 106 Stat. 73, note following 28 U.S.C. § 1350, identifying such a norm is only the beginning of defining a cause of action. See *id.*, § 3 (providing detailed definitions for extrajudicial killing and torture); *id.*, § 2 (specifying who may be liable, creating a rule of exhaustion, and establishing a statute of limitations). Each of these decisions carries with it significant foreign policy implications.

The principles underlying the presumption against extraterritoriality thus constrain courts exercising their power under the ATS.

III

Petitioners contend that even if the presumption applies, the text, history, and purposes of the ATS rebut it for causes of action brought under that statute. It is true that Congress, even in a jurisdictional provision, can indicate that it intends federal law to apply to conduct occurring abroad. See, *e.g.,* 18 U.S.C. § 1091(e) (providing jurisdiction over the offense of genocide "regardless of where the offense is committed" if the alleged offender is, among other things, "present in the United States"). But to rebut the presumption, the ATS would need to evince a "clear indication of extraterritoriality." *Morrison,* 130 S.Ct., at 2883. It does not.

To begin, nothing in the text of the statute suggests that Congress intended causes of action recognized under it to have extraterritorial reach. The ATS covers actions by aliens for violations of the law of nations, but that does not imply extraterritorial reach—such violations affecting aliens can occur either within or outside the United States. Nor does the fact that the text reaches "*any* civil action" suggest application to torts committed abroad; it is well established that generic terms like "any" or "every" do not rebut the presumption against extraterritoriality.

Petitioners make much of the fact that the ATS provides jurisdiction over civil actions for "torts" in violation of the law of nations. They claim that in using that word, the First Congress "necessarily meant to provide for jurisdiction over extraterritorial transitory torts that could arise on foreign soil." For support, they cite the common-law doctrine that allowed courts to assume jurisdiction over such "transitory torts," including actions for personal injury, arising abroad. See *Mostyn v. Fabrigas,* 98 Eng. Rep. 1021, 1030 (1774) (Mansfield, L.) ("[A]ll actions of a transitory nature that arise abroad may be laid as happening in an English county"); *Dennick v. Railroad Co.,* 103 U.S. 11, 18 (1881) ("Wherever, by either the common law or the statute law of a State, a right of action has become fixed and a legal liability incurred, that liability may be enforced and the right of action pursued in any court which has jurisdiction of such matters and can obtain jurisdiction of the parties").

Under the transitory torts doctrine, however, "the only justification for allowing a party to recover when the cause of action arose in another civilized jurisdiction is a well founded belief that it was a cause of action in that place." *Cuba R. Co. v. Crosby,* 222 U.S. 473, 479 (1912) (majority opinion of Holmes, J.). The question under *Sosa* is not whether a federal court has jurisdiction to entertain a cause of action provided by foreign or even international law. The question is instead whether the court has authority to recognize a cause of action under U.S. law to enforce a norm of international law. The reference to "tort" does not demonstrate that the First Congress "necessarily meant" for those causes of action to reach conduct in the territory of a foreign sovereign. In the end, nothing in the text of the ATS evinces the requisite clear indication of extraterritoriality.

Nor does the historical background against which the ATS was enacted overcome the presumption against application to conduct in the territory of another sovereign. We explained in *Sosa* that when Congress passed the ATS, "three principal offenses against the law of nations" had been identified by Blackstone: violation of safe conducts, infringement of the rights of ambassadors, and piracy. 542 U.S., at 723, 724; see 4 W. Blackstone, Commentaries on the Laws of England 68 (1769). The first two offenses have no necessary extraterritorial application. Indeed, Blackstone—in describing them—did so in terms of conduct occurring within the forum nation. See *ibid.* (describing the right of safe conducts for those "who are here"); 1 *id.,* at 251 (1765) (explaining that safe conducts grant a member of one society "a right to intrude into another"); *id.,* at 245–248 (recognizing the king's power to "receiv[e] ambassadors at home" and detailing their rights in the state "wherein they are appointed to reside"); see also E. De Vattel, Law of Nations 465 (J. Chitty et al. transl. and ed. 1883) ("[O]n his entering the country to which he is sent, and making himself known, [the ambassador] is under the protection of the law of nations . . .").

Two notorious episodes involving violations of the law of nations occurred in the United States shortly before passage of the ATS. Each concerned the rights of ambassadors, and each involved conduct within the Union. In 1784, a French adventurer verbally and physically assaulted Francis Barbe Marbois—the Secretary of the French Legion—in Philadelphia. The assault led the French Minister Plenipotentiary to lodge a formal protest with the Continental Congress and threaten to leave the country unless an adequate remedy were provided. *Respublica v. De Longchamps,* 1 Dall. 111 (O.T.Phila.1784). And in 1787, a New York constable entered the Dutch Ambassador's house and arrested one of his domestic servants. See Casto, The Federal Courts' Protective Jurisdiction over Torts Committed in Violation of the Law of Nations, 18 Conn. L. Rev. 467, 494 (1986). At the request of Secretary of Foreign Affairs John Jay, the Mayor of New York City arrested the constable in turn, but cautioned that because " 'neither Congress nor our [State] Legislature have yet passed any act respecting a breach of the privileges of Ambassadors,' " the extent of any available relief would depend on the common law. See Bradley, The Alien Tort Statute and Article III, 42 Va. J. Int'l L. 587, 641–642 (2002) (quoting 3 Dept. of State, The Diplomatic Correspondence of the United States of America 447 (1837)). The two cases in which the ATS was invoked shortly after its passage also concerned conduct within the territory of the United States. See *Bolchos,* 3 F. Cas. 810 (wrongful seizure of slaves from a vessel while in port in the United States); *Moxon,* 17 F. Cas. 942 (wrongful seizure in United States territorial waters).

These prominent contemporary examples—immediately before and after passage of the ATS—provide no support for the proposition that Congress expected causes of action to be brought under the statute for violations of the law of nations occurring abroad.

The third example of a violation of the law of nations familiar to the Congress that enacted the ATS was piracy. Piracy typically occurs on the high seas, beyond the territorial jurisdiction of the United States or any other country. See 4 Blackstone, *supra,* at 72 ("The offence of piracy, by common law, consists of committing those acts of robbery and depredation upon the high seas, which, if committed upon land, would have amounted to felony there"). * * * Petitioners contend that because Congress surely intended the ATS to provide jurisdiction for actions against pirates, it necessarily anticipated the statute would apply to conduct occurring abroad.

Applying U.S. law to pirates, however, does not typically impose the sovereign will of the United States onto conduct occurring within the territorial jurisdiction of another sovereign, and therefore carries less direct foreign policy consequences. Pirates were fair game wherever found, by any nation, because they generally did not operate within any jurisdiction. We do not think that the existence of a cause of action against them is a sufficient basis for concluding that other causes of action under the ATS reach conduct that does occur within the territory of another sovereign; pirates may well be a category unto themselves. See *Morrison,* 130 S.Ct., at 2883 ("[W]hen a statute provides for some extraterritorial application, the presumption against extraterritoriality operates to limit that provision to its terms.") * * *

Finally, there is no indication that the ATS was passed to make the United States a uniquely hospitable forum for the enforcement of international norms. As Justice Story put it, "No nation has ever yet pretended to be the custos morum of the whole world. . . ." *United States v. The La Jeune Eugenie,* 26 F. Cas. 832, 847 (No. 15,551) (C.C.Mass.1822). It is implausible to suppose that the First Congress wanted their fledgling Republic—struggling to receive international recognition—to be the first. Indeed, the parties offer no evidence that any nation, meek or mighty, presumed to do such a thing.

The United States was, however, embarrassed by its potential inability to provide judicial relief to foreign officials injured in the United States. Such offenses against ambassadors violated the law of nations, "and if not adequately redressed could rise to an issue of war." *Sosa,* 542 U.S., at 715; cf. The Federalist No. 80, p. 536 (J. Cooke ed. 1961) (A. Hamilton) ("As the denial or perversion of justice . . . is with reason classed among the just causes of war, it will follow that the federal judiciary ought to have cognizance of all causes in which the citizens of other countries are concerned"). The ATS ensured that the United States could provide a forum for adjudicating such incidents. See *Sosa, supra,* at 715–718, and n. 11. Nothing about this historical context suggests that Congress also intended federal common law under the ATS to provide a cause of action for conduct occurring in the territory of another sovereign.

Indeed, far from avoiding diplomatic strife, providing such a cause of action could have generated it. Recent experience bears this out. See *Doe v. Exxon Mobil Corp.,* 654 F.3d 11, 77–78 (C.A.D.C. 2011) (Kavanaugh, J., dissenting in part) (listing recent objections to extraterritorial applications of the ATS by Canada, Germany, Indonesia, Papua New Guinea, South Africa, Switzerland, and the United Kingdom). Moreover, accepting petitioners' view would imply that other nations, also applying the law of nations, could hale our citizens into their courts for alleged violations of the law of nations occurring in the United States, or anywhere else in the world. The presumption against extraterritoriality guards against our courts triggering such serious foreign policy consequences, and instead defers such decisions, quite appropriately, to the political branches.

We therefore conclude that the presumption against extraterritoriality applies to claims under the ATS, and that nothing in the statute rebuts that presumption. "[T]here is no clear indication of extraterritoriality here," *Morrison,* 130 S.Ct., at 2883, and petitioners' case seeking relief for violations of the law of nations occurring outside the United States is barred.

IV

On these facts, all the relevant conduct took place outside the United States. And even where the claims touch and concern the territory of the United States, they must do so with sufficient force to displace the presumption against extraterritorial application. See *Morrison,* 130 S.Ct., at 2883–2888. Corporations are often present in many countries, and it would reach too far to say that mere corporate presence suffices. If Congress were to determine otherwise, a statute more specific than the ATS would be required.

The judgment of the Court of Appeals is affirmed.

It is so ordered.

Justice KENNEDY, concurring.

The opinion for the Court is careful to leave open a number of significant questions regarding the reach and interpretation of the Alien Tort Statute. In my view that is a proper disposition. Many serious concerns with respect to human rights abuses committed abroad have been addressed by Congress in statutes such as the Torture Victim Protection Act of 1991 (TVPA), 106 Stat. 73, and that class of cases will be determined in the future according to the detailed statutory scheme Congress has enacted. Other cases may arise with allegations of serious violations of international law principles protecting persons, cases covered neither by the TVPA nor by the reasoning and holding of today's case; and in those disputes the proper implementation of the presumption against extraterritorial application may require some further elaboration and explanation.

Justice ALITO, with whom Justice THOMAS joins, concurring.

I concur in the judgment and join the opinion of the Court as far as it goes. Specifically, I agree that when Alien Tort Statute (ATS) "claims touch and concern the territory of the United States, they must do so with sufficient force to displace the presumption against extraterritorial application." This formulation obviously leaves much unanswered, and perhaps there is wisdom in the Court's preference for this narrow approach. I write separately to set out the broader standard that leads me to the conclusion that this case falls within the scope of the presumption.

In *Morrison v. National Australia Bank Ltd.,* 130 S.Ct. 2869 (2010), we explained that "the presumption against extraterritorial application would be a craven watchdog indeed if it retreated to its kennel whenever *some* domestic activity is involved in the case." *Id.*, at 2884. We also reiterated that a cause of action falls outside the scope of the presumption—and thus is not barred by the presumption—only if the event or relationship that was "the `focus' of congressional concern" under the relevant statute takes place within the United States. *Ibid.* (quoting *EEOC v. Arabian American Oil Co.,* 499 U.S. 244, 255 (1991)).

[O]nly conduct that satisfies *Sosa*'s requirements of definiteness and acceptance among civilized nations can be said to have been "the 'focus' of congressional concern," when Congress enacted the ATS. As a result, a putative ATS cause of action will fall within the scope of the presumption against extraterritoriality—and will therefore be barred—unless the domestic conduct is sufficient to violate an international law norm that satisfies *Sosa*'s requirements of definiteness and acceptance among civilized nations.

Justice BREYER, with whom Justice GINSBURG, Justice SOTOMAYOR and Justice KAGAN join, concurring in the judgment.

I agree with the Court's conclusion but not with its reasoning. * * *

Unlike the Court, I would not invoke the presumption against extraterritoriality. Rather, guided in part by principles and practices of foreign relations law, I would find jurisdiction under this statute where (1) the alleged tort occurs on American soil, (2) the defendant is an American national, or (3) the defendant's conduct substantially and adversely affects an important American national interest, and that includes a distinct interest in preventing the United States from becoming a safe harbor (free of civil as well as criminal liability) for a torturer or other common enemy of mankind. See *Sosa v. Alvarez-Machain,* 542 U.S. 692, 732. ("'[F]or purposes of civil liability, the torturer has become—like the pirate and slave trader before him—*hostis humani generis,* an enemy of all mankind.'" (quoting *Filartiga v. Pena-Irala,* 630 F.2d 876, 890 (C.A.2 1980)). See also 1 Restatement (Third) of Foreign Relations Law of the United States §§ 402, 403, 404 (1986). In this case, however, the parties and relevant conduct lack sufficient ties to the United States for the ATS to provide jurisdiction.

I

A

Our decision in *Sosa* frames the question. * * *

In this case we must decide the extent to which this jurisdictional statute [the ATS] opens a federal court's doors to those harmed by activities belonging to the limited class that *Sosa* set forth *when those activities take place abroad.* To help answer this question here, I would refer both to *Sosa* and, as in *Sosa,* to norms of international law. See Part II, *infra.*

B

In my view the majority's effort to answer the question by referring to the "presumption against extraterritoriality" does not work well. That presumption "rests on the perception that Congress ordinarily legislates with respect to domestic, not foreign matters." *Morrison v. National Australia Bank Ltd.,* 130 S.Ct. 2869, 2877–2888 (2010). The ATS, however, was enacted with "foreign matters" in mind. The statute's text refers explicitly to "alien[s]," "treat[ies]," and "the law of nations." 28 U.S.C. § 1350. The statute's purpose was to address "violations of the law of nations, admitting of a judicial remedy and at the same time threatening serious consequences in international affairs." *Sosa,* 542 U.S., at 715. And at least one of the three kinds of activities that we found to fall within the statute's scope, namely piracy, normally takes place abroad. See 4 W. Blackstone, Commentaries on the Law of England 72 (1769).

The majority cannot wish this piracy example away by emphasizing that piracy takes place on the high seas. That is because the robbery and murder that make up piracy do not normally take place in the water; they take place on a ship. And a ship is like land, in that it falls within the jurisdiction of the nation whose flag it flies. See *McCulloch v. Sociedad Nacional de Marineros de Honduras,* 372 U.S. 10, 20–21 (1963); 2 Restatement § 502, Comment *d* ("[F]lag state has jurisdiction to prescribe with respect to any activity aboard the ship"). Indeed, in the early 19th century Chief Justice Marshall described piracy as an "offenc[e] against the nation under whose flag the vessel sails, and within whose particular jurisdiction all on board the vessel are." *United States v. Palmer,* 3 Wheat. 610, 632 (1818). See *United States v. Furlong,* 5 Wheat. 184, 197 (1820) (a crime committed "within the jurisdiction" of a foreign state and a crime committed "in the vessel of another nation" are "the same thing"). * * *

The majority * * * writes, "Pirates were fair game wherever found, by any nation, because they generally did not operate within any jurisdiction." I very much agree that pirates were fair game "wherever found." Indeed, that is the point. That is why we asked, in *Sosa,* who are today's pirates? Certainly today's pirates include torturers and perpetrators of genocide. And today, like the pirates of old, they are "fair game" where they are found. Like those pirates, they are "common enemies of all mankind and all nations have an equal interest in their apprehension and punishment." 1 Restatement § 404 Reporters' Note 1, p. 256 (quoting *In re Demjanjuk,* 612 F.Supp. 544, 556 (N.D.Ohio 1985) (internal quotation marks omitted)). And just as a nation that harbored pirates provoked the concern of other nations in past centuries, so harboring "common enemies of all mankind" provokes similar concerns today. * * *

In any event, as the Court uses its "presumption against extraterritorial application," it offers only limited help in deciding the question presented, namely "'under what circumstances the Alien Tort Statute . . . allows courts to recognize a cause of action for violations of the law of nations occurring within the territory of a sovereign other than the United States.'" 132 S.Ct. 472 (2012). The majority echoes in this jurisdictional context *Sosa*'s warning to use "caution" in shaping federal common-law causes of action. But it also makes clear that a statutory claim might sometimes "touch and concern the territory of the United States . . . with sufficient force to displace the presumption." It leaves for another day the determination of just when the presumption against extraterritoriality might be "overcome."

II

In applying the ATS to acts "occurring within the territory of a[nother] sovereign," I would assume that Congress intended the statute's jurisdictional reach to match the statute's underlying substantive grasp. That grasp, defined by the statute's purposes set forth in *Sosa,* includes compensation for those injured by piracy and its modern-day equivalents, at least where allowing such compensation avoids "serious" negative international "consequences" for the United States. 542 U.S., at 715. And just as we have looked to established international substantive norms to help determine the statute's substantive reach, *id.,* at 729, so we should look to international jurisdictional norms to help determine the statute's jurisdictional scope.

The Restatement (Third) of Foreign Relations Law is helpful. Section 402 recognizes that, subject to § 403's "reasonableness" requirement, a nation may apply its law (for example, federal common law, see 542 U.S., at 729–730, not only (1) to "conduct" that "takes place [or to persons or things] within its territory" but also (2) to the "activities, interests, status, or relations of its nationals outside as well as within its territory," (3) to "conduct outside its territory that has or is intended to have substantial effect within its territory," and (4) to certain foreign "conduct outside its territory . . . that is directed against the security of the state or against a limited class of other state interests." In addition, § 404 of the Restatement explains that a "state has jurisdiction to define and prescribe punishment for certain offenses recognized by the community of nations as of universal concern, such as piracy, slave trade," and analogous behavior.

Considering these jurisdictional norms in light of both the ATS's basic purpose (to provide compensation for those injured by today's pirates) and *Sosa*'s basic caution (to avoid international friction), I believe that the statute provides jurisdiction where (1) the alleged tort occurs on American soil, (2) the defendant is an American national, or (3) the defendant's conduct substantially and adversely affects an important American national interest, and that includes a distinct interest in preventing the United States from becoming a safe harbor (free of civil as well as criminal liability) for a torturer or other common enemy of mankind.

I would interpret the statute as providing jurisdiction only where distinct American interests are at issue. Doing so reflects the fact that Congress adopted the present statute at a time when, as Justice Story put it, "No nation ha[d] ever yet pretended to be the custos morum of the whole world." *United States v. La Jeune Eugenie,* 26 F. Cas. 832, 847 (No. 15,551) (C.C.D.Mass.1822). That restriction also should help to minimize international friction. Further limiting principles such as exhaustion, *forum non conveniens,* and comity would do the same. So would a practice of courts giving weight to the views of the Executive Branch.

As I have indicated, we should treat this Nation's interest in not becoming a safe harbor for violators of the most fundamental international norms as an important jurisdiction-related interest justifying application of the ATS in light of the statute's basic purposes—in particular that of compensating those who have suffered harm at the hands of, *e.g.,* torturers or other modern pirates. Nothing in the statute or its history suggests that our courts should turn a blind eye to the plight of victims in that "handful of heinous actions." *Tel-Oren v. Libyan Arab Republic,* 726 F.2d 774, 781 (C.A.D.C. 1984) (Edwards, J., concurring). See generally Leval, The Long Arm of International Law: Giving Victims of Human Rights Abuses Their Day in Court, 92 Foreign Affairs 16

(Mar./Apr. 2013). To the contrary, the statute's language, history, and purposes suggest that the statute was to be a weapon in the "war" against those modern pirates who, by their conduct, have "declar[ed] war against all mankind." 4 Blackstone 71. * * *

III

Applying these jurisdictional principles to this case, however, I agree with the Court that jurisdiction does not lie. The defendants are two foreign corporations. Their shares, like those of many foreign corporations, are traded on the New York Stock Exchange. Their only presence in the United States consists of an office in New York City (actually owned by a separate but affiliated company) that helps to explain their business to potential investors. The plaintiffs are not United States nationals but nationals of other nations. The conduct at issue took place abroad. And the plaintiffs allege, not that the defendants directly engaged in acts of torture, genocide, or the equivalent, but that they helped others (who are not American nationals) to do so.

Under these circumstances, even if the New York office were a sufficient basis for asserting general jurisdiction, it would be farfetched to believe, based solely upon the defendants' minimal and indirect American presence, that this legal action helps to vindicate a distinct American interest, such as in not providing a safe harbor for an "enemy of all mankind." Thus I agree with the Court that here it would "reach too far to say" that such "mere corporate presence suffices."

I consequently join the Court's judgment but not its opinion.

NOTES AND QUESTIONS

1. *From* Filartiga *to* Sosa *to* Kiobel. It has been quite a jurisprudential ride from *Filartiga* in 1980 to *Sosa* in 2004 to *Kiobel* in 2013. What happened? In brief, *Filartiga* inaugurated modern Alien Tort Statute litigation, tens of cases were litigated in the federal district courts, and some reached the federal courts of appeal. Many, though not all, courts followed *Filartiga* and were "friendly" toward international human rights cases brought under the ATS. However, in the 1990s ATS litigation began to change. Suits broadened from those brought against individual foreign aliens to include new claims against large corporations—"Barclay National Bank, Chevron, Del Monte, Ford, IBM, Rio Tinto, Talisman Energy, and Unocal"—and plaintiffs' lawyers were no longer only those working for non-governmental human rights organizations, but also "private, for-profit lawyers working on a contingency fee." Ingrid Woerth, "International Decision: *Kiobel v. Royal Dutch Petroleum Co.*: The Supreme Court and the Alien Tort Statute," 107 *American Journal of International Law* 601, 604 (2013). How might the perception of the public policy value of ATS litigation change with these new defendants and these new plaintiffs' lawyers? Had the ATS envelope been pushed too far? Not remarkably, those defending a

corporate point of view applauded *Kiobel*, while human rights advocates deplored the judgment. Mark Walsh, "Global Warning: High Court Limits the Alien Tort Statute, Slowing Suits Against U.S. Companies for Action Overseas," 99 *ABA Journal,* July 2013, at 17, 17–18. See "Agora: Reflections on *Kiobel*," 107 *American Journal of International Law* 829 (2013).

2. *The Way We Are Now*. Following two Supreme Court judgments, the Alien Tort Statute is more clearly defined. What do we know now? At least four conclusions stand out. First, *Sosa*, as confirmed by *Kiobel*, decided that the ATS as a statute is jurisdictional. Second, the ATS has been held to support certain substantive causes of action from 1789 found in Blackstone. Third, the ATS is read to permit new customary norms of international law as modern causes of action, but only if each is defined as definitely as was an original cause of action in 1789. Fourth, *Kiobel* has ruled that the ATS is limited by a presumption against extraterritoriality that the Court applies to statutes without an explicit legislative extraterritorial extension.

Would *Filartiga* be saved under the present statutory construction? Torture would probably meet the substantive test of customary international law, but would the facts in *Filartiga* satisfy the presumption against extraterritoriality? Would Pena-Irala's presence in the United States, where he was served process, be enough for Chief Justice Roberts's measure? For that of Justice Breyer? And, perhaps crucially, for that of Justice Kennedy?

3. *The* Custos Morum *of the Whole World.* Both Chief Justice Roberts and Justice Breyer relied in part on language from Justice Story in *The La Jeune Eugenie* in 1822: "No nation has ever yet pretended to be the custos morum of the whole world." Roughly translated, "*custos morum*" means the guardian of morals. Is Story's principle at all dated? We explore in Chapter 6 how Nazi atrocities and the Nuremberg Judgment transformed international law, sparking a modern law of international human rights based on the notion that foreign states ought, to a degree at least, be committed to protecting all individuals from human rights violations, even when committed by their own governments within their own territory. Should the Supreme Court have taken modern international human rights law more into account in *Kiobel*?

Another way of posing the *custos morum* question is to ask who, if not the courts, should guard the world's morals? Should we rely on the political branches of governments, *e.g.*, the U.S. President and State Department or the Congress? Or might it better be the job of countries acting together in international organizations, *e.g.*, the United Nations or the Council of Europe, institutions also considered in Chapter 6?

4. *The Fate of the Alien Tort Statute*. 5–4 the Supreme Court in *Kiobel* has applied the presumption against extraterritoriality to the ATS. Even the more liberal international-law-based approach of the minority did not save the case for Kiobel. All nine judges ruled that, by one test or another, the alleged cause of action was not closely enough tied to the United States to warrant U.S. jurisdiction. Professor Woerth was pessimistic about the fate of

the ATS: "if courts apply a strong version of the presumption [against extraterritoriality] and only permit claims based on conduct in the United States allegedly in violation of a norm of international law that meets the *Sosa* standard, then ATS litigation as we know it today is effectively dead." Woerth, *supra* Note 1, at 603. Even before the final judgment in *Kiobel* was handed down, scholars were debating whether state rather than federal courts might be a better choice for some international human rights law suits in the United States. See Christopher A. Whytock, Donald Earl Childress III & Michael D. Ramsey, "After *Kiobel*—International Human Rights Litigation in State Courts and Under State Law," 3 *UC Irvine Law Review* 1 (2013). Why had the plaintiff's lawyers in *Filartiga* gone to federal court in the first place? Does their logic still hold true?

5. *Interpreting the Constitution Using International Law.* Should international and foreign law be used to interpret provisions of the U.S. Constitution that do not, on their face, relate to international affairs? This question has become much-debated in U.S. constitutional law. Cases in which international and foreign law have been used by one or more judges in rendering their opinions on such issues as the juvenile death penalty, the death penalty in general, and regulation of homosexuality include: Coker v. Georgia, 433 U.S. 584, 596 n.10 (1977) (according to Justice White, "[i]t is * * * not irrelevant here that out of 60 major nations in the world surveyed in 1965, only 3 retained the death penalty for rape where death did not ensue"); Foster v. Florida, 537 U.S. 990, 991–92 (2002) (the debate between Justices Thomas and Breyer respecting delays in execution); Lawrence v. Texas, 539 U.S. 558, 573 (2003) (Justice Kennedy, looking to the judgment of the European Court of Human Rights in Dudgeon v. United Kingdom, 45 Eur. Ct. H.R. (1981), respecting consensual homosexual conduct); and Roper v. Simmons, 543 U.S. 551, 578 (2005) (according to Justice Kennedy, "[t]he opinion of the world community, while not controlling our outcome, does provide respected and significant confirmation for our own conclusions" concerning the unconstitutionality of the juvenile death penalty). In 2010 in *Graham v. Florida*, Justice Kennedy wrote: "There is support for our conclusion" that imposing life without parole sentences on juveniles who did not commit homicide is unconstitutional in "the fact that * * * the United States adheres to a sentencing practice rejected the world over." Although "[t]he judgments of other nations and the international community are not dispositive as to the meaning of the Eighth Amendment," they are also "not irrelevant." 560 U.S. 48, 80 (2010). See "Agora: The United States Constitution and International Law," 98 *American Journal of International Law* 42 (2004), especially Roger P. Alford, "Misusing International Sources to Interpret the Constitution," *id.* at 57, and Michael D. Ramsey, "International Materials and Domestic Rights: Reflections on *Atkins* and *Lawrence*," *id.* at 69; Sarah H. Cleveland, "Our International Constitution," 31 *Yale Journal of International Law* 1 (2006).

The use of international law to interpret the U.S. Constitution is long-standing. For example, in the infamous case of Dred Scott v. Sandford, 60 U.S. (19 How.) 393 (1857), the Justices of the Supreme Court employed international law extensively as they bitterly divided in a 7–2 judgment holding that African-Americans could never be U.S. citizens and that Congress had not had constitutional power to abolish slavery in the territories in the 1820 Missouri Compromise. See Mark W. Janis, "*Dred Scott* and International Law," 43 *Columbia Journal of Transnational Law* 763 (2005). "[A]t no time in U.S. history was the gap between our human rights rhetoric and our human rights practice so great." *Id.* at 810.

CHAPTER 5

INTERNATIONAL COURTS AND TRIBUNALS

■ ■ ■

The process of interpreting, applying, and enforcing international law employs not only municipal courts but also various forms of international courts and tribunals. In the first two parts of this chapter, we introduce both public international arbitration and the one more or less universal international court, the International Court of Justice (ICJ). The ICJ and its immediate predecessor, the Permanent Court of International Justice (PCIJ), have never had a heavy caseload: two, three, or four adjudicated cases a year have been typical. However, PCIJ and ICJ cases have been a very influential source of international law in the 20th and 21st centuries. Finally, in the last part of this chapter, we look at some of the questions raised by the proliferation of new international courts and tribunals.

While reading the cases excerpted below, keep in mind the question: when and why do states agree to submit disputes to international arbitration or adjudication? As infrequent as such submissions are, there is no doubt that governments sometimes do wish for their disagreements to be settled by international arbiters or judges. What makes an international dispute "court-friendly" or "court-unfriendly"? An intelligent answer to this question might help us determine not only what international disputes are likely to go to formal international dispute settlement procedures but also which international decisions once rendered will be respected by states in practice.

A. PUBLIC INTERNATIONAL ARBITRATION

Our story begins with public international arbitration and the 1872 *Alabama Claims* arbitration between the United States and the United Kingdom, the pinnacle of 19th-century aspirations for international law and international adjudication. Among other things, *Alabama Claims* inspired the creation of the Permanent Court of Arbitration (PCA), established in 1899 in The Hague, The Netherlands. A 1905 PCA case, *Dogger Bank* between the United Kingdom and Russia, comes next, a good example of the kind of cases that that permanent arbitral institution decided in the years before the First World War. Following are two decisions related to the *Rainbow Warrior* incident between New Zealand and France, modern examples of the continuing utility of public international arbitration.

MARK WESTON JANIS, "THE *ALABAMA* ARBITRATION"

America and the Law of Nations 1776–1939, at 131–34 (2010)

After the Civil War, some Americans thought that war's days might well be numbered. The great codifier, David Dudley Field remarked at the 1876 Centennial Celebration in Philadelphia:

> The history of international law since July 4, 1776, shows that, not withstanding the prevalence of almost universal war during the last quarter of the past century and the first fifteen years of the present, there has been a general tendency of the nations to approach each other more closely, to avoid war as much as possible, and to diminish its severity, when it occurs.

In 1910, John W. Foster, Benjamin Harrison's Secretary of State and grandfather of Dwight Eisenhower's Secretary of State, John Foster Dulles, opined that all three of America's nineteenth-century foreign wars—the War of 1812, the 1846 Mexican War, and the 1898 Spanish-American War—could have been avoided if the disputes precipitating them had "been submitted to arbitration and decided without recourse to war." * * *

Field and Foster seemed not to be merely pipe-dreaming. International arbitration had had a remarkable record in the nineteenth-century. Beginning with the 536 awards of the Jay Treaty arbitrations between 1799 and 1804, there had been hundreds of international arbitrations, many involving the United States. America was a party to the establishment of international arbitral tribunals along the lines of those introduced in the Jay Treaty with Ecuador, Mexico, Peru, Spain, and Venezuela. The busiest of these, the United States-Mexican Mixed Claims Commission of 1868, heard more than 2,000 claims between 1871 and 1876. As Foster noted in a little book in 1904, "[t]he nineteenth century was more fruitful than any similar era in the submission to the adjudication of special arbitration tribunals of the differences of nations insolvable by diplomatic methods."

Most important of all for the optimism of the time was the judgment of the *Alabama* arbitral tribunal, probably the most influential event of nineteenth-century American international law. Delivered in 1872, * * * the *Alabama* judgment was the work of an *ad hoc* tribunal composed of five judges * * * named by each of the United States, Great Britain, Italy, Switzerland, and Brazil. The panel had been empowered by Great Britain and America in 1871 to decide whether Britain had violated international law when it permitted British companies to build Confederate warships, notably the cruisers *Alabama, Florida,* and *Shenandoah*, which preyed on Union shipping during the American Civil War.

[T]he *Alabama* tribunal ruled that though Britain had owed the United States a duty of "active due diligence" to prevent private parties from supplying the southern rebels, she had failed to observe her international obligations as a neutral state. In relevant part, the judgment read:

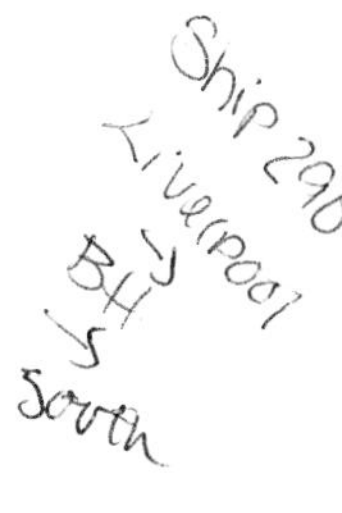

> And whereas, with respect to the vessel called the *Alabama*, it clearly results from all the facts relative to the construction of the ship, at first designated by the number '290,' in the port of Liverpool, and its equipment and armament in the vicinity of Terceira, through the agency of the vessels called the *Agrippina* and the *Bahama*, dispatched from Great Britain to that end, that the British Government failed to use due diligence in the performance of its neutral obligations, and especially that it omitted, notwithstanding the warnings and official representations made by the diplomatic agents of the United States during the construction of the said number '290,' to take in due time any effective measures of prevention, and that those orders which it did give at last, for the detention of the vessel, were issued so late that their execution was not practicable;
>
> And whereas, after the escape of that vessel, the measures taken for its pursuit and arrest were so imperfect as to lead to no result, and therefore cannot be considered sufficient to release Great Britain from the responsibility already incurred;
>
> And whereas, in despite of the violations of the neutrality of Great Britain, committed by the '290,' this same vessel, later known as the Confederate cruiser *Alabama*, was on several occasions freely admitted into the ports of the colonies of Great Britain, instead of being proceeded against as it ought to have been in any and every port within British jurisdiction in which it might have been found;
>
> And whereas the Government of Her Britannic Majesty cannot justify itself for a failure in due diligence on the plea of insufficiency of the legal means of action which it possessed;
>
> Four of the arbitrators for the reasons above assigned, and the fifth, for reasons separately assigned by him, are of opinion that Great Britain has in this case failed, by omission, to fulfill the duties prescribed in the first and the third of the rules, established by the sixth article of the treaty of Washington. [These rules specify the due diligence obligations of neutrals.]

The United States claimed about $21 million in direct and $4 million in indirect damages caused by the attacks of the *Alabama* and her sister Confederate raiders; the United Kingdom acknowledged only about $8 million in direct damages. The arbitrators split the difference, ordering the United Kingdom to pay the United States some $15,500,000. The full sum was proffered in British Treasury Bonds on September 9, 1873. The American receipt was framed and hung in 10 Downing Street.

The *Alabama* arbitration was an exceptionally encouraging development for American international law enthusiasts. Some years earlier, in 1865, Lord Russell, the British Foreign Secretary, had refused to arbitrate the *Alabama* claims on the grounds that the British government were "sole guardians of their own honor." War between the two countries was not an outlandish possibility. The United States and Great Britain had already fought twice—the Revolutionary War (1775–1783) and the War of 1812 (1812–1815). It seemed credible that a third Anglo-American conflict might break out, a struggle not only about compensation for the Confederate maritime attacks, but also to settle possession of Canada, a part of the British Empire much coveted by some Americans.

The eventual success of the *Alabama* arbitration became an important popular demonstration that it was possible for powerful states to arbitrate important disputes and thereby avoid war. General Ulysses S. Grant (1822–1885), President of the United States during the *Alabama* arbitration, was so encouraged by the tribunal's deeds that the old warrior predicted "an epoch when a court recognized by all nations will settle international differences instead of keeping large standing armies." David Dudley Field turned to the *Alabama* proceedings to demonstrate the probability of the eventual success of international arbitration. The *Alabama* judgment, now largely forgotten, was at the time profoundly influential. In the words of Samuel Eliot Morison, "never before had disputes involving such touchy subjects of national honor been submitted to the majority vote of an international tribunal."

RICHARD NED LEBOW, "ACCIDENTS AND CRISES: THE DOGGER BANK AFFAIR"

31 *Naval War College Review*, No. 1, at 66 (Summer 1978)

Russian expansion into Manchuria in the latter part of the 19th century brought her into conflict with Japan. Russian penetration of Korea, which directly challenged Japan's economic and political primacy in that country, brought the conflict to a head. St. Petersburg's intransigence made a mockery of negotiations and Japan broke relations with Russia on 8 February 1904.

That very morning Japanese torpedo boats and destroyers launched a daring surprise attack against the Russian Pacific Squadron in its moorings at Port Arthur. The attack was followed up the next day by a long-range naval bombardment of the Russian anchorage. When the smoke had cleared the Japanese Navy was supreme in the Far East. They inflicted a further defeat upon the Russians at Chemulpo in August. On land, the Japanese were equally successful. Their army moved into Manchuria and forced the Russians to retreat down the Liaotung Peninsula. By 14 May they had invested Port Arthur.

The relief of Port Arthur became Moscow's most urgent objective. General Kuropatkin, the Russian Commander-in-Chief, ordered the navy to ready its idle Baltic Fleet for service in the Pacific. Departure of the armada awaited completion of four new battleships, during which time the Baltic Fleet, considered to be the least seaworthy component of the navy, received special training. The deteriorating military situation in the Far East forced Admiral Rozhestvensky to cut his training exercises short and on 14 October 1904 the 42 ships of the hastily assembled Second Pacific Squadron departed the Baltic port of Libau for the 10,000 mile journey to Port Arthur.

As the fleet steamed through the Baltic it was warned to be on the lookout for Japanese torpedo boats disguised as trawlers which were planning an ambush somewhere between The Skaw and English Channel. This far-fetched notion had gained credence in St. Petersburg because of the reports of a Captain Hartling, sent to Copenhagen sometime earlier to organize a Russian counterintelligence network. Hartling's agents, anxious to justify their expense, had reported the existence of suspicious vessels in isolated Danish and Norwegian harbors. Rumors of a Japanese "suicide squadron" had also been picked up by the European press which speculated about the effect of Britain's assumed collusion with her Japanese ally upon Anglo-Russian relations.

According to all reports the prospect of a torpedo attack reduced Admiral Rozhestvensky, a man with no command experience, to a state of extreme anxiety. He doubled all watches, arranged to have searchlights sweep the surrounding sea at night and instructed guncrews to remain by their stations around the clock. The admiral ordered that "No vessel of any sort whatsoever must be allowed to get in amongst the fleet." Approaching merchantmen were warned away, often by a shot across their bows. Tension rose on the evening of 20 October, following receipt of a warning that unidentified torpedo boats had departed from secret bases in Norway. Later that night, *Navarin* reported sighting enemy reconnaissance balloons.

The expected attack failed to materialize and as morning broke the fleet steamed into the North Sea, ominously shrouded by fog. More alarming intelligence came in during the day warning of floating mines and trawlers with torpedo tubes preparing to attack the fleet. At dusk, the cruiser *Kamchatka*, which had become separated from the main body of the fleet, reported that it was under attack by eight torpedo boats and was returning fire. Ninety minutes later action stations were sounded abroad the flagship *Suvorov* in response to two flares sighted from the bridge. Shortly thereafter the order to engage the enemy was flashed down the line as searchlights revealed ships barely a half mile away. Battleships and cruisers opened fire and kept up an intensive barrage for 20 minutes until the admiral could discern only a few battered trawlers bobbing hopelessly in the water. The fleet steamed off concluding that the torpedo boats had fled from the scene.

The "enemy" engaged by Russian gunners was the Gamecock fleet of fishing boats which had left Hull for the Dogger Bank 2 days before and was then 200 miles northeast of the Spurn. They were identifiable as trawlers by their sails and red, white and green lights. These lights were probably the flares sighted on the bridge of *Suvorov*. When the firing began, one of the deckhands, illuminated by the searchlights, held up a plaice while his mate displayed a large haddock in the hope of signaling their peaceful intent. Their efforts were unsuccessful and when the barrage finally ceased one trawler had been sent to the bottom and five damaged. Two seamen were dead and six seriously wounded. Fortunately for the fishermen Russian gunnery had proven extremely inaccurate.

News of the incident reached London on Monday, 23 October. The next day the M.P. from Hull brought a deputation of fishermen to the Foreign Office where they produced shell splinters to substantiate their story. The Wednesday morning papers carried a more detailed account of the incident and public opinion was so incensed that the Russian Ambassador needed a police escort to leave his Embassy. Trafalgar Square was filled with protesters and the evening papers demanded strong action. The *Standard* raised the question that was on everybody's mind: was the "wretched Baltic fleet with its inefficient commanders, its drafts of raw landsmen, its blundering navigators and incompetent engineers" to be permitted to continue on its journey? The czarist regime was unpopular in England and as more details were released to the press public sentiment was adamant in favor of going after the Russian Fleet. Valentine Chirol, foreign editor of *The Times*, warned the foreign office that "the feeling in this country is such that no government can trifle with it."

The Balfour government, about to face an election, was particularly susceptible to popular pressure. However, the Cabinet did not act solely in response to public opinion. The majority were hostile to Russia and quite prepared to retaliate against her fleet. The Earl of Selbourne, First Lord of the Admiralty, was the most bellicose but Walter Long and Gerald Balfour, neither of whom normally displayed any interest in foreign affairs, also urged military action unless the Russians put into port and removed the officers responsible for the outrage. Admiral Fisher, who had recently been promoted to First Sea Lord, thought it a superb opportunity to destroy the Russian Fleet. It "is ours," he informed Selbourne, "whenever we like to take it." The King himself referred to the incident as "a most dastardly outrage" and urged a military response although he later moderated his position, fearing that war with Russia would only be in Germany's interest.

Lord Lansdowne, the Foreign Secretary, would have had support for any action against Russia he proposed. But he was an advocate of détente with Russia and was intent on resolving the incident peaceably. Lansdowne was nevertheless as outraged as his colleagues and thought Rozhestvensky's failure to stop and search for survivors particularly reprehensible. He was not convinced of the accidental nature of the incident, attributing it instead to the Russian propensity to "shoot first and ask questions later." In his opinion this trigger happy policy made a mockery of maritime law which Britain more than any other nation was dependent upon for her survival. Lansdowne believed that such incidents were likely to recur unless Russia was compelled to adhere to the established rules and customs that governed maritime behavior. Like other members of the Cabinet he also believed that Britain's reputation as a great power was at stake.

* * * Unwilling to let the hostage fleet escape the prime minister and foreign secretary agreed that Russia must be sent an ultimatum demanding that Rozhestvensky call at the Spanish port of Vigo and put ashore the officers responsible for the incident along with witnesses. The Russians were also to give satisfaction that the investigation of the incident would be complete and impartial. * * *

The Royal Navy had already begun preparations for a showdown. Six battleships of the Home Fleet had been ordered to Gibraltar and the reserve fleet of six battleships was being readied for action. Cruisers were sent to shadow the Russian Fleet, Gibraltar was put on a war footing, and the powerful Mediterranean Fleet was hurriedly recalled from the Austrian and Italian ports it was visiting. By the evening of 26 October, 28 battleships, 44 cruisers and their supporting vessels stood poised off Gibraltar ready to intercept the Russian Fleet which in the graphic words of First Sea Lord Fisher had become the "ham of a strategic sandwich."

On 27 October, [Russian Foreign Minister] Lamsdorff called on Hardinge [the British Minister in St. Petersburg] to warn that "he considered the general purport [of the ultimatum] to be humiliating and unacceptable to a Great Power." Lansdowne and Balfour, in receipt of Hardinge's report that afternoon, were pessimistic about the chances for peace. Their hopes plummeted in response to a second cable from St. Petersburg containing Rozhestvensky's account of the incident. The Russian admiral claimed that his fleet had been set upon by two torpedo boats but that he had tried to avoid firing on the trawlers even though they were in apparent complicity with the torpedo boats. Lansdowne told the Russian Ambassador that the admiral's version "seemed to bristle with improbabilities" and did not alter the situation.

Figure 5.A

The Dogger Bank

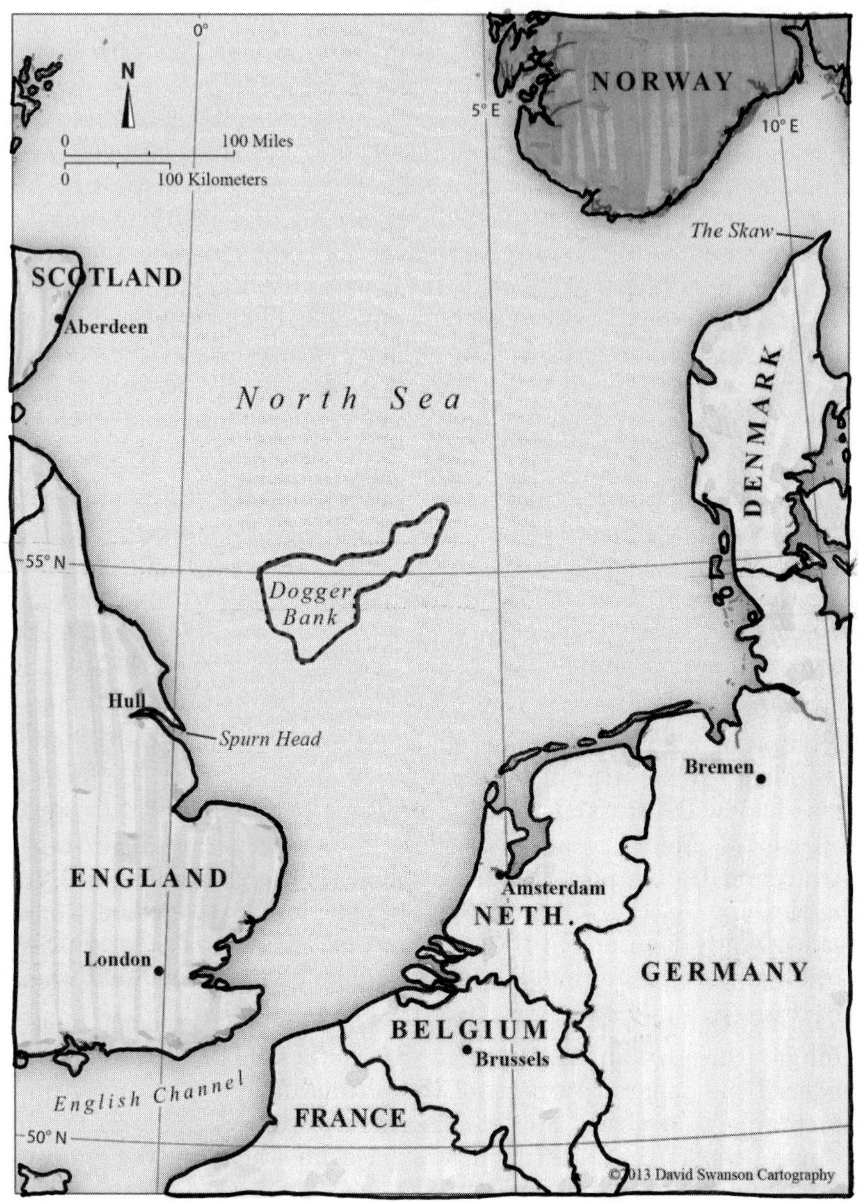

Lansdowne and [Russian Ambassador] Benckendorff conferred at length exploring possible ways out of the crisis. Paul Cambon, the French Ambassador, also participated in these talks. As the representative of France, Russia's ally, and the architect of the Anglo-French Entente, Cambon shared the trust of both sides. He acted as translator, as Benckendorff spoke Russian and French but Lansdowne knew only

English, and attempted to bridge the gap between the two men created by their uncomplementary personalities. "Benckendorff is too vague, Lansdowne too reserved," he confided to his son, "and when I am not between them, they inhabit different planets."

The main impediment to a solution was the British demand for an inquiry in which British officers would participate. This was seen as humiliating by the Russians. Cambon nevertheless urged acceptance as did the French Foreign Minister in Paris. On the 27th, the three men agreed that an inquiry conducted by some august international body might be more palatable to the Czar as he had urged the creation of boards of arbitration at the Hague Conference. The suggestion, attributed by Benckendoff to Cambon, was cabled to Lamsdorff who cleverly presented it to the Czar as his own idea in order to secure the autocrat's approval.

No word had been received from St. Petersburg when it came time for Balfour to depart for Southampton on the morning of the 28th. The mood at the Foreign Office was gloomy and remained so until a cable arrived from Hardinge reporting that the Czar approved of an international court of inquiry. A second cable contained the welcome news that Rozhestvensky had received orders to send the ships involved in the attack on the fishing boats to Vigo, that the guilty parties, as determined by the international board of inquiry, would be punished by Russian courts and that measures would be implemented to prevent further incidents. In return Lamsdorff requested that Balfour give credit to Russia in his speech for having expressed its prompt regrets and offering to pay proper compensation.

Upon his arrival at Southampton Balfour was handed a telegram reporting the Russian capitulation. Much relieved, the Prime Minister deleted those parts of his speech which were the equivalent to a declaration of war and told the good news to the cheering crowd. The Royal Navy remained on a war footing until her cruisers had "escorted" Rozhestvensky's fleet half way down the coast of Africa.

THE DOGGER BANK CASE

Great Britain v. Russia, Report of February 26, 1905,
The Hague Court Reports 403 (James Brown Scott ed. 1916)

1. The commissioners [five admirals from Britain, Russia, the United States, France, and Austria], after a minute and prolonged examination of the whole of the facts brought to their knowledge in regard to the incident submitted to them for inquiry by the declaration of St. Petersburg of the 12th (25th) November, 1904, have proceeded to make, in this report, an analysis of these facts in their logical sequence. * * *

9. Toward 1 o'clock in the morning of 9th (22d) October, 1904, the night was rather dark, a slight, low fog partly clouding the air. The moon only showed intermittently between the clouds. A moderate wind blew from the southeast, raising a long swell, which gave the ships a roll of 5° on each side.

The course followed by the squadron toward the southwest would have taken the last two divisions, as the event proved, close past the usual fishing ground of the fleet of Hull trawlers, which was composed of some thirty of these small steamboats, and was spread over an area of several miles.

It appears from the concordant testimony of the British witnesses that all these boats carried their proper lights, and were trawling in accordance with their usual rules, under the direction of their "admiral," and in obedience to the signals given by the conventional rockets.

10. Judging from the communications received by wireless telegraphy, the divisions which preceded that of Admiral Rojdestvensky across these waters had signaled nothing unusual.

It became known afterward, in particular, that Admiral Folkersam, having been led to pass round the fishing fleet on the north, threw his electric searchlight on the nearest trawlers at close quarters, and, having seen them to be harmless vessels, quietly continued his voyage.

11. A short time afterwards the last division of the squadron, led by the *Souvoroff* flying Admiral Rojdestvensky's flag, arrived in its run close to the spot where the trawlers were fishing.

The direction in which this division was sailing led it nearly toward the main body of the fleet of trawlers, round which and to the south of which it would therefore be obliged to sail, when the attention of the officers of the watch on the bridges of the *Souvoroff* was attracted by a green rocket, which put them on their guard. This rocket, sent up by the "admiral" of the fishing fleet, indicated in reality, according to regulation, that the trawlers were to trawl on the starboard tack.

Almost immediately after this first alarm, and as shown by the evidence, the lookout men, who, from the bridges of the *Souvoroff*, were scanning the horizon with their night glasses, discovered "on the crest of the waves on the starboard bow, at an approximate distance of 18 to 20 cables," a vessel which aroused their suspicions because they saw no light, and because she appeared to be bearing down upon them.

When the suspicious-looking vessel was shown up by the searchlight, the lookout men thought they recognized a torpedo boat proceeding at great speed.

It was on account of these appearances that Admiral Rojdestvensky ordered fire to be opened on this unknown vessel.

The majority of the commissioners express the opinion, on this subject, that the responsibility for this action and the results of the fire to which the fishing fleet was exposed are to be attributed to Admiral Rojdestvensky.

12. Almost immediately after fire was opened to starboard, the *Souvoroff* caught sight of a little boat on her bow barring the way, and was obliged to turn sharply to the left to avoid running it down. This boat, however, on being lit up by the searchlight, was seen to be a trawler.

To prevent the fire of the ships being directed against this harmless vessel, the searchlight was immediately thrown up at an angle of 45°.

The admiral then made the signal to the squadron "not to fire on the trawlers."

But at the same time that the searchlight had lit up this fishing vessel, according to the evidence of witnesses, the lookout men on board the *Souvoroff* perceived to port another vessel, which appeared suspicious from the fact of its presenting the same features as were presented by the object of their fire to starboard.

Fire was immediately opened on this second object, and was, therefore, being kept up on both sides of the ship, the line of ships having resumed their original course by a correcting movement without changing speed.

13. According to the standing orders of the fleet, the Admiral indicated the objects against which the fire should be directed by throwing his searchlight upon them; but as each vessel swept the horizon in every direction with her own searchlights to avoid being taken by surprise, it was difficult to prevent confusion.

The fire, which lasted from ten to twelve minutes, caused great loss to the trawlers. Two men were killed and six others wounded; the *Crane* sank; the *Snipe*, the *Mino*, the *Moulmein*, the *Gull*, and the *Majestic* were more or less damaged.

On the other hand, the cruiser *Aurora* was hit by several shots.

The majority of the commissioners observe that they have not sufficiently precise details to determine what was the object fired on by the vessels; but the commissioners recognize unanimously that the vessels of the fishing fleet did not commit any hostile act; and, the majority of the commissioners being of opinion that there were no torpedo boats either among the trawlers nor anywhere near, the opening of the fire by Admiral Rojdestvensky was not justifiable.

The Russian commissioner, not considering himself justified in sharing this opinion, expresses the conviction that it was precisely the suspicious-looking vessels approaching the squadron with hostile intent which provoked the fire.

NOTES AND QUESTIONS

1. *Incentives to Arbitrate.* Looking at *Alabama* and *Dogger Bank*, what were the inducements for Britain to go to international arbitration? For the United States and Russia? In *Dogger Bank* why did France seek to bring Britain and Russia together? What role did public opinion play in facilitating arbitral solutions to the conflicts?

2. *The Composition of the Arbitral Panels.* Note that the arbitral panel in *Dogger Bank* was composed not of lawyers or judges but of naval officers. What would have been the advantages and disadvantages of employing admirals instead of jurists as arbitrators? Would it have been probably Britain or Russia that would have preferred admirals rather than international lawyers on the panel?

The fact that states choose their arbitrators was and remains an ordinary feature of public international arbitration. Indeed, party choice of the tribunal is probably the most important general distinction between arbitration and adjudication as forms of dispute settlement, whether public (as in much of international law) or private (as in most commercial disputes). Sometimes, arbitrators are less bound than judges to apply strict rules of law to the case before them, but, other times, arbitrators are just as rule-minded as judges. Did the *Alabama* and *Dogger Bank* arbitrators see their role as being appliers of strict rules of international law or more as being appliers of some sort of "common sense"?

3. *Compensation.* In *Alabama*, Britain paid the full award of $15,500,000, a sum that corresponds to approximately $290,000,000 in 2005 dollars. See Tom Bingham, "The *Alabama* Claims Arbitration," 54 *International and Comparative Law Quarterly* 1 (2005). In *Dogger Bank*, James Brown Scott, the editor of the *Reports* of the Permanent Court of Arbitration, noted that "Russia accepted the decision and paid damages to the extent of about $300,000." *Hague Court Reports* 403 (James Brown Scott ed. 1916). Were Britain's and Russia's misgivings about permitting the arbitrations justified? Would both countries have been better off to have simply paid damages at the outset? Or did the lapse of time and the decision of an arbitral panel make the payment of damages more palatable?

4. *Avoiding War.* *Alabama* and *Dogger Bank* were the kinds of disputes 19th-century international arbitration enthusiasts hoped would be settled by law rather than by war. Tom Bingham, Lord Chief Justice of England and Wales between 1996 and 2000, described the *Alabama* arbitration "as the greatest the world had ever seen." Bingham, *supra* Note 3, at 1.

> The *Alabama* arbitration is * * * one of the very few instances in history when the world's leading nation, in the plenitude of its power, has agreed to submit an issue of great national moment to the decision of a body in which it could be, as it was, heavily outvoted. [British Prime Minister William] Gladstone did not see the arbitration as righting a wrong. Rather, "[h]e saw the process as

exemplifying the means by which two civilized nations could settle differences, without either having to admit being in the wrong."

Id. at 24. Similarly, Professor Merrills observed, "The *Dogger Bank* episode furnishes a striking example of the value of the international inquiry commission as an instrument of dispute settlement. Had the issue been investigated by two national inquiries, it is almost certain that * * * they would have exacerbated matters by coming to opposite conclusions." J.G. Merrills, *International Dispute Settlement* 43 (5th ed. 2011).

However, neither *Alabama* nor *Dogger Bank* lived up to expectations as harbingers of the substitution of courtrooms for battlefields. Lord Bingham concluded that *Alabama* "did not, regrettably, herald a century in which judicial arbitration of international differences became the norm." Bingham, *supra* Note 3, at 24. Koopmans found that *Dogger Bank*, formally a commission of inquiry, engendered just a few subsequent commissions, mostly employed "for technical aspects of maritime disputes." Sven M.G. Koopmans, *Diplomatic Dispute Settlement: The Use of Inter-State Conciliation* 28–29 (2008).

5. *The Permanent Court of Arbitration.* Founded by the 1899 Hague Peace Conference, the Permanent Court of Arbitration was the world's first permanent and universal court of arbitration. See Mark Weston Janis, *International Law* 119–26 (6th ed. 2012). Did the availability of permanent international arbitral machinery at The Hague make it more likely that the parties in *Dogger Bank* would go to arbitration? What might be done to make it even more likely that states use a form of international arbitration in a time of crisis?

After the International Court was established in 1921, the Permanent Court of Arbitration fell into desuetude. It administered only 34 cases during its first century. Lately, however, the PCA has reinvented itself. In its capacity as an arbitral registry, it provided administrative assistance for some 88 cases in 2012 alone. Six of these cases were state-to-state arbitrations, while others involved states or state-controlled entities as at least one of the parties. Some of the arbitrations have been politically charged. In 2008–2009, for example, the PCA administered an arbitration between Sudan and an armed movement operating in the country (the Sudan People's Liberation Movement). The PCA's Secretary-General also acts as the appointing authority under many arbitral agreements.

The Permanent Court has updated its rules and programs. In 2012 it adopted new procedural rules applicable to disputes involving at least one state, state-controlled entity, or international organization. A fund assists developing states using PCA services, and the PCA has concluded host country agreements with Argentina, Chile, Costa Rica, India, Lebanon, Mauritius, Singapore, and South Africa to support PCA-run proceedings conducted in those countries. See Permanent Court of Arbitration, *Annual Report 2012, available at* http://www.pca-cpa.org/ (last visited Dec. 7, 2013).

6. *Public and Private International Arbitration.* Good examples of modern public international law arbitration are the two rulings below involving the *Rainbow Warrior* incident; they illustrate the flexibility in form and function of international third-party dispute settlement. Private or commercial international arbitration (between private litigants) and mixed international arbitration (between a state and a private litigant) are even more frequent nowadays. There are several thousands of such cases a year. We have already seen examples of mixed international arbitrations in the *CMS Case* in Chapter 2 and the *Texaco/Libya Case* in Chapter 3. A private international arbitration is at issue in the *Scherk Case* in Chapter 11, where we discuss party choice in international conflict of laws.

THE RAINBOW WARRIOR CASE (1986)

Ruling [of July 6, 1986, by the U.N. Secretary-General] Pertaining to the Differences Between France and New Zealand Arising from the Rainbow Warrior Affair, 19 *Reports of International Arbitral Awards* 199 (2006), 26 *International Legal Materials* 1349 (1987)

[On June 19, 1986, following an appeal by Prime Minister Lubbers of the Netherlands, France and New Zealand asked the U.N. Secretary-General for an "equitable and principled" ruling in matters arising from the sinking of the *Rainbow Warrior*.]

INTRODUCTION

1. On 10 July 1985 a civilian vessel, the *Rainbow Warrior*, not flying the New Zealand flag, was sunk at its moorings in Auckland Harbor, New Zealand, as a result of extensive damage caused by two high explosive devices. One person, a Netherlands citizen, Mr. Fernando Pereira, was killed as a result of this action; he drowned when the ship sank.

2. On 12 July, two agents of the French Directorate General of External Security (DGSE) were interviewed by the New Zealand Police and subsequently arrested and prosecuted. On 4 November they pleaded guilty in the District Court in Auckland, New Zealand, to charges of manslaughter and wilful damage to a ship by means of an explosive. They were sentenced to ten years imprisonment each; they are presently serving their sentences in New Zealand prisons.

3. A communiqué issued on 22 September 1985 by the Prime Minister of France confirmed that the *Rainbow Warrior* had been sunk by agents of the DGSE upon instructions. On the same day, the Minister of External Affairs of France pointed out to the Prime Minister of New Zealand that France was ready to undertake reparations for the consequences of that action. He also declared he was ready, as the Prime Minister of New Zealand had already suggested, to meet with the Deputy Prime Minister of New Zealand on 23 and 25 September in New York. Such a meeting did take place for the purpose of discussing the possible ways to find a solution to the problems arising from the *Rainbow Warrior* affair.

4. A number of subsequent meetings took place between officials of the two countries in the months that followed, but it did not prove possible to reach a settlement.

5. In June 1986 I was formally approached by the Governments of France and New Zealand, who referred to me all the problems between them arising from the *Rainbow Warrior* affair for a ruling which both sides agreed to abide by. I then informed both Governments that I was prepared to undertake such a task. On 19 June, in Paris and in Wellington, both Governments made public announcements to that effect, and in New York on the same day I publicly confirmed that I was willing to undertake that task[.]

PROCEDURE * * *

After I had received * * * written statements of the New Zealand and French positions, I then made contact, through diplomatic channels, with each of the two Governments. I did so in order to satisfy myself that I had a full and complete understanding of their respective positions and to be sure that I am able to produce a ruling on all aspects of the affair which in terms of the agreement announced in Paris, Wellington and New York on 19 June, is both equitable and principled.

RULING

The issues that I need to consider are limited in number. I set out below my ruling on them which takes account of all the information available to me. My ruling is as follows:

1. Apology

New Zealand seeks an apology. France is prepared to give one. My ruling is that the Prime Minister of France should convey to the Prime Minister of New Zealand a formal and unqualified apology for the attack, contrary to international law, on the *Rainbow Warrior* by French service agents which took place on 10 July 1985.

2. Compensation

New Zealand seeks compensation for the wrong done to it and France is ready to pay some compensation. The two sides, however, are some distance apart on quantum. New Zealand has said that the figure should not be less than US Dollars 9 million, France that it should not be more than US Dollars 4 million. My ruling is that the French Government should pay the sum of US Dollars 7 million to the Government of New Zealand as compensation for all the damage it has suffered.

3. The Two French Service Agents

It is on this issue that the two Governments plainly had the greatest difficulty in their attempts to negotiate a solution to the whole issue on a bilateral basis before they took the decision to refer the matter to me.

The French Government seeks the immediate return of the two officers. It underlines that their imprisonment in New Zealand is not justified, taking into account in particular the fact that they acted under military orders and that France is ready to give an apology and to pay compensation to New Zealand for the damage suffered.

The New Zealand position is that the sinking of the *Rainbow Warrior* involved not only a breach of international law, but also the commission of a serious crime in New Zealand for which the two officers received a lengthy sentence from a New Zealand court. The New Zealand side states that their release to freedom would undermine the integrity of the New Zealand judicial system. In the course of bilateral negotiations with France, New Zealand was ready to explore possibilities for the prisoners serving their sentences outside New Zealand.

But it has been, and remains, essential to the New Zealand position that there should be no release to freedom, that any transfer should be to custody, and that there should be a means of verifying that.

The French response to that is that there is no basis either in international law or in French law on which the two could serve out any portion of their New Zealand sentence in France, and that they could not be subjected to new criminal proceedings after a transfer into French hands.

On this point, if I am to fulfil my mandate adequately, I must find a solution in respect of the two officers which both respects and reconciles these conflicting positions.

My ruling is as follows:

(*a*) The Government of New Zealand should transfer Major Alain Mafart and Captain Dominique Prieur to the French military authorities. Immediately thereafter, Major Mafart and Captain Prieur should be transferred to a French military facility on an isolated island outside of Europe for a period of three years.

(*b*) They should be prohibited from leaving the island for any reason, except with the mutual consent of the two Governments. They should be isolated during their assignment on the island from persons other than military or associated personnel and immediate family and friends. They should be prohibited from any contact with the press or other media whether in person or in writing or in any other manner. These conditions should be strictly complied with and appropriate action should be taken under the rules governing military discipline to enforce them.

(*c*) The French Government should every three months convey to the New Zealand Government and to the Secretary-General of the United Nations, through diplomatic channels, full reports on the situation of Major Mafart and Captain Prieur in terms of the two preceding paragraphs in order to allow the New Zealand Government to be sure that they are being implemented.

(*d*) If the New Zealand Government so requests, a visit to the French military facility in question may be made, by mutual agreement by the two Governments, by an agreed third party.

(*e*) I have sought information on French military facilities outside Europe. On the basis of that information, I believe that the transfer of Major Mafart and Captain Prieur to the French military facility on the isolated island of Hao in French Polynesia would best facilitate the enforcement of the conditions which I have laid down in paragraphs (*a*) to (*d*) above. My ruling is that that should be their destination immediately after their transfer.

4. Trade Issues

The New Zealand Government has taken the position that trade issues have been imported into the affair as a result of French action, either taken or in prospect. The French Government denies that, but it has indicated that it is willing to give some undertakings relating to trade, as sought by the New Zealand Government. I therefore rule that France should:

(*a*) Not oppose continuing imports of New Zealand butter into the United Kingdom in 1987 and 1988 at levels proposed by the Commission of the European Communities in so far as these do not exceed those mentioned in document COM(83)574 of 6 October 1983 that is to say, 77,000 tonnes in 1987 and 75,000 tonnes in 1988; and

(*b*) Not take measures that might impair the implementation of the agreement between New Zealand and the European Economic Community on Trade in Mutton, Lamb and Goatmeat which entered into force on 20 October 1980 (as complemented by the exchange of letters of 12 July 1984).

5. Arbitration

The New Zealand Government has argued that a mechanism should exist to ensure that any differences that may arise about the implementation of the agreements concluded as a result of my ruling can be referred for binding decision to an arbitral tribunal. The Government of France is not averse to that. My ruling is that an agreement to that effect should be concluded and provide that any dispute concerning the interpretation or application of the other agreements, which it has not been possible to resolve through the diplomatic channel, shall, at the request of either of the two Governments, be submitted to an arbitral tribunal under the following conditions:

(a) Each Government shall designate a member of the tribunal within 30 days of the date of the delivery by either Government to the other of a written request for arbitration of the dispute, and the two Governments shall, within 60 days of that date, appoint a third member of the tribunal who shall be its chairman;

(*b*) If, within the times prescribed, either Government fails to designate a member of the tribunal or the third member is not agreed, the Secretary-General of the United Nations shall be requested to make the necessary appointment after consultations with the two Governments by choosing the member or members of the tribunal;

(*c*) A majority of the members of the tribunal shall constitute a quorum and all decisions shall be made by a majority vote;

(*d*) The decisions of the tribunal, including all rulings concerning its constitution, procedure and jurisdiction, shall be binding on the two Governments.

6. The two Governments should conclude and bring into force as soon as possible binding agreements incorporating all of the above rulings. These agreements should provide that the undertaking relating to an apology, the payment of compensation and the transfer of Major Mafart and Captain Prieur should be implemented at the latest on 25 July 1986.

7. On one matter I find no need to make a ruling. New Zealand, in its written statement of position, has expressed concern regarding compensation for the family of the individual whose life was lost in the incident and for Greenpeace. The French statement of position contains an account of the compensation arrangements that have been made; I understand that those assurances constitute the response that New Zealand was seeking.

THE RAINBOW WARRIOR CASE (1990)

New Zealand v. France, France-New Zealand Arbitration Tribunal,
82 *International Law Reports* 500 (1990)

[On July 9, 1986, three days after the U.N. Secretary-General made his rulings, France and New Zealand entered three agreements to implement those rulings, including the transfer of Major Mafart and Captain Prieur to the island of Hao. This 1990 arbitration concerns France's decision to evacuate Mafart and Prieur from Hao to France before their three-year detention period had run. France sought New Zealand's consent to Major Mafart's transfer on December 11, 1987, for health-related reasons. New Zealand asked that its doctors examine Mafart, but France refused to permit a New Zealand military plane carrying New Zealand doctors to land in Hao. Mafart left Hao for France on December 14, 1987, without New Zealand's consent, and France allowed Mafart to remain in France after his treatment, despite New Zealand doctors' conclusions that he could be safely returned to Hao. Prieur left Hao for France in May 1988 after France sought New

Zealand's consent on the ground that she was pregnant. France agreed to an independent examination of Prieur in Hao by New Zealand doctors, but Prieur left the day before the doctors arrived, France claiming that Prieur's father was dying. Prieur also never returned to Hao.

New Zealand unilaterally instituted this arbitration pursuant to one of its 1986 agreements with France that incorporated paragraph 5 of the Secretary-General's decision. New Zealand argued that the Mafart's and Prieur's departure from Hao was illegal. The two countries then in 1989 concluded a Supplementary Agreement designating three arbitrators (one appointed by each state and one appointed jointly by both states) and specifying Tribunal procedures. Article 2 of the Supplementary Agreement indicated that the Tribunal's decisions would be based on the 1986 France-New Zealand agreements and on "applicable rules and principles of international law."]

75. [F]or the decision of the present case, both the customary Law of Treaties and the customary Law of State Responsibility are relevant and applicable. The customary Law of Treaties, as codified in the Vienna Convention proclaimed in Article 26, under the title "*Pacta sunt servanda*" that

> Every treaty in force is binding upon the parties to it and must be performed by them in good faith.

This fundamental provision is applicable to the determination whether there have been violations of that principle and in particular, whether material breaches of treaty obligations have been committed.

Moreover, certain specific provisions of customary law in the Vienna Convention are relevant in this case such as Article 60 which gives a precise definition of the concept of a material breach of a treaty, and Article 70, which deals with the legal consequences of the expiry of a treaty.

On the other hand, the legal consequences of a breach of a treaty, including the determination of the circumstances that may exclude wrongfulness (and render the breach only apparent) and the appropriate remedies for breach, are subjects that belong to the customary Law of State Responsibility.

The reason is that the general principles of International Law concerning State responsibility are equally applicable in the case of breach of treaty obligation, since in the international law field there is no distinction between contractual and tortious responsibility, so that any violation by a State of any obligation, of whatever origin, gives rise to State responsibility and consequently, to the duty of reparation. * * *

76. Under the title "Circumstances Precluding Wrongfulness" the International Law Commission proposed in Articles 29 to 35 a set of rules

which include three provisions on *force majeure* and fortuitous event (Article 31), distress (Article 32), and state of necessity (Article 33), which may be relevant to the decision on this case. * * *

77. * * * New Zealand is right in asserting that the excuse of *force majeure* is not of relevance in this case because the test of its applicability is of absolute and material impossibility, and because a circumstance rendering performance more difficult or burdensome does not constitute a case of *force majeure*. Consequently, this excuse is of no relevance in the present case.

78. Article 32 of the Articles drafted by the International Law Commission deals with another circumstance which may preclude wrongfulness in international law, namely, that of the "distress" of the author of the conduct which constitutes the act of State whose wrongfulness is in question. * * *

The question therefore is to determine whether the circumstances of distress in a case of extreme urgency involving elementary humanitarian considerations affecting the acting organs of the State may exclude wrongfulness in this case.

[T]he International Law Commission explains that " 'distress' means a situation of extreme peril in which the organ of the State which adopts that conduct has, at that particular moment, no means of saving himself or persons entrusted to his care other than to act in a manner not in conformity with the requirements of the obligation in question."

[The Tribunal also notes the "controversial doctrine" of necessity.] Article 33, which allegedly authorizes a State to take unlawful action invoking a state of necessity, refers to situations of grave and imminent danger to the State as such and to its vital interests. * * *

79. In accordance with the previous legal considerations, three conditions would be required to justify the conduct followed by France in respect to Major Mafart and Captain Prieur:

1) The existence of very exceptional circumstances of extreme urgency involving medical or other considerations of an elementary nature, provided always that a prompt recognition of the existence of those exceptional circumstances is subsequently obtained from the other interested party or is clearly demonstrated.

2) The reestablishment of the original situation of compliance with the assignment in Hao as soon as the reasons of emergency invoked to justify the repatriation had disappeared.

Figure 5.B

Hao and New Zealand

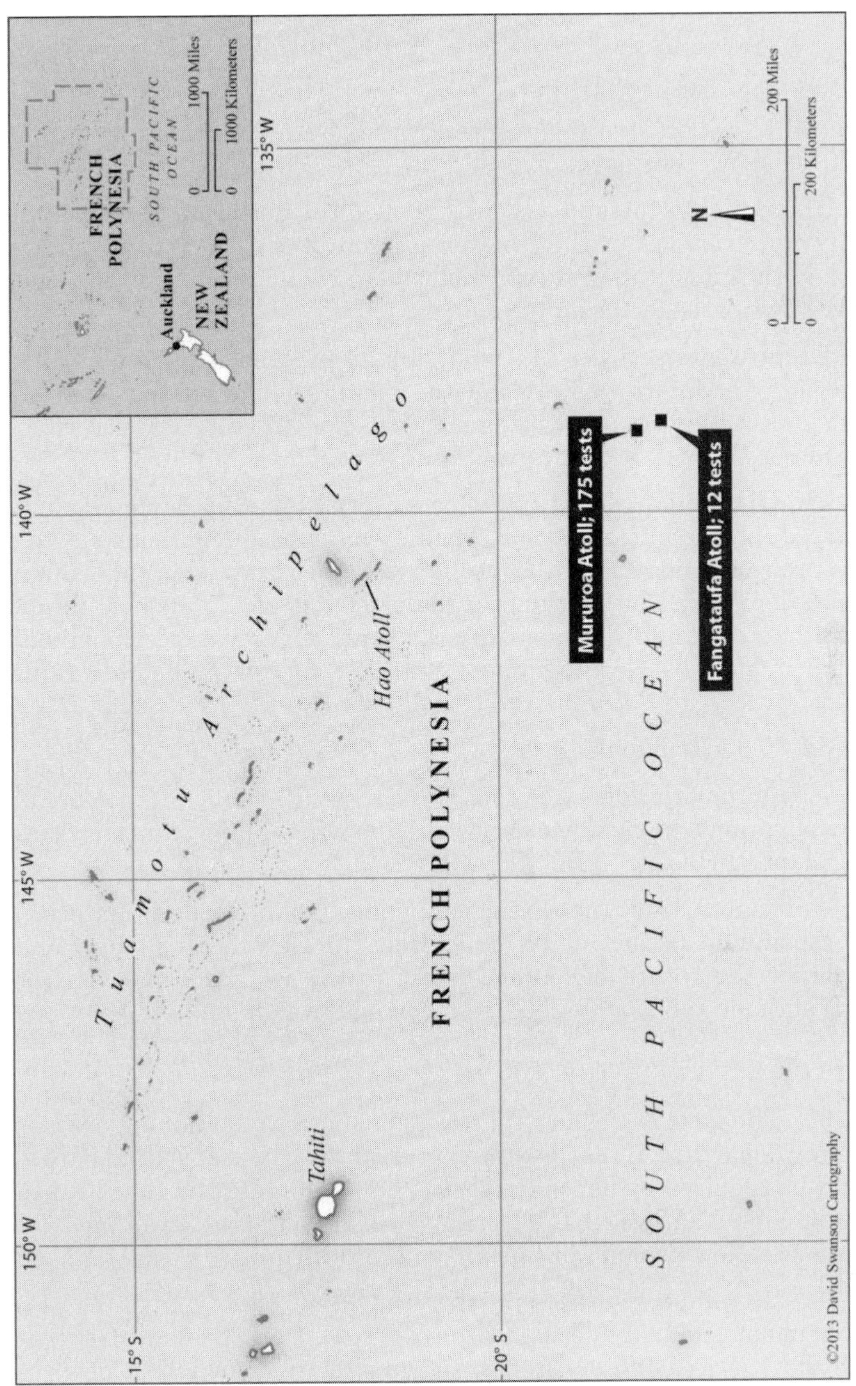

3) The existence of a good faith effort to try to obtain the consent of New Zealand in terms of the 1986 Agreement.

THE CASE OF MAJOR MAFART

80. The New Zealand reaction to the French initiative for the removal of Major Mafart appears to have been conducted in conformity with the above considerations.

The decision to send urgently a medical doctor to Hao in order to verify the existence of the invoked ground of serious risk to life clearly implied that if the alleged conditions were confirmed, then the requested consent would be forthcoming.

Unfortunately, it proved impossible to proceed with that verification while Major Mafart was still on the island. [N]one of the parties is to blame for the failure in carrying out the very difficult task of verifying *in situ* Major Mafart's health during that weekend.

81. [H]aving accepted the offer to verify whether Major Mafart had required an urgent sanitary evacuation, subsequent consent to that measure would necessarily be implied unless there was an immediate and formal denial by New Zealand of the existence of the medical conditions which had determined Major Mafart's urgent removal, accompanied by a formal request by New Zealand authorities for his immediate return to Hao, or at least to Papeete. And this did not occur. * * *

88. [T]he Tribunal:

– by a majority declares that the French Republic did not breach its obligations to New Zealand by removing Major Mafart from the island of Hao on 13 December 1987;

– declares that the French Republic committed a material and continuing breach of its obligations to New Zealand by failing to order the return of Major Mafart to the island of Hao as from 12 February 1988[, when he had recovered from his illness.]

THE CASE OF CAPTAIN PRIEUR

93. The facts * * * show that New Zealand would not oppose Captain Prieur's departure, if that became necessary because of special care which might be required by her pregnancy. They also indicated that France and New Zealand agreed that Captain Prieur would be examined by Dr. Brenner, a New Zealand physician, before returning to Paris. * * *

94. [I]t appears that during the day of 5 May the French Government suddenly decided to present the New Zealand Government with the *fait accompli* of Captain Prieur's hasty return for a new reason, the health of Mrs. Prieur's father, who was seriously ill, hospitalized for cancer. Indisputably the health of Mrs. Prieur's father, who unfortunately

would die on 16 May, and the concern for allowing Mrs. Prieur to visit her dying father constitute humanitarian reasons worthy of consideration by both Governments under the 1986 Agreement. But the events of 5 May (French date) prove that the French Republic did not make efforts in good faith to obtain New Zealand's consent. First of all, it must be remembered that France and New Zealand agreed that Captain Prieur would be examined in Hao on 6 May, which would allow her to return to France immediately. For France, in this case, it was only a question of gaining 24 or 36 hours. Of course, the health of Mrs. Prieur's father, who had been hospitalized for several months, could serve as grounds for such acute and sudden urgency: but, in this case, New Zealand would have had to be informed very precisely and completely, and not be presented with a decision that had already been made.

* * * New Zealand was really not asked for its approval, as compliance with France's obligations required even under extremely urgent circumstances: it was indeed demanded so firmly that it was bound to provoke a strong reaction from New Zealand.

101. [T]he Tribunal:

– declares that the French Republic committed a material breach of its obligations to New Zealand by not endeavoring in good faith to obtain on 5 May 1988 New Zealand's consent to Captain Prieur's leaving the island of Hao;

– declares that as a consequence the French Republic committed a material breach of its obligations by removing Captain Prieur from the island of Hao on 5 and 6 May 1988;

– declares that the French Republic committed a material and continuing breach of its obligations to New Zealand by failing to order the return of Captain Prieur to the island of Hao. * * *

110. In the present case the Tribunal must find that the infringement of the special regime designed by the Secretary-General to reconcile the conflicting views of the Parties has provoked indignation and public outrage in New Zealand and caused a new, additional non-material damage. This damage is of a moral, political and legal nature, resulting from the affront to the dignity and prestige not only of New Zealand as such, but of its highest judicial and executive authorities as well.

111. It follows from the foregoing findings that New Zealand is entitled to appropriate remedies. It claims certain declarations, to the effect that France has breached the First Agreement. But New Zealand seeks as well an order for the return of the agents. * * *

112. For its part, the French Republic maintains that adequate reparation for moral or legal damage can only take the form of

satisfaction, generally considered as the remedy *par excellence* in cases of non-material damage. Invoking the decisions of the International Court of Justice, France maintains that whenever the damage suffered amounts to no more than a breach of the law, a declaration by the judge of this breach constitutes appropriate satisfaction. France points out, moreover, that, rather than *restitutio*, what New Zealand is demanding is the cessation of the denounced behaviour[.]

114. * * * The recent jurisprudence of the International Court of Justice confirms that an offer for the cessation or discontinuance of wrongful acts or omissions is only justified in case of continuing breaches of international obligations which are still in force at the time the judicial order is issued (*The United States Diplomatic and Consular Staff in Teheran Case,* I.C.J. Reports, 1979, p. 21, para. 38 to 41, and 1980, para. 95, No. 1; *The Case Concerning Military and Paramilitary Activities in and Against Nicaragua*, I.C.J. Reports, 1984, p. 187, and 1986, para. 292, p. 149). * * *

It would be * * * illogical to issue the order requested by New Zealand, which is really an order for the cessation or discontinuance of a certain French conduct, rather than a *restitutio*. The reason is that this conduct, namely to keep the two agents in Paris, is no longer unlawful, since the international obligation expired on 22 July 1989. Today, France is no longer obliged to return the two agents to Hao and submit them to the special regime. * * *

115. On the other hand, the French contention that satisfaction is the only appropriate remedy for non-material damage is also not justified in the circumstances of the present case.

The granting of a form of reparation other than satisfaction has been recognized and admitted in the relations between the parties by the Ruling of the Secretary-General of 9 July 1986, which has been accepted and implemented by both Parties to this case.

In the Memorandum presented to the Secretary-General, the New Zealand Government requested compensation for non-material damage, stating that it was "entitled to compensation for the violation of sovereignty and the affront and insult that involved."

The French Government opposed this claim, contending that the compensation "could concern only the material damage suffered by New Zealand, the moral damage being compensated by the offer of apologies."

But the Secretary-General did not make any distinction, ruling instead that the French Government "should pay the sum of U.S. dollars 7 million to the Government of New Zealand as *compensation for all the damage it has suffered.*"

[T]he compensation constituted a reparation not just for material damage—such as the cost of the police investigation—but for non-material damage as well, regardless of material injury and independent therefrom. * * *

119. New Zealand has not however requested the award of monetary compensation—even as a last resort should the Tribunal not make the declarations and orders for the return of the agents.

120. [T]he Tribunal has decided not to make an order for monetary compensation. * * *

122. There is a long established practice of States and international Courts and Tribunals of using satisfaction as a remedy or form of reparation (in the wide sense) for the breach of an international obligation. This practice relates particularly to the case of moral or legal damage done directly to the State, especially as opposed to the case of damage to persons involving international responsibilities. * * *

Satisfaction in this sense can take and has taken various forms. Arangio-Ruiz [in his 1989 report for the International Law Commission on state responsibility] mentions regrets, punishment of the responsible individuals, safeguards against repetition, the payment of symbolic or nominal damages or of compensation on a broader basis, and a decision of an international tribunal declaring the unlawfulness of the State's conduct.

123. It is to the last of these forms of satisfaction for an international wrong that the Tribunal now turns. * * * The Tribunal accordingly decides to make four declarations of material breach of its obligations by France and further decides in compliance with Article 8 of the Agreement of 14 February 1989 to make public the text of its Award. For the foregoing reasons the Tribunal:

– declares that the condemnation of the French Republic for its breaches of its treaty obligations to New Zealand, made public by the decision of the Tribunal, constitutes in the circumstances appropriate satisfaction for the legal and moral damage caused to New Zealand. * * *

126. Th[e] important relationship [between New Zealand and France], the nature of the decisions made by the Tribunal, and the earlier discussion of monetary compensation lead the Tribunal to make a recommendation. The recommendation, addressed to the two Governments, is intended to assist them in putting an end to the present unhappy affair. * * *

128. The power of an arbitral tribunal to address recommendations to the parties to a dispute, in addition to the formal finding and obligatory

decisions contained in the award, has been recognized in previous arbitral decisions. * * *

For the foregoing reasons the Tribunal:

– in light of the above decisions, recommends that the Governments of the French Republic and of New Zealand set up a fund to promote close and friendly relations between the citizens of the two countries, and that the Government of the French Republic make an initial contribution equivalent to US Dollars 2 million to that fund.

NOTES AND QUESTIONS

1. *The Political Context.* France's sinking of the *Rainbow Warrior*, a Greenpeace vessel, was prompted by that organization's protests against French nuclear testing in the South Pacific. France's nuclear testing program had begun well before the *Rainbow Warrior* was sunk in July 1985. Indeed, New Zealand and Australia had challenged the legality of France's nuclear testing before the International Court of Justice in 1973. France refused to appear in the cases, but its public statements that its 1974 series of atmospheric tests would be its last persuaded the Court to dismiss the cases. The Court concluded that "the objective of the Applicant has in effect been accomplished, inasmuch as the Court finds that France has undertaken the obligation to hold no further nuclear tests in the South Pacific." Nuclear Tests Case (New Zealand v. France), 1974 I.C.J. 457, 475; Nuclear Tests Case (Australia v. France), 1974 I.C.J. 253, 270. France subsequently withdrew its acceptance of the compulsory jurisdiction of the ICJ and resumed nuclear testing, albeit underground.

France conducted a nuclear test at Mororua atoll in the South Pacific just two months before the sinking of the *Rainbow Warrior*. Greenpeace was planning to sail the vessel to the French nuclear testing area in protest later in 1985. France admitted the attack on the *Rainbow Warrior*. French President François Mitterand apparently personally approved the attack. Henry Samuel, "Sinking of the Rainbow Warrior was personally sanctioned by Mitterand," *The Telegraph* (London), July 11, 2005, at 12. On September 22, 1985, the French Prime Minister confirmed that agents of the French secret service had acted on official orders and had sunk the vessel.

French officials at the time expressed regret and indicated France's readiness to make reparations to New Zealand. According to France's submission to the Secretary-General, France "recognize[d] that the attack carried out against the *Rainbow Warrior* took place in violation of the territorial sovereignty of New Zealand and that it was therefore committed in violation of international law."

Greenpeace's political activism has continued to upset governments. In September 2013, Russia seized a Greenpeace vessel, the *Arctic Sunrise*, that was protesting at a Russian offshore oil rig in the Arctic Ocean. See Steven Lee Myers, "Russia Seizes Greenpeace Ship and Crew for Investigation," *New York Times*, Sept. 21, 2013, at A8. In November 2013 the International

Tribunal for the Law of the Sea (ITLOS) ordered Russia to release the ship and her crew on the posting of a bond. Arctic Sunrise Case (Netherlands v. Russia), ITLOS Case No. 22, *available at* http://www.itlos.org (last visited Dec. 10, 2013). For more on the ITLOS, see Chapter 10.

2. *Recourse to International Legal Process.* Why in 1986 did France and New Zealand determine that an international legal proceeding was more desirable than alternatives? Why did the two countries ask the Secretary-General of the United Nations, Perez de Cuellar, formerly a professor of international law, to make a binding, "equitable and principled" ruling on the *Rainbow Warrior* incident? France and New Zealand in fact negotiated many of the provisions of the Secretary-General's ruling behind the scenes, and the Secretary-General endorsed them. One unsettled issue was compensation. France argued that compensation should be limited to material damage, *e.g.*, New Zealand's costs for cleaning up Auckland harbor and for the police inquiry, trial, and detention of the two French agents. New Zealand submitted that, in addition, it was "entitled to compensation for the violation of sovereignty and the affront and insult that that involved." The Secretary-General decided the amount of compensation, and, as noted in paragraph 115 of the 1990 arbitration, he included some compensation for non-material damage. See Sir Geoffrey Palmer, "Adjudication, Politics, and International Law," 17 *Temple International Law and Comparative Law Journal* 523, 525–26 (2003).

What did New Zealand hope to gain by the 1990 arbitration? Why did it not seek compensation? How do the roles and functions of the U.N. Secretary-General in his 1986 decision and the tribunal in the 1990 *Rainbow Warrior* arbitration compare with those of the tribunals in the *Alabama* and *Dogger Bank* disputes?

3. *The Legal Complexity of* Rainbow Warrior. Besides the two proceedings excerpted above, note how many other legal processes were engaged by one aspect or another of the *Rainbow Warrior* incident. First, there was the 1974 ICJ *Nuclear Test Case* between New Zealand and France. Second, New Zealand brought domestic criminal proceedings against the French secret agents. Third, individuals pursued five claims against France, including a 1985–1986 negotiated settlement whereby France paid 2.3 million French francs to the widow, children, and parents of the crew member killed aboard the *Rainbow Warrior*, as well as a 1995 challenge to France in the European Court of Human Rights. Fourth, there were four claims brought by Greenpeace, a non-governmental organization, against France, including a 1987 arbitration resulting in an order for France to pay Greenpeace $8.1 million, and legal challenges to France made by Greenpeace in 1995 at Euratom and at the French Conseil d'Etat. Fifth, France and New Zealand each made or threatened trade reprisals, involving both the World Trade Organization and the European Union. See Christopher Harding, "Vingt Ans Après: *Rainbow Warrior*, Legal Ordering and Legal Complexity," 10 *Singapore Yearbook of International Law* 99 (2006). The multiplicity of

legal proceedings raises questions about how to reconcile conflicting legal systems, questions further addressed in Chapters 11 and 12.

4. *The Aftermath.* France complied almost immediately with the arbitral tribunal's recommendation to contribute $2 million to a fund to promote friendly relations. J. Scott Davidson, "The Rainbow Warrior Arbitration Concerning the Treatment of the French Agents Mafart and Prieur," 40 *International and Comparative Law Quarterly* 446, 456 (1991). Michael Rocard, the French Prime Minister, also visited New Zealand in May 1991 and formally apologized for the 1985 bombing. Nevertheless, tensions continued. France resumed its nuclear testing in the South Pacific, and New Zealand expressed outrage when, in July 1991, France awarded Alain Mafart a medal for distinguished service. Richard Long, "New Zealand Disgust as France Honours Bomber," *The Times* (London), July 6, 1991, at 9. A new round of French nuclear testing in 1995 led New Zealand and other Pacific states to protest anew. New Zealand complained to the International Court that the testing was contrary to the *Nuclear Tests Case* described in Note 1. The Court disagreed, however, noting that the earlier case concerned atmospheric testing, whereas the more recent French testing was non-atmospheric. See Request for an Examination of the Situation in Accordance with Paragraph 63 of the Court's Judgment of 20 December 1974 in the Nuclear Tests (New Zealand v. France) Case, 1995 I.C.J. 288.

France finally halted its nuclear program in 1996 after conducting over 140 tests at Pacific atolls. See Craig R. Whitney, "France Ending Nuclear Tests That Caused Broad Protests," *New York Times*, Jan. 30, 1996, at A1. In 1998 France ratified the 1996 Comprehensive Test Ban Treaty, 35 *International Legal Materials* 1439 (1996).

5. *Compromissory Clauses in Treaties.* Many different types of treaties contain compromissory clauses, which authorize arbitrators to hear disputes concerning the treaty in question. The July 9, 1986 agreement that France and New Zealand entered to implement paragraph 5 of the Secretary-General's ruling served a compromissory function with respect to the two other July 9th agreements that carried out the substantive provisions of his decision.

A separate *compromis* to arbitrate has been employed in many modern interstate arbitrations, even when a compromissory clause authorizes the submission of disputes arising under a treaty to arbitral tribunals. See Christine Gray & Benedict Kingsbury, "Inter-State Arbitration Since 1945: Overview and Evaluation," in *International Courts for the Twenty-first Century* 55, 61 (Mark W. Janis ed. 1992). Why should states conclude such separate *compromis* when there already are compromissory clauses? What functions do compromissory clauses serve, other than providing the basis for consent to arbitral proceedings? See John E. Noyes, "The Functions of Compromissory Clauses in U.S. Treaties," 34 *Virginia Journal of International Law* 831, 898–900 (1994).

Does a compromissory clause preclude measures other than third-party proceedings to counteract the breach of a treaty? Could New Zealand legally have taken steps other than instituting arbitration to respond to France's alleged breach of its obligation to confine Mafart and Prieur to Hao? Once a state has instituted an arbitration, should it be permitted to pursue countermeasures against the state with which it has a dispute? See Case Concerning the Air Services Agreement of 27 March 1946 (United States v. France), 54 *International Law Reports* 304 (1975), and the discussion of countermeasures in Chapter 9.B.

B. THE INTERNATIONAL COURT

The failure of diplomacy and the Permanent Court of Arbitration (PCA) to solve the problems prompting the 1914 outbreak of the First World War inspired the 1919 Paris Peace Conference to create the Permanent Court of International Justice (PCIJ) as the judicial arm of the new League of Nations. When the League and the PCIJ in their turn failed to arrest the onset of the Second World War, the new peace-makers in 1944–1945 established both the United Nations and a new judicial institution, the International Court of Justice (ICJ). In form and function, there are few differences between the PCIJ (1921–1945) and the ICJ (1945 on). Together they are commonly known as the "International Court" or the "World Court." Both have been housed at The Hague in the Netherlands in the Peace Palace, also still the home of the PCA.

1. THE JURISDICTION OF THE INTERNATIONAL COURT

We can better understand the kinds of disputes that come before the International Court of Justice by carefully reading the exact delegations of jurisdiction made to the Court by its constituting treaty. There is a contentious jurisdiction based on Article 36 of the Court's Statute, which is an integral part of the United Nations Charter. Only states may be parties in contentious cases. The Court also has jurisdiction to render advisory opinions to some international organizations pursuant to Article 65 of its Statute and Article 96 of the U.N. Charter itself.

STATUTE OF THE INTERNATIONAL COURT OF JUSTICE, ARTICLES 36, 65

June 26, 1945, 59 Stat. 1031, T.S. No. 993

Article 36

1. The jurisdiction of the Court comprises all cases which the parties refer to it and all matters specially provided for in the Charter of the United Nations or in treaties and conventions in force.

2. The states parties to the present Statute may at any time declare that they recognize as compulsory *ipso facto* and without special agreement, in relation to any other state accepting the same obligation, the jurisdiction of the Court in all legal disputes concerning:

a. the interpretation of a treaty;

b. any question of international law;

c. the existence of any fact which, if established, would constitute a breach of an international obligation;

d. the nature or extent of the reparation to be made for the breach of an international obligation.

3. The declarations referred to above may be made unconditionally or on condition of reciprocity on the part of several or certain states, or for a certain time. * * *

6. In the event of a dispute as to whether the Court has jurisdiction, the matter shall be settled by the decision of the Court.

Article 65

1. The Court may give an advisory opinion on any legal question at the request of whatever body may be authorized by or in accordance with the Charter of the United Nations to make such a request.

2. Questions upon which the advisory opinion of the Court is asked shall be laid before the Court by means of a written request containing an exact statement of the question upon which an opinion is required, and accompanied by all documents likely to throw light upon the question.

CHARTER OF THE UNITED NATIONS, ARTICLE 96

June 26, 1945, 59 Stat. 1031, T.S. No. 993

1. The General Assembly or the Security Council may request the International Court of Justice to give an advisory opinion on any legal question.

2. Other organs of the United Nations and specialized agencies, which may at any time be so authorized by the General Assembly, may also request advisory opinions of the Court on legal questions arising within the scope of their activities.

NOTES AND QUESTIONS

1. *Types of Jurisdiction*. In addition to hearing contentious cases and advisory proceedings pursuant to the provisions quoted above, the ICJ also exercises various types of "incidental jurisdiction." For example, before a final judgment, the International Court may "indicate, if it considers that circumstances so require, any provisional measures which ought to be taken

to preserve the respective rights of either party." ICJ Statute, art. 41. The Court has determined that such interim measures are legally binding. LaGrand (Germany v. United States), 2001 I.C.J. 466, 501–03. In addition, the Court exercises incidental jurisdiction with respect to: the intervention by third states in contentious cases; the interpretation or revision of its own judgments; and counterclaims presented by respondent states in contentious cases. See ICJ Statute, arts. 60–63; Rules of the International Court of Justice, Rule 80. For an introduction to incidental jurisdiction, see J.G. Merrills, *International Dispute Settlement* 124–32 (5th ed. 2011).

2. *Compulsory Jurisdiction and Mutual Consent in Contentious Cases.* What does it mean to say that the ICJ sometimes may exercise "compulsory" jurisdiction, a term used in Article 36(2) of the Court's Statute? Does it mean that the ICJ will have jurisdiction any time one member state of the United Nations brings a suit against any other member state? During the 19th and early 20th centuries, members of popular peace societies and many European and U.S. leaders favored not only the codification of international law but the development of a world court with jurisdiction to hear cases brought unilaterally by states. See Mark Weston Janis, *America and the Law of Nations 1776–1939*, at 72–91 (2010). According to a 1920 proposal of the Committee of Jurists, which prepared the Statute of the Permanent Court of International Justice, the Court should be able to exercise jurisdiction in a contentious case when one state unilaterally applied to it. The Committee's proposal was not adopted. The idea of such true compulsory jurisdiction resurfaced during the drafting of the U.N. Charter and the Statute of the International Court of Justice. Many delegations favored subjecting U.N. member states to such compulsory jurisdiction. See 2 Shabtai Rosenne, *The Law and Practice of the International Court 1920–2005*, at 701–06 (4th ed. 2006). As finally adopted, however, the U.N. Charter, although providing (Article 93(1)) that member states are *ipso facto* parties to the Statute of the International Court, requires that states take some additional action if the Court is to obtain jurisdiction over them in a contentious case. As you read the cases below, consider how the states involved consented to ICJ jurisdiction.

2. CONTENTIOUS CASES AT THE INTERNATIONAL COURT

As with our discussion of public international arbitration and the *Alabama, Dogger Bank*, and *Rainbow Warrior* cases, keep in mind some key questions here, as we explore the International Court. When and why do sovereign states agree to submit disputes to third-party legal settlement? When and why are governments willing to be bound by the decisions of international tribunals? Note, in *Minquiers and Ecrehos,* that France's and Britain's consent to the jurisdiction of the ICJ came *after* the dispute had already arisen. Look carefully at their Special Agreement, a form of *compromis*, submitting their case to the Court.

THE MINQUIERS AND ECREHOS CASE

France/United Kingdom, 1953 I.C.J. 47

By a letter dated December 5th, 1951, the British Ambassador to the Netherlands transmitted to the Registry on behalf of his Government a certified copy of a Special Agreement concluded between the Government of the United Kingdom of Great Britain and Northern Ireland and the Government of the French Republic, signed on December 29th, 1950, the instruments of ratification in respect of which were exchanged at Paris on September 24th, 1951. * * *

By Article I of the Special Agreement, signed on December 29th, 1950, the Court is requested

> to determine whether the sovereignty over the islets and rocks (in so far as they are capable of appropriation) of the Minquiers and Ecrehos groups respectively belongs to the United Kingdom or the French Republic.

Having thus been requested to decide whether these groups belong either to France or to the United Kingdom, the Court has to determine which of the Parties has produced the more convincing proof of title to one or the other of these groups, or to both of them. By the formulation of Article I the Parties have excluded the status of *res nullius* as well as that of *condominium*. * * *

By the Special Agreement the Court is requested to determine the sovereignty over the islets and rocks in so far as they are capable of appropriation. These words must be considered as relating to islets and rocks which are physically capable of appropriation. The Court is requested to decide in general to which Party sovereignty over each group as a whole belongs, without determining in detail the facts relating to the particular units of which the groups consist.

These groups lie between the British Channel Island of Jersey and the coast of France and consist each of two or three habitable islets, many smaller islets and a great number of rocks. The Ecrehos group lies north-east of Jersey, 3.9 sea-miles from that island, measured from the rock nearest thereto and permanently above water, and 6.6 sea-miles from the coast of France, measured in the same way. The Minquiers group lies south of Jersey, 9.8 sea-miles therefrom and 16.2 sea-miles from the French mainland, measured in the same way. This group lies 8 sea-miles from the Chausey Islands which belong to France.

Both Parties contend that they have respectively an ancient or original title to the Ecrehos and the Minquiers, and that their title has always been maintained and was never lost. The present case does not therefore present the characteristics of a dispute concerning the acquisition of sovereignty over *terra nullius*.

The United Kingdom Government derives the ancient title invoked by it from the conquest of England in 1066 by William Duke of Normandy. By this conquest England became united within the Duchy of Normandy, including the Channel Islands, and this union lasted until 1204 when King Philip Augustus of France drove the Anglo-Norman forces out of Continental Normandy. But his attempts to occupy also the Islands were not successful, except for brief periods when some of them were taken by French forces. On this ground the United Kingdom Government submits the view that all of the Channel Islands, including the Ecrehos and the Minquiers, remained, as before, united with England and that this situation of fact was placed on a legal basis by subsequent Treaties concluded between the English and French Kings.

The French Government does not dispute that the Islands of Jersey, Guernsey, Alderney, Sark, Herm and Jethou continued to be held by the King of England; but it denies that the Ecrehos and Minquiers groups were held by him after the dismemberment of the Duchy of Normandy in 1204. After that event, these two groups were, it is asserted, held by the King of France together with some other islands close to the continent, and reference is made to the same medieval Treaties as those which are invoked by the United Kingdom Government.

In such circumstances it must be examined whether these Treaties, invoked by both Parties, contain anything which might throw light upon the status of the Ecrehos and the Minquiers.

The Treaty of Lambeth of 1217, to which the Parties have referred, cannot be said to contain anything which might elucidate this question. The Treaty of Paris of 1259, which appears to be the principal Treaty on which the Parties rely, enumerates in Article 4 all the lands which the King of England should hold in fee of the King of France in Saintonge beyond the river Charente as well as Bordeaux, Bayonne and Gascony and "all the land which he holds on this side of the Sea of England in fee and in demesne and the islands, if any there be, which the king of England holds which are of the realm of france, and he shall hold of us as peer of france and duke of Aquitaine." These terms seem to refer to islands which the King of England held as Duke of Aquitaine, and not to the Channel Islands. But even assuming that these Islands were also included, the article refers in any case only to islands, if any there be, which are held by the English King. It does not say which islands were at that time held by him. [Similarly, the Court finds that neither the Treaty of Calais of 1360 nor the Treaty of Tropes of 1420 refers specifically to the Minquiers and Ecrehos.]

There are, however, other documents which provide some indication as to the possession of the islets in dispute.

By a Charter of January 14th, 1200, King John of England granted to one of his Barons, Piers des Préaux, the Islands of Jersey, Guernsey and

Alderney "to have and to hold of us by service of three knights' fees." Three years later, by a Charter of 1203, Piers des Pr´eaux granted to the Abbey of Val–Richer "the island of Escrehou in entirety," stating that the King of England "gave me the islands" (*insulas mihi dedit*). This shows that he treated the Ecrehos as an integral part of the fief of the Islands which he had received from the King. In an Order from the English King of July 5th, 1258, the Sub–Warden of the Islands was ordered "to guard the islands of Gernere and Geresey, and the king's other islands in his keeping." In Letters Patent of the English King, dated June 28th, 1360, it was provided that the "keeper of the islands of Gernseye, Jerseye, Serk and Aurneye, and the other islands adjacent thereto" may have the keeping for a further period. The Truce of London of 1471 provided in Article 3 that the King of France would not make any hostile act against the Kingdom of England and other lands specially mentioned, including the Islands "of guernsey, Jersey and alderney [and] other territories, islands, lands and lordships, which are, or will be, held and possessed by the said lord King of England or by his subjects." A Papal Bull of January 20th, 1500, transferring the Channel Islands from the Diocese of Coutances to the Diocese of Winchester, mentioned "the islands of Jersey and Guernsey, Chausey, Alderney, Herm and Sark," while two commercial Treaties of 1606 and 1655 mentioned only Jersey and Guernsey.

[The Court reviews the political history of the Channel Islands and concludes:] What is of decisive importance, in the opinion of the Court, is not indirect presumptions deduced from events in the Middle Ages, but the evidence which relates directly to the possession of the Ecrehos and Minquiers groups.

[The Court turns first to the Ecrehos.]

It has already been mentioned that the Charter of 1200 of the English King, whereby he granted the fief of the Channel Islands to Piers des Préaux, and the Charter of 1203, whereby the latter in turn granted the Ecrehos to the Abbey of Val-Richer, show that the Ecrehos were treated by him as an integral part of his fief.

The grant of the Ecrehos was in frankalmoin. The French Government contends that such a grant had the effect of severing the feudal link between Piers des Préaux and the Abbey, so that the Ecrehos no longer formed a part of the fief of the Channel Islands. The view submitted by that Government is that the Ecrehos remained subject to the Duke of Normandy through the intermediary of the Abbey of Val-Richer, which was situated on the French mainland, and that, when the King of France succeeded to the rights of the Duke after the occupation of Continental Normandy in 1204, the Abbey "passed under his protection, as did the Ecrehos, whose overlord he became."

Figure 5.C

The Channel Islands

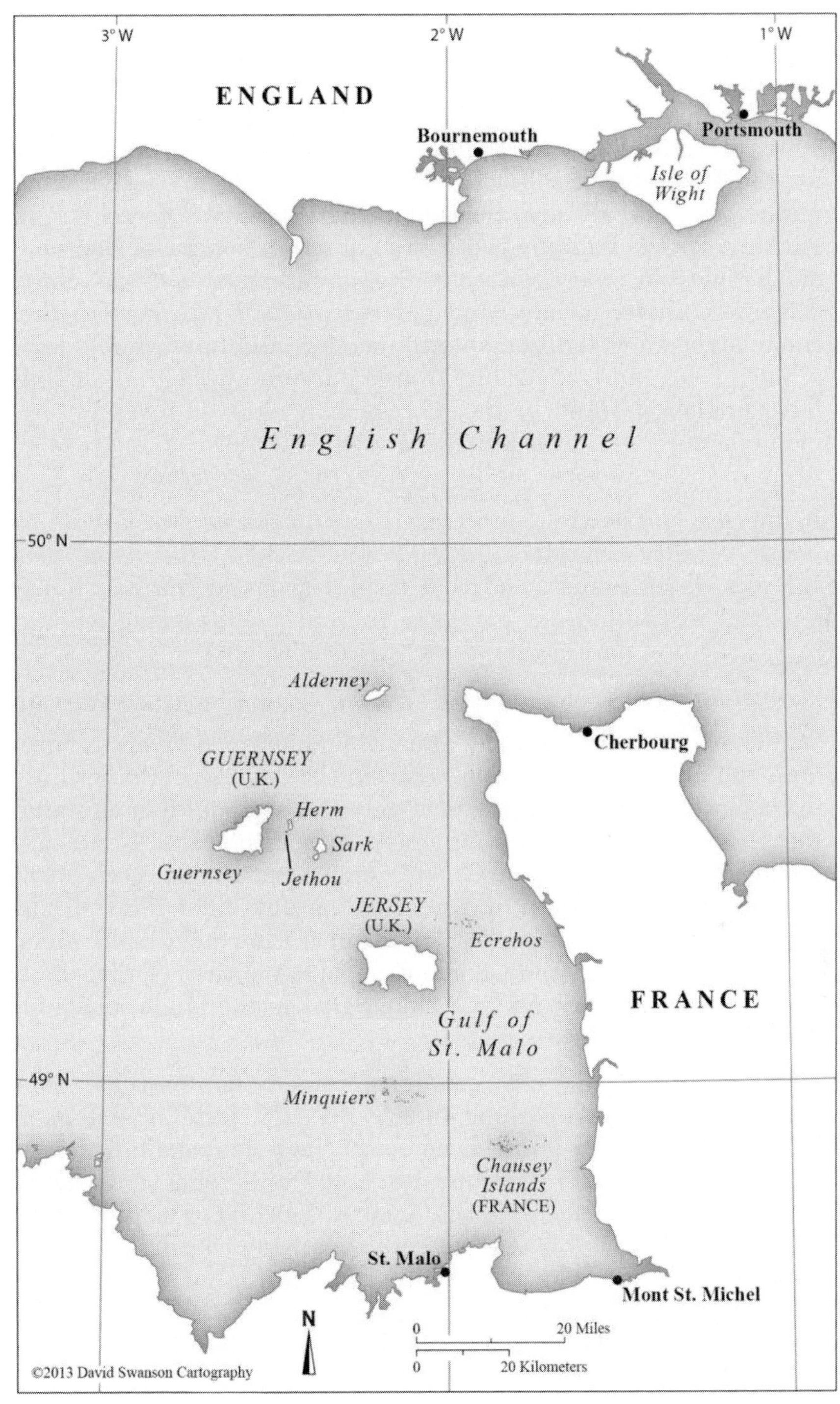

This contention renders it necessary to consider the Charter of 1203 more closely. It provided the following: * * *

> .... Know ye all that I, having regard to the mercy of God, have granted and given and by my present charter have confirmed to God and to the church of St. Mary of Val-Richer and to the monks there serving God, for the salvation of the soul of John, illustrious king of England, who gave me the islands, and for the salvation of the souls of myself and of my father and mother and of all my ancestors, the island of Escrehou in entirety, for the building there of a church in honour of God and of the blessed Mary, so that the divine mysteries be daily celebrated there, to have and possess [it] and whatever in the same island they shall be able to increase and build, freely and quietly, fully and honourably, in free pure and perpetual alms. I have further granted to the aforesaid monks whatever by my men of Jersey, and of Guernsey, and of Alderney, having regard to charity, shall be reasonably given to them, saving my right.

It appears clearly from the *Grand Coutumier de Normandie* of the thirteenth century, chapters XXVIII and XXXII, that land held in frankalmoin was a tenure, and that such a grant in frankalmoin to an ecclesiastical institution did not have the effect of severing feudal ties. The text of the first part of Chapter XXXII is as follows:

[*Translation*]

> They are said to hold by alms who hold lands given in pure alms to God and his servants, wherein the donors retain nothing to themselves or their heirs save only the patronal domain; and they hold from them by alms only, as from patrons. None can make alms out of any land, save only that which is his own therein. Wherefore note that neither the duke, nor barons, nor anyone, ought to sustain any detriment if their men make alms of the lands which they hold of them; and their lords shall exercise their justice and levy their rights in the lands so put in alms, notwithstanding.

This text shows that the grantor retained the "patronal domain" (*dominium patronale*). According to this ancient Norman custom, Piers des Préaux did not by his grant drop out of the feudal chain as far as the Ecrehos was concerned. He continued to hold the Ecrehos as a part of his fief of the Channel Islands, with the Abbot of Val-Richer as his vassal and the King of England as his overlord, and the King continued to exercise his justice and levy his rights in the land so put in alms. By granting the Ecrehos in frankalmoin to the Abbey, Piers des Préaux did not, and could not, alienate the island from the fief of the Channel Islands; it remained a part of that fief.

This view is contested by the French Government on the ground that Piers des Préaux had not in the Charter reserved any feudal service and that he therefore had not created any feudal tenure. It seems that no such condition for the creation of a "*teneure par omosne*," or frankalmoin, was required by the ancient Norman custom, as described in the *Coutumier*. But even assuming that a condition or reservation was required, the grant to the Abbey did contain such a condition or reservation. As is seen from the text of the Charter, the Abbey was to build a church in the Ecrehos "so that the divine mysteries be daily celebrated there," and when the grant was said to be given "for the salvation of the soul of John, illustrious king of England . . . and for the salvation of the souls of myself and of my father and mother and all my ancestors," this could, in view of the custom at that time, only mean that a service of prayers was reserved in the Charter. That this must also have been the view of the Abbot himself and of his successors is seen from the records of certain *Quo Warranto* proceedings held in Jersey in 1309 before the King's itinerant Justices. The Assize Rolls show that a chapel had in fact been built in the Ecrehos, and that the Prior of that chapel, appearing before the Justices, gave evidence that he and his fellow monk, dwelling in the chapel throughout the whole year, "always celebrate for the lord the King and his progenitors." These records show that the Prior himself as well as the Justices called the grant a *tenura*.

Shortly after his grant of 1203 Piers de Préaux forfeited the fief of the Channel Islands, which thereupon reverted to the English King and were administered by Wardens appointed by that King, except for certain periods in the thirteenth and the beginning of the fourteenth century, when the Islands were again granted in fee. Up to 1309, there is no indication that any change had occurred as to the connection of the Ecrehos with the Channel Islands.

The object of the *Quo Warranto* proceedings of 1309 mentioned above was to enquire into the property and revenue of the English King. These proceedings, which were numerous, took the form of calling upon persons to justify their possession of property. The Abbot of Val-Richer was summoned before the King's Justices to answer regarding a mill and the *advocatio* of the Priory of the Ecrehos as well as a rent. * * * When therefore the Abbot of Val-Richer was summoned before the King's Justices in Jersey to answer for this *advocatio*, it must have been on the ground that the Ecrehos, to which the *advocatio* was attached, was within the domain of the English King. And when the Prior of the Ecrehos appeared as the Abbot's attorney in answer to the summons, jurisdiction in respect of the Ecrehos was exercised by the Justices, who decided that "it is permitted to the said Prior to hold the *premissa* as he holds them as long as it shall please the lord the King."

[The Court reviews more of the history of the Priory and finds that later in the Middle Ages, the Priory "was abandoned and the chapel fell into ruins. The close relationship between the Ecrehos and Jersey ceased and for a considerable period thereafter the islets were only occasionally visited by Jerseymen for the purpose of fishing and collecting seaweed." From the 16th through the 18th centuries, the Ecrehos were more or less abandoned.]

From the beginning of the nineteenth century the connection between the Ecrehos and Jersey became closer again because of the growing importance of the oyster fishery in the waters surrounding the islets, and Jersey authorities took, during the subsequent period, action in many ways in respect of the islets. Of the manifold facts invoked by the United Kingdom Government, the Court attaches, in particular, probative value to the acts which relate to the exercise of jurisdiction and local administration and to legislation.

In 1826 criminal proceedings were instituted before the Royal Court in Jersey against a Jerseyman for having shot at a person on the Ecrehos. Similar judicial proceedings in Jersey in respect of criminal offences committed on the Ecrehos took place in 1881, 1883, 1891, 1913 and 1921. On the evidence produced the Court is satisfied that the Courts of Jersey, in criminal cases such as these, have no jurisdiction in the matter of a criminal offence committed outside the Bailiwick of Jersey, even though the offence be committed by a British subject resident in Jersey, and that Jersey authorities took action in these cases because the Ecrehos were considered to be within the Bailiwick. These facts show therefore that Jersey courts have exercised criminal jurisdiction in respect of the Ecrehos during nearly a hundred years.

Evidence produced shows that the law of Jersey has for centuries required the holding of an inquest on corpses found within the Bailiwick where it was not clear that death was due to natural causes. Such inquests on corpses found at the Ecrehos were held in 1859, 1917 and 1948 and are additional evidence of the exercise of jurisdiction in respect of these islets.

Since about 1820, and probably earlier, persons from Jersey have erected and maintained some habitable houses or huts on the islets of the Ecrehos, where they have stayed during the fishing season. Some of these houses or huts have, for the purpose of parochial rates, been included in the records of the Parish of St. Martin in Jersey, which have been kept since 1889, and they have been assessed for the levying of local taxes. Rating schedules for 1889 and 1950 were produced in evidence.

A register of fishing boats for the port of Jersey shows that the fishing boat belonging to a Jersey fisherman, who lived permanently on an islet of the Ecrehos for more than forty years, was entered in that register in 1872, the port or place of the boat being indicated as "Ecrehos

Rocks," and that the licence of that boat was cancelled in 1882. According to a letter of June, 1876, from the Principal Customs Officer of Jersey, an official of that Island visited occasionally the Ecrehos for the purpose of endorsing the licence of that boat.

It is established that contracts of sale relating to real property on the Ecrehos islets have been passed before the competent authorities of Jersey and registered in the public registry of deeds of that island. Examples of such registration of contracts are produced for 1863, 1881, 1884 and some later years.

In 1884, a custom-house was established in the Ecrehos by Jersey customs authorities. The islets have been included by Jersey authorities within the scope of their census enumerations, and in 1901 an official enumerator visited the islets for the purpose of taking the census.

These various facts show that Jersey authorities have in several ways exercised ordinary local administration in respect of the Ecrehos during a long period of time.

By a British Treasury Warrant of 1875, constituting Jersey as a Port of the Channel Islands, the "Ecrehou Rocks" were included within the limits of that port. This legislative Act was a clear manifestation of British sovereignty over the Ecrehos at a time when a dispute as to such sovereignty had not yet arisen. The French Government protested in 1876 on the ground that this Act derogated from the Fishery Convention of 1839. But this protest could not deprive the Act of its character as a manifestation of sovereignty.

Of other facts which throw light upon the dispute, it should be mentioned that Jersey authorities have made periodical official visits to the Ecrehos since 1885, and that they have carried out various works and constructions there, such as a slipway in 1895, a signal post in 1910 and the placing of a mooring buoy in 1939.

The French Government, in addition to the alleged original feudal title considered above, has invoked the fact that the States of Jersey in 1646 prohibited the inhabitants of Jersey from fishing without special permission at the Ecrehos and the Chausey Islands, and that they restricted visits to the Ecrehos in 1692 because of the war between England and France. This shows, it is contended, that the Ecrehos were not considered as British territory. But the Court does not consider that this is the necessary or natural inference to be drawn from these facts.

In the course of the diplomatic exchanges between the two Governments in the beginning of the nineteenth century concerning fisheries off the coast of Cotentin, the French Ambassador in London addressed to the Foreign Office a Note, dated June 12th, 1820, attaching two charts sent from the French Ministry of Marine to the French Ministry of Foreign Affairs purporting to delimit the areas within which the fishermen of each country were entitled to exclusive rights of fishery. In these charts a blue line marking territorial waters was drawn along the coast of the French mainland and round the Chausey Islands, which were indicated as French, and a red line marking territorial waters was drawn round Jersey, Alderney, Sark and the Minquiers, which were indicated as British. No line of territorial waters was drawn round the Ecrehos group, one part of which was included in the red line for Jersey and consequently marked as belonging to Great Britain and the other part apparently treated as *res nullius*. When the French Government in 1876 protested against the British Treasury Warrant of 1875 and challenged British sovereignty over the Ecrehos, it did not itself claim sovereignty, but continued to treat the Ecrehos as *res nullius*. In a letter of March 26th, 1884, from the French Ministry of Foreign Affairs to the French Minister of Marine, it was stated that the British Government had not ceased to claim the Ecrehos as a dependency to the Channel Islands, and it was suggested that French fishermen should be prohibited access to the Ecrehos. It does not appear that any such measure was taken, and subsequently, in a Note to the Foreign Office of December 15th, 1886, the French Government claimed for the first time sovereignty over the Ecrehos "*à la lumière des nouvelles données historiques et géologiques*."

The Court being now called upon to appraise the relative strength of the opposing claims to sovereignty over the Ecrehos in the light of the facts considered above, finds that the Ecrehos group in the beginning of the thirteenth century was considered and treated as an integral part of the fief of the Channel Islands which were held by the English King, and that the group continued to be under the dominion of that King, who in the beginning of the fourteenth century exercised jurisdiction in respect thereof. The Court further finds that British authorities during the greater part of the nineteenth century and in the twentieth century have exercised State functions in respect of the group. The French Government, on the other hand, has not produced evidence showing that it has any valid title to the group. In such circumstances it must be concluded that the sovereignty over the Ecrehos belongs to the United Kingdom.

[The Court examines the claims to the Minquiers in similar detail.]

THE COURT,

unanimously,

finds that the sovereignty over the islets and rocks of the Ecrehos and Minquiers groups, in so far as these islets and rocks are capable of appropriation, belongs to the United Kingdom.

NOTES AND QUESTIONS

1. *International Law and the Acquisition of Territory*. Questions about the acquisition of territory have long troubled interstate relations. We met the issue in the Cession of Alaska and the *Eastern Greenland Case* in Chapter 2, and see it again in Chapters 7 (discussing self-determination), 8 (Antarctica), and 9 (use of force). International law recognizes several ways in which states may acquire new territory: discovery and occupation of *terra nullius*, a label used to describe uninhabited territory such as newly discovered islands; cession from another state; accretion, *i.e.*, the increase of land, as through new geological formations; and acquiescence or prescription, *i.e.*, a continuous, uncontested display of control. Subjugation—conquest followed by annexation—was historically another method of territorial acquisition, but today may violate the U.N. Charter's proscription against the use of force. See 1 *Oppenheim's International Law* 677–709 (Robert Jennings & Arthur Watts eds., 9th ed. 1992). Which theories of territorial acquisition did France and the United Kingdom employ in *Minquiers and Ecrehos*?

2. *The Decision to Adjudicate*. Why was the Minquiers and Ecrehos dispute susceptible to resolution by the International Court? What did the governments of the United Kingdom and France each gain and lose by suspending diplomatic negotiations while the Court heard the case? Did each believe it had the better claim? Does hope of success or fear of failure affect a state's willingness to submit a case to the ICJ?

Sovereignty over even small islands may be significant. The sovereign state is entitled to offshore zones in which it may control fishing and exercise other rights. See Chapter 10. Before the ICJ was notified about the Special Agreement to submit the *Minquiers and Echrehos Case*, France and the United Kingdom had already concluded a treaty allocating important fishing rights off the islets, "without prejudice to the determination of the question of sovereignty" over the islets themselves. Agreement Regarding Rights of Fishery in Areas of the Ecrehos and Minquiers, Jan. 30, 1951, 121 U.N.T.S. 97. Did this Agreement facilitate the decision to adjudicate?

3. *The Choice of Forum*. Why did France and the United Kingdom choose the International Court rather than an *ad hoc* panel of international arbitrators? In delimiting the continental shelf a quarter century later, the same two countries appointed an arbitral tribunal unrelated to the ICJ. See Arbitration between the United Kingdom of Great Britain and Northern Ireland and the French Republic on the Delimitation of the Continental Shelf, Decisions of the Court of Arbitration, June 30, 1977, Mar. 14, 1978, 18 *International Legal Materials* 397 (1979). Another procedural option is to submit a case to a chamber of the ICJ, typically composed of five judges and constituted at the request of the parties. See the discussion about the *ELSI Case* below.

4. *Territorial Dispute Settlement*. Territorial disputes seem a favorite kind of issue for international adjudication. Are such disputes especially amenable to legal argument and arbitral or judicial settlement? In *Minquiers*

and Ecrehos, what kind of proof did the lawyers need to collect and argue? How did the Court, which acts both as fact finder and as final arbiter, weigh the evidence and apply legal rules to reach its judgment? Are territorial disputes good legal fodder because of the nature of their facts?

5. *The Judges.* Who sits on the International Court? How are its judges elected? See Articles 2–15 of the ICJ Statute, reproduced in the Appendix. As of 2013, four of the ICJ's 15 judges were from the "Western Europe and Other Group" (including one from New Zealand), two were from Eastern Europe, three from Asia, three from Africa, two from Latin America, and one from the United States. By tradition, a national of each permanent member of the U.N. Security Council (China, France, Russia, the United Kingdom, and the United States) always serves as a member of the Court. For a critical evaluation of the selection of judges to the ICJ and the International Criminal Court, which we introduce in Chapter 6, see Ruth Mackenzie *et al.*, *Selecting International Judges: Principle, Process, and Politics* (2010).

If the Court's judges do not include a national of a party to a contentious case, that state may appoint an *ad hoc* judge to sit on the case. See ICJ Statute, art. 31. What explains this rule? Is the appointment of *ad hoc* judges consistent with the independent judicial character of the Court? A judge of the nationality of a state party usually sides with that state. However, the French judge in the *Minquiers and Echrehos Case* voted against France.

6. *Compliance with ICJ Decisions.* Why are states likely to comply with ICJ decisions like those in *Minquiers and Ecrehos*? Did both states mean to comply with any eventual judgment when they consented to the *compromis*? Note how France and the United Kingdom formulated the question the Court was authorized to decide. By minimizing the possibility that the Court would find the islets to be either *terra nullius* or subject to a joint condominium regime, the parties seemingly maximized the possibility that the Court would rule that only one or the other state had sovereignty over the islets. If either France or the United Kingdom ran a significant risk of losing the case in the ICJ, was this risk worth running because it would be easier politically for the government to give up the islets in a court case than in diplomatic negotiations? Does the ICJ sometimes serve a "scapegoat function"?

7. *The Norman Invasion.* On July 10, 1994, the Ecrehos were "invaded" by 150 French citizens from Normandy who sought to reopen the dispute about the ownership of the islets at a time when Jersey was seeking to extend its territorial waters from three to 12 miles. Despite assurances from the government of Jersey that traditional French fishing rights would not be impaired, the Norman party came to the Ecrehos to protest. They were restrained from tearing down the Union Jack, but Jersey authorities permitted them to hold a mass and to plant a Norman flag of two yellow lions rampant on a red ground beside a temporary altar. Marcus Binney & Michael Hornsby, "Jersey Police Outwit Norman Invasion," *The Times* (London), July 11, 1994, at 5.

8. *"Consensual" Submissions.* Although in a formal sense all contentious cases submitted to the ICJ are "consensual," sometimes consent is given after, sometimes before, the dispute arises. In *Minquiers and Ecrehos* consent was given after the dispute arose, and both France and Britain were agreeable at the time about going to court. Note how different "consent" is in the *Diplomatic and Consular Staff Case* below. Iran's consent was given prior to any dispute with the United States, and, at the time of the case, Iran resisted the ICJ proceedings.

THE DIPLOMATIC AND CONSULAR STAFF CASE

United States v. Iran, 1980 I.C.J. 3

1. On 29 November 1979, the Legal Adviser of the Department of State of the United States of America handed to the Registrar an Application instituting proceedings against the Islamic Republic of Iran in respect of a dispute concerning the seizure and holding as hostages of members of the United States diplomatic and consular staff and certain other United States nationals.

[The United States also applied for provisional measures to protect the hostages. Iran refused to plead or argue before the International Court. On December 15, 1979, the ICJ delivered an order instructing Iran to release the hostages immediately, 1979 I.C.J. 7, but Iran failed to comply. The case went forward on the merits.]

10. No pleadings were filed by the Government of Iran, which also was not represented at the oral proceedings, and no submissions were therefore presented on its behalf. The position of that Government was, however, defined in two communications addressed to the Court by the Minister for Foreign Affairs of Iran; the first of these was a letter dated 9 December 1979 and transmitted by telegram the same day * * *; the second was a letter transmitted by telex dated 16 March 1980 and received on 17 March 1980, the text of which followed closely that of the letter of 9 December 1979 and reads as follows:

[*Translation from French*]

> I have the honour to acknowledge receipt of the telegram concerning the meeting of the International Court of Justice to be held on 17 March 1980 at the request of the Government of the United States of America, and to set forth to you below, once again, the position of the Government of the Islamic Republic of Iran in that respect:
>
> The Government of the Islamic Republic of Iran wishes to express its respect for the International Court of Justice, and for its distinguished Members, for what they have achieved in the quest for a just and equitable solution to legal conflicts between States, and respectfully draws the attention of the Court to the

> deep-rootedness and the essential character of the Islamic Revolution of Iran, a revolution of a whole oppressed nation against its oppressors and their masters, the examination of whose numerous repercussions is essentially and directly a matter within the national sovereignty of Iran.
>
> The Government of the Islamic Republic of Iran considers that the Court cannot and should not take cognizance of the case which the Government of the United States of America has submitted to it, and in the most significant fashion, a case confined to what is called the question of the "hostages of the American Embassy in Tehran."
>
> For this question only represents a marginal and secondary aspect of an overall problem, one such that it cannot be studied separately, and which involves, *inter alia*, more than 25 years of continual interference by the United States in the internal affairs of Iran, the shameless exploitation of our country, and numerous crimes perpetrated against the Iranian people, contrary to and in conflict with all international and humanitarian norms.
>
> The problem involved in the conflict between Iran and the United States is thus not one of the interpretation and the application of the treaties upon which the American Application is based, but results from an overall situation containing much more fundamental and more complex elements. Consequently, the Court cannot examine the American Application divorced from its proper context, namely the whole political dossier of the relations between Iran and the United States over the last 25 years.
>
> With regard to the request for provisional measures, as formulated by the United States, it in fact implies that the Court should have passed judgment on the actual substance of the case submitted to it, which the Court cannot do without breach of the norms governing its jurisdiction. Furthermore, since provisional measures are by definition intended to protect the interest of the parties, they cannot be unilateral, as they are in the request submitted by the American Government.

[Despite Iran's refusal to participate, the Court rules it has enough information to decide the case. The Court then examines the factual background respecting the seizure of the hostages.]

17. At approximately 10:30 a.m. on 4 November 1979, during the course of a demonstration of approximately 3,000 persons, the United States Embassy compound in Tehran was overrun by a strong armed group of several hundred people. The Iranian security personnel are

reported to have simply disappeared from the scene; at all events it is established that they made no apparent effort to deter or prevent the demonstrators from seizing the Embassy's premises. The invading group (who subsequently described themselves as "Muslim Student Followers of the Imam's Policy," and who will hereafter be referred to as "the militants") gained access by force to the compound and to the ground floor of the Chancery building. Over two hours after the beginning of the attack, and after the militants had attempted to set fire to the Chancery building and to cut through the upstairs steel doors with a torch, they gained entry to the upper floor; one hour later they gained control of the main vault. The militants also seized the other buildings, including the various residences, on the Embassy compound. In the course of the attack, all the diplomatic and consular personnel and other persons present in the premises were seized as hostages, and detained in the Embassy compound; subsequently other United States personnel and one United States private citizen seized elsewhere in Tehran were brought to the compound and added to the number of hostages.

18. During the three hours or more of the assault, repeated calls for help were made from the Embassy to the Iranian Foreign Ministry, and repeated efforts to secure help from the Iranian authorities were also made through direct discussions by the United States Chargé d'affaires, who was at the Foreign Ministry at the time, together with two other members of the mission. From there he made contact with the Prime Minister's Office and the Foreign Ministry officials. A request was also made to the Iranian Chargé d'affaires in Washington for assistance in putting an end to the seizure of the Embassy. Despite these repeated requests, no Iranian security forces were sent in time to provide relief and protection to the Embassy. In fact when Revolutionary Guards ultimately arrived on the scene, despatched by the Government "to prevent clashes," they considered that their task was merely to "protect the safety of both the hostages and the students," according to statements subsequently made by the Iranian Government's spokesman, and by the operations commander of the Guards. No attempt was made by the Iranian Government to clear the Embassy premises, to rescue the persons held hostage, or to persuade the militants to terminate their action against the Embassy. * * *

21. The premises of the United States Embassy in Tehran have remained in the hands of the militants; and the same appears to be the case with the Consulates at Tabriz and Shiraz. Of the total number of United States citizens seized and held as hostages, 13 were released on 18–20 November 1979, but the remainder have continued to be held up to the present time. The release of the 13 hostages was effected pursuant to a decree by the Ayatollah Khomeini addressed to the militants dated 17 November 1979, in which he called upon the militants to "hand over the

blacks and the women, if it is proven they did not spy, to the Ministry of Foreign Affairs so that they may be immediately expelled from Iran."

22. The persons still held hostage in Iran include, according to the information furnished to the Court by the United States, at least 28 persons having the status, duly recognized by the Government of Iran, of "member of the diplomatic staff" within the meaning of the Vienna Convention on Diplomatic Relations of 1961; at least 20 persons having the status, similarly recognized, of "member of the administrative and technical staff" within the meaning of that Convention; and two other persons of United States nationality not possessing either diplomatic or consular status. Of the persons with the status of member of the diplomatic staff, four are members of the Consular Section of the Mission.

23. Allegations have been made by the Government of the United States of inhumane treatment of hostages; the militants and Iranian authorities have asserted that the hostages have been well treated, and have allowed special visits to the hostages by religious personalities and by representatives of the International Committee of the Red Cross. The specific allegations of ill-treatment have not however been refuted. Examples of such allegations, which are mentioned in some of the sworn declarations of hostages released in November 1979, are as follows: at the outset of the occupation of the Embassy some were paraded bound and blindfolded before hostile and chanting crowds; at least during the initial period of their captivity, hostages were kept bound, and frequently blindfolded, denied mail or any communication with their government or with each other, subjected to interrogation, threatened with weapons.

24. Those archives and documents of the United States Embassy which were not destroyed by the staff during the attack on 4 November have been ransacked by the militants. Documents purporting to come from this source have been disseminated by the militants and by the Government-controlled media. * * *

28. * * * On 25 November 1979, the Secretary-General of the United Nations addressed a letter to the President of the Security Council referring to the seizure of the United States Embassy in Tehran and the detention of its diplomatic personnel, and requesting an urgent meeting of the Security Council "in an effort to seek a peaceful solution to the problem." The Security Council met on 27 November and 4 December 1979; on the latter occasion, no representative of Iran was present, but the Council took note of a letter of 13 November 1979 from the Supervisor of the Iranian Foreign Ministry to the Secretary-General. The Security Council then adopted resolution 457 (1979), calling on Iran to release the personnel of the Embassy immediately, to provide them with protection and to allow them to leave the country. The resolution also called on the two Governments to take steps to resolve peacefully the remaining issues between them, and requested the Secretary-General to lend his good

offices for the immediate implementation of the resolution, and to take all appropriate measures to that end. It further stated that the Council would "remain actively seized of the matter" and requested the Secretary-General to report to it urgently on any developments with regard to his efforts. * * *

33. It is to be regretted that the Iranian Government has not appeared before the Court in order to put forward its arguments on the questions of law and of fact which arise in the present case; and that, in consequence, the Court has not had the assistance it might have derived from such arguments or from any evidence adduced in support of them. Nevertheless, in accordance with its settled jurisprudence, the Court, in applying Article 53 of its Statute, must first take up, *proprio motu*, any preliminary question, whether of admissibility or of jurisdiction, that appears from the information before it to arise in the case and the decision of which might constitute a bar to any further examination of the merits of the Applicant's case. The Court will, therefore, first address itself to the considerations put forward by the Iranian Government in its letters of 9 December 1979 and 16 March 1980, on the basis of which it maintains that the Court ought not to take cognizance of the present case.

34. The Iranian Government in its letter of 9 December 1979 drew attention to what it referred to as the "deep rootedness and the essential character of the Islamic Revolution of Iran, a revolution of a whole oppressed nation against its oppressors and their masters." The examination of the "numerous repercussions" of the revolution, it added, is "a matter essentially and directly within the national sovereignty of Iran." However, as the Court pointed out in its Order of 15 December 1979,

> a dispute which concerns diplomatic and consular premises and the detention of internationally protected persons, and involves the interpretation or application of multilateral conventions codifying the international law governing diplomatic and consular relations, is one which by its very nature falls within international jurisdiction.

36. The Court * * * in its Order of 15 December 1979, made it clear that the seizure of the United States Embassy and Consulates and the detention of internationally protected persons as hostages cannot be considered as something "secondary" or "marginal," having regard to the importance of the legal principles involved. It also referred to a statement of the Secretar-General of the United Nations, and to Security Council resolution 457 (1979), as evidencing the importance attached by the international community as a whole to the observance of those principles in the present case as well as its concern at the dangerous level of tension between Iran and the United States. The Court, at the same time, pointed out that no provision of the Statute or Rules contemplates that the Court

should decline to take cognizance of one aspect of a dispute merely because that dispute has other aspects, however important. It further underlined that, if the Iranian Government considered the alleged activities of the United States in Iran legally to have a close connection with the subject-matter of the United States' Application, it was open to that Government to present its own arguments regarding those activities to the Court either by way of defence in a Counte-Memorial or by way of a counter-claim.

37. The Iranian Government, notwithstanding the terms of the Court's Order, did not file any pleadings and did not appear before the Court. By its own choice, therefore, it has forgone the opportunities offered to it under the Statute and Rules of Court to submit evidence and arguments in support of its contention in regard to the "overall problem." Even in its later letter of 16 March 1980, the Government of Iran confined itself to repeating what it had said in its letter of 9 December 1979, without offering any explanations in regard to the points to which the Court had drawn attention in its Order of 15 December 1979. It has provided no explanation of the reasons why it considers that the violations of diplomatic and consular law alleged in the United States' Application cannot be examined by the Court separately from what it describes as the "overall problem" involving "more than 25 years of continual interference by the United States in the internal affairs of Iran." Nor has it made any attempt to explain, still less define, what connection, legal or factual, there may be between the "overall problem" of its general grievances against the United States and the particular events that gave rise to the United States' claims in the present case which, in its view, precludes the separate examination of those claims by the Court. This was the more necessary because legal disputes between sovereign States by their very nature are likely to occur in political contexts, and often form only one element in a wider and long-standing political dispute between the States concerned. Yet never has the view been put forward before that, because a legal dispute submitted to the Court is only one aspect of a political dispute, the Court should decline to resolve for the parties the legal questions at issue between them. Nor can any basis for such a view of the Court's functions or jurisdiction be found in the Charter or the Statute of the Court; if the Court were, contrary to its settled jurisprudence, to adopt such a view, it would impose a far-reaching and unwarranted restriction upon the role of the Court in the peaceful solution of international disputes.

38. It follows that the considerations and arguments put forward in the Iranian Government's letters of 9 December 1979 and 16 March 1980 do not, in the opinion of the Court, disclose any ground on which it should conclude that it cannot or ought not to take cognizance of the present case. * * *

45. Article 53 of the Statute requires the Court, before deciding in favour of an Applicant's claim, to satisfy itself that it has jurisdiction, in accordance with Articles 36 and 37, empowering it to do so. In the present case the principal claims of the United States relate essentially to alleged violations by Iran of its obligations to the United States under the Vienna Conventions of 1961 on Diplomatic Relations and of 1963 on Consular Relations. With regard to these claims the United States has invoked as the basis for the Court's jurisdiction Article I of the Optional Protocols concerning the Compulsory Settlement of Disputes which accompany these Conventions. The United Nations publication *Multilateral Treaties in respect of which the Secretary-General Performs Depository Functions* lists both Iran and the United States as parties to the Vienna Conventions of 1961 and 1963, as also to their accompanying Protocols concerning the Compulsory Settlement of Disputes, and in each case without any reservation to the instrument in question. The Vienna Conventions, which codify the law of diplomatic and consular relations, state principles and rules essential for the maintenance of peaceful relations between States and accepted throughout the world by nations of all creeds, cultures and political complexions. Moreover, the Iranian Government has not maintained in its communications to the Court that the two Vienna Conventions and Protocols are not in force as between Iran and the United States. Accordingly, as indicated in the Court's Order of 15 December 1979, the Optional Protocols manifestly provide a possible basis for the Court's jurisdiction, with respect to the United States' claims under the Vienna Conventions of 1961 and 1963. It only remains, therefore, to consider whether the present dispute in fact falls within the scope of their provisions.

46. The terms of Article I, which are the same in the two Protocols, provide:

> Disputes arising out of the interpretation or application of the Convention shall lie within the compulsory jurisdiction of the International Court of Justice and may accordingly be brought before the Court by an application made by any party to the dispute being a Party to the present Protocol.

The United States' claims here in question concern alleged violations by Iran of its obligations under several articles of the Vienna Conventions of 1961 and 1963 with respect to the privileges and immunities of the personnel, the inviolability of the premises and archives, and the provision of facilities for the performance of the functions of the United States Embassy and Consulates in Iran. In so far as its claims relate to two private individuals held hostage in the Embassy, the situation of these individuals falls under the provisions of the Vienna Convention of 1961 guaranteeing the inviolability of the premises of embassies, and of Article 5 of the 1963 Convention concerning the consular functions of assisting nationals and protecting and safeguarding their interests. By their very nature all these claims concern the interpretation or application of one or other of the two Vienna Conventions. * * *

50. However, the United States also presents claims in respect of alleged violations by Iran * * * of the Treaty of Amity, Economic Relations, and Consular Rights of 1955 between the United States and Iran, which entered into force on 16 June 1957. With regard to these claims the United States has invoked paragraph 2 of Article XXI of the Treaty as the basis for the Court's jurisdiction. The claims of the United States under this Treaty overlap in considerable measure with its claims under the two Vienna Conventions and more especially the Convention of 1963. * * *

54. No suggestion has been made by Iran that the 1955 Treaty was not in force on 4 November 1979 when the United States Embassy was overrun and its nationals taken hostage, or on 29 November when the United States submitted the dispute to the Court. The very purpose of a treaty of amity * * * is to promote friendly relations between the two countries concerned, and between their two peoples, more especially by mutual undertakings to ensure the protection and security of their nationals in each other's territory. It is precisely when difficulties arise that the treaty assumes its greatest importance, and the whole object of Article XXI, paragraph 2, of the 1955 Treaty was to establish the means for arriving at a friendly settlement of such difficulties by the Court or by other peaceful means. It would, therefore, be incompatible with the whole purpose of the 1955 Treaty if recourse to the Court under Article XXI, paragraph 2, were now to be found not to be open to the parties precisely at the moment when such recourse was most needed. Furthermore, although the machinery for the effective operation of the 1955 Treaty has, no doubt, now been impaired by reason of diplomatic relations between the two countries having been broken off by the United States, its provisions remain part of the corpus of law applicable between the United States and Iran. * * *

56. * * * The events which are the subject of the United States' claims fall into two phases which it will be convenient to examine separately.

57. The first of these phases covers the armed attack on the United States Embassy by militants on 4 November 1979, the overrunning of its premises, the seizure of its inmates as hostages, the appropriation of its property and archives and the conduct of the Iranian authorities in the face of those occurrences. The attack and the subsequent overrunning, bit by bit, of the whole Embassy premises, was an operation which continued over a period of some three hours without any body of police, any military unit or any Iranian official intervening to try to stop or impede it from being carried through to its completion. The result of the attack was

considerable damage to the Embassy premises and property, the forcible opening and seizure of its archives, the confiscation of the archives and other documents found in the Embassy and, most grave of all, the seizure by force of its diplomatic and consular personnel as hostages, together with two United States nationals.

58. No suggestion has been made that the militants, when they executed their attack on the Embassy, had any form of official status as recognized "agents" or organs of the Iranian State. Their conduct in mounting the attack, overrunning the Embassy and seizing its inmates as hostages cannot, therefore, be regarded as imputable to that State on that basis. Their conduct might be considered as itself directly imputable to the Iranian State only if it were established that, in fact, on the occasion in question the militants acted on behalf of the State, having been charged by some competent organ of the Iranian State to carry out a specific operation. The information before the Court does not, however, suffice to establish with the requisite certainty the existence at that time of such a link between the militants and any competent organ of the State.

59. Previously, it is true, the religious leader of the country, the Ayatollah Khomeini, had made several public declarations inveighing against the United States as responsible for all his country's problems. In so doing, it would appear, the Ayatollah Khomeini was giving utterance to the general resentment felt by supporters of the revolution at the admission of the former Shah to the United States. The information before the Court also indicates that a spokesman for the militants, in explaining their action afterwards, did expressly refer to a message issued by the Ayatollah Khomeini, on 1 November 1979. In that message the Ayatollah Khomeini had declared that it was "up to the dear pupils, students and theological students to expand with all their might their attacks against the United States and Israel, so they may force the United States to return the deposed and criminal shah, and to condemn this great plot" (that is, a plot to stir up dissension between the main streams of Islamic thought). In the view of the Court, however, it would be going too far to interpret such general declarations of the Ayatollah Khomeini to the people or students of Iran as amounting to an authorization from the State to undertake the specific operation of invading and seizing the United States Embassy. To do so would, indeed, conflict with the assertions of the militants themselves who are reported to have claimed credit for having devised and carried out the plan to occupy the Embassy. Again, congratulations after the event, such as those reportedly telephoned to the militants by the Ayatollah Khomeini on the actual evening of the attack, and other subsequent statements of official approval, though highly significant in another context shortly to be considered, do not alter the initially independent and unofficial character of the militants' attack on the Embassy.

60. The first phase, here under examination, of the events complained of also includes the attacks on the United States Consulates at Tabriz and Shiraz. Like the attack of the Embassy, they appear to have been executed by militants not having an official character, and successful because of lack of sufficient protection.

61. The conclusion just reached by the Court, that the initiation of the attack on the United States Embassy on 4 November 1979, and of the attacks on the Consulates at Tabriz and Shiraz the following day, cannot be considered as in itself imputable to the Iranian State does not mean that Iran is, in consequence, free of any responsibility in regard to those attacks; for its own conduct was in conflict with its international obligations. By a number of provisions of the Vienna Conventions of 1961 and 1963, Iran was placed under the most categorical obligations, as a receiving State, to take appropriate steps to ensure the protection of the United States Embassy and Consulates, their staffs, their archives, their means of communication and the freedom of movement of the members of their staffs.

62. Thus, after solemnly proclaiming the inviolability of the premises of a diplomatic mission, Article 22 of the 1961 Convention continues in paragraph 2:

> *The receiving State is under a special duty to take all appropriate steps to protect the premises of the mission against any* intrusion or damage and to prevent any disturbance of the peace of the mission or impairment of its dignity. (Emphasis added.)

So, too, after proclaiming that the person of a diplomatic agent shall be inviolable, and that he shall not be liable to any form of arrest or detention, Article 29 provides:

> The receiving State shall treat him with due respect and *shall take all appropriate steps to prevent any attack on his person, freedom or dignity*. (Emphasis added.)

The obligation of a receiving State to protect the inviolability of the archives and documents of a diplomatic mission is laid down in Article 24, which specifically provides that they are to be "inviolable at any time and wherever they may be." Under Article 25 it is required to "accord full facilities for the performance of the functions of the mission," under Article 26 to "ensure to all members of the mission freedom of movement and travel in its territory," and under Article 27 to "permit and protect free communication on the part of the mission for all official purposes." Analogous provisions are to be found in the 1963 Convention regarding the privileges and immunities of consular missions and their staffs. In the view of the Court, the obligations of the Iranian Government here in question are not merely contractual obligations established by the Vienna

Conventions of 1961 and 1963, but also obligations under general international law.

63. The facts * * * establish to the satisfaction of the Court that on 4 November 1979 the Iranian Government failed altogether to take any "appropriate steps" to protect the premises, staff and archives of the United States' mission against attack by the militants, and to take any steps either to prevent this attack or to stop it before it reached its completion. They also show that on 5 November 1979 the Iranian Government similarly failed to take appropriate steps for the protection of the United States Consulates at Tabriz and Shiraz. In addition they show, in the opinion of the Court, that the failure of the Iranian Government to take such steps was due to more than mere negligence or lack of appropriate means. * * *

67. This inaction of the Iranian Government by itself constituted clear and serious violation of Iran's obligations to the United States under the provisions of Article 22, paragraph 2, and Articles 24, 25, 26, 27 and 29 of the 1961 Vienna Convention on Diplomatic Relations, and Articles 5 and 36 of the 1963 Vienna Convention on Consular Relations. Similarly, with respect to the attacks on the Consulates at Tabriz and Shiraz, the inaction of the Iranian authorities entailed clear and serious breaches of its obligations under the provisions of several further articles of the 1963 Convention on Consular Relations. So far as concerns the two private United States nationals seized as hostages by the invading militants, that inaction entailed, albeit incidentally, a breach of its obligations under Article II, paragraph 4, of the 1955 Treaty of Amity, Economic Relations, and Consular Rights which, in addition to the obligations of Iran existing under general international law, requires the parties to ensure "the most constant protection and security" to each other's nationals in their respective territories. * * *

69. The second phase of the events which are the subject of the United States' claims comprises the whole series of facts which occurred following the completion of the occupation of the United States Embassy by the militants, and the seizure of the Consulates at Tabriz and Shiraz. The occupation having taken place and the diplomatic and consular personnel of the United States' mission having been taken hostage, the action required of the Iranian Government by the Vienna Conventions and by general international law was manifest. Its plain duty was at once to make every effort, and to take every appropriate step, to bring these flagrant infringements of the inviolability of the premises, archives and diplomatic and consular staff of the United States Embassy to a speedy end, to restore the Consulates at Tabriz and Shiraz to United States control, and in general to re-establish the status quo and to offer reparation for the damage.

70. No such step was, however, taken by the Iranian authorities. At a press conference on 5 November the Foreign Minister, Mr. Yazdi, conceded that "according to international regulations the Iranian Government is dutybound to safeguard the life and property of foreign nationals." But he made no mention of Iran's obligation to safeguard the inviolability of foreign embassies and diplomats; and he ended by announcing that the action of the students "enjoys the endorsement and support of the government, because America herself is responsible for this incident." As to the Prime Minister, Mr. Bazargan, he does not appear to have made any statement on the matter before resigning his office on 5 November. * * *

73. The seal of official government approval was finally set on this situation by a decree issued on 17 November 1979 by the Ayatollah Khomeini. His decree began with the assertion that the American Embassy was "a centre of espionage and conspiracy" and that "those people who hatched plots against our Islamic movement in that place do not enjoy international diplomatic respect." He went on expressly to declare that the premises of the Embassy and the hostages would remain as they were until the United States had handed over the former Shah for trial and returned his property to Iran. This statement of policy the Ayatollah qualified only to the extent of requesting the militants holding the hostages to "hand over the blacks and the women, if it is proven that they did not spy, to the Ministry of Foreign Affairs so that they may be immediately expelled from Iran." As to the rest of the hostages, he made the Iranian Government's intentions all too clear:

> The noble Iranian nation will not give permission for the release of the rest of them. Therefore, the rest of them will be under arrest until the American Government acts according to the wish of the nation. * * *

79. The Court moreover cannot conclude its observations on the series of acts which it has found to be imputable to the Iranian State and to be patently inconsistent with its international obligations under the Vienna Conventions of 1961 and 1963 without mention also of another fact. This is that judicial authorities of the Islamic Republic of Iran and the Minister of Foreign Affairs have frequently voiced or associated themselves with, a threat first announced by the militants, of having some of the hostages submitted to trial before a court or some other body. These threats may at present merely be acts in contemplation. But the Court considers it necessary here and now to stress that, if the intention to submit the hostages to any form of criminal trial or investigation were to be put into effect, that would constitute a grave breach by Iran of its obligations under Article 31, paragraph 1, of the 1961 Vienna Convention. This paragraph states in the most express terms: "A diplomatic agent shall enjoy immunity from the criminal jurisdiction of the receiving

State." Again, if there were an attempt to compel the hostages to bear witness, a suggestion renewed at the time of the visit to Iran of the Secretary-General's Commission, Iran would without question be violating paragraph 2 of that same Article of the 1961 Vienna Convention which provides that: "A diplomatic agent is not obliged to give evidence as a witness."

80. The facts of the present case, viewed in the light of the applicable rules of law, thus speak loudly and clearly of successive and still continuing breaches by Iran of its obligations to the United States under the Vienna Conventions of 1961 and 1963, as well as under the Treaty of 1955. * * *

90. On the basis of the foregoing detailed examination of the merits of the case, the Court finds that Iran, by committing successive and continuing breaches of the obligations laid upon it by the Vienna Conventions of 1961 and 1963 on Diplomatic and Consular Relations, the Treaty of Amity, Economic Relations, and Consular Rights of 1955, and the applicable rules of general international law, has incurred responsibility towards the United States. As to the consequences of this finding, it clearly entails an obligation on the part of the Iranian State to make reparation for the injury thereby caused to the United States. Since however Iran's breaches of its obligations are still continuing, the form and amount of such reparation cannot be determined at the present date.

91. At the same time the Court finds itself obliged to stress the cumulative effect of Iran's breaches of its obligations when taken together. A marked escalation of these breaches can be seen to have occurred in the transition from the failure on the part of the Iranian authorities to oppose the armed attack by the militants on 4 November 1979 and their seizure of the Embassy premises and staff, to the almost immediate endorsement by those authorities of the situation thus created, and then to their maintaining deliberately for many months the occupation of the Embassy and detention of its staff by a group of armed militants acting on behalf of the State for the purpose of forcing the United States to bow to certain demands. Wrongfully to deprive human beings of their freedom and to subject them to physical constraint in conditions of hardship is in itself manifestly incompatible with the principles of the Charter of the United Nations, as well as with the fundamental principles enunciated in the Universal Declaration of Human Rights. But what has above all to be emphasized is the extent and seriousness of the conflict between the conduct of the Iranian State and its obligations under the whole corpus of the international rules of which diplomatic and consular law is comprised, rules the fundamental character of which the Court must here again strongly affirm. In its Order of 15 December 1979, the Court made a point of stressing that the obligations laid on States by the two Vienna Conventions are of cardinal

importance for the maintenance of good relations between States in the interdependent world of today. "There is no more fundamental prerequisite for the conduct of relations between States," the Court there said, "than the inviolability of diplomatic envoys and embassies, so that throughout history nations of all creeds and cultures have observed reciprocal obligations for that purpose." The institution of diplomacy, the Court continued, has proved to be "an instrument essential for effective co-operation in the international community, and for enabling States, irrespective of their differing constitutional and social systems, to achieve mutual understanding and to resolve their differences by peaceful means."

92. It is a matter of deep regret that the situation which occasioned those observations has not been rectified since they were made. Having regard to their importance the Court considers it essential to reiterate them in the present Judgment. The frequency with which at the present time the principles of international law governing diplomatic and consular relations are set at naught by individuals or groups of individuals is already deplorable. But this case is unique and of very particular gravity because here it is not only private individuals or groups of individuals that have disregarded and set at naught the inviolability of a foreign embassy, but the government of the receiving State itself. Therefore in recalling yet again the extreme importance of the principles of law which it is called upon to apply in the present case, the Court considers it to be its duty to draw the attention of the entire international community, of which Iran itself has been a member since time immemorial, to the irreparable harm that may be caused by events of the kind now before the Court. Such events cannot fail to undermine the edifice of law carefully constructed by mankind over a period of centuries, the maintenance of which is vital for the security and well-being of the complex international community of the present day, to which it is more essential than ever that the rules developed to ensure the ordered progress of relations between its members should be constantly and scrupulously respected.

93. Before drawing the appropriate conclusions from its findings on the merits in this case, the Court considers that it cannot let pass without comment the incursion into the territory of Iran made by the United States military units on 24–25 April 1980[.] No doubt the United States Government may have had understandable preoccupations with respect to the well-being of its nationals held hostage in its Embassy for over five months. No doubt also the United States Government may have had understandable feelings of frustration at Iran's long-continued detention of the hostages, notwithstanding two resolutions of the Security Council as well as the Court's own Order of 15 December 1979 calling expressly for their immediate release. Nevertheless, in the circumstances of the present proceedings, the Court cannot fail to express its concern in regard

to the United States' incursion into Iran. When, as previously recalled, this case had become ready for hearing on 19 February 1980, the United States Agent requested the Court, owing to the delicate stage of certain negotiations, to defer setting a date for the hearings. Subsequently, on 11 March, the Agent informed the Court of the United States Government's anxiety to obtain an early judgment on the merits of the case. The hearings were accordingly held on 18, 19 and 20 March, and the Court was in course of preparing the present judgment adjudicating upon the claims of the United States against Iran when the operation of 24 April 1980 took place. The Court therefore feels bound to observe that an operation undertaken in those circumstances, from whatever motive, is of a kind calculated to undermine respect for the judicial process in international relations; and to recall that in * * * its Order of 15 December 1979 the Court had indicated that no action was to be taken by either party which might aggravate the tension between the two countries.

94. At the same time, however, the Court must point out that neither the question of the legality of the operation of 24 April 1980, under the Charter of the United Nations and under general international law, nor any possible question of responsibility flowing from it, is before the Court. It must also point out that this question can have no bearing on the evaluation of the conduct of the Iranian Government over six months earlier, on 4 November 1979, which is the subject-matter of the United States' Application. It follows that the findings reached by the Court in this Judgment are not affected by that operation.

95. For these reasons,

THE COURT,

1. By thirteen votes to two,

Decides that the Islamic Republic of Iran, by the conduct which the Court has set out in this Judgment, has violated in several respects, and is still violating, obligations owed by it to the United States of America under international conventions in force between the two countries, as well as under long-established rules of general international law;

IN FAVOUR: *President* Sir Humphrey Waldock; *Vice-President* Elias; *Judges* Forster, Gros, Lachs, Nagendra Singh, Ruda, Mosler, Oda, Ago, El-Erian, Sette-Camara and Baxter.

AGAINST: *Judges* Morozov and Tarazi.

2. By thirteen votes to two,

Decides that the violations of these obligations engage the responsibility of the Islamic Republic of Iran towards the United States of America under international law;

IN FAVOUR: *President* Sir Humphrey Waldock; *Vice-President* Elias; *Judges* Forster, Gros, Lachs, Nagendra Singh, Ruda, Mosler, Oda, Ago, El-Erian, Sette-Camara and Baxter.

AGAINST: *Judges* Morozov and Tarazi.

3. Unanimously,

Decides that the Government of the Islamic Republic of Iran must immediately take all steps to redress the situation resulting from the events of 4 November 1979 and what followed from these events, and to that end:

(*a*) must immediately terminate the unlawful detention of the United States Chargé d'affaires and other diplomatic and consular staff and other United States nationals now held hostage in Iran, and must immediately release each and every one and entrust them to the protecting Power (Article 45 of the 1961 Vienna Convention on Diplomatic Relations);

(*b*) must ensure that all the said persons have the necessary means of leaving Iranian territory, including means of transport;

(*c*) must immediately place in the hands of the protecting Power the premises, property, archives and documents of the United States Embassy in Tehran and of its Consulates in Iran;

4. Unanimously,

Decides that no member of the United States diplomatic or consular staff may be kept in Iran to be subjected to any form of judicial proceedings or to participate in them as a witness;

5. By twelve votes to three,

Decides that the Government of the Islamic Republic of Iran is under an obligation to make reparation to the Government of the United States of America for the injury caused to the latter by the events of 4 November 1979 and what followed from these events;

IN FAVOUR: *President* Sir Humphrey Waldock; *Vice-President* Elias; *Judges* Forster, Gros, Nagendra Singh, Ruda, Mosler, Oda, Ago, El-Erian, Sette-Camara and Baxter.

AGAINST: *Judges* Lachs, Morozov and Tarazi.

6. By fourteen votes to one,

Decides that the form and amount of such reparation, failing agreement between the Parties, shall be settled by the Court, and reserves for this purpose the subsequent procedure in the case.

IN FAVOUR: *President* Sir Humphrey Waldock; *Vice-President* Elias; *Judges* Forster, Gros, Lachs, Nagendra Singh, Ruda, Mosler, Tarazi, Oda, Ago, El-Erian, Sette-Camara and Baxter.

AGAINST: *Judge* Morozov.

NOTES AND QUESTIONS

1. *Background to the Hostages Crisis.* Former U.S. Secretary of State Warren Christopher and former Iran-U.S. Claims Tribunal Judge Richard Mosk summarized events leading up to the hostages crisis:

> In 1925 Reza Khan, a semi-literate military officer, ousted the existing dynasty of Iran and had himself enthroned as Reza Shah Pahlavi. Early in World War II, British and Soviet troops, in effect, occupied Iran and secured the Iranian oil fields for Allied use. The Shah had become too pro German for the Allies. So they had Mohammad Reza Pahlavi, Reza Shah Pahlavi's son, replace him at the age of 22.
>
> In the early 1950s, Mohammed Mossadegh, an elected leftist prime minister, nationalized British and American oil operations in Iran and refused to pay compensation. The Shah did not back Mossadegh, and mobs called for the Shah's removal. He fled Iran.
>
> In 1953, the Iranian military, with C.I.A. support, overthrew Mossadegh, and the Shah was restored to the throne. With a grateful Shah in power, the United States and Iran signed a Treaty of Amity.
>
> In 1963, the Shah began his "White Revolution" of reform. Clerics led by Ayatollah Khomeini challenged the Shah's reform programs. Rioting in Qom was suppressed, and in 1964, Ayatollah Khomeini was exiled to Iraq.
>
> By 1972, the United States decided to allow Iran access to U.S. military weapons. In return, the Shah became a strong ally of the United States in the Gulf region. Meanwhile, American businesses invested heavily, and did substantial business in Iran. The Shah began to increase his powers and used a feared secret police apparatus, SAVAK.
>
> President Carter had criticized the Shah's abuses of human rights but determined that his value as a military ally outweighed his autocratic measures. * * *
>
> After the Government-controlled press published an article [in 1978] ridiculing Khomeini, rioting erupted in Qom. * * *
>
> In January 1979, the Shah left Iran on an "extended vacation[.]" On February 1, the Ayatollah Khomeini triumphantly returned to Iran and was deemed the Imam. The revolution was completed as the Islamic Republic of Iran was declared. * * * The revolution can be traced to the repressive and corrupt regime of the Shah, the perception of Iranians that the Shah was a threat to their culture and religion, and the real and perceived intervention by foreign powers into Iranian internal affairs.

> On October 22, 1979, the exiled Shah left Mexico and arrived in New York to undergo treatment for cancer at New York Hospital-Cornell Medical Center. On November 1, 1979, Khomeini's office in Qom issued a statement encouraging Iranian students to "expand their attacks" against the United States to force the U.S. to return the deposed Shah.

Warren Christopher & Richard M. Mosk, "The Iranian Hostage Crisis and the Iran-U.S. Claims Tribunal: Implications for International Dispute Resolution and Diplomacy," 7 *Pepperdine Dispute Resolution Law Journal* 165, 165–67 (2007). The movie *Argo*, winner of the 2013 Oscar for best picture, is a Hollywood dramatization of the Iranian hostage crisis.

2. *Attribution and the Law of State Responsibility*. How do we know that the acts about which the United States complained in the *Diplomatic and Consular Staff Case* were attributable to Iran? In modern international law, attribution is one aspect of the law of state responsibility. We considered state responsibility in the *CMS Case* in Chapter 2 and in the 1990 *Rainbow Warrior Case* earlier in this chapter; we explore the topic in more depth in Chapter 6.

3. *The Decision to Litigate*. Why did the United States bring the *Diplomatic and Consular Staff Case* to the International Court? According to Professor Merrills, in bringing the case the United States may have been signaling its willingness to "depoliticise" the hostages dispute, seeking settlement through peaceful judicial means. J.G. Merrills, *International Dispute Settlement* 160 (5th ed. 2011). But was it likely that Iran would comply with an adverse judgment? Was the legal issue ever in much doubt? What could the United States gain if Iran disregarded the judgment? What could the U.S. lose? According to Roberts B. Owen, State Department Legal Adviser during the Carter administration, "it was generally recognized that * * * it was unlikely that Iran would obey." "[W]e nonetheless believed strongly * * * that quick condemnatory action by the World Court would help us mobilize world opinion against Iran's irresponsible action." *Quoted in* Michael P. Scharf & Paul R. Williams, *Shaping Foreign Policy in Times of Crisis: The Role of International Law and the State Department Legal Adviser* 49 (2010). It could be that "the United States agreed to use the Court's decision as a means for translating a dispute between Iran and the United States specifically into one between Iran and the international community generally." M.W. Janis, "The Role of the International Court in the Hostages Crisis," 13 *Connecticut Law Review* 263, 280 (1981). Was the U.S. public also being shown that something was being done to free the hostages?

4. *Resolving the Hostages Crisis*. Efforts to resolve the hostages crisis proceeded through diplomatic channels, at the U.N. Security Council, before the ICJ, by a failed U.S. helicopter rescue mission, and by the freezing of Iranian assets in the United States and abroad. Might the United States have responded by seizing the Iranian embassy in Washington, DC and taking Iranian diplomats hostage? See Scharf & Williams, *supra* Note 3, at 50–51. Ultimately, in January 1981, a U.S.-Iranian treaty, negotiated

through the good offices of Algeria, resulted in the release of the U.S. hostages, the unfreezing of Iranian assets, and the establishment of the Iran-U.S. Claims Tribunal to decide disputes among Iran, the United States, and nationals of those countries. *Dames & Moore*, a U.S. case related to the creation of the Iran-U.S. Claims Tribunal and the unfreezing of Iranian assets, appears in Chapter 4.

5. *Compliance with ICJ Decisions.* Iran eventually released the hostages, but would you say that Iran "complied" with the Court's judgment? How can we measure compliance? Should losing states be counted as complying with a judgment if they significantly delay or take only some of the steps required by the Court? The ICJ has no formal mechanism for monitoring compliance.

How strong is the correlation between the basis for ICJ jurisdiction and compliance? Will a losing state almost always resist complying with an ICJ decision if the parties have mutually agreed on jurisdiction in advance of the dispute, as in the *Diplomatic and Consular Staff Case*? In 2006 Argentina brought a case against Uruguay challenging the legality of Uruguay's planned and actual construction of mills; jurisdiction was based on a provision in a 1975 treaty, the Statute of the River Uruguay. The ICJ found that Uruguay failed to provide notice about its plans for the mills and also failed to negotiate with Argentina, as required by the 1975 Statute. Pulp Mills on the River Uruguay (Argentina v. Uruguay), 2010 I.C.J. 14. According to one commentator, "[t]he Court's decision appears to have helped resolve the diplomatic dispute between the two countries," leading to "an agreement to monitor pollution levels." Jacob Katz Cogan, "The 2010 Judicial Activity of the International Court of Justice," 105 *American Journal of International Law* 477, 478 n.10 (2011). Was it easier for Uruguay to change its behavior because it was found to have breached procedural rather than substantive obligations? What factors may prompt states to comply with ICJ decisions, even when consent to jurisdiction is given well in advance of a case? The clarity of the jurisdictional authorization? A lack of political tension between the disputing parties? The subject matter of the case? See Constanze Schulte, *Compliance with Decisions of the International Court of Justice* (2004).

What are the prospects for formal institutional enforcement of ICJ judgments? The U.N. Security Council may impose legally binding measures, such as trade sanctions, to pressure a state to comply with an ICJ judgment. See Articles 25 and 94 of the United Nations Charter in the Appendix. However, the Council has never exercised this authority. See Karin Oehlers-Frahm, "Article 94 UN Charter," in *The Statute of the International Court of Justice: A Commentary* 186 (Andreas Zimmerman *et al.* eds., 2d ed. 2012). We explore Security Council decisions further in Chapter 9. May ICJ judgments also be enforced in national courts? See *Medellín* in Chapter 4.

6. *The ICJ as a Public Forum.* Should the Court be concerned if it is being used as a forum in which to appeal to and influence public opinion? Should the Court turn away cases where it seems likely that a state will refuse to appear and to comply with the orders of the Court? Iran is not the

only state to have boycotted an ICJ case. France, Iceland, Turkey, and the United States have also refused to appear before the Court in cases in which the Court found that the parties had consented in advance to jurisdiction. Does the practice of non-appearing states reflect a lack of respect for the Court and undercut its ability to perform essential judicial functions? See Mark W. Janis, "Somber Reflections on the Compulsory Jurisdiction of the International Court," 81 *American Journal of International Law* 144 (1987).

When the Court is used as a public forum, can it still serve a judicial role? May ICJ decisions have efficacy even if the losing party does not comply with them? Is it enough to say that, whatever the circumstances, the Court can usefully add the words of a new judgment to the corpus of international law doctrine? In the *Diplomatic and Consular Staff Case* the ICJ emphasized fundamental precepts of international law protecting diplomats, consular officials, and diplomatic premises, norms that have been important in international law since antiquity. See the *De Longchamps Case* in Chapter 4. The *Diplomatic and Consular Staff Case* also concerned the law of state responsibility (see Note 2) and the succession of the international obligations of a state following a radical change in its government, a topic discussed further in Chapter 7.

DECLARATION OF MALAWI RECOGNIZING THE COMPULSORY JURISDICTION OF THE ICJ

International Court of Justice, *Yearbook 2006–2007*, No. 61, at 146 (2007)

On behalf of the Government of Malawi, I declare under Article 36, paragraph 2, of the Statute of the International Court of Justice that I recognize as compulsory *ipso facto* and without special agreement, in relation to any other State accepting the same obligation, on condition of reciprocity, the jurisdiction of the International Court of Justice in all legal disputes which may arise in respect of facts or situations subsequent to this declaration concerning:

(a) the interpretation of a treaty;

(b) any question of international law;

(c) the existence of any fact which, if established, would constitute a breach of an international obligation;

(d) the nature or extent of the reparation to be made for the breach of an international obligation:

Provided that this declaration shall not apply to—

(i) disputes with regard to matters which are essentially within the domestic jurisdiction of the Republic of Malawi as determined by the Government of Malawi;

(ii) disputes in regard to which the parties of the dispute have agreed or shall agree to have recourse to some other method of peaceful settlement; or

(iii) disputes concerning any question relating to or arising out of belligerent or military occupation.

The Government of Malawi also reserves the right at any time, by means of a notification addressed to the Secretary-General of the United Nations, to add to, amend, or withdraw any of the foregoing reservations or any that may hereafter be added. Such notification shall be effective on the date of their receipt by the Secretary-General of the United Nations.

Given under my hand in Zomba this 22nd day of November 1966.

(SIGNED) H. KAMUZU BANDA,
President and
Minister for External Affairs.

NOTES AND QUESTIONS

1. *The Utility of Compulsory Jurisdiction.* What is the utility of the ICJ's compulsory jurisdiction clause, Article 36(2) of the ICJ Statute, reproduced in Section 1 above? Only about one-third of all states have joined Malawi in filing declarations with the Court accepting its compulsory jurisdiction. Are prior treaty submissions like that in the *Diplomatic and Consular Staff Case* also not useful? Would it be better if the ICJ relied solely on *ad hoc* submissions on the lines of *Minquiers and Ecrehos*?

2. *Attaching Conditions to 36(2) Declarations.* As Malawi's declaration illustrates, some states attach conditions to their 36(2) declarations. Concerns with reciprocity have led the Court to allow a respondent state to invoke material "reservations" attached to an applicant state's declaration to deprive the Court of jurisdiction, even if the respondent state's own 36(2) declaration would otherwise subject it to jurisdiction.

Note especially Malawi's self-judging domestic jurisdiction reservation. Should the Court accept such a reservation as valid at all? If the Court were to reject a self-judging domestic reservation, should the rest of the 36(2) declaration containing such a reservation be deemed valid or invalid? Should the Court subject invocations of such a reservation to a test of reasonableness? In Certain Norwegian Loans (France v. Norway), 1957 I.C.J. 9, the Court allowed Norway to rely on a self-judging domestic reservation attached to France's then-in-effect 36(2) declaration.

3. *The United States and 36(2) Jurisdiction.* On August 14, 1946, President Harry S. Truman signed a declaration accepting the Article 36(2) jurisdiction of the International Court of Justice. The declaration contained three reservations. The first provided that acceptance would not apply to "disputes the solution of which the parties shall entrust to other tribunals by virtue of agreements already in existence or which may be concluded in the future." The second was a self-judging domestic reservation, labeled the

Connally Amendment after U.S. Senator Tom Connally, who had proposed it; Malawi's self-judging domestic exception was modeled on this U.S. reservation. Because of the reciprocity concerns discussed in Note 2 above, the Connally Amendment prevented the United States from using Article 36(2) to bring claims to the International Court. For example, when Bulgaria attacked a commercial airliner with U.S. passengers on board and the United States sought to bring a case to the ICJ, Bulgaria relied on the U.S. Connally Amendment. See Leo Gross, "Bulgaria Invokes the Connally Amendment," 56 *American Journal of International Law* 357 (1962). The third reservation, known as the Vandenberg Amendment (after another U.S. senator), provided that the U.S. 36(2) declaration would not apply to "disputes arising under a multilateral treaty, unless (1) all parties to the treaty affected by the decision are also parties to the case before the Court, or (2) the United States of America specially agrees to jurisdiction." In an ICJ case brought by Nicaragua against the United States in 1984, challenging U.S. military activities and support for rebels in Nicaragua, the Vandenberg Amendment precluded claims brought under the U.N. Charter; Nicaragua could pursue only claims for violations of customary international law and of a bilateral treaty. See Case Concerning Military and Paramilitary Activities In and Against Nicaragua (Nicaragua v. United States), 1986 I.C.J. 14, 29–38, 92–97, 115–16 (Merits).

On October 7, 1985, following the ICJ's determination that it had jurisdiction in the *Nicaragua Case*, the United States terminated its Article 36(2) declaration, effective six months later, the period of notice specified in the 1946 U.S. declaration. 24 *International Legal Materials* 1742 (1985). The United States is not the only Western power that has terminated a 36(2) declaration. France took the same step following cases brought to the International Court by Australia and New Zealand in the 1970s that challenged the legality of French nuclear testing in the Pacific. See International Court of Justice, *Yearbook 1973–1974*, No. 28, at 49 (1974). Should the United States reaccept the Article 36(2) compulsory jurisdiction of the ICJ? If so, what reservations, if any, should it attach to its acceptance?

The United States remains bound by numerous treaties containing clauses that authorize a state party to refer to the ICJ a dispute relating to the interpretation or application of the treaty. For a list, see Medellín v. Texas, 552 U.S. 491, 569–75 (2008) (Appendix B) (Breyer, J., dissenting).

3. CHAMBERS AT THE INTERNATIONAL COURT

Sometimes the Court is willing to hear contentious interstate cases submitted to it via chambers pursuant to Article 26 of its Statute. One of these chambers cases, *ELSI*, is excerpted below. Ask whether the chambers procedure makes it more likely that states will turn to the ICJ.

STATUTE OF THE INTERNATIONAL COURT OF JUSTICE, ARTICLE 26

June 26, 1945, 59 Stat. 1031, T.S. No. 993

1. The Court may from time to time form one or more chambers, composed of three or more judges as the Court may determine, for dealing with particular categories of cases; for example, labour cases and cases relating to transit and communications.

2. The Court may at any time form a chamber for dealing with a particular case. The number of judges to constitute such a chamber shall be determined by the Court with the approval of the parties.

3. Cases shall be heard and determined by the chambers provided for in this article if the parties so request.

THE ELSI CASE

United States v. Italy, 1989 I.C.J. 15.

1. By a letter dated 6 February 1987, filed in the Registry of the Court the same day, the Secretary of State of the United States of America transmitted to the Court an Application instituting proceedings against the Republic of Italy in respect of a dispute arising out of the requisition by the Government of Italy of the plant and related assets of Raytheon-Elsi S.p.A., previously known as Elettronica Sicula S.p.A. (ELSI), an Italian company which was stated to have been 100 per cent owned by two United States corporations. By the same letter, the Secretary of State informed the Court that the Government of the United States requested, pursuant to Article 26 of the Statute of the Court, that the dispute be resolved by a Chamber of the Court. * * *

4. [T]he Court * * * decided to accede to the request of the Governments of the United States of America and Italy to form a special Chamber of five judges to deal with the case and declared that at an election held on that day President Nagendra Singh and Judges Oda, Ago, Schwebel and Sir Robert Jennings had been elected to the Chamber, and declared a Chamber to deal with the case to have been duly constituted by the Order, with the composition indicated. * * *

6. On 11 December 1988 Judge Nagendra Singh, President of the Chamber, died. Following further consultations with the Parties[,] the Court, by Order dated 20 December 1988, declared that Judge Ruda, President of the Court, had that day been elected a Member of the Chamber to fill the vacancy left by the death of Judge Nagendra Singh. * * * President Ruda became President of the Chamber. * * *

12. The claim of the United States in the present case is that Italy has violated the international legal obligations which it undertook by the Treaty of Friendship, Commerce and Navigation between the two

countries concluded on 2 February 1948 ("the FCN Treaty") and the Supplementary Agreement thereto concluded on 26 September 1951, by reason of its acts and omissions in relation to, and its treatment of, two United States corporations, the Raytheon Company ("Raytheon") and The Machlett Laboratories Incorporated ("Machlett"), in relation to the Italian corporation Raytheon-Elsi S.p.A. (previously Elettronica Sicuia S.p.A. (ELSI)), which was wholly owned by the two United States corporations. * * *

13. [Between 1956 and 1967] ELSI was established in Palermo, Sicily, where it had a plant for the production of electronic components; in 1967 it had a workforce of slightly under 900 employees. Its five major product lines were microwave tubes, cathode-ray tubes, semiconductor rectifiers, X-ray tubes and surge arresters.

14. During the fiscal years 1964 to 1966 inclusive, ELSI made an operating profit, but this profit was insufficient to offset its debt expense or accumulated losses, and no dividends were ever paid to its shareholders. * * *

16. The management of ELSI took the view that one of the reasons for its lack of success was that it had trained and was employing an excessively large labour force. In June 1967 it was decided to dismiss some 300 employees; under an Italian union agreement this involved a procedure of notifications and negotiations. [A]n alternative plan was agreed to whereby 168 workers would be suspended from 10 July 1967, with limited pay by ELSI for a period not exceeding six weeks. After a training programme during which the workers were paid by the Sicilian Government, it was contemplated that ELSI would endeavour to re-employ the suspended employees. The necessary additional business to make this possible was not forthcoming, and the suspended employees were dismissed early in March 1968. * * *

17. * * * General planning for the potential liquidation of ELSI began in the latter part of 1967, and in early 1968 detailed plans were made for a shut-down and liquidation at any time after 16 March 1968. * * *

30. On 1 April 1968 the Mayor of Palermo issued an order, effective immediately, requisitioning ELSI's plant and related assets for a period of six months. The text of this order, in the translation supplied by the United States, was as follows:

> *The Mayor of the Municipality of Palermo,*
>
> *Taking into consideration* that Raytheon-Elsi of Palermo has decided to close its plant located in this city at Via Villagrazia, 79, because of market difficulties and lack of orders;

That the company has furthermore decided to send dismissal letters to the personnel consisting of about 1,000 persons;

Taking notice that ELSI's actions, beside provoking the reaction of the workers and of the unions giving rise to strikes (both general and sectional) has caused a wide and general movement of solidarity of all public opinion which has strongly stigmatized the action taken considering that about 1,000 families are suddenly destituted;

That, considering the fact that ELSI is the second firm in order of importance in the District, because of the shutdown of the plant a serious damage will be caused to the District, which has been so severely tried by the earthquakes had during the month of January 1968;

Considering also that the local press is taking a great interest in the situation and that the press is being very critical toward the authorities and is accusing them of indifference to this serious civic problem;

That, furthermore, the present situation is particularly touchy and unforeseeable disturbances of public order could take place;

Taking into consideration that in this particular instance there is sufficient ground for holding that there is a grave public necessity and urgency to protect the general economic public interest (already seriously compromised) and public order, and that these reasons justify requisitioning the plant and all equipment owned by Raytheon-Elsi located here at Via Villagrazia 79[.]

32. On 9 April 1968 ELSI addressed a telegram to the Mayor of Palermo, with copies to other Government authorities, claiming (*inter alia*) that the requisition was illegal and expressing the company's intention to take all legal steps to have it revoked and to claim damages. On 12 April 1968 the company served on the Mayor a formal document dated 11 April 1968 inviting him to revoke the requisition order. The Mayor did not respond and the order was not revoked[.]

44. In the bankruptcy proceedings, creditors presented claims against ELSI totalling some 13,000 million lire; these did not include amounts due to Raytheon and Raytheon Service Company[.] The bankruptcy proceedings closed in November 1985. According to the bankruptcy reports, the bankruptcy realized only some 6,370 million lire for ELSI's assets, as compared with the minimum liquidation value estimated by ELSI's management in March 1968 at 10,840 million lire. Of the amount realized, some 6,080 million lire went to pay banks, employees, and other

creditors. The remainder went to pay bankruptcy administration, tax, registry, and customs charges. All of the secured and preferred creditors who filed claims in the bankruptcy were paid in full. The unsecured creditors received less than one per cent of their claims; accordingly no surplus remained for distribution to the shareholders, Raytheon and Machlett. * * *

56. The damage claimed in this case to have been caused to Raytheon and Machlett is said to have resulted from the "losses incurred by ELSI's owners as a result of the involuntary change in the manner of disposing of ELSI's assets": and it is the requisition order that is said to have caused this change, and which is therefore at the core of the United States complaint. * * *

65. The acts of the Respondent which are thus alleged to violate its treaty obligations were described by the Applicant's counsel in terms which it is convenient to cite here:

> First, the Respondent violated its legal obligations when it unlawfully requisitioned the ELSI plant on 1 April 1968 which denied the ELSI stockholders their direct right to liquidate the ELSI assets in an orderly fashion. Second, the Respondent violated its obligations when it allowed ELSI workers to occupy the plant. Third, the Respondent violated its obligations when it unreasonably delayed ruling on the lawfulness of the requisition for 16 months until immediately after the ELSI plant, equipment and work-in-process had all been acquired by ELTEL [a subsidiary of a holding company controlled by Italy]. Fourth and finally, the Respondent violated its obligations when it interfered with the ELSI bankruptcy proceedings, which allowed the Respondent to realize its previously expressed intention of acquiring ELSI for a price far less than its fair market value. * * *

67. The Chamber is faced with a situation of mixed fact and law of considerable complexity, wherein several different strands of fact and law have to be examined both separately and for their effect on each other: the meaning and effect of the relevant Articles of the FCN Treaty and Supplementary Agreement; the legal status of the Mayor's requisition of ELSI's plant and assets; and the legal and practical significance of the financial position of ELSI at material times, and its effect, if any, upon ELSI's plan for orderly liquidation of the company.

[With respect to the FCN Treaty, much of the debate concerned the interpretation of Article III(2), which permitted "nationals, corporations and associations of either High Contracting Party," in conformity with laws and regulations applicable in the territory of the other party, to "control and manage corporations and associations of" that other High party.]

85. Did ELSI, in this precarious position at the end of March 1968, still have the practical possibility to proceed with an orderly liquidation plan? The successful implementation of a plan of orderly liquidation would have depended upon a number of factors not under the control of ELSI's management. Since the company's coffers were dangerously low, funds had to be forthcoming to maintain the cash flow necessary while the plan was being carried out. Evidence has been produced by the Applicant that Raytheon was prepared to supply cash flow and other assistance necessary to effect the orderly liquidation, and the Chamber sees no reason to question that Raytheon had entered or was ready to enter into such a commitment. Other factors governing the matter however give rise to some doubt.

86. First, for the success of the plan it was necessary that the major creditors (i.e., the banks) would be willing to wait for payment of their claims until the sale of the assets released funds to settle them: and this applied not only to the capital sums outstanding, which may not at the time have yet been legally due for repayment, but also the agreed payments of interest or installments of capital. Though the Chamber has been given no specific information on the point, this is of the essence of such a liquidation plan: the creditors had to be asked to give the company time. If ELSI had been confident of continuing to meet all its obligations promptly and regularly while seeking a buyer for its assets, no negotiations with creditors, and no elaborate calculations of division of the proceeds, on different hypotheses, such as have been produced to the Chamber, would have been needed.

87. Secondly, the management were by no means certain that the sale of the assets would realize enough to pay all creditors in full; in fact, the existence of the calculation of a "quick-sale value" suggests perhaps more than uncertainty. Thus the creditors had to be asked to give time in return for an assurance, not that 100 per cent would be paid, but that a minimum of 50 per cent would be paid. While in general it might be in the creditors' interest to agree to such a proposal, this does not mean in this case that ELSI could count on such agreement.* * *

88. Nor should it be overlooked that the dismissed employees of ELSI ranked as preferential creditors for such sums as might be due to them for severance pay or arrears. * * *

89. Thirdly, the plan as formulated by ELSI's management involved a potential inequality among creditors: unless enough was realized to cover the liabilities fully, the major creditors were to be content with some 50 per cent of their claims; but the smaller creditors were still to be paid in full. [This] was an additional factor which might have caused a major creditor to hesitate to agree.* * *

90. Fourthly, the assets of the company had to be sold with the minimum delay and at the best price obtainable—desiderata which are

often in practice irreconcilable. The United States has emphasized the damaging effect of the requisition on attempts to realize the assets; after the requisition it was no longer possible for prospective buyers to view the plant, nor to assure them that if they bought they would obtain immediate possession. It is however not at all certain that the company could have counted on unfettered access to its premises and plant, and the opportunity of showing it to buyers without disturbance, even if the requisition had not been made. There has been argument between the Parties on the question whether and to what extent the plant was occupied by employees of ELSI both before and after the requisition; but what is clear is that the company was expecting trouble at the plant when its closure plans became known: the books had been removed to Milan, according to the evidence given at the hearings, "so that if we did have problems we could at least control the books" and "we had moved quite a lot of inventory [to Milan] so that we could sell it from there if we had to."

91. Fifthly, there was the attitude of the Sicilian administration: the company was well aware that the administration was strongly opposed to a closure of the plant, or more specifically, to a dismissal of the workers. True, the measure used to try to prevent this—the requisition order—was found by the Prefect to have lacked the "juridical cause which might justify it and make it operative[.]" But ELSI's management in March 1968 could not have been certain that the hostility of the local authorities to their plan of closure and dismissals would not take practical form in a legal manner. The company's management had been told before the staff dismissal letters were sent out that such dismissals would lead to a requisition of the plant.

92. All these factors point towards a conclusion that the feasibility at 31 March 1968 of a plan of orderly liquidation, an essential link in the chain of reasoning upon which the United States claim rests, has not been sufficiently established. * * *

137. For these reasons,

THE CHAMBER, * * *

(2) By four votes to one,

Finds that the Italian Republic has not committed any of the breaches, alleged in the said Application, of the Treaty of Friendship, Commerce and Navigation between the Parties signed at Rome on 2 February 1948, or of the Agreement Supplementing that Treaty signed by the Parties at Washington on 26 September 1951.

IN FAVOUR: *President* Ruda; *Judges* Oda, Ago and Sir Robert Jennings;

AGAINST: *Judge* Schwebel. * * *

DISSENTING OPINION OF JUDGE SCHWEBEL * * *

The Chamber's Judgment concludes that "the possibility" of an orderly liquidation by ELSI "is purely a matter of speculation." I agree that an orderly liquidation would have been beset with uncertainties, but those uncertainties go not so much to ELSI's ability and entitlement to liquidate its assets as to the calculability of the damages which may be found to flow from the denial of that ability and entitlement by the requisition imposed upon ELSI.

In my view, it is unpersuasive for the Chamber to say, in effect, that ELSI would have gone into bankruptcy later if not sooner, and accordingly that the requisition did not matter. It is in this respect that I believe that the Chamber muddles what it finds to be the facts with time factors. At the time the requisition took place, it did matter, it did have the economic effects, or some of the economic effects, just described; and at the time it took place, it deprived Raytheon and Machlett of their right to control and manage and hence liquidate ELSI and it deprived ELSI of its right to be liquidated by a management responsible to Raytheon and Machlett. Accordingly the requisition placed Italy in violation of its obligation under Article III of the Treaty to permit Raytheon and Machlett to "control and manage" ELSI.

NOTES AND QUESTIONS

1. *The Decision to Use Chambers*. The United States brought the *ELSI Case* with Italy to the ICJ shortly after the U.S. backed away from participating in the merits stage of the *Nicaragua Case* and after it withdrew its consent to the Court's Article 36(2) compulsory jurisdiction. Previously, the United States and Italy had been planning to take the ELSI dispute to an arbitral tribunal. See W. Michael Reisman, *Systems of Control in International Adjudication and Arbitration* 43 (1992). Having decided to go to the International Court, why would the United States and Italy choose to employ a five-judge chamber? Why would the Court have agreed to proceedings by a chamber rather than by its full membership?

2. *Fact or Law?* Rather than a legal problem, was it the facts that lost the case for Raytheon and the United States? Did they fail to establish that ELSI was sufficiently financed at the time of requisition to permit an orderly liquidation of its assets? See Sean D. Murphy, "The ELSI Case: An Investment Dispute at the International Court of Justice," 16 *Yale Journal of International Law* 391 (1991). Was the *ELSI* chamber realistic in expecting that the course of any international bankruptcy could be accurately foreseen? In a note generally critical of the majority opinion in *ELSI*, F.A. Mann urged "the United States and United Kingdom governments—indeed, all governments concerned with foreign investments, probably even Italy—to look afresh at the standard form of agreement in the light of the disheartening experience of the United States at the hands of the International Court of Justice." F.A. Mann, "Foreign Investment in the International Court of Justice: The *ELSI* Case," 86 *American Journal of*

International Law 92, 100 (1992). Should entirely new investment treaties be developed to address difficulties of the sort experienced by the United States, Raytheon, Matchlett, and ELSI? See Kenneth J. Vandevelde, *U.S. International Investment Agreements* (2009). Compare the protections for foreign investors discussed in the *CMS Case* in Chapter 2.

3. *Access to the International Court.* Note that Raytheon itself had no standing to bring suit in the ICJ. The Statute of the ICJ provides that "only states may be parties in cases before the Court." Why was the U.S. government willing to forward Raytheon's case to the Hague Court? What would be objections the U.S. government might have had to so "internationalizing" the ELSI dispute? International adjudications in which one country takes up the claims of its nationals are often referred to as "espousal cases." In the *ELSI Case*, the United States espoused the claim of Raytheon and Machlett, U.S. companies that were shareholders of the Italian company ELSI. Are any of the other principal cases in Chapter 5 espousal cases? *Nottebohm* and *Barcelona Traction* in Chapter 6, Section A are examples of espousal. Certainly, if private litigants like Raytheon could bring cases themselves to the ICJ, there would be far more cases for the ICJ. Is this an argument for or against a right of private parties to sue in the ICJ?

4. *Exhaustion of Local Remedies.* In espousal cases, or in cases brought directly by corporations or individuals to an international court (such as the *McCann Case* in Chapter 1), international law may require an individual to exhaust domestic remedies before an international panel takes up a case. The doctrine of exhaustion of local remedies raises difficult issues: Is exhaustion required in an espousal case if the applicant country is seeking to recover for "its own" injuries, sufficiently distinct from its espousal claims? At what point in the domestic legal process are remedies to be deemed exhausted? When will pursuing local remedies be considered futile, so that no domestic proceedings are necessary? When are an individual's domestic claims sufficiently "like" the international court claim, such that local remedies must be pursued before the international court is allowed to proceed with the merits? If an international claim is based on a treaty violation, and the respondent country does not allow treaty claims to be brought directly in its courts—recall the self-executing treaty doctrine in U.S. law in Chapter 4—is exhaustion required? In the *ELSI Case*, "there ha[d] in fact been much resort to the municipal courts," and "Italy ha[d] not been able to satisfy the Chamber that there clearly remained some remedy which Raytheon and Machlett, independently of ELSI, and of ELSI's trustee in bankruptcy, ought to have pursued and exhausted." Para. 63. See Matthew H. Adler, "The Exhaustion of the Local Remedies Rule After the International Court of Justice's Decision in *ELSI*," 39 *International and Comparative Law Quarterly* 641 (1990). Why is exhaustion of local remedies generally required in international law? Should the rule apply if an injured individual has not voluntarily established a link or territorial connection with the state allegedly violating international law? See *Report of the International Law Commission, Fifty-eighth Session*, U.N. Doc. A/61/10, at 70–86 (2006) (Draft Articles on Diplomatic Protection, arts. 14–15 and commentary).

5. *The Use of Chambers.* Since the first *ad hoc* Article 26(2) ICJ chamber was constituted in 1982, there have only been six chambers cases before the ICJ. Of these, *ELSI*, brought in 1987, was the third. The others were Delimitation of the Maritime Boundary in the Gulf of Maine Area (Canada/United States, 1982), Frontier Dispute (Burkina Faso/Mali, 1985), Land, Island and Maritime Frontier Dispute (El Salvador/Honduras, 1987), Frontier Dispute (Benin/Niger, 2002), and Land, Island and Maritime Frontier Dispute (El Salvador/Honduras, 2002). All have had five-member panels. International Court of Justice, "Chambers and Committees," http://www.icj-cij.org/court (last visited Dec. 7, 2013). Why has this flexible chambers procedure not been employed more often? Would it be desirable to amend the ICJ's Statute to create permanent regional chambers, allowing more convenient access for states from different parts of the world? See Rudolf Ostrihansky, "Chambers of the International Court of Justice," 37 *International and Comparative Law Quarterly* 30, 36–38 (1988).

Is one reason for the lack of chamber business at the ICJ simply that there are many other ways in which parties can now go to international dispute settlement? We explore the proliferation of international courts and tribunals in Part C of this chapter.

4. ADVISORY OPINIONS AT THE INTERNATIONAL COURT

As we saw in Section 1, the ICJ has authority pursuant to Article 96 of the U.N. Charter and Article 65 of its Statute to render advisory opinions. These are only given at the request of designated international organizations and, unlike judgments in the ICJ's contentious cases, are not legally binding. In practice, however, many advisory opinions have served functions rather similar to Court judgments. One such example is the *Wall Case* below. Ask why states sought to persuade the U.N. General Assembly to request an advisory opinion from the Court.

LEGAL CONSEQUENCES OF THE CONSTRUCTION OF A WALL IN THE OCCUPIED PALESTINIAN TERRITORY

2004 I.C.J. 136

THE COURT * * * *gives the following Advisory Opinion:*

1. The question on which the advisory opinion of the Court has been requested is set forth in resolution ES–10/14 adopted by the General Assembly of the United Nations (hereinafter the "General Assembly") on 8 December 2003 at its Tenth Emergency Special Session. * * * The resolution reads as follows: * * *

The General Assembly * * *

> *Decides*, in accordance with Article 96 of the Charter of the United Nations, to request the International Court of Justice,

pursuant to Article 65 of the Statute of the Court, to urgently render an advisory opinion on the following question:

> What are the legal consequences arising from the construction of the wall being built by Israel, the occupying Power, in the Occupied Palestinian Territory, including in and around East Jerusalem, as described in the report of the Secretary-General, considering the rules and principles of international law, including the Fourth Geneva Convention of 1949, and relevant Security Council and General Assembly resolutions? * * *

9. Within the time-limit fixed by the Court for that purpose, written statements were filed by, in order of their receipt: Guinea, Saudi Arabia, League of Arab States, Egypt, Cameroon, Russian Federation, Australia, Palestine, United Nations, Jordan, Kuwait, Lebanon, Canada, Syria, Switzerland, Israel, Yemen, United States of America, Morocco, Indonesia, Organization of the Islamic Conference, France, Italy, Sudan, South Africa, Germany, Japan, Norway, United Kingdom, Pakistan, Czech Republic, Greece, Ireland on its own behalf, Ireland on behalf of the European Union, Cyprus, Brazil, Namibia, Malta, Malaysia, Netherlands, Cuba, Sweden, Spain, Belgium, Palau, Federated States of Micronesia, Marshall Islands, Senegal, Democratic People's Republic of Korea. * * *

13. When seised of a request for an advisory opinion, the Court must first consider whether it has jurisdiction to give the opinion requested and whether, should the answer be in the affirmative, there is any reason why it should decline to exercise any such jurisdiction. * * *

15. It is for the Court to satisfy itself that the request for an advisory opinion comes from an organ or agency having competence to make it. In the present instance, the Court notes that the General Assembly, which seeks the advisory opinion, is authorized to do so by Article 96, paragraph 1, of the Charter, which provides: "The General Assembly or the Security Council may request the International Court of Justice to give an advisory opinion on any legal question."

16. Although the above-mentioned provision states that the General Assembly may seek an advisory opinion "on any legal question," the Court has sometimes in the past given certain indications as to the relationship between the question the subject of a request for an advisory opinion and the activities of the General Assembly.

17. The Court will so proceed in the present case. The Court would observe that Article 10 of the Charter has conferred upon the General Assembly a competence relating to "any questions or any matters" within the scope of the Charter, and that Article 11, paragraph 2, has specifically provided it with competence on "questions relating to the maintenance of

international peace and security brought before it by any Member of the United Nations . . . " and to make recommendations under certain conditions fixed by those Articles. [T]he question of the construction of the wall in the Occupied Palestinian Territory was brought before the General Assembly by a number of Member States in the context of the Tenth Emergency Special Session of the Assembly, convened to deal with what the Assembly, in its resolution ES–10/2 of 25 April 1997, considered to constitute a threat to international peace and security. * * *

21. On 27 October 2003, the General Assembly adopted resolution ES–10/13, by which it demanded that "Israel stop and reverse the construction of the wall in the Occupied Palestinian Territory, including in and around East Jerusalem, which is in departure of the Armistice Line of 1949 and is in contradiction to relevant provisions of international law." * * *

22. [O]n 19 November 2003, the Security Council adopted resolution 1515 (2003), by which it "*Endorse[d]* the Quartet Performance-based Roadmap to a Permanent Two-State Solution to the Israeli-Palestinian Conflict." The Quartet consists of representatives of the United States of America, the European Union, the Russian Federation and the United Nations. That resolution "*Call[ed] on* the parties to fulfil their obligations under the Roadmap in cooperation with the Quartet and to achieve the vision of two States living side by side in peace and security." Neither the "Roadmap" nor resolution 1515 (2003) contained any specific provision concerning the construction of the wall, which was not discussed by the Security Council in this context. * * *

25. * * * Article 12, paragraph 1, of the Charter provides that: "While the Security Council is exercising in respect of any dispute or situation the functions assigned to it in the present Charter, the General Assembly shall not make any recommendation with regard to that dispute or situation unless the Security Council so requests." A request for an advisory opinion is not in itself a "recommendation" by the General Assembly "with regard to [a] dispute or situation." It has however been argued in this case that the adoption by the General Assembly of resolution ES–10/14 was *ultra vires* as not in accordance with Article 12. The Court thus considers that it is appropriate for it to examine the significance of that Article, having regard to the relevant texts and the practice of the United Nations.

26. Under Article 24 of the Charter the Security Council has "primary responsibility for the maintenance of international peace and security." In that regard it can impose on States "an explicit obligation of compliance if for example it issues an order or command . . . under Chapter VII" and can, to that end, "require enforcement by coercive action" (*Certain Expenses of the United Nations (Article 17, paragraph 2, of the Charter), Advisory Opinion, I.C.J. Reports 1962,* p. 163). However,

the Court would emphasize that Article 24 refers to a primary, but not necessarily exclusive, competence. The General Assembly does have the power, *inter alia,* under Article 14 of the Charter, to "recommend measures for the peaceful adjustment" of various situations. * * *

27. [T]he interpretation of Article 12 has evolved[.] In response to a question posed by Peru during the twenty-third session of the General Assembly, the Legal Counsel of the United Nations confirmed that the Assembly interpreted the words "is exercising the functions" in Article 12 of the Charter as meaning "is exercising the functions at this moment." Indeed, the Court notes that there has been an increasing tendency over time for the General Assembly and the Security Council to deal in parallel with the same matter concerning the maintenance of international peace and security. * * *

28. The Court considers that the accepted practice of the General Assembly, as it has evolved, is consistent with Article 12, paragraph 1, of the Charter. The Court is accordingly of the view that the General Assembly, in adopting resolution ES–10/14, seeking an advisory opinion from the Court, did not contravene the provisions of Article 12, paragraph 1, of the Charter. The Court concludes that by submitting that request the General Assembly did not exceed its competence.

[The Court rejects other challenges to its jurisdiction, including assertions that the question posed was "political" and that it was imprecise and overly abstract. The Court notes that it "has often been requested to broaden, interpret and even reformulate the questions put" in advisory opinion proceedings.]

42. The Court accordingly has jurisdiction to give the advisory opinion requested by resolution ES–10/14 of the General Assembly.

43. It has been contended in the present proceedings, however, that the Court should decline to exercise its jurisdiction because of the presence of specific aspects of the General Assembly's request that would render the exercise of the Court's jurisdiction improper and inconsistent with the Court's judicial function.

44. The Court has recalled many times in the past that Article 65, paragraph 1, of its Statute, which provides that "The Court *may* give an advisory opinion . . . " (emphasis added), should be interpreted to mean that the Court has a discretionary power to decline to give an advisory opinion even if the conditions of jurisdiction are met. The Court however is mindful of the fact that its answer to a request for an advisory opinion "represents its participation in the activities of the Organization, and, in principle, should not be refused." Given its responsibilities as the "principal judicial organ of the United Nations" (Article 92 of the Charter), the Court should in principle not decline to give an advisory

opinion. In accordance with its consistent jurisprudence, only "compelling reasons" should lead the Court to refuse its opinion.

The present Court has never, in the exercise of this discretionary power, declined to respond to a request for an advisory opinion. * * *

46. The first such argument is to the effect that the Court should not exercise its jurisdiction in the present case because the request concerns a contentious matter between Israel and Palestine, in respect of which Israel has not consented to the exercise of that jurisdiction. According to this view, the subject-matter of the question posed by the General Assembly "is an integral part of the wider Israeli-Palestinian dispute concerning questions of terrorism, security, borders, settlements, Jerusalem and other related matters." Israel has emphasized that it has never consented to the settlement of this wider dispute by the Court or by any other means of compulsory adjudication; on the contrary, it contends that the parties repeatedly agreed that these issues are to be settled by negotiation, with the possibility of an agreement that recourse could be had to arbitration. It is accordingly contended that the Court should decline to give the present Opinion, on the basis *inter alia* of the precedent of the [1923] decision of the Permanent Court of International Justice on the *Status of Eastern Carelia.*

47. [T]he Court explained in its Advisory Opinion on *Western Sahara* that[:]

> In certain circumstances . . . the lack of consent of an interested State may render the giving of an advisory opinion incompatible with the Court's judicial character. An instance of this would be when the circumstances disclose that to give a reply would have the effect of circumventing the principle that a State is not obliged to allow its disputes to be submitted to judicial settlement without its consent. (*Western Sahara, I.C.J. Reports 1975,* p. 25.)

In applying that principle to the request concerning *Western Sahara*, the Court found that a legal controversy did indeed exist, but one which had arisen during the proceedings of the General Assembly and in relation to matters with which the Assembly was dealing. It had not arisen independently in bilateral relations. * * *

49. [T]he Court does not consider that the subject-matter of the General Assembly's request can be regarded as only a bilateral matter between Israel and Palestine. Given the powers and responsibilities of the United Nations in questions relating to international peace and security, it is the Court's view that the construction of the wall must be deemed to be directly of concern to the United Nations. The responsibility of the United Nations in this matter also has its origin in the Mandate and the Partition Resolution concerning Palestine (see paragraphs 70 and 71

below). This responsibility has been described by the General Assembly as "a permanent responsibility towards the question of Palestine until the question is resolved in all its aspects in a satisfactory manner in accordance with international legitimacy" (General Assembly resolution 57/107 of 3 December 2002). Within the institutional framework of the Organization, this responsibility has been manifested by the adoption of many Security Council and General Assembly resolutions, and by the creation of several subsidiary bodies specifically established to assist in the realization of the inalienable rights of the Palestinian people.

50. The object of the request before the Court is to obtain from the Court an opinion which the General Assembly deems of assistance to it for the proper exercise of its functions. The opinion is requested on a question which is of particularly acute concern to the United Nations, and one which is located in a much broader frame of reference than a bilateral dispute. In the circumstances, the Court does not consider that to give an opinion would have the effect of circumventing the principle of consent to judicial settlement, and the Court accordingly cannot, in the exercise of its discretion, decline to give an opinion on that ground.

51. The Court now turns to another argument raised in the present proceedings in support of the view that it should decline to exercise its jurisdiction. Some participants have argued that an advisory opinion from the Court on the legality of the wall and the legal consequences of its construction could impede a political, negotiated solution to the Israeli-Palestinian conflict. More particularly, it has been contended that such an opinion could undermine the scheme of the "Roadmap," which requires Israel and Palestine to comply with certain obligations in various phases referred to therein. The requested opinion, it has been alleged, could complicate the negotiations envisaged in the "Roadmap," and the Court should therefore exercise its discretion and decline to reply to the question put. * * *

53. The Court is conscious that the "Roadmap," which was endorsed by the Security Council in resolution 1515 (2003), constitutes a negotiating framework for the resolution of the Israeli-Palestinian conflict. It is not clear, however, what influence the Court's opinion might have on those negotiations: participants in the present proceedings have expressed differing views in this regard. The Court cannot regard this factor as a compelling reason to decline to exercise its jurisdiction.

54. It was also put to the Court by certain participants that the question of the construction of the wall was only one aspect of the Israeli-Palestinian conflict, which could not be properly addressed in the present proceedings. The Court does not however consider this a reason for it to decline to reply to the question asked. The Court is indeed aware that the question of the wall is part of a greater whole, and it would take this circumstance carefully into account in any opinion it might give. At the

same time, the question that the General Assembly has chosen to ask of the Court is confined to the legal consequences of the construction of the wall, and the Court would only examine other issues to the extent that they might be necessary to its consideration of the question put to it.

55. Several participants in the proceedings have raised the further argument that the Court should decline to exercise its jurisdiction because it does not have at its disposal the requisite facts and evidence to enable it to reach its conclusions. In particular, Israel has contended * * * that the Court could not give an opinion on issues which raise questions of fact that cannot be elucidated without hearing all parties to the conflict. According to Israel, if the Court decided to give the requested opinion, it would be forced to speculate about essential facts and make assumptions about arguments of law. More specifically, Israel has argued that the Court could not rule on the legal consequences of the construction of the wall without enquiring, first, into the nature and scope of the security threat to which the wall is intended to respond and the effectiveness of that response, and, second, into the impact of the construction for the Palestinians. This task, which would already be difficult in a contentious case, would be further complicated in an advisory proceeding, particularly since Israel alone possesses much of the necessary information and has stated that it chooses not to address the merits. Israel has concluded that the Court, confronted with factual issues impossible to clarify in the present proceedings, should use its discretion and decline to comply with the request for an advisory opinion.
* * *

57. In the present instance, the Court has at its disposal [the report of the Secretary-General issued on November 24, 2003, and prepared pursuant to General Assembly resolution ES–10/13 (hereinafter the "report of the Secretary-General")], as well as a voluminous dossier submitted by him to the Court, comprising not only detailed information on the route of the wall but also on its humanitarian and socio-economic impact on the Palestinian population. The dossier includes several reports based on on-site visits by special rapporteurs and competent organs of the United Nations. The Secretary-General has further submitted to the Court a written statement updating his report, which supplemented the information contained therein. Moreover, numerous other participants have submitted to the Court written statements which contain information relevant to a response to the question put by the General Assembly. The Court notes in particular that Israel's Written Statement, although limited to issues of jurisdiction and judicial propriety, contained observations on other matters, including Israel's concerns in terms of security, and was accompanied by corresponding annexes; many other documents issued by the Israeli Government on those matters are in the public domain.

58. The Court finds that it has before it sufficient information and evidence to enable it to give the advisory opinion requested by the General Assembly. Moreover, the circumstance that others may evaluate and interpret these facts in a subjective or political manner can be no argument for a court of law to abdicate its judicial task. There is therefore in the present case no lack of information such as to constitute a compelling reason for the Court to decline to give the requested opinion.

59. In their written statements, some participants have also put forward the argument that the Court should decline to give the requested opinion on the legal consequences of the construction of the wall because such opinion would lack any useful purpose. They have argued that the advisory opinions of the Court are to be seen as a means to enable an organ or agency in need of legal clarification for its future action to obtain that clarification. In the present instance, the argument continues, the General Assembly would not need an opinion of the Court because it has already declared the construction of the wall to be illegal and has already determined the legal consequences by demanding that Israel stop and reverse its construction, and further, because the General Assembly has never made it clear how it intended to use the opinion. * * *

62. [T]he Court cannot decline to answer the question posed based on the ground that its opinion would lack any useful purpose. The Court cannot substitute its assessment of the usefulness of the opinion requested for that of the organ that seeks such opinion, namely the General Assembly. Furthermore, and in any event, the Court considers that the General Assembly has not yet determined all the possible consequences of its own resolution. The Court's task would be to determine in a comprehensive manner the legal consequences of the construction of the wall, while the General Assembly—and the Security Council—may then draw conclusions from the Court's findings. * * *

65. In the light of the foregoing, the Court concludes not only that it has jurisdiction to give an opinion on the question put to it by the General Assembly, but also that there is no compelling reason for it to use its discretionary power not to give that opinion. * * *

70. Palestine was part of the Ottoman Empire. At the end of the First World War, a class "A" Mandate for Palestine was entrusted to Great Britain by the League of Nations, pursuant to paragraph 4 of Article 22 of the Covenant, which provided that:

> Certain communities, formerly belonging to the Turkish Empire have reached a stage of development where their existence as independent nations can be provisionally recognized subject to the rendering of administrative advice and assistance by a Mandatory until such time as they are able to stand alone.

The Court recalls that in its Advisory Opinion on the *International Status of South West Africa,* speaking of mandates in general, it observed that "The Mandate was created in the interest of the inhabitants of the territory, and of humanity in general, as an international institution with an international object—a sacred trust of civilization." (*I.C.J. Reports 1950,* p. 132.) The Court also held in this regard that "two principles were considered to be of paramount importance: the principle of non-annexation and the principle that the well-being and development of . . . peoples [not yet able to govern themselves] form[ed] 'a sacred trust of civilization' " (*ibid.,* p. 131).

The territorial boundaries of the Mandate for Palestine were laid down by various instruments, in particular on the eastern border by a British memorandum of 16 September 1922 and an Anglo-Transjordanian Treaty of 20 February 1928.

71. In 1947 the United Kingdom announced its intention to complete evacuation of the mandated territory by 1 August 1948, subsequently advancing that date to 15 May 1948. In the meantime, the General Assembly had on 29 November 1947 adopted resolution 181(II) on the future government of Palestine, which "*Recommends* to the United Kingdom . . . and to all other Members of the United Nations the adoption and implementation . . . of the Plan of Partition" of the territory, as set forth in the resolution, between two independent States, one Arab, the other Jewish, as well as the creation of a special international régime for the City of Jerusalem. The Arab population of Palestine and the Arab States rejected this plan, contending that it was unbalanced; on 14 May 1948, Israel proclaimed its independence on the strength of the General Assembly resolution; armed conflict then broke out between Israel and a number of Arab States and the Plan of Partition was not implemented.

72. By resolution 62 (1948) of 16 November 1948, the Security Council decided that "an armistice shall be established in all sectors of Palestine" and called upon the parties directly involved in the conflict to seek agreement to this end. In conformity with this decision, general armistice agreements were concluded in 1949 between Israel and the neighbouring States through mediation by the United Nations. In particular, one such agreement was signed in Rhodes on 3 April 1949 between Israel and Jordan. Articles V and VI of that Agreement fixed the armistice demarcation line between Israeli and Arab forces (often later called the "Green Line" owing to the colour used for it on maps; hereinafter the "Green Line").

73. In the 1967 armed conflict, Israeli forces occupied all the territories which had constituted Palestine under British Mandate (including those known as the West Bank, lying to the east of the Green Line).

74. On 22 November 1967, the Security Council unanimously adopted resolution 242 (1967), which emphasized the inadmissibility of acquisition of territory by war and called for the "Withdrawal of Israel armed forces from territories occupied in the recent conflict," and "Termination of all claims or states of belligerency."

75. From 1967 onwards, Israel took a number of measures in these territories aimed at changing the status of the City of Jerusalem. The Security Council, after recalling on a number of occasions "the principle that acquisition of territory by military conquest is inadmissible," condemned those measures and, by resolution 298 (1971) of 25 September 1971, confirmed in the clearest possible terms that: "all legislative and administrative actions taken by Israel to change the status of the City of Jerusalem, including expropriation of land and properties, transfer of populations and legislation aimed at the incorporation of the occupied section, are totally invalid and cannot change that status."

Later, following the adoption by Israel on 30 July 1980 of the Basic Law making Jerusalem the "complete and united" capital of Israel, the Security Council, by resolution 478 (1980) of 20 August 1980, stated that the enactment of that Law constituted a violation of international law and that "all legislative and administrative measures and actions taken by Israel, the occupying Power, which have altered or purport to alter the character and status of the Holy City of Jerusalem . . . are null and void." It further decided "not to recognize the 'basic law' and such other actions by Israel that, as a result of this law, seek to alter the character and status of Jerusalem."

76. Subsequently, a peace treaty was signed on 26 October 1994 between Israel and Jordan. That treaty fixed the boundary between the two States "with reference to the boundary definition under the Mandate as is shown in Annex 1*(a)* . . . without prejudice to the status of any territories that came under Israeli military government control in 1967" (Article 3, paragraphs 1 and 2). Annex 1 provided the corresponding maps and added that, with regard to the "territory that came under Israeli military government control in 1967," the line indicated "is the administrative boundary" with Jordan.

77. Lastly, a number of agreements have been signed since 1993 between Israel and the Palestine Liberation Organization imposing various obligations on each Party. Those agreements *inter alia* required Israel to transfer to Palestinian authorities certain powers and responsibilities exercised in the Occupied Palestinian Territory by its military authorities and civil administration. Such transfers have taken place, but, as a result of subsequent events, they remained partial and limited.

78. The Court would observe that, under customary international law as reflected in Article 42 of the Regulations Respecting the Laws and

Customs of War on Land annexed to the Fourth Hague Convention of 18 October 1907 (hereinafter "the Hague Regulations of 1907"), territory is considered occupied when it is actually placed under the authority of the hostile army, and the occupation extends only to the territory where such authority has been established and can be exercised.

The territories situated between the Green Line and the former eastern boundary of Palestine under the Mandate were occupied by Israel in 1967 during the armed conflict between Israel and Jordan. Under customary international law, these were therefore occupied territories in which Israel had the status of occupying Power. Subsequent events in these territories have done nothing to alter this situation. All these territories (including East Jerusalem) remain occupied territories and Israel has continued to have the status of occupying Power.

79. It is essentially in these territories that Israel has constructed or plans to construct the works described in the report of the Secretary-General. The Court will now describe those works, basing itself on that report. For developments subsequent to the publication of that report, the Court will refer to complementary information contained in the Written Statement of the United Nations, which was intended by the Secretary-General to supplement his report (hereinafter "Written Statement of the Secretary-General").

80. The report of the Secretary-General states that "The Government of Israel has since 1996 considered plans to halt infiltration into Israel from the central and northern West Bank. . . . " According to that report, a plan of this type was approved for the first time by the Israeli Cabinet in July 2001. Then, on 14 April 2002, the Cabinet adopted a decision for the construction of works, forming what Israel describes as a "security fence," 80 kilometres in length, in three areas of the West Bank.

81. According to the Written Statement of the Secretary-General, the first part of these works (Phase A), which ultimately extends for a distance of 150 kilometres, was declared completed on 31 July 2003. It is reported that approximately 56,000 Palestinians would be encompassed in enclaves. During this phase, two sections totalling 19.5 kilometres were built around Jerusalem. * * *

82. According to the description in the report and the Written Statement of the Secretary-General, the works planned or completed have resulted or will result in a complex consisting essentially of:

(1) a fence with electronic sensors;

(2) a ditch (up to 4 metres deep);

(3) a two-lane asphalt patrol road;

(4) a trace road (a strip of sand smoothed to detect footprints) running parallel to the fence;

(5) a stack of six coils of barbed wire marking the perimeter of the complex.

The complex has a width of 50 to 70 metres, increasing to as much as 100 metres in some places. "Depth barriers" may be added to these works.

The approximately 180 kilometres of the complex completed or under construction as of the time when the Secretary-General submitted his report included some 8.5 kilometres of concrete wall. These are generally found where Palestinian population centres are close to or abut Israel (such as near Qalqiliya and Tulkarm or in parts of Jerusalem).

83. According to the report of the Secretary-General, in its northernmost part, the wall as completed or under construction barely deviates from the Green Line. It nevertheless lies within occupied territories for most of its course. The works deviate more than 7.5 kilometres from the Green Line in certain places to encompass Settlements, while encircling Palestinian population areas. A stretch of 1 to 2 kilometres west of Tulkarm appears to run on the Israeli side of the Green Line. Elsewhere, on the other hand, the planned route would deviate eastward by up to 22 kilometres. In the case of Jerusalem, the existing works and the planned route lie well beyond the Green Line and even in some cases beyond the eastern municipal boundary of Jerusalem as fixed by Israel.

84. On the basis of that route, approximately 975 square kilometres (or 16.6 per cent of the West Bank) would, according to the report of the Secretary-General, lie between the Green Line and the wall. This area is stated to be home to 237,000 Palestinians. If the full wall were completed as planned, another 160,000 Palestinians would live in almost completely encircled communities, described as enclaves in the report. As a result of the planned route, nearly 320,000 Israeli settlers (of whom 178,000 in East Jerusalem) would be living in the area between the Green Line and the wall.

85. Lastly, it should be noted that the construction of the wall has been accompanied by the creation of a new administrative régime. Thus in October 2003 the Israeli Defence Forces issued Orders establishing the part of the West Bank lying between the Green Line and the wall as a "Closed Area." Residents of this area may no longer remain in it, nor may non-residents enter it, unless holding a permit or identity card issued by the Israeli authorities. According to the report of the Secretary-General, most residents have received permits for a limited period. Israeli citizens, Israeli permanent residents and those eligible to immigrate to Israel in accordance with the Law of Return may remain in, or move freely to, from and within the Closed Area without a permit. Access to and exit from the Closed Area can only be made through access gates, which are opened infrequently and for short periods.

86. The Court will now determine the rules and principles of international law which are relevant in assessing the legality of the measures taken by Israel. Such rules and principles can be found in the United Nations Charter and certain other treaties, in customary international law and in the relevant resolutions adopted pursuant to the Charter by the General Assembly and the Security Council.

[The Court examines the obligations of occupying powers under international humanitarian law. The Court also considers legal principles relating to human rights, the self-determination of peoples, self-defense, and necessity.]

121. Whilst the Court notes the assurance given by Israel that the construction of the wall does not amount to annexation and that the wall is of a temporary nature, it nevertheless cannot remain indifferent to certain fears expressed to it that the route of the wall will prejudge the future frontier between Israel and Palestine, and the fear that Israel may integrate the settlements and their means of access. The Court considers that the construction of the wall and its associated régime create a "fait accompli" on the ground that could well become permanent, in which case, and notwithstanding the formal characterization of the wall by Israel, it would be tantamount to *de facto* annexation.

122. [T]he route chosen for the wall gives expression *in loco* to the illegal measures taken by Israel with regard to Jerusalem and the settlements, as deplored by the Security Council. There is also a risk of further alterations to the demographic composition of the Occupied Palestinian Territory resulting from the construction of the wall inasmuch as it is contributing * * * to the departure of Palestinian populations from certain areas. That construction, along with measures taken previously, thus severely impedes the exercise by the Palestinian people of its right to self-determination, and is therefore a breach of Israel's obligation to respect that right. * * *

134. To sum up, the Court is of the opinion that the construction of the wall and its associated régime impede the liberty of movement of the inhabitants of the Occupied Palestinian Territory (with the exception of Israeli citizens and those assimilated thereto) as guaranteed under Article 12, paragraph 1, of the International Covenant on Civil and Political Rights. They also impede the exercise by the persons concerned of the right to work, to health, to education and to an adequate standard of living as proclaimed in the International Covenant on Economic, Social and Cultural Rights and in the United Nations Convention on the Rights of the Child. Lastly, the construction of the wall and its associated régime, by contributing to the demographic changes referred to * * * above, contravene Article 49, paragraph 6, of the Fourth Geneva Convention and [various] Security Council resolutions[.]

Figure 5.D

The Israeli Wall/Security Fence on the West Bank

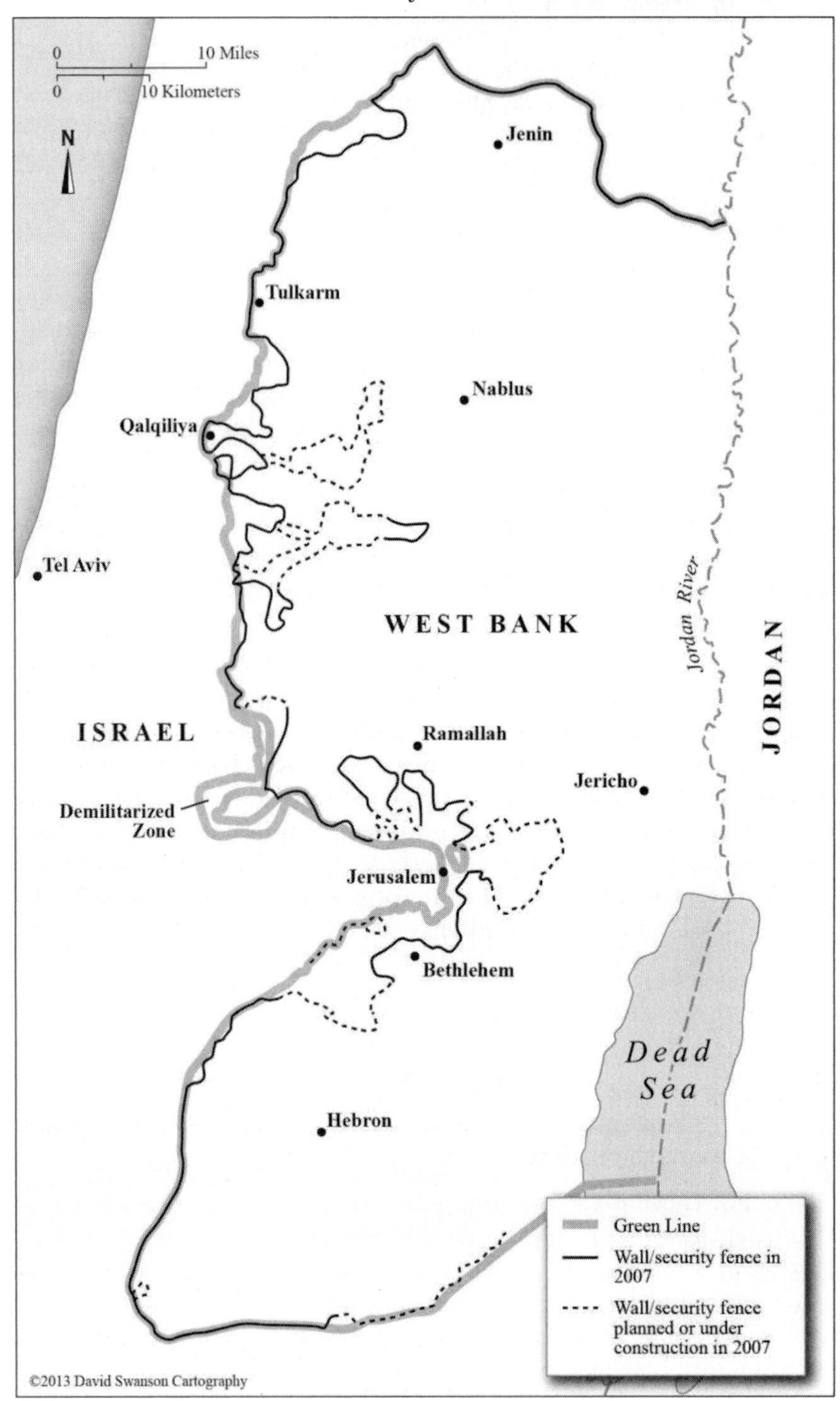

137. To sum up, the Court, from the material available to it, is not convinced that the specific course Israel has chosen for the wall was necessary to attain its security objectives. The wall, along the route chosen, and its associated régime gravely infringe a number of rights of Palestinians residing in the territory occupied by Israel, and the infringements resulting from that route cannot be justified by military exigencies or by the requirements of national security or public order. The construction of such a wall accordingly constitutes breaches by Israel of various of its obligations under the applicable international humanitarian law and human rights instruments. * * *

141. The fact remains that Israel has to face numerous indiscriminate and deadly acts of violence against its civilian population. It has the right, and indeed the duty, to respond in order to protect the life of its citizens. The measures taken are bound nonetheless to remain in conformity with applicable international law.

142. In conclusion, the Court considers that Israel cannot rely on a right of self-defence or on a state of necessity in order to preclude the wrongfulness of the construction of the wall resulting from the considerations mentioned in paragraphs 122 and 137 above. The Court accordingly finds that the construction of the wall, and its associated régime, are contrary to international law. * * *

162. * * * The Court would emphasize that both Israel and Palestine are under an obligation scrupulously to observe the rules of international humanitarian law, one of the paramount purposes of which is to protect civilian life. Illegal actions and unilateral decisions have been taken on all sides, whereas, in the Court's view, this tragic situation can be brought to an end only through implementation in good faith of all relevant Security Council resolutions, in particular resolutions 242 (1967) and 338 (1973). The "Roadmap" approved by Security Council resolution 1515 (2003) represents the most recent of efforts to initiate negotiations to this end. The Court considers that it has a duty to draw the attention of the General Assembly, to which the present Opinion is addressed, to the need for these efforts to be encouraged with a view to achieving as soon as possible, on the basis of international law, a negotiated solution to the outstanding problems and the establishment of a Palestinian State, existing side by side with Israel and its other neighbours, with peace and security for all in the region.

163. For these reasons,

THE COURT

(1) Unanimously,

Finds that it has jurisdiction to give the advisory opinion requested;

(2) By fourteen votes to one,

Decides to comply with the request for an advisory opinion;

IN FAVOUR: *President* Shi; *Vice-President* Ranjeva; *Judges* Guillaume, Koroma, Vereshchetin, Higgins, Parra-Aranguren, Kooijmans, Rezek, Al-Khasawneh, Elaraby, Owada, Simma, Tomka;

AGAINST: *Judge* Buergenthal;

(3) *Replies* in the following manner to the question put by the General Assembly:

A. By fourteen votes to one,

The construction of the wall being built by Israel, the occupying Power, in the Occupied Palestinian Territory, including in and around East Jerusalem, and its associated régime, are contrary to international law;

IN FAVOUR: *President* Shi; *Vice-President* Ranjeva; *Judges* Guillaume, Koroma, Vereshchetin, Higgins, Parra-Aranguren, Kooijmans, Rezek, Al-Khasawneh, Elaraby, Owada, Simma, Tomka;

AGAINST: *Judge* Buergenthal;

B. By fourteen votes to one,

Israel is under an obligation to terminate its breaches of international law; it is under an obligation to cease forthwith the works of construction of the wall being built in the Occupied Palestinian Territory, including in and around East Jerusalem, to dismantle forthwith the structure therein situated, and to repeal or render ineffective forthwith all legislative and regulatory acts relating thereto[;]

IN FAVOUR: *President* Shi; *Vice-President* Ranjeva; *Judges* Guillaume, Koroma, Vereshchetin, Higgins, Parra-Aranguren, Kooijmans, Rezek, Al-Khasawneh, Elaraby, Owada. Simma, Tomka;

AGAINST: *Judge* Buergenthal;

C. By fourteen votes to one,

Israel is under an obligation to make reparation for all damage caused by the construction of the wall in the Occupied Palestinian Territory, including in and around East Jerusalem;

IN FAVOUR: *President* Shi; *Vice-President* Ranjeva; *Judges* Guillaume, Koroma, Vereshchetin, Higgins, Parra-Aranguren, Kooijmans, Rezek, Al-Khasawneh, Ellaraby, Owada, Simma, Tomka;

AGAINST: *Judge* Buergenthal;

D. By thirteen votes to two,

All States are under an obligation not to recognize the illegal situation resulting from the construction of the wall and not to render aid or assistance in maintaining the situation created by such construction;

all States parties to the Fourth Geneva Convention relative to the Protection of Civilian Persons in Time of War of 12 August 1949 have in addition the obligation, while respecting the United Nations Charter and international law, to ensure compliance by Israel with international humanitarian law as embodied in that Convention;

IN FAVOUR: *President* Shi; *Vice-President* Ranjeva; *Judges* Guillaume, Koroma, Vereshchetin, Higgins, Parra-Aranguren, Rezek, Al-Khasawneh, Elaraby, Owada, Simma, Tomka;

AGAINST: *Judges* Kooijmans, Buergenthal;

E. By fourteen votes to one,

The United Nations, and especially the General Assembly and the Security Council, should consider what further action is required to bring to an end the illegal situation resulting from the construction of the wall and the associated régime, taking due account of the present Advisory Opinion.

IN FAVOUR: *President* Shi; *Vice-President* Ranjeva; *Judges* Guillaume, Koroma, Vereshchetin, Higgins, Parra-Aranguren, Kooijmans, Rezek, Al-Khasawneh, Elaraby, Owada, Simma, Tomka;

AGAINST: *Judge* Buergenthal.

NOTES AND QUESTIONS

1. *The Political Context and the Efficacy of the Court's Judgment.* The Wall Case was decided in a highly politicized context. Palestinians and Israelis held radically different and deeply-felt views. At the 2004 ICJ hearings on the *Wall Case*, Nasser al-Kidwa, a Palestinian observer at the United Nations, argued that the Palestinian people "have too long been denied the right to self-determination and sovereignty over their land." The Palestinians, "half of whom remain refugees[,] have been subject to a military occupation for almost 37 years. They have been dehumanized and demonized, humiliated and demeaned, dispossessed and dispersed, and brutally punished by their occupier." Since September 2000, "Israeli occupying forces have directly killed, including many by extrajudicial execution, a total of 2,770 Palestinian civilians, including children, women and men." Introductory Statement, Verbatim Record, Feb. 23, 2004, ¶¶ 2, 20, ICJ Doc. CR 2004/1, *available at* http://unispal.un.org/UNISPAL.NSF/0/94E8ED18CFA868C585256E4A00582D91 (last visited Dec. 7, 2013).

Israeli officials viewed the circumstances far differently, stressing that the "security fence" was a necessary response to "Palestinian terrorism." An "evil campaign" had since 2000 "taken the lives of nearly 1,000 Israelis in over 20,000 attacks" and wounded "thousands more, leaving broken families, widows, and orphans." As long as such terrorism continued, Israel had "a moral and legal obligation" to defend its citizens. "Israel calls on the international community not to lend its hand to the ongoing Palestinian attempts to use international forums to avoid fulfilling their own commitment to fight terrorism." Israeli Statement on ICJ Advisory Opinion on Israel's Security Fence, July 9, 2004, *available at* http://www.mfa.gov.il/mfa/pressroom/2004/pages/statement%20on%20icj%20advisory%20opinion%209-july-2004.aspx (last visited Dec. 7, 2013). More recently, much controversy attended the methodology and conclusions of the Report of the United Nations Fact Finding Mission on the Gaza Conflict, U.N. Doc. A/HRC/12/48 (2009), which was mandated by the U.N. Human Rights Council (the Goldstone Report).

Should or could the ICJ have refused to render an advisory opinion in the *Wall Case* on the grounds that the dispute involved highly sensitive and complex political questions not susceptible to legal resolution? Might the *Wall* opinion complicate efforts to negotiate a political solution to the Israeli-Palestinian conflict? Was it important that the Court rule on the legal issues to help ensure that any future political settlement conform to the requirements of international law?

What is likely to be the efficacy of the Court's opinion? Do the functions of the decision in the *Wall Case* differ from those in a contentious case such as the *Diplomatic and Consular Staff Case*?

2. *A Contentious Case?* Should the Court have refused to decide the *Wall Case* on the grounds that it was really a contentious bilateral dispute in advisory opinion disguise? Why did this objection not persuade the Court to exercise its discretion to refuse to render an advisory opinion? Did the Court's multilateral emphasis lead it to fail to address bilateral factors important to a more complete understanding of the issues? Should Israel have had the right to name its own *ad hoc* judge, as it would have had in a contentious case?

3. *The Factual Record.* As we saw in the *Diplomatic and Consular Staff Case*, when a party fails to appear and does not present evidence in a contentious case, the ICJ may still render an opinion, although the Court must satisfy itself "that the claim is well founded in fact and law." ICJ Statute, art. 53(2). In advisory proceedings, the Court shall be "guided by" the Statute's provisions that "apply in contentious cases to the extent to which [the Court] recognizes them to be applicable." *Id.* art. 68.

Advisory proceedings have no parties, but Israel could have presented the Court with facts related to threats to its security and the placement of the wall/security fence. Israel chose not to do so. Should the ICJ have refused to render an advisory opinion on the grounds that important facts were missing? The U.S. judge on the Court, Thomas Buergenthal, the sole dissenting judge on most of the Court's conclusions, was troubled by what he saw as an insufficient factual record:

> It may well be * * * that on a thorough analysis of all relevant facts, a finding could well be made that some or even all segments of the wall being constructed by Israel on the Occupied Palestinian Territory violate international law. But to reach that conclusion

with regard to the wall as a whole without having before it or seeking to ascertain all relevant facts bearing directly on issues of Israel's legitimate right of self-defence, military necessity and security needs, given the repeated deadly terrorist attacks in and upon Israel proper coming from the Occupied Palestinian Territory to which Israel has been and continues to be subjected, cannot be justified as a matter of law. The nature of these cross-Green Line attacks and their impact on Israel and its population are never really seriously examined by the Court, and the dossier provided the Court by the United Nations on which the Court to a large extent bases its findings barely touches on that subject. I am not suggesting that such an examination would relieve Israel of the charge that the wall it is building violates international law, either in whole or in part, only that without this examination the findings made are not legally well founded.

Declaration of Judge Buergenthal, ¶ 3.

The sufficiency of a factual record does not pose the same major concern in every advisory proceeding. Sometimes the ICJ has ruled on rather abstract legal questions. See, *e.g.*, the *Reservations to the Genocide Convention Case* (Chapter 2). In other cases, the Court has applied international law to facts that could be relatively easily determined. See, *e.g.*, Constitution of the Maritime Safety Committee of the Inter-Governmental Maritime Consultative Organization, 1960 I.C.J. 150.

4. *The Substantive Issues.* The ICJ's analysis and conclusions concerning the substantive issues in the *Wall Case* have been much debated. The fact that 14 of 15 judges agreed on a wide range of conclusions represents a significant consensus. However, some ICJ judges and other experts have complained that the Court should more thoroughly have explained its reasoning concerning difficult legal issues. For example, Judge Rosalyn Higgins, in her separate opinion, concluded that the Court's analysis of international humanitarian law was insufficiently detailed. She chided the ICJ for not "follow[ing] the tradition of using advisory opinions as an opportunity to elaborate and develop international law." Separate Opinion of Judge Higgins, ¶ 23.

As discussed in Note 3, the Court's legal conclusions might have been more persuasive had the Court relied on a more extensive factual record. The Israeli Supreme Court, in a decision handed down just days before the ICJ's advisory opinion, applied customary international law to an extensive factual record and ruled that portions of the wall/security fence, though intended to protect Israeli security, were illegal because they disproportionately affected Palestinian civilians. HCJ/2056/04, Beit Sourik Village Council v. Israel, 43 *International Legal Materials* 1099 (2004).

The *Wall Case* involved several complex questions related to subjects we explore in later chapters: international human rights law (Chapter 6); the law of self-determination (Chapter 7); international humanitarian law, which applies in armed conflicts and to occupying powers (Chapter 9); and the law governing self-defense and resort to use of force (Chapter 9). More on the relationship between the U.N. General Assembly and Security Council—a topic the Court addressed in paragraphs 25–28 of its opinion in the *Wall Case*—appears in Chapters 8 and 9. For discussion of various aspects of the *Wall Case*, see the ten articles in "Agora: ICJ Advisory Opinion on Construction of a Wall in the Occupied Palestinian Territory," 99 *American Journal of International Law* 1 (2005).

5. *The Infrequency of Advisory Proceedings*. During the two-thirds century of its existence, 1945 to 2012, the ICJ has delivered only 23 advisory opinions, about one every three years. Why has resort to advisory proceedings been so rare? One of the questions we consider in Part C is whether changes should be made to the ICJ's advisory jurisdiction to allow referrals from other courts on questions of international law.

C. THE PROLIFERATION OF INTERNATIONAL COURTS AND TRIBUNALS

International courts have multiplied in the later 20th and early 21st centuries. Here we introduce this development and some associated challenges. The principal case, a decision of the Appellate Body of the World Trade Organization, shows the work of a specialized international tribunal created by multilateral treaty.

MARK WESTON JANIS, INTERNATIONAL LAW

164–65 (6th ed. 2012)

[One] reason why the work of the ICJ has not expanded in recent times is the creation of other international courts with a regional or a specialized jurisdiction. When the PCIJ was established in 1921, there were no other permanent international tribunals, save the [Permanent Court of Arbitration], which the PCIJ largely supplanted. The ICJ, too, had a virtually exclusive position as *the* international court until late in the 1950s. Since then, new international courts have been added at an ever-quickening pace. * * *

Faced with these new international courts, some, like President Guillaume of the ICJ, fear that international law will become fragmented unless the ICJ is recognized as a kind of supreme court for international law. However, it is doubtful that the world community would ever agree to such a hierarchy. Not only would it be politically unlikely that agreement could be reached on such a proposal, but establishing the international judicial supremacy of the ICJ would undermine many of the advantages of the new regional and international courts, such as their more limited state memberships and more expert areas of competence. Thus, it seems inevitable that these new international courts will develop their own areas of the law with a resulting diversity of international legal jurisprudence.

NOTES AND QUESTIONS

1. *The Variety of International Courts and Tribunals.* There are now several dozen international courts and tribunals. See the listing of the Project on International Courts and Tribunals at http://www.pict-pcti.org/ (last visited Dec. 7, 2013). Several global tribunals address only specific subject matters, such as international trade (*e.g.*, the World Trade Organization's Dispute Settlement Body) or the law of the sea (the International Tribunal for the Law of the Sea). There are also regional courts, such as the European Court of Human Rights and the Inter-American Court of Human Rights. One might differentiate international courts not only by region and subject matter, but also by function. Some help to resolve disputes between parties, while others, instead or in addition, apply international criminal law and impose criminal penalties, or review the consistency of national laws and actions with international law. See Karen J. Alter, "Delegating to International Courts: Self-Binding vs. Other-Binding Delegation," 71 *Law and Contemporary Problems*, Winter 2008, at 37; David D. Caron, "Towards a Political Theory of International Courts and Tribunals," 24 *Berkeley Journal of International Law* 401 (2006). International courts and tribunals also reflect significant procedural differences. Some permit only states to be parties, while others allow suits to be brought by or against individuals. The busiest international courts and tribunals boast appellate structures or other procedures to handle hundreds or thousands of cases. For example, the European Court of Human Rights and the European Court of Justice have two-tier structures to manage their heavy caseloads.

We explore several different international courts and tribunals in this book, including the European Court of Human Rights in Chapters 1 and 6, the European Court of Justice in Chapters 3 and 8, the Nuremberg Tribunal and the International Criminal Court in Chapter 6, the International Criminal Tribunal for the former Yugoslavia in Chapters 3 and 9, the Inter-American Commission on Human Rights in Chapter 3, the International Tribunal for the Law of the Sea and its Seabed Disputes Chamber in Chapter 10, and various arbitral tribunals in Chapters 2, 3, 5, 9, and 11. The *Shrimp-Turtle Case* below is from the Appellate Body operating under the dispute settlement system of the World Trade Organization.

THE SHRIMP-TURTLE CASE

United States-Import Prohibition of Certain Shrimp and Shrimp Products,
World Trade Organization, Report of the Appellate Body, WT/DS58/AB/R (1998),
38 *International Legal Materials* 118 (1999)

1. This is an appeal by the United States from certain issues of law and legal interpretations in the Panel Report, *United States-Import Prohibition of Certain Shrimp and Shrimp Products*. Following a joint request for consultations by India, Malaysia, Pakistan and Thailand on 8

October 1996, Malaysia and Thailand requested in a communication dated 9 January 1997, and Pakistan asked in a communication dated 30 January 1997, that the Dispute Settlement Body (the "DSB") establish a panel to examine their complaint regarding a prohibition imposed by the United States on the importation of certain shrimp and shrimp products by Section 609 of Public Law 101–162 ("Section 609") and associated regulations and judicial rulings. On 25 February 1997, the DSB established two panels in accordance with these requests and agreed that these panels would be consolidated into a single Panel, pursuant to Article 9 of the *Understanding on Rules and Procedures Governing the Settlement of Disputes* (the "DSU"), with standard terms of reference. On 10 April 1997, the DSB established another panel with standard terms of reference in accordance with a request made by India in a communication dated 25 February 1997, and agreed that this third panel, too, would be merged into the earlier Panel established on 25 February 1997. The Report rendered by the consolidated Panel was circulated to the Members of the World Trade Organization (the "WTO") on 15 May 1998.

2. * * * The United States issued regulations in 1987 pursuant to the Endangered Species Act of 1973 requiring all United States shrimp trawl vessels to use approved Turtle Excluder Devices ("TEDs") or tow-time restrictions in specified areas where there was a significant mortality of sea turtles in shrimp harvesting. These regulations, which became fully effective in 1990, were modified so as to require the use of approved TEDs at all times and in all areas where there is a likelihood that shrimp trawling will interact with sea turtles, with certain limited exceptions.

3. Section 609 was enacted on 21 November 1989. Section 609(a) calls upon the United States Secretary of State, in consultation with the Secretary of Commerce, *inter alia*, to "initiate negotiations as soon as possible for the development of bilateral or multilateral agreements with other nations for the protection and conservation of . . . sea turtles" and to "initiate negotiations as soon as possible with all foreign governments which are engaged in, or which have persons or companies engaged in, commercial fishing operations which, as determined by the Secretary of Commerce, may affect adversely such species of sea turtles, for the purpose of entering into bilateral and multilateral treaties with such countries to protect such species of sea turtles[.]" Section 609(b)(1) imposed, not later than 1 May 1991, an import ban on shrimp harvested with commercial fishing technology which may adversely affect sea turtles. Section 609(b)(2) provides that the import ban on shrimp will not apply to harvesting nations that are certified. * * *

7. In the Panel Report, the Panel [concluded]

> that the import ban on shrimp and shrimp products as applied by the United States on the basis of Section 609 of Public Law

> 101–162 is not consistent with Article XI:1 of GATT 1994, and cannot be justified under Article XX of GATT 1994.

and made this recommendation:

> The Panel *recommends* that the Dispute Settlement Body request the United States to bring this measure into conformity with its obligations under the WTO Agreement.

8. On 13 July 1998, the United States notified the DSB of its decision to appeal certain issues of law covered in the Panel Report and certain legal interpretations developed by the Panel, pursuant to paragraph 4 of Article 16 of the DSU, and filed a notice of appeal with the Appellate Body pursuant to Rule 20 of the *Working Procedures for Appellate Review*. * * *

10. In the view of the United States, the Panel erred in finding that Section 609 was outside the scope of Article XX. The United States stresses that under the Panel's factual findings and undisputed facts on the record, Section 609 is within the scope of the Article XX chapeau and Article XX(g) and, in the alternative, Article XX(b), of the GATT 1994. The Panel was also incorrect in finding that Section 609 constitutes "unjustifiable discrimination between countries where the same conditions prevail." The Panel interprets the chapeau of Article XX as requiring panels to determine whether a measure constitutes a "threat to the multilateral trading system." This interpretation of Article XX has no basis in the text of the GATT 1994, has never been adopted by any previous panel or Appellate Body Report, and would impermissibly diminish the rights that WTO Members reserved under Article XX. * * *

A. The Panel's Findings and Interpretative Analysis * * *

113. Article XX of the GATT 1994 reads, in its relevant parts:

> ARTICLE XX
>
> *General Exceptions*
>
> Subject to the requirement that such measures are not applied in a manner which would constitute a means of arbitrary or unjustifiable discrimination between countries where the same conditions prevail, or a disguised restriction on international trade, nothing in this Agreement shall be construed to prevent the adoption or enforcement by any Member of measures: . . .
>
> (b) necessary to protect human, animal or plant life or health; . . .

> (g) relating to the conservation of exhaustible natural resources if such measures are made effective in conjunction with restrictions on domestic production or consumption[.]

116. * * * Maintaining, rather than undermining, the multilateral trading system is necessarily a fundamental and pervasive premise underlying the *WTO Agreement*; but it is not a right or an obligation, nor is it an interpretative rule which can be employed in the appraisal of a given measure under the chapeau of Article XX. * * *

118. In *United States—Gasoline*, we enunciated the appropriate method for applying Article XX of the GATT 1994:

> In order that the justifying protection of Article XX may be extended to it, the measure at issue must not only come under one or another of the particular exceptions—paragraphs (a) to (j)—listed under Article XX; it must also satisfy the requirements imposed by the opening clauses of Article XX. *The analysis is*, in other words, *two-tiered: first, provisional justification by reason of characterization of the measure under XX(g); second, further appraisal of the same measure under the introductory clauses of Article XX*. (emphasis added)

121. * * * The Panel formulated a broad standard and a test for appraising measures sought to be justified under the chapeau; it is a standard or a test that finds no basis either in the text of the chapeau or in that of either of the two specific exceptions claimed by the United States. The Panel, in effect, constructed an *a priori* test that purports to define a category of measures which, *ratione materiae*, fall outside the justifying protection of Article XX's chapeau. In the present case, the Panel found that the United States measure at stake fell within that class of excluded measures because Section 609 conditions access to the domestic shrimp market of the United States on the adoption by exporting countries of certain conservation policies prescribed by the United States. It appears to us, however, that conditioning access to a Member's domestic market on whether exporting Members comply with, or adopt, a policy or policies unilaterally prescribed by the importing Member may, to some degree, be a common aspect of measures falling within the scope of one or another of the exceptions (a) to (j) of Article XX. Paragraphs (a) to (j) comprise measures that are recognized as *exceptions to substantive obligations* established in the GATT 1994, because the domestic policies embodied in such measures have been recognized as important and legitimate in character. It is not necessary to assume that requiring from exporting countries compliance with, or adoption of, certain policies (although covered in principle by one or another of the exceptions) prescribed by the importing country, renders a measure *a priori* incapable of justification under Article XX. Such an interpretation

renders most, if not all, of the specific exceptions of Article XX inutile, a result abhorrent to the principles of interpretation we are bound to apply.

122. We hold that the findings of the Panel * * * and the interpretative analysis embodied therein, constitute error in legal interpretation and accordingly reverse them.

B. Article XX(g): Provisional Justification of Section 609

125. In claiming justification for its measure, the United States primarily invokes Article XX(g). * * *

1. *"Exhaustible Natural Resources"* * * *

128. * * * Textually, Article XX(g) is not limited to the conservation of "mineral" or "non-living" natural resources. [L]iving species, though in principle, capable of reproduction and, in that sense, "renewable," are in certain circumstances indeed susceptible of depletion, exhaustion and extinction, frequently because of human activities. Living resources are just as "finite" as petroleum, iron ore and other non-living resources.

129. The words of Article XX(g), "exhaustible natural resources," were actually crafted more than 50 years ago. They must be read by a treaty interpreter in the light of contemporary concerns of the community of nations about the protection and conservation of the environment. While Article XX was not modified in the Uruguay Round, the preamble attached to the *WTO Agreement* shows that the signatories to that Agreement were, in 1994, fully aware of the importance and legitimacy of environmental protection as a goal of national and international policy. The preamble of the *WTO Agreement*—which informs not only the GATT 1994, but also the other covered agreements—explicitly acknowledges "the objective of *sustainable development*[.]"

130. From the perspective embodied in the preamble of the *WTO Agreement*, we note that the generic term "natural resources" in Article XX(g) is not "static" in its content or reference but is rather "by definition, evolutionary." It is, therefore, pertinent to note that modern international conventions and declarations make frequent references to natural resources as embracing both living and non-living resources. [The Appellate Body reviews various sources that refer to the conservation and management of living resources, including the 1982 United Nations Convention on the Law of the Sea, the 1992 Convention on Biological Diversity, Agenda 21 adopted at the 1992 Rio Conference, the Resolution on Assistance to Developing Countries adopted in conjunction with the 1973 Convention on the Conservation of Migratory Species of Wild Animals, and GATT panel reports.]

131. * * * We hold that * * * measures to conserve exhaustible natural resources, whether *living or non-living*, may fall within Article XX(g).

132. We turn next to the issue of whether the living natural resources sought to be conserved by the measure are "exhaustible" under Article XX(g). That this element is present in respect of the five species of sea turtles here involved appears to be conceded by all the participants and third participants in this case. The exhaustibility of sea turtles would in fact have been very difficult to controvert since all of the seven recognized species of sea turtles are today listed in Appendix 1 of the Convention on International Trade in Endangered Species of Wild Fauna and Flora ("CITES"). The list in Appendix 1 includes "all species *threatened with extinction* which are or may be affected by trade." (emphasis added).

133. Finally, we observe that sea turtles are highly migratory animals, passing in and out of waters subject to the rights of jurisdiction of various coastal states and the high seas. * * * The sea turtle species here at stake, i.e., covered by Section 609, are all known to occur in waters over which the United States exercises jurisdiction. Of course, it is not claimed that *all* populations of these species migrate to, or traverse, at one time or another, waters subject to United States jurisdiction. Neither the appellant nor any of the appellees claims any rights of exclusive ownership over the sea turtles, at least not while they are swimming freely in their natural habitat—the oceans. We do not pass upon the question of whether there is an implied jurisdictional limitation in Article XX(g), and if so, the nature or extent of that limitation. We note only that in the specific circumstances of the case before us, there is a sufficient nexus between the migratory and endangered marine populations involved and the United States for purposes of Article XX(g).

134. For all the foregoing reasons, we find that the sea turtles here involved constitute "exhaustible natural resources" for purposes of Article XX(g) of the GATT 1994.

[The Appellate Body also holds that "Section 609 is a measure 'relating' to the conservation of an exhaustible natural resource within the meaning of Article XX(g) of the GATT 1994," and that Section 609 is "made effective in conjunction with the restrictions on domestic harvesting of shrimp, as required by Article XX(g)."]

C. *The Introductory Clauses of Article XX: Characterizing Section 609 under the Chapeau's Standards* * * *

147. Although provisionally justified under Article XX(g), Section 609, if it is ultimately to be justified as an exception under Article XX, must also satisfy the requirements of the introductory clauses—the "chapeau"—of Article XX, that is,

ARTICLE XX

General Exceptions

> Subject to the requirement that such measures are *not applied in a manner which would constitute a means of arbitrary or unjustifiable discrimination between countries where the same conditions prevail, or a disguised restriction on international trade*, nothing in this Agreement shall be construed to prevent the adoption or enforcement by any Member of measures: (emphasis added)

We turn, hence, to the task of appraising Section 609, and specifically the manner in which it is applied under the chapeau of Article XX; that is, to the second part of the two-tier analysis required under Article XX.

1. *General Considerations* * * *

157. In our view, the language of the chapeau makes clear that each of the exceptions in paragraphs (a) to (j) of Article XX is a *limited and conditional* exception from the substantive obligations contained in the other provisions of the GATT 1994, that is to say, the ultimate availability of the exception is subject to the compliance by the invoking Member with the requirements of the chapeau. This interpretation of the chapeau is confirmed by its negotiating history. * * *

158. The chapeau of Article XX is, in fact, but one expression of the principle of good faith. * * * One application of this general principle, the application widely known as the doctrine of *abus de droit*, prohibits the abusive exercise of a state's rights and enjoins that whenever the assertion of a right "impinges on the field covered by [a] treaty obligation, it must be exercised bona fide, that is to say, reasonably." * * *

159. The task of interpreting and applying the chapeau is, hence, essentially the delicate one of locating and marking out a line of equilibrium between the right of a Member to invoke an exception under Article XX and the rights of the other Members under varying substantive provisions (e.g., Article XI) of the GATT 1994,* so that neither of the competing rights will cancel out the other and thereby distort and nullify or impair the balance of rights and obligations constructed by the Members themselves in that Agreement. The location of the line of equilibrium, as expressed in the chapeau, is not fixed and unchanging;

---

* Article XI(1) contains the general rule of GATT 1994 eliminating quantitative restrictions:

> No prohibitions or restrictions other than duties, taxes or other charges, whether made effective through quotas, import or export licences or other measures, shall be instituted or maintained by any contracting party on the importation of any product of the territory of any other contracting party or on the exportation or sale for export of any product destined for the territory of any other contracting party.

—Eds.

the line moves as the kind and the shape of the measures at stake vary and as the facts making up specific cases differ. * * *

2. "*Unjustifiable Discrimination*"

161. We scrutinize first whether Section 609 has been applied in a manner constituting "unjustifiable discrimination between countries where the same conditions prevail." Perhaps the most conspicuous flaw in this measure's application relates to its intended and actual coercive effect on the specific policy decisions made by foreign governments, Members of the WTO. * * *

163. The actual *application* of the measure, through the implementation of the 1996 Guidelines and the regulatory practice of administrators, *requires* other WTO Members to adopt a regulatory program that is not merely *comparable*, but rather *essentially the same*, as that applied to the United States shrimp trawl vessels. Thus, the effect of the application of Section 609 is to establish a rigid and unbending standard by which United States officials determine whether or not countries will be certified, thus granting or refusing other countries the right to export shrimp to the United States. Other specific policies and measures that an exporting country may have adopted for the protection and conservation of sea turtles are not taken into account, in practice, by the administrators making the comparability determination.

164. We understand that the United States also applies a uniform standard throughout its territory, regardless of the particular conditions existing in certain parts of the country. * * * However, it is not acceptable, in international trade relations, for one WTO Member to use an economic embargo to *require* other Members to adopt essentially the same comprehensive regulatory program, to achieve a certain policy goal, as that in force within that Member's territory, *without* taking into consideration different conditions which may occur in the territories of those other Members.

165. Furthermore, when this dispute was before the Panel and before us, the United States did not permit imports of shrimp harvested by commercial shrimp trawl vessels using TEDs comparable in effectiveness to those required in the United States if those shrimp originated in waters of countries not certified under Section 609. In other words, *shrimp caught using methods identical to those employed in the United States* have been excluded from the United States market solely because they have been caught in waters of *countries that have not been certified by the United States.* The resulting situation is difficult to reconcile with the declared policy objective of protecting and conserving sea turtles. This suggests to us that this measure, in its application, is more concerned with effectively influencing WTO Members to adopt essentially the same comprehensive regulatory regime as that applied by the United States to its domestic shrimp trawlers, even though many of

those Members may be differently situated. We believe that discrimination results not only when countries in which the same conditions prevail are differently treated, but also when the application of the measure at issue does not allow for any inquiry into the appropriateness of the regulatory program for the conditions prevailing in those exporting countries.

166. Another aspect of the application of Section 609 that bears heavily in any appraisal of justifiable or unjustifiable discrimination is the failure of the United States to engage the appellees, as well as other Members exporting shrimp to the United States, in serious, across-the-board negotiations with the objective of concluding bilateral or multilateral agreements for the protection and conservation of sea turtles, before enforcing the import prohibition against the shrimp exports of those other Members. * * *

167. * * * First, [a]part from the negotiation of the Inter-American Convention for the Protection and Conservation of Sea Turtles which concluded in 1996, the record before the Panel does not indicate any serious, substantial efforts to carry out [the] express directions of Congress [to initiate negotiations with other states to develop treaties protecting sea turtles].

168. Second, the protection and conservation of highly migratory species of sea turtles, that is, the very policy objective of the measure, demands concerted and cooperative efforts on the part of the many countries whose waters are traversed in the course of recurrent sea turtle migrations. The need for, and the appropriateness of, such efforts have been recognized in the WTO itself as well as in a significant number of other international instruments and declarations. * * * Of particular relevance is Principle 12 of the Rio Declaration on Environment and Development, which states, in part:

> Unilateral actions to deal with environmental challenges outside the jurisdiction of the importing country should be avoided. *Environmental measures addressing transboundary or global environmental problems should, as far as possible, be based on international consensus.* (emphasis added)

[The Appellate Body notes similar language in Agenda 21, the 1992 Convention on Biological Diversity, the 1979 Convention on the Conservation of Migratory Species of Wild Animals, and a 1996 Report of the WTO's Committee on Trade and Environment.]

171. [T]he record does not, however, show that serious efforts were made by the United States to negotiate similar agreements with any other country or group of countries before (and, as far as the record shows, after) Section 609 was enforced on a world-wide basis on 1 May 1996. Finally, the record also does not show that the appellant, the

United States, attempted to have recourse to such international mechanisms as exist to achieve cooperative efforts to protect and conserve sea turtles[174] before imposing the import ban.

172. Clearly, the United States negotiated seriously with some, but not with other Members (including the appellees), that export shrimp to the United States. The effect is plainly discriminatory and, in our view, unjustifiable. [T]he policies relating to the necessity for use of particular kinds of TEDs in various maritime areas, and the operating details of these policies, are all shaped by the Department of State, without the participation of the exporting Members. The system and processes of certification are established and administered by the United States agencies alone. The decision-making involved in the grant, denial or withdrawal of certification to the exporting Members, is, accordingly, also unilateral. The unilateral character of the application of Section 609 heightens the disruptive and discriminatory influence of the import prohibition and underscores its unjustifiability.

[The Appellate Body also finds additional differential treatment among countries desiring certification under Section 609. For example, the United States gave some countries a longer time than others to phase in the use of TEDs. In addition, the United States made "[f]ar greater efforts to transfer" required technology "to certain exporting countries * * * than to other exporting countries, including the appellees."]

176. When the foregoing differences in the means of application of Section 609 to various shrimp exporting countries are considered in their cumulative effect, we find, and so hold, that those differences in treatment constitute "unjustifiable discrimination" between exporting countries desiring certification in order to gain access to the United States shrimp market within the meaning of the chapeau of Article XX.

3. "*Arbitrary Discrimination*"

177. We next consider whether Section 609 has been applied in a manner constituting "arbitrary discrimination between countries where the same conditions prevail." * * *

180. * * * The certification processes under Section 609 consist principally of administrative *ex parte* inquiry or verification by staff of the Office of Marine Conservation in the Department of State with staff of the United States National Marine Fisheries Service. [T]here is no formal opportunity for an applicant country to be heard, or to respond to any

---

[174] While the United States is a party to [the Convention on International Trade in Endangered Species of Wild Flora and Fauna (CITES), Mar. 3, 1973, 27 U.S.T. 1087, 993 U.N.T.S. 243,] it did not make any attempt to raise the issue of sea turtle mortality due to shrimp trawling in the CITES Standing Committee as a subject requiring concerted action by states. In this context, we note that the United States, for example, has not signed the Convention on the Conservation of Migratory Species of Wild Animals or [the 1982 Convention of the Law of the Sea], and has not ratified the Convention on Biological Diversity.

arguments that may be made against it, in the course of the certification process before a decision to grant or to deny certification is made. Moreover, no formal written, reasoned decision, whether of acceptance or rejection, is rendered on applications for * * * certification[.] Countries which are granted certification are included in a list of approved applications published in the Federal Register; however, they are not notified specifically. Countries whose applications are denied also do not receive notice of such denial (other than by omission from the list of approved applications) or of the reasons for the denial. No procedure for review of, or appeal from, a denial of an application is provided.

181. The certification processes followed by the United States thus appear to be singularly informal and casual, and to be conducted in a manner such that these processes could result in the negation of rights of Members. There appears to be no way that exporting Members can be certain whether the terms of Section 609, in particular, the 1996 Guidelines, are being applied in a fair and just manner by the appropriate governmental agencies of the United States. It appears to us that, effectively, exporting Members applying for certification whose applications are rejected are denied basic fairness and due process, and are discriminated against, *vis-à-vis* those Members which are granted certification.

182. The provisions of Article X:3[191] of the GATT 1994 bear upon this matter. [R]igorous compliance with the fundamental requirements of due process should be required in the application and administration of a measure which purports to be an exception to the treaty obligations of the Member imposing the measure and which effectively results in a suspension *pro hac vice* of the treaty rights of other Members.

183. * * * Article X:3 of the GATT 1994 establishes certain minimum standards for transparency and procedural fairness in the administration of trade regulations which, in our view, are not met here. The non-transparent and *ex parte* nature of the internal governmental procedures applied by the competent officials in the Office of Marine Conservation, the Department of State, and the United States National Marine Fisheries Service throughout the certification processes under Section 609, as well as the fact that countries whose applications are denied do not receive formal notice of such denial, nor of the reasons for the denial, and the fact, too, that there is no formal legal procedure for review of, or

---

[191] Article X:3 states, in part:

(a) Each Member shall administer in a uniform, impartial and reasonable manner all its laws, regulations, decisions and rulings of the kind described in paragraph 1 of this Article.

(b) Each Member shall maintain, or institute as soon as practicable, judicial, arbitral or administrative tribunals or procedures for the purpose, inter alia, of the prompt review and correction of administrative action relating to customs matters . . . .

appeal from, a denial of an application, are all contrary to the spirit, if not the letter, of Article X:3 of the GATT 1994.

184. We find, accordingly, that the United States measure is applied in a manner which amounts to a means not just of "unjustifiable discrimination," but also of "arbitrary discrimination" between countries where the same conditions prevail, contrary to the requirements of the chapeau of Article XX. The measure, therefore, is not entitled to the justifying protection of Article XX of the GATT 1994. Having made this finding, it is not necessary for us to examine also whether the United States measure is applied in a manner that constitutes a "disguised restriction on international trade" under the chapeau of Article XX.

185. In reaching these conclusions, we wish to underscore what we have not decided in this appeal. We have *not* decided that the protection and preservation of the environment is of no significance to the Members of the WTO. Clearly, it is. We have *not* decided that the sovereign nations that are Members of the WTO cannot adopt effective measures to protect endangered species, such as sea turtles. Clearly, they can and should. And we have *not* decided that sovereign states should not act together bilaterally, plurilaterally or multilaterally, either within the WTO or in other international fora, to protect endangered species or to otherwise protect the environment. Clearly, they should and do.

186. What we *have* decided in this appeal is simply this: although the measure of the United States in dispute in this appeal serves an environmental objective that is recognized as legitimate under paragraph (g) of Article XX of the GATT 1994, this measure has been applied by the United States in a manner which constitutes arbitrary and unjustifiable discrimination between Members of the WTO, contrary to the requirements of the chapeau of Article XX. * * * WTO Members are free to adopt their own policies aimed at protecting the environment as long as, in so doing, they fulfill their obligations and respect the rights of other Members under the *WTO Agreement*. * * *

188. The Appellate Body *recommends* that the DSB request the United States to bring its measure found in the Panel Report to be inconsistent with Article XI of the GATT 1994, and found in this Report to be not justified under Article XX of the GATT 1994, into conformity with the obligations of the United States under that Agreement.

NOTES AND QUESTIONS

1. *The GATT and the WTO.* The General Agreement on Tariffs and Trade (GATT), Oct. 30, 1947, 61 Stat. A3, 55 U.N.T.S. 187, is a multilateral treaty adopted to further the goal of reducing tariffs and other barriers to trade. The GATT was one of several post-World War II initiatives relating to trade and development. The International Monetary Fund and the World Bank were also created in the 1940s to promote investment and economic

growth. See the discussion of the ICSID Convention in the *CMS Case* in Chapter 2. A guiding principle of the GATT is "national treatment," which provides for equal taxation and regulation of foreign and domestic goods after foreign goods have been imported. Another important GATT principle is "most favored nation treatment," according to which a GATT Contracting Party must, when it grants a privilege to a product imported from one state, accord the same privilege to similar products from all GATT Contracting Parties. However, the GATT Generalized System of Preferences gives temporary preferences to specific goods imported from developing states. GATT Article XI(1), the 1994 version of which was at issue in the *Shrimp-Turtle Case*, prohibits discriminatory import restrictions based on standards related to the means of producing a product. Tariffs and various non-tariff trade barriers have been progressively lowered or eliminated in a series of GATT negotiating "rounds" held since 1947.

The World Trade Organization came into existence on January 1, 1995, a result of the so-called Uruguay Round. Unlike the original GATT, which simply established a treaty framework, the WTO is an international organization, headquartered in Switzerland and charged with administering WTO trade agreements, including the GATT. The WTO serves as a forum for trade negotiations, provides technical assistance to developing states, and hears trade disputes. As of December 2013, the WTO had 159 members.

2. *The WTO and Dispute Settlement*. Annex II of the 1994 Agreement Establishing the World Trade Organization, Apr. 15, 1994, 1867 U.N.T.S. 3, contains a Dispute Settlement Understanding (DSU), 1869 *id.* 401, which establishes a formal dispute settlement mechanism. The original GATT contemplated that consultation, good offices, or conciliation would resolve many disputes. In case such informal mechanisms proved unavailing, many GATT disputes could be submitted to panels selected by the parties, which would issue reports containing recommendations. Although a panel report could be submitted to the Council of the GATT Contracting Parties in an effort to have it adopted as an authoritative ruling, a party to a dispute could block Council adoption.

The WTO's DSU replaced the GATT panel process with a more formal third-party mechanism that can lead to legally binding decisions. A disadvantaged party can no longer unilaterally block a report from being adopted. A panel report (including any changes made on appeal by a seven-member Appellate Body) is adopted by the WTO's Dispute Settlement Body (DSB) unless that Body decides by consensus not to adopt it. The DSU also contains detailed enforcement provisions. These concern surveillance of compliance by the DSB, a call for negotiated compensation, and a provision under which parties to a dispute that are affected by an illegal trade measure ultimately may suspend trade concessions or other GATT obligations toward the violating WTO member. See Marco Bronckers & Freya Baetens, "Reconsidering Financial Remedies in WTO Dispute Settlement," 16 *Journal of International Economic Law* 281 (2013).

The WTO's caseload has been heavy. During the first 18 years of the WTO's existence, over 450 cases have been brought. See "Chronological List of Disputes Cases," http://www.wto.org/english/tratop_e/dispu_e/dispu_status_e.htm (last visited Dec. 10, 2013). What has been gained by making the WTO's dispute settlement mechanism more formal? Has anything been lost? Are developing states, with small trade matters at stake and perhaps without the resources necessary to litigate trade disputes, disadvantaged by the third-party WTO DSU process? Should the process be made more formal still, *e.g.*, by creating a standing judicial body to decide trade disputes? See Susan Esserman & Robert Howse, "The WTO on Trial," *Foreign Affairs*, Jan.-Feb. 2003, at 130; Håkan Nordström & Gregory Shaffer, "Access to Justice in the World Trade Organization: A Case for a Small Claims Procedure?," 7 *World Trade Review* 587 (2008).

3. *The Aftermath of the* Shrimp-Turtle Case. In November 1998 the WTO's DSB formally adopted the Appellate Body's report in the *Shrimp-Turtle Case* and issued corresponding recommendations and rulings. Would you expect the United States to comply with them? The U.S. State Department, "in response to recommendations of the Dispute Settlement Body of the World Trade Association," adopted new shrimp import certification guidelines. These new guidelines were intended to "introduc[e] greater flexibility in considering the comparability of foreign programs and the U.S. program, * * * increase the transparency and predictability of the certification process and * * * afford foreign governments seeking certification a greater degree of due process." 64 *Federal Register* 36,946 (1999). The United States also, in 2000, entered into a memorandum of understanding with states in the Indian Ocean region to protect sea turtles there, and the U.S. government offered to supply TEDs and technical training to states affected by the U.S. shrimp import ban. See 2001 *Digest of United States Practice in International Law* 761–62. Had the United States taken sufficient steps to comply with the 1998 ruling of the WTO's Dispute Settlement Body? The Appellate Body thought so. Appellate Body Report, *United States-Import Prohibition of Certain Shrimp and Shrimp Products; Recourse to Article 21.5 of the DSU by Malaysia*, ¶ 122, WT/DS58/AB/RW (2001). See Louise de La Fayette, "International Decision," 96 *American Journal of International Law* 685 (2002); 2001 *Digest of United States Practice in International Law* 752–56. For discussion of U.S. litigation and the WTO proceedings concerning the U.S. shrimp import restrictions, see Turtle Island Restoration Network v. Evans, 284 F.3d 1282 (Fed. Cir. 2002), *cert. denied*, 538 U.S. 960 (2003).

4. *Overlapping Legal Regimes.* GATT 1994 and the World Trade Organization establish a global regime for international trade. We study international organizations and international regimes—treaty-based arrangements involving international organizations—in more depth in Chapter 8. For now, note the complexities, illustrated by the *Shrimp-Turtle Case*, that arise when a regime created for one purpose, *e.g.*, trade, comes into competition with rules or principles from another regime, *e.g.*, international environmental law. What techniques did the Appellate Body in the *Shrimp-*

Turtle Case use to reconcile the competing regimes? How satisfactory was the result?

Despite the *Shrimp-Turtle Case*, questions remain about how to coordinate environmental measures with the GATT. Should the United States unilaterally be able to impose environmental measures respecting sea turtles found beyond its boundaries and in the international commons? Are unilateral measures objectionable only if they are applied against particular countries (or processes?) in a discriminatory manner? Must a country seeking to impose unilateral restrictions to promote environmental goals negotiate with other countries? When and how should such negotiations be conducted? Are unilateral import bans more acceptable when they protect species such as sea turtles that have been recognized as endangered in an international treaty (*e.g.*, CITES, noted in the *Shrimp-Turtle Case*), even though no international agreement requires that shrimp be harvested in ways safe for sea turtles? How might the WTO system best accommodate environmental measures authorized by environmental treaties? See Jeffrey Atik, "Two Hopeful Readings of *Shrimp-Turtle*," 9 *Yearbook of International Environmental Law* 6 (1998); Daniel Bodansky, "What's So Bad About Unilateral Action to Protect the Environment?," 11 *European Journal of International Law* 339 (2000); and Kuei-Jung Ni, "Redefinition and Elaboration of an Obligation to Pursue International Negotiations for Solving Global Environmental Problems in Light of the WTO *Shrimp/Turtle* Compliance Adjudication between Malaysia and the United States," 14 *Minnesota Journal of Global Trade* 111 (2004).

5. *Advantages and Disadvantages of Multiple International Courts and Tribunals.* Why are there so many international courts and tribunals? Are there too many opportunities for forum shopping? Recall from Note 3 following the *Rainbow Warrior* decisions earlier in this chapter just how many different forums were called on to address aspects of the incident. Even when we consider only interstate disputes in international courts and tribunals, multiple forums may be available. For example, four different international courts and tribunals—the International Tribunal for the Law of the Sea, an arbitral tribunal constituted under the Convention on the Law of the Sea, Dec. 10, 1982, 1833 U.N.T.S 3, the European Court of Justice, and an arbitral tribunal created pursuant to the Convention for the Protection of the Marine Environment of the North-East Atlantic (OSPAR Convention), Sept. 22, 1992, 32 *International Legal Materials* 1069 (1993)—heard aspects of a dispute between Ireland and the United Kingdom concerning pollution in the Irish Sea. See Nikolaos Lavranos, "Protecting Its Exclusive Jurisdiction: The MOX Plant Judgment of the ECJ," 5 *Law and Practice of International Courts and Tribunals* 479 (2006). What mechanisms or techniques might moderate conflicts between international courts? Conflicts between the judicial jurisdictions of municipal courts or between national laws have long been a concern in domestic legal systems; we study such conflicts in Chapters 11 and 12.

With so many tribunals, is there a risk of divergent interpretations of international law? If so, is that undesirable? Jonathan Charney, after examining the case law of several international courts, concluded that international law "remains, at its core, relatively coherent," with different international "tribunals operat[ing] within the same dialectic and reach[ing] relatively compatible conclusions." Jonathan I. Charney, "Is International Law Threatened by Multiple International Tribunals?," 271 *Recueil des Cours* 101, 352 (1998). Others disagree. See Chester Brown, "Review Essay: The Proliferation of International Courts and Tribunals: Finding Your Way Through the Maze," 3 *Melbourne Journal of International Law* 453 (2002). The growth of international tribunals is explored in *International Courts for the Twenty-first Century* (Mark W. Janis ed. 1992), and Yuval Shany, *The Competing Jurisdictions of International Courts and Tribunals* (2003).

6. *The International Court of Justice and the Proliferation of International Courts.* What role should the International Court of Justice—the principal judicial organ of the United Nations—play in this complex institutional world of multiple courts and tribunals? Should municipal courts be allowed to refer questions about international law to the ICJ? There is such a mechanism, called a preliminary ruling, in European Union law. See Article 267 of the Consolidated Versions of the Treaty on European Union and the Treaty on the Functioning of the European Union, Oct. 26, 2012, 2012 O.J. (326) 164, and the *Friends of the Earth Case* in Chapter 8. The Andean Tribunal of Justice has a similar jurisdiction, and since 1985 has rendered over 1,300 decisions on requests from national courts about regional international law. See Laurence R. Helfer, Karen J. Alter & M. Florencia Guerzovich, "Islands of Effective International Adjudication: Constructing an Intellectual Property Rule of Law in the Andean Community," 103 *American Journal of International Law* 1 (2009).

Should international courts also be authorized to refer legal questions to the ICJ? See Tullio Treves, "Advisory Opinions of the International Court of Justice on Questions Raised by Other International Tribunals," 4 *Max Planck Yearbook of United Nations Law* 215 (2000). Should referrals from the Secretary-General of the United Nations be permitted? See Stephen M. Schwebel, "Authorizing the Secretary-General of the United Nations to Request Advisory Opinions of the International Court of Justice," 78 *American Journal of International Law* 869 (1984). Should individuals be allowed to bring cases or questions to the ICJ? See Mark W. Janis, "Individuals and the International Court," in *The International Court of Justice: Its Future Role After Fifty Years* 205, 210–15 (A.S. Muller, D. Raic & J.M. Thuránszky eds. 1997). See also Andrew Strauss, "Cutting the Gordian Knot: How and Why the United Nations Should Vest the International Court of Justice with Referral Jurisdiction," 44 *Cornell International Law Journal* 603 (2011). What would be lost and what would be gained by moving toward a hierarchical system of judicial review, with the ICJ at the apex?

Should the International Court of Justice make changes on its own—changes not involving formal amendments to the U.N. Charter or the Court's

Statute—to enhance its influence? For example, when the ICJ is hearing a case, should it become more proactive, reaching out to pronounce on substantive legal issues of great importance? See Pieter Kooijmans, "The ICJ in the 21st Century: Judicial Restraint, Judicial Activism, or Proactive Judicial Policy," 56 *International and Comparative Law Quarterly* 741 (2007). Would becoming more proactive help or hurt the ICJ's influence?

Would other, perhaps procedural, changes help the Court function more efficiently, increasing its attractiveness? When he was President of the ICJ, Gilbert Guillaume of France termed the modernization of the Court's antiquated procedures the ICJ's "foremost challenge." "Press Conference of Judge Gilbert Guillaume, President of the International Court of Justice," *ICJ Communiqué* No. 2000/5, Feb. 16, 2000. Several recent amendments to the Court's rules and practices have improved its proceedings. See *Amendments to the Rules of Court*, ICJ Press Release 2005/9. In addition, complaints of understaffing and underfunding have been at least partially addressed. The ICJ's budget, $20,261,700 for the two-year period 2000–2001, increased to $47,766,400 for the 2012–2013 biennium. See *Report of the International Court of Justice, 1 August 2000–31 July 2001*, at 63–65, U.N. Doc. A/56/4 (2001); *Report of the International Court of Justice, 1 August 2011–31 July 2012*, at 63–65, U.N. Doc. A/67/4 (2012).

CHAPTER 6

INDIVIDUALS AND INTERNATIONAL LAW

■ ■ ■

The legal status of individuals has long been a controversial topic in international law. The classical law of nations of the 17th and 18th centuries gave individuals legal rights and duties, but, as we explore in Part A below, the narrow positivist doctrine of the 19th and early 20th centuries treated individuals as mere objects of international law. Part B introduces the modern concept of individuals as subjects of international law, a theme developed in Part C, which provides an overview of the development of international human rights law in the later 20th and early 21st centuries. Finally follow cases and commentary on two of the most important modern aspects of the rights and duties of individuals in international law: European human rights law in Part D and the International Criminal Court in Part E.

A. INDIVIDUALS AS OBJECTS OF INTERNATIONAL LAW

In the traditional positivistic international law of the 19th and early 20th centuries, individuals were viewed as "objects" of international law. Although individuals were not deemed to be "subjects" of international law (and so had neither international legal rights nor duties), they could be objects of state versus state litigation. So grew up doctrines of state protection of individuals and state responsibility for injuries done to individuals. However, the traditional doctrines of state protection and state responsibility have at least three significant limitations. First, as we see in *Nottebohm* below, individuals may only be protected by their national states; national links may be elusive. Second, when the notion of national links is extended to corporations, even more confusion can result, as *Barcelona Traction* illustrates. Finally and most importantly, the objective view of individuals leaves nationals open to abuse by their own states, since it is impractical to conceive of a state protecting its own nationals against itself in international law.

THE NOTTEBOHM CASE

Liechtenstein v. Guatemala, 1955 I.C.J. 4

[Nottebohm, born German, obtained Liechtenstein citizenship in 1939, but nonetheless was treated as a German enemy alien during the Second World War. As a consequence, Guatemala deported Nottebohm to the United States where he was interned; his Guatemalan properties were expropriated. Liechtenstein sued Guatemala on Nottebohm's behalf in the ICJ, but Guatemala objected that Liechtenstein was not a state that could legitimately protect Nottebohm before the Court.]

Nottebohm was born at Hamburg on September 16th, 1881. He was German by birth, and still possessed German nationality when, in October 1939, he applied for naturalization in Liechtenstein.

In 1905 he went to Guatemala. He took up residence there and made that country the headquarters of his business activities, which increased and prospered; these activities developed in the field of commerce, banking and plantations. Having been an employee in the firm of Nottebohm Hermanos, which had been founded by his brothers Juan and Arturo, he became their partner in 1912 and later, in 1937, he was made head of the firm. After 1905 he sometimes went to Germany on business and to other countries for holidays. He continued to have business connections in Germany. He paid a few visits to a brother who had lived in Liechtenstein since 1931. Some of his other brothers, relatives and friends were in Germany, others in Guatemala. He himself continued to have his fixed abode in Guatemala until 1943, that is to say, until the occurrence of the events which constitute the basis of the present dispute.

In 1939, after having provided for the safeguarding of his interests in Guatemala by a power of attorney given to the firm of Nottebohm Hermanos on March 22nd, he left that country at a date fixed by Counsel for Liechtenstein as at approximately the end of March or the beginning of April, when he seems to have gone to Hamburg, and later to have paid a few brief visits to Vaduz where he was at the beginning of October 1939. It was then, on October 9th, a little more than a month after the opening of the second World War marked by Germany's attack on Poland, that his attorney, Dr. Marxer, submitted an application for naturalization on behalf of Nottebohm.

The Liechtenstein Law of January 4th, 1934, lays down the conditions for the naturalization of foreigners, specifies the supporting documents to be submitted and the undertakings to be given and defines the competent organs for giving a decision and the procedure to be followed. The Law specifies certain mandatory requirements, namely, that the applicant for naturalization should prove: (1) "that the acceptance into the Home Corporation (*Heimatverband*) of a Liechtenstein commune has been promised to him in case of acquisition of the nationality of the State;" (2) that he will lose his former nationality as a result of naturalization, although this requirement may be waived under stated conditions. It further makes naturalization conditional upon compliance with the requirement of residence for at least three years in the territory of the Principality, although it is provided that "this requirement can be dispensed with in circumstances deserving special consideration and by way of exception." In addition, the applicant for naturalization is required to submit a number of documents, such as evidence of his residence in the territory of the Principality, a certificate of good conduct issued by the competent authority of the place of residence, documents relating to his property and income and, if he is not a resident in the Principality, proof that he has concluded an agreement with the Revenue authorities, "subsequent to the revenue commission of the presumptive home commune having been heard." The Law further provides for the payment by the applicant of a naturalization fee, which is fixed by the Princely Government and amounts to at least one half of the sum payable by the applicant for reception into the Home Corporation of a Liechtenstein commune, the promise of such reception constituting a condition under the Law for the grant of naturalization. * * *

On October 9th, 1939, Nottebohm, "resident in Guatemala since 1905 (at present residing as a visitor with his brother, Hermann Nottebohm, in Vaduz)," applied for admission as a national of Liechtenstein and, at the same time, for the previous conferment of citizenship in the Commune of Mauren. He sought dispensation from the condition of three years' residence as prescribed by law, without indicating the special circumstances warranting such waiver. He submitted a statement of the *Crédit Suisse* in Zurich concerning his assets, and undertook to pay 25,000 Swiss francs to the Commune of Mauren, 12,500 Swiss francs to the State, to which was to be added the payment of dues in connection with the proceedings. He further stated that he had made "arrangements with the Revenue Authorities of the Government of Liechtenstein for the conclusion of a formal agreement to the effect that he will pay an annual tax of naturalization amounting to Swiss francs 1,000 of which Swiss francs 600 are payable to the Commune of Mauren and Swiss francs 400 are payable to the Principality of Liechtenstein, subject to the proviso that the payments of these taxes will be set off against ordinary taxes which will fall due if the applicant takes up residence in one of the Communes of the Principality." He further undertook to deposit as security a sum of 30,000 Swiss francs. He also gave certain general information as to his financial position and indicated that he would never become a burden to the Commune whose citizenship he was seeking.

Lastly, he requested "that naturalization proceedings be initiated and concluded before the Government of the Principality and before the Commune of Mauren without delay, that the application be then placed before the Diet with a favourable recommendation and, finally, that it be submitted with all necessary expedition to His Highness the Reigning Prince."

On the original typewritten application which has been produced in a photostatic copy, it can be seen that the name of the Commune of Mauren and the amounts to be paid were added by hand, a fact which gave rise to some argument on the part of Counsel for the Parties. There is also a reference to the "*Vorausverständnis*" of the Reigning Prince obtained on October 13th, 1939, which Liechtenstein interprets as showing the decision to grant naturalization, which interpretation has, however, been questioned. Finally, there is annexed to the application an otherwise blank sheet bearing the signature of the Reigning Prince, "Franz Josef," but without any date or other explanation.

A document dated October 15th, 1939, certifies that on that date the Commune of Mauren conferred the privilege of its citizenship upon Mr. Nottebohm and requested the Government to transmit it to the Diet for approval. A certificate of October 17th, 1939, evidences the payment of the taxes required to be paid by Mr. Nottebohm. On October 20th, 1939, Mr. Nottebohm took the oath of allegiance and a final arrangement concerning liability to taxation was concluded on October 23rd.

This was the procedure followed in the case of the naturalization of Nottebohm.

A certificate of nationality has also been produced, signed on behalf of the Government of the Principality and dated October 20th, 1939, to the effect that Nottebohm was naturalized by Supreme Resolution of the Reigning Prince dated October 13th, 1939.

Having obtained a Liechtenstein passport, Nottebohm had it visa-ed by the Consul General of Guatemala in Zurich on December 1st, 1939, and returned to Guatemala at the beginning of 1940, where he resumed his former business activities and in particular the management of the firm of Nottebohm Hermanos.

Relying on the nationality thus conferred on Nottebohm, Liechtenstein considers itself entitled to seize the Court of its claim on his behalf, and its Final Conclusions contain two submissions in this connection. Liechtenstein requests the Court to find and declare, first, "that the naturalization of Mr. Frederic Nottebohm in Liechtenstein on October 13th, 1939, was not contrary to international law," and secondly, "that Liechtenstein's claim on behalf of Mr. Nottebohm as a national of Liechtenstein is admissible before the Court."

The Final Conclusions of Guatemala, on the other hand, request the Court "to declare that the claim of the Principality of Liechtenstein is inadmissible," and set forth a number of grounds relating to the nationality of Liechtenstein granted to Nottebohm by naturalization.

Thus, the real issue before the Court is the admissibility of the claim of Liechtenstein in respect of Nottebohm. * * *

In order to decide upon the admissibility of the Application, the Court must ascertain whether the nationality conferred on Nottebohm by Liechtenstein by means of a naturalization which took place in the circumstances which have been described, can be validly invoked as against Guatemala, whether it bestows upon Liechtenstein a sufficient title to the exercise of protection in respect of Nottebohm as against Guatemala and therefore entitles it to seize the Court of a claim relating to him. * * *

Since no proof has been adduced that Guatemala has recognized the title to the exercise of protection relied upon by Liechtenstein as being derived from the naturalization which it granted to Nottebohm, the Court must consider whether such an act of granting nationality by Liechtenstein directly entails an obligation on the part of Guatemala to recognize its effect, namely, Liechtenstein's right to exercise its protection. In other words, it must be determined whether that unilateral act by Liechtenstein is one which can be relied upon against Guatemala in regard to the exercise of protection. The Court will deal with this question without considering that of the validity of Nottebohm's naturalization according to the law of Liechtenstein.

It is for Liechtenstein, as it is for every sovereign State, to settle by its own legislation the rules relating to the acquisition of its nationality, and to confer that nationality by naturalization granted by its own organs in accordance with that legislation. It is not necessary to determine whether international law imposes any limitations on its freedom of decision in this domain. Furthermore, nationality has its most immediate, its most far-reaching and, for most people, its only effects within the legal system of the State conferring it. Nationality serves above all to determine that the person upon whom it is conferred enjoys the rights and is bound by the obligations which the law of the State in question grants to or imposes on its nationals. This is implied in the wider concept that nationality is within the domestic jurisdiction of the State.

But the issue which the Court must decide is not one which pertains to the legal system of Liechtenstein. It does not depend on the law or on the decision of Liechtenstein whether that State is entitled to exercise its protection, in the case under consideration. To exercise protection, to apply to the Court, is to place oneself on the plane of international law. It is international law which determines whether a State is entitled to exercise protection and to seize the Court.

The naturalization of Nottebohm was an act performed by Liechtenstein in the exercise of its domestic jurisdiction. The question to be decided is whether that act has the international effect here under consideration.

International practice provides many examples of acts performed by States in the exercise of their domestic jurisdiction which do not necessarily or automatically have international effect, which are not necessarily and automatically binding on other States or which are binding on them only subject to certain conditions: this is the case, for instance, of a judgment given by the competent court of a State which it is sought to invoke in another state.

In the present case it is necessary to determine whether the naturalization conferred on Nottebohm can be successfully invoked against Guatemala, whether, as has already been stated, it can be relied upon as against that State, so that Liechtenstein is thereby entitled to exercise its protection in favour of Nottebohm against Guatemala. * * *

International arbitrators have decided * * * numerous cases of dual nationality, where the question arose with regard to the exercise of protection. They have given their preference to the real and effective nationality, that which accorded with the facts, that based on stronger factual ties between the person concerned and one of the States whose nationality is involved. Different factors are taken into consideration, and their importance will vary from one case to the next: the habitual residence of the individual concerned is an important factor, but there are other factors such as the centre of his interests, his family ties, his participation in public life, attachment shown by him for a given country and inculcated in his children, etc.

Similarly, the courts of third States, when they have before them an individual whom two other States hold to be their national, seek to resolve the conflict by having recourse to international criteria and their prevailing tendency is to prefer the real and effective nationality.

The same tendency prevails in the writings of publicists and in practice. This notion is inherent in the provisions of Article 3, paragraph 2, of the Statute of the Court. National laws reflect this tendency when, *inter alia*, they make naturalization dependent on conditions indicating the existence of a link, which may vary in their purpose or in their nature but which are essentially concerned with this idea. The Liechtenstein Law of January 4th, 1934, is a good example.

The practice of certain States which refrain from exercising protection in favour of a naturalized person when the latter has in fact, by his prolonged absence, severed his links with what is no longer for him anything but his nominal country, manifests the view of these States that, in order to be capable of being invoked against another State, nationality must correspond with the factual situation. A similar view is manifested in the relevant provisions of the bilateral nationality treaties concluded between the United States of America and other States since 1868, such as those sometimes referred to as the Bancroft Treaties, and in the Pan-American Convention, signed at Rio de Janeiro on August 13th, 1906, on the status of naturalized citizens who resume residence in their country of origin.

The character thus recognized on the international level as pertaining to nationality is in no way inconsistent with the fact that international law leaves it to each State to lay down the rules governing the grant of its own nationality. The reason for this is that the diversity of demographic conditions has thus far made it impossible for any general agreement to be reached on the rules relating to nationality, although the latter by its very nature affects international relations. It has been considered that the best way of making such rules accord with the varying demographic conditions in different countries is to leave the fixing of such rules to the competence of each State. On the other hand, a State cannot claim that the rules it has thus laid down are entitled to recognition by another State unless it has acted in conformity with this general aim of making the legal bond of nationality accord with the individual's genuine connection with the State which assumes the defence of its citizens by means of protection as against other States. * * *

According to the practice of States, to arbitral and judicial decisions and to the opinions of writers, nationality is a legal bond having as its basis a social fact of attachment, a genuine connection of existence, interests and sentiments, together with the existence of reciprocal rights and duties. It may be said to constitute the juridical expression of the fact that the individual upon whom it is conferred, either directly by the law or as the result of an act of the authorities, is in fact more closely connected with the population of the State conferring nationality than with that of any other State. Conferred by a State, it only entitles that State to exercise protection vis-à-vis another State, if it constitutes a translation into juridical terms of the individual's connection with the State which has made him its national.

Diplomatic protection and protection by means of international judicial proceedings constitute measures for the defence of the rights of the State. As the Permanent Court of International Justice has said and has repeated, "by taking up the case of one of its subjects and by resorting to diplomatic action or international judicial proceedings on his behalf, a State is in reality asserting its own rights—its right to ensure, in the person of its subjects, respect for the rules of international law."

Since this is the character which nationality must present when it is invoked to furnish the State which has granted it with a title to the exercise of protection and to the institution of international judicial proceedings, the Court must ascertain whether the nationality granted to Nottebohm by means of naturalization is of this character or, in other words, whether the factual connection between Nottebohm and Liechtenstein in the period preceding, contemporaneous with and following his naturalization appears to be sufficiently close, so preponderant in relation to any connection which may have existed between him and any other State, that it is possible to regard the nationality conferred upon him as real and effective, as the exact juridical expression of a social fact of a connection which existed previously or came into existence thereafter.

Naturalization is not a matter to be taken lightly. To seek and to obtain it is not something that happens frequently in the life of a human being. It involves his breaking a bond of allegiance and his establishment of a new bond of allegiance. It may have far-reaching consequences and involve profound changes in the destiny of the individual who obtains it. It concerns him personally, and to consider it only from the point of view of its repercussions with regard to his property would be to misunderstand its profound significance. In order to appraise its international effect, it is impossible to disregard the circumstances in which it was conferred, the serious character which attaches to it, the real and effective, and not merely the verbal preference of the individual seeking it for the country which grants it to him.

At the time of his naturalization does Nottebohm appear to have been more closely attached by his tradition, his establishment, his interests, his activities, his family ties, his intentions for the near future to Liechtenstein than to any other State? * * *

The essential facts are as follows:

At the date when he applied for naturalization Nottebohm had been a German national from the time of his birth. He had always retained his connections with members of his family who had remained in Germany and he had always had business connections with that country. His country had been at war for more than a month, and there is nothing to indicate that the application for naturalization then made by Nottebohm was motivated by any desire to dissociate himself from the Government of his country.

He had been settled in Guatemala for 34 years. He had carried on his activities there. It was the main seat of his interests. He returned there shortly after his naturalization, and it remained the centre of his interests and of his business activities. He stayed there until his removal as a result of war measures in 1943. He subsequently attempted to return there, and he now complains of Guatemala's refusal to admit him. There, too, were several members of his family who sought to safeguard his interests.

In contrast, his actual connections with Liechtenstein were extremely tenuous. No settled abode, no prolonged residence in that country at the time of his application for naturalization: the application indicates that he was paying a visit there and confirms the transient character of this visit by its request that the naturalization proceedings should be initiated and concluded without delay. No intention of settling there was shown at that time or realized in the ensuing weeks, months or years—on the contrary, he returned to Guatemala very shortly after his naturalization and showed every intention of remaining there. If Nottebohm went to Liechtenstein in 1946, this was because of the refusal of Guatemala to admit him. No indication is given of the grounds warranting the waiver of the condition of residence, required by the 1934 Nationality Law, which waiver was implicitly granted to him. There is no allegation of any economic interests or of any activities exercised or to be exercised in Liechtenstein, and no manifestation of any intention whatsoever to transfer all or some of his interests and his business activities to Liechtenstein. It is unnecessary in this connection to attribute much importance to the promise to pay the taxes levied at the time of his naturalization. The only links to be discovered between the Principality and Nottebohm are the short sojourns already referred to and the presence in Vaduz of one of his brothers: but his brother's presence is referred to in his application for naturalization only as a reference to his good conduct. Furthermore, other members of his family have asserted Nottebohm's desire to spend his old age in Guatemala.

These facts clearly establish, on the one hand, the absence of any bond of attachment between Nottebohm and Liechtenstein and, on the other hand, the existence of a long-standing and close connection between him and Guatemala, a link which his naturalization in no way weakened. That naturalization was not based on any real prior connection with Liechtenstein, nor did it in any way alter the manner of life of the person upon whom it was conferred in exceptional circumstances of speed and accommodation. In both respects, it was lacking in the genuineness requisite to an act of such importance, if it is to be entitled to be respected by a State in the position of Guatemala. It was granted without regard to the concept of nationality adopted in international relations.

Naturalization was asked for not so much for the purpose of obtaining a legal recognition of Nottebohm's membership in fact in the population of Liechtenstein, as it was to enable him to substitute for his status as a national of a belligerent State that of a national of a neutral State, with the sole aim of thus coming within the protection of Liechtenstein but not of becoming wedded to its traditions, its interests, its way of life or of assuming the obligations—other than fiscal obligations—and exercising the rights pertaining to the status thus acquired.

Guatemala is under no obligation to recognize a nationality granted in such circumstances. Liechtenstein consequently is not entitled to extend its protection to Nottebohm vis-à-vis Guatemala and its claim must, for this reason, be held to be inadmissible.

The Court is not therefore called upon to deal with the other pleas in bar put forward by Guatemala or the Conclusions of the Parties other than those on which it is adjudicating in accordance with the reasons indicated above.

For these reasons,

THE COURT,

by eleven votes to three,

Holds that the claim submitted by the Government of the Principality of Liechtenstein is inadmissible.

NOTES AND QUESTIONS

1. *Nottebohm.* Friedrich Nottebohm, born in Hamburg in 1881, moved to Guatemala in 1905. There he worked with his brothers, Arturo and Juan, in a family company engaged in commerce, banking, and growing coffee. It was "one of the oldest, wealthiest, and most influential families in Guatemala and Central America." Cindy C. Buys, "Nottebohm's Nightmare: Have We Exorcized the Ghosts of WWII Detention Programs or Do They Still Haunt Guantanamo?," 11 *Chicago-Kent Journal of International & Comparative Law* 1, 4 (2011). For more on confiscation of German assets in Latin America during World War II, see J. Fred Rippy, "German Investments in Guatemala," 20 *Journal of Business of the University of Chicago* 212 (1947), and Max Paul Friedman, *Nazis and Good Neighbors: The United States Campaign Against the Germans of Latin America in World War II* (2003).

2. *State Responsibility and State Protection.* Guatemala's alleged violation of international law in *Nottebohm* involved a duty often characterized as state responsibility, in this instance a state's responsibility to protect a foreign investor. State responsibility is a complex and multifaceted legal concept, deserving of its own substantive note. This follows these Notes and Comments devoted to *Nottebohm* itself. A counterpart of state responsibility is state protection, a doctrine permitting but not obliging a state to protect its nationals. State protection of individuals in international proceedings is especially common in investment disputes. Despite the negative outcome for Nottebohm himself, there are in practice a great many examples of successful state protection of individuals not only in the International Court, but in *ad hoc* commissions and tribunals. See Timothy G. Nelson, "Passport, S'il Vous Plaît?: Investment Treaty Protection and the Individual Investor's Citizenship," 32 *Suffolk Transnational Law Review* 451 (2009).

Given that Liechtenstein in the *Nottebohm Case* was under no legal obligation to protect Nottebohm, what reasons would there have been for Liechtenstein to go to the trouble and expense of suing Guatemala in the International Court? Was it because of the government's concern for Nottebohm? Because of the threat to Liechtenstein's reputation as a safe haven? If Liechtenstein had refused to pursue Nottebohm's claim, how else could Nottebohm have sought redress? What were his chances for real success in Guatemala's courts? Liechtenstein's courts? Diplomatic negotiations? International arbitration?

The ICJ was careful to state that Nottebohm's Liechtenstein nationality was not "opposable" to Guatemala, and that Liechtenstein could not "extend its protection to Nottebohm vis-à-vis Guatemala." Did this leave open the possibility that Liechtenstein might have effectively espoused Nottebohm's claims against other states?

When one state successfully claims that another state is responsible for injuring the claimant state's national, does the notion that the claimant state is "in reality asserting its own right" extend to issues of reparation? For example, if Liechtenstein had been successful in obtaining compensation from Guatemala for injuries done to Nottebohm, should Liechtenstein have had to turn the proceeds it obtained over to Nottebohm?

In 2012, the ICJ ruled in favor of claims made by the Republic of Guinea on behalf of its national, Ahmadon Sadio Diallo, against the Democratic Republic of the Congo (the DRC). ICJ Judgment of June 19, 2012. This was the ICJ's first judgment awarding damages in a human rights case. The Court had previously found that Diallo had been illegally arrested by the DRC and that the DRC had wrongfully seized Diallo's property. Although Guinea sought reparations of more than $11.5 million, the ICJ ordered the DRC to pay only a total of $95,000 for both non-material and material injury. Mads Adenas, "International Decision: Ahmadon v. Democratic Republic of Congo," 107 *American Journal of International Law* 178 (2013). Is this a landmark ruling? Or does it show a continued reluctance of the ICJ to act meaningfully to protect human rights?

3. *Stateless Persons*. Do stateless people have rights? How can stateless individuals pursue claims against states for violating their rights? In Trop v. Dulles, 356 U.S. 86 (1958), the U.S. Supreme Court found that depriving a military deserter of his U.S. citizenship was a violation of the Eighth Amendment's protection against cruel and unusual punishment:

> There may be involved no physical mistreatment, no primitive torture. There is instead the total destruction of the individual's status in organized society. It is a form of punishment more primitive than torture, for it destroys for the individual the political existence that was centuries in the development. The punishment strips the citizen of his status in the national and international political community. His very existence is at the sufferance of the country in which he happens to find himself. * * * In short, the expatriate has lost the right to have rights.
>
> This punishment * * * subjects the individual to a fate of ever-increasing fear and distress. He knows not what discriminations may be established against him, what proscriptions may be directed against him, and when and for what cause his existence in his native land may be terminated. He may be subject to banishment, a fate universally decried by civilized people. He is stateless, a condition deplored in the international community of democracies. * * *

> The civilized nations of the world are in virtual unanimity that statelessness is not to be imposed as punishment for crime.

Id. at 101–02.

As reproduced in the Appendix, in 1948, the U.N. General Assembly resolved in Article 15 of the Universal Declaration of Human Rights that "[e]veryone has the right to a nationality" and that "[n]o one shall be arbitrarily deprived of his nationality nor denied the right to change his nationality."

4. *Multiple Nationality.* Is there an exclusive relationship between an individual and a state, or may an individual be eligible to be a dual national? Or a national of many states? See Linda Bosniak, "Multiple Nationality and the Postnational Transformation of Citizenship," 42 *Virginia Journal of International Law* 979 (2002). Professor Sloane has concluded that *Nottebohm's* "genuine link theory [is] anachronistic today." Robert D. Sloane, "Breaking the Genuine Link: The Contemporary International Legal Regulation of Nationality," 50 *Harvard International Law Journal* 1 (2009). He suggested:

> For many purposes, reserving [nationality's] legal regulation to the internal competence of states remains sound international policy. But at the international level, nationality serves more and more diverse functions in the twenty-first century than at any time in history. Relative to some of these functions, it undoubtedly needs to be regulated by international, not only internal, law. But it is past time to liberate international law in this area from the fiction of the genuine link as a generic, broadly applicable norm regulating the ascription of nationality. Rather, in each field, the form that the international legal regulation of nationality takes today should be responsive to its diverse contemporary functions.

Id. at 60. Is this more relativistic approach a sensible guideline? How would it, for example, be applied in the *Nottebohm Case* itself? Would it lead to more equitable, but less predictable, results?

NOTE: STATE RESPONSIBILITY

There is no easy definition of "state responsibility" in international law—the term is used to describe several related concepts—but it might help to begin with a little history. Professor Brownlie identified seven "strands" to the doctrine, marking a rough chronology: (1) the emergence of the law of nations in the 16th century necessitated, albeit obscurely, a consideration of "the issue of liability"; (2) the close connection between natural law and the law of nations in the 17th and 18th centuries meant that the law of nations turned to "concepts of responsibility for injuries inflicted"; (3) Roman law and national law in the 16th and 17th centuries were concerned with issues of "fault"; (4) just war, a medieval concept, was important to Vittoria in the 16th century, Grotius in the 17th century, and Vattel in the 18th century, all of whom viewed war as a legal procedure to redress "injuries sustained or complained of"; (5) hence followed the doctrine that a denial of justice enabled "the issue of letters of reprisal by princes in cases where their subjects had failed to obtain redress for legal wrongs in the domestic forum of principality"; (6) after the Jay Treaty arbitrations, the United States engaged in 17 more commissions and courts of international arbitration between 1794 and 1871, "which gave rise to an articulate and reasonably sophisticated law of international claims"; and (7) led by the United States, there was increasing reference "to legal bases of claim[s] in [19th-century] diplomatic correspondence." Ian Brownlie, *State Responsibility (Part I)*, at 2–6 (1983).

Much of the modern international law of state responsibility developed from state practice and tribunal decisions relating to states taking up the claims of their citizens for harm done to those citizens by another state; the *Nottebohm Case* is an example, as is *ELSI* in Chapter 5. In the Mavrommatis Palestine Concessions Case, 1924 P.C.I.J., Ser. A, No. 2, the Greek government sued the United Kingdom for denial of contractual rights of a Greek national to operate public works in Jerusalem and Jaffa in the British mandate of Palestine. Answering the British objection that Mavrommatis was merely a private person, the Permanent Court of International Justice held:

> [I]t is true that the dispute was at first between a private person and a State—i.e. between M. Mavrommatis and Great Britain. Subsequently the Greek Government took up the case. The dispute then entered upon a new phase; it entered into the domain of international law, and became a dispute between two States.

Id. at 12. A helpful historical account of the traditional international law of state responsibility is Georg Nolte, "From Dionisio Anzilotti to Roberto Ago: The Classical International Law of State Responsibility and the Traditional Primacy of a Bilateral Conception of Inter-State Relations," 13 *European Journal of International Law* 1083 (2002).

In the latter part of the 20th century, new procedural mechanisms developed allowing individuals to pursue claims at international law in international tribunals against states directly on their own behalf. We have already seen several examples, *e.g., McCann* in Chapter 1, *CMS* in Chapter 2, and the *Texaco/Libya Arbitration* and the *Domingues Case* in Chapter 3. We see more examples later in this chapter.

Issues of state responsibility may also concern general questions of the liability of states, arising in contexts other than cases of injuries to aliens. States may be responsible for violating the territorial integrity of other states, as in the *Rainbow Warrior Case* in Chapter 5, or for unlawfully using force against another state (Chapter 9). States may be

responsible for harm to the environment (Chapter 8, Part C and Chapter 10, Part E) or for breaching their treaty obligations (Chapter 2). And states now may be responsible for violating the rights of their own citizens, *e.g.*, when states breach certain *erga omnes* obligations (Chapter 3) or when they violate international conventions, *e.g.*, the European Human Rights Convention considered in Part D.

Since 1949, the International Law Commission (ILC), a body of experts of various nationalities that works within the United Nations system on the codification and progressive development of international law, has extensively studied basic principles of the law of state responsibility. The task has been politically sensitive. Philip Allott, a notable critic of the ILC's effort, maintained there was a clash between Western international lawyers who viewed the ILC's work as "codifying the obligations of states in the treatment of aliens" and Third World international lawyers who saw it as "a matter of confirming the diplomatic protection of aliens within limits that respected the sovereignty of all states." Philip Allott, "State Responsibility and the Unmasking of International Law," 29 *Harvard International Law Journal* 1, 10 (1988). A political impasse was broken in 1963 when Roberto Ago, the newly selected Rapporteur for the project, decided not to focus on "primary" rules concerning, *e.g.*, protections for aliens. Ago decided instead to set out principles of responsibility at a rather high level of generality. This decision calmed some opposition, and the ILC project continued, culminating in the adoption in 2001 of its Draft Articles on the Responsibility of States for Internationally Wrongful Acts.

The ILC's General Commentary sets out the Commission's basic approach, which is to treat matters of state responsibility at a high level of generality:

> These articles seek to formulate, by way of codification and progressive development, the basic rules of international law concerning the responsibility of States for their internationally wrongful acts. The emphasis is on the secondary rules of State responsibility: that is to say, the general conditions under international law for the State to be considered responsible for wrongful actions or omissions, and the legal consequences which flow therefrom. The articles do not attempt to define the content of international obligations, the breach of which gives rise to responsibility. This is the function of the primary rules, whose codification would involve restating most of substantive customary and conventional international law.

Report of the International Law Commission on the Work of its Fifty-third Session, U.N. Doc. A/56/10 (2001), in 2 *Yearbook of the International Law Commission*, U.N. Doc. A/CN.4/SER.A/2001/Add.1 (Part 2), at 20, 31 (2001). Reviews of this ILC effort appear in "Symposium: The ILC's State

Responsibility Articles," 96 *American Journal of International Law* 773 (2002), and in "Symposium: Assessing the Work of the International Law Commission on State Responsibility," 13 *European Journal of International Law* 1053 (2002).

However, it may well be that the ILC has only added to the confusion surrounding the doctrine of state responsibility. Philip Allott commented: "There is reason to believe that the Commission's long and laborious work on state responsibility is doing serious long-term damage to international law and international society." Allott, *supra*, at 10. For Allott, even trying to define state responsibility has become a "dangerous fiction," both because it assigns legal responsibility to "legal persons known as states" rather than to "human beings" who should be morally responsible and because the ILC's concept of state responsibility leaves too much room for unnecessary argument about "every conceivable case of potential responsibility." *Id.* at 14–15.

Looking, for example, at the *CMS Case* in Chapter 2, does Allott have a point? How exactly is ILC Draft Article 25 on necessity, quoted in *CMS*, to be construed and applied in a situation of harm to an investor? See Robert D. Sloane, "On the Use and Abuse of Necessity in the Law of State Responsibility," 106 *American Journal of International Law* 447 (2012). Is it appropriate to use a "one size fits all" approach for issues of international responsibility? Are the ILC's Draft Articles on State Responsibility sufficiently nuanced to take account of the conflicting interests and values underlying the wide range of situations to which they may apply—not just to injuries to foreign investors, but also to matters as varied as violation of the territorial integrity of other countries (see the *Rainbow Warrior Case* in Chapter 5), injuries to diplomats (the *Diplomatic and Consular Staff Case*, also in Chapter 5), environmental harm, use of force, and human rights? See *id.* at 503. Furthermore, how do we know that each of the ILC's Draft Articles represents a rule of law? For example, the doctrine of necessity originally applied only when a state's existence was threatened, see *id.* at 453–71, and not until 1997 did the International Court of Justice suggest that conditions of necessity set forth in the ILC's formulation "reflect customary international law." Gabčíkovo-Nagymaros Project (Hungary-Slovakia), 1997 I.C.J. 3, 41. Commentators have noted that the "seductive clarity, seeming concreteness, and treatylike form [of the ILC's 2001 Draft Articles on State Responsibility], together with the paucity of other sources on some important issues, may tempt decision makers to apply the articles verbatim, rather than treat them only as evidence of the relevant international rule." Daniel Bodansky & John R. Crook, "Symposium: The ILC's State Responsibility Articles: Introduction and Overview," 96 *American Journal of International Law* 773, 775 (2002) (summarizing the cautionary view of David Caron); see David D. Caron, "The ILC Articles on State Responsibility: The Paradoxical Relationship Between Form and Authority," 96 *American Journal of International Law* 857 (2002).

The ILC's 2001 Draft Articles address general topics in addition to necessity and other "circumstances precluding wrongfulness." Among them are "invocation of the responsibility of a state," relating in part to the issue of standing that arose in *Nottebohm* and below in *Barcelona Traction*, and "countermeasures," a principle we meet in Chapter 9.

We close this Note on State Responsibility by highlighting some traditional issues of state responsibility: attribution, due diligence, and reparation. Attribution raises the question, for whose acts is a state responsible? The case law illustrates the considerable reach of the state responsibility doctrine. The United Kingdom was held responsible in the Union Bridge Co. Case (1924), 6 *Reports of International Arbitral Awards* 138 (2006), for the acts of a low-level railway official in South Africa who wrongly interfered with property belonging to a U.S. citizen in 1900 when the United States was a neutral during the Anglo-Boer War. The ILC, after surveying state practice, judicial decisions, and the writings of publicists, concluded that a state may be held responsible for the acts of all of its organs—executive, legislative, and judicial. *Report of the International Law Commission on the Work of Its Fifty-third Session*, *supra*, at 26 (Article 4), 40–42. Some cases pose difficult questions about whether the actions of individuals or groups may be attributed to a state. In Yeager v. Iran, 17 Iran-U.S. Claims Tribunal Reports 92 (1987), Iran was held responsible for the actions of Revolutionary Guards when they harassed U.S. citizens out of their employment in the country. See also the *Diplomatic and Consular Staff Case* in Chapter 5.

Tribunals sometimes have relied on notions of due diligence to find states responsible for failing to prevent individuals from harming foreign nationals, or for failing to apprehend or punish the perpetrators. For example, in Janes (U.S.A.) v. United Mexican States (1925), 4 *Reports of International Arbitral Awards* 82 (2006), an international arbitral tribunal found Mexico responsible for the failure of Mexican authorities to exercise due diligence in their efforts to apprehend a mine company employee who in 1918 shot and killed Byron Janes, a U.S. citizen who was a superintendent of mines.

Within the law of state responsibility, every breach of a state's legal obligations gives rise to a duty to make full reparation. Reparation may take the form, alternatively or in combination, of restitution, compensation, or satisfaction. As we saw in the *Rainbow Warrior Case* in Chapter 5, satisfaction may include, for example, apology or a declaration that a responsible state engaged in wrongdoing. For discussion of reparation for injury and other consequences of wrongful acts, see, *e.g.*, *Report of the International Law Commission on the Work of Its Fifty-third*

Session, *supra*, at 28–29 (Articles 28–41), 86–116; Christine Gray, *Judicial Remedies in International Law* (1987).

THE BARCELONA TRACTION CASE

Case Concerning the Barcelona Traction, Light and Power Co., Limited, Second Phase, Belgium v. Spain, 1970 I.C.J. 3

8. The Barcelona Traction, Light and Power Company, Limited, is a holding company incorporated in 1911 in Toronto (Canada), where it has its head office. For the purpose of creating and developing an electric power production and distribution system in Catalonia (Spain), it formed a number of operating, financing, and concession-holding subsidiary companies. Three of these companies, whose shares it owned wholly or almost wholly, were incorporated under Canadian law and had their registered offices in Canada (Ebro Irrigation and Power Company, Limited, Catalonian Land Company, Limited and International Utilities Finance Corporation, Limited); the others were incorporated under Spanish law and had their registered offices in Spain. At the time of the outbreak of the Spanish Civil War the group, through its operating subsidiaries, supplied the major part of Catalonia's electricity requirements.

9. According to the Belgian Government, some years after the First World War Barcelona Traction's share capital came to be very largely held by Belgian nationals—natural or juristic persons—and a very high percentage of the shares has since then continuously belonged to Belgian nationals, particularly the Société Internationale d'Energie Hydro-Electrique (Sidro), whose principal shareholder, the Société Financière de Transports et D'Entreprises Industrieles (Sofina), is itself a company in which Belgian interests are preponderant. The fact that large blocks of shares were for certain periods transferred to American nominees, to protect these securities in the event of invasion of Belgian territory during the Second World War, is not, according to the Belgian contention, of any relevance in this connection, as it was Belgian nationals, particularly Sidro, who continued to be the real owners. For a time the shares were vested in a trustee, but the Belgian Government maintains that the trust terminated in 1946. The Spanish Government contends, on the contrary, that the Belgian nationality of the shareholders is not proven and that the trustee or the nominees must be regarded as the true shareholders in the case of the shares concerned.

[Barcelona Traction issued bonds, most in pounds sterling. It serviced the bonds through funds transferred to it from its subsidiaries operating in Spain. Interest payments were disrupted in 1936 by the Spanish Civil War. The Spanish Government refused to allow transfers of foreign currency, and interest payments on the sterling bonds were never resumed. Three Spanish holders of Barcelona Traction bonds obtained a bankruptcy declaration against Barcelona Traction in Spanish court because of its failure to pay interest on the bonds. A bankruptcy receiver seized the assets of Barcelona Traction, Ebro, and a Spanish subsidiary. Barcelona Traction, which did not receive proper notice of the proceedings, failed to enter a plea opposing the bankruptcy judgment, as was required under Spanish law, within the requisite time period. In 1949, trustees in bankruptcy created new shares of the subsidiaries, cancelled the shares located outside Spain, and decreed that the head offices of Ebro and Catalonian Land were in Barcelona rather than Toronto. In 1952, the trustees, operating under court authorization, sold all the shares of the subsidiaries at public auction.]

20. The British Government made representations to the Spanish Government on 23 February 1948 concerning the bankruptcy of Barcelona Traction and the seizure of its assets as well as those of Ebro and Barcelonesa, stating its interest in the situation of the bondholders resident in United Kingdom. It subsequently supported the representations made by the Canadian Government.

21. The Canadian Government made representations to the Spanish Government in a series of diplomatic notes, the first being dated 27 March 1948 and the last 21 April 1952; in addition, approaches were made on a less official level in July 1954 and March 1955. The Canadian Government first complained of the denials of justice said to have been committed in Spain towards Barcelona Traction, Ebro and National Trust, but it subsequently based its complaints more particularly on conduct towards the Ebro company said to be in breach of certain treaty provisions applicable between Spain and Canada. The Spanish Government did not respond to a Canadian proposal for the submission of the dispute to arbitration and the Canadian Government subsequently confined itself, until the time when its interposition entirely ceased, to endeavoring to promote a settlement by agreement between the private groups concerned.

22. The United States Government made representations to the Spanish Government on behalf of Barcelona Traction in a note of 22 July 1949, in support of a note submitted by the Canadian Government the previous day. It subsequently continued its interposition through the diplomatic channel and by other means. Since references were made by the United States Government in these representations to the presence of American interests in Barcelona Traction, the Spanish Government draws the conclusion that, in the light of the customary practice of the United States Government to protect only substantial American investments abroad, the existence must be presumed of such large American interests as to rule out a preponderance of Belgian interests. The Belgian Government considers that the United States Government was motivated by a more general concern to secure equitable treatment of

foreign investments in Spain, and in this context cites, *inter alia*, a note of 5 June 1967 from the United States Government.

23. The Spanish Government having stated in a note of 26 September 1949 that Ebro had not furnished proof as to the origin and genuineness of the bond debts, which justified the refusal of foreign currency transfers, the Belgian and Canadian Governments considered proposing to the Spanish Government the establishment of a tripartite committee to study the question. Before this proposal was made, the Spanish Government suggested in March 1950 the creation of a committee on which, in addition to Spain, only Canada and the United Kingdom would be represented. This proposal was accepted by the United Kingdom and Canadian Governments. The work of the committee led to a joint statement of 11 June 1951 by the three Governments to the effect, *inter alia*, that the attitude of the Spanish administration in not authorizing the transfers of foreign currency was fully justified. The Belgian Government protested against the fact that it had not been invited to nominate an expert to take part in the enquiry, and reserved its rights; in the proceedings before the Court it contended that the joint statement of 1951, which was based on the work of the committee, could not be set up against it, being *res inter alios acta*.

24. The Belgian Government made representations to the Spanish Government on the same day as the Canadian Government, in a note of 27 March 1948. It continued its diplomatic intervention until the rejection by the Spanish Government of a Belgian proposal for submission to arbitration (end of 1951). After the admission of Spain to membership in the United Nations (1955), which, as found by the Court in 1964, rendered operative again the clause of compulsory jurisdiction contained in the 1927 Hispano-Belgian Treaty of Conciliation, Judicial Settlement and Arbitration, the Belgian Government attempted further representations. After the rejection of a proposal for a special agreement, it decided to refer the dispute unilaterally to this Court.

[The Spanish Government objected, *inter alia*, that the Belgian Government "lacked capacity to submit any claim in respect of wrongs done to a Canadian company, even if the shareholders were Belgian." The Court joined that objection to the merits.]

28. * * * The claim is presented on behalf of natural and juristic persons, alleged to be Belgian nationals and shareholders in the Barcelona Traction, Light and Power Company, Limited. The submissions of the Belgian Government make it clear that the object of its Application is reparation for damage allegedly caused to these persons by the conduct, said to be contrary to international law, of various organs of the Spanish State towards that company and various other companies in the same group. * * *

30. The States which the present case principally concerns are Belgium, the national State of the alleged shareholders, Spain, the State whose organs are alleged to have committed the unlawful acts complained of, and Canada, the State under whose law Barcelona Traction was incorporated and in whose territory it has its registered office ("head office" in the terms of the by-laws of Barcelona Traction). * * *

32. In these circumstances it is logical that the Court should first address itself to what was originally presented as the subject-matter of the third preliminary objection: namely the question of the right of Belgium to exercise diplomatic protection of Belgian shareholders in a company which is a juristic entity incorporated in Canada, the measures complained of having been taken in relation not to any Belgian national but to the company itself.

33. When a State admits into its territory foreign investments or foreign nationals, whether natural or juristic persons, it is bound to extend to them the protection of the law and assumes obligations concerning the treatment to be afforded them. These obligations, however, are neither absolute nor unqualified. In particular, an essential distinction should be drawn between the obligations of a State towards the international community as a whole, and those arising vis-à-vis another State in the field of diplomatic protection. By their very nature the former are the concern of all States. In view of the importance of the rights involved, all States can be held to have a legal interest in their protection; they are obligations *erga omnes*.

34. Such obligations derive, for example, in contemporary international law, from the outlawing of acts of aggression, and of genocide, as also from the principles and rules concerning the basic rights of the human person, including protection from slavery and racial discrimination. Some of the corresponding rights of protection have entered into the body of general international law (*Reservations to the Convention on the Prevention and Punishment of the Crime of Genocide, Advisory Opinion, I.C.J. Reports 1951*, p. 23); others are conferred by international instruments of a universal or quasi-universal character.

35. Obligations the performance of which is the subject of diplomatic protection are not of the same category. It cannot be held, when one such obligation in particular is in question, in a specific case, that all States have a legal interest in its observance. * * * In the present case it is therefore essential to establish whether the losses allegedly suffered by Belgian shareholders in Barcelona Traction were the consequence of the violation of obligations of which they were the beneficiaries. In other words: has a right of Belgium been violated on account of its nationals' having suffered infringement of their rights as shareholders in a company not of Belgian nationality?

36. Thus it is the existence or absence of a right, belonging to Belgium and recognized as such by international law, which is decisive for the problem of Belgium's capacity.

> This right is necessarily limited to intervention [by a State] on behalf of its own nationals because, in the absence of a special agreement, it is the bond of nationality between the State and the individual which alone confers upon the State the right of diplomatic protection, and it is as a part of the function of diplomatic protection that the right to take up a claim and to ensure respect for the rules of international law must be envisaged. (*Panevezys-Saldutiskis Railway, Judgment, 1939, P.C.I.J., Series A/B, No. 76,* p. 16.)

It follows that the same question is determinant in respect of Spain's responsibility towards Belgium. Responsibility is the necessary corollary of a right. In the absence of any treaty on the subject between the Parties, this essential issue has to be decided in the light of the general rules of diplomatic protection. * * *

38. In this field international law is called upon to recognize institutions of municipal law that have an important and extensive role in the international field. This does not necessarily imply drawing any analogy between its own institutions and those of municipal law, nor does it amount to making rules of international law dependent upon categories of municipal law. All it means is that international law has had to recognize the corporate entity as an institution created by States in a domain essentially within their domestic jurisdiction. This in turn requires that, whenever legal issues arise concerning the rights of States with regard to the treatment of companies and shareholders, as to which rights international law has not established its own rules, it has to refer to the relevant rules of municipal law. Consequently, in view of the relevance to the present case of the rights of the corporate entity and its shareholders under municipal law, the Court must devote attention to the nature and interrelation of those rights.

39. Seen in historical perspective, the corporate personality represents a development brought about by new and expanding requirements in the economic field, an entity which in particular allows of operation in circumstances which exceed the normal capacity of individuals. As such it has become a powerful factor in the economic life of nations. Of this, municipal law has had to take due account, whence the increasing volume of rules governing the creation and operation of corporate entities, endowed with a specific status. These entities have rights and obligations peculiar to themselves. * * *

41. Municipal law determines the legal situation not only of such limited liability companies but also of those persons who hold shares in them. Separated from the company by numerous barriers, the

shareholder cannot be identified with it. The concept and structure of the company are founded on and determined by a firm distinction between the separate entity of the company and that of the shareholder, each with a distinct set of rights. The separation of property rights as between company and shareholder is an important manifestation of this distinction. So long as the company is in existence the shareholder has no right to the corporate assets.

42. It is a basic characteristic of the corporate structure that the company alone, through its directors or management acting in its name, can take action in respect of matters that are of a corporate character. The underlying justification for this is that, in seeking to serve its own best interests, the company will serve those of the shareholder too. Ordinarily, no individual shareholder can take legal steps, either in the name of the company or in his own name. If the shareholders disagree with the decisions taken on behalf of the company they may, in accordance with its articles or the relevant provisions of the law, change them or replace its officers, or take such action as is provided by law. Thus to protect the company against abuse by its management or the majority of shareholders, several municipal legal systems have vested in shareholders (sometimes a particular number is specified) the right to bring an action for the defence of the company, and conferred upon the minority of shareholders certain rights to guard against decisions affecting the rights of the company vis-à-vis its management or controlling shareholders. Nonetheless the shareholders' rights in relation to the company and its assets remain limited, this being, moreover, a corollary of the limited nature of their liability. * * *

44. Notwithstanding the separate corporate personality, a wrong done to the company frequently causes prejudice to its shareholders. But the mere fact that damage is sustained by both company and shareholder does not imply that both are entitled to claim compensation. * * * Thus whenever a shareholder's interests are harmed by an act done to the company, it is to the latter that he must look to institute appropriate action; for although two separate entities may have suffered from the same wrong, it is only one entity whose rights have been infringed. * * *

47. The situation is different if the act complained of is aimed at the direct rights of the shareholder as such. It is well known that there are rights which municipal law confers upon the latter distinct from those of the company, including the right to any declared dividend, the right to attend and vote at general meetings, the right to share in the residual assets of the company on liquidation. Whenever one of his direct rights is infringed, the shareholder has an independent right of action. * * *

48. The Belgian Government claims that shareholders of Belgian nationality suffered damage in consequence of unlawful acts of the Spanish authorities and, in particular, that the Barcelona Traction

shares, though they did not cease to exist, were emptied of all real economic content. It accordingly contends that the shareholders had an independent right to redress, notwithstanding the fact that the acts complained of were directed against the company as such. Thus the legal issue is reducible to the question of whether it is legitimate to identify an attack on company rights, resulting in damage to shareholders, with the violation of their direct rights. * * *

52. International law may not, in some fields, provide specific rules in particular cases. In the concrete situation, the company against which allegedly unlawful acts were directed is expressly vested with a right, whereas no such right is specifically provided for the shareholder in respect of those acts. Thus the position of the company rests on a positive rule of both municipal and international law. As to the shareholder, while he has certain rights expressly provided for him by municipal law[,] appeal can, in the circumstances of the present case, only be made to the silence of international law. Such silence scarcely admits of interpretation in favour of the shareholder. * * *

56. [Municipal] law, confronted with economic realities, has had to provide protective measures and remedies in the interests of those within the corporate entity as well as of those outside who have dealings with it: the law has recognized that the independent existence of the legal entity cannot be treated as an absolute. It is in this context that the process of "lifting the corporate veil" or "disregarding the legal entity" has been found justified and equitable in certain circumstances. * * *

64. * * * In this connection two particular situations must be studied: the case of the company having ceased to exist and the case of the company's national State lacking capacity to take action on its behalf.

65. As regards the first of these possibilities the Court observes that * * * Barcelona Traction has lost all its assets in Spain, and was placed in receivership in Canada, a receiver and manager having been appointed. [F]rom the economic viewpoint the company has been entirely paralyzed. It has been deprived of all its Spanish sources of income, and the Belgian Government has asserted that the company could no longer find the funds for its legal defence, so that these had to be supplied by the shareholders.

66. It cannot however, be contended that the corporate entity of the company has ceased to exist, or that it has lost its capacity to take corporate action. [A] precarious financial situation cannot be equated with the demise of the corporate entity, which is the hypothesis under consideration: the company's status in law is alone relevant, and not its economic condition[.] Only in the event of the legal demise of the company are the shareholders deprived of the possibility of a remedy available through the company; it is only if they became deprived of all such possibility that an independent right of action for them and their government could arise.

67. In the present case, Barcelona Traction is in receivership in the country of incorporation. Far from implying the demise of the entity or of its rights, this much rather denotes that those rights are preserved for so long as no liquidation has ensued. Though in receivership, the company continues to exist. Moreover, it is a matter of public record that the company's shares were quoted on the stock-market at a recent date.

68. [E]ven if the company is limited in its activity after being placed in receivership, there can be no doubt that it has retained its legal capacity and that the power to exercise it is vested in the manager appointed by the Canadian courts. The Court is thus not confronted with the first hypothesis contemplated in paragraph 64, and need not pronounce upon it.

69. The Court will now turn to the second possibility, that of the lack of capacity of the company's national State to act on its behalf. The first question which must be asked here is whether Canada—the third apex of the triangular relationship—is, in law, the national State of Barcelona Traction.

70. In allocating corporate entities to States for purposes of diplomatic protection, international law is based, but only to a limited extent, on an analogy with the rules governing the nationality of individuals. The traditional rule attributes the right of diplomatic protection of a corporate entity to the State under the laws of which it is incorporated and in whose territory it has its registered office. These two criteria have been confirmed by long practice and by numerous international instruments. This notwithstanding, further or different links are at times said to be required in order that a right of diplomatic protection should exist. Indeed, it has been the practice of some States to give a company incorporated under their law diplomatic protection solely when it has its seat (*siège social*) or management or centre of control in their territory, or when a majority or a substantial proportion of the shares has been owned by nationals of the State concerned. Only then, it has been held, does there exist between the corporation and the State in question a genuine connection of the kind familiar from other branches of international law. However, in the particular field of the diplomatic protection of corporate entities, no absolute test of the "genuine connection" has found general acceptance. Such tests as have been applied are of a relative nature, and sometimes links with one State have had to be weighed against those with another. In this connection reference has been made to the *Nottebohm* case. * * * However, given both the legal and factual aspects of protection in the present case the Court is of the opinion that there can be no analogy with the issues raised or the decision given in that case.

71. In the present case, it is not disputed that the company was incorporated in Canada and has its registered office in that country. The

incorporation of the company under the law of Canada was an act of free choice. Not only did the founders of the company seek its incorporation under Canadian law but it has remained under that law for a period of over 50 years. It has maintained in Canada its registered office, its accounts and its share registers. Board meetings were held there for many years; it has been listed in the records of the Canadian tax authorities. Thus a close and permanent connection has been established, fortified by the passage of over half a century. This connection is in no way weakened by the fact that the company engaged from the very outset in commercial activities outside Canada, for that was its declared object. Barcelona Traction's links with Canada are thus manifold.

72. Furthermore, the Canadian nationality of the company has received general recognition. Prior to the institution of proceedings before the Court, three other governments apart from that of Canada (those of the United Kingdom, the United States and Belgium) made representations concerning the treatment accorded to Barcelona Traction by the Spanish authorities. The United Kingdom Government intervened on behalf of bondholders and of shareholders. Several representations were also made by the United States Government, but not on behalf of the Barcelona Traction company as such. * * *

74. * * * The Belgian Government admitted the Canadian character of the company in the course of the present proceedings. It explicitly stated that Barcelona Traction was a company of neither Spanish nor Belgian nationality but a Canadian company incorporated in Canada. The Belgian Government has even conceded that it was not concerned with the injury suffered by Barcelona Traction itself, since that was Canada's affair.

76. [F]rom 1948 onwards the Canadian Government made to the Spanish Government numerous representations which cannot be viewed otherwise than as the exercise of diplomatic protection in respect of the Barcelona Traction company. Therefore this was not a case where diplomatic protection was refused or remained in the sphere of fiction. It is also clear that over the whole period of its diplomatic activity the Canadian Government proceeded in full knowledge of the Belgian attitude and activity.

77. It is true that at a certain point the Canadian Government ceased to act on behalf of Barcelona Traction, for reasons which have not been fully revealed, though a statement made in a letter of 19 July 1955 by the Canadian Secretary of State for External Affairs suggests that it felt the matter should be settled by means of private negotiations. The Canadian Government has nonetheless retained its capacity to exercise diplomatic protection; no legal impediment has prevented it from doing so: no fact has arisen to render this protection impossible. It has discontinued its action of its own free will.

78. The Court would here observe that, within the limits prescribed by international law, a State may exercise diplomatic protection by whatever means and to whatever extent it thinks fit, for it is its own right that the State is asserting. Should the natural or legal persons on whose behalf it is acting consider that their rights are not adequately protected, they have no remedy in international law. All they can do is to resort to municipal law, if means are available, with a view to furthering their cause or obtaining redress. The municipal legislator may lay upon the State an obligation to protect its citizens abroad, and may also confer upon the national a right to demand the performance of that obligation, and clothe the right with corresponding sanctions. However, all these questions remain within the province of municipal law and do not affect the position internationally.

79. The State must be viewed as the sole judge to decide whether its protection will be granted, to what extent it is granted, and when it will cease. It retains in this respect a discretionary power the exercise of which may be determined by considerations of a political or other nature, unrelated to the particular case. Since the claim of the State is not identical with that of the individual or corporate person whose cause is espoused, the State enjoys complete freedom of action. Whatever the reasons for any change of attitude, the fact cannot in itself constitute a justification for the exercise of diplomatic protection by another government, unless there is some independent and otherwise valid ground for that.

80. This cannot be regarded as amounting to a situation where a violation of law remains without remedy: in short, a legal vacuum. There is no obligation upon the possessors of rights to exercise them. Sometimes no remedy is sought, though rights are infringed. To equate this with the creation of a vacuum would be to equate a right with an obligation. * * *

92. Since the general rule on the subject does not entitle the Belgian Government to put forward a claim in this case, the question remains to be considered whether nonetheless, as the Belgian Government has contended during the proceedings, considerations of equity do not require that it be held to possess a right of protection. [A] theory has been developed to the effect that the State of the shareholders has a right of diplomatic protection when the State whose responsibility is invoked is the national State of the company. Whatever the validity of this theory may be, it is certainly not applicable to the present case, since Spain is not the national State of Barcelona Traction.

93. On the other hand, the Court considers that, in the field of diplomatic protection as in all other fields of international law, it is necessary that the law be applied reasonably. It has been suggested that if in a given case it is not possible to apply the general rule that the right of diplomatic protection of a company belongs to its national State,

considerations of equity might call for the possibility of protection of the shareholders in question by their own national State. This hypothesis does not correspond to the circumstances of the present case.

94. In view, however, of the discretionary nature of diplomatic protection, considerations of equity cannot require more than the possibility for some protector State to intervene, whether it be the national State of the company, by virtue of the general rule mentioned above, or, in a secondary capacity, the national State of the shareholders who claim protection. In this connection, account should also be taken of the practical effects of deducing from considerations of equity any broader right of protection for the national State of the shareholders. It must first of all be observed that it would be difficult on an equitable basis to make distinctions according to any quantitative test: it would seem that the owner of 1 per cent. and the owner of 90 per cent. of the share-capital should have the same possibility of enjoying the benefit of diplomatic protection. The protector State may, of course, be disinclined to take up the case of the single small shareholder, but it could scarcely be denied the right to do so in the name of equitable considerations. In that field, protection by the national State of the shareholders can hardly be graduated according to the absolute or relative size of the shareholding involved.

95. The Belgian Government, it is true, has also contended that as high a proportion as 88 per cent. of the shares in Barcelona Traction belonged to natural or juristic persons of Belgian nationality, and it has used this as an argument for the purpose not only of determining the amount of the damages which it claims, but also of establishing its right of action on behalf of the Belgian shareholders. Nevertheless, this does not alter the Belgian Government's position * * * which implies, in the last analysis, that it might be sufficient for one single share to belong to a national of a given State for the latter to be entitled to exercise its diplomatic protection.

96. The Court considers that the adoption of the theory of diplomatic protection of shareholders as such, by opening the door to competing diplomatic claims, could create an atmosphere of confusion and insecurity in international economic relations. The danger would be all the greater inasmuch as the shares of companies whose activity is international are widely scattered and frequently change hands. It might perhaps be claimed that, if the right of protection belonging to the national States of the shareholders were considered as only secondary to that of the national State of the company, there would be less danger of difficulties of the kind contemplated. However, the Court must state that the essence of a secondary right is that it only comes into existence at the time when the original right ceases to exist. As the right of protection vested in the national State of the company cannot be regarded as extinguished

because it is not exercised, it is not possible to accept the proposition that in case of its non-exercise the national States of the shareholders have a right of protection secondary to that of the national State of the company. * * *

99. [T]he promoters of a company whose operations will be international must take into account the fact that States have, with regard to their nationals, a discretionary power to grant diplomatic protection or to refuse it. When establishing a company in a foreign country, its promoters are normally impelled by particular considerations; it is often a question of tax or other advantages offered by the host State. It does not seem to be in any way inequitable that the advantages thus obtained should be balanced by the risks arising from the fact that the protection of the company and hence of its shareholders is thus entrusted to a State other than the national State of the shareholders.

100. In the present case, it is clear from what has been said above that Barcelona Traction was never reduced to a position of impotence such that it could not have approached its national State, Canada, to ask for its diplomatic protection, and that, as far as appeared to the Court, there was nothing to prevent Canada from continuing to grant its diplomatic protection to Barcelona Traction if it had considered that it should do so.

101. For the above reasons, the Court is not of the opinion that, in the particular circumstances of the present case, *jus standi* is conferred on the Belgian Government by considerations of equity. * * *

102. * * * The Court fully appreciates the importance of the legal problems raised by the allegation, which is at the root of the Belgian claim for reparation, concerning the denials of justice allegedly committed by organs of the Spanish State. However, the possession by the Belgian Government of a right of protection is a prerequisite for the examination of these problems. Since no *jus standi* before the Court has been established, it is not for the Court in its Judgment to pronounce upon any other aspect of the case, on which it should take a decision only if the Belgian Government had a right of protection in respect of its nationals, shareholders in Barcelona Traction.

103. Accordingly,

THE COURT rejects the Belgian Government's claim by fifteen votes to one, twelve votes of the majority being based on the reasons set out in the present Judgment.

NOTES AND QUESTIONS

1. *Expropriation. Barcelona Traction* illustrates some of the problems involved in protecting a foreign branch or subsidiary from discriminatory treatment by the host country, even from out-right expropriation. A foreign

expropriation can be blatant, for example, the expropriation by Libya in the *Texaco/Libya Case* in Chapter 3 or by Cuba of U.S. sugar interests in *Banco Nacional de Cuba v. Sabbatino*, which we explore in Chapter 12. Also see *ELSI* in Chapter 5.

A tale of *Barcelona Traction* put a face to a more subtle expropriation: "Juan March—the former smuggler who in the nineteen-twenties had become one of the richest men in Spain and in the nineteen-thirties had been the chief private financier of the counter-revolution that had put Francisco Franco in power." John Brooks, "Annals of Finance: Privateer—II," *The New Yorker*, May 28, 1979, at 42. Juan March's maneuvers led a court in a small town in Spain to declare the Barcelona Traction Company bankrupt, in 1948, despite the fact that the company had shown net profits of $3.7 million in the previous year and had sufficient cash on hand to pay off its debts. "[L]ater evidence strongly suggested [that] the complainants, the trustees in bankruptcy, and the judge himself were all allies of the man seeking to seize the company, Juan March." John Brooks, "Annals of Finance: Privateer—I," *The New Yorker*, May 21, 1979, at 42, 42–43.

2. *State Protection.* The Barcelona Traction, Light and Power Co., Limited, was incorporated in Canada, as were some, though not all, of its subsidiaries. Its operating assets were, however, virtually all in Spain. What were the advantages and disadvantages of Canadian incorporation for foreign investors? Certainly, one advantage would be the possibility of triggering the diplomatic intercession of the Canadian government in any investment dispute with Spain. How did Canada actually come to the aid of the expropriated company?

May the nationality of a person or a corporation change for the purposes of state protection from the date of the alleged injury to the date of the resolution of the claim? Does permitting such a change encourage legal manipulations? For some of the debate about this issue in the International Law Commission, see Michael J. Matheson, "The Fifty-Eighth Session of the International Law Commission," 101 *American Journal of International Law* 407, 413–21 (2007).

3. *The Jurisdiction of the ICJ.* Unlike Belgium, which could rely on a treaty with Spain providing for the submission of disputes to the International Court of Justice, Canada had no way to bring Spain before the ICJ. See Chapter 5's discussion of grounds for ICJ jurisdiction. Was it any wonder that Spain would not agree to an *ad hoc* case between it and Canada? Can the Belgian suit in the ICJ be viewed as a way to circumvent the obstacle posed by Spain's unwillingness to litigate with Canada? Did the ICJ's judgment take this obstacle of non-consent at all into account?

4. *Obtaining Justice for Barcelona Traction.* Was it equitable for Spain to, first, prevent a solvent Spanish company from paying its obligations denominated in foreign currency, second, through its judicial process declare the company bankrupt, and, third, sell the company's assets to domestic purchasers, thereby depriving the foreign shareholders of their stake in the

company? Besides going to the ICJ, how did the foreign shareholders complain both inside and outside Spain? What other avenues of protest, legal or political, might they have followed? Would Barcelona Traction have been better served with a bilateral treaty protecting foreign investment like that in *ELSI* in Chapter 5?

5. *Genuine Link.* Should the ICJ have adopted a *Nottebohm* genuine link requirement with respect to corporations? Some corporations are only technically incorporated in one state. They may have their headquarters and many operations in a second state, with shareholders and managers domiciled there. Which state should be able to pursue an international claim on the corporation's behalf for injury caused by a third state?

Judge Jessup, who wrote a concurring opinion in *Barcelona Traction*, accepted the genuine link theory, and rejected Great Britain, the United States, and Canada as claimants because their connections with Barcelona Traction were transitory and nominal. Belgium, he found, might have had a "genuine link" with the company because Belgian nationals beneficially owned 88 per cent of the company's shares. Nevertheless, Belgium's claim failed because there was no continuous Belgian interest between the time injury was inflicted and the date Belgium espoused the claim. See 1970 I.C.J. at 200, 203. On the date of injury—which Judge Jessup deemed to be February 12, 1948, the date of the bankruptcy decree—the Belgian shares were still held in trust by a U.S. corporation, which had legal title to and full control of the shares. He therefore concluded that the claim was not Belgian in character on the critical date of injury. Does this suggest a flaw in the use of a "genuine link" approach? Are the problems with allowing all interested states—the state of incorporation and the states of any shareholders—to exercise rights of protection before the Court in fact insoluble?

Note that in some forms of international legal process, no "genuine link" between a state and a private party is required. In European human rights law, for example, states may protect private parties against other states regardless of the nationality of the victim. See Part D below.

6. *The Debate About* Barcelona Traction *Still Rages.* The debate about *Barcelona Traction* and how to determine the nationality of a corporation or other legal entities for purposes of diplomatic protection still rages. In 2003, the International Law Commission, considering a report on the protection of corporations, divided among "different approaches found in common law and civil law systems * * * including concepts of 'genuine link,' *siege social* or domicile, and economic control." Michael J. Matheson & Sara Bickler, "The Fifty-Fifth Session of the International Law Commission," 98 *American Journal of International Law* 317, 318 (2004). The International Tribunal for the Law of the Sea, see Chapter 10, was criticized for rendering "the ITLOS equivalent of the *Barcelona Traction* case" when, in 2001 in the *Grand Prince Case*, 125 *International Law Reports* 272 (2001), it decided that Belize had failed to demonstrate that it was, at the time of its judicial application, the flag state of a fishing vessel seized by France. Vaughn Lowe & Robin

Churchill, "The International Tribunal for the Law of the Sea: Survey for 2001," 17 *International Journal of Marine and Coastal Law* 463, 467 (2002).

7. *Obligations* Erga Omnes. Paragraphs 33 and 34 of the *Barcelona Traction Case* helped introduce obligations *erga omnes* into modern international law. Review the material about this concept in Chapter 3. As you read the rest of this chapter, consider how obligations *erga omnes* relate to the rights and duties of individuals in international law.

B. INDIVIDUALS AS SUBJECTS OF INTERNATIONAL LAW

MARK W. JANIS, "INDIVIDUALS AS SUBJECTS OF INTERNATIONAL LAW"

17 *Cornell International Law Journal* 61 (1984)

Legal positivism has long provided the usual theory for comprehending international law. The typical positivist definition of international law is grounded on a subject-based differentiation between international and municipal rules. Positivism views international law as a set of rules with states as its subjects. Municipal law is thought of as pertaining to individuals who are subjects of a single state. * * *

Before positivism, there was no theoretical insistence that the rules of the law of nations applied only to states. William Blackstone reflected the sentiment of the middle eighteenth century. For Blackstone, individuals and states were both proper subjects of the law of nations. He drew no dividing line between what later came to be called public and private international law. Blackstone distinguished his law of nations from other sorts of law not on the basis of its subjects but because of its sources. He saw the rules of the law of nations as universal, emanating either from natural justice or from the practice of many states. Municipal legal rules, however, emanated from a single state.

In 1789, Jeremy Bentham created the term "international law" in his *Introduction to the Principles of Morals and Legislation*. Bentham defined the new concept as the law which relates to "the mutual transactions between sovereigns as such." He thought that "as to any transactions which may take place between individuals who are subjects of different states, these are regulated by the internal laws, and decided upon by the internal tribunals" of individual sovereign states. Categorizing laws on the basis of "the persons whose conduct is the object of the law," Bentham concluded that international law had only states as its subjects. While categorizing rules on the basis of the subjects to be governed is logical enough, it plainly was wrong for Bentham to assume that international law so defined was equivalent to the traditional law of nations. There were significant differences between the two.

Two early nineteenth century positivists promoted the notion that the individual was not a proper subject of international law. Joseph Story, complaining that no treatises existed on the subject, crafted "private" international law to parallel Bentham's "public" international law. Public international law went to international matters affecting states, while private international law concerned international matters between individuals. John Austin argued that because public international law claimed to regulate matters between sovereign states which as sovereigns could not be regulated by any outside authority, international law was just a form of "positive morality" and not really law at all.

Legal positivism had taken the eighteenth century law of nations, a law common to individuals and states, and transformed it into public and private international law. The former was deemed to apply to states, the latter to individuals. Positivists scorned both sides of the discipline. Public international law was "international" but not really "law." Private international law was "law" but not really "international." Even so insightful a modern positivist as H.L.A. Hart assumed that the essence of international law was that it addressed states. Although Hart saw persuasive similarities between international and municipal law, he accepted uncritically Bentham's subject-based approach to the field.

The positivist definition of international law has had an enormous impact on modern perceptions concerning the individual and international law. With few exceptions, the theory rejects the notion that individuals are proper subjects of public international law. Originally, the subject-based approach was merely Bentham's attempt to provide a rational way of explaining that law may have different subjects: individuals and states. While law can be categorized on the basis of its subjects, in practice the law of nations and international law have concerned more than the legal rights of states. * * *

A prominent example of the failure of positivism to describe adequately the reality of the individual as a subject of international law comes from the time of Bentham himself. In *Respublica v. De Longchamps*, an American municipal court indicted the defendant for assaulting the Consul General of France to the new United States. It was held that the case "must be determined on the principles of the laws of nations." There was, following Blackstone, no doubt that an individual could be guilty of an infraction of the law of nations. De Longchamps, for his violation of the law of nations, was ordered to pay a fine of one hundred French crowns to the Commonwealth of Pennsylvania and to be imprisoned for "a little more" than two years.

Even during the high tide of positivism, the United States Supreme Court had no difficulty seeing individuals as subjects of international law. In *The Paquete Habana*, the United States Navy had seized two Cuban fishing smacks in the opening days of the Spanish-American War. A lower federal court condemned the boats as prizes of war. The masters for themselves, their crews, and their owners, argued before the Supreme Court that peaceful fishing craft were exempt from seizure under the rules of international law. In perhaps the most famous statement ever made about international law by a United States court, the Supreme Court held that "[i]nternational law is part of our law, and must be ascertained and administered by the courts of justice of appropriate jurisdiction, as often as questions of right depending upon it are duly presented for their determination." The Court held that:

> By an ancient usage among civilized nations, beginning centuries ago, and gradually ripening into a rule of international law, coast fishing vessels, pursuing their vocation of catching and bringing in fresh fish, have been recognized as exempt, with their cargoes and crews, from capture as prize of war.

Individuals had a right to rely on this rule as against the United States. The Court ordered the government to pay over the proceeds of the sale of the vessels and their cargoes to the individual claimants.

However inadequately subject-based theory accounted for individual rights and obligations in international law in the eighteenth and nineteenth centuries, positivism has done an even poorer job in explaining the practices of the twentieth century. The trials of Nazi war criminals after the Second World War highlighted the limitations of positivism. Faced with the excesses of a seemingly "civilized" state, those formulating and applying international law discarded any pretense that international rules applied only to state behavior.

The Charter of the International Military Tribunal at Nuremberg explicitly made individuals subject to international rules relating to crimes against peace, war crimes, and crimes against humanity. At Nuremberg and in other war trials, thousands of individuals were tried and convicted; hundreds were executed. Nuremberg re-established plainly and forcefully that the rules of international law should and do apply to individuals. The Nuremberg Tribunal held that "[c]rimes against international law are committed by men, not by abstract entities, and only by punishing individuals who commit such crimes can the provisions of international law be enforced." * * *

All of these examples—*De Longchamps*, *Paquete Habana*, the Nuremberg trials, the European and American human rights systems, the European [Union], and *Filartiga*—demonstrate that a large and important part of international law practice establishes individual rights and obligations and provides international and municipal procedures for enforcing these rights and obligations. The reality of practice contradicts the positivist insistence that international law applies only to relations among states. Insofar as the purpose of theory is to describe reality, the positivist, subject-based theory is inadequate.

Furthermore, restricting international law to states fails a second test by which positivism may be measured—its prescriptive worth. Surely, it is counter to the proper values of international law to prescribe that individuals may not be the subjects of international law. It was, at the time of the Nuremberg trials, politically and morally unacceptable to say that individuals within the German State between 1933 and 1945 were subjects only of German law to whom international rights and obligations could not pertain. In light of the atrocities of Nazi Germany, it would have been reprehensible to leave victims without legal rights and perpetrators without legal obligations. The lesson of Nuremberg is that there are individual international rights and obligations that transcend state boundaries.

Similar considerations pertain to international communities such as the Council of Europe and the European [Union]. These groups have recognized the need to extend certain basic human and economic rights and obligations directly to individuals even though these rights and obligations emanate not from municipal law but from international law. Given the difficulty of addressing some issues, such as human rights and economic development, through municipal legal systems alone, such an extension of international law rules to individuals makes sense. It is impressive that, with the European Human Rights system and the legal system of the [European Union], the Europeans have begun to open international legal processes to individuals.

It is wrong, both in terms of describing reality and in terms of preferential expression, for the theory of international law to hold that individuals are outside the ambit of international law rules. Individuals are and should be within this realm. The positivist notion that individuals are not fit subjects for international law springs not from a description of reality, but from a jurisprudential philosophy most concerned with a subject-based categorization of types of law. In so categorizing international law, the positivist theorists simply discarded the more inclusive notions of the law of nations. Whatever the impact of positivist theory, it never absolutely represented the practice of any time. Today, reality and preference have so revealed the weakness and obsolescence of subject-based theory that the sooner we rid ourselves of it the better. * * *

If we reject the positivist's subject-based definition of international law, then what should be our new concept of the nature of international law? What are the objections to reverting to Blackstone's understanding that the discipline should be characterized by its reliance on universal and multinational sources?

One might say that, so characterized, international law is not properly "inter-national," but this is a rather superficial problem. Bentham supposed international law to be the equivalent of the law of nations, but it was not. So, the fault, if any, in matching the term and the content of international law must rest with its creator. We could easily use the old term, law of nations, and eliminate the linguistic quibble. But the term "international law" is too much in use to abandon it now. I suggest that we continue using the word international but understand "nation" to mean not only the national state but also the individuals who are the nationals of state. This meaning is both true to the word "nation" and finally makes sense of Bentham's equivalence between the law of nations and international law.

NOTES AND QUESTIONS

1. *Individuals, International Law, and U.S. Law.* U.S. law has been relatively favorable over time in recognizing and prescribing the international rights and duties of individuals—*e.g.*, *De Longchamps*, *Smith*, *Paquete Habana*, *Asakura*, *Filartiga*, *Sosa*. Why did U.S. law more or less resist the restrictive notions of 19th and early 20th-century legal positivism? Was it because U.S. lawyers and judges were common lawyers, moving along in the conservative stream of case law and judicial precedent, while their European counterparts were civil lawyers, more likely to be affected by the changing currents of legal philosophy and academic doctrine? Whatever the cause, the readiness of the classical 18th-century law of nations to acknowledge individuals as subjects of its law was better preserved in U.S. law than in civil law, which had to rediscover individual rights and duties in modern international law. Note how important U.S. precedent on this matter was in the Nuremberg judgment below.

2. *Individual Rights and State Sovereignty.* Are individual rights at international law a challenge to the sovereignty of states? We saw in the Treaty of Westphalia in Chapter 2 that one of the cornerstones of the Westphalian system of international relations was the principle that sovereign states should be free of outside interference in regulating their own citizens in their own territories. Individual rights at international law, of course, permeate state sovereignty, permitting outsiders to evaluate how well a state does protecting the rights of individuals, citizens as well as aliens, in its own territory. The challenge is particularly acute with respect to international human rights law, the topic to which we now turn.

C. INTERNATIONAL HUMAN RIGHTS LAW

The concept that individuals can be subjects, as well as objects, of international law logically divides into individual *rights* at international law and individual *duties*. The next two parts primarily explore individual human rights—Part C looks at international human rights law in general, and Part D addresses the particularly successful European regional international human rights legal system. Part E then turns to individual duties with an introduction to international criminal law. Note how much progress has been made over the last seven decades in establishing individuals as true subjects of international law.

Part C's Section 1 is a short introduction to the antecedents of international human rights law in municipal (domestic) human rights law. Section 2 examines the Nuremberg Trial, which helped inaugurate modern international human rights law in the 1940's. Section 3 discusses the evolution of international human rights law, using a sample case, *Damian Thomas*, before the U.N. Human Rights Committee to show some of the strengths and weaknesses of general international human rights law under the auspices of the United Nations.

1. HUMAN RIGHTS AND MUNICIPAL LAW

The principle that law should protect the rights of individuals against the abuses of governments can at least be dated back to John Locke's *Two Treatises of Government,* published in 1690. Locke believed that human rights, not governments, came first in the natural order of things. Locke's prose celebrated the rights to life, liberty, and property of the English under the limited government won by the Glorious Revolution of 1688. The particular advantages of England's unwritten constitution in the 18th century, especially the separation and balance of powers among the executive, legislative and judicial branches of government, were elaborated and popularized by the French political philosopher, Montesquieu, in the *Spirit of the Laws* in 1748. In 1762, the revolutionary potential of human rights—"Man is born free; and everywhere he is in chains"—was proclaimed by Jean Jacques Rousseau. Democratic revolutions soon followed in America and throughout Europe.

On July 4, 1776, the American Declaration of Independence issued from Philadelphia. The intellectual influences of Locke, Montesquieu, and Rousseau on Thomas Jefferson's document were plain to see. In a ringing affirmation of human rights and the duty of governments to protect them, the delegates of the 13 United States of America proclaimed:

> We hold these truths to be self-evident, that all men are created equal, that they are endowed by their Creator with certain unalienable Rights, that among these are Life, Liberty and the pursuit of Happiness. That to secure these rights, Governments are instituted among Men, deriving their just powers from the consent of the governed. That whenever any Form of Government becomes destructive of these ends, it is the Right of the People to alter or to abolish it, and to institute new Government, laying its foundation on such principles and organizing its powers in such form, as to them shall seem most likely to effect their Safety and Happiness.

The last decades of the 18th century were a good time for political affirmations of human rights. As the constitutions of the newly independent American states were drafted in 1776, bills of rights enumerating specific rights were directly incorporated therein, even, as for Virginia, making up its first part. The fashion of bills of rights spread to Europe. Jefferson wrote James Madison from Paris on January 12, 1789: "Everybody here is trying their hands at forming declarations of rights." Thomas Jefferson, Letter of Jan. 12, 1789, 14 *The Papers of Thomas Jefferson* 436, 437 (Julian P. Boyd ed. 1958). Jefferson continued to play his part, reading and critiquing Lafayette's draft of what on August 27, 1789, a few weeks after the fall of the Bastille, would become the National Assembly's Declaration of the Rights of Man and Citizen. Thomas Jefferson, Letter of June 3, 1789, to Rabaut de St. Etienne, 15 *id.* at 166. The French Declaration's indebtedness to Rousseau's philosophy and Philadelphia's practice was widely acknowledged.

On September 25, 1789, less than a month after the promulgation of the French Declaration, the first Congress of the new Federal Government of the United States of America proposed the first ten amendments to the United States Constitution. These amendments, which are reproduced in the Appendix, came into force following the tenth state ratification (Virginia's) on December 15, 1791.

Many of the rights enunciated in the French Declaration and the U.S. Bill of Rights are similar. For example, Article 11 of the French Declaration reads: "Free communication of ideas and opinions is one of the most precious of the rights of man. Consequently, every citizen may speak, write, and print freely subject to responsibility for the abuse of such liberty in the cases determined by law;" while Article 1 of the U.S. Bill of Rights provides: "Congress shall make no law * * * abridging the freedom of speech, or of the press[.]"

Close in kinship, the American Declaration of Independence, the French Declaration of the Rights of Man and Citizen, and the U.S. Bill of Rights make up the 18th-century documentary foundation on which two centuries of legal protection of human rights in municipal law have been built. Constitutional guarantees of human rights are now widespread. In many countries, such as the United Kingdom, the principal responsibility for protecting human rights has ordinarily been vested in a democratically elected legislature. In others, such as the United States, that role has been assumed by the courts.

2. THE NUREMBERG JUDGMENT

The idea that human rights could be protected by international, as well as municipal, law developed slowly. Throughout the 19th and early 20th centuries, the prevalent conception of state sovereignty proved a stumbling block to efforts to impose international legal obligations on states to protect individuals. Instead, the doctrine of state responsibility examined above in *Nottebohm* and *Barcelona Traction* provided partial protection, but only so long as the claim of a foreign national injured by a state was effectively espoused at the international level by that individual's national state. However, neither the doctrine of state sovereignty nor its counterpart, the doctrine of state protection, could shield individuals from abuses committed by their own governments. In practice, this fault excluded international review of most instances of governmental violations of human rights.

The turning point for this traditional approach in international law came in the 1940s in the midst of the extreme human rights abuses in war-torn Europe. In the Moscow Declaration of German Atrocities of October 30, 1943, the United States, the United Kingdom, France, and the Soviet Union declared that individual Germans would be held responsible for their violations of international law. U.N. Doc. A/CN.4/5, at 87–88 (1949). In the August 8, 1945, Charter of the International Military Tribunal, the same four Allies established the Nuremberg Tribunal.

THE NUREMBERG JUDGMENT

The United States of America, the French Republic, the United Kingdom of Great Britain and Northern Ireland, and the Union of Soviet Socialist Republics v. Hermann Wilhelm Goering, Rudolf Hess, Joachim von Ribbentrop [and 24 Other Named Defendants], 6 F.R.D. 69 (1946)

The Court:

On the 8th August 1945, the Government of the United Kingdom of Great Britain and Northern Ireland, the Government of the United States of America, the Provisional Government of the French Republic, and the Government of the Union of Soviet Socialist Republics entered into an agreement establishing this Tribunal for the trial of War Criminals whose offences have no particular geographical location. In accordance with Article 5, the following Governments of the United Nations have expressed their adherence to the Agreement:

Greece, Denmark, Yugoslavia, the Netherlands,

Czechoslovakia, Poland, Belgium, Ethiopia, Australia,

Honduras, Norway, Panama, Luxemburg, Haiti, New Zealand,

India, Venezuela, Uruguay, and Paraguay.

By the Charter annexed to the Agreement, the constitution, jurisdiction and functions of the Tribunal were defined.

The Tribunal was invested with power to try and punish persons who had committed crimes against peace, war crimes and crimes against humanity as defined in the Charter.

The Charter also provided that at the trial of any individual member of any group or organization the Tribunal may declare (in connection with any act of which the individual may be convicted) that the group or organization of which the individual was a member was a criminal organization.

In Berlin, on the 18th October 1945, in accordance with Article 14 of the Charter, an indictment was lodged against the defendants named in the caption above, who had been designated by the Committee of the Chief Prosecutors of the signatory Powers as major war criminals.

A copy of the indictment in the German language was served upon each defendant in custody at least thirty days before the Trial opened.

This indictment charges the defendants with crimes against peace by the planning, preparation, initiation and waging of wars of aggression, which were also wars in violation of international treaties, agreements and assurances; with war crimes; and with crimes against humanity. The defendants are also charged with participating in the formulation or execution of a common plan or conspiracy to commit all these crimes. The Tribunal was further asked by the Prosecution to declare all the named groups or organizations to be criminal within the meaning of the Charter.
* * *

In accordance with Articles 16 and 23 of the Charter, Counsel were either chosen by the defendants in custody themselves, or at their request were appointed by the Tribunal. In his absence the Tribunal appointed Counsel for the defendant Bormann, and also assigned Counsel to represent the named groups or organizations.

The trial which was conducted in four languages—English, Russian, French and German—began on the 20th November 1945, and pleas of "Not Guilty" were made by all the defendants except Bormann.

The hearing of evidence and the speeches of Counsel concluded on 31st August 1946.

403 open sessions of the Tribunal have been held. 33 witnesses gave evidence orally for the Prosecution against the individual defendants, and 61 witnesses, in addition to 19 of the defendants, gave evidence for the Defense.

A further 143 witnesses gave evidence for the Defense by means of written answers to interrogatories.

The Tribunal appointed Commissioners to hear evidence relating to the organizations, and 101 witnesses were heard for the Defense before the Commissioners, and 1,809 affidavits from other witnesses were submitted. Six reports were also submitted, summarizing the contents of a great number of further affidavits.

38,000 affidavits signed by 155,000 people were submitted on behalf of the Political Leaders, 136,213 on behalf of the SS, 10,000 on behalf of the SA, 7,000 on behalf of the SD, 3,000 on behalf of the General Staff and OKW, and 2,000 on behalf of the Gestapo.

The Tribunal itself heard 22 witnesses for the organizations. The documents tendered in evidence for the prosecution of the individual defendants and the organizations numbered several thousands. A complete stenographic record of everything said in court has been made, as well as an electrical recording of all the proceedings. * * *

Much of the evidence presented to the Tribunal on behalf of the Prosecution was documentary evidence, captured by the Allied armies in German army headquarters, Government buildings, and elsewhere. Some of the documents were found in salt mines, buried in the ground, hidden behind false walls and in other places thought to be secure from discovery. The case, therefore against the defendants rests in a large measure on documents of their own making, the authenticity of which has not been challenged except in one or two cases.

THE CHARTER PROVISIONS

The individual defendants are indicted under Article 6 of the Charter, which is as follows:

> Article 6. The Tribunal established by the Agreement referred to in Article 1 hereof for the trial and punishment of the major war criminals of the European Axis countries shall have the power to try and punish persons who, acting in the interests of the European Axis countries, whether as individuals or as members of organizations, committed any of the following crimes.
>
> The following acts, or any of them, are crimes coming within the jurisdiction of the Tribunal for which there shall be individual responsibility;
>
> (a) Crimes Against Peace: namely planning, preparation, initiation or waging a war of aggression, or a war in violation of international treaties, agreements or assurances, or participation in a common plan or conspiracy for the accomplishment of any of the foregoing:
>
> (b) War Crimes: namely, violations of the laws or customs of war. Such violations shall include, but not be limited to, murder, ill-treatment or deportation to slave labor or for any other purpose of civilian population of or in occupied territory, murder or ill-treatment of prisoners of war or persons on the seas, killing of hostages, plunder of public or private property, wanton destruction of cities, towns or villages, or devastation not justified by military necessity;

(c) Crimes Against Humanity: namely, murder, extermination, enslavement, deportation, and other inhumane acts committed against any civilian population, before or during the war, or persecutions on political, racial or religious grounds in execution of or in connection with any crime within the jurisdiction of the Tribunal, whether or not in violation of the domestic law of the country where perpetrated.

Leaders, organizers, instigators and accomplices participating in the formulation or execution of a common plan or conspiracy to commit any of the foregoing crimes are responsible for all acts performed by any persons in execution of such plan. * * *

THE LAW OF THE CHARTER

The jurisdiction of the Tribunal is defined in the Agreement and Charter, and the crimes coming within the jurisdiction of the Tribunal, for which there shall be individual responsibility, are set out in Article 6. The law of the Charter is decisive, and binding upon the Tribunal.

The making of the Charter was the exercise of the sovereign legislative power by the countries to which the German Reich unconditionally surrendered; and the undoubted right of these countries to legislate for the occupied territories has been recognized by the civilized world. The Charter is not an arbitrary exercise of power on the part of the victorious nations, but in the view of the Tribunal, as will be shown, it is the expression of international law existing at the time of its creation; and to that extent is itself a contribution to international law.

The Signatory Powers created this Tribunal, defined the law it was to administer, and made regulations for the proper conduct of the Trial. In doing so, they have done together what any one of them might have done singly; for it is not to be doubted that any nation has the right thus to set up special courts to administer law. With regard to the constitution of the court, all that the defendants are entitled to ask is to receive a fair trial on the facts and the law.

The Charter makes the planning or waging of a war of aggression or a war in violation of international treaties a crime; and it is therefore not strictly necessary to consider whether and to what extent aggressive war was a crime before the execution of the London Agreement. But in view of the great importance of the questions of law involved, the Tribunal has heard full argument from the Prosecution and the Defense, and will express its view on the matter.

It was urged on behalf of the defendants that a fundamental principle of all law—international and domestic—is that there can be no punishment of crime without a pre-existing law. *Nullum crimen sine lege, nulla poena sine lege.* It was submitted that *ex post facto* punishment is abhorrent to the law of all civilized nations, that no sovereign power had made aggressive war a crime at the time the alleged criminal acts were committed, that no statute had defined aggressive war, that no penalty had been fixed for its commission, and no court had been created to try and punish offenders.

In the first place, it is to be observed that the maxim *nullum crimen sine lege* is not a limitation of sovereignty, but is in general a principle of justice. To assert that it is unjust to punish those who in defiance of treaties and assurances have attacked neighboring states without warning is obviously untrue, for in such circumstances the attacker must know that he is doing wrong, and so far from it being unjust to punish him, it would be unjust if his wrong were allowed to go unpunished. Occupying the positions they did in the government of Germany, the defendants, or at least some of them must have known of the treaties signed by Germany, outlawing recourse to war for the settlement of international disputes; they must have known that they were acting in defiance of all international law when in complete deliberation they carried out their designs of invasion and aggression. On this view of the case alone, it would appear that the maxim has no application to the present facts.

This view is strongly reinforced by a consideration of the state of international law in 1939, so far as aggressive war is concerned. The General Treaty for the Renunciation of War of August 27th 1928, more generally known as the Pact of Paris or the Kellogg-Briand Pact, was binding on sixty-three nations, including Germany, Italy and Japan at the outbreak of war in 1939. In the preamble, the signatories declared that they were:—

> Deeply sensible of their solemn duty to promote the welfare of mankind; persuaded that the time has come when a frank renunciation of war as an instrument of national policy should be made to the end that the peaceful and friendly relations now existing between their peoples should be perpetuated . . . all changes in their relations with one another should be sought only be pacific means . . . thus uniting civilised nations of the world in a common renunciation of war as an instrument of their national policy . . .

The first two articles are as follows:

> Article I: the High Contracting Parties solemnly declare in the names of their respective peoples that they condemn recourse to war for the solution of international controversies and renounce it as an instrument of national policy in their relations to one another.

> Article II: The High Contracting Parties agree that the settlement or solution of all disputes or conflicts of whatever nature or of whatever origin they may be, which may arrive among them, shall never be sought except by pacific means.

The question is, what was the legal effect of this pact? The nations who signed the pact or adhered to it unconditionally condemned recourse to war for the future as an instrument of policy, and expressly renounced it. After the signing of the pact, any nation resorting to war as an instrument of national policy breaks the pact. In the opinion of the Tribunal, the solemn renunciation of war as an instrument of national policy necessarily involves the proposition that such a war is illegal in international law and that those who plan and wage such a war, with its inevitable and terrible consequences, are committing a crime in so doing. War for the solution of international controversies undertaken as an instrument of national policy certainly includes a war of aggression, and such a war is therefore outlawed by the pact. As Mr. Henry L. Stimson, then Secretary of State of the United States, said in 1932:

> War between nations was renounced by the signatories of the Kellogg-Briand Treaty. This means that it has become throughout practically the entire world . . . an illegal thing. Hereafter, when nations engage in armed conflict, either one or both of them must be termed violators of this general treaty law. . . . We denounce them as law breakers.

But it is argued that the pact does not expressly enact that such wars are crimes, or set up courts to try those who make such wars. To that extent the same is true with regard to the laws of war contained in the Hague Convention. The Hague Convention of 1907 prohibited resort to certain methods of waging war. These included the inhumane treatment of prisoners, the employment of poisoned weapons, the improper use of flags of truce, and similar matters. Many of these prohibitions had been enforced long before the date of the Convention; but since 1907 they have certainly been crimes, punishable as offences against the laws of war; yet the Hague Convention nowhere designates such practices as criminal, nor is any sentence prescribed, nor any mention made of a court to try and punish offenders. For many years past, however, military tribunals have tried and punished individuals guilty of violating the rules of land warfare laid down by this Convention. In the opinion of the Tribunal, those who wage aggressive war are doing that which is equally illegal, and of much greater moment than a breach of one of the rules of the Hague Convention. In interpreting the words of the Pact, it must be remembered that international law is not the product of an international legislature, and that such international agreements as the Pact of Paris have to deal with general principles of law, and not with administrative matters of procedure. The law of war is to be found not only in treaties, but in the customs and practices of states which gradually obtained universal recognition and from the general principles of justice applied by jurists and practised by military courts. This law is not static, but by continual adaptation follows the needs of a changing world. Indeed, in many cases treaties do no more than express and define for more accurate reference the principles of law already existing. * * *

It was submitted that international law is concerned with the actions of sovereign states, and provides no punishment for individuals; and further, that where the act in question is an act of state, those who carry it out are not personally responsible, but are protected by the doctrine of the sovereignty of the State. In the opinion of the Tribunal, both these submissions must be rejected. That international law imposes duties and liabilities upon individuals as well as upon states has long been recognized. In the recent case of Ex parte Quirin (1942, 317 U.S. 1), before the Supreme Court of the United States, persons were charged during the war with landing in the United States for purposes of spying and sabotage. The late Chief Justice Stone, speaking for the Court, said:

> From the very beginning of its history this Court has applied the law of war as including that part of the law of nations which prescribes for the conduct of war, the status, rights and duties of enemy nations as well as enemy individuals.

He went on to give a list of cases tried by the Courts, where individual offenders were charged with offences against the laws of nations, and particularly the laws of war. Many other authorities could be cited, but enough has been said to show that individuals can be punished for violations of international law. Crimes against international law are committed by men, not by abstract entities, and only by punishing individuals who commit such crimes can the provisions of international law be enforced.

The provisions of Article 228 of the Treaty of Versailles * * * illustrate and enforce this view of individual responsibility.

The principle of international law, which under certain circumstances, protects the representatives of a state, cannot be applied to acts which are condemned as criminal by international law. The authors of these acts cannot shelter themselves behind their official position in order to be freed from punishment in appropriate proceedings. Article 7 of the Charter expressly declares:

> The official position of defendants, whether as heads of state, or responsible officials in government departments, shall not be considered as freeing them from responsibility, or mitigating punishment.

On the other hand the very essence of the Charter is that individuals have international duties which transcend the national obligations of obedience imposed by the individual state. He who violates the laws of war cannot obtain immunity while acting in pursuance of the authority of the state if the state in authorizing action moves outside its competence under International Law.

It was also submitted on behalf of most of these defendants that in doing what they did they were acting under the orders of Hitler, and therefore cannot be held responsible for the acts committed by them in carrying out these orders. The Charter specifically provides in Article 3:

> The fact that the defendant acted pursuant to orders of his Government or of a superior shall not free him from responsibility, but may be considered in mitigation of punishment.

The provisions of this article are in conformity with the law of all nations. That a soldier was ordered to kill or torture in violation of the international law of war has never been recognized as a defense to such acts of brutality, though, as the Charter here provides, the order may be urged in mitigation of the punishment. The true test, which is found in varying degrees in the criminal law of most nations, is not the existence of the order, but whether moral choice was in fact possible.

NOTES AND QUESTIONS

1. *The Nuremberg Judgment.* The 1946 judgment of the Nuremberg Tribunal confirmed the classical norm that individuals, as well as states, were proper subjects of international law. The Nuremberg judgment has come to stand not only for the moral and political imperative that individuals be made legally responsible for violations of international law but also for the proposition that individual human rights ought to be protected at the level of international law. In the words of Professor Henry King, one of the prosecuting attorneys at Nuremberg: "Nuremberg was designed to change the anarchic context in which the nations and peoples of the world related to one another." Henry T. King, "The Meaning of Nuremberg," 30 *Case Western Journal of International Law* 143, 143–44 (1998).

As the Judgment emphasized, punishment of individuals for war crimes by military tribunals was long-standing. For U.S. practice, see John Fabian Witt, *Lincoln's Code: The Laws of War in American History* (2012). Is this kind of legal argument more a matter of general principles of law than of customary international law? See both in Chapter 3.

Though some, like George Kennan, lamented the effect of Nuremberg on the United States' post-war relations with Germany, see George F. Kennan, *Memoirs 1925–1950*, at 175 (1967), nowadays most applaud the Tribunal's work. The very term "Nuremberg" has become a shorthand for both modern international criminal law and international human rights law. Professor Sadat described what she called the "Nuremberg principles":

> Following the Second World War, the United States promoted the view that criminal trials of the Nazi leaders should be held and the Nuremberg trials were the result. The so-called Nuremberg principles that resulted from the Charter of the Nuremberg Tribunal and its judgment were adopted by the General Assembly immediately upon the establishment of the United Nations. They eschew collective responsibility in favor of individual criminal responsibility; provide that no human being (even a head of state or other responsible government official) is above the law with respect to the most serious crimes of concern to humanity as a whole: war crimes, crimes against humanity, and the crime of aggressive war; and that reliance upon internal law is no defense to a crime for which an individual may have responsibility under international law. The corollary to the notion that individuals may have duties under international law is that they have rights thereunder. Thus, the Nuremberg principles provided a foundation for the emergence of international human rights law.

Leila Nadya Sadat, "Shattering the Nuremberg Consensus: U.S. Rendition Policy and International Criminal Law," *Yale Journal of International Affairs,* Winter 2008, at 65, 66–67. For additional background on the creation of the Nuremberg Tribunal, the trials there, and their lasting significance, see Theodor Meron & Jean Galbraith, "Nuremberg and Its Legacy," in *International Law Stories* 13 (John E. Noyes, Laura A. Dickinson & Mark W. Janis eds. 2007).

2. *Human Rights and the U.N. Charter.* In the Preamble of the 1945 Charter of the United Nations, the People of the United Nations reaffirm their "faith in fundamental human rights." Charter Article 55 calls on the Organization to promote "universal respect for, and observance of, human rights and fundamental freedoms for all without distinction as to race, sex, language, or religion." We saw that these norms were held not self-executing in U.S. law by the California Supreme Court in *Sei Fujii* in Chapter 4.

3. *Human Rights After Nuremberg.* The emergence of international human rights law in the mid-20th century has been described as the most "radical development in the whole history of international law" since it so speedily reestablished individuals as well as states as subjects of international law. John P. Humphrey, "The Revolution in the International Law of Human Rights," 4 *Human Rights* 205, 208 (1975). Is it any surprise that it was the experience of Nazi-occupied Europe that destroyed the moral foundations of the positivist theory that international law and legal process should not be available to individuals?

However rapid the emergence of the rules of international human rights law, the development of effective international human rights legal process has been much more gradual. Need there necessarily be a greater political consensus to create effective legal machinery than to promulgate rules of substantive law? In cases where there is no formal international legal process, *i.e.*, no court or executive to enforce international human rights law, how is international human rights law to be made efficacious? What is the influence of public pronouncements by critical governments or private groups? How can such pronouncements be made more forceful, *e.g.*, by economic or political sanctions? As we see below, some progress has been made in creating enforcement mechanisms at the level of the United Nations. More progress, however, is to be seen in regional human rights systems, especially in Europe, explored in Part D.

3. HUMAN RIGHTS AND THE UNITED NATIONS

The transformation of the substantive norms of human rights law from national to international law was made complete in 1948 in the Universal Declaration of Human Rights, where the U.N. General Assembly followed in the footsteps of Jefferson and the drafters of the French Declaration of the Rights of Man and Citizen and the U.S. Bill of Rights. The Universal Declaration, reproduced in the Appendix, is generally said to enumerate human rights norms at the level of international law. Among the sources of international law surveyed in Chapters 2 and 3, which would most strongly support the assertion that the various articles in the Universal Declaration constitute international legal norms? Is the fact that the norms are embodied in a General Assembly resolution that was adopted unanimously (the vote was 48 states in favor, none against, and 8 abstaining) itself sufficient? Does every article of the Universal Declaration have an equal claim to be an international legal norm?

The system of human rights law at the United Nations has evolved from a preoccupation with the development of norms to an emphasis on procedures for implementing those norms, an evolution traced in the first excerpt in this section. Following this excerpt is an opinion in the *Damian Thomas Case* brought to one of the forums available at the United Nations for pursuing complaints of human rights abuses, along with discussion of the efficacy of the U.N. human rights system.

THOMAS BUERGENTHAL, "THE NORMATIVE AND INSTITUTIONAL EVOLUTION OF INTERNATIONAL HUMAN RIGHTS"

19 *Human Rights Quarterly* 703 (1997)

I. INTRODUCTION * * *

The starting point of this analysis is the Charter of the United Nations (Charter), which laid the foundation of modern international human rights law. While it is true that international law recognized some forms of international human rights protection prior to the [1945] entry into force of the UN Charter, "the internationalization of human rights and the humanizaton of international law" begins with the establishment of the United Nations. The Charter ushered in a worldwide movement in which states, intergovernmental, and nongovernmental organizations are the principal players in an ongoing struggle over the role the international community should play in promoting and protecting human rights. * * *

II. STAGE ONE: THE NORMATIVE FOUNDATION

The first stage in this process begins with the entry into force of the UN Charter and continues at least through the adoption in 1966 of the International Covenants on Human Rights. By this time, the Universal Declaration of Human Rights had been adopted by the United Nations, as had the Genocide Convention and the Convention on the Elimination of All Forms of Racial Discrimination, to mention only the principal human rights instruments. During this same period, the European Convention on Human Rights entered into force; the Organization of American States proclaimed the American Declaration on the Rights and Duties of Man; and UNESCO [the United Nations Educational, Social and Cultural Organization] and the ILO [International Labor Organization], respectively, promulgated the Convention against Discrimination in Education and the Convention Concerning Discrimination in Respect of Employment and Occupation.

This period, in short, witnessed the normative consolidation of international human rights law. It is true, of course, that this process continues to this day. It is equally true, however, that in these first 20 years following the establishment of the UN the process had become irreversible. * * *

III. STAGE TWO: INSTITUTION BUILDING

The second stage in the evolution of international human rights begins in the late 1960s and continues for the next fifteen to twenty years. This is the era of institution building. During these years we find two distinct developments taking place within the UN framework. The first focused on the nature or scope of the human rights obligations that Articles 55 and 56 imposed on the Member States. Only after this issue had been resolved could the UN begin to create institutions and mechanisms to enforce their obligations. * * *

The period here under consideration also saw the emergence and consolidation of universal and regional treaty-based institutions for the protection of human rights. In the mid to late 1970s the UN Human Rights Committee and the Committee on the Elimination of Racial Discrimination (CERD) came into being with the entry into force of the International Covenant on Civil and Political Rights and the International Convention on the Elimination of All Forms of Racial Discrimination. The entry into force in 1978 of the American Convention on Human Rights brought with it the establishment of the Inter-

American Commission and Court of Human Rights. Although the European Convention of Human Rights came into effect as early as 1953, it was not until the late 1960s and early 1970s that the institutions it created, particularly the Court, began to play an important role in the implementation of the Convention. In 1978, moreover, UNESCO adopted a special mechanism for dealing with human rights violations falling within its sphere of competence. ILO institutions for dealing with human rights issues predate those referred to above, whereas those established under the African Charter on Human and Peoples' Rights did not come into being until after the entry into force of that instrument in 1986. * * *

IV. STAGE THREE: IMPLEMENTATION IN THE POST COLD WAR ERA

The institutions referred to in the preceding section did not come fully into their own until the mid to late 1980s when they could begin to focus on adopting effective measures to ensure state compliance with their international obligations. This process continues to this day. It is one thing to establish institutions on the international plane to promote and protect human rights, it is quite another to give them the authority and tools they need to achieve their objective. States are more likely to agree to the creation of human rights institutions than to cooperate with these institutions when they or their allies are charged with human rights violations. It must be recognized, however, that the political factors which contributed in large measure to the creation of human rights institutions in the first place—the ideas that inspired the international human rights movement and captured the imagination of mankind—make it increasingly more difficult for states not to comply with their human rights obligations.

During the period here under consideration, the world underwent dramatic changes to which the human rights revolution contributed significantly and from which the revolution also benefitted significantly. The end of the Cold War freed many nations in Europe from Communist rule, permitting them to embark on a process of democratic transformation. What is more, it liberated international efforts to promote human rights from the debilitating ideological conflicts and political sloganeering of the past. These developments have enabled the UN to focus increasingly on obstacles to the implementation of human rights. * * *

In some regions of the world considerable progress has * * * been made in the implementation of human rights. During the period here under consideration the human rights system established under the European Convention of Human Rights gained institutional maturity. In fact, by the time the Soviet Union collapsed, the European Court of Human Rights had for all practical purposes become the constitutional court of Western Europe. The recent accession to the European

Convention of the former Eastern and Central European allies of the Soviet Union as well as some of the new Soviet Republics has the potential of transforming the Court into the constitutional court of all Europe. This process may take longer, however, than one might assume at first glance because the newer members face many serious political, economic and social problems that few, if any, of the Western European members confronted when they first joined the Convention system.

The inter-American human rights system, which came into being later than its European counterpart, was unable for many years to play a major role in improving the human rights situation in the Americas. For decades the region was in the grips of oppressive regimes that engaged in massive violations of human rights behind a veil of impunity sustained at the height of the Cold War by superpower protection. With the onset of the process of transition to democracy in that region, which began in the mid-1980s, the inter-American human rights system could finally focus on implementation. The judgments of the Inter-American Court of Human Rights in the late 1980s, exposing the heinous practice of disappearances for all the world to see, opened the way for the Court and the Inter-American Commission on Human Rights to play a much more active role in protecting human rights in the Americas. Unlike Western Europe, however, the Americas is a region still very much in the process of development, with serious social and economic problems, poverty, and corruption. Moreover, there are some countries where the military, while ostensibly no longer in power, remains a real force to be reckoned with. Transition to democracy has a long way to go in the region, despite the impressive progress made in the past few years. It is clear, though, that those who believed in the 1960s and 1970s that oppressive military regimes were the only obstacle to the effective protection of human rights and genuine democracy in the region proved to be only partially right. By the same token, it is probably true that the process of democratization is now irreversible. Moreover, while the human rights problems of the region cannot be solved by merely substituting a freely elected government for a military regime, the inter-American human rights system has in recent years been able to point to some real successes.

The same cannot be said as yet of the African human rights system. It still faces many of the problems that afflicted the inter-American system two decades ago as far as repressive regimes are concerned and even greater economic, social, and political obstacles. The poverty, corruption, underdevelopment, disease, tribal conflicts, and many other scourges that affect African society today make the task of the African Commission on Human and Peoples' Rights extremely difficult. The liberation of South Africa from apartheid—in itself probably the greatest victory to date of the human rights revolution—and that country's emergence as the foremost democratic nation on the African continent, as well as some promising trends towards democracy in the region, cannot in the long run do anything but strengthen the role of the African Commission.

The African Commission, the human rights organs of the inter-American system, and the treaty bodies established within the UN framework all suffer from a very serious lack of financial resources. This fact has very harmful consequences for their ability to discharge their responsibilities. The real tragedy here is that at precisely the moment in history when conditions are, on the whole, more favorable than ever before for the implementation of human rights on the global and regional levels, the institutions assigned the task of promoting and supervising this process are for financial reasons not able to do so satisfactorily. Here it should be said that while resources are scarce everywhere, the real reasons for at least some budget-cutting activities affecting human rights bodies have more to do with a desire of certain governments to limit the power of these institutions than with genuine budgetary concerns. Given the contemporary human rights revolution, it is politically easier today to cut the budget of a human rights body by pointing to a lack of funds than by suggesting that its activities are not important.

DAMIAN THOMAS V. JAMAICA

U.N. Human Rights Committee Communication No. 800/1998,
U.N. Doc. CCPR/65/D/800/1998,
7 *International Human Rights Report* 326 (2000)

The Human Rights Committee, established under article 28 of the International Covenant on Civil and Political Rights, [m]eeting on 8 April 1999 [a]dopts the following:

VIEWS UNDER ARTICLE 5, PARAGRAPH 4, OF THE OPTIONAL PROTOCOL

1. The author of the communication is Damian Thomas, a Jamaican minor (16 years old at the time of submission of the communication), currently at St. Catherine's District Prison, Jamaica. The author was born on 21 November 1980. * * * He is not represented by counsel.

2.1. The author was arrested on 9 May 1995 and convicted on 3 May 1996. On 5 May 1996 he was placed in the General Penitentiary, Kingston.

2.2. By a further submission the author informed the Committee that he was 15 years old when he was arrested. He was brought before the Gun Court for two murders, where only one of those allegations was sent to trial. He was tried before the Home Circuit Court, convicted and sentenced to be detained during her Majesty's pleasure. * * *

3. While at the General Penitentiary, the author wrote to the Commissioner for Prisons requesting that he be removed from the adult prison. It appears that someone within the prison system, one Mr.

Dawkins, informed him that he was to be moved to a juvenile institution. However, when the author was moved it was to St. Catherine District Prison, once again among adults. The author claims that he is being held in a prison with adult inmates in violation of the Covenant.

4.1. By submission dated 23 March 1998, the State party contends that the circumstances under which the author is being held are not clear. It requests that the author provide information on the offence for which he was convicted, as well as any other relevant information, e.g. how old was he at the time of his sentence and whether the judicial authorities were made aware of his age.

4.2. It undertakes to investigate the circumstances of the author's detention and would advise the Committee as soon as the results were available.

5.1. The author in a letter dated 11 May 1998, informed the Committee that he was tried at the Gun Court for two murders, that he lost his appeal, being sentenced to detention during her Majesty's pleasure. He informs the Committee that he was born on 21 November 1980, and was only 15 at the time of his arrest.

5.2. He further submits that since he has been in detention both at the General Penitentiary and at St. Catherine District Prison he has been systematically beaten by warders. He refers to several incidents; one on 8 November 1996, where he was kicked by several warders; Mr. Norris, Mr. Dwight and Sergeant Brown. On 20 March 1997 a warder called Mr. Waugh boxed him round the ears and threatened him. On 16 December 1997 he was thumped on the back and beaten by a Mr. Campbell and a corporal Ferguson while taking him to the overseer's office. They told the overseer that they were taking him to the hospital allegedly because he had lice. He was never taken to the hospital but rather he was beaten and kicked about by the warders and a warder called Mr. Mcdermatt cut off his Rastafarian hair. On 20 July 1997, he was beaten by several warders including a Mr. Gardener allegedly because the author was from the same area where the warder's aunt had been killed.

5.3. These new allegations were transmitted to the State party with a request that any comments be submitted to the Committee before 30 January 1999, since the case would be put before the Committee at its 65th session. To date, 25 March 1999, no response has been received from the State party. * * *

6.3. With regard to the author's alleged ill-treatment at the General Penitentiary and St. Catherine District Prison, the Committee notes that the author has made precise allegations that he was brutalized by several wardens on 8 November 1996; 20 March 1997; 16 December 1997 and 20 July 1997. The Committee also notes that the author has complained to the prison authorities. His claims have not been refuted by the State party, which has promised to investigate these, but has failed to forward to the Committee its findings, eleven months after promising to do so, in spite of a reminder sent on 30 October 1998. The Committee recalls that a State party is under the obligation to investigate seriously allegations of violations of the Covenant made under the Optional Protocol. However, in the present case the Committee notes that these allegations were transmitted to the State party after Jamaica's denunciation of the Optional Protocol came into force on 23 January 1998. Consequently, the Committee considers that these claims are inadmissible under article 1 of the Optional Protocol.

6.4. With respect to the remaining allegations the Committee observes that the State party has not raised objections to the admissibility of the communication. It further observes that, given the name, date of birth, date of arrest and of conviction and the location in 1998 in St. Catherine's District Prison, all in relation to the author, the State party should have no difficulty in identifying the details relevant to this matter. Accordingly the Committee decides that the remaining allegations are admissible and proceeds, without further delay, to an examination of the substance of the author's claims, in the light of all the information made available to it by the parties, as required by article 5, paragraph 1 of the Optional Protocol.

6.5. With respect to the non segregation of the author from adult prisoners both at the General Penitentiary and at St. Catherine's District Prison, the Committee once again regrets the State party's lack of cooperation in this matter. The Committee considers that it is incumbent upon the State party where a complaint such as this is submitted to it in respect of a serving prisoner, to verify whether that prisoner is, or has at any relevant stage, been a minor. The Committee notes from the information before it and not refuted by the State party, that the author was born in November 1980, making him seventeen years old when his communication was submitted to the Committee and 15, when he was sentenced. The Committee considers that the State party has failed to discharge its obligations under the Covenant in respect of Damian Thomas, in so far as he has been kept among adult prisoners when still a minor, and consequently, finds that there has been a violation of article 10, paragraphs 2 and 3.

6.6. The Committee further observes that the facts as described in the present case, also constitute a violation of article 24 of the Covenant, since the State party has failed to provide to Damian Thomas such measures of protection as are required by his status as a minor.

7. The Human Rights Committee, acting under article 5, paragraph 4, of the Optional Protocol to the International Covenant on Civil and Political Rights, is of the view that the facts before it disclose a violation of articles 10, paragraphs 2 and 3, and 24 of the Covenant.

8. In accordance with article 2, paragraph 3(a), of the Covenant, the State party is under an obligation to provide Mr. Thomas with an effective remedy, entailing his placement in a juvenile institution, separated from adult prisoners if Jamaican legislation authorises it, and including compensation for his non segregation from adult prisoners while a minor. The State party is under an obligation to ensure that similar violations do not occur in the future.

9. On becoming a State party to the Optional Protocol, Jamaica recognized the competence of the Committee to determine whether there has been a violation of the Covenant or not. This case was submitted for consideration before Jamaica's denunciation of the Optional Protocol became effective on 23 January 1998; in accordance with article 12(2) of the Optional Protocol it is subject to the continued application of the Optional Protocol. Pursuant to article 2 of the Covenant, the State party has undertaken to ensure to all individuals within its territory or subject to its jurisdiction the rights recognized in the Covenant and to provide an effective and enforceable remedy in case a violation has been established. The Committee wishes to receive from the State party, within 90 days, information about the measures taken to give effect to the Committee's views.

NATALIA SCHIFFRIN, "JAMAICA WITHDRAWS THE RIGHT OF INDIVIDUAL PETITION UNDER THE INTERNATIONAL COVENANT ON CIVIL AND POLITICAL RIGHTS"

92 *American Journal of International Law* 563 (1998)

In October 1997, a little-noticed event took place at the United Nations that may roll back the international legal protection of human rights. Jamaica became the first country to denounce the Optional Protocol to the International Covenant on Civil and Political Rights (ICCPR), and thus withdrew the right of individual petition to the UN Human Rights Committee (Committee). Although it is provided for under the Protocol's Article 12, no state has previously made such a denunciation.

Jamaica's action runs counter to the steady growth in ratifications of the Optional Protocol, expanding from twenty-two nations (including Jamaica) on the day it entered into force of March 23, 1976, to ninety-two by the time of denunciation this past fall. In the more than twenty years since the Committee has been rendering decisions (or "adopting views") under the Optional Protocol, hundreds of decisions have been issued concerning a vast array of human rights issues across the globe.

Jamaica's decision is particularly troublesome because, it is feared in some quarters, this action may serve as a catalyst for other countries in the Commonwealth Caribbean and elsewhere to follow suit. It is no secret that several other nations have been considering the same move. * * *

The background to Jamaica's unprecedented move is complex. The story begins in the late 1980's, when lawyers representing death row litigants in Jamaica started making petitions to the Committee as an integral part of a campaign against the use of capital punishment. This legal maneuver contributed to the success of that campaign; though the death penalty is considered to enjoy wide public support in Jamaica, there have been no executions on the island since 1988.

The first case against Jamaica before the Committee was filed in 1984, the 165th case received by that body. At that time, communications had been filed against only a few states, with Uruguay and Canada receiving the most complaints. In the late 1980s and 1990s, an ever-growing number of cases were filed against Jamaica concerning the death penalty, eventually rendering that state one of the most frequent respondents before the Committee. Many of the Committee's most important judgments in the field of liberty and security of the person have been adopted in relation to Jamaica, exposing various serious human rights violations left unremedied by the domestic courts. In terms of the death penalty, the Committee has principally ruled against it on the grounds that execution of an individual when the Covenant's fair trial guarantees (contained in Article 14) have not been met violates the Covenant's guarantee of the right to life (contained in Article 6). Without review by the Committee, for example, individuals in Jamaica could be sentenced to death without the benefit of counsel present at trial, with only a few moments to consult counsel before trial, and without a written judgment upon which to base an appeal.

At first, the strategy of taking cases to the Committee worked as well in Jamaica as it does in most countries. In other words, it was hard to say exactly how effective the strategy was. Since its inception, enforcement of the Covenant, like that of all international human rights agreements, has been problematic. Some countries file the required periodic state reports years late,[10] while others never file at all.[11] The individual petition system is considered to be one of the most effective enforcement mechanisms within the international human rights legal framework, and yet even it boasts a state compliance rate of only about 25 percent. Jamaica, like most states, does not readily admit when an action is taken directly in response to a decision by the Committee, but, on the other hand, Jamaica has never executed an individual where the Committee has recommended that it should not.[13] * * *

---

[10] For example, Cyprus, Mali, Jamaica and Vietnam have all been half a dozen years late or more in the submission of their state reports to the Human Rights Committee.

[11] For example, Equatorial Guinea, Gabon and Somalia.

[13] Unfortunately, this cannot be said of two of Jamaica's Commonwealth Caribbean neighbors. Trinidad and Tobago executed Glen Ashby in 1994 despite a request by the Committee under Rule 86 of its Rules of Procedure for an interim stay of execution pending consideration of Mr. Ashby's application to the Committee. Shortly after acceding to the Optional Protocol, Guyana executed Rockliffe Ross in 1996 under similar circumstances.

Resuming capital punishment in a manner consistent with Jamaica's legal obligations is no easy task. Jamaica's decision to pull out of the Optional Protocol will not of itself achieve this goal, while it will potentially cause great harm. Jamaica's action has taken away an important avenue of redress and may encourage other states to follow suit. Until now, the individual petitions procedure has worked at least to some extent because it represents an attempt by state parties to participate in a growing community of nations trying to create and adhere to a universal set of human rights standards, irrespective of whether it suits those nations on a case-by-case basis. The system is only as strong as its members. Its effectiveness will be significantly reduced if countries pull out whenever they perceive the Committee as posing an obstacle to domestic practice. When Jamaica withdrew from the Optional Protocol, it was thus, in the words of the Human Rights Committee member Christine Chanet of France, a sad day for human rights and a sad day for the community of nations that adhere to the Covenant.

To be sure, Jamaica remains a party to the Covenant itself, and to that end the rights enshrined in it are still guaranteed to its people. But without the right of individual petition, enforcement will be even more difficult than it has been thus far. And, clearly, without the Optional Protocol, an important avenue of redress has been shut off. Its absence will be felt especially by the residents of death row in St. Catherine's district prison.

NOTES AND QUESTIONS

1. *Human Rights Norms, Institutions, and Implementation.* Professor Buergenthal, from 2000 to 2010 the U.S. judge on the International Court of Justice, divided the history of international human rights law into three eras: norm-building between 1945 and 1966, institution-building between 1966 and 1989, and implementation-building since 1989. Of course, not all international human rights systems have developed at the same pace. On the one hand, the most effective system of all, European human rights law, explored in Section D below, was effectively implementing the European Human Rights Convention at least by the 1970s. On the other hand, most U.N.-based human rights systems, the Human Rights Committee being just one example, seem to be still well short of effective implementation.

2. *Accounting for the Weakness of the U.N. Human Rights System.* Professor Mutua has criticized "official international human rights bodies such as the Human Rights Committee [as] basically weak and ineffectual." Makau wa Mutua, "Looking Past the Human Rights Committee: An Argument for De-Marginalizing Enforcement," 4 *Buffalo Human Rights Law Review* 211 (1998). The causes are many, including poor funding, "organizational and bureaucratic constraints," and a choice of "the UN institutional culture which emphasizes compromise, consensus and

diplomacy" rather than a disinterested "application of norm to fact." *Id.* at 223.

The Human Rights Committee set up under the International Covenant on Civil and Political Rights (ICCPR) is not the only U.N. human rights body to be criticized for its lack of efficacy. A 53-member U.N. Commission on Human Rights, established in 1946 to hear and respond to human rights complaints, had been roundly condemned, and in 2006 the U.N. General Assembly replaced it with a new 47-member Human Rights Council. See U.N. Doc. A/60/251 (2006); http://www.ohchr.org/en/hrbodies/hrc/Pages/HRCIndex.aspx (last visited Dec. 8, 2013). Although immediately acknowledged to be imperfect, the new Human Rights Council, with its system of "Universal Periodic Review" of every country's human rights practices, was hoped to be "transparent, fair and impartial." Scott R. Lyons, "The New United Nations Human Rights Council," 10 *ASIL Insights,* Issue 7 (2006). However, within a year the Council was criticized for "again fail[ing] to address many egregious human-rights abuses around the world," even declining to condemn Sudan for its conduct in Darfur. "Human Rights: Bad Counsel: The UN Adrift on Human Rights," *The Economist*, Apr. 7, 2007, at 58. The Council on Foreign Relations reported in 2009:

> Despite a high-profile effort to reform the world's top human rights panel, the new UN Human Rights Council continues to face the same criticisms that plagued its predecessor, the Commission on Human Rights. Experts say bloc voting, loose membership standards, and bias against Israel are keeping the two-year-old council from living up to expectations as a responsible watchdog over global human rights norms. It is earning a failing grade from a broad range of groups, including human rights advocates, international law experts, and democracy activists. Experts say the Council's condemnation of the human rights situations in Darfur, Myanmar, and the Democratic Republic of Congo are steps in the right direction, and there is also a broad expectation that a new U.S. administration in Washington could change the contentious relationship between the Council and the United States, which is not a member. But in a year during which the world marked the sixtieth anniversary of the Universal Declaration of Human Rights, many see the new rights council as a stain on the UN's reputation.

Lauren Vriens, "Troubles Plague UN Human Rights Council," Council on Foreign Relations, *Backgrounder*, May 13, 2009, at 1. The United States was elected to the Council in 2009, but in 2010, seven of the 14 countries elected to the Human Rights Council—Libya, Angola, Malaysia, Thailand, Uganda, Mauritania, and Qatar—were criticized by human rights organizations for poor human rights records. All 14 ran unopposed. Edith M. Lederer, "UN Elects Rights Violators to Human Rights Council," Associated Press, May 13, 2010, http://www.boston.com (last visited Dec. 8, 2013). Does the fault really rest with the United Nations? Can a more or less universal institution be expected to surmount the ideological and cultural divides among states with at all as much success as regional institutions such as the Council of Europe and the European Court of Human Rights explored below?

3. *A Confusion of Norms and Institutions.* Is it fair to say that the United Nations has too often substituted words and bureaucracies for action on human rights? There are "literally several hundred" U.N. human rights treaties and, besides the U.N. Human Rights Committee, tens of U.N. institutions charged with monitoring human rights. See Gudmundur Alfredsson, "The United Nations and Human Rights," 25 *International Journal of Legal Information* 17 (1997). For discussion of possible steps to improve the effectiveness of U.N. human rights efforts, see Report of the High-Level Panel on Threats, Challenges and Change, *A More Secure World: Our Shared Responsibility* ¶¶ 82–91, U.N. Doc. A/59/565 (2004). For more on the origins and structure of the United Nations, see Chapter 8, Part A.

4. *Shaming.* Unlike some of the regional human rights systems, most U.N.-based bodies lack any enforcement power; their decisions are not even legally binding. The U.N. Human Rights Committee can only hope to "shame" a government with bad publicity. See Markus Schmidt, "Treaty-Based Human Rights Complaints Procedures in the UN—Remedy or Mirage for Victims of Human Rights Violations?," 1998 *Human Rights*, No. 2, at 13, 15–16. "Shaming" can, of course, still sometimes be an important goal in human rights litigation, as we saw in *Filartiga* in Chapter 1. When might a government be more or less susceptible to pressure from an adverse opinion of an international body such as the U.N. Human Rights Committee?

What has Jamaica lost by repudiating the right of individual petition to the U.N. Human Rights Committee? Will criticism, such as that from Natalia Schiffrin, Senior Legal Officer at the International Centre for the Legal Protection of Human Rights (Interights), a non-governmental organization based in London, have an international economic or political impact? Will it encourage domestic dissatisfaction with government policies?

5. *The Efficacy of International Human Rights Treaties.* Critics from different ideological perspectives now wonder whether international human rights treaties necessarily encourage better governmental behavior. Professor Hathaway has documented how frequently governments that have ratified such treaties still flout their obligations. Oona Hathaway, "Do Human Rights Treaties Make a Difference?," 111 *Yale Law Journal* 1935 (2002). However, Professor Hathaway has been challenged:

> Public international law desperately needs work like Hathaway's—studies that connect the law to events on the ground. There is a real danger that, absent such efforts, international lawyers will act in ways that have negligible or perverse effects on the injustices they seek to combat. But because the stakes are so high, it is important that we make accurate connections between what the law does and what happens on the ground. Those connections cannot be ascertained through the research design that Hathaway employed. Perhaps the answer is to discard this type of

> statistical modelling and adopt a softer kind of empiricism, something more sociological than economic. Perhaps it's something else. We certainly have not given up hope for statistical approaches in this area, as there are many devices that can be employed to help conduct such studies. In any event, this much is clear: we still do not satisfactorily know the full effects of human rights treaties. Absent such knowledge, the best assumption remains the conventional one: human rights treaties advance the cause they seek to promote, not the other way around.

Ryan Goodman & Derek Jinks, "Measuring the Effects of Human Rights Treaties," 14 *European Journal of International Law* 171, 182–83 (2003).

6. *Regional Protection of International Human Rights*. Besides the universal international human rights law of the United Nations and the protection of human rights in domestic legal systems, there are, as Professor Buergenthal noted, several regional international human rights stories to be told. For example, the African Charter on Human and Peoples' Rights and an African Commission on Human and Peoples' Rights date from 1981. In 2006, a new 11-judge African Court on Human and Peoples' Rights based in Arusha, Tanzania, was sworn in. Scott Lyons, "The African Court on Human and Peoples' Rights," 10 *ASIL Insights*, Issue 24 (2006). However, Professor Heyns has concluded that the "African regional human rights system is faced with almost insurmountable challenges: massive violations on a continent of immense diversity, where a tradition of domestic compliance with human rights norms is still to be established." Christof Heyns, "The African Regional Human Rights System: The African Charter," 108 *Penn State Law Review* 679, 701 (2004).

There is somewhat more regional success in the Americas where there are two overlapping regional international human rights systems, one based on the Charter of the Organization of American States, the other created by the American Convention on Human Rights. See Mark Weston Janis, *International Law* 287–94 (6th ed. 2012). However, the workload and efficacy of the Inter-American Court of Human Rights, which sits in Costa Rica, by no means rival that of the European Court of Human Rights, which we examine below. *Id.* at 293. Some scholars have doubted that the Inter-American system actually does much to improve the protection of human rights in the Americas. James L. Cavallaro & Stephanie Erin Brewer, "Reevaluating Regional Human Rights Litigation in the Twenty-First Century: The Case of the Inter-American Court," 102 *American Journal of International Law* 768 (2008). Another wondered why domestic courts are so reluctant to respect the judgments of the Inter-American Court. Alexandra Huneeus, "Courts Resisting Courts: Lessons from the Inter-American Court's Struggle to Enforce Human Rights," 44 *Cornell International Law Journal* 493 (2011).

Why do states choose to participate in international organizations protecting human rights? How far are governments willing to bend state sovereignty to permit international supervision of domestic human rights practices? A comprehensive review of many academic studies concluded that state participation is motivated by diverse reasons, sometimes because of a deep commitment to human rights, but othertimes to "lock in" domestic reforms, or to "reduce pressure for real change." In most cases the explanation comes from very differing domestic political processes. Emilie M. Hafner-Burton, "International Regimes for Human Rights," 15 *Annual Review of Political Science* 265, 271 (2012).

7. *The United States and Human Rights Law.* Sadly, the United States has never itself joined the Inter-American Court of Human Rights. An American Bar Association group, the World Justice Project, concluded in 2009 that though "the courts and other legal institutions in the U.S. generally meet a high standard in most of 15 key measures of adherence to the rule of law," the United States "lags behind its peer nations in its adherence to international rule of law principles." James Podgers, "Survey Says—Study Measures Adherence to Rule of Law by U.S. and Other Nations," 96 *ABA Journal,* Jan. 2010, at 61. American ambivalence toward international law is long-standing, see Mark Weston Janis, *America and the Law of Nations 1776–1939* (2010), but some problems are of recent origin. Writing in 2005, Professor Ignatieff lamented that "[t]o date, the Bush Administration has paid no political price [in domestic politics] for its flouting of the Geneva Convention and other treaties." Michael Ignatieff, "America the Mercurial," *Legal Affairs*, Mar./Apr. 2005, at 68. The Obama administration promised to do better. In the words of Secretary of State Hillary Clinton: "Our human rights agenda for the 21st century is to make human rights a human reality." Hillary Rodham Clinton, "Remarks on the Human Rights Agenda for the 21st Century," Address on Dec. 14, 2009, http://www.state.gov (last visited Dec. 8, 2013).

We have already seen some of the ways in which U.S. courts do and do not apply international human rights law—*Filartiga, Asakura, Sei Fujii, Medellín, Sosa*, and *Kiobel*. Judge Fletcher of the U.S. Ninth Circuit Court of Appeals, after reviewing the judicial record, concluded:

> International human rights, as we understand them today, are a recent creation, and the Court's decision in *Sosa* is but a way station in what promises to be a long journey. To some slight degree *Sosa* has clarified the law of human rights in American courts, but it has left us with more questions than answers. The answers to those questions may be suggested by nineteenth century jurisprudential categories. But those questions can be fully and properly answered only by adapting our jurisprudence to the modern world, just as those who came before us adapted their jurisprudence to what was, for them, their modern world.

William A. Fletcher, "International Human Rights in American Courts," 93 *Virginia Law Review* 653, 672–73 (2007).

Why is it that democratic, as well as totalitarian, governments sometimes skirt international human rights law? How much depends on the regard in which international human rights law is held domestically, *e.g.*, by the general public, the political leaders, the lawyers and judges?

D. EUROPEAN HUMAN RIGHTS LAW

The proceedings at Nuremberg had special meaning for those who had witnessed the awful abuses of human rights in Nazi-occupied Europe. For the Europeans pressing for political union, human rights became an important priority. The European Convention for the Protection of Human Rights and Fundamental Freedoms was signed on November 4, 1950, and came into force on September 3, 1953. Merely as a European bill of rights, the Convention provided little exceptional on the international scene. The heart of the Convention rested in what were, until 1998, two optional clauses, the crucial aspects of the system's enforcement machinery: Article 25 (now mandatory Article 34) gave individuals as well as states the right to petition the European human rights system, and Article 46 (now mandatory Article 32) gave the European Court of Human Rights jurisdiction to hear and try cases already reported on by a Commission to which petitions were submitted.

Historically, the Europeans were familiar with bills of rights, but they were unfamiliar with judicial enforcement of those rights. Domestically, they trusted the legislative and executive branches of government rather than the judiciary to protect fundamental freedoms. Only over time have they been willing to empower international institutions to safeguard the Convention's rights.

Nowadays, the European Court of Human Rights in Strasbourg, France, is the most successful of all the international human rights courts or commissions. Its jurisdiction extends to 47 states, about one-quarter of all the world's nations: Albania, Andorra, Armenia, Austria, Azerbaijan, Belgium, Bosnia and Herzegovina, Bulgaria, Croatia, Cyprus, Czech Republic, Denmark, Estonia, Finland, France, Georgia, Germany, Greece, Hungary, Iceland, Ireland, Italy, Latvia, Liechtenstein, Lithuania, Luxembourg, Malta, Moldova, Monaco, Montenegro, Netherlands, Norway, Poland, Portugal, Romania, Russia, San Marino, Serbia, Slovakia, Slovenia, Spain, Sweden, Switzerland, The former Yugoslav Republic of Macedonia, Turkey, Ukraine, and the United Kingdom.

Looking at the history of the system, it can be said that each of the six decades of the European Convention on Human Rights has told its own distinctive tale. The 1950s spoke of institutional development but had little actual case law about which to boast. The Convention was signed in 1950 and, ratified by eight states, came into force in 1953. In 1955 the Commission was granted the right to hear individual petitions against consenting states. The Court was constituted in 1958. Only on June 2, 1956, was an application declared admissible by the Commission (by Greece against the United Kingdom respecting Cyprus). Altogether only five applications (two government, three individual) were deemed admissible in the 1950s. No case was heard by the Court.

The 1960s saw both modest triumph and disquieting disobedience. There were some 54 applications admitted by the Commission (five government and 49 individual), and the Court rendered its first ten decisions in seven cases. However, in 1969, following adverse reports by the Commission, Greece withdrew from the Council of Europe and denounced the European Convention on Human Rights. This reduced the total membership in the system from 16 to 15 at the end of the decade. The number of states accepting the right of individual petition had grown to 11. The same number (though not always the same states) accepted the jurisdiction of the Court.

The 1970s showed a solid maturation of the system. Greece rejoined the Convention in 1974. By the end of the decade some 20 countries belonged, 14 accepting individual petition and 17 consenting to the jurisdiction of the Court. One hundred sixty-eight applications (five government, 163 individual) were deemed admissible by the Commission. Twenty-four cases were decided by the Court.

The 1980s witnessed an explosion of activity under the Convention. As of December 31, 1989, 22 states were parties to the Convention. All had accepted the right of individual petition and the jurisdiction of the Court. Four hundred and fifty-five applications were deemed admissible by the Commission. One hundred and sixty-nine cases were decided by the Court.

The 1990s evidenced the continuing growth of the system. As of the end of the decade, 41 countries had ratified the European Human Rights Convention and thus accept the Convention's now mandatory right of individual petition and jurisdiction of the Court. New member states included many nations from the former Communist bloc: Hungary, Bulgaria, Poland, Romania, Slovenia, the Czech Republic, Slovakia, Slovenia, Lithuania, Estonia, Albania, The former Yugoslav Republic of Macedonia, Ukraine, Latvia, Moldova, Croatia, Russia, and Georgia. In the first eight years of the decade (1990–1997), the Commission admitted 3,491 applications. Between 1990 and 1999, the Court delivered 995 judgments, more in those ten years than in the previous four decades. On November 1, 1998, the Convention was significantly amended by Protocol No. 11, which not only transformed the two critical optional clauses into mandatory provisions, but merged the part-time European Commission and Court of Human Rights into a single full-time European Court of Human Rights.

In the new millenium, the European Court of Human Rights has become a real work horse. As of September 2013, the Strasbourg judges are charged to review the practice of some 47 member states of the European Convention on Human Rights and Fundamental Freedoms. In the ten years 2000–2009, the Strasbourg Court received more than 330,000 applications, roughly 33,000 each year. During 2000–2009, the Court rendered more than 11,000 judgments, an average of more than one thousand judgments every year. Altogether, the Strasbourg Court delivered more than 90 per cent of all its judgments in that one decade than in the previous 50 years. Lately, the Court has joined more applications and hence delivered fewer judgments: 1,499 in 2010, 1,157 in 2011, and 1,099 in 2012, all still impressive totals. As of September 30, 2013, the Court had more than 111,000 applications pending. See http://www.echr.coe.int (last visited Nov. 2, 2013).

The story of the success of the European human rights law system is the story of what were the two optional clauses. In 1950, it may have seemed that opponents had "gutted" the Convention by making the right of individual petition and the jurisdiction of the Court optional, but, over time, the nations "opted into" both procedures. What strategies did the Commission and the Court use to induce states to accept the optional clauses and to maintain their acceptances? Did the example of some European governments accepting the optional clauses make it difficult for other European governments to opt out? Were European governments influenced by human rights abuses in other parts of the world, and did they seek to underline their own commitments to human rights? See Mark W. Janis, Richard S. Kay & Anthony W. Bradley, *European Human Rights Law* 12–23, 103–16 (3d ed. 2008).

THE SUNDAY TIMES CASE

European Court of Human Rights,
Judgment of 26 April 1979, Series A, Vol. 30

8. Between 1958 and 1961 Distillers Company (Biochemicals) Limited ("Distillers") manufactured and marketed under license in the United Kingdom drugs containing an ingredient initially developed in the Federal Republic of Germany and known as thalidomide. The drugs were prescribed as sedatives for, in particular, expectant mothers. In 1961 a number of women who had taken the drugs during pregnancy gave birth to children suffering from severe deformities; in the course of time there were some 250 such births in all. Distillers withdrew all drugs containing thalidomide from the British market in November of the same year. * * *

10. [B]y 1971, three hundred and eighty-nine claims in all were pending against Distillers. Apart from a statement of claim in one case and a defence delivered in 1969, no further steps were taken in those actions where writs had been issued. Distillers had announced in February 1968 that they would provide a substantial sum for the benefit of the remaining three hundred and eighty-nine claimants and both sides were anxious to arrive at a settlement out of court. The case in fact raised legal issues of considerable difficulty under English law. Had any of the

actions come on for trial, they would have been heard by a professional judge sitting without a jury.

In 1971 negotiations began on a proposal by Distillers to establish a charitable trust fund for all the deformed children other than those covered by the 1968 settlement. The proposal was made subject to the condition that all parents accepted but five refused, one, at least, because payments out of the fund would have been based on need. An application, on behalf of the parents who would have accepted, to replace those five by the Official Solicitor as next friend was refused by the Court of Appeal in April 1972. During subsequent negotiations, the original condition was replaced by a requirement that "a substantial majority" of the parents consented. By September 1972 a settlement involving the setting-up of a £3,250,000 trust fund had been worked out and was expected to be submitted in October to the court for approval.

11. Reports concerning the deformed children had appeared regularly in *The Sunday Times* since 1967 and in 1968 it had ventured some criticism of the settlement concluded in that year. There had also been comment on the children's circumstances in other newspapers and on television. In particular, in December 1971, the *Daily Mail* published an article which prompted complaints from parents that it might jeopardize the settlement negotiations in hand; the *Daily Mail* was "warned off" by the Attorney-General in a formal letter threatening sanctions under the law of contempt of court but contempt proceedings were not actually instituted. On 24 September 1972, *The Sunday Times* carried an article entitled "Our Thalidomide Children: A Cause for National Shame": this examined the settlement proposals then under consideration, describing them as "grotesquely out of proportion to the injuries suffered," criticized various aspects of English law on the recovery and assessment of damages in personal injury cases, complained of the delay that had elapsed since the births and appealed to Distillers to make a more generous offer. The article contained the following passage:

> . . . the thalidomide children shame Distillers . . . there are times when to insist on the letter of the law is as exposed to criticism as infringement of another's legal rights. The figure in the proposed settlement is to be £3.25 million, spread over 10 years. This does not shine as a beacon against pre-tax profits last year of £64.8 million and company assets worth £421 million. Without in any way surrendering on negligence, Distillers could and should think again.

A footnote in the article announced that "in a future article *The Sunday Times* [would] trace how the tragedy occurred." On 17 November 1972, the Divisional Court of the Queen's Bench Division granted the Attorney-General's application for an injunction restraining publication of this future article on the ground that it would constitute contempt of court[.]

17. The unpublished article which was the subject of the injunction opened with a suggestion that the manner of marketing thalidomide in Britain left a lot to be desired. It stated that Distillers:

—relied heavily on the German tests and had not completed full trials of its own *before* marketing the drug;

—failed to uncover in its research into medical and scientific literature the fact that a drug related to thalidomide could cause monster births;

—before marketing the drug did no animal tests to determine the drug's effect on the foetus;

—accelerated the marketing of the drug for commercial reasons. Were not deflected by a warning from one of its own staff that thalidomide was far more dangerous than had been supposed;

—were not deflected by the discovery that thalidomide could damage the nervous system, in itself a hint that it might damage the foetus;

—continued to advertise the drug as safe for pregnant women up to a month from when it was withdrawn.

The body of the article described how, after their apparently disappointing initial ventures into pharmaceutics, Distillers learned in 1956 that the German firm of *Chemie Gruenenthal* had developed a sedative considered harmless and unique—thalidomide. The very large market existing at the time for sedatives was becoming overcrowded and Distillers thought it necessary to act quickly. Their decision to market the drug was taken before they had seen technical information, other than the transcript of a German symposium, and before carrying out independent tests. Indeed, they seemed to believe that thalidomide would not need elaborate tests. Distillers put in hand a search of scientific literature but failed to discover the results of research in 1950 by a Dr. Thiersch showing that a chemical related to thalidomide could cause monster births; opinions differed as to whether his work should have been found.

Sales of thalidomide began in Germany in October 1957 and Distillers were committed under their licensing agreement to commence marketing in April 1958. They put the programme for the drug's launch in hand even though clinical trials were behind. Results of the first British trials were published in January 1958: it had been found that thalidomide suppressed the work of the thyroid gland and that its method of action was unknown; the researcher warned that more tests were needed. Distillers did not rely on this advice, basing their decision on "flimsy" evidence, namely other trials in the United Kingdom and assurances concerning the results of research in Germany. The warning about anti-thyroid effects was particularly relevant since it was known that drugs affecting the thyroid could affect unborn children; it was reasonable to argue that Distillers should have delayed launching the drug pending further tests.

On 14 April 1958, continued the article, thalidomide went on sale in Britain, advertised as "completely safe." At the end of 1959, Distillers' pharmacologist discovered that thalidomide in liquid form was highly poisonous and that an overdose might be lethal, but his report was never published and the liquid product went on sale in July 1961. In December 1960, it was reported that patients who had taken thalidomide in the tablet form in which it had firstly been on sale showed symptoms of peripheral neuritis; this news had the result of holding up an application to market thalidomide in the United States of America where it was, in fact, never sold. Further cases of peripheral neuritis were reported in 1961 but Distillers' advertising continued to stress the drug's safety.

Early in 1961 children were born in the United Kingdom with deformities, but there was at the time nothing to connect them with thalidomide. However, between May and October, a doctor in Australia discovered that the common factor in a number of monster births was that the mothers had taken thalidomide during pregnancy. This was reported to *Chemie Gruenenthal* on 24 November who withdrew the drug two days later following newspaper disclosures. Distillers ended the public sale of thalidomide immediately afterwards. Tests on animals, published in April 1962, confirmed that thalidomide caused deformities, but sales to hospitals were not ended until December 1962.

The draft article concluded as follows:

> So the burden of making certain that thalidomide was safe fell squarely on [Distillers]. How did the company measure up to this heavy responsibility? It can be argued that:
>
> 1. [Distillers] should have found all the scientific literature about drugs related to thalidomide. It did not.
>
> 2. It should have read Thiersch's work on the effects on the nervous system of drugs related to thalidomide, have suspected the possible action on unborn babies and therefore have done tests on animals for teratogenic effect. It did not.
>
> 3. It should have done further tests when it discovered that the drug had anti-thyroid activity and unsuspected toxicity. It did not.
>
> 4. It should have had proof before advertising the drug as safe for pregnant women that this was in fact so. It did not.

> For [Distillers] it could be argued that it sincerely believed that thalidomide was free from any toxicity at the time it was first put on the market in Britain; that peripheral neuritis did not emerge as a side effect until the drug had been on sale in Britain for two years; that testing for teratogenic effects was not general in 1958; that if tests had been done on the usual laboratory animals nothing would have shown because it is only in the New Zealand white rabbit that thalidomide produces the same effects as in human beings; and, finally, that in the one clinical report of thalidomide being given to pregnant women no serious results followed (because thalidomide is dangerous only during the first 12 weeks of pregnancy). * * *
>
> There appears to be no neat set of answers[.]

21. Distillers made a formal complaint to the Attorney-General that the *Sunday Times* article of 24 September 1972 constituted contempt of court in view of the litigation still outstanding and, on 27 September, the Solicitor-General, in the absence of the Attorney-General, wrote to the editor of *The Sunday Times* to ask him for his observations. The editor, in his reply, justified that article and also submitted the draft of the proposed future article for which he claimed complete factual accuracy. The Solicitor-General enquired whether the draft had been seen by any of the parties to the litigation, as a consequence of which a copy of the draft was sent by *The Sunday Times* to Distillers on 10 October. On the previous day, *The Sunday Times* had been advised that the Attorney-General had decided to take no action in respect of the matter already published in September and October; Distillers also took no action. On 11 October, the Attorney-General's Office informed *The Sunday Times* that, following representations by Distillers, the Attorney-General had decided to apply to the High Court in order to obtain a judicial decision on the legality of the publication of the proposed article. On the following day, he issued a writ against Times Newspapers Ltd. in which he claimed an injunction "to restrain the defendants . . . by themselves, their servants or agents or otherwise, from publishing or causing or authorizing to be published or printed an article in draft dealing, *inter alia*, with the development, distribution and use of the drug thalidomide, a copy of which article had been supplied to the Attorney-General by the defendants."

22. The Attorney-General's application was heard by three judges of the Queen's Bench Division from 7 to 9 November 1972; on 17 November the court granted the injunction.

In its judgment the court remarked:

> the article does not purport to express any views as to the legal responsibility of Distillers . . . but . . . is in many respects critical of Distillers and charges them with neglect in regard to

> their own failure to test the product, or their failure to react sufficiently sharply to warning signs obtained from the tests by others. No one reading the article could . . . fail to gain the impression that the case against Distillers on the footing of negligence was a substantial one.

The editor of the *Sunday Times* had indicated that any libel proceedings following publication would be defended by a plea that the contents of the article were true and the court approached the article on the footing that it was factually accurate.

23. The reasoning in the court's judgment may be summarised as follows. The objection to unilateral comment, prior to conclusion of the court hearing, was that it might prevent the due and impartial administration of justice by affecting and prejudicing the mind of the tribunal itself, by affecting witnesses who were to be called or by prejudicing the free choice and conduct of a party to the litigation. It was the third form of prejudice that was relevant to the present case. * * *

24. An appeal by Times Newspapers Ltd. against the Divisional Court's decision was heard by the Court of Appeal from 30 January to 2 February 1973. The court had before it an affidavit by the editor of the Sunday Times setting out developments in the intervening period both in the case itself and in public discussion thereof. With the leave of the court, counsel for Distillers made submissions on the contents of the proposed article, pointing to errors he said it contained. On 16 February, the Court of Appeal discharged the injunction. * * *

25. Lord Denning said that the proposed article:

> . . . contains a detailed analysis of the evidence against Distillers. It marshals forcibly the arguments for saying that Distillers did not measure up to their responsibility. Though, to be fair, it does summarise the arguments which could be made for Distillers. * * *

"Trial by newspaper," continued Lord Denning, must not be allowed. However, the public interest in a matter of national concern had to be balanced against the interest of the parties in a fair trial or settlement; in the present case the public interest in discussion outweighed the potential prejudice to a party. The law did not prevent comment when litigation was dormant and not being actively pursued. * * *

28. Following the Court of Appeal's decision, the *Sunday Times* refrained from publishing the proposed article so as to enable the Attorney-General to appeal. [L]eave to appeal * * * was granted by the House of Lords on 1 March 1973. The hearing before the House of Lords was held in May 1973. On 18 July 1973, the House gave judgment unanimously allowing the appeal and subsequently directed the

Divisional Court to grant an injunction in the terms set out in paragraph 34 below. * * *

29. Lord Reid said that the House must try to remove the uncertainty which was the main objection to the present law. The law of contempt had to be founded entirely on public policy; it was not there to protect the rights of parties to a litigation but to prevent interference with the administration of justice and should be limited to what was reasonably necessary for the purpose. Freedom of speech should not be limited more than was necessary but it could not be allowed where there would be real prejudice to the administration of justice. * * *

The Court of Appeal had wrongly described the actions as "dormant" since settlement negotiations were in hand and improper pressure on a litigant to settle could constitute contempt. As for the Court of Appeal's balancing of competing interests, Lord Reid said:

> . . . contempt of court has nothing to do with the private interests of litigants. I have already indicated the way in which I think that a balance must be struck between the public interest in freedom of speech and the public interest in protecting the administration of justice from interference. I do not see why there should be any difference in principle between a case which is thought to have news value and one which is not. Protection of the administration of justice is equally important whether or not the case involves important general issues.

Lord Reid concluded that publication of the article should be postponed for the time being in the light of the circumstances then prevailing; however, if things dragged on indefinitely, there would have to be a reassessment of the public interest in a unique situation.

[A summary of the concurring opinion of Lord Morris of Booth-y-Gest in the English House of Lords is omitted.]

31. Lord Diplock said that contempt of court was punishable because it undermined the confidence of the parties and of the public in the due administration of justice. The due administration of justice required that all citizens should have unhindered access to the courts; that they should be able to rely on an unbiased decision based only on facts proved in accordance with the rules of evidence; that, once a case was submitted to a court, they should be able to rely upon there being no usurpation by any other person, for example in the form of "trial by newspaper," of the function of the court. Conduct calculated to prejudice any of these requirements or to undermine public confidence that they would be observed was contempt of court.

[Summaries of the concurring opinions of Lord Simon of Glaisdale and Lord Cross of Chelsea in the English House of Lords are omitted.]

34. On 25 July 1973, the House of Lords ordered that the cause be remitted to the Divisional Court with a direction to grant the following injunction:

> That . . . Times Newspapers Ltd., by themselves, their servants, agents or otherwise, be restrained from publishing, or causing or authorising or procuring to be published or printed, any article or matter which prejudges the issues of negligence, breach of contract or breach of duty, or deals with the evidence relating to any of the said issues arising in any actions pending or imminent against Distillers . . . in respect of the development, distribution or use of the drug "thalidomide."

The defendants were granted liberty to apply to the Divisional Court for discharge of the injunction.

The Divisional Court implemented the above direction on 24 August 1973.

35. On 23 June 1976, the Divisional Court heard an application by the Attorney-General for the discharge of the injunction. It was said on behalf of the Attorney-General that the need for the injunction no longer arose: most of the claims against Distillers had been settled and there were only four extant actions which could by then have been brought before the courts if they had been pursued diligently. As there was a conflicting public interest in the *Sunday Times* being allowed to publish "at the earliest possible date," the Attorney-General submitted the matter to the court as one where the public interest no longer required the restraint. The court, considering that the possibility of pressure on Distillers had completely evaporated, granted the application.

[A discussion of the Phillimore Report on the Law of Contempt, issued in December 1974, is omitted.]

38. In their application, lodged with the Commission on 19 January 1974, the applicants claimed that the injunction, issued by the High Court and upheld by the House of Lords, to restrain them from publishing an article in the *Sunday Times* dealing with thalidomide children and the settlement of their compensation claims in the United Kingdom constituted a breach of Article 10 of the Convention. They further alleged that the principles upon which the decision of the House of Lords was founded amounted to a violation of Article 10 and asked the Commission to direct or, alternatively, to request the Government to introduce legislation overruling the decision of the House of Lords and bringing the law of contempt of court into line with the Convention.

39. In its decision of 21 March 1975, the Commission, after describing the question before it as "whether the rules of contempt of court as applied in the decision of the House of Lords granting the

injunction are a ground justifying the restriction under Article 10 § 2," declared admissible and accepted the application.

[Additional allegations were made by the applicant under Articles 14 and 18 of the Convention; though considered by the Commission and by the Court, neither additional allegation is held by either body to have demonstrated a violation of the Convention.]

41. In its report of 18 May 1977, the Commission * * * expressed the opinion:

> —by eight votes to five, that the restriction imposed on the applicant's right to freedom of expression was in breach of Article 10 of the Convention[.]

42. The applicants claim to be the victims of a violation of Article 10 of the Convention which provides:

> 1. Everyone has the right to freedom of expression. This right shall include freedom to hold opinions and to receive and impart information and ideas without interference by public authority and regardless of frontiers. This Article shall not prevent States from requiring the licensing of broadcasting, television or cinema enterprises.
>
> 2. The exercise of these freedoms, since it carries with it duties and responsibilities, may be subject to such formalities, conditions, restrictions or penalties as are prescribed by law and are necessary in a democratic society, in the interests of national security, territorial integrity or public safety, for the prevention of disorder or crime, for the protection of health or morals, for the protection of the reputation or rights of others, for preventing the disclosure of information received in confidence, or for maintaining the authority and impartiality of the judiciary. * * *

45. It is clear that there was an "interference by public authority" in the exercise of the applicants' freedom of expression which is guaranteed by paragraph 1 of Article 10. Such an interference entails a "violation" of Article 10 if it does not fall within one of the exceptions provided for in paragraph 2. The Court, therefore, has to examine in turn whether the interference in the present case was "prescribed by law," whether it had an aim or aims that is or are legitimate under Article 10 § 2 and whether it was "necessary in a democratic society" for the aforesaid aim or aims.

[The European Court holds that there had been an "interference with the applicants' freedom of expression," that it was "prescribed by law," and that "the interference with the applicants' freedom of expression had an aim that is legitimate under Article 10 § 2." The crucial part of the case then follows: "Was the interference 'necessary in a democratic society' for maintaining the authority of the judiciary?"]

65. * * * As the Court remarked in its Handyside judgment, freedom of expression constitutes one of the essential foundations of a democratic society; subject to paragraph 2 of Article 10, it is applicable not only to information or ideas that are favourably received or regarded as inoffensive or as a matter of indifference, but also to those that offend, shock or disturb the State or any sector of the population.

These principles are of particular importance as far as the press is concerned. They are equally applicable to the field of the administration of justice, which serves the interests of the community at large and requires the co-operation of an enlightened public. There is general recognition of the fact that the courts cannot operate in a vacuum. Whilst they are the forum for the settlement of disputes, this does not mean that there can be no prior discussion of disputes elsewhere, be it in specialized journals, in the general press or amongst the public at large. Furthermore, whilst the mass media must not overstep the bounds imposed in the interests of the proper administration of justice, it is incumbent on them to impart information and ideas concerning matters that come before the courts just as in other areas of public interest. Not only do the media have the task of imparting such information and ideas: the public also has a right to receive them.

To assess whether the interference complained of was based on "sufficient" reasons which rendered it "necessary in a democratic society," account must thus be taken of any public interest aspect of the case. The Court observes in this connection that, following a balancing of the conflicting interests involved, an absolute rule was formulated by certain of the Law Lords to the effect that it was not permissible to prejudge issues in pending cases: it was considered that the law would be too uncertain if the balance were to be struck anew in each case. Whilst emphasising that it is not its function to pronounce itself on an interpretation of English law adopted in the House of Lords, the Court points out that it has to take a different approach. The Court is faced not with a choice between two conflicting principles but with a principle of freedom of expression that is subject to a number of exceptions which must be narrowly interpreted. In the second place, the Court's supervision under Article 10 covers not only the basic legislation but also the decision applying it. It is not sufficient that the interference involved belongs to that class of the exceptions listed in Article 10 § 2 which has been invoked; neither is it sufficient that the interference was imposed because its subject-matter fell within a particular category or was caught by a legal rule formulated in general or absolute terms: the Court has to be satisfied that the interference was necessary having regard to the facts and circumstances prevailing in the specific case before it.

66. The thalidomide disaster was a matter of undisputed public concern. It posed the question whether the powerful company which had marketed the drug bore legal or moral responsibility towards hundreds of individuals experiencing an appalling personal tragedy or whether the victims could demand or hope for indemnification only from the community as a whole; fundamental issues concerning protection against and compensation for injuries resulting from scientific developments were raised and many facets of the existing law on these subjects were called in question.

As the Court has already observed, Article 10 guarantees not only the freedom of the press to inform the public but also the right of the public to be properly informed[.]

In the present case, the families of numerous victims of the tragedy, who were unaware of the legal difficulties involved, had a vital interest in knowing all the underlying facts and the various possible solutions. They could be deprived of this information, which was crucially important for them, only if it appeared absolutely certain that its diffusion would have presented a threat to the "authority of the judiciary."

Being called upon to weigh the interests involved and assess their respective force, the Court makes the following observations:

In September 1972, the case had, in the words of the applicants, been in a "legal cocoon" for several years and it was, at the very least, far from certain that the parents' actions would have come on for trial. There had also been no public enquiry[.]

The Government and the minority of the Commission point out that there was no prohibition on discussion of the "wider issues," such as the principles of the English law of negligence, and indeed it is true that there had been extensive discussion in various circles especially after, but also before, the Divisional Court's initial decision[.] However, the Court considers it rather artificial to attempt to divide the "wider issues" and the negligence issue. The question of where responsibility for a tragedy of this kind actually lies is also a matter of public interest.

It is true that, if the *Sunday Times* article had appeared at the intended time, Distillers might have felt obliged to develop in public, and in advance of any trial, their arguments on the facts of the case[;] however, those facts did not cease to be a matter of public interest merely because they formed the background to pending litigation. By bringing to light certain facts, the article might have served as a brake on speculative and unenlightened discussion.

67. Having regard to all the circumstances of the case on the basis of the approach described in paragraph 65 above, the Court concludes that the interference complained of did not correspond to a social need sufficiently pressing to outweigh the public interest in freedom of

expression within the meaning of the Convention. The Court therefore finds the reasons for the restraint imposed on the applicants not to be sufficient under Article 10 § 2. That restraint proves not to be proportionate to the legitimate aim pursued; it was not necessary in a democratic society for maintaining the authority of the judiciary.

68. There has accordingly been a violation of Article 10. * * *

FOR THESE REASONS, THE COURT

1. *holds* by eleven votes to nine that there has been a breach of Article 10 of the Convention[.]

NOTES AND QUESTIONS

1. *Balancing the Issues.* In *Sunday Times*, there was no doubt that the balancing of the legal issues—weighing the public's right to know and the *Sunday Times'* right to freedom of expression against Distillers' right to a trial by the courts, not by the media, and the interest of the English government in the integrity of the judicial process—was a very close one. Eight English judges (three at the trial level and five in the House of Lords), five European Human Rights commissioners, and nine European Human Rights judges felt that the scales tilted toward granting an injunction against the *Sunday Times*. Three English judges (in the Court of Appeal), eight European Human Rights commissioners, and eleven European Human Rights judges felt that the balance went for permitting the *Sunday Times* to publish the thalidomide article. Of 44 judges and commissioners who considered the case, half went one way and half the other. Reasonable men and women could and did differ. What is the difference between the standards applied in English law and those in European human rights law?

2. *The Boldness of the Court.* A distinguished British international lawyer, F.A. Mann, felt that the European Court of Human Rights had gone too far:

> However uncertain its definition and scope may be in some respects, contempt of court is undoubtedly one of the great contributions the common law has made to the civilised behaviour of a large part of the world beyond the continent of Europe where the institution is unknown. * * * Yet it is that very branch of the law which the European Court of Human Rights has seriously undermined by, in effect, overturning the unanimous decision of the House of Lords in the *Sunday Times* case—a unique event in the history of English law. In fact it is probably no exaggeration to say that the gravest blow to the fabric of English law has been dealt by the majority of eleven judges coming from Cyprus, Denmark, Eire, France, Germany, Greece, Italy, Portugal, Spain, Sweden and Turkey, who, over the dissent of nine judges from Austria, Belgium, Holland, Iceland, Luxembourg, Malta, Norway, Switzerland and the United Kingdom, decided in favor of the *Sunday Times*. * * *

> The reader will have to make up his or her own mind * * * whether the Strasbourg Court arrogated to itself powers of factual appreciation which it cannot possibly exercise convincingly * * * and ask whether according to the standards and traditions of English law and English public life it is the decision of the House of Lords or that of the European Court of Human Rights which more correctly assesses the "social need" and "the legitimate aim" of a civilised society * * * and whether the level of judicial reasoning is higher in London or Strasbourg.

F.A. Mann, "Contempt of Court in the House of Lords and the European Court of Human Rights," 95 *Law Quarterly Review* 348, 348–49, 352 (1979).

One can understand Mann's discomfort with the "overturning" of the House of Lords by the Strasbourg Court, but did *Sunday Times* really raise the question of which court's "judicial reasoning" was "higher"? As another observer remarked about another judgment against the United Kingdom, the *Golder Case*: "Membership of a European institution, and submission to the jurisdiction of its organs, means the acceptance of a European way of thinking. The European Commission and Court of Human Rights are likely to construe texts in the 'continental,' not the common law, manner." William Dale, "Human Rights in the United Kingdom—International Standards," 25 *International and Comparative Law Quarterly* 292, 302 (1976).

3. *Continued Acceptance of the Optional Clauses*. The United Kingdom was at the time not obliged to accept forever "a European way of thinking." However, states continued to accept both Article 25 and Article 46. At the time of the *Sunday Times Case* 14 of the 21 Council of Europe states had already accepted Article 25 individual petition, and 16 had consented to Article 46 jurisdiction of the Court. Not only did the United Kingdom continue to renew its pledges to both Article 25 and Article 46, but so did the other then-consenting states. Now, the once optional clauses are mandatory. Far from discouraging governments, the *Sunday Times* judgment and cases like it did not slow the accession of states to the legal machinery of European human rights law.

4. *The Efficacy of European Human Rights Law*. How far can the Court go without upsetting the apple cart of state consent? Writing just after the *Sunday Times Case*, Ralph Beddard remarked on the caution exercised by the system's institutions up to that time:

> It is, and always has been, obvious that winning the confidence of the parties and the public was a first step in any attempt to establish judicial determination of the protection of human rights. The last 27 years have not been free of difficulties, however, and the confidence of the parties was won, particularly in the early days, by very careful treading on the part of the Commission. There are cases which, if presented to the Commission today, would probably make greater progress than they did at the time of application.

> However, a Commission leaning heavily in favor of governments would have lost the confidence of the public.

Ralph Beddard, *Human Rights and Europe* 4 (1980).

Such caution paid off. In 1980, Sir Humphrey Waldock, then President of the International Court of Justice but previously President of both the European Commission and the European Court of Human Rights, could conclude that "the system set up by the European Convention on Human Rights is, in general, effective is not, I believe, today open to serious question." Humphrey Waldock, "The Effectiveness of the System Set Up by the European Convention on Human Rights," 1 *Human Rights Law Journal* 1 (1980).

How easy is it to judge the "efficacy" of law? Does it matter whether one is testing (1) the efficacy of a particular legal decision, (2) the efficacy of legal rules in practice, or (3) the efficacy of the legal system in the society in general? Most studies evaluating the "efficacy" of European human rights law focus on the efficacy of the judgments of the European Court of Human Rights, but avoid broader efficacy questions. See Mark W. Janis, "The Efficacy of Strasbourg Law," 15 *Connecticut Journal of International Law* 39 (2000).

5. *The Efficacy of International Law.* Regional international law, and especially judgments of regional international courts like the European Court of Human Rights or the European Union's European Court of Justice, can become so effective that some commentators unused to a really efficacious system of international law may think it has become a form of municipal law. Some, for example, have viewed the law of the European Union as "federal" law. See John Bridge, "American Analogues in the Law of the European Community," 11 *Anglo-American Law Review* 130 (1982). Others have felt European Union law is still fundamentally international law. See Derrick Wyatt, "New Legal Order or Old," 7 *European Law Review* 147 (1982). Does it really matter whether a legal system is denominated "federal law" or "regional international law"? Does one or the other have a more impressive connotation?

6. *Remedies at Strasbourg.* Sometimes, as in *Sunday Times*, the Court's declaration of a violation of the European Human Rights Convention is the only remedy provided by the Court. Other times, as in the *McCann Case* in Chapter 1, the Court awards damages. However, these damages are ordinarily small or nominal, most typically an award of some of the costs of litigating the case. Recently, the Court has begun experimenting, occasionally ordering the restitution of property or paying applicants its fair market value. See Mark W. Janis, Richard S. Kay & Anthony W. Bradley, *European Human Rights Law* 89–103 (3d ed. 2008). If the Strasbourg Court becomes bolder in awarding damages or in ordering restitution, will this boldness help or hurt the system's efficacy? Will it demonstrate that Strasbourg has clout, or will it induce states to disregard costly judgments?

7. *The Victim of Its Own Success?* Is the European Court of Human Rights now a victim of its own success? We noted at the outset of this part how Strasbourg's case load has grown from a handful of rendered judgments in each of its first decades to more than a thousand judgments a year in the last few years. Even so, the European Court of Human Rights is falling behind. In 2009, for example, the Strasbourg Court received about 57,000 applications but was able to deliver "only" about 1,600 judgments. What has accounted for the explosion in applications? Is it due more to "deepening," *i.e.*, that lawyers are more acquainted with the Strasbourg system and, hence, are more likely to apply for review of domestic governmental action, or to "widening," *i.e.*, that the number of member states has grown to more than twice the total less than 20 years ago? What can be done to handle the onslaught of new applications? Some have suggested that the Court be given new powers "to decline to examine in detail applications that raise no substantial issue under the Convention." Jean-Paul Costa, "The European Court of Human Rights and Its Recent Case Law," 38 *Texas International Law Journal* 455, 467 (2003). Others have proposed that the Court sometimes render a "pilot" judgment instead of issuing a great many similar decisions against a repetitively transgressing state. Steven Greer, "Reforming the European Convention on Human Rights: Towards Protocol 14," 2003 *Public Law* 663, 665–66. Whatever the solution to the problem of too much work, Strasbourg's difficulty with its success would be a happy prospect to face for most other international legal tribunals.

THE SOERING CASE

European Court of Human Rights,
Judgment of 7 July 1989, Series A, Vol. 161

AS TO THE FACTS

I. *Particular circumstances of the case*

11. The applicant, Mr. Jens Soering, was born on 1 August 1966 and is a German national. He is currently detained in prison in England pending extradition to the United States of America to face charges of murder in the Commonwealth of Virginia.

12. The homicides in question were committed in Bedford County, Virginia, in March 1985. The victims, William Reginald Haysom (aged 72) and Nancy Astor Haysom (aged 53), were the parents of the applicant's girlfriend, Elizabeth Haysom, who is a Canadian national. Death in each case was the result of multiple and massive stab and slash wounds to the neck, throat and body. At the time the applicant and Elizabeth Haysom, aged 18 and 20 respectively, were students at the University of Virginia. They disappeared together from Virginia in October 1985, but were arrested in England in April 1986 in connection with cheque fraud.

13. The applicant was interviewed in England between 5 and 8 June 1986 by a police investigator from the Sheriff's Department of Bedford

County. In a sworn affidavit dated 24 July 1986 the investigator recorded the applicant as having admitted to killings in his presence and in that of two United Kingdom police officers. The applicant had stated that he was in love with Miss Haysom but that her parents were opposed to the relationship. He and Miss Haysom had therefore planned to kill them. They rented a car in Charlottesville and traveled to Washington where they set up an alibi. The applicant then went to the parents' house, discussed the relationship with them and, when they told him they would do anything to prevent it, a row developed during which he killed them with a knife.

On 13 June 1986 a grand jury of the Circuit Court of Bedford County indicted him on charges of murdering the Haysom parents. The charges alleged capital murder of both of them and the separate non-capital murders of each.

14. On 11 August 1986 the Government of the United States of America requested the applicant's and Miss Haysom's extradition under the terms of the Extradition Treaty of 1972 between the United States and the United Kingdom * * *. On 12 September a Magistrate at Bow Street Magistrates' Court was required by the Secretary of State for Home Affairs to issue a warrant for the applicant's arrest under the provisions of section 8 of the Extradition Act 1870[.] The applicant was subsequently arrested on 30 December at HM Prison Chelmsford after serving a prison sentence for cheque fraud.

15. On 29 October 1986 the British Embassy in Washington addressed a request to the United States' authorities in the following terms:

> Because the death penalty has been abolished in Great Britain, the Embassy has been instructed to seek an assurance, in accordance with the terms of . . . the Extradition Treaty, that, in the event of Mr. Soering being surrendered and being convicted of the crimes for which he has been indicted . . . , the death penalty, if imposed, will not be carried out.
>
> Should it not be possible on constitutional grounds for the United States Government to give such an assurance, the United Kingdom authorities ask that the United States Government undertake to recommend to the appropriate authorities that the death penalty should not be imposed or, if imposed, should not be executed.

16. On 30 December 1986 the applicant was interviewed in prison by a German prosecutor (*Staatsanwalt*) from Bonn. In a sworn witness statement the prosecutor recorded the applicant as having said, *inter alia*, that "he had never had the intention of killing Mr. and Mrs. Haysom and . . . he could only remember having inflicted wounds at the neck on

Mr. and Mrs. Haysom which must have had something to do with their dying later;" and that in the immediately preceding days "there had been no talk whatsoever [between him and Elizabeth Haysom] about killing Elizabeth's parents." * * *

On 11 February 1987 the local court in Bonn issued a warrant for the applicant's arrest in respect of the alleged murders. On 11 March the Government of the Federal Republic of Germany requested his extradition to the Federal Republic under the Extradition Treaty of 1872 between the Federal Republic and the United Kingdom[.]

17. In a letter dated 20 April 1987 to the Director of the Office of International Affairs, Criminal Division, United States Department of Justice, the Attorney for Bedford County, Virginia (Mr. James W. Updike, Jr.) stated that, on the assumption that the applicant could not be tried in Germany on the basis of admissions alone, there was no means of compelling witnesses from the United States to appear in a criminal court in Germany. On 23 April the United States, by diplomatic note, requested the applicant's extradition to the United States in preference to the Federal Republic of Germany.

18. On 8 May 1987 Elizabeth Haysom was surrendered for extradition to the United States. After pleading guilty on 22 August as an accessory to the murder of her parents, she was sentenced on 6 October to 90 years' imprisonment (45 years on each count of murder).

19. On 20 May 1987 the Government of the United Kingdom informed the Federal Republic of Germany that the United States had earlier "submitted a request, supported by *prima facie* evidence, for the extradition of Mr. Soering." The United Kingdom Government notified the Federal Republic that they had "concluded that, having regard to all the circumstances of the case, the court should continue to consider in the normal way the United States' request." They further indicated that they had sought an assurance from the United States' authorities on the question of the death penalty and that "in the event that the court commits Mr. Soering, his surrender to the United States' authorities would be subject to the receipt of satisfactory assurances on this matter."

20. On 1 June 1987 Mr. Updike swore an affidavit in his capacity as Attorney for Bedford County, in which he certified as follows:

> I hereby certify that should Jens Soering be convicted of the offence of capital murder as charged in Bedford County, Virginia . . . a representation will be made in the name of the United Kingdom to the judge at the time of sentencing that it is the wish of the United Kingdom that the death penalty should not be imposed or carried out.

This assurance was transmitted to the United Kingdom Government under cover of a diplomatic note on 8 June. It was repeated in the same terms in a further affidavit from Mr. Updike sworn on 16 February 1988 and forwarded to the United Kingdom by diplomatic note on 17 May 1988. In the same note the Federal Government of the United States undertook to ensure that the commitment of the appropriate authorities of the Commonwealth of Virginia to make representations on behalf of the United Kingdom would be honored.

During the course of the present proceedings the Virginia authorities have informed the United Kingdom Government that Mr. Updike was not planning to provide any further assurances and intended to seek the death penalty in Mr. Soering's case because the evidence, in his determination, supported such action.

21. On 16 June 1987 at the Bow Street Magistrates' Court committal proceedings took place before the Chief Stipendiary Magistrate.

The Government of the United States adduced evidence that on the night of 30 March 1985 the applicant killed William and Nancy Haysom at their home in Bedford County, Virginia. In particular, evidence was given of the applicant's own admissions as recorded in the affidavit of the Bedford County police investigator (see paragraph 13 above).

On behalf of the applicant psychiatric evidence was adduced from a consultant forensic psychiatrist (report dated 15 December 1986 by Dr. Henrietta Bullard) that he was immature and inexperienced and had lost his personal identity in a symbiotic relationship with his girlfriend—a powerful, persuasive and disturbed young woman. * * *

22. On 29 June 1987 Mr. Soering applied to the Divisional Court for a writ of habeas corpus in respect of his committal and for leave to apply for judicial review. On 11 December both applications were refused by the Divisional Court (Lord Justice Lloyd and Mr. Justice Macpherson).

In support of his application for leave to apply for judicial review, Mr. Soering had submitted that the assurance received from the United States' authorities was so worthless that no reasonable Secretary of State could regard it as satisfactory under Article IV of the Extradition Treaty between the United Kingdom and the United States[.] In his judgment Lord Justice Lloyd agreed that "the assurance leaves something to be desired":

> Article IV of the Treaty contemplates an assurance that the death penalty will not be carried out. That must presumably mean an assurance by or on behalf of the Executive Branch of Government, which in this case would be the Governor of the Commonwealth of Virginia. The certificate sworn by Mr. Updike, far from being an assurance on behalf of the Executive, is nothing more than an undertaking to make representations on behalf of the United Kingdom to the judge. I cannot believe that this is what was intended when the Treaty was signed. But I can

> understand that there may well be difficulties in obtaining more by way of assurance in view of the federal nature of the United States Constitution.

Leave to apply for judicial review was refused because the claim was premature. Lord Justice Lloyd stated:

> The Secretary of State has not yet decided whether to accept the assurance as satisfactory and has certainly not yet decided whether or not to issue a warrant for Soering's surrender. Other factors may well intervene between now and then. This court will never allow itself to be put in the position of reviewing an administrative decision before the decision has been made.

As a supplementary reason, he added:

> Secondly, even if a decision to regard the assurance as satisfactory had already been made by the Secretary of State, then on the evidence currently before us I am far from being persuaded that such a decision would have been irrational in the Wednesbury sense. (As to "irrationality" in the Wednesbury sense, see paragraph 35 below.) [There it is explained that "The test in an extradition case would be that no reasonable Secretary of State could have made an order for return in the circumstances."]

23. On 30 June 1988 the House of Lords rejected the applicant's petition for leave to appeal against the decision of the Divisional Court.

24. On 14 July 1988 the applicant petitioned the Secretary of State, requesting him to exercise his discretion not to make an order for the applicant's surrender under section 11 of the Extradition Act 1870[.]

This request was rejected, and on 3 August 1988 the Secretary of State signed a warrant ordering the applicant's surrender to the United States' authorities. However, the applicant has not been transferred to the United States by virtue of the interim measures indicated in the present proceedings firstly by the European Commission and then by the European Court[.]

[The European Court of Human Rights reviews the laws relating to murder in England and Virginia and then turns to the prison conditions in Virginia facing Soering.]

61. There are currently 40 people under sentence of death in Virginia. The majority are detained in Mecklenburg Correctional Center, which is a modern maximum security institution with a total capacity of 335 inmates. Institutional Operating Procedures establish uniform operating procedures for the administration, security, control and delivery of necessary services to death row in Mecklenburg. In addition conditions of confinement are governed by a comprehensive consent

decree handed down by the United States District Court in Richmond in the case of *Alan Brown et al. v. Allyn R. Sielaff et al.* (5 April 1985). Both the Virginia Department of Corrections and the American Civil Liberties Union monitor compliance with the terms of the consent decree. The United States District Court also retains jurisdiction to enforce compliance with the decree. * * *

63. The size of a death row inmate's cell is 3m by 2.2m. Prisoners have an opportunity for approximately 7 1/2 hours' recreation per week in summer and approximately 6 hours' per week, weather permitting, in winter. The death row area has two recreation yards, both of which are equipped with basketball courts and one of which is equipped with weights and weight benches. Inmates are also permitted to leave their cells on other occasions, such as to receive visits, to visit the law library or to attend the prison infirmary. In addition, death row inmates are given one hour out-of-cell time in the morning in a common area. Each death row inmate is eligible for work assignments, such as cleaning duties. When prisoners move around the prison they are handcuffed with special shackles around the waist.

When not in their cells, death row inmates are housed in a common area called "the pod." The guards are not within this area and remain in a box outside. In the event of disturbance or inter-inmate assault, the guards are not allowed to intervene until instructed to do so by the ranking officer present.

64. The applicant adduced much evidence of extreme stress, psychological deterioration and risk of homosexual abuse and physical attack undergone by prisoners on death row, including Mecklenburg Correctional Center. This evidence was strongly contested by the United Kingdom Government on the basis of affidavits sworn by administrators from the Virginia Department of Corrections. * * *

68. A death row prisoner is moved to the death house 15 days before he is due to be executed. The death house is next to the death chamber where the electric chair is situated. Whilst a prisoner is in the death house he is watched 24 hours a day. He is isolated and has no light in his cell. The lights outside are permanently lit. A prisoner who utilizes the appeals process can be placed in the death house several times. * * *

AS TO THE LAW

I. *Alleged Breach of Article 3*

80. The applicant alleged that the decision by the Secretary of State for the Home Department to surrender him to the authorities of the United States of America would, if implemented, give rise to a breach by the United Kingdom of Article 3 of the Convention, which provides:

No one shall be subjected to torture or to inhuman or degrading treatment or punishment.

A. Applicability of Article 3 in cases of extradition

81. The alleged breach derives from the applicant's exposure to the so-called "death row phenomenon." This phenomenon may be described as consisting in a combination of circumstances to which the applicant would be exposed if, after having been extradited to Virginia to face a capital murder charge, he was sentenced to death.

82. In its report the Commission reaffirmed "its case-law that a person's deportation or extradition may give rise to an issue under Article 3 of the Convention where there are serious reasons to believe that the individual will be subjected, in the receiving State, to treatment contrary to that Article."

The Government of the Federal Republic of Germany supported the approach of the Commission, pointing to a similar approach in the case-law of the German courts.

The applicant likewise submitted that Article 3 not only prohibits the Contracting States from causing inhuman or degrading treatment or punishment to occur within their jurisdiction but also embodies an associated obligation not to put a person in a position where he will or may suffer such treatment or punishment at the hands of other States. For the applicant, at least as far as Article 3 is concerned, an individual may not be surrendered out of the protective zone of the Convention without the certainty that the safeguards which he would enjoy are as effective as the Convention standard.

83. The United Kingdom Government, on the other hand, contended that Article 3 should not be interpreted so as to impose responsibility on a Contracting State for acts which occur outside its jurisdiction. In particular, in their submission, extradition does not involve the responsibility of the extraditing State for inhuman or degrading treatment or punishment which the extradited person may suffer outside the State's jurisdiction. To begin with, they maintained, it would be straining the language of Article 3 intolerably to hold that by surrendering a fugitive criminal the extraditing State has "subjected" him to any treatment or punishment that he will receive following conviction and sentence in the receiving State. Further arguments advanced against the approach of the Commission were that it interferes with international treaty rights; it leads to a conflict with the norms of international judicial process, in that it in effect involves adjudication on the internal affairs of foreign States not Parties to the Convention or to the proceedings before the Convention institutions; it entails grave difficulties of evaluation and proof in requiring the examination of alien systems of law and of conditions in foreign States; the practice of national courts and the

international community cannot reasonably be invoked to support it; it causes a serious risk of harm in the Contracting State which is obliged to harbour the protected person, and leaves criminals untried, at large and unpunished.

In the alternative, the United Kingdom Government submitted that the application of Article 3 in extradition cases should be limited to those occasions in which the treatment or punishment abroad is certain, imminent and serious. In their view, the fact that by definition the matters complained of are only anticipated, together with the common and legitimate interest of all States in bringing fugitive criminals to justice, requires a very high degree of risk, proved beyond reasonable doubt, that ill-treatment will actually occur.

84. The Court will approach the matter on the basis of the following considerations.

85. As results from Article 5 § 1(f), which permits "the lawful . . . detention of a person against whom action is being taken with a view to . . . extradition," no right not to be extradited is as such protected by the Convention. Nevertheless, in so far as a measure of extradition has consequences adversely affecting the enjoyment of a Convention right, it may, assuming that the consequences are not too remote, attract the obligations of a Contracting State under the relevant Convention guarantee. What is at issue in the present case is whether Article 3 can be applicable when the adverse consequences of extradition are, or may be, suffered outside the jurisdiction of the extraditing State as a result of treatment or punishment administered in the receiving State.

86. Article 1 of the Convention, which provides that "the High Contracting Parties shall secure to everyone within their jurisdiction the rights and freedoms defined in Section I," sets a limit, notably territorial, on the reach of the Convention. In particular, the engagement undertaken by a Contracting State is confined to "securing" ("*reconnaître*" in the French text) the listed rights and freedoms to persons within its own "jurisdiction." Further, the Convention does not govern the actions of States not Parties to it, nor does it purport to be a means of requiring the Contracting States to impose Convention standards on other States. Article 1 cannot be read as justifying a general principle to the effect that, notwithstanding its extradition obligations, a Contracting State may not surrender an individual unless satisfied that the conditions awaiting him in the country of destination are in full accord with each of the safeguards of the Convention. Indeed, as the United Kingdom Government stressed, the beneficial purpose of extradition in preventing fugitive offenders from evading justice cannot be ignored in determining the scope of application of the Convention and of Article 3 in particular.

In the instant case it is common ground that the United Kingdom has no power over the practices and arrangements of the Virginia authorities which are the subject of the applicant's complaints. It is also true that in other international instruments cited by the United Kingdom Government—for example the 1951 United Nations Convention relating to the Status of Refugees (Article 33), the 1957 European Convention on Extradition (Article 11) and the 1984 United Nations Convention against Torture and Other Cruel, Inhuman and Degrading Treatment or Punishment (Article 3)—the problems of removing a person to another jurisdiction where unwanted consequences may follow are addressed expressly and specifically.

These considerations cannot, however, absolve the Contracting Parties from responsibility under Article 3 for all and any foreseeable consequences of extradition suffered outside their jurisdiction.

87. In interpreting the Convention regard must be had to its special character as a treaty for the collective enforcement of human rights and fundamental freedoms. Thus, the object and purpose of the Convention as an instrument for the protection of individual human beings require that its provisions be interpreted and applied so as to make its safeguards practical and effective. In addition, any interpretation of the rights and freedoms guaranteed has to be consistent with "the general spirit of the Convention, an instrument designed to maintain and promote the ideals and values of a democratic society."

88. Article 3 makes no provision for exceptions and no derogation from it is permissible under Article 15 in time of war or other national emergency. This absolute prohibition of torture and of inhuman or degrading treatment or punishment under the terms of the Convention shows that Article 3 enshrines one of the fundamental values of the democratic societies making up the Council of Europe. It is also to be found in similar terms in other international instruments such as the 1966 International Covenant on Civil and Political Rights and the 1969 American Convention on Human Rights and is generally recognised as an internationally accepted standard.

The question remains whether the extradition of a fugitive to another State where he would be subjected or be likely to be subjected to torture or to inhuman or degrading treatment or punishment would itself engage the responsibility of a Contracting State under Article 3. That the abhorrence of torture has such implications is recognised in Article 3 of the United Nations Convention Against Torture and Other Cruel, Inhuman or Degrading Treatment or Punishment, which provides that "no State Party shall . . . extradite a person where there are substantial grounds for believing that he would be in danger of being subjected to torture." The fact that a specialised treaty should spell out in detail a specific obligation attaching to the prohibition of torture does not mean that an essentially similar obligation is not already inherent in the general terms of Article 3 of the European Convention. It would hardly be compatible with the underlying values of the Convention, that "common heritage of political traditions, ideals, freedom and the rule of law" to which the Preamble refers, were a Contracting State knowingly to surrender a fugitive to another State where there were substantial grounds for believing that he would be in danger of being subjected to torture, however heinous the crime allegedly committed. Extradition in such circumstances, while not explicitly referred to in the brief and general wording of Article 3, would plainly be contrary to the spirit and intendment of the Article, and in the Court's view this inherent obligation not to extradite also extends to cases in which the fugitive would be faced in the receiving State by a real risk of exposure to inhuman or degrading treatment or punishment proscribed by that Article.

89. What amounts to "inhuman or degrading treatment or punishment" depends on all the circumstances of the case (see paragraph 100 below). Furthermore, inherent in the whole of the Convention is a search for a fair balance between the demands of the general interest of the community and the requirements of the protection of the individual's fundamental rights. As movement about the world becomes easier and crime takes on a larger international dimension, it is increasingly in the interest of all nations that suspected offenders who flee abroad should be brought to justice. Conversely, the establishment of safe havens for fugitives would not only result in danger for the State obliged to harbour the protected person but also tend to undermine the foundations of extradition. These considerations must also be included among the factors to be taken into account in the interpretation and application of the notions of inhuman and degrading treatment or punishment in extradition cases.

90. It is not normally for the Convention institutions to pronounce on the existence or otherwise of potential violations of the Convention. However, where an applicant claims that a decision to extradite him would, if implemented, be contrary to Article 3 by reason of its foreseeable consequences in the requesting country, a departure from this principle is necessary, in view of the serious and irreparable nature of the alleged suffering risked, in order to ensure the effectiveness of the safeguard provided by that Article (see paragraph 87 above).

91. In sum, the decision by a Contracting State to extradite a fugitive may give rise to an issue under Article 3, and hence engage the responsibility of that State under the Convention, where substantial grounds have been shown for believing that the person concerned, if extradited, faces a real risk of being subjected to torture or to inhuman or degrading treatment or punishment in the requesting country. The establishment of such responsibility inevitably involves an assessment of conditions in the requesting country against the standards of Article 3 of the Convention. Nonetheless, there is no question of adjudicating on or

establishing the responsibility of the receiving country, whether under general international law, under the Convention or otherwise. In so far as any liability under the Convention is or may be incurred, it is liability incurred by the extraditing Contracting State by reason of its having taken action which has as a direct consequence the exposure of an individual to proscribed ill-treatment.

B. Application of Article 3 in the particular circumstances of the present case

[The Court first determines that it was not unlikely that Soering would be charged with and convicted of a crime that would expose him to the "death row phenomenon."]

2. Whether in the circumstances the risk of exposure to the "death row phenomenon" would make extradition a breach of Article 3

(a) General considerations

100. As is established in the Court's case-law, ill-treatment, including punishment, must attain a minimum level of severity if it is to fall within the scope of Article 3. The assessment of this minimum is, in the nature of things, relative; it depends on all the circumstances of the case, such as the nature and context of the treatment or punishment, the manner and method of its execution, its duration, its physical or mental effects and, in some instances, the sex, age and state of health of the victim.

Treatment has been held by the Court to be both "inhuman" because it was premeditated, was applied for hours at a stretch and "caused, if not actual bodily injury, at least intense physical and mental suffering," and also, "degrading" because it was "such as to arouse in [its] victims feelings of fear, anguish and inferiority capable of humiliating and debasing them and possibly breaking their physical or moral resistance." In order for a punishment or treatment associated with it to be "inhuman" or "degrading," the suffering or humiliation involved must in any event go beyond that inevitable element of suffering or humiliation connected with a given form of legitimate punishment. In this connection, account is to be taken not only of the physical pain experienced but also, where there is a considerable delay before execution of the punishment, of the sentenced person's mental anguish of anticipating the violence he is to have inflicted on him.

101. Capital punishment is permitted under certain conditions by Article 2 § 1 of the Convention, which reads:

> Everyone's right to life shall be protected by law. No one shall be deprived of his life intentionally save in the execution of a sentence of a court following his conviction of a crime for which this penalty is provided by law.

In view of this wording, the applicant did not suggest that the death penalty *per se* violated Article 3. He, like the two Government Parties, agreed with the Commission that the extradition of a person to a country where he risks the death penalty does not in itself raise an issue under either Article 2 or Article 3. On the other hand, Amnesty International in their written comments * * * argued that the evolving standards in Western Europe regarding the existence and use of the death penalty required that the death penalty should now be considered as an inhuman and degrading punishment within the meaning of Article 3.

102. Certainly, "the Convention is a living instrument which . . . must be interpreted in the light of present-day conditions;" and, in assessing whether a given treatment or punishment is to be regarded as inhuman or degrading for the purposes of Article 3, "the Court cannot but be influenced by the developments and commonly accepted standards in the penal policy of the member States of the Council of Europe in this field." *De facto* the death penalty no longer exists in time of peace in the Contracting States to the Convention. In the few Contracting States which retain the death penalty in law for some peacetime offences, death sentences, if ever imposed, are nowadays not carried out. This "virtual consensus in Western European legal systems that the death penalty is, under current circumstances, no longer consistent with regional standards of justice," to use the words of Amnesty International, is reflected in Protocol No. 6 to the Convention, which provides for the abolition of the death penalty in time of peace. Protocol No. 6 was opened for signature in April 1983, which in the practice of the Council of Europe indicates the absence of objection on the part of any of the Member States of the Organization; it came into force in March 1985 and to date has been ratified by thirteen Contracting States to the Convention, not however including the United Kingdom.

Whether these marked changes have the effect of bringing the death penalty *per se* within the prohibition of ill-treatment under Article 3 must be determined on the principles governing the interpretation of the Convention.

103. The Convention is to be read as a whole and Article 3 should therefore be construed in harmony with the provisions of Article 2. On this basis Article 3 evidently cannot have been intended by the drafters of the Convention to include a general prohibition of the death penalty since that would nullify the clear wording of Article 2 § 1.

Subsequent practice in national penal policy, in the form of a generalized abolition of capital punishment, could be taken as establishing the agreement of the Contracting States to abrogate the exception provided for under Article 2 § 1 and hence to remove a textual limit on the scope for evolutive interpretation of Article 3. However, Protocol No. 6, as a subsequent written agreement, shows that the intention of the Contracting Parties as recently as 1983 was to adopt the normal method of amendment of the text in order to introduce a new obligation to abolish capital punishment in time of peace and, what is more, to do so by an optional instrument allowing each State to choose the moment when to undertake such an engagement. In these conditions, notwithstanding the special character of the Convention (see paragraph 87 above), Article 3 cannot be interpreted as generally prohibiting the death penalty.

104. That does not mean however that circumstances relating to a death sentence can never give rise to an issue under Article 3. The manner in which it is imposed or executed, the personal circumstances of the condemned person and a disproportionality to the gravity of the crime committed, as well as the conditions of detention awaiting execution, are examples of factors capable of bringing the treatment or punishment received by the condemned person within the proscription under Article 3. Present-day attitudes in the Contracting States to capital punishment are relevant for the assessment whether the acceptable threshold of suffering or degradation has been exceeded.

(b) The particular circumstances

105. The applicant submitted that the circumstances to which he would be exposed as a consequence of the implementation of the Secretary of State's decision to return him to the United States, namely the "death row phenomenon," cumulatively constitute such serious treatment that his extradition would be contrary to Article 3. He cited in particular the delays in the appeal and review procedures following a death sentence, during which time he would be subject to increasing tension and psychological trauma; the fact, so he said, that the judge or jury in determining sentence is not obliged to take into account the defendant's age and mental state at the time of the offence; the extreme conditions of his future detention on "death row" in Mecklenburg Correctional Center, where he expects to be the victim of violence and sexual abuse because of his age, color and nationality; and the constant spectre of the execution itself, including the ritual of execution. He also relied on the possibility of extradition or deportation, which he would not oppose, to the Federal Republic of Germany as accentuating the disproportionality of the Secretary of State's decision.

The Government of the Federal Republic of Germany took the view that, taking all the circumstances together, the treatment awaiting the applicant in Virginia would go so far beyond treatment inevitably connected with the imposition and execution of a death penalty as to be "inhuman" within the meaning of Article 3.

On the other hand, the conclusion expressed by the Commission was that the degree of severity contemplated by Article 3 would not be attained.

The United Kingdom Government shared this opinion. In particular, they disputed many of the applicant's factual allegations as to the conditions on death row in Mecklenburg and his expected fate there.

i. Length of detention prior to execution

106. The period that a condemned prisoner can expect to spend on death row in Virginia before being executed is on average six to eight years[.] This length of time awaiting death is, as the Commission and the United Kingdom Government noted, in a sense largely of the prisoner's own making in that he takes advantage of all avenues of appeal which are offered to him by Virginia law. The automatic appeal to the Supreme Court of Virginia normally takes no more than six months[.] The remaining time is accounted for by collateral attacks mounted by the prisoner himself in habeas corpus proceedings before both the State and Federal courts and in applications to the Supreme Court of the United States for certiorari review, the prisoner at each stage being able to seek a stay of execution[.] The remedies available under Virginia law serve the purpose of ensuring that the ultimate sanction of death is not unlawfully or arbitrarily imposed.

Nevertheless, just as some lapse of time between sentence and execution is inevitable if appeal safeguards are to be provided to the condemned person, so it is equally part of human nature that the person will cling to life by exploiting those safeguards to the full. However well-intentioned and even potentially beneficial is the provision of the complex of post-sentence procedures in Virginia, the consequence is that the condemned prisoner has to endure for many years the conditions on death row and the anguish and mounting tension of living in the ever-present shadow of death.

ii. Conditions on death row

107. As to conditions in Mecklenburg Correctional Center, where the applicant could expect to be held if sentenced to death, the Court bases itself on the facts which were uncontested by the United Kingdom Government, without finding it necessary to determine the reliability of the additional evidence adduced by the applicant, notably as to the risk of homosexual abuse and physical attack undergone by prisoners on death row.

The stringency of the custodial regime in Mecklenburg, as well as the services (medical, legal and social) and the controls (legislative, judicial and administrative) provided for inmates, are described in some detail above. In this connection, the United Kingdom Government drew attention to the necessary requirement of extra security for the safe custody of prisoners condemned to death for murder. Whilst it might thus well be justifiable in principle, the severity of a special regime such as that operated on death row in Mecklenburg is compounded by the fact of inmates being subject to it for a protracted period lasting on average six to eight years.

iii. The applicant's age and mental state

108. At the time of the killings, the applicant was only 18 years old and there is some psychiatric evidence, which was not contested as such, that he "was suffering from [such] an abnormality of mind . . . as substantially impaired his mental responsibility for his acts."

Unlike Article 2 of the Convention, Article 6 of the 1966 International Covenant on Civil and Political Rights and Article 4 of the 1969 American Convention on Human Rights expressly prohibit the death penalty from being imposed on persons aged less than 18 at the time of commission of the offence. Whether or not such a prohibition be inherent in the brief and general language of Article 2 of the European Convention, its explicit enunciation in other, later international instruments, the former of which has been ratified by a large number of States Parties to the European Convention, at the very least indicates that as a general principle the youth of the person concerned is a circumstance which is liable, with others, to put in question the compatibility with Article 3 of measures connected with a death sentence.

It is in line with the Court's case-law (as summarised above at paragraph 100) to treat disturbed mental health as having the same effect for the application of Article 3.

109. Virginia law, as the United Kingdom Government and the Commission emphasised, certainly does not ignore these two factors. Under the Virginia Code account has to be taken of mental disturbance in a defendant, either as an absolute bar to conviction if it is judged to be sufficient to amount to insanity or, like age, as a fact in mitigation at the sentencing stage[.] Additionally, indigent capital murder defendants are entitled to the appointment of a qualified mental health expert to assist in the preparation of their submissions at the separate sentencing proceedings[.] These provisions in the Virginia Code undoubtedly serve, as the American courts have stated, to prevent the arbitrary or capricious imposition of the death penalty and narrowly to channel the sentencer's discretion[.] They do not however remove the relevance of age and mental condition in relation to the acceptability, under Article 3, of the "death row phenomenon" for a given individual once condemned to death.

Although it is not for this Court to prejudge issues of criminal responsibility and appropriate sentence, the applicant's youth at the time of the offence and his then mental state, on the psychiatric evidence as it stands, are therefore to be taken into consideration as contributory factors tending, in his case, to bring the treatment on death row within the terms of Article 3.

iv. Possibility of extradition to the Federal Republic of Germany

110. For the United Kingdom Government and the majority of the Commission, the possibility of extraditing or deporting the applicant to face trial in the Federal Republic of Germany, where the death penalty has been abolished under the Constitution[,] is not material for the present purposes. Any other approach, the United Kingdom Government submitted, would lead to a "dual standard" affording the protection of the Convention to extraditable persons fortunate enough to have such an alternative destination available but refusing it to others not so fortunate.

This argument is not without weight. Furthermore, the Court cannot overlook either the horrible nature of the murders with which Mr. Soering is charged or the legitimate and beneficial role of extradition arrangements in combating crime. The purpose for which his removal to the United States was sought, in accordance with the Extradition Treaty between the United Kingdom and the United States, is undoubtedly a legitimate one. However, sending Mr. Soering to be tried in his own country would remove the danger of a fugitive criminal going unpunished as well as the risk of intense and protracted suffering on death row. It is therefore a circumstance of relevance for the overall assessment under Article 3 in that it goes to the search for the requisite fair balance of interests and to the proportionality of the contested extradition decision in the particular case.

(c) Conclusion

111. For any prisoner condemned to death, some element of delay between imposition and execution of the sentence and the experience of severe stress in conditions necessary for strict incarceration are inevitable. The democratic character of the Virginia legal system in general and the positive features of Virginia trial, sentencing and appeal procedures in particular are beyond doubt. The Court agrees with the Commission that the machinery of justice to which the applicant would be subject in the United States is in itself neither arbitrary nor unreasonable, but, rather, respects the rule of law and affords not inconsiderable procedural safeguards to the defendant in a capital trial. Facilities are available on death row for the assistance of inmates, notably through provision of psychological and psychiatric services[.]

However, in the Court's view, having regard to the very long period of time spent on death row in such extreme conditions, with the ever present and mounting anguish of awaiting execution of the death penalty, and to the personal circumstances of the applicant, especially his age and mental state at the time of the offence, the applicant's extradition to the United States would expose him to a real risk of treatment going beyond the threshold set by Article 3. A further consideration of relevance is that in the particular instance the legitimate purpose of extradition could be achieved by another means which would not involve suffering of such exceptional intensity or duration.

Accordingly, the Secretary of State's decision to extradite the applicant to the United States would, if implemented, give rise to a breach of Article 3.

This finding in no way puts in question the good faith of the United Kingdom Government, who have from the outset of the present proceedings demonstrated their desire to abide by their Convention obligations, firstly by staying the applicant's surrender to the United States authorities in accord with the interim measures indicated by the Convention institutions and secondly by themselves referring the case to the Court for a judicial ruling[.]

For These Reasons, the Court Unanimously

1. *Holds* that, in the event of the Secretary of State's decision to extradite the applicant to the United States of America being implemented, there would be a violation of Article 3[.]

NOTES AND QUESTIONS

1. *Soering's Fate.* Soon after the judgment of the Court, the United States represented to the United Kingdom that Soering would not be tried for a crime for which the death penalty could be imposed. Soering was then extradited to the United States, tried in Virginia, and found guilty on two counts of first-degree murder; it was recommended by the jury that he serve two life terms. Richard Lillich & Hurst Hannum, *International Human Rights* 768 (3d ed. 1995). Jens Soering tells his own version of the murders, his conviction, and his life in prison at http://www.jenssoering.com (last visited Dec. 12, 2013). Might the Court have differed from the Commission because it thought that Virginia would be willing to reduce the charge only if the United Kingdom were ordered *not* to extradite Soering?

2. *The United Kingdom's Predicament.* If Virginia had refused to try Soering for a charge where the death penalty could not be imposed, then the United Kingdom might have been caught between a rock and a hard place in international law. If by the terms of the U.K.-U.S. extradition treaty the U.K. government thought it ought to extradite Soering, but by the terms of the European Convention for the Protection of Human Rights and Fundamental Freedoms the United Kingdom was obligated to follow the judgment of the European Court of Human Rights, what should the United Kingdom have done? Should the U.K. government follow the extradition treaty because it is the international agreement later in time? Or should the U.K. government follow the European Human Rights Convention because the Convention concerns more fundamental rights? Is the answer linked to notions about *jus cogens*? See Chapter 3 and look back to *Filartiga* in Chapter 1. As it turned out, Virginia let the United Kingdom off the hook. There is more about international conflict of laws in general in Chapter 11 and about the specific

conflict in *Soering* in David Seymour & Jennifer Tooze, "The *Soering* Case: The Long Reach of the European Convention on Human Rights," in *International Law Stories* 115 (John E. Noyes, Laura A. Dickinson & Mark W. Janis eds. 2007).

3. *The Extraterritorial Effect of the* Soering *Judgment.* Is it fair to impose the human rights obligations of the European Convention on a non-party such as the United States? See Christine Van den Wyngaert, "Applying the European Convention on Human Rights to Extradition: Opening Pandora's Box?" 39 *International and Comparative Law Quarterly* 757 (1990). According to one extradition expert, the *Soering* decision "is having an impact on U.S. domestic criminal procedure at a very basic level;" officials of U.S. states seeking to extradite from Europe a fugitive accused of murder must essentially "prove to the Departments of State and Justice that the document [seeking extradition] is signed by the state official who has authority to bind the state to the commitment not to pursue or impose the death penalty." Christopher L. Blakesley, "The *Pinochet Extradition Case* and Beyond: Human Rights Clauses Compared to Traditional Derivative Protections Such as Double Criminality," 1999–2000 *Proceedings of the American Branch of the International Law Association* 370, 402. Why should U.S. death row conditions be a fit topic for consideration by the Strasbourg Court? The aftermath of *Soering* is treated in John Dugard & Christine Van den Wyngaert, "Reconciling Extradition with Human Rights," 92 *American Journal of International Law* 187 (1998), and Hemme Battjes, "In Search of a Fair Balance: The Absolute Character of the Prohibition of Refoulement under Article 3 ECHR Reassessed," 22 *Leiden Journal of International Law* 583 (2009). The European Court of Human Rights chose not to extend the logic of *Soering* to possible sentences in Maryland to life imprisonment without parole. Harkins and Edwards v. United Kingdom, Judgment of 17 January 2012. How easy is it to distinguish such a sentence from the death row phenomenon in *Soering*?

E. INTERNATIONAL CRIMINAL LAW

Besides rights individuals may also have duties at international law. Indeed, as we have seen, the modern transformation of the role of individuals in international law began after World War II with the Nuremberg criminal trials of individual defendants. After Nuremberg, it was the hope of many to establish a permanent international criminal tribunal. It took a long time, though, for the International Criminal Court (ICC) to emerge. Only in 1998 did states draft the Rome Statute, which, coming into force in 2002, finally established the ICC. The readings below introduce the negotiations leading to the Rome Statute and one of the first decisions of the ICC, the *Dyilo Case*. The Notes review developments at the ICC and at some of the other new international criminal tribunals.

LEILA NADYA SADAT & S. RICHARD CARDEN, "THE NEW INTERNATIONAL CRIMINAL COURT: AN UNEASY REVOLUTION"

88 *Georgetown Law Journal* 381 (2000)

I. PROLOGUE: THE LAST INTERNATIONAL INSTITUTION OF THE TWENTIETH CENTURY

From June 15 through July 17, 1998, representatives of 160 countries, closely watched by 250 non-governmental organizations (NGOs), met in Rome to negotiate a Treaty that would establish a permanent international criminal court. The Conference was held in the United Nations Food and Agricultural Organization building ("la FAO" in Italian), a large, rather plebeian structure from the Mussolini period, with a splendid view of *Il Palatino* from the top floor terrace. The weather was hot, the mood alternated between exhilaration and anxiety, the work was hard. Issues that had been debated for more than two years during the Preparatory Committee meetings leading up to the Rome Conference (PrepComI) remained on the table unresolved. The starting point of the negotiations was a complex consolidated text containing 116 articles, including some 1300 phrases in brackets. It was extremely difficult to read, let alone understand. As is by now well known, after five weeks of grueling negotiations, the Diplomatic Conference adopted a Statute for the Court in an emotional vote of 120 to 7, with 21 countries abstaining. The United States, whose delegation was instrumental in the development of the Statute throughout the PrepComI meetings and the Rome Conference, was one of the seven countries voting against the Treaty.

The adoption of the International Criminal Court (ICC) Statute is the result of more than seventy-five years of hard work and false starts. As the Preamble to the Treaty notes, the purpose of the Court is to end impunity for the perpetrators of "atrocities that deeply shock the conscience of humanity." And the Twentieth Century witnessed atrocities on a truly unprecedented scale. The estimate of 170 million dead in 250 conflicts that have occurred since World War II is a grim testament to the failure of the international community to create a viable mechanism to prevent aggression and enforce international humanitarian law.

It was thus appropriate and somehow fortuitous that the Diplomatic Conference was held in Rome. Once the center of an empire that stretched, during the Hadrianic period, across an area the size of the Continental United States and Alaska, Rome is a city rich in historic and cultural treasures. It has also been repeatedly devastated by war. And what delegate, gazing out over *Il Palatino* and the ruins of the Forum, or seeing *Castel Sant'Angelo*, where Pope Clement was besieged for months while soldiers looted the city and tormented and killed its inhabitants, could not feel the weight of history upon him or her, or understand the historic purpose for which all were gathered? Indeed, what better place in which to argue, on behalf of humanity, that the excesses of war should be restrained by the Rule of Law?

The International Criminal Court is the last great international institution of the Twentieth Century. It is no exaggeration to suggest that its creation has the potential to reshape our thinking about international law. For if many aspects of the Rome Treaty demonstrate the tenacity of traditional Westphalian notions of State sovereignty, there are nonetheless elements of supranationalism and efficacy (in spite of the complementarity principle [under which states may try individuals for crimes within the ICC's jurisdiction, in place of the ICC]) in the Statute that could prove extremely powerful. Not only does the Statute place State and non-State actors side-by-side in the international arena, but the Court will put real people in real jails. Indeed, the establishment of the Court raises hopes that the lines between international law on the one hand, and world order, on the other, are blurring and that the normative structure being created by international law might influence or even restrain the Hobbesian order established by the politics of States.

Given the unsuccessful history of previous efforts to establish an international criminal court, and the tepid support of many of the major powers during the Preparatory Committee meetings leading up to the Diplomatic Conference, the adoption of the Statute by the Diplomatic Conference comes as a surprise. It can be credited, at least in part, to the enormous lobbying and informational efforts of NGO's, which conducted a tireless campaign in support of the Court and came together as new evidence of global civil society. Another important factor was the emergence of a so-called "like-minded" group of States, which, although individually holding quite divergent views on many issues, were united in their view that the Court's ultimate establishment was a priority. Moreover, strong support from European countries and other traditional U.S. allies rallied the West behind the Court even without U.S. participation. * * *

But classic ideas about sovereignty die hard, and if the road to Rome was long and difficult, the journey to the seat of the Court at the Hague may be even more arduous. First, sixty States must ratify the Treaty before the Court can come into existence. In addition, before the Court can exercise its functions, the Preparatory Commission, established by the Diplomatic Conference at Rome, must prepare draft texts of Rules of Procedure and Evidence, Elements of Crimes, a relationship agreement between the Court and the United Nations, basic principles of the headquarters agreement, financial regulations and rules, an agreement on the privileges and immunities of the Court, a budget for the first financial year, and the rules of procedure for the Assembly of States

Parties. Much of this work will be the subject of Preparatory Commission meetings held over the next two years.

NOTES AND QUESTIONS

1. *Developments at the International Criminal Court.* The Rome Statute came into force in July 2002. Judges, 18 in all, were elected to serve on the International Criminal Court (ICC) in March 2003. As of November 1, 2013, there were 122 states parties to the Rome Statute. According to the President of the ICC, over its first two and a half years, the ICC built "the Court's physical structure" and established "the Court's judicial structure," *e.g.*, "the adoption by the judges of the Regulations of the Court." Philippe Kirsch, "Building an Effective & Efficient Court," *ICC Newsletter #3*, Feb. 2005, at 1. The pace has picked up a little. By late 2013, the ICC Office of the Prosecutor was conducting investigations in eight situations, all in Africa. There were also preliminary examinations of situations in Afghanistan, Cambodia, Colombia, the Comoros, Georgia, Greece, Guinea, Honduras, the Republic of Korea, and Nigeria. The ICC Secretary-General in 2013 hinted at some practical challenges when he stressed it was "particularly crucial that States provide timely and full cooperation to the Court in accordance with their legal obligations, and that appropriate action be taken in cases of non-cooperation." *Report of the International Criminal Court for 2012–13*, U.N. Doc. A/68/314, at 2, 21 (2013). The Court has submitted that its caseload is "considerable" and that the "system set up by the States in the Rome Statute continued to operate effectively in practice." *Report of the International Criminal Court for 2008/09*, U.N. Doc. A/64/356, at 2, 18 (2009). Do you agree?

2. *U.S. Hostility Toward the International Criminal Court.* The United States, with its many international military engagements exposing overseas U.S. personnel to possible prosecution, has been especially doubtful about turning over prosecutorial and adjudicatory powers to the ICC. Although President Clinton did finally authorize the signing of the Rome Statute, he did so only on December 31, 2000, the last day that the treaty was open to signature and very near the end of his term in office. And rather than submit the treaty to the Senate for its advice and consent to ratification, President Clinton emphasized what he saw as the treaty's "significant flaws." Sean D. Murphy, "Contemporary Practice of the United States Relating to International Law," 95 *American Journal of International Law* 387, 399 (2001). Even less friendly to the ICC, President Bush's administration notified the United Nations on May 6, 2002, "that the United States does not intend to become a party to the [Rome] treaty [and that accordingly] the United States has no legal obligations arising from its signature on December 31, 2001." Sean D. Murphy, "Contemporary Practice of the United States Relating to International Law," 96 *American Journal of International Law* 706, 724 (2002). See Article 18 of the Vienna Convention on the Law of Treaties, in the Appendix. President Obama's administration seems divided about joining the ICC.

What has motivated U.S. hostility to the ICC? Central to U.S. opposition is American "policy of ensuring that no U.S. national will ever be tried before the International Criminal Court." John F. Murphy, "Gulliver No Longer Quivers: U.S. Views on and the Future of the International Criminal Court," 44 *International Lawyer* 1123, 1128 (2010). Besides this, there have been doubts expressed about the constitutionality of U.S. adherence to the Rome Statute. For a comprehensive review, see David Scheffer & Ashley Cox, "The Constitutionality of the Rome Statute of the International Criminal Court," 98 *Journal of Criminal Law & Criminology* 983 (2008).

Important, too, is the preference the United States has for *ad hoc* rather than permanent international criminal tribunals. The *ad hoc* tribunals established at The Hague for the former Yugoslavia in 1993 and at Arusha for Rwanda in 1994 were created by the U.N. Security Council and thus much more sure to be controlled by the Council's permanent members—the United States, China, France, Russia, and the United Kingdom—than a permanent international criminal court. See William A. Schabas, "United States Hostility to the International Criminal Court: It's All About the Security Council," 15 *European Journal of International Law* 701 (2004). Adding to U.S. anxieties, ICC Chief Prosecutor Luis Moreno Campo warned that international corporate officers could face charges at The Hague if they facilitate government or insurgent conduct that violates international human rights law. James Podgers, "Corporations in Line of Fire: International Prosecutors Says Corporate Officials Could Face War Crimes Charges," 90 *ABA Journal,* Jan. 2004, at 13.

Even given these drawbacks, Professor Sievert has argued that the United States ought to modify its opposition to the ICC: "it is far better that the U.S. controls the process in the future and use it to its advantage than stand alone as its own rogue state against ninety-nine civilized nations." Ron Sievert, "A New Perspective on the International Criminal Court: Why the Right Should Embrace the ICC and How America Can Use It," 63 *University of Pittsburgh Law Review* 77, 129 (2006).

Has the United States tempered its opposition to the International Criminal Court? In 2005, the George W. Bush administration did not oppose a U.N. Security Council resolution referring the situation in Darfur, in the Sudan, to the ICC Prosecutor. In 2011, the United States under the Obama administration joined a unanimous Security Council vote referring the situation in Libya after February 15, 2011 to the Prosecutor. See U.N. Doc. S/RES/1595 (2005); U.N. Doc. S/RES/1970 (2011). More on the U.N. Security Council appears in Chapters 8 and 9. Is a critical issue for the United States the extent of discretion of the ICC Office of the Prosecutor to investigate situations and pursue cases without Security Council authorization? If a Security Council resolution were the only route to ICC jurisdiction, any permanent member of the Council, including the United States, could block ICC investigations or cases.

3. *The Jurisdiction of the ICC.* Referral from the Security Council acting under Chapter VII of the U.N. Charter is not the only basis for the

Court's exercise of jurisdiction. State parties may refer cases to the ICC, and the Prosecutor may also investigate proceedings *proprio motu*, if authorized by the Pre-Trial Chamber. See Rome Statute, arts. 13–15. As of November 2013, four countries—Uganda, the Democratic Republic of the Congo, the Central African Republic, and Mali—had referred situations in their territories to the ICC Prosecutor for investigation. The Prosecutor has also been authorized to conduct *proprio motu* investigations in Kenya and the Ivory Coast. The Court may exercise jurisdiction only with respect to war crimes, crimes against humanity, and the crime of aggression, and then "only with respect to crimes committed after the entry into force of" the Rome Statute. *Id.* art. 10.

4. *The Utility of International Criminal Courts.* There seem to be four kinds of goals advanced for the creation of international criminal courts: (1) justice and punishment, (2) deterrence, (3) record-keeping, and (4) the progressive development of international law. So far, practice shows that achievement of the first two goals—justice/punishment and deterrence—has been spotty at best. However, the utility of international criminal tribunals has been surer for the other two aims—record-keeping and the progressive development of international law. See Mark W. Janis, "The Utility of International Criminal Courts," 12 *Connecticut Journal of International Law* 161 (1997). See also Mark A. Drumbl, "Collective Violence and Individual Punishment: The Criminality of Mass Atrocity," 99 *Northwestern University Law Review* 539 (2005). When reading the *Lubanga Case* below, ask which of these four goals may or may not be advanced by the ICC proceeding and judgment.

SITUATION IN THE DEMOCRATIC REPUBLIC OF THE CONGO IN THE CASE OF THE PROSECUTOR V. THOMAS LUBANGA DYILO (2007)

Decision on the Confirmation of Charges, International Criminal Court
Pre-trial Chamber I, ICC–01/04–01/06, Jan. 29, 2007

I. INTRODUCTION

A. Factual Background

1. The District of Ituri before 1 July 2002

1. Ituri is a district in the Orientale Province of the Democratic Republic of the Congo (the DRC). It is bordered by Uganda to the east and Sudan to the north. Its population is between 3.5 and 5.5 million people, of whom only about 100,000 live in Bunia, the district capital. Ituri's population consists of some 20 different ethnic groups, the largest being the Hemas, the Alurs, the Biras, the Lendus and their southern sub-group, the Ngitis.

2. Ituri is rich in natural resources, such as gold, oil, timber, coltan and diamonds. For example, the Mongwalu mine, which is located about

forty-five kilometres north-west of Bunia, is the most important gold mine in the DRC and one of the most important in Central Africa.

3. The majority of the population of Ituri makes its living from agriculture, and the rest from trade, animal husbandry and fishing. Agriculture is the principal economic activity of the Lendus, while the Hemas are more active in livestock farming.

4. In the summer of 1999, tensions developed as a result of disputes over the allocation of land in Ituri and the appropriation of natural resources. During the second half of 2002, there was renewed violence in various parts of the district.

2. Thomas Lubanga Dyilo

5. Thomas Lubanga Dyilo was born in 1960 in Jiba (Djugu territory of Ituri, Orientale Province, DRC), and belongs to the Hema ethnic group. He studied at the University of Kisangani, where he obtained a degree in psychology. From 1986 to 1997, he allegedly headed an organisation called "Votura." From 1990 to 1994, he was also allegedly assistant at the CEPROMAD University. Throughout that period, he also engaged in other income-generating activities, ranging from farming to gold trading.

6. On the evidence presented for the purpose of the confirmation hearing, it would appear that Thomas Lubanga Dyilo entered politics between late 1999 and early 2000. Soon thereafter, he was elected to the Ituri District Assembly.

7. On 15 September 2000, the statutes of the *Union des Patriotes Congolais* (UPC) were signed by Thomas Lubanga Dyilo, as the first signatory, and several other persons who subsequently held leadership positions within the party and its armed military wing, the *Forces Patriotiques pour la Liberation du Congo* (FPLC). In August 2002, the UPC took control of Bunia.

8. In early September 2002, the UPC was renamed *Union des Patriotes Congolais/Reconciliation et Paix* (UPC/RP) and Thomas Lubanga Dyilo appointed its President. A few days later, in Bunia, Thomas Lubanga Dyilo signed the decree appointing the members of the first UPC/RP executive for the Ituri District. At the same time, a second decree officially established the FPLC. Immediately after the establishment of the FPLC, Thomas Lubanga Dyilo became its Commander-in-Chief.

3. Prosecution allegations against Thomas Lubanga Dyilo

9. In the "Document Containing the Charges, Article 61(3)(a)," filed on 28 August 2006, the Prosecution charges Thomas Lubanga Dyilo under articles 8(2)(e)(vii) and 25(3)(a) of the [ICC] Statute with the war crimes of conscripting and enlisting children under the age of fifteen years into an armed group (in this case, the FPLC, military wing of the

UPC since September 2002) and using them to participate actively in hostilities. The Prosecution submits that "the crimes occurred in the context of an armed conflict not of an international character."

10. The Prosecution asserts that even prior to the founding of the FPLC, the UPC actively recruited children under the age of fifteen years in significant numbers and subjected them to military training in its military training camp in Sota, amongst other places.

11. The Prosecution further submits that, after its founding and until the end of 2003, the FPLC continued to systematically enlist and conscript children under the age of fifteen years in large numbers in order to provide them with military training, and use them subsequently to participate actively in hostilities, including as bodyguards for senior FPLC military commanders. The FPLC military training camps included camps in Centrale, Mandro, Rwampara, lrumu and Bule.

12. The Prosecution submits that Thomas Lubanga Dyilo is criminally responsible for the crimes listed in the Document Containing the Charges as a co-perpetrator, jointly with other FPLC officers and UPC members and supporters. * * *

379. [T]he Chamber has concluded that * * * there was sufficient evidence to establish substantial grounds to believe that from early September 2002 to the end of 2003:

i. the FPLC repeatedly admitted into its ranks young recruits, including children under the age of fifteen years, who wished to voluntarily join the FPLC;

ii. the FPLC repeatedly forcibly recruited into its ranks young recruits, including children under the age of fifteen years;

iii. the FPLC encouraged the practice whereby each Hema family was to contribute to the war effort, in particular, by supplying young recruits, including children under the age of fifteen years;

iv. the FPLC sent its young recruits, including children under the age of fifteen years, to the FPLC military training camps in Centrale, Rwampara, Mandro, lrumu, Bule, Bogoro, and Sota;

v. the aim of the military training was to prepare the young FPLC recruits, including those under the age of fifteen years, to participate actively in military operations; the training lasted up to two months, and included physical exercises like learning to salute, march, run, take up positions and use firearms;

vi. the young FPLC recruits, including those under the age of fifteen years, were subject to strict military discipline and the instructors sought to boost their morale by making them sing aggressive military songs;

vii. the most senior FPLC commanders—Thomas Lubanga Dyilo, Floribert Kisembo and Bosco Ntaganda—regularly visited FPLC military training camps where young recruits, including those under the age of fifteen years, were being trained;

viii. upon completion of their military training, Floribert Kisembo and Bosco Ntaganda and other senior commanders (such as Tchalingonza) provided the young recruits, including those under the age of fifteen years, with a military uniform and a personal weapon (usually a firearm), and soon thereafter ordered them into combat on the front line in military operations conducted in Libi and Mbau in October 2002, in Largu in early 2003, in Lipri and Bogoro in February and March 2003, in Bunia in May 2003 and in Djugu and Mongwalu in June 2003;

ix. it was common practice among the most senior FPLC commanders (i.e. Thomas Lubanga Dyilo, Floribert Kisembo and Bosco Ntaganda) and other senior commanders (such as Tchalingonza) to use young recruits, including those under the age of fifteen years, as bodyguards to protect military objectives, such as their physical safety (including during military operations) and FPLC military quarters. * * *

410. [T]he Chamber finds that there is sufficient evidence to establish substantial grounds to believe that from early September 2002 to 13 August 2003, Thomas Lubanga Dyilo incurred criminal responsibility as a co-perpetrator within the meaning of article 25(3)(a) of the Statute for the crimes referred to in Section IV of this decision.

SITUATION IN THE DEMOCRATIC REPUBLIC OF THE CONGO IN THE CASE OF THE PROSECUTOR V. THOMAS LUBANGA DYILO (2012)

Judgment Pursuant to Article 74 of the Statute, International Criminal Court Trial Chamber I, ICC-01/04–01/06, Mar. 14, 2012

1270. The Chamber concludes beyond reasonable doubt that the accused, by virtue of his position as President and Commander-in-Chief from September 2002 onwards, was able to shape the policies of the

UPC/FPLC and to direct the activities of his alleged co-perpetrators. The established reporting structures; the lines of communication within the UPC/FPLC; and the meetings and close contact between the accused and at least some of the alleged co-perpetrators, support the conclusion that he was kept fully informed throughout the relevant period and he issued instructions relating to the implementation of the common plan. Thomas Lubanga personally assisted in the military affairs of the UPC/FPLC in a variety of ways. He was involved in planning military operations and he exercised a key role in providing logistical support, by ensuring weapons, ammunition, food, uniforms and military rations and other supplies were available for the troops. * * *

1271. Viewed in its entirety, the evidence demonstrates that the accused and his alleged co-perpetrators, including particularly Floribert Kisembo, Chief Kahwa and Bosco Ntaganda, worked together and each of them made an essential contribution to the common plan that resulted in the enlistment, conscription and use of children under the age of 15 to participate actively in hostilities.

1272. In light of the evidence above, the Chamber is persuaded beyond reasonable doubt that the accused made an essential contribution to the common plan for the purposes of Article 25(3)(a). * * *

1351. The accused and his co-perpetrators agreed to, and participated in a common plan to build an army for the purpose of establishing and maintaining political and military control over Ituri. This resulted, in the ordinary course of events, in the conscription and enlistment of boys and girls under the age of 15, and their use to participate actively in hostilities. * * *

1354. The accused and at least some of his co-perpetrators were involved in the takeover of Bunia in August 2002. Thomas Lubanga, as the highest authority within the UPC, appointed Chief Kahwa, Floribert Kisembo and Bosco Ntaganda to senior positions within theUPC/FPLC. The evidence has established that during this period, the leaders of the UPC/FPLC, including Chief Kahwa, and Bosco Ntaganda, and Hema elders such as Eloy Mafuta, were active in mobilization and recruitment campaigns aimed at persuading Hema families to send their children to join the UPC/FPLC. Those children recruited before the formal creation of the FPLC were incorporated into that group, and a number of training camps were added to the original facility at Mandro. The Chamber has concluded that between 1 September 2002 and 13 August 2003, a significant number of high-ranking members of the UPC/FPLC and other personnel conducted a large-scale recruitment exercise directed at young people, including children under the age of 15, whether voluntarily or by coercion.

1355. The Chamber is satisfied beyond reasonable doubt that as a result of the implementation of the common plan to build an army for the purpose of establishing and maintaining political and military control over Ituri, boys and girls under the age of 15 were conscripted and enlisted into the UPC/FPLC between 1 September 2002 and 13 August 2003. Similarly, the Chamber is satisfied beyond reasonable doubt that the UPC/FPLC used children under the age of 15 to participate actively in hostilities, including during battles. They were also used, during the relevant period, as soldiers and as bodyguards for the senior officials, including the accused.

1356. Thomas Lubanga was the President of the UPC/FPLC, and the evidence demonstrates that he was simultaneously the Commander-in-Chief of the army and its political leader. He exercised an overall coordinating role over the activities of the UPC/FPLC. He was informed, on a substantive and continuous basis, of the operations of the FPLC. He was involved in planning military operations, and he played a critical role in providing logistical support, including as regards weapons, ammunition, food, uniforms, military rations and other general supplies for the FPLC troops. He was closely involved in making decisions on recruitment police and he actively supported recruitment initiatives, for instance by giving speeches to the local population and the recruits. In his speech at the Rwampara camp, he encouraged children, including those under the age of 15 years, to join the army and to provide security for the populace once deployed in the field following their military training. Furthermore, he personally used children below the age of 15 amongst his bodyguards and he regularly saw guards of other UPC/FPLC members of staff who were below the age of 15. The Chamber has concluded that these contributions by Thomas Lubanga, taken together, were essential to a common plan that resulted in the conscription and enlistment of girls and boys below the age of 15 in to the UPC/FPLC and their use to actively participate in hostilities.

1357. The Chamber is satisfied beyond reasonable doubt, as set out above, that Thomas Lubanga acted with the intent and knowledge necessary to establish the charges (the mental element required by Article 30). He was aware of the factual circumstances that established the existence of the armed conflict. Furthermore, he was aware of the nexus between those circumstances and his own conduct, which resulted in the enlistment, conscription and use of children below the age of 15 to participate actively in hostilities.

1358. For the foregoing reasons and on the basis of the evidence submitted and discussed before the Chamber at trial, and the entire proceedings, pursuant to Article 74(2) of the Statute, the Chamber finds Mr. Thomas Lubanga Dyilo:

GUILTY of the crimes of conscripting and enlisting children under the age of fifteen years into the FPLC and using them to participate actively in hostilities within the meaning of Articles 8(2)(e)(vii) and 25(3)(a) of the Statute from early September 2002 to 13 August 2003.

NOTES AND QUESTIONS

1. Lubanga*: The Belated First Judgment.* The 2012 *Lubanga* judgment was long-anticipated. As early as 2008, a newspaper columnist lamented: "as it celebrates its 10th anniversary, the ICC is facing its own indictment. Its critics charge that its work is often counter-productive, politicised and plain incompetent." Among the criticisms: that the ICC had not completed a prosecution, that its defendants were all African, and that its work complicated peace efforts. Gideon Rachman, "When Peace and Justice Collide," *Financial Times*, July 7, 2008. The slow progress of the *Lubanga Case* illustrates some of the ICC's problems. In 2003, the ICC's Chief Prosecutor underlined that the Ituri situation in the Democratic Republic of the Congo ought to be "the most urgent situation to be followed" by the ICC. Lubanga, who had been arrested by the Congolese government in 2005, was transferred to The Hague in 2006. In 2007, as we see, a pre-trial chamber decided there was sufficient evidence for the Prosecutor to proceed. In 2009, the trial finally began. Marlies Glasius, "What is Global Justice and Who Decides? Civil Society and Victim Responses to the International Criminal Court's First Investigations," 31 *Human Rights Quarterly* 496, 498–99 (2009). In July 2010, however, the trial chamber stayed the proceedings, ruling that "because of the Prosecutor's clearly evinced intention not to implement the Chamber's orders[,] the fair trial of the accused is no longer possible." Decision of July 8, 2010, ¶ 31. The trial chamber's order to release Lubanga was reversed on appeal, and the trial recommenced in December 2010—only to be interrupted again to hear (and ultimately reject) a defense motion to dismiss the case on the grounds that the Office of the Prosecutor had allegedly bribed and coached witnesses.

When the ICC finally did deliver its first judgment in 2012, it was not generally praised. There were three ICC decisions altogether, numbering hundreds of pages: the verdict convicting Lubanga, a ruling on his sentence, and an outline on awarding reparations to victims. Diane Marie Amann, "International Decision: *Prosecutor v. Lubanga*," 106 *American Journal of International Law* 809 (2012). "[P]rovoking concern was the fact that it took the ICC six years to render a trial verdict in a case involving a single defendant accused only of the war crime of child soldiering." *Id.* at 815. Moreover, despite its length, "the decision did not meet the bar * * * of 'a fully reliable record' established 'so that future generations can remember and be made fully cognizant of what happened.'" *Id.* at 817. Nevertheless, one observer commended the ICC for "shedding light on the conscription, enlistment, and use of child soldiers." Triestino Mariniello, "*Prosecutor v. Thomas Lubanga Dyilo*: The First Judgment of the International Criminal Court's Trial Chamber," 1 *International Human Rights Law Review* 137, 138 (2012). But even this triumph was warped: "[T]he [ICC] was not satisfied that even a single one of the witnesses whom the prosecution called purporting to be victims had, in fact, been child soldiers. In other words, not a single one of Lubanga's victims ever got a chance to tell his or her story to the Court and have it count." Caroline Buisman, "Delegating Investigations: Lessons to be Learned from the *Lubanga* Judgment," 11 *Northwestern Journal of International Human Rights* 30, 82 (2013). Why has the ICC been so slow, and so relatively unsuccessful?

2. *The Fate of the International Criminal Court.* What will be the fate of the ICC? There has been considerable opposition to one of the ICC's most high-profile prosecutions, the 2009 indictment of Omar Hassan Ahmad Al Bashir, the President of the Sudan, for war crimes and crimes against humanity in Darfur. Among those opposed are the African Union parties to the Rome Statute, the League of Arab States, Russia, and China. Manisuli Ssenyonjo, "The International Criminal Court Warrant Decision for President Al Bashir of Sudan," 59 *International and Comparative Law Quarterly* 205, 206–07, 224–25 (2010). Can the ICC work effectively facing such wide-spread attack? What, if anything, can be done to make the ICC a more acceptable forum within the international community?

3. Ad Hoc *International Criminal Tribunals.* Although a permanent international criminal court is an innovation, *ad hoc* international criminal courts set up for a specific region or problem are longstanding. Besides the Nuremberg trials explored above, there have been *ad hoc* international criminal tribunals in Tokyo for the trial of Japanese World War II war criminals, in The Hague (beginning in 1993) for crimes in the former Yugoslavia, and in Arusha (beginning in 1994) for crimes in Rwanda. There are significant differences among the four *ad hoc* tribunals. Among other things, the Nuremberg and Tokyo trials, following the Allied defeat of Germany and Japan, proceeded immediately against the principal leaders of those governments; the Hague and Arusha trials, with no conquests in hand, had to begin with proceedings against figures of lesser consequence. Louis B. Sohn, "From Nazi Germany and Japan to Yugoslavia and Rwanda: Similarities and Differences," 12 *Connecticut Journal of International Law* 209 (1997).

Much criticism has been launched at the Arusha proceedings of the International Criminal Tribunal for Rwanda (ICTR). See Paul J. Magnarella, *Justice in Africa: Rwanda's Genocide, Its Courts, and the UN Criminal Tribunal* (2000). In four short months in 1994, Hutus in Rwanda killed almost three quarters of the country's Tutsi minority population. Tutsi exiles in Uganda then invaded Rwanda, overthrew the Hutu regime, and, in turn, committed mass killings. Leslie Haskell & Lars Waldorf, "The Impunity Gap of the International Criminal Tribunal for Rwanda: Causes and Consequences," 34 *Hastings International and Comparative Law Review* 49, 49–50 (2011). As of 2009, all the ICTR prosecutions—90 in all—were of individuals from the overthrown Hutu regime. As one commentator has remarked, "the tribunal's failure to prosecute the [present Tutsi government] would inevitably lead to the objective conclusion that the ICTR was a form of victor's justice." Thierry Cruvellier, *Court of Remorse: Inside the International Criminal Tribunal for Rwanda* 164 (2010).

More progress has been made at the International Criminal Tribunal for the former Yugoslavia (ICTY). The ICTY reached out to try some, though not all, of the principal suspected actors, including former Yugoslav President Slobodan Milošević. Milošević's trial was criticized for taking so long—he died in March 2006, when his trial had been underway for more than four years—and for its high costs and procedural confusions. See "Former Yugoslavia: Justice on Trial," *The Economist*, Feb. 28, 2004, at 47. The ICTY is still criticized for being unwilling to rein in "truculent defendants." See Marlise Simons, "As a Defendant Bullies and Boasts, Questions Arise on a Court's Limits," *New York Times*, Apr. 17, 2012, at A3. One commentator concluded: The ICTY "weaves a sad end to the story of a court that was founded by little hope, encouraged some, then jettisoned it all." Eric Gordy, "What Happened to the Hague Tribunal?," *International Herald Tribune*, June 3, 2013, at 6. Adding to its woes, one of its 18 judges, Frederick Harhoff of Denmark, has complained about the President of the Court, Judge Theodor Meron. Marlise Simons, "Hague Court was Pressured in Recent Verdicts, Judge Says," *International Herald Tribune*, June 15–16, 2013, at 1. Nonetheless, the ICTY proceedings constitute the most significant example of an international criminal court's prosecutions since Nuremberg. ICTY case law is already voluminous. See the several collections of cases, largely ICTY, compiled in *Annotated Leading Cases of International Criminal Tribunals*, vols. 1–40 (André Klip & Göran Sluiter eds. 1999–2013); and the essays in *International Criminal Law Developments in the Case Law of the ICTY* (Gideon Boas & William A. Schabas eds. 2003). This casebook excerpts two cases drawn from the ICTY, in Chapters 3 (*Furundžija*) and 9 (*Tadić*).

Besides the permanent international criminal court and the *ad hoc* international criminal courts at The Hague and Arusha, there is a new *ad hoc* international criminal tribunal for Sierra Leone based in The Hague. Although the Special Court for Sierra Leone has been criticized for its slow and expensive pace, it has prosecuted and convicted a number of military leaders for crimes against humanity, war crimes, and violations of international humanitarian law. Charles Chernor Jalloh, "Special Court for Sierra Leone: Achieving Justice," 32 *Michigan Journal of International Law* 395, 445–48 (2010–2011). And significantly, in 2012, the Special Court for Sierra Leone found Charles Taylor, the former President of Liberia, to be guilty of aiding and abetting war crimes and crimes against humanity. Taylor was the first African president to be prosecuted by an international court. Owen Bowcott & Monica Mark, "Charles Taylor Found Guilty of Abetting Sierra Leone War Crimes," *The Guardian*, Apr. 26, 2012. The British Foreign Secretary, William Hague, termed the Taylor conviction as a "landmark verdict." *Quoted in id.*

4. *National and Hybrid International Criminal Law.* A variety of national and hybrid courts, special and ordinary, are also used to prosecute international crimes. See the review of available procedures in Leila Nadya

Sadat, "Exile, Amnesty and International Law," 81 *Notre Dame Law Review* 955 (2006). We include several examples of prosecutions and tort claims in U.S. courts here—*Filartiga* in Chapter 1, *Smith* in Chapter 3, and *De Longchamps, Sosa,* and *Kiobel* in Chapter 4. Other countries have been active as well, notably Belgium. See Marlise Simons, "Human Rights Cases Begin to Flood Into Belgian Courts," *New York Times International*, Dec. 27, 2001, at A8; Pieter H.F. Bekker, "World Court Orders Belgium to Cancel an Arrest Warrant Issued Against the Congolese Foreign Minister," *ASIL Newsletter*, Jan./Feb. 2002, at 1. In Spain, a prominent investigating judge, Baltasar Garzón, indicted, among others, the 9/11 terrorist, Osama bin Laden, and Chile's dictator, Augusto Pinochet. However, Garzón himself was indicted in a Spanish court when he opened an investigation into the disappearance of tens of thousands of people during the Spanish Civil War and General Franco's dictatorship. Spanish authorities complained that Garzón's investigation would violate an amnesty granted after Franco's death in 1975 that sought to promote national reconciliation. Graham Keeley, "Judge Baltasar Garzón in the Dock Over Inquiry Into Franco-Era Killings," *The Times Online*, Sept. 10, 2009, http://www.timesonline.co.uk (last visited Dec. 8, 2013).

Apparently bolder, a trial court in Guatemala convicted the former dictator of the country for crimes against humanity and genocide for massacres of Ixil villagers in the early 1980s. Elisabeth Malkin, "Former Leader of Guatemala is Guilty of Genocide Against Mayan Group," *New York Times*, May 11, 2013, at A6. However, Guatemala's Constitutional Court vacated the judgment and ordered a retrial. Tracey Wilkinson, "Guatemalan Court Overturns Rios Montt Conviction," *Los Angeles Times*, May 20, 2013. Another national approach to reconciliation is the South African process of "transitional justice," involving "truth commissions" that assess allegations of mass violations of human rights by former officials of an ousted government. Truth commissions have also been employed in Latin America and elsewhere. See Ruti G. Teitel, *Transitional Justice* (2000). Such national prosecutions of international crimes are sometimes ordered and supervised by regional human rights courts such as the European and Inter-American courts of human rights. See Alexandra Huneeus, "International Law by Other Means: The Quasi-Criminal Jurisdiction of Human Rights Courts," 107 *American Journal of International Law* 1 (2013).

A new approach created in Bosnia-Herzegovina, East Timor, and Kosovo, "hybrid courts," mixes national and foreign judges on hybrid national/international criminal tribunals. See Omer Ibrahimagic, "The Aggression Upon Bosnia and the Judicial Protection of Human Rights," 12 *Connecticut Journal of International Law* 171 (1997); Laura A. Dickinson, "The Promise of Hybrid Courts," 97 *American Journal of International Law* 295 (2003). Another new hybrid tribunal, the Special Tribunal for Lebanon, addresses certain Lebanese crimes, including terrorism, rather than international law crimes. See Olivia Swaak-Goldman, "Introductory Note to Security Council Resolution 1757 Establishing the Special Tribunal for Lebanon," 46 *International Legal Materials* 989 (2007). And yet another national/international hybrid court, the Extraordinary Chambers in the Courts of Cambodia, was established in 2005 to try former leaders of the Khmer Rouge, accused of killing an estimated 1.7 million Cambodians between 1975 and 1979. For its, at best, mixed record, see Abby Seif, "Seeking Justice in the Killing Fields," 99 *ABA Journal*, Mar. 2013, at 50.

5. *A Toothless Tiger?* Forecasting dire consequences in anticipation of the Supreme Court's opinion in *Kiobel* (see Chapter 4), Second Circuit Judge Pierre Leval lamented, "over 65 years after Nuremberg, although the world remains awash in these atrocities, the prohibitions of international law are largely toothless." Pierre N. Leval, "The Long Arm of International Law: Giving Victims of Abuse Their Day in Court," 92 *Foreign Affairs*, Mar./Apr. 2013, at 16. After your study of the various courts and processes devoted to international human rights and criminal law, do you agree? For an excellent up-to-date review of the work of the ad hoc criminal tribunals and the ICC, see Leila Nadya Sadat, "Crimes Against Humanity in the Modern Era," 107 *American Journal of International Law* 334 (2013).

CHAPTER 7

STATES AND INTERNATIONAL LAW

■ ■ ■

As we have seen, individuals are now usually treated as subjects of international law, but states, at least since 1648, have been viewed as the principal actors in making international legal rules and coordinating international legal process. Moreover, states remain the most important subjects of international law and relations. But what exactly is a state?

In Part A of this chapter, we examine the concept of sovereignty, a hallmark of statehood. Part B introduces the complicated theories of the recognition and succession of states and governments. Questions of recognition and succession link to problems concerning the transformation of states and governments. Do the legal obligations of a state continue when its government changes radically, or when the state breaks apart? Finally, in Part C we consider the principle of self-determination, which has been invoked with respect to the creation of new states.

A. THE SOVEREIGN STATE

What does it mean to say that a state is "sovereign"? How can we reconcile state sovereignty with the notion that states both exercise rights and are subject to duties under international law? Is state sovereignty itself a product of international law? To explore these questions, we look at the work of Emer de Vattel, an influential 18th-century international law theorist.

E. DE VATTEL, THE LAW OF NATIONS

3–7, 11 (1758 ed., Charles G. Fenwick trans. 1916; reprinted 1964)

Nations or States are political bodies, societies of men who have united together and combined their forces, in order to procure their mutual welfare and security.

Such a society has its own affairs and interests; it deliberates and takes resolutions in common, and it thus becomes a moral person having an understanding and a will peculiar to itself, and susceptible at once of obligations and of rights.

[L]iberty and independence belong to man by his very nature, and * * * they can not be taken from him without his consent. Citizens of a State, having yielded them in part to the sovereign, do not enjoy them to their full and absolute extent. But the whole body of the Nation, the State, so long as it has not voluntarily submitted to other men or other Nations, remains absolutely free and independent.

As men are subject to the laws of nature, and as their union in civil society can not exempt them from the obligation of observing those laws, since in that union they remain none the less men, the whole Nation, whose common will is but the outcome of the united wills of the citizens, remains subject to the laws of nature and is bound to respect them in all its undertakings. * * *

Such is man's nature that he is not sufficient unto himself and necessarily stands in need of the assistance and intercourse of his fellows, whether to preserve his life or to perfect himself and live as befits a rational animal. * * * Therefore, since nature has constituted men thus, it is a clear proof that it means them to live together and mutually to aid and assist one another.

[W]hen men have agreed to act in common, and have given up their rights and submitted their will to the whole body as far as concerns their common good, it devolves thenceforth upon that body, the State, and upon its rulers, to fulfill the duties of humanity towards outsiders in all matters in which individuals are no longer at liberty to act, and it peculiarly rests with the State to fulfill these duties towards other States.

* * * Hence the end of the great society established by nature among all nations is likewise that of mutual assistance in order to perfect themselves and their condition.

The first general law, which is to be found in the very end of the society of Nations, is that each Nation should contribute as far as it can to the happiness and advancement of other Nations.

But as its duties towards itself clearly prevail over its duties towards others, a Nation owes to itself, as a prime consideration, whatever it can do for its own happiness and advancement. (I say whatever it *can* do, not meaning *physically* only, but *morally* also, what it can do lawfully, justly, and honestly.) * * *

Since Nations are free and independent of one another as men are by nature, the second general law of their society is that each Nation should be left to the peaceable enjoyment of that liberty which belongs to it by nature. The natural society of nations can not continue unless the rights which belong to each by nature are respected. * * *

Since men are by nature equal, and their individual rights and obligations the same, as coming equally from nature, Nations, which are composed of men and may be regarded as so many free persons living together in a state of nature, are by nature equal and hold from nature the same obligations and the same rights. Strength or weakness, in this case, counts for nothing. A dwarf is as much a man as a giant is; a small Republic is no less a sovereign State than the most powerful Kingdom.

From this equality it necessarily follows that what is lawful or unlawful for one Nation is equally lawful or unlawful for every other Nation. * * *

From the fact that [individuals form] a society in which they have common interests and must act in concert it is necessary that a public authority be set up, which shall regulate and prescribe the duties of each member with respect to the object of the association. This public authority constitutes the *sovereignty*; and he, or they, in whom it is vested is the *sovereign*. * * *

Every Nation which governs itself, under whatever form, and which does not depend on any other Nation, is a *sovereign State*. Its rights are, in the natural order, the same as those of every other State. Such is the character of the moral persons who live together in a society established by nature and subject to the Law of Nations. To give a Nation the right to a definite position in this great society, it need only be truly sovereign and independent; it must govern itself by its own authority and its own laws.

NOTES AND QUESTIONS

1. *The Concept of "State."* How do we conceive of states? Has the concept changed over time? Jean Bodin, writing in 1576, conceptualized European political authority in terms of the unified control of monarchs. Bodin identified "markes of Soveraignetie" that concerned especially a monarch's internal authority. These "markes" included the rights, subject to "the lawes of God and nature," to make laws, name magistrates, hear final appeals, grant pardons, coin money, set weights and measures, impose taxes, wage war, and exact "liege fealtie and homage." See Jean Bodin, *The Six Bookes of a Commonweale* (1606 English trans. of *République,* Kenneth Douglas McRae ed. 1962).

Later scholars devoted more attention to the external relationships of states. One, Emer de Vattel, was frequently cited in 18th- and 19th-century U.S. legal argument. For example, in Dred Scott v. Sandford, 60 U.S. (19 How.) 393 (1857), the Supreme Court's most infamous judgment, Mr. Justice Daniel, writing in support of the Court's pro-slavery decision, relied heavily on Vattel. See Mark W. Janis, "*Dred Scott* and International Law," 43 *Columbia Journal of Transnational Law* 763 (2005).

Which of the features that Vattel associated with the state continue to have currency? Are there additional or different features that, today, we identify with the sovereign state? See Stéphane Beaulac, "Emer de Vattel and the Externalization of Sovereignty," 5 *Journal of the History of International Law* 237 (2003); Penelope Simons, "The Emergence of the Idea of the Individualized State in the International Legal System," *id.* at 293.

2. *Sovereignty and International Law*. Review the Peace of Westphalia and the notes on Hobbes, Grotius, and the Thirty Years War in Chapter 2. What measures of autonomy and authority did the Peace of Westphalia grant to states? How did it limit state autonomy and authority? What limits did Vattel identify?

Is state sovereignty consistent with the notion that international law regulates when and how a state may use force against another state? Does the acquiescence of each independent state in rules of international law concerning territorial integrity and protections for diplomats and citizens travelling abroad help to establish and preserve the rights of every other state? Does international law limit a sovereign state's freedom of action even with respect to its own "internal" affairs? Does international law restrict how a state may treat is own citizens within its own territory? How can such limits be consistent with the concept of sovereignty? See Chapter 6.

According to the Permanent Court of International Justice in the S.S. Wimbledon, 1923 P.C.I.J. Ser. A, No. 1, at 15, 25, "the right of entering into international engagements is an attribute of state sovereignty." Does non-consensual international law also help define state sovereignty? Consider the following views: "[S]overeignty is the term for 'the totality of international rights and duties recognized by international law' as residing in an independent territorial unit—the State." James Crawford, *The Creation of States in International Law* 32 (2d ed. 2006). "[W]e cannot deduce the extent of a state's freedom of action from the mere fact of its statehood. Sovereignty is, as the Permanent Court of International Justice noted in 1923, an 'essentially relative question'—dependent on whatever law there is to curtail it." Martti Koskenniemi, "The Future of Statehood," 32 *Harvard International Law Journal* 397, 408 (1991). In order to decide disputes between competing state claims to freedom of action "without violating sovereign equality, we are limited to criteria that are hierarchically more important than statehood to provide a justification for drawing its limit in some particular way." *Id.*

3. *The Development of the State System*. Following the Peace of Westphalia, states with defined boundaries became the predominant form of political organization in Europe. Outside of Europe as well, states evolved from other forms of political relationships. In some regions, territorially bounded states are modern phenomena. Until the late 19th century, for example, the rulers of Siam (Thailand):

> controlled a set of specific, non-adjacent places according to their proximity and usefulness to Bangkok; [rulers] controlled specific resources, trade routes or populations [but] did not conceive of * * * authority in terms of territory. * * * Hierarchical relations between various rulers and subjects, not control over continuous territory, defined Siam.

> [B]oundaries were not thin demarcating lines but rather substantial regions or zones. Moreover, boundaries were indeterminate, even potentially mobile.

Richard T. Ford, "Law's Territory (A History of Jurisdiction)," 97 *Michigan Law Review* 843, 868–69 (1999), *citing* Thongchai Winichakul, *Siam Mapped: A History of the Geo-Body of a Nation* (1994). Decolonization in the 20th century resulted in the creation of many states; we explore decolonization and self-determination in Part C.

4. *The Jurisdiction of States.* International lawyers are often concerned with the "jurisdiction" of sovereign states, *e.g.*, the authority of states to determine and affect legal relationships involving private parties. We examine jurisdiction and how to resolve conflicts among the laws, courts, and executives of different states in Chapters 11 and 12.

5. *The Equality of States.* Vattel asserted that each state has the same legal rights as other states. In making this claim, was Vattel drawing on some precept of natural law? The principle of juridical equality of states is enshrined in Article 4 of the Montevideo Convention, reproduced in Part B below, and in Article 2(1) of the United Nations Charter. According to Chief Justice Marshall of the U.S. Supreme Court, "No principle of general law is more universally acknowledged, than the perfect equality of nations." The Antelope, 23 U.S. (10 Wheat.) 66, 122 (1825). Does the equality principle simply mean that the weakness of a state provides no legal justification for violating its legal rights? Should this fundamental principle ever be varied? If so, when and why? For example, how well does the principle of equality of states fit with the right of the five permanent members at the U.N. Security Council to veto resolutions? See Chapters 8 and 9. See also Benedict Kingsbury, "Sovereignty and Inequality," 9 *European Journal of International Law* 599 (1998).

6. *"Civilized" States?* Recall from Chapter 3 that the ICJ Statute, echoing language in the 1920 Statute of the Permanent Court of International Justice, lists as a source of international law "general principles of law recognized by civilized nations." The "civilized" limitation is rarely invoked today. In the 19th and early 20th centuries, however, European international law doctrine generally considered that the "family of nations" was open only to European states and to those entities outside Europe that achieved a certain degree of civilization and of interaction with states that were already part of the "family." In the decades after the American Revolution, the United States was eager to demonstrate that it was part of that European "family of nations." See Mark Weston Janis, *America and the Law of Nations 1776–1939*, at 49–91 (2010). As you read the Montevideo Convention in Part B, consider whether its "declaratory" treatment of recognition is consistent with the notion of a family of nations.

7. *Challenges to State Sovereignty.* The sovereign state has been criticized on many fronts. Some, for example, stressing the importance of economics in the modern world, see states as imposing artificial boundaries

that impede the efficient operation of markets. Others argue that states may be either too large or too small to respond well to current challenges; management problems may require structures larger than the state, while entities smaller than the state may more effectively produce political legitimacy. In light of such criticisms of the state, what justifies its continuing central role in international law? Do states retain legitimate authority today only insofar as they act as "trustees for the people committed to their care," operating to further a "peaceful and ordered world"? Jeremy Waldron, "The Rule of International Law," 30 *Harvard Journal of Law and Public Policy* 15, 24 (2006). Should international law adopt a functional view of authority, under which the state competes as just one of several actors in efforts to regulate international activities? Or do you agree with Professor Kingsbury that "discarding sovereignty in favour of a functional approach will intensify inequality, weakening restraints on coercive intervention, diminishing critical roles of the state as a locus of identity and an autonomous zone of politics, and redividing the world into zones"? Benedict Kingsbury, "Sovereignty and Inequality," 9 *European Journal of International Law* 599 (1998). See "Theoretical Perspectives on the Transformation of Sovereignty," 1994 *American Society of International Law Proceedings* 1.

As we saw in Chapter 6, individuals have rights and duties under international law. Part C of this chapter suggests that certain groups ("peoples") enjoy the right of self-determination. And as we explore in Chapter 8, international organizations possess "international personality." How broadly should we extend the concept of international personality to non-state entities?

B. THE RECOGNITION AND SUCCESSION OF STATES AND GOVERNMENTS

Just what is a state? To say that it is an entity possessing sovereignty leaves us to debate what entities are entitled to sovereignty. To what extent does a state's very existence depend on recognition by other states or international organizations? And what legal issues arise when existing states break apart or merge?

Examining the succession of states helps us understand some of the ways states are created and sheds light on the legal functions of recognition. At times in history, changes in states have been dramatic. Between 1990 and 1993, for example, East and West Germany united, as did North and South Yemen; Eritrea seceded from Ethiopia; Czechoslovakia split in two; and Yugoslavia and the Soviet Union each broke apart into several new states. Namibia also gained full independence during this period, and a United Nations Trusteeship over the Marshall Islands ended. Some transitions are peaceful, agreed to by all concerned, while other changes are the product of violence. Changes in governments are even more common than changes in states. New governments may be radically different from their predecessors when, for example, new constitutions are adopted or governments fall in coups. International lawyers must grapple with legal issues related to the transformation of states and governments.

We explore the issues in this part by considering a treaty, municipal court cases, an international arbitral decision, and 1991 European Community Guidelines on the recognition of new states.

THE MONTEVIDEO CONVENTION

Convention on Rights and Duties of States,
Dec. 26, 1933, 49 Stat. 3097, 165 L.N.T.S. 19

Article 1

The state as a person of international law should possess the following qualifications: *a*) a permanent population; *b*) a defined territory; *c*) government; and *d*) capacity to enter into relations with the other states.

Article 2

The federal state shall constitute a sole person in the eyes of international law.

Article 3

The political existence of the state is independent of recognition by the other states. Even before recognition the state has the right to defend its integrity and independence, to provide for its conservation and prosperity, and consequently to organize itself as it sees fit, to legislate upon its interests, administer its services, and to define the jurisdiction and competence of its courts.

The exercise of these rights has no other limitation than the exercise of the rights of other states according to international law.

Article 4

States are juridically equal, enjoy the same rights, and have equal capacity in their exercise. The rights of each one do not depend upon the power which it possesses to assure its exercise, but upon the simple fact of its existence as a person under international law.

Article 5

The fundamental rights of states are not susceptible of being affected in any manner whatsoever.

Article 6

The recognition of a state merely signifies that the state which recognizes it accepts the personality of the other with all the rights and duties determined by international law. Recognition is unconditional and irrevocable.

Article 7

The recognition of a state may be express or tacit. The latter results from any act which implies the intention of recognizing the new state.

Article 8

No state has the right to intervene in the internal or external affairs of another.

NOTES AND QUESTIONS

1. *The Montevideo Convention.* The years after World War I saw a growth in multilateral codification promoting broad principles of interstate relations. See Thomas D. Grant, "Defining Statehood: The Montevideo Convention and its Discontents," 37 *Columbia Journal of International Law* 403, 447–48 (1999), and recall the Kellogg-Briand Pact in Chapter 2. The Montevideo Convention was adopted in 1933 at the 7th International Conference of American States. The Convention reflected Latin American concerns with the intervention of major powers in the internal and external affairs of Latin American states. In a similar vein, the 1930 "Estrada Doctrine," proclaimed by Mexico's Secretary of Foreign Relations, provided that Mexico would end the "insulting practice" of recognizing new governments:

> [I]n addition to the fact that it offends the sovereignty of other nations, [this practice] implies that judgment of some sort may be passed upon the internal affairs of those nations by other governments, inasmuch as the latter assume, in effect, an attitude of criticism, when they decide, favorably or unfavorably, as to the legal qualifications of foreign régimes.

2 Marjorie Whiteman, *Digest of International Law* 85 (1963). The United States, for its part, was turning away from interventionism in Central America and South America when the Montevideo Convention was concluded. See E.H. Carr, *International Relations Between the Two World Wars* 250–51 (1966). The United States and 15 Latin American states accepted the Montevideo Convention.

2. *The Constitutive and Declaratory Theories of Recognition.* The Montevideo Convention rejected the view that recognition by already-existing states was necessary in order to "constitute" a new state. The constitutive theory was the preference of the British scholar Lassa Oppenheim, writing in the early 20th century. According to Oppenheim, "a new State before its recognition cannot claim any right which a member of the Family of Nations has towards other members. * * * Through recognition only and exclusively a State becomes an International Person and a subject of International Law." 1 Lassa Oppenheim, *International Law* § 71 (1905). What difficulties does the constitutive theory of recognition create? Would the view that recognition is

"constitutive" of statehood mean, for example, that international law rules forbidding transborder use of force do not apply to invasions of unrecognized "states"? How many, or what categories of, existing states need to recognize an entity before it legally becomes a state?

An alternative to the constitutive view is to consider recognition as merely "declaratory" of statehood. This is the position reflected in Articles 3 and 6 of the Montevideo Convention. But who determines whether an entity is a state? If an existing state is the decision maker, would not its recognition or nonrecognition of statehood shape its conclusion as to whether a state exists? Do you favor the position of Hersh Lauterpacht, who urged that existing states owe a legal duty to recognize an entity that has attained the objective characteristics of a state? See H. Lauterpacht, *Recognition in International Law* 73–76 (1947). When existing states grant or withhold recognition based on national policies, does recognition lose value as a means to determine the existence of a new state? What values does the constitutive theory of recognition reflect? The declaratory theory?

Even if formal recognition is not a prerequisite of statehood, why might a new state—even one whose government appears stable and in control of the population—care about recognition? How well can a new state function if other states refuse to acknowledge its existence or enter into relations with it? Was it of practical importance to the new United States, on concluding the Peace of Paris with Britain at the end of the Revolutionary War (see Chapter 2), to be recognized by European powers? Or, to pick an example from the early 1990s, why might The former Yugoslav Republic of Macedonia have been concerned about recognitions when it declared its independence during the dissolution of Yugoslavia? Very few states initially recognized the Republic, their reluctance probably reflecting Greek complaints over Macedonia's use of the name of Greece's northern region and Greek fears that Macedonia might assert territorial claims there. See Paul C. Szasz, "Introductory Note," 34 *International Legal Materials* 1461 (1995).

There are also constitutive and declaratory theories about the recognition of governments. See the *Tinoco Arbitration* below.

3. *States and Admission to the United Nations.* Is admission to the United Nations a proxy for statehood? Is admission an example of "collective recognition"? "States" cannot unilaterally accede to the U.N. Charter. According to Article 4 of the U.N. Charter, "peace-loving states" that accept the Charter's obligations and "are able and willing to carry out" those obligations may be admitted by action of the U.N. Security Council and General Assembly. Virtually every state belongs to the United Nations, which as of December 2013 had 193 members. Does U.N. membership assure statehood status? Were the Byelorussian S.S.R. and the Ukrainian S.S.R.—Union Republics in the Soviet Union that were among the 51 original members of the United Nations—really states in the international sense? The Soviet Constitution did formally accord Union Republics "the right to enter into relations with foreign states, conclude treaties with them, exchange diplomatic and consular representatives, and to be part in the work of

international organizations." John N. Hazard, *Constitutions of the Countries of the World: Union of Soviet Socialist Republics* 33 (1978). See Henn-Jüri Uibopuu, "International Legal Personality of Union Republics of U.S.S.R.," 24 *International and Comparative Law Quarterly* 811 (1975). Does nonmembership in the United Nations necessarily mean that an entity is not a state? Note that Switzerland did not join the United Nations until 2002.

IN RE DUCHY OF SEALAND

Case No. 9 K 2565/77 (Federal Republic of Germany, Administrative Court of Cologne, 1978), 80 *International Law Reports* 683

On 14 November 1975 the plaintiff, a German citizen by birth, received a document issued on 26 August 1975 which granted him citizenship of the so-called "Duchy of Sealand." The "Duchy" is a former British anti-aircraft platform situated approximately eight nautical miles off the southern coast of Great Britain. After the end of the Second World War the British abandoned this platform. It constitutes a small island which is situated outside the British three-mile zone. In 1967 a British Major, R.B., occupied the former anti-aircraft platform and proclaimed the "Duchy of Sealand." This "Duchy" is connected to the sea-bed by strong concrete pillars and has a surface area of approximately 1300 square metres. At present 106 persons possess the so-called "citizenship of Sealand." In 1975 R.B. issued a constitution for the former anti-aircraft platform, designating himself as "Roy of Sealand." The plaintiff holds the post of "Foreign Secretary" and "Chairman of the Council of State" of the "Duchy."

On 2 August 1976 the plaintiff [applied] to the defendant for the determination of his citizenship. After the defendant had established the date on which the plaintiff had been issued with the so-called "naturalization document" by the "Duchy of Sealand," the plaintiff was notified that he had not lost his German citizenship because the "Duchy of Sealand" did not constitute a State within the meaning of international law. * * *

The plaintiff instituted proceedings challenging the decision on the basis that the "Duchy of Sealand" was an independent State. * * * The island was permanently inhabited by between thirty and forty persons who were responsible for the defence of the miniature island and the maintenance of the community. Furthermore, he contended, his island was on the verge of being recognized as a State by Ceylon, Paraguay and Cyprus. The plaintiff seeks a declaration that he has lost his German citizenship as a result of his acquisition of the citizenship of the so-called "Duchy of Sealand" from 14 November 1975.

The plaintiff's action for a declaration * * * is unfounded. * * *

According to [German law] a German who is neither domiciled nor permanently resident within the country loses his citizenship if he acquires a foreign citizenship, if the acquisition of the new citizenship is at his own request. * * * Although, since 28 October 1975, [the plaintiff] has been neither domiciled nor permanently resident in the Federal Republic of Germany, nevertheless he has not lost his German citizenship since he has not acquired any foreign citizenship.

Since the so-called "Duchy of Sealand" does not constitute a State within the meaning of international law, the plaintiff did not acquire foreign nationality when he was issued with a document by the "Duchy of Sealand" on 14 November 1975.

International law lays down three essential attributes for Statehood. The State must have a territory, that territory must be inhabited by a people and that people must be subject to the authority of a Government.

The "Duchy of Sealand" fails to satisfy even the first condition as it does not possess a State territory within the meaning of international law.

The former anti-aircraft platform is not situated on any fixed point of the surface of the earth. Rather, the miniature island has been constructed on concrete pillars.

* * * State territory within the meaning of international law must be either "mother earth" or something standing directly thereon. * * *

In addition to the lack of State territory, the so-called "Duchy" also lacks a State people within the meaning of international law. At present the "Duchy" has 106 "citizens." [T]he size of a people is irrelevant to the question of whether or not it constitutes a State. Nevertheless, in the case of the "Duchy of Sealand" it cannot be accepted that there is a "people" within the meaning of international law since the life of a community is lacking.

The State, as an amalgamation of many individuals, complements the family * * * and has the duty to promote community life. This duty does not merely consist of the promotion of a loose association aimed at the furtherance of common hobbies and interests. Rather it must be aimed at the maintenance of an essentially permanent form of communal life in the sense of sharing a common destiny.

The so-called "nationals" of the "Duchy of Sealand" do not satisfy these criteria for community life. Apart from the 30 to 40 persons permanently living on the platform, who are responsible for its defence and the maintenance of its installations, the presence of the other so-called "nationals" is limited to occasional visits. The territorial extent of the "Duchy" of merely 1300 square metres does not satisfy the requirements for the permanent residence of all its "nationals." Even if the plans of "Roy of Sealand" to extend the size of the platform to approximately 13,000 square metres were to come to fruition, there would still not be suitable living space for all "nationals." The life of the State is not limited to the provision of casinos and places of entertainment. Rather a State community must play a more decisive role in serving the other vital human needs of people from their birth to their death. These needs include education and professional training, assistance in all the eventualities of life and the provision of subsistence allowances where necessary. The so-called "Duchy of Sealand" fails to satisfy any of these requirements.

[T]he "nationals" of the "Duchy" * * * have not acquired their "nationality" in order to live with one another and handle all aspects of their lives on a collective basis, but on the contrary they continue to pursue their individual interests outside the "Duchy." The common purpose of their association is limited to a small part of their lives, namely their commercial and tax affairs. This degree of common interest cannot be regarded as sufficient for the recognition of a "people" within the meaning of international law.

NOTES AND QUESTIONS

1. *New "States" at Sea.* Sealand is only one of several would-be states situated outside the territorial sea, a narrow band of the oceans over which a coastal state exercises sovereignty. Other candidates have included: the Grand Capri Republic and Atlantis, Isle of Gold, off the Florida coast; the Republic of Minerva, planned for coral reefs in the Pacific Ocean; the short-lived Republic of Rose Island in the Adriatic Sea; Abalonia, envisioned for the Cortes Bank 110 nautical miles off the coast of southern California; and the Dominion of Melchizedek, which claims several Pacific islands. See Samuel P. Menefee, " 'Republics of the Reefs': Nation-Building on the Continental Shelf and in the World's Oceans," 25 *California Western International Law Journal* 81 (1994); Marjorie Miller & Richard Boudreaux, "A Nation for Friend and Faux," *Los Angeles Times*, June 7, 2000, at A1. Some innovators pursue "seasteading" in communities on the high seas. See "Cities on the Ocean," *The Economist*, Dec. 3, 2011, at 14; http://www.seasteading.org (website of the Seasteading Institute) (last visited Dec. 7, 2013).

Why is Sealand not a state? Does Sealand meet the criteria of the Montevideo Convention? Why must Sealand's inhabitable territory be a part of the surface of the earth rather than connected to that surface by pillars at sea? Indeed, why must a state have any defined territory at all? Should Sealand's small population preclude it from being a state? Note that the Republic of Nauru, an eight-square-mile South Pacific island with a population of approximately 9,400 (as of 2012), joined the United Nations in 1999. See Thomas D. Grant, "Micro States," in 7 *Encyclopedia of Public International Law* 133 (Rüdiger Wolfrum ed. 2012). Does most of a state's population have to live in its territory? Is Sealand's statehood precluded if its citizens do not share a "common identity," so long as they in fact subject themselves to the authority of the Duchy? And is it in any event clear that

Sealand's nationals lack a community of interests? For more on the concept and importance of "peoples" in international law, see Part C. When might Germany be bound at international law to recognize a foreign nationality? See the discussion of "genuine link" in the *Nottebohm Case* in Chapter 6.

Is it wrong to analyze statehood simply by applying the Montevideo Convention's criteria? Can we assess whether a new state exists without considering the reactions of existing states? Would a state of Sealand inevitably interfere with British rights to coastal waters, in a way that Britain would not tolerate? See the discussion of coastal zones in Chapter 10. Would other states be willing to challenge British prerogatives by recognizing Sealand? Does Sealand simply lack sufficient political power to effectively carry out the national and international legal obligations expected of any state? For more on Sealand, see James Grimmelmann, "Sealand, HavenCo, and the Rule of Law," 2012 *University of Illinois Law Review* 405.

2. *The Variety of "States."* One survey article found it "surprisingly difficult" to determine the number and identity of countries in the world. "Defining What Makes a Country: In Quite a State," *The Economist*, Apr. 10, 2010, at 62. What makes statehood problematic in some of the following situations? Is it concern with the Montevideo Convention's Article 1 criteria of "government" and "capacity to enter into relations with other states"? Or with lack of recognition? Or with other factors? Are the Montevideo Convention's criteria for statehood exclusive? Do the following examples suggest that state sovereignty is a flexible concept, not requiring that each state possess the same bundle of rights?

a. *Dependent "States."* International law historically regarded some states as not fully independent. These dependent states, although often maintaining some independent relations with third states, were largely under the control of one "protecting power" or "suzerain." The precise status of dependent states varied. According to the Permanent Court of International Justice, "[t]he extent of the powers of a protecting state * * * depends, first, upon the treaties between the protecting state and the protected state establishing the protectorate, and, secondly, upon the conditions under which the protectorate has been recognized by third powers[.]" Protectorates "have individual legal characteristics resulting from the special conditions under which they were created, and the stage of their development." Nationality Decrees in Tunis and Morocco, 1923 P.C.I.J. Ser. B, at 4, 27. Today, some states or entities have elected to rely on more powerful countries to conduct their foreign relations. For example, the Cook Islands (91 square miles; population 10,750), a former British colony, in 1965 chose the status of self-government in free association with New Zealand. The Principality of Liechtenstein (62 square miles; population 36,700), which was admitted to the United Nations in 1990, has delegated to Switzerland much responsibility for its defense, customs affairs, and diplomatic relations with other states.

b. *Subjugated "States."* Is the Navajo Nation a state? Approximately 200,000 Navajos live within a large, clearly bounded territory in the southwestern United States. In 1849, the Navajos acknowledged that the tribe "was lawfully placed under the exclusive jurisdiction and protection" of the United States. Treaty between the United States of America and the Navajo Tribe of Indians, Sept. 9, 1849, art. I, 9 Stat. 974. The Navajo Nation has its own constitution, however, and exercises domestic self-governance within boundaries set by an 1868 treaty. Treaty Between the United States of America and the Navajo Tribe of Indians, June 1, 1868, 15 Stat. 667.

Compare the status of Kuwait after it was overrun by Iraq in 1990, an event we consider in Chapter 9 in connection with legal proscriptions against the use of force. Or consider Estonia, which became independent in 1918, was overrun and annexed by the Soviet Union in 1940, and regained its independence in 1991. Was Estonia a state between 1940 and 1991? Consider too the status of colonies, where transition to full independence may be more or less gradual. See the discussion of self-determination in Part C.

c. *"Failed States."* In 1991, Somalia's central government collapsed, contributing to widespread pillage and fighting among rival clans. In 1992, the United States and other states sent troops to Somalia. These forces were deployed, pursuant to U.N. Security Council Resolution 794, to provide humanitarian relief to displaced persons, to help restore peace and stability, and to act with "a view to facilitating the process of a political settlement under the auspices of the United Nations." Efforts to negotiate an end to this civil war proved unavailing, and the involvement of the United Nations and other non-Somali entities in efforts to rebuild Somalia has been controversial. See Ruth Gordon, "Saving Failed States: Sometimes a Neocolonialist Notion," 12 *American University Journal of International Law and Policy* 903 (1997). Somalia continues to be plagued by violence, and clan militias control various regions of Somalia. By 2012, a transitional government, bolstered by hundreds of millions of dollars of U.N. and U.S. aid and by the presence of thousands of African Union troops, had made progress in unseating the Shabab, a fundamentalist Islamic group, from many cities and towns. See Jeffrey Gettleman, "Last Somali Militant Bastion Falls, Kenya Claims," *New York Times*, Sept. 28, 2012. Does the situation in Somalia over the last two decades suggest the extinction of that state, or rather "merely" a crisis of government? See Neyire Akpinarli, *The Fragility of the "Failed State" Paradigm* (2010).

d. *States in Economic and Strategic Unions.* The best known example of a functioning, highly integrated economic union of states is the European Union, but numerous other looser unions also exist. For instance, the Commonwealth of Independent States (C.I.S.), formed in 1991 when the Soviet Union disintegrated, is composed of Azerbaijan, Armenia, Belarus, Kazakhstan, Kyrgystan, Moldova, the Russian Federation, Tajikistan, Turkmenistan, Uzbekistan, and Ukraine; Georgia, an original member, withdrew from the C.I.S. in 2008 following Russia's invasion of the South Ossetia region of Georgia. The C.I.S. contemplates unified command of strategic military forces, joint control over nuclear weapons, joint decisions on military training and the use of peacekeeping forces, and an economic union.

See the Alma Ata Declaration, Dec. 21, 1991, 31 *International Legal Materials* 138 (1992); C.I.S. Charter, June 22, 1993, 34 *International Legal Materials* 1279 (1995); C.I.S. Treaty on Creation of Economic Union, Sept. 24, 1993, 34 *International Legal Materials* 1298 (1995); C.I.S. Council of Heads of State Decisions on Settlement of Conflicts, Peace-keeping Forces and Military Training, Jan. 19, 1996, 35 *International Legal Materials* 783 (1996); Gennady M. Danilenko, "The Economic Court of the Commonwealth of Independent States," 31 *New York University Journal of International Law and Politics* 893 (1999). According to the Alma Ata Declaration, the C.I.S. itself "is neither a State nor a supra-State entity."

e. *Federal States.* Australia, Brazil, Canada, Germany, India, the Russian Federation, Switzerland, and the United States are all examples of federal states. May the components of a federal state themselves be deemed "states" under international law? Professor Opeskin has distinguished "the accommodations that may be made for federal States at the time of negotiating or ratifying a treaty, on the one hand, and modern international law's insistence on treating federal and non-federal States alike in the law of State responsibility, on the other." Brian R. Opeskin, "Federal States in the International Legal Order," 43 *Netherlands International Law Review* 353, 384 (1996). Was this distinction respected in the United States in *Medellín*? See Chapter 4. Federalism issues have also toubled other states. Consider the Republic of Tatarstan, one of 21 republics in the Russian Federation. Tatarstan has an area of over 26,000 square miles and is home to approximately four million predominantly Muslim people. In March 1992, over 60 percent of voters in a referendum in Tatarstan agreed "that the Republic of Tatarstan is a sovereign state, a subject of international law, developing its relations with the Russian federation and other republics and states on the basis of equal treaties." "Russia; Ta-tar?," *The Economist*, Mar. 28, 1992, at 49. As of the late 1990s Tatarstan retained its own constitution, passed legislation that sometimes contradicted federal law, and maintained its own diplomatic ties with over 15 foreign governments. See Babak Nikravesh, "Quebec and Tatarstan in International Law," 23 *Fletcher Forum of World Affairs,* Winter-Spring 1999, at 227; Sam Nunn & Adam Stulberg, "The Many Faces of Modern Russia," 79 *Foreign Affairs*, Mar.–Apr. 2000, at 48. In 2004, Russia tightened its control over Tatarstan, prohibiting the direct election of governors. See "Tatarstan: The Survivor," *The Economist*, June 2, 2007, at 56. Although relations between Tatarstan and Russia have stabilized, other component republics strongly resist Russia's assertions of power. See "Beyond the Kremlin's Reach," *The Economist*, Jan. 28, 2010.

f. *Palestine.* Palestine, or the Palestinian Territories, adjoin Israel and comprise the Gaza Strip and the West Bank. See the *Wall Case* in Chapter 5. Is Palestine a state? What is the significance of the October 2011 resolution by the United Nations Educational, Scientific and Cultural Organization, one of the specialized agencies of the United Nations, to admit Palestine as a member state? 51 *International Legal Materials* 610 (2012). In November 2012, the U.N. General Assembly also accorded Palestine the status of a non-member observer state (replacing its former status as an observer "entity");

the vote was 138 to 9, with 41 states abstaining. See John Cerone, "Legal Implications of the UN General Assembly Vote to Accord Palestine the Status of Observer State," 16 *ASIL Insights*, Issue 37 (2012). Palestine has not, however, been admitted as a member state of the United Nations. May Palestine now become a party to treaties or bring cases to the International Criminal Court? See Chapter 6 and Articles 81–83 of the Vienna Convention on the Law of Treaties, in the Appendix.

g. *The Holy See*. The Holy See refers to the seat of Saint Peter, occupied by successive Popes of the Roman Catholic Church. The Holy See is located territorially in the 325-square-mile Vatican City, an entity created by a 1929 treaty between Italy and the Holy See. The Holy See is not solely a religious entity. It maintains diplomatic relations with almost all states, has permanent observer status at the United Nations, is a full member of several other international organizations, and negotiates and enters treaties. See Robert John Araujo, "The International Personality and Sovereignty of the Holy See," 50 *Catholic University Law Review* 291 (2001). Even if Palestine and the Holy See are not states, do they possess "international personality"? We explore that concept in Chapter 8.

GUIDELINES ON THE RECOGNITION OF NEW STATES IN EASTERN EUROPE AND IN THE SOVIET UNION

Dec. 16, 1991, 31 *International Legal Materials* 1486 (1992)

The [European] Community and its Member States confirm their attachment to the principles of the Helsinki Final Act and the Charter of Paris, in particular the principle of self-determination. They affirm their readiness to recognise, subject to the normal standards of international practice and the political realities in each case, those new states which, following the historic changes in the region, have constituted themselves on a democratic basis, have accepted the appropriate international obligations and have committed themselves in good faith to a peaceful process and to negotiations.

Therefore, they adopt a common position on the process of recognition of these new states, which requires:

–respect for the provisions of the Charter of the United Nations and the commitments subscribed to in the Final Act of Helsinki and in the Charter of Paris, especially with regard to the rule of law, democracy and human rights;

–guarantees for the rights of ethnic and national groups and minorities in accordance with the commitments subscribed to in the framework of the [Conference on Security and Co-operation in Europe];

–respect for the inviolability of all frontiers which can only be changed by peaceful means and by common agreement;

–acceptance of all relevant commitments with regard to disarmament and nuclear non-proliferation as well as to security and regional stability;

–commitment to settle by agreement, including where appropriate by recourse to arbitration, all questions concerning state succession and regional disputes.

The Community and its Member States will not recognise entities which are the result of aggression. They would take account of the effects of recognition on neighbouring states.

The commitment to these principles opens the way to recognition by the Community and its Member States and to the establishment of diplomatic relations. It could be laid down in agreements.

NOTES AND QUESTIONS

1. *The Break-up of Yugoslavia.* The Guidelines on the Recognition of New States, adopted by the Council of the European Community in late 1991, were a response to the dissolution of the Soviet Union and the break-up of Yugoslavia. Yugoslavia, originally known as the "Serb-Croat-Slovene State," was recognized as independent in treaties following World War I. That new country unified Macedonia, Croatia, Slovenia, and Bosnia and Herzegovina, all of which had been under the control of the Austrian-Hungarian Empire, independent Serbia, and nominally independent Montenegro. Following World War II, the government of Marshall Tito headed the Socialist Federal Republic of Yugoslavia (SFRY), which in 1946 became one of the original member states of the United Nations. Tito died in 1980. During 1991–1992, the SFRY broke up into Croatia, Bosnia-Herzegovina, Slovenia, and The former Yugoslav Republic of Macedonia; two other Yugoslav republics within the SFRY, Serbia and Montenegro, formed yet another state, which itself broke in two following Montenegro's 2006 declaration of independence. See Figure 7.A. The current status of Kosovo, which we explore in Part C of this chapter, is much debated.

2. *New States and the Recognition Guidelines.* When the Council of the European Community adopted the Guidelines on the Recognition of New States, it also invited the Yugoslav Republics to apply for recognition, with an Arbitration Commission of the Conference on Yugoslavia to provide advice on those applications. In 1992 the Arbitration Commission rendered a series of opinions related to the dissolution of Yugoslavia. 31 *International Legal Materials* 1488 (1992). See Matthew C.R. Craven, "The European Community Arbitration Commission on Yugoslavia," 66 *British Yearbook of International Law* 333 (1996). In its Opinion No. 3 the Commission found that the former internal boundaries of the Yugoslav Republics within the SFRY would

become the external boundaries of new states, absent agreement to the contrary.

Should the January 1992 resolution of an assembly of Serbian people in Bosnia-Herzegovina proclaiming the so-called "Serbian Republic of Bosnia-Herzegovina"—also known as Srpska—have sufficed to establish its independence? What were the implications of that resolution for the recognition of a larger Bosnia-Herzegovina? Consider the Arbitration Commission's Opinion No. 4, the reference in the Recognition Guidelines to self-determination, and the discussion of self-determination in Part C below.

In 1995 the U.S. Second Circuit Court of Appeals decided Kadic v. Karadžić, 70 F.3d 232 (2d Cir. 1995), *cert. denied*, 518 U.S. 1005 (1996), a case brought by Croat and Muslim citizens of Bosnia-Herzegovina, an "internationally recognized" state, against Radovan Karadžić, "President of the self-proclaimed Bosnian-Serb republic of 'Srpska.'" *Id.* at 236. The case was brought under the Alien Tort Claims Act, 28 U.S.C. § 1350, which we studied in *Filartiga* (Chapter 1) and in *Sosa* and *Kiobel* (Chapter 4); it provides U.S. federal courts with jurisdiction in cases involving "any civil action by an alien for a tort only, committed in violation of the law of nations." The plaintiffs claimed, *inter alia*, that Karadžić was responsible for torture and summary execution, acts that "when not perpetrated in the course of genocide or war crimes * * * are proscribed by international law only when committed by state officials or under color of law." *Id.* at 243. The Second Circuit found that plaintiffs were entitled "to prove that Karadžić's regime satisfies the criteria for a state":

> Srpska is alleged to control defined territory, control populations within its power, and to have entered into agreements with other governments. It has a president, a legislature, and its own currency. These circumstances readily appear to satisfy the criteria for a state in all aspects of international law.

Id. at 245. Viewed in light of *Kiobel*, was the Second Circuit's exercise of jurisdiction valid in *Kadic*? Should the court have considered Srpska a state? Would other forums also view Srpska as a state, especially with regard to issues other than those being litigated in *Kadic*, *e.g.*, admission to the United Nations? Might the same entity be considered a state for some purposes but not for others? As of 2013, Republika Srpska exercised significant authority as one of the two main political entities comprising the state of Bosnia-Herzegovina.

Figure 7.A

States Following the Breakup of the Socialist Federal Republic of Yugoslavia

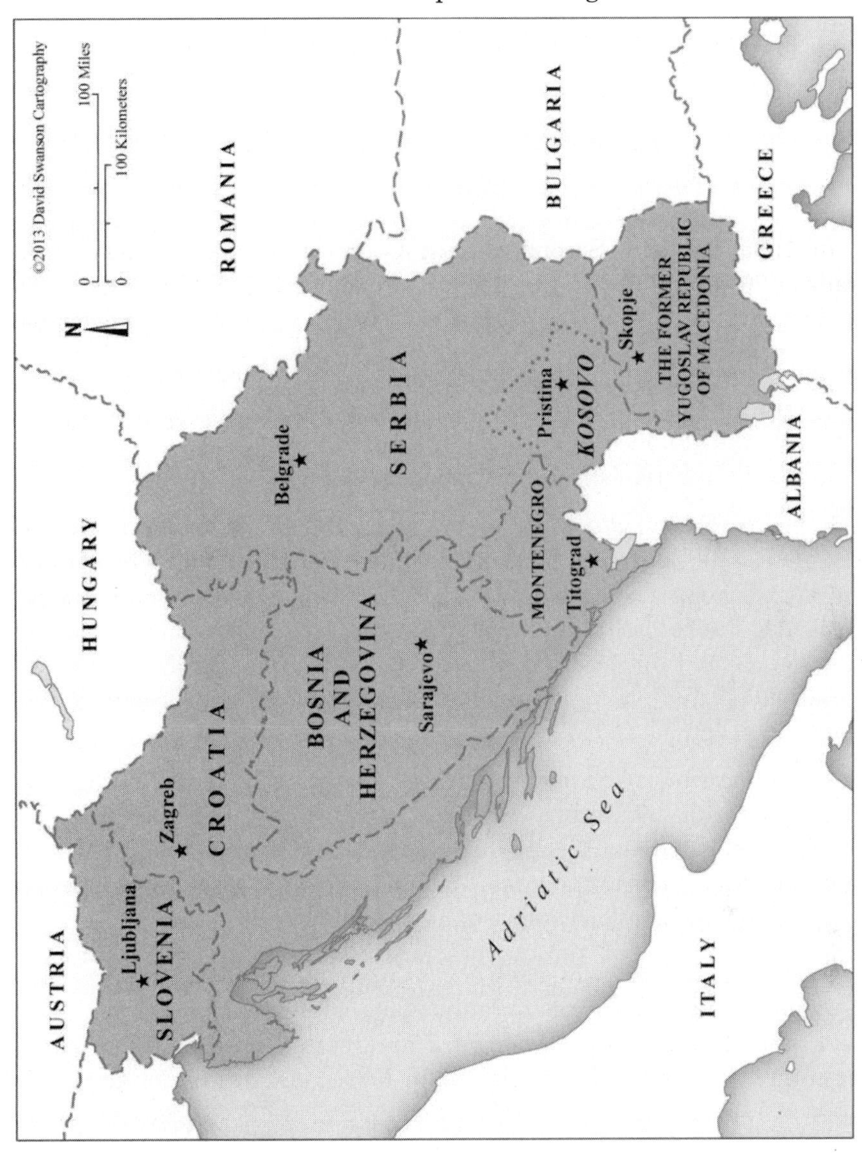

3. *Evaluating the Guidelines.* As a formal matter, the Guidelines set a policy for one regional organization—the European Community—concerning the recognition of certain new states. Should recognition of statehood depend on a potential state's respecting borders with its neighbors or accepting arms control commitments? Should recognition depend on internal compliance with norms concerning human rights and the protection of minorities? See Roland Bieber, "European Community Recognition of Eastern European States: A New Perspective for International Law?," 1992 *American Society of International Law Proceedings* 374. Should recognition be refused a state that has forcefully seized territory from an existing country, violating the U.N. Charter's prohibition on the use of force? Compare *Goldberg* and *Tinoco* below.

According to Professor Shaw, because recognition is "interlinked" with the criteria for statehood, the Guidelines may be "interpreted as additions to [those] criteria." Malcolm N. Shaw, *International Law* 207 (6th ed. 2008). What are the implications if the Guidelines' values supplement the Montevideo Convention's statehood criteria?

4. *New States and Customary International Law.* Decision makers regard new states as bound by customary international law. Why should any of the Yugoslav republics within the SFRY be bound by customary rules that were formed before they gained the status of states? Customary international law is considered in Chapter 3. See Ram P. Anand, "New States and International Law," in 7 *Encyclopedia of Public International Law* 672 (Rüdiger Wolfrum ed. 2012).

5. *Succession of States and Governments.* When new states emerge after an older state disintegrates, as was true in the case of the SFRY, or when new governments take control of a state following a revolution, a range of difficult legal questions arise. What happens to the former regime's treaties, contracts, property, and memberships in international organizations? The next three cases focus on succession to contracts and property rights. Pay close attention in these cases to the significance of recognition.

REPUBLIC OF CROATIA ET AL. V. GIROCREDIT BANK A.G. DER SPARKASSEN

Supreme Court of Austria, Dec. 17, 1996,
36 *International Legal Materials* 1520 (1997)

[The Republic of Croatia and the Republic of Macedonia, among others, sued GiroCredit Bank, an Austrian bank, "to cease and desist and render accounts." The Supreme Court of Austria upholds 1996 lower court decisions concerning the Republic of Croatia and the Republic of Macedonia.]

The National Bank of the Socialist Federal Republic of Yugoslavia (hereinafter SFRY) had concluded banking contracts with the Defendant, on the basis of which funds were invested upon interest in Austria and assets were deposited.

The SFRY has been dissolved by "dismembratio." The successor States of Croatia, Macedonia, Slovenia, Bosnia-Herzegovina and the Federal Republic of Yugoslavia have so far not reached any agreement on the distribution of the assets and liabilities of the SFRY. The National Bank of the Federal Republic of Yugoslavia, founded in 1993, claims to be the sole lawful successor to the former National Bank of the SFRY. * * *

In order to secure their claims made * * * to cease and desist and to render accounts, the Plaintiffs applied for an interim injunction[.] [Plaintiffs obtained an injunction, which the Court of Appeal upheld.]

While the rights and obligations resulting from the banking contract itself are to be judged under the law of the place of the establishment of the credit institution, *i.e.*, under Austrian law, the question as to whether the assets invested by the National Bank of the SFRY in Austria were held by the National Bank as an independent legal entity or constituted State property (in terms of international law) are to be assessed according to the then domestic law of the SFRY.

It is in this sense that Art. 8 of the 1983 "Vienna Convention on Succession of States in Respect of State Property, Archives and Debts," prepared by the International Law Commission, defines "State property of the predecessor State" as property and rights which, at the date of the succession of States, were, according to the internal law of the predecessor State, owned by that State. The purpose of this codification was to formulate existing customary international law.

[According to the National Bank Act of the SFRY] the National Bank of the SFRY * * * was a "socialized" legal person, which is to be seen in contrast to a legal person under private law. Its organs were appointed by the Federal Parliament and responsible to it. The Parliament also adopted the Statutes of the National Bank as the basis of its organization. The National Bank performed its activities in political dependence, it had no political autonomy. It was directly subject to political influence.

All these provisions taken together show that the assets of the National Bank of the SFRY—although it enjoyed legal personality as a "socialized company"—formed part of State property of the SFRY according to international law, which in the case of a "dismembratio" has to be distributed among the successor States. * * *

While the Federal Republic of Yugoslavia considers itself to be the sole successor State to the SFRY and identical with it, the international community unanimously views the disintegration of the SFRY as a case of "dismembratio." In international law this means the complete dissolution of the predecessor State and replacement by several successor States.

The opinion of the international community is expressed in the following documents:

In Security Council Resolution 757 (1992) it was stated that the claim of the successor States of Serbia and Montenegro to continue automatically the membership of the former SFRY in the United Nations was not recognized.

In Security Council Resolution 777 (1992) the view was expressed that the SFRY had ceased to exist, that there was no identity of the Federal Republic of Yugoslavia, consisting of Serbia and Montenegro, with the former State of the SFRY. The Federal Republic of Yugoslavia could not participate in the General Assembly of the United Nations and would have first to apply for membership.

Pursuant to a recommendation of the Security Council, the General Assembly of the United Nations decided in a Resolution of 22 September 1992 that the Federal Republic of Yugoslavia should apply for membership and could not participate in the work of the General Assembly.

The Arbitration Commission set up by the Members of the European Community and chaired by Badinter also dealt with the question of State succession and in its Opinions No. 1, 8 and 10 (1992) held the view that the SFRY had been dissolved and had ceased to exist, that the Federal Republic of Yugoslavia was one of the successor States and not the sole legal successor. This view was also supported in a declaration of the European Political Cooperation of 20 July 1992 as well as the EU Declaration of 9 April 1996 on the Recognition of the Federal Republic of Yugoslavia as a successor State.

On the basis of this, Austria recognized the Federal Republic of Yugoslavia as one of the successor States of the SFRY and as an independent and sovereign Member of the community of States.

In terms of international law, the disintegration of the SFRY therefore is to be regarded as a case of "dismembratio." The SFRY as a subject of international law has ceased to exist, its State territory has been divided among five successor States, which have in the meantime been recognized by Austria.

Under customary international law, in the case of "dismembratio," State property is to be distributed according to the international principle of "equity." In such a case Art. 18 of the "Vienna Convention on Succession of States in Respect of State Property, Archives and Debts" of 1983 prepared by the International Law Commission provides for the passing of movable State property to the successor States in "equitable proportions." Thus, the successor States have an international law title to distribution recognized by the community of States.

Resolution 1022 of the [Security Council] of the United Nations, leaving it to the Member States to release funds and assets frozen pursuant to Security Council Resolutions 757 and 820, specifically points out in operative paragraph 6 that these funds and assets had to be released without prejudice to claims of the successor States to such property. Moreover, operative paragraph 5 provides (this being binding on Members) that property being subject to legal action shall remain frozen until released in accordance with applicable law.

Also the EU Arbitration Commission chaired by Badinter states in its Opinion No. 9 that State property of the SFRY located in third countries must be distributed equitably among the successor States in accordance with an agreement to be reached among them.

The requirement of an agreement among the successor States on the distribution [of assets] is also evident from the EU Declaration of 9 April 1996. * * *

As a result of the disintegration of the SFRY by "dismembratio," the legal personalities of that State and its National Bank ceased to exist. The property attributable to the State (of the SFRY) is to be distributed among the successor States in accordance with international agreements still to be concluded. As far as funds and assets deposited with Austrian banks are concerned, surrendering the joint property to only one of the successor States—ignoring the claims of the other members of such a community—would even more amount to the recognition of an expropriation without compensation in the State of the actual administrative seat, as the Federal Republic of Yugoslavia claims to be the sole successor State to the SFRY, if not identical with it. As the confiscation of property, being contrary to *ordre public*, does not extend to property located in Austria of a legal person the extinction of which has to be recognized in Austria under § 12 of the [Austrian] Federal Statute on Private International Law, such property constitutes a "communio incidens" [under Austrian law,] *i.e.*, a joint-ownership community of all successor States. Each member of this community thus has only a joint-ownership claim vis-a-vis the Defendant, which would be—illegally—infringed upon by any unilateral acts of disposal by one of them. Hence, each member of this community has a private law claim to the maintenance of the status quo, thus also a legal claim against the

Defendant to desist from any disposal of such property as long as the successor States do not jointly dispose of such funds and assets.

This right can be secured by an interim injunction according to § 381(1) of the [Austrian] Enforcement Code.

[T]he Court of Appeal was right in assuming an actual risk to the claims of [the Republic of Croatia and the Republic of Macedonia] as members of the communio incidens. It is a fact that the Defendant had, by reference to the existing banking contracts, refused to (continue to) freeze the accounts and deposits as demanded by the Plaintiffs and had thus made payments to the Federal Republic of Yugoslavia appear probable as soon as the latter would raise such claims based on the banking contracts concluded between the former National Bank of the SFRY and the Defendant[.]

NOTES AND QUESTIONS

1. *The Interplay of International and Municipal Law.* A distinguishing and sometimes confusing feature of international transactional law is the need to master both international law and the law of one or more municipal legal systems. The court in the *GiroCredit Bank Case* applied Austrian law to determine rights and obligations pertaining to contracts between the Austrian bank and the National Bank of the SFRY. In order to ascertain whether the Austrian assets of the National Bank of the SFRY were "state property," however, the court referred to the terms of a 1983 treaty. That treaty in turn defined state property of a predecessor state by reference to the municipal law of the predecessor state, thus requiring the court to look to the law of the SFRY. To determine the appropriate remedy for the plaintiff successor states, the court relied on Austrian law and its theory of *communio incidens*; however, as one commentator noted, a similar remedy could have been identified in international law and applied in the case in accordance with principles of Austrian constitutional law regarding the use of international law. See Konrad G. Bühler, "Two Recent Austrian Supreme Court Decisions on State Succession from an International Law Perspective," 2 *Austrian Review of International and European Law* 213, 233–38 (1997).

How did Austria's implementation of United Nations Security Council decisions affect the timing of the lawsuit against GiroCredit Bank? The National Bank of the SFRY had deposited funds with Austrian commercial banks before the break-up of Yugoslavia began in 1991. However, Croatia and Macedonia did not seek an injunction to keep the National Bank from turning over the funds to the Serbian-dominated Federal Republic of Yugoslavia until February 1996. Before then, Austria had frozen Yugoslav accounts in Austria in accordance with U.N. Security Council Resolutions 757 (1992), 31 *International Legal Materials* 1453 (1992), and 820 (1993), 47

United Nations Yearbook of International Law 471 (1993), resolutions adopted to reduce the amount of hard currency available to Yugoslav President Milošević. Just prior to this lawsuit, Austria repealed its freezing orders, implementing Security Council Resolution 1022 (1995), 35 *International Legal Materials* 259 (1996), which endorsed the 1995 General Framework Agreement for Peace in Bosnia and Herzegovina (the Dayton Accords), 35 *International Legal Materials* 75 (1996). More on the legal effect of U.N. Security Council decisions appears in Chapter 9.

Finally, the Austrian court looked to international legal sources to determine the critical issue of whether Yugoslavia had entirely dissolved into new states, or whether the Federal Republic of Yugoslavia was the successor state to the SFRY. What was the significance of recognition with respect to this conclusion? Should the court have considered the objective characteristics stressed by the Federal Republic, and asked whether the Federal Republic retained a substantial percentage of the SFRY's territory, resources, and population, as well as its seat of government?

2. *The Variety of Succession Issues.* According to one court, "[t]he problem of State succession is one of the most disputed areas of international law." Espionage Prosecution Case (Case No. 2 BGs 38/91), 94 *International Law Reports* 68, 77–78 (Ger. Fed. Sup. Ct., 1991). The variety of state succession issues makes generalizations about this area of law difficult. Succession may affect, *e.g.*, contractual obligations (as in the *Tinoco Arbitration* below, albeit that case involved a succession of governments), liability for non-contractual wrongs, state property (as in the *GiroCredit Bank Case*), archives and cultural heritage (as in the *Goldberg Case* below), treaties, membership in international organizations, and nationality of citizens. Review how like matters were treated in the 1867 Cession of Alaska in Chapter 2.

Complexity also results from the different ways in which states may appear, disappear, and change. Sometimes states dissolve into entirely new states, as the *GiroCredit Bank* court concluded was true of the SFRY, and other times states secede from a state that continues to exist. New states, invoking the principle of self-determination, have emerged as a result of decolonization, as discussed in Part C. States may merge, forming an entirely new state, or one state may absorb another. Sometimes a state is enlarged when a neighboring state cedes some of its territory (as in the Cession of Alaska) or loses it in a war. For a survey of state practice, see James Crawford & Alan Boyle, "Opinion: Referendum on the Independence of Scotland—International Law Aspects" ¶¶ 53–65, 74–92, 99–108, in *Scotland Analysis: Devolution and the Implications of Scottish Independence*, Annex A, Cm. 8554 (Feb. 2013).

In the absence of agreements addressing succession issues, the applicable legal rules may be much debated. Municipal courts may provide guidance on some succession issues, as in the *GiroCredit Bank Case*, and international financial institutions may play a significant role in reallocating loan obligations in state succession situations. The issues frequently arise in highly politicized contexts. See Committee on Aspects of the Law of State Succession, "Final Report," in International Law Association, *Report of the Seventy-Third Conference (Rio de Janiero)* 250 (2008).

3. *Succession to Assets.* The *GiroCredit Bank* court concluded that, following the dissolution of the SFRY, international law required that the National Bank's accounts be distributed equitably among the successor states pursuant to agreement. What does equity mean in this context? See the *North Sea Cases* and the discussion of equity in Chapter 3. What factors ought to be taken into account in negotiating an agreement? Should state property be divided on a per capita basis, or according to historical shares of tax revenues received from different regions of the predecessor state? Should real property of the predecessor state be allocated based on its physical location? See Daniel S. Blum, "The Apportionment of Public Debt and Assets During State Secession," 29 *Case Western Reserve Journal of International Law* 263 (1997).

The Federal Republic of Yugoslavia eventually abandoned its claim to being the continuator state of the SFRY. In 2001, following nine years of negotiations, the states that had comprised the SFRY concluded an agreement to govern succession to state property, financial assets and liabilities, and archives. See Agreement on Succession Issues, June 29, 2001, 41 *International Legal Materials* 3 (2002); Carsten Stahn, "The Agreement on Succession Issues of the Former Socialist Federal Republic of Yugoslavia," 96 *American Journal of International Law* 379 (2002).

4. *Succession to Treaties.* When a new state emerges, it may enter agreements with the treaty partners of its predecessor state to confirm the continuing effect of treaties. See, *e.g.*, Marian Nash (Leich), "Contemporary Practice of the United States Relating to International Law: Succession of States," 89 *American Journal of International Law* 761 (1995). Could a devolution agreement between a predecessor and successor state, specifying which of the predecessor state's treaties the successor state will accept, bind third-state treaty parties? If not, what is the practical significance of such devolution agreements? See Gerhard Hafner & Gregor Novak, "State Succession in Respect of Treaties," in *The Oxford Guide to Treaties* 396, 408–09 (Duncan B. Hollis ed. 2012). And what happens if the new state does not indicate the treaties to which it is willing to be bound? Should only some new states, *e.g.*, those emerging from colonialism, be entitled to begin life with a "clean state," not bound by a predecessor state's treaties? See Vienna Convention on Succession of States in Respect of Treaties, arts. 2(f), 16, 34, Aug. 23, 1978, 17 *International Legal Materials* 1488 (1978). What values and practical reasons support a general presumption that treaties should continue in force for all successor states?

Does the type of treaty affect succession? Treaties that establish international boundaries or other territorial regimes generally continue in existence in cases of state succession. See Case Concerning the Frontier Dispute (Burkina Faso/Mali), 1986 I.C.J. 554, 566. What about human rights treaties? Do those treaties "attach" to individuals, as territorial treaties attach to land? According to an Appeals Chamber of the International Tribunal for the former Yugoslavia, international law has now accepted "automatic State succession to multilateral humanitarian treaties" such as the Geneva Conventions, *i.e.*, "treaties of universal character which express fundamental human rights." Prosecutor v. Delalić, Case No. IT–96–21–A, ¶ 111 (2001). Should treaties concerning alliances and diplomatic exchanges continue in effect? Should the same presumptions concerning succession apply to bilateral and multilateral treaties? One survey concluded that "a universally applicable rule of international law for treaty succession does not yet exist * * * (although a certain tendency towards the continuity theory cannot be denied). Rather, different rules and practices have emerged for the [different] categories of State succession * * * and with respect to particular kinds of treaties." Hafner & Novak, *supra*, at 407–08.

5. *Succession to Membership in International Organizations.* Succession to membership in an international organization requires satisfying membership standards prescribed by the organization's charter and practice. The *GiroCredit Bank* court described the United Nations' treatment of the membership of the Federal Republic of Yugoslavia. What explains the U.N. action, given that Russia was allowed to retain the U.N. membership of the Soviet Union when it broke apart, and India was permitted to keep the U.N. membership of British India when Pakistan and India separated in 1947? See Michael P. Scharf, "Musical Chairs: The Dissolution of States and Membership in the United Nations," 28 *Cornell International Law Journal* 29 (1995). Croatia, Bosnia-Herzegovina, Slovenia, and The former Yugoslav Republic of Macedonia were all admitted as U.N. members in 1992 and 1993. The Federal Republic of Yugoslavia was admitted in 2000, when Yugoslav President Slobadan Milošević was voted out of office. The Federal Republic officially changed its name to Serbia and Montenegro in 2003; Montenegro declared its independence in 2006 and gained U.N. membership that same year; and the Republic of Serbia has continued to hold the seat of Serbia and Montenegro.

THE TINOCO ARBITRATION

Arbitration Between Great Britain and Costa Rica, Opinion and Award of William H. Taft, Sole Arbitrator, Washington, D.C., Oct. 18, 1923, 18 *American Journal of International Law* 147 (1924),1 *Reports of International Arbitral Awards* 369 (2006)

This is a proceeding under a treaty of arbitration between Great Britain and Costa Rica. * * *

In January, 1917, the Government of Costa Rica, under President Alfredo Gonzalez, was overthrown by Frederico Tinoco, the Secretary of War. Gonzalez fled. Tinoco assumed power, called an election, and established a new constitution in June, 1917. His government continued until August, 1919, when Tinoco retired, and left the country. His government fell in September following. [T]he old constitution was restored and elections held under it. The restored government is a signatory to this treaty of arbitration.

On the 22nd of August, 1922, the Constitutional Congress of the restored Costa Rican Government passed a law known as Law of Nullities No. 41. It invalidated all contracts between the executive power and private persons, made with or without approval of the legislative power between January 27, 1917 and September 2, 1919, covering the period of the Tinoco government. It also nullified the legislative decree No. 12 of the Tinoco government, dated June 28, 1919, authorizing the issue of the 15 million colones currency notes. The colon is a Costa Rican gold coin or standard nominally equal to 46 1/12 cents of an American dollar, but it is uncoined and the exchange value of the paper colon actually in circulation is much less. The Nullities Law also invalidated the legislative decree of the Tinoco government of July 8, 1919, authorizing the circulation of notes of the nomination of 1000 colones, and annulled all transactions with such colones bills between holders and the state, directly or indirectly, by means of negotiation or contract, if thereby the holders received value as if they were ordinary bills of current issue.

The claim of Great Britain is that the Royal Bank of Canada and the Central Costa Rica Petroleum Company are Britain corporations whose shares are owned by British subjects; that the Banco Internacional of Costa Rica and the Government of Costa Rica are both indebted to the Royal Bank in the sum of 998,000 colones, evidenced by 998 one thousand colones bills held by the Bank; that the Central Costa Rica Petroleum Company owns, by due assignment, a grant by the Tinoco government in 1918 of the right to explore for and exploit oil deposits in Costa Rica, and that both the indebtedness and the concession have been annulled without right by the Law of Nullities and should be excepted from its operation. She asks an award that she is entitled on behalf of her subjects to have the claim of the bank paid, and the concession recognized and given effect by the Costa Rican Government.

The Government of Costa Rica denies its liability for the acts or obligations of the Tinoco government and maintains that the Law of Nullities was a legitimate exercise of its legislative governing power. It further denies the validity of such claims on the merits, unaffected by the Law of Nullities.

It is convenient to consider first the general objections to both claims of Great Britain, urged by Costa Rica, and then if such general objections cannot prevail, to consider the merits of each claim and Costa Rica's special defenses to it.

Coming now to the general issues applicable to both claims, Great Britain contends, first, that the Tinoco government was the only government of Costa Rica *de facto* and *de jure* for two years and nine months; that during that time there is no other government disputing its sovereignty, that it was in peaceful administration of the whole country, with the acquiescence of its people.

Second, that the succeeding government could not by legislative decree avoid responsibility for acts of that government affecting British subjects, or appropriate or confiscate rights and property by that government except in violation of international law; that the act of Nullities is as to British interests, therefore itself a nullity, and is to be disregarded, with the consequence that the contracts validly made with the Tinoco government must be performed by the present Costa Rican Government, and that the property which has been invaded or the rights nullified must be restored.

To these contentions the Costa Rican Government answers: First, that the Tinoco government was not a *de facto* or *de jure* government according to the rules of international law. This raises an issue of fact.

Second, that the contracts and obligations of the Tinoco government, set up by Great Britain on behalf of its subjects, are void, and do not create a legal obligation, because the government of Tinoco and its acts were in violation of the constitution of Costa Rica of 1871.

Third, that Great Britain is stopped by the fact that it did not recognize the Tinoco government during its incumbency, to claim on behalf of its subjects that Tinoco's was a government which could confer rights binding on its successor. * * *

Dr. John Bassett Moore, now a member of the Permanent Court of International Justice, in his *Digest of International Law,* Volume I, p. 249, announces the general principle which has had such universal acquiescence as to become well settled international law:

> Changes in the government or the international policy of a state do not as a rule affect its position in international law. A monarchy may be transformed into a republic or a republic into a monarchy; absolute principles may be substituted for constitutional, or the reverse; but though the government changes, the nation remains, with rights and obligations unimpaired. . . .
>
> The principle of the continuity of states has important results. The state is bound by engagements entered into by governments that have ceased to exist; the restored government is generally liable for the acts of the usurper. The governments of Louis XVIII and Louis Philippe so far as practicable indemnified the citizens of foreign states for losses caused by the government of Napoleon; and the King of the Two Cicilies made compensation to citizens of the United States for the wrongful acts of Murat.

Again Dr. Moore says:

> The origin and organization of government are questions generally of internal discussion and decision. Foreign powers deal with the existing *de facto* government, when sufficiently established to give reasonable assurance of its permanence, and of the acquiescence of those who constitute the state in its ability to maintain itself, and discharge its internal duties and its external obligations. * * *

First, what are the facts to be gathered from the documents and evidence submitted by the two parties as to the *de facto* character of the Tinoco government?

In January, 1917, Frederico A. Tinoco was Secretary of War under Alfredo Gonzalez, the then President of Costa Rica. On the ground that Gonzalez was seeking reelection as President in violation of a constitutional limitation, Tinoco used the army and navy to seize the government, assume the provisional headship of the Republic and become Commander-in-Chief of the army. Gonzalez took refuge in the American Legation, thence escaping to the United States. Tinoco constituted a provisional government at once and summoned the people to an election for deputies to a constituent assembly on the first of May, 1917. At the same time he directed an election to take place for the Presidency and himself became a candidate. An election was held. Some 61,000 votes were cast for Tinoco and 259 for another candidate. Tinoco then was inaugurated as the President to administer his powers under the former constitution until the creation of a new one. A new constitution was adopted June 8, 1917, supplanting the constitution of 1871. For a full two years Tinoco and the legislative assembly under him peaceably administered the affairs of the Government of Costa Rica, and there was no disorder of a revolutionary character during that interval. No other government of any kind asserted power in the country. The courts sat, Congress legislated, and the government was duly administered. Its power was fully established and peaceably exercised. The people seemed to have accepted Tinoco's government with great good will when it came in, and to have welcomed the change. [T]hroughout the record as made by the case and counter case, there is no substantial evidence that Tinoco was not in actual and peaceable administration without resistance or conflict or contest by anyone until a few months before the time when he retired and resigned.

Speaking of the resumption of the present government, this passage occurs in the argument on behalf of Costa Rica:

> Powerful forces in Costa Rica were opposed to Tinoco from the outset, but his overthrow by ballot or unarmed opposition was impossible and it was equally impossible to organize armed opposition against him in Costa Rican territory.

It is true that action of the supporters of those seeking to restore the former government was somewhat delayed by the influence of the United States with Gonzalez and his friends against armed action, on the ground that military disturbances in Central America during the World War would be prejudicial to the interests of the Allied Powers. It is not important, however, what were the causes that enabled Tinoco to carry on his government effectively and peaceably. The question is, must his government be considered a link in the continuity of the Government of Costa Rica? I must hold that from the evidence that the Tinoco government was an actual sovereign government.

But it is urged that many leading Powers refused to recognize the Tinoco government, and that recognition by other nations is the chief and best evidence of the birth, existence and continuity of succession of a government. Undoubtedly recognition by other Powers is an important evidential factor in establishing proof of the existence of a government in the society of nations. What are the facts as to this? The Tinoco government was recognized by Bolivia on May 17, 1917; by Argentina on May 22, 1917; by Chile on May 22, 1917; by Haiti on May 22, 1917; by Guatemala on May 28, 1917; by Switzerland on June 1, 1917; by Germany on June 10, 1917; by Denmark on June 18, 1917; by Spain on June 18, 1917; by Mexico on July 1, 1917; by Holland on July 11, 1917; by the Vatican on June 9, 1917; by Colombia on August 9, 1917; by Austria on August 10, 1917; by Portugal on August 14, 1917; by El Salvador on September 12, 1917; by Romania on November 15, 1917; by Brazil on November 28, 1917; by Peru on December 15, 1917; and by Ecuador on April 23, 1917.

What were the circumstances as to the other nations?

The United States, on February 9, 1917, two weeks after Tinoco had assumed power, took this action:

> The Government of the United States has viewed the recent overthrow of the established government in Costa Rica with the gravest concern and considers that illegal acts of this character tend to disturb the peace of Central America and to disrupt the unity of the American continent. In view of its policy in regard to the assumption of power through illegal methods, clearly enunciated by it on several occasions during the past four years, the Government of the United States desires to set forth in an emphatic and distinct manner its present position in regard to the actual situation in Costa Rica which is that it will not give recognition or support to any government which may be established unless it is clearly proven that it is elected by legal and constitutional means.

And again on February 24, 1917:

> In order that citizens of the United States may have definite information as to the position of this Government in regard to any financial aid which they may give to, or any business transaction which they may have with those persons who overthrew the constitutional Government of Costa Rica by an act of armed rebellion, the Government of the United States desires to advise them that it will not consider any claims which may in the future arise from such dealings, worthy of its diplomatic support.

[The U.S. State Department reaffirmed its nonrecognition of the Tinoco regime in April 1918.]

Probably because of the leadership of the United States in respect to a matter of this kind, her then Allies in the war, Great Britain, France and Italy, declined to recognize the Tinoco government. Costa Rica was, therefore, not permitted to sign the Treaty of Peace at Versailles, although the Tinoco government had declared war against Germany.

The merits of the policy of the United States in this non-recognition it is not for the arbitrator to discuss, for the reason that in his consideration of this case, he is necessarily controlled by principles of international law, and however justified as a national policy non-recognition on such a ground may be, it certainly has not been acquiesced in by all the nations of the world, which is a condition precedent to considering it as a postulate of international law.

The non-recognition by other nations of a government claiming to be a national personality, is usually appropriate evidence that it has not attained the independence and control entitling it by international law to be classed as such. But when recognition *vel non* of a government is by such nations determined by inquiry, not into its *de facto* sovereignty and complete governmental control, but into its illegitimacy or irregularity of origin, their non-recognition loses something of evidential weight on the issue with which those applying the rules of international law are alone concerned. What is true of the non-recognition of the United States in its bearing upon the existence of a *de facto* government under Tinoco for thirty months is probably in a measure true of the non-recognition by her Allies in the European War. Such non-recognition for any reason, however, cannot outweigh the evidence disclosed by this record before me as to the *de facto* character of Tinoco's government, according to the standard set by international law.

Second. It is ably and earnestly argued on behalf of Costa Rica that the Tinoco government cannot be considered a *de facto* government, because it was not established and maintained in accord with the constitution of Costa Rica of 1871. To hold that a government which establishes itself and maintains a peaceful administration, with the acquiescence of the people for a substantial period of time, does not become a *de facto* government unless it conforms to a previous constitution would be to hold that within the rules of international law a revolution contrary to the fundamental law of the existing government cannot establish a new government. This cannot be, and is not, true. The change by revolution upsets the rule of the authorities in power under the then existing fundamental law, and sets aside the fundamental law in so far as the change of rule makes it necessary. To speak of a revolution creating a *de facto* government, which conforms to the limitations of the old constitution is to use a contradiction in terms. The same government continues internationally, but not the internal law of its being. * * * The question is, has [the new government] really established itself in such a way that all within its influence recognize its control, and that there is no opposing force assuming to be a government in its place? Is it discharging its functions as a government usually does, respected within its own jurisdiction? * * *

Third. It is further objected by Costa Rica that Great Britain by her failure to recognize the Tinoco government is estopped now to urge claims of her subjects dependent upon the acts and contracts of the Tinoco government. The evidential weight of such non-recognition against the claim of its *de facto* character I have already considered and admitted. The contention here goes further and precludes a government which did not recognize a *de facto* government from appearing in an international tribunal in behalf of its nationals to claim any rights based on the acts of such government.

To sustain this view a great number of decisions in English and American courts are cited to the point that a municipal court cannot, in litigation before it, recognize or assume the *de facto* character of a foreign government which the executive department of foreign affairs of the government of which the court is a branch has not recognized. This is clearly true. It is for the executive to decide questions of foreign policy and not courts. It would be most unseemly to have a conflict of opinion in respect to foreign relations of a nation between its department charged with the conduct of its foreign affairs and its judicial branch. But such cases have no bearing on the point before us. Here the executive of Great Britain takes the position that the Tinoco government which it did not recognize, was nevertheless a *de facto* government that could create rights in British subjects which it now seeks to protect. Of course, as already emphasized, its failure to recognize the *de facto* government can be used against it as evidence to disprove the character it now attributes to that government, but this does not bar it from changing its position. Should a case arise in one of its own courts after it has changed its position, doubtless that court would feel it incumbent upon it to note the change in its further rulings. * * *

I do not understand the arguments on which an equitable estoppel in such case can rest. The failure to recognize the *de facto* government did not lead the succeeding government to change its position in any way upon the faith of it. Non-recognition may have aided the succeeding government to come into power; but subsequent presentation of claims based on the *de facto* existence of the previous government and its dealings does not work an injury to the succeeding government in the nature of a fraud or breach of faith. An equitable estoppel to prove the truth must rest on previous conduct of the person to be estopped, which has led the person claiming the estoppel into a position in which the truth will injure him. There is no such case here.

* * * It may be urged that it would be in the interest of the stability of governments and the orderly adjustment of international relations, and so a proper rule of international law, that a government in recognizing or refusing to recognize a government claiming admission to the society of nations should thereafter be held to an attitude consistent with its deliberate conclusion on this issue. * * * I have not been cited to text writers of authority or to decisions of significance indicating a general acquiescence of nations in such a rule. Without this, it cannot be applied here as a principle of international law.

It is urged that the subjects of Great Britain knew of the policy of their home government in refusing to recognize the Tinoco régime and cannot now rely on protection by Great Britain. This is a question solely between the home government and its subjects. That government may take the course which the United States had done and refuse to use any diplomatic offices to promote such claims and thus to leave its nationals to depend upon the sense of justice of the existing Costa Rican Government, as they were warned in advance would be its policy, or it may change its conclusion as to the *de facto* existence of the Tinoco government and offer its subjects the protection of its diplomatic intervention. It is entirely a question between the claimants and their own government. It should be noted that Great Britain issued no such warning to its subjects as did the United States to its citizens in this matter.

* * * The decision [on the merits] must be governed by the answer to the question whether the claims would have been good against the Tinoco government as a government, unaffected by the Law of Nullities, and unaffected by the Costa Rican Constitution of 1871.

[The arbitrator first addresses the claim brought on behalf of the Royal Bank of Canada. Costa Rican law provided for a Costa Rican bank to issue credit, to be used for such purposes as rural farm loans, payments to army veterans, and road construction and repair. This bank deposited credit instruments ("bills") in the Royal Bank of Canada on which the Costa Rican government could draw. Taft finds that the Royal Bank honored some requests for funds from Tinoco government officials that the British government, espousing the claim of the Royal Bank, should not now be entitled to recover:]

It thus appears that the present claim of the bank rests on its payment of $200,000 to the Tinocos, $100,000 to Frederico Tinoco, "for expenses of representation of the Chief of State in his approaching trip abroad," and $100,000 to Jose Joaquin Tinoco, as Minister of Costa Rica to Italy for four years' salary and expenses of the Legation of Costa Rica in Italy, to which post the latter had been appointed by his brother. The Royal Bank cannot here claim the benefit of the presumptions which might obtain in favor of a bank receiving a deposit in regular course of business and paying it out in the usual way upon checks bearing no indication on their face of the purpose. The whole transaction here was full of irregularities. There was no authority of law, in the first place for making the Royal Bank the depositary of a revolving credit fund. * * * The case of the Royal Bank depends not on the mere form of the transaction but upon the good faith of the bank in the payment of money for the real use of the Costa Rican Government under the Tinoco régime. It must make out its case of actual furnishing of money to the government for its legitimate use. It has not done so. The bank knew that this money was to be used by the retiring president, F. Tinoco, for his personal support after he had taken refuge in a foreign country. It could not hold his own government for the money paid to him for this purpose.

The case of the money paid to the brother, the Secretary of War, and the appointed Minister to Italy, is much the same. The government book entry charges him with this as a payment for expenses to be incurred in the establishment of a legation in Italy. It includes the salaries and expenses for four years. To pay salaries for four years in advance is a most unusual and absurd course of business. All the circumstances should have advised the Royal Bank that this second draft, too, was for personal and not for legitimate government purposes. It must have known that Jose Joaquin Tinoco in the fall of his brother's government, which was pending, could not expect to represent the Costa Rican Government as its Minister to Italy for four years, that the reasons given for the payment of the money were a mere pretense and that it was only, as in the case of his brother Frederico, an abstraction of the money from the public treasury to support a refugee abroad. * * *

The claim of the Royal Bank against the Costa Rican Government has, however, been given a better status than as decided above, to the extent of one-half of it, by the act of the existing Government of Costa Rica in December, 1922. [Jose Joaquin Tinoco was killed during anti-Tinoco protests in August 1919. The current government sued his estate for $100,000 in Costa Rican court, and in 1922 secured a mortgage for $100,000.] This should enure to the benefit of the Royal Bank. Proceeding in this matter *ex aequo et bono*, therefore, I must hold that the bank is subrogated to the title of Costa Rica in the mortgage[.]

My award, therefore, is that the Law of Nullities in its operation upon the validity of the 998 one thousand colones bills and the claim in behalf of the Royal Bank, will work no injury of which Great Britain can complain, if Costa Rica assigns all her interest in the mortgage for $100,000 upon Jose Joaquin Tinoco's estate executed by his widow, together with all interest paid thereon to the Royal Bank, and that, upon Costa Rica's executing this assignment and delivering the mortgage, the Royal Bank should deliver to the Government of Costa Rica the 998 one thousand colones bills held by it.

[With respect to the petroleum concession, the arbitrator disallows recovery because the concession violated Costa Rica's 1917 constitution. Because of this violation, even Tinoco's government could have defeated the concession. Thus, when the Law of Nullities deemed the concession to be invalid, it worked no injury to the British companies of which Great Britain could complain.]

NOTES AND QUESTIONS

1. *The Arbitrator in the* Tinoco Case. William Howard Taft, the sole arbitrator in the *Tinoco Case*, was President of the United States during 1909–1913 and Chief Justice of the U.S. Supreme Court during 1921–1930. As President, he, along with other leading public figures, supported treaties of general arbitration, applicable even to questions of "vital interests" and "national honor." See John E. Noyes, "William Howard Taft and the Taft Arbitration Treaties," 106 *Villanova Law Review* 535 (2011).

2. *The* Tinoco Case *and the Creation of New States*. Does the *Tinoco Case* demonstrate that even a radical change in government will not by itself affect the identity of a state? The state of Costa Rica survived when Tinoco seized power, and continued when he was deposed. Does the continued existence of Costa Rica settle the question whether the contract obligations of the Tinoco regime must be honored?

3. *Government Succession to Obligations*. Taft's basic position was that, as a matter of international law, a new government is generally bound by the legal commitments of an old government. Could there be any practical alternative to this rule? It is difficult to see how there could be any legally binding commitments of states if international obligations could be repudiated simply by forming or declaring a new government. Should an exception be made to permit the repudiation of national commitments when there has been a radical change in government? If so, who determines whether the change is radical enough?

Today, should the contracts of a government that seized control in an extraconstitutional coup, in violation of the wishes of the people who are governed, be considered binding? Professor Reisman has suggested that the

Tinoco decision, although "consistent with the law of its time" and supported by "policy reasons [that] may still have some cogency," is now "anachronistic, for it stands in stark contradiction to the new constitutive, human rights-based conception of popular sovereignty." W. Michael Reisman, "Sovereignty and Human Rights in Contemporary International Law," in *Democratic Governance and International Law* 239, 244 (Gregory H. Fox & Brad R. Roth eds. 2000). Did Taft occupy a middle, "rule of law" ground between, on the one hand, finding all obligations of a predecessor government binding, and, on the other, refusing to enforce any foreign contracts of an undemocratic predecessor government? See Odette Lienau, "Who Is the 'Sovereign' in Sovereign Debt: Reinterpreting a Rule-of-Law Framework from the Early Twentieth Century," 33 *Yale Journal of International Law* 63 (2008). How sensible is Taft's approach today?

Are some government debts so "odious" that a successor state or government should not have to repay them? Even if the government contracting for the original debt has been popularly elected? In the *Tinoco Case*, note how Taft treated the claim of the Royal Bank of Canada. Are equitable limits on the sanctity of contract particularly applicable when governments or states are in transition? See Robert Howse, *The Concept of Odious Debt in Public International Law*, UNCTAD/OSG/DP 2007/4 (2007).

4. De Facto *and* De Jure *Governments*. Taft needed to establish whether the Tinoco regime was the actual government of Costa Rica when it entered into the banking and oil concession arrangements with the British companies. He discussed the categories of *de facto* and *de jure* governments. What is the difference between them? Taft seemed to look most at the factor of popular acquiescence to determine whether the Tinoco regime was the *de facto* government of Costa Rica. What evidences would a judge or lawyer consider in evaluating the popular support for a government? If Taft had found that the Tinoco regime lacked popular support, would he necessarily have concluded it was not the *de facto* government?

There were about 50 governments world-wide in 1917; the Tinoco regime was recognized by 20 of them. Was this number of recognitions enough to establish Tinoco as the *de jure* government of Costa Rica? Would the answer depend on the degree to which non-recognizing foreign governments opposed the Tinoco regime and still supported the old Gonzalez regime?

5. *The Relative Importance of* De Facto *Control and* De Jure *Recognition*. What if the evidences of *de facto* control conflict with the evidences of *de jure* recognition? Which should govern in determining the legitimate government of a state? Could there be different answers to this question depending on the forum and depending on whether the forum looks to an answer in international law or one or another municipal law? Is the distinction between *de facto* and *de jure* governments another way of stating the conflict between declaratory and constitutive theories of recognition? See Stefan Talmon, *Recognition of Governments in International Law* (1998).

6. *Estoppel.* How persuasive was Taft in his estoppel argument? Should Great Britain have been permitted to insist that the Tinoco regime was the government of Costa Rica when it had failed to recognize the Tinoco regime? The Tinoco regime probably could not have availed itself of the British courts because it was unrecognized. Should there be one answer as to the status of the Tinoco regime *vis-à-vis* Great Britain in British municipal courts and another in an international tribunal?

7. *Comparing the Succession of States and the Succession of Governments.* Is it always easy to distinguish changes in states from changes in governments? Should different consequences attach to changes in governments and changes in states? In the view of Professor Daniel O'Connell,

> the solution of the problem raised by political change cannot be left to the hazard of characterizing the event as a succession of States or a succession of governments. There is evident at the present time a developing pressure in the direction of assimilating these two categories of events, and as the nineteenth-century theory of the State, with its concomitant metaphysics of political personality, loses its cogency, legal theory will tend more and more to return to its eighteenth-century position.

1 D.P. O'Connell, *State Succession in Municipal Law and International Law* 7 (1967). The 18th-century position to which O'Connell referred called for a succession to commitments without drawing a distinction between states and governments.

AUTOCEPHALOUS GREEK-ORTHODOX CHURCH OF CYPRUS v. GOLDBERG & FELDMAN FINE ARTS, INC.

917 F.2d 278 (7th Cir. 1990), *cert. denied*, 502 U.S. 941 (1991)

BAUER, CHIEF JUDGE.

* * * In this appeal, we consider the fate of several tangible victims of Cyprus' turbulent history: specifically, four Byzantine mosaics created over 1400 years ago. The district court awarded possession of these extremely valuable mosaics to plaintiff-appellee, the Autocephalous Greek-Orthodox Church of Cyprus ("Church of Cyprus" or "Church"). *Autocephalous Greek-Orthodox Church of Cyprus v. Goldberg & Feldman Fine Arts, Inc.*, 717 F. Supp. 1374 (S.D. Ind. 1989). Defendants-appellants, Peg Goldberg and Goldberg & Feldman Fine Arts, Inc. (collectively "Goldberg"), claim that in so doing, the court committed various reversible errors. We affirm.

I. BACKGROUND

In the early sixth century, A.D., a large mosaic was affixed to the apse of the Church of the Panagia Kanakaria ("Kanakaria Church") in the village of Lythrankomi, Cyprus. The mosaic, made of small bits of colored glass, depicted Jesus Christ as a young boy in the lap of his mother, the Virgin Mary, who was seated on a throne. Jesus and Mary were attended by two archangels and surrounded by a frieze depicting the twelve apostles. The mosaic was displayed in the Kanakaria Church for centuries, where it became, under the practices of Eastern Orthodox Christianity, sanctified as a holy relic. It survived both the vicissitudes of history, *see Autocephalous*, 717 F. Supp. at 1377 (discussing the period of Iconoclasm during which many religious artifacts were destroyed), and, thanks to restoration efforts, the ravages of time.

Testimony before Judge Noland established that the Kanakaria mosaic was one of only a handful of such holy Byzantine relics to survive into the twentieth century. Sadly, however, war came to Cyprus in the 1970s, from which the mosaic could not be spared.

The Cypriot people have long been a divided people, approximately three-fourths being of Greek descent and Greek-Orthodox faith, the other quarter of Turkish descent and Muslem [*sic*] faith. No sooner had Cyprus gained independence from British rule in 1960 than this bitter division surfaced. Civil disturbances erupted between Greek and Turkish Cypriots, necessitating the introduction of United Nations peacekeeping forces in 1964. (U.N. forces still remain in Cyprus.) Through the 1960s, the Greek Cypriots, concentrated in the southern part of the island, became increasingly estranged from the Turkish Cypriots, concentrated in the north.

The tensions erupted again in 1974, this time with more violent results. In July, 1974, the civil government of the Republic of Cyprus was replaced by a government controlled by the Greek Cypriot military. In apparent response, on July 20, 1974, Turkey invaded Cyprus from the north. By late August, the Turkish military forces had advanced to occupy approximately the northern third of the island. The point at which the invading forces stopped is called the "Green Line." To this day, the heavily-guarded Green Line bisects Nicosia, the capital of the Republic, and splits the island from east to west.

The Turkish forces quickly established their own "government" north of the Green Line. In 1975, they formed what they called the "Turkish Federated State of Cyprus" ("TFSC"). In 1983, that administration was dissolved, and the "Turkish Republic of Northern Cyprus" ("TRNC") was formed. These "governments" were recognized immediately by Turkey, but all other nations in the world—including the United States—have never recognized them, and continue to recognize the Republic of Cyprus ("Republic"), plaintiff-appellee in this action, as the only legitimate government for all Cypriot people.

The Turkish invasion led to the forced southern exodus of over 100,000 Greek Cypriots who lived in northern Cyprus. Turkish Cypriots living in southern Cyprus (and tens of thousands of settlers from mainland Turkey) likewise flooded into northern Cyprus, resulting in a massive exchange of populations.

Lythrankomi is in the northern portion of Cyprus that came under Turkish rule. Although the village and the Kanakaria Church were untouched by the invading forces in 1974, the villagers of Greek ancestry were soon thereafter "enclaved" by the Turkish military. Despite the hostile environment, the pastor and priests of the Kanakaria Church continued for two years to conduct religious services for the Greek Cypriots who remained in Lythrankomi. Hardy as they must have been, these clerics, and virtually all remaining Greek Cypriots, were forced to flee to southern Cyprus in the summer of 1976. Church of Cyprus officials testified that they intend to re-establish the congregation at the Kanakaria Church as soon as Greek Cypriots are permitted to return safely to Lythrankomi. (Thirty-five thousand Turkish troops remain in northern Cyprus.)

When the priests evacuated the Kanakaria Church in 1976, the mosaic was still intact. In the late 1970s, however, Church of Cyprus officials received increasing reports that Greek Cypriot churches and monuments in northern Cyprus were being attacked and vandalized, their contents stolen or destroyed. * * * In November, 1979, a resident of northern Cyprus brought word to the Republic's Department of Antiquities that this fate had also befallen the Kanakaria Church and its mosaic. Vandals had plundered the church, removing anything of value from its interior. The mosaic, or at least its most recognizable and valuable parts, had been forcibly ripped from the apse of the church. Once a place of worship, the Kanakaria Church had been reduced to a stable for farm animals.

Upon learning of the looting of the Kanakaria Church and the loss of its mosaics (made plural by the vandals' axes), the Republic of Cyprus took immediate steps to recover them. [T]hese efforts took the form of contacting and seeking assistance from many organizations and individuals, including the United Nations Educational, Scientific and Cultural Organization ("UNESCO"); the International Council of Museums; the International Council of Museums and Sites; Europa Nostra (an organization devoted to the conservation of the architectural heritage of Europe); the Council of Europe; international auction houses such as Christie's and Sotheby's; Harvard University's Dumbarton Oaks Institute for Byzantine Studies; and the foremost museums, curators and Byzantine scholars throughout the world. The Republic's United States Embassy also routinely disseminated information about lost cultural properties to journalists, U.S. officials and scores of scholars, architects and collectors in this country, asking for assistance in recovering the mosaics. The overall strategy behind these efforts was to get word to the

Figure 7.B

Divided Cyprus

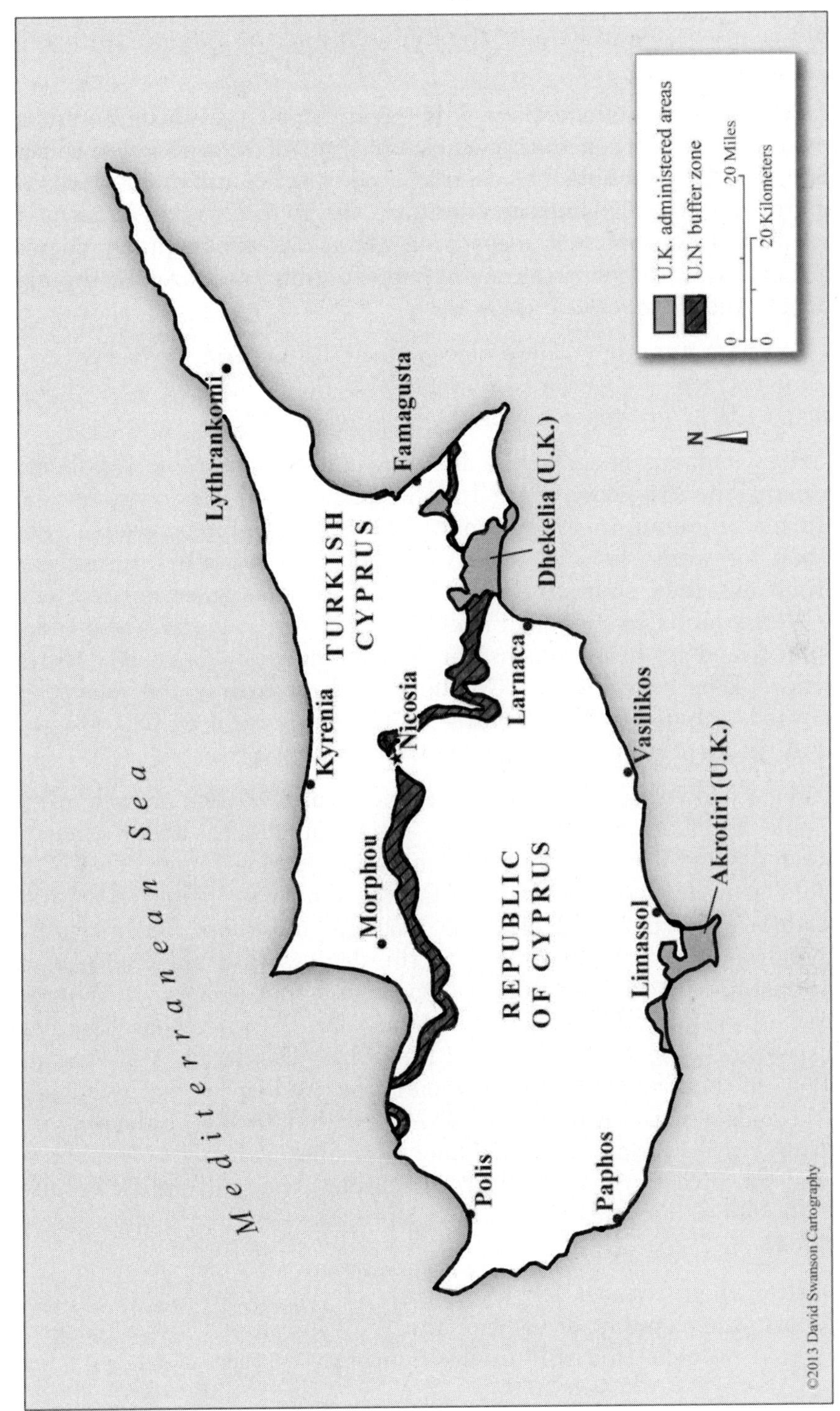

experts and scholars who would probably be involved in any ultimate sale of the mosaics. These individuals, it was hoped, would be the most likely (only?) actors in the chain of custody of stolen cultural properties who would be interested in helping the Republic and Church of Cyprus recover them.

The Republic's efforts have paid off. In recent years, the Republic has recovered and returned to the Church of Cyprus several stolen relics and antiquities. The Republic has even located frescoes and other works taken from the Kanakaria Church, including the four mosaics at issue here. These four mosaics, each measuring about two feet square, depict the figure of Jesus, the busts of one of the attending archangels, the apostle Matthew and the apostle James.

To understand how these pieces of the Kanakaria mosaic resurfaced, we must trace the actions of appellant Peg Goldberg and the other principals through whose hands they passed in 1988.

Peg Goldberg is an art dealer and gallery operator. Goldberg and Feldman Fine Arts, Inc., is the Indiana corporation that owns her gallery in Carmel, Indiana. In the summer of 1988, Peg Goldberg went to Europe to shop for works for her gallery. Although her main interest is 20th century paintings, etchings and sculptures, Goldberg was enticed while in The Netherlands by Robert Fitzgerald, another Indiana art dealer and "casual friend" of hers, to consider the purchase of "four early Christian mosaics." [The court details Goldberg's efforts to buy the mosaics. The sale was concluded by the exchange of the mosaics for $1,080,000 in $100 bills at the airport in Geneva, Switzerland.]

Peg Goldberg's efforts soon turned to * * * the resale of these valuable mosaics. She worked up sales brochures about them, and contacted several other dealers to help her find a buyer. Two of these dealers' searches led them both to Dr. Marion True of the Getty Museum in California. When told of these mosaics and their likely origin, the aptly-named Dr. True explained to the dealers that she had a working relationship with the Republic of Cyprus and that she was duty-bound to contact Cypriot officials about them. Dr. True called Dr. Vassos Karageorghis, the Director of the Republic's Department of Antiquities and one of the primary Cypriot officials involved in the worldwide search for the mosaics. Dr. Karageorghis verified that the Republic was in fact hunting for the mosaics that had been described to Dr. True, and he set in motion the investigative and legal machinery that ultimately resulted in the Republic learning that they were in Goldberg's possession in Indianapolis.

After their request for the return of the mosaics was refused by Goldberg, the Republic of Cyprus and the Church of Cyprus (collectively "Cyprus") brought this suit in the Southern District of Indiana for the recovery of the mosaics. * * * Judge Noland awarded possession of the mosaics to the Church of Cyprus. Goldberg filed a timely appeal.

II. ANALYSIS

[The court concludes that no statute of limitations bars the action, and that applicable rules of replevin allow the plaintiff Church to recover the mosaics.]

Finally, Goldberg argues that several decrees of the TFSC (the entity established in northern Cyprus by the Turkish military immediately after the 1974 invasion) divested the Church of title to the mosaics. Goldberg asks us to honor these decrees under the notion that in some instances courts in the United States can give effect to the acts of nonrecognized but "*de facto*" regimes if the acts relate to purely local matters. *See Restatement (Third) of the Foreign Relations Law of the United States ("Third Restatement")* § 205(3) (1987);[15] *Salimoff v. Standard Oil Co.*, 262 N.Y. 220, 186 N.E. 679 (1933) (under Soviet law, U.S.S.R. nationalization decree effective to pass title to oil within Russia despite fact that U.S.S.R. was not yet recognized by the U.S.). The TFSC decrees at issue, all propagated in 1975, are principally these: 1) the "Abandoned Movable Property Law," which provided that all movable property within the boundaries of the TFSC abandoned by its owner because of the owner's "departure" from northern Cyprus "as a result of the situation after 20th July 1974" now belongs to the TFSC "in the name of the Turkish Community" and that the TFSC "is responsible for the possession and control of such property;" and 2) the "Antiquities Ordinance," which provided that all religious buildings and antiquities, including specifically "synagogues, basilicas, churches, monasteries and the like," located north of the Green Line, as well as any and all "movable antiquities" contained therein, are now the property of the TFSC. Because these decrees were enacted before the Kanakaria Church was looted and its mosaics stolen, the argument concludes, the Church cannot here claim to hold title to the mosaics.

It is helpful to note at the outset what is *not* being claimed here. First, Goldberg does not (and cannot) suggest that this court should pass on the validity of the Turkish administration in northern Cyprus. We repeat here precepts that are well-established in the law of this country:

> [T]he conduct of foreign relations was committed by the Constitution to the political departments of the government, and the propriety of what may be done in the exercise of this political power [is] not subject to judicial inquiry or decision, . . . [and]

---

[15] This Restatement section provides:

> [C]ourts in the United States ordinarily give effect to acts of a regime representing an entity not recognized as a state, or of a regime not recognized as the government of a state, if those acts apply to territory under the control of that regime and relate to domestic matters only.

> who is the sovereign of a territory is not a judicial question, but one the determination of which by the political departments conclusively binds the courts[.]

United States v. Belmont, 301 U.S. 324, 328 (1937). Indeed, Goldberg herself supports the district court's decision to deny the TRNC's motion to intervene in this case, which decision was based on the TRNC's continued status as a nonrecognized entity. *See Third Restatement* § 205(1) (entity not recognized as a state ordinarily denied access to U.S. courts).

Second, this is not a case in which one party is claiming title under the laws of a state that has been entirely displaced, and the other is claiming title under the laws of the new, displacing regime. All Goldberg can hope to gain from the invocation of these TFSC edicts is a finding that the Church's claim of title is defective; she has no plausible claim of valid title in herself based on these edicts. This fact sets this case apart from the cases cited by Goldberg, including *Salimoff*, 186 N.E. 679 (plaintiff Russian nationals claimed title to property under laws of the old Russian Empire and defendant U.S. companies claimed title due to purchase from Soviet government, which seized the property pursuant to nationalization decree)[.]

What Goldberg is claiming is that the TFSC's confiscatory decrees, adopted only one year after the Turkish invasion, should be given effect by this court because the TFSC and its successor TRNC should now be viewed as the "*de facto*" government north of the Green Line. This we are unwilling to do. We draw on two lines of precedent as support for our decision. First, we note that, contrary to the New York court's decision in *Salimoff*, several courts of the same era refused to give effect to the nationalization decrees of the as-yet-unrecognized Soviet Republics. These courts relied on a variety of grounds, including especially the fact that the political branches of our government still refused to recognize these entities. *See, e.g., Latvian State Cargo & Passenger S.S. Line v. McGrath*, 188 F.2d 1000, 1002–04 (D.C. Cir. 1951) (also stating as a possible alternative ground the following view: "since the nationalization decrees here involved were confiscatory and thus contrary to the public policy of this country, our courts would in no event give them effect," and citing cases); *The Maret*, 145 F.2d 431, 442 (3d Cir. 1944) ("[N]o valid distinction can be drawn between the political or diplomatic act of nonrecognition of a sovereign and nonrecognition of the decrees or acts of that sovereign. . . . Nonrecognition of a foreign sovereign and nonrecognition of its decrees are to be deemed to be as essential a part of the power confided by the Constitution to the Executive for the conduct of foreign affairs as recognition."). Similarly, as regards the Turkish administration in northern Cyprus, the United States government (like the rest of the non-Turkish world) has not recognized its legitimacy, nor does our government "recognize that [the Turkish administration] has functioned as a de facto or quasi government . . . , ruling within its own borders."

Second, we are guided in part by the post-Civil War cases in which courts refused to give effect to property-affecting acts of the Confederate state legislatures. In one such case, *Williams v. Bruffy*, 96 U.S. 176 (1878), the Supreme Court drew a helpful distinction between two kinds of "*de facto*" governments. The first kind "is such as exists after it has expelled the regularly constituted authorities from the seats of power and the public offices, and established its own functionaries in their places, so as to represent in fact the sovereignty of the nation." This kind of *de facto* government, the Court explained, "is treated as in most respects possessing rightful authority, . . . [and] its legislation is in general recognized." The second kind of *de facto* government "is such as exists where a portion of the inhabitants of a country have separated themselves from the parent State and established an independent government. The validity of its acts, both against the parent State and its citizens or subjects, depends entirely upon its ultimate success. . . . If it succeed, and become recognized, its acts from the commencement of its existence are upheld as those of an independent nation." (The Court held that the Confederacy was a government of the second type that ultimately failed.) Goldberg argues that the TFSC and its successor TRNC have achieved the level of "ultimate success" contemplated by this standard, because they have maintained control of the territory north of the Green Line for over fifteen years. We will not thus equate simple longevity of control with "ultimate success." The Turkish forces, despite their best efforts, did not completely supplant the Republic nor its officers. Instead, the TFSC and the TRNC, neither of which has ever been recognized by the non-Turkish world, only acceded to the control of the northern portion of Cyprus. The Republic of Cyprus remains the only recognized Cypriot government, the sovereign nation for the entire island. [W]e conclude that the confiscatory decrees proffered by Goldberg do not divest the Church of its claim of title.

III. CONCLUSION

* * * Those who plundered the churches and monuments of war-torn Cyprus, hoarded their relics away, and are now smuggling and selling them for large sums, are * * * blackguards. The Republic of Cyprus, with diligent effort and the help of friends like Dr. True, has been able to locate several of these stolen antiquities; items of vast cultural, religious (and, as this case demonstrates, monetary) value. Among such finds are the pieces of the Kanakaria mosaic at issue in this case. Unfortunately, when these mosaics surfaced they were in the hands not of the most guilty parties, but of Peg Goldberg and her gallery. Correctly applying Indiana law, the district court determined that Goldberg must return the mosaics to their rightful owner: the Church of Cyprus. Goldberg's tireless

attacks have not established reversible error in that determination, and thus, for the reasons discussed above, the district court's judgment is AFFIRMED.

[T]hose who wish to purchase art work on the international market, undoubtedly a ticklish business, are not without means by which to protect themselves. Especially when circumstances are as suspicious as those that faced Peg Goldberg, prospective purchasers would do best to do more than make a few last-minute phone calls. * * * In such cases, dealers can (and probably should) take steps such as a formal IFAR [International Foundation for Art Research] search; a documented authenticity check by disinterested experts; a full background search of the seller and his claim of title; insurance protection and a contingency sales contract; and the like. If Goldberg would have pursued such methods, perhaps she would have discovered in time what she has now discovered too late: the Church has a valid, superior and enforceable claim to these Byzantine treasures, which therefore must be returned to it.

CUDAHY, CIRCUIT JUDGE, concurring * * *

A second * * * aspect of this case involves the treatment of the cultural heritage of foreign nations under international and United States law. The United States has both acceded to international agreements and enacted its own statutes regarding the importation of cultural property. These regulatory efforts have encompassed transfers of property during both wartime and peacetime and apply whether the property was originally stolen or "merely" illegally exported from the country of origin. The two most significant international agreements that attempt to protect cultural property are the 1954 Convention on the Protection of Cultural Property in the Event of Armed Conflict (the "1954 Hague Convention"), 249 U.N.T.S. 215 (1956), and the UNESCO Convention on the Means of Prohibiting and Preventing the Illicit Transport, Export and Transfer of Ownership of Cultural Property (the "UNESCO Convention"), 823 U.N.T.S. 231 (1972). Under both these multinational treaties, as well as under the United States' Convention on Cultural Property Implementation Act, 19 U.S.C. § 2601 *et seq.* (1983), the Cypriot mosaics would be considered cultural property warranting international protection. * * *

The 1954 Hague Convention may be applicable to the case before us given the incursion of Turkish armed forces into Cyprus in 1974 and our ongoing refusal to recognize the government established in the northern part of Cyprus. The 1954 Hague Convention, which is but the most recent multilateral agreement in a 200-year history of international attempts to protect cultural property during wartime, prohibits the destruction or seizure of cultural property during armed conflict, whether international or civil in nature, and during periods of belligerent occupation. The

Hague Convention also applies to international trafficking during peacetime in cultural property unlawfully seized during an armed conflict. The attempt of the government established in northern Cyprus by the Turkish military to divest the Greek Cypriot church of ownership of the mosaics might be viewed as an interference of the sort contemplated by the 1954 Hague Convention. If this were the case, the acts and decrees of the northern Cyprus government divesting title to this cultural property would not demand the deference of American courts.

The second international agreement, the UNESCO Convention, focuses on private conduct, primarily during peacetime, and thus is also applicable to the theft and removal of the mosaics from Cyprus. Article 7 of that Convention requires signatory nations:

> (a) To take the necessary measures, consistent with national legislation, to prevent museums and similar institutions within their territories from acquiring cultural property originating in another State Party which has been illegally exported . . . ;
>
> (b)(i) to prohibit the import of cultural property stolen from a museum or a religious or secular public monument or similar institution in another State Party . . . , provided that such property is documented as appertaining to the inventory of that institution;
>
> (ii) at the request of the State Party of origin, to take appropriate steps to recover and return any such cultural property . . . , provided, however, that the requesting State shall pay just compensation to an innocent purchaser or to a person who has valid title to that property. . . .

It is clear that the mosaics in the case before us were stolen (under any reasonable definition of that word) from a religious institution and that the mosaics were extensively documented by the Dumbarton Oaks publication as belonging to the Kanakaria Church. While the UNESCO Convention seems to contemplate primarily measures to be implemented by the executive branch of a government through its import and export rules and policies, the judicial branch should certainly attempt to reflect in its decisionmaking the spirit as well as the letter of an international agreement to which the United States is a party.

NOTES AND QUESTIONS

1. *Illicit Trafficking in Cultural Property*. Those who steal art and antiquities often destroy archaeological and other significant cultural information. Moreover, the economic losses from illicit trafficking in cultural property, although difficult to measure, are enormous. "[T]he annual illicit flow of cultural property totals well above $1 billion." James A.R. Nafziger, "Protection of Cultural Property," in 1 *International Criminal Law* 977, 1011

(M. Cherif Bassiouni ed., 3d ed. 2008). For perspective on the economics of the antiquities market, see Ricardo J. Elia, "Looting, Collecting, and the Destruction of Archaeological Resources," 6 *Nonrenewable Resources*, No. 2, at 85 (1997).

Countries have sometimes persuaded museums to return some stolen art treasures, and have also sued individuals allegedly conspiring in illegal art transactions. Dr. Marion True, the chief antiquities curator at the Getty Museum from 1986–2005 who contacted Cypriot officials in the *Goldberg Case*, has herself been a defendant in criminal cases in Greece and Italy. See Anthee Carassava, "Greek Court Dismisses Case Against Ex-Curator," *New York Times*, Nov. 28, 2007, at E1. For more about the *Goldberg Case* and the depredation of Cypriot cultural heritage, see Dan Hofstadter, *Goldberg's Angel* (1994); Mark Rose, "From Cyprus to Munich," *Archaeology*, Apr. 20, 1998, *available at* http://www.archive.archaeology.org/online/features/cyprus/ (last visited Dec. 7, 2013). For good overviews of legal issues, see Nafziger, *supra*, and "Symposium: International Legal Dimensions of Art and Cultural Property," 38 *Vanderbilt Journal of Transnational* Law 921 (2005).

2. *Divided Cyprus*. How should we characterize the Turkish Republic of Northern Cyprus (TRNC), labeled "Turkish Cyprus" in Figure 7.B? Is it a state? The widespread refusal of existing states to recognize the Turkish Federated State of Cyprus (TFSC) or its successor, the TRNC, has been explained as a reaction to Turkey's unlawful use of force in northern Cyprus. See Ian Brownlie, "The United Nations Charter and the Use of Force, 1945–1985," in *The Current Legal Regulation of the Use of Force* 491, 492 (A. Cassese ed. 1986); S.C. Res. 541 (1983); S.C. Res. 550 (1984). The European Court of Human Rights has imputed to Turkey various human rights violations in northern Cyprus. Cyprus v. Turkey, 2001–IV Eur. Ct. H.R. 1. This judgment further "weakens the Turkish Cypriots' claim that the TRNC operates as an independent state." Frank Hoffmeister, "International Decision," 96 *American Journal of International Law* 445, 450 (2002).

There have been proposals to establish a federal Cypriot government, with the northern and southern regions of the island each exercising extensive internal competences. However, such efforts to end the division of Cyprus have proved unsuccessful. See "The Insoluble Cyprus Problem: Sad Island Story," *The Economist*, Apr. 2, 2011, at 51. The Greek-dominated Republic of Cyprus joined the European Union in 2004.

3. *Giving Effect to the Laws of Unrecognized States and Governments*. How does the *Goldberg* court's treatment of recognition compare to that of Arbitrator Taft in the *Tinoco Case*? In *Goldberg*, we see some effects of non-recognition in a municipal court. The U.S. Seventh Circuit Court of Appeals refused to give effect to a law of an entity that the United States had not recognized as a state. If the TFSC and the TRNC had been recognized by many states, but not by the United States, would the court have given effect to the confiscatory TFSC decrees? Or did the *Goldberg* court refuse to give effect to the TFSC's decrees simply because the court found them objectionable? Should acts taken under *un*objectionable laws of an

unrecognized state—perhaps laws specifying rules of intestate succession—be denied effect in U.S. courts?

4. *Access of Unrecognized States and Governments to U.S. Courts*. The *Goldberg* district court also refused to allow the TRNC to intervene directly in the case, stating that to do so "would create the incongruous result of having the Judicial Branch implicitly recognize that entity as a legitimate government in the face of explicit nonrecognition by the Executive Branch." Autocephalous Greek-Orthodox Church of Cyprus v. Goldberg & Feldman Fine Arts, Inc., No. IP 89–304–C (S.D. Ind. May 31, 1989), *quoted in* 86 *American Journal of International Law* 128, 129 (1992). Other decisions also have denied unrecognized states or governments access to U.S. courts. In Russian Socialist Federated Soviet Republic v. Cibrario, 235 N.Y. 255, 139 N.E. 259 (1923), the court concluded that foreign powers appeared in U.S. courts only as a matter of comity. The court defined comity as "that reciprocal courtesy which one member of the family of nations owes to the others," a concept that presupposed friendship. No comity was due a foreign government appearing as a plaintiff in U.S. court, the *Cibrario* court found, unless the United States had recognized that government. More on comity appears in Chapter 11.

Yet U.S. courts have not always refused to allow unrecognized entities to pursue their claims. In National Petrochemical Co. v. M/T Stolt Sheaf, 860 F.2d 551 (2d Cir. 1988), *cert. denied*, 489 U.S. 1081 (1989), the Second Circuit reversed the district court's dismissal of a suit brought by a corporation wholly owned by the government of Iran. Although the United States did not recognize Iran at the time, the court accepted the view of the U.S. Justice and State Departments, which argued in an *amicus* brief that this plaintiff should have access to U.S. courts:

> Two reasons support this holding. First, as this century draws to a close, the practice of extending formal recognition to new governments has altered: The United States Department of State has sometimes refrained from announcing recognition of a new government because grants of recognition have been misinterpreted as pronouncements of approval. As a result, the absence of formal recognition cannot serve as the touchstone for determining whether the Executive Branch has "recognized" a foreign nation for the purpose of granting that government access to United States courts.
>
> Second, the power to deal with foreign nations outside the bounds of formal recognition is essential to a president's implied power to maintain international relations. *Cf. United States v. Curtiss-Wright Export Corp.*, 299 U.S. 304, 318–20 (1936). As part of this power, the Executive Branch must have the latitude to permit a foreign nation access to U.S. courts, even if that nation is not formally recognized by the U.S. government.

Id. at 554–55. Should unrecognized governments be permitted to litigate in U.S. courts unless the executive branch expressly objects?

5. *Recognition and the Maintenance of Diplomatic Relations.* Recognition by the executive branch is ordinarily a prerequisite for the establishment of diplomatic relations. As noted above, nonrecognition traditionally meant that the unrecognized state or government could not sue in U.S. court. Should a government with which the United States does not maintain diplomatic relations be similarly barred? The U.S. Supreme Court addressed the issue in Banco Nacional de Cuba v. Sabbatino, 376 U.S. 398, 410 (1964):

> Respondents, pointing to the severance of diplomatic relations, commercial embargo, and freezing of Cuban assets in this country, contend that relations between the United States and Cuba manifest such animosity that unfriendliness is clear, and that the courts should be closed to the Cuban Government. We do not agree. This Court would hardly be competent to undertake assessments of varying degrees of friendliness or its absence, and, lacking some definite touchstone for determination, we are constrained to consider any relationship, short of war, with a recognized sovereign power as embracing the privilege of resorting to United States courts. * * * Severance [of diplomatic relations] may take place for any number of political reasons, its duration is unpredictable, and whatever expression of animosity it may imply does not approach that implicit in a declaration of war.

C. SELF-DETERMINATION AND THE CREATION OF STATES

This part examines the concept of self-determination and its relevance to the creation of states. Self-determination also concerns the rights of "peoples," one category of non-state entity. Article 1(2) of the U.N. Charter provides that one purpose of the United Nations is "to develop friendly relations among nations based on respect for the principle of equal rights and self-determination of peoples," a goal that has been elaborated in widely accepted treaties and U.N. General Assembly declarations.

Although self-determination took on particular importance in the U.N. system, its international law roots trace back at least to World War I, as discussed in the following Note. The 1998 *Secession of Quebec Case* then analyzes the international law of self-determination as it evolved in U.N. instruments and practice, which focused especially on decolonization. The last reading, a 2010 International Court of Justice advisory opinion concerning Kosovo, allows us to explore the legal relevance of self-determination for non-colonies in the 21st century.

NOTE: SELF-DETERMINATION IN THE AFTERMATH OF WORLD WAR I

Self-determination gained prominence in international relations at the Paris Peace Conference concluding World War I. U.S. President Woodrow Wilson believed that national self-determination was important in maintaining a peaceful international society. For Wilson, self-determination had both an internal aspect (promotion of democratic institutions, in order to respect the consent of the governed) and an external aspect (freedom from alien rule). Wilson particularly championed self-determination in breaking up the Austro-Hungarian and Ottoman empires. The Soviet leader, Vladimir Lenin, also forcefully espoused a right of self-determination, at least on the international level. Lenin condemned colonialism, arguing that peoples under colonial rule had the right to gain their independence, a position closely tied to his more fundamental goal of advancing socialism on a global basis. While Wilson also thought that self-determination should be taken into account in settling colonial claims, he sought to balance self-determination concerns with the interests of colonial powers, and to achieve self-determination in an orderly, nonviolent manner.

The states at the Paris Peace Conference consulted with various European groups seeking self-determination. The Conference agreed to allow residents along some borders to hold plebiscites to help determine new boundaries between states. Belief in self-determination also facilitated the establishment of Poland and Czechoslovakia as independent states. However, the economic, strategic, and geopolitical interests of the principal Allied powers proved more important than self-determination as the shape of Europe was decided after World War I. When it proved impossible to divide all of Europe up into perfectly homogenous states, the Allies concluded peace treaties requiring that new states protect the rights of ethnic, religious, and linguistic minorities. See, *e.g.*, Minorities Treaty Between the Principal Allied and Associated Powers and Poland, June 28, 1919, 225 Consol. T.S. 412.

The League of Nations, also a product of the Paris Peace Conference (see Chapter 8), grappled with self-determination issues in the 1920s and 1930s. For example, a League-designated Committee of Jurists investigated the status of the Åland Islands, asking whether the Ålands, which had previously been controlled by Finland, "should, according to International Law, be entirely left to the domestic jurisdiction of Finland." "Report of the International Committee of Jurists on the Legal Aspects of the Aaland Islands Question," *League of Nations Official Journal*, Special Supp. No. 3, at 3 (1920). Åland inhabitants sought to align with Sweden because of linguistic, cultural, and ethnic ties. According to the Committee of Jurists, the principle of self-determination, though recognized in some treaties, did not rest "upon the same footing as a positive rule of the Law of Nations." *Id.* at 5. Nonetheless, self-determination was an important, though not necessarily dispositive, consideration in this case, because Finland, emerging from under Russian control, itself faced an unsettled political situation. The Åland Island situation suggested to some observers that a right to self-determination during this period applied only in "abnormal" situations. See Nathaniel Berman, "Sovereignty in Abeyance: Self-determination and International Law," 7 *Wisconsin Journal of International Law* 51, 72–76 (1988). Ultimately, the Ålands remained part of Finland, although the Islanders were accorded significant autonomy.

In another act of deference to self-determination, the Covenant of the League of Nations created "mandates," authorizing European powers to govern certain territories under certain conditions. Pursuant to Article 22 of the Covenant, colonies that had been governed by states defeated in World War I and that were "inhabited by peoples not yet able to stand by themselves under the strenuous conditions of the modern world" could be administered under this system, subject to "the principle that the well-being and development of such peoples form a sacred trust of civilization." Class A mandates, for territories closest to statehood, comprised "[c]ertain communities formerly belonging to the Turkish Empire"—Mesopotamia (later Iraq), Syria, and Palestine—that had "reached a stage of development where their existence as independent nations can be provisionally recognized subject to the rendering of administrative advice and assistance by a Mandatory until such time as they are able to stand alone." Other classes of mandates, located in Africa and the South Pacific, were deemed to require more control by a Mandatory. See Ruth Gordon, "Mandates," in 6 *Max Planck Encyclopedia of Public International Law* 989 (Rüdiger Wolfrum ed. 2012).

Mandates ended with the dissolution of the League of Nations after World War II. In their place, the United Nations established so-called "trust territories" and took action to implement the legal principle of self-determination, enshrined in the U.N. Charter and treaty law.

REFERENCE RE SECESSION OF QUEBEC

Supreme Court of Canada, Aug. 20, 1998,
37 *International Legal Materials* 1340 (1998)

[The Canadian Supreme Court finds that a "reference," or request for an advisory opinion, from the Canadian Governor in Council properly presented questions about the potential secession of Quebec from Canada. The Court first determines that Canadian constitutional law does not permit unilateral secession, although a constitutional duty to negotiate would arise if Quebecers voted for secession by "a clear majority on a clear question." The Court then turns to the second question:

Does international law give the National Assembly, legislature or government of Quebec the right to effect the secession of Quebec from Canada unilaterally? In this regard, is there a right to self-determination under international law that would give the National Assembly, legislature or government of Quebec the right to effect the secession of Quebec from Canada unilaterally?]

(1) *Secession at International Law*

111. [I]nternational law does not specifically grant component parts of sovereign states the legal right to secede unilaterally from their "parent" state. * * * Given the lack of specific authorization for unilateral secession, proponents of the existence of such a right at international law are therefore left to attempt to found their argument (i) on the proposition that unilateral secession is not specifically prohibited and that what is not specifically prohibited is inferentially permitted; or (ii) on the implied duty of states to recognize the legitimacy of secession brought about by the exercise of the well-established international law right of "a people" to self-determination. * * *

(a) *Absence of a Specific Prohibition*

112. International law contains neither a right of unilateral secession nor the explicit denial of such a right, although such a denial is, to some extent, implicit in the exceptional circumstances required for secession to be permitted under the right of a people to self-determination, e.g., the right of secession that arises in the exceptional situation of an oppressed or colonial people, discussed below. As will be seen, international law places great importance on the territorial integrity of nation states and, by and large, leaves the creation of a new state to be determined by the domestic law of the existing state of which the seceding entity presently forms a part. Where, as here, unilateral secession would be incompatible with the domestic Constitution, international law is likely to accept that conclusion subject to the right of peoples to self-determination, a topic to which we now turn.

(b) *The Right of a People to Self-determination*

113. While international law generally regulates the conduct of nation states, it does, in some specific circumstances, also recognize the "rights" of entities other than nation states—such as the right of a *people* to self-determination.

114. The existence of the right of a people to self-determination is now so widely recognized in international conventions that the principle has acquired a status beyond "convention" and is considered a general principle of international law (A. Cassese, *Self-determination of peoples: A legal reappraisal* (1995), at pp. 171–72; K. Doehring, "Self-

Determination," in B. Simma, ed., *The Charter of the United Nations: A Commentary* (1994), at p. 70).

115. Article 1[(2)] of the *Charter of the United Nations* states in part that one of the purposes of the United Nations (U.N.) is:

> To develop friendly relations among nations based on respect for the principle of equal rights and self-determination of peoples, and to take other appropriate measures to strengthen universal peace[.]

116. Article 55 of the U.N. *Charter* further states that the U.N. shall promote goals such as higher standards of living, full employment and human rights "[w]ith a view to the creation of conditions of stability and well-being which are necessary for peaceful and friendly relations among nations based on respect for the principle of equal rights and self-determination of peoples." * * *

118. * * * Article 1 of both the U.N.'s *International Covenant on Civil and Political Rights*, 999 U.N.T.S. 171, and its *International Covenant on Economic, Social and Cultural Rights*, 993 U.N.T.S. 3, states:

> All peoples have the right of self-determination. By virtue of that right they freely determine their political status and freely pursue their economic, social and cultural development.

119. Similarly, the U.N. General Assembly's *Declaration on Principles of International Law Concerning Friendly Relations and Co-operation Among States in Accordance with the Charter of the United Nations*, GA Res. 2625 (XXV), 24 October 1970, states:

> By virtue of the principle of equal rights and self-determination of peoples enshrined in the Charter of the United Nations, all peoples have the right freely to determine, without external interference, their political status and to pursue their economic, social and cultural development, and every State has the duty to respect this right in accordance with the provisions of the Charter. * * *

122. As will be seen, international law expects that the right to self-determination will be exercised by peoples within the framework of existing sovereign states and consistently with the maintenance of the territorial integrity of those states. Where this is not possible, in the exceptional circumstances discussed below, a right of secession may arise.

(i) Defining "Peoples"

123. International law grants the right to self-determination to "peoples." Accordingly, access to the right requires the threshold step of characterizing as a people the group seeking self-determination. However, * * * the precise meaning of the term "people" remains somewhat uncertain.

124. It is clear that "a people" may include only a portion of the population of an existing state. The right to self-determination has developed largely as a human right, and is generally used in documents that simultaneously contain references to "nation" and "state." The juxtaposition of these terms is indicative that the reference to "people" does not necessarily mean the entirety of a state's population. To restrict the definition of the term to the population of existing states would render the granting of a right to self-determination largely duplicative, given the parallel emphasis within the majority of the source documents on the need to protect the territorial integrity of existing states, and would frustrate its remedial purpose.

125. While much of the Quebec population certainly shares many of the characteristics (such as a common language and culture) that would be considered in determining whether a specific group is a "people," as do other groups within Quebec and/or Canada, it is not necessary to explore this legal characterization to resolve Question 2 appropriately. Similarly, it is not necessary for the Court to determine whether, should a Quebec people exist within the definition of public international law, such a people encompasses the entirety of the provincial population or just a portion thereof. Nor is it necessary to examine the position of the aboriginal population within Quebec. As the following discussion of the scope of the right to self-determination will make clear, whatever be the correct application of the definition of people(s) in this context, their right of self-determination cannot in the present circumstances be said to ground a right to unilateral secession.

(ii) Scope of the Right to Self-determination

126. The recognized sources of international law establish that the right to self-determination of a people is normally fulfilled through *internal* self-determination—a people's pursuit of its political, economic, social and cultural development within the framework of an existing state. A right to *external* self-determination (which in this case potentially takes the form of the assertion of a right to unilateral secession) arises in only the most extreme of cases and, even then, under carefully defined circumstances. *External* self-determination can be defined as in the following statement from the *Declaration on Friendly Relations, supra*, as

> The establishment of a sovereign and independent State, the free association or integration with an independent State or the emergence into any other political status freely determined by a *people* constitute modes of implementing the right of self-determination by *that people*. (Emphasis added.)

127. The international law principle of self-determination has evolved within a framework of respect for the territorial integrity of existing states. The various international documents that support the existence of a people's right to self-determination also contain parallel

statements supportive of the conclusion that the exercise of such a right must be sufficiently limited to prevent threats to an existing state's territorial integrity or the stability of relations between sovereign states.

128. The *Declaration on Friendly Relations, supra,* [the U.N. General Assembly's *Declaration on the Occasion of the Fiftieth Anniversary of the United Nations*, G.A. Res. 50/6 (1995), and the *Vienna Declaration and Programme of Action*, A/Conf.157/24 (1993), which was adopted by the U.N. World Conference on Human Rights,] are specific. They state, immediately after affirming a people's right to determine political, economic, social and cultural issues, that such rights are *not* to ["]be construed as authorizing or encouraging any action which would dismember or *impair, totally or in part, the territorial integrity or political unity of sovereign and independent States conducting themselves in compliance with the principle of equal rights and self-determination of peoples* as described above and thus possessed of a government representing the whole people belonging to the territory without distinction. . . . " (Emphasis added.)

129. Similarly, while the concluding document of the Vienna Meeting in 1989 of the Conference on Security and Co-operation in Europe on the follow-up to the *Helsinki Final Act* again refers to peoples having the right to determine "their internal and *external* political status" (emphasis added), that statement is immediately followed by express recognition that the participating states will at all times act, as stated in the *Helsinki Final Act*, "in conformity with the purposes and principles of the Charter of the United Nations and with the relevant norms of international law, *including those relating to territorial integrity of states*" (emphasis added).

[T]he reference in the *Helsinki Final Act* to a people determining its external political status is interpreted to mean the expression of a people's external political status through the government of the existing state, save in the exceptional circumstances discussed below. As noted by Cassese, *supra*, at p. 287, given the history and textual structure of this document, its reference to external self-determination simply means that "no territorial or other change can be brought about by the central authorities of a State that is contrary to the will of the whole people of that State."

130. While the *International Covenant on Economic, Social and Cultural Rights, supra,* and the *International Covenant on Civil and Political Rights, supra,* do not specifically refer to the protection of territorial integrity, they both define the ambit of the right to self-determination in terms that are normally attainable within the framework of an existing state. There is no necessary incompatibility between the maintenance of the territorial integrity of existing states, including Canada, and the right of a "people" to achieve a full measure of

self-determination. A state whose government represents the whole of the people or peoples resident within its territory, on a basis of equality and without discrimination, and respects the principles of self-determination in its own internal arrangements, is entitled to the protection under international law of its territorial integrity.

(iii) Colonial and Oppressed Peoples

131. Accordingly, the general state of international law with respect to the right to self-determination is that the right operates within the overriding protection granted to the territorial integrity of "parent" states. However, as noted by Cassese, *supra*, at p. 334, there are certain defined contexts within which the right to the self-determination of peoples does allow that right to be exercised "externally," which, in the context of this Reference, would potentially mean secession:

> . . . the right to external self-determination, which entails the possibility of choosing (or restoring) independence, has only been bestowed upon two classes of peoples (those under colonial rule or foreign occupation), based upon the assumption that both classes make up entities that are inherently distinct from the colonialist Power and the occupant Power and that their "territorial integrity," all but destroyed by the colonialist or occupying Power, should be fully restored[.]

132. The right of colonial peoples to exercise their right to self-determination by breaking away from the "imperial" power is now undisputed, but is irrelevant to this Reference.

133. The other clear case where a right to external self-determination accrues is where a people is subject to alien subjugation, domination or exploitation outside a colonial context. This recognition finds its roots in the *Declaration on Friendly Relations, supra*[.]

134. A number of commentators have further asserted that the right to self-determination may ground a right to unilateral secession in a third circumstance. Although this third circumstance has been described in several ways, the underlying proposition is that, when a people is blocked from the meaningful exercise of its right to self-determination internally, it is entitled, as a last resort, to exercise it by secession. The *Vienna Declaration, supra*, requirement that governments represent "the whole people belonging to the territory without distinction of any kind" adds credence to the assertion that such a complete blockage may potentially give rise to a right of secession.

135. * * * Even assuming that the third circumstance is sufficient to create a right to unilateral secession under international law, the current Quebec context cannot be said to approach such a threshold. * * *

136. The population of Quebec cannot plausibly be said to be denied access to government. Quebecers occupy prominent positions within the government of Canada. Residents of the province freely make political choices and pursue economic, social and cultural development within Quebec, across Canada, and throughout the world. The population of Quebec is equitably represented in legislative, executive and judicial institutions. In short, to reflect the phraseology of the international documents that address the right to self-determination of peoples, Canada is a "sovereign and independent state conducting itself in compliance with the principle of equal rights and self-determination of peoples and thus possessed of a government representing the whole people belonging to the territory without distinction."

137. [W]e cannot conclude under current circumstances that [the Canadian constitutional arrangements presently in effect] place Quebecers in a disadvantaged position within the scope of the international law rule.

138. In summary, the international law right to self-determination only generates, at best, a right to external self-determination in situations of former colonies; where a people is oppressed, as for example under foreign military occupation; or where a definable group is denied meaningful access to government to pursue their political, economic, social and cultural development. In all three situations, the people in question are entitled to a right to external self-determination because they have been denied the ability to exert internally their right to self-determination. Such exceptional circumstances are manifestly inapplicable to Quebec under existing conditions. Accordingly, neither the population of the province of Quebec, even if characterized in terms of "people" or "peoples," nor its representative institutions, the National Assembly, the legislature or government of Quebec, possess a right, under international law, to secede unilaterally from Canada.

139. We would not wish to leave this aspect of our answer to Question 2 without acknowledging the importance of the submissions made to us respecting the rights and concerns of aboriginal peoples in the event of a unilateral secession, as well as the appropriate means of defining the boundaries of a seceding Quebec with particular regard to the northern lands occupied largely by aboriginal peoples. However, the concern of aboriginal peoples is precipitated by the asserted right of Quebec to unilateral secession. In light of our finding that there is no such right applicable to the population of Quebec, either under the Constitution of Canada or at international law, but that on the contrary a clear democratic expression of support for secession would lead under the Constitution to negotiations in which aboriginal interests would be taken into account, it becomes unnecessary to explore further the concerns of the aboriginal peoples in this Reference.

(2) *Recognition of a Factual/Political Reality: the "Effectivity" Principle*

140. [A]n argument advanced by the *amicus curiae* * * * was that, while international law may not ground a positive right to unilateral secession in the context of Quebec, international law equally does not prohibit secession and, in fact, international recognition would be conferred on such a political reality if it emerged, for example, via effective control of the territory of what is now the province of Quebec.

141. It is true that international law may well, depending on the circumstances, adapt to recognize a political and/or factual reality, regardless of the legality of the steps leading to its creation. However, * * * effectivity, as such, does not have any real applicability to Question 2, which asks whether a right to unilateral secession exists.

142. No one doubts that legal consequences may flow from political facts[.] Secession of a province from Canada, if successful in the streets, might well lead to the creation of a new state. Although recognition by other states is not, at least as a matter of theory, necessary to achieve statehood, the viability of a would-be state in the international community depends, as a practical matter, upon recognition by other states. * * * However, international recognition * * * does not relate back to the date of secession to serve retroactively as a source of a "legal" right to secede in the first place. Recognition occurs only after a territorial unit has been successful, as a political fact, in achieving secession.

143. [O]ne of the legal norms which may be recognized by states in granting or withholding recognition of emergent states is the legitimacy of the process by which the *de facto* secession is, or was, being pursued. The process of recognition, once considered to be an exercise of pure sovereign discretion, has come to be associated with legal norms. See, e.g., *European Community Declaration on the Guidelines on the Recognition of New States in Eastern Europe and in the Soviet Union*, 31 *International Legal Materials* 1485 (1992), at p. 1487. While national interest and perceived political advantage to the recognizing state obviously play an important role, foreign states may also take into account their view as to the existence of a right to self-determination on the part of the population of the putative state, and * * * an examination of the legality of the secession according to the law of the state from which the territorial unit purports to have seceded. [A]n emergent state that has disregarded legitimate obligations arising out of its previous situation can potentially expect to be hindered by that disregard in achieving international recognition, at least with respect to the timing of that recognition. * * * The notion that what is not explicitly prohibited is implicitly permitted has little relevance where (as here) international law refers the legality of secession to the domestic law of the seceding state and the law of that state holds unilateral secession to be unconstitutional. * * *

146. The principle of effectivity * * * proclaims that an illegal act may eventually acquire legal status if, as a matter of empirical fact, it is recognized on the international plane. Our law has long recognized that through a combination of acquiescence and prescription, an illegal act may at some later point be accorded some form of legal status. In the law of property, for example, it is well-known that a squatter on land may ultimately become the owner if the true owner sleeps on his or her right to repossess the land. In this way, a change in the factual circumstances may subsequently be reflected in a change in legal status. It is, however, quite another matter to suggest that a subsequent condonation of an initially illegal act retroactively creates a legal right to engage in the act in the first place. The broader contention is not supported by the international principle of effectivity or otherwise and must be rejected.

NOTES AND QUESTIONS

1. *The* Secession of Quebec Case *in Context.* In October 1995, a proposal calling for Quebec's secession from Canada was narrowly defeated in a provincial referendum. Canadian political leaders, upset at the close vote, determined they had been insufficiently attentive to separatist arguments in Quebec. The national government countered aggressively, stressing the social and economic disadvantages of secession and questioning whether a referendum on the future of Canada in which only Quebecers would vote could ever be legitimate. The request for an advisory opinion on the legality of Quebec's secession was part of the national government's strategy. "[T]he federal Government wanted to reassert the relevance of law to the shaping of democratic governance within Canada. Less charitably, the Government may also have hoped that Quebecers"—who showed little sympathy for revolutionary movements—would "be frightened by a judicial declaration that secession by the province would be an 'illegal' act." Stephen J. Troope, "International Decision," 93 *American Journal of International Law* 519, 520 (1999). Quebec's Attorney General refused to participate in the case, and the Court appointed a separatist lawyer as an *amicus curiae.*

Note the phrasing of the international law questions the Court addressed in the *Secession of Quebec Case.* How might the Court have dealt with the question, "If Quebec were to secede from Canada, would it be a state in international law?" Or with the question suggested by Professor Troope: "According to prevailing normative criteria, would a unilateral secession attract the recognition of Quebec by the international community as a sovereign state?" *Id.* at 522.

According to Professor Crawford, the Court's unanimous opinion, which found no legal right of unilateral secession but a constitutional duty to negotiate for independence if Quebecers clearly voted for secession, achieved an "astute balance" that helped "reduce tension." James Crawford, *The Creation of States in International Law* 412 (2d ed. 2006). In light of the Court's determination that Quebec had no right to secede under either Canadian constitutional law or international law, the Court did not address another question that was asked of it: would the Canadian Constitution or international law have priority in case of a conflict? See Anne F. Bayefsky, "Introduction," in *Self-determination in International Law: Quebec and Lessons Learned* 1 (Anne F. Bayefsky ed. 2000).

2. *External Self-determination, Decolonization, and the United Nations.* The United Nations has supported the right of self-determination of "peoples" in the context of decolonization. See, *e.g.*, the 1970 Declaration on Friendly Relations, cited in the *Secession of Quebec Case*, and the Declaration on the Granting of Independence to Colonial Countries and Peoples, G.A. Res. 1514 (XV) (1960), which was adopted with no dissenting votes. In Resolution 1514, the U.N. General Assembly declared that "subjection of peoples to alien subjugation, domination and exploitation" violates the U.N. Charter, and that "[a]ll peoples have the right to self-determination." Resolution 1514 also called for the immediate transfer of "all powers to the peoples" in "territories which have not yet attained independence," in order to enable such peoples "to enjoy complete independence and freedom." The territories of concern were colonies designated as "non-self-governing territories" pursuant to General Assembly Resolution 1541 (XV) (1960). A non-self-governing territory was one both geographically separate and ethnically or culturally distinct from its administering power. According to the International Court of Justice, "the right of peoples to self-determination, as it evolved from the Charter and from United Nations practice, has an *erga omnes* character." Case Concerning East Timor (Portugal v. Australia), 1995 I.C.J. 90, 102. See Chapter 3 for discussion of obligations *erga omnes*.

When a right of external self-determination applies, what consequences follow? The ICJ has stressed that self-determination "requires a free and genuine expression of the will of the peoples concerned." Advisory Opinion on the Western Sahara, 1975 I.C.J. 12, 32. How should the "will of the peoples" in non-self-governing territories be ascertained? Since 1954, the United Nations has organized and supervised plebiscites or elections in many such territories. The ultimate result most often has been independence: 70 non-self-governing territories became independent between 1945 and 1979, with a few more gaining independence since then.

Not all of these new states gained their independence peacefully. What was the role of self-determination in situations involving violence against colonial powers? When a white minority government in Southern Rhodesia seized power and proclaimed independence from Britain in 1965, the Security Council immediately called on all states not to assist or recognize the "illegal racist minority régime," S.C. Res. 216 (1965), 5 *International Legal Materials* 167 (1966), and then imposed comprehensive economic sanctions against Southern Rhodesia. *E.g.*, S.C. Res. 232 (1966), 6 *International Legal Materials* 141 (1967); S.C. Res. 253 (1968), 7 *International Legal Materials* 897 (1968). Should a colonial power be condemned for using force to suppress liberation forces in the territory of its "own" colony? When rebels in Portuguese Guinea declared independence in 1973 in the face of continued opposition by Portugal, the U.N. General Assembly invoked the right of self-determination, welcomed the independence of "the sovereign State of the Republic of Guinea-Bissau," and condemned Portugal for its "illegal occupation" and "repeated acts of aggression" in Guinea-Bissau. G.A. Res. 3061 (XXVIII). Many states had recognized Guinea-Bissau even before this General Assembly resolution. Do the Montevideo Convention criteria for statehood, considered in Part B, capture all of the defining characteristics of new states emerging from decolonization?

Almost all non-self-governing territories that achieved independence did so without any changes in their territorial boundaries. Should the United Nations have sought changes in those boundaries, many of which were drawn by European powers in the late 19th century? Or, should the United Nations have more actively promoted autonomy for sub-state ethnic groups within newly independent states? For critical views of the legacies of colonial administrators and colonial boundaries, see Kwasi Kwarteng, *Ghosts of Empire: Britain's Legacies in the Modern World* (2011); Makua Wa Mutua, "Why Redraw the Map of Africa: A Moral and Legal Inquiry," 16 *Michigan Journal of International Law* 1113 (1995).

The U.N. Trusteeship Council also helped promote self-government or independence for territories that were run by "administering authorities" pursuant to the U.N. Charter. Article 76 of the Charter sets out the trusteeship system's goals, which include "to promote the political, economic, social, and educational advancement of the inhabitants of the trust territories, and their progressive development towards self-government or independence," and "to encourage respect for human rights and for fundamental freedoms for all without distinction as to race, sex, language, or religion." Trust territories included some former colonies of Italy and Japan —countries defeated in World War II—as well as territories previously administered under League of Nations mandates. When Palau became independent in 1994, the last U.N. Trusteeship was dissolved. The U.N. Trusteeship Council is now dormant. The situation in Kosovo, discussed below, has revived arguments about the appropriate role of the United Nations in assisting regions that seek independence.

3. *Internal Self-determination*. In paragraph 126 of its opinion in the *Secession of Quebec Case*, the Court noted the concept of "internal self-determination," which echoes President Woodrow Wilson's promotion of democratic institutions at the end of World War I. Internal self-determination was also emphasized in the European Community's 1991 Guidelines on Recognition of New States, noted in paragraph 143 of the *Secession of Quebec Case* and reproduced in Part B. According to Professor Cassese, the EC was "prepared to endorse the achievement of independent statehood, i.e., external self-determination, only on condition that the breakaway republics fully respected the principle of representative democracy, that is, internal self-determination." Antonio Cassese, *Self-Determination of Peoples: A Legal Reappraisal* 268 (1998).

4. *Self-determination and the Rights of Indigenous Peoples*. Should the aboriginal peoples of northern Quebec, which the Canadian Supreme Court

mentioned in paragraph 139, have a right of self-determination? If so, how should such a right be implemented? The international status and rights of indigenous peoples were long the subject of negotiations within the U.N. system. Drafts of a U.N. declaration concerning rights for indigenous peoples were developed with input from the governing bodies of indigenous groups, human rights experts, and non-governmental organizations. The U.N. Human Rights Council adopted the U.N. Declaration on the Rights of Indigenous Peoples in 2006, and the General Assembly gave its approval in 2007 over the objection of Australia, Canada, New Zealand, and the United States. See Stefania Errico, "The UN General Assembly Adopts the Declaration on the Rights of Indigenous Peoples," 11 *ASIL Insights*, Issue 19 (2007). The Declaration provides in part:

Article 3

> Indigenous peoples have the right to self-determination. By virtue of that right they freely determine their political status and freely pursue their economic, social and cultural development.

Article 4

> Indigenous peoples, in exercising their right to self-determination, have the right to autonomy or self-government in matters relating to their internal and local affairs, as well as ways and means for financing their autonomous functions. * * *

Article 46

> Nothing in this Declaration may be interpreted as implying for any State, people, group or person any right to engage in any activity or to perform any act contrary to the Charter of the United Nations or construed as authorizing or encouraging any action which would dismember or impair, totally or in part, the territorial integrity or political unity of sovereign and independent States.

U.N. Doc. A/61/L.67 (2007). What is the legal force of this Declaration? Does the Declaration emphasize internal or external self-determination? Is the situation of indigenous peoples comparable to peoples in overseas colonies? Does any normative concept unify the various situations in which a right of self-determination exists? Does self-determination reinforce statehood or destabilize existing states? See Karen Knop, "Statehood: Territory, People, Government," in *The Cambridge Companion to International Law* 95, 101–04 (James Crawford & Martti Koskenniemi eds. 2012).

In 2000, the U.N. Economic and Social Council established a Permanent Forum on Indigenous Issues, an ECOSOC subsidiary organ that functions as an advisory body. This Forum "formally integrates indigenous peoples and their representatives into the structure of the United Nations" and "marks the first time that representatives of states and non-state actors have been accorded parity in a permanent representative body within the United Nations Organization proper." John Carey & Siegfried Wiessner, "A New United Nations Subsidiary Organ: The Permanent Forum on Indigenous

Issues," *ASIL Insights*, Apr. 2001. See also Committee on Rights of Indigenous Peoples, "Final Report," in International Law Association, *Report of the Seventy-Fifth Conference (Sofia)* 503 (2012).

ACCORDANCE WITH INTERNATIONAL LAW OF THE UNILATERAL DECLARATION OF INDEPENDENCE IN RESPECT OF KOSOVO

Advisory Opinion, 2010 I.C.J. 403

[Kosovo, whose population is largely Albanian, has been an autonomous province in Serbia and its predecessor states. The Serbian government of Slobadan Milošević rescinded Kosovo's autonomy beginning in 1989. Massive Serbian attacks on Kosovars, and failed attempts to resolve Kosovo's status by negotiation, led to a 1999 NATO bombing campaign against Serbia. Following the bombing, the U.N. Security Council in Resolution 1244 (1999), 38 *International Legal Materials* 1451 (1999), authorized an international security force in Kosovo, made up largely of contingents from NATO member states. The Council also approved interim international civil administration of Kosovo to establish "provisional institutions for democratic and autonomous self-government." *Id.* ¶ 11(c). This international administration—the United Nations Mission in Kosovo (UNMIK)—has held local parliamentary elections, coordinated humanitarian aid, helped maintain law and order, and exercised functions related to health, education, banking, and commerce. A Comprehensive Proposal for the Kosovo Status Settlement, the so-called Ahtisaari Plan, submitted by a U.N. Special Envoy in 2007, envisioned Kosovo's independence following a transition period of international supervision. However, Serbia rejected the plan, and attempts at international mediation concerning the status of Kosovo floundered.

In February 2008, members of Kosovo's legislative Assembly declared "Kosovo to be an independent and sovereign state." Their declaration also pledged that any action would respect the values of democracy, human rights, protection of minorities, and the rule of law, consistent with Security Council Resolution 1244 and "principles of international law." See Colin Warbrick, "Kosovo: The Declaration of Independence," 57 *International and Comparative Law Quarterly* 675 (2008).

In October 2008, the U.N. General Assembly, by a vote of 77 to 6, with 74 states abstaining, referred a question about Kosovo to the International Court of Justice in a request for an advisory opinion.]

49. The Court will now turn to the scope and meaning of the question on which the General Assembly has requested that it give its opinion. The General Assembly has formulated that question in the following terms: "Is the unilateral declaration of independence by the

Provisional Institutions of Self-Government of Kosovo in accordance with international law?"

50. The Court recalls that in some previous cases it has departed from the language of the question put to it where the question was not adequately formulated or where the Court determined, on the basis of its examination of the background to the request, that the request did not reflect the "legal questions really in issue." * * *

51. In the present case, the question posed by the General Assembly is clearly formulated. The question is narrow and specific; it asks for the Court's opinion on whether or not the declaration of independence is in accordance with international law. [I]n past requests for advisory opinions, the General Assembly and the Security Council, when they have wanted the Court's opinion on the legal consequences of an action, have framed the question in such a way that this aspect is expressly stated (see, for example, *Legal Consequences of the Construction of a Wall in the Occupied Palestinian Territory, Advisory Opinion, I.C.J. Reports 2004 (I)*, p. 136). Accordingly, the Court does not consider that it is necessary to address such issues as whether or not the declaration has led to the creation of a State or the status of the acts of recognition in order to answer the question put by the General Assembly. The Court accordingly sees no reason to reformulate the scope of the question. * * *

56. * * * The answer to [the General Assembly's] question turns on whether or not the applicable international law prohibited the declaration of independence. * * *

79. During the eighteenth, nineteenth and early twentieth centuries, there were numerous instances of declarations of independence, often strenuously opposed by the State from which independence was being declared. * * * State practice during this period points clearly to the conclusion that international law contained no prohibition of declarations of independence. * * *

80. Several participants in the proceedings before the Court have contended that a prohibition of unilateral declarations of independence is implicit in the principle of territorial integrity. [T]he principle of territorial integrity is an important part of the international legal order and is enshrined in the Charter of the United Nations, in particular in Article 2, paragraph 4, which provides that: "All Members shall refrain in their international relations from the threat or use of force against the territorial integrity or political independence of any State, or in any other manner inconsistent with the Purposes of the United Nations." In General Assembly resolution 2625 (XXV), entitled "Declaration on Principles of International Law concerning Friendly Relations and Co-operation among States in Accordance with the Charter of the United Nations," which reflects customary international law, the General Assembly reiterated "[t]he principle that States shall refrain in their

international relations from the threat or use of force against the territorial integrity or political independence of any State." This resolution then enumerated various obligations incumbent upon States to refrain from violating the territorial integrity of other sovereign States. In the same vein, the Final Act of the Helsinki Conference on Security and Co-operation in Europe of 1 August 1975 (the Helsinki Conference) stipulated that "[t]he participating States will respect the territorial integrity of each of the participating States" (Art. IV). Thus, the scope of the principle of territorial integrity is confined to the sphere of relations between States.

81. Several participants have invoked resolutions of the Security Council condemning particular declarations of independence: see, *inter alia*, Security Council resolutions 216 (1965) and 217 (1965), concerning Southern Rhodesia; Security Council resolution 541 (1983), concerning northern Cyprus; and Security Council resolution 787 (1992), concerning the Republika Srpska. [I]n all of those instances * * * the illegality attached to the declarations of independence * * * stemmed not from the unilateral character of these declarations as such, but from the fact that they were, or would have been, connected with the unlawful use of force or other egregious violations of norms of general international law, in particular those of a peremptory character (*jus cogens*). In the context of Kosovo, the Security Council has never taken this position. The exceptional character of the resolutions enumerated above appears to the Court to confirm that no general prohibition against unilateral declarations of independence may be inferred from the practice of the Security Council.

82. A number of participants in the present proceedings have claimed, although in almost every instance only as a secondary argument, that the population of Kosovo has the right to create an independent State either as a manifestation of a right to self-determination or pursuant to what they described as a right of "remedial secession" in the face of the situation in Kosovo. [O]ne of the major developments of international law during the second half of the twentieth century has been the evolution of the right of self-determination. Whether, outside the context of non-self-governing territories and peoples subject to alien subjugation, domination and exploitation, the international law of self-determination confers upon part of the population of an existing State a right to separate from that State is, however, a subject on which radically different views were expressed by those taking part in the proceedings and expressing a position on the question. Similar differences existed regarding whether international law provides for a right of "remedial secession" and, if so, in what circumstances. There was also a sharp difference of views as to whether the circumstances which some participants maintained would give rise to a right of "remedial secession" were actually present in Kosovo.

83. The Court considers that it is not necessary to resolve these questions in the present case. The General Assembly has requested the Court's opinion only on whether or not the declaration of independence is in accordance with international law. Debates regarding the extent of the right of self-determination and the existence of any right of "remedial secession," however, concern the right to separate from a State. [T]hat issue is beyond the scope of the question posed by the General Assembly. To answer that question, the Court need only determine whether the declaration of independence violated either general international law or the *lex specialis* created by Security Council resolution 1244 (1999).

84. For the reasons already given, the Court considers that general international law contains no applicable prohibition of declarations of independence. Accordingly, it concludes that the declaration of independence of 17 February 2008 did not violate general international law.

[The Court also concludes that the Kosovo declaration of independence does not violate the *lex specialis* of Security Council Resolution 1244 (1999) and the UNMIK Constitutional Framework Created Thereunder.]

123. For these reasons,

THE COURT, * * *

(3) By ten votes to four,

Is of the opinion that the declaration of independence of Kosovo adopted on 17 February 2008 did not violate international law.

IN FAVOUR: *President* Owada; *Judges* Al-Khasawneh, Buergenthal, Simma, Abraham, Keith, Sepúlveda-Amor, Cançado Trindade, Yusuf, Greenwood;

AGAINST: *Vice-President* Tomka; *Judges* Koroma, Bennouna, Skotnikov.

NOTES AND QUESTIONS

1. *The Advisory Opinion.* The status of Kosovo has been, and remains, controversial. Should the International Court of Justice have exercised its discretion not to render an opinion at all? Compare the *Wall Case* in Chapter 5. Having decided to proceed, should the Court have construed the question more broadly? For example, in the *Western Sahara Case*, another ICJ advisory opinion related to self-determination (discussed in Note 2 in the previous set of Notes), the Court was asked about the status of the Western Sahara at the time of its colonization and "[w]hat *were* the legal ties between [the Western Sahara] and the Kingdom of Morocco and the Mauritanian entity" (emphasis added). Rather than merely providing historical answers, the Court noted that it was important to guide the United Nations in its

ongoing debates about self-determination and determined that the peoples of the Western Sahara were entitled to a referendum about their future. Should the ICJ in the *Kosovo Case* have articulated and developed the law concerning self-determination, recognition, and secession? The Court might, for example, have considered whether Kosovo was a state, whether the people of Kosovo had a right to self-determination in 1998, or whether it was legal to recognize Kosovo's statehood in light of Serbia's concerns with its territorial integrity.

Was the ICJ, by construing the question as narrowly as it did, trying to preserve the status quo, allowing both Kosovo and Serbia (and their allies) to point to favorable aspects of the decision? If so, is that an appropriate concern for an international court exercising its advisory jurisdiction? Compare the *Wall Case*, where the Court characterized the legal issues as of concern to the international community, instead of focusing on the bilateral dispute between Israel and Palestine. See Hurst Hannum, "The Advisory Opinion on Kosovo: An Opportunity Lost, or a Poisoned Chalice Refused?," 24 *Leiden Journal of International Law* 155 (2011); Daphné Richemond-Barak, "The International Court of Justice on Kosovo: Missed Opportunity or Dispute 'Settlement'?," 23 *Hague Yearbook of International Law* 1 (2010).

2. *Self-determination Beyond the Colonial Context.* Had the ICJ addressed the legality of Kosovo's secession, what should the Court have said? Does or should a right of secession exist at international law if any group chooses it? Or should the right apply to any "nation" possessing some common ethnic, cultural, religious, or linguistic identity, along with a relationship to a given territory? If so, should the "nation" be defined by objective criteria, or in terms of its members' subjective feelings of identity? Or, instead, does a right to secession exist as a remedy for some particular wrong?

The *Secession of Quebec* Court, in paragraph 134, noted the possibility that "when a people is blocked from the meaningful exercise of its right to self-determination internally, it is entitled, as a last resort, to exercise it by secession." That is, a denial of internal self-determination to some group within a state might give rise to a right of external self-determination. Should we conclude that the right to internal self-determination has been blocked when a "people" constituting less than the entire population is entitled to participate in governance through democratic processes, but is consistently and systematically outvoted and denied the ability to express its distinctive cultural identity, or to share in a state's power and resources? What if, in addition, the group in question has been brutally oppressed? For a discussion of factors contributing to secessionist movements, see Jerry Z. Muller, "Us and Them: The Enduring Power of Ethnic Nationalism," *Foreign Affairs*, Mar.–Apr. 2008, at 18.

If there is a right to self-determination in cases of lack of representation or oppression, would that right necessarily give rise to a right of secession? One can envision a range of possible self-determination remedies. See Paul H. Brietzke, "Self-Determination, or Jurisprudential Confusion: Exacerbating

Political Conflict," 14 *Wisconsin International Law Journal* 69, 122–23 (1995).

3. *Recognizing Kosovo*. When the U.N. General Assembly approved the request for an advisory opinion on October 8, 2008, 48 states had recognized Kosovo. As of December 2013, 105 of the 193 U.N. member states recognized Kosovo. See http://www.kosovothanksyou.com/ (last visited Dec. 12, 2013). How significant is this trend for Kosovo's claim to statehood? Is it important to consider whether powerful states or neighboring states are among those recognizing Kosovo? The United States and France recognized Kosovo the day after the declaration of independence; Japan, the United Kingdom, Germany, several other European countries, and several neighbors—Albania, The former Yugoslav Republic of Macedonia, and Montenegro—have done so as well. China, Russia, and, of course, Serbia, are among the non-recognizing states.

4. *Self-determination and Territorial Integrity*. The situation in Kosovo raises questions concerning the right to territorial integrity. Is one concern with approving a right of remedial secession in the case of Kosovo the possibility that such approval might serve as "precedent" for separatist movements elsewhere, threatening the territorial integrity of existing states? Note, however, the ICJ's statement, in paragraph 80 of the *Kosovo Case*, that "the scope of the principle of territorial integrity is confined to the sphere of relations between States." Is it only other states that may threaten a country's territorial integrity? If a country's right to territorial integrity is not opposable to groups inside the state, does it make any *legal* difference whether a right to external self-determination exists? That is, whose rights would secession violate?

5. *Self-determination and International Administration of Territory*. Kosovo has been labeled an internationally administered territory. Does the U.N. Security Council's international oversight system for Kosovo make the situation there legally unique? Is such international administration one way new states can be created—a modern parallel to post-World War I mandates or post-World War II trust territories? In Chapters 8 and 9 we further explore the principle of territorial integrity of states, as well as U.N. efforts at peacekeeping and rebuilding civilian administrations.

6. *Self-determination Human Rights, and Group Rights*. As noted in paragraph 118 of the *Secession to Quebec Case*, the right of self-determination is enshrined in human rights treaties. How does self-determination relate to the sorts of human rights we considered in Chapter 6? Is self-determination a human right?

One feature distinguishing self-determination from many human rights is that self-determination appears to be a group or collective right, applicable to "peoples," rather than solely an individual right. As you review the materials in this part, who do you see as the "peoples" entitled to self-determination? Are they only, with respect to external self-determination, the entire populations of non-self-governing or occupied territories, and, with respect to internal self-determination, the entire populations of states? May the term also refer to ethnic, cultural, or religious groups within a state? Is the population of Kosovo a "people"?

Despite the uncertainty about the exact contours of the concept of "peoples," the law of self-determination suggests that some groups—entities other than individuals and states—have rights at international law. What additional entities have international legal rights and duties? In Chapter 8, we consider the "international personality" of international organizations formed by states, such as the United Nations, as well as roles of non-governmental organizations.

CHAPTER 8

INTERNATIONAL ORGANIZATIONS, NON-GOVERNMENTAL ORGANIZATIONS, AND TREATY REGIMES

■ ■ ■

Along with states and individuals, other entities and groups participate in the international legal arena. Part A of this chapter examines international organizations, which are created by treaties among states. Part B introduces non-governmental organizations. NGOs, organized or chartered under municipal law, increasingly influence international law and process. In Part C we explore international regimes. These are issue-oriented international legal systems, typically created by treaty, often involving international organizations, and sometimes providing roles for non-governmental organizations.

A. INTERNATIONAL ORGANIZATIONS

Early international organizations were often designed to develop and administer common standards for specialized and largely technical matters. Among the several such organizations created in the 19th century were the 1856 European Danube Commission, the 1865 Universal Telegraphic Union (now the International Telecommunications Union), and the 1874 Universal Postal Union. Many of today's hundreds of international organizations focus on specialized subject areas, providing continuity and expertise with respect to the issues within their mandates.

Global international organizations designed to address broader issues, such as the use of force, were in practice though not in theory slower to develop. Ideas about peaceful universal unions of people can be found in the writings of ancient Greek and Roman thinkers. Subsequent European political philosophers, including Erasmus, Thomas More, Jean-Jacques Rousseau, Immanuel Kant, and Jeremy Bentham, all devised and espoused utopian proposals involving international organizations. The League of Nations, formed in 1919 after World War I, was the first general association of states concerned with dispute settlement and the promotion of peace.

Section 1 of this Part A introduces the League of Nations and the United Nations, the successor to the League. Section 2 asks what sort of "international personality" international organizations and other non-state entities may have. More on the United Nations and its roles with respect to collective security appears in Chapter 9.

1. AN OVERVIEW OF INTERNATIONAL ORGANIZATIONS

MARK WESTON JANIS, INTERNATIONAL LAW
214–17 (6th ed. 2012)

In the nineteenth century, alongside the movement for an international court, there emerged a popular enthusiasm for an international government. One of the most important publications promoting the idea was the *Essay on a Congress of Nations*, written in 1840 by the president of the American Peace Society, William Ladd (1778–1841). * * * Reviewing Ladd's *Essay*, Georg Schwarzenberger in 1935 decided that there was "a direct line" in the history of ideas about international organization "from Ladd to the achievements of Geneva, and even further, on the foundations of his Equity Tribunal, to a real League of Nations."

American enthusiasm for international government, at least in theory, ran high in the early years of the twentieth century. The onset of the Great War in 1914 only quickened the pace. Notables at a meeting of the First Annual National Assemblage of the League to Enforce Peace in Washington, D.C., in 1916 included the former President of the United States, William Howard Taft; the president of Harvard, A. Lawrence Lowell; the director of the Chamber of Commerce of the United States, Edward Filene; the president of the American Federation of Labor, Samuel Gompers; the senator from Massachusetts, Henry Cabot Lodge; the president of the Federal Council of Churches of Christ in America, Shailer Matthews; and the former president of Princeton and the then-President of the United States, Woodrow Wilson. It was Wilson who put the longstanding aspirations for international government into concrete form, proposing in the last of his Fourteen Points on January 8, 1918, that "[a] general association of nations must be formed under specific covenants for the purpose of affording mutual guarantees of political independence and territorial integrity to great and small States alike." Wilson and others believed that an international organization devoted to collective security could better guarantee the peace than could traditional balance-of-power politics, which not only had failed to prevent the outbreak of war in 1914, but also, because of its triggering system of alliances, had contributed to the expansion of the conflict.

The Versailles Treaty establishing the League "had been constructed on the assumption that the United States would be not merely a contracting but an actively executant party." Unfortunately, or as put politely by a Frenchman, "by a strange paradox," the U.S. Senate refused to consent to the ratification of the Treaty, and the United States stayed out of its own plan to keep the peace.

For a decade, from 1920 to 1930, the League, based in Geneva, even without the United States and also without the new Soviet Union, made real contributions to international law, world health, the protection of minorities, and the settlement of international disputes (for example, the pacific settlement of the dispute between Greece and Bulgaria in 1925). Unfortunately, the next decade was disastrous for the League. The turning point was probably the Japanese invasion of Manchuria on September 18, 1931, which the League proved powerless to stop. The League finally condemned the Japanese occupation of Manchuria on February 24, 1933, and Japan simply left the League the next month. Dedicated to the prevention of aggression, the League watched helplessly as Italy invaded Ethiopia in 1934 and as Germany marched into the Rhineland, Austria, and Czechoslovakia between 1936 and 1938. Finally, when Germany and Russia attacked Poland in 1939, Britain and France took action, but it was too late. Poland was lost, then France itself, and the nations descended into the twentieth century's second world war.

By the time of the invasion of Poland in 1939, the League was, in large measure, already a forgotten institution. Poland, France, and Great Britain made no attempt to involve the League in the new world war. For a year, the functionaries of the League carried on in Geneva, a situation described by the Deputy Secretary-General of the League as a "situation of abnormal normality." In the summer and autumn of 1940, the League's officials departed Geneva, where they feared a German or Italian invasion, for safer locations. A large part of the Secretariat was based at Princeton University, a fitting, if ironic, twist on the origins of the League with Woodrow Wilson. Almost a year after the foundation of the United Nations in June 1945, diplomats reconvened at Geneva, where on April 8, 1946, Lord Robert Cecil closed his speech to the League Assembly as follows: "The League is dead, Long live the United Nations." Ten days later, the Assembly unanimously voted to dissolve the League and to transfer its powers, functions, buildings, library, and archives to the United Nations.

RICHARD EDIS, "A JOB WELL DONE: THE FOUNDING OF THE UNITED NATIONS REVISITED"

6 *Cambridge Review of International Affairs* 29 (1992)

There was no inevitability that there would be a world organisation at the end of the Second World War, or indeed about the form that it should take. [A]n exclusive directorate of the principal victors to call the shots in the post-war world was a distinct possibility, and indeed was contemplated. On the other hand, the League could have been revived; or a regionally-based system might have been tried.

The UN Charter as it emerged in June 1945 reflected many strands, layers and influences[:] the agendas of the leading anti-Axis powers; the views and idiosyncracies of their leaders, especially Franklin Delano Roosevelt and Winston Churchill; the perceptions and pre-conceptions of their advisers and officials; public opinion as expressed by legislatures, the media and NGO's; and, to a greater extent than is often appreciated, the demands of the medium and smaller powers, who were by no means all "western" in outlook. * * *

The three major Allies brought different agendas to the question of a future world organisation. The British approach could be characterised as a blend of national self-interest and pragmatism admixed with a measure of decency and even vision. The primary British aim was to involve the United States fully in a post-war security system. * * *

The American approach was undoubtedly the most idealistic of the Three, even though the military intruded hard-headed considerations at times. Although Roosevelt thought initially in terms of an Anglo-American condominium, later expanded to include the other two leading anti-Axis powers—the famous "Four Policemen" concept—it was the idea of a worldwide "New Deal" that soon gripped American imagination. There was a crusading wish to end the rotten old system of "balance of power" and "spheres of influence." Concepts such as human rights, freedom for colonial peoples (especially in Asia) and free trade (on the grounds that economic nationalism bred conflict) were prominent in American thinking. Roosevelt became increasingly obsessed with the need to win [Soviet leader Joseph] Stalin's engagement in the new venture, even at the expense of British interests and his relations with Churchill. The US was also a strong supporter of a leading role for China, which was regarded with less than enthusiasm by the British and Russians.

A major factor in the American approach was domestic public opinion which after the experience of the Senate's rejection of the Covenant of the League of Nations in 1920 despite President Woodrow Wilson's key role, was judged to be hostile to or at least suspicious of foreign entanglements. * * *

Although little has emerged about the thinking behind the Soviet approach to the new world organisation, it is not hard to surmise that their agenda was more limited and more motivated by *realpolitik* than either the Americans or the British. The nature of the Soviet system and Stalin's style in particular left little scope for idealism. The main Russian aim was to prevent the revival of Germany and to establish Soviet security and influence more widely. * * *

The Dumbarton Oaks meeting took place in Washington in the Georgetown house of the same name during five weeks in August and September 1944. It was attended at senior official level by representatives of the US, UK and USSR[.]

The basic structure of the new organisation had already been thought through and caused little debate. The framework of the League of Nations with its Council, Assembly, Secretariat and International Court was regarded as sound and new nomenclature readily agreed. The Russians saw no need for an economic and social role for the organisation which they envisaged as having a purely security role. The Americans and the British, however, argued that security issues could not be divorced from the overall economic and social background, and also that the new organisation needed a positive and progressive element which would offer the prospect of human development. * * *

By far the most important question which had to be settled was how to maintain * * * "international peace and security." The League of Nations security system set out in the Covenant, which had been designed to prevent a reoccurrence of 1914 by a process of mediation, cooling-off periods, and voluntary sanctions, had patently failed. It was common ground that the new system needed to be given "teeth" but how? The basic concept was that the executive arm of the new organisation needed to be a policeman rather than as under the League a magistrate and a mediator. In Roosevelt's memorable description "a policeman would not be a very effective policeman if, when he saw a felon break into a house, he had to go down to the town hall and call a town meting to issue a warrant before the felon could be arrested."

To achieve this, the role of the Security Council was clearly differentiated from that of the General Assembly. In contrast to the situation under the Covenant, the Council was to be given the ability to act quickly and effectively by avoiding elaborate preliminary procedures, including largely cutting out a role for legal mechanisms, and by introducing the device of majority voting in place of the League Council's requirement of unanimity. The Council was also to be given real power to enforce its decisions by being able to require armed forces to be put at its disposal. These forces were to consist of national military contingents, including airforce units on immediate standby, rather than a mixed international force which was regarded as unworkable. Coordination and control [were] to be exercised by the Chiefs of Staff of the major military powers through a Military Staff Committee. * * * There was no truck with the notion of disarmament, which had been so prominent in the Covenant's scheme of things.

* * * It was envisaged that the strongest military powers, that is the leading Allied nations acting in concert, would provide the muscle to enforce the decisions of the Council. It was regarded as only realistic to accept that the major powers would not be willing to bear the burden of combating future threats to international peace and security, as they were carrying the brunt of the struggle against the Axis powers, unless there were adequate safeguards for their perceived essential interests.

All the Big Three at Dumbarton Oaks were agreed that the Great Powers who would be Permanent Members of the Security Council should have the powers of veto over its decisions in certain cases. But in what cases? Britain argued strongly that if the new system was to attract the adherence of the other powers, the veto could only be used in restricted circumstances and not, for example, in situations to which a Permanent Member was a party. The Soviet Union, on the other hand, maintained that Permanent Members' right to veto should apply to any and all activity in the Security Council. The US, initially undecided, came round to the British position. Despite strenuous efforts, the meeting proved unable to resolve the issue, to the despair of Western participants. * * *

The San Francisco conference which was to finalise the drafting of the United Nations Charter opened on April 25th 1945 and was attended by the fifty countries who were signatories of the UN Declaration or "associated powers." * * *

If the Great Powers were under any illusion that the other powers would show their gratitude by muting their demands, this was soon dissipated. * * * The San Francisco conference, which took two months from beginning to end, cannot in any sense be described as a rubber stamp.

* * * The main issues at the conference were:

—the position of the Permanent Members in the Security Council and in particular the scope of the veto;

—the role of the General Assembly and of the Economic and Social Council;

—the status of bilateral and regional arrangements;

—the question of domestic jurisdiction;

—the handling of Trusteeship and colonial matters.

The non-great powers accepted, albeit somewhat grudgingly, the basic concept that the leading powers in the victorious Allied coalition should be accorded a special position in the new international security system. However, they subjected the proposed veto power to detailed scrutiny and applied considerable ingenuity to efforts to whittle it down, as well as to accord themselves a greater influence. * * *

The onslaught by the non-great powers on the veto privilege took a number of forms. A move to take away its applicability from the pacific settlements of disputes procedure was only voted down fairly narrowly after the sponsoring powers mustered every effort to defeat it. There was a proposal to increase the number of non-Permanent Members on the Security Council and also to give a vote to parties to a dispute. There was even an idea of adding new Permanent Members such as Brazil. Another line of attack was to limit the duration of the veto privilege for a fixed period of time and, allied to this, to set a date by which the whole system would be subject for review.

While ready to make concessions in other areas, the sponsoring powers were adamant in opposing any significant lessening of the veto power and in the end made it clear that without the veto there would be no United Nations. * * * However, there was one significant change to the proposed security system as a result of the discussion at San Francisco, which was the addition to the enforcement procedure of a range of measures falling short of the use of force, i.e. economic and diplomatic sanctions, military demonstrations and blockade.

Other issues which reflected the particular concerns of the non-great powers related to the powers of the Security Council were the status of existing and future regional arrangements and the protection of national sovereignty. * * * The outcome was some primarily cosmetic changes to the existing regional provisions of the draft but much more significantly the addition of a new article [51] which reserved the right of individual and collective defence.

A similarly important addition was a clause [Article 2(7)] designed to protect domestic jurisdiction. [T]he Australians and South Africans * * * took the lead on the issue because of their fears of attacks on their racial policies. * * *

Foiled in their attempt to diminish the position of the Great Powers in the Security Council, the other states were more successful in extending the status and responsibilities of those parts of the organisation in which all members were on the same footing. The right of the General Assembly to discuss all matters within the scope of the Charter, including those relating to international peace and security unless the Security Council was formally seized of the issue, was established. And the Economic and Social Council's role was enhanced. It was given the status of a principal organ and ambitious hopes were entertained for its activities in the economic and social field. Greater prominence was also attached to human rights and to social issues such as the status of women.

The deferred issue of Trusteeship and colonial territories was settled by a series of compromises. [L]ed by Britain the colonial powers refused to make explicit the notion of full independence for colonial territories, preferring the term "self-government." This option was however recognised for Trusteeship territories and a separate Trusteeship Council on which neither the Great Powers nor the colonial powers had any special privilege was set up as a principal organ.

In the judicial area, the existing Permanent Court of International Justice was effectively maintained under a new name as the

International Court of Justice[.] Finally, Russian attempts to neuter the Secretary General's independence were unsuccessful. * * *

In establishing a system of international peace and security it was realistic of the founding fathers to recognise that great powers will not be prepared to participate in an organisation in which they have to shoulder much of the burden without safeguards for their essential interests. Without the veto, who can doubt that the Soviet Union and the United States would not have been tempted to walk out of the UN as great powers had done from the League? At the same time, there was no question of giving such states unbridled power. Even in the Security Council, the non-permanent members could if united constitute a sixth veto and had in any case to form part of a voting majority. And the Permanent Members were given no privileged role in the other parts of the organisation.

The pragmatic approach was matched by a wider vision. The Preamble of the Charter sets out an inspirational world view which speaks to men and women everywhere today as much as it did in 1945.

CHARTER OF THE UNITED NATIONS

June 26, 1945, 59 Stat. 1031, T.S. No. 993, 3 Bevans 1153

WE THE PEOPLES OF THE UNITED NATIONS DETERMINED

to save succeeding generations from the scourge of war, which twice in our lifetime has brought untold sorrow to mankind, and

to reaffirm faith in fundamental human rights, in the dignity and worth of the human person, in the equal rights of men and women and of nations large and small, and

to establish conditions under which justice and respect for the obligations arising from treaties and other sources of international law can be maintained, and

to promote social progress and better standards of life in larger freedom,

AND FOR THESE ENDS

to practice tolerance and live together in peace with one another as good neighbors, and

to unite our strength to maintain international peace and security, and

to ensure, by the acceptance of principles and the institution of methods, that armed force shall not be used, save in the common interest, and to employ international machinery for the promotion of the economic and social advancement of all peoples,

HAVE RESOLVED TO COMBINE OUR EFFORTS TO ACCOMPLISH THESE AIMS.

Accordingly, our respective Governments, through representatives assembled in the city of San Francisco, who have exhibited their full powers found to be in good and due form, have agreed to the present Charter of the United Nations and do hereby establish an international organization to be known as the United Nations.

Article 1

The Purposes of the United Nations are:

1. To maintain international peace and security, and to that end: to take effective collective measures for the prevention and removal of threats to the peace, and for the suppression of acts of aggression or other breaches of the peace, and to bring about by peaceful means, and in conformity with the principles of justice and international law, adjustment or settlement of international disputes or situations which might lead to a breach of the peace;

2. To develop friendly relations among nations based on respect for the principle of equal rights and self-determination of peoples, and to take other appropriate measures to strengthen universal peace;

3. To achieve international cooperation in solving international problems of an economic, social, cultural, or humanitarian character, and in promoting and encouraging respect for human rights and for fundamental freedoms for all without distinction as to race, sex, language, or religion; and

4. To be a center for harmonizing the actions of nations in the attainment of these common ends.

Article 25

The Members of the United Nations agree to accept and carry out the decisions of the Security Council in accordance with the present Charter.

Article 103

In the event of a conflict between the obligations of the Members of the United Nations under the present Charter and their obligations under any other international agreement, their obligations under the present Charter shall prevail.

NOTES AND QUESTIONS

1. *The United Nations.* In the second decade of the 21st century, more than two-thirds of a century after the establishment of the United Nations,

are the U.N. Charter's goals and purposes still essential? Should the Organization's ambitions be modified? Might any of the purposes of the United Nations be achieved nowadays without this form of global cooperation?

The U.N. Security Council, now composed of 15 members, with China, France, Russia, the United Kingdom, and the United States as permanent members, is one of the six "principal organs" created by the U.N. Charter. Does it still make sense to accord legal supremacy to the decisions of the U.N. Security Council in accordance with Articles 25 and 103 of the U.N. Charter? The other five principal U.N. organs are the General Assembly, the Secretariat (headed by the Secretary-General), the International Court of Justice, the Economic and Social Council, and the now-dormant Trusteeship Council. Many other U.N. subsidiary organs and committees were subsequently created. For example, the General Assembly's subsidiary bodies include the United Nations Environment Programme, the United Nations Conference on Trade and Development, and the Office of the United Nations High Commissioner for Refugees. In addition, Articles 57 and 63 of the U.N. Charter provide for relationships between the United Nations and various "specialized agencies," created by separate treaties and addressing a range of subject matters. The International Monetary Fund, the International Maritime Organization, the Food and Agriculture Organization, and the World Health Organization are some of the specialized agencies. Hence, the term "U.N. system" actually refers to more than just one integrated international organization.

We have already referred to various U.N. activities in previous chapters. Recall the debate over General Assembly resolutions as a potential source of international law in the *Texaco/Libya Case* (Chapter 3), the Secretary-General's role in helping to settle the *Rainbow Warrior* dispute (Chapter 5), the decisions of the International Court of Justice (Chapter 5 and elsewhere), the U.N.'s work with respect to human rights and international criminal law (Chapter 6), and the Organization's efforts concerning decolonization (Chapter 7). The International Law Commission (ILC), a body of legal experts appointed by the General Assembly pursuant to Article 13 of the U.N. Charter, helps to codify international law. For example, the ILC prepared drafts of Vienna Convention on the Law of Treaties (discussed in Chapter 2) and the 2001 Draft Articles on State Responsibility (Chapter 6 and elsewhere). The relationship between the United Nations and the use of force, introduced in this chapter, is explored more thoroughly in Chapter 9. U.N. organs and agencies have also contributed significantly to international environmental law and the international law of the sea. See especially Part C of this chapter and Chapter 10. For an excellent introduction to U.N. law and its underlying themes and principles, see *Law and Practice of the United Nations* (Simon Chesterton, Thomas M. Franck & David M. Malone eds. 2008).

2. *The U.N. Budget.* As of 2012, approximately 43,000 people from most of the 193 U.N. Member States worked for the Secretariat. See

"Composition of the Secretariat," U.N. Doc. A/67/329 (2012). The U.N. budget is proposed by the Secretary-General, reviewed by budgetary committees, and approved by the General Assembly pursuant to Article 17 of the U.N. Charter. Paying for U.N. staff, basic infrastructure, and Organization activities, the U.N. budget was $5.153 billion for the 2012–2013 biennium, or slightly over $2.5 billion per year, funded through Member States' assessed and voluntary contributions. U.N. peacekeeping operations, which we introduce in Section 2 below and in Chapter 9, are financed through a separate system of Member State assessments. The peacekeeping budget for the 2013–2014 fiscal year was approximately $7.54 billion. See "Financing Peace-keeping," http://www.un.org/en/peacekeeping/operations/financing.shtml (last visited Dec. 9, 2013).

3. *Changes to the U.N. Charter*. It is possible to amend the U.N. Charter pursuant to Articles 108 or 109, and—as indicated by footnotes to Charter articles in the Appendix—a few amendments have been adopted. Consistent practice may also effectively change the Charter. For example, an abstention by a permanent member of the Security Council is not now regarded as a veto of a Council decision, despite the literal language of Article 27(3) of the Charter. How else may the Charter change? What changes should be made? For discussions of possible U.N. reforms, see Report of the High-Level Panel on Threats, Challenges and Change, *A More Secure World: Our Shared Responsibility*, U.N. Doc. A/59/586 (2004); Anne-Marie Slaughter, "Secruity, Solidarity, and Sovereignty: The Grand Themes of UN Reform," 99 *American Journal of International Law* 619 (2005).

One theme in the cases and readings in the next section and in Chapter 9 is the constitutional evolution of the United Nations. Constitutional law is always a complex subject. It becomes even more so in an international context with so many states and legal cultures involved.

2. INTERNATIONAL PERSONALITY

Does an international organization have an "international personality"? Are its powers limited to those expressly delegated by its member states in the organization's charter? The International Court of Justice addressed such matters in its advisory opinion in the *Reparation Case*, which follows. The second reading, an excerpt from an International Law Commission report, discusses the legal responsibilities of international organizations. Consider throughout this section whether it is international law or municipal law that answers questions about the rights and duties of international organizations.

THE REPARATION CASE

Reparation for Injuries Suffered in the Service of the United Nations, 1949 I.C.J. 174

[In April 1947 the United Kingdom, which administered a League of Nations Mandate over Palestine (formerly part of the Ottoman Empire), asked the U.N. General Assembly to consider the future of Palestine. The

General Assembly recommended that Palestine be divided into independent Arab and Jewish states; Jerusalem was to be administered under international control. Skirmishes in the region led the U.N. Security Council, in April 1948, to call for a ceasefire in Palestine and to establish a Truce Commission. See S.C. Res. S/273, S/727. The U.N. General Assembly appointed Count Folke Bernadotte, a Swedish national, to be U.N. Mediator in Palestine. On September 17, 1948, several months after the Provisional Government of Israel proclaimed Israel to be a state, Count Bernadotte and another U.N. observer, Colonel Serot of France, were assassinated in the Israeli-held zone of Jerusalem by men in Israeli army uniform. The assassins were members of the Stern Gang, an extremist group opposed to outside interference in Israel.

On December 3, 1948, the U.N. General Assembly decided to ask the International Court of Justice for an advisory opinion:

> In the event of an agent of the United Nations in the performance of his duties suffering injury in circumstances involving the responsibility of a State, has the United Nations, as an Organization, the capacity to bring an international claim against the responsible *de jure* or *de facto* government with a view to obtaining the reparation due in respect of the damage caused (*a*) to the United Nations, (*b*) to the victim or to persons entitled through him?]

Competence to bring an international claim is, for those possessing it, the capacity to resort to the customary methods recognized by international law for the establishment, the presentation and the settlement of claims. Among these methods may be mentioned protest, request for an enquiry, negotiation, and request for submission to an arbitral tribunal or to the Court in so far as this may be authorized by the Statute. * * *

But, in the international sphere, has the Organization such a nature as involves the capacity to bring an international claim? In order to answer this question, the Court must first enquire whether the Charter has given the Organization such a position that it possesses, in regard to its Members, rights which it is entitled to ask them to respect. In other words, does the Organization possess international personality? This is no doubt a doctrinal expression, which has sometimes given rise to controversy. But it will be used here to mean that if the Organization is recognized as having that personality, it is an entity capable of availing itself of obligations incumbent upon its Members.

To answer this question, which is not settled by the actual terms of the Charter, we must consider what characteristics it was intended thereby to give to the Organization.

The subjects of law in any legal system are not necessarily identical in their nature or in the extent of their rights, and their nature depends upon the needs of the community. Throughout its history, the development of international law has been influenced by the requirements of international life, and the progressive increase in the collective activities of States has already given rise to instances of action upon the international plane by certain entities which are not States. This development culminated in the establishment in June 1945 of an international organization whose purposes and principles are specified in the Charter of the United Nations. But to achieve these ends the attribution of international personality is indispensable.

The Charter has not been content to make the Organization created by it merely a centre "for harmonizing the actions of nations in the attainment of these common ends" (Article I, para. 4). It has equipped that centre with organs, and has given it special tasks. It has defined the position of the Members in relation to the Organization by requiring them to give it every assistance in any action undertaken by it (Article 2, para. 5), and to accept and carry out the decisions of the Security Council; by authorizing the General Assembly to make recommendations to the Members; by giving the Organization legal capacity and privileges and immunities in the territory of each of its Members; and by providing for the conclusion of agreements between the Organization and its Members. Practice—in particular the conclusion of conventions to which the Organization is a party—has confirmed this character of the Organization, which occupies a position in certain respects in detachment from its Members, and which is under a duty to remind them, if need be, of certain obligations. It must be added that the Organization is a political body, charged with political tasks of an important character, and covering a wide field namely, the maintenance of international peace and security, the development of friendly relations among nations, and the achievement of international co-operation in the solution of problems of an economic, social, cultural or humanitarian character (Article I); and in dealing with its Members it employs political means. The "Convention on the Privileges and Immunities of the United Nations" of 1946 creates rights and duties between each of the signatories and the Organization (see, in particular, Section 35). It is difficult to see how such a convention could operate except upon the international plane and as between parties possessing international personality.

In the opinion of the Court, the Organization was intended to exercise and enjoy, and is in fact exercising and enjoying, functions and rights which can only be explained on the basis of the possession of a large measure of international personality and the capacity to operate upon an international plane. It is at present the supreme type of international organization, and it could not carry out the intentions of its founders if it was devoid of international personality. It must be acknowledged that its Members, by entrusting certain functions to it, with the attendant duties and responsibilities, have clothed it with the competence required to enable those functions to be effectively discharged.

Accordingly, the Court has come to the conclusion that the Organization is an international person. That is not the same thing as saying that it is a State, which it certainly is not, or that its legal personality and rights and duties are the same as those of a State. Still less is it the same thing as saying that it is "a super-State," whatever that expression may mean. It does not even imply that all its rights and duties must be upon the international plane, any more than all the rights and duties of a State must be upon that plane. What it does mean is that it is a subject of international law and capable of possessing international rights and duties, and that it has capacity to maintain its rights by bringing international claims.

The next question is whether the sum of the international rights of the Organization comprises the right to bring the kind of international claim described in the Request for this Opinion. That is a claim against a State to obtain reparation in respect of the damage caused by the injury of an agent of the Organization in the course of the performance of his duties. Whereas a State possesses the totality of international rights and duties recognized by international law, the rights and duties of an entity such as the Organization must depend upon its purposes and functions as specified or implied in its constituent documents and developed in practice. The functions of the Organization are of such a character that they could not be effectively discharged if they involved the concurrent action, on the international plane, of fifty-eight or more Foreign Offices, and the Court concludes that the Members have endowed the Organization with capacity to bring international claims when necessitated by the discharge of its functions.

What is the position as regards the claims mentioned in the request for an opinion? Question I is divided into two points, which must be considered in turn.

* * * It cannot be doubted that the Organization has the capacity to bring an international claim against one of its Members which has caused injury to it by a breach of its international obligations towards it. The damage specified in Question I (*a*) means exclusively damage caused to the interests of the Organization itself, to its administrative machine, to its property and assets, and to the interests of which it is the guardian. It is clear that the Organization has the capacity to bring a claim for this damage. As the claim is based on the breach of an international obligation on the part of the Member held responsible by the Organization, the Member cannot contend that this obligation is governed by municipal

law, and the Organization is justified in giving its claim the character of an international claim.

When the Organization has sustained damage resulting from a breach by a Member of its international obligations, it is impossible to see how it can obtain reparation unless it possesses capacity to bring an international claim. It cannot be supposed that in such an event all the Members of the Organization, save the defendant State, must combine to bring a claim against the defendant for the damage suffered by the Organization. * * *

Question I (*b*) is as follows:

> . . . has the United Nations, as an Organization, the capacity to bring an international claim . . . in respect of the damage caused . . . (*b*) to the victim or to persons entitled through him? * * *

The traditional rule that diplomatic protection is exercised by the national State does not involve the giving of a negative answer to Question I (*b*). * * *

The Court is here faced with a new situation. The questions to which it gives rise can only be solved by realizing that the situation is dominated by the provisions of the Charter considered in the light of the principles of international law.

The question lies within the limits already established; that is to say it presupposes that the injury for which the reparation is demanded arises from a breach of an obligation designed to help an agent of the Organization in the performance of his duties. It is not a case in which the wrongful act or omission would merely constitute a breach of the general obligations of a State concerning the position of aliens; claims made under this head would be within the competence of the national State and not, as a general rule, within that of the Organization.

The Charter does not expressly confer upon the Organization the capacity to include, in its claim for reparation, damage caused to the victim or to persons entitled through him. The Court must therefore begin by enquiring whether the provisions of the Charter concerning the functions of the Organization, and the part played by its agents in the performance of those functions, imply for the Organization power to afford its agents the limited protection that would consist in the bringing of a claim on their behalf for reparation for damage suffered in such circumstances. Under international law, the Organization must be deemed to have those powers which, though not expressly provided in the Charter, are conferred upon it by necessary implication as being essential to the performance of its duties. * * *

Having regard to its purposes and functions already referred to, the Organization may find it necessary, and has in fact found it necessary, to entrust its agents with important missions to be performed in disturbed parts of the world. Many missions, from their very nature, involve the agents in unusual dangers to which ordinary persons are not exposed. For the same reason, the injuries suffered by its agents in these circumstances will sometimes have occurred in such a manner that their national State would not be justified in bringing a claim for reparation on the ground of diplomatic protection, or, at any rate, would not feel disposed to do so. Both to ensure the efficient and independent performance of these missions and to afford effective support to its agents, the Organization must provide them with adequate protection. * * *

For this purpose, the Members of the Organization have entered into certain undertakings, some of which are in the Charter and others in complementary agreements. The content of these undertakings need not be described here; but the Court must stress the importance of the duty to render to the Organization "every assistance" which is accepted by the Members in Article 2, paragraph 5, of the Charter. It must be noted that the effective working of the Organization—the accomplishment of its task, and the independence and effectiveness of the work of its agents—require that these undertakings should be strictly observed. For that purpose, it is necessary that, when an infringement occurs, the Organization should be able to call upon the responsible State to remedy its default, and, in particular, to obtain from the State reparation for the damage that the default may have caused to its agent.

In order that the agent may perform his duties satisfactorily, he must feel that this protection is assured to him by the Organization, and that he may count on it. To ensure the independence of the agent, and, consequently, the independent action of the Organization itself, it is essential that in performing his duties he need not have to rely on any other protection than that of the Organization (save of course for the more direct and immediate protection due from the State in whose territory he may be). In particular, he should not have to rely on the protection of his own State. If he had to rely on that State, his independence might well be compromised, contrary to the principle applied by Article 100 of the Charter. And lastly, it is essential that—whether the agent belongs to a powerful or to a weak State; to one more affected or less affected by the complications of international life; to one in sympathy or not in sympathy with the mission of the agent—he should know that in the performance of his duties he is under the protection of the Organization. This assurance is even more necessary when the agent is stateless.

Upon examination of the character of the functions entrusted to the Organization and of the nature of the missions of its agents, it becomes clear that the capacity of the Organization to exercise a measure of functional protection of its agents arises by necessary intendment out of the Charter.

The obligations entered into by States to enable the agents of the Organization to perform their duties are undertaken not in the interest of the agents, but in that of the Organization. When it claims redress for a breach of these obligations, the Organization is invoking its own right, the right that the obligations due to it should be respected. On this ground, it asks for reparation of the injury suffered, for "it is a principle of international law that the breach of an engagement involves an obligation to make reparation in an adequate form;" as was stated by the Permanent Court in its Judgment No. 8 of July 26th, 1927. In claiming reparation based on the injury suffered by its agent, the Organization does not represent the agent, but is asserting its own right, the right to secure respect for undertakings entered into towards the Organization.

Having regard to the foregoing considerations, and to the undeniable right of the Organization to demand that its Members shall fulfill the obligations entered into by them in the interest of the good working of the Organization, the Court is of the opinion that, in the case of a breach of these obligations, the Organization has the capacity to claim adequate reparation, and that in assessing this reparation it is authorized to include the damage suffered by the victim or by persons entitled through him.

The question remains whether the Organization has "the capacity to bring an international claim against the responsible *de jure* or *de facto* government with a view to obtaining the reparation due in respect of the damage caused (*a*) to the United Nations, (*b*) to the victim or to persons entitled through him" when the defendant State is not a member of the Organization.

In considering this aspect of Question I (*a*) and (*b*), it is necessary to keep in mind the reasons which have led the Court to given an affirmative answer to it when the defendant State is a Member of the Organization. It has now been established that the Organization has capacity to bring claims on the international plane, and that it possesses a right of functional protection in respect of its agents. Here again the Court is authorized to assume that the damage suffered involves the responsibility of a State, and it is not called upon to express an opinion upon the various ways in which that responsibility might be engaged. Accordingly the question is whether the Organization has capacity to bring a claim against the defendant State to recover reparation in respect of that damage or whether, on the contrary, the defendant State, not being a member, is justified in raising the objection that the Organization lacks the capacity to bring an international claim. On this point, the Court's opinion is that fifty States, representing the vast majority of the members of the international community, had the power, in conformity with international law, to bring into being an entity possessing objective international personality, and not merely personality recognized by them alone, together with capacity to bring international claims.

Accordingly, the Court arrives at the conclusion that an affirmative answer should be given to Question I (*a*) and (*b*) whether or not the defendant State is a Member of the United Nations. * * *

FOR THESE REASONS,

The Court is of opinion

*On Question I (*a*):*

(i) unanimously,

That, in the event of an agent of the United Nations in the performance of his duties suffering injury in circumstances involving the responsibility of a Member State, the United Nations as an Organization has the capacity to bring an international claim against the responsible *de jure* or *de facto* government with a view to obtaining the reparation due in respect of the damage caused to the United Nations.

(ii) unanimously,

That, in the event of an agent of the United Nations in the performance of his duties suffering injury in circumstances involving the responsibility of a State which is not a member, the United Nations as an Organization has the capacity to bring an international claim against the responsible *de jure* or *de facto* government with a view to obtaining the reparation due in respect of the damage caused to the United Nations.

*On Question I (*b*):*

(i) by eleven votes against four,

That, in the event of an agent of the United Nations in the performance of his duties suffering injury in circumstances involving the responsibility of a Member State, the United Nations as an Organization has the capacity to bring an international claim against the responsible *de jure* or *de facto* government with a view to obtaining the reparation due in respect of the damage caused to the victim or to persons entitled through him.

(ii) by eleven votes against four,

That, in the event of an agent of the United Nations in the performance of his duties suffering injury in circumstances involving the responsibility of a State which is not a member, the United Nations as an Organization has the capacity to bring an international claim against the responsible *de jure* or *de facto* government with a view to obtaining the reparation due in respect of the damage caused to the victim or to persons entitled through him.

NOTES AND QUESTIONS

1. *The Aftermath of the* Reparation Case. Following the ICJ's opinion in the *Reparation Case*, the U.N. General Assembly authorized the Secretary-General to bring a claim for reparations against allegedly responsible states for injuries incurred in the service of the United Nations. Arbitration was contemplated if negotiation did not lead to a settlement. G.A. Res. 365 (IV) (1949). Israel paid over $50,000 in reparations for the deaths of Count Bernadotte and Colonel Serot. 1 *Public Papers of the Secretaries-General of the United Nations* 163–65, 227–35 (Andrew W. Cordier & Wilder Foote eds. 1969); Louis B. Sohn, *Cases on United Nations Law* 47–50 (2d rev. ed. 1967). For more background on the *Reparation Case*, see David J. Bederman, "The *Reparation for Injuries* Case: The Law of Nations is Transformed into International Law," in *International Law Stories* 307 (John E. Noyes, Laura A. Dickinson & Mark W. Janis eds. 2007).

2. *International Personality.* According to Professor Bederman, the opinion in the *Reparation Case*:

> conclusively ushered in a new era of international law, fully diversified with multiple subjects and objects. Indeed, what the *Reparation* opinion achieved was a fusion between the subjects and objects of international law. Any entity, thing or person bound by international legal rules was an international legal person. The distinction between active subjects and passive objects of the law was no longer relevant.

David J. Bederman, "The Souls of International Organizations: Legal Personality and the Lighthouse at Cape Spartel," 36 *Virginia Journal of International Law* 275, 367 (1996). Why did the Court find that the United Nations had "international personality"? If, as the ICJ suggested, international personality depends on a subject being "capable of possessing international rights and duties" and having "capacity to maintain its rights by bringing international claims," what is the source of that capability and capacity? Do the United Nations and other international organizations have international legal rights only because they are authorized in treaties? What underpins the "international personality" of other entities, such as states or individuals? See José E. Alvarez, *International Organizations as Law-makers* 129–39 (2005); Janne E. Nijman, "Non-State Actors and the International Rule of Law: Revisiting the 'Realist Theory' of International Legal Personality," in *Non-State Actor Dynamics in International Law* 91 (Math Noortmann ed. 2010).

3. *Capacity of the United Nations to Bring International Claims.* In the *Reparation Case*, the capacity of the United Nations to bring a claim for the death of Count Bernadotte did not follow automatically once the Court concluded the Organization had international personality. The Court separately found that the United Nations could bring an international claim against a responsible government to obtain reparations on behalf of a U.N. employee or his survivors. Why did the Court reach this result? Should the

ICJ have left it to Sweden, Count Bernadotte's state of nationality, to pursue any claims related to his death? See the *Nottebohm Case* in Chapter 6. Was the Court persuasive in arguing that the intention of Article 100 of the U.N. Charter (see Appendix) would be compromised if the employee must rely only on protection from his own state?

Judge Hackworth dissented from the part of the Court's opinion finding that the United Nations had the capacity to sponsor an international claim on behalf of one of its agents. He said in part:

> [T]he Organization is one of delegated and enumerated powers. It is to be presumed that such powers as the Member States desired to confer upon it are stated either in the Charter or in complementary agreements concluded by them. Powers not expressed cannot freely be implied. Implied powers flow from a grant of expressed powers, and are limited to those that are "necessary" to the exercise of powers expressly granted. No necessity for the exercise of the power here in question has been shown to exist. There is no impelling reason, if any at all, why the Organization should become the sponsor of claims on behalf of its employees, even though limited to those arising while the employee is in line of duty. These employees are still nationals of their respective countries, and the customary methods of handling such claims are still available in full vigour.

1949 I.C.J. at 198. Should the Court have advised that the U.N. Charter be amended to authorize the United Nations to espouse claims on behalf of nationals of Member States in service of the Organization? In interpreting the U.N. Charter, did the ICJ follow the approach to treaty interpretation later set out in Articles 31–32 of the Vienna Convention on the Law of Treaties (reproduced in the Appendix)? See Chapter 2. Does it make a difference that the U.N. Charter is the "constitution" of the United Nations, creating the Organization? Should "constitutional" treaties such as the U.N. Charter be interpreted differently from other interstate treaties?

4. *Other Types of Legal Capacity*. What other international legal rights does the United Nations have, in addition to the right to make claims for injuries to the Organization and its agents? Although Articles 1 and 2 of the Vienna Convention on the Law of Treaties do not define "treaties" to include agreements made by international organizations, the United Nations may enter into international agreements. For example, as discussed in Note 6 below, the United States and the United Nations have a Headquarters Agreement. There is a Vienna Convention on the Law of Treaties between States and International Organizations or between International Organizations, Mar. 21, 1986, 25 *International Legal Materials* 543 (1986), modeled on the Vienna Convention on the Law of Treaties. However, the United Nations does not have all the rights of a state. For example, the Organization is not permitted to be a party in contentious cases before the International Court of Justice.

Does every international organization have the same legal attributes? The Permanent Court of International Justice, in its *Advisory Opinion of February 7, 1923, on Nationality Decrees in Tunis and Morocco*, suggested that the legal authority of apparently similar entities may differ. The Court, while noting some common features of protectorates under international law, also stressed that "they have individual legal characteristics resulting from the special conditions under which they were created, and the stage of their development." 1923 P.C.I.J., Ser. B, No. 4, at 27.

5. *The United Nations and Nonmember States*. One issue in the *Reparation Case* was whether the United Nations had legal rights *vis-à-vis* nonmember states. What supports the Court's conclusion that the United Nations had the capacity to bring international claims even against a nonmember state? May the Organization take other steps with respect to nonmember states, such as sanctioning them for conduct that threatens international peace and security? See Article 2(6) of the U.N. Charter.

6. *The United Nations and Municipal Legal Systems*. The United Nations relies on its Member States to accord the Organization and its employees and agents certain rights, privileges, and immunities. On the international level, these measures are furthered by treaties, such as Articles 104 and 105 of the U.N. Charter and the Convention on the Privileges and Immunities of the United Nations, Feb. 13, 1946, 21 U.S.T. 1418, 1 U.N.T.S. 16. On the municipal level, a state defines the "legal personality" of international organizations for municipal legal purposes. States enact legislation to provide privileges, immunities, and protections to U.N. missions, to U.N. officials, and to diplomats representing their states at U.N. offices. The United States, for example, enacted the International Organizations Immunities Act, 22 U.S.C. §§ 288–288f, in 1945, and the Act for the Prevention and Punishment of Crimes Against Internationally Protected Persons, 18 U.S.C. § 112, in 1976 (implementing a convention that addresses such crimes). The bilateral U.S.-U.N. Agreement Regarding the Headquarters of the United Nations, June 26, 1947, 61 Stat. 3416, 11 U.N.T.S. 11, was implemented by a 1947 joint congressional resolution.

A state may not always take the same view of its obligations *vis-à-vis* U.N. officials as does the United Nations. Consider the case of Dato Param Cumaraswamy, a Malaysian jurist, who was named in 1994 as Special Rapporteur on the Independence of Judges and Lawyers by the U.N. Commission on Human Rights (a subsidiary organ of ECOSOC) to investigate the independence of judges, lawyers, and court officials in Malaysia. Cumaraswamy was sued for defamation in Malaysian court for his comments during an interview about matters relating to judicial corruption, which were published in an article in a 1995 issue of the magazine *International Commercial Litigation*. Despite the U.N. Secretary-General's finding that Cumaraswamy spoke in his official capacity as Special Rapporteur during the interview, and that he therefore was immune from legal process pursuant to the Convention on Privileges and Immunities of the United Nations, the Malaysian High Court rejected Cumaraswamy's absolute immunity in 1997.

MBf Capital Bhd. v. Cumaraswamy, 121 *International Law Reports* 368. ECOSOC then requested an advisory opinion from the International Court of Justice, which ruled in April 1999 that Cumaraswamy was "entitled to immunity from legal process of every kind" for his words during the interview in question. Difference Relating to Immunity from Legal Process of a Special Rapporteur of the Commission on Human Rights (Advisory Opinion), 1999 I.C.J. 1. Article VIII, Section 30 of the Privileges and Immunities Convention varies the normal rule that ICJ advisory opinions are not legally binding, by providing that advisory opinions concerning the Convention "shall be accepted as decisive by the parties." Counsel for plaintiffs argued to the Malaysian High Court, however, that the ICJ's decision was not binding in a defamation case between private litigants, and that the ICJ's decision breached "rules of natural justice." "Counsel: ICJ's Decision Was in Breach of the Rules of Natural Justice," *New Straits Times (Malaysia)*, May 12, 2000, at 19. In July 2000, the Malaysian High Court noted with "great concern" that Cumaraswamy "was able to make damaging and disparaging statements," and opined that the defendant had "shown a total disregard to the meaning of the word 'impartial' " with respect to his views concerning the Malaysian legal system. Insas Bhd. v. Cumaraswamy, 121 *International Law Reports* 464, 471. The High Court nevertheless ruled that Malaysia's agreement to be bound by the ICJ's advisory opinion required that the defendant be accorded immunity from all legal process. See Charles H. Brower, II, "International Immunities: Some Dissident Views on the Roles of Municipal Courts," 41 *Virginia Journal of International Law* 1 (2000).

7. *Responsibility of International Organizations*. If international organizations have rights at international law, do they also have duties? The International Court of Justice, in its advisory opinion in the *Immunity from Legal Process Case* discussed in Note 6, although affirming the immunity of the U.N. agent, found that "the United Nations may be required to bear responsibility for the damage arising from" acts performed by the Organization "or by its agents acting in their official capacity." 1999 I.C.J. at 88–89. The next excerpt examines the responsibility of international organizations.

DRAFT ARTICLES ON THE RESPONSIBILITY OF INTERNATIONAL ORGANIZATIONS

Report of the International Law Commission on its Sixty-third Session, U.N. GAOR, 66th Sess., Supp. No. 10, U.N. Doc. A/66/10, at 52 (2011)

[In 2001 the International Law Commission (ILC) completed its Draft Articles on State Responsibility, which we discuss elsewhere, especially in Chapter 6. In 2002 the ILC decided to pursue the parallel topic of responsibility of international organizations. In 2011 the ILC adopted Draft Articles on that topic, excerpted below.]

Article 4

Elements of an internationally wrongful act of an international organization

There is an internationally wrongful act of an international organization when conduct consisting of an action or omission:

(a) is attributable to the international organization under international law; and

(b) constitutes a breach of an international obligation of that international organization.

Commentary

1. [T]he attribution of conduct to an international organization is one of the two essential elements for an internationally wrongful act to occur. * * *

2. A second essential element * * * is that conduct constitutes the breach of an obligation under international law. The obligation may result either from a treaty binding the international organization or from any other source of international law applicable to the organization. As the International Court of Justice noted in its advisory opinion on the *Interpretation of the Agreement of 25 March 1951 between the WHO and Egypt*, international organizations

> are bound by any obligations incumbent upon them under general rules of international law, under their constitutions or under international agreements to which they are parties.

A breach is thus possible with regard to any of these international obligations.

[The Commission's general commentary concerning attribution of conduct to an international organization includes the following text:]

4. Although it may not frequently occur in practice, dual or even multiple attribution of conduct cannot be excluded. Thus, attribution of a certain conduct to an international organization does not imply that the same conduct cannot be attributed to a State; nor does attribution of conduct to a State rule out attribution of the same conduct to an international organization. * * *

5. [T]he present draft articles * * * do not point to cases in which conduct cannot be attributed to the organization. For instance, the articles do not say, but only imply, that conduct of military forces of States or international organizations is not attributable to the United Nations when the Security Council authorizes States or international organizations to take necessary measures outside a chain of command linking those forces to the United Nations.

Article 6

Conduct of organs or agents of an international organization

1. The conduct of an organ or agent of an international organization in the performance of functions of that organ or agent shall be considered as an act of that organization under international law whatever position the organ or agent holds in respect of the organization. * * *

Article 7

Conduct of organs of a State or organs or agents of an international organization placed at the disposal of another international organization

The conduct of an organ of a State or an organ or agent of an international organization that is placed at the disposal of another international organization shall be considered under international law an act of the latter organization if the organization exercises effective control over that conduct.

Commentary

1. When an organ of a State is placed at the disposal of an international organization, the organ may be fully seconded to that organization. In this case the organ's conduct would clearly be attributable only to the receiving organization [and] the general rule set out in Article 6 would apply. Article 7 deals with the different situation in which the seconded organ or agent still acts to a certain extent as organ of the seconding State or as organ or agent of the seconding organization. This occurs for instance in the case of military contingents that a State places at the disposal of the United Nations for a peacekeeping operation, since the State retains disciplinary powers and criminal jurisdiction over the members of the national contingent. In this situation the problem arises whether a specific conduct of the seconded organ or agent is to be attributed to the receiving organization or to the seconding State or organization. * * *

3. The seconding State or organization may conclude an agreement with the receiving organization over placing an organ or agent at the latter organization's disposal. The agreement may state which State or organization would be responsible for conduct of that organ or agent. [T]his type of agreement is not conclusive because it governs only the relations between the contributing State or organization and the receiving organization and could thus not have the effect of depriving a third party of any right that that party may have towards the State or organization which is responsible under the general rules.

4. The criterion for attribution of conduct either to the contributing State or organization or to the receiving organization is based according to article 7 on the factual control that is exercised over the specific

conduct taken by the organ or agent placed at the receiving organization's disposal. * * *

6. The United Nations assumes that in principle it has exclusive control of the deployment of national contingents in a peacekeeping force. This premise led the United Nations Legal Counsel to state:

> As a subsidiary organ of the United Nations, an act of a peacekeeping force is, in principle, imputable to the Organization, and if committed in violation of an international obligation entails the international responsibility of the Organization and its liability in compensation.

This statement sums up United Nations practice relating to the United Nations Operation in the Congo (ONUC), the United Nations Peace-keeping Force in Cyprus (UNFICYP) and later peacekeeping forces. In a [2011] comment, the United Nations Secretariat observed that "[f]or a number of reasons, notably political," the practice of the United Nations had been that of "maintaining the principle of United Nations responsibility vis-à-vis third parties" in connection with peacekeeping operations.

7. Practice relating to peacekeeping forces is particularly significant in the present context because of the control that the contributing State retains over disciplinary and criminal matters. This may have consequences with regard to attribution of conduct. For instance, the Office of Legal Affairs of the United Nations took the following line with regard to compliance with obligations under the 1973 Convention on International Trade in Endangered Species of Wild Fauna and Flora:

> Since the Convention places the responsibility for enforcing its provisions on the States parties and since the troop-contributing States retain jurisdiction over the criminal acts of their military personnel, the responsibility for enforcing the provisions of the Convention rests with those troop-contributing States which are parties to the Convention.

Attribution of conduct to the contributing State is clearly linked with the retention of some powers by that State over its national contingent and thus on the control that the State possesses in the relevant respect.

8. As has been held by several scholars, when an organ or agent is placed at the disposal of an international organization, the decisive question in relation to attribution of a given conduct appears to be who has effective control over the conduct in question. * * *

10. The European Court of Human Rights considered, [in 2007] in *Behrami and Behrami v. France* and *Saramati v. France, Germany and Norway*, its jurisdiction *ratione personae* in relation to the conduct of forces placed in Kosovo at the disposal of the United Nations (United

Nations Interim Administration Mission in Kosovo (UNMIK)) or authorized by the United Nations (Kosovo Force (KFOR)). The Court referred to the present work of the International Law Commission and in particular to the criterion of "effective control" that had been provisionally adopted by the Commission. While not formulating any criticism to this criterion, the Court considered that the decisive factor was whether "the United Nations Security Council retained ultimate authority and control so that operational command only was delegated." While acknowledging "the effectiveness or unity of NATO command in *operational* matters" concerning KFOR, the Court noted that the presence of KFOR in Kosovo was based on a resolution adopted by the Security Council and concluded that "KFOR was exercising lawfully delegated Chapter VII powers of the UNSC so that the impugned action was, in principle, 'attributable' to the UN within the meaning of the word outlined [in article 4 of the present articles]." [W]hen applying the criterion of effective control, "operational" control would seem more significant than "ultimate" control, since the latter hardly implies a role in the act in question. It is therefore not surprising that in his report of June 2008 on the United Nations Interim Administration Mission in Kosovo, the United Nations Secretary-General distanced himself from the latter criterion and stated: "It is understood that the international responsibility of the United Nations will be limited in the extent of its effective operational control." * * *

12. Also the decision of the House of Lords in *Al-Jedda* [R (on the application of Al-Jedda) v. Secretary of State for Defence, [2008] 1 A.C. 332 (House of Lords, 2007)] contained ample references to the current work of the Commission. One of the majority opinions stated that "[i]t was common ground between the parties that the governing principle [was] that expressed by the International Law Commission in article [7] of its draft articles on Responsibility of International Organizations." The House of Lords was confronted with a claim arising from the detention of a person by British troops in Iraq. In its resolution 1546 (2004) the Security Council had previously authorized the presence of the multinational force in that country. The majority opinions appeared to endorse the views expressed by the European Court of Human Rights in *Behrami and Saramati*, but distinguished the facts of the case and concluded that it could not "realistically be said that US and UK forces were under the effective command and control of the UN, or that UK forces were under such command and control when they detained the appellant." This conclusion appears to be in line with the way in which the criterion of effective control was intended.

13. After the judgment of the House of Lords an application was made by Mr. Al-Jedda to the European Court of Human Rights. In *Al-Jedda v. United Kingdom* this Court quoted several texts concerning attribution, including the article (identical to the present article) which had been adopted by the Commission at first reading and some

paragraphs of the commentary. The Court considered that "the United Nations Security Council had neither effective control nor ultimate authority and control over the acts and omissions of foreign troops within the Multi-National Force and that the applicant's detention was not, therefore, attributable to the United Nations." The Court unanimously concluded that the applicant's detention had to be attributed to the respondent State.

NOTES AND QUESTIONS

1. *Peacekeeping*. The question of responsibility for the conduct of U.N. peacekeepers arises in situations as mundane as negligent driving and as egregious as rape or sexual abuse. We explore peacekeeping operations, along with U.N. Security Council-authorized enforcement measures to respond to threats to international peace and security, in the next chapter.

2. *International Organizations and Breaches of International Obligations*. For what sorts of international obligations may an international organization be responsible? The U.N. Secretary-General in 1999 instructed forces under U.N. command and control to respect international humanitarian law. The United Nations also accepted responsibility, subject to certain temporal and financial limitations, for tortious damage caused by U.N. peacekeepers while performing their official duties. See Committee on Accountability of International Organizations, "Final Report," in International Law Association, *Report of the Seventy-First Conference (Berlin)* 164 (2004); Daphne Shraga, "UN Peacekeeping Operations: Applicability of International Humanitarian Law and Responsibility for Operations-Related Damage," 94 *American Journal of International Law* 406 (2000). The United Nations has been criticized, however, for failing to assume responsibility for the contributions of Nepalese peacekeepers to a cholera epidemic in Haiti. See Transnational Development Clinic, Yale Law School *et al.*, *Peacekeeping Without Accountability* (Aug. 2013), *available at* http://www.law.yale.edu/documents/pdf/Clinics/Haiti_TDC_Final_Report.pdf (last visited Dec. 9, 2013). Are international organizations in breach only when their agents violate the organization's rules or governing treaty? May the United Nations be liable for violating international human rights law or customary international law? See Tom Dannenbaum, "Translating the Standard of Effective Control into a System of Effective Accountability: How Liability Should be Apportioned for Violations of Human Rights by Member State Troop Contingents Serving as United Nations Peacekeepers," 51 *Harvard Journal of International Law* 113, 134–39 (2010).

3. *Attributing Responsibility to International Organizations*. The European Court of Human Rights relied on the notion of "ultimate control" rather than "effective control" in attributing conduct to the United Nations in the *Behrami* and *Saramati Cases* discussed in the excerpt above. Behrami and Behrami v. France; Saramati v. France, Germany and Norway, App. Nos. 71412/01 & 78166/01 (Grand Chamber, 2007). Which approach is preferable? How should we determine who exercises "effective control" in peacekeeping

situations? In *Behrami* children were killed and injured when they played with undetonated cluster bombs left over from a 1999 North Atlantic Treaty Organization (NATO) bombing in Kosovo; members of the U.N. Mission in Kosovo (UNMIK), a U.N. peacekeeping force, had not cleaned up the bombs. *Saramati* involved an individual who was detained by KFOR, a NATO operation authorized by the United Nations to maintain order in Kosovo. Alleging violations of the European Convention on Human Rights, the applicants in *Behrami* brought a claim against France, which led UNMIK in the relevant sector of Kosovo, while Saramati sought recovery from the governments whose nationals had ordered his detention.

Commentators criticized the European Court's conclusion that the conduct was attributable to the United Nations:

> The [U.N. Security] Council most certainly did not exercise [effective control] in relation to KFOR. The fact that home States did retain substantial powers over their troops is evidence of their effective control over the specific conduct. KFOR troops were directly answerable to their national commanders and fell exclusively within the jurisdiction of their home State which decided on waiver of immunities; moreover, home States retained jurisdiction in disciplinary, civil and criminal matters and KFOR personnel were immune from arrest and detention other than by their State; rules of engagement were national, deployment decisions were national, as was the financing of the troops.

Marko Milanović & Tatjana Papić, "As Bad as It Gets: The European Court of Human Rights's *Behrami and Saramati* Decisions and General International Law," 58 *International and Comparative Law Quarterly* 267, 286 (2009). Why did the Court find the conduct at issue attributable to the United Nations? The Court's decision meant that the conduct of such personnel was not attributable to the states, and thus that the European Court lacked jurisdiction over those state actors.

Attributing responsibility to an international organization has meant that injured claimants could not obtain relief in some ocases. Consider, for example, J.H. Rayner Ltd. v. Department of Trade and Industry, [1990] 2 App. Cas. 418, 81 *International Law Reports* 671 (House of Lords, 1989), and related litigation involving the International Tin Council (ITC). In the 1980s the ITC, an international organization established to buy and sell tin to stabilize the price of that commodity, ran out of funds to pay for tin it had purchased. Creditors sued the ITC and tried to implead its member states. The British House of Lords ruled that, given the ITC's separate international personality, its member states were not responsible for the ITC's debts. Should states be able to shield themselves from liability by operating through an international organization? See Romana Sadurska & C.M. Chinkin, "The Collapse of the International Tin Council: A Case of State Responsibility?," 30 *Virginia Journal of International Law* 845 (1990); Andrew Stumer, Note, "Liability of Member States for Acts of International Organizations:

Reconsidering the Policy Objections," 48 *Harvard International Law Journal* 553 (2007).

Some courts have decided that the United Nations did not exercise effective control over the actions of its peacekeeping forces and instead attributed control to the troop-contributing state. See the *Al-Jedda* decisions of the British House of Lords and the European Court of Human Rights discussed in the ILC commentary above, and Marko Milanovic, "*Al Skeini* and *Al-Jedda* in Strasbourg," 23 *European Journal of International Law* 121 (2012). In 2013 the Dutch Supreme Court found the Netherlands responsible for actions of Dutch forces (the Dutchbat) assigned to a U.N. peacekeeping mission. Operating in the former Yugoslavia in 1995, the Dutchbat had refused to allow male family members of a Yugoslav translator to take refuge in a Dutch military compound; those family members were murdered by Bosnian Serbs at Srebenica. Netherlands v. Nuhanović, Case 12/03324 (Supreme Court of the Netherlands, 2013). The Court relied on the ILC's Draft Articles on Responsibility of International Organizations to determine that the Netherlands exercised effective control over the Dutchbat, concluding that Article 7 applied where, as in the *Nuhanović Case*, "a State places troops at the disposal of the United Nations in the context of a UN peace mission, and command and control is transferred to the United Nations, but the disciplinary powers and criminal jurisdiction (the 'organic command') remain vested in the seconding State." *Id.* ¶ 3.10.2. Ought the conduct of the Dutchbat forces also be attributed to the United Nations? The Dutch court left open the possibility of such dual attribution. See *id.* ¶ 3.11.2 and Article 48(1) of the ILC Draft Articles.

4. *Preventing and Redressing Violations of International Law by International Organizations*. Is it appropriate to develop general articles applicable across the board to all international organizations? Is it reasonable to presume that the same definitions and standards for responsibility should apply to international organizations as varied as the United Nations, regional self-defense organizations such as NATO, and economic organizations like the World Bank? For analyses of the ILC's initiative, see *Responsibility of International Organizations* (Maurizio Ragazzi ed. 2103), and Kristen E. Boon, "New Directions in Responsibility: Assessing the International Law Commission's Draft Articles on the Responsibility of International Organizations," 37 *Yale Journal of International Law Online*, Spring 2010, at 1, http://www.yjil.org/docs/pub/o-37-boon-new-directions-in-responsibility.pdf (last visited Dec. 9, 2013). What other mechanisms are available to hold international organizations accountable? How might international organizations themselves prevent their agents from violating international law?

What forums are available to redress violations? The previous set of Notes discussed the *Immunity from Legal Process Case*, which concluded that a U.N. agent was immune from jurisdiction in municipal court. See Jacob Katz Cogan, "International Decision: *Stichting Mothers of Srebrenica v. Netherlands*," 107 *American Journal of International Law* 884 (2013);

Elizabeth F. Defeis, "U.N. Peacekeepers and Sexual Abuse and Exploitation: An End to Impunity," 7 *Washington University Global Studies Law Review* 185 (2008).

B. NON-GOVERNMENTAL ORGANIZATIONS

Non-governmental organizations (NGOs) are created under municipal law rather than by interstate agreement. There are thousands of "international NGOs" working on a wide range of economic, social, human rights, and environmental issues of international concern. Although some NGOs have links to governments or receive government grants, most are private, not-for-profit entities, receiving all their support from individual members or private contributions. As we saw in the *Texaco-Libya Arbitration* in Chapter 3 and the *Barcelona Traction Case* in Chapter 6, business corporations, which are also creatures of municipal law, may use international law and international legal process to try to obtain redress when their economic interests have been harmed. International NGOs, by contrast, often have as primary goals the development of international legal norms and the implementation and enforcement of those norms on the international and municipal levels.

In this part, we look at some of the roles of NGOs in international law and process. We first consider the International Committee of the Red Cross, a private organization that provides assistance to victims of armed conflicts. The last reading concerns actual and potential functions of NGOs in developing and enforcing international environmental law. These materials explore questions about the international legal personality of NGOs and their recognition by other entities.

GABOR RONA, "THE ICRC'S STATUS: IN A CLASS OF ITS OWN"

Feb. 2004, *available at* http://www.icrc.org (last visited Dec. 9, 2013)

NGOs are private organizations such as associations, federations, unions, institutes, and other groups; they are not established by a government or by intergovernmental agreement. NGOs can play a role in international affairs by virtue of their activities, but they do not necessarily possess any official status, nor do they have a mandate for their existence or activities.

Where an organization's membership or activity is limited to a specific country, it's considered a national NGO; if its activities cross borders, it becomes an international NGO. Some of the best-known international NGOs include Médécins Sans Frontières, Amnesty International, Human Rights Watch, Oxfam, and so on.

* * * Unlike NGOs, intergovernmental organizations by definition have a mandate from governments for their existence and activities and

enjoy certain working facilities known in diplomatic parlance as "privileges and immunities."

The ICRC has a hybrid nature. As a private association formed under the Swiss Civil Code, its existence is not in itself mandated by governments. And yet its functions and activities—to provide protection and assistance to victims of conflict—are mandated by the international community of States and are founded on international law, specifically the Geneva Conventions, which are among the most widely ratified treaties in the world.

Because of this the ICRC, like any intergovernmental organization, is recognized as having an "international legal personality" or status of its own. It enjoys working facilities (privileges and immunities) comparable to those of the United Nations, its agencies, and other intergovernmental organizations. Examples of these facilities include exemption from taxes and customs duties, inviolability of premises and documents, and immunity from judicial process.

The ICRC can only do its job of providing protection and assistance to conflict victims if its working principles of impartiality, independence and neutrality are respected. It is through recognition of the ICRC's privileges and immunities that States and international organizations acknowledge their respect for those principles. Thus, in line with its international legal mandate, the ICRC's privileges and immunities are widely recognized by governments, by the United Nations and by other organizations. This means that the ICRC is * * * treated as * * * an intergovernmental organization for the work it does under its international mandate.

The legal basis for the ICRC's essential privileges and immunities [is] recognized in various ways, including:

- *Headquarters Agreements between the ICRC and governments, or state legislation.* In the nearly 80 countries in which the ICRC carries out significant operations, its international legal personality, judicial immunity and testimonial privilege (right not to be called as a witness) [are] recognized either by treaty or by legislation.

- *Judicial decisions.* Several domestic and international tribunals have ruled on the ICRC's judicial immunity and testimonial privileges. Recently, the International Criminal Tribunal for the former Yugoslavia (ICTY) distinguished the ICRC from NGOs by citing its international legal mandate and status, including its right to decline to testify. The rules of procedure and evidence of the newly established International Criminal Court also reflect the position of the more than one hundred states that drafted the document, that the ICRC enjoys testimonial immunity.

- *The United Nations and other international organizations.* The ICRC has been granted observer status at the UN General Assembly [pursuant to General Assembly Resolution 45/6 (1990)] and enjoys similar status with other international, intergovernmental organizations.

NOTES AND QUESTIONS

1. *The ICRC and the International Red Cross and Red Crescent Movement.* The founding of the International Committee of the Red Cross was largely due to the efforts of Henry Dunant, who observed the suffering of thousands of wounded troops during an 1859 battle in the War of Italian Unification. The ICRC was formed under Swiss law in 1863, and its governing body is composed of Swiss nationals. See http://www.icrc.org (last visited Dec. 9, 2013).

The ICRC is one component of what is known as the International Red Cross and Red Crescent Movement. Another part is the International Federation of Red Cross and Red Crescent Societies (formerly the League of Red Cross Societies), an NGO founded in 1919 and, like the ICRC, headquartered in Geneva. The Federation supports the activities of national societies, promoting and coordinating relief operations for natural or technological disasters. As of December 2013, there were 189 national Red Cross and Red Crescent societies, of which the American Red Cross—a corporation formed and supported by the U.S. government (see 36 U.S.C. §§ 300101–300113)—is one. The ICRC itself has multiple functions: assessing whether new national societies meet conditions for recognition; providing international relief services to soldiers and civilians in armed conflicts; assisting national societies in such situations; and developing and promoting international humanitarian law. See "The International Committee of the Red Cross (ICRC): Its Mission and Work," 91 *International Review of the Red Cross*, No. 824 (2009). In 1977 the "International Red Cross" was described as "a transnational movement with two heads and many arms. [T]he heads do not control the arms, and the heads are not always looking in the same direction." David P. Forsythe, *Humanitarian Politics: The International Committee of the Red Cross* 5 (1977). The Agreement on the Organization of the International Activities of the Components of the International Red Cross and Red Crescent Movement (Seville Agreement), Nov. 26, 1997, *reprinted in International Review of the Red Cross*, No. 322, at 159, addresses the functions of the Movement's components and recognizes the ICRC's lead role with respect to armed conflicts. Even after that Agreement, however, the Movement continued to grapple with issues of fragmentation and decentralization. See David P. Forsythe, *The Humanitarians: The International Committee of the Red Cross* 125–28, 304–07 (2005).

2. *The ICRC and the Geneva Conventions.* The ICRC has contributed to the negotiation of international humanitarian law treaties, including the four 1949 Geneva Conventions, which concern the protection and humane treatment of prisoners of war (POWs), of wounded and sick members of the armed forces in the field and at sea, and of civilians in time of war. Treaties also explicitly provide roles for the Committee. For example, according to

Article 5 of Protocol Additional (No. I) to the Geneva Conventions, June 8, 1977, 1125 U.N.T.S. 3, the ICRC may serve as a "Protecting Power," monitoring implementation, *e.g.*, by visiting POWs or conflict zones. See also *id.* art. 81. Similar authority is granted to the ICRC under the four Geneva Conventions. Why might a government prefer to have the ICRC, rather than a neutral government or the United Nations, act as a Protecting Power? Has the ICRC's confidentiality helped or harmed its ability to fulfill humanitarian functions? See David P. Forsythe, "Who Guards the Guardians: Third Parties and the Law of Armed Conflict," 70 *American Journal of International Law* 41 (1976); Steven R. Ratner, "Behind the Flag of Dunant: Secrecy and the Compliance Mission of the International Committee of the Red Cross," in *Transparency in International Law* 297 (Andrea Bianchi & Anne Peters eds. 2013). More on the Geneva Conventions and international humanitarian law (also known as *jus in bello*) appears in Chapter 9, Part A.

3. *The ICRC's International Personality*. Gabor Rona, in the excerpt above, noted other aspects of the ICRC's international personality. For example, the ICRC has entered into headquarters agreements with states where the Committee conducts its activities. These agreements give the ICRC much the same sorts of privileges and immunities that international organizations enjoy pursuant to agreement. For instance, the Agreement Between the International Committee of the Red Cross and the Swiss Federal Council To Determine the Legal Status of the Committee in Switzerland, Mar. 1, 1993, *reprinted in International Review of the Red Cross*, No. 293, at 152, provides that the ICRC's premises and archives are inviolable and that the ICRC is, with certain exceptions, immune from legal process and execution. According to Article 1 of the Agreement, Switzerland "recognizes the international juridical personality and the legal capacity in Switzerland" of the ICRC.

4. *The International Personality of NGOs*. As you read the following excerpt and Notes, consider whether NGOs generally possess some degree of international personality. What differences among international organizations, peoples (discussed in Chapter 7, Part C), individuals (Chapter 6), and NGOs help explain the status of NGOs at international law? If all have important roles with respect to international law, should we stop attempting to classify entities as either "subjects" with international legal personality or "objects" without it? Should we instead characterize all influential entities as "participants" in a global legal process? See Rosalyn Higgins, *Problems and Process: International Law and How We Use It* 49–50 (1994).

THE FRIENDS OF THE EARTH CASE

Bund für Umwelt und Naturschutz Deutschland, Landesverband Nordrhein-Westfalen eV v. Bezirksregierung Arnsberg, [2011] EUECJ C-115/09 (European Court of Justice, Fourth Chamber) (translated from German)

1. This reference for a preliminary ruling concerns the interpretation of Council Directive 85/337/EEC of 27 June 1985 on the assessment of the

effects of certain public and private projects on the environment, as amended by Directive 2003/35/EC of the European Parliament and of the Council of 26 May 2003 ("Directive 85/337").

2. The reference has been made in proceedings between the Bund für Umwelt und Naturschutz Deutschland, Landesverband Nordrhein-Westfalen eV (the Nordrhein-Westfalen branch of Friends of the Earth, Germany; "Friends of the Earth") and the Bezirksregierung Arnsberg, concerning the authorisation granted by the latter to Trianel Kohlekraftwerk GmbH & Co. KG ("Trianel") for the construction and operation of a coal-fired power station in Lünen.

LEGAL CONTEXT

International law

3. The Convention on Access to Information, Public Participation in Decision-making and Access to Justice in Environmental Matters, known as "the Aarhus Convention," was signed on 25 June 1998 and approved on behalf of the European Community by Council Decision 2005/370/EC of 17 February 2005[.]

4. Article 9 of the Aarhus Convention provides: ...

> 2. Each Party shall, within the framework of its national legislation, ensure that members of the public concerned:
>
> (a) having a sufficient interest or, alternatively,
>
> (b) maintaining impairment of a right, where the administrative procedural law of a Party requires this as a precondition,
>
> have access to a review procedure before a court of law and/or another independent and impartial body established by law, to challenge the substantive and procedural legality of any decision, act or omission subject to the provisions of Article 6 and, where so provided for under national law and without prejudice to paragraph 3 below, of other relevant provisions of this Convention.
>
> What constitutes a sufficient interest and impairment of a right shall be determined in accordance with the requirements of national law and consistently with the objective of giving the public concerned wide access to justice within the scope of this Convention. To this end, the interest of any non-governmental organisation meeting the requirements referred to in Article 2(5) shall be deemed sufficient for the purpose of subparagraph (a) above. Such organisations shall also be deemed to have rights capable of being impaired for the purpose of subparagraph (b) above.

The provisions of this paragraph 2 shall not exclude the possibility of a preliminary review procedure before an administrative authority and shall not affect the requirement of exhaustion of administrative review procedures prior to recourse to judicial review procedures, where such a requirement exists under national law.

3. In addition and without prejudice to the review procedures referred to in paragraphs 1 and 2 above, each Party shall ensure that, where they meet the criteria, if any, laid down in its national law, members of the public have access to administrative or judicial procedures to challenge acts and omissions by private persons and public authorities which contravene provisions of its national law relating to the environment.

4. In addition and without prejudice to paragraph 1 above, the procedures referred to in paragraphs 1, 2 and 3 above shall provide adequate and effective remedies, including injunctive relief as appropriate, and be fair, equitable, timely and not prohibitively expensive. Decisions under this article shall be given or recorded in writing. Decisions of courts, and whenever possible of other bodies, shall be publicly accessible.

European Union ("EU") law

Directive 2003/35

5. Recital 5 in the preamble to Directive 2003/35 states that Community law should be properly aligned with the Aarhus Convention with a view to the ratification of that Convention by the Community. * * *

7. Recital 11 to Directive 2003/35 states that Directive 85/337 should be amended to ensure that it is fully compatible with the provisions of the Aarhus Convention[.]

9. Article 1(1) of Directive 85/337 provides:

This Directive shall apply to the assessment of the environmental effects of those public and private projects which are likely to have significant effects on the environment.

10. Article 1(2) of Directive 85/337 sets out the definitions * * * of the concepts of "the public" and "the public concerned":

For the purposes of this Directive: ...

"the public" means: one or more natural or legal persons and, in accordance with national legislation or practice, their associations, organisations or groups;

"the public concerned" means: the public affected or likely to be affected by, or having an interest in, the environmental decision-

> making procedures referred to in Article 2(2); for the purposes of this definition, non-governmental organisations promoting environmental protection and meeting any requirements under national law shall be deemed to have an interest.

11. * * * Article 10a of Directive 85/337, also inserted by Directive 2003/35 [provides that "Member States shall ensure that" they meet the obligations set out in Article 9 of the Aarhus Convention. Article 10a tracks exactly the language of Article 9 of the Aarhus Convention, as set out in paragraph 4 above].

Directive 92/43/EC

12. Article 6(3) of Council Directive 92/43/EC of 21 May 1992 on the conservation of natural habitats and of wild fauna and flora, as amended by Directive 2006/105/EC of 20 November 2006 ("the Habitats Directive") provides as follows:

> Any plan or project not directly connected with or necessary to the management of the site but likely to have a significant effect thereon, either individually or in combination with other plans or projects, shall be subject to appropriate assessment of its implications for the site in view of the site's conservation objectives. In the light of the conclusions of the assessment of the implications for the site and subject to the provisions of paragraph 4, the competent national authorities shall agree to the plan or project only after having ascertained that it will not adversely affect the integrity of the site concerned and, if appropriate, after having obtained the opinion of the general public.

National law

[The Court sets out in detail relevant German law, key provisions of which are summarized in the discussion that follows.]

BACKGROUND AND QUESTIONS REFERRED

24. Trianel—the intervener in the main proceedings—intends to construct and operate a coal-fired power station in Lünen. The power station, which will deliver heat output to a maximum of 1705 megawatts and 750 megawatts of electricity output, will enter service in 2012. Within eight kilometers of the project site, there are five areas designated as special areas of conservation within the meaning of the Habitats Directive.

25. On 6 May 2008, in the context of the environmental impact assessment of that project, the Bezirksregierung Arnsberg (Arnsberg District Administration)—the defendant in the main proceedings—issued Trianel with a preliminary decision and a partial permit for the project.

The preliminary decision stated that there were no legal objections to the project.

26. On 16 June 2008, Friends of the Earth initiated proceedings for the annulment of those measures before the Oberverwaltungsgericht für das Land Nordrhein-Westfalen (Higher Administrative Court for the Nordrhein-Westfalen Land; "the referring court"). Friends of the Earth relied, in particular, on an infringement of the provisions transposing into German law the Habitats Directive and, in particular, Article 6 thereof.

27. According to the referring court, those measures infringe Article 6(3) of the Habitats Directive inasmuch as the environmental impact assessment of the project at issue did not show that it was unlikely to have a significant effect on the special areas of conservation located nearby.

28. The referring court finds that, on the basis of domestic law, an environmental protection organisation is not entitled to rely on infringement of the law for the protection of water and nature or on the precautionary principle laid down in [the 2002 German Anti-pollution Law].

29. It states that, accordingly, the right of action accorded to non-governmental organisations * * * will be admissible only if the administrative measure affects the claimant's rights, that is to say, his individual public law rights. * * *

31. The referring court finds [that relevant German] anti-pollution law * * * concerns the general public and not the protection of individual rights. * * *

33. Since [the referring court] considers that such a restriction on access to justice could nevertheless undermine the useful effect of Directive 85/337, the referring court wonders whether the action brought by Friends of the Earth ought not to be allowed on the basis of Article 10a of that directive.

[The German court referred three detailed questions to the European Court of Justice, the first two of which are summarized in paragraph 35.]

Questions 1 and 2

35. By its first two questions, which it is appropriate to examine together, the referring court asks essentially whether Article 10a of Directive 85/337 precludes legislation which does not permit non-governmental organisations promoting environmental protection, as referred to in Article 1(2) of Directive 85/337 ("environmental protection organizations"), to rely before the courts, in an action contesting a decision authorising projects likely to have "significant effects on the environment" for the purposes of Article 1(1) of Directive 85/337, on the

infringement of a rule which protects only the interests of the general public and not the interests of individuals. * * *

37. [T]he first paragraph of Article 10a of Directive 85/337 provides that the decisions, acts or omissions referred to in that article must be actionable before a court of law through a review procedure "to challenge [their] substantive or procedural legality," without in any way limiting the pleas that could be put forward in support of such an action.

38. With regard to the conditions for the admissibility of such actions, Article 10a of Directive 85/337 provides for two possibilities: the admissibility of an action may be conditional on "a sufficient interest in bringing the action" or on the applicant alleging "the impairment of a right," depending on which of those conditions is adopted in the national legislation. * * *

42. [W]hichever option a Member State chooses for the admissibility of an action, environmental protection organisations are entitled, pursuant to Article 10a of Directive 85/337, to have access to a review procedure before a court of law or another independent and impartial body established by law, to challenge the substantive or procedural legality of decisions, acts or omissions covered by that article.

43. [W]here * * * Member State[s] lay down the detailed procedural rules governing actions for safeguarding rights which individuals derive from EU law, those detailed rules must not be less favourable than those governing similar domestic actions (principle of equivalence) and must not make it in practice impossible or excessively difficult to exercise rights conferred by EU law (principle of effectiveness). * * *

46. If, as is clear from [Article 10a of Directive 85/337, non-governmental] organisations must be able to rely on the same rights as individuals, it would be contrary to the objective of giving the public concerned wide access to justice and at odds with the principle of effectiveness if such organisations were not also allowed to rely on the impairment of rules of EU environment law solely on the ground that those rules protect the public interest. As the dispute in the main proceedings shows, that very largely deprives those organisations of the possibility of verifying compliance with the rules of that branch of law, which, for the most part, address the public interest and not merely the protection of the interests of individuals as such.

47. It follows first that the concept of "impairment of a right" cannot depend on conditions which only other physical or legal persons can fulfil, such as the condition of being a more or less close neighbour of an installation or of suffering in one way or another the effects of the installation's operation.

48. * * * Article 10a of Directive 85/337 must be read as meaning that the "rights capable of being impaired" which the environmental

protection organisations are supposed to enjoy must necessarily include the rules of national law implementing EU environment law and the rules of EU environment law having direct effect.

49. [A] plea raised against a contested decision which alleges infringement of the rules of national law flowing from Article 6 of the Habitats Directive must be capable of being relied on by an environmental protection organisation.

NOTES AND QUESTIONS

1. *NGOs and International Law Litigation.* What role should international law play in authorizing NGOs to participate in litigation concerning the environment or human rights? The *Friends of the Earth Case* concerned one such initiative: the Convention on Access to Information, Public Participation in Decision-making and Access to Justice in Environmental Matters (the Aarhus Convention), June 25, 1998, 2161 U.N.T.S. 447. The Convention, negotiated within the United Nations Economic Commission for Europe, entered into force on October 30, 2001, and as of December 2013 numbered 46 parties. Core principles of the Aarhus Convention include citizen access to environmental information, public participation in environmental decision making, and access to judicial or administrative procedures to promote adherence to environmental law and the Convention's principles. See Vera Rodenhoff, "The Aarhus Convention and its Implications for the 'Institutions' of the European Community," 11 *Review of European Community and International Environmental Law* 343 (2002); and generally Philippe J. Sands, "The Environment, Community and International Law," 30 *Harvard International Law Journal* 393 (1988). Pursuant to the *Friends of the Earth Case*, the German Parliament amended German law, giving effect to the judgment. See John Blain & Sharon Long, "Standing of Environmental NGOs: New Measures to Fast-track Proceedings," *Lexology*, Mar. 5, 2013, *available at* http://www.lexology.com/library/detail.aspx?g=aa288c7e-41a6-480c-b413-aba68ddfdfcf (last visited Dec. 9, 2013).

What was the jurisdiction of the European Court of Justice to hear the *Friends of the Earth Case*? Should this sort of referral jurisdiction be employed more widely to help promote national compliance with international law? Should the International Court of Justice have referral jurisdiction or a broader scope of advisory jurisdiction? See the discussion of this issue in Note 6 at the end of Chapter 5.

Should NGOs be able to participate directly in international law cases brought before international tribunals concerning international environmental or human rights law? For a review of practice concerning NGO participation in international environmental litigation, see Tim Stephens, *International Courts and Environmental Protection* 252–64 (2009). Stephens noted "a host of political impediments in commencing environmental litigation in the community interest." Although efforts by non-state actors to gain access to international litigation "have begun to yield results," these results "have been relatively modest in comparison with gains in environmental diplomacy generally, where civil society groups have become active and valued participants." *Id.* at 269–70.

Even without the impetus of a treaty such as the Aarhus Convention, municipal legal rules sometimes allow non-governmental organizations to participate in litigation. For example, Amnesty International was allowed to intervene in a case before the British House of Lords, in support of Spain's effort to extradite Chile's former dictator, General Augusto Pinochet, in order to prosecute him for human rights offenses. The House of Lords' 1998 decision denying Pinochet immunity with respect to alleged instances of torture and hostage-taking was, however, set aside when it was discovered that one of the Law Lords sitting on the case had links to Amnesty International (as chair and a director of a separate organization, Amnesty International Charity Limited). Following hearings before a new panel of judges, the House of Lords ruled that Pinochet could be extradited to Spain. Although the British government released him on medical grounds, he faced trial in Chile following his return there. See William J. Aceves, "Liberalism and International Legal Scholarship: The Pinochet Case and the Move Toward a Universal System of Transnational Law Litigation," 41 *Harvard Journal of International Law* 129 (2000). Human rights NGOs also participate in cases in municipal courts in which international human rights law is litigated by filing *amicus curiae* briefs, which courts sometimes cite in their judgments. See, *e.g.*, Ma v. Reno, 208 F.3d 815, 829–30 (9th Cir. 2000).

2. *The Contributions of NGOs to International Law.* By gathering facts, lobbying, and providing technical expertise, NGOs contribute to the development and implementation of treaties and other international legal norms, to the work of international organizations, and to the international legal activities of national governments. See Steve Charnovitz, "Two Centuries of Participation: NGOs and International Governance," 18 *Michigan Journal of International Law* 183 (1997). Treaties occasionally specify a direct role for NGOs in international organizations. For example, the Constitution of the International Labor Organization, established in 1919, provides for direct NGO participation. Each ILO member state is represented in the ILO's plenary body by two representatives from government, one representative from management, and one from labor. For the United States, the United States Council for International Business represents employers, and the AFL–CIO represents workers. Does this tripartite ILO structure help achieve consensus positions? See Recommendation and Report on the International Labor Organization, in *The United Nations at 50: Proposals for Improving Its Effectiveness* 107 (John E. Noyes ed. 1997). International organizations may also allow non-governmental organizations to participate in their work even absent explicit "constitutional" authorization. The International Atomic Energy Agency (IAEA), a U.N. specialized agency created in 1957, has long accorded consultative status to NGOs with "special competence in the field," allowing those NGOs to observe meetings, submit certain statements, and gain access

to some IAEA documents. See IAEA, Rules on Consultative Status of Non-governmental Organizations with the Agency, IAEA Doc. INFCIRC/14 (1959); Sheel Kant Sharma, "The IAEA and the UN Family: Networks of Nuclear Co-operation," *IAEA Bulletin*, No. 373 (1995), *available at* http://www.iaea.org/Publications/Magazines/Bulletin/Bull373/sharma.html (last visited Dec. 9, 2013).

3. *Accountability and Recognition of NGOs*. It is sometimes easy to form an NGO, a step typically accomplished by satisfying a state's requirements for forming a not-for-profit entity. A small group of individuals may make decisions on behalf of an NGO. Will an NGO be accountable to its membership? Are NGOs more or less accountable than states? Should NGOs be externally accountable to other international actors for their roles in international systems? See the essays by Paul Wapner, Peter J. Spiro, Debora Spar and James Dail, and Benedict Kingsbury in Vol. 3, No. 1 of the *Chicago Journal of International Law* (2002), and Kenneth Anderson, "Review Essay: What NGO Accountability Means—and Does Not Mean," 103 *American Journal of International Law* 170 (2009) (reviewing *NGO Accountability: Politics, Principles & Innovations* (Lisa Jordan & Peter van Tuijl eds. 2006)). Are concerns about input from members, the accuracy and impartiality of positions espoused, and transparency in decision making assuaged if there is competition from other groups and individuals? Are such concerns adequately addressed if an NGO is "recognized" by an international legal person with which it deals?

The U.N. Economic and Social Council, acting pursuant to Article 71 of the U.N. Charter, has adopted criteria for establishing consultative relationships with NGOs. ECOSOC Res. 1996/31. These provide that an NGO must focus on matters within ECOSOC's competence, have purposes in conformity with the U.N. Charter, and disclose its sources of revenue to ECOSOC. Furthermore:

> The organization shall be of recognized standing within the particular field of its competence or of a representative character. Where there exist a number of organizations with similar objectives, interests and basic views in a given field, they may, for the purposes of consultation with the Council, form a joint committee or other body authorized to carry on such consultation for the group as a whole.
>
> The organization * * * shall have a democratically adopted constitution, * * * which shall provide for the determination of policy by a conference, congress or other representative body, and for an executive organ responsible to the policy-making body. * * *
>
> The organization shall have a representative structure and possess appropriate mechanisms of accountability to its members, who shall exercise effective control over its policies and actions through the exercise of voting rights or other appropriate democratic and transparent decision-making processes.

Id. ¶¶ 9–10, 12. Consultative status with ECOSOC will be suspended or withdrawn:

> (a) If an organization, either directly or through its affiliates or representatives acting on its behalf, clearly abuses its status by engaging in a pattern of acts contrary to the purposes and principles of the Charter of the United Nations including unsubstantiated or politically motivated acts against Member States of the United Nations incompatible with those purposes and principles;
>
> (b) If there exists substantiated evidence of influence from proceeds resulting from internationally recognized criminal activities such as the illicit drugs trade, money-laundering or the illegal arms trade;
>
> (c) If, within the preceding three years, an organization did not make any positive or effective contribution to the work of the United Nations and, in particular, of the Council or its commissions or other subsidiary organs.

Id. ¶ 57. As of September 2013, over 3,700 NGOs had entered into consultative status with ECOSOC. See the website of the NGO Branch of the U.N. Department of Economic and Social Affairs at http://www.csonet.org (last visited Dec. 9, 2013).

4. *Global Civil Society.* How should the activities of NGOs be taken into account in international law and legal process? Do NGOs contribute to the development of a global or world civil society, a concept competing with a state-centric view of international law and relations? Professor Christenson defined global civil society as comprising "individuals and groups in voluntary association without regard to their identities as citizens of any particular country, and outside the political and public dominion of the community of nations." Gordon A. Christenson, "World Civil Society and the International Rule of Law," 19 *Human Rights Quarterly* 724, 731 (1997). Do the media, academia, and transnational corporations also contribute to an emerging global civil society? See *Our Global Neighborhood: The Report of the Commission on Global Governance* (1995). It has been suggested that the origins of the concept of global civil society may be found in the American missionary movement of the 19th century. Walter Russell Mead, *Special Providence: American Foreign Policy and How It Changed the World* 145–46 (2001).

NGOs, interacting with each other and with other entities, form networks of advocacy groups. As noted in Chapter 6, NGOs collaborated to promote the International Criminal Court. Networking has been aided by developments in information technology. Web sites facilitate communication and cooperative endeavors, especially with respect to human rights and environmental issues. See, *e.g.*, http://www.derechos.net (last visited Dec. 9, 2013). For thoughtful discussions of advocacy networks and the governance contributions of NGOs, see Ann Florini, *The Coming Democracy* (2003); Margaret E. Keck & Kathryn Sikkink, *Activists Beyond Borders* (1998); Julie

Mertus, "Considering Nonstate Actors in the New Millenium: Toward Expanded Participation in Norm Generation and Norm Application," 32 *New York University Journal of International Law and Politics* 537 (2000). For proposals to improve interactions between NGOs and the United Nations, see *We the Peoples: Civil Society, the United Nations and Global Governance*, U.N. Doc. A/58/817 (2004) (Report of the Panel of Eminent Persons on United Nations-Civil Society Relations).

C. TREATY REGIMES

International lawyers and international relations theorists sometimes refer to "regimes" when discussing formal and informal international political arrangements. According to one international relations definition, regimes are

> sets of implicit principles, norms, rules and decision-making procedures around which actors' expectations converge in a given area of international relations. Principles are beliefs of fact, causation and rectitude. Norms are standards of behavior defined in terms of rights and obligations. Rules are specific prescriptions or proscriptions for action. Decision-making procedures are prevailing practices for making and implementing collective choice.

Stephen D. Krasner, "Structural Causes and Regime Consequences: Regimes as Intervening Variables," in *International Regimes* 1, 2 (Stephen D. Krasner ed. 1983). Under this definition, non-binding soft law declarations—such as the Rio Principles excerpted in Chapter 3—may be elements of regimes. More formal international legal regimes are treaty-based, typically employing both general standards and precise rules. International organizations often play roles in administering international legal regimes. And some regimes provide roles for technical or limited-role "treaty bodies" that do not have international personality. In this part we explore two examples of regimes, governing Antarctica and ozone depletion. As you read these materials, consider how and why these regimes evolved, the roles that international organizations or institutions play in them, and potential alternatives.

1. ANTARCTICA

This section reproduces excerpts from the foundational 1959 Antarctic Treaty, a U.N. General Assembly debate from the 1980s concerning governance of Antarctica, and a recent resolution authorized by the Antarctic Treaty. We close with a Note concerning the "Antarctic Treaty System," which incorporates several additional treaties applicable to activities on the continent and in offshore waters.

THE ANTARCTIC TREATY

Dec. 1, 1959, 12 U.S.T. 794, 402 U.N.T.S. 71

The Governments of Argentina, Australia, Belgium, Chile, the French Republic, Japan, New Zealand, Norway, the Union of South Africa, the Union of Soviet Socialist Republics, the United Kingdom of Great Britain and Northern Ireland, and the United States of America,

Recognizing that it is in the best interest of all mankind that Antarctica shall continue forever to be used exclusively for peaceful purposes and shall not become the scene or object of international discord;

Acknowledging the substantial contributions to scientific knowledge resulting from international cooperation in scientific investigation in Antarctica;

Convinced that the establishment of a firm foundation for the continuation and development of such cooperation on the basis of freedom of scientific investigation in Antarctica as applied during the International Geophysical Year accords with the interests of science and progress of all mankind;

Convinced also that a treaty ensuring the use of Antarctica for peaceful purposes only and the continuance of international harmony in Antarctica will further the purposes and principles embodied in the Charter of the United Nations;

Have agreed as follows:

Article I

1. Antarctica shall be used for peaceful purposes only. There shall be prohibited, *inter alia*, any measures of a military nature, such as the establishment of military bases and fortifications, the carrying out of military maneuvers, as well as the testing of any type of weapons.

2. The present Treaty shall not prevent the use of military personnel or equipment for scientific research or for any other peaceful purpose.

Article II

Freedom of scientific investigation in Antarctica and cooperation toward that end, as applied during the International Geophysical Year, shall continue, subject to the provisions of the present Treaty.

Article III

1. In order to promote international cooperation in scientific investigation in Antarctica, as provided for in Article II of the present Treaty, the Contracting Parties agree that, to the greatest extent feasible and practicable:

(a) information regarding plans for scientific programs in Antarctica shall be exchanged to permit maximum economy and efficiency of operations;

(b) scientific personnel shall be exchanged in Antarctica between expeditions and stations;

(c) scientific observations and results from Antarctica shall be exchanged and made freely available.

2. In implementing this Article, every encouragement shall be given to the establishment of cooperative working relations with those Specialized Agencies of the United Nations and other international organizations having a scientific or technical interest in Antarctica.

Article IV

1. Nothing contained in the present Treaty shall be interpreted as:

(a) a renunciation by any Contracting Party of previously asserted rights of or claims to territorial sovereignty in Antarctica;

(b) a renunciation or diminution by any Contracting Party of any basis of claim to territorial sovereignty in Antarctica which it may have whether as a result of its activities or those of its nationals in Antarctica, or otherwise;

(c) prejudicing the position of any Contracting Party as regards its recognition or nonrecognition of any other State's right of or claim or basis of claim to territorial sovereignty in Antarctica.

2. No acts or activities taking place while the present Treaty is in force shall constitute a basis for asserting, supporting or denying a claim to territorial sovereignty in Antarctica or create any rights of sovereignty in Antarctica. No new claim, or enlargement of an existing claim, to territorial sovereignty in Antarctica shall be asserted while the present Treaty is in force.

Article V

1. Any nuclear explosions in Antarctica and the disposal there of radioactive waste material shall be prohibited.

2. In the event of the conclusion of international agreements concerning the use of nuclear energy, including nuclear explosions and the disposal of radioactive waste material, to which all of the Contracting Parties whose representatives are entitled to participate in the meetings provided for under Article IX are parties, the rules established under such agreements shall apply in Antarctica.

Article VI

The provisions of the present Treaty shall apply to the area south of 60° South Latitude, including all ice shelves, but nothing in the present Treaty shall prejudice or in any way affect the rights, or the exercise of the rights, of any State under international law with regard to the high seas within that area.

Article VII

1. In order to promote the objectives and ensure the observance of the provisions of the present Treaty, each Contracting Party whose representatives are entitled to participate in the meetings referred to in Article IX of the Treaty shall have the right to designate observers to carry out any inspection provided for by the present Article. Observers shall be nationals of the Contracting Parties which designate them. The names of observers shall be communicated to every other Contracting Party having the right to designate observers, and like notice shall be given of the termination of their appointment.

2. Each observer designated in accordance with the provisions of paragraph 1 of this Article shall have complete freedom of access at any time to any or all areas of Antarctica.

3. All areas of Antarctica, including all stations, installations and equipment within those areas, and all ships and aircraft at points of discharging or embarking cargoes or personnel in Antarctica, shall be open at all times to inspection by any observers designated in accordance with paragraph 1 of this Article.

4. Aerial observation may be carried out at any time over any or all areas of Antarctica by any of the Contracting Parties having the right to designate observers.

5. Each Contracting Party shall, at the time when the present Treaty enters into force for it, inform the other Contracting Parties, and thereafter shall give them notice in advance, of

(a) all expeditions to and within Antarctica, on the part of its ships or nationals, and all expeditions to Antarctica organized in or proceeding from its territory;

(b) all stations in Antarctica occupied by its nationals; and

(c) any military personnel or equipment intended to be introduced by it into Antarctica subject to the conditions prescribed in paragraph 2 of Article I of the present Treaty. * * *

Article IX

1. Representatives of the Contracting Parties named in the preamble to the present Treaty shall meet at the City of Canberra within two months after the date of entry into force of the Treaty, and thereafter at

suitable intervals and places, for the purpose of exchanging information, consulting together on matters of common interest pertaining to Antarctica, and formulating and considering, and recommending to their Governments, measures in furtherance of the principles and objectives of the Treaty, including measures regarding:

(a) use of Antarctica for peaceful purposes only;

(b) facilitation of scientific research in Antarctica;

(c) facilitation of international scientific cooperation in Antarctica;

(d) facilitation of the exercise of the rights of inspection provided for in Article VII of the Treaty;

(e) questions relating to the exercise of jurisdiction in Antarctica;

(f) preservation and conservation of living resources in Antarctica.

2. Each Contracting Party which has become a party to the present Treaty by accession under Article XIII shall be entitled to appoint representatives to participate in the meetings referred to in paragraph 1 of the present Article, during such time as that Contracting Party demonstrates its interest in Antarctica by conducting substantial scientific research activity there, such as the establishment of a scientific station or the despatch of a scientific expedition.

3. Reports from the observers referred to in Article VII of the present Treaty shall be transmitted to the representatives of the Contracting Parties participating in the meetings referred to in paragraph 1 of the present Article.

4. The measures referred to in paragraph 1 of this Article shall become effective when approved by all the Contracting Parties whose representatives were entitled to participate in the meetings held to consider those measures. * * *

Article X

Each of the Contracting Parties undertakes to exert appropriate efforts, consistent with the Charter of the United Nations, to the end that no one engages in any activity in Antarctica contrary to the principles or purposes of the present Treaty.

Article XI

1. If any dispute arises between two or more of the Contracting Parties concerning the interpretation or application of the present Treaty, those Contracting Parties shall consult among themselves with a view to having the dispute resolved by negotiation, inquiry, mediation,

conciliation, arbitration, judicial settlement or other peaceful means of their own choice.

2. Any dispute of this character not so resolved shall, with the consent, in each case, of all parties to the dispute, be referred to the International Court of Justice for settlement; but failure to reach agreement on reference to the International Court shall not absolve parties to the dispute from the responsibility of continuing to seek to resolve it by any of the various peaceful means referred to in paragraph 1 of this Article. * * *

NOTES AND QUESTIONS

1. *Acquisition of Territory*. One generally accepted way for states to acquire new territory is by discovery and occupation of *terra nullius*, a label used to describe uninhabited territory such as Antarctica. Jurists in the early 20th century argued that discovery alone provided only an "inchoate" title, which in order to become effective against other states had to be followed by occupation and concrete acts exercising authority. See, *e.g.*, T.J. Lawrence, *The Principles of International Law* § 74 (1915). However, in the 19th and early 20th centuries, European explorers, engaged in surveying and conducting scientific investigations, laid claim to parts of Antarctica on behalf of their states, without establishing permanent settlements in that harsh environment. For example, in 1929 Great Britain's King George commissioned explorer Douglas Mawson to lead an expedition to Antarctica, "plant the British flag wherever * * * practicable to do so, * * * read the proclamation of annexation[,] attach a copy of the proclamation to the flagstaff, and place a second copy of the proclamation in a tin at the foot of the flagstaff." *Reprinted in* A. Grenfell Price, *The Winning of Australian Antarctica: Mawson's B.A.N.Z.A.R.E. Voyages 1929–31*, at 22–24 (1962). In light of the practical difficulties of establishing permanent settlements in Antarctica, should discovery alone have sufficed to establish state sovereignty?

More controversial than discovery plus effective occupation as grounds for asserting sovereignty over portions of Antarctica are the contiguity theory, propounded by several states geographically close to Antarctica, and the sector theory. Under the sector theory, Antarctic territorial boundaries ought to correspond to longitudinal lines that converge on the South Pole. The longitudinal lines either are extensions of the mainland boundaries of a nearby claimant state, or are drawn from the ends of a stretch of coast claimed by the state.

By the 1950s, Argentina, Australia, Chile, France, New Zealand, Norway, and the United Kingdom exercised or claimed territorial sovereignty over "pie slice" sectors of Antarctica that meet at the South Pole. The United States and the Soviet Union made no claims to territory in Antarctica but reserved their right to assert claims in the future. These "nonclaimant states" also refused to recognize the territorial claims of other states. As shown in Figure 8.A, one area of Antarctica remains unclaimed. For more about international law and the acquisition of territory, see the *Minquiers and Echrehos Case* and its accompanying Notes in Chapter 5.

2. *Disputed Claims, the International Geophysical Year, and the Antarctic Treaty.* After laying claim to portions of Antarctica, governments occasionally debated the nature and validity of their asserted sovereignty. For example, the British ambassador in Washington and the U.S. Secretary of State exchanged diplomatic notes on the issue in 1934 and 1935. 1 Hackworth, *Digest of International Law* 457–59 (1940). Initially, Britain expressed concern about U.S. airplane flights over, and the establishment of a wireless station and postal facilities in, the Ross Dependency, now an area of Antarctica claimed by New Zealand. If the United States were to establish a post office in this area or to sanction the use of U.S. postage stamps there without permission, the British ambassador claimed, "such acts could not be regarded otherwise than as infringing the British sovereignty." The United States responded that discovery—the basis of the British Antarctic claim—could not, "unaccompanied by occupancy and use," lead to sovereignty. The British replied that they had no objection to a U.S. expedition to the Antarctic and its associated commemorative postal activities. The United States in turn noted the British reply and stated that it "reserves all rights which this country or its citizens may have with respect to the matter." Was this diplomatic exchange part of the claim-counterclaim process used in the formation of customary international law we studied in Chapter 3?

Some disputes over territory in Antarctica led to tense incidents. The claims of Argentina, Chile, and the United Kingdom overlap, and in the areas of overlap there were occasional displays of naval power and even the firing of shots by military personnel. For discussion about claims to Antarctica before the Antarctic Treaty, and conflicts and diplomatic maneuvers concerning those claims, see David Day, *Antarctica: A Biography* (2013).

The 1957 International Geophysical Year (IGY), a cooperative effort of 66 states including all the major powers except the People's Republic of China, provided impetus for the Antarctic Treaty. IGY scientists allocated scientific stations in Antarctica to states and arranged cooperative ventures concerning mapping, collection of weather data, and exchanges of scientific personnel. The entry of the Soviet Union into Antarctic activities beginning in 1955 contributed to an international arrangement for Antarctica that helped preserve the continent as a laboratory for cooperative scientific research and as a region to be used only for peaceful purposes. Following the IGY, representatives of the 12 states active in the Antarctic work of the IGY met regularly in Washington, D.C., for preparatory treaty talks and a formal negotiating conference. The Antarctic Treaty was signed on December 1, 1959, and entered into force June 23, 1961. See Christopher C. Joyner, "U.S.-Soviet Cooperative Diplomacy: The Case of Antarctica," in *U.S.-Soviet Cooperation* 39 (Nish Jamgotch ed. 1989); Walter Sullivan, "Antarctica," in *The International Geophysical Year* 318 (International Conciliation No. 521, Jan. 1959). The Treaty helped stabilize the situation on the continent, providing the foundation of the Antarctic regime. According to the Treaty, what principles underlie this regime?

Figure 8.A

Map of National Claims in Antarctica

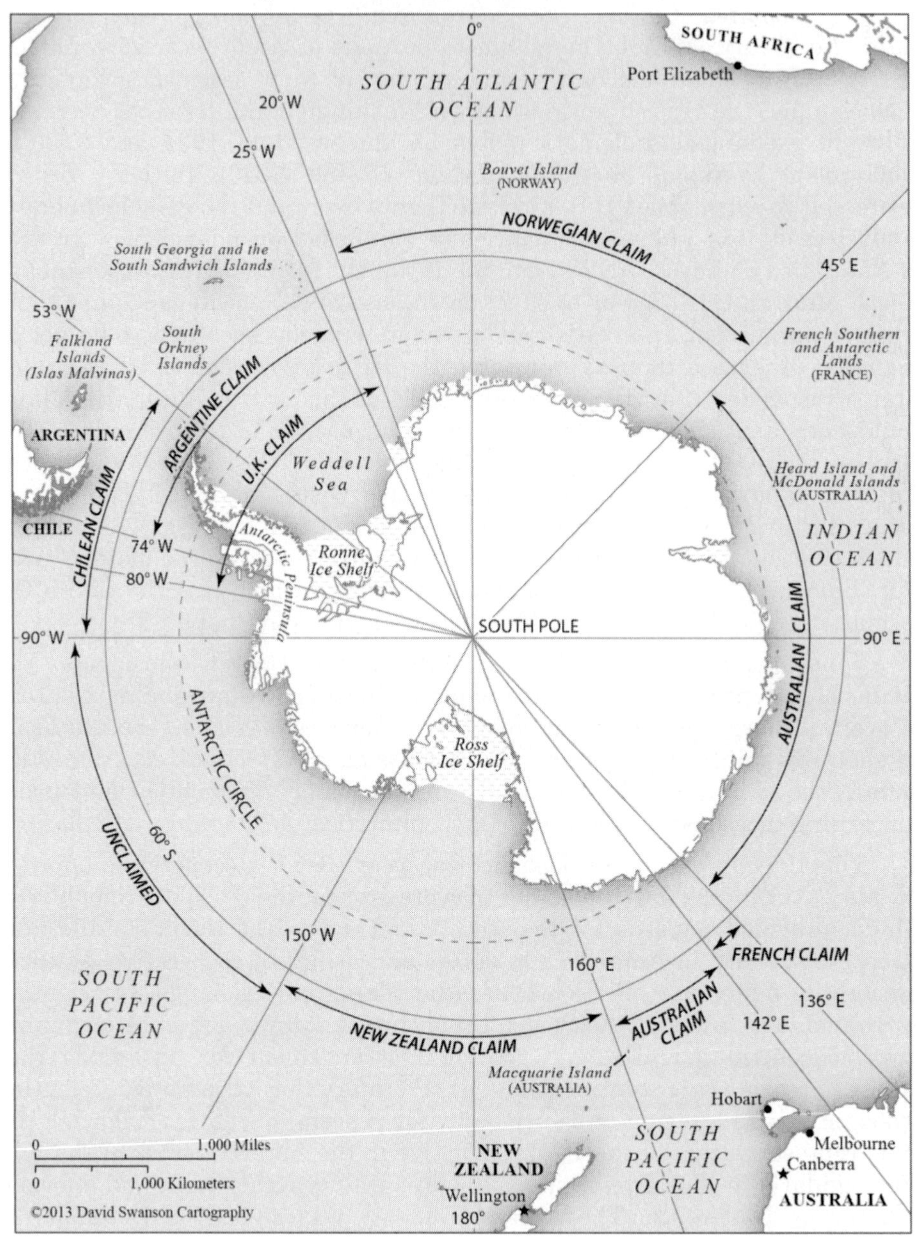

3. *Freezing Territorial Claims.* One core principle is set forth in Article IV, which "freezes" territorial and sovereignty claims. Why have states found this arrangement acceptable? What problems might be anticipated as time goes on?

4. *Effect on Nonparties.* Does the Antarctic Treaty create legal obligations for nonparties? Would such obligations be *erga omnes*? See Chapter 3 and the *Reparation Case* in Part A of this chapter. What would be the reaction if a nonparty to the Antarctic Treaty were to claim sovereignty over the "unclaimed sector" or some other portion of Antarctica? To dispose of radioactive waste anywhere on the continent? See Article X of the Treaty.

5. *Classes of Parties to the Antarctic Treaty.* The Antarctic Treaty distinguishes between Consultative Parties and other parties. The 12 original parties to the Antarctic Treaty joined as Consultative Parties, entitled to decision-making roles in periodic international meetings. As of December 2013, 50 states were parties to the Antarctic Treaty, but only 28 of them were Consultative Parties. What justifies the Treaty's two-tiered system? Among the Consultative Parties, should some special status be accorded those states that have asserted territorial claims? The following excerpt addresses some of these concerns.

UNITED NATIONS GENERAL ASSEMBLY DEBATES ON ANTARCTICA

A/C.1/38/PV.42 (1983), Thirty-Eighth Session, First Committee, Summary Record of the 42nd Meeting, Nov. 28, 1983; A/C.1/38/PV.44 (1983), Thirty-Eighth Session, First Committee, Summary Record of the 44th Meeting, Nov. 29, 1983; A/C.1/38/PV.5(1984), Thirty-Eighth Session, First Committee, Verbatim Record of the 45thMeeting, Nov. 30, 1983; A/C.1/39/PV.54 (1984), Thirty-Ninth Session, First Committee, Verbatim Record of the 54th Meeting, Nov. 30, 1984

MR. ZAINAL ABIDIN (Malaysia)

* * * The [Antarctic] Treaty at its inception could have been considered as an unusually enlightened experiment in international co-operation.

In our view, however, the Treaty and its system have become mired in the obsession to maintain a *status quo* régime advantageous to the privileged few. * * * My delegation would like to draw the attention of the Committee to two crucial areas in which the Treaty has not kept pace with current international reality.

My delegation would like first to address the obvious structural flaw inherent in the Treaty system. The Treaty provides for a two-tier membership structure, characterized by gross inequality. This is evident from the relevant Treaty articles pertaining to membership [Articles XIII(1) and IX(2)]. * * *

This means that while every State is welcome and encouraged to accede to the Treaty only the original 12 can participate in decision-making, along with such other States as, in the unanimous judgement of the original Contracting Parties, have demonstrated significant interest in Antarctica by conducting substantial scientific research activity there. Thus, a State acceding to the Treaty formalizes its willingness to abide by the Treaty provisions without any role to play whatsoever, as voting and regulatory control are reserved for the full—or "consultative"—members only. States are, in actual fact, called upon to accede to the Treaty without any right to participate in the decision-making process. It is clear that this undemocratic arrangement which the Treaty perpetuates goes against the grain of current international reality. Most States would find accession without representation extremely difficult to accept, while the representation requirement of a significant capacity for research would be beyond their means. They are thus effectively frozen out of meaningful participation in the Antarctic Treaty system.

The second major flaw of the Treaty system, in the view of my delegation, pertains to the limitations on its efficacy. The Treaty purports to be an international régime that serves the interests of all mankind, yet it benefits only the few. [Despite Article III(2) of the Antarctic Treaty, which encourages cooperative working relations with international organizations,] the Consultative Parties have actually rejected co-operation with the Food and Agriculture Organization of the United Nations (FAO), the United Nations Environment Programme (UNEP), the Committee on Natural Resources and other international organizations. Furthermore, the * * * flow of information about Antarctica * * * is very much limited to the Consultative Parties and is not even made available to ordinary parties of the Treaty, let alone the international community at large.

The efficacy of the Treaty system is especially questionable with regard to environmental and ecological management. [T]o forestall any destruction of Antarctica's invaluable and irreplaceable endowments, environmentalists world-wide have advocated the designation of Antarctica as a world park. [Because international non-governmental organizations are denied access,] even as observers, to ATCP [Antarctic Treaty Consultative Party] meetings[,] the world community is entitled to entertain serious doubts on the effective management of Antarctica's present and future environment, especially as the Treaty system lacks a centralized environmental review body and enforcement is left to individual States. * * *

We note that several closed-door meetings have been held to devise a new and exclusive minerals régime in Antarctica among the few parties enjoying consultative status within the Antarctic Treaty framework.

[S]afeguarding of the interests of all mankind * * * requires the creation of international mechanisms that are not only truly representative in membership but also truly committed to serving all of its constituents. The philosophy that guides those mechanisms must be such as to command unquestioned moral authority amongst the nations of the world. In this respect the concepts of common benefit and common heritage come to mind.

The common heritage approach * * * should be considered in a future international design for Antarctica. The elements of the common heritage concept—peaceful use, non-appropriation, preservation for future generations, including environmental protection and conservation of resources, international management and benefit-sharing—are of great relevance to Antarctica. * * *

In conclusion, may I be permitted to sum up the conviction of my delegation as follows. First, the world is in a process of evolution and there is an urgent need for all to display the necessary political will to make adaptations and adjustments to rapidly changing circumstances in order to build a structure of international peace and a just international order.

Secondly, the world of 1959, when the Antarctic Treaty was first formulated, is different from that of 1983. There are now 158 States Members of the United Nations, most of which are categorized as developing countries. Their rights, interests, aspirations and, not least, their views have to be accommodated by any purportedly international régime on Antarctica.

Thirdly, there is a growing and an inexorable demand by this articulate and growing majority for greater involvement in international decision-making. No longer can a handful of countries arrogate unto themselves the prerogative of representing humanity in matters of common concern when the majority of humanity is not directly involved.

Fourthly, the movement for a just and a balanced world order for the cause of mankind is irresistible. Significant areas of the world beyond national jurisdiction, and the celestial bodies in outer space, must be viewed in the context of the common heritage of mankind, and for the benefit of mankind as a whole.

And, fifth, Antarctica constitutes one such significant and vital area, because what happens in this region will have a direct effect on the rest of the world. * * * It is time that a proper and representative international régime beyond the Antarctic Treaty be explored within the framework of the United Nations.

MR. HEAP (United Kingdom)

[T]he Antarctic Treaty system was an exercise in prudent forethought. [A] number of notable "firsts" * * * have been achieved by agreement between States within the Treaty system. The Antarctic Treaty was the first international agreement to demilitarize a whole continent, to provide for on-site inspection of all activities on a continent, to outlaw nuclear explosions or the dumping of radioactive waste, to ensure freedom of scientific investigation and require that the results be freely available and to set aside, in favour of co-operation, conflicting views about the legal basis which should underlie the management of affairs over a whole continent.

[T]hese firsts * * * are totally consistent with the Charter of the United Nations.

Since the Antarctic Treaty came into force in 1961 the development of a large number of agreements through its consultative mechanism has given rise to a number of other "firsts," among which are: the Agreed Measures for the Conservation of Antarctic Fauna and Flora, the first international agreement to prohibit the killing of any native mammal or native bird in Antarctica without a permit and to arrange for details on the permits issued to be internationally exchanged; the Convention for the Conservation of Antarctic Seals, the first and, I believe, so far the only international agreement to regulate the utilization of a living resource before any industry has developed to exploit it; the Convention for the Conservation of Antarctic Marine Living Resources, the first international agreement to require that regulation of the utilization of target species shall have regard to the effect that utilization has on the ecosystem as a whole. More generally, certain pioneering recommendations of the Treaty's consultative procedures require that the first consideration to be applied to a new activity in Antarctica is not whether it is profitable or in the interests of one or more Governments. Instead, prior consideration has to be given to whether or not it will have adverse effects on the Antarctic environment. This test, itself a notable first, is unparalleled anywhere else in the world.

[A]ll these "firsts," and note especially those measures taken to protect Antarctic marine living resources, are in marked contrast to what happened before the Treaty system came into being. * * *

None of these "firsts" give substantive rights to the parties to the agreements. They all circumscribe the freedom of action of all parties. Overwhelmingly, they consist of obligations and not of rights. This record of achievement should go far to put right the misconception that the Antarctic Treaty Consultative Parties are carving up Antarctica for their own benefit.

MR. WOOLCOTT (Australia)

* * * There seems to be a desire, at least on the part of some delegations, to have Antarctic resources, whatever these are or may be, declared the common heritage of mankind, like those of outer space and the deep sea-bed, beyond national jurisdiction. Australia is, of course, in favour of this principle in the Law-of-the-Sea context, but we do not

consider it relevant or appropriate in Antarctica. First, for Australia and six other countries that maintain national territorial claims and, let me add, national settlements, Antarctica is not beyond national jurisdiction. Antarctica has instead been the subject of exploration, settlement and claims to sovereignty by a number of countries over many years. So there can be no international consensus that a common-heritage approach to Antarctica is acceptable.

Secondly, the common-heritage concept embodies a developmental purpose, which is not now, and we hope will never be, dominant in Antarctica, where the environment is, as some of the sponsors of this draft resolution have stressed, extremely vulnerable to the activity of man and must be safeguarded by those pursuing activity there in the interest of all mankind.

* * * The Treaty is not exclusive. Any State may join, and 28 countries with diverse economic and political interests have already done so. In 1983, two new members, China and India, joined the Treaty, and Finland only yesterday signified its intention to do so. * * *

What about the status of Consultative Parties? Claims have been made here which reveal a misunderstanding of the operation of the Treaty. Any State carrying out substantial scientific activities may become a Consultative Party to the Treaty. In 1983 Brazil and India took this step. There are now 16 Treaty members that are also Consultative Parties.

It is not unnatural that those heavily involved in scientific research should wish to consult together and then to make available to the international community the fruits of their consultations.

Claims that the deliberations of the Consultative Parties are conducted in secret and that consultative Parties meet as a cabal to take secret decisions, sometimes contrary to the interest of the acceding parties and the international community are quite simply untrue. Acceding parties, for their own good reasons, have presumably wished to limit their commitment to the Antarctic, short of that implied by consultative status. * * *

Australia, when it determines its approach to a regional question, invariably gives weight to the views of the regional countries closest to, and most directly concerned with, the particular issue under consideration. * * * A glance at the map will show that Antarctica lies to Australia's immediate south. This is the basis of our own clear and legitimate concern that the present satisfactory situation there should not be disturbed. * * *

In current international circumstances it would simply, in the view of my delegation, not be realistic to expect that a new instrument could have the same provisions for total demilitarization of the region, verified by on-site inspection, for the setting aside of potential disputes over territorial sovereignty and for harmonious international co-operation in scientific research and environmental protection. In short, any new instrument would not as effectively protect important international interests in the Antarctic as does the current Treaty, and any attempt to revise this situation would, in our view, risk reopening the very contention and competition which the Treaty was created to do away with.

MR. JESUS (Cape Verde)

* * * During this debate I have not heard anybody question the principles established in the Antarctic Treaty relating to the peaceful use of Antarctica, the preservation of flora, fauna and the environment in general or its declaration as an area free from military activities, or even the freedom of scientific research. In this respect, it seems to my delegation that we are all in agreement with one another. What therefore, we, the majority of members of the international community, are in disagreement with is the fact that a few countries which have consultative status, however powerful they might be, can ascribe to themselves the right to decide what is right or wrong for the whole of mankind.

[O]nly a party to the Treaty which demonstrates its interest in Antarctica by conducting substantial scientific research activity there, such as the establishment of a scientific station or the dispatch of a scientific expedition, is entitled to become a Consultative Party.

In other words, the majority of third world countries, even if they became parties to the Antarctic Treaty, would not be able to participate fully on an equal footing with any other State Consultative Party in establishing the policies for the activities of Antarctica for the simple reason that they cannot afford to send a scientific expedition to Antarctica or to establish a scientific station there. It is evident that the principle of equality of States established in the Charter, upon which the Antarctic Treaty is said to be based, cannot allow that its observance be limited with regard to co-operation on Antarctica merely because of lack of resources of third world countries.

The Antarctic Treaty can become a basis for universal co-operation in Antarctica, subject to the following provisos: the extension of the right of equal treatment to all States parties, irrespective of their conduct of substantial scientific research activity in Antarctica; that in all activities related to Antarctica decisions be taken by all States parties on the basis of one State, one vote; that provision be made to make it plain that Antarctica is free from national appropriation and therefore no territorial claim there should ever be recognized.

NOTES AND QUESTIONS

1. *The Common Heritage Principle.* Mr. Abidin summarized features typically associated with the common heritage principle: "peaceful use, non-appropriation, preservation for future generations, including environmental protection and conservation of resources, international management and benefit-sharing." Should the U.N. General Assembly declare that Antarctica is the "common heritage of mankind"? What would be the legal implications of such a resolution? Would it be effective? Does the *Texaco/Libya Case* in Chapter 3 provide some answers? The common heritage principle is most often associated with the deep seabed mining regime of the seabed beyond the limits of national jurisdiction, a topic we explore in Chapter 10, Part E. For more on this principle, see Kemal Baslar, *The Concept of the Common Heritage of Mankind in International Law* (1998); Christopher C. Joyner, *Governing the Frozen Commons: The Antarctic Regime and Environmental Protection* 250–58 (1998); John E. Noyes, "The Common Heritage of Mankind: Past, Present, and Future," 40 *Denver Journal of International Law and Policy* 447 (2011).

2. *The United Nations and Antarctica.* The issue of U.N. involvement with Antarctica was first posed shortly after World War II. India raised the question again in 1956, and Malaysia brought the issue before the U.N. General Assembly in 1982. In 1989 the General Assembly resolved that regimes to protect the Antarctic environment "must be negotiated with the full participation of all members of the international community," urged bans on prospecting and mining in Antarctica, and asked all members of the international community to ensure that activities in Antarctica "are for the benefit of all mankind." G.A. Res. 44/124, ¶¶ 4–5 (1989) (adopted by a vote of 108 states in favor, 0 opposed, and 6 abstaining). This resolution was one of a series expressing regret that the U.N. Secretary-General had not been invited to Antarctic Treaty Consultative Party (ATCP) meetings, and calling on the Consultative Parties "to invite the Secretary-General or his representative to all meetings." *Id.* ¶ 2. In 1996 the General Assembly welcomed "invitations to the Executive Director of the United Nations Environment Programme to attend Antarctic Treaty Consultative Meetings in order to assist such meetings" and "also the practice whereby the Antarctic Treaty Consultative Parties regularly provide the Secretary-General with information on the consultative meetings and on their activities in Antarctica." G.A. Res. 51/56, ¶¶ 3–4 (1996). But in 2005 Malaysia abandoned its attempt to involve the United Nations more in Antarctic territorial matters. "As a result * * * the Question of Antarctica was made a sleeping beauty on the UN agenda." Marie Jacobsson, "The Antarctic Treaty System: Legal and Environmental Issues—Future Challenges for the Antarctic Treaty System," in *Antarctica: Legal and Environmental Challenges for the Future* 1, 3 (Gillian Triggs & Anna Riddell eds. 2008). What might spur non-ATCP states again to press for alternative governance arrangements for Antarctica? See Peter J. Beck, "The United Nations and Antarctica, 2005: The End of the 'Question of Antarctica'?," 42 *Polar Records* 217 (2006).

3. *NGOs and Antarctica.* What roles may non-governmental organizations usefully play with respect to Antarctica? NGO access to meetings and NGO participation concerning Antarctic issues has increased over the years. One regular and respected NGO observer at ATCP meetings is the Scientific Committee on Antarctic Science. See Richard A. Herr, "The Changing Roles of Non-governmental Organisations in the Antarctic Treaty System," in *Governing the Antarctic: The Effectiveness and Legitimacy of the Antarctic Treaty System* 91 (Olav Schram Stokke & Davor Vidas eds. 1996); Lee Kimball, "The Role of Non-Governmental Organizations in Antarctic Affairs," in *The Antarctic Legal Regime* 32 (Christopher C. Joyner & Sudhir K. Chopra eds. 1988).

GENERAL GUIDELINES FOR VISITORS TO THE ANTARCTIC

Resolution 3 (2011), ATCM XXXIV—CEP XIV, Buenos Aires

The Representatives, * * *

Recommend that:

1. their Governments endorse the annexed General Guidelines for Visitors to the Antarctic;

2. the Guidelines be placed on the website of the Antarctic Treaty Secretariat;

3. their Governments urge all those intending to visit sites in Antarctica to ensure that they are fully conversant with and adhere to the advice in these General Guidelines for Visitors to the Antarctic; and

4. Parties work to make Recommendation XVIII-1 (1994) effective as soon as possible.

NOTES AND QUESTIONS

1. *Governing Antarctica.* How is Antarctica managed under the 1959 Antarctic Treaty? The ATCPs meet each year and, pursuant to Article IX of the Antarctic Treaty, adopt non-binding "resolutions" such as the one reproduced above, "measures" that become legally binding once all the ATCPs approve them in their municipal legal systems, and "decisions" concerning internal organizational matters. (Prior to 1995, resolutions, measures, and decisions were collectively known as recommendations.) In 2012, for example, the ATCPs adopted four decisions, 11 measures concerning Antarctic historic sites and management plans, and 11 resolutions concerning such matters as cooperation in expeditions, vessel safety, and coordination in search and rescue operations, as well as guidelines for visitors. See 1 *Final Report of the Thirty-fifth Antarctic Treaty Consultative Meeting* (2012), *available at* http://www.ats.aq/documents/ATCM35/fr/ATCM35_fr001_e.pdf (last visited Dec. 9, 2013).

Resolution 3 from 2011, reproduced above, contains a two-and-a-half-page appendix with guidelines for visitors, concerning respect for Antarctic animals, vegetation, and historic sites, non-interference with scientific research, waste disposal, safety, and landing and transport requirements. Is Resolution 3 an example of "soft law"? See Chapter 3, Part D. How effective would you expect such a resolution to be? See Kees Bastmeijer and Ricardo Roura, "Recent Development: Regulating Antarctic Tourism and the Precautionary Principle," 98 *American Journal of International Law* 763 (2004).

What laws govern individuals' activities in Antarctica? Article VIII of the Antarctic Treaty suggests a partial answer, providing that, "in respect of" their Antarctic activities, observers and scientific personnel "shall be subject only to the jurisdiction of the Contracting Party of which they are nationals." In Chapter 11 we consider territoriality, nationality, and other bases states rely on to exercise jurisdiction over individuals.

2. *The Antarctic Secretariat.* The Antarctic Treaty is silent about any role for international organizations or institutions. After much debate, the ATCPs decided to form an Antarctic Secretariat to assist with preparing Consultative Meetings, maintaining records, preparing reports, circulating information among the ATCPs, and disseminating information about activities in Antarctica. See ATCP Measure XXVI-1 and Decisions XXVI-1 to 4 (2003); http://www.ats.aq (last visited Dec. 9, 2013). The Secretariat, described as an "organ without a body," Patrizia Vigni, "The Secretariat of the Antarctic Treaty: Achievements and Weaknesses Three Years After its Establishment," in *Antarctia: Legal and Environmental Challenges for the Future* 17, 18 (Gillian Triggs & Anna Riddell eds. 2007), began operating in 2004 and is headquartered in Buenos Aires, Argentina. Why have the ATCPs narrowly circumscribed the activities of the Secretariat, denying this treaty body international personality? Might a stronger institutional structure promote the legitimacy of the international legal system applicable to Antarctica? See Karen Scott, "Institutional Developments Within the Antarctic Treaty System," 52 *International and Comparative Law Quarterly* 473 (2003).

3. *Alternatives for Governing Antarctica.* What are alternatives to the current system or to international administration of Antarctica as a common heritage regime? What would be the advantages and disadvantages of, for example, a territorial regime in which claimant states asserted control over their pie-shaped claims? Of a condominium regime, pursuant to which the Antarctic Treaty parties establish a system of joint sovereignty over the continent? Of turning Antarctica into a "world park"? For an overview of alternatives, see S.K.N. Blay, R.W. Piotrowicz & B.M. Tsamenyi, *Antarctica After 1991: The Legal and Policy Options* 13–19 (1989).

Assuming that no fundamental change is made to the framework established by the Antarctic Treaty, what steps should be taken to respond to increased international interest in Antarctica? As you think about this question, consider additional components of the current "Antarctic Treaty System," which we explore in the following Note.

NOTE: THE ANTARCTIC TREATY SYSTEM

In addition to the 1959 Antarctic Treaty, several other treaties address issues in Antarctica, collectively forming what is known as the Antarctic Treaty System (ATS). Notable environmental instruments include the Agreed Measures for the Conservation of Antarctic Flora and Fauna, June 13, 1964, 17 U.S.T. 991 (now Annex II to the more comprehensive Protocol on Environmental Protection to the Antarctic Treaty (Environment Protocol), Oct. 4, 1991, 30 *International Legal Materials* 1455 (1991)), the Convention for the Conservation of Antarctic Seals, Feb. 11, 1972, 29 U.S.T. 441, 1080 U.N.T.S. 175, and the Convention for the Conservation of Antarctic Marine Living Resources (CCAMLR), May 20, 1980, 33 U.S.T. 3476, 1329 U.N.T.S. 47. These treaties complement the 1959 Antarctic Treaty. Article 4(1) of the Environment Protocol, for example, provides that it "shall supplement the Antarctic Treaty" but "neither modify nor amend" it. According to Article III of CCAMLR, parties "agree that they will not engage in any activities in the Antarctic Treaty area contrary to the principles and purposes of that Treaty and that, in their relations with each other, they are bound by the obligations contained in Article I and V of the Antarctic Treaty." What is the commitment of a state to the ATS if it has accepted the Antarctic Treaty but not related conventions? See Arthur Watts, International Law and the Antarctic Treaty System 293–94 (1992).

Treaties in the ATS reflect the concern of states, scientists, and non-governmental organizations with protecting the fragile Antarctic environment. Antarctica and its seas are home to numerous birds, fish, whales, and seals. Antarctica's environment affects the Earth's ocean circulation and weather patterns. The Antarctic Treaty itself contains several provisions relating to the environment, notably Article V's prohibition on nuclear explosions and the disposal of radioactive waste and Article IX(1)(f)'s call for consultations on the preservation and conservation of living resources. Many of the ATCP resolutions and measures also relate to protection of the environment.

CCAMLR has as its goal a comprehensive management scheme to maintain ecological relationships among all populations of Antarctic living resources. Whereas many fisheries treaties seek to insure the maximum sustainable yield of a particular species, CCAMLR (which applies to birds and other creatures as well as to fish) follows an "ecosystem approach." Under CCAMLR, a Commission composed of Contracting States to the Convention is to gather data, study environmental issues, and formulate and adopt conservation measures "on the basis of the best scientific evidence available." Reviews of how well CCAMLR has protected the environment have been mixed. See Stuart B. Kaye, *International Fisheries Management* 355–460 (2001); Olav Schramm Stokke, "The Effectiveness of CCAMLR," in *Governing the*

Antarctic: The Effectiveness and Legitimacy of the Antarctic Treaty System 120 (Olav Schram Stokke & Davor Vidas eds. 1996). Cutting against the adoption and implementation of strong environmental measures have been the requirement that the CCAMLR Commission act by consensus, the fact that CCAMLR leaves it up to each Contracting State to "take appropriate measures within its competence to ensure compliance," and the possibility that nonparties to CCAMLR may overfish there. States have failed to establish marine protected areas in the Southern Ocean to protect fish species. See "No Deal on Huge Antarctic Marine Reserves," *BBC News*, July 16, 2013, http://www.bbc.co.uk/news/science-environment-23327315 (last visited Dec. 9, 2013).

Faced with new challenges to the Antarctic environment, some states have taken measures to unilaterally protect the area and its fauna, *e.g.*, Australia has enjoined a Japanese company whaling in a whale sanctuary. Does such unilateral action endanger the Antarctic Treaty? See Donald K. Anton, "Environmental Change in Polar Regions: False Sanctuary: The Australian Whale Sanctuary and Long-term Stability in Antarctica," 8 *Sustainable Development Law & Policy*, Spring 2008, at 17; Christopher Joyner, "Challenges to the Antarctic Treaty: Looking Back to See Ahead," 6 *New Zealand Yearbook of International Law* 25, 49–61 (2008). In June 2010, Australia also instituted proceedings against Japan in the International Court of Justice, alleging that Japan's large-scale program of whaling violated its international legal obligations. See ICJ Press Release No. 2010/16. In 2013 the ICJ approved New Zealand's application to intervene in the case. See ICJ Press Release No. 2013/2.

Environmental considerations have also been important in negotiations relating to the use of mineral resources in Antarctica. Between 1982 and 1988—not coincidentally, a period of great interest in Antarctica at the United Nations—the ATCPs negotiated a regime to regulate mineral exploration and exploitation. The product of these negotiations, the Convention on the Regulation of Antarctic Mineral Resource Activities (CRAMRA), June 2, 1988, 27 *International Legal Materials* 859 (1988), called for a regulatory framework to govern minerals activities. It provided for inspection, monitoring, reporting, obligatory dispute settlement, and the suspension of any activities that caused unacceptable damage to the environment. A new international institution, the Antarctic Minerals Resources Commission, was to decide whether to open an area for minerals exploration and development, and any activities were to be overseen by a Regulatory Committee.

In the summer of 1989, however, Australia and France rejected CRAMRA, which did not enter into force. Contributing to the demise of CRAMRA were the efforts of international non-governmental organizations concerned about the environment. They argued the Convention would promote prospecting and eventual exploitation, criticized the fact that enforcement ultimately remained with individual governments, and objected to the structure and powers of some of the proposed new institutions. Sovereignty concerns also undercut support for CRAMRA. Australia feared that agreeing to a treaty-based Antarctica minerals arrangement would be viewed as an admission that Australia's "claim of sovereignty was soft and could be compromised." Furthermore, CRAMRA's failure "to provide any royalties to claimant states for other states' exploration or exploitation activities in claimed sectors * * * could be read as tacit admission that claimant states were willing to give up full administrative control over *their* territory." Christopher C. Joyner, "Antarctic Treaty Diplomacy: Problems, Prospects, and Policy Implications," in *The Diplomatic Record 1989–1990*, at 155, 163 (David D. Newsom ed. 1991).

Following the rejection of CRAMRA, states negotiated the 1991 Madrid Protocol on Environmental Protection. Article 2 of this Environment Protocol designates Antarctica a "natural reserve, devoted to peace and science." According to Articles 7 and 24(2), "[a]ny activity relating to mineral resources, other than scientific research," is prohibited for at least 50 years. The focus of the Protocol is thus on preventing environmental harm by banning mining, rather than, as under CRAMRA, on permitting activities but protecting against harm. The Protocol also created a Committee on Environmental Protection that advises the ATCPs on implementing the Protocol, provides for mandatory dispute settlement, and authorizes any party to inspect, unannounced, any area of the continent. Five detailed Annexes to the Environment Protocol also address other environmental issues: (1) environmental impact assessments must be prepared in advance of almost all activity in Antarctica; (2) the 1964 Agreed Measures for Flora and Fauna is strengthened; (3) the production, storage, and disposal of wastes are regulated, and the introduction of pesticides and other chemicals into Antarctica is prohibited; (4) ship discharges of oil, other noxious substances, garbage, and sewage are regulated according to standards based on the International Convention for the Prevention of Pollution from Ships (MARPOL 73/78); and (5) sites of "outstanding environmental, scientific, historic, aesthetic and/or wilderness values" are protected. The Environment Protocol entered into force in January 1998, following its acceptance by all states that were ATCPs when Protocol negotiations concluded in 1991. The ATCP governments must implement the Protocol in their municipal laws.

It has been difficult to negotiate a treaty on liability for environmental damage in Antarctica. Many issues have proven controversial, including how natural resource damages should be measured, the standard for liability, financial limits on liability, whether damages caused by certain scientific activities or other causes should be excluded from the scope of liability, how response actions should be coordinated and funded, and the shape of a dispute settlement system. Liability arising from environmental emergencies is addressed in the 2005 Annex VI to the Environment Protocol, 45 *International Legal Materials* 5 (2006), which as of December 2013 had not entered into force. Is negotiation of principles of liability intrinsically more difficult than negotiation of a regulatory regime?

New uses of Antarctic resources also pose challenges. Antarctic genetic resources are of both scientific and commercial interest, but the ATS does not directly regulate their bioprospecting. How should Antarctic biodiversity be protected in light of this new interest? How should revenues from any bioprospecting be shared? See Joyner, "Challenges to the Antarctic Treaty," *supra*, at 37–49.

Environmental, mineral, and bioprospecting resource issues lead one to wonder how adaptable the Antarctic legal regime will prove to be. Is it possible to achieve a satisfactory system of environmental protection in Antarctica by leaving so much control with states, some of which claim sovereignty over portions of the continent? Can states effectively regulate the Antarctic environment, mineral resources, and bioprospecting without a significant restructuring of the existing Antarctic Treaty regime?

2. THE OZONE REGIME

Many regulatory regimes address international environmental issues. This section explores the regime designed to limit the production and consumption of chlorofluorocarbons (CFCs) and other ozone-depleting substances. Scientists have concluded that the release of such substances, which were used in refrigerants, air conditioners, aerosol cans, and fire extinguishers, results in the destruction of ozone in the stratosphere. This ozone filters out shortwave ultraviolet radiation; when the amount of ozone diminishes, more ultraviolet radiation reaches the earth. Increased ultraviolet radiation may, among other things, increase the incidence of skin cancer, cause cataracts, suppress the immune system, stunt crop growth, and lead to a drop in the productivity of phytoplankton, an important marine food source. Scientists first postulated the process of ozone depletion in 1974. Losses in the ozone layer over Antarctica were documented in the 1980s, and ozone depletion has affected the middle and high latitudes of both hemispheres as well. As you read the material in this section, ask whether the ozone regime requires universal or near-universal participation to be effective, what techniques promote participation and compliance, and whether international organizations and treaty bodies are essential to the success of this regime.

DAVID D. CARON, "PROTECTION OF THE STRATOSPHERIC OZONE LAYER AND THE STRUCTURE OF INTERNATIONAL ENVIRONMENTAL LAWMAKING"

14 *Hastings International and Comparative Law Review* 755 (1991)

II. STRATOSPHERIC OZONE DEPLETION: THE PROBLEM AND A BRIEF HISTORY OF THE INTERNATIONAL RESPONSE * * *

C. UNEP and the 1985 Vienna Framework Convention

Even as the national debates proceeded, the groundwork for an international approach was laid. The United Nations Environment Programme (UNEP) in 1977 convened a meeting to begin the international process. The meeting resulted in the adoption of the "World Plan of Action on the Ozone Layer" and the establishment of a Global Coordinating Committee on the Ozone Layer.

* * * In 1981 UNEP established an Ad Hoc Working Group of Legal and Technical Experts charged with the task of drafting a framework convention for the protection of the ozone layer. A framework convention is a document that aims not at substantive norms, but rather at establishment of the institutional framework that will result in such norms. [T]he Vienna Conference in March 1985 * * * ultimately adopted a framework convention.

Adoption of the Vienna Convention was bittersweet, however, because several states had sought more from the Conference. * * * Ultimately a compromise was reached in the form of a Resolution of the Conference calling for the states to reassemble for the purpose of concluding a protocol regulating CFCs.

D. A Growing Sense of Urgency and the 1987 Montreal Protocol

Even as work proceeded in anticipation of a second meeting to adopt a protocol, two important trends were occurring. First, a British research group in May 1985 announced that huge losses in Antarctic ozone had occurred in the springs of 1982, 1983, and 1984. By late summer 1985 American satellite measurements, free of certain previous interpretational errors, confirmed the British findings. [T]he Antarctic hole was significant because, even before the scientific community could confirm that chlorine was responsible for the hole, the public had what in it view was tangible and comprehensible evidence that humanity could fundamentally alter the Earth's atmosphere. As the public increasingly voiced its concern, the states participating in the international negotiations became increasingly receptive not only to a ban on aerosol use, but more generally, to across the board phased reductions in CFC and halon consumption and production.

The second trend also facilitated the inclination to adopt across the board phased reductions. Specifically, the major producers of CFCs had come to believe that environmentally safe substitutes for CFCs existed and that it was for each of them in their individual interest to be the first to develop and offer such substitutes. Although it was thought that such substitutes would be several times more expensive than CFCs, it was also thought that there would be a market for them in a world that called for limits on the use of CFCs. Simultaneously, numerous large users of CFCs moved to eliminate their reliance on such substances.

For these reasons, the Montreal meeting was quite different from the one held only two years earlier in Vienna in that virtually all of the interested parties were now in agreement that some amount of phased reductions was appropriate. Thus, even though the final report of the international study of the Antarctic hole was not yet released, a Protocol to the Vienna Convention calling for a 50 percent reduction in the production and consumption of specified CFCs over an approximately ten year period was adopted in Montreal in September 1987.

E. The Antarctic Ozone Hole and the Race to 1990 London Adjustments and Amendments

But even as states adopted the Montreal Protocol in September 1987, two major concerns were present regarding the instrument. First, the startling findings regarding the Antarctic ozone hole, officially confirmed only after the meeting in Montreal, had not been taken fully into account in the Protocol. The negotiators were frustrated by their apparent inability to draft regimes that kept up with the revelations emerging from the scientific community. They had taken a step forward in Montreal, but they felt that they were always two steps behind in their own understanding of the problem, and at least two steps behind in their response to the problem. Thus, there was a widespread feeling that the Protocol was inadequate and would require revision.

Second, the early indications by China and India, representing over one-third of humanity, that they would not become parties to the Protocol because of its failure to provide adequate assistance to developing countries, suggested that the international community might not be sufficiently cohesive to comprehensively regulate the matter. * * * It was apparent that any regime relating to protection of the ozone layer must include highly populated states, whether or not they presently were significant consumers or producers of ozone-depleting substances. This development was particularly important because it marked one of the few times that the industrialized world needed the cooperation and participation of the Third World. This need allowed the Third World to raise development and international equity concerns they believed had been unaddressed for too long.

[P]lanning for * * * adjustment and amendment [of the Montreal Protocol] began almost immediately. The political focus on the global environment in general, and on the protection of the ozone layer in particular, was intense from the 1987 Montreal Conference of Parties to the 1990 London Meeting of the Parties to the Montreal Protocol. Of particular importance at this time, although less publicly dramatic than the Antarctic ozone hole, was the release of a study by the U.S. Environmental Protection Agency asserting that even assuming 100 percent global participation in the Protocol, the presence of chlorine in the stratosphere would, by the year 2075, increase by a factor of three.

Amidst these new revelations, the entry into force of the Montreal Protocol on January 1, 1989, was anticlimactic and hardly noticed. At that time, one nation after another was calling for swifter and deeper cuts in the production and consumption of ozone-depleting substances, and in some cases unilaterally adopting such measures. By the opening of the London Meeting in June 1990, the negotiating parties were in agreement not merely on accelerating the phased reductions, but on phasing out entirely the substances specified by the Montreal Protocol. The primary issue was whether this phaseout should be accomplished by the year 1997 or the year 2000, the latter representing the adjustment ultimately made to the Montreal schedules. Simultaneously, evolving scientific knowledge regarding the threat posed by other substances led to the consensus to amend the Protocol so that it would require phaseouts of other [substances by 2000 or] 2005. Increased understanding that the substitutes thought to exist at the time of the Montreal Protocol might also be ozone-depleting and significant contributors to the greenhouse effect, resulted in the designation of these substitutes as "transitional ozone-depleting substances," and in the conclusion that the transitional substances should be phased out by the year 2040, or, if possible, by the year 2020.

The apparent willingness of nonparticipating countries such as China and India to operate outside of what they perceived to be an unjust regime, was pitted against the reluctance of some developed countries such as the United States, to construct new international structures, to recognize a right of such countries to assistance and technology transfer, and to encourage linkages between participation in regimes like the Protocol and recognition of the special situation of developing countries. This reluctance was particularly strong since, at this same time, the developing world was making analogous demands for a global climate change fund. * * * Ultimately, the London meeting adopted amendments to the Protocol that provided for technology transfer, and established a fund under the supervision of a fourteen member committee drawn from the developed and developing world. At the conclusion of the London Meeting, the representatives of China and India indicated their countries would sign the Protocol in 1992. * * *

III. A RESTATEMENT OF THE REGIME

A. The Organization of the Regime

There are two main strands to the international organizational scheme created by the Vienna Convention and the Montreal Protocol, as amended and adjusted. First, there are state parties (to the Convention, to the Protocol, and to the Protocol as amended) who meet on a regular basis and who in smaller groups meet more regularly for particular tasks. Second, there is a Secretariat which fulfills a number of duties, occasionally through ad hoc working groups, assigned to it by the state parties in the Convention and Protocol.

[O]nly Parties to the Protocol, and not those who are solely members of the Conference of the Parties to the Convention, can vote on amendments to the Protocol. Similarly, membership on the Executive Committee, which is responsible for the Multilateral Fund established by the London Amendments to the Protocol is limited to Parties to the Protocol as amended. * * *

Finally, the organizational structure created by the Convention and Protocol necessarily has extensive relations with two other organizational clusters. First, in order to provide a better foundation for the timely making of policy, there are relations with the public international scientific community (namely, the World Meteorological Organization and the World Health Organization), leading national scientific agencies, and private international scientific organizations. Second, in order to provide financial and technical assistance, there are relations with organizations such as the World Bank.

B. The Lawmaking Process

A number of innovative steps in lawmaking are contained in the Montreal Protocol. * * *

The Protocol anticipates that continued revision may be necessary, and calls for the Parties periodically to assess the adequacy of the measures taken in the Protocol. The Protocol provides that the Parties, on the basis of such an assessment, may decide to adjust the reductions called for in the controlled substances, and if the Parties are unable to reach agreement on such adjustments, two-thirds majority adoption of adjustments shall be binding upon all Parties to the Protocol. Thus, the Parties to the Protocol have limited legislative power in this area with an objector's recourse being withdrawal generally from the Protocol. Some of the actions taken at the London Meeting were adjustments.

In contrast to this legislative-like adjustment process, there is also the more commonly encountered amendment process that becomes binding only upon those states who accept such amendments. In this regard, it is particularly important to see that although the parties may make adjustments to the controlled substances already designated, they cannot use an adjustment to designate a new controlled substance. As a consequence, the actions taken at the London Meeting were in part also amendments. Many of the amendments relate to the creation of a financial mechanism, but many others relate to the addition of new controlled substances. The crucial implication, however, is that since amendments must be consented to in order to have application to any particular party, a confusing array of regimes may arise.

C. The Normative Scheme

1. The Obligation to Phase Out Designated Ozone-Depleting Chemicals

The basic regulatory approach of the Montreal Protocol in 1987 was to require the Parties to the Protocol to reduce their production and consumption of five chlorofluorocarbons * * * and three halons[.] The London Adjustments to the Protocol accelerated this timetable and deepened the cuts by requiring the parties to phase out production and consumption entirely by the year 2000. * * *

The London Amendments to the Protocol added new chemicals to the regulatory scheme[.]

[T]he scheduled reductions, leading ultimately to phaseouts, are expressed in terms of percentages of calculated national levels of consumption and production in either 1986, in the case of the substances originally regulated by the Protocol, or in 1989, for the substances added to the scope of the Protocol by the London Amendments. The national calculated levels are * * * particularly important benchmarks for the purpose of the regulatory scheme. * * * It is up to each state to decide how they will mix reductions of [various groups of ozone-depleting substances] so as to meet any scheduled reduction in the overall calculated level. To avoid false incentives in this scheme the formula for the calculated level places all of the various designated chemicals on the same level by multiplying the amount of each chemical produced, imported, and exported by its "ozone-depleting potential[.]" * * *

The use of national calculated levels is also significant because it inherently gives value to historical usage and avoids the difficult issue of equitably allocating between states a limited resource, the right to emit ozone-depleting substances. Thus, the United States could be viewed as particularly advantaged under the Montreal Protocol since a fifty percent reduction in its production and consumption would still leave it with a disproportionate per capita share of such use. This significance of course diminished greatly when the Protocol was adjusted and amended so as to require phaseouts rather than mere reductions. * * *

2. Recognition of the Special Situation of Developing Countries

The special situation of certain developing countries is recognized through the possibility of a delayed phaseout schedule for such countries [in order to satisfy " 'basic domestic needs."]

3. The Resolution of States to Act Beyond the Requirements of the Protocol as Adjusted and Amended

[T]he reduction schedule set forth in the Protocol as adjusted and amended represents only the baseline. A number of states have accepted greater obligations, and the Protocol urges the parties to act with greater dispatch when possible. * * *

D. Encouraging Participation and Facilitating Implementation

From the beginning, it was recognized that the shared nature of the ozone-depletion problem required widespread participation in the regime to be established by the Convention and Protocol. Encouragement of participation by developing countries, in particular India and China, required mechanisms to aid implementation of the regime by those countries. Thus, encouragement of participation and facilitation of implementation were and remain linked.

The regime encourages participation in a number of ways. First, because the reduction schedules are tied to either 1986 or 1989 levels of consumption and production, there is no advantage to waiting to join the regime. Second, although the parties to the regime during the phaseout periods may trade the controlled substances with one another, the Protocol, as adjusted and amended, progressively restricts trade involving controlled substances between parties and nonparties. Thus, for example, by January 1, 1993, the parties, having agreed upon a list of products containing the controlled substances specified in the Montreal Protocol, shall bar the import of those products from any state not party to the Protocol.

Third, the Protocol not only attempts to limit the advantages of remaining outside, but for developing countries, also provides incentives to join. * * * In response to the positions of India and China in particular, more specific and detailed provisions for financial assistance and technology transfer were adopted at the London Meeting.

E. Noncompliance, Enforcement, and Dispute Settlement

Thus far, the Parties to the Convention and the Protocol have been concerned primarily with elaboration of and formal participation in the regime. As a result, enforcement procedures at this point are not particularly developed.

The key monitoring and enforcement device at present is the requirement for parties to provide to the Secretariat statistics on production, on imports and exports to parties and nonparties, and on amounts destroyed or recycled as feedstocks. Such reports will aid

Secretariat and party monitoring, and will also further nongovernmental organization involvement since such data is not regarded as confidential. Unfortunately, not all parties have made such reports, or have submitted incomplete reports. The London meeting of the parties, noting these reporting difficulties, established an ad hoc group of experts to consider the reasons for the difficulties and to recommend solutions.

Investigatory and dispute settlement provisions are quite limited. [Article 11 of the] Convention, with application to the Protocol, provides that in the event of a dispute concerning interpretation or application of a provision, the parties (1) shall negotiate; (2) failing that, seek the good offices of, or request mediation by, a third party; and (3) failing that, submit the dispute to conciliation. The parties, in accepting the Convention also may declare that they accept as a means of dispute settlement either arbitration or submission to the International Court of Justice, or both. Against that backdrop, the Parties to the Protocol have been considering procedures and institutional mechanisms for determining noncompliance and for treatment of parties found to be in noncompliance. Interim noncompliance provisions adopted at the London Meeting essentially provide for parties with reservations regarding implementation by other parties to report such concerns in writing to the Secretariat. The Secretariat shall transmit the submission to an Implementation Committee established by these same interim procedures, and that Committee shall consider the record with a view to securing an amicable resolution. The Committee shall report on its work to the Meeting of the Parties and the parties "may . . . decide upon and call for steps to bring about full compliance . . . including measures to assist the Party's compliance . . . ."

IV. THE EVOLVING STRUCTURE OF INTERNATIONAL ENVIRONMENTAL LAWMAKING * * *

A. Lawmaking Amidst Uncertainty: The Process as the Solution * * *

In the case of stratospheric ozone depletion, the international community initially confronted great debate as to whether there was a problem at all, followed by debate regarding the extent of the problem. [T]he nature of many environmental problems requires action by the relevant community before it has proof of the theory. In other words, the international community, despite uncertainty about the theory, must act to confront the danger indicated by the theory. Moreover, it must act knowing that its knowledge will continue to evolve and suggest further actions. These aspects of uncertainty and evolving knowledge lead to two major differences in international environmental lawmaking efforts from lawmaking efforts generally. Both of these differences evidence an emphasis on an ongoing process of lawmaking rather than, as ordinarily the case, the one time negotiation of a treaty at a particular conference.

The first difference is the explicit incorporation of scientific inquiry into the lawmaking process. Dealing with the uncertainty necessarily present in environmental problems requires that the process not only increase the shared knowledge of the parties, but that such knowledge also accurately reflects the state of scientific understanding of the problem. This requires much greater cooperation between the lawmaking community attempting to draft a response and the scientific community seeking to understand the phenomena. Imbedding this scientific effort in an international organizational structure or in international efforts that coordinate national efforts increases the perceived legitimacy, and hence shared nature, of the resulting description of the problem. Making the scientific inquiry an integral part of an ongoing lawmaking process serves both to educate the lawmakers and to speed up the incorporation of such knowledge into the process. In the case of the ozone regime, the Protocol institutionalizes this cooperation by requiring the convening of "appropriate panels of experts" (scientific, environmental, technical, and economic) at least one year before the parties meet to reassess the sufficiency of the Protocol's controls on ozone-depleting substances.

The second major difference is that the lawmaking effort that accommodates evolving knowledge through the establishment of an ongoing process of lawmaking continuously incorporates new knowledge and revises previous responses. In this sense, the Protocol calls for the parties to periodically "assess the control measures provided for in Article 2 on the basis of available scientific, environmental, technical, and economic information." Thus, we see a transition from a one-conference effort to an ongoing process and from "two steps behind" to action on the basis of evolving knowledge. In this sense, cooperation and education are recognized as important aspects of the lawmaking process in the environmental area. For all these reasons, the solution to a threat such as ozone depletion is not the particular requirements of the Montreal Protocol or the London Adjustments and Amendments to the Protocol. Rather, the solution is the process which yielded the Protocol and which already looks ahead to the next adjustments and amendments.

B. Consensual Lawmaking on Transcendent Problems

International environmental lawmaking is also distinct in that the nature of many environmental problems requires that at least those countries primarily contributing, or potentially contributing; to the problem participate in the regime. * * *

In encouraging participation, the tools of the lawmaker are sticks and carrots. In other words, states either may be penalized for not joining the regime or rewarded for doing so. In the ozone protection regime, developing countries were encouraged to join through the recognition of their special needs. Moreover, although there are no sticks per se, the treaty does attempt to prevent those who remain outside from benefitting by doing so. First, there is no advantage in waiting to join the treaty since the baseline calculation from which reductions are to be made is fixed. Second, there is no trade advantage in remaining outside the convention since it restricts members from trading in areas involving the regulated substances with those outside the regime.

The more subtle implication of needing widespread participation, as discussed above, was the demand by China, India, and others for a linkage between their agreement to participate in the regime and satisfaction of other concerns, particularly, development assistance for the Third World. In the case of stratospheric ozone protection, linkage ultimately was made in the London amendments. The amendments provide for technology transfer and establish a fund to aid implementation of the Protocol by facilitating nonozone-depleting paths for growth in developing countries. * * *

C. The Tension Between Manageability of Negotiations and Systemic Thinking

One of the first lessons of environmental studies is the need to approach the environment as a system, an indivisible process. The lawmaker, however, cannot approach the development of an environmentally sound relationship between humanity and the world all at once. Rather, negotiations must be limited so that the number of issues and interests involved remain at a manageable level. The danger with the slicing off of what appears to be a somewhat separable and manageable problem, however, is that systemic thinking may be lost. The question thus becomes how to best reconcile the need for manageable negotiations with the need for holistic thinking.

NOTES AND QUESTIONS

1. *The Negotiating Context.* Richard Benedick, the chief U.S. negotiator for the 1987 Montreal Protocol, characterized the diplomatic challenges:

> [In 1986] I was asked by Secretary of State George Shultz and Ambassador John Negroponte, then Assistant Secretary of State for Oceans, Environmental, and Scientific Affairs (OES), to lead negotiations for a protocol on controlling CFCs. Very few gamblers would have wagered at that time that such negotiations could succeed. CFCs were virtually synonymous with modern standards of living, finding new uses in thousands of products and processes. Billions of dollars of international investment and hundreds of thousands of jobs worldwide were involved. Technological alternatives were nonexistent or considered too costly or unfeasible. Powerful governments and global economic interests were aligned in adamant opposition to controls, as were ideological elements within the administration of President Reagan. Still other

> governments and publics were unaware or indifferent to an arcane threat. Perhaps most significant of all, the arguments for control rested on unproven scientific theories: throughout the protocol negotiations there was firm evidence neither of the predicted ozone layer depletion nor of any harmful effects.
>
> Yet, in September 1987 an international accord was signed in Montreal that made headlines around the globe. By 1989, protection of the ozone layer figured prominently in discussions among the world's political leaders. Within a short time, whole classes of hitherto indispensable chemicals were being phased out and industries were being transformed. * * *
>
> The heads of the World Meteorological Organization (WMO) and UNEP later wrote that "the action to defend the ozone layer will rank as one of the great international achievements of the century." * * * The protocol also set a number of important precedents that influenced the great wave of environmental diplomacy of subsequent years[.]
>
> Final success on the control schedules at Montreal was attributable to a combination of factors, including: the American diplomatic and information campaign, which prompted Japan and the Soviet Union, among others, to agree on the need for stronger controls; the vigorous efforts of such delegations as Canada, Austria, Denmark, Egypt, Finland, New Zealand, Norway and others; the growing influence of the Federal Republic of Germany within [European Community] councils; and the personal interventions by UNEP's Executive Director Tolba at the negotiating table and behind the scenes with key developing country governments.

Richard Elliot Benedick, "The Improbable Montreal Protocol: Science, Diplomacy, and Defending the Ozone Layer," at 1–2, 14, *available at* https://www.ametsoc.org/atmospolicy/documents/Benedickcasestudy_000.pdf (last visited Dec. 10, 2013). For a full account of the negotiations, see, by the same author, *Ozone Diplomacy* (enlarged ed. 1998).

Other global initiatives were also focusing on problems facing the international environment in the 1980s. UNEP was established in 1972 in conjunction with the Stockholm Conference on the Human Environment, which also promulgated the Stockholm Declaration, a soft law instrument similar to the Rio Declaration excerpted in Chapter 3, Part D. The Stockholm Declaration "was the first major international document that cast environmental concerns as global concerns and that highlighted development issues as integral to these concerns." Jutta Brunnée, "The Stockholm Declaration and the Structure and Processes of International Environmental Law," in *The Future of Ocean Regime-Building* 41, 42 (Aldo Chircop, Ted L. McDorman & Susan J. Rolston eds. 2008).

2. *Sustainable Development.* When the Montreal Protocol was being negotiated, a new doctrine of sustainable development was gaining recognition. In 1987 the World Commission on Environment and Development, created by the United Nations in 1983, released its report titled *Our Common Future* (known as the Brundtland Report after the Commission's chairman, former Norwegian Prime Minister Gro Harlem Brundtland). The Brundtland Report stressed sustainable development, defining it as:

> development that meets the needs of the present without compromising the ability of future generations to meet their own needs. It contains within it two key concepts:
>
> –the concept of "needs," in particular the essential needs of the world's poor, to which overriding priority should be given; and
>
> –the idea of limitations imposed by the state of technology and social organization on the environment's ability to meet present and future needs.

U.N. Doc. A/42/427, Annex, Chapter 2, at 54 (1987). Overall, "sustainable development is not a fixed state of harmony, but rather a process of change in which the exploitation of resources, the direction of investments, the orientation of technological development, and institutional change are made consistent with future as well as present needs." *Id.* Overview ¶ 29. Sustainable development became a central theme of the 1992 U.N. Conference on Environment and Development in Rio de Janeiro. For more on the concept, see Committee on Legal Aspects of Sustainable Development, "Report," in International Law Association, *Report of the Seventieth Conference (New Delhi)* 380 (2002); G.A. Res. 60/1, ¶¶ 48–56 (2005) (adopting the World Summit Outcome).

3. *The Success of the Ozone Regime.* The ozone regime has been remarkably successful, attracting virtually universal participation. As of December 2013, 197 states had accepted the 1985 Vienna Convention on Substances that Deplete the Ozone Layer, 1513 U.N.T.S. 293, the 1987 Montreal Protocol, 1522 U.N.T.S. 3, and the 1990 London Amendment to the Montreal Protocol, 1598 U.N.T.S. 469. Additional amendments to the Montreal Protocol were adopted in Copenhagen in 1992 (197 parties as of December 2013), in Montreal in 1997 (197 parties), and in Beijing in 1999 (193 parties). According to a 2010 UNEP summary:

> Global observations have verified that atmospheric levels of key ozone depleting substances are going down and it is believed that with implementation of the Protocol's provisions the ozone layer should return to pre-1980 levels by the middle of this century; * * *
>
> [T]he Parties to the Montreal Protocol have achieved a compliance rate of over 98%. Further, in the process of phasing-out, many countries, both developed and developing, have met their phase-out targets well ahead of schedule; * * *

> In terms of health benefits, controls implemented under the Montreal Protocol have enabled the global community to avoid millions of cases of fatal skin cancer and tens of millions of cases of non fatal skin cancer and cataracts. The United States estimates that by the year 2165 more than 6.3 million skin cancer deaths will have been avoided in that country alone and that efforts to protect the ozone layer will have saved it an estimated $4.2 trillion in health care costs over the period 1990–2165. This year, the U.S. Environmental Protection Agency (EPA) estimated that more than 22 million additional cataract cases will be avoided for Americans born between 1985–2100 due to [the] Montreal Protocol; * * *
>
> The Protocol has also delivered substantial climate benefits. Because ozone depleting substances are also global warming gases, the reduction in ozone depleting substances between 1990, when they reached peak levels, and the year 2000 has yielded a net integrated reduction of approximately 25 billion tonnes of CO2 weighted global warming gases.

Key Achievements of the Montreal Protocol to Date (Sept. 2010), *available at* http://ozone.unep.org/Publications/MP_Key_Achievements-E.pdf (last visited Dec. 9, 2013). Remaining challenges include a black market trade in ozone-depleting substances and implementation difficulties in some developing countries. See Anne Luciea Plein, "A Story between Success and Challenge—20th Anniversary of the Montreal Protocol," 11 *New Zealand Journal of Environmental Law* 67, 78–95 (2007).

4. *The Framework Convention-Protocol Approach.* The Vienna Convention on Substances that Deplete the Ozone Layer and its 1987 Montreal Protocol exemplify a framework convention-protocol approach to international regulation. What are the advantages and disadvantages of such an approach in addressing environmental concerns?

What is the difference between adjustments and amendments to the Montreal Protocol? The Montreal Protocol's Conference of the Parties (COP), after evaluating the success of previous measures and the implications of new scientific evidence, may itself adjust reductions of controlled chemicals; adjustments agreed to by a two-thirds vote are binding on all parties to the Protocol. Is the ozone regime's distinction between adjustments and amendments sensible? Would it be desirable to increase the scope of the decisions that parties to the Montreal Protocol can, by majority or supermajority vote, make binding on all parties? See Geoffrey Palmer, "New Ways to Make International Environmental Law," 86 *American Journal of International Law* 259 (1992).

5. *Encouraging Widespread Participation in the Ozone Regime.* Note the various incentives the Vienna Convention and the Montreal Protocol employed to encourage participation by many states. As one example, states parties are prohibited from trading ozone-depleting chemicals with non-parties. See Article 4 of the Montreal Protocol. Was this prohibition on trade

consistent with the rules of the World Trade Organization? See the *Shrimp-Turtle Case* in Chapter 5. What other techniques could help prevent states from becoming "free riders," benefitting from widespread implementation of an international environmental regime without themselves becoming parties?

6. *Developing States and the Ozone Regime.* Why was it important to apply the ozone regime to developing states and their populations? In the 1980s, when the Vienna Convention and Montreal Protocol were being negotiated, developed states produced virtually all CFCs. And those developed states, with less than a quarter of the earth's population, were consuming upwards of eighty percent of CFCs.

Should developing states have been accorded a "special status" in the ozone regime? What practical and conceptual arguments support differentiated responsibilities for developing states? According to Principle 7 of the 1992 Rio Declaration on Environment and Development:

> In view of the different contributions to global environmental degradation, States have common but differentiated responsibilities. The developed countries acknowledge the responsibility that they bear in the international pursuit of sustainable development in view of the pressures their societies place on the global environment and of the technologies and financial resources they command.

UNCED Doc. /CONF.151/5/Rev. 1, 31 *International Legal Materials* 874 (1992). See Duncan French, "Developing States and International Environmental Law: The Importance of Differentiated Responsibilities," 49 *International and Comparative Law Quarterly* 35 (2000), and the discussion of soft law in Chapter 3, Part D.

The 1990 London Amendment to the Montreal Protocol reflected the concerns of developing states. According to Article 10 of the London Amendment, the financial mechanism for assisting developing states "shall meet all agreed incremental costs" of those states "in order to enable their compliance with the control measures of the [Montreal] Protocol." Developing states that submit a detailed program for reducing their production and consumption of ozone-depleting substances may be eligible for grants and technical assistance to help them switch to safer substances and technologies. The financial mechanism includes a Multilateral Fund to be funded by industrialized states. An Executive Committee, on which developing and developed states are equally represented, administers the Fund. Establishing this Fund helped persuade China and India to accept the Vienna Convention and the Montreal Protocol. As of May 2013, 53 countries had contributed over $2.69 billion to the Fund. See Executive Committee of the Multilateral Fund for the Implementation of the Montreal Protocol, Seventieth Meeting, *Status of Contributions and Disbursements*, U.N. Doc. UNEP/OzL.Pro/ExCom/70/3, Annex I (2013); http://www.multilateralfund.org (last visited Dec. 9, 2013). What do you see as the advantages and disadvantages of the Multilateral Fund?

7. *The Roles of International Organizations and Treaty Bodies.* How well could the ozone regime function if the only entities involved were states? Note the range of roles that international organizations play in the ozone regime. UNEP helped negotiate the regime. The United Nations and its specialized agencies participate as observers at meetings of the COP. Vienna Convention, art. 6(5). As Professor Caron noted in the principal reading, there are links with international scientific organizations such as the World Health Organization and international financial organizations such as the World Bank.

Several organs or treaty bodies that are less formal than international organizations or international courts have roles in the ozone regime. For example, the Vienna Convention and the Montreal Protocol created the Ozone Secretariat, headquartered in Nairobi, Kenya, to arrange meetings of parties, carry out certain decisions reached at meetings, report on implementation of the Convention and Protocol, provide information to governments and individuals, and analyze data. See http://www.ozone.unep.org (last visited Dec. 9, 2013). The COP highlighted in Note 4, the Executive Committee of the Multilateral Fund considered in Note 6, and the Implementation Committee discussed in Note 9 are other examples of treaty bodies associated with the ozone regime. See generally Robin R. Churchill & Geir Ulfstein, "Autonomous Institutional Arrangements in Multilateral Agreements: A Little-Noticed Phenomenon in International Law," 94 *American Journal of International Law* 623 (2000); Geir Ulfstein, "Treaty Bodies and Regimes," in *The Oxford Guide to Treaties* 428 (Duncan B. Hollis ed. 2012). The complexity of decision-making authority in many international regimes, involving treaty bodies and experts as well as more traditional international organizations and states, has led scholars to postulate the emergence of "global administrative law." See 37 *New York University Journal of International Law and Politics*, No. 4 (2005), and "Symposium: Global Governance and Global Administrative Law in the International Legal Order," 17 *European Journal of International Law*, No. 1 (2006).

8. *The Roles of Non-governmental Organizations.* Non-governmental organizations provide scientific advice and gather information important in the negotiation of environmental treaties. What other roles do and should NGOs play? Article 6(5) of the Vienna Convention allows NGOs "qualified in fields relating to the protection of the ozone layer" to sit as observers at COP meetings "unless at least one-third of the Parties present object." 26 *International Legal Materials* 1529, 1532 (1987). NGOs may also obtain reports that are submitted to an Implementation Committee (see Note 9), allowing them to monitor states' compliance with the ozone regime.

9. *Compliance with the Ozone Regime.* What mechanisms should be used to promote compliance with the Montreal Protocol to the Vienna Convention? Negotiators concentrated first on elaborating the framework-protocol structure and on participation, rather than on compliance. Professor Caron, in the excerpt above, reported on an interim non-compliance procedure, which has now been revised and implemented. See Annex II to the

Report of the Tenth Meeting of the Parties to the Montreal Protocol on Substances that Deplete the Ozone Layer, U.N. Doc. UNEP/OzL.Pro.10/9, at 47 (1998). This procedure, which creates an elected ten-member Implementation Committee, allows any party to raise concerns about another party's compliance; a state may also bring its own record of data reporting and compliance with substantive obligations to the Implementation Committee. The Committee reports its recommendations to the COP, which may call for steps to bring about full compliance. Non-complying states may be eligible to receive financial assistance to assist with compliance. As David Hunter, James Salzman, and Durwood Zaelke have written, the non-compliance procedure "facilitates compliance by encouraging Parties to self-police themselves. By coming to the Implementation Committee, Parties can ask for assistance from other parties. Facilitating compliance as opposed to mandating it through sanctions is a growing trend in international environmental law." *International Environmental Law and Policy* 575 (4th ed. 2011). Should an institutional monitoring system also be mandated, in order to determine instances of non-compliance? Monitoring was discussed but not adopted at the 1990 London conference. For discussion of the ozone regime's procedures concerning implementation and compliance, see Gilbert M. Bankobeza, *Ozone Protection: The International Legal Regime* 218–301 (2005).

The non-compliance procedures "shall apply without prejudice to the operation of the settlement of disputes procedure laid down in Article 11 of the Vienna Convention," which, as outlined by Professor Caron, includes the possibility of formal interstate third-party dispute settlement. Are traditional interstate dispute settlement procedures (see Chapter 5) consistent with the non-compliance mechanism, or might they work at cross purposes with it? Are interstate dispute resolution mechanisms well suited for promoting compliance in collective action contexts such as the ozone regime? The formal mechanisms of Article 11 of the Vienna Convention have not been invoked.

10. *Evaluating the Ozone Regime*. Treaty-based regimes respecting the international environment vary significantly as to whether they seek to impose liability or prevent harm, how flexible they are in defining commitments, and whether states or private actors are bound by obligations. Some treaty-based regimes establish general objectives but leave it to participating states to determine how to achieve those objectives. See, *e.g.*, U.S.-Canada Air Quality Agreement, Mar. 13, 1991, 30 *International Legal Materials* 676 (1991). In contrast, other treaty arrangements precisely define the measures states must undertake. See, *e.g.*, the Convention on International Trade in Endangered Species of Wild Flora and Fauna, Mar. 3, 1973, 27 U.S.T. 1087, 993 U.N.T.S. 243, which specifies what species to protect and how they must be protected (through a system of import and export permits and certificates). Other regimes focus attention on private actors, providing for their liability in the event of environmental harm. See, *e.g.*, Protocol of 1992 to Amend the International Convention on Civil Liability for Oil Pollution Damage of 29 November 1969, Nov. 27, 1992, 1956 U.N.T.S. 285. Should the Vienna Convention/Montreal Protocol system add

provisions on the liability of private actors, in an effort to force entities using CFCs to absorb the cost of damage caused by their pollution? Would any other changes to the current ozone regime improve it?

It can be extraordinarily difficult to fashion international regimes to protect the global commons. What explains the significant efficacy of the ozone regime? Why was near-universal participation achieved? Do the framework-protocol approach and the roles of various treaty bodies facilitate interactions that promote shared commitments?

11. *Climate Change*. The vast majority of climate scientists have concluded that climate change is likely attributable in significant measure to human emissions of carbon dioxide and other greenhouse gases, and that it poses significant risks. Although the precise consequences of climate change are not known, the risks include higher global temperatures, sea level rise that could inundate lowlands and displace millions of people, and more severe storms, droughts, heat waves, and floods. The work of the Intergovernmental Panel on Climate Change has received much attention. See http://www.ipcc.ch (last visited Dec. 9, 2013).

Does the ozone regime hold lessons for a climate change regime? Both provide a framework-protocol arrangement. In the late 1980s and early 1990s, when scientific studies began to document the potentially severe consequences of climate change, countries negotiated the United Nations Framework Convention on Climate Change (UNFCCC), May 9, 1992, 1771 U.N.T.S. 107. As of December 2013, the UNFCCC numbered 195 parties, including the United States. The UNFCCC establishes foundational principles, including sustainable development; sets out some commitments applicable to all parties, such as reporting national inventories of emission sources; requires developed states to undertake other steps, including financially assisting developing countries; and proclaims the "aim" of having developed states reduce their greenhouse gas emissions to 1990 levels. One product of the Framework Convention's Conference of the Parties was the Kyoto Protocol, Dec. 10, 1997, 2203 U.N.T.S. 162, which sets out a complicated system of emissions permit trading and binding commitments by developed states to reduce their greenhouse gas emissions. The Kyoto Protocol entered into force in 2005 and as of September 2013 had 192 parties, but the United States has not accepted it, and it has not led to significant reductions in emissions of greenhouse gases. Why has it been so difficult to achieve an effective legal climate change regime? The relevant science is complex; greenhouse gases are emitted from a huge number and variety of sources around the world; and the costs and benefits of various strategies to address climate change have proved highly contentious. For developments concerning the UNFCCC-Kyoto Protocol regime, see http://www.unfccc.org/ (last visited Dec. 9, 2013), and for a comparison with the ozone regime, see Chris Peloso, "Crafting an International Climate Change Protocol: Applying the Lessons Learned from the Success of the Montreal Protocol and the Ozone Depletion Problem," 25 *Journal of Land Use* 305 (2010).

As questions have arisen about the efficacy of the UNFCCC-Kyoto Protocol regime, states, international organizations, and other regimes have taken actions or considered policies related to climate change. These include bilateral initiatives, policies of multilateral development assistance agencies such as the World Bank, sub-national measures (*e.g.*, California's emission trading system), rules to facilitate or manage adaptation to climate-related problems, intellectual property and investment rules that include clean energy provisions, possible initiatives in the international trade regime, and even the ozone regime's Montreal Protocol. See Justin Gillis, "The Little Treaty that Could," *New York Times*, Dec. 10, 2013, at D3. According to Professors Keohane and Victor, "[t]he international institutions that regulate issues related to climate change are diverse in membership and content. They have been created at different times, and by different groups of countries." These institutions "are not integrated, comprehensive, or arranged in a clear hierarchy. They form a loosely-linked regime complex rather than a single international regime." Robert O. Keohane & David G. Victor, "The Regime Complex for Climate Change," 9 *Perspectives on Politics*, No. 1, at 7, 19 (Mar. 2011).

CHAPTER 9

INTERNATIONAL LAW AND THE USE OF FORCE

■ ■ ■

Rules about the use of force are among the oldest in international law. Classical categories are *jus in bello*, *i.e.*, laws concerning the conduct of hostilities, and *jus ad bellum*, *i.e.*, laws about when it is legal to resort to force at all. In Part A we consider *jus in bello*, also known as international humanitarian law and sometimes as the law of war. Part B introduces traditional law about *jus ad bellum*. Part C explores when states may legally use force under the U.N. Charter absent the authorization of the Security Council with a focus on the Cold War era, 1945–1989. Finally, Part D turns to new developments in the law of armed force since 1989, including responses to terrorism.

A. JUS IN BELLO

Jus in bello, or international humanitarian law, asks how states and their armed forces ought to treat combatants, civilians, and prisoners during armed conflicts. The law of nations historically called on armies to protect civilian populations. Numerous widely accepted conventions now specify protections for civilians during hostilities and proscribe conduct that would cause unnecessary suffering for combatants and prisoners. These treaties emerged from the Hague Peace Conferences of 1899 and 1907, as well as from 1864, 1906, 1929, and 1949 codification efforts in Geneva, Switzerland. "Hague law" is generally associated with the methods of conducting hostilities and permissible types of armaments, while 1949 "Geneva law" focuses on protecting victims of armed conflict. The four Geneva Conventions of 1949, responses to the atrocities of World War II, detail protections due: (1) the wounded and sick in armed forces in the field; (2) wounded, sick, and shipwrecked members of the armed forces at sea; (3) prisoners of war; and (4) civilians in times of war or armed conflict. Two 1977 Protocols to these 1949 Conventions, applicable respectively to "international armed conflicts" and "armed conflicts not of an international character," update international humanitarian law. The statutes of international criminal tribunals—for example, the International Criminal Tribunal for the former Yugoslavia, the International Criminal Tribunal for Rwanda, and the International Criminal Court (see Chapter 6, Part E)—also specify the content of this body of law.

The first two readings in this part explore the development of international humanitarian law, its links to international human rights law, and challenges to making international humanitarian law effective. Next, the *Tadić Case* from the International Criminal Tribunal for the former Yugoslavia discusses the doctrine of "armed conflict" and the distinction between international and internal armed conflicts. The Notes following it have more to say about categories of armed conflicts, as well as whether suspected terrorists are entitled to protection under international humanitarian law.

THEODOR MERON, "THE HUMANIZATION OF HUMANITARIAN LAW"

94 *American Journal of International Law* 239 (2000)

I. LIMITATIONS ON HUMANIZATION AND ITS CONTRADICTIONS

[I]t has become common in some quarters to conflate human rights and the law of war/international humanitarian law. Nevertheless, despite the growing convergence of various protective trends, significant differences remain. Unlike human rights law, the law of war allows, or at least tolerates, the killing and wounding of innocent human beings not directly participating in an armed conflict, such as civilian victims of lawful collateral damage. It also permits certain deprivations of personal freedom without convictions in a court of law. It allows an occupying power to resort to internment and limits the appeal rights of detained persons. It permits far-reaching limitations of freedoms of expression and assembly.

The law of armed conflict regulates aspects of a struggle for life and death between contestants who operate on the basis of formal equality. Derived as it is from the medieval tradition of chivalry, it guarantees a modicum of fair play. As in a boxing match, pummeling the opponent's upper body is fine; hitting below the belt is proscribed. As long as the rules of the game are observed, it is permissible to cause suffering, deprivation of freedom, and death. This is a narrow, technical vision of legality.

Human rights laws protect physical integrity and human dignity in all circumstances. They apply to relationships between unequal parties, protecting the governed from their governments. Under human rights law, no one may be deprived of life except in pursuance of a judgment by a competent court. The two systems, human rights and humanitarian norms, are thus distinct and, in many respects, different.

To speak of the humanization of humanitarian law or the law of war is thus in many ways a contradiction in terms. Consider, for example, the law of war term "unnecessary suffering."

To genuinely humanize humanitarian law, it would be necessary to put an end to all kinds of armed conflict. But wars have been a part of the human condition since the struggle between Cain and Abel, and regrettably they are likely to remain so. * * *

The separation between *jus ad bellum* and *jus in bello* results in the uniform, neutral application of the latter, without reference to its distinctions between the rights and obligations of the parties. This separation thus contributes to the practicality of the law of war, the avoidance of preliminary disputes on the character of the war as just or aggressive, and the fair treatment of combatants in judicial proceedings involving allegations of war crimes. * * *

The parameters of humanization need to be drawn so that it can be related to the reality of armed conflicts. * * *

II. AN OVERVIEW OF DEVELOPMENTS

The law of war has always contained rules based on chivalry, humanity, and religious values that were designed to protect noncombatants, especially women, children, and old men, who were presumed incapable of bearing arms and committing acts of hostility. It has also incorporated rules protecting combatants (in matters such as quarter, perfidy, and unnecessary suffering). Moreover, the law of war has increasingly encompassed rules on accountability and protection, such as those on protecting powers, the International Committee of the Red Cross, criminal responsibility, and international criminal tribunals. Nevertheless, this law has inevitably been animated by considerations of military strategy and victory, and reciprocity has historically been central to its development. Reciprocity served as a key rationale for the formation of the norms and as a major factor in securing respect for them and discouraging their violation. The law of war was paradigmatically interstate law, driven by reciprocity, and thus, as Georges Abi-Saab put it, by "collective responsibility, with the attendant collective sanctions of classical international law: belligerent reprisals *durante bello* and war reparations *post bellum*."

Chivalry and principles of humanity created a counterbalance to military necessity, serving as a competing inspiration for the law of armed conflict. Indeed, tension between military necessity and restraint on the conduct of belligerents is the hallmark of that law. * * *

Calamitous events and atrocities have repeatedly driven the development of international humanitarian law. The more offensive or painful the suffering, the greater the pressure for accommodating humanitarian restraints. The American Civil War generated the Lieber Code, which ultimately spawned the branch of international humanitarian law that governs the conduct of hostilities, commonly known as Hague law. The battle of Solferino and Henry Dunant's moving portrayal of the suffering and bloodshed there (*A Memory of Solferino* (1862)) inspired the creation of the Red Cross movement and Geneva law, the other branch of humanitarian law, which emphasizes protection of the victims of war, the sick, the wounded, prisoners, and civilians. Nazi atrocities led to the Nuremberg Charter, the 1949 Geneva Conventions, and the Genocide Convention, and helped shift some state-to-state aspects of international humanitarian law to individual criminal responsibility, which contributed to changing its emphasis from the interests of states to the rights of individuals and populations. The atrocities of the last decade in the former Yugoslavia, Rwanda, and elsewhere owed their impact not to their unprecedented nature—there is unfortunately nothing new in atrocities—but to the media's rapid sensitization of public opinion, which reduced the time between commission of the tragedies and responses by the international community. One result was the establishment of the ad hoc criminal tribunals for the former Yugoslavia and Rwanda, which continue to exert broad influence on both the development of international humanitarian law and its humanization. Commenting on these events, George Aldrich concludes that "the development of international humanitarian law since the second world war has made individual criminal liability an explicit part of the law."

* * * Although the prospects for compliance with humanitarian norms may be less auspicious than for other norms of public international law, they enjoy stronger moral support. Judges, scholars, governments, and nongovernmental organizations are often prepared to accept a rather large gap between practice and the norms concerned without questioning their binding character. In many cases, gradual and partial compliance has been accepted as fulfilling the requirements for the formation of customary law, and contrary practice downplayed. Courts and tribunals have frequently ignored operational or battlefield practice. Without formally abandoning the dual requirements (practice and *opinio juris*) for the formation of customary international law, they have tended to weigh statements both as evidence of practice and as articulations of *opinio juris*. They have relied on this *opinio juris*, or general principles of humanitarian law distilled in part from the Geneva, Hague, and other humanitarian conventions, in reaching their decisions. The methodology thus resembles that applied in the human rights field more than that used in other areas of international law. * * *

III. FROM AN INTERSTATE TO AN INDIVIDUAL-RIGHTS PERSPECTIVE: RECIPROCITY AND REPRISALS

The extent to which humanitarian law has already departed from the purely interstate character of reliance on reciprocity can be seen by revisiting the now-obsolete *si omnes* clause[.]

The *si omnes* clause found in early law of war treaties provided that if one party to a conflict was not party to the instrument, it would not apply to relations between all parties to the conflict. * * *

Common Article 2(3) of the 1949 Geneva Conventions went further. [Echoing 1929 treaties, it provides] for the application of the Conventions between parties involved in a conflict, even if one of the belligerents is not a party to the Convention[.] [Common Article 2(3) also] specifies that the belligerents "shall furthermore be bound by the Convention in relation to["] [a power accepting] the Convention for the specific conflict only. This idea had been broached in 1929 but rejected.

The International Court of Justice held common Article 1 to the 1949 Geneva Conventions to be declaratory of customary law. The article provides that "the High Contracting Parties undertake to respect and ensure respect for the present Convention *in all circumstances*," epitomizing the rejection of reciprocity and insistence on the automatic application of the Conventions. The [ICRC's] *Commentary* to the First Convention emphasizes the unconditional and nonreciprocal character of the obligations: "A State does not proclaim the principle of the protection due to wounded and sick combatants in the hope of saving a certain number of its own nationals. It does so out of respect for the human person as such."

Another aspect of common Article 1, similarly derived from the rejection of reciprocity, goes to the heart of accountability for violations of international humanitarian law. Although it may well have first been intended to address the obligations of a party to comply with and ensure respect for the Convention by its entire civilian and military apparatus, and perhaps even by its entire population, Article 1 has subsequently been interpreted as creating standing for states parties vis-à-vis violating states. [Although] the exact scope of third-party rights under common Article 1 remains unclear, [it] can already be seen as the humanitarian law analogue to the human rights *erga omnes* principle. * * *

XI. LIMITATIONS TO THE EFFECTIVENESS OF LAWS

* * * The normative progress in humanization brings into sharp relief the contrast between the normative framework and the harsh, often barbaric reality of the battlefield. The events in Bosnia, Kosovo, Sierra Leone, Congo, Somalia, Afghanistan, and, not so long ago, Cambodia, Kuwait, and elsewhere represent a horrific series of massacres, rapes, and mutilations. In the confrontations between racial, ethnic, religious, and state interests of various kinds, it is the normative that has been eroding. International and national criminal tribunals have thus far engendered little demonstrable deterrence. Humanization may have triumphed, but mostly rhetorically.

A recent report by the U.S. National Intelligence Council states that civilians have become key targets for combatants on all sides; that war now involves displacing people as much as moving borders; and that combatants are employing starvation, slaughter, and various civilian and military technologies to expel or kill civilians, including "demonstration killings and maimings." * * *

The gap between the norms and the reality in human rights and humanitarian law has always been wide. Today the visibility and immensity of violations of international humanitarian law highlight issues of compliance that raise cynicism and doubt. In the long run, humanitarian norms must become a part of public consciousness everywhere. Education, training, persuasion, and emphasis on values * * * such as ethics, honor, mercy, and shame, must be vigorously pursued. This job cannot be left to the law alone. Public opinion and the social consensus that have proved so effective in the development of the law should be geared to transforming practice as well. For that, the creation of a culture of values is indispensable. Until such a culture becomes a reality, the international community may have no alternative, in some instances, to intervention, in its infinite varieties, to stop atrocities wherever they occur.

NOTES AND QUESTIONS

1. *International Humanitarian Law as* Lex Specialis. International humanitarian law, or the law of armed conflict, has traditionally been regarded as *lex specialis*, displacing rules of general international law during wars and other armed conflicts. International lawyers have long believed that the legality of acts should be judged by different rules in times of war than in times of peace. Hugo Grotius published his famous *De Jure Belli ac Pacis (On the Law of War and Peace)* in 1625, and for scholars thereafter the law of war and the law of peace have been fundamental organizing constructs. Today the phrase "law of armed conflict" is more commonly used than "law of war," reflecting the fact that modern "wars" are rarely formally declared. May international human rights law still apply during armed conflicts? Is there anything undesirable about interjecting more of human rights law into humanitarian law? See Geoffrey S. Corn, "Mixing Apples and Hand Grenades: The Logical Limit of Applying Human Rights Norms to Armed Conflict," 1 *Journal of International Humanitarian Legal Studies* 52 (2010).

2. *Basic Principles of International Humanitarian Law.* In its advisory opinion, Legality of the Threat or Use of Nuclear Weapons, 1996 I.C.J. 226, 257, the International Court of Justice identified two "cardinal principles" of international humanitarian law:

> The first is aimed at the protection of the civilian population and civilian objects and establishes the distinction between combatants and non-combatants; States must never make civilians the object of attack and must consequently never use weapons that are incapable

of distinguishing between civilian and military targets. According to the second principle, it is prohibited to cause unnecessary suffering to combatants: it is accordingly prohibited to use weapons causing them such harm or uselessly aggravating their suffering. In application of that second principle, States do not have unlimited freedom of choice of means in the weapons they use.

What are the implications of the principle never to "make civilians the object of attack"? Does it mean that any killing of civilians by a military force during an armed conflict violates the laws of war? The Council of the International Institute of Humanitarian Law, a non-governmental organization based in Italy, has suggested some corollaries of this cardinal principle, including "the prohibition of attacks on dwellings and other installations which are used only by the civilian population" and "the prohibition to attack, destroy, remove or render useless objects indispensable to the survival of the civilian population." Declaration on the Rules of International Humanitarian Law Governing the Conduct of Hostilities in Non-International Armed Conflicts, *International Review of the Red Cross*, Sept.–Oct. 1990, at 404, 406.

3. *International Criminal Courts and International Humanitarian Law.* Judge Meron concluded that "[i]nternational and national criminal tribunals have thus far engendered little demonstrable deterrence." Do you agree? In what circumstances might such tribunals deter violations of international humanitarian law? What other functions do such tribunals serve?

Various international criminal tribunals have elaborated the content of international humanitarian law. Recall from Chapter 6 the Nuremberg proceedings. Core parts of international humanitarian law are incorporated in the Statute of the International Criminal Tribunal for the former Yugoslavia, 32 *International Legal Materials* 1192 (1993). The Rome Statute of the International Criminal Court (ICC), July 17, 1998, 2187 U.N.T.S. 3, proscribes war crimes over which that Court may exercise jurisdiction. These crimes include "[g]rave breaches of the [1949] Geneva Conventions," such as "[t]orture or inhuman treatment, including biological experiments" and "[w]ilfully depriving a prisoner of war or other protected person of the rights of fair and regular trial." *Id.* art. 8(2)(a)(ii), (vi). Grave breaches are particularly significant, not only substantively but because of procedural obligations in the Geneva Conventions. For example, Article 146 of the Fourth Geneva Convention, which protects civilians, provides that each contracting party must "search for persons alleged to have committed" grave breaches and bring such persons before its own courts or transfer them for trial to another contracting party.

The Rome Statute also specifies 26 "[o]ther serious violations of the laws and customs applicable in international armed conflict," ICC Statute, art. 8(2)(b), along with 12 "[o]ther serious violations of the laws and customs applicable in armed conflicts not of an international character." *Id.* art. 8(2)(e). Some acts—such as intentionally directing attacks against civilians, using children under age 15 to participate in hostilities, and refusing quarter to opposing forces—are within the Court's war crimes jurisdiction regardless of whether they occur in international or non-international armed conflicts. *Id.* arts. 8(2)(b)(ii), (xii), (xxvi) and 8(2)(e)(ii), (vii), (x).

4. *The Efficacy of International Humanitarian Law.* What mechanisms, other than national and international judicial proceedings, could promote the efficacy of international humanitarian law? Do concerns of reciprocity still influence compliance with the *jus in bello*? What are the roles of the International Committee on the Red Cross, discussed in Chapter 8, Part B? Possibilities for humanitarian interventions by states, or for decisions by the U.N. Security Council seeking to avert humanitarian disasters during armed conflicts, are addressed in Parts C and D of this chapter. Consider, as you read the next excerpt, what roles military lawyers play in promoting compliance with the *jus in bello*.

MIKE NEWTON, "THE MILITARY LAWYER: NUISANCE OR NECESSITY?"

in *Human Dignity Protection in Armed Conflict: Strengthening Measures for the Respect and Implementation of International Humanitarian Law and Other Rules Protecting Human Dignity in Armed Conflict* 107 (International Institute of Humanitarian Law, Guido Ravasi & Gian Luca Beruto eds. 2006)

LAWYERS AS A MILITARY NECESSITY

Military commanders and their lawyers do not approach the law of armed conflict as an esoteric intellectual exercise. The necessity for military lawyers grew from the requirements of commanders across the world for guidance. [C]ommanders have relied on sound legal advice precisely *because* of their need to accomplish the mission rather than as an unfortunate impediment. Military lawyers and good commanders develop a very special relationship of trust precisely because the lawyer provides necessary technical advice that the commander relies upon in solving some of the most complex problems posed by the military mission itself.

For example, even during [the U.S. Civil War], the tactical uncertainty faced by Union forces in waging a campaign against the rebel forces thrust lawyers into the spotlight. The first comprehensive effort to describe the law of war in a written code (the Lieber Code) began as a request from the General-in-Chief of the Union Armies, based on his confusion over the distinction between lawful and unlawful combatants. General Henry Wager Halleck recognized that the law of armed conflict never accorded combatant immunity to every person who conducted hostilities, but could provide no pragmatic command response to the changing tactics of war. On August 6, 1862, General Halleck wrote to Dr. Francis Lieber, a highly regarded law professor at the then Columbia College in New York, to request his assistance in defining guerrilla warfare. This request, which can justly be described as the catalyst that precipitated more than one hundred years of legal effort resulting in the modern web of international agreements regulating the conduct of hostilities, read as follows:

> My Dear Doctor: Having heard that you have given much attention to the usages and customs of war as practiced in the present age, and especially to the matter of guerrilla war, I hope you may find it convenient to give to the public your views on that subject. The rebel authorities claim the right to send men, in the garb of peaceful citizens, to waylay and attack our troops, to burn bridges and houses and to destroy property and persons within our lines. They demand that such persons be treated as ordinary belligerents, and that when captured they have extended to them the same rights as other prisoners of war; they also threaten that if such persons be punished as marauders and spies they will retaliate by executing our prisoners of war in their possession. I particularly request your views on these questions.

Based on the stimulus of Confederate conduct, the Union Army issued a disciplinary code governing the conduct of hostilities (known worldwide as the Lieber Code) as "General Orders 100: Instructions for the Government of the Armies of the United States in the Field" in April 1863. This was the first comprehensive military code of discipline that sought to define the precise parameters of permissible conduct during conflict. The principle endures in the law today that persons who do not enjoy lawful combatant status are not entitled to the benefits of legal protections derived from the laws of war (including prisoner of war status) and are subject to punishment for their warlike acts. The law of war is therefore integral to the very notion of military professionalism because it defines the class of persons against whom professional military forces can lawfully apply violence based on principles of military necessity and reciprocity. * * *

Though the detailed prescriptions of the law of armed conflict evolved in response to the demands of military pragmatism and the impetus of changing technology, lawyers were also a necessary ingredient in developing the norms that have come to define the very essence of professionalism. Commanders must balance the need to accomplish the mission against an internalized awareness of the larger legal and ethical context for their actions. As a consequence, military professionals developed legal codes in order to increase military efficiency by defining appropriate bounds that served to facilitate the accomplishment of the mission. * * * Any unit that is ripped apart by allegations of illegality and indiscipline cannot be combat effective simply because its members are focused on the details of sworn statements, self preservation, and self interest rather than the overall accomplishment of operational goals. Lawyers who are enforcing the law through comprehensive investigations and appropriate prosecutions will likely affect the unit's mission posture, but the underlying indiscipline can be justly blamed for undercutting the mission-first focus of a good, cohesive military organization.

[T]he modern law of armed conflict * * * serves as the firebreak between being a hero in the service of your nation and a criminal who brings disgrace to your nation, dishonor to the unit, and disruption to the military mission.

In the wake of the Lieber Code, other states issued similar manuals: Prussia, 1870; The Netherlands, 1871; France, 1877; Russia, 1877 and 1904; Serbia, 1878; Argentina, 1881; Great Britain, 1883 and 1904; and Spain, 1893. Over time, military codes and the more thorough military manuals that followed served to communicate the "gravity and importance" of behavioral norms to commanders and soldiers. Legal norms continue to form the rallying point of moral and professional clarity that guides soldiers in the midst of incredibly nuanced missions, no matter how tired they are, or how much adrenaline is flowing in the impetus of the moment. * * *

THE LAW OF LAWYERS

As the law became more complex, and its implementation on the battlefield more problematic, it is unsurprising and perhaps inevitable that the role for lawyers became embedded in the law itself. [T]he lawyer help[s] to ensure that the obligations of the law are not seen as a hindrance, but as an essential component of a professional military balancing the legitimate use of power against the terror and pain that conflict causes. These principles form the practical foundation which warrants the textual mandate of Protocol I, Article 82:

> The High Contracting Parties at all times, and the Parties to the conflict in time of armed conflict, shall ensure that legal advisors are available, when necessary, to advise military commanders at the appropriate level on the application of the Conventions and this Protocol and on the appropriate instruction to be given the armed forces on this subject.

For those states party to the Protocol, Article 82 imposes an affirmative obligation to provide legal advisors to military forces. From my perspective, the concept of legal advisor for military forces should be largely synonymous with the concept of military lawyer. Who better to understand and represent both professional military obligations with the requirements of the law than a professional soldier? The professionalism of the military lawyer is also an extremely important component in gaining the credibility and respect of both commanders and soldiers that is necessary to properly implement the constraints of the law.

* * * The unstated but necessary corollary to [Article 82] is that the Parties to the Protocol have an obligation to ensure that the selected legal advisors "get the appropriate training." In addition, the creation of an office or section exclusively devoted to international law applicable in armed conflict is an "apparently essential prerequisite for the implementation of Article 82."

The Additional Protocol expanded on earlier provisions of the law with regard to concrete obligations for its training and dissemination. Article 83 included more sweeping provisions focused on closing the gap between the textual provisions of law and their realization in practice:

> 1. The High Contracting Parties undertake, in time of peace as in time of armed conflict, to disseminate the Conventions and this Protocol as widely as possible in their respective countries and, in particular, to include the study thereof in their programmes of military instruction and to encourage the study thereof by the civilian population, so that those instruments may become known to the armed forces and to the civilian population.
>
> 2. Any military or civilian authorities who, in time of armed conflict, assume responsibilities in respect of the application of the Conventions and this Protocol shall be fully acquainted with the text thereof.

Taken together, these provisions are intended to effect a comprehensive mechanism for training military professionals in the obligations inherent in the law of armed conflict as well as a systematic and authoritative implementation of those principles.

BACK TO THE FUTURE: THE CONTINUED NECESSITY FOR MILITARY LAWYERS

The Lawyer as Trainer—Recent events in Iraq serve as a stark reminder that the efforts of commanders and lawyers to achieve a well-trained and disciplined force can never be taken for granted. Unfortunately, this is not a new lesson. Lieutenant General William R. Peers reported that one of the contributing factors to the crimes committed at My Lai was that "[n]either units nor individual members of Task Force Barker and the 11th Brigade received the proper training in the Law of War (Hague and Geneva conventions), the safeguarding of noncombatants, or the Rules of Engagement." * * *

In practice, the lawyer must have a hand in the drafting, training, dissemination, inspection, and enforcement of the Rules of Engagement and command policies that provide the linkage from the classroom to the field. This, in turn, requires that lawyers work closely with commanders and staffs to ensure proper targeting in the deliberate process. The Rules of Engagement must be disseminated to every corner of the command; equally important, the lawyer must be constantly on the move to reinforce the legal component of the Rules of Engagement, answer questions, and help fill the gaps in soldiers' minds regarding the interface of law and tactics.

Some soldiers from the Vietnam era reported that a lackadaisical approach to legal training caused them to take the otherwise sound command guidance they received on pocket cards and put the cards into their pockets unread and hence ignored. The United States Army continues to develop and disseminate such cards, as do many of our allies. The card is not an end in itself, but serves as the commander's tool to help instill compliance with legal norms, which is in turn reinforced by the active role of military lawyers.

In contrast to simply preparing a card for distribution to soldiers, lawyers with the Third Infantry Division during Operation Iraqi Freedom developed a matrix that was disseminated and used at command levels down to the smallest tactical force. The matrix (*see Figure 1 below*) gave commanders and soldiers a quick and ready reference with which to consider and implement the obligations of international humanitarian law. Anecdotal evidence shows that the Third Infantry Division filled out these cards and kept records of their efforts to comply with the law as long as it was physically possible given the demands of the battle.

The Lawyer as Negotiator—Military lawyers must continue to play a central role in the negotiation of new legal norms. The Official ICRC Commentary on Protocol I notes with some understatement, "a good military legal advisor should have some knowledge of military problems." In a similar vein, the law cannot be allowed to drift into an atrophied state in which its objectives are seen as romanticized and unattainable in the operational context. If Humanitarian Law becomes separated from the everyday experience and practice of professional military forces around the world, it is in danger of being relegated to the remote pursuit of ethereal goals. As the Third Infantry Division matrix illustrates so well, the law takes form and shape in the practice of soldiers and the thinking of commanders on the ground rather than in the textbooks and scholarly opinions.

* * * Failure to keep the legal norms anchored in the real world of practice would create a great risk of superimposing the humanitarian goals of the law as the dominant and perhaps only legitimate objective in times of conflict. This trend could result in principles and documents that would become increasingly divorced from military practice and therefore increasingly irrelevant to the actual conduct of operations. * * *

Figure 1

Commanders are responsible for assessing proportionality before authorizing indirect fire into a populated area or protected place (NFA/RFA). Refer to ROE; seek legal advice; copy SJA, G5 and FSE.

POPULATED AREA TARGETING RECORD
(Military Necessity – Collateral Damage – Proportionality Assessment)

I. MILITARY NECESSITY – What are we shooting at and why?

1. DTG of mission: ____________
2. Location – Grid Coordinates: ____________
3. Enemy Target (WMD, CHEM, SCUD, ARTY, ARMOR, C2, LOG)
   a. Type and Unit: ____________
   b. Importance to Mission: ____________
4. Target Intel:
   a. How Observed: UAV, FIST, SOF, other: ____________
   b. Unobserved: Q36, Q37, ELINT, other: ____________
   c. Last Known DTG of Observation or Detection: ____________
5. Other Concerns as applicable:
   a. US Casualties: Number: ______ Location: ____________
   b. Receiving Enemy Fire: Unit: ______ Location: ____________

II. COLLATERAL DAMAGE – Who or what is there now?

6. City: ____________ Original Population: ____________
7. Estimated Population Now in Target Area (if known): ____________
8. Cultural, Economic, or Other Significance and Effects:

____

III. MUNITIONS SELECTION – Mitigate civilian casualties and civilian property destruction

9. Available Delivery Systems Within Range:
   155, MLRS, ATACMS, AH64, CAS, other: ____________
10. Munitions: DPICM, Precision-Guided Munitions (PGM),
   other: ____________

IV. COMMANDER'S AUTHORIZATION TO FIRE – Proportionality analysis

11. Legal Advisor's Rank and Name: ____________
12. Civil Affairs/G5 Advisor: ____________
13. Is the anticipated loss of life and damage to civilian property acceptable in relation to the military advantage expected to be gained? ____________ Yes/No ______
14. Commander or Representative's Rank, Name, and Position:

____
15. Optional Comments: ____________
16. DTG of Decision: ____________

The Lawyer as Enforcer—The importance of enforcing the substantive body of norms through criminal investigations and prosecutions when appropriate cannot be overstated. As early as 1842, Secretary of State Daniel Webster articulated the idea that a nation's sovereignty also entails "the strict and faithful observance of all those principles, laws, and usages which have obtained currency among civilized states, and which have for their object the mitigation of the miseries of war." Military lawyers are at the forefront of such efforts precisely because they are in the best position to evaluate the culpability of commanders in light of the "reasonable commander" standard that is built into the law of armed conflict. Moreover, the same experts who advise commanders on the proper implementation of the law should find a great deal of professional satisfaction in helping to ensure that the law retains its influence and credibility. Their expertise forms the basis of effective prosecutions that are legally sound, but fair and credible from the perspective of soldiers in the field.

The events at Abu Ghraib have served to remind military professionals of the visceral linkage between their actions and the achievement of the mission. Abu Ghraib represents a sharp departure from American ideals precisely because some soldiers forgot about their overarching mission to defend justice and human dignity. At the same time, it is worth recalling that the crimes were made public because one young soldier, Specialist Joseph Darby, alerted appropriate authorities when he became aware of the activities inside Abu Ghraib.

The investigation and administration of appropriate discipline against culpable individuals serves an important deterrent purpose in the legal regime by helping to strengthen the resolve of the next Joseph Darby who may be forced to choose between loyalty to his comrade-in-arms and the principles of law and professionalism.

[M]any of the prosecutions of those who strayed so far from accepted professional norms in Iraq are based on the principle of dereliction of duty. Reflecting a concept of military law recognized around the world, Article 92 of the Uniform Code of Military Justice makes it a crime to fail to perform a known duty, either willfully or through neglect. The necessary base of knowledge that supports subsequent enforcement efforts was built by the military lawyers who taught the units, rehearsed them, and integrated legal considerations into the operational flow.

The Lawyer as Reporter—Lawyers who advise commanders on the proper application of Humanitarian Law have a vested interest in helping to ensure that those norms are respected and implemented in the future. In order to achieve that fundamental objective, legal advisors must be engaged at all levels to bring the light of truth and proper legal analysis to allegations of war crimes. * * *

Lawyers must be proactive in responding to allegations that humanitarian norms have been violated by collecting the relevant facts and eyewitness accounts, and analyzing them in light of their particular expertise in the law. * * *

For example, no responsible commander intentionally targets civilian populations, and the law on this matter is clear and fundamental. In the era of mass communications, the media often creates a perception that the normative content of the law is meaningless by conveying an automatic presumption that any instance of collateral damage is based on illegal conduct by military commanders. This perception is, of course, completely without foundation in Humanitarian Law. [N]othing would erode compliance with Humanitarian Law faster than false reports of what the other side has done, or distorted allegations that permissible conduct in fact represents willful defiance of international norms.

* * * If the exposure of illegal acts on the part of the adversary helps sway social and political opinion away from supporting lawless thugs, they may in turn recognize that their unlawful actions are a barrier to achieving their ends. * * * The legal advisor plays a critical role in getting to the scene quickly at the behest of the commander and ensuring that the facts are accurate so that the legal analysis is correct and timely.

NOTES AND QUESTIONS

1. *Individual Responsibility for Violations of the* Jus in Bello. Professor Newton's discussion of the military lawyer's role as "enforcer" indicates that individuals—both soldiers and their commanders—may be responsible for violating the law of war. Individual responsibility may attach to prohibited acts directed at combatants on the battlefield, prisoners of war, and civilians outside of combat.

What sorts of excuses might individuals who have committed an act that violates international humanitarian law appropriately invoke? If, for example, a commanding officer were to order a soldier to violate the law of war, could a soldier who complied with that order be held accountable? According to the Nuremberg judgment (see Chapter 6), "[t]hat a soldier was ordered to kill or torture in violation of the international law of war has never been recognized as a defense to such acts of brutality, though * * * the order may be urged in mitigation of the punishment." The same standard is incorporated in Article 7(4) of the Statute of the International Criminal Tribunal for the former Yugoslavia (ICTY), 32 *International Legal Materials* 1192, 1194 (1993), and in Article 6(4) of the Statute of the International Criminal Tribunal for Rwanda (ICTR), 33 *International Legal Materials* 1602, 1605 (1994); to the same effect is Article 33 of the Rome Statute of the International Criminal Court (ICC). What if the officer made it clear that the soldier receiving an order that violated international humanitarian law would be shot if he did not follow the order? See Prosecutor v. Erdemović, Case No. IT–96–22–A (Appeals Chamber, ICTY, 1997), *available at* http://www.icty.org (last visited Dec. 8, 2013).

The Nuremberg judgment and decisions of the ICTY and the ICTR provide numerous examples of commanding military officers themselves being tried and convicted for violating the law of war. Could a commanding officer be liable if that officer did not actually commit a proscribed act? Consider Article 6(3) of the Statute of the ICTR:

> The fact that any of the acts referred to in articles 2 to 4 of the present Statute was committed by a subordinate does not relieve his or her superior of criminal responsibility if he or she knew or had reason to know that the subordinate was about to commit such acts

> or had done so and the superior failed to take the necessary and reasonable measures to prevent such acts or to punish the perpetrators thereof.

33 *International Legal Materials* at 1604–05.

Should civilian leaders also be liable for violations of international humanitarian law? Under what circumstances? See Prosecutor v. Musema, No. 96–13–1 (ICTR, 2000), *available at* http://www.unictr.org (last visited Dec. 7, 2013).

2. *Process.* Although international courts may be able to try individuals for violations of the law of war in some situations in which municipal procedures are unavailable, international humanitarian law is most often implemented at the state level. Rules of international humanitarian law may be incorporated into municipal law. In the United States, these rules are set out in U.S. military manuals, *e.g.*, *The Law of Land Warfare* (FM 27–10, 1976), and *Human Intelligence Collector Operations* (FM 2–22.3 (FM 34–52), 2006), and soldiers and commanders may be prosecuted for proscribed conduct under the Uniform Code of Military Justice, 10 U.S.C. §§ 801 *et seq.* As Professor Newton noted, soldiers may be found liable for "dereliction of duty" under their own state's military disciplinary procedures if they have violated military orders that incorporate rules of international humanitarian law. Is not some such incorporation mechanism necessary if this body of law is ever to be truly effective? Unfortunately, as suggested by Professor Newton's references to the My Lai incident in Vietnam and to the abuses at Abu Ghraib in Iraq, not all violations have been deterred. Can participation by national military lawyers along the lines suggested by Professor Newton help prevent, as well as punish, violations of international humanitarian law? Professor Dickinson, while noting that "the mere existence of military lawyers does not guarantee that legal norms will be obeyed," has emphasized the importance of "organizational structure and institutional culture" for compliance with international humanitarian law. Laura A. Dickinson, "Military Lawyers on the Battlefield: An Empirical Account of International Law Compliance," 104 *American Journal of International Law* 1, 27 (2010). What additional measures at the national level are possible and desirable? See also Michal R. Belknap, *The Vietnam War on Trial: The My Lai Massacre and Court-Martial of Lieutenant Calley* (2002); Seymour M. Hersch, *Chain of Command: The Road from 9/11 to Abu Ghraib* (2004).

3. *Characterization Issues.* Applying the *jus in bello* requires classifying groups of people and types of conflicts. According to Professor Newton, the law of war "defines the class of persons against whom professional military forces can lawfully apply violence." It is essential, for example, to know who is a civilian and who is a combatant. Professor Dinstein has concluded that "the hallmark of civilians is that they are neither members of the armed forces nor do they actively participate in hostilities." Yoram Dinstein, *The Conduct of Hostilities under the Law of International Armed Conflict* 113 (2004). Compare Charles Garraway, "Interoperability and

the Atlantic Divide—A Bridge Over Troubled Waters," 34 *Israel Yearbook on Human Rights* 105, 107–17 (2004).

The *Tadić Case*, next, discussed other problems of characterization. According to the 1977 Protocols to the 1949 Geneva Conventions and current conceptions of customary international law, international humanitarian law only relates to "armed conflicts," and it is thus important to determine what constitutes an armed conflict. Since legal obligations may vary depending on whether an armed conflict is "international" or "not of an international character," it is also important to consider that distinction.

PROSECUTOR V. TADIĆ

Decision on the Defense Motion for Interlocutory Appeal on Jurisdiction,
Case No. IT–94–1
(Appeals Chamber, International Criminal Tribunal for the former Yugoslavia, 1995),
35 *International Legal Materials* 32 (1996)

66. Appellant now asserts the new position that there did not exist a legally cognizable armed conflict—either internal or international—at the time and place that the alleged offences were committed. * * *

67. International humanitarian law governs the conduct of both internal and international armed conflicts. Appellant correctly points out that for there to be a violation of this body of law, there must be an armed conflict. The definition of "armed conflict" varies depending on whether the hostilities are international or internal but, contrary to Appellant's contention, the temporal and geographical scope of both internal and international armed conflicts extends beyond the exact time and place of hostilities. With respect to the temporal frame of reference of international armed conflicts, each of the four Geneva Conventions contains language intimating that their application may extend beyond the cessation of fighting. For example, both Conventions I and III apply until protected persons who have fallen into the power of the enemy have been released and repatriated.

68. Although the Geneva Conventions are silent as to the geographical scope of international "armed conflicts," * * * at least some of the provisions of the Conventions apply to the entire territory of the Parties to the conflict, not just to the vicinity of actual hostilities. * * * With respect to prisoners of war, the Convention applies to combatants in the power of the enemy; it makes no difference whether they are kept in the vicinity of hostilities. In the same vein, Geneva Convention IV protects civilians anywhere in the territory of the Parties. [T]he very nature of the Conventions—particularly Conventions III and IV—dictates their application throughout the territories of the parties to the conflict; any other construction would substantially defeat their purpose.

69. The geographical and temporal frame of reference for internal armed conflicts is similarly broad. This conception is reflected in the fact

that beneficiaries of common Article 3 of the Geneva Conventions are those taking no active part (or no longer taking active part) in the hostilities. This indicates that the rules contained in Article 3 also apply outside the narrow geographical context of the actual theatre of combat operations. [The Tribunal discusses other examples involving detainee protections, which continue even after the end of hostilities.]

70. On the basis of the foregoing, we find that an armed conflict exists whenever there is a resort to armed force between States or protracted armed violence between governmental authorities and organized armed groups or between such groups within a State. International humanitarian law applies from the initiation of such armed conflicts and extends beyond the cessation of hostilities until a general conclusion of peace is reached; or, in the case of internal conflicts, a peaceful settlement is achieved. Until that moment, international humanitarian law continues to apply in the whole territory of the warring States or, in the case of internal conflicts, the whole territory under the control of a party, whether or not actual combat takes place there.

Applying the foregoing concept of armed conflicts to this case, we hold that the alleged crimes were committed in the context of an armed conflict. Fighting among the various entities within the former Yugoslavia began in 1991, continued through the summer of 1992 when the alleged crimes are said to have been committed, and persists to this day. * * * These hostilities exceed the intensity requirements applicable to both international and internal armed conflicts. There has been protracted, large-scale violence between the armed forces of different States and between governmental forces and organized insurgent groups. * * *

77. [W]e conclude that the conflicts in the former Yugoslavia have both internal and international aspects, that the members of the Security Council clearly had both aspects of the conflicts in mind when they adopted the Statute of the International Tribunal, and that they intended to empower the International Tribunal to adjudicate violations of humanitarian law that occurred in either context. To the extent possible under existing international law, the Statute should therefore be construed to give effect to that purpose. * * *

96. Whenever armed violence erupted in the international community, in traditional international law the legal response was based on a stark dichotomy: belligerency or insurgency. The former category applied to armed conflicts between sovereign States (unless there was recognition of belligerency in a civil war), while the latter applied to armed violence breaking out in the territory of a sovereign State. Correspondingly, international law treated the two classes of conflict in a markedly different way: interstate wars were regulated by a whole body of international legal rules, governing both the conduct of hostilities and

the protection of persons not participating (or no longer participating) in armed violence (civilians, the wounded, the sick, shipwrecked, prisoners of war). By contrast, there were very few international rules governing civil commotion, for States preferred to regard internal strife as rebellion, mutiny and treason coming within the purview of national criminal law and, by the same token, to exclude any possible intrusion by other States into their own domestic jurisdiction. This dichotomy was clearly sovereignty-oriented and reflected the traditional configuration of the international community, based on the coexistence of sovereign States more inclined to look after their own interests than community concerns or humanitarian demands.

97. Since the 1930s, however, the aforementioned distinction has gradually become more and more blurred, and international legal rules have increasingly emerged or have been agreed upon to regulate internal armed conflict. There exist various reasons for this development. First, civil wars have become more frequent, not only because technological progress has made it easier for groups of individuals to have access to weaponry but also on account of increasing tension, whether ideological, inter-ethnic or economic; as a consequence the international community can no longer turn a blind eye to the legal regime of such wars. Secondly, internal armed conflicts have become more and more cruel and protracted, involving the whole population of the State where they occur: the all-out resort to armed violence has taken on such a magnitude that the difference with international wars has increasingly dwindled (suffice to think of the Spanish civil war, in 1936–39, of the civil war in the Congo, in 1960–1968, the Biafran conflict in Nigeria, 1967–70, the civil strife in Nicaragua, in 1981–1990, or El Salvador, 1980–1993). Thirdly, the large-scale nature of civil strife, coupled with the increasing interdependence of States in the world community, has made it more and more difficult for third States to remain aloof: the economic, political and ideological interests of third States have brought about direct or indirect involvement of third States in this category of conflict, thereby requiring that international law take greater account of their legal regime in order to prevent, as much as possible, adverse spill-over effects. Fourthly, the impetuous development and propagation in the international community of human rights doctrines, particularly after the adoption of the Universal Declaration of Human Rights in 1948, has brought about significant changes in international law, notably in the approach to problems besetting the world community. A State-sovereignty-oriented approach has been gradually supplanted by a human-being-oriented approach. * * * It follows that in the area of armed conflict the distinction between interstate wars and civil wars is losing its value as far as human beings are concerned. Why protect civilians from belligerent violence, or ban rape, torture or the wanton destruction of hospitals, churches, museums or private property, as well as proscribe weapons causing

unnecessary suffering when two sovereign States are engaged in war, and yet refrain from enacting the same bans or providing the same protection when armed violence has erupted "only" within the territory of a sovereign State? If international law, while of course duly safeguarding the legitimate interests of States, must gradually turn to the protection of human beings, it is only natural that the aforementioned dichotomy should gradually lose its weight. * * *

129. [T]he violations at issue here * * * entail individual criminal responsibility, regardless of whether they are committed in internal or international armed conflicts. Principles and rules of humanitarian law reflect "elementary considerations of humanity" widely recognized as the mandatory minimum for conduct in armed conflicts of any kind. No one can doubt the gravity of the acts at issue, nor the interest of the international community in their prohibition.

NOTES AND QUESTIONS

1. *The International Criminal Tribunal for the former Yugoslavia.* The U.N. Security Council established the International Criminal Tribunal for the former Yugoslavia (ICTY) in Security Council Resolution 827 (1993). The Tribunal's Statute confers jurisdiction to prosecute individuals for certain international law offenses alleged to have been committed in the territory of the former Yugoslavia since January 1, 1991. Article 2 of the Statute provides that the Tribunal has "the power to prosecute persons committing or ordering to be committed grave breaches of the Geneva Conventions of 12 August 1949." Article 3 provides for "the power to prosecute persons violating the laws or customs of war," and Article 5 "the power to prosecute persons responsible for" specified crimes against humanity "when committed in armed conflict, whether international or internal in character." Dusko Tadić challenged the Tribunal's jurisdiction in part on the grounds that the offenses listed in Articles 2, 3, and 5 could only be committed during an armed conflict; he argued that no such conflict was ongoing in the region of Prijedor, where he was alleged to have committed crimes. For the text of the Tribunal's Statute, see 32 *International Legal Materials* 1192 (1993), and for an overview of the work of the Tribunal, see http://www.icty.org (last visited Dec. 8, 2013). For discussion of other international criminal tribunals, see Chapter 6.

2. *Armed Conflicts.* Deciding whether an armed conflict exists is critical in determining whether international humanitarian law applies. The status of armed conflict may also be important, *e.g.*, with respect to rights of asylum, the law of neutrality, the activities of U.N. peacekeepers, and the interpretation of arms control treaties. What features characterize armed conflicts? According to Article 1(2) of Protocol II to the 1977 Geneva Conventions, "situations of internal disturbances and tensions, such as riots [and] isolated and sporadic acts of violence" are not covered. How about "sporadic" international violence? Did France's sinking of the *Rainbow Warrior* (Chapter 5) constitute an armed conflict? Would an international

border incident, such as occurred in the *Naulilaa Case* in Part B below, constitute an "armed conflict"? What about the "Cod Wars" between the United Kingdom and Iceland, considered in the *Fisheries Jurisdiction Case* in Chapter 10? Are criteria of intensity and duration equally significant in determining the existence of an armed conflict? According to the International Tribunal for the former Yugoslavia in Prosecutor v. Haradinaj, Judgment, Case No. IT–04–84–T, ¶ 49 (Trial Chamber I, 2008), "[t]he criterion of protracted armed violence" refers "more to the intensity of the armed violence than to its duration." What factors should be used to judge intensity? When does an armed conflict begin and end?

The *Haradinaj Case* recognized that "an armed conflict can exist only between parties that are sufficiently organized to confront each other with military means." *Id.* ¶ 60. When is a group sufficiently well organized to engage in armed conflict? See Prosecutor v. Boškoski, Judgment, Case No. IT–04–82–A, ¶¶ 19–24 (Appeals Chamber, ICTY, 2010); International Law Association Committee on Use of Force, "Final Report on the Meaning of Armed Conflict in International Law," in International Law Association, *Report of the Seventy-Fourth Conference (The Hague)* 676 (2010); "How is the Term 'Armed Conflict' Defined in International Humanitarian Law?," International Committee of the Red Cross Opinion Paper, Mar. 2008, *available at* http://www.icrc.org (last visited Dec. 8, 2013).

3. *International Versus Internal Armed Conflicts.* The distinction between international and internal armed conflicts remains significant. As a matter of treaty law, for example, Protocol I to the Geneva Conventions (accepted by 173 parties, not including the United States, as of February 2013) applies to international armed conflicts, while Protocol II (167 parties, not including the United States) applies only to armed conflicts "not of an international character," *e.g.,* civil wars. With respect to customary international law, the Tribunal in the 1995 *Tadić Case* found that "(i) only a number of rules and principles governing international armed conflicts have gradually been extended to apply to internal conflicts; and (ii) this extension has not taken place in the form of a full and mechanical transplant of those rules to internal conflicts." 35 *International Legal Materials* at 69. The International Committee of the Red Cross (ICRC) and U.S. government officials have debated the customary international law status of rules of international humanitarian law. See 1–2 International Committee of the Red Cross, *Customary International Humanitarian Law* (Jean-Marie Henckaerts & Louise Doswald-Beck eds. 2005), and the exchange between U.S. government lawyers and the ICRC at 46 *International Legal Materials* 514, 959 (2007).

What distinguishes an international conflict from an internal one? Is it too simplistic to say that all international armed conflicts are fought between states? The distinction between internal and international armed conflicts was addressed in a later phase of the *Tadić Case.* A trial chamber convicted Tadić, who served with Bosnian Serb forces in Bosnia-Herzegovina where the crimes were committed, of some offenses, but not of "grave breaches of the

Geneva Conventions" under Article 2 of the Tribunal's Statute. Those grave breaches applied to protected persons (victims) in international armed conflicts, and, according to the trial chamber, the conflict inside Bosnia was internal. On a cross-appeal of Tadić's conviction, the ICTY Appeals Chamber concluded that even though Tadić and his victims were Bosnian, the Bosnian Serb forces of which Tadić was a part

> acted as *de facto* organs of another State, namely, the [Federal Republic of Yugoslavia]. Thus the requirements set out in Article 4 of Geneva Convention IV are met: the victims were "protected persons" as they found themselves in the hands of armed forces of a State of which they were not nationals.

Prosecutor v. Tadić, Case No. IT–94–1–A (Appeals Chamber, 1999), 38 *International Legal Materials* 1518, 1550 (1999). This conclusion was true "regardless of any specific instructions by the controlling State concerning the commission of" acts by the Bosnian Serb forces:

> The control required by international law may be deemed to exist when a State (or, in the context of an armed conflict, the Party to the conflict) *has a role in organising, coordinating or planning the military actions* of the military group, in addition to financing, training and equipping or providing operational support to that group.

Id. at 1545 (emphasis in original). The International Criminal Court in the *Lubanga Case* (Chapter 6) used this *Tadić* "overall control" test when it ruled that an internal armed conflict could become international not only when another state directly intervened, but when "some of the participants in the internal armed conflict act on behalf of that other State (indirect intervention)." Case No. ICC-01/04–01/06, Decision on the Confirmation of Charges ¶¶ 209, 211 (2007). See also Human Rights Council, *Report of the International Commission of Inquiry to Investigate All Alleged Violations of International Human Rights Law in the Libyan Arab Jamahiriya*, U.N. Doc. A/HRC/17/44, at 11, ¶¶ 60–66 (2011).

4. *Armed Conflict and Terrorists.* Is the struggle against global terrorism an armed conflict? To answer yes, must the fight be with a well-organized group? Could there be an armed conflict with an individual terrorist? If the struggle is an armed conflict, is it an international armed conflict, an armed conflict "not of an international character," or an armed conflict of some different sort?

In Hamdan v. Rumsfeld, 548 U.S. 557 (2006), the Supreme Court ruled on whether the Geneva Conventions applied to the conflict with Al Qaeda. The case involved a *habeas corpus* petition by Salim Ahmed Hamdan, a Yemeni national who was seized in Afghanistan after the September 11, 2001 terrorist attacks and held in custody at the U.S. prison in Guantánamo Bay, Cuba. He was to be tried for conspiracy by a U.S. military commission convened by the President. The alleged conspiracy involved Hamdan's transporting weapons and working as Osama bin Laden's bodyguard and personal driver. The Supreme Court ruled for Hamdan, concluding "that the military commission convened to try Hamdan lacks power to proceed because its structure and procedures"—*e.g.*, the authority to exclude the defendant and his counsel from the trial, and to allow use of hearsay evidence and evidence obtained through coercion—"violate both the [U.S. Uniform Code of Military Justice (UCMJ), 10 U.S.C. §§ 801 *et seq.*] and the Geneva Conventions." *Id.* at 567.

The Court ruled that the 1949 Geneva Conventions are, "as the Government does not dispute, part of the law of war. And compliance with the law of war is the condition upon which the authority set forth in Article 21 [of the UCMJ, authorizing a presidential order to establish a military commission] is granted." *Id.* at 628. It then turned to the nature of the "armed conflict" with Al Qaeda:

> The conflict with al Qaeda is not, according to the Government, a conflict to which the full protections afforded detainees under the 1949 Geneva Conventions apply because Article 2 of those Conventions (which appears in all four Conventions) renders the full protections applicable only to "all cases of declared war or of any other armed conflict which may arise between two or more of the High Contracting Parties." Since Hamdan was captured and detained incident to the conflict with al Qaeda and not the conflict with the Taliban, and since al Qaeda, unlike Afghanistan, is not a "High Contracting Party" * * * the protections of those Conventions are not, it is argued, applicable to Hamdan.
>
> We need not decide the merits of this argument because there is at least one provision of the Geneva Conventions that applies here even if the relevant conflict is not one between signatories. Article 3, often referred to as Common Article 3 because, like Article 2, it appears in all four Geneva Conventions, provides that in a "conflict not of an international character occurring in the territory of one of the High Contracting Parties, each Party to the conflict shall be bound to apply, as a minimum," certain provisions protecting "[p]ersons taking no active part in the hostilities, including members of armed forces who have laid down their arms and those placed *hors de combat* by . . . detention." One such provision prohibits "the passing of sentences and the carrying out of executions without previous judgment pronounced by a regularly constituted court affording all the judicial guarantees which are recognized as indispensable by civilized peoples."
>
> The Court of Appeals thought, and the Government asserts, that Common Article 3 does not apply to Hamdan because the conflict with al Qaeda, being " 'international in scope,' " does not qualify as a " 'conflict not of an international character.' " That reasoning is erroneous. The term "conflict not of an international character" is used here in contradistinction to a conflict between nations. * * * Common Article 3 * * * affords some minimal

protection, falling short of full protection under the Conventions, to individuals associated with neither a signatory nor even a nonsignatory "Power" who are involved in a conflict "in the territory of" a signatory. The latter kind of conflict is distinguishable from the conflict described in Common Article 2 chiefly because it does not involve a clash between nations (whether signatories or not). In context, then, the phrase "not of an international character" bears its literal meaning. See, *e.g.*, J. Bentham, Introduction to the Principles of Morals and Legislation 6, 296 (J. Burns & H. Hart eds. 1970) (using the term "international law" as a "new though not inexpressive appellation" meaning "betwixt nation and nation"; defining "international" to include "mutual transactions between sovereigns as such"); Int'l Comm. of Red Cross Commentary on the Additional Protocols to the Geneva Conventions of 12 August 1949, p 1351 (1987) ("[A] non-international armed conflict is distinct from an international armed conflict because of the legal status of the entities opposing each other").

Although the official commentaries accompanying Common Article 3 indicate that an important purpose of the provision was to furnish minimal protection to rebels involved in one kind of "conflict not of an international character," *i.e.*, a civil war, the commentaries also make clear "that the scope of application of the Article must be as wide as possible." * * *

Common Article 3, then, is applicable here and, as indicated above, requires that Hamdan be tried by a "regularly constituted court affording all the judicial guarantees which are recognized as indispensable by civilized peoples." * * * At a minimum, a military commission "can be 'regularly constituted' by the standards of our military justice system only if some practical need explains deviations from court-martial practice." [N]o such need has been demonstrated here. * * *

Common Article 3 obviously tolerates a great degree of flexibility in trying individuals captured during armed conflict; its requirements are general ones, crafted to accommodate a wide variety of legal systems. But *requirements* they are nonetheless. The commission that the President has convened to try Hamdan does not meet those requirements.

Id. at 628–33, 635.

If the *Hamdan* Court had accepted the government's argument that the "war" with Al Qaeda was neither an "international armed conflict" (because not between states) nor a "non-international armed conflict" (because not a civil war), would there have been a gap in the law? The Supreme Court avoided that outcome by finding that Common Article 3 had a broad scope of application. Was the Court's rationale convincing? Common Article 3 by its terms applies to "the case of armed conflict not of an international character occurring in the territory of one of the High Contracting Parties," but terrorist activities are not always localized in one territory. Did the Supreme Court interpret the term "international" too restrictively? Should we welcome the Court's invocation of Jeremy Bentham's 18th-century conception of international law? See M.W. Janis, "Jeremy Bentham and the Fashioning of 'International Law,'" 78 *American Journal of International Law* 405 (1984). Did the Court grapple sufficiently with the possibility that the "global war on terror" might be a new sort of armed conflict—international in scope, although not between nation states? If existing international humanitarian law did not apply in this global war, would other international law apply? See the "Cleveland Principles of International Law on the Detention & Treatment of Persons in Connection with 'The Global War on Terror,'" Principle 1 (2005), *available at* http://www.law.case.edu/centers/cox/content.asp?content_id=85 (last visited Dec. 8, 2013); John B. Bellinger III & Vijay M. Padmanabahn, "Detention Operations in Contemporary Conflicts: Four Challenges for the Geneva Conventions and Other Existing Law," 105 *American Journal of International Law* 201 (2011); Geoffrey S. Corn, "*Hamdan*, Lebanon, and the Regulation of Hostilities: The Need to Recognize a Hybrid Category of Armed Conflict," 40 *Vanderbilt Journal of Transnational Law* 295 (2007).

5. *Types of Combatants.* International humanitarian law accords different protections to different categories of individuals, distinguishing combatants from civilians. During international armed conflicts, lawful combatants may be targeted based on their status; they may not be prosecuted for acts of war during military operations (except for violations of international humanitarian law such as war crimes); and, when captured, they enjoy prisoner of war status (see Note 6 below). Many would also distinguish "lawful" from "unlawful" combatants. "[T]he term unlawful combatant describes all persons taking a direct part in hostilities without being entitled to do so." Knut Dörmann, "Combatants, Unlawful," in 2 *Max Planck Encyclopedia of Public International Law* 360, ¶ 4 (Rüdiger Wolfrum ed. 2012). What criteria determine whether a civilian is "taking a direct part in hostilities"? See Nils Melzer, *Interpretive Guidance on the Notion of Direct Participation in Hostilities Under International Humanitarian Law* (International Committee for the Red Cross, 2009), *available at* http://www.icrc.org/ (last visited Dec. 8, 2013); "Forum: The ICRC Interpretive Guidance on the Notion of Direct Participation in Hostilities Under International Humanitarian Law," 42 *New York University Journal of International Law and Politics* 637 (2010). Was Hamdan—allegedly Osama bin Laden's bodyguard and personal driver—an unlawful combatant? Do combatants include financiers, recruiters, trainers, those collecting intelligence, or those selling goods or providing services to Al Qaeda? See David Glazier, "Playing by the Rules: Combating Al Qaeda within the Law of War," 51 *William and Mary Law Review* 957, 996–1015 (2009); Faiza Patel, "Who Can Be Detained in the 'War on Terror'? The Emerging Answer," 13 *ASIL Insights*, Issue 18 (2009).

6. *Prisoners of War.* A lawful combatant is entitled to prisoner of war (POW) status when captured, and hence to the full protections of the (Third) 1949 Geneva Convention Relative to the Treatment of Prisoners of War, 3 U.S.T. 3316, 75 U.N.T.S. 135. These protections include the right not to be interrogated without consent, and the associated rights not to be subjected to torture or coercion to secure information, or to be subjected to "any unpleasant or disadvantageous treatment of any kind" for failure to answer questions. *Id.* art. 17. The view that lawful combatants have committed no legal wrong merely by fighting in an armed conflict suggests their detention is not penal. As the U.S. Supreme Court stated in Hamdi v. Rumsfeld, 542 U.S. 507, 518 (2004): "The purpose of detention is to prevent captured individuals from returning to the field of battle and taking up arms once again. [Under] the law of war * * * detention may last no longer than active hostilities. See Article 118 of the [Third Geneva Convention]." When POWs are alleged to have committed an offense, they generally have the right to be tried for an offence "only by a military court" offering "essential guarantees of independence and impartiality." Third Geneva Convention, art. 84.

Are all combatants entitled to POW status? Article 4(A)(1) of the Third Geneva Convention provides that POWs include "[m]embers of the armed forces of a Party to [an international armed] conflict as well as members of militias or volunteer corps forming part of such armed forces," once they "have fallen into the power of the enemy." Members of militia "belonging to" a party to an international armed conflict may also qualify for POW status under Article 4(A)(2) if they meet additional criteria: openly carrying arms; wearing a uniform or a distinctive sign; being under the command of a leader responsible for his subordinates; and conducting "operations in accordance with the laws and customs of war."

President George W. Bush unilaterally determined that none of the Guantánamo detainees seized after the 9/11 terrorist attacks—including alleged members of Al Qaeda, a non-state organization, and individuals fighting for the Taliban, the then-government of Afghanistan—was entitled to POW status. Was that determination consistent with the Third Geneva Convention? Article 5 of the Convention provides in part:

> Should any doubt arise as to whether persons, having committed a belligerent act and having fallen into the hands of the enemy, belong to any of the categories [of prisoners of war] enumerated in Article 4, such persons shall enjoy the protection of the present Convention until such time as their status has been determined by a competent tribunal.

According to one commentator, "the most difficult element to defend of the decisions made by President Bush in February [2002] with respect to the status of prisoners taken in Afghanistan is the blanket nature of the decision to deny POW status to the Taliban prisoners." George H. Aldrich, "The Taliban, Al Qaeda, and the Determination of Illegal Combatants," 96 *American Journal of International Law* 891, 897 (2002). See also John F. Murphy, "Is US Adherence to the Rule of Law in International Affairs

Feasible?," in *International Law and Armed Conflict: Exploring the Faultlines* 197, 214–20 (Michael Schmitt & Jelena Pejic eds. 2007). Should some entity also have determined whether any of those seized were civilians who had not "committed a belligerent act" at all?

7. *The Treatment of Detainees in the "War on Terror."* Assuming a suspected Al Qaeda terrorist is captured and detained, what legal standards apply to his treatment? Should he be treated in accordance with domestic criminal procedures? Do the risks to the prosecution of revealing sources, the difficulties of proving a case against a suspected terrorist who may have resided abroad, and the dangers of releasing suspected terrorists from prison suggest that a due process, criminal justice model cannot work? Is a "prisoner of war model" preferable? According to Professor Franck,

> [t]he logic behind the Geneva Conventions * * * is, first, that humane treatment of prisoners of war will encourage other combatants to surrender peaceably. Second, it is assumed that, when one party to a conflict treats its prisoners humanely, the other will reciprocate. Third, it is probably an unspoken conjecture that ordinary prisoners of war do not have much information that is likely, whether revealed or unrevealed, to have a great impact on the outcome of the conflict. Simply stating these underlying assumptions of the law of war is to suggest that they are not so evidently applicable to an international terrorist conspiracy like Al Qaeda.

Thomas M. Franck, "Criminals, Combatants, or What? An Examination of the Role of Law in Responding to the Threat of Terror," 98 *American Journal of International Law* 686, 687 (2004). If Al Qaeda members are neither treated as criminals in a domestic legal system, nor given full protections as POWs, what international legal standards apply to them?

Before the *Hamdan* decision, some officials in the George W. Bush administration, including Justice Department attorneys, argued that "enemy combatants"—a term neither defined in the Geneva Conventions nor commonly used in international humanitarian law—were not entitled to the protection of Common Article 3 of the Geneva Conventions. This Article, which has been called a "mini-convention," provides in part:

> In the case of armed conflict not of an international character occurring in the territory of one of the High Contracting Parties, each Party to the conflict shall be bound to apply, as a minimum, the following provisions:
>
> > 1. Persons taking no active part in the hostilities, including members of armed forces who have laid down their arms and those placed "hors de combat" by sickness, wounds, detention, or any other cause, shall in all circumstances be treated humanely, without any adverse distinction founded on race, colour, religion or faith, sex, birth or wealth, or any other similar criteria.

To this end, the following acts are and shall remain prohibited at any time and in any place whatsoever with respect to the above-mentioned persons:

(a) violence to life and person, in particular murder of all kinds, mutilation, cruel treatment and torture;

(b) taking of hostages;

(c) outrages upon personal dignity, in particular humiliating and degrading treatment;

(d) the passing of sentences and the carrying out of executions without previous judgment pronounced by a regularly constituted court, affording all the judicial guarantees which are recognized as indispensable by civilized peoples.

In February 2002, President George W. Bush determined that enemy combatants should be granted some protections: "[a]s a matter of policy, the United States Armed Forces shall continue to treat detainees humanely and, to the extent appropriate and consistent with military necessity, in a manner consistent with the principles of" the Third Geneva Convention of 1949. *Reprinted in The Torture Papers: The Road to Abu Ghraib* 134, 135 (Karen J. Greenberg & Joshua L. Dratel eds. 2005). Did this amount to a recognition that Common Article 3 applied to all detainees?

8. *Government Attorneys.* Was it ethical for U.S. Justice Department lawyers to prepare memoranda supporting President Bush's decision to deny POW status to all Guantánamo detainees, a decision discussed in Note 6 above? In addition, some government attorneys broadly construed presidential authority and narrowly interpreted prohibitions on torture and inhumane interrogation techniques, prohibitions mandated for example in the Convention Against Torture and Other Cruel, Inhuman or Degrading Treatment or Punishment, Dec. 10, 1984, 23 *International Legal Materials* 1027 (1984). See Sean D. Murphy, "Contemporary Practice of the United States Relating to International Law," 98 *American Journal of International Law* 820 (2004); *The Torture Papers, supra* Note 7. Justice Department memoranda allegedly contributed to abuses of U.S. detainees in Guantánamo and Iraq. See Laura A. Dickinson, "Abu Ghraib: The Battle Over Institutional Culture and Respect for International Law within the U.S. Military," in *International Law Stories* 405 (John E. Noyes, Laura A. Dickinson & Mark W. Janis eds. 2007). Other U.S. practices have been controversial as well. Was it legal to engage in "extraordinary renditions," *i.e.*, sending detainees to countries where they might well be tortured? See Leila Nadya Sadat, "Ghost Prisoners and Black Sites: Extraordinary Rendition under International Law," 37 *Case Western Reserve Journal of International Law* 309 (2006). May the United States escape its legal responsibilities by delegating military functions to private contractors who engage in abuses? See Laura A. Dickinson, *Outsourcing War and Peace: Preserving Public Values in a World of Privatized Foreign Affairs* (2011). See

generally Thomas Michael McDonnell, *The United States, International Law, and the Struggle against Terrorism* (2010).

The Justice Department memoranda did not go unchallenged. Other U.S. government lawyers found them "legally and morally unsupportable, likely to endanger our own military personnel, and damaging to our country's reputation and national interest." Richard B. Bilder & Detlev F. Vagts, "Speaking Law to Power: Lawyers and Torture," 98 *American Journal of International Law* 689, 690 (2004). In 2004, the U.S. Department of Justice withdrew and then modified one notorious memorandum narrowly interpreting the definition of torture. U.S. Department of Justice, Office of Legal Counsel, Memorandum for James B. Comey, Deputy Attorney General, from Acting Assistant Attorney General Daniel Levin, Dec. 30, 2004, *available at* http://www.justice.gov/olc/18usc23402340a2.htm (last visited Dec. 8, 2013).

Were the Justice Department attorneys insufficiently familiar with historical links between international law and U.S. foreign policy? Should the President instead have relied on advice from State Department and military lawyers, who more routinely face issues of international law? Consider the views of William H. Taft IV, who served as Legal Adviser to the U.S. Department of State from 2001 to 2005:

> [B]oth the civilian and military leadership of the Department of Defense proposed to follow the U.S. practice in Vietnam of treating all detainees in accordance with the [Geneva] Conventions, regardless of whether they were entitled to such treatment or not. It was the lawyers from the Department of Justice who pressed for a determination that the Conventions and other standards of international law and practice did not govern the conflict. Bearing an abstract hostility to international law, developed in the sheltered environment of academic journals, and equally unfamiliar and unconcerned with our broader policy interests in promoting respect for the rule of law among states as well as within them, these lawyers proposed to create a regime in which detainees were deprived of all legal rights and the conditions of their treatment were a matter of unreviewable executive discretion. Why lawyers, of all people, should want to establish the point that such a lawless regime could legally exist, even as a theoretical matter, much less recommend that one actually be created, is, I confess, beyond me, and in itself is a sad commentary on the extent to which sophistry has penetrated what used to be widely regarded as an honorable and learned profession.
>
> [I]t was a mistake to disconnect as large an organization as the U.S. Army from a system of rules under which it had been operating for many years, tell it that there are no legal requirements for its future conduct, and give it no more guidance than to act humanely. Even when rules for how to treat detainees are well settled and troops are trained and disciplined to comply with them, the tension

> and the high passion involved in combat can easily result in abuses. When the rules are changing and their legal authority is in doubt, such abuses are virtually inevitable. * * *
>
> [During the Bush] Administration's consideration of how to treat detainees in the conflict with al Qaeda * * * lawyers effectively turned what should have been, as it was in Vietnam, a question of how we wanted to treat the detainees into a debate about what our minimal obligations were under the law. The nation's foreign policy on which our liberty and prosperity depend * * * became simply the occasion for lawyers with but slight experience in and no responsibility for these matters to obtain official endorsement of an exotic legal proposition. Even if the proposition had been correct, which the Supreme Court determined it was not, this abstract exercise would have been a mistake. Of course, it's important to know what the law is, but it's even more important to know what it is in your interest to do. When you know that, it is time to ask the lawyers whether it is lawful, and if it is, you go ahead with it. This is the way foreign and national security policy have generally been made and carried out in the past, and international law has developed consistent with state practice determined by policymaking officials.

William H. Taft IV, "A View from the Top: American Perspectives on International Law After the Cold War," 31 *Yale Journal of International Law* 503, 509–10 (2006). John Bellinger, the State Department Legal Adviser during President Bush's second term (2005–2009) agreed "that the United States should have provided all detainees in the conflict with Al Qaeda and the Taliban the protections of common Article 3 * * * from the outset of the conflict." Bellinger & Padmanabahn, *supra* Note 4, at 207.

9. *Enforcing International Humanitarian Law*. Detainees in the "war on terror" have challenged their detention and treatment in U.S. and foreign courts. Cases reaching the U.S. Supreme Court included Boumediene v. Bush, 553 U.S. 723 (2008), Hamdi v. Rumsfeld, 542 U.S. 507 (2004), Rasul v. Bush, 542 U.S. 466 (2004), and Rumsfeld v. Padilla, 542 U.S. 426 (2004), as well as *Hamdan*. After the *Hamdan* decision, the U.S. Department of Defense affirmed that all armed service members "shall observe the requirements of the law of war, and shall apply, without regard to a detainee's legal status, at a minimum the standards articulated in Common Article 3." Directive 2310.01E, "The Department of Defense Detainee Program," ¶ 4.2 (2006), *quoted in* Gary D. Solis, *The Law of Armed Conflict* 166–67 (2010). *Hamdan* also prompted Congress to enact a new Military Commission Act of 2006. In *Boumediene* the Supreme Court ruled unconstitutional portions of that Act that suspended the *habeas corpus* right of detainees at Guantánamo to challenge their detentions. The United States has further modified its laws concerning detainees in the Military Commission Act of 2009 and the National Defense Authorization Act for Fiscal Year 2012. See Jennifer K.

Elsea & Michael John Garcia, "The National Defense Authorization Act for FY 2012 and Beyond: Detainee Matters," *CRS Report for Congress* (2013).

U.S. cases stemming from the "war on terror" have addressed issues we consider elsewhere in this book. All concerned the foreign affairs responsibilities of the President, Congress, and the judiciary, topics introduced in Chapter 4. Some also considered the extraterritorial application of U.S. law (see Chapter 11). Other cases, including *Hamdan*, involved the relationship between treaties and U.S. law. Are the Geneva Conventions self-executing? Why did the *Hamdan* Court apply Common Article 3 of the Geneva Conventions? See Chapter 4 and Note 4 above.

What forum can best help ensure respect for international humanitarian law? Should the military be left to enforce this law? See the essay by Professor Newton above. How efficacious are national courts? Are international courts, such as the International Tribunal for the former Yugoslavia, which decided *Tadić*, better able to promote compliance with the law of war? See Chapters 5 and 6.

10. Jus Cogens. The proscription against official torture has often been cited as an example of a *jus cogens* norm. Why is it important to determine whether an alleged act of torture also constitutes a violation of international humanitarian law? For discussion of *jus cogens*, see Chapter 3.

B. JUS AD BELLUM: TRADITIONAL LIMITS ON RESORT TO FORCE

For centuries, theologians and jurists have worked to define legal and moral limits on the use of force. St. Augustine, writing in the 5th century, developed a concept of *just war*, war pursued to avenge injuries against an enemy who "has neglected either to punish wrongs committed by its own citizens or to restore what has been unjustly taken by it. Further that kind of war is undoubtedly just which God Himself ordains." *Quoted in* Ian Brownlie, *International Law and the Use of Force by States* 5 (1963). The 16th-century Spanish Catholic jurists Vitoria and Suarez, along with the Dutch Protestant theorist Hugo Grotius, who wrote at the time of the Thirty Years War (1618–1648), were among those who refined the just war doctrine, believing there ought to be both humane means and right ends in the prosecution of war.

Just war doctrine eventually fell into disfavor in many international legal circles. In the 19th and early 20th centuries, international law commentators often regarded war—a formal status that depended on the declaration or intention of one of the parties—as a legitimate exercise of sovereign power. Writing in the late 19th century, William Hall claimed that international law has "no alternative but to accept war, independently of the justice of its origin, as a relation which the parties to it may set up, if they choose." W.E. Hall, *A Treatise on International Law* § 16, at 64–65 (4th ed. 1895). According to Charles Hyde, "[i]t always lies within the power of a State to endeavor to obtain redress for wrongs, or to gain political or other advantages over another * * * by direct recourse to war." 2 *International Law Chiefly as Interpreted and Applied by the United States* § 597, at 189 (1922). Indeed, a traditional way for a state to acquire territory was by conquest followed by occupation and effective control, a method consistent with discretionary unilateral use of force. Nowadays, as we see in Parts C and D, the legality of recourse to force is suspect, except in cases of self-defense or when authorized by the United Nations Security Council.

Yet even when recourse to war was generally regarded as legal, some international law rules limited resort to force. Two types of limits were notable during the 19th and early 20th centuries. First, some treaties constrained states in their resort to force. For example, parties to the 1907 Hague Convention No. II agreed "not to have recourse to armed force for the recovery of contract debts claimed from the Government of one country by the Government of another country as being due to its nationals," although the limitation was not applicable if the debtor state refused to submit to arbitration or to comply with a resulting arbitral award. Art. 1, 36 Stat. 2241, 2251 (1907). Other agreements limited the size of forces that could be placed along borders, while still others protected neutral states.

Second, significant authority suggested that general international law limited the use of force short of war. The arbitral tribunal in the *Naulilaa Case*, excerpted below, discussed limits on the use of force in a reprisal, an act of self-help by an injured state. The 19th-century diplomatic exchange in the *Caroline* dispute, the second reading in this part, concerned limits on the use of force in self-defense.

THE NAULILAA CASE

Portugal v. Germany, Special Arbitral Tribunal, Judgment of 31 July 1928,
8 *Recueil des Décisions des Tribunaux Arbitrales Mixtes* 409,
2 *Reports of International Arbitral Awards* 1011 (2006)
(authors' translation from the French)

[In October 1914, a delegation from the German colony of Southwest Africa (present-day Namibia) crossed to the border post of Naulilaa in Angola, then a Portuguese colony, to discuss importing food into Southwest Africa. A series of misunderstandings, originating with translation difficulties on the part of the German interpreter, led the Portuguese garrison to kill three Germans and to confine two others. In retaliation, the German authorities in Southwest Africa attacked Naulilaa and other Portuguese outposts in Angola, resulting in numerous casualties and serious property damage. The Portuguese retreated to the north, the Germans withdrew back into Southwest Africa, and the indigenous Cuanhama peoples then pillaged the evacuated region. Portugal recaptured the evacuated territory in the spring of 1915. An arbitral tribunal, composed of three Swiss arbitrators, was constituted to consider Portugal's claim for the damages resulting from Germany's attack.]

The arbitrators conclude as follows:

a) The Naulilaa incident was not the result of acts contrary to the law of nations imputable to German or Portuguese civil or military authorities. In particular, it is necessary to rule out, on the part of the [German] Schultze-Jena mission, any intentional penetration of Portuguese territory with the secret goal of beginning or preparing an invasion, and on the part of the regional Portuguese military authorities, any premeditated intention to lure the German detachment to Naulilaa in order to destroy or capture it.

b) The deplorable occurrence, which took place at the fort itself, was clearly fortuitous. It was the result of a series of misunderstandings, due initially to the inadequacy of the interpreter Jensen, next to some imprudence on the part of Dr. Schultze-Jena, and lastly to an unfortunate gesture, perhaps wrongly interpreted, which could have led [Portuguese] Lieutenant Sereno to believe that he was being threatened and that he found himself in a condition calling for legitimate defense.

THE QUESTION OF REPRISALS

The most recent doctrine, notably German doctrine, defines a reprisal in these terms:

The *reprisal* is an act of self-help (*Selbsthilfehandlung*) on the part of the injured state—*after an unsatisfied demand*—responding to an act contrary to the law of nations on the part of the offending state. [The reprisal] has the effect of momentarily suspending, in the relations of the two states, the observance of one or another rule of international law. It is *limited* by considerations of humanity and rules of good faith, applicable in interstate relations. *It would be illegal if a prior act, contrary to international law, had not furnished the reason for it.* It tends to impose, on the offending state, the duty to make reparation for the offense or to return to legality, while avoiding new offenses.

This definition does not require that a reprisal be *proportionate* to the offense. On this point, authors, unanimous until a few years ago, are beginning to be divided in their opinions. Most take the view that a certain proportionality between offense and reprisal is necessary for the legitimacy of the latter. Others, among the most modern, no longer demand this condition. As for international law, presently developing in the light of the last war, it certainly seems to restrict the notion of legitimate reprisal and to prohibit excess.

[T]he deaths of Dr. Schultze-Jena and the two officers who accompanied him were not the result of any act contrary to the law of nations by the Portuguese authorities.

A neutral state has the right to disarm and to intern armed belligerents who enter its territory. The internment of the interpreter Jensen and the soldier Kimmel were thus, in principle, authorized by the positive law of nations. * * * The German authorities * * * could not * * * consider such internment or its continuance as an act contrary to the law of nations, giving them a fair motive to conduct armed reprisals.

[The German vice-consul Schoess was expelled from Portuguese territory after the German attacks.] Furthermore, expulsion of a consular agent, against whom a state believes it has a complaint, may constitute an "unfriendly" act, giving rise to diplomatic representations[.] [B]ut [such an expulsion] cannot be, in similar circumstances where the sovereign authority of a neutral state is asserted, an act contrary to the law of nations, justifying, in the name of reprisal, an attack accompanied by all the severities of war.

The first condition—*sine qua non*—of the right to take reprisals is a reason furnished by a prior act contrary to the law of nations. This condition—the necessity of which is acknowledged by Germany—is lacking[.]

Even if the arbitrators had found that the Portuguese authorities had acted contrary to the law of nations, providing, in principle, justification for reprisals, the German case would nevertheless fail for two other reasons, each of them decisive:

1. A reprisal is only lawful when it has been preceded by an unsatisfied *demand*. The use of force is justified, indeed, only by its character of necessity. * * * There was, on the part of the authorities of [German] South-West Africa, resort to force, without a prior attempt to obtain satisfaction by way of legal means, which, again, precludes the legality of the reprisals taken.

2. The necessity of *proportionality* between the reprisal and the offense seems to be recognized in the German response. Even if one were to admit that the law of nations required that a reprisal correlate only approximately to an offense, one certainly ought to consider as excessive, and hence illegal, reprisals beyond all proportion with the act that motivated them. [T]here was evident disproportion between the incident at Naulilaa and the six acts of reprisals that followed it.

The arbitrators thus reach the conclusion that the German aggressions in October, November and December 1914 at the Angolan border cannot be considered as legal reprisals for the Naulilaa incident or for the subsequent acts of the Portuguese authorities, because of the lack of a prior demand and of acceptable proportionality between the alleged offense and the reprisals taken. * * *

Some of the damages for which Portugal demands reparation are the immediate consequence of the unjustified acts of aggression committed by Germany: soldiers or civilians killed or wounded in the fighting with the German troops, destruction by enemy fire of forts or outposts and all they contained, supplies, war material, etc. * * *

As for the remainder [of the damages], the Portuguese claims relate to damages for which the German attacks are not in all cases the sole cause. The Portuguese troops having fallen back after the battle of Naulilaa, and the forts and outposts of the Cunene line having been evacuated, the indigenous peoples rebelled. [The tribunal determines that the damage during this rebellion was attributable in part to Germany, in part to Portugal, whose local commander decided to evacuate a wide area although not under immediate pressure from German forces, and in part to the indigenous Cuanhama peoples.]

In conclusion, it is necessary to distinguish two categories of damages: the immediate damages caused by the German attacks, for which the respondent state is held fully liable, * * * and other damages which * * * the arbitrators will take into account, in a very limited measure, by fixing a supplemental equitable indemnity, noting the greater part of the causes foreign to Germany.

NOTES AND QUESTIONS

1. *The Naulilaa Arbitral Tribunal*. To establish the tribunal, Portugal invoked a provision of the 1919 Treaty of Versailles, 225 Consolidated Treaty Series 189, 332. This provision authorized arbitration of claims of nationals of Allied or Associated Powers, of which Portugal was one, "growing out of acts committed by" Germany after July 31, 1914, but before the Allied or Associated Power in question entered World War I.

2. *Neutrality*. Although World War I was already underway in 1914 when the Naulilaa incident occurred, Portugal was then neutral and did not go to war with Germany until 1916. The arbitrators referred to the rights of neutral states, itself a detailed field of traditional international law. See generally Michael Bothe, "Neutrality, Concept and General Rules," in 7 *Max Planck Encyclopedia of Public International Law* 617 (Rüdiger Wolfrum ed. 2012).

3. *Reprisals*. A reprisal is a state act taken in response to another state's internationally wrongful act. Reprisals would themselves be illegal acts, except for the prior violation by the other state. Reprisals need not necessarily involve the use of force. Detentions of foreign vessels in port, pacific blockades against the movement of foreign vessels, and seizures of foreign vessels or their cargoes on the high seas were typical forms of reprisals. The early practice of "special reprisal," whereby a state would issue

a "letter of marque" to one of its citizens who was wronged by another state, authorizing that citizen to seize property of citizens of the wrongdoing state, has long been discontinued. See Article I(8) of the U.S. Constitution, in the Appendix.

Nowadays, the legality of the use of force as a reprisal is suspect. The U.N. General Assembly's 1970 Declaration on Principles of International Law concerning Friendly Relations and Co-operation among States in accordance with the Charter of the United Nations, G.A. Res. 2625 (XXV), adopted by consensus, provides that "States have a duty to refrain from acts of reprisal involving the use of force." According to the ICJ in its advisory opinion in the *Legality of the Threat or Use of Nuclear Weapons Case*, "armed reprisals in time of peace * * * are considered to be unlawful." 1996 I.C.J. 226, 246. Article 33 of the 1949 Fourth Geneva Convention and Article 51(6) of 1977 Protocol I explicitly prohibit reprisals against civilians during international armed conflicts. See Derek Bowett, "Reprisals Involving Recourse to Armed Force," 66 *American Journal of International Law* 1 (1972); Theodor Meron, "The Humanization of Humanitarian Law," 94 *American Journal of International Law* 239, 249–50 (2000). As you read about the *Caroline* dispute below, and about the modern law of self-defense in Parts C and D, consider what distinguishes the use of force in reprisals from the use of force in self-defense.

4. *Other Forms of Self-help*. A retorsion, like a reprisal, is a form of self-help. A retorsion is an act that, though unfriendly, would have been legal even if not taken in response to another state's action. For example, if one state cuts off longstanding economic assistance to another state or breaches a bilateral treaty, the adversely affected state might reply by withdrawing its ambassador from the first state. Self-help also encompasses self-defense, addressed later in this chapter.

International lawyers today often use the term "countermeasures" rather than referring to either reprisals or retorsions. A countermeasure was at issue in the Case Concerning the Air Services Agreement of 27 March 1946 (U.S.-France), 54 *International Law Reports* 304 (1978). France refused to allow passengers travelling to Paris on a U.S. airline to disembark because the airline had switched them to a smaller plane in London en route from the U.S. west coast. The United States argued that this "change in gauge" was legal, and France's action illegal, under a 1946 U.S.-French Air Services Agreement, 139 U.N.T.S. 253, and a 1960 U.S.-French Exchange of Notes, 458 U.N.T.S. 292. Responding to France's refusal to allow passengers to disembark in Paris, the United States took steps to prohibit certain flights by French carriers to the U.S. west coast. This U.S. move would have been illegal under the 1946 Agreement, but the United States submitted that it was a valid countermeasure. The arbitral tribunal first ruled that the U.S. carrier had the right to operate its U.S. west coast—Paris service with a change in gauge in London, and then turned to the U.S. countermeasure. In line with the decision in the *Naulilaa Case*, the tribunal emphasized that a countermeasure must be proportionate to the prior illegal act, both in terms of the damages it causes and in terms of the importance of the principle at stake.

Should a party have to make use of dispute settlement mechanisms, such as arbitration, before taking countermeasures? The *Air Services Agreement* tribunal found that the United States was not precluded from taking countermeasures before concluding an arbitral *compromis.* The International Law Commission, in its study of state responsibility, debated a proposal requiring recourse to international dispute settlement procedures as a condition for lawful countermeasures. See Oscar Schachter, "Dispute Settlement and Countermeasures in the International Law Commission," 88 *American Journal of International Law* 471 (1994). The ILC's 2001 Draft Articles on the Responsibility of States for Internationally Wrongful Acts did not adopt this proposal. *Report of the International Law Commission on the Work of its Fifty-third Session,* U.N. Doc. A/56/10 (2001), in 2 *Yearbook of the International Law Commission*, U.N. Doc. A/CN.4/SER.A/2001/Add.1 (Part 2), at 20 (2001). Article 52 of the Draft Articles instead provides that "[c]ountermeasures may not be taken, and if already taken must be suspended [if:] [t]he internationally wrongful act has ceased; and [t]he dispute is pending before a court or tribunal which has the authority to make decisions binding on the parties." See David J. Bederman, "Counterintuiting Countermeasures," 96 *American Journal of International Law* 817 (2002).

THE CAROLINE DISPUTE

29 *British and Foreign State Papers* 1129;
30 *British and Foreign State Papers* 195

[During an 1837 Canadian insurrection against the British government, rebels urged Americans to help their cause. Despite the efforts of U.S. authorities to prevent U.S. citizens from cooperating with the uprising, many volunteers from the Buffalo, N.Y. area were recruited. In December 1837 a force of 800–1000 men, mostly U.S. citizens, took possession of Navy Island, a Canadian island in the Niagara River, which formed the boundary between the United States and Canadian territory. This base was used to fire on houses and vessels. The *Caroline*, a privately owned American ship, delivered ammunition and supplies from U.S. territory to Navy Island. One night in late December 1837, British forces attacked the *Caroline*, which at the time was docked on the U.S. shore. At least one American was killed. The British lit the ship on fire and then set it adrift; it broke apart.

This incident gave rise to diplomatic exchanges between the U.S. and British governments during the period 1838–1842. U.S. Secretary of State Daniel Webster sent the April 1841 letter excerpted below to Henry Fox, the British Minister in Washington. The second excerpt is from the reply of Lord Ashburton to a note from Daniel Webster dated July 27, 1842, with which Webster enclosed a copy of his April 1841 letter. Lord Ashburton had been sent from Britain to the United States as a special minister to address several outstanding disputes between the two countries.]

Mr. Webster to Mr. Fox. Washington, April 24, 1841.

[T]he act of destroying the *Caroline* [cannot] be justified by any reasonable application or construction of the right of self-defence under the laws of nations. It is admitted that a just right of self-defence attaches always to nations as well as to individuals, and is equally necessary for the preservation of both. But the extent of this right is a question to be judged of by the circumstances of each particular case, and when its alleged exercise has led to the commission of hostile acts within the territory of a Power at peace, nothing less than a clear and absolute necessity can afford ground of justification.

[I]t will be for Her Majesty's Government * * * to show a necessity of self-defence, instant, overwhelming, leaving no choice of means, and no moment for deliberation. It will be for it to show, also, that the local authorities of Canada, even supposing the necessity of the moment authorized them to enter the territories of The United States at all, did nothing unreasonable or excessive; since the act, justified by the necessity of self-defence, must be limited by that necessity, and kept clearly within it. It must be shown that admonition or remonstrance to the persons on board the Caroline was impracticable, or would have been unavailing; it must be shown that day-light could not be waited for; that there could be no attempt at discrimination between the innocent and the guilty; that it would not have been enough to seize and detain the vessel; but that there was a necessity, present and inevitable, for attacking her in the darkness of the night, while moored to the shore, and while unarmed men were asleep on board, killing some and wounding others, and then drawing her into the current, above the cataract, setting her on fire, and, careless to know whether there might not be in her the innocent with the guilty, or the living with the dead, committing her to a fate which fills the imagination with horror. A necessity for all this, the Government of the United States cannot believe to have existed.

Lord Ashburton to Mr. Webster. Washington, July 28, 1842. * * *

It is so far satisfactory to perceive that we are perfectly agreed as to the general principles of international law applicable to this unfortunate case. Respect for the inviolable character of the territory of independent nations is the most essential foundation of civilization. It is useless to strengthen a principle so generally acknowledged by any appeal to authorities on international law, and you may be assured, Sir, that Her Majesty's Government set the highest possible value on this principle, and are sensible of their duty to support it by their conduct and example for the maintenance of peace and order in the world.

Figure 9.A

The Niagara River and Navy Island

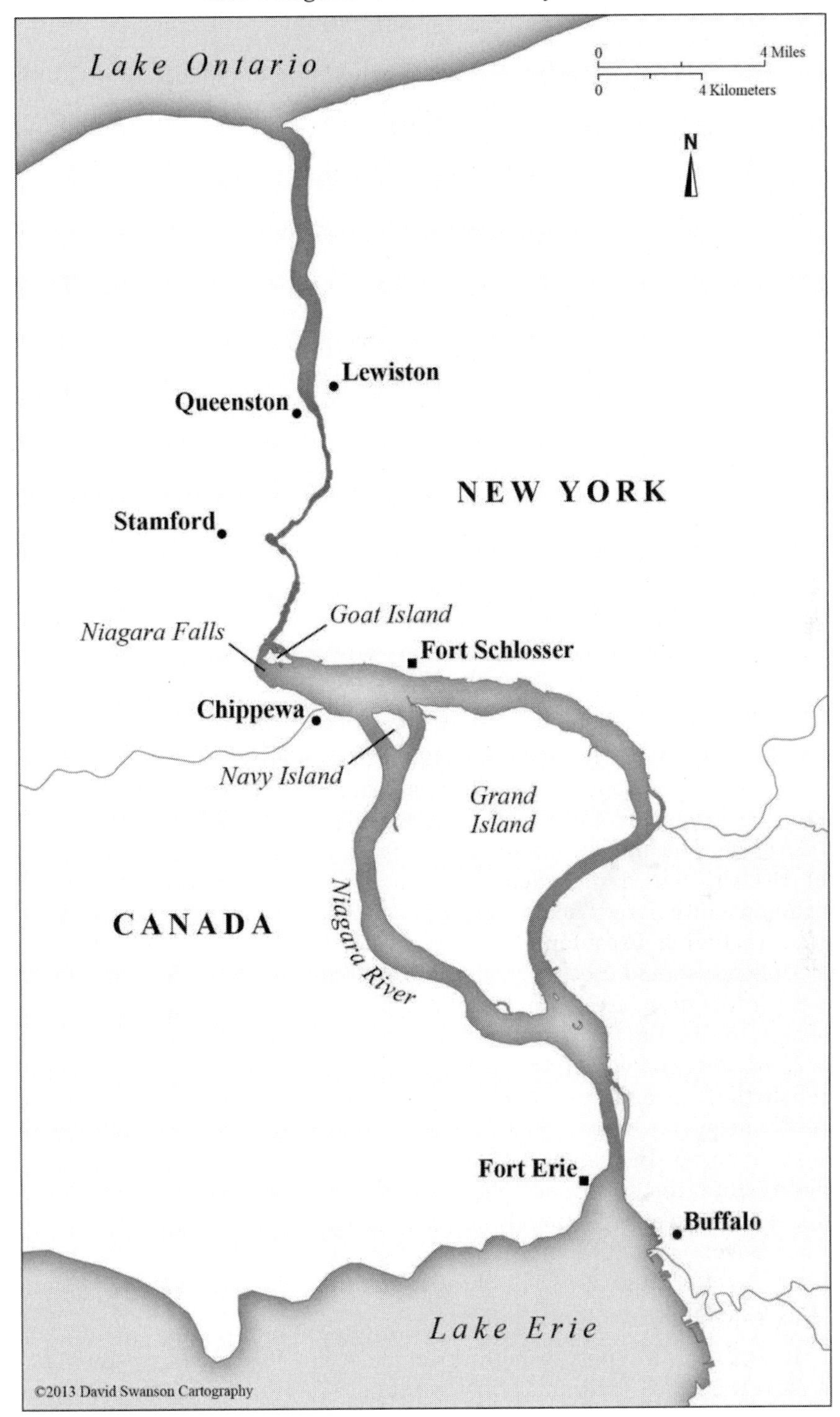

[But] a strong overpowering necessity may arise when this great principle may and must be suspended. It must be so for the shortest possible period during the continuance of an admitted overruling necessity, and strictly confined within the narrowest limits imposed by that necessity. "Self" defence is the first law of our nature, and it must be recognized by every code which professes to regulate the conditions and relations of man. Upon this modification, if I may so call it, of the great general principle, we seem also to be agreed[.]

NOTES AND QUESTIONS

1. *The Outcome of the* Caroline *Dispute.* In parts of his July 1842 letter not reproduced above, Lord Ashburton attempted, in good lawyerly fashion, to justify the attack on the *Caroline* within the framework of the rules Webster had set forth. Ashburton also expressed regret for the need to violate U.S. territory, and apologized for not expressing that regret earlier. Webster replied on August 6, 1842. He accepted the apology, noting "with pleasure that your Lordship fully admits those great principles of public law, applicable to cases of this kind, which this government has expressed; and that on your part, as on ours, respect for the inviolable character of the territory of independent states is the most essential foundation of civilization." *Quoted in* 2 Moore, *Digest of International Law* § 217, at 412 (1906). According to Webster, President Tyler found Ashburton's letter "sufficient to warrant forbearance from any further remonstrance against what took place[.]" *Quoted in id.* at 413.

2. *The Trial of Alexander McLeod.* The trial of Alexander McLeod contributed significantly to U.S.-British tensions over the *Caroline* affair. McLeod, a British deputy sheriff, was arrested in New York in 1840 and charged with murder and arson for allegedly participating in the attack on the *Caroline*. His imprisonment and trial in New York state court greatly upset Britain, which regarded the attack on the *Caroline* as a necessary government-authorized act. Secretary of State Webster and other U.S. leaders, including Presidents Harrison and Tyler, agreed with the British that McLeod should not be individually responsible if he was following British orders to attack the *Caroline*. Nevertheless, federal officials were powerless to stop the trial, and conceded that any defenses had to be raised in state court. McLeod was ultimately acquitted when the prosecution could not establish that he had even been present when the *Caroline* was destroyed. McLeod's acquittal helped pave the way for the diplomatic resolution of the *Caroline* dispute. In response to McLeod's case, Congress enacted a statute providing that the federal courts could hear *habeas corpus* petitions from foreigners who were in custody for acts done under orders "of any foreign State or Sovereignty, the validity and effect whereof depend upon the law of nations[.]" Act of Aug. 29, 1842, 5 Stat. 539 (now codified, as amended, at 28 U.S.C. § 2241(c)(4)).

McLeod, for his part, sought compensation for his imprisonment and trial. An 1853 U.S.-British treaty established a binational commission to consider "unsettled" claims of U.S. citizens against the British government, and of British citizens against the United States. 10 Stat. 988. The commissioners found that since matters related to the *Caroline* affair had been settled by the diplomatic exchanges of 1841–1842, they could not reach the merits of McLeod's claim. See 3 John Bassett Moore, *History and Digest of the International Arbitrations to Which the United States Has Been a Party* 2419–28 (1898; reprinted 1995). The British government awarded McLeod an annual £200 pension (equivalent to approximately $20,000 today) for deprivations he suffered during his 11 months in prison in New York. For more background on McLeod's trial and the *Caroline* affair, see John E. Noyes, "*The Caroline*: International Law Limits on Resort to Force," in *International Law Stories* 263 (John E. Noyes, Laura A. Dickinson & Mark W. Janis eds. 2007).

3. *Self-defense.* When Daniel Webster formulated the *Caroline* rule, he was well aware of a natural law tradition that, according to Professor Totten, recognized that states could, in narrow circumstances, use force defensively before they had actually been attacked. See Mark Totten, *First Strike: America, Terrorism, and Moral Tradition* (2010). Webster, in formulating this rule so restrictively, also emphasized the respect due U.S. neutrality in a conflict between rebels and the British government. See Noyes, *supra* Note 2, at 274–78. Scholars, political leaders, and a few jurists have continued to invoke the *Caroline* rule in the 20th and 21st centuries, albeit in different political and legal contexts. The Nuremberg Tribunal cited the *Caroline* rule when rejecting German leaders' arguments that it was legitimate to attack Norway in self-defense. International Military Tribunal (Nuremberg), Judgment and Sentences, Oct. 1, 1946, *reprinted in* 41 *American Journal of International Law* 172, 205–07 (1947). Is the *Caroline* rule still legally relevant after adoption of Article 51 of the U.N. Charter, considered below? Which aspects, if any, of the rule are suited to today's world?

C. ARTICLE 2(4) AND THE USE OF FORCE: THE COLD WAR

States reacted to the excesses of World War I by adopting new legal constraints on the use of force. For example, the Kellogg-Briand Pact, reproduced in Chapter 2, condemned "recourse to war for the solution of international controversies" and renounced war "as an instrument of national policy." The Covenant of the League of Nations provided procedural mechanisms encouraging a cooling-off period before hostilities could commence. Members of the League promised to submit "any dispute likely to lead to a rupture" to arbitration or judicial settlement, or to the League's Council for inquiry. They also agreed "in no case to resort to war until three months after the award by the arbitrators or the judicial decision, or the report by the Council." League of Nations Covenant, arts. 12(1), 15(1). These restraints proved futile in the 1930's and during the Second World War.

Following the carnage of World War II, the United Nations Charter in 1945 introduced a general prohibition on the unilateral use of force by states. Articles 2(3) and 33 of the Charter oblige Member States to settle disputes by peaceful means. Article 2(4), which limits the threat or use of force by states, and Article 51, which preserves a right of self-defense, are set out below. However, the Charter's promise of an active multilateral form of collective security proved more or less a dead letter during the 45 years of the Cold War, 1945–1989. Divided into opposing camps, the West led by the United States and the East led by the Soviet Union, the world's states stymied most collective security efforts attempted during the period. Below, following Articles 4(2) and 51, is an excerpt from Professor Franck who recounts the ways in which the United Nations tried to help keep the peace during the Cold War. We also introduce the ICJ's *Certain Expenses Case*, where in 1962 the International Court considered some of the financial implications of these somewhat improvised measures. Finally, in this part we ask the question what, given the circumstances, has been the real legal force of Charter Article 2(4). Reproduced are essays by Professors Louis Henkin and Michael Reisman, who take different views of the meaning of Article 2(4) and its importance.

UNITED NATIONS CHARTER, ARTICLES 2(4), 51

June 26, 1945, 59 Stat. 1031, T.S. No. 993, 3 Bevans 1153

Article 2(4)

All Members shall refrain in their international relations from the threat or use of force against the territorial integrity or political independence of any state, or in any manner inconsistent with the Purposes of the United Nations.

Article 51

Nothing in the present Charter shall impair the inherent right of individual or collective self-defense if an armed attack occurs against a Member of the United Nations until the Security Council has taken the measures necessary to maintain international peace and security. Measures taken by Members in the exercise of this right of self-defense shall be immediately reported to the Security Council and shall not in any way affect the authority and responsibility of the Security Council under the present Charter to take at any time such action as it deems necessary in order to maintain or restore international peace and security.

NOTES AND QUESTIONS

1. *The United Nations During the Cold War*. The first and probably most important purpose of the United Nations, as set forth in the Preamble to the U.N. Charter, is to "save succeeding generations from the scourge of war." The Organization's principal mission, listed in Article 1, is "to maintain

international peace and security." Although various U.N. organs have addressed use of force issues, Article 24 of the U.N. Charter provides that the Security Council has "primary responsibility for the maintenance of international peace and security." Under Chapter VII of the Charter (reproduced in the Appendix), the Security Council is charged with taking action with respect to threats to the peace, breaches of the peace, and acts of aggression. As we saw in Chapter 8, Chapter VII of the Charter was based on the premise that the world's major powers would agree on sanctions, and ultimately approve the use of force, to counter threats to the peace and breaches of the peace.

The original vision of the U.N. Charter concerning the maintenance of international peace and security was challenged by Cold War politics. The Security Council's permanent members—China, France, the Soviet Union, the United Kingdom, and the United States—were often divided, and the veto blocked many possible Council measures. The United Nations developed the institution of peacekeeping early in its history as a response to some instances of tension and violence in the world. The United Nations was involved in many peacekeeping operations between 1945 and 1989. These operations are not explicitly set out in the U.N. Charter.

THOMAS M. FRANCK, NATION AGAINST NATION

38–42 (1985)

[T]he Korean conflict * * * eventually prompted a significant shift in responsibility for collective security from the Security Council to the General Assembly. This occurred when, after the Inchon landing, United Nations forces appeared to have routed the North. New instructions were needed as General Douglas MacArthur's army neared the 38th parallel. But, with the Russians back at the circular table, instructions could not come from the veto-bound Council.

Washington wanted to pursue the remnants of the Northern army beyond the 38th parallel, despite serious misgivings among allies with contingents under MacArthur's command. On October 7, 1950, at U.S. insistence, the General Assembly authorized the pursuit of the aggressor into its own territory. The resolution passed on that date by a vote of 47 to 5, with seven abstentions, approving "[a]ll appropriate steps . . . to ensure stability throughout Korea . . . including the holding of elections, under the auspices of the United Nations, for the establishment of a unified, independent and democratic government in the sovereign State of Korea[,]" also authorized the U.N. forces to occupy as much of Korea "as necessary for achieving the objectives specified[.]" [U.S. Secretary of State] Dean Acheson thought that this "might be construed to mean something more than the prevention of a new attack."

This new and wider mandate for the U.N. force replaced the earlier one spelled out in the Security Council resolution of June 25, which had only called for pushing North Korean forces back to the 38th parallel. Whatever its tactical wisdom, the resolution of October 7 had the most far-reaching implications for the distribution of functions and powers within the U.N.: the Assembly had been used to circumvent the Council. This was fully understood by Secretary-General Lie, who declared himself elated at the ability of the organization to neutralize obstacles: "This was Korea, not Manchuria," he wrote; "this was the United Nations, not the League of Nations." To make sure that this was not an isolated victory, Washington, with the Secretary-General's support, persuaded the Assembly to establish simplified procedures for convening that body to sidestep the Council in future.

The British had not been nearly as enthusiastic as Trygve Lie. Wiser heads at the Foreign Office had correctly prophesied, in a warning to the U.S. Department of State, that any move to increase the power of the General Assembly would present dangers to the West once its majority gave way before the surge of new nations being created in Africa and Asia. Acheson disagreed, arguing that "present difficulties outweighed possible future ones, and we pressed on." The U.S. proceeded at full speed to secure the Assembly's adoption of what became known as the Uniting for Peace resolution, or Acheson Plan. Acheson personally introduced it, claiming it would increase the effectiveness of the United Nations against aggression. He urged the Assembly not to allow the Soviet veto to render the organization impotent. In good lawyerly fashion he argued that articles 10, 11, and 14 of the Charter made the Assembly the Council's partner in wielding "authority and responsibility for matters affecting international peace." The U.S.'s ambassador Benjamin Cohen added the uniquely American argument that the U.N. should follow our Supreme Court's practice of construing the Constitution flexibly, allowing the system to invent new ways of overcoming unanticipated difficulties without formal amendment of the basic compact. He cited the invention of the Presidential "executive agreement" as an example of how the U.S. had worked around the awkward constitutional requirement of a two-thirds Senatorial majority for the ratification of treaties, and urged the undoubtedly bemused Assembly delegates to study the creative U.S. Supreme Court decision in *McCulloch v. Maryland*. There the Justices had inferred from the Constitution's enumerated federal powers certain additional "implied" powers not spelled out in the text.

Advocates of the Acheson Plan pointed out that it meticulously adhered to the fundamental difference between the powers of the General Assembly—which may only *recommend* collective action—and those of the Security Council—which may *order* member states to participate in enforcing collective security. Even so, the Uniting for Peace resolution does envisage circumstances in which the Assembly, convened on 24 hours' notice after a veto in the Council, would step in to organize the collective use of force against an aggressor. Such was certainly not the intent of the drafters at San Francisco. Article 10 allows the Assembly to discuss "any questions or any matters within the scope of the present Charter" and "make recommendations to the Members" except when the matter is being considered by the Security Council. But this is qualified by article 11, which says that when the issue relates "to the maintenance of peace and security" and "action is necessary," the matter "shall be referred to the Security Council." U.S. Ambassador Ernest Gross has rightly written that the effect of the Acheson Plan is to transfer to the Assembly "major, rather than merely 'residual . . .'" authority "in relation to peace and security."

* * * Although the Uniting for Peace resolution had formalized the new rules, they had been evolving almost from the first, when it became clear that optimistic prophecies about Soviet restraint in using the veto were wrong. In 1946, the first Assembly had called on members to implement diplomatic sanctions against Franco's Spain, after the sanctions had drawn a veto in the Council. In 1949, in response to another veto, the Assembly had asked its members to embargo military supplies for communist guerrillas in Greece. Even the Assembly's resolution of October 7, 1950, redefining the mission of U.N. forces in Korea, antedated the Acheson Plan.

* * * Uniting for Peace was adopted on November 3, 1950, by a handy 40-to-5 (with 12 abstentions, including India and Argentina)[.]

The Israeli, British, and French invasion of Egypt, late in 1956, led to the formation of the United Nations Emergency Force (UNEF). Unlike U.N. contingents in Korea, UNEF was not created to repel an ongoing breach of the peace with a collective use of armed might, but as a legion of peacekeepers to oversee a decision of the combatants to disengage. Unlike the Korean force, UNEF was genuinely international, commanded by an officer appointed on the initiative of the Secretary-General. It deliberately excluded contributions from any of the Big Five. Instead, UNEF was made up of small units from a broad assortment of states. * * * UNEF was authorized not by the Security Council, but by the General Assembly acting on the basis of the Uniting for Peace resolution.

The Suez crisis began when Egypt's President Gamal Abdel Nasser nationalized the Suez Canal Company on July 26, 1956. After inconclusive negotiations to establish international guarantees for unfettered use of the Canal, Israel attacked Egypt on October 29. The next day a prearranged British and French ultimatum demanded that Egypt and Israel both withdraw from the area of the Canal. When Egypt demurred, British aircraft stationed in Cyprus began bombing Egyptian targets. On November 5 British and French paratroops were dropped near Port Said.

British and French vetoes effectively immobilized the Security Council, but not the Soviets, who began threatening direct retaliation against London and Paris. * * *

With matters approaching [a] dangerous pass, the Yugoslav member of the Security Council, specifically invoking the Uniting for Peace resolution, introduced a resolution to convene an Emergency Session of the General Assembly. Since the resolution was procedural, the negative British and French votes did not constitute a veto. The Soviets, who had bitterly opposed the Acheson Plan, now voted with the U.S. to implement it.

After much behind-the-scenes maneuvering—in which Canada's foreign minister Lester B. Pearson and Secretary-General Dag Hammarskjold played leading roles—an agreement was reached. British, French, and—somewhat later—Israeli forces were to withdraw from the Canal and be replaced by UNEF. A few weeks later, the Assembly authorized UNEF "to assist in achieving situations conducive to the maintenance of peaceful conditions in the area" and gave the Secretary-General wide discretion "to take steps to carry out these measures." Hammarskjold negotiated personally with President Nasser to create the agreed framework for UNEF's operations in Egypt, which was duly approved by the Assembly.

At its zenith the UNEF force, with contingents from ten nations chosen by the Secretary-General after consulting with Egypt, consisted of some 6000 officers and men. Stationed along the Egyptian side of the armistice line, the force became a major factor in preventing the renewal of fedayeen raids from Egypt into Israel and in maintaining peace along that previously afflicted boundary. Not only did the Suez crisis further enhance the peacekeeping and conflict-resolving role of the General Assembly, but it also thrust forward Hammarskjold, whose skill in setting up UNEF earned him the respect of world leaders, including President Eisenhower and Secretary of State Dulles.

The Suez crisis thus confirmed the United Nations in its most fruitful line of endeavor: the stationing of international peacekeeping forces between mutually hostile antagonists at that crucial moment in a dispute when both sides perceive disengagement as preferable to continued hostilities.

NOTES AND QUESTIONS

1. *Traditional Peacekeeping.* According to a former U.N. Under-Secretary-General for Political Affairs, "[t]he technique of peacekeeping is a distinctive innovation by the United Nations. The Charter does not mention it. It was discovered, like penicillin. We came across it, while looking for something else, during an investigation of the guerrilla fighting in northern Greece in 1947." Brian Urquhart, "The United Nations, Collective Security,

and International Peacekeeping," in *Negotiating World Order: The Artisanship and Architecture of Global Diplomacy* 59, 62 (Alan K. Henrikson ed. 1986), *quoted in* Frederic L. Kirgis, Jr., "The Security Council's First Fifty Years," 89 *American Journal of International Law* 506, 532 (1995). Is there sufficient U.N. Charter authority for peacekeeping operations in Chapter VII's Article 40, under which the Security Council may call on states to comply with "provisional measures"? Or could we analogize peacekeeping to "peacemaking" and rely on provisions in Chapter VI, concerning the pacific settlement of disputes? Is it important to identify specific authority for peacekeeping in the text of the Charter? U.N. Secretary-General Dag Hammerskjold said that, in truth, peacekeeping derived from a Chapter "six-and-a-half" of the Charter, since it bridged Chapter VII, dealing with enforcement measures, and Chapter VI. See John F. Murphy, "Force and Arms," in 1 *United Nations Legal Order* 247, 292–96 (Oscar Schachter & Christopher C. Joyner eds. 1995).

Between 1948 and 1978, the United Nations authorized 13 peacekeeping bodies, which, since there was and is no standing U.N. army, utilized forces contributed by U.N. Member States. Early peacekeeping operations followed a traditional pattern: U.N. peacekeepers were stationed along a cease-fire line, interposed between belligerents, or assigned to observe boundaries; they could use force only to defend themselves or to remain in positions taken in accordance with U.N. authorization; they operated under U.N. command; and they included no representatives from any of the permanent members of the Security Council. UNEF was an example of U.N. peacekeepers undertaking traditional functions. Such peacekeeping operations were established only with the consent of the states in which they were to be deployed. See Eric Suy, "Peace-Keeping Operations," in *A Handbook on International Organizations* 539 (René-Jean Dupuy ed., 2d ed. 1998). Is such consent important legally or politically? Does such consent necessarily signal a willingness to support the operations of peacekeepers?

2. *The General Assembly and Peacekeeping.* In the 1950 Uniting for Peace Resolution, the General Assembly asserted its authority to help maintain international peace and security if the Security Council failed "to discharge its responsibilities." Some states regarded UNEF, along with another peacekeeping operation in the Congo sanctioned by the Security Council, as not in conformity with the U.N. Charter. These states refused to pay their share of General Assembly-authorized expenditures for these operations. In response, the General Assembly requested an advisory opinion from the International Court of Justice concerning the legality of these expenditures.

THE CERTAIN EXPENSES CASE

Certain Expenses of the United Nations (Article 17, Paragraph 2 of the Charter), Advisory Opinion of 20 July 1962, 1962 I.C.J. 151

The question on which the Court is asked to give its opinion is whether certain expenditures which were authorized by the General

Assembly to cover the costs of the United Nations operations in the Congo (hereinafter referred to as ONUC) and of the operations of the United Nations Emergency Force in the Middle East (hereinafter referred to as UNEF), "constitute 'expenses of the Organization' within the meaning of Article 17, paragraph 2, of the Charter of the United Nations."

* * * In determining whether the actual expenditures authorized constitute "expenses of the Organization within the meaning of Article 17, paragraph 2, of the Charter," the Court agrees that such expenditures must be tested by their relationship to the purposes of the United Nations in the sense that if an expenditure were made for a purpose which is not one of the purposes of the United Nations, it could not be considered an "expense of the Organization."

The purposes of the United Nations are set forth in Article 1 of the Charter. The first two purposes as stated in paragraphs 1 and 2, may be summarily described as pointing to the goal of international peace and security and friendly relations. The third purpose is the achievement of economic, social, cultural and humanitarian goals and respect for human rights. The fourth and last purpose is: "To be a center for harmonizing the actions of nations in the attainment of these common ends."

The primary place ascribed to international peace and security is natural, since the fulfilment of the other purposes will be dependent upon the attainment of that basic condition. These purposes are broad indeed, but neither they nor the powers conferred to effectuate them are unlimited. Save as they have entrusted the Organization with the attainment of these common ends, the Member States retain their freedom of action. But when the Organization takes action which warrants the assertion that it was appropriate for the fulfilment of one of the stated purposes of the United Nations, the presumption is that such action is not *ultra vires* the Organization.

If it is agreed that the action in question is within the scope of the functions of the Organization but it is alleged that it has been initiated or carried out in a manner not in conformity with the division of functions among the several organs which the Charter prescribes, one moves to the internal plane, to the internal structure of the Organization. If the action was taken by the wrong organ, it was irregular as a matter of that internal structure, but this would not necessarily mean that the expense incurred was not an expense of the Organization. Both national and international law contemplate cases in which the body corporate or politic may be bound, as to third parties, by an *ultra vires* act of an agent.

In the legal systems of States, there is often some procedure for determining the validity of even a legislative or governmental act, but no analogous procedure is to be found in the structure of the United Nations. Proposals made during the drafting of the Charter to place the ultimate authority to interpret the Charter in the International Court of Justice were not accepted; the opinion which the Court is in course of rendering is an *advisory* opinion. As anticipated in 1945, therefore, each organ must, in the first place at least, determine its own jurisdiction.

[I]t is apparent that the operations were undertaken to fulfil a prime purpose of the United Nations, that is, to promote and to maintain a peaceful settlement of the situation. This being true, the Secretary-General properly exercised the authority given him to incur financial obligations of the Organization and expenses resulting from such obligations must be considered "expenses of the Organization within the meaning of Article 17, paragraph 2."

NOTES AND QUESTIONS

1. *Interpreting the U.N. Charter.* Does the U.N. Charter merely assign functions to different U.N. organs, or does it, in addition, establish legal limits on the authority of such organs? Is it appropriate, as the ICJ suggested in the *Certain Expenses Case*, to adopt a presumption against finding U.N. acts *ultra vires* "when the Organization takes action which warrants the assertion that it was appropriate for the fulfilment of one of the stated purposes of the United Nations"? Should the Court have refused to rule on this matter of Charter interpretation at all, on the grounds that it was a "political question" better left to other U.N. institutions? See the discussion of ICJ advisory opinions in Chapter 5.

In the *Certain Expenses Case*, the Court contrasted the constitutional structure of the United Nations with the legal systems of states. In general, how analogous is the U.N. Charter to a municipal constitution? What differences are explained by the fact that most municipal constitutions draw their authority from the people, while the U.N.'s constitution is based on authority delegated by states?

2. *Peacekeeping and Chapter VII Enforcement Actions.* In portions of the *Certain Expenses Case* not reproduced above, the International Court emphasized a distinction between "Chapter VII enforcement actions," which the Security Council alone could take, and other measures relating to international peace and security, such as the authorization of peacekeeping operations. As with UNEF, the General Assembly has sometimes approved peacekeeping operations when the Security Council refused to act. What limits the General Assembly's authority with respect to peacekeeping? One limit is found in Article 12 of the U.N. Charter, echoed by the ICJ's *Certain Expenses Case* ruling that "the Assembly should not recommend measures while the Security Council is dealing with the same matter unless the Council requests it to do so." 1962 I.C.J. at 163. Also see the *Wall Case* in Chapter 5. In recent decades the Security Council has asserted full control over the approval of peacekeeping operations.

3. *Modern Peacekeeping.* States have called on the U.N. Security Council to send peacekeepers to conduct a variety of tasks, and the Council has approved many operations, particularly after the end of the Cold War in

1989. Many recent missions have involved so-called "second-generation" peacekeeping, *i.e.*, "preventive diplomacy and peacemaking" or "post-conflict peace-building." As of October 2013 more than 98,000 U.N. peacekeepers, contributed by 119 countries, were deployed on 16 different missions. "United Nations Peacekeeping Fact Sheet," Oct. 2013, *available at* www.un.org/en/peacekeepingresources/statistics/factsheet.shtml (last visited Dec. 11, 2013). The Security Council now invokes Chapter VII of the U.N. Charter as authority for these operations. The invocation of Chapter VII, which obviates the formal need for consent from the state to which U.N. peacekeepers are deployed, blurs the distinction between Chapter VII enforcement actions and traditional peacekeeping.

Some U.N. peacekeeping operations have been generally acknowledged as successful. These include both traditional cease-fire and border monitoring and some modern endeavors, including observing elections in El Salvador and helping to implement the comprehensive negotiated settlement of the conflict in Namibia. Furthermore, since 1990 U.N. peacekeeping has reportedly contributed to an overall significant decline in global violence. See Human Security Centre, *Human Security Report 2005: War and Peace in the 21st Century* 8–9 (2005). In many modern operations, *e.g.*, nation-building functions in East Timor and Cambodia, however, the challenges have been daunting. For example, in the early 1990s the U.N. Transitional Authority in Cambodia (UNTAC), along with the U.N. High Commissioner for Refugees, coordinated the repatriation of more than 360,000 refugees living in camps in Thailand. UNTAC also was charged with controlling the civil administration of Cambodia's government (in particular in the areas of defense, public security, finance, information, and foreign affairs), developing a civilian police force, and organizing and monitoring free elections. With respect to military issues, UNTAC's mandate included the demobilization and disarming of the armed forces of the various Cambodian factions. During its 18 months of operation, UNTAC employed about 22,000 international personnel and cost about $1.7 billion. For assessments of UNTAC's successes and failures, see Michael W. Doyle, *UN Peacekeeping in Cambodia: UNTAC's Civil Mandate* (1995), and Steven R. Ratner, *The New UN Peacekeeping* 135–206 (1995). Other modern operations, such as the U.N. Protection Force (UNPROFOR) sent to Bosnia-Herzegovina during the break-up of Yugoslavia, have been judged clear failures. See John F. Murphy, *The Evolving Dimensions of International Law* 125–26 (2010).

What could be done to make complex peacekeeping or peace-building operations more effective? Challenges include assuring reliable funding and national support for broad U.N. mandates. Dr. John Hillen, a member of the U.S. Commission on National Security/21st Century bluntly criticized the United States for "push[ing] an unwilling UN into a hugely ambitious nation-building mission" in Somalia without providing necessary support. *Hearing on United Nations Peacekeeping Missions and Their Proliferation Before the Subcommittee on International Operations of the Senate Committee on Foreign Relations*, 106th Cong., *quoted in* John F. Murphy, *The United States and the Rule of Law in International Affairs* 187 (2004). In 2005 the U.N.

General Assembly and Security Council established the U.N. Peacebuilding Commission, an intergovernmental advisory body operating with input from non-governmental organizations. G.A. Res. 60/180 (2005); S.C. Res. 1645 (2005). The Commission's mandate encompasses bringing together relevant actors to marshal resources for peacebuilding, advising on strategies, and helping to ensure financing. See http://www.un.org/peace/peacebuilding/index.shtml (last visited Dec. 11, 2013). What else should be done? Should states negotiate agreements with the United Nations under Article 43 of the U.N. Charter to make armed forces, facilities, and other assistance immediately available to the Organization? Would this mechanism provide a ready source of logistical support for the U.N. Security Council to use when a crisis develops, dispensing with the need to wait for states to contribute troops and supplies? Or, should the Council itself establish a globally recruited volunteer force, using its authority under Article 29 of the U.N. Charter? See Thomas Franck, "The United Nations as Guarantor of International Peace and Security: Past, Present and Future," in *The United Nations at Age Fifty: A Legal Perspective* 25, 33–35 (Christian Tomuschat ed. 1995). For discussion of a recent Security Council decision authorizing a peacekeeping force in the Congo to use force offensively, see the last set of Notes in Part D below. For more information on peacekeeping and proposals for change, see *A More Secure World: Our Shared Responsibility* ¶¶ 210–30, 261–69, U.N. Doc. A/59/565 (2004) (Report of the High-Level Panel on Threats, Challenges and Change); http://globalpolicy.org/security-council/peacekeeping.html (last visited Dec. 12, 2013); http://www.un.org/en/peacekeeping (last visited Dec. 12, 2013).

LOUIS HENKIN, "USE OF FORCE: LAW AND U.S. POLICY"

Right v. Might: International Law and the Use of Force 37 (1989)

* * * The Charter remains the authoritative statement of the law on the use of force. It is the principal norm of international law of this century.

The crucial norm is set forth in article 2(4). * * *

The Charter reflected universal agreement that the status quo prevailing at the end of World War II was not to be changed by force. Even justified grievances and a sincere concern for "national security" or other "vital interests" would not warrant any nation's initiating war. Peace was the paramount value. The Charter and the organization were dedicated to realizing other values as well—self-determination, respect for human rights, economic and social development, justice, and a just international order. But those purposes could not justify the use of force between states to achieve them; they would have to be pursued by other means. Peace was more important than progress and more important than justice. The purposes of the United Nations could not in fact be achieved by war. War inflicted the greatest injustice, the most serious violations of human rights, and the most violence to self-determination and to economic and social development. War was inherently unjust. In the future, the only "just war" would be war against an aggressor—in self-defense by the victim, in collective defense of the victim by others, or by all. Nations would be assured independence, the undisturbed enjoyment of autonomy within their territory, and their right to be let alone. Change—other than internal change through internal forces—would have to be achieved peacefully by international agreement. Henceforth there would be order so that international society could concentrate on meeting better the needs of justice and human welfare.

EFFORTS TO RECONSTRUE THE CHARTER

During the early postwar years there was general agreement as to what the prescriptions of article 2(4) meant. Clearly, the article outlaws war and other acts of armed aggression by one state against another; it also forbids lesser forms of intervention by force by one state in the territory of another. Apart from collective action under the auspices of the United Nations to enforce the peace, the only lawful use of force by a state is that contemplated under the limited exception in article 51 permitting the use of force in self-defense against an armed attack. In time, the language of article 2(4) proved to be not without ambiguities and not invulnerable to claims that intervention by force is permitted for certain "benign" purposes.

One initial ambiguity appears on the face of article 2(4). Does the prohibition of the use of force against "the territorial integrity" of another state forbid only a use of force designed to deprive that state of territory, or does it also prohibit force that violates the territorial borders of that state, however temporarily and for whatever purpose? Does the prohibition of the use of force against "the political independence" of another state outlaw only a use of force that aims to end that state's political independence by annexing it or rendering it a puppet, or does it also prohibit force designed to coerce that state to follow a particular policy or take a particular decisions? In what other circumstances would a use or threat of force be "inconsistent with the purposes of the United Nations"? Another debate concerned whether economic pressure—an oil embargo, a boycott, or other sanctions—designed to derogate from a state's territorial integrity or political independence is a "use of force" prohibited by article 2(4).

An effective United Nations system, or a court with comprehensive jurisdiction and recognized authority, might have answered these and other questions by developing the law of the Charter through construction and case-by-case application. In the absence of such authoritative interpretation, the meaning of the Charter has been shaped by the actions and reactions of states and by the opinions of publicists and scholars. Scholars have debated the ambiguities of the Charter that I have cited and other questions of interpretation; a government occasionally has sought to shape the law to justify an action it has taken. But governments generally have insisted on the interpretations most restrictive of the use of force: the Charter outlaws war for any reason; it prohibits the use of armed force by one state on the territory of another or against the forces, vessels, or other public property of another state located anywhere, for any purpose, in any circumstances. Virtually every use of force in the years since the Charter was signed has been clearly condemned by virtually all states. Virtually every putative justification of a use of force has been rejected. Over the years since the Charter's adoption, even states that have perpetrated acts of force, when seeking to justify their acts, have not commonly urged a relaxed interpretation of the prohibition. Rather, they have asserted facts and circumstances that might have rendered their actions not unlawful. For example, in 1950, North Korea claimed that the South Korean army had initiated hostilities, permitting North Korea to act in self-defense; in Czechoslovakia in 1948 and 1968, and in Hungary in 1956, the USSR claimed that its troops had been invited by the legitimate authorities to help preserve order.

Indeed, the community of states has acted formally to tighten the Charter's restrictions. The Declaration on Principles of International Law concerning Friendly Relations and Cooperation among States in Accordance with the Charter of the United Nations, adopted by consensus in the General Assembly in 1970, and the Definition of Aggression, adopted by consensus in 1974, have restated and expanded the law of the Charter as prohibiting armed intervention and aggression, broadly conceived. The resolution defining aggression made it clear that prohibited forms of aggression include not only invasion, but also attack or military occupation, however temporary; sending armed bands or mercenaries that carry out grave acts of armed force; bombarding a state's territory; blocking its ports; and attacking the forces of another state (wherever they are).

SUGGESTED EXCEPTIONS TO THE PROHIBITIONS OF ARTICLE 2(4)

In time, however, some states claimed exceptions to the absolute prohibitions of article 2(4), as permitting intervention by force for certain "benign" purposes (in addition to the self-defense exception under article 51). None of the "benign exceptions" has been formally accepted; only one has brought wide acquiescence.

Humanitarian intervention. On several occasions states have claimed the right to use force in "humanitarian intervention." The paradigmatic case was the action of Israel in 1976 to extricate hostages held on a hijacked plane at Entebbe (Uganda). The United States claimed its unsuccessful attempt in 1980 to liberate the diplomatic hostages held in Teheran also came within the exception. States have been reluctant to adopt this exception to article 2(4) formally, but the legal community has widely accepted that the Charter does not prohibit humanitarian intervention by use of force strictly limited to what is necessary to save lives.

The exception, I believe, is not restricted to actions by a state on behalf of its own nationals. But it is a right to liberate hostages if the territorial state cannot or will not do so. It has not been accepted, however, that a state has a right to intervene by force to topple a government or occupy its territory even if that were necessary to terminate atrocities or to liberate detainees. Entebbe was acceptable, but the occupation of Cambodia by Vietnam was not. The U.S. invasion and occupation of Grenada, even if in fact designed to protect the lives of U.S. nationals, also was widely challenged.

Intervention to support self-determination. The suggestion that a state may intervene by force to help a people achieve "self-determination" in some circumstances has received some support.

Self-determination is a powerful political dogma that has been accepted as a principle of international law. It is incorporated in widely accepted treaties, including both the International Covenant on Civil and Political Rights and the International Covenant on Economic, Social and Cultural Rights. The concept of self-determination cries for definition, and few agree on its content, but all agree that it includes at least the right of peoples in Asia and Africa to be free from colonial domination, Western style.

Neither article 2(4) of the Charter nor any other provision of international law forbids authentic revolution and wars of independence. Indeed, there is a strong case that it is now unlawful for a state to maintain an unwilling people in colonial status, and such unlawfulness is compounded if a colony is maintained by force. A very different question, however, is whether an external power is permitted to intervene by force to help expel the colonial power or hasten its departure.

On various theories, many states have supported the right to intervene by force to help an entity achieve independence from colonial rule. The United States has firmly rejected any such right. In addressing India's invasion and occupation of Goa (Portuguese India) in 1961, Ambassador Adlai Stevenson said:

> What is at stake today is not colonialism; it is a bold violation of one of the most basic principles in the United Nations Charter. . . . But if our Charter means anything, it means that states are obligated to renounce the use of force, are obligated to seek a solution of their differences by peaceful means.

India used force to end Portuguese control in Goa and claimed the territory for itself; later, other states asserted a general right to intervene by force to help a people achieve independence. In a famous statement, attributed to Leonid Brezhnev, defending the Soviet invasion of Czechoslovakia in 1968, the USSR decried those who "regard the notion of sovereignty as prohibiting support for the struggle of progressive forces." He added: "Genuine revolutionaries, being internationalists, cannot but support progressive forces in their just struggle for national and social liberation."

The world rejected Brezhnev's invasion of Czechoslovakia; even the Third World was not persuaded by the "national liberation" justification. General Assembly resolutions, however, have confirmed the right of colonial peoples to achieve independence by force if necessary and included ambiguous declarations that suggested a right of other states to intervene to help them.

With colonialism no longer an important concern, the pressure for a "self-determination exception" to the law of the Charter has subsided, and the potential significance of such an exception, if recognized, is sharply reduced.

Intervention for socialism: The Brezhnev Doctrine. The Brezhnev regime also asserted generally the right of any socialist state to intervene in another when socialism there is threatened. It said:

> Just as, in Lenin's words, a man living in a society cannot be free from the society, a particular socialist state, staying in a system of other states composing the socialist community, cannot be free from the common interests of that community.
>
> The sovereignty of each socialist country cannot be opposed to the interests of the world of socialism, of the world revolutionary movement. . . .
>
> Discharging their internationalist duty toward the fraternal peoples of Czechoslovakia and defending their own socialist gains, the U.S.S.R. and other socialist states had to act decisively and they did act against the antisocialist forces in Czechoslovakia.

The Brezhnev Doctrine has been generally condemned. The USSR itself appears to have disavowed it in the Helsinki accords.

Intervention for democracy. Self-determination as a justification for the use of force to end colonialism has lost its raison d'être, but some have invoked a people's right to "internal self-determination" to support the use of force by one state to preserve or impose democracy in another. One suggestion, for example, is that article 2(4) permits the use of force to "enhance opportunities of ongoing self-determination . . . to increase the probability of the free choice of peoples about their government and political structure." Some see this view as the foundation of the so-called

Reagan Doctrine, construed as including a claim of the right to intervene by force in another state to preserve or impose democracy.

The claim has received no support by any other government. Like the use of force to impose or maintain socialism or any other ideology, the use of force for democracy clearly would be contrary to the language of article 2(4), to the intent of its framers, and to the construction long given to that article by the United States.

At bottom, all suggestions for exceptions to article 2(4) imply that, contrary to the assumptions of the Charter's framers, there are universally recognized values higher than peace and the autonomy of states. In general, the claims of peace and state autonomy have prevailed.

SELF-DEFENSE UNDER THE CHARTER * * *

The original intent of article 51 seems clear: despite the prohibition on the unilateral use of force in article 2(4), a victim of an armed attack may use force to defend itself, and others may join to use force in collective self-defense of the victim, pending action by the Security Council. No one has doubted that the right of individual or collective self-defense against armed attack continues to apply if the Security Council does not act, or if—as later proved to be the case—the Security Council becomes generally incapable of acting. It has also been accepted that the right of self-defense, individual or collective, is subject to limitations of "necessity" and "proportionality," but that self-defense includes a right both to repel the armed attack and to take the war to the aggressor state in order effectively to terminate the attack and prevent a recurrence. It is generally accepted, too, that states are permitted to organize themselves in advance in bona fide collective self-defense arrangements (such as the North Atlantic Treaty Organization) for possible response if one of the members should become the victim of an armed attack.

The right of self-defense is available "if an armed attack occurs." In the wake of Suez-Sinai (1956), however, some publicists began to argue that the "inherent right of self-defense" recognized by article 51 is the traditional right of self-defense, predating the Charter, which was not limited to defense against "armed attack." They argued that the right of self-defense "if an armed attack occurs" does not mean "only if an armed attack occurs." The only limitation on self-defense, they said, was that implied in the famous *Caroline* dictum: that the right of self-defense was available only when "the necessity of that self-defense is instant, overwhelming, and leaving no choice of means, and no moment for deliberation."

This more permissive interpretation of article 51 found favor with some commentators, but little with governments. The United States rejected it when its allies in effect invoked it at Suez (1956). During the Cuban missile crisis (1962), the United States, though eager to justify its blockade of Cuba, pointedly refrained from adopting the "loose" construction of article 51 and did not claim as justification a right to act in "inherent self-defense." To this day, the United States has not claimed a right to act in self-defense where no armed attack has occurred. In 1985, however, the United States interpreted the concept of armed attack to include certain terrorist activities. Declaring the Libyan government responsible for terrorist acts in Europe, including the bombing of a Berlin nightclub frequented by U.S. servicemen in which one was killed and many wounded, the United States launched a bomb attack on targets in Libyan territory. President Reagan described the attack as "fully consistent with Article 51 of the UN Charter," presumably because, in the American view, the terrorist act was an "armed attack" justifying the bombing as a use of force in self-defense.

* * * Publicists have debated whether, under article 51, a state may use force in * * * "anticipatory" self-defense, particularly in the context of nuclear strategy. Some have suggested that if a state has strong reasons to believe it is about to be the target of a nuclear strike, the "armed attack has occurred" and the victim need not wait but may "respond" in "anticipatory self-defense." Fortunately, that issue has remained academic. [T]he attack on Libya * * * was not designed to "beat Libya to the punch," but, President Reagan said, it "will not only diminish Colonel Quadhafi's capacity to export terror, it will provide him with incentives and reasons to alter his criminal behavior."

The bombing of Libya by the United States was widely condemned and the claimed justification widely rejected.

INTERVENTION AND COUNTERINTERVENTION

Before the UN Charter, the law seemed to be that a state may provide military assistance to the government of another state, even to help it suppress rebellion, but a state could not assist rebels against the incumbent government of another state. If rebellion succeeded sufficiently to achieve the status of "belligerent" and constitute a civil war, the law probably forbade assistance to either side. That law, confirmed by special Non-Intervention Agreements in the 1930s, was battered during the Spanish Civil War as states intervened on both sides. The United States, however, honored the principle of nonintervention, helping neither side.

The United Nations Charter did not expressly address intervention in civil wars. Nothing in article 2(4) forbids sending military assistance to an incumbent government, but the use of force in support of rebels against an incumbent government would be a use of force against the territorial integrity of the state and, presumably, against its political independence. Under the Charter, a state probably may not send troops into the territory of another state to support either side in a civil war, since that too would violate the latter's territorial integrity and compromise its political independence. Assistance not involving the use of force, however—for example, providing advice, selling arms, or giving financial assistance to one (or both) sides in a civil war—seems not to be covered by article 2(4), but may violate norms against nonintervention that predate the Charter and have been strongly restated in numerous General Assembly resolutions.

W. MICHAEL REISMAN, "CRITERIA FOR THE LAWFUL USE OF FORCE IN INTERNATIONAL LAW"

10 *Yale Journal of International Law* 279 (1985)

Law includes a system of authorized coercion in which force is used to maintain and enhance public order objectives and in which unauthorized coercions are prohibited. * * * Law acknowledges the utility and the inescapability of the use of coercion in social processes, but seeks to organize, monopolize, and economize it.

The international legal system diverges from these general legal features only in terms of degree of organization and centralization of the use of coercion. In national systems, coercion is organized, relatively centralized, and, for the most part, monopolized by the apparatus of the state. In the international system, it is not. Individual actors historically have reserved the right to use force unilaterally to protect and vindicate legal entitlements.

Political and jurisprudential principles such as these must be kept in mind in an examination and rational interpretation of Article 2(4) of the United Nations Charter. Its sweeping prohibition of the threat or use of force in international politics was not an autonomous ethical affirmation of nonviolence[.] Article 2(4) was embedded in and made initially plausible by a complex security scheme, established and spelled out in the United Nations Charter. If the scheme had operated, it would have obviated the need for the unilateral use of force. States with a grievance could have repaired to the Security Council, which could then apply the appropriate quantum and form of authoritative coercion and thereby vindicate collectively the rights it found had been violated. Under these circumstances, the need for and justification of a unilateral resort to force ceased. Even then, * * * the Charter acknowledged the inherent limits of its structures in the prevailing international politics by reserving to states the right of self-defense.

But the security system of the United Nations was premised on a consensus between the permanent members of the Security Council. Lamentably, that consensus dissolved early in the history of the organization. Thereafter, for almost all cases but those in which there was a short-term interest in collaboration, the Security Council could not operate as originally planned. Part of the systemic justification for the theory of Article 2(4) disappeared. At the same time, the Soviet Union announced, in effect, that it did not accept Article 2(4): "Wars of national liberation," an open-textured conception essentially meaning wars the Soviets supported, were not, in the Soviet conception, violations of Article 2(4). * * *

The international political system has largely accommodated itself to the indispensability of coercion in a legal system, on the one hand, and the deterioration of the Charter system, on the other, by developing a nuanced code for appraising the lawfulness of individual unilateral uses of force. The net result is not the value sterility of nineteenth century international legal conceptions of coercion, but neither is it Article 2(4). Some sense of the complexity of the code can be gained by examining, in a single time period, 1979, forceful unilateral interventions without the prior authorization of the United Nations.

In 1979, forces of Tanzania invaded Uganda, expelled the government of Idi Amin, and ultimately restored the government of Milton Obote. In the same year, French forces, in a quick and bloodless coup, expelled the government of Jean-Bedel Bokassa from the Central African Republic and installed a different president. In the same year, forces of the government of Vietnam entered Cambodia and sought to unseat the Pol Pot government and to replace it with a Vietnamese-backed government led by Heng Samrin. And in the same year, Soviet forces entered Afghanistan to support a government which, it seemed, would not have survived had it not been for the timely intervention and continued presence and operation of a foreign military force. * * *

Although efforts were made to arouse the United Nations to criticize the first two of these interventions, the organization resisted. But the organization condemned the latter two. Since all of these interventions, like all unilateral actions, were motivated in key part by the self-interest of the actors concerned, we must assume that there were some additional ingredients that rendered some of them internationally acceptable. I submit that it is in the identification of those factors that one can begin to describe the contemporary international law on the use of force.

The deterioration of the Charter security regime has stimulated a partial revival of a type of unilateral *jus ad bellum*. But in sharp contrast to the nineteenth century conception, which was value-neutral and ultimately power-based, the contemporary doctrine relates only to the vindication of rights which the international community recognizes but has, in general or in a particular case, demonstrated an inability to secure or guarantee. Hence, appraisals of state resort to coercion can no longer simply condemn them by invoking Article 2(4), but must test permissibility or lawfulness by reference to a number of factors, including the objective and the contingency for which coercion is being applied.

Nine basic categories appear to have emerged in which one finds varying support for unilateral uses of force. They are self-defense, which has been construed quite broadly; self-determination and decolonization; humanitarian intervention by the military instrument to replace an elite in another state; uses of the military instrument within spheres of influence and critical defense zones; treaty-sanctioned interventions within the territory of another state; use of the military instrument for the gathering of evidence in international proceedings; use of the military instrument to enforce international judgments; and counter-measures such as reprisals and retorsions. The categories themselves, however, are not determinative. * * *

In the determination of any action, a key and constant factor—less a criterion of lawfulness and more a sine qua non of survival—is the need for the maintenance of minimum order in a precarious international system. Will a particular use of force, whatever its justification otherwise, enhance or undermine world order?

When this requirement is met, attention may be directed to the fundamental principle of political legitimacy in contemporary international politics. It is, as anyone familiar with the UN Charter and with such key constitutive decisions as *Namibia* and *Western Sahara* knows, the enhancement of the ongoing right of peoples to determine their own political destinies. That obvious point bears renewed emphasis, for it is, in my view, the main purpose of contemporary international law: Article 2(4) is the means. The basic policy of contemporary international law has been to maintain the political independence of territorial communities so that they can continue to be able to express their ongoing desire for political organization in a form appropriate to them. Article 2(4), like so much in the Charter and in contemporary international politics, supports and must be interpreted in terms of this key postulate. Each application of Article 2(4) must enhance opportunities for ongoing self-determination. Though all interventions are lamentable, the fact is that some may serve, in terms of aggregate consequences, to increase the probability of the free choice of peoples about their government and political structure. Others have the manifest objective and consequence of doing exactly the opposite.

There is, thus, neither need nor justification for treating in a mechanically equal fashion, Tanzania's intervention in Uganda to overthrow the Amin despotism, on the one hand, and Soviet intervention in Hungary or Czechoslovakia to overthrow popular governments and to impose an undesired regime on a coerced population, on the other. Nor should the different appraisal of these cases by the international legal system occasion any surprise.

It is important to remember that norms are instruments devised by human beings to precipitate desired social consequences. One should not seek a point-for-point conformity to a rule without constant regard for the policy or principle that animated its prescription, with appropriate regard for the factual constellation in the minds of the drafters. * * * The expression of Article 2(4), in the form of a rule, is premised, I submit, on a political context and a technological environment which has been changing inexorably since the end of the nineteenth century. The rule assumes that the only threat to or usurpation of the right of political independence of a people within a particular territorial community is from external and overt invasion. It makes a historicist assumption as well: internal changes are deemed to be personnel changes in the composition of an elite which do not bring about basic changes in systems of public order within the country or in its external political alignments; governments come and go but the life of the people continues in its traditional fashion. Most important, it does not presuppose division, maintained by a precarious nuclear equipoise, between two contending public order systems, either of which might find itself substantially disadvantaged and pressed to intense coercion by the defection of a particular community from its own critical defense zone.

The rule-formulation of Article 2(4) is oblivious to these factors. * * *

The net effect of a mechanical interpretation of Article 2(4) may be to superimpose on an unwilling polity an elite, an ideology, and an external alignment alien to its wishes. This may entail far-reaching social and economic changes and grave deprivations of human rights for substantial numbers and strata of the population.

NOTES AND QUESTIONS

1. *Article 2(4).* Contrast the views of Professors Henkin and Reisman, both written near the end of the Cold War, concerning the international law governing the use of force. What for each is the role of Article 2(4)? What are permissible exceptions to 2(4)? What instances of the use of force would both regard as illegal? How does each explain the fact that there have been many examples of the use of force involving territorial incursions since World War II? As we see in Part D below, the United Nations Security Council has become more directly involved in authorizing the use of force since then.

2. *Categorizing Use of Force Issues.* As emphasized by Professor Henkin and the readings below, the use of force in self-defense must, according to traditional formulations, be both necessary for defensive purposes and proportional to the threatened injury. The International Court of Justice in the *Legality of the Threat or Use of Nuclear Weapons Case* suggested that "a use of force that is proportionate under the law of self-defense, must, in order to be lawful, also meet the requirements of the law applicable in armed conflict which comprise in particular the principles and rules of humanitarian law." 1996 I.C.J. 226, 245. Could it ever be "proportional" to respond in self-defense to a non-nuclear attack by using nuclear weapons? How else might the *jus ad bellum* intersect with the *jus in bello*?

3. *The Relevance of International Law.* When is the international law relating to the use of force really taken into account? Debates over the use of force are often carried out in diplomatic or political fora, with states making opposing assertions about the legality of each other's recourse to armed force. In such highly political contexts, is the law on the use of force irrelevant? Are the legal rules too indeterminate to matter? Do they sometimes provide at least a framework for debate and perhaps a structure for the formulation of policy positions?

In the United States, as in many other countries, government lawyers advise political leaders about international law. Recall the role of lawyers advising President Franklin Roosevelt in the Hull-Lothian negotiations in Chapter 2. What is the efficacy of legal advice concerning recourse to force? Several former U.S. State Department Legal Advisers recently shared their views on that question. Abraham D. Sofaer, Legal Adviser from 1985–1990 during the administrations of Ronald Reagan and George H.W. Bush, recalled occasions—"once at the very highest level imaginable"—when he advised against the use of force and his advice was taken. *Quoted in* Michael P. Scharf & Paul R. Williams, *Shaping Foreign Policy in Times of Crisis: The Role of International Law and the State Department Legal Adviser* 165 (2010). Conrad Harper, Legal Adviser from 1993–1996 during the Clinton administration, recounted discussions he had about a proposed use of force with the General Counsel of the Central Intelligence Agency and lawyers from the Departments of Justice and Defense. Although these government lawyers found it difficult to "go back to our principals and say that the proposed action 'probably wasn't a good idea,'" they became persuaded that the action would have been illegal. "And having been persuaded, we all went back to our principals and convinced them—and the action was never taken." *Quoted in id.* Michael J. Matheson, Legal Adviser during part of the George H.W. Bush administration, found it unrealistic "to think Presidents are often going to refrain from the use of force on what they consider to be essential security grounds because of the views of the Legal Adviser." However,

> there are important things that Legal Advisers can do with respect to the use of force. One is to see to it that the modalities used are as consistent with international law as possible. For example, the actions we took in Nicaragua, which were gratuitously in violation of international law need not necessarily have been so. [Also,] when the decision is made to use force, it's important what argument is made to justify that decision. There are some ways of justifying which will open up entirely new open-ended doctrines. There are others that are more consistent with past practices; the Legal Adviser can have a considerable amount of influence on what arguments are made, which in turn greatly influences what precedential effect that use of force might have.

Quoted in id. at 164–65.

How else might international law relating to the use of force be relevant? As suggested in the Notes following the *Goldberg Case* in Chapter 7, states sometimes have refused to recognize a government that has come into existence because of an illegal use of force. Professor Brownlie concluded that the international law on the use of force has influenced such varied matters as the law of treaties, the content of treaties, rules of engagement written by states for their armed forces, and the content of municipal laws and constitutions. See Ian Brownlie, "The United Nations Charter and the Use of Force, 1945–1985," in *The Current Legal Regulation of the Use of Force* 491 (A. Cassese ed. 1986). Furthermore, as we shall see in Part D of this chapter, a state's illegal use of force also may trigger a response of the U.N. Security Council toward that state.

4. *Judicial Interpretations*. International courts and arbitral tribunals occasionally address the legality of uses of force and self-defense. The International Court of Justice has done so on several occasions: the 1986 *Nicaragua Case*, Case Concerning Military and Paramilitary Activities In and Against Nicaragua (Nicaragua v. United States), 1986 I.C.J. 14; Legality of the Threat or Use of Nuclear Weapons, Advisory Opinion, 1996 I.C.J. 226; Oil Platforms (Iran v. United States), 2003 I.C.J. 161; the 2004 *Wall Case* (see Chapter 5); and Armed Activities on the Territory of the Congo (Congo v. Uganda), 2005 I.C.J. 168. Recent arbitral pronouncements on the use of force include *Jus ad Bellum* (Ethiopia v. Eritrea), Ethiopia's Claims 1–8, Partial Award (Eritrea-Ethiopia Claims Commission, 2005), 45 *International Legal Materials* 430 (2006), and Delimitation of Maritime Boundary (Guyana v. Suriname) ¶¶ 78–81, 140–44, 165 (Law of the Sea Convention Annex VII Arbitral Tribunal, 2007), *available at* www.pca-cpa.org (last visited Dec. 11, 2013). What are the advantages and disadvantages of the ICJ or international arbitral tribunals hearing and deciding cases involving the use of force and intervention? Compare the ICJ decisions in Chapter 5, as well as the Permanent Court of Arbitration's *Dogger Bank Case* in the same chapter.

5. *Armed Attack*. Article 51 of the U.N. Charter authorizes the use of force in self-defense "if an armed attack occurs." What constitutes an "armed attack"? The International Court of Justice considered that question in the *Nicaragua Case* cited in Note 4 when it ruled that U.S. use of force against Nicaragua could not be justified as an exercise of collective self-defense. The ICJ defined "armed attack" as follows:

> [A]n armed attack must be understood as including not merely action by regular armed forces across an international border, but also "the sending by or on behalf of a State of armed bands, groups, irregulars or mercenaries, which carry out acts of armed force against another State of such gravity as to amount to" (*inter alia*) an actual armed attack conducted by regular forces, "or its substantial involvement therein." [T]he prohibition of armed attacks may apply to the sending by a State of armed bands to the territory of another State, if such an operation, because of its scale and effects, would have been classified as an armed attack rather than as a mere frontier incident had it been carried out by regular armed forces. But the Court does not believe that the concept of "armed

> attack" includes not only acts by armed bands where such acts occur on a significant scale but also assistance to rebels in the form of the provision of weapons or logistical or other support.

1986 I.C.J. at 103–04.

What may be done in response to force that falls short of an armed attack? One of the *Nicaragua* Court's more controversial rulings concerned that issue:

> While an armed attack would give rise to an entitlement to collective self-defence, a use of force of a lesser degree of gravity cannot * * * produce any entitlement to take collective counter-measures involving the use of force. The acts of which Nicaragua is accused * * * could not justify counter-measures taken by a third State, the United States, and particularly could not justify intervention involving the use of force.

Id. at 127. For discussion of the ICJ's perspective on self-defense, see Sean D. Murphy, "The United States and the International Court of Justice: Coping with Antinomies," in *The Sword and the Scales: The United States and International Courts and Tribunals* 46 (Cesare P.R. Romano ed. 2009); John E. Noyes, "Unit Self-defense at Sea: Views from the United States and the International Court of Justice," in *The Exercise of Jurisdiction over Vessels: New Developments in the Fields of Pollution, Fisheries, Crimes at Sea and Trafficking of Weapons of Mass Destruction* 185 (Erik Franckx & Philippe Gautier eds. 2010).

D. THE USE OF FORCE AFTER THE COLD WAR

1. IRAQ'S 1990 INVASION OF KUWAIT

When the Berlin Wall fell in 1989, it tolled the bell for the Cold War. East Germany, along with Poland, Czechoslovakia, Hungary, Romania, and Bulgaria left the Soviet bloc. The Soviet Union itself began to disintegrate. More than a dozen Soviet republics—Estonia, Latvia, Lithuania, the Ukraine, Armenia, and Kazakhstan among them—declared their independence. Yugoslavia, too, crumbled into six (or maybe seven; we explore the status of Kosovo in Chapter 7, Part C) new sovereign states. All this loosened the logjam in the U.N. Security Council, which was now freer to act, to recover perhaps its original promise in 1945 to provide for collective security. The "new" Security Council's first major test was not long in coming.

On August 2, 1990, over 100,000 Iraqi troops attacked neighboring Kuwait. The greatly outnumbered Kuwaiti forces were routed, and the Emir of Kuwait fled the country. The invasion followed the collapse of talks in which Iraq had asserted financial and territorial claims. On the same day as the invasion, the U.N. Security Council voted 14–0, with Yemen abstaining, to condemn the invasion and to demand immediate and unconditional withdrawal of all Iraqi forces. S.C. Res. 660 (1990), 29 *International Legal Materials* 1325 (1990). In Resolution 661, adopted on August 6, 1990 by a vote of 13–0 (Cuba and Yemen abstaining), the Council "decide[d] that all States shall" prevent Iraqi imports and impose other economic sanctions on Iraq. Three days later the Council voted unanimously to declare Iraq's asserted annexation of Kuwait null and void. S.C. Res. 662 (1990), 29 *International Legal Materials* 1327 (1990).

The readings in this section illustrate the scope of Security Council actions under Chapter VII of the U.N. Charter. We begin with Security Council Resolution 678, which followed a massive buildup of U.S. and other military forces in Saudi Arabia and the region. Beginning on January 16, 1991, when Iraq refused to comply with a U.S. deadline for withdrawing from Kuwait, the air strikes and ground assault of "Operation Desert Storm" began. These led, by the end of February, to the restoration of Kuwaiti sovereignty within the territory of Kuwait. Was Operation Desert Storm an exercise of collective self-defense or a proper exercise of Security Council authority under Chapter VII of the U.N. Charter? The readings that follow Resolution 678 debate the question. The section concludes with an examination of Security Council Resolution 687, one of the significant resolutions passed after Iraq was driven out of Kuwait.

SECURITY COUNCIL RESOLUTION 678

Nov. 28, 1990, 29 *International Legal Materials* 1565 (1990)

The Security Council,

Recalling, and reaffirming its resolutions 660 (1990) of 2 August 1990, 661 (1990) of 6 August 1990, 662 (1990) of 9 August 1990, 664 (1990) of 18 August 1990, 665 (1990) of 25 August, 1990, 666 (1990) of 13 September 1990, 667 (1990) of 16 September 1990, 669 (1990) of 24 September 1990, 670 (1990) of 25 September 1990, 674 (1990) of 29 October 1990 and 677 (1990) of 28 November 1990,

Noting that, despite all efforts by the United Nations, Iraq refuses to comply with its obligation to implement resolution 660 (1990) and the above mentioned subsequent relevant resolutions, in flagrant contempt of the Security Council,

Mindful of its duties and responsibilities under the Charter of the United Nations for the maintenance and preservation of international peace and security,

Determined to secure full compliance with its decisions,

Acting under Chapter VII of the Charter,

1. *Demands* that Iraq comply fully with resolution 660 (1990) and all subsequent relevant resolutions, and decides, while maintaining all its

decisions, to allow Iraq one final opportunity, as a pause of goodwill, to do so;

2. *Authorizes* Member States co-operating with the government of Kuwait, unless Iraq on or before 15 January 1991 fully implements, as set forth in paragraph 1 above, the foregoing resolutions, to use all necessary means to uphold and implement resolution 660 (1990) and all subsequent relevant resolutions and to restore international peace and security in the area;

3. *Requests* all States to provide appropriate support for the actions undertaken in pursuance of paragraph 2 of the present resolution[.]

THOMAS M. FRANCK & FAIZA PATEL, "UN POLICE ACTION IN LIEU OF WAR: 'THE OLD ORDER CHANGETH' "

85 *American Journal of International Law* 63 (1991)

The United Nations system is an elegant, carefully crafted instrument to make war illegal and unnecessary. To this end, in Article 2(4) of the UN Charter, members are required to "refrain . . . from the threat or use of force against the territorial integrity or political independence of any state." * * *

The new alternative to traditional wars of self-defense is collective police actions by the members of the international community. Exceptionally, these could be implemented by regional organizations. Usually, they would take the form of global action. Either way, the police action must be authorized specifically by the Security Council under Article 53 (for regional action) or Article 42 (for global action).

If states use armed force under the self-defense rubric of Article 51, their individual activities are subsumed by, or incorporated into, the global police response once it is activated. That is, the old way is licensed only until the new way begins to work: "until," in the words of Article 51, "the Security Council has taken the necessary measures to maintain international peace and security."

[T]he argument that the *war* power of member states was not intended to be restricted, but only augmented, by the Charter's creation of a new *police* power [is erroneous]. This interpretation flies in the face of common sense and the literal text. A new-style, UN-authorized police action functioning alongside a traditional sovereign exercise of war powers is conceptually and operationally untenable, the more so when states seeking the freedom to act unilaterally have forces committed alongside others in a Security Council police action. As a textual matter, it is obvious on its face that the Charter, in creating the new police power, intended to establish an exclusive alternative to the old war system. * * *

The delegates to the San Francisco Conference recognized that the enforcement provisions of chapter VII of the Charter provided "the teeth of the United Nations." The committee considering its military enforcement measures adopted Article 42 unanimously. In so doing, delegates intended to give the Security Council "the power, when diplomatic, economic, or other measures are considered by the Council to be inadequate, to undertake such aerial, naval, or other operations as may be necessary to maintain or restore international peace and security." This article was thought to remedy the principal defect of the League Covenant and the committee's rapporteur observed that "this unanimous vote . . . renders sacred the obligation of all states to participate in the operations." Thus, "[m]ilitary assistance, in case of aggression, ceases to be a *recommendation* made to member states; it becomes for us an *obligation* which none can shirk."

This record is entirely inconsistent with the notion that, once the Security Council has taken measures, individual members are supposed to remain free to design their own military responses. * * *

Any effort to ascertain the intent of the drafters is somewhat clouded by the large amount of attention given by the drafters and ratifiers of the Charter to one provision pertaining to police action, which, historically, has proven to be something of a red herring. Just as Congress nowadays does not grant letters of marque and reprisal (Constitution, Article I, section 8(11)) or establish post roads (Article I, section 8(7)), so the Security Council has not made use of Article 43 of the Charter, which authorizes it to negotiate agreements with consenting member states that, preemptively, would have placed designated national military contingents at the Council's disposal. That no such agreements were made, owing to the Cold War, does not signify a lapse in the Organization's general police power, set out in Article 42, any more than the abstinence by Congress in matters of post roads signifies a lapse in its power to legislate on other matters pertaining to the Postal Service. Rather, the practice of the Security Council has evolved other means for taking coercive measures, including the use of police forces raised ad hoc in response to a specific threat to the peace. Both the Korean and the Kuwaiti situations are examples. What emerges from the institutional history of the years of stasis is not evidence that the Council's policing functions have fallen into desuetude but, on the contrary, that the central idea of a globally sanctioned police action was never abandoned; that the failure to implement Article 43 merely led to organic growth and the alternative creation of police action through invocation of Article 42, which does not require special agreements.

This is as one would expect. The UN Charter is not merely a treaty, but also the constitutive instrument of a living global organization. Its organs were designed both to implement important tasks and to interpret their own authority. Such organic growth is desirable and inevitable.

EUGENE V. ROSTOW, "UNTIL WHAT? ENFORCEMENT ACTION OR COLLECTIVE SELF-DEFENSE?"

85 *American Journal of International Law* 506 (1991)

Should the Persian Gulf war of 1990–1991 be characterized as an "international enforcement action" of the United Nations Security Council or as a campaign of collective self-defense approved, encouraged, and blessed by the Security Council?

This is not simply a nice and rather metaphysical legal issue, but an extremely practical one. The question it presents is whether the control and direction of hostilities in the gulf, their termination, and the substance of the settlement they produce were handled by the Council as the Korean War was handled, that is, as a campaign of collective self-defense, or as the United Nations' first "international enforcement action." * * *

On paper, the powers of the UN Security Council go beyond those possessed by the League of Nations. The Council can call on the members to apply measures not involving the use of armed force in order to deal with situations of aggression, and, if such measures are deemed inadequate, it "may take such action by air, sea, or land forces as may be necessary to maintain or restore international peace and security." Provision was made for the formation of a standing United Nations force, and of a Military Staff Committee to advise and assist the Security Council on these and cognate questions. The Military Staff Committee exists in a state of suspended animation at the present time, although it may be revived. Military actions to restore peace taken under Article 42 and 43 of the Charter are called "international enforcement actions."

Finally, after the Charter outlined the peacekeeping procedures of the Security Council under chapter VII in Articles 39–50, it provided in Article 51 that "[n]othing in the present Charter shall impair the inherent right of individual or collective self-defense if an armed attack occurs . . . until the Security Council has taken measures necessary to maintain international peace and security." In the narrowest sense, the present controversy is about the meaning of the word "until" in Article 51.

The coercive powers conferred on the Security Council have not yet become a working part of the process for managing the state system. The fate of these coercive powers thus far reflects the nature of the United Nations as a hybrid political entity superimposed on the system of sovereign states: not a superpower or a world government, but an instrumentality for achieving cooperation among the nations in the interest of peace; an instrumentality, a catalyst, to which certain powers have been tentatively delegated by those nations. Diplomacy and conciliation are the normal methods of the Security Council. * * *

While some eminent authorities consider the Korean War to have been a Security Council "enforcement action," they press the term too hard. In the Korean episode, the Security Council was able to function for two months because the Soviet Union was boycotting the Organization at the time. Even under those circumstances, however, the Council did not use the language of "decision" which would have activated Article 25. The Council's resolutions simply recommended that the members refrain from helping North Korea and urged them to "furnish such assistance to the Republic of Korea as may be necessary to repel the armed attack and to restore international peace and security in the area." For all their symbolic panoply of the United Nations flag and other emblems, the forces which finally prevailed in Korea were national forces carrying out a mission of collective self-defense under American direction, not a Security Council enforcement action. * * *

In the Persian Gulf crisis, Security Council Resolution 678 "[*a*]*uthorizes* Member States co-operating with the Government of Kuwait . . . to use all necessary means to uphold [the earlier resolutions] and to restore international peace and security in the area." Except for the word "authorizes," the resolution is clearly one designed to encourage and support a campaign of collective self-defense, and therefore not a Security Council enforcement action. Instead of attempting to direct such an operation itself, the Council "requests the States concerned" to keep it regularly informed about their progress. The Security Council held no meetings on the gulf crisis between November 29, 1990, when Resolution 678 was adopted, and February 14, 1991, when it met in secret session to discuss the political aspects of the end of the war. And the initial cease-fire in the gulf war was achieved as a practical matter not by an agreed Security Council resolution but by President Bush's ultimatum of February 28, 1991. * * *

During the period of active hostilities, neither the Secretary-General nor any other part of the United Nations Secretariat attempted to exercise control over military operations, although a committee of the Council actively supervised the program of economic sanctions.

Thus, the practice followed in implementing Resolution 678 and in terminating hostilities has been that of an allied military campaign in defense of Kuwait directed by officers of the United States and the associated nations. Does the word "authorized" in Resolution 678 mean that the member states which cooperated with Kuwait in driving Iraq out of that country could not have done so without the Council's "authority"? As Professor Glennon points out, Resolution 678 is in fact permissive, like Resolution 83 of June 27, 1950, adopted by the Security Council during the Korean War. It imposes no legally binding obligation under Article 25 of the Charter. In Glennon's words, it "merely exhorts, authorizes or recommends," leaving to the member states the decision whether to cooperate in the effort of the allied coalition to liberate Kuwait. The word "authorizes" in Resolution 678 should not therefore be considered to transform a military campaign of self-defense into an enforcement action.

Thus far, the nominal authority of the Security Council to engage in military "enforcement actions" has not been tested. This is not a state of affairs to be deplored. Political relations among the members of the Council—permanent and temporary alike—are not sufficiently stable to make so radical a step politically feasible or desirable. Although the diplomacy of the gulf crisis in 1990 and 1991 has shown some movement in a promising direction, it remains to be seen whether these hints of progress are followed by more substantial changes.

NOTES AND QUESTIONS

1. *Chapter VII and Security Council Decisions.* What were the legal grounds for the Security Council's resolutions related to the Gulf War? According to Resolution 661, for example, the Security Council acted generally under Chapter VII of the U.N. Charter when it decided that states were to impose economic sanctions on Iraq. Must the Security Council find explicit authority to justify Chapter VII actions in a particular article of the Charter?

A Security Council "decision" has particular legal significance. According to Article 25 of the U.N. Charter, "Members of the United Nations agree to accept and carry out the decisions of the Security Council in accordance with the present Charter." See also Article 48. Furthermore, Article 103 of the Charter provides: "In the event of a conflict between the obligations of the Members of the United Nations under the present Charter and their obligations under any other international agreement, their obligations under the present Charter shall prevail." The Security Council may make decisions on procedural matters by an affirmative vote of any nine of the Council's 15 members, but decisions on other matters require nine votes, "including the concurring votes of the permanent members." U.N. Charter, art. 27. The requirement of "concurring votes" has long been interpreted to be satisfied if no permanent member of the Council (China, France, Russia, the United Kingdom, and the United States) votes against a measure.

2. *Collective Self-defense v. Chapter VII Enforcement Action.* Did Security Council Resolution 678 authorize a type of Chapter VII enforcement action, as Franck and Patel suggested? Or was the use of force against Iraq an exercise of collective self-defense in accordance with Article 51 of the U.N. Charter? How comparable is the debate between Franck/Patel and Rostow to that between Henkin and Reisman in Part C?

If the use of force against Iraq was an exercise of collective self-defense, why did the United States and other members of the Security Council find it necessary to approve Resolution 678? Why might such a choice of justifications make a difference?

According to Article 51 of the U.N. Charter, the right of self-defense is preserved "until the Security Council has taken measures necessary to maintain international peace and security." When is the right of states to use force in self-defense suspended? When the Security Council passes any resolutions under Chapter VII? When the Security Council decides U.N. Member States should impose comprehensive mandatory sanctions against a state that has used force? Once the Security Council has taken measures sufficient to suspend the right of self-defense, how long should the suspension continue? Security Council Resolution 661 explicitly affirmed "the inherent right of individual or collective self-defense, in response to the armed attack by Iraq against Kuwait, in accordance with Article 51 of the Charter." But what if references to Article 51 were absent in a comprehensive sanctions resolution? Who decides whether any Security Council measures satisfy the "necessary to maintain international peace and security" clause of Article 51?

SECURITY COUNCIL RESOLUTION 687

Apr. 3, 1991, 30 *International Legal Materials* 846 (1991)

The Security Council,

Recalling its resolutions 660 (1990) of 2 August 1990, 661 (1990) of 6 August 1990, 662 (1990) of 9 August 1990, 664 (1990) of 18 August 1990, 665 (1990) of 25 August 1990, 666 (1990) of 13 September 1990, 667 (1990) of 16 September 1990, 669 (1990) of 24 September 1990, 670 (1990) of 25 September 1990, 674 (1990) of 29 October 1990, 677 (1990) of 28 November 1990, 678 (1990) of 29 November 1990 and 686 (1991) of 2 March 1991,

Welcoming the restoration to Kuwait of its sovereignty, independence and territorial integrity and the return of its legitimate Government, * * *

Bearing in mind its objective of restoring international peace and security in the area as set out in recent resolutions of the Security Council,

Conscious of the need to take the following measures acting under Chapter VII of the Charter,

1. *Affirms* all thirteen resolutions noted above, except as expressly changed below to achieve the goals of this resolution, including a formal cease-fire;

[The Security Council "decides to guarantee the inviolability of" the international boundary between Iraq and Kuwait in accordance with the terms of a 1963 bilateral agreement, calling for a process to demarcate that boundary. The Council also provides for deployment of a U.N. observer unit to monitor a demilitarized zone between Iraq and Kuwait.]

6. *Notes* that as soon as the Secretary-General notifies the Security Council of the completion of the deployment of the United Nations observer unit, the conditions will be established for the Member States cooperating with Kuwait in accordance with resolution 678 (1990) to bring their military presence in Iraq to an end consistent with resolution 686 (1991);

[The Council decides Iraq will accept the destruction or removal of certain weapons, submit to on-site inspections of its weapons systems, and take other steps related to its military capabilities. The Council calls on the Secretary-General and the International Atomic Energy Agency to carry out measures concerning Iraqi weapons, nuclear material, and nuclear facilities. In addition, the Council requests a report concerning steps to return Kuwaiti property seized by Iraq, reaffirms debts and obligations of Iraq, decides to create a compensation fund for damage suffered by governments, individuals, and corporations as a result of Iraq's invasion and occupation of Kuwait, and decides that prohibitions on transactions with Iraq shall not apply to certain foodstuffs and other materials required for essential civilian needs.]

22. *Decides* that upon the approval by the Security Council of the [claims compensation] programme called for in paragraph 19 above and upon Council agreement that Iraq has completed all actions contemplated in paragraphs 8, 9, 10, 11, 12 and 13 above [concerning Iraqi weapons and on-site inspections], the prohibitions against the import of commodities and products originating in Iraq and the prohibitions against financial transactions related thereto contained in resolution 661 (1990) shall have no further force or effect; * * *

24. *Decides* that, in accordance with resolution 661 (1990) and subsequent related resolutions and until a further decision is taken by the Security Council, all States shall continue to prevent the sale or supply, or the promotion or facilitation of such sale or supply, to Iraq by their nationals, or from their territories or using their flag vessels or aircraft, of [military equipment, arms, and related technology and support services.]

[The Council, in paragraph 29, decides that all states shall ensure that no person shall have a claim in connection with any contract affected by the measures taken in Resolution 661. The Council also decides that Iraq shall cooperate with the International Committee of the Red Cross in repatriating Kuwaiti and other foreign nationals, and requires that Iraq commit not to support international terrorism.]

33. *Declares* that, upon official notification by Iraq to the Secretary-General and to the Security Council of its acceptance of the provisions above, a formal cease-fire is effective between Iraq and Kuwait and the Member States cooperating with Kuwait in accordance with resolution 678 (1990);

34. *Decides* to remain seized of the matter and to take such further steps as may be required for the implementation of the present resolution and to secure peace and security in the area.

NOTES AND QUESTIONS

1. *Post-Desert Storm Security Council Resolutions.* Resolution 687 was one of several significant Security Council resolutions passed after Iraq was driven out of Kuwait. Many of its provisions were bold. For example, states normally settle boundary disputes by agreement or by authorizing a tribunal to decide them, but in Resolution 687 the Security Council itself seemed to impose a settlement to an Iraq-Kuwait boundary dispute. See also S.C. Res. 833 (1993), 32 *International Legal Materials* 1463 (1993). In paragraph 29 of Resolution 687, the Security Council effectively required all states to apply a *force majeure* defense to Iraqi claims in connection with otherwise valid transactions that were not carried out because of the Security Council's economic sanctions against Iraq, a type of "legislation" directed at the practices of municipal courts. And Resolution 687 also contemplated a Compensation Commission to assess Iraq's liability for damages due to the invasion of Kuwait. This Commission, formally created as a subsidiary organ of the Security Council under Article 29 of the U.N. Charter, S.C. Res. 692 (1991), 30 *International Legal Materials* 864 (1991), operated as a fact-finding and quasi-adjudicatory body. The Commission completed its work in 2005, resolving over 2.6 million claims, awarding approximately $52.4 billion to successful claimants, and paying out about $21.8 billion from a fund created by taking proceeds of Iraq's sales of its oil exports. See http://www.uncc.ch. (last visited Dec. 11, 2013); Arthur W. Rovine, "The United Nations Compensation Commission," in 35 *International Law News*, No. 2, at 10 (2006). Was Resolution 687 an appropriate exercise of the Security Council's authority? Did the Council, although a political institution, provide "institutionalized countermeasures" as a means of responding to Iraq's illegal actions and thus enforcing international law? See Vera Gowlland-Debbas, "Security Council Enforcement Action and Issues of State Responsibility," 43 *International and Comparative Law Quarterly* 55 (1994).

Some paragraphs of Resolution 687 related to humanitarian measures, as did Security Council Resolution 688, 30 *International Legal Materials* 858 (1991), which condemned Iraq's repression of Kurds in northern Iraq. The Security Council continued to emphasize the significance of humanitarian concerns in Iraq in the years following Desert Storm. See, *e.g.*, S.C. Res. 1284 (1999), 39 *International Legal Materials* 760 (2000).

The various sanctions against Iraq met with mixed success. Iraq expelled U.N. weapons inspectors in 1998 and resisted the return of inspectors under a revised inspection regime. See Barbara Crossette & Stephen Lee Myers, "U.N. Readies Team to Check Weapons Held by the Iraqis," *New York Times*, Aug. 22, 2000, at 1. Some states resumed civilian air travel to Iraq, avoiding the Security Council's economic sanctions, and smugglers also evaded some sanctions. See Barbara Crossette, "French Flight

Tests Ban Against Iraq," *New York Times*, Sept. 23, 2000, at A7. And a U.N. program authorizing Iraq to sell oil to raise funds to purchase humanitarian goods was beset by fraud. See the 2005 Reports of the Independent Inquiry Committee into the United Nations Oil-for-Food Programme concerning the manipulation and management of that Programme, available at http://www.iic-offp.org (last visited Dec. 11, 2013). For an overview of the efficacy of U.N. sanctions against Iraq during the 1990s, see David Cartright & George A. Lopez, *The Sanctions Decade: Assessing UN Strategies in the 1990s*, at 37–61 (2000). As we see in Section 2 below, some states used force against Iraq during the 1990s and early 2000s and, most notably, there was a U.S.- and British-led invasion in 2003.

2. *Terminating Security Council Decisions*. Paragraph 24 of Resolution 687 provided that some Security Council sanctions imposed against Iraq were to continue in effect "until a further decision is taken by the Security Council." Since one of the Council's permanent members could veto any proposal to lift sanctions, should the Council require that any sanctions it imposes expire if they are not renewed by some date certain? Or require that an initial sanctions resolution include a modified voting procedure to determine when the sanctions can be lifted? See David D. Caron, "The Legitimacy of the Collective Authority of the Security Council," 87 *American Journal of International Law* 552, 577–88 (1993).

2. THE 2003 INVASION OF IRAQ

When the United States, the United Kingdom, and others invaded Iraq in March 2003 and toppled the regime of Saddam Hussein, the invading states justified their action as consistent with Security Council resolutions. The Security Council had unanimously passed Resolution 1441, which is reproduced below, on November 8, 2002. That Resolution, along with Resolutions 678 and 687, which appear in Section 2 above, have been invoked as legal justifications for the invasion. Following Resolution 1441 is an excerpt that sets out arguments for and against the legality of the 2003 invasion. The invasion also raises broader questions about the efficacy of the U.N. Charter's system of collective security.

SECURITY COUNCIL RESOLUTION 1441

Nov. 8, 2002, 42 *International Legal Materials* 250 (2003)

The Security Council,

Recalling all its previous relevant resolutions, in particular its resolutions 661 (1990) of 6 August 1990, 678 (1990) of 29 November 1990, 686 (1991) of 2 March 1991, 687 (1991) of 3 April 1991, 688 (1991) of 5 April 1991, 707 (1991) of 15 August 1991, 715 (1991) of 11 October 1991, 986 (1995) of 14 April 1995, and 1284 (1999) of 17 December 1999, and all the relevant statements of its President, * * *

Recognizing the threat Iraq's non-compliance with Council resolutions and proliferation of weapons of mass destruction and long-range missiles poses to international peace and security,

Recalling that its resolution 678 (1990) authorized Member States to use all necessary means to uphold and implement its resolution 660 (1990) of 2 August 1990 and all relevant resolutions subsequent to resolution 660 (1990) and to restore international peace and security in the area,

Further recalling that its resolution 687 (1991) imposed obligations on Iraq as a necessary step for achievement of its stated objective of restoring international peace and security in the area,

Deploring the fact that Iraq has not provided an accurate, full, final, and complete disclosure, as required by resolution 687 (1991), of all aspects of its programmes to develop weapons of mass destruction and ballistic missiles with a range greater than one hundred and fifty kilometres, and of all holdings of such weapons, their components and production facilities and locations, as well as all other nuclear programmes, including any which it claims are for purposes not related to nuclear-weapons-usable material,

Deploring further that Iraq repeatedly obstructed immediate, unconditional, and unrestricted access to sites designated by the United Nations Special Commission (UNSCOM) and the International Atomic Energy Agency (IAEA), failed to cooperate fully and unconditionally with UNSCOM and IAEA weapons inspectors, as required by resolution 687 (1991), and ultimately ceased all cooperation with UNSCOM and the IAEA in 1998,

Deploring the absence, since December 1998, in Iraq of international monitoring, inspection, and verification, as required by relevant resolutions, of weapons of mass destruction and ballistic missiles[,]

Deploring also that the Government of Iraq has failed to comply with its commitments pursuant to resolution 687 (1991) with regard to terrorism, pursuant to resolution 688 (1991) to end repression of its civilian population and to provide access by international humanitarian organizations to all those in need of assistance in Iraq, and pursuant to resolutions 686 (1991), 687 (1991), and 1284 (1999) to return or cooperate in accounting for Kuwaiti and third country nationals wrongfully detained by Iraq, or to return Kuwaiti property wrongfully seized by Iraq,

Recalling that in its resolution 687 (1991) the Council declared that a ceasefire would be based on acceptance by Iraq of the provisions of that resolution, including the obligations on Iraq contained therein,

Determined to ensure full and immediate compliance by Iraq without conditions or restrictions with its obligations under resolution 687 (1991)

and other relevant resolutions and recalling that the resolutions of the Council constitute the governing standard of Iraqi compliance, * * *

Reaffirming the commitment of all Member States to the sovereignty and territorial integrity of Iraq, Kuwait, and the neighbouring States, * * *

Determined to secure full compliance with its decisions,

Acting under Chapter VII of the Charter of the United Nations,

1. *Decides* that Iraq has been and remains in material breach of its obligations under relevant resolutions, including resolution 687 (1991), in particular through Iraq's failure to cooperate with United Nations inspectors and the IAEA, and to complete the actions required under paragraphs 8 to 13 of resolution 687 (1991);

2. *Decides*, while acknowledging paragraph 1 above, to afford Iraq, by this resolution, a final opportunity to comply with its disarmament obligations under relevant resolutions of the Council; and accordingly decides to set up an enhanced inspection regime with the aim of bringing to full and verified completion the disarmament process established by resolution 687 (1991) and subsequent resolutions of the Council;

3. *Decides* that, in order to begin to comply with its disarmament obligations, in addition to submitting the required biannual declarations, the Government of Iraq shall provide to [the United Nations Monitoring, Verification and Inspection Commission (UNMOVIC), the successor organization to UNSCOM], the IAEA, and the Council, not later than 30 days from the date of this resolution, a currently accurate, full, and complete declaration of all aspects of its programmes to develop chemical, biological, and nuclear weapons, ballistic missiles, and other delivery systems such as unmanned aerial vehicles and dispersal systems designed for use on aircraft, including any holdings and precise locations of such weapons, components, subcomponents, stocks of agents, and related material and equipment, the locations and work of its research, development and production facilities, as well as all other chemical, biological, and nuclear programmes, including any which it claims are for purposes not related to weapon production or material;

4. *Decides* that false statements or omissions in the declarations submitted by Iraq pursuant to this resolution and failure by Iraq at any time to comply with, and cooperate fully in the implementation of, this resolution shall constitute a further material breach of Iraq's obligations and will be reported to the Council for assessment in accordance with paragraphs 11 and 12 below;

5. *Decides* that Iraq shall provide UNMOVIC and the IAEA immediate, unimpeded, unconditional, and unrestricted access to any and all, including underground, areas, facilities, buildings, equipment,

records, and means of transport which they wish to inspect, as well as immediate, unimpeded, unrestricted, and private access to all officials and other persons whom UNMOVIC or the IAEA wish to interview in the mode or location of UNMOVIC's or the IAEA's choice pursuant to any aspect of their mandates; * * *

11. *Directs* the Executive Chairman of UNMOVIC and the Director-General of the IAEA to report immediately to the Council any interference by Iraq with inspection activities, as well as any failure by Iraq to comply with its disarmament obligations, including its obligations regarding inspections under this resolution;

12. *Decides* to convene immediately upon receipt of a report in accordance with paragraphs 4 or 11 above, in order to consider the situation and the need for full compliance with all of the relevant Council resolutions in order to secure international peace and security;

13. *Recalls*, in that context, that the Council has repeatedly warned Iraq that it will face serious consequences as a result of its continued violations of its obligations;

14. *Decides* to remain seized of the matter.

NOTES AND QUESTIONS

1. *Weapons Inspections and the Invasion of Iraq*. The U.N.'s "enhanced inspection regime" called for in paragraph 2 of Resolution 1441, which was led by Hans Blix, had not found any proscribed Iraqi weapons by early 2003. The United States criticized the inspection effort, along with the sufficiency of the Iraqi information provided in response to the decision in paragraph 3 of Resolution 1441. U.S. efforts to marshal enough votes for another Security Council resolution that specifically authorized the use of force against Iraq nevertheless fell short. See Steven R. Weisman & Felicity Barringer, "Powell Attacks Validity of the Work by Weapons Inspectors in Iraq," *New York Times*, Mar. 6, 2003, at A17. U.S. and British forces, along with forces from a few other states, invaded Iraq on March 20, 2003, and ousted the Iraqi leader, Saddam Hussein.

The U.S. Central Intelligence Agency concluded, following a comprehensive search for weapons of mass destruction in Iraq, that Iraq had "essenticccddddr55ally destroyed" all of its chemical and biological weapons and its nuclear weapons program by the end of 1991 and had destroyed its last biological weapons plant in 1996. See *Comprehensive Report of the Special Advisor to the DCI [Director of Central Intelligence] on Iraq's WMD* (2004), *available at* https://www.cia.gov/library/reports/general-reports-1/iraq_wmd_2004/ (last visited Dec. 11, 2013). See also Roula Khalaf & Mark Turner, "Blix Found No Sign of Non-Compliance," *Financial Times (London)*, Apr. 28, 2005, at 2. However, the CIA also found that several countries—including China, France, and Russia—and their nationals helped to subvert the U.N. sanctions against Iraq, even supplying Iraq with conventional weapons and, on occasion, material that might be useful for chemical or biological weapons production. See John F. Murphy, *The Evolving Dimensions of International Law* 126–32 (2010). For his part, Iraq's Saddam Hussein reportedly sought to undermine the U.N. sanctions, although he recognized that maintaining WMDs while the sanctions were in place might harm his efforts to have sanctions lifted. He also projected ambiguity about whether Iraq possessed illegal weapons, believing such ambiguity would deter Iran and Israel from attacking Iraq. See Douglas Jehl, "U.S. Report Finds Iraqis Eliminated Illicit Arms in 90's," *New York Times*, Oct. 7, 2004, at A1; Kevin Woods, James Lacey & Williamson Murray, "Saddam's Delusions: The View from the Inside," *Foreign Affairs*, May–June 2006, at 2, 5–11.

2. *Other Post-Desert Storm Uses of Force Against Iraq*. During the 1990s and early 2000s, after Iraq was driven out of Kuwait, the United States and other states used armed force against Iraq. The uses of force responded to Iraq's failure to allow the weapons inspectors called for in Resolution 687 free movement, to Iraqi attacks on civilians, and to Iraqi violations of "no-fly zones" proclaimed over portions of Iraq. These no-fly zones had not been specifically established by any Security Council resolution. Many of the questions raised about the legality of the uses of force in Iraq after the liberation of Kuwait and prior to the March 2003 invasion were similar to questions raised about the 2003 invasion itself. See, *e.g.*, Christine Gray, "From Unity to Polarisation: International Law and the Use of Force Against Iraq," 13 *European Journal of International Law* 1 (2002).

MEMO FROM BRITISH ATTORNEY-GENERAL GOLDSMITH TO PRIME MINISTER TONY BLAIR

Mar. 7, 2003, *available at* http://www.iraqinquirydigest.org/?page_id=154 (last visited Dec. 10, 2013)

1. You have asked me for advice on the legality of military action against Iraq without a further resolution of the Security Council. * * *

Possible legal bases for the use of force

2. [T]here are generally three possible bases for the use of force:

(a) self-defence (which may include collective self-defence);

(b) exceptionally, to avert overwhelming humanitarian catastrophe; and

(c) authorisation by the Security Council acting under Chapter VII of the UN Charter.

3. Force may be used in self-defence if there is an actual or imminent threat of an armed attack; the use of force must be necessary, i.e. the only means of averting an attack; and the force used must be a proportionate response. It is now widely accepted that an imminent armed attack will justify the use of force if the other conditions are met. The concept of what

is imminent may depend on the circumstances. Different considerations may apply, for example, where the risk is of attack from terrorists sponsored or harbored by a particular State, or where there is a threat of an attack by nuclear weapons. However, in my opinion there must be some degree of imminence. I am aware that the USA has been arguing for recognition of a broad doctrine of a right to use force to pre-empt danger in the future. If this means more than a right to respond proportionately to an imminent attack (and I understand that the doctrine is intended to carry that connotation) this is not a doctrine which, in my opinion, exists or is recognized in international law.

4. The use of force to avert overwhelming humanitarian catastrophe has been emerging as a further, and exceptional, basis for the use of force. * * * The doctrine remains controversial, however. I know of no reason why it would be an appropriate basis for action in present circumstances.

5. Force may be used where this [is] authorised by the UN Security Council acting under Chapter VII of the UN Charter. The key question is whether resolution 1441 has the effect of providing such authorisation.

Resolution 1441

6. [T]he argument that resolution 1441 itself provides the authorisation to use force depends on the revival of the express authorisation to use force given in 1990 by Security Council resolution 678. This in turn gives rise to two questions:

(a) is the so-called "revival argument" a sound legal basis in principle?

(b) is resolution 1441 sufficient to revive the authorisation in resolution 678?

[I]f the answer to these two questions is "yes," the use of force will have been authorised by the United Nations and not in defiance of it.

The revival argument

7. Following its invasion and annexation of Kuwait, the Security Council authorised the use of force against Iraq in resolution 678 (1990). This resolution authorised coalition forces to use all necessary means to force Iraq to withdraw from Kuwait and to restore international peace and security in the area. The resolution gave a legal basis for Operation Desert Storm, which was brought to an end by the cease-fire set out by the Council in resolution 687 (1991). The conditions for the cease-fire in that resolution (and subsequent resolutions) imposed obligations on Iraq with regard to the elimination of WMD and monitoring of its obligations. Resolution 687 suspended, but did not terminate, the authority to use force in resolution 678. Nor has any subsequent resolution terminated the authorisation to use force in resolution 678. It has been the UK's view that a violation of Iraq's obligations under resolution 687 which is

sufficiently serious to undermine the basis of the cease-fire can revive the authorisation to use force in resolution 678. * * *

9. [T]he UK has consistently taken the view * * * that, as the cease-fire conditions were set by the Security Council in resolution 687, it is for the Council to assess whether any such breach of those obligations has occurred. The US has a rather different view: they maintain that the fact of whether Iraq is in breach is a matter of objective fact which may therefore be assessed by individual Member States. I am not aware of any other state which supports this view. This is an issue of critical importance when considering the effect of resolution 1441.

10. [I] believe that the arguments in support of the revival argument are stronger following adoption of resolution 1441. That is because of the terms of the resolution and the course of the negotiations which led to its adoption. * * *

11. I disagree, therefore, with those commentators and lawyers, who assert that nothing less than an *explicit* authorisation to use force in a Security Council resolution will be sufficient.

Sufficiency of resolution 1441

12. [Operative paragraph (OP) 2 of resolution 1441] has the effect * * * of suspending the legal consequences of the OP 1 determination of material breach which would otherwise have triggered the revival of the authorisation in resolution 678. The narrow but key question is: on the true interpretation of resolution 1441, what has the Security Council decided will be the consequences of Iraq's failure to comply with the enhanced regime.

13. The provisions relevant to determining whether or not Iraq has taken the final opportunity given by the Security Council are contained in OPs 4, 11 and 12 of the resolution. * * * It is clear from the text of the resolution, and is apparent from the negotiating history, that if Iraq fails to comply, there will be a further Security Council discussion. The text is, however, ambiguous and unclear on what happens next.

14. There are two competing arguments:

(i) that provided there is a Council discussion, if it does not reach a conclusion, there remains an authorisation to use force;

(ii) that nothing short of a further Council decision will be a legitimate basis for the use of force.

The first argument

15. The first argument is based on the following steps:

(a) OP 1, by stating that Iraq "has been and remains in material breach" of its obligations under relevant resolutions, including resolution 687 amounts to a determination by the

Council that Iraq's violations of resolution 687 are sufficiently serious to destroy the basis of the cease-fire and therefore, in principle, to revive the authorisation to use force in resolution 678;

(b) the Council decided, however, to give Iraq "a final opportunity" (OP 2) but because of the clear warning that it faced "serious consequences as a result of its continued violations" (OP 13) was warning that a failure to take that "final opportunity" would lead to such consequences;

(c) further, by OP 4, the Council decided *in advance* that false statements or omissions in its declaration and "failure by Iraq *at any time* to comply with, and cooperate fully in the implementation of, this resolution" would constitute "a further material breach"; the argument is that the Council's determination in advance that particular conduct would constitute a material breach (thus reviving the authorisation to use force) is as good as its determination *after* the event;

(d) in either event, the Council must meet (OP 12) "to consider the situation and the need for full compliance with all of the relevant Council resolutions in order to secure international peace and security," but the resolution singularly does *not* say that the Council must decide what action to take. The Council knew full well, it is argued, the difference between "consider" and "decide" and so the omission is highly significant. * * * On this view, therefore, while the Council has the opportunity to take a further decision, the determinations of material breach in OPs 1 and 4 remain valid even if the Council does not act.

The second argument

16. The second argument focuses, by contrast, on two provisions in particular of the resolution: first, the final words in OP 4 ("and will be reported to the Council for assessment in accordance with paragraphs 11 and 12 below") and, second, the requirement in OP 12 for the Council to "consider the situation and the need for full compliance with all of the relevant Council resolutions in order to secure international peace and security." Taken together, it is argued, these provisions indicate that the Council decided in resolution 1441 that in the event of continued Iraqi non-compliance, the issue should return to the Council for a further decision on what action should be taken at that stage.

Discussion * * *

21. [T]he language of OP 12 was a compromise by the US from their starting position that the Council should authorise in advance the use of all necessary means to enforce the cease-fire resolution in the event of continued violations by Iraq.

It is equally clear, however, that the language does not expressly provide that a further Council decision is necessary to authorise the use of force. The paragraph indicates that in the event of a report of a further material breach (whether under OP 4 or OP 11) there will be a meeting of the Council to consider the situation and the need for compliance in order to secure international peace and security. * * * The resolution does not state what is to happen [if the Council fails to act.] My view is that different considerations apply in different circumstances. The OP 12 discussion might make clear that the Council's view is that military action is appropriate but that no further decision is required because of the terms of resolution 1441. In such a case, there would be good grounds for relying on the existing resolution as the legal basis for any subsequent military action. The more difficult scenario is if the views of Council members are divided and a further resolution is not adopted either because it fails to attract 9 votes or because it is vetoed. * * *

Summary * * *

27. [T]he safest legal course would be to secure the adoption of a further resolution to authorise the use of force. I have already advised that I do not believe that such a resolution need be explicit in its terms. The key point is that it should establish that the Council has concluded that Iraq has failed to take the final opportunity offered by resolution 1441.

28. Nevertheless, having regard to the information on the negotiating history which I have been given and to the arguments of the US Administration which I heard in Washington, I accept that a reasonable case can be made that resolution 1441 is capable in principle of reviving the authorisation in 678 without a further resolution.

29. However, the argument that resolution 1441 alone has revived the authorisation to use force in resolution 678 will only be sustainable if there are strong factual grounds for concluding that Iraq has failed to take the final opportunity. In other words, we would need to be able to demonstrate hard evidence of non-compliance and non-cooperation. * * *

Proportionality

36. Finally, I must stress that the lawfulness of military action depends not only on the existence of a legal basis, but also on the question of proportionality. Any force used pursuant to the authorisation in resolution 678 (whether or not there is a second resolution):

> —must have as its objective the enforcement the terms of the cease-fire contained in resolution 687 (1990) and subsequent relevant resolutions;
>
> —be limited to what is necessary to achieve that objective; and

—must be a proportionate response to that objective, i.e. securing compliance with Iraq's disarmament obligations.

[R]egime change cannot be the objective of military action. This should be borne in mind in considering the list of military targets and in making public statements about any campaign.

NOTES AND QUESTIONS

1. *Government Legal Advisors.* The United Kingdom has a tradition that government officials should provide independent legal advice about international law. Was Attorney-General Goldsmith politically pressured not to give objective advice? Several previously classified documents, released by Britain's Iraq Inquiry Commission (established in 2009) and available at http://www.iraqinquiry.org.uk (last visited Dec. 12, 2013), provide insight into Goldsmith's views on the legality of using force against Iraq in 2003. In paragraph 13 of a draft memorandum handed to the Prime Minister on January 14, 2003, Goldsmith concluded that "resolution 1441 does not revive the authorisation to use of force contained in resolution 678 in the absence of a further decision of the Security Council." Goldsmith then met with Sir Jeremy Greenstock, the British Ambassador to the United Nations, to discuss the negotiating history of Resolution 1441 and the U.S. legal position. Following that meeting, Goldsmith "remain[ed] of the view that the correct legal interpretation of resolution 1441 is that it does not authorise the use of military force without a further determination by the Security Council." Memo of Jan. 30, 2003, ¶ 4. However, in the March 7 memo reproduced above, Goldsmith equivocated. Although he thought "the safest legal course would be to secure the adoption of a further resolution to authorise the use of force," he also "accept[ed] that a reasonable case can be made that resolution 1441" could "reviv[e] the authorisation in 678 without a further resolution." On March 17, 2003, in his public response to a question raised in the House of Lords, the Attorney-General was of the view that "the authority to use force under Resolution 678 has revived," and that all "1441 requires is reporting to and discussion by the Security Council of Iraq's failures, but not an express further decision to authorise force." *Reprinted in* 52 *International and Comparative Law Quarterly* 811 (2003).

There were repercussions. Foreign and Commonwealth Office Deputy Legal Adviser Elizabeth Wilmhurst tendered her resignation in a letter dated March 18, 2003:

> I regret that I cannot agree that it is lawful to use force against Iraq without a second Security Council resolution to revive the authorisation given in SCR 678. * * * My views accord with the views that have been given consistently in this Office before and after the adoption of SCR 1441 and with what the Attorney General gave us to understand was his view prior to his letter of 7 March. (The view in that letter has of course changed again into what is now the official line.) I cannot in conscience go along with advice—

within the Office or to the public or Parliament—which asserts the legitimacy of military action without such a resolution, particularly since an unlawful use of force on such a scale amounts to the crime of aggression; nor can I agree with such action in circumstances which are so detrimental to the international order and the rule of law.

Did Goldsmith modify his legal advice because of pressure from Prime Minister Tony Blair, who supported the invasion of Iraq? See Chris Ames, "Iraq Inquiry Is All About Political Context," *The Guardian*, July 1, 2010; Kim Sengupta, "Documents Lay Bare How Goldsmith Changed His Advice on Legality of War," *Independent UK*, July 1, 2010, at 2. Should government legal advisors provide independent, objective legal advice? Or should they make the strongest possible legal case to support whatever position the political leadership wants to take? For discussion of the roles of government legal advisors, see Michael P. Scharf & Paul R. Williams, *Shaping Foreign Policy in Times of Crisis: The Role of International Law and the State Department Legal Adviser* (2010), and materials in Chapters 2.B and 9.A.

2. *Evaluating the Revival Argument.* Is it ever legally plausible for the Security Council to authorize the use of force implicitly? If it is possible in theory to revive prior Security Council authorization to use force, did Council Resolution 1441 revive Resolution 678? If there were revival, what exactly would be revived? Resolution 678, adopted in 1990, addressed both Iraqi compliance with Council resolutions related to Iraq's invasion of Kuwait and "restor[ing]" (rather than "establishing" or "maintaining") "international peace and security in the area." If authority to use force to uphold 678's mandates could be revived, would that revival justify toppling Iraq's government in 2003? Did Resolution 687 preserve the use of force authorization in Resolution 678? Or did 687 instead, by expressly setting remedies for Iraq's noncompliance, effectively displace the use of force authorization of 678? Is Resolution 687 a "cease-fire agreement"? When one state breaches a cease-fire treaty, another affected state party may resume hostilities. Are bilateral or multilateral treaties providing for cease-fires different from legally binding Security Council resolutions, under which the Council determines what should be done (and by whom) in the event of a breach? Under the U.S. interpretation of Resolution 1441, would the use of force already be authorized to uphold *any* future Council resolution related to Iraq? See Sean D. Murphy, "Assessing the Legality of Invading Iraq," 92 *Georgetown Law Journal* 173 (2004). For the U.S. government's view, see Letter dated 20 March 2003 from the Permanent Representative of the United States of America to the United Nations to the President of the Security Council, U.N. Doc. S/2003/351 (2003); William H. Taft, IV & Todd F. Buchwald, "Preemption, Iraq and International Law," 97 *American Journal of International Law* 557 (2003).

3. *The U.N. System of Collective Security.* According to Professor Michael Glennon, such developments as NATO's bombing of Kosovo in 1999 and U.S. attitudes toward the 2003 invasion of Iraq demonstrate that "the

Charter provisions governing use of force are simply no longer regarded as binding international law. [T]he Charter has, tragically, gone the way of the 1928 Kellogg-Briand pact which purported to outlaw war." Michael J. Glennon, "How War Left the Law Behind," *New York Times*, Nov. 21, 2002, at A33. Is it a sufficient response to argue that the U.N. Security Council was never intended to restrain the actions of the major powers, but that it has always been available to counter threats to the peace by lesser powers? Or, does the U.N. system of collective security present such a compelling normative vision that occasional (or frequent) violations of its requirements leave the edifice in place? Did this U.N. system in fact affect U.S. decisions concerning the 2003 invasion of Iraq? Is the system ineffective if many international actors continue to believe that U.N. Security Council approval confers legitimacy on uses of force not undertaken in self-defense? Is skepticism about the continued legal validity of the U.N.'s collective security system a product of a particular strand of U.S. views about law and international relations—a position that does not resonate in other parts of the world? See the essays by Edward C. Luck, Anne-Marie Slaughter, and Ian Hurd in "Stayin' Alive: The Rumors of the UN's Death Have Been Exaggerated," *Foreign Affairs*, July–Aug. 2003, at 201; John E. Noyes, "American Hegemony, U.S. Political Leaders, and General International Law," 19 *Connecticut Journal of International Law* 293, 304–08 (2004); Richard H. Pildes, "Conflicts Between American and European Views of Law: The Dark Side of Legalism," 44 *Virginia Journal of International Law* 145 (2003).

4. Jus in Bello. International humanitarian law imposes obligations on "occupying powers" after fighting has ended in an international armed conflict. For example, Article 2(2) of the Fourth 1949 Geneva Convention on the protection of civilians explicitly provides for its application during an occupation following an international armed conflict. Has the United States been an occupying power in Iraq? Did its obligations as an occupying power end when Iraq held elections to elect a new government in June 2004? See Mayur Patel, "The Legal Status of Coalition Forces in Iraq After the June 30 Handover," 8 *ASIL Insights*, Mar. 2004; Philip James Walker, "Iraq, Failed States, and the Law of Occupation," 33 *International Law News*, No. 1, at 1 (2004).

3. TERRORISM

This section raises questions about the legal approaches of the United Nations and United States to the problems posed by international terrorism. The Security Council has made some broad "legislative" decisions, in response to instances of terrorism. What should be appropriate limits on the Council's activity? What changes, if any, could make the Security Council and the United Nations more respected and more effective? After exploring the response of the United Nations, we turn to legal issues respecting the response of the United States to the challenges of terrorism.

PAUL C. SZASZ, "THE SECURITY COUNCIL STARTS LEGISLATING"

96 *American Journal of International Law* 901 (2002)

With its recent resolution to counter the threat of terrorism [S.C. Res. 1373, Sept. 28, 2001, 40 *International Legal Materials* 1278 (2001)], the United Nations Security Council broke new ground by using, for the first time, its Chapter VII powers under the Charter to order all states to take or to refrain from specified actions in a context not limited to disciplining a particular country.

[U]nder Charter Articles 25 and 48(1), the Security Council can adopt decisions that are binding on UN members. Although nonmembers are not directly bound by the Charter, its Article 2(6) requires the Organization to "ensure that" such states act in accordance with the principles set out in Article 2 "so far as may be necessary for the maintenance of international peace and security"—and for decades the Security Council has routinely made a practice of addressing resolutions to "all States." These decisions, of course, must be taken in exercise of the Council's "primary responsibility for the maintenance of international peace and security" under Article 24(1), and their potentially binding nature is clearest when taken under Charter Chapter VII upon a determination by the Council that there exists "a threat to the peace, breach of the peace, or act of aggression."

These constraints, as well as the Security Council's practice in exercising its powers for over five decades, have created the impression that those powers are to be exercised almost exclusively with respect to particular conflicts or situations. In this regard the Council has frequently, especially since the end of the Cold War, imposed economic sanctions or other restrictions requiring compliance by all states—expressed by stating that the "Council decides that all States shall. . . ." By their nature these restrictions are imposed for a limited purpose—to secure compliance by a target state—and explicitly or implicitly are limited in time until that purpose is accomplished. These decisions of the Council cannot, therefore, be considered as establishing new rules of international law.

In recent years, however, the Security Council has increasingly adopted decisions that deal not with any particular conflict or situation but, rather, with conflicts in general. Thus, it has addressed the protection of children and civilians, the role of women with respect to peace and security, humanitarian questions, and even international terrorism. Nevertheless, the operative paragraphs of these resolutions that are addressed to states are not formulated in compulsory terms but, for the most part, merely "call upon" states or parties to a conflict, or even more weakly just "urge" them—terminology that is understood as not implying compulsion. Other provisions "condemn" certain practices but, again, without requiring states to refrain from them. Consequently, these decisions of the Council also cannot be considered as establishing new rules of international law.

On September 28, 2001, the Security Council, reacting to the events of September 11, departed from its previous limited and cautious practice. Acting on a draft proposed by the United States and explicitly referring to Chapter VII of the Charter, the Council adopted Resolution 1373 (2001), by which it decided in two operative paragraphs "that all States shall" take certain actions against the financing of terrorist activities, as well as a miscellany of other actions designed to prevent any support for terrorists and terrorist activities. A further operative paragraph "calls upon all States" to take certain additional actions. Furthermore, the resolution established a plenary committee of the Council (since referred to as the "Counter-Terrorism Committee") to monitor implementation of the resolution and called on all states to report on their compliance with it, initially within ninety days and thereafter according to a timetable to be proposed by the committee. [A]s Resolution 1373, while inspired by the attacks of September 11, 2001, is not specifically related to these (though they are mentioned in the preamble) and lacks any explicit or implicit time limitation, a significant portion of the resolution can be said to establish new binding rules of international law—rather than mere commands relating to a particular situation—and, moreover, even creates a mechanism for monitoring compliance with them.

[T]he substantive rules that the Security Council thus imposed on all states were not suddenly invented by the Council but were based, albeit somewhat loosely, on prior resolutions of the General Assembly adopted unanimously or by overwhelming majorities largely during the past decade.

Of particular interest are the provisions of operative paragraph 1 of Resolution 1373, designed to cut off financing for terrorists. These are clearly based on the International Convention for the Suppression of the Financing of Terrorism, adopted by the General Assembly without a vote on December 9, 1999. At the time the Council acted on September 28, 2001, only four states had ratified the Convention (Botswana, Sri Lanka, the United Kingdom, and Uzbekistan) and forty-six others had signed it[.] By making only a few substantive provisions of the 1999 Convention obligatory, the Security Council refrained from imposing on states various other substantive requirements of that treaty, in particular its many detailed administrative provisions, most of which relate to the prosecution or extradition of offenders. In principle, however, it would seem that it could have done so, either by making participation in the Convention obligatory rather than optional, or by providing that all the provisions of the Convention (except the final clauses) are binding on all states. * * *

During the past decade, the Security Council, suddenly freed from its Cold War deadlock, has greatly expanded the repertory of devices available to it under Charter Chapter VII. It has determined proprio motu the boundary between two states, and has established a highly intrusive arms control regime for a state, a claims commission, and two international criminal tribunals—all actions not explicitly provided for in the Charter. The addition of a legislative capacity would appear to be another such enhancement, the bounds of which it may be worth exploring, at least tentatively.

The basic legal limitation on the legislative capacity of the Security Council is evidently that its exercise must relate to the maintenance of international peace and security: thus, its scope clearly includes subjects such as international terrorism and other violations of the obligation to maintain friendly relations among states, as set out in the General Assembly's declaration on the subject, as well as all questions relating to armaments, disarmament, and arms control. * * * The Council might even consider extreme violations of human rights or humanitarian law, or massive assaults on the international environment, to constitute unacceptable threats to the peace, and legislate accordingly. [E]ventually the question might arise as to whether the Council's appreciation of what constitutes a threat to the peace, and thus justifies the exercise of its special lawmaking powers, is entirely unchallengeable. In this connection, two of the other principal UN organs come to mind: the General Assembly, whose role is discussed in the following paragraph; and the International Court of Justice, which so far has avoided invitations to challenge the Council but has indicated that the latter's decisions may be subject to judicial review.

Probably more formidable than the need to comply with the legal requirements of the Charter are the political obstacles that inhibit any excessive legislative activity by the Security Council. In the first place, of course, is the requirement of securing nine votes in the Council, and of not attracting a veto from any of the permanent members. The latter will naturally in the first instance protect their own perceived interests, whether of a political or a legal nature (e.g., resisting international legislation that might conflict with constitutional requirements). They are also likely to protect the interests of close allies (e.g., a permanent member might resist the imposition of the Nuclear Non-Proliferation Treaty to allow an ally to acquire or retain nuclear arms). When legislating, the Council would also be well advised to do so only to the extent that it reflects the general will of the world community, as expressed by the General Assembly, though this procedure is not required for the adoption of Council resolutions. * * * In principle, the Security Council could adopt formally binding rules even without the approval of most of the world's states, but such "laws" would probably remain empty letters if widely disapproved and therefore disregarded, since the Council would obviously have no way of enforcing unpopular decrees; on the other hand, if the Council's legislation were to meet with general approval, pressure could be brought to bear on any few recalcitrant states.

NOTES AND QUESTIONS

1. *Defining Terrorism.* Agreement on an international law definition of terrorism has proven elusive. The 2004 report of the U.N. Secretary-General's High-Level Panel on Threats, Challenges and Change, however, highlighted features of terrorism that may help future efforts to arrive at a generally applicable definition. The Panel regarded terrorism as:

> any action, in addition to actions already specified by the existing conventions on aspects of terrorism, the Geneva Conventions and Security Council resolution 1566 (2004), that is intended to cause death or serious bodily harm to civilians or non-combatants, when the purpose of such an act, by its nature or context, is to intimidate a population or to compel a government or an international organization to do or to abstain from doing any act.

A More Secure World: Our Shared Responsibility ¶ 164(d), U.N. Doc. A/59/565 (2004). Resolution 1566 provided in part:

> that criminal acts, including against civilians, committed with the intent to cause death or serious bodily injury, or taking of hostages, with the purpose to provoke a state of terror in the general public or in a group of persons or particular persons, intimidate a population or compel a government or an international organization to do or to abstain from doing any act, which constitute offences within the scope of and as defined in the international conventions and protocols relating to terrorism, are under no circumstances justifiable by considerations of a political, philosophical, ideological, racial, ethnic, religious or other similar nature.

In 2011, the Special Tribunal for Lebanon, a hybrid criminal court established by the U.N. Security Council in 2007 (see Chapter 6, Part E), though acknowledging that "many scholars and other legal experts" believe "that no widely accepted definition of terrorism has evolved in the world society," nevertheless unanimously concluded:

> 85. [A] number of treaties, UN resolutions, and the legislative and judicial practice of States evince the formation of a general *opinio juris* in the international community, accompanied by a practice consistent with such *opinio,* to the effect that a customary rule of international law regarding the international crime of terrorism, at least *in time of peace,* has indeed emerged. This customary rule requires the following three key elements: (i) the perpetration of a criminal act (such as murder, kidnapping, hostage-taking, arson, and so on), or threatening such an act; (ii) the intent to spread fear among the population (which would generally entail the creation of public danger) or directly or indirectly coerce a

> national or international authority to take some action, or to refrain from taking it; (iii) when the act involves a transnational element.

Ayyash *et al.*, Interlocutory Decision on the Applicable Law: Terrorism, Conspiracy, Homicide, Perpetration, Cumulative Charging, Case No. STL-11-01/I (Feb. 16, 2011).

How successful have been these attempts to define terrorism? See "Council Comment: Defining Terrorism," *ASIL Newsletter*, Jan.–Feb. 2005, at 6. Is it important to arrive at a general international law definition of terrorism? The 2005 World Summit Outcome, adopted by over 150 heads of state and government and then by the U.N. General Assembly, did not call for a definition of terrorism. See G.A. Res. 60/1 (2005); Frederic L. Kirgis, "International Law Aspects of the 2005 World Summit Outcome Document," 9 *ASIL Insights*, Oct. 2005.

2. *Resolution 1373 and U.N. Counterterrorism Efforts.* Each of the U.N.'s then 191 Member States submitted the initial reports called for in Security Council Resolution 1373, discussed in the Szasz excerpt—an astounding record of compliance. What challenges arise in attempting to achieve continuing compliance with the requirements of Resolution 1373? See Eric Rosand, "Security Council Resolution 1373, the Counter-Terrorism Committee, and the Fight Against Terrorism," 97 *American Journal of International Law* 333 (2003).

A Security Council sanctions regime, established in 1999 to respond to the Taliban in Afghanistan, S.C. Res. 1267 (1999), 39 *International Legal Materials* 235 (2000), was expanded to encompass Al Qaeda and Osama bin Laden. Under this regime, a "1267 Committee," composed of representatives from states on the Security Council, lists individuals and entities believed to support terrorism. U.N. member states are required to implement specified sanctions against those on the list, such as freezing their assets and imposing travel bans. Is listing just an administrative procedure? Should those on the list have due process protections? In the mid-2000s the Security Council added some protections for individuals. See S.C. Res. 1452 (2003) (allowing states to exclude from frozen assets funds used for food, housing, medical treatment, and other "extraordinary expenses"); S.C. Res. 1617 (2005) (requiring states proposing listings to file explanatory "statements of case"); S.C. Res. 1730 (2006) (establishing a procedure allowing designated parties to submit delisting petitions).

Individuals and organizations subject to the Council's "targeted sanctions" filed judicial challenges. For example, in Joined Cases C–402/05 P and C–415/05 P, Kadi & Al Barakaat International Foundation v. Council of the European Union & European Commission, 2008 E.C.R. I–06351 (European Court of Justice, Grand Chamber, 2008), 47 *International Legal Materials* 927 (2008), the appellants disputed their listing under a European Community (EC) regulation that implemented the 1267 Committee's measures. Kadi and Al Barakaat alleged violations of fundamental individual rights under EC law, including the right to property, the right to be heard by a court, and the right of effective judicial review. The *Kadi* court noted that, as of early 2007, the 1267 Committee's procedures were "still in essence diplomatic and intergovernmental," with the "[C]ommittee taking its decisions by consensus, each of its members having a right of veto." Furthermore, listees could not be represented before the Committee, but had to rely on their governments to make observations. The Committee also need not "communicate to the applicant the reasons and evidence justifying his appearance in the summary list," or "give him access, even restricted, to that information," or provide reasons when rejecting a delisting request. *Id.* at 961.

Despite these concerns, should the European Court of Justice have deferred to the targeted sanctions of the 1267 Committee, because all states are legally required to comply with Security Council decisions? See Articles 25, 48, and especially 103 of the U.N. Charter, reproduced in the Appendix. The court found that it could not review the lawfulness of Security Council resolutions adopted under Chapter VII of the U.N. Charter, even if its review were "limited to examination of the compatibility of that resolution with jus cogens." *Id.* at 958. However, the ECJ's own jurisdiction, based on its governing treaty, provided "no immunity" for the contested Community regulation on the grounds that it implemented Security Council resolutions. *Id.* at 959. In sum:

> 316. [T]he review by the Court of the validity of any Community measure in the light of fundamental rights must be considered to be the expression, in a community based on the rule of law, of a constitutional guarantee stemming from the EC Treaty as an autonomous legal system which is not to be prejudiced by an international agreement. * * *
>
> 327. The Court of First Instance erred in law, therefore, when it held * * * that the contested regulation, since it is designed to give effect to a resolution adopted by the Security Council under Chapter VII of the Charter of the United Nations affording no latitude in that respect, must enjoy immunity from jurisdiction so far as concerns its internal lawfulness save with regard to its compatibility with the norms of jus cogens.

Id. at 961–62. The *Kadi* court then found a violation of appellants' fundamental rights under EC law. See Miša Zgonec-Rozej, "*Kadi & Al Barakaat v. Council of the EU & EC Commission*: European Court of Justice Quashes a Council of the EU Regulation Implementing UN Security Council Resolutions," 12 *ASIL Insights*, Issue 22 (2008). Is *Kadi* an example of dualism? Did the ECJ's decision undermine respect for the U.N. Charter? Compare the *Medellín Case* in Chapter 4. See Gráinne de Búrca, "The European Court of Justice and the International Legal Order After *Kadi*," 51 *Harvard Journal of International Law* 1 (2010). The U.N. Security Council, for its part, has further modified the 1267 Committee's procedures. For more on U.N. counterterrorism efforts and the work of the 1267 Committee, see John F. Murphy, *The Evolving Dimensions of International Law* 216–26

(2010); *UN Counter-Terrorism Online Handbook, available at* http://www.un.org/terrorism/cthandbook/; http://www.un.org/sc/committees/1267/index.shtml (last visited Dec. 11, 2013). For further developments in Kadi's litigation, see Clemens A. Feinägle, "International Decision: *Commission v. Kadi*," 107 *American Journal of International Law* 878 (2013).

3. *Limits on the Security Council's Legislative Authority.* Is there a risk that the Security Council may, at least with respect to economic sanctions and other measures not endorsing or authorizing the use of force, become too active as a legislative body? Another broad "legislative" Council resolution is Resolution 1540 (2004), 43 *International Legal Materials* 1237 (2004), requiring states to take steps to prevent the proliferation of weapons of mass destruction. What formal and informal constraints limit the Security Council's ability to act as a legislature? See Stefan Talmon, "The Security Council as World Legislature," 99 *American Journal of International Law* 175 (2005).

4. *ICJ Review of Security Council Decisions?* Does the International Court of Justice have the authority to judicially review the legality of Security Council decisions? In what circumstances could there be a problem with the legality of a Security Council decision? What form would judicial review take? For example, if the ICJ determined that a Security Council decision presented some legal difficulty, should the Court necessarily declare the decision invalid?

Some judges in the Case Concerning Questions of Interpretation and Application of the 1971 Montreal Convention Arising From the Aerial Incident at Lockerbie (Libya v. United States), 1992 I.C.J. 114 (Request for Provisional Measures), and in a companion case against the United Kingdom (1992 I.C.J. 231), raised the possibility of judicial review. The *Lockerbie Case* involved Libya's challenge to a Security Council decision requiring that Libya hand over to the United States or Britain two Libyan nationals suspected of bombing a Pan Am flight that crashed near Lockerbie, Scotland, in 1988. The Council imposed economic sanctions on Libya until the suspects were handed over. Libya claimed it had satisfied the 1971 Montreal Convention for the Suppression of Unlawful Acts Against the Safety of Civil Aviation, to which it, the United States, and the United Kingdom were parties. The Convention required Libya to submit the case to its own authorities "for the purpose of prosecution" if it chose not to extradite suspects. The United States and the United Kingdom argued that a Security Council decision trumped the Montreal Convention under Article 103 of the U.N. Charter. The ICJ refused to grant Libya the provisional measures it had requested (see Article 41 of the Court's Statute, in the Appendix), but Judge Shahabuddeen in his Separate Opinion wondered whether there was "any conceivable point beyond which a legal issue may properly arise as to the competence of the Security Council to produce" overriding results; and if there were any limits, "what are those limits and what body, if other than the Security Council, is competent to say what those limits are." 1992 I.C.J. at 142. Judge Lachs commented that the ICJ was "the guardian of legality for the international community as a whole," and that the intention of the U.N. Charter's framers was to encourage "a fruitful interaction" between the "different U.N. organs." *Id.* at 138. For discussion, see Jose E. Alvarez, "Judging the Security Council," 90 *American Journal of International Law* 1 (1996); Bernd Martenczuk, "The Security Council, the International Court and Judicial Review: What Lessons from Lockerbie?," 10 *European Journal of International Law* 517 (1999).

Following the *Lockerbie Case*, Libya agreed to a trial of two Libyan suspects in the Netherlands under Scottish law. One of the suspects was convicted and sent to prison in Scotland, and the case was removed from the ICJ's list of cases in 2003. For more background, see Khalil I. Matar & Robert W. Thabit, *Lockerbie and Libya: A Study in International Relations* (2003); Michael P. Scharf, "The Lockerbie Model of Transfer of Proceedings," in 2 *International Criminal Law* 521 (M. Cherif Bassiouni ed., 3d ed. 2008). In 2008 Libya completed paying $1.5 billion to resolve claims related to Lockerbie and other terrorist attacks in which Libya had been implicated. John R. Crook, "Contemporary Practice of the United States Relating to International Law," 103 *American Journal of International Law* 132, 165–66 (2009). A 2009 British decision to release the convicted Lockerbie bomber on medical grounds, after he had served eight years of his life sentence in Scottish prison, provoked considerable controversy. See John F. Burns, "Senate Hearing on Lockerbie Sets Off More Finger-Pointing," *New York Times*, July 26, 2010, at A4.

MARY ELLEN O'CONNELL, "LAWFUL SELF-DEFENSE TO TERRORISM"

63 *University of Pittsburgh Law Review* 889 (2002)

On October 7, 2001, the United States and the United Kingdom launched operation Enduring Freedom. Enduring Freedom was a massive aerial and land operation on the territory of Afghanistan in response to the September 11 terror attacks on the United States. The two governments justified Enduring Freedom as an exercise of lawful self-defense. * * * At the outset, Enduring Freedom did indeed meet the conditions of lawful self-defense, but later stages of the operation may have gone beyond the bounds of proportionality.

The right to take military action on the territory of another state is at the core of a self-defense and why it is of concern to international society. Governments have decided they cannot eliminate the right to use force in self-defense in all cases. Nevertheless, they have, through international law, limited force in self-defense to the most exigent circumstances. Unless a state has received United Nations Security Council authorization, it must meet four conditions to engage in lawful self-defense: First, the defending state must be the victim of a significant armed attack. Second, the armed attack must be either underway or the victim of an attack must have at least clear and convincing evidence that more attacks are planned. Third, the defending state's target must be responsible for the significant armed attack in progress or planned. Fourth, the force used by the defending state must be necessary for the purpose of defense and it must be proportional to the injury threatened.

I. THE VICTIM OF SIGNIFICANT ARMED ATTACK

Articles 2(4) and 51 of the United Nations Charter prohibit the unauthorized use of force except in self-defense against an armed attack, and, even then, only until the Security Council acts. * * *

With regard to September 11, Security Council resolutions adopted in the wake of the attacks refer to the right of self-defense. In particular, Resolution 1373 (September 28) reveals the Council's consensus as to self-defense and terrorism shortly before Enduring Freedom was launched[.] [Resolution 1373 in part "[r]eaffirm[ed] the inherent right of individual or collective self-defence as recognized by the Charter of the United Nations as reiterated in resolution 1368" of September 12, 2001. Resolution 1373] does not authorize the use of armed force, nor does it explicitly authorize the United States to use armed force in self-defense to the September 11 attacks. Nevertheless, the Resolution does support the conclusion that the September 11 attacks were significant enough to trigger the right of self-defense, if the other conditions of legality are met. In several subsequent resolutions relating to terrorism and the situation in Afghanistan, neither the Security Council nor the General Assembly condemned Enduring Freedom as a violation of the Charter. Moreover, it is quite clear that the Resolutions did not intend to displace self-defense by the United States with measures by the Security Council. Therefore, we can conclude that the first condition for lawful self-defense was met. The United States was the victim of a significant armed attack.

II. TO DETER THE NEXT ATTACK

Armed force in self-defense must have defense as its object. Force in self-defense must aim at stopping an attack in progress, defending against a future attack once an attack has occurred, or ending an unlawful occupation. Lawful self-defense cannot be a mere act of punishment or revenge. Armed force to "send a message" or to generally deter is unlawful. Armed counter-attack must have the aim of more specific defense. Where a significant armed attack has already occurred but is not on-going, the defending state must show at least by clear and convincing evidence that future attacks are planned. In the case where no actual attack has yet struck its intended target, the defending state may act only where it has clear and convincing evidence of an incipient attack—one that is underway, requiring an instant response. * * *

In addition to the views of scholars, judicial decisions, and the U.S. position, as a matter of policy, the standard for self-defense should be at least clear and convincing. * * *

In the case of Enduring Freedom, both the United States and United Kingdom have argued that the September 11 attacks were part of a series of attacks that began in 1993 on the United States. Both have argued that future attacks in the same series were planned. The series began with the first attack on the World Trade Center. It included the embassy bombings in Tanzania and Kenya, and very likely included the attack on the USS Cole. Almost immediately following the September 11 attacks, the United States and several European states apprehended individuals who indicated more attacks were planned. The evidence was presented to NATO members and was called "compelling." Thus, based on publicly available material, the United States and United Kingdom appeared to have clear and convincing evidence that the U.S. faced on-going attacks. Subsequent to the launch of Enduring Freedom, the United States found documentary evidence in Afghanistan confirming that more attacks in the series were indeed being planned.

III. BY THE RESPONSIBLE STATE

Establishing the need for taking defensive action can only justify fighting on the territory of another state if that state is responsible for the on-going attacks. It may well be that in a world of non-state actors, a group launching significant, on-going armed attacks has no link to a state and so no state can be the target of defensive counter-attack. In those cases, measures other than self-defense on the territory of a state must be taken by the victim. * * *

In the case of Enduring Freedom, the Taliban, Afghanistan's *de facto* government, developed such close links to the known terrorist organization al Qaeda that it became responsible for the acts of al Qaeda. With that responsibility came the right of the United States and United Kingdom to take the fight to Afghanistan. U.K. lawyers understood the facts they needed to show: the U.K.'s paper of 4 October carefully detailed links between al Qaeda and the Taliban.

The British paper states most significantly, that:

> 11. In 1996 Osama Bin Laden moved back to Afghanistan. He established a close relationship with Mullah Omar, and threw his support behind the Taliban. Osama Bin Laden and the Taliban regime have a close alliance on which both depend for their continued existence. They also share the same religious values and vision.
>
> 12. Osama bin Laden has provided the Taliban regime with troops, arms and money to fight the Northern Alliance. He is closely involved with Taliban military training, planning and operations. He has representatives in the Taliban military command structure. He has also given infrastructure assistance and humanitarian aid. Forces under the control of Osama bin

Laden have fought alongside the Taliban in the civil war in Afghanistan.

13. Omar has provided bin Laden with a safe haven in which to operate, and has allowed him to establish terrorist training camps in Afghanistan. They jointly exploit the Afghan drugs trade. In return for active al-Qaida support, the Taliban allow al-Qaida to operate freely, including planning, training and preparing for terrorist activity. In addition the Taliban provide security for the stockpiles of drugs.

An independent expert concluded that the "[t]he Taliban Army . . . includes al Qaeda[.]" International society appears to accept the Taliban's responsibility. Little criticism has been heard against the United States or United Kingdom for holding the Taliban responsible for the acts of al Qaeda. * * *

IV. USING ONLY NECESSARY AND PROPORTIONAL FORCE

Once the requisite armed attack occurs and is linked to a responsible state, the right of self-defense includes taking the defense to the territory of that state, if necessary to the defense and proportional to the injury threatened. Armed force used in self-defense must be necessary for the objective of defense, and it must be proportional to the injury threatened. * * * Necessity refers to military necessity, and the obligation that force be used only if necessary to accomplish a reasonable military objective. * * * The military objective of self-defense is to repel on-going and future attacks. Proportionality, which is closely related to necessity, prohibits force "which may be expected to cause incidental loss of civilian life, injury to civilians, damage to civilian objects, or a combination thereof, which would be excessive in relation to concrete and direct military advantage anticipated." * * *

Enduring Freedom began consistently with the principles of necessity and proportionality. [U.S. Secretary of State Colin] Powell indicated that the U.S. would not aim to eliminate the Taliban entirely. Events seemed to have overtaken the United States, however, when suddenly the Northern Alliance continued to Kabul and completely routed the Taliban from power. Judging from Powell's indications, the U.S. apparently did not intend this, and thus it may not be responsible for a disproportionate use of force. Nevertheless, several governments, including Afghanistan's new interim government, criticized the United States for continuing to bomb after the Taliban fell in December 2001. Continuing to use that amount and type of force may have exceeded both necessity and proportionality. The shift to more ground troops starting in January to respond to al Qaeda fighters in the Afghan hills was arguably closer to the necessity and proportionality standards, though bombing continued, with tragic consequences.

NOTES AND QUESTIONS

1. *State Responsibility*. Was Afghanistan, which in 2001 was governed by the Taliban, responsible at international law for the attacks of September 11th? What standard should be used to determine whether conduct is attributable to a state? In the *Nicaragua Case* the United States was found not to be responsible for violations of international humanitarian law allegedly committed by the *contras* in Nicaragua. According to the International Court of Justice, "[f]or this conduct to give rise to legal responsibility of the United States, it would in principle have to be proved that that State had effective control of the military or paramilitary operations in the course of which the alleged violations were committed." 1986 I.C.J. at 65. The ICJ similarly considered the responsibility of Iran for the acts of student militants in the *Diplomatic and Consular Staff Case* (Chapter 5). The International Criminal Tribunal for the former Yugoslavia in *Tadić* (see Part A), set out a different test of control: "The control required by international law may be deemed to exist when a State * * * *has a role in organising, coordinating or planning the military actions* of the military group, in addition to financing, training and equipping or providing operational support to that group." 38 *International Legal Materials* 1518, 1545 (1999) (emphasis in original). Did the Taliban meet either test? With respect to the use of force in self-defense, which test, if either, should be used to determine the Taliban's responsibility for the conduct of Al Qaeda? See Derek Jinks, "State Responsibility for Sponsorship of Terrorist and Insurgent Groups: State Responsibility for the Acts of Private Armed Groups," 4 *Chicago Journal of International Law* 83 (2003).

2. *Self-Defense in Response to Terrorist Attacks*. Must one take an expansive view of self-defense to legally justify the use of force against terrorist threats abroad? May a non-state actor commit an "armed attack" within the meaning of Article 51 of the U.N. Charter, giving rise to a right to use force in self-defense? See Sean D. Murphy, "Terror and the Concept of 'Armed Attack' in Article 51 of the U.N. Charter," 43 *Harvard International Law Journal* 41 (2002). May a series of small terrorist incidents be aggregated to satisfy the threshold requirement of an "armed attack" that would justify using force in self-defense? See Christopher Greenwood, "International Law and the United States' Air Operation Against Libya", 89 *West Virginia Law Review* 933, 954–56 (1987). Suppose the government of Afghanistan opposed the activities of Al Qaeda, but could not suppress those activities. Do the fact situation and legal test used in the *Caroline* dispute (see Part B) suggest that a U.S. attack against Al Qaeda in Afghanistan would be a legal use of force in self-defense? For an intriguing account of the continuing importance of guerilla warfare, see Max Boot, "The Evolution of Irregular War: Insurgents and Guerillas from Akkadia to Afghanistan," 92 *Foreign Affairs*, Mar./Apr. 2013, at 100.

3. *Targeted Killings*. Could U.S. authorization of "secret military missions against suspected Al Qaeda targets in as many as twenty countries," including attacks by unmanned drone aircraft, be legally justified

under "an expansive interpretation of the right of self-defense"? John R. Crook, "Contemporary Practice of the United States Relating to International Law," 103 *American Journal of International Law* 132, 161 (2009). Does the legality of such missions, or continued U.S. military activity against Al Qaeda in Afghanistan and elsewhere, necessarily depend on the consent of the government in whose territory the United States is operating? If a drone attack were a legal use of force in self-defense, would violations of international humanitarian law or human rights law, caused by the attack, be excused? See *Report of the Special Rapporteur on Extrajudicial, Summary or Arbitrary Executions, Philip Alston: Study on Targeted Killings*, U.N. Doc. A/HRC/14/24/Add.6 (2010); Thomas Michael McDonnell, "Sow What You Reap: Using Predator and Reaper Drones to Carry Out Assassinations of Suspected Islami Terrorists," 44 *George Washington International Law Journal* 243 (2012). What steps other than the unilateral use of force could one state legally take against terrorists situated in another state?

THE 2002 NATIONAL SECURITY STRATEGY OF THE UNITED STATES OF AMERICA

Sept. 17, 2002, *available at* http://georgewbush-whitehouse.archives.gov/nsc/nss/2002 (last visited Dec. 11, 2013)

The United States of America is fighting a war against terrorists of global reach. The enemy is not a single political regime or person or religion or ideology. The enemy is terrorism—premeditated, politically motivated violence perpetrated against innocents. * * *

Our priority will be first to disrupt and destroy terrorist organizations of global reach and attack their leadership; command, control, and communications; material support; and finances. This will have a disabling effect upon the terrorists' ability to plan and operate.

* * * We will disrupt and destroy terrorist organizations by:

—direct and continuous action using all the elements of national and international power[;]

—defending the United States, the American people, and our interests at home and abroad by identifying and destroying the threat before it reaches our borders. While the United States will constantly strive to enlist the support of the international community, we will not hesitate to act alone, if necessary, to exercise our right of self defense by acting preemptively against such terrorists, to prevent them from doing harm against our people and our country; and

—denying further sponsorship, support, and sanctuary to terrorists by convincing or compelling states to accept their sovereign responsibilities.

We will also wage a war of ideas to win the battle against international terrorism. This includes:

—using the full influence of the United States, and working closely with allies and friends, to make clear that all acts of terrorism are illegitimate so that terrorism will be viewed in the same light as slavery, piracy, or genocide: behavior that no respectable government can condone or support and all must oppose[.]

In the Cold War, especially following the Cuban missile crisis, we faced a generally status quo, risk-averse adversary. Deterrence was an effective defense. But deterrence based only upon the threat of retaliation is less likely to work against leaders of rogue states more willing to take risks, gambling with the lives of their people, and the wealth of their nations. * * *

—Traditional concepts of deterrence will not work against a terrorist enemy whose avowed tactics are wanton destruction and the targeting of innocents; whose so-called soldiers seek martyrdom in death and whose most potent protection is statelessness. The overlap between states that sponsor terror and those that pursue [weapons of mass destruction] compels us to action.

For centuries, international law recognized that nations need not suffer an attack before they can lawfully take action to defend themselves against forces that present an imminent danger of attack. Legal scholars and international jurists often conditioned the legitimacy of preemption on the existence of an imminent threat—most often a visible mobilization of armies, navies, and air forces preparing to attack.

We must adapt the concept of imminent threat to the capabilities and objectives of today's adversaries. Rogue states and terrorists do not seek to attack us using conventional means. They know such attacks would fail. Instead, they rely on acts of terror and, potentially, the use of weapons of mass destruction—weapons that can be easily concealed, delivered covertly, and used without warning. * * *

The United States has long maintained the option of preemptive actions to counter a sufficient threat to our national security. The greater the threat, the greater is the risk of inaction—and the more compelling the case for taking anticipatory action to defend ourselves, even if uncertainty remains as to the time and place of the enemy's attack. To forestall or prevent such hostile acts by our adversaries, the United States will, if necessary, act preemptively.

A MORE SECURE WORLD: OUR SHARED RESPONSIBILITY

Report of the High-Level Panel on Threats, Challenges and Change, U.N. Doc. A/59/565 (2004)

188. The language of [Article 51] is restrictive: "Nothing in the present Charter shall impair the inherent right of individual or collective self-defense if an armed attack occurs against a member of the United Nations, until the Security Council has taken measures to maintain international peace and security." However, a threatened State, according to long established international law, can take military action as long as the threatened attack is *imminent*, no other means would deflect it and the action is proportionate. The problem arises where the threat in question is not imminent but still claimed to be real: for example the acquisition, with allegedly hostile intent, of nuclear weapons-making capability.

189. Can a State, without going to the Security Council, claim in these circumstances the right to act, in anticipatory self-defence, not just pre-emptively (against an imminent or proximate threat) but preventively (against a non-imminent or non-proximate one)? Those who say "yes" argue that the potential harm from some threats (e.g., terrorists armed with a nuclear weapon) is so great that one simply cannot risk waiting until they become imminent, and that less harm may be done (e.g., avoiding a nuclear exchange or radioactive fallout from a reactor destruction) by acting earlier.

190. The short answer is that if there are good arguments for preventive military action, with good evidence to support them, they should be put to the Security Council, which can authorize such action if it chooses to. If it does not so choose, there will be, by definition, time to pursue other strategies, including persuasion, negotiation, deterrence and containment—and to visit again the military option.

191. For those impatient with such a response, the answer must be that, in a world full of perceived potential threats, the risk to the global order and the norm of non-intervention on which it continues to be based is simply too great for the legality of unilateral preventive action, as distinct from collectively endorsed action, to be accepted. Allowing one to so act is to allow all.

192. We do not favour the rewriting or reinterpretation of Article 51.

NOTES AND QUESTIONS

1. *Preemptive Self-Defense.* Does the "Bush doctrine" of preemptive (or preventive) self-defense represent a claim that customary international law governing the use of force in self-defense be changed? See Chapter 3. Should all states have the right to engage in preemptive self-defense? May Russia

invoke a "right" of preemptive self-defense to launch attacks anywhere in the world against those supporting rebels in Chechnya? Would the United States have been better advised not to have articulated the policy of preemptive self-defense but to have reaffirmed U.N. Charter-based rules governing the use of force in self-defense? See Jane G. Dalton, "The United States National Security Strategy: Yesterday, Today, and Tomorrow," 52 *Naval Law Review* 60 (2005).

President Obama's first National Security Strategy, issued in May 2010, avoided explicit reference to "preemptive actions." It provides that: "The United States must reserve the right to act unilaterally if necessary to defend our nation and our interests, yet we will also seek to adhere to standards that govern the use of force. Doing so strengthens those who act in line with international standards, while isolating and weakening those who do not." *National Security Strategy* 22 (2010), *available at* http://www.whitehouse.gov (last visited Dec. 11, 2013).

2. *Modifying Legal Proscriptions Against the Use of Force.* Are the legal standards relating to the use of force and self-defense either inappropriate or unacceptably vague? How might they be changed or clarified? For a restatement of the law of self-defense in light of modern threats, based on a survey of British international law academics, practitioners, and international relations scholars, see "The Chatham House Principles of International Law on the Use of Force in Self-Defence," 55 *International and Comparative Law Quarterly* 963 (2006). Would it be preferable to evaluate a state's recourse to force not in terms of its legality, but instead its "legitimacy"? If so, what factors should determine whether a use of force is legitimate? See Abraham D. Sofaer, "The Best Defense?," *Foreign Affairs*, Jan.–Feb. 2010, at 109. Should states choose to act unilaterally, providing "state practice" useful for the formation of customary international law? What are the prospects for bilateral agreements restricting intervention or the use of force? For regional understandings? For steps by the United Nations?

4. HUMANITARIAN INTERVENTION

An important test for the collective security system of the United Nations has been when to use force to promote humanitarian causes, notably during the so-called "Arab Spring" of 2010. Following is an introduction to some of the key legal questions arising out of recent developments in Libya and Syria.

SIMON CHESTERMAN, " 'LEADING FROM BEHIND': THE RESPONSIBILITY TO PROTECT, THE OBAMA DOCTRINE, AND HUMANITARIAN INTERVENTION AFTER LIBYA"

25 *Ethics & International Affairs* 279 (2011)

Humanitarian intervention has always been more popular in theory than in practice. In the face of unspeakable acts, the desire to do something, *anything,* is understandable. States have tended to be reluctant to act on such desires, however, leading to the present situation in which there are scores of books and countless articles articulating the contours of a right—or even an obligation—of humanitarian intervention, while the number of cases that might be cited as models of what is being advocated can be counted on one hand.

So is Libya such a case? It depends on why one thinks that precedent is important. From an international legal perspective, debates have tended to focus on whether one or more states have the *right* to intervene in another for human protection purposes. From the standpoint of international relations and domestic politics, the question is whether states have the *will* to intervene. From a military angle, a key dilemma is whether states have the *ability* to intervene effectively. This essay considers these three issues in turn. The legal significance of Libya is minimal, though the international response does show how the politics of humanitarian intervention has shifted to the point where it is harder to do nothing in the face of atrocities. At the same time, however, military action to the end of May 2011 suggested a continuing disjunction between ends and means.

For an international lawyer, the intervention in Libya is interesting but not exactly groundbreaking. Security Council Resolution 1973 (2011) was consistent with resolutions passed in the heady days of the immediate post-cold war era. As early as December 1992 (Somalia) and April 1993 (Srebrenica) the Council had authorized the use of "all necessary means" to establish secure conditions for humanitarian relief and create safe havens in situations of internal conflict. Though there are nuances of difference, the question of consent to an operation is not legally significant when it is authorized under Chapter VII of the UN Charter. Tellingly, there was no need to include language that the situation was "unique," "exceptional," or "unique and exceptional"—phrases used in resolutions in the early 1990s to ensure abstentions by China and others on resolutions that significantly broadened the Security Council's international peace and security mandate.

From a legal standpoint, then, Resolution 1973 was hardly groundbreaking. Yet the complications of implementing those two resolutions of the early 1990s—in Somalia and Srebrenica—suggest that the problems have never been limited only to what the law allows, but also include what politics permits and what is militarily possible.

This is not to say that the emergence of the "responsibility to protect" (RtoP) has not been normatively important. In order to get consensus in the commission that coined the term and the UN General Assembly that embraced it, however, compromises were necessary. First, the 2001 International Commission on Intervention and State Sovereignty (ICISS) sandwiched the military question between the "white bread" of prevention and post-conflict peacebuilding. Second, by the time RtoP was endorsed by the World Summit in 2005, its normative content had been emasculated to the point where it essentially provided that the Security Council could authorize, on a case-by-case basis, things that it had been authorizing for more than a decade.

There is evident hesitation on the part of the Council to embrace the RtoP doctrine fully. Resolution 1973 refers only to the "responsibility *of the Libyan authorities* to protect the Libyan population." This is consistent with earlier Council resolutions that had used variants of the phrase, but limited it to that first pillar of RtoP, national protection. Two later resolutions went further, touching on the responsibility of the international community, but confined themselves to "reaffirming" the provisions of the 2005 Outcome Document. (Interestingly, a series of resolutions on Georgia beginning in 2002 "recalled" that the Abkhaz side bore "a particular responsibility to protect" returnees. This was arguably distinct from RtoP, but was repeated in subsequent extensions of the United Nations Observer Mission in Georgia [UNOMIG]. Perhaps coincidentally, the phrase was dropped in the eight resolutions on UNOMIG adopted after the 2005 World Summit.)

Nonetheless, the significance of RtoP was never, in a strict sense, legal. Rather, it was political—and, importantly, *rhetorical.* The ICISS was funded in significant part by Canada and Britain, both of which had participated in military action in Kosovo in 1999 that appeared to violate the UN Charter. Article 2(4) of the Charter prohibits the threat or use of force against member states. There are only two exceptions: self-defense and action authorized by the Security Council. Neither applied to Kosovo; and the dubious possibility of a General Assembly resolution in support of intervention—which would have required the support of two-thirds of member states and, for all that, would not have been binding—had been rejected by Britain.

It is noteworthy that in Kosovo—and virtually every other case of so-called humanitarian intervention—states were reluctant to justify their actions in legal terms. In particular, states chose not to articulate a legal argument that might be used by other states to justify other interventions. In relation to Kosovo, for example, the German government atypically used the phrase "humanitarian intervention" but emphasized that Operation Allied Force should not be a precedent for further action. U.S. Secretary of State Madeleine Albright stressed that the air strikes were a "unique situation *sui generis* in the region of the Balkans." British Prime Minister Tony Blair retreated from his initial enthusiasm for the intervention to emphasize the exceptional nature of the air campaign. Kosovo was also unusual in that it was a case of alleged humanitarian intervention that actually made it to the International Court of Justice. In proceedings brought by Yugoslavia against ten NATO members, however, only Belgium presented a formal legal justification for the intervention. The case was ultimately dismissed on technical grounds.

Such reticence was emulated in two major commissions on the topic. Richard Goldstone's Kosovo Commission obfuscated the issue by concluding that NATO's action was, in the now famous phrase, "illegal but legitimate." The ICISS report acknowledged that, as a matter of "political reality," it would be impossible to find consensus around any set of proposals for military intervention not authorized by the Security Council, but questioned where the greater harm lay: in the damage to international order if the Council is bypassed, or in the damage if civilians are slaughtered while the Council stands idly by. The commissioners pointedly failed to answer that question. From a legal standpoint, then, neither RtoP in general nor Resolution 1973 in particular [has] changed the standing prohibition on the use of force outside self-defense and Security Council-authorized enforcement action.

[A]lthough RtoP does not create rights or impose legal obligations, it may nonetheless be understood as conferring public power and allocating jurisdiction. Seen through such a lens, the vague formulations embraced by the 2005 Summit do not invoke "responsibility" in the strict legal sense of an obligation to act in a specific way, but rather in the sense of an allocation of responsibility to respond to a situation. This may be compared to the function played by Article 99 of the UN Charter, which allows the UN secretary-general to bring to the attention of the Security Council "any matter which in his opinion may threaten the maintenance of international peace and security." It is no coincidence that much of the energy behind the adoption and, now, implementation of RtoP has come from the office of the secretary-general. Much like Article 99, the true significance of RtoP is not in creating new rights or obligations to do "the right thing"; rather, it is in making it harder to do the wrong thing or nothing at all.

Such a dynamic appears to have had some success at the international level, facilitated by the unusual clarity of the situation in Libya. State leaders are usually more circumspect in the threats they make against their populations than was Qaddafi; impending massacres are rarely so easy to foresee. Combined with the support of African states and the Arab League for intervention, this left most states on the Council unwilling to allow atrocities to occur—and others unwilling to be seen as the impediment to action.

Such clarity of intent influenced the Obama administration in particular. Within a twenty-four-hour period the United States pivoted from skepticism about intervention in Libya to forceful advocacy. That change of policy was partly driven by external events—in particular the imminent possibility of thousands being killed by Qaddafi's troops—but also by the internal advocacy of Secretary of State Hillary Rodham Clinton, Ambassador to the UN Susan Rice, and National Security Council staffer

Samantha Power. Rice in particular had used her first statement in the UN Security Council to endorse RtoP; Power, who also served as a special advisor to the president, is the author of the Pulitzer Prize-winning book *A Problem from Hell: America and the Age of Genocide.*

Nevertheless, when President Obama articulated the reasons for the United States acting in Libya—at a time of upheaval in many other countries across the Arab world—those reasons were carefully confined to the Libyan case. As he noted:

> America cannot use our military wherever repression occurs. And given the costs and risks of intervention, we must always measure our interests against the need for action. But that cannot be an argument for never acting on behalf of what's right. In this particular country—Libya—at this particular moment, we were faced with the prospect of violence on a horrific scale. We had a unique ability to stop that violence: an international mandate for action, a broad coalition prepared to join us, the support of Arab countries, and a plea for help from the Libyan people themselves. We also had the ability to stop Qaddafi's forces in their tracks without putting American troops on the ground.

Such a pragmatic assessment of individual cases can hardly be described as a "doctrine," and it was swiftly condemned by some for its passivity or naivete, the unfortunate quote from an administration official that the United States was "leading from behind" came to be a subject of ridicule—particularly when a lead role in the initial air strikes was assumed by France and the entire operation was later handed over to NATO, with operational command in the hands of a Canadian. Bluster aside, however, and after a decade of belligerent and unsuccessful leadership from the front, the cautious policy implied by such a phrase seemed more closely tied to U.S. capacities and interests at a time when its relative power is declining, and when in certain parts of the world the United States continues to be reviled.

The lingering question, of course, is the military one. Jennifer Welsh rightly points out in her contribution to this roundtable that the disjunction between stated political objectives and available military means would have Clausewitz turning in his grave. As in many previous cases, the commitment of leaders to confining their countries' involvement to air strikes alone and for a limited duration was transparently a political rather than military decision. The commencement of military action, as in many previous cases, swiftly showed that air strikes alone were unlikely to be effective. The potential tragedy of Benghazi soon devolved into farce as the Libyan rebels were revealed to be a disorganized rabble.

The sixteenth-century proverb about the road to Hell is frequently invoked by critics of humanitarian intervention. The intentions behind the decision to intervene in Libya were good—as they were in Somalia, in Srebrenica, and in other efforts to respond to mass atrocity. Yet the difficulty in following through on those intentions in Srebrenica allowed the killing of 8,000 men and boys, and severely undermined the credibility of NATO; the decision to withdraw from Somalia led to the failed, pirate-ridden state of today, and indirectly to the mass graves of Rwandans, where genocide took place less than a year later.

BARACK OBAMA, "STATEMENT BY THE PRESIDENT ON SYRIA"

The White House, Office of the Press Secretary, Aug. 31, 2013, *available at* http://www.whitehouse.gov (last visited Dec. 11, 2013)

THE PRESIDENT: Good afternoon, everybody. Ten days ago, the world watched in horror as men, women and children were massacred in Syria in the worst chemicals attack of the 21st century. Yesterday the United States presented a powerful case that the Syrian government was responsible for this attack on its own people.

Our intelligence shows the Assad regime and its forces preparing to use chemical weapons, launching rockets in the highly populated suburbs of Damascus, and acknowledging that a chemical attack took place. And all of this corroborates what the world can plainly see—hospitals overflowing with victims, terrible images of the dead. All told well over 1,000 people were murdered. Several hundred of them were children—young girls and boys gassed to death by their own government.

This attack is an assault on human dignity[;] it also presents a serious danger to our national security. It risks making a mockery of the global prohibition on the use of chemical weapons. It endangers our friends and our partners along Syria's borders, including Israel, Jordan. Turkey, Lebanon and Iraq. It could lead to escalating use of chemical weapons, or their proliferation to terrorist groups who would do our people harm.

In a world with many dangers, this menace must be confronted.

Now after careful deliberation, I have decided that the United States should take military action against Syrian regime targets. This would not be an open-ended intervention. We would not put boots on the ground. Instead, our action would be designed to be limited in duration and scope. But I am confident we can hold the Assad regime accountable for their use of chemical weapons, deter this kind of behavior, and degrade their capacity to carry it out.

Our military has positioned assets in the region. The Chairman of the Joint Chiefs has informed me that we are prepared to strike whenever we choose. Moreover, the Chairman has indicated to me that our capacity to execute this mission is not time-sensitive: it will be effective tomorrow, or neat week, or one month from now. And I'm prepared to give that order.

But having made my decision as Commander-in-Chief based on what I am convinced is our national security interests. I'm also mindful that I'm the President of the world's eldest constitutional democracy. I've long believed that our power is rooted not just in our military might but in our example as a government of the people, by the people, and for the people. And that's why I've made a second decision: I will seek authorization for the use of force from the American people's representatives in Congress.

Over the last several days, we've heard from members of Congress who want their voices to be heard. I absolutely agree. So this morning, I spoke with all four congressional leaders, and they've agreed to schedule a debate and then a vote as soon as Congress comes back into session

In the coming days, my administration stands ready to provide every member with the information they need to understand what happened in Syria and why it has such profound implications for America's national security. And all of us should be accountable as we move forward, and that can only be accomplished with a vote.

I'm confident in the case our government has made without waiting for U.N. inspectors. I'm comfortable going forward without the approval of a United Nations Security Council that, so far, has been completely paralyzed and unwilling to hold Assad accountable. As a consequence, many people have advised against taking this decision to Congress, and undoubtedly, they were impacted by what we saw happen in the United Kingdom this week when the Parliament of our closest ally failed to pass a resolution with a similar goal, even as the Prime Minister supported taking action.

Yet, while I believe I have the authority to carry cut this military action without specific congressional authorization. I know that the country will be stronger if we take this course, and our actions will be even more effective. We should have this debate, because the issues are too big for business as usual And this morning, John Boehner, Harry Reid, Nancy Pelosi and Mitch McConnell agreed that this is the right thing to do for our democracy

A country faces few decisions as grave as using military force, even when that force is limited. I respect the views of those who call for caution, particularly as our country emerges from a time of war that I was elected in part to end. But if we really do want to turn away from taking appropriate action in the face of such an unspeakable outrage, then we must acknowledge the costs of doing nothing

Here's my question for every member of Congress and every member of the global community: What message will we send if a dictator can gas hundreds of children to death in plain sight and pay no price? What's the purpose of the international system that we've built if a prohibition on the use of chemical weapons that has been agreed to by the governments of

98 percent of the world's people and approved overwhelmingly by the Congress of the United States is not unforced?

Make no mistake—this has implications beyond chemical warfare. If we won't enforce accountability in the face of this heinous act, what does it say about our resolve to stand up to others who flout fundamental international rules? To governments who would choose to build nuclear arms? To terrorist who would spread biological weapons? To armies who carry out genocide?

We cannot raise our children in a world where we will not follow through on the things we say, the accords we sign, the values that define us.

So just as I will take this case to Congress, I will also deliver this message to the world. While the U.N. investigation has some time to report on its findings, we will insist that an atrocity committed with chemical weapons is not simply investigated, it must be confronted.

I don't expect every nation to agree with the decision we have made. Privately we've heard many expressions of support from our friends. But I will ask those who care about the writ of the international community to stand publicly behind our action.

And finally, let me say this to the American people. I know well that we are weary of war. We've ended one war in Iraq. We're ending another in Afghanistan. And the American people have the good sense to know we cannot resolve the underlying conflict in Syria with our military. In that part of the world, there are ancient sectarian differences, and the hopes of the Arab Spring have unleashed forces of change that are going to take many years to resolve. And that's why we're not contemplating putting our troops in the middle of someone else's war.

Instead, we'll continue to support the Syrian people through our pressure on the Assad regime, our commitment to the opposition, our care for the displaced, and our pursuit of a political resolution that achieves a government that respects the dignity of its people.

But we are the United States of America, and we cannot and must not turn a blind eye to what happened in Damascus. Out of the ashes of world war, we built an international order and enforced the rules that gave it meaning And we did so because we believe that the rights of individuals to live in peace and dignity depends on the responsibilities of nations. We aren't perfect, but this nation more than any other has been willing to meet those responsibilities.

So to all members of Congress of both parties, I ask you to take this vote for our national security. I am looking forward to the debate. And in doing so, I ask you, members of Congress, to consider that some things are more important than partisan differences or the politics of the moment.

Ultimately, this is not about who occupies this office at any given time, it's about who we are as a country. I believe that the people's representatives must be invested in what America does abroad, and now is the time to show the world that America keeps our commitments. We do what we say. And we lead with the belief that right makes might—not the other way around. We all know there are no easy options. But I wasn't elected to avoid hard decisions. And neither were the members of the House and the Senate. I've told you what I believe, that our security and our valuess demand that we cannot turn away from the massacre of countless civilians with chemical weapons. And our democracy is stronger when the President and the people's representatives stand together.

I'm ready to act in the face of this outrage. Today I'm asking Congress to send a message to the world that we are ready to move forward together as one nation.

Thanks very much.

NOTES AND QUESTIONS

1. *Humanitarian Intervention.* When, if ever, should unilateral use of force be permitted in the interest of humanitarian intervention? What conditions need be satisfied? For example, how extensive should human rights violations have to be in order to justify a humanitarian intervention? Should humanitarian intervention be precluded if an intervening state also has significant interests of its own that would be furthered by the intervention? Does humanitarian intervention gain legitimacy when undertaken by a group of states, rather than by a single state? More legitimacy if the states are democratic? Should there be a requirement of proportionality? Must humanitarian intervention have a reasonable chance of ameliorating the situation? Recall Professor Henkin's views on the restrictive scope of a humanitarian intervention exception to the prohibition on the use of force, in Part C above. See also Louis Henkin, "Kosovo and the Law of 'Humanitarian Intervention,' " 93 *American Journal of International Law* 824 (1999). Should we treat humanitarian intervention "not as a new legal right * * * but as a mitigating circumstance that does not create law and which is recognized as purely circumstantial and discretionary relief, rather like the early uses of equity"? Thomas M. Franck, *Recourse to Force* 190 (2002). See generally Dino Kritsiotis, "Reappraising Policy Objections to Humanitarian Intervention," 19 *Michigan Journal of International Law* 1005 (1998); James A.R. Nafziger, "Self-Determination and Humanitarian Intervention in a Community of Power," 20 *Denver Journal of International Law and Policy* 9 (1991), and *id.* "Part II," 22 *Denver Journal of International Law and Policy* 219 (1994).

2. *The Security Council and the Responsibility to Protect.* Does the U.N. Security Council alone, rather than an individual state or group of

states acting unilaterally, have both the authority and the responsibility to approve the use of force to avert a humanitarian disaster? According to the U.N. Secretary-General's High-Level Panel on Threats, Challenges and Change:

> 201. The successive humanitarian disasters in Somalia, Bosnia and Herzegovina, Rwanda, Kosovo and now Darfur, Sudan, have concentrated attention not on the immunities of sovereign Governments but their responsibilities, both to their own people and to the wider international community. [T]here is a growing acceptance that while sovereign Governments have the primary responsibility to protect their own citizens from such catastrophes, when they are unable or unwilling to do so that responsibility should be taken up by the wider international community—with it spanning a continuum involving prevention, response to violence, if necessary, and rebuilding shattered societies. * * *
>
> 203. We endorse the emerging norm that there is a collective international responsibility to protect, exercisable by the Security Council authorizing military intervention as a last resort, in the event of genocide and other large-scale killing, ethnic cleansing or serious violations of international humanitarian law which sovereign Governments have proved powerless or unwilling to prevent.

A More Secure World: Our Shared Responsibility, U.N. Doc. A/59/565 (2004). The U.N. General Assembly and Security Council have affirmed "R2P." G.A. Res. 60/1, ¶¶ 138–39 (2005) (adopting the 2005 World Summit Outcome); S.C. Res. 1674, ¶ 4 (2006). What aspects of R2P are controversial? What could be done to help assure that this responsibility is carried out effectively? See *Implementing the Responsibility to Protect: Report of the Secretary-General*, U.N. Doc. A/63/677 (2009).

3. *Libya.* A week after President Obama spoke about Libya, as quoted in the Chesterman excerpt, Harold Hongju Koh, the Legal Adviser to the U.S. Department of State, argued that "United States military actions rest on ample legal authority." He cited to Chapter VII of the U.N. Charter, specifically to Articles 39, 41, and 42. He also noted that Security Council Resolution 1973 authorized states to take "all necessary measures" to enforce a no-fly zone over Libya, to protect Libyan civilians, and to carry out inspections for an arms embargo. Koh also submitted that U.S. policy was "aimed at preventing an imminent humanitarian catastrophe." Harold Hongju Koh, "Statement Regarding Use of Force in Libya," American Society of International Law Annual Meeting, Washington, DC, Mar. 26, 2011, *available at* http://www.state.gov (last visited Dec. 11, 2013). Punished by the air strikes of the United States, United Kingdom, and France, the Qaddafi government in Libya fell, and Qaddafi himself was killed by opposing Libyan forces.

Was the Libyan intervention as much about regime change as it was about humanitarianism? If so, who gets to decide which government's humanitarian abuses justify and trigger outside intervention? As Chesterman pointed out, was Qaddafi particularly vulnerable to outside intervention first because he was so forthright about an "impending massacre" and second because he had lost support not only in the West but among the African and Arab states and was thus politically isolated?

The Libya intervention was costly for the United States—more than $1 billion. Moreover, there was heated opposition to President Obama's use of force without Congressional approval. It was noted that "previous cases involved peacekeeping missions in which the United States had been invited in, and there were only infrequent outbreaks of violence as in Lebanon, Somalia and Bosnia. The Libyan operation, by contrast, [was] an offensive mission involving substantial bombardment of a government's forces." Charlie Savage & Mark Landler, "White House Defends Continuing U.S. Role in Libya Operation," *New York Times*, June 16, 2011, at A16.

4. *Syria.* As this book goes to press, the troubles in Syria are far from resolved. President Obama backtracked on his September 2013 pledge to intervene in Syria when the British Parliament refused to authorize the use of force and U.S. Congressional support seemed doubtful. A Russian-U.S. agreement—the Framework for Elimination of Syrian Chemical Weapons—quickly ensued, however, calling for procedures to destroy those weapons; and the U.N. Security Council decided "to impose measures under Chapter VII" should Syria use chemical weapons or transfer them without authorization. S.C. Res. 2118, ¶ 21 (2013). See John R. Crook, "Contemporary Practice of the United States Relating to International Law," 107 *American Journal of International Law* 899, 900-07 (2013). Syria—one of the few countries in the world not to have accepted the 1992 Chemical Weapons Convention, 1974 U.N.T.S. 45, which prohibits the development, production, stockpiling, and use of such weapons, and which authorizes inspections—ratified the Convention on September 14, 2013. See the website of the Organization for the Prohibition of Chemical Weapons (OPCW), http://www.opcw.org (last visited Dec. 12, 2013). Inspectors from the United Nations and the OPCW verified the destruction of Syrian chemical weapons sites and equipment. See Alan Cowell & Rick Gladstone, "Inspectors in Syria Have Only One Site Left to Check," *New York Times*, Nov. 8, 2013, at A13. However, plans to ship chemical weapons out of Syria and destroy them were delayed. See Rick Gladstone & Nick Cumming-Bruce, "Delay in Chemical Arms Pledge Criticized," *New York Times*, Jan. 31, 2014, at A8.

One interesting debate is whether a use of force in Syria not authorized by the Security Council would be either wise or legal. David Cameron, the British Prime Minister, and President Obama pondering whether to use force for Libya-like regime change in Syria, faced Russian and Chinese opposition in the Security Council. Some commentators felt that U.S.-U.K. intervention would be unwise but lawful. See Joshua Rozenberg, "Syria Intervention: It may not be Wise, but Using Force may be Lawful," *The Guardian* (London),

Aug. 28, 2013. Others felt that such action might not be lawful, but it would be wise. Professor Hurd argued that "[t]here are moral reasons for disregarding the law." Ian Hurd, "Bomb Syria, Even if It is Illegal," *New York Times*, Aug. 28, 2013, at A23. Do you agree that morality should sometimes trump international law when making national policy decisions? If so, who should judge the morality of such acts? Was President Obama right or wrong to apparently give up on his moral argument of humanitarian intervention? U.N. Secretary-General Ban Ki-Moon lamented that the stalemate over Syria in the Security Council had harmed both the Syrian people and the reputation of the United Nations: "We cannot look the other way while the increasing sectarian violence spirals out of control, the humanitarian emergency escalates and the crisis spills over borders." Michele Nichols, "U.N. Chief Says Security Council Paralysis Harming Syrian People," Reuters, Sept. 5, 2012, *available at* http://www.reuters.com (last visited Dec. 9, 2013). Might U.S. use of force in Syria be justified on the grounds of collective self-defense? See Case Concerning Military and Paramilitary Activitites In and Against Nicaragua (Nicaragua v. United States), 1986 I.C.J. 226.

5. *The Congo*. On March 28, 2013, the Security Council decided to authorize, for the first time, its own offensive war. Dismayed by the on-going conflict in the Democratic Republic of the Congo and the "summary executions, sexual and gender based violence and large scale recruitment and use of children" by armed groups there, S.C. Res. 2098, ¶ 8 (2013), the Council sent in a military force of 3,000 from South Africa, Tanzania, and Malawi. See *id.* ¶¶ 9-10, 12(b). Previous Security Council decisions had not authorized peacekeepers to use force offensively; and in other situations, such as Iraq's 1990 invasion of Iraq considered in Section 1, the Council had simply authorized member states to use "all necessary means" to achieve U.N. collective security goals. Is the Congo action a wise expansion of United Nations use of force? See "The United Nations in Congo: Art of Darkness," *The Economist*, June 15, 2013, at 14; "Democratic Republic of Congo: Bigger Guns are on the Way," *The Economist*, June 15, 2013, at 50. Is the United Nations in the Congo now independently responsible to follow the rules of international humanitarian law? See Bruce "Ossie" Oswald, "The Security Council and the Intervention Brigade: Some Legal Issues," 17 *ASIL Insights*, Issue 15 (2013), and the discussion of the responsibility of international organizations in Chapter 8, Part A.

CHAPTER 10

THE LAW OF THE SEA

■ ■ ■

Much of the oceans—the high seas—has long been regarded as common space, subject to no state's sovereignty. For many years, international law recognized coastal state rights only in internal waters, such as ports, and in a narrow band of oceans near the coast known as the territorial sea. In the mid-20th century, however, what had been a relatively stable customary legal system for the oceans began to disintegrate. Some states asserted jurisdiction over broad coastal zones, seeking to take advantage of advances in technology that allowed mining and drilling for oil and gas on the continental shelf. The ability of foreign trawlers and factory ships to capture and process huge quantities of fish near the shores of coastal states also contributed to proclamations of wide coastal zones. Such coastal state assertions disquieted maritime powers, which feared infringements on traditional navigational freedoms.

The modern law of the sea was molded by the Third United Nations Conference on the Law of the Sea (UNCLOS III), which officially convened in 1973, following six years of studies and preparatory work by U.N. bodies. After numerous formal negotiating sessions and intersessional meetings, the Conference generated the 1982 Convention on the Law of the Sea. The Convention codified many principles previously accepted in customary and treaty law. It also introduced or affirmed new concepts, concerning the exclusive economic zone, fishing rights, the continental shelf, marine scientific research, pollution, transit passage through straits, the breadth of the territorial sea, and rights of landlocked states. Controversial provisions about mining the seabed beyond national jurisdiction delayed the entry into force of the Convention until November 1994, but as of December 2013, there were 166 parties, including most developed states though not the United States.

The concept of regimes, introduced in Chapter 8, is useful in thinking about the law of the sea. International lawyers do not usually speak of a single regime governing the oceans. Law of the sea issues are too diverse. It probably is more helpful to think about one regime governing warships, for example, and another governing seabed mining. In each, the forums available to resolve legal problems and the relative importance of municipal and international law may vary. The 1982 Convention, customary international law, other treaties, and regulations of many international organizations (*e.g.*, the International Maritime

Organization) shape much of the law. State agencies, including municipal courts, also regularly deal with law of the sea matters.

This chapter begins with two traditional law of the sea topics—the high seas in Part A and vessels in Part B. Part C then explores assertions of coastal state jurisdiction over parts of the commons and over resources on the continental shelf, in exclusive economic zones, and in fisheries zones. Part D addresses the territorial sea and straits. Part E turns to the regime governing deep seabed mining.

A. THE HIGH SEAS

The high seas have traditionally been regarded as international common space, open to all vessels and subject to the sovereignty of no state. The readings in this part span many centuries. Hugo Grotius's 1633 treatise was influential in shaping conceptions of the legal status of the high seas. The excerpts from the 1982 Law of the Sea Convention provide a modern vantage point from which to assess some of the changes in the law governing the high seas.

HUGO GROTIUS, THE FREEDOM OF THE SEAS (1633)

Ralph van Deman Magoffin trans. & James Brown Scott ed. 1916; reprinted 2001

The delusion is as old as it is detestable with which many men, especially those who by their wealth and power exercise the greatest influence, * * * try to persuade themselves, that justice and injustice are distinguishable the one from the other not by their own nature, but in some fashion merely by the opinion and custom of mankind. * * *

But * * * there have stood forth in every age independent and wise and devout men able to root out this false doctrine from the minds of the simple, and to convict its advocates of shamelessness. * * *

My intention is to demonstrate briefly and clearly that the Dutch—that is to say, the subjects of the United Netherlands—have the right to sail to the East Indies, as they are now doing, and to engage in trade with the people there. I shall base my argument on the following most specific and unimpeachable axiom of the Law of Nations, called a primary rule or first principle, the spirit of which is self-evident and immutable, to wit; Every nation is free to travel to every other nation, and to trade with it.

God Himself says this speaking through the voice of nature; and inasmuch as it is not His will to have Nature supply every place with all the necessaries of life, He ordains that some nations excel in one art and others in another. Why is this His will, except it be that He wished human friendships to be engendered by mutual needs and resources, lest individuals deeming themselves entirely sufficient unto themselves should for that very reason be rendered unsociable? * * * Those therefore who deny this law, destroy this most praiseworthy bond of human fellowship, remove the opportunities for doing mutual service, in a word do violence to Nature herself. For do not the ocean[s], navigable in every direction with which God has encompassed all the earth, and the regular and the occasional winds which blow now from one quarter and now from another, offer sufficient proof that Nature has given to all peoples a right of access to all other peoples? * * *

[L]et us consider whether [Portugal has] been able to obtain exclusive jurisdiction over the sea and its navigation or over trade. Let us first consider the case of the sea.

Now, in the legal phraseology of the Law of Nations, the sea is called indifferently the property of no one (*res nullius*), or a common possession (*res communis*), or public property (*res publica*). It will be most convenient to explain the signification of these terms if we follow the practice of all the poets since Hesiod, of the philosophers and jurists of the past, and distinguish certain epochs, the divisions of which are marked off perhaps not so much by intervals of time as by obvious logic and essential character. And we ought not to be criticized if in our explanation of a law deriving from nature, we use the authority and definition of those whose natural judgment admittedly is held in the highest esteem.

[C]ommon possession relates to use, as is seen from a quotation from Seneca:

> Every path was free, All things were used in common.

According to his reasoning there was a kind of sovereignty, but it was universal and unlimited. For God had not given all things to this individual or to that, but to the entire human race, and thus a number of persons, as it were *en masse*, were not debarred from being substantially sovereigns or owners of the same thing, which is quite contradictory to our modern meaning of sovereignty. For it now implies particular or private ownership, a thing which no one then had. * * *

It seems certain that the transition to the present distinction of ownerships did not come violently, but gradually, nature herself pointing out the way. For since there are some things, the use of which consists in their being used up, either because having become part of the very substance of the user they can never be used again, or because by use they become less fit for future use, it has become apparent, especially in dealing with the first category, such things as food and drink for example, that a certain kind of ownership is inseparable from use. For "own" implies that a thing belongs to some one person, in such a way that it cannot belong to any other person. By the process of reasoning this was next extended to things of the second category, such as clothes and movables and some living things. * * *

This occupation or possession, however, in the case of things which resist seizure, like wild animals for example, must be uninterrupted or perpetually maintained, but in the case of other things it is sufficient if after physical possession is once taken the intention to possess is maintained. Possession of movables implies seizure, and possession of immovables either the erection of buildings or some determination of boundaries, such as fencing in. * * *

Two conclusions may be drawn from what has thus far been said. The first is, that which cannot be occupied, or which never has been occupied, cannot be the property of any one, because all property has arisen from occupation. The second is, that all that which has been so constituted by nature that although serving some one person it still suffices for the common use of all other persons, is today and ought in perpetuity to remain in the same condition as when it was first created by nature. * * *

The air * * * is not susceptible of occupation; and * * * its common use is destined for all men. For the same reasons the sea is common to all, because it is so limitless that it cannot become a possession of any one, and because it is adapted for the use of all, whether we consider it from the point of view of navigation or of fisheries. * * *

These things therefore are what the Romans call "common" to all men by natural law, or as we have said, "public" according to the law of nations; and indeed they call their use sometimes common, sometimes public. Nevertheless, although those things are with reason said to be *res nullius*, so far as private ownership is concerned, still they differ very much from those things which, though also *res nullius*, have not been marked out for common use, such for example as wild animals, fish, and birds. For if any one seizes those things and assumes possession of them, they can become objects of private ownership, but the things in the former category by the consensus of opinion of all mankind are forever exempt from such private ownership on account of their susceptibility to universal use; and as they belong to all they cannot be taken away from all by any one person any more than what is mine can be taken away from me by you. * * *

The nature of the sea * * * differs from that of the shore, because the sea, except for a very restricted space, can neither easily be built upon, nor inclosed; if the contrary were true yet this could hardly happen without hindrance to the general use. Nevertheless, if any small portion of the sea can be thus occupied, the occupation is recognized. * * *

Now Celsus holds that piles driven into the sea belong to the man who drove them. But such an act is not permissible if the use of the sea be thereby impaired. * * * Labeo * * * holds that in case any * * * construction should be made in the sea, the following injunction is to be enforced: "Nothing may be built in the sea whereby the harbor, the roadstead, or the channel be rendered less safe for navigation."

Now the same principle which applies to navigation applies also to fishing, namely, that it remains free and open to all. Nevertheless there shall be no prejudice if any one shall by fencing off with stakes an inlet of the sea make a fish pond for himself, and so establish a private preserve.

* * * But outside of an inlet this will not hold, for then the common use of the sea might be hindered.

* * * The Portuguese claim as their own the whole expanse of the sea which separates two parts of the world so far distant the one from the other, that in all the preceding centuries neither one has so much as heard of the other. Indeed, if we take into account the share of the Spaniards, whose claim is the same as that of the Portuguese, only a little less than the whole ocean is found to be subject to two nations, while all the rest of the peoples in the world are restricted to the narrow bounds of the northern seas. * * * If in a thing so vast as the sea a man were to reserve to himself from general use nothing more than mere sovereignty, still he would be considered a seeker after unreasonable power. If a man were to enjoin other people from fishing, he would not escape the reproach of monstrous greed. But the man who even prevents navigation, a thing which means no loss to himself, what are we to say of him?

* * * For it is most outrageous for you to appropriate a thing, which both by ordinance of nature and by common consent is as much mine as yours, so exclusively that you will not grant me a right of use in it which leaves it no less yours than it was before. * * *

The last defense of injustice is usually a claim or plea based on prescription or on custom. To this defense therefore the Portuguese have resorted. But the best established reasoning of the law precludes them from enjoying the protection of either plea.

[I]t is impossible to acquire by usucaption or prescription things which cannot become property, that is, which are not susceptible of possession or of quasi-possession, and which cannot be alienated. All of which is true of the sea and its use.

[S]ince the law of nature arises out of Divine Providence, it is immutable; but a part of this natural law is the primary or primitive law of nations, differing from the secondary or positive law of nations, which is mutable. For if there are customs incompatible with the primary law of nations, then, according to the judgment of Vasquez, they are not customs belonging to men, but to wild beasts, customs which are corruptions and abuses, not laws and usages. Therefore those customs cannot become prescriptions by mere lapse of time, cannot be justified by the passage of any law, cannot be established by the consent, the protection, or the practice even of many nations. * * *

The conclusion of the whole matter therefore is that the Portuguese are in possession of no right whereby they may interdict to any nation whatsoever the navigation of the Ocean to the East Indies.

UNITED NATIONS CONVENTION ON THE LAW OF THE SEA, ARTICLES 86–90, 301

Dec. 10, 1982, Senate Treaty Doc. No. 103–39 (1994), 1833 U.N.T.S. 3

High Seas

Article 86

Application of the provisions of this Part

The provisions of this Part apply to all parts of the sea that are not included in the exclusive economic zone, in the territorial sea or in the internal waters of a State, or in the archipelagic waters of an archipelagic State. This article does not entail any abridgement of the freedoms enjoyed by all States in the exclusive economic zone in accordance with article 58.

Article 87

Freedom of the high seas

1. The high seas are open to all States, whether coastal or land-locked. Freedom of the high seas is exercised under the conditions laid down by this Convention and by other rules of international law. It comprises, *inter alia,* both for coastal and land-locked States:

(a) freedom of navigation;

(b) freedom of overflight;

(c) freedom to lay submarine cables and pipelines, subject to Part VI;

(d) freedom to construct artificial islands and other installations permitted under international law, subject to Part VI;

(e) freedom of fishing, subject to the conditions laid down in section 2;

(f) freedom of scientific research, subject to Parts VI and XIII.

2. These freedoms shall be exercised by all States with due regard for the interests of other States in their exercise of the freedom of the high seas, and also with due regard for the rights under this Convention with respect to activities in the Area.

Article 88

Reservation of the high seas for peaceful purposes

The high seas shall be reserved for peaceful purposes.

Article 89

Invalidity of claims of sovereignty over the high seas

No State may validly purport to subject any part of the high seas to its sovereignty.

Article 90

Right of navigation

Every State, whether coastal or land-locked, has the right to sail ships flying its flag on the high seas.

* * *

Article 301

Peaceful uses of the seas

In exercising their rights and performing their duties under this Convention, States Parties shall refrain from any threat or use of force against the territorial integrity or political independence of any State, or in any other manner inconsistent with the principles of international law embodied in the Charter of the United Nations.

NOTES AND QUESTIONS

1. *Hugo Grotius*. Grotius was a prodigy. He knew Latin and Greek by age 8, entered university at age 11, edited an encyclopedia at 15, was a lawyer pleading cases in the highest court of the Netherlands at 16, and became Attorney General of the Netherlands by the time he was 24. Grotius gained fame not only as a lawyer, but as a diplomat and a political and legal theorist. He is one of the most important figures in the history of international law; we have noted his fundamental contributions to a state-oriented conception of international law in the Notes following the 1648 Peace of Westphalia in Chapter 2. Grotius's *De Mare Liberum* (*The Freedom of the Seas*) was originally a chapter of *De Jure Praede* (*Commentary on the Law of Prize and Booty*), a work written in 1604–1605. Grotius's most famous work, *De Jure Belli ac Pacis* (*On the Law of War and Peace*), was published in 1625.

2. *Grotius and High Seas Freedoms*. Grotius wrote *De Jure Praede* to support Dutch access to the East Indian trade and to dispute Spanish and Portuguese claims over the high seas. *De Mare Liberum* was separately published in 1609, probably in anticipation of a proclamation by King James I of England that prohibited foreigners from fishing in "British seas" unless they obtained a British license. How did Grotius envision the legal regime of the high seas? How did he support his position? Recall the discussion of natural law, one of the traditional sources of international law, in Chapter 3.

3. *John Selden and Closed Seas*. Grotius's views did not go unchallenged. The best-known response was that of the Englishman John Selden, who published *Mare Clausum* in 1635. Selden argued that the seas

could be appropriated, and that various uses of the oceans could diminish the owner's rights. Selden's work supported such British practices as requiring foreigners to obtain fishing licenses, demanding that foreign ships strike their flags in salute to British ships in "British seas," stopping hostilities by foreign ships in those seas, and imposing certain tolls on the passage of foreign vessels. See Edward Gordon, "Grotius and the Freedom of the Seas in the Seventeenth Century," 16 *Willamette Journal of International Law and Dispute Resolution* 252 (2008); Ruth Lapidoth, "Freedom of Navigation—Its Legal History and Its Normative Basis," 6 *Journal of Maritime Law and Commerce* 259 (1975).

4. *British Sea Power and High Seas Freedoms.* Grotius's notion of the high seas as not subject to exclusive sovereignty came to be generally accepted:

> During the 19th century, British sea power, then supreme, helped consolidate an international maritime regime based on the freedoms of the high seas, freedoms to travel and to fish without coastal state regulation outside a 3-mile territorial sea. This was a customary legal regime, not written in any convention or treaty. It was, however, remarkably effective, respected by most states in times of peace from the end of the Napoleonic Wars in 1815 to the end of World War II in 1945. As a result, for over a century, navies and other users of the oceans could sail freely on seas covering some 70 percent of the earth's surface. Only within a narrow band of 3 miles, the territorial sea, did coastal states put some legal limits on the mobility of naval forces.

Mark W. Janis, *Sea Power and the Law of the Sea* xiii–xiv (1976).

5. *Modern Conceptions of High Seas Freedoms.* Article 2 of the 1958 Geneva Convention on the High Seas explicitly designated navigation, fishing, overflight, and the laying of submarine cables and pipelines as high seas freedoms. These are repeated in Article 87 of the 1982 Convention on the Law of the Sea, which added the freedom of scientific research and the freedom to build artificial islands and other installations permitted under international law to the list of high seas freedoms. Are other, unenumerated uses legitimate? For example, states have, from time to time, employed the high seas for military purposes. Would it be legitimate for a state to declare a military test site in the oceans? To place weapons or military detection devices on the sea bed, invoking traditional high seas freedoms? What do you make of Articles 88 and 301 of the 1982 Convention? For discussion of international law limits on recourse to force, see Chapter 9. Overall, what modifications of the Grotian conception of *mare liberum* do Articles 86–90 of the 1982 Convention on the Law of the Sea reflect?

6. *Controlling Activities on the High Seas.* If the high seas are generally open to ships for a variety of purposes, who is responsible for maintaining order there? What if a vessel is in an unsafe operating condition, or threatens other vessels or the environment? Or if a ship engages in such

egregious practices as slave trading, piracy, or the dumping of dangerous chemicals? Some answers are provided in the next part.

B. VESSELS

Jurisdiction and control over the actions of and activities on board vessels on the high seas have traditionally been left to the ship's "flag state," the state of the vessel's nationality. The first reading in this part, an excerpt from a 1905 arbitral decision, explores the concept of vessel nationality. Both that decision and the second reading, taken from a British government report about oil spills from ships, also suggest some of the problems that arise when flag states do not effectively exercise control. What steps have and should be taken to solve these problems? The Notes and the last three readings—a decision by the International Tribunal for the Law of the Sea, an article from the 1982 Law of the Sea Convention, and a modern U.S. piracy case—explore that question.

CASE OF THE MUSCAT DHOWS

France-Great Britain, 1905,
in *The Hague Arbitration Cases* 64 (George G. Wilson ed. 1915), *available at* http://www.haguejusticeportal.net/index.php?id=6128 (last visited Dec. 8, 2013)

[Great Britain and France agreed to arbitrate a dispute that arose after Muscat (referred to nowadays as Oman) quarantined five Muscat subjects for medical reasons. The five men escaped, and the British, acting at the request of the Sultan of Muscat, recaptured them. These Muscat subjects held French papers that, according to France, gave France the right to exercise jurisdiction over them; France demanded their release. In negotiations with France, Britain agreed to advise the Sultan that he release the men if France agreed to arbitrate several matters, including the rights of ships flying the French flag (considered in the excerpt below) and the rights of individuals holding French papers. The case was set against the broader background of efforts to suppress the slave trade and competing French and British assertions of authority in the Persian Gulf.]

The Tribunal of Arbitration constituted in virtue of the Compromis concluded at London on October 13, 1904 between Great Britain and France;

Whereas the Government of His Britannic Majesty and that of the French Republic have thought it right by the Declaration of March 10, 1862 "to engage reciprocally to respect the independence" of His Highness the Sultan of Muscat,

Whereas difficulties as to the scope of that Declaration have arisen in relation to the issue, by the French Republic, to certain subjects of His Highness the Sultan of Muscat of papers authorizing them to fly the

French flag, and also as to the nature of the privileges and immunities claimed by subjects of His Highness who are owners or masters of dhows and in possession of such papers or are members of the crew of such dhows and their families, especially as to the manner in which such privileges and immunities affect the jurisdiction of His Highness the Sultan over his said subjects,

Whereas the two Governments have agreed by the Compromis of October 13, 1904 that these questions shall be determined by reference to arbitration[;]

AS TO THE FIRST QUESTION:

Whereas generally speaking it belongs to every Sovereign to decide to whom he will accord the right to fly his flag and to prescribe the rules governing such grants, and whereas therefore the granting of the French flag to subjects of His Highness the Sultan of Muscat in itself constitutes no attack on the independence of the Sultan,

Whereas nevertheless a Sovereign may be limited by treaties in the exercise of this right, and * * * whereas therefore the question arises, under what conditions Powers which have acceded to the General Act of the Brussels Conference of July 2, 1890 relative to the African Slave Trade, especially to article 32 of this Act, are entitled to authorize native vessels to fly their flags,

Whereas by article 32 of this Act the faculty of the Signatory Powers to grant their flag to native vessels has been limited for the purpose of suppressing slave trading and in the general interests of humanity, irrespective of whether the applicant for the flag may belong to a state signatory of this Act or not, and whereas at any rate France is in relation to Great Britain bound to grant her flag only under the conditions prescribed by this Act,

Whereas in order to attain the above mentioned purpose, the Signatory Powers of the Brussels Act have agreed in its article 32 that the authority to fly the flag of one of the Signatory Powers shall in future only be granted to such native vessels, which shall satisfy all the three following conditions:

1. Their fitters-out or owners must be either subjects of or persons protected by [protégés of] the Power whose flag they claim to fly,

2. They must furnish proof that they possess real estate situated in the district of the authority to whom their application is addressed, or supply a solvent security as a guarantee for any fines to which they may eventually become liable,

3. Such fitters-out or owners, as well as the captain of the vessel, must furnish proof that they enjoy a good reputation, and

especially that they have never been condemned for acts of slave trade,

Whereas in default of a definition of the term "protégé" in the General Act of the Brussels Conference this term must be understood in the sense which corresponds best as well to the elevated aims of the Conference and its Final Act, as to the principles of the law of nations, as they have been expressed in treaties existing at that time, in internationally recognized legislation and in international practice,

Whereas the aim of the said article 32 is to admit to navigation in the seas infested by slave trade only those native vessels which are under the strictest surveillance of the Signatory Powers, a condition which can only be secured if the owners, fitters-out and crews of such vessels are exclusively subjected to the sovereignty and jurisdiction of the State, under whose flag they are sailing,

[The tribunal examines the meaning of the term "protégé." It reviews several instruments, including an 1863 French treaty and an 1863 municipal statute that limited France's rights to create new protégés.]

Whereas the fact of having granted before the ratification of the Brussels Act on January 2, 1892 authorizations to fly the French flag to native vessels not satisfying the conditions prescribed by article 32 of this Act was not in contradiction with any international obligation of France,

FOR THESE REASONS,

decides and pronounces as follows:

1. before the 2nd of January 1892 France was entitled to authorize vessels belonging to subjects of His Highness the Sultan of Muscat to fly the French flag, only bound by her own legislation and administrative rules;

2. owners of dhows, who before 1892 have been authorized by France to fly the French flag, retain this authorization as long as France renews it to the grantee;

3. after January 2, 1892 France was not entitled to authorize vessels belonging to subjects of His Highness the Sultan of Muscat to fly the French flag, except on condition that their owners or fitters-out had established or should establish that they had been considered and treated by France as her "protégés" before the year 1863;

AS TO THE 2ND QUESTION:

Whereas the legal situation of vessels flying foreign flags and of the owners of such vessels in the territorial waters of an Oriental State is determined by the general principles of jurisdiction, by * * * treaties and by the practice resulting therefrom,

Whereas the terms of the Treaty of Friendship and Commerce between France and the Iman of Muscat of November 17, 1844, [preclude visits by the authorities of the Sultan to French vessels without the consent of such vessels],

Whereas, although it cannot be denied that by admitting the right of France to grant under certain circumstances her flag to native vessels and to have these vessels exempted from visitation by the authorities of the Sultan or in his name, slave trade is facilitated, because slave traders may easily abuse the French flag, for the purpose of escaping from search, the possibility of this abuse, which can be entirely suppressed by the accession of all Powers to article 42 of the Brussels Convention, cannot affect the decision of this case, which must only rest on juridical grounds, * * *

FOR THESE REASONS,

decides and pronounces as follows:

1. dhows of Muscat authorized as aforesaid to fly the French flag are entitled in the territorial waters of Muscat to the inviolability provided by the French-Muscat Treaty of November 17, 1844[.]

Done at The Hague, in the Permanent Court of Arbitration, August 8, 1905.

SAFER SHIPS, CLEANER SEAS

Report of Lord Donaldson's Inquiry Into the Prevention of Pollution From Merchant Shipping, Cm. 2560 (1994)

1.1. On 5 January 1993 one of the Shetland Islanders' worst nightmares became a reality. The MV *BRAER* went onto the rocks at Garths Ness. She was fully laden with 84,700 tonnes of Norwegian Gullfaks crude oil and some 1,600 tonnes of heavy fuel oil bunkers. The weather was atrocious—storm force winds and mountainous seas. There were all the makings of a major economic and ecological disaster for the local community.

1.2. In the event the consequences were serious but miraculously less catastrophic than might have been expected. * * *

1.29. [T]he *BRAER* was registered in Liberia[.]

1.31. It must not be forgotten that on 3 December 1992, only a month before the *BRAER* was wrecked off Shetland, the tanker *AEGEAN SEA* was wrecked off La Coruña in northern Spain. * * *

6.1. In an ideal world Flag States, whose flags are worn by the world's shipping, would lay down, and enforce upon their own shipowners, standards of design, maintenance and operation which would ensure a very high standard of safety at sea. Coastal States, along whose coasts shipping passes, and Port States, at whose ports or anchorages shipping calls, would have no cause to concern themselves with the maintenance of such standards.

6.2. The present system of Flag State Control falls well short of this ideal. At any one time the fleet of any Flag State will be scattered throughout the world. No Flag State has the resources to police its fleet on a continuous and all-embracing basis. The most that it can do is to insist upon periodic surveys and to undertake *ad hoc* inspection if it learns that a ship has suffered a casualty or, for some other reason such as a Port State Control inspection, it suspects that its ship no longer complies with internationally agreed standards. Good shipowners will maintain the seaworthiness of their ships regardless of whether a Flag State periodical survey is imminent. Regrettably, bad shipowners regard the imminence of such a survey as the only reason for spending money on maintenance or repairs and then only if satisfied that the survey will be thorough.

6.3. In this situation, even if Flag States were to comply to the full with their responsibilities, Coastal and Port States would have a part to play. They would, in their own interests, be concerned to detect the few unseaworthy ships which had escaped the Flag State net. Their role would be to supplement and support Flag State Control, but not to substitute for it.

6.4. Regrettably it is beyond argument that not all Flag States live up to their responsibilities. Figures for deficiencies and detections revealed by Port State Control inspections show that, for example, of 61 Indian registered ships inspected over one in four were so seriously deficient that they had to be detained in port. Over 85 per cent of the inspections of Indian registered ships uncovered deficiencies. India, although a striking example, is by no means alone and a number of other Flag States also have a poor record.

[The Report demonstrates that the United Kingdom's percentage of the world's shipping has declined significantly, and that the U.K. depends heavily on foreign-flag vessels to move its goods.]

6.8. A State which confers its nationality upon a ship, and thus authorizes it to fly its flag, has an unfettered right to subject that ship to its laws. This enables it to impose and maintain standards of design, construction, equipment, maintenance and operation. Whilst there is no upper limit to these standards, there are lower limits. These stem from the various international Conventions to which Flag States are parties, such as the SOLAS, MARPOL 73/78 and Load Line Conventions, under which Flag States are required to establish that ships flying their flags comply with the provisions of those Conventions and to issue the necessary certificates of compliance. * * *

6.9. Economic and competitive considerations effectively prevent Flag States from imposing standards which are higher than those internationally agreed and any improvement in standards is thus only achievable by international agreement. The machinery for such agreement is provided by the International Maritime Organization (IMO). * * *

6.12. It is for Flag States individually to decide how to give effect to their international obligations. In some cases the international Conventions specify precise requirements. SOLAS, for example, requires minimum pressures at fire hydrants and MARPOL includes precise formulae for the calculation of positions of ballast tanks. But in other cases, the Conventions merely specify that equipment must be "approved" by the Flag State or be "to the satisfaction of the Flag State." Sometimes such lack of precision is necessary for technical reasons or to allow for innovation. Regrettably in others it is merely designed to conceal differences of view between the members of IMO. * * *

6.18. When the international Conventions were originally drafted, most of the world's merchant fleet was owned by, and flew the flags of, the world's major maritime and trading powers. These States had already established survey and inspection of their ships as a matter of public policy aimed at protecting the safety of crews and passengers. While the setting of such standards was not immune from commercial pressures from shipowning interests, their enforcement was not subject to such pressures. This was presumably in reflection of the fact that in the UK, for example, there had been a long history of regulation through the Board of Trade and the fact that most UK trade was carried in UK ships which were subject to the same standards and accordingly competed fairly with one another. States had little or no direct financial interest in shipping and could apply and enforce standards in the interests of public policy without feeling any pressure to maintain or enhance their merchant fleets.

6.19. All that has changed. Today few States regard it as consistent with their national status and dignity to be without a register of national shipping of as large a size as possible. Some also regard such a register as a useful source of income. In seeking to achieve this aim, some see no need to limit eligibility to ships whose owners or operators have any connection with the State. They maintain what are called "open" registers. A few such States are landlocked and have no connection with the sea. Rather more include ships which are never likely to call at a national port. Perhaps in recognition of this fact one of the largest and, it has to be said, one of the most efficient, Liberia, maintains its register and discharges its responsibilities from an office in the USA. Relatively few Liberian ships ever call at Monrovia, their usual port of registry.

Another example is Vanuatu, which has few foreign exports and whose register is run from the USA and London.

6.20. All this might be unobjectionable if, despite the very considerable difficulties in enforcing standards on ships (and shipowners) which have no real connection with the State whose flag the ships fly, agreed international standards were universally enforced. However they are not. The vice of "open" registers is twofold. First, in practice they lead to varying standards of safety. This is easily demonstrated by [statistics on] the incidence of total losses by flag. Second, the existence of "open" registers and the consequent ease with which ships can be transferred to a different register and flag has led to some shipowners shopping around for the registers which have the lowest standards of enforcement and which, in consequence, involve them in the least expense. This is positively encouraged by some of the Flag States concerned which have even been known to advertise competitive "prices" for their survey and certification work.

NOTES AND QUESTIONS

1. *The* Muscat Dhows *Arbitration*. The *Muscat Dhows Case* was litigated in the Permanent Court of Arbitration, which is discussed in Chapter 5. Note that Muscat (Oman) was not a party to the arbitration. The Sultan was reportedly dissuaded from sending a Muscat representative to The Hague because of the cost involved, and he asked Britain to act on Muscat's behalf. France, however, was not willing to arbitrate with Muscat if the British acted as Muscat's agent. This French objection led to Muscat not being named as a party in the case. Following the arbitral decision, it took France and Britain over three years to agree on which particular French protégés and dhows were "grandfathered" under the French flag. For accounts of the arbitration and events leading up to it, see Briton Cooper Busch, *Britain and the Persian Gulf, 1894–1914*, at 154–86 (1967), and Dolliver Nelson, "The Muscat Dhows," in 7 *Max Planck Encyclopedia of Public International Law* 426 (Rüdiger Wolfrum ed. 2013).

2. *The Nationality of Ships*. During the *Muscat Dhows* arbitration, Great Britain argued that "Frenchifying" the dhows infringed on the independence of the Sultan of Muscat, because dhows owned by Muscat nationals were "thereby withdrawn from their natural jurisdiction" and could not be searched by Muscat warships. *The Times* (London), July 25, 1905, at 5. The arbitral tribunal, however, affirmed the general rule that a state may authorize any vessel to fly its flag. The flag that a ship is entitled to fly is a symbol of its nationality. States normally register ships to establish their nationality, issuing documents that those ships can use as proof of their nationality. See Article 91 of the 1982 Convention on the Law of the Sea.

Why is it important for ships to have nationality? What state would protect a stateless vessel from attacks or interference? Why else does statelessness matter? Consider the following passage from United States v.

Marino-Garcia, 679 F.2d 1373, 1382 (11th Cir. 1982), in which the court discussed stateless vessels:

> Vessels without nationality are international pariahs. They have no internationally recognized right to navigate freely on the high seas. Moreover, flagless vessels are frequently not subject to the laws of a flag-state. As such they represent "floating sanctuaries from authority" and constitute a potential threat to the order and stability of navigation on the high seas.
>
> The absence of any right to navigate freely on the high seas coupled with the potential threat to order on international waterways has led various courts to conclude that international law places no restrictions upon a nation's right to subject stateless vessels to its jurisdiction.

3. *Flag State Jurisdiction.* On the high seas, a ship is generally immune from the exercise of jurisdiction except by the authorities of the ship's flag state. There are only limited exceptions to the principle of exclusive flag state jurisdiction and control on the high seas. One exception concerns piracy, the subject of the *Dire Case* below.

4. *Coastal State Control of Foreign Flag Vessels.* The second question discussed in the *Muscat Dhows Case* suggests that a coastal state may visit foreign flag vessels while they are in the territorial sea, a zone of coastal state sovereignty that today may extend up to 12 nautical miles—one nautical mile equals 1.15078 miles; in this chapter "miles" refer to nautical miles—from a state's coastal baselines. The coastal state may by treaty limit its rights in this regard, as Muscat had done in this case. We further address coastal state jurisdiction in the territorial sea, as well as the right of foreign flag vessels to "innocent passage" through the territorial sea, in Part D of this chapter.

With respect to pollution issues, coastal states today have considerable rights to set standards and to take enforcement measures in their offshore zones. These measures may affect foreign flag ships. See Articles 210–211 and 220–221 of the 1982 Convention on the Law of the Sea. Should coastal states have the right to take steps to prevent pollution from foreign flag ships on the high seas? What additional steps could be taken to help insure compliance with the obligations of international environmental law?

5. *Port State Control of Foreign Flag Vessels.* As noted in paragraph 6.4 of Lord Donaldson's Report, port states may exercise some control over substandard ships by detaining them until essential repairs are made. Should the standards used to detain ships in port be subject to uniform international law? Many matters concerning port state inspections and detentions of vessels, including communications among states about substandard ships, are regulated by regional port state memoranda of understanding. See Tatjana Keselj, "Port State Jurisdiction in Respect of Pollution from Ships: The 1982 United Nations Convention on the Law of the

Sea and the Memoranda of Understanding," 30 *Ocean Development and International Law* 127 (1999).

6. *Open Registry*. A system of flag state control poses particular difficulties if a flag state cannot or will not control its ships. The *Muscat Dhows* tribunal expressed concern that "slavetraders may easily abuse the French flag, for the purpose of escaping from search." Modern challenges relate to unsafe labor conditions on board ships and threats of oil spills, *e.g.*, when the Liberian-flag *Braer* spilled huge quantities of crude oil when it ran aground off the Shetlands. The *Braer*'s largely Filipino crew complained to the International Transport Workers' Federation in 1992 that the aging ship was undermanned. Jason Benetto, "The Shetland Oil Disaster: Cut-price Recipe for Catastrophe," *Independent on Sunday*, Jan. 10, 1993, at 22. Although vessels registered in "open registry" (also known as "flag of convenience") states certainly are not responsible for all vessel safety and pollution problems—the *Exxon Valdez*, which caused a massive oil spill off Alaska in 1989, was registered in the United States—the safety record of many such vessels has been questionable. Massive oil spills off the coasts of France and Spain from the Maltese-flagged *Erika* (in 1999) and the Bahamian-flagged *Prestige* (in 2001) raised anew questions about how to regulate the practice of open registry.

A 1970 British committee headed by Lord Rochdale identified six features common to open registry:

> (i) The country of registry allows ownership and/or control of its merchant vessels by non-citizens;
>
> (ii) Access to the registry is easy. A ship may usually be registered at a consul's office abroad. Equally important, transfer from the registry at the owner's option is not restricted;
>
> (iii) Taxes on the income from the ships are not levied locally or are low. A registry fee and an annual fee, based on tonnage, are normally the only charges made. A guarantee or acceptable understanding regarding future freedom from taxation may also be given;
>
> (iv) The country of registry is a small power with no national requirement under any foreseeable circumstances for all the shipping registered, but receipts from very small charges on a large tonnage may produce a substantial effect on its national income and balance of payments;
>
> (v) Manning of ships by non-nationals is freely permitted; and
>
> (vi) The country of registry has neither the power nor the administrative machinery effectively to impose any government or international regulations; nor has the country the wish or the power to control the companies themselves.

Committee of Inquiry into Shipping, *Report* 51, Cmnd. 4337 (1970). As of 2011, flag of convenience vessels, registered in such states as the Bahamas,

Honduras, Liberia, Malta, Mongolia, Panama, Saint Vincent and the Grenadines, and Vanuatu, accounted for an estimated 71.5 percent of the world shipping tonnage. U.N. Conference on Trade and Development, *Review of Maritime Transport 2012*, at 45, UNCTAD/RMT/2012 (U.N. Sales No. E.12.II.D.17, 2012).

7. *Limiting Flag State Grants of Nationality*. In the *Muscat Dhows Case*, should France have had an unqualified right to determine the conditions under which a ship was entitled to fly the French flag? Would conditions such as those set forth in Article 32 of the General Act of the Brussels Conference of 1890 make sense today? States generally have not accepted significant limitations on their right to grant nationality to vessels. One limited response to open registry is the "genuine link" requirement, explored in the next excerpt.

THE M/V "SAIGA" (NO. 2)

Saint Vincent and the Grenadines v. Guinea, International Tribunal for the Law of the Sea, http://www.itlos.org (last visited Dec. 8, 2013), 38 *International Legal Materials* 1323 (1999)

[The *Saiga*, a tanker flying the flag of Saint Vincent and the Grenadines, was engaged in supplying fuel oil to fishing boats inside Guinea's 200-mile exclusive economic zone but outside the 24-mile limit of the contiguous zone, a zone in which international law recognizes the customs authority of coastal states. We discuss the EEZ and the contiguous zone in Part C. On October 28, 1997, a Guinean patrol craft attacked the *Saiga*, arrested it, and brought the vessel and its crew to port in Conakry, Guinea, where the master was detained and the cargo of fuel oil was discharged. Guinea claimed that supplying fuel to fishing vessels violated Guinean customs laws. Criminal charges were brought against the master of the *Saiga*, who received a suspended sentence of six months imprisonment and a fine. In this case, Saint Vincent and the Grenadines claimed, *inter alia*, that Guinea interfered with the navigation rights of a Vincentian vessel and used excessive force in stopping and arresting the vessel. The International Tribunal for the Law of the Sea, in this judgment of July 1, 1999, ultimately rules in favor of Saint Vincent and the Grenadines on several issues, awarding that state $2,123,357 as compensation.

The Tribunal also addresses arguments raised by Guinea urging that, as a threshold matter, the claims of Saint Vincent and the Grenadines were inadmissible. One of the admissibility arguments, concerning the issue of "genuine link," is considered here.]

75. The next objection to admissibility raised by Guinea is that there was no genuine link between the *Saiga* and Saint Vincent and the Grenadines. Guinea contends that "without a genuine link between Saint Vincent and the Grenadines and the M/V '*Saiga*,' Saint Vincent and the

Grenadines' claim concerning a violation of its right of navigation and the status of the ship is not admissible before the Tribunal *vis-à-vis* Guinea, because Guinea is not bound to recognize the Vincentian nationality of the M/V '*Saiga*,' which forms a prerequisite for the mentioned claim in international law."

76. Guinea further argues that a State cannot fulfill its obligations as a flag State under the [1982] Convention [on the Law of the Sea] with regard to a ship unless it exercises prescriptive and enforcement jurisdiction over the owner or, as the case may be, the operator of the ship. Guinea contends that, in the absence of such jurisdiction, there is no genuine link between the ship and Saint Vincent and the Grenadines and that, accordingly, it is not obliged to recognize the claims of Saint Vincent and the Grenadines in relation to the ship.

77. Saint Vincent and the Grenadines maintains that there is nothing in the Convention to support the contention that the existence of a genuine link between a ship and a State is a necessary precondition for the grant of nationality to the ship, or that the absence of such a genuine link deprives a flag State of the right to bring an international claim against another State in respect of illegal measures taken against the ship.

78. Saint Vincent and the Grenadines also challenges the assertion of Guinea that there was no genuine link between the *Saiga* and Saint Vincent and the Grenadines. It claims that the requisite genuine link existed between it and the ship. Saint Vincent and the Grenadines calls attention to various facts which, according to it, provide evidence of this link. These include the fact that the owner of the *Saiga* is represented in Saint Vincent and the Grenadines by a company formed and established in that State and the fact that the *Saiga* is subject to the supervision of the Vincentian authorities to secure compliance with the International Convention for the Safety of Life at Sea (SOLAS), 1960 and 1974, the International Convention for the Prevention of Pollution from Ships, 1973, as modified by the Protocol of 1978 relating thereto (MARPOL 73/78), and other conventions of the International Maritime Organization to which Saint Vincent and the Grenadines is a party. In addition, Saint Vincent and the Grenadines maintains that arrangements have been made to secure regular supervision of the vessel's seaworthiness through surveys, on at least an annual basis, conducted by reputable classification societies authorized for that purpose by Saint Vincent and the Grenadines. Saint Vincent and the Grenadines also points out that, under its laws, preference is given to Vincentian nationals in the manning of ships flying its flag. It further draws attention to the vigorous efforts made by its authorities to secure the protection of the *Saiga* on the international plane before and throughout the present dispute.

79. Article 91, paragraph 1, of the [1982 Law of the Sea] Convention provides: "There must exist a genuine link between the State and the ship." Two questions need to be addressed in this connection. The first is whether the absence of a genuine link between a flag State and a ship entitles another State to refuse to recognize the nationality of the ship. The second question is whether or not a genuine link existed between the *Saiga* and Saint Vincent and the Grenadines at the time of the incident.

80. With regard to the first question, the Tribunal notes that the provision in article 91, paragraph 1, of the Convention, requiring a genuine link between the State and the ship, does not provide the answer. Nor do articles 92 and 94 of the Convention, which together with article 91 constitute the context of the provision, provide the answer. The Tribunal, however, recalls that the International Law Commission, in article 29 of the Draft Articles on the Law of the Sea adopted by it in 1956, proposed the concept of a "genuine link" as a criterion not only for the attribution of nationality to a ship but also for the recognition by other States of such nationality. After providing that "ships have the nationality of the State whose flag they are entitled to fly," the draft article continued: "Nevertheless, for purposes of recognition of the national character of the ship by other States, there must exist a genuine link between the State and the ship." This sentence was not included in article 5, paragraph 1, of the Convention on the High Seas of 29 April 1958 (hereinafter "the 1958 Convention"), which reads, in part, as follows:

> There must exist a genuine link between the State and the ship; in particular, the State must effectively exercise its jurisdiction and control in administrative, technical and social matters over ships flying its flag.

Thus, while the obligation regarding a genuine link was maintained in the 1958 Convention, the proposal that the existence of a genuine link should be a basis for the recognition of nationality was not adopted.

81. The [1982 Law of the Sea] Convention follows the approach of the 1958 Convention. Article 91 retains the part of the third sentence of article 5, paragraph 1, of the 1958 Convention which provides that there must be a genuine link between the State and the ship. The other part of that sentence, stating that the flag State shall effectively exercise its jurisdiction and control in administrative, technical and social matters over ships flying its flag, is reflected in article 94 of the Convention, dealing with the duties of the flag State.

82. Paragraphs 2 to 5 of article 94 of the Convention outline the measures that a flag State is required to take to exercise effective jurisdiction as envisaged in paragraph 1. Paragraph 6 sets out the procedure to be followed where another State has "clear grounds to believe that proper jurisdiction and control with respect to a ship have not been exercised." That State is entitled to report the facts to the flag State

which is then obliged to "investigate the matter and, if appropriate, take any action necessary to remedy the situation." There is nothing in article 94 to permit a State which discovers evidence indicating the absence of proper jurisdiction and control by a flag State over a ship to refuse to recognize the right of the ship to fly the flag of the flag State.

83. The conclusion of the Tribunal is that the purpose of the provisions of the Convention on the need for a genuine link between a ship and its flag State is to secure more effective implementation of the duties of the flag State, and not to establish criteria by reference to which the validity of the registration of ships in a flag State may be challenged by other States. * * *

86. In the light of the above considerations, the Tribunal concludes that there is no legal basis for the claim of Guinea that it can refuse to recognize the right of the *Saiga* to fly the flag of Saint Vincent and the Grenadines on the ground that there was no genuine link between the ship and Saint Vincent and the Grenadines.

87. With regard to the second question, the Tribunal finds that, in any case, the evidence adduced by Guinea is not sufficient to justify its contention that there was no genuine link between the ship and Saint Vincent and the Grenadines at the material time. * * *

183. For the above reasons, the Tribunal * * *

(4) By 18 votes to 2,

Rejects the objection to the admissibility of the claims of Saint Vincent and the Grenadines based on Guinea's contention that there was no genuine link between Saint Vincent and the Grenadines and the *Saiga* at the time of its arrest[.]

UNITED NATIONS CONVENTION ON THE LAW OF THE SEA, ARTICLE 94

Dec. 10, 1982, Senate Treaty Doc. No. 103–39 (1994), 1833 U.N.T.S. 3

Duties of the flag state

1. Every State shall effectively exercise its jurisdiction and control in administrative, technical and social matters over ships flying its flag.

2. In particular, every State shall:

(a) maintain a register of ships containing the names and particulars of ships flying its flag, except those which are excluded from generally accepted international regulations on account of their small size; and

(b) assume jurisdiction under its internal law over each ship flying its flag and its master, officers and crew in respect of administrative, technical and social matters concerning the ship.

3. Every State shall take such measures for ships flying its flag as are necessary to ensure safety at sea with regard, *inter alia*, to:

(a) the construction, equipment and seaworthiness of ships;

(b) the manning of ships, labour conditions and the training of crews, taking into account the applicable international instruments;

(c) the use of signals, the maintenance of communications and the prevention of collisions.

4. Such measures shall include those necessary to ensure:

(a) that each ship, before registration and thereafter at appropriate intervals, is surveyed by a qualified surveyor of ships, and has on board such charts, nautical publications and navigational equipment and instruments as are appropriate for the safe navigation of the ship;

(b) that each ship is in the charge of a master and officers who possess appropriate qualifications, in particular in seamanship, navigation, communications and marine engineering, and that the crew is appropriate in qualifications and numbers for the type, size, machinery and equipment of the ship;

(c) that the master, officers and, to the extent appropriate, the crew are fully conversant with and required to observe the applicable international regulations concerning the safety of life at sea, the prevention of collisions, the prevention, reduction and control of marine pollution, and the maintenance of communications by radio.

5. In taking the measures called for in paragraphs 3 and 4 each State is required to conform to generally accepted international regulations, procedures and practices and to take any steps which may be necessary to secure their observance.

6. A State which has clear grounds to believe that proper jurisdiction and control with respect to a ship have not been exercised may report the facts to the flag State. Upon receiving such a report, the flag State shall investigate the matter and, if appropriate, take any action necessary to remedy the situation.

7. Each State shall cause an inquiry to be held by or before a suitably qualified person or persons into every marine casualty or incident of navigation on the high seas involving a ship flying its flag and causing loss of life or serious injury to nationals of another State or serious damage to ships or installations of another State or to the marine environment. The flag State and the other State shall cooperate in the

conduct of any inquiry held by that other State into any such marine casualty or incident of navigation.

NOTES AND QUESTIONS

1. Saiga *and the International Tribunal for the Law of the Sea.* The 1982 Convention on the Law of the Sea provides for obligatory reference of certain disputes to third-party tribunals if negotiated settlements fail. If states parties to a dispute do not agree on the same forum, or fail to indicate a preferred forum, the dispute will usually go to binding arbitration. However, when a flag state seeks only the prompt release of a vessel and crew being detained by a coastal state for specific fishing or pollution offenses, or when provisional relief is sought, the International Tribunal for the Law of the Sea (ITLOS), a court created by the Law of the Sea Convention, may have jurisdiction. The *Saiga* dispute led to three different decisions by the ITLOS. First, on December 4, 1997, the ITLOS ordered the prompt release of the *Saiga* and its crew on the posting of a $400,000 bond. Second, on March 11, 1998, the Tribunal prescribed provisional measures, ordering Guinea to refrain from taking certain enforcement measures. Third, the Tribunal decided the merits of the case on July 1, 1999; jurisdiction at the merits stage was grounded on an agreement between Guinea and Saint Vincent and the Grenadines. The case excerpt reproduced above is from the merits decision.

2. *The "Genuine Link" Requirement.* What does "genuine link" mean? Does the absence of a genuine link between a flag state and a vessel allow another state to refuse to recognize the nationality of that vessel? Compare the *Nottebohm* and *Barcelona Traction* cases in Chapter 6. For further discussion, see Doris König, "Flag of Ships," in 4 *Max Planck Encyclopedia of Public International Law* 98 (Rüdiger Wolfrum ed. 2012); John E. Noyes, "Interpreting the 1982 Law of the Sea Convention and Defining its Terms," in *Definitions for the Law of the Sea: Terms Not Defined by the 1982 Convention* 45, 69–77 (George K. Walker ed. 2012).

3. *The Responsibilities of Flag States.* States have accepted treaty provisions mandating that each state exercise administrative and supervisory responsibilities with respect to ships flying its flag. Article 94 of the 1982 Convention on the Law of the Sea is one example. Is Article 94 overly vague? Does it provide a reasonable approach to the challenges posed by open registry? How else could international law and process respond to such challenges? Would a system of inspections and approvals of ship safety by an international regulatory body be preferable?

4. *Multiple Treaty Obligations.* Besides the 1982 Convention on the Law of the Sea, numerous other treaties set rules governing ships and shipboard activities. Many contain specific substantive standards. The Law of the Sea Tribunal in the *Saiga Case* and Lord Donaldson's Report mentioned a few examples.

In taking the measures listed in Article 94(3) and (4) of the 1982 Law of the Sea Convention, a flag state must, per Article 94(5), "conform to generally accepted international regulations, procedures and practices." Such regulations may be embodied in a growing number of international conventions adopted primarily under the auspices of the International Maritime Organization (IMO). The reference to "generally accepted" standards, which also appears elsewhere in the 1982 Convention (*e.g.*, Article 21, reproduced in Part D of this chapter), apparently means that a State Party to the Convention may be legally obligated to apply detailed standards developed by the IMO even if that state is not a party to the specific treaty that sets the standards. But what determines whether a regulation has been "generally accepted"? Is the inquiry identical to whether the standard has been accepted as customary international law? See *Paquete Habana* and the other cases about custom in Chapter 3. Is the practice of ship owners or other private entities relevant in determining "general acceptance"? For discussion, see Committee on Coastal State Jurisdiction Relating to Marine Pollution, "Final Report," in International Law Association, *Report of the Sixty-Ninth Conference (London)* 443, 473-81 (2000), *reprinted in Vessel-source Pollution and Coastal State Jurisdiction* 75, 105–13 (Erik Franckx ed. 2001).

5. *Nationality of Claims.* If a vessel's crew members, owners, and cargo interests suffer injury through actions of a non-flag state, may the vessel's flag state represent those various entities if they are not of the same nationality as the flag state? In the *Saiga Case*, Saint Vincent and the Grenadines alleged that Guinea had illegally seized the ship and used excessive force against it, damaging the vessel and its cargo and injuring some of those on board. Although the *Saiga* was flying the flag of Saint Vincent and the Grenadines, a corporation from Cyprus owned the vessel, a Scottish corporation managed it, a Swiss corporation chartered it, its master and crew were Ukrainians, and some Senegalese nationals were employed on board. Guinea argued that Saint Vincent and the Grenadines was not entitled to represent the interests of the *Saiga*'s employees, crew, or cargo owners. The ITLOS disagreed:

> 106. [T]he [1982 Law of the Sea] Convention considers a ship as a unit, as regards the obligations of the flag State with respect to the ship and the right of a flag State to seek reparation for loss or damage. * * * Thus the ship, every thing on it, and every person involved or interested in its operations are treated as an entity linked to the flag State. The nationalities of these persons are not relevant.
>
> 107. The Tribunal must * * * call attention to * * * two basic characteristics of modern maritime transport: the transient and multinational composition of ships' crews and the multiplicity of interests that may be involved in the cargo on board a single ship. A container vessel carries a large number of containers, and the persons with interests in them may be of many different nationalities. This may also be true in relation to cargo on board a

> break-bulk carrier. Any of these ships could have a crew comprising persons of several nationalities. If each person sustaining damage were obliged to look for protection from the State of which such person is a national, undue hardship would ensue.

http://www.itlos.org (last visited Dec. 8, 2013), 38 *International Legal Materials* at 1347.

Suppose that a company with a nationality different from that of the flag state owns cargo on a vessel of the flag state, and that the cargo has been damaged by another state's illegal act. Should the company, or the state of the company's nationality, be precluded from pursuing a claim for that damage? Is only the flag state entitled to pursue the claim? What if the flag state is unwilling to do so? The International Law Commission in its 2006 Draft Articles on Diplomatic Protection concluded that

> [t]he right of the State of nationality of the members of the crew of a ship to exercise diplomatic protection is not affected by the right of the State of nationality of a ship to seek redress on behalf of such crew members, irrespective of their nationality, when they have been injured in connection with an injury to the vessel resulting from an internationally wrongful act.

Report of the International Law Commission on the Work of its Fifty-eighth Session, art. 18, U.N. Doc. A/61/10 (2006). Compare *Nottebohm* and *Barcelona Traction* in Chapter 6, and see generally Bernard H. Oxman, "Human Rights and the United Nations Convention on the Law of the Sea," 36 *Columbia Journal of Transnational Law* 399 (1997), and Tullio Treves, "Human Rights and the Law of the Sea," 28 *Berkeley Journal of International Law* 1 (2010).

UNITED STATES V. DIRE

680 F.3d 446 (4th Cir. 2012), *cert. denied*, 133 S. Ct. 982 (2013)

Opinion by Judge King:

In the early morning hours of April 1, 2010, on the high seas between Somalia and the Seychelles (in the Indian Ocean off the east coast of Africa), the defendants * * * imprudently launched an attack on the USS Nicholas, having confused that mighty Navy frigate for a vulnerable merchant ship. The defendants, all Somalis, were swiftly apprehended and then transported to the Eastern District of Virginia, where they were convicted of the crime of piracy, as proscribed by 18 U.S.C. § 1651, plus myriad other criminal offenses. In this appeal, the defendants challenge their convictions and life plus-eighty-year sentences on several grounds, including that their fleeting and fruitless strike on the Nicholas did not, as a matter of law, amount to a § 1651 piracy offense. As explained below, we reject their contentions and affirm.

According to the trial evidence, the USS Nicholas was on a counter-piracy mission in the Indian Ocean when, lit to disguise itself as a merchant vessel, it encountered the defendants shortly after midnight on April 1, 2010. The Nicholas was approached by an attack skiff operated by defendant Hasan and also carrying defendants Dire and Ali, while defendants Umar and Gurewardher remained with a larger mother-ship some distance away. From their posts on the Nicholas, crew members could see by way of night-vision devices that Hasan was armed with a loaded rocket-propelled grenade launcher (commonly referred to as an "RPG"), and that Dire and Ali carried AK-47 assault rifles.

* * * When the defendants' attack skiff was within sixty feet of the Nicholas's fantail (its lowest and thus most accessible point), Dire and Ali discharged the first shots—bursts of rapid, automatic fire from their AK-47s aimed at the Nicholas and meant to attain its surrender. The Nicholas's crew responded in kind, resulting in an exchange of fire that lasted less than thirty seconds. Bullets from Dire and Ali's AK-47s struck the Nicholas near two of its crew members, but the defendants' brief attack was (thankfully) casualty-free. Dire, Ali, and Hasan then turned their skiff and fled, with the Nicholas in pursuit.

* * * Dire, Ali, and Hasan threw various items from the skiff overboard into the Indian Ocean, discarding the RPG, the AK-47s, and a ladder that would have enabled them to board the Nicholas. About thirty minutes into the pursuit, the Nicholas captured the three defendants in the skiff. Thereafter, the Nicholas chased and captured the two defendants in the mothership. * * *

The defendants' strike on the USS Nicholas was consistent with an accustomed pattern of Somali pirate attacks, designed to seize a merchant ship and then return with the vessel and its crew to Somalia, where a ransom would be negotiated and secured. Indeed, on April 4, 2010, during questioning aboard the Nicholas, the defendants separately confessed to participating willingly in a scheme to hijack a merchant vessel, and they provided details about their operation. * * *

In these consolidated appeals, the defendants first contend that their ill-fated attack on the USS Nicholas did not constitute piracy under 18 U.S.C. § 1651, which provides in full:

> Whoever, on the high seas, commits the crime of piracy as defined by the law of nations, and is afterwards brought into or found in the United States, shall be imprisoned for life.

According to the defendants, the crime of piracy has been narrowly defined for purposes of § 1651 as robbery at sea, i.e., seizing or otherwise robbing a vessel. Because they boarded the Nicholas only as captives and indisputably took no property, the defendants contest their convictions on Count One [piracy], as well as the affixed life sentences.

[The district court, in United States v. Hasan, 747 F. Supp. 2d 599, 602 (E.D. Va. 2010), referred to here as *Hasan I*, denied the defendants' motion to dismiss the piracy count, concluding that "piracy under the law of nations" encompassed acts of violence committed on the high seas for private ends.]

The *Hasan I* opinion was issued on the heels of the August 17, 2010 published opinion in *United States v. Said*, 757 F. Supp. 2d 554 (E.D. Va. 2010), wherein a different judge of the Eastern District of Virginia essentially took these defendants' view of the piracy offense by recognizing a robbery element. Like these defendants, the *Said* defendants have been charged with piracy under 18 U.S.C. § 1651 for attacking—but not seizing or otherwise robbing—a United States Navy ship. The *Said* court granted the defendants' pretrial motion * * * to dismiss the piracy count from the indictment because no taking of property was alleged.

As the *Said* court recognized, article I of the Constitution accords Congress the power "[t]o define and punish Piracies and Felonies committed on the high Seas, and Offences against the Law of Nations." * * * Examining the Act of 1819 [the predecessor of 18 U.S.C. § 1651] in its *United States v. Smith* decision of 1820, the Supreme Court recognized:

> There is scarcely a writer on the law of nations, who does not allude to piracy, as a crime of a settled and determinate nature; and whatever may be the diversity of definitions, in other respects, all writers concur, in holding, that robbery, or forcible depredations upon the sea, animo furandi [*i.e.*, with intent to steal] is piracy.

18 U.S. (5 Wheat.) 153, 161 (1820). Accordingly, the *Smith* Court, through Justice Story, articulated "no hesitation in declaring, that piracy, by the law of nations, is robbery upon the sea." *Id.* at 162.

Invoking the principle that a court "must interpret a statute by its ordinary meaning at the time of its enactment," the *Said* court deemed *Smith* to be the definitive authority on the meaning of piracy under 18 U.S.C. § 1651. * * *

The *Said* court * * * noted, "the only substantive change to § 1651 since its enactment has been the removal of the death penalty for the offense as opposed to the current penalty of life imprisonment."

[A]lthough the *Said* court acknowledged contemporary international law sources defining piracy to encompass the *Said* defendants' violent conduct, the court deemed such sources to be too "unsettled" to be authoritative. The court further determined that relying on those international law sources would violate due process, explaining that, if "the definition of piracy [were adopted] from [the] debatable international sources whose promulgations evolve over time, defendants in United States courts would be required to constantly guess whether their conduct is proscribed by § 1651[,] render[ing] the statute unconstitutionally vague." Thereby undeterred from employing the "clear and authoritative" definition in *Smith* "of piracy as sea robbery," the court dismissed the piracy count from the *Said* indictment.

[In *Hasan I*] the district court took a different tack, * * * denying these defendants' pretrial motion to dismiss the Count One piracy charge from their Indictment. That is, the court focused on piracy's unusual status as a crime defined by the law of nations and subject to universal jurisdiction.

The district court began by recognizing that, "[f]or centuries, pirates have been universally condemned as *hostis humani generis*—enemies of all mankind—because they attack vessels on the high seas, and thus outside of any nation's territorial jurisdiction, . . . with devastating effect to global commerce and navigation."

[According to the district court in *Hasan I*,] "general piracy can be prosecuted by any nation, irrespective of the presence of a jurisdictional nexus." (citing *Sosa v. Alvarez-Machain*, 542 U.S. 692, 762 (2004) (Breyer, J., concurring in part and concurring in the judgment) ("[I]n the 18th century, nations reached consensus not only on the substantive principle that acts of piracy were universally wrong but also on the jurisdictional principle that any nation that found a pirate could prosecute him.")). Importantly, though, "because it is created by international consensus, general piracy is restricted in substance to those offenses that the international community agrees constitute piracy."

[A]s the district court recounted, "Congress passed the Act of 1819 to make clear that it wished to proscribe not only piratical acts that had a nexus to the United States, but also piracy as an international offense subject to universal jurisdiction." * * *

Having noted that "[n]o other Supreme Court decision since *Smith* has directly addressed the definition of general piracy," and recognizing the necessity of looking to foreign sources to determine the law of nations, the district court then focused on case law from other countries. The court deemed the Privy Council of England's 1934 decision in *In re Piracy Jure Gentium*, [1934] A.C. 586 (P.C.), to be "[t]he most significant foreign case dealing with the question of how piracy is defined under international law."

[T]he Privy Council [ruled]: "Actual robbery is not an essential element in the crime of piracy jure gentium. A frustrated attempt to commit a piratical robbery is equally piracy jure gentium." *Id.* [at 588.]

[T]he district court in *Hasan I* [also] examined Kenya's 2006 *Republic v. Ahmed* prosecution of "ten Somali suspects captured by the United

States Navy on the high seas"—"[t]he most recent case on [general piracy] outside the United States of which [the district court was] aware." The High Court of Kenya affirmed the *Ahmed* defendants' convictions for piracy *jure gentium*, culling from international treaties a modern definition of piracy that encompasses acts of violence and detention.

As detailed in *Hasan I,* "there are two prominent international agreements that have directly addressed, and defined, the crime of general piracy." The first of those treaties is the Geneva Convention on the High Seas (the "High Seas Convention"), which was adopted in 1958 and ratified by the United States in 1961, rendering the United States one of today's sixty-three parties to that agreement. * * *

The second pertinent treaty is the United Nations Convention on the Law of the Sea (the "UNCLOS"), which has amassed 162 parties since 1982—albeit not the United States, which has not ratified the UNCLOS "but has recognized that its baseline provisions reflect customary international law." [Article 101 of] the UNCLOS provides that

> [p]iracy consists of any of the following acts:
>
> (a) any illegal acts of violence or detention, or any act of depredation, committed for private ends by the crew or the passengers of a private ship or a private aircraft, and directed:
>
> (i) on the high seas, against another ship or aircraft, or against persons or property on board such ship or aircraft;
>
> (ii) against a ship, aircraft, persons or property in a place outside the jurisdiction of any State;
>
> (b) any act of voluntary participation in the operation of a ship or of an aircraft with knowledge of facts making it a pirate-ship or aircraft;
>
> (c) any act of inciting or of intentionally facilitating an act described in subparagraph (a) or (b).

[T]he UNCLOS * * * "defines piracy in exactly the same terms as the [High Seas Convention], with only negligible stylistic changes." The court also observed that the UNCLOS "represents the most recent international statement regarding the definition . . . of piracy."

"Having concluded that Congress's proscription of 'piracy as defined by the law of nations' in 18 U.S.C. § 1651 necessarily incorporates modern developments in international law," the district court next endeavored to "discern the definition of piracy under the law of nations at the time of the alleged offense in April 2010." In so doing, the court observed that the law of nations is ascertained today via the same path followed in 1820 by the Supreme Court in *Smith*: consultation of " 'the works of jurists, writing professedly on public law[s]' "; consideration of " 'the general usage and practice of nations' "; and contemplation of " 'judicial decisions recognising and enforcing that law.' " (quoting *Smith*, 18 U.S. (5 Wheat.) at 160–61). Engaging in that analysis, the court concluded:

> As of April 1, 2010, the law of nations, also known as customary international law, defined piracy to *include* acts of violence committed on the high seas for private ends without an actual taking. More specifically, . . . the definition of general piracy under modern customary international law is, at the very least, reflected in Article 15 of the 1958 High Seas Convention and Article 101 of the 1982 UNCLOS.

([The *Hasan* I court also concluded that] "[t]oday, 'the law of nations has become synonymous with the term "customary international law," which describes the body of rules that nations in the international community universally abide by, or accede to, out of a sense of legal obligation and mutual concern.' ") Narrowing customary international law to one of those two treaties, the court chose the UNCLOS, which—in addition to "contain[ing] a definition of general piracy that is, for all practical purposes, identical to that of the High Seas Convention"—"has many more states parties than the High Seas Convention" and "has been much more widely accepted by the international community than the High Seas Convention."

* * * According to the court, "[w]hile all treaties shed some light on the customs and practices of a state, 'a treaty will only constitute sufficient proof of a norm of customary international law if an overwhelming majority of States have ratified the treaty, and those States uniformly and consistently act in accordance with its principles.' " [T]he court recognized: "UNCLOS's definition of general piracy has a norm-creating character and reflects an existing norm of customary international law that is binding on even those nations that are not a party to the Convention, including the United States."

[E]ven accepting that "actual robbery on the high seas" was once an essential element of general piracy, "the view that general piracy does not require an actual robbery on the sea has certainly gained traction since the Nineteenth Century, as evidenced by [intervening case law], the Harvard Draft Convention on Piracy, the High Seas Convention, and UNCLOS." Additionally, the court recognized that "[c]ontemporary scholarly sources . . . appear to agree that the definition of piracy in UNCLOS represents customary international law." "While writers on the issue do present disagreements regarding the definition of general piracy," the court acknowledged, "such disagreements do not implicate the core definition provided in UNCLOS" (explaining that "writers [instead] disagree about the outer boundaries of the definition of general piracy, such as whether UNCLOS's requirement of 'private ends' prohibits its application to terrorist activities, or whether piracy can arise in situations involving just one ship rather than two"). * * *

The *Hasan I* opinion further rejected the *Said*-approved theory "that applying the contemporary customary international law definition of general piracy violates fundamental due process protections." According to *Hasan I,* "§ 1651's express incorporation of the definition of piracy provided by 'the law of nations,' which is today synonymous with customary international law, provides fair warning of what conduct is proscribed by the statute." In support of that conclusion, the district court in *Hasan I* recapped the Supreme Court's 1820 holding in *Smith* "that, by incorporating the definition of piracy under the law of nations, Congress had proscribed general piracy as clearly as if it had enumerated the elements of the offense in the legislation itself." * * *

The district court then reaffirmed that, as of the alleged offense date of April 2010, the definition of piracy under the law of nations was found in the substantively identical High Seas Convention and UNCLOS[.]

[The district court in *Hasan I* concluded that the facts supported an allegation of piracy against the defendants. At trial, all defendants were convicted of piracy, and they appealed their convictions.]

We * * * agree with the district court that the definition of piracy under the law of nations, at the time of the defendants' attack on the USS Nicholas and continuing today, had for decades encompassed their violent conduct. That definition, spelled out in the UNCLOS, as well as the High Seas Convention before it, has only been reaffirmed in recent years as nations around the world have banded together to combat the escalating scourge of piracy. For example, in November 2011, the United Nations Security Council adopted Resolution 2020, recalling a series of prior resolutions approved between 2008 and 2011 "concerning the situation in Somalia"; expressing "grave[ ] concern[ ] [about] the ongoing threat that piracy and armed robbery at sea against vessels pose"; and emphasizing "the need for a comprehensive response by the international community to repress piracy and armed robbery at sea and tackle its underlying causes." Of the utmost significance, Resolution 2020 reaffirmed "that international law, as reflected in the [UNCLOS], sets out the legal framework applicable to combating piracy and armed robbery at sea." Because the district court correctly applied the UNCLOS definition of piracy as customary international law, we reject the defendants' challenge to their Count One piracy convictions, as well as their mandatory life sentences.

NOTES AND QUESTIONS

1. *Municipal Courts and the Law of the Sea.* The *Dire Case* is but one of many examples of municipal courts deciding issues related to the international law of the sea. Municipal courts traditionally have been a force in developing and articulating a uniform maritime law, applicable to a wide

range of issues. We see another example later in this chapter, in *Regina v. Keyn*.

Cases arising in municipal courts may involve maritime treaties or municipal statutes embodying such treaties. As the *Dire Case* reminds us, these courts may also apply the law of nations. For other examples of U.S. courts interpreting the law of nations or customary international law, see *Filartiga*, which we studied in Chapter 1, *Paquete Habana* and *United States v. Smith* in Chapter 3, and *De Longchamps*, *Charming Betsy*, and *Sosa v. Alvarez-Machain* in Chapter 4. Do you agree with the *Dire* district court and court of appeals that the meaning of "piracy in violation of the law of nations" as proscribed in 18 U.S.C. § 1651 may change over time? Or, as the *Said* district court ruled, should piracy be limited to its 1819 definition? Was *Dire* correct in concluding that customary international law is equivalent to the law of nations?

2. *Exceptions to Flag State Jurisdiction*. Many treaties, particularly bilateral ones, authorize countries to exercise some degree of jurisdiction over foreign flag vessels on the high seas with respect to fishing, immigration, drug trafficking, and terrorist-related activities. Article 110 of the 1982 Law of the Sea Convention also provides for a limited right to board and inspect documents where "there is reasonable ground for suspecting" that a ship flying a foreign flag is engaged in the slave trade or unauthorized broadcasting, is stateless, or in reality has the same nationality as a boarding warship. For discussion of flag state jurisdiction and these exceptions, see Louis B. Sohn, Kristen Gustafson Juras, John E. Noyes & Erik Franckx, *Law of the Sea in a Nutshell* 70–96 (2d ed. 2010). Should the list in Article 110 be expanded to encompass additional subjects, such as drug trafficking or transporting weapons of mass destruction? Why was additional authority not approved when the Law of the Sea Convention was negotiated?

As *Dire* indicated, when a vessel is suspected of piracy, a warship may do more than merely board and inspect documents. According to Article 105 of the Law of the Sea Convention, on the high seas, "every State may seize a pirate ship[,] arrest the persons and seize the property on board[, and] decide upon the penalties to be imposed[.]" States may, in short, exercise universal jurisdiction over pirates. We met the concept of universal jurisdiction when we studied *Filartiga* (Chapter 1), *Smith, Furundžija*, and *jus cogens* (Chapter 3), and *Sosa* and *Kiobel* (Chapter 4); in Chapter 11 we study jurisdiction in depth. Should piracy be subject to more severe enforcement measures than other egregious conduct at sea?

Although *Dire* affirmed that modern piracy is not limited to "robbery at sea," the scope of piracy is nonetheless restricted. What are the characteristics of modern piracy? Read carefully Article 101 of the Law of the Sea Convention, quoted in *Dire*. Why is the definition of piracy so narrow? When in 1985 terrorists boarded the passenger ship *Achille Lauro* in port, took control of the vessel on the high seas, and threw a passenger overboard, many observers concluded no act of piracy had been committed. In response, the International Maritime Organization prepared the Convention for the

Suppression of Unlawful Acts against the Safety of Maritime Navigation, Mar. 10, 1988, which does apply to such conduct. As of December 2013, this SUA Convention had been accepted by 161 contracting parties representing 94.51 of the world's shipping tonnage.

3. *Piracy and Armed Conflict.* When pirates are seized, then tried and convicted in municipal courts, they are treated as criminals. Why should international law not regard pirate attacks—which justify responses by military forces—as armed attacks and invoke the law of war? If there were a "war on piracy," would pirates be entitled to prisoner of war status or other rights under international humanitarian law? Compare the treatment of terrorists under international humanitarian law, considered in Chapter 9.

Historically, the United States and other countries commissioned private ships as privateers, issuing letters of marque and reprisal that authorized them to attack and capture enemy vessels as well as pirates. A privateer acting within the scope of its commission could itself avoid charges of piracy, certainly in the courts of its commissioning country. See Article I, Section 8 of the U.S. Constitution in the Appendix and the 1804 *Charming Betsy Case* (Chapter 4), which involved protections accorded ships of neutral powers.

The Paris Declaration Respecting Maritime Law, Apr. 16, 1856, 1 *American Journal of International Law Supplement* 89 (1907), proclaimed that "[p]rivateering is, and remains abolished," and governments have abandoned its use. Why is privateering no longer tolerated? Why are only government warships authorized to seize pirate or enemy vessels? See Dino Kritsiotis, "The Contingencies of Piracy," 41 *California Western International Law Journal* 305 (2011); Nicholas Parrillo, "The Deprivatization of American Warfare: How the U.S. Government Used, Regulated, and Ultimately Abandoned Privateering in the Nineteenth Century," 19 *Yale Journal of Law and Humanities* 1 (2007).

4. *Contemporary Piracy.* Recent decades have seen an upsurge in piracy, along with what is known as "armed robbery against ships," a phrase referring to piratical acts committed in internal waters or the territorial sea. Hundreds of pirate attacks have occurred off the coast of Somalia, off West Africa, and in the waters of southeast Asia. Efforts to respond to piracy involve complex legal and foreign policy issues related to arms trafficking, networks used to finance pirates, human rights, international development aid, insurance law, criminal law, and the use of military forces, as well as law of the sea issues. International organizations have been involved in anti-piracy efforts. For example, the United Nations Security Council has adopted resolutions authorizing foreign warships to enter the territorial waters of Somalia to repress acts of piracy; the International Maritime Organization has developed anti-piracy guidelines for flag states and shippers; and various U.N. agencies have provided assistance to African countries to train prosecutors and build prisons for pirates. Several treaties and declarations set out cooperative measures to deter or punish acts of piracy. For background, see James Kraska, *Contemporary Maritime Piracy* (2011), and "Agora: Piracy Prosecutions," 104 *American Journal of International Law* 397

(2010). Useful websites include those of the International Maritime Bureau Piracy Reporting Centre of the International Chamber of Commerce, the IMO, which regularly prepares piracy reports, and Piracy Studies, which provides academic research and commentary. See respectively http://www.icc-ccs.org/piracy-reporting-centre, http://imo.org, and http://piracy-studies.org (all last visited Dec. 6, 2013).

C. THE CONTINENTAL SHELF, FISHERIES ZONES, AND THE EXCLUSIVE ECONOMIC ZONE

In the middle of the 20th century, coastal states began to make claims with respect to zones of the oceans beyond the narrow territorial sea over which states traditionally had asserted sovereignty. See Figure 10.A. In this part, we first examine the regime of the continental shelf, initiated through unilateral proclamation but now developed as treaty law. We then look at coastal state claims to fisheries zones. These claims contributed to acceptance of coastal state rights over fisheries in the exclusive economic zone (EEZ). The seaward extension of national jurisdiction has affected both access to and management of ocean resources. The materials at the end of this part explore attempts to devise international legal regimes to conserve and manage fisheries, both within and outside national zones of authority.

THE TRUMAN PROCLAMATION

Proclamation 2667, Policy of the United States With Respect to the Natural Resources of the Subsoil and Sea Bed of the Continental Shelf, Sept. 28, 1945 3 C.F.R. 67 (1943–1948 Compilation)

WHEREAS the Government of the United States of America, aware of the long range world-wide need for new sources of petroleum and other minerals, holds the view that efforts to discover and make available new supplies of these sources should be encouraged; and

WHEREAS its competent experts are of the opinion that such resources underlie many parts of the continental shelf off the coasts of the United States of America, and that with modern technological progress their utilization is already practicable or will become so at an early date; and

WHEREAS recognized jurisdiction over these resources is required in the interest of their conservation and prudent utilization when and as development is undertaken; and

WHEREAS it is the view of the Government of the United States that the exercise of jurisdiction over the natural resources of the subsoil and sea bed of the continental shelf by the contiguous nation is reasonable and just, since the effectiveness of measures to utilize or conserve those resources would be contingent upon cooperation and protection from the shore, since the continental shelf may be regarded as an extension of the land-mass of the coastal nation and thus naturally appurtenant to it, since these resources frequently form a seaward extension of a pool or deposit lying within the territory, and since self-protection compels the coastal nation to keep close watch over activities off its shores which are of the nature necessary for utilization of these resources;

NOW, THEREFORE, I, HARRY S. TRUMAN, President of the United States of America, do hereby proclaim the following policy of the United States of America with respect to the natural resources of the subsoil and sea bed of the continental shelf.

Having concern for the urgency of conserving and prudently utilizing its natural resources, the Government of the United States regards the natural resources of the subsoil and sea bed of the continental shelf beneath the high seas but contiguous to the coasts of the United States as appertaining to the United States, subject to its jurisdiction and control. In cases where the continental shelf extends to the shores of another State, or is shared with an adjacent State, the boundary shall be determined by the United States and the State concerned in accordance with equitable principles. The character as high seas of the waters above the continental shelf and the right to their free and unimpeded navigation are in no way thus affected.

UNITED NATIONS CONVENTION ON THE LAW OF THE SEA, ARTICLES 77–78

Dec. 10, 1982, Senate Treaty Doc. No. 103–39 (1994), 1833 U.N.T.S. 3

Article 77

Rights of the coastal State over the continental shelf

1. The coastal State exercises over the continental shelf sovereign rights for the purpose of exploring it and exploiting its natural resources.

2. The rights referred to in paragraph 1 are exclusive in the sense that if the coastal State does not explore the continental shelf or exploit its natural resources, no one may undertake these activities without the express consent of the coastal State.

3. The rights of the coastal State over the continental shelf do not depend on occupation, effective or notional, or on any express proclamation.

Figure 10.A

Coastal Zones Under the 1982 Convention on the Law of the Sea

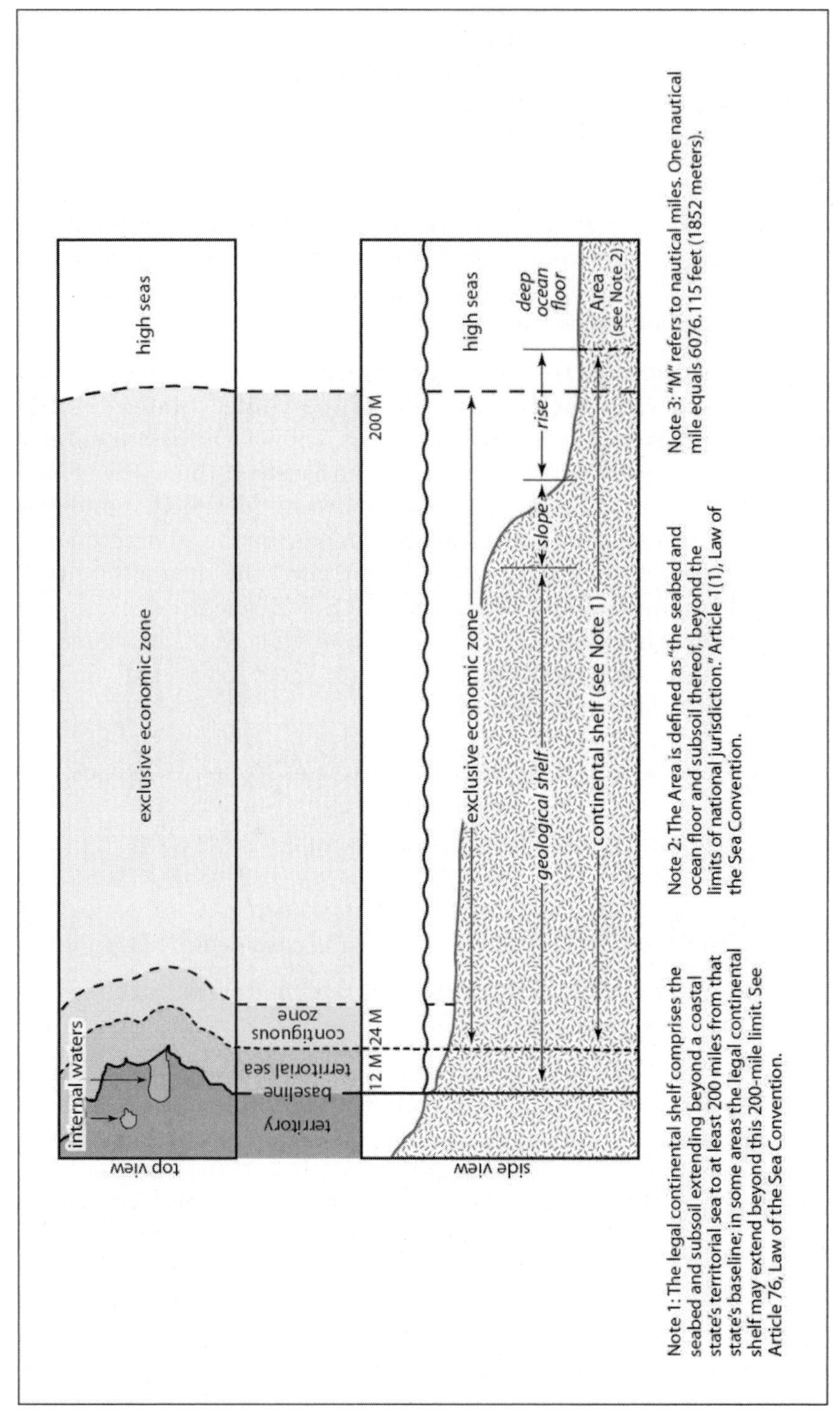

4. The natural resources referred to in this Part consist of the mineral and other non-living resources of the sea-bed and subsoil together with living organisms belonging to sedentary species, that is to say, organisms which, at the harvestable stage, either are immobile on or under the sea-bed or are unable to move except in constant physical contact with the sea-bed or the subsoil.

Article 78

Legal status of the superjacent waters and airspace and the rights and freedoms of other States

1. The rights of the coastal State over the continental shelf do not affect the legal status of the superjacent waters or of the air space above those waters.

2. The exercise of the rights of the coastal State over the continental shelf must not infringe or result in any unjustifiable interference with navigation and other rights and freedoms of other States as provided for in this Convention.

NOTES AND QUESTIONS

1. *The Truman Proclamation on the Continental Shelf.* The Truman Proclamation on the continental shelf was a significant event in the 20th-century movement toward extended coastal state jurisdiction. In June 1943, U.S. Secretary of the Interior Harold Ickes wrote to President Franklin Roosevelt:

> The war has impressed us with the necessity for an augmented supply of natural resources. In this connection I draw your attention to the importance of the Continental Shelf not only to the defense of our country, but more particularly as a storehouse of natural resources. The extent of these resources can only be guessed at and needs careful investigating.
>
> The Continental Shelf extending some 100 or 150 miles from our shores forms a fine breeding place for fish of all kinds; it is an excellent hiding place for submarines; and since it is a continuation of our continent, it probably contains oil and other resources similar to those found in our States.
>
> I suggest the advisability of laying the ground work now for availing ourselves fully of the riches in this submerged land and in the waters over them. The legal and policy problems involved, both international and domestic, are many and complex. In the international field, it may be necessary to evolve new concepts of maritime territorial limits beyond three miles, and of rights to occupy and exploit the surface and the subsoil of the open sea.

[1945] 2 *Foreign Relations of the United States* 1481. Ickes referred to "maritime territorial limits beyond three miles" because the United States, like many other states, already claimed sovereignty over a three-mile territorial sea. In 1988 the United States extended its territorial sea to 12 miles, a step consistent with Article 3 of the 1982 Convention on the Law of the Sea. See John E. Noyes, "United States of America Presidential Proclamation No. 5298: A 12-Mile U.S. Territorial Sea," 4 *International Journal of Estuarine and Coastal Law* 142 (1989).

President Roosevelt reacted favorably to Ickes's suggestion regarding the continental shelf in a memorandum to Secretary of State Cordell Hull:

> I think Harold Ickes has the right slant on this. For many years I have felt that the old three-mile limit * * * should be superseded by a rule of common sense. For instance, the Gulf of Mexico is bounded on the south by Mexico and on the north by the United States. In parts of the Gulf, shallow water extends very many miles offshore. It seems to me that the Mexican Government should be entitled to drill for oil in the southern half of the Gulf and we in the northern half of the Gulf. That would be far more sensible than allowing some European nation, for example, to come in there and drill.

[1945] 2 *Foreign Relations of the United States* 1482. The State Department's Office of Economic Affairs, reviewing Ickes's proposal and another proposal to establish U.S. fisheries conservation zones, argued that the proposals constituted "so significant a departure from past practices under the law of nations" that they "could, if proper precautions were not taken, lead to misunderstanding, suspicion, and opposition on the part of many other countries." *Id.* at 1485–86. The Office argued for international consultation with, and the "concurrence" of, various states. One or both of the U.S. proposals were in fact informally communicated to Canada, Cuba, Denmark, France, Iceland, Mexico, the Netherlands, Norway, Portugal, the Soviet Union, and the United Kingdom. See *id.* at 1510. Some states suggested negotiating international agreements concerning resources outside the territorial sea, but the United States proceeded unilaterally. Was this appropriate?

2. *Latin American Coastal Zones.* Following the Truman Proclamation, Mexico issued a proclamation claiming sovereign rights over its adjacent continental shelf and the superjacent resources. Several other Latin American countries, including Argentina, Chile, Costa Rica, El Salvador, and Peru, soon claimed such rights up to 200 miles from their coasts. Although other states cited U.S. action as precedent for their assertions of authority over broad coastal zones, each responded to its own set of national goals. Chile, for example, was particularly concerned to protect its new offshore

whaling industry when it issued its proclamation, and Peru sought primarily to reserve rich offshore fisheries for its own citizens. See Ann Hollick, "The Origins of 200-Mile Offshore Zones," 71 *American Journal of International Law* 994 (1977). The states making these various claims typically disavowed any intention of interfering with freedom of navigation. After the Truman Proclamation, could the United States persuasively object to assertions by other coastal states of extensive authority over coastal zones?

3. *Evolution of the Legal Concept of the Continental Shelf.* The several unilateral proclamations contributed to a process by which the regime of the continental shelf ultimately gained acceptance in international law. In Petroleum Dev't Ltd. v. Abu Dhabi, 18 *International Law Reports* 144, 155 (1951), the arbitrator concluded "that in no form can the doctrine [of the continental shelf] claim as yet to have assumed * * * the hard lineaments or the definitive status of an established rule of International Law." Also in 1951, however, the International Law Commission adopted draft articles on the continental shelf, and the ILC's work contributed significantly to the 1958 Geneva Convention on the Continental Shelf, Apr. 29, 1958, 15 U.S.T. 471, 499 U.N.T.S. 311. The International Court of Justice addressed the contribution of the 1958 Convention to the crystallization of customary international law in the 1969 *North Sea Continental Shelf Cases*, which appear at the end of Chapter 3. The ICJ's decisions also emphasized that the continental shelf was to be considered the "natural prolongation" of the land territory of a state.

4. *The Continental Shelf and the 1982 Law of the Sea Convention*. The continental shelf was one of many issues addressed during the Third United Nations Conference on the Law of the Sea, which led to the 1982 Convention on the Law of the Sea. One matter in controversy was the definition of the continental shelf. Article 1 of the 1958 Convention on the Continental Shelf defined the continental shelf as the seabed and subsoil "adjacent to the coast" but beyond the territorial sea, extending "to a depth of 200 metres or, beyond that limit, to where the depth of the superjacent waters admits of the exploitation of the natural resources" of the seabed or subsoil. What ambiguities does that definition embody?

Article 76 of the 1982 Convention on the Law of the Sea provides a more certain definition. According to Article 76, each coastal state is entitled to a continental shelf, beyond its territorial sea, of at least 200 miles from its baselines. A state with a physically broader shelf must, in setting the legal limits of the shelf beyond 200 miles, apply detailed scientific criteria set out in Article 76. Article 76(8) requires a state seeking to establish an outer limit beyond 200 miles to submit supporting data to the Commission on the Limits of the Continental Shelf (CLCS), a technical body created by the 1982 Convention. If the coastal state sets the outer limit of its continental shelf "on the basis of" recommendations of the CLCS, Article 76(8) provides that the outer limit is "final and binding." In no case may the outer limit of the continental shelf extend beyond the further seaward of (a) 350 miles from the baseline, or (b) 100 miles beyond the point at which the ocean depth reaches 2,500 meters. For a detailed analysis of Article 76, see Committee on the Legal Issues of the Outer Continental Shelf, "Second Report," in International Law Association, *Report of the Seventy-Second Conference (Toronto)* 215 (2006).

In addition to debating the outer limit of the continental shelf, the delegates to UNCLOS III also addressed the legal status of the shelf. According to Articles 77 and 78 of the 1982 Convention, what is the balance struck between coastal state rights and the rights of other states with regard to the continental shelf and activities on and above it?

5. *Baselines.* The lines from which the breadth of a state's coastal zones are measured are known as "baselines." In general, the baseline follows the low-water line along the coast. See Convention on the Law of the Sea, art. 5; Committee on Baselines Under the International Law of the Sea, "Committee Report," in International Law Association, *Report of the Seventy-Fifth Conference (Sofia)* 385 (2012).

Some states have proclaimed lengthy straight baselines rather than baselines that closely follow the low-water marks of the coastline. In 1951 the International Court of Justice approved Norway's decision to draw a straight baseline along a fringe of islands and rocks, known as a skjærgaard, that generally follows the direction of the coast. "Where a coast is deeply indented and cut into, as is that of Eastern Finnmark," the Court stated, "or where it is bordered by an archipelago such as in the 'skjærgaard'[,] the base line becomes independent of the low-water mark, and can only be determined by means of a geometric construction." Anglo-Norwegian Fisheries Case, 1951 I.C.J. 116, 128–29. The Court also suggested that important economic interests in a region, "clearly evidenced by a long usage," were a relevant consideration supporting straight baselines, in addition to the geographical criteria. *Id.* at 133. Article 7 of the 1982 Convention on the Law of the Sea, reflecting factors articulated in the *Anglo-Norwegian Fisheries Case*, describes conditions under which a state may draw straight baselines.

More than 75 states have drawn straight baselines along all or part of their coasts since 1951. Some of these baselines are many miles distant from the coast. See J. Ashley Roach & Robert W. Smith, *Excessive Maritime Claims* § 4.6 (3d ed. 2012). What are the implications of the practice of drawing straight baselines? What mechanisms are available to challenge assertions of straight baselines?

6. *Maritime Boundary Delimitations.* Since many law of the sea issues turn on the allocation of rights and responsibilities in coastal zones, it is

important to determine the maritime boundaries between adjacent and opposite states. The expansion of coastal zones has precipitated many new maritime boundary delimitation disputes. These are often settled by negotiation, conciliation, or adjudication. Recall the *North Sea Continental Shelf Cases* in Chapter 3. See the multi-volume *International Maritime Boundaries* (Jonathan I. Charney *et al.* eds. 1993–2005). Territorial sovereignty disputes may complicate the determination of maritime boundaries. Recall the *Minquiers and Echrehos Case* in Chapter 5.

7. *U.S. Fisheries Zones*. A companion to President Truman's continental shelf proclamation was Proclamation No. 2,668, Policy of the United States with Respect to Coastal Fisheries in Certain Areas of the High Seas, Sept. 28, 1945, 3 C.F.R. 68 (1943–1948 Compilation). The fisheries proclamation asserted sole U.S. authority to conserve and manage fisheries in areas contiguous to U.S. coasts where U.S. nationals historically had fished exclusively, and called for joint regulatory agreements in areas where both U.S. and foreign nationals fished. The United States, however, never established conservation zones under this proclamation, and foreign states were not eager to enter agreements that would limit their fishing practices. The Exclusive Fisheries Zone Act of 1966, 16 U.S.C. §§ 1091–1094, established a 12-mile exclusive U.S. fisheries zone. That statute was repealed by the 1976 Fishery Conservation and Management Act, 16 U.S.C. §§ 1801–1882, which established a 200-mile fisheries conservation zone. The American Fisheries Promotion Act of 1980, 16 U.S.C. § 1821(e), phased out foreign fishing in this 200-mile zone. The following case excerpt and its Notes examine the expansion of coastal fishing zones in international law.

THE FISHERIES JURISDICTION CASE

United Kingdom v. Iceland, 1974 I.C.J. 3 (Merits)

[In 1948, Iceland's Parliament passed a law authorizing the Ministry of Fisheries to set "conservation zones within the limits of the continental shelf of Iceland; wherein all fisheries shall be subject to Icelandic rules and control." In 1952, Iceland established a fisheries zone extending four miles from straight baselines and prohibited foreign fishing within the zone. In 1958, Iceland proclaimed a 12-mile fisheries zone, again prohibiting foreign fishing within the new limit. British efforts to continue fishing in the 12-mile zone led to "incidents on the fishing grounds." In a 1961 exchange of notes, the United Kingdom acknowledged Iceland's dependence on coastal fisheries for its livelihood and economic development and agreed not to object to the 12-mile zone. Iceland, for its part, agreed to give the United Kingdom six months' notice of any further extension of Icelandic fisheries jurisdiction and agreed to refer any dispute over such an extension to the International Court of Justice.

When Iceland extended its fisheries jurisdiction to 50 miles in 1972, the United Kingdom brought a claim to the Court. Iceland refused to appear before the Court.]

11. In the course of the written proceedings, the following submissions were presented on behalf of the Government of the United Kingdom: * * *

> The United Kingdom asks the Court to adjudge and declare:
>
> (*a*) That there is no foundation in international law for the claim by Iceland to be entitled to extend its fisheries jurisdiction by establishing a zone of exclusive fisheries jurisdiction extending to 50 nautical miles from the baselines[;] and that its claim is therefore invalid; and
>
> (*b*) that questions concerning the conservation of fish stocks in the waters around Iceland are not susceptible in international law to regulation by the unilateral extension by Iceland of its exclusive fisheries jurisdiction to 50 nautical miles from the aforesaid baselines but are matters that may be regulated, as between Iceland and the United Kingdom, by arrangements agreed between those two countries[.]

50. The Geneva Convention on the High Seas of 1958, which was adopted "as generally declaratory of established principles of international law," defines in Article 1 the term "high seas" as "all parts of the sea that are not included in the territorial sea or in the internal waters of a State." Article 2 then declares that "The high seas being open to all nations, no State may validly purport to subject any part of them to its sovereignty" and goes on to provide that the freedom of the high seas comprises, *inter alia*, both for coastal and non-coastal States, freedom of navigation and freedom of fishing. The freedoms of the high seas are however made subject to the consideration that they "shall be exercised by all States with reasonable regard to the interests of other States in their exercise of the freedom of the high seas."

51. * * * At the 1958 Conference, the main differences on the breadth of the territorial sea were limited at the time to disagreements as to what limit, not exceeding 12 miles, was the appropriate one. The question of the breadth of the territorial sea and that of the extent of the coastal State's fishery jurisdiction were left unsettled at the 1958 conference. These questions were referred to the Second Conference on the Law of the Sea, held in 1960. Furthermore, the question of the extent of the fisheries jurisdiction of the coastal State, which had constituted a serious obstacle to the reaching of an agreement at the 1958 Conference, became gradually separated from the notion of the territorial sea. This was a

development which reflected the increasing importance of fishery resources for all States.

52. The 1960 Conference failed by one vote to adopt a text governing the two questions of the breadth of the territorial sea and the extent of fishery rights. However, after that Conference the law evolved through the practice of States on the basis of the debates and near-agreements at the Conference. Two concepts have crystallized as customary law in recent years arising out of the general consensus revealed at that Conference. The first is the concept of the fishery zone, the area in which a State may claim exclusive fishery jurisdiction independently of its territorial sea; the extension of that fishery zone up to a 12-mile limit from the baselines appears now to be generally accepted. The second is the concept of preferential rights of fishing in adjacent waters in favour of the coastal State in a situation of special dependence on its coastal fisheries, this preference operating in regard to other States concerned in the exploitation of the same fisheries, and to be implemented in the way indicated in paragraph 57 below.

53. In recent years the question of extending the coastal State's fisheries jurisdiction has come increasingly to the forefront. The Court is aware that a number of States has asserted an extension of fishery limits. The Court is also aware of present endeavours, pursued under the auspices of the United Nations, to achieve in a third Conference on the Law of the Sea the further codification and progressive development of this branch of the law, as it is of various proposals and preparatory documents produced in this framework, which must be regarded as manifestations of the views and opinions of individual States and as vehicles of their aspirations, rather than as expressing principles of existing law. The very fact of convening the third Conference on the Law of the Sea evidences a manifest desire on the part of all States to proceed to the codification of that law on a universal basis, including the question of fisheries and conservation of the living resources of the sea. * * * In the circumstances, the Court, as a court of law, cannot render judgment *sub specie legis ferendae*, or anticipate the law before the legislator has laid it down.

54. The concept of a 12-mile fishery zone * * * has been accepted with regard to Iceland in the substantive provisions of the 1961 Exchange of Notes, and the United Kingdom has also applied the same fishery limit to its own coastal waters since 1964; therefore this matter is no longer in dispute between the Parties. At the same time, * * * the Applicant has expressly recognized Iceland's preferential rights in the disputed waters and at the same time has invoked its own historic fishing rights in these same waters, on the ground that reasonable regard must be had to such traditional rights by the coastal State, in accordance with the generally

recognized principles embodied in Article 2 of the High Seas Convention. * * *

57. * * * The contemporary practice of States leads to the conclusion that the preferential rights of the coastal State in a special situation are to be implemented by agreement between the States concerned, either bilateral or multilateral, and, in case of disagreement, through the means for the peaceful settlement of disputes provided for in Article 33 of the Charter of the United Nations. * * *

58. State practice on the subject of fisheries reveals an increasing and widespread acceptance of the concept of preferential rights for coastal States, particularly in favour of countries or territories in a situation of special dependence on coastal fisheries. Both [a resolution at the 1958 conference] and [a] 1960 joint amendment concerning preferential rights were approved by a large majority of the Conferences, thus showing overwhelming support for the idea that in certain special situations it was fair to recognize that the coastal State had preferential fishing rights. After these Conferences, the preferential rights of the coastal State were recognized in various bilateral and multilateral international agreements. * * *

59. There can be no doubt of the exceptional dependence of Iceland on its fisheries. That exceptional dependence was explicitly recognized by the Applicant in the Exchange of Notes of 11 March 1961, and the Court has also taken judicial notice of such recognition[.]

60. The preferential rights of the coastal State come into play only at the moment when an intensification in the exploitation of fishery resources makes it imperative to introduce some system of catch-limitation and sharing of those resources, to preserve the fish stocks in the interests of their rational and economic exploitation. This situation appears to have been reached in the present case. * * *

61. The Icelandic regulations challenged before the Court have been issued and applied by the Icelandic authorities as a claim to exclusive rights thus going beyond the concept of preferential rights. Article 2 of the Icelandic Regulations of 14 July 1972 states:

> Within the fishery limits all fishing activities by foreign vessels shall be prohibited in accordance with the provisions of Law No. 33 of 19 June 1922, concerning Fishing inside the Fishery Limits.

Article 1 of the 1922 Law provides: "Only Icelandic citizens may engage in fishing in the territorial waters of Iceland, and only Icelandic boats or ships may be used for such fishing." * * *

62. The concept of preferential rights is not compatible with the exclusion of all fishing activities of other States. A coastal State entitled

to preferential rights is not free, unilaterally and according to its own uncontrolled discretion, to determine the extent of those rights. The characterization of the coastal State's rights as preferential implies a certain priority, but cannot imply the extinction of the concurrent rights of other States, and particularly of a State which, like the Applicant, has for many years been engaged in fishing in the waters in question, such fishing activity being important to the economy of the country concerned. * * *

63. In this case, the Applicant has pointed out that its vessels have been fishing in Icelandic waters for centuries and that they have done so in a manner comparable with their present activities for upwards of 50 years. Published statistics indicate that from 1920 onwards, fishing of demersal species by United Kingdom vessels in the disputed area has taken place on a continuous basis from year to year, and that, except for the period of the Second World War, the total catch of those vessels has been remarkably steady. Similar statistics indicate that the waters in question constitute the most important of the Applicant's distant-water fishing grounds for demersal species.

64. The Applicant further states that in view of the present situation of fisheries in the North Atlantic, which has demanded the establishment of agreed catch-limitations of cod and haddock in various areas, it would not be possible for the fishing effort of United Kingdom vessels displaced from the Icelandic area to be diverted at economic levels to other fishing grounds in the North Atlantic. Given the lack of alternative fishing opportunity, it is further contended, the exclusion of British fishing vessels from the Icelandic area would have very serious adverse consequences, with immediate results for the affected vessels and with damage extending over a wide range of supporting and related industries. It is pointed out in particular that wide-spread unemployment would be caused among all sections of the British fishing industry and in ancillary industries and that certain ports—Hull, Grimsby and Fleetwood—specially reliant on fishing in the Icelandic area, would be seriously affected. * * *

67. The provisions of the Icelandic Regulations of 14 July 1972 and the manner of their implementation disregard the fishing rights of the Applicant. Iceland's unilateral action thus constitutes an infringement of the principle enshrined in Article 2 of the 1958 Geneva Convention on the High Seas which requires that all States, including coastal States, in exercising their freedom of fishing, pay reasonable regard to the interests of other States. It also disregards the rights of the Applicant as they result from the Exchange of Notes of 1961. The Applicant is therefore justified in asking the Court to give all necessary protection to its own rights, while at the same time agreeing to recognize Iceland's preferential position. Accordingly, the Court is bound to conclude that the Icelandic

Regulations of 14 July 1972 establishing a zone of exclusive fisheries jurisdiction extending to 50 nautical miles from baselines around the coast of Iceland, are not opposable to the United Kingdom, and the latter is under no obligation to accept the unilateral termination by Iceland of United Kingdom fishery rights in the area. * * *

71. * * * Due recognition must be given to the rights of both Parties, namely the rights of the United Kingdom to fish in the waters in dispute, and the preferential rights of Iceland. Neither right is an absolute one: the preferential rights of a coastal State are limited according to the extent of its special dependence on the fisheries and by its obligation to take account of the rights of other States and the needs of conservation; the established rights of other fishing States are in turn limited by reason of the coastal State's special dependence on the fisheries and its own obligation to take account of the rights of other States, including the coastal State, and of the needs of conservation.

72. It follows that even if the court holds that Iceland's extension of its fishery limits is not opposable to the Applicant, this does not mean that the Applicant is under no obligation to Iceland with respect to fishing in the disputed waters in the 12-mile to 50-mile zone. On the contrary, both States have an obligation to take full account of each other's rights and of any fishery conservation measures the necessity of which is shown to exist in those waters. It is one of the advances in maritime international law, resulting from the intensification of fishing, that the former *laissez-faire* treatment of the living resources of the sea in the high seas has been replaced by a recognition of a duty to have due regard to the rights of other States and the needs of conservation for the benefit of all. Consequently, both Parties have the obligation to keep under review the fishery resources in the disputed waters and to examine together, in the light of scientific and other available information, the measures required for the conservation and development, and equitable exploitation, of those resources, taking into account any international agreement in force between them, such as the North-East Atlantic Fisheries Convention of 24 January 1959, as well as such other agreements as may be reached in the matter in the course of further negotiation.

73. The most appropriate method for the solution of the dispute is clearly that of negotiation. Its objectives should be the delimitation of the rights and interests of the Parties, the preferential rights of the coastal State on the one hand and the rights of the Applicant on the other, to balance and regulate equitably questions such as those of catch-limitation, share allocations and "related restrictions concerning areas closed to fishing, number and type of vessels allowed and forms of control of the agreed provisions" (*Fisheries Jurisdiction (United Kingdom v. Iceland), Interim Measures, Order of 12 July 1973, I.C.J. Reports 1973*, p.

303, para. 7). This necessitates detailed scientific knowledge of the fishing grounds. It is obvious that the relevant information and expertise would be mainly in the possession of the Parties. The Court would, for this reason, meet with difficulties if it were itself to attempt to lay down a precise scheme for an equitable adjustment of the rights involved. * * *

78. In the fresh negotiations which are to take place on the basis of the present Judgment, the Parties will have the benefit of the above appraisal of their respective rights, and of certain guidelines defining their scope. The task before them will be to conduct their negotiations on the basis that each must in good faith pay reasonable regard to the legal rights of the other in the waters around Iceland outside the 12-mile limit, thus bringing about an equitable apportionment of the fishing resources based on the facts of the particular situation, and having regard to the interests of other States which have established fishing rights in the area. It is not a matter of finding simply an equitable solution, but an equitable solution derived from the applicable law. * * *

79. For these reasons,

THE COURT,

by ten votes to four,

(1) finds that the Regulations concerning the Fishery Limits off Iceland * * * promulgated by the Government of Iceland on 14 July 1972 and constituting a unilateral extension of the exclusive fishing rights of Iceland to 50 nautical miles from the baselines specified therein are not opposable to the Government of the United Kingdom;

(2) finds that, in consequence, the Government of Iceland is not entitled unilaterally to exclude United Kingdom fishing vessels from areas between the fishery limits agreed to in the Exchange of Notes of 11 March 1961 and the limits specified in the Icelandic Regulations of 14 July 1972, or unilaterally to impose restrictions on the activities of those vessels in such areas;

by ten votes to four,

(3) holds that the Government of Iceland and the Government of the United Kingdom are under mutual obligations to undertake negotiations in good faith for the equitable solution of their differences concerning their respective fishery rights in the areas specified in subparagraph 2;

(4) holds that in these negotiations the Parties are to take into account, *inter alia*:

(*a*) that in the distribution of the fishing resources in the areas specified in subparagraph 2 Iceland is entitled to a preferential share to the extent of the special dependence of its people upon the fisheries in the seas around its coasts for their livelihood and economic development;

(*b*) that by reason of its fishing activities in the areas specified in subparagraph 2, the United Kingdom also has established rights in the fishery resources of the said areas on which elements of its people depend for their livelihood and economic well-being;

(*c*) the obligation to pay due regard to the interests of other States in the conservation and equitable exploitation of these resources;

(*d*) that the above-mentioned rights of Iceland and of the United Kingdom should each be given effect to the extent compatible with the conservation and development of the fishery resources in the areas specified in subparagraph 2 and with the interests of other States in their conservation and equitable exploitation;

(*e*) their obligation to keep under review those resources and to examine together, in the light of scientific and other available information, such measures as may be required for the conservation and development, and equitable exploitation, of those resources, making use of the machinery established by the North-East Atlantic Fisheries Convention or such other means as may be agreed upon as a result of international negotiations.

NOTES AND QUESTIONS

1. *The Cod Wars.* In the "Cod Wars," Iceland boarded British vessels, arrested British fishermen, and cut the nets of British trawlers. The United Kingdom deployed naval frigates to escort and protect British trawlers off Iceland. There were shooting and ramming incidents. Tensions were particularly high during 1958–1961, when Iceland extended its fisheries zone from four to 12 miles, and in 1972–1973, when Iceland declared a 50-mile fisheries zone. Iceland's 1972 decisions to extend its fisheries zone and to denounce its 1961 agreement with Great Britain followed the 1971 Icelandic election; the Agrarian Progressive Party, which had made fisheries jurisdiction a major campaign issue, emerged as the head of a new coalition government.

Rejecting the decision in the *Fisheries Jurisdiction Case*, Iceland extended its fishing limits from 50 to 200 miles in 1975. Regulations Concerning the Fishery Limits off Iceland, July 15, 1975, 14 *International Legal Materials* 1282 (1975). How does this action by Iceland compare to the reception accorded the ICJ decisions we studied in Chapter 5? This extension of Icelandic fishing limits resulted in further clashes involving British and Icelandic naval units. Other states became concerned that the controversy might lead Iceland to withdraw from the North Atlantic Treaty Organization and to shut down a NATO military base in the country that was used to monitor the Soviet Navy. In June 1976, Iceland and the United Kingdom finally reached an agreement allowing limited British fishing within the 200-mile zone. Iceland-United Kingdom: Agreement Concerning British Fishing in Icelandic Waters, June 1, 1976, 15 *International Legal Materials* 878 (1976). Iceland also concluded bilateral fishing agreements with Belgium, the Federal Republic of Germany, and Norway. *Id.* at 1, 43, 875. For discussion of the Cod Wars, see Hannes Jónsson, *Friends in Conflict: The Anglo-Icelandic Cod Wars and the Law of the Sea* (1982), and Andrew Welch, *The Royal Navy in the Cod Wars: Britain and Iceland in Conflict* (2006).

2. *The ICJ's View of Rights to Fisheries.* The ICJ concluded that Iceland had no unilateral right to extend its fisheries zone to 50 miles. Why did the ICJ not simply rule that British vessels had the freedom to fish outside Iceland's 12-mile fisheries zone? Is the Court's reasoning persuasive? How does the Court's invocation of equity compare with its use of equity in the *North Sea Continental Shelf Cases* in Chapter 3? The Court concluded that Iceland and the United Kingdom should negotiate a settlement of their differences over rights to fisheries. Did this procedural recourse suggest that, at base, there was a lack of consensus on the substantive values that would shape any norm of international law on this issue? If the Court wanted to help Britain and Iceland resolve this particular dispute, why did it not elaborate a general rule of law?

3. *Customary International Law and Coastal State Fisheries Jurisdiction.* Judges Forster, Bengzon, Jimenez de Arechaga, Nagendra Singh, and Ruda concurred separately in the *Fisheries Jurisdiction Case.* Although the judges agreed with the result in the majority opinion and found that a 12-mile fisheries zone was generally accepted in international law, they felt that no general rule of customary international law established 12 miles as the obligatory maximum limit. The judges argued that 30 to 35 coastal states had extended their fisheries jurisdiction beyond 12 miles, and noted the general lack of protests to such extensions and the existence of public pronouncements inconsistent with making any protest. The concurring judges also cited declarations and proposals made at the then-ongoing Third United Nations Conference on the Law of the Sea (UNCLOS III). They questioned whether, on "a subject where practice was contradictory and lacks precision," it was "reasonable to discard entirely as irrelevant the evidence of what States are prepared to claim and to acquiesce in, as gathered from the positions taken by them in view of or in preparation for a conference for the codification and progressive development of the law on the subject." 1974 I.C.J. at 48. Finally, the judges lamented the legal uncertainty at the time regarding the maximum limit of coastal state fisheries jurisdiction, and expressed the hope that the matter would be clarified at UNCLOS III.

4. *Multilateral Efforts to Codify the Law of the Sea.* The *Fisheries Jurisdiction* decision noted multilateral efforts prior to UNCLOS III to codify the international law of the sea. The excerpt above refers specifically to two of the five 1958 treaties concluded at the First United Nations Conference on the Law of the Sea: the Convention on the High Seas, Apr. 29, 1958, 13 U.S.T. 2312, 450 U.N.T.S. 82, and the Convention on the Territorial Sea and the Contiguous Zone, Apr. 29, 1958, 15 U.S.T. 1606, 516 U.N.T.S. 205. The other three are: the Convention on the Continental Shelf, Apr. 29, 1958, 15

U.S.T. 471, 499 U.N.T.S. 311; the Convention on Fishing and Conservation of the Living Resources of the High Seas, Apr. 29, 1958, 17 U.S.T. 138, 559 U.N.T.S. 285, and the Optional Protocol of Signature concerning the Compulsory Settlement of Disputes, Apr. 29, 1958, 459 U.N.T.S. 169. The United Kingdom, but not Iceland, was party to those five treaties.

NOTE: UNCLOS III NEGOTIATIONS CONCERNING THE EXCLUSIVE ECONOMIC ZONE

At the 1974 Caracas session of UNCLOS III, delegates from over 100 states favored a 200-mile coastal state exclusive economic zone (EEZ). That is not to say that all issues relating to the EEZ were resolved early in the Conference. Negotiating many of these issues—the legal status of the EEZ, the applicability of the EEZ to archipelagic states and small islands, the relationship between the EEZ and the continental shelf, boundary delimitation, dispute settlement, and coastal state responsibilities concerning fish in their EEZs—took years. Compare the complex negotiations of the 1982 Convention on the Law of the Sea to the relatively simpler bilateral treaty negotiations we examined in Chapter 2, Part B.

The 1974 debates revealed considerable variety in the positions of states. Just a few examples: Honduras's delegate claimed "inherent rights" over resources in its adjacent zones, and argued that foreign states had no competence there absent agreement with the coastal state. UNCLOS III, 2nd Sess., 2nd Comm., 22nd Mtg., July 31, 1974, in 2 UNCLOS III Official Records 171 (U.N. Sales No. E.75.V.4, 1975). Kenya and Ecuador, along with many developing countries, favored complete coastal state sovereignty in the EEZ; their delegates advocated 200-mile territorial seas. Somalia's delegate thought that the traditional law of the sea favored the major maritime powers, and that developing coastal states should not "sign away their territorial sovereignty in exchange for lesser rights." Id. at 210 (26th Mtg., Aug. 5, 1974).

Island states and archipelagic states had particular interests in fisheries. New Zealand's delegate criticized a suggestion that the economic zone of islands should be restricted. Archipelagic states also strongly supported the concept of an EEZ, but did not necessarily favor complete coastal state "sovereignty" over the EEZ.

For other countries, the EEZ concept represented a significant concession. Mr. Ogiso, Japan's delegate, argued that "[f]reedom of access to fishery resources, if it was retained only beyond 200 miles, would become practically meaningless." *Id.* at 217 (28th Mtg., Aug. 6, 1974). He urged respect for traditional distant water fishing states whose economies depended on fishing.

Maritime powers, including states in the Soviet bloc, also stressed the importance of coastal states not exercising rights in their EEZs that would interfere with navigational freedoms. The concern was that extensive coastal state EEZ rights or 200-mile territorial seas might well allow coastal states to disrupt navigation by exercising control over pollution, scientific research, or customs, fiscal, immigration, and health matters. The delegate of the Ukrainian Soviet Socialist Republic worried that "[u]nder the pretext of exercising such controls, a coastal State might at any time detain a foreign vessel and reduce to nothing the freedom of navigation in the zone." Id. at 201 (25th Mtg., Aug. 5, 1974).

Land-locked and geographically disadvantaged states also voiced concerns. Upper Volta (now Burkina Faso) argued for assured access to the sea by land-locked countries and for their right to participate in the exploitation of EEZ resources. Mr. Ballah, the delegate from the Caribbean nation of Trinidad and Tobago, said his country "conditioned its acceptance of the concept of the 200-mile exclusive economic zone on recognition by the Conference of preferential or equal rights for every State within a region or subregion to the living resources of the economic zones of the other States of the region." *Id.* at 179 (22nd Mtg., July 31, 1974). Turkey noted that, although it was surrounded on three sides by seas, those seas were semi-enclosed and not well stocked with fish. The delegate of the Federal Republic of Germany stressed dual needs—the effective conservation of fisheries and the equitable allocation of those resources—and found "no justification for the reallocation of available resources for the benefit of a limited number of geographically advantaged States." *Id.* at 192 (24th Mtg., Aug. 1, 1974). Germany was one of several countries stressing the importance of an obligatory dispute settlement mechanism to review the actions of coastal states.

UNITED NATIONS CONVENTION ON THE LAW OF THE SEA, ARTICLES 55–59, 121

Dec. 10, 1982, Senate Treaty Doc. No. 103–39 (1994), 1833 U.N.T.S. 3

Exclusive Economic Zone

Article 55

Specific legal regime of the exclusive economic zone

The exclusive economic zone is an area beyond and adjacent to the territorial sea, subject to the specific legal regime established in this Part, under which the rights and jurisdiction of the coastal State and the rights and freedoms of other States are governed by the relevant provisions of this Convention.

Article 56

Rights, jurisdiction and duties of the coastal State in the exclusive economic zone

1. In the exclusive economic zone, the coastal State has:

(a) sovereign rights for the purpose of exploring and exploiting, conserving and managing the natural resources, whether living or non-living, of the waters superjacent to the seabed and of the seabed and its subsoil, and with regard to other activities for the economic exploitation and exploration of the zone, such as the production of energy from the water, currents and winds;

(b) jurisdiction as provided for in the relevant provisions of this Convention with regard to:

(i) the establishment and use of artificial islands, installations and structures;

(ii) marine scientific research;

(iii) the protection and preservation of the marine environment;

(c) other rights and duties provided for in this Convention.

2. In exercising its rights and performing its duties under this Convention in the exclusive economic zone, the coastal State shall have due regard to the rights and duties of other States and shall act in a manner compatible with the provisions of this Convention.

3. The rights set out in this article with respect to the seabed and subsoil shall be exercised in accordance with Part VI [concerning the continental shelf].

Article 57

Breadth of the exclusive economic zone

The exclusive economic zone shall not extend beyond 200 nautical miles from the baselines from which the breadth of the territorial sea is measured.

Article 58

Rights and duties of other States in the exclusive economic zone

1. In the exclusive economic zone, all States, whether coastal or land-locked, enjoy, subject to the relevant provisions of this Convention, the freedoms referred to in article 87 of navigation and overflight and of the laying of submarine cables and pipelines, and other internationally lawful uses of the sea related to these freedoms, such as those associated

with the operation of ships, aircraft and submarine cables and pipelines, and compatible with the other provisions of this Convention.

2. Articles 88 to 115 and other pertinent rules of international law apply to the exclusive economic zone in so far as they are not incompatible with this Part.

3. In exercising their rights and performing their duties under this Convention in the exclusive economic zone, States shall have due regard to the rights and duties of the coastal State and shall comply with the laws and regulations adopted by the coastal State in accordance with the provisions of this Convention and other rules of international law in so far as they are not incompatible with this Part.

Article 59

Basis for the resolution of conflicts regarding the attribution of rights and jurisdiction in the exclusive economic zone

In cases where this Convention does not attribute rights or jurisdiction to the coastal State or to other States within the exclusive economic zone, and a conflict arises between the interests of the coastal State and any other State or States, the conflict should be resolved on the basis of equity and in the light of all the relevant circumstances, taking into account the respective importance of the interests involved to the parties as well as to the international community as a whole.

* * *

Article 121

Regime of islands

1. An island is a naturally formed area of land, surrounded by water, which is above water at high tide.

2. Except as provided for in paragraph 3, the territorial sea, the contiguous zone, the exclusive economic zone and the continental shelf of an island are determined in accordance with the provisions of this Convention applicable to other land territory.

3. Rocks which cannot sustain human habitation or economic life of their own shall have no exclusive economic zone or continental shelf.

NOTES AND QUESTIONS

1. *Acceptance of the EEZ as Customary International Law.* In March 1983 President Reagan proclaimed a 200-mile exclusive economic zone for the United States, asserting that "international law recognizes that * * * a coastal State may assert certain sovereign rights over natural resources and related jurisdiction" in such a zone. Presidential Proclamation No. 5,030, Mar. 10, 1983, 22 *International Legal Materials* 465 (1983). In 1985 the International Court of Justice found it "incontestable that * * * the

institution of the exclusive economic zone * * * is shown by the practice of states to have become part of customary law." Continental Shelf (Libya v. Malta) Case, 1985 I.C.J. 13, 33. As of October 1993, according to paragraph 16 of the U.N. Secretary-General's 1993 annual *Report* on the law of the sea, 91 states had claimed a 200-mile EEZ (or one up to a median line with opposite states), and an additional 15 states had claimed a 200-mile fisheries zone; eleven states still claimed a 200-mile territorial sea. Had the 1982 Convention's EEZ regime gained general acceptance as customary international law even before the Convention entered into force in November 1994? What additional information, if any, might be needed to answer the question?

2. *Beneficiaries of the EEZ.* Which states benefit most from the concept of the EEZ? Some states that have long coastlines, are located far from other states, or possess distant territories or dependencies may claim huge exclusive economic zones. The United States has the largest area, approximately 3,000,000 square miles. France's EEZ is next with approximately 2,000,000 square miles. Several relatively small states, including Japan, Kiribati, New Zealand, and Papua New Guinea, have extensive EEZs. Indonesia, with its many islands, has an EEZ measuring approximately 1,500,000 square miles. Note the significance, under Article 121 of the Law of the Sea Convention, whether a piece of land surrounded by water is an "island" or a "rock" that "cannot sustain human habitation or economic life of [its] own."

It is not merely the size of an EEZ that is important. According to Article 56(a), reproduced above, coastal states have sovereign rights over the living resources of the EEZ, but EEZs differ significantly in terms of the amount of fish they support. Among the states noted in the preceding paragraph, the United States and Indonesia topped the list in 2007, with, respectively, an estimated 4,800,000 and 4,900,000 metric tons of fish caught in their EEZs. France's EEZ catch lagged far behind at 500,000 metric tons. See Louis B. Sohn, Kristen Juras, John E. Noyes & Erik Franckx, *Law of the Sea in a Nutshell* 248 (2d ed. 2010).

3. *Conflicting Interests in the EEZ.* How does the Law of the Sea Convention resolve the Grotius/Selden *mare liberum/mare clausum* debate with regard to the EEZ? Is the EEZ still a part of the high seas?

Access to and control over coastal fisheries was an issue of tremendous importance in the debate over the EEZ. Does the 1982 Convention adhere to the same conception of rights concerning fisheries that the ICJ articulated in the *Fisheries Jurisdiction Case*? Article 56 of the Convention provides generally that the coastal state has "sovereign rights" over EEZ natural resources, while Articles 61 (on conservation) and 62 (on utilization) contain more details about the EEZ fisheries regime. In general, Article 61 requires the coastal state to "ensure through proper conservation and management measures that the maintenance of [EEZ fisheries] is not endangered by over-exploitation," and Article 62 requires the coastal state to "promote the objective of optimum utilization of" EEZ fisheries. In their particulars, however, the two Articles give the coastal state great discretion. According to Article 61, the coastal state "shall determine the allowable catch of the living resources" in its EEZ and shall adopt conservation and management measures designed to "produce the maximum sustainable yield, as qualified by relevant environmental and economic factors, including the economic needs of coastal fishing communities and the special requirements of developing states[.]" Under Article 62, the coastal state determines its capacity to harvest the living resources in the EEZ, and where it lacks "the capacity to harvest the entire allowable catch, it shall, through agreements * * * and pursuant to the terms, conditions, laws and regulations referred to in paragraph 4, give other States access to the surplus of the allowable catch." The Article 62(4) laws and regulations "may relate, *inter alia*," to licensing, fees, fishing areas and seasons, catch quotas, gear, fish species, vessel reports, transfer of fisheries technology, catch landing requirements, and enforcement procedures. For discussion of Articles 61 and 62, see William T. Burke, *The New International Law of Fisheries* 26–81 (1994).

Do the interests and values associated with EEZ fisheries solely concern coastal states and distant water fishing states? Has giving coastal states "sovereign rights" with respect to EEZ fisheries effectively promoted conservation and management of the 90 percent of fish stocks found in EEZs? According to Professor Christie,

> The premise that coastal state jurisdiction over marine living resources to 200 miles offshore would prevent the overexploitation of marine fisheries has proved to be flawed. Scientific information and management methodologies continue to be inadequate; entry into domestic fisheries has largely not been controlled; enforcement and reporting remain questionable; and the EEZ as a management area has not been an adequate zone for ecosystem management[.] Simply changing jurisdictional zones did not substantially benefit the resources.

Donna R. Christie, "It Don't Come EEZ: The Failure and Future of Coastal State Fisheries Management," 14 *Journal of Transnational Law and Policy* 1, 34 (2004). See also Harry N. Scheiber, "Ocean Governance and the Marine Fisheries Crisis: Two Decades of Innovation—and Frustration," 20 *Virginia Environmental Law Journal* 119 (2001). How might international law more effectively promote EEZ fisheries conservation and management?

Were the United States and each country named in the above "Note: UNCLOS III Negotiations Concerning the Exclusive Economic Zone" pleased with Articles 55–59 and 61–62 of the 1982 Convention on the Law of the Sea? If a state was not satisfied with the Convention's EEZ provisions, why might it still accept the Convention? Different parts of the Convention address protection of the marine environment, marine scientific research, and a wide range of other oceans topics. U.S. complaints about the Convention focused on its deep seabed mining provisions, explored in Part E of this chapter.

4. *Obligatory Third-party Dispute Resolution.* Many categories of disputes are subject to the Law of the Sea Convention's provisions for obligatory third-party arbitration or adjudication. Excluded from such provisions, however, are disputes relating to a coastal state's "sovereign rights with respect to the living resources in the exclusive economic zone or their exercise, including its discretionary powers for determining allowable catch, its harvesting capacity, the allocation of surpluses to other States and the terms and conditions established in its conservation and management laws and regulations." Convention on the Law of the Sea, art. 297(3). What are the implications of this exclusion for the balance of rights and obligations set out in Part V of the Convention, which concerns the EEZ?

5. *Comparing the EEZ and the Continental Shelf.* Article 56 of the 1982 Convention, which is contained in Part V on the EEZ, refers to sovereign rights of coastal states to explore, exploit, conserve, and manage non-living, as well as living, natural resources. Why, then, does the Convention include a separate Part VI on the continental shelf?

6. *Comparing the EEZ and the Contiguous Zone.* The 1958 Convention on the Territorial Sea and the Contiguous Zone provides that states may assert a zone contiguous to the territorial sea. This contiguous zone may extend 12 miles from the baseline; Article 33 of the 1982 Convention increases the limit to 24 miles. Within this zone, according to Article 33, a coastal state "may exercise the control necessary to (a) prevent infringement of its customs, fiscal, immigration or sanitary laws and regulations within its territory or territorial sea; (b) punish infringement of the above laws and regulations committed within its territory or territorial sea." Does the EEZ render the concept of the contiguous zone superfluous?

In the *Saiga Case* excerpted above, Guinea attempted to justify its arrest of a foreign-flag vessel outside a 24-mile zone. Guinea argued that the vessel's actions in Guinea's EEZ—supplying fuel oil to fishing vessels ("bunkering")—circumvented Guinean customs laws, and that arrest of the vessel was consistent with Article 58(3) of the Law of the Sea Convention. The International Tribunal for the Law of the Sea rejected Guinea's assertion:

> 130. The main public interest which Guinea claims to be protecting by applying its customs laws to the exclusive economic zone is said to be the "considerable fiscal losses a developing country like Guinea is suffering from illegal off-shore bunkering in its exclusive economic zone." * * * In effect, Guinea's contention is that the customary international law principle of "public interest" gives it the power to impede "economic activities that are undertaken [in its EEZ] under the guise of navigation but are different from communication."
>
> 131. According to article 58, paragraph 3, of the Convention, the "other rules of international law" which a coastal State is entitled to apply in the exclusive economic zone are those which are

> not incompatible with Part V of the Convention. In the view of the Tribunal, recourse to the principle of "public interest," as invoked by Guinea, would entitle a coastal State to prohibit any activities in the exclusive economic zone which it decides to characterize as activities which affect its economic "public interest" or entail "fiscal losses" for it. This would curtail the rights of other States in the exclusive economic zone. The Tribunal is satisfied that this would be incompatible with the provisions of articles 56 and 58 of the Convention regarding the rights of the coastal State in the exclusive economic zone.

http://www.itlos.org (last visited Dec. 8, 2013), 38 *International Legal Materials* at 1351. An arrest of a foreign flag vessel in the EEZ for customs violations may, however, be valid under international law if the arrest follows "hot pursuit" from the territorial sea or the contiguous zone. See Article 111 of the Convention on the Law of the Sea.

NOTE: THE CONSERVATION AND MANAGEMENT OF HIGH SEAS FISHERIES

As 200-mile EEZs gained acceptance, distant water fishing vessels that previously fished up to the limit of a narrow foreign territorial sea faced new problems. They were sometimes precluded altogether from fishing in a coastal state's EEZ, or could fish there only by paying a license fee and subjecting themselves to coastal state restrictions affecting, *e.g.*, catch limits, allowable fishing gear, and fishing seasons. Even though the vast majority of fish stocks are found in EEZs, some distant water fleets chose to concentrate their fishing activities outside the EEZs, and sometimes just outside. This tactic gave rise to controversies over fish stocks that swim between the EEZ and the high seas. In 1995 Canada, which had regulated fishing for turbot in its EEZ, arrested the *Estai*, a Spanish vessel that was fishing for turbot on a portion of the Grand Banks that extended outside Canada's 200-mile limit. Compare the "Cod Wars" associated with the *Fisheries Jurisdiction Case* above. The *Estai* incident was settled by negotiation, but it illustrated the need for effective conservation and management measures concerning high seas fisheries.

Regional fisheries management organizations have long had regulatory authority over some high seas fisheries. For example, the Northwest Atlantic Fisheries Organization (NAFO), established by the Convention on Future Multilateral Cooperation in the Northwest Atlantic Fisheries, Oct. 24, 1978, Sen. Exec. Doc. T, 96th Cong., 1st Sess., 1135 U.N.T.S. 369, has authority to set catch quotas. Although both Canada and the European Union were parties to NAFO at the time of the seizure of the *Estai*, and NAFO had set quotas for the catch of turbot, the EU had opted out from the quotas—a move that was legal under the Convention.

The 1982 Law of the Sea Convention addresses high seas fisheries only generally, for example requiring states to "cooperate with each other in the conservation and management of living resources in the areas of the high seas." Convention on the Law of the Sea, art. 118. Separate articles apply to fish that range between the EEZ and the high seas, such as straddling stocks, highly migratory species (*e.g.*, tuna), and anadramous species (*e.g.*, salmon), which hatch in a coastal state's rivers, swim out beyond the EEZ, and return to the same rivers to spawn. These articles too are generally worded. Article 63(2) of the 1982 Convention, concerning straddling stocks, simply provides that "the coastal State and the States fishing for such stocks in the [area adjacent to the EEZ] shall seek, either directly or through appropriate subregional or regional organizations, to agree upon the measures necessary for the conservation of these stocks in the adjacent area."

The 1992 Rio Conference on the Environment and Development, noted in our discussion of soft law in Chapter 3, prompted efforts to improve the conservation and management of high seas fisheries. The Food and Agriculture Organization (FAO), a specialized agency associated with the United Nations, developed the Agreement to Promote Compliance with International Conservation and Management Measures by Fishing Vessels on the High Seas, Nov. 24, 1993, Sen. Treaty Doc. No. 103–24, 2221 U.N.T.S. 91, which specifies flag state obligations and created an FAO register for reporting vessels that violated their obligations. The FAO has also adopted several important soft law instruments, including its Code of Conduct for Responsible Fisheries (1995), *available at* http://www.fao.org/docrep/005/v9878e/v9878e00.htm (last visited Dec. 10, 2013), its International Guidelines for the Management of Deep-sea Fisheries in the High Seas, 47 *International Legal Materials* 998 (2008), and its Voluntary Guidelines for Flag State Performance (2013), *available at* ftp://ftp.fao.org/FI/DOCUMENT/tc-fsp/2013/VolGuidelines_adopted.pdf (last visited Dec. 8, 2013). What are the legal significance and efficacy of such soft law instruments?

An innovative treaty is the Agreement for the Implementation of the Provisions of the United Nations Convention on the Law of the Sea of 10 December 1982 relating to the Conservation and Management of Straddling Fish Stocks and Highly Migratory Fish Stocks, Dec. 4, 1995, 2167 U.N.T.S. 88, accepted by the United States and 80 other parties as of December 2013. This Fish Stocks Agreement, in addition to specifying flag state obligations, contains several significant new features. First, it draws on new international environmental principles. The Agreement incorporates a version of the precautionary approach (see the *Responsibilities and Obligations Case* in Part E below) and highlights such goals as ecosystem management, sustainable use, and protection of biodiversity. Second, the Fish Stocks Agreement obliges parties to cooperate in a regional fisheries management organization's conservation measures, even if they are not members of the regional organization. Third, the Agreement goes beyond flag state enforcement, creating some rights for members of a regional fisheries management organization to board and inspect and, in extreme cases, bring to port vessels flying the flag of any state that is a party to the Fish Stocks Agreement. The Agreement also authorizes port states to inspect documents, fishing gear, and catches of foreign fishing vessels voluntarily entering ports. Fourth, the Fish Stocks Agreement incorporates by reference the obligatory dispute settlement provisions of the Law of the Sea Convention.

Despite these efforts, recent reports indicate that high seas fisheries lack an effective management regime, and that illegal, unreported, and unregulated (IUU) fishing on the high seas is threatening the sustainability of many fish stocks. See High Seas Task Force, *Closing the Net: Stopping Illegal Fishing on the High Seas* (2006). What else can and should be done? Does the Fish Stocks Agreement authorize measures against flag of convenience vessels whose flag states are not parties either to the Agreement or a regional fisheries management organization? What steps may legally be taken against such vessels? What else could regional fisheries organizations do, in addition to limiting possibilities for member states to opt out from fishing quotas? Should regional fisheries organizations coordinate their measures, so that fish stocks that swim between the areas of such organizations are subject to a uniform governance regime?

If regulatory treaties and soft law initiatives have not succeeded in curbing illegal fishing, might international litigation engage the responsibility of coastal or fishing states? The *Fisheries Jurisdiction Case* excerpted above provides one example. In the *Southern Bluefin Tuna Cases*, Australia and New Zealand challenged Japan's "experimental fishing" for tuna as illegal under the Convention for the Conservation of Southern Bluefin Tuna, May 10, 1993, 1819 U.N.T.S. 360. Australia and New Zealand obtained provisional relief from the International Tribunal for the Law of the Sea, ITLOS Cases Nos. 3 and 4 (Order on Requests for Provisional Measures, 1999), 38 *International Legal Materials* 1624 (1999), but an arbitral tribunal concluded that it lacked jurisdiction to rule on the merits. Arbitral Tribunal Constituted Under Annex VII of the United Nations Convention on the Law of the Sea (Award on Jurisdiction and Admissibility, 2000), 39 *International Legal Materials* 1359 (2000). Australia has also challenged Japan's whaling in the Southern Ocean in an International Court of Justice case filed in 2010, with hearings held in June and July 2013. Prompted by reports of IUU fishing in West African coastal waters, the Sub-Regional Fisheries Organization has requested an ITLOS advisory opinion, seeking clarification of the rights and duties of flag states, international organizations, and coastal states under international fisheries instruments; as of December 2013, the case is pending. See Request for an Advisory Opinion Submitted by the Sub-

Regional Fisheries Commission (SRFC), ITLOS Case No. 21, http://www.itlos.org (last visited Dec. 10, 2013); Michael A. Becker, "Sustainable Fisheries and the Obligations of Coastal States: The Request by the Sub-Regional Fisheries Commission for an ITLOS Advisory Opinion," 17 *ASIL Insights*, Issue 19 (2013).

How else may states be held responsible for failing to prevent IUU fishing by vessels flying their flags? Are unilateral measures appropriate? The U.S. Magnuson-Stevens Reauthorization Act of 2006, Pub. L. No. 109–479, § 401–408, 120 Stat. 3575 (2007), contained provisions that could lead to such sanctions as denying port access to, or prohibiting imports from, countries whose vessels are engaged in IUU fishing. See 16 U.S.C. §§ 1826h–1826j. Might trade sanctions target IUU fishing? See the *Shrimp-Turtle Case* in Chapter 5.

D. THE TERRITORIAL SEA AND STRAITS

International law today provides that a coastal state has sovereignty over a narrow band of waters adjacent to its coastline, known as the territorial sea. As you read this part, ask what are the relative rights and responsibilities of coastal states and flag states in the territorial sea. We start with a case and a treaty excerpt relating to the exercise of criminal jurisdiction by a coastal state over a person on board a foreign flag vessel in the territorial sea. Subsequent excerpts concern the rights of vessels to innocent passage through the territorial sea and to transit passage through straits, issues that have been particularly sensitive with respect to warships.

REGINA V. KEYN

Great Britain, Court for Crown Cases Reserved,
2 Law Reports (Exchequer Division) 63 (1876)

[The *Franconia*, a German merchant ship, accidentally struck and sunk the *Strathclyde*, a British vessel, less than three miles from the British coast, resulting in the drowning of a woman aboard the *Strathclyde*. Ferdinand Keyn, the German captain of the *Franconia*, was tried for manslaughter in a British criminal court and convicted. The Court for Crown Cases Reserved then addressed the issue of the jurisdiction of British courts over acts by foreign nationals aboard foreign vessels in British coastal waters. The Court's 13 judges voted, 7 to 6, that British courts had no jurisdiction. The majority held that Parliament could grant the courts jurisdiction over acts committed in a marginal belt of the oceans, but concluded that Parliament had not yet done so. The following excerpt contains brief excerpts from two of the lengthy opinions in this case.]

SIR R. PHILLIMORE

[W]ithin [the] term "territory" are certainly comprised the ports and harbours, and the space between the flux and reflux of tide, or the land up to the furthest point at which the tide recedes. But it is at this point that the difficulty presented by the case before us begins, and here the following questions present themselves for solution:

1. Is a state entitled to any extension of dominion beyond low-water mark?

2. If so, how far does this territory, or do these territorial waters, as they are usually called, extend?

3. Has a state the same dominion over these territorial waters as over the territory of her soil and in her ports, or is it of a more limited character and confined to certain purposes?

With respect to the first of these questions the answer may be given without doubt or hesitation, namely, that a state is entitled to a certain extension of territory, in a certain sense of that word, beyond low-water mark.

With respect to the second question, the distance to which the territorial waters extend, it appears on an examination of the authorities that the distance has varied (setting aside even more extravagant claims) from 100 to 3 miles, the present limit. * * *

The third question * * * remains to be substantively considered; it is one of much importance, viz., whether, admitting that the state has a dominion over three miles of adjacent water, it is the same dominion which the possessor has over her land and her ports, or is it of a more limited character—limited to the purpose of protecting the adjacent shore, for which it was granted, and not extending to a general sovereignty over all passing vessels[.]

The consensus of civilised independent states has recognised a maritime extension of frontier to the distance of three miles from low-water mark, because such a frontier or belt of water is necessary for the defence and security of the adjacent state.

It is for the attainment of these particular objects that a dominium has been granted over this portion of the high seas.

This proposition is materially different from the proposition contended for, namely, that it is competent to a state to exercise within these waters the same rights of jurisdiction and property which appertain to it in respect to its lands and its ports. There is one obvious test by which the two sovereignties may be distinguished.

According to modern international law, it is certainly a right incident to each state to refuse a passage to foreigners over its territory by land, whether in time of peace or war. But it does not appear to have the same right with respect to preventing the passage of foreign ships over this portion of the high seas. * * *

The reason of the thing, that is, the defence and security of the state, does not require or warrant the exclusion of peaceable foreign vessels from passing over these waters; and the custom and usage of nations has not sanctioned it.

Consequences fraught with mischief and injustice might flow from the opposite doctrine, which would render applicable to a foreign vessel while in itinere from one foreign port to another, passing over these waters, all the criminal law of the adjacent territory. No single instance has been brought to our notice of the practical exercise by any nation of this jurisdiction.

The authorities cited in order to shew that a foreign vessel is subject to the laws of the foreign port which she enters appear to me inapplicable to the present case.

A foreign merchant vessel going into the port of a foreign state subjects herself to the ordinary law of the place during the period of her commorancy [*i.e.,* stopping] there; she is as much a subditus temporaneus as the individual who visits the interior of the country for the purposes of pleasure or business. * * *

If, indeed, as has been contended, there be no difference between the jurisdiction by the adjacent state over vessels in ports and over passing and commorant vessels, then the whole criminal law of England was applicable to the crew and those on board the German vessel, so long as she was within a marine league of the English shore.

The consequences of such a position of law appear to me, especially in the absence of any precedent, sufficient to render it untenable.

There is yet another argument, already partially adverted to, which appears to me entitled to great weight in an English court of justice.

Upon the subject of the three-miles belt of territorial water, Parliament has frequently legislated. It might perhaps be not impertinently asked, why, if these waters are territorial in the same sense as the land, and those who traverse them are already subject to the law. But, passing by this observation, it will be found on examination of the statutes that the provisions in them are either framed exclusively for British subjects and ships, or that they relate to the protection and peace of the state. * * *

Upon the whole, I am of opinion that the Court had no jurisdiction over this foreigner for an offence committed on board a foreign ship on the high seas, though within three miles of the coast; that he is governed by the law of the state to which his flag belongs; and that the conviction cannot be sustained. * * *

COCKBURN, C.J.

* * * There can be no doubt that the suggestion of Bynkershoek, that the sea surrounding the coast to the extent of cannon-range should be treated as belonging to the state owning the coast, has, with but very few exceptions, been accepted and adopted by the publicists who have followed him during the last two centuries. But it is equally clear that, in the practical application of the rule, in respect of the particular of distance, as also in the still more essential particular of the character and degree of sovereignty and dominion to be exercised, great difference of opinion and uncertainty have prevailed, and still continue to exist. * * *

One set of writers * * * ascribe to the state territorial property and sovereignty over the three miles of sea, to the extent of the right of excluding the ships of all other nations, even for the purpose of passage—a doctrine flowing immediately from the principle of territorial property, but which is too monstrous to be admitted. Another set concede territorial property and sovereignty, but make it subject to the right of other nations to use these waters for the purpose of navigation. Others * * * deny any right of territorial property, but concede "jurisdiction;" by which I understand them to mean the power of applying the law, applicable to persons on the land, to all who are within the territorial water, and the power of legislating in respect of it, so as to bind every one who comes within the jurisdiction, whether subjects or foreigners. Some * * * would confine this jurisdiction to purposes of "safety and police"—by which I should be disposed to understand measures for the protection of the territory, and for the regulation of the navigation, and the use of harbours and roadsteads, and the maintenance of order among the shipping therein, rather than the general application of the criminal law.

Other authors * * * would restrict the jurisdiction to certain specified purposes in which the local state has an immediate interest, namely, the protection of its revenue and fisheries, the exacting of harbour and light dues, and the protection of its coasts in time of war.

Some of these authors * * * make a most important distinction between a commorant and a passing ship. According to [one] author, while the commorant ship is subject to the general law of the local state, the passing ship is liable to the local jurisdiction only in matters of "military and police regulations, made for the safety of the territory and population of the coast." None of these writers, it should be noted, discuss the question, or go the length of asserting that a foreigner in a foreign ship, using the waters in question for the purpose of navigation solely, on its way to another country, is liable to the criminal law of the adjoining country for an offence committed on board.

Now, when it is remembered that it is mainly on the statements and authority of these writers, and to opinions founded upon them, that we are called upon to hold that foreigners on the so-called territorial sea are subject to the general law of this country, the discrepancy of opinion which I have been pointing out becomes very material.

* * * This unanimity of opinion that the littoral sea is, at all events for some purposes, subject to the dominion of the local state, may go far to shew that, by the concurrence of other nations, such a state may deal with these waters as subject to its legislation. But it wholly fails to show that, in the absence of such legislation, the ordinary law of the local state will extend over the waters in question—which is the point which we have to determine.

UNITED NATIONS CONVENTION ON THE LAW OF THE SEA, ARTICLE 27

Dec. 10, 1982, Senate Treaty Doc. No. 103–39 (1994), 1833 U.N.T.S. 3

Criminal jurisdiction on board a foreign ship

1. The criminal jurisdiction of the coastal State should not be exercised on board a foreign ship passing through the territorial sea to arrest any person or to conduct any investigation in connection with any crime committed on board the ship during its passage, save only in the following cases:

(a) if the consequences of the crime extend to the coastal State;

(b) if the crime is of a kind to disturb the peace of the country or the good order of the territorial sea;

(c) if the assistance of the local authorities has been requested by the master of the ship or by a diplomatic agent or consular officer of the flag State; or

(d) if such measures are necessary for the suppression of illicit traffic in narcotic drugs or psychotropic substances.

2. The above provisions do not affect the right of the coastal State to take any steps authorized by its laws for the purpose of an arrest or investigation on board a foreign ship passing through the territorial sea after leaving internal waters.

3. In the cases provided for in paragraphs 1 and 2, the coastal State shall, if the master so requests, notify a diplomatic agent or consular officer of the flag State before taking any steps, and shall facilitate contact between such agent or officer and the ship's crew. In cases of emergency this notification may be communicated while the measures are being taken.

4. In considering whether or in what manner an arrest should be made, the local authorities shall have due regard to the interests of navigation.

5. Except as provided in Part XII [concerning protection of the marine environment] or with respect to violations of laws and regulations adopted in accordance with Part V [concerning the exclusive economic zone], the coastal State may not take any steps on board a foreign ship passing through the territorial sea to arrest any person or to conduct any investigation in connection with any crime committed before the ship entered the territorial sea, if the ship, proceeding from a foreign port, is only passing through the territorial sea without entering internal waters.

NOTES AND QUESTIONS

1. *Coastal State Sovereignty and Exercise of Criminal Jurisdiction on Board Foreign Ships in the Territorial Sea.* What supports coastal state sovereignty over the territorial sea? Are there justifications for sovereign authority valid today that were not present or not recognized in 1876?

Who exercises jurisdiction over criminal activity in the territorial sea? Coastal states may defer to a flag state's exercise of jurisdiction with respect to criminal activities on board a foreign flag vessel. The circumstances in which such deference is appropriate are debatable. The narrow reason precluding the British courts from prosecuting Captain Keyn was cured within two years, when Parliament enacted a law authorizing, *inter alia*, Britain's exercise of criminal jurisdiction over acts in a marginal sea. Territorial Waters Jurisdiction Act, 41 and 42 Victoria, c. 73 (1878). Would Britain's exercise of criminal jurisdiction over Keyn have been appropriate under Article 27 of the 1982 Law of the Sea Convention? Is it sensible, for purposes of the exercise of a coastal state's criminal jurisdiction, to distinguish among vessels passing through the territorial sea on their way to or from one of the coastal state's ports, vessels simply passing by the coastal state's shores, and vessels stopping in the territorial sea?

2. *The Breadth of the Territorial Sea.* As the opinions in *Regina v. Keyn* indicate, the breadth of the territorial sea has historically been the subject of disagreement. In the mid-20th century, some Latin American states unilaterally asserted 200-mile territorial seas, and the delegates to the 1958 First U.N. Conference on the Law of the Sea could reach no agreement on the maximum permissible breadth of the territorial sea. In 1960, the Second U.N. Conference on the Law of the Sea failed by one vote to adopt a proposal for a six-mile territorial sea and an additional six-mile fisheries zone. Now, almost all states accept that the territorial sea may extend up to 12 miles from a state's baselines. See Convention on the Law of the Sea, art. 3. States favoring very broad territorial seas in order to protect their access to living resources were largely satisfied by the acceptance of a 200-mile EEZ in the 1982 Convention. For an overview of the historical development of the territorial sea, see John E. Noyes, "The Territorial Sea," in 4 *The Oxford Encyclopedia of Maritime History* 125 (John B. Hattendorf ed. 2007).

3. *Internal Waters.* Waters landward of a state's baselines (noted in Part C above) are deemed internal waters, unambiguously within a state's

sovereignty. A foreign merchant vessel in internal waters, in Phillimore's words, "subjects herself to the ordinary law of the place during the period of her commorancy there."

However, international law is still relevant in internal waters. For example, Articles 218 and 219 of the 1982 Law of the Sea Convention specify the enforcement measures port states may take with respect to pollution violations by foreign flag vessels voluntarily in port. International law may limit or specify port state rights with respect to other issues as well. Some have argued that international law provides a right of access to ports for foreign flag vessels, subject to those vessels' compliance with port state laws and regulations relating to health and security. See Saudi Arabia v. Aramco, 27 *International Law Reports* 117 (1963); *Restatement (Third) of the Foreign Relations Law of the United States* § 512, Reporters' Note 3 (1988). At least when a vessel enters a foreign port in distress, "all writers agree" that such access is permissible under international law. Louise de La Fayette, "Access to Ports in International Law," 11 *International Journal of Marine and Coastal Law* 1, 11 (1996). And port states often refrain from exercising their jurisdiction with regard to shipboard matters that do not "disturb the public tranquility," leaving such matters to flag state authorities. This peace of the port doctrine may be regulated by bilateral treaties. See Wildenhus's Case, 120 U.S. 1 (1887).

4. *Conflicts of Jurisdiction*. The peace of the port doctrine just noted is but one of many examples in the law of the sea of a conflict of jurisdiction between a flag state and a coastal or port state. Failing a treaty resolving such a conflict, how are we to determine whether to apply the flag state's law when it differs from the coastal or port state's law? The U.S. Supreme Court in Lauritzen v. Larsen, 345 U.S. 571 (1953), asked whether the U.S. Jones Act, 46 U.S.C. § 30104, which governs personal injuries to "[a]ny seaman" injured "in the course of his employment," applied to a sailor who was hired in New York, in his suit against a vessel owner whose ships frequently stopped at U.S. ports. The Court applied a multi-factor balancing test and, emphasizing that both plaintiff and defendant were Danish nationals and that the injury occurred on board a Danish flag ship in Cuban waters, concluded that the Jones Act did not apply. The Court's decision has had significance beyond the law of the sea, as it was important in the development of modern approaches to the field of conflict of laws (sometimes known as private international law). There is more on *Lauritzen* and conflicts of jurisdiction in Chapter 11.

UNITED NATIONS CONVENTION ON THE LAW OF THE SEA, ARTICLES 17, 19–21, 24–25

Dec. 10, 1982, Senate Treaty Doc. No. 103–39 (1994), 1833 U.N.T.S. 3

Article 17

Right of innocent passage

Subject to this Convention, ships of all States, whether coastal or land-locked, enjoy the right of innocent passage through the territorial sea.

Article 19

Meaning of innocent passage

1. Passage is innocent so long as it is not prejudicial to the peace, good order or security of the coastal State. Such passage shall take place in conformity with this Convention and with other rules of international law.

2. Passage of a foreign ship shall be considered to be prejudicial to the peace, good order or security of the coastal State if in the territorial sea it engages in any of the following activities:

(a) any threat or use of force against the sovereignty, territorial integrity or political independence of the coastal State, or in any other manner in violation of the principles of international law embodied in the Charter of the United Nations;

(b) any exercise or practice with weapons of any kind;

(c) any act aimed at collecting information to the prejudice of the defence or security of the coastal State;

(d) any act of propaganda aimed at affecting the defence or security of the coastal State;

(e) the launching, landing or taking on board of any aircraft;

(f) the launching, landing or taking on board of any military device;

(g) the loading or unloading of any commodity, currency or person contrary to the customs, fiscal, immigration or sanitary laws and regulations of the coastal State;

(h) any act of wilful and serious pollution contrary to this Convention;

(i) any fishing activities;

(j) the carrying out of research or survey activities;

(k) any act aimed at interfering with any systems of communication or any other facilities or installations of the coastal State;

(*l*) any other activity not having a direct bearing on passage.

Article 20

Submarines and other underwater vehicles

In the territorial sea, submarines and other underwater vehicles are required to navigate on the surface and to show their flag.

Article 21

Laws and regulations of the coastal state relating to innocent passage

1. The coastal State may adopt laws and regulations, in conformity with the provisions of this Convention and other rules of international law, relating to innocent passage through the territorial sea, in respect of all or any of the following:

(a) the safety of navigation and the regulation of maritime traffic;

(b) the protection of navigational aids and facilities and other facilities or installations;

(c) the protection of cables and pipelines;

(d) the conservation of the living resources of the sea;

(e) the prevention of infringement of the fisheries laws and regulations of the coastal State;

(f) the preservation of the environment of the coastal State and the prevention, reduction and control of pollution thereof;

(g) marine scientific research and hydrographic surveys;

(h) the prevention of infringement of the customs, fiscal, immigration or sanitary laws and regulations of the coastal State.

2. Such laws and regulations shall not apply to the design, construction, manning or equipment of foreign ships unless they are giving effect to generally accepted international rules or standards.

3. The coastal State shall give due publicity to all such laws and regulations.

4. Foreign ships exercising the right of innocent passage through the territorial sea shall comply with all such laws and regulations and all generally accepted international regulations relating to the prevention of collisions at sea.

Article 24

Duties of the coastal State

1. The coastal State shall not hamper the innocent passage of foreign ships through the territorial sea except in accordance with this Convention. In particular, in the application of this Convention or of any laws or regulations adopted in conformity with this Convention, the coastal State shall not:

(a) impose requirements on foreign ships which have the practical effect of denying or impairing the right of innocent passage; or

(b) discriminate in form or in fact against the ships of any State or against ships carrying cargoes to, from or on behalf of any State.

2. The coastal State shall give appropriate publicity to any danger to navigation, of which it has knowledge, within its territorial sea.

Article 25

Rights of protection of the coastal State

1. The coastal State may take the necessary steps in its territorial sea to prevent passage which is not innocent.

2. In the case of ships proceeding to internal waters or a call at a port facility outside internal waters, the coastal State also has the right to take the necessary steps to prevent any breach of the conditions to which admission of those ships to internal waters or such a call is subject.

3. The coastal State may, without discrimination in form or in fact among foreign ships, suspend temporarily in specified areas of its territorial sea the innocent passage of foreign ships if such suspension is essential for the protection of its security, including weapons exercises. Such suspension shall take effect only after having been duly published.

R.P. ANAND, "TRANSIT PASSAGE AND OVERFLIGHT IN INTERNATIONAL STRAITS"

26 *Indian Journal of International Law* 72 (1986)

Since the doctrine of innocent passage came to be established in the middle of the nineteenth century, the question of right of passage of warships has remained controversial and coastal states have been reluctant to permit passage without previous authorization or at least notification. * * * At the [Hague Codification] Conference in 1930, * * * the United States, for one, bluntly denied that there was such a right, because innocent passage existed primarily for commerce, and, so far as warships were concerned, it was wholly a question of usage and comity. * * *

The International Law Commission, in its 1956 draft presented to the 1958 UN Conference on the Law of the Sea, suggested that:

> The coastal state may make the passage of warships through the territorial sea subject to previous authorization or notification. Normally it shall grant innocent passage[.]

The International Law Commission's text, as it was presented to the conference, favoured the policies of the Soviet bloc. However, the United States, which until the Second World War was always opposed to the passage of warships through [the] territorial sea without authorization, had changed its stance. Having emerged as the greatest maritime power, it was now interested in the widest freedom of navigation even for its warships. The United States and its allies in NATO were strongly opposed to any limitation on the freedom of the seas, whether in the form of an extension of the territorial sea or a limitation on the passage of warships. Such a limitation, they thought, favoured the Soviet Union which possessed the largest fleet of submarines which could operate undetected for long periods in neutral states' territorial waters without surfacing. Extension of territorial waters coupled with restrictions on free passage of warships, they felt, would have the effect of exposing the mobility of NATO warships and aircraft to crippling jurisdictional restrictions.

[Anand traces diplomatic maneuvering at the 1958 Conference, related to the adoption of the ILC's proposed article.]

The bizarre result of this diplomatic struggle at Geneva was that the 1958 Convention contains no provision on the subject of passage of warships through the territorial sea, but includes Article 23 as suggested by the International Law Commission, which states that if a warship does not comply with the regulations of the coastal state, the latter may require it to leave the territorial sea. This provision survived because the Commission had fortuitously made it a separate article rather than a part of the composite article on straits.

The absence of an article on innocent passage of warships is sometimes interpreted by scholars and diplomats to mean that no restrictions are permissible on the passage of warships. This is said to be supported by Article 14 in which "all ships," including warships, it is asserted, are given the right of innocent passage. Furthermore, Article 23 is said to permit the coastal state to regulate the use of the territorial sea by foreign warships, but not to require previous permission for their transit.

On the other hand, it is argued by some countries and publicists that the expression "ships" in Article 14 means merchant ships because the inclusion of warships, in the light of long-standing customary law, would have required express provision; that Article 23 authorized the coastal state to insist on prior permission as part of its regulatory competence; and that this interpretation is supported by customary law which authorized the coastal state to exclude foreign warships from the territorial sea at will. * * *

With this historical record, it is difficult to conclude that warships have an untrammeled right of innocent passage through territorial waters. Because the 1958 Convention is silent on the subject, it must be interpreted in the light of customary law * * * which did permit coastal states to require notification and authorization before such passage was permitted. * * *

During the Third UN Conference on the Law of the Sea (UNCLOS III), the Soviet Union and its allies quietly dropped their strong objections to innocent passage of warships through territorial waters. The new identity of interest among the major naval powers led to substantially identical proposals by NATO and Warsaw Pact countries to include warships in the rules relating to innocent passage. * * *

The opposition to the right of innocent passage of warships shifted during the Conference from the Soviet bloc to a few Third World countries which were both afraid of the super powers and wanted to protect their coastal areas from becoming involved with their military maneuvers.

[A]lthough the 1982 Convention defines innocent passage in the same terms as the 1958 Convention as a passage that "is not prejudicial to the peace, good order or security of the coastal state" (Article 19(1)), unlike the 1958 Convention, it contains a catalogue of actions, applicable to all ships, that render the passage non-innocent. * * * The adoption of this catalogue to some extent presumes the right of innocent passage for warships, because the activities generally concern the mode of passage of warships.

[T]he 1958 Convention, like past practice dealt with the question of straits in the context of innocent passage in the territorial sea. * * *

The assimilation of the regime of straits with that of the territorial sea in the 1958 Convention was a step backward for all those supporting a special regime for straits. * * *

After the failure of the 1958 and 1960 Conferences to reach an agreement on the limits of the territorial sea, extension by many states of coastal state maritime zone jurisdiction to 12 miles threatened to enclose within * * * territorial sea limits another 116 straits. The three mile rule would have left a strip of high seas between them. Freedom of navigation through several strategic straits, such as the Dover Strait, the Strait of Gibraltar, the Bering Straits, Babel-Mandeb, the Strait of Hormuz, became more precarious, because they came under the coastal states' problematic territorial sea jurisdiction and discretion. The territorial seas regime requires submarines to come up to the surface and show their flag, and there is no right of innocent passage for aircraft through the airspace above the territorial sea.

* * * Before the Second World War, most of the strategic and vital straits, especially in Asia and the Middle East, were under the control of the maritime power[s] interested in keeping them open (and claiming narrow territorial sea of three miles). With the collapse of colonialism, new states emerged which were more concerned about their own security and economic interests and were not enamored by the "freedom of the seas" doctrine which had for a long time been used and abused to their disadvantage. Indeed, feeling that unlimited freedom of the seas was against their interests, they wanted to curb it. Some of these newly independent states were strait states now able and willing to control these important waterways to protect their vital interests. The threat of oil spills, dumping on the high seas, and other sources of pollution in a period of growing ecological concern, added still another reason for expanded jurisdictional claims by coastal states. As the trend to extend territorial waters gathered momentum after 1960, most of these straits became part of the territorial seas subject to numerous controls and limitations imposed by the coastal states. In fact, some of these states went further and sought to make certain important straits internal waters subject to their absolute sovereignty. * * * Indonesia enjoys a monopoly over all deep water straits between the Asian mainland and Australia connecting the Pacific and the Indian Oceans. The closure of those straits like Sunda, Lombok, Ombai-Wetar or Macassar would necessitate a diversion of traffic around Australia or through the Panama Canal resulting in time delays, higher consumer prices, and the reduced mobility and flexibility of naval forces.

This trend was totally unacceptable to the maritime powers. * * *

The United States representative said in Sub-committee of the Seabed Committee that "in addition to the importance of sea navigation for their international trade, many states depended upon air and sea mobility in order to exercise their inherent right of individual and collective self-defence." He pointed out that "the security of the United States and its allies depended to a very large extent on the freedom of navigation and on the overflight of the high seas. More extensive territorial seas, without the right to free transit of straits, would threaten that security." The United States maintained that the invulnerability of its nuclear missile submarines (SSBNs)—currently the Polaris/Poseidon fleet—and hence their indispensable role in an adequate second strike force depended on their right to pass through straits submerged and unannounced. In the U.S. view, the right of free transit through straits was "an indispensable adjunct to the freedom of navigation and that of overflight on the high seas themselves." Moreover, the regime of innocent passage provided for in the 1958 Convention on the Territorial Sea was "inadequate when applied to international straits" because it was a subjective standard subject to abuse. Some states, he said, had in fact claimed that certain types of passage—by nuclear-powered ships and super tankers—should be considered as non-innocent *per se.*

The United States made it clear time and again that it would not accept any extension of the territorial sea from three miles to twelve miles unless the right of *free passage* through international straits was accepted. It demanded freedom of unobstructed passage for warships, including nuclear submarines, on the surface or submerged, without notification and irrespective of mission. Further, it wanted freedom of civilian and military flights through the superjacent airspace. All these rights were claimed not only in those straits that were wider than six miles and were supposed to have, at least theoretically, a corridor of high seas in their midst, but in *all straits irrespective of their breadth or importance.*

The United States was willing to accept and "observe reasonable traffic safety and marine pollution regulations," that is to say, regulations that were "consistent with the basic right of transit." The safety standards to be applied in straits, however, should be established by international agreement and should not be unilaterally imposed by the coastal state.

As to the free transit of aircraft, the United States stated that civil aircraft already enjoyed transit rights over national territory of other states, under the Convention on International Civil Aviation and the International Air Service Transit Agreement. But such rights were not available to state aircraft. The United States demanded a right of free transit for all aircraft over straits, but also stated that such aircraft need not be routed over the strait itself but, at the coastal state's discretion, could be directed through "suitable corridors over land areas."

The United States was supported on this issue not only by the western maritime powers, like the United Kingdom, France, West Germany and others but also by the Soviet Union and Communist bloc countries which also insisted that the limited right of "innocent passage" was not sufficient and "had never been and could never be applied to such straits as those of Gibraltar, Dover, Malacca, Singapore and Bab-el-Mandeb, where freedom of navigation had always been enjoyed."

* * * Refusal to recognize the principle of free passage would mean, according to the Soviet Union, "establishing the domination of only 12 to 15 states adjacent to straits over the passage of vessels of some 130 states of the world." The reversal of the Soviet policy from its stand in 1958 was, of course, the result of the emergence of the Soviet military capability—naval, fishing and merchant marine—during the subsequent two decades.

Skeptical of the true intentions of the maritime powers and fearful for their own security and sovereignty, the small coastal and strait states strongly objected to the right of "free passage" (instead of "innocent passage") through international straits. By "championing a superficial freedom of navigation," their representatives decried, the big powers were actually seeking authority to "interfere in the domestic affairs of states situated thousands of miles away from their shores." * * *

The principle of "free transit," they contended, might lead to a variety of unfortunate results. For instance, coastal state patrols might misinterpret the presence of military vessels and become involved in a confrontation. Foreign warships might meet other unfriendly warships with results detrimental to the coastal state. Moreover, a foreign military presence could cause domestic consternation and political upheaval, or create misunderstandings between the coastal state and its neighbors. If warships and submarines are engaged in harmless innocent passage there should be no reason for them not to let the coastal state know of their presence. If free transit were permitted, it was contended, military vessels and aircraft passing through international straits would enjoy freedom from law or regulation, a status never enjoyed by any navigator.

Despite all the misgivings and apprehensions of the smaller coastal and strait states[,] the maritime powers * * * left no one in doubt that "unless unimpeded passage on, over and under straits used for international navigation was conceded to all commercial vessels and warships, including submarines, there was simply no possibility of coming to an agreement on the subject of national jurisdiction and other issues." They were prepared to make concessions on other issues, e.g., the exploitation of deep seabed resources and to accept wide coastal jurisdiction, even the claims of archipelagic states, provided their naval mobility was not affected.

* * * As finally adopted, the Convention provides for a guaranteed non-suspendable transit passage through straits and archipelagic waters, subject only to the power of the coastal state to make certain rules related to navigational safety, pollution, and fishing. For the first time the Convention provides separate regimes for "innocent passage" through [the] territorial sea, laid down in Part II, Section 3 (Articles 17 to 32), and "transit passage" through international straits, laid down in Part III, Section 2 (Articles 37 to 44), and Section 3 (Article 45), the latter applicable only to special straits. The right of transit passage applies to "straits which are used for international navigation between one part of the high seas or an exclusive economic zone and another part of the high seas or an exclusive economic zone" [Article 37]. But transit passage does not apply to:

(1) Straits formed by an island of a state bordering the strait and its mainland if there exists seaward of the island a route through

the high seas or through an EEZ of similar convenience with respect to navigational and hydrographical characteristics [Article 38(1)].

(2) Straits used for international navigation between one area of the high seas or an EEZ and the territorial sea of a foreign state [Article 45(1)(b)].

For these two categories the right of "innocent passage" is deemed sufficient which however cannot be suspended [Article 45(2)].

Transit passage is defined as:

the exercise in accordance with this part of the freedom of navigation and overflight solely for the purpose of continuous and expeditious transit of the strait between one part of the high seas or an EEZ and another part of the high seas or an EEZ. However, the requirement of continuous and expeditious transit does not preclude passage through the strait for the purpose of entering, leaving or returning from a state bordering the strait, subject to the conditions of entry to that state [Art. 38(2)].

Article 39 lays down the duties of ships and aircraft while exercising the right of transit passage, such as, [(1)] to proceed without delay through or over the strait; (2) refrain from use of force against the sovereignty, integrity or independence of the bordering states, or in any manner in violation of the principles of international law; (3) refrain from any activities other than those incidental to their normal modes of continuous and expeditious transit unless rendered necessary by *force majeure* or by distress. The ships and aircraft are also expected to comply with the generally accepted international regulations, procedures, and practices for preventing collision and avoiding collisions and aircraft must comply with the rules of the air established by [the International Civil Aviation Organization] or otherwise [Article 34(2)(3)].

The coastal states have been authorized under Article 41 to designate sea lanes and prescribe traffic separation schemes for navigation after receiving the approval of the IMO. They may also adopt rules and regulations regarding navigation, pollution, fishing, and loading and unloading in transit.

NOTES AND QUESTIONS

1. *Innocent Passage.* The existence of a right of innocent passage demonstrates that a coastal state's sovereignty over its territorial sea is not absolute in international law. For discussion of state sovereignty, see Chapter 7, Part A. The coastal state has no right to exclude foreign vessels engaged in innocent passage. The innocent passage articles of the 1982 Convention reflect an effort to make the standards for innocent passage more objective than was the case under the 1958 Convention on the Territorial Sea

and Contiguous Zone. That Convention, in Article 14(4), simply defined innocent passage in the same terms that were later repeated in Article 19(1) of the 1982 Convention. The 1982 Convention articles certainly are more detailed than those in earlier treaties. In addition to the articles reproduced above, the Convention defines "passage," which must be "continuous and expeditious" (Article 18), allows the coastal state to designate sea lanes and traffic separation schemes in the territorial sea (Article 22), and authorizes special precautionary measures with respect to nuclear-powered ships or ships with particularly dangerous cargoes (Article 28). But are the 1982 Convention's standards for innocent passage all that objective? Who decides whether passage is innocent?

Does the 1982 Convention treat the passage of foreign warships through the territorial sea, as opposed to the passage of merchant ships, as "innocent"? Is a coastal state legally entitled to be notified, or to give its authorization, before a foreign warship may pass through its territorial sea? In 1989, the United States and the former Soviet Union concluded a bilateral agreement providing that "neither prior notification or authorization" is a precondition to warships' enjoying the right of innocent passage. Uniform Interpretation of Norms of International Law Governing Innocent Passage, Sept. 23, 1989, 28 *International Legal Materials* 1444 (1989). However, several states still maintain that passage of warships through the territorial sea requires the prior consent of the coastal state. See Donald R. Rothwell & Tim Stephens, *The International Law of the Sea* 270–71 (2010).

2. *The* Corfu Channel Case. As Professor Anand indicated, maritime powers tried to assure free navigation of their warships in territorial seas and through straits well before UNCLOS III. State practice and treaty negotiations largely shaped the law in this area, but an early decision by the International Court of Justice also was influential. In the Corfu Channel Case (United Kingdom v. Albania), 1949 I.C.J. 4, the Court found Albania responsible for damage done to British warships by mines in the Corfu Strait, a strait 31 miles long between Albania and the Greek island of Corfu. The Court held:

> * * * States in time of peace have a right to send their warships through straits used for international navigation between two parts of the high seas without the previous authorization of a coastal State, provided that the passage is *innocent*. Unless otherwise prescribed in an international convention, there is no right for a coastal State to prohibit such passage through straits in time of peace. * * *
>
> It may be asked whether the test [for what constitutes an international strait] is to be found in the volume of traffic passing through the Strait or in its greater or lesser importance for international navigation. But in the opinion of the Court the decisive criterion is rather its geographical situation as connecting two parts of the high seas and the fact of its being used for international navigation. Nor can it be decisive that this Strait is

> not a necessary route between two parts of the high seas, but only an alternative passage between the Ægean and the Adriatic Seas. It has nevertheless been a useful route for international maritime traffic. * * *
>
> Having regard to these various considerations, the Court has arrived at the conclusion that the North Corfu Channel should be considered as belonging to the class of international highways through which passage cannot be prohibited by a coastal State in time of peace.
>
> On the other hand, it is a fact that the two coastal States did not maintain normal relations, that Greece had made territorial claims precisely with regard to a part of Albanian territory bordering on the Channel, that Greece had declared that she considered herself technically in a state of war with Albania, and that Albania, invoking the danger of Greek incursions, had considered it necessary to take certain measures of vigilance in this region. The Court is of opinion that Albania, in view of these exceptional circumstances, would have been justified in issuing regulations in respect of the passage of warships through the Strait, but not in prohibiting such passage or in subjecting it to the requirement of special authorization.

Id. at 28–29.

3. *Transit Passage Through Straits*. How does the right of transit passage through straits, as set out in the 1982 Convention on the Law of the Sea, differ from the right of innocent passage? How, with respect to the issue of transit passage through straits, does the Convention strike a balance between coastal states' claims of sovereignty and maritime powers' claims to high seas freedoms? How can compliance with Convention provisions on transit passage through straits best be assured? Rights of innocent passage and of archipelagic sea lanes passage, which is similar to transit passage through straits, apply in archipelagic waters of archipelagic states. See Convention on the Law of the Sea, arts. 52–54.

4. *The Regime of Warships*. Permitting warships to navigate or conduct exercises in zones of the oceans other than the territorial sea and straits has been also, of course, of concern to maritime powers. Professor Oxman found "nothing surprisingly new in the regime of warships under the 1982 Convention":

> The demilitarization pressures were deflected by liberal use of "peaceful purposes" clauses and cross-references to the prohibitions on the threat or use of force in the U.N. Charter that have little, if any, effect on the legal regime. With respect to all the new regimes or geographical expansions of existing regimes, effects on activities of warships are expressly eliminated or mitigated in each case:
>
> —there is a liberal right of archipelagic sea lanes passage in broad sealanes traversing the newly recognized archipelagic waters;

—the regime of innocent passage in the expanded territorial sea is made more objective and is replaced by a more liberal regime of transit passage in straits;

—high seas freedoms of navigation, overflight and the laying of submarine cables and pipelines, and other internationally lawful uses of the sea related to those freedoms, are expressly preserved in the economic zone;

—high seas freedoms are given more explicit protection from infringement by the coastal State in its exercise of continental shelf rights;

—warships are excluded from all environmental provisions;

—regulation of the deep seabeds depends on a definition of the term "activities in the Area" that does not cover military activities or marine scientific research.

Bernard H. Oxman, "The Regime of Warships Under the United Nations Convention on the Law of the Sea," 24 *Virginia Journal of International Law* 809, 861–62 (1984).

5. *A Package Deal?* International lawyers debate whether various new provisions in the 1982 Convention amount to customary international law, or whether they are binding only as treaty law. Some argue that acceptance of provisions at UNCLOS III, coupled with state practice, provide the necessary consensus for the bulk of the Convention to be considered customary international law. Others maintain that the Convention is a "package deal," the product of numerous compromises and trade-offs, and that a state cannot claim particular rights concerning the oceans while rejecting certain obligations. Note that the Convention, in Article 309, generally prohibits reservations and exceptions to its provisions. See, *e.g.*, Hugo Caminos & Michael R. Molitor, "Progressive Development of International Law and the Package Deal," 74 *American Journal of International Law* 871 (1985).

UNCLOS III negotiations concerning innocent passage and transit passage through straits were not carried out in isolation from negotiations on other issues. Some maritime powers, whose interests, according to many observers, were well-served by the outcome of the negotiations on transit passage through straits, were less pleased by other negotiated compromises. In particular, some developed states criticized the deep seabed mining regime that evolved at UNCLOS III. That regime, which now incorporates significant 1994 changes favored by developed states, is explored in Part E.

6. *The United States and the Law of the Sea Convention.* As of December 2013, the United States is not one of the 166 parties to the Law of the Sea Convention. What then are the legal rights of the United States with respect to innocent passage and transit passage through straits? Is the United States, a party to the 1958 Convention on the Territorial Sea, bound by that Convention's navigation provisions in its relations with other 1958 Convention parties, such as Spain and Iran? In light of the "package deal"

arguments outlined in Note 5, may the provisions of the 1982 Law of the Sea Convention on innocent passage and transit passage through straits be considered customary international law? Might customary international law differ from the provisions of the Law of the Sea Convention?

To promote U.S. navigational freedoms, should the United States negotiate bilateral agreements, rely on assertions of customary international law, or instead assert U.S. military might? Note that the U.S. Department of Defense and every U.S. administration since 1994—when the Convention's deep seabed mining regime was changed (see Part E)—have advocated U.S. accession to the Law of the Sea Convention. In 2012 testimony before the U.S. Senate Foreign Relations Committee, John Bellinger, Legal Adviser to the State Department during the second term of President George W. Bush, noted that the Bush administration in February 2002 concluded there was an "urgent need for Senate approval" of the Law of the Sea Convention:

> [T]he Bush Administration did not decide to support the Law of the Sea Convention out of a blind commitment to multilateral treaties or international organizations. No one has ever accused the Bush Administration of an over-abundance of enthusiasm for the United Nations or multilateralism. * * * And the Bush Administration was especially committed to defending U.S. sovereignty and international freedom of action, particularly after September 11.
>
> The Bush Administration decided to support the Law of the Sea Convention [because we] concluded that, on balance, the treaty was clearly in the U.S. national security, economic, and environmental interests.
>
> First and foremost, the Bush Administration concluded that the Convention was beneficial to the United States military, especially during a time of armed conflict, because it provided clear treaty-based navigational rights for our Navy, Coast Guard, and aircraft. This was especially important for the Bush Administration as we asked our military to take on numerous new missions after the 9-11 attacks during the Global War on Terrorism; several countries had challenged U.S. military activities in their territorial waters, and the Administration concluded that it was vital to have a treaty-based legal right to support our freedom of movement and activities.

The Law of the Sea Convention (Treaty Doc. 103–39): Hearing Before the Senate Committee on Foreign Relations, 112th Cong. 181, 184–85 (2013). Some have denounced the United States for hypocrisy when it has criticized parties to the Law of the Sea Convention for not complying with its freedom of navigation provisions, since the United States itself has not accepted the Convention. See, *e.g.*, Alan M. Wachman, "Playing by or Playing with the Rules of UNCLOS?," in *Military Activities in the EEZ: A U.S.-China Dialogue on Security and International Law in the Maritime Commons*, U.S. Naval

War College, China Maritime Studies Institute No. 7, at 107, 113 (Peter Dutton ed. 2010) (summarizing the comments of Shen Dingli, Vice Dean of the Department of International Studies at China's Fudan University). What difference would it make if the United States were to accept the Convention on the Law of the Sea?

E. THE DEEP SEABED

The contours of a legal regime to govern the seabed beyond the limits of national jurisdiction have taken shape only in the past half century. In 1967, Arvid Pardo, Malta's Ambassador to the United Nations, addressed the General Assembly on the uses and resources of the seabed. In a seminal speech, he discussed underseas archaeological treasures, offshore natural gas and petroleum, ocean floor sediments, marine scientific research, missile systems and other fixed military installations, and pollution. He stirred the most interest, however, when he turned to the exploitation of the "incredibly vast" mineral resources on and beneath the ocean floor beyond the boundaries of national jurisdiction. U.N. Doc. A/C.1/PV1515 (1967) (speech by Dr. Pardo in U.N. General Assembly, First Committee, Nov. 1, 1967). Although Pardo underestimated the extent of national jurisdiction over the continental shelf that came to be accepted, many at UNCLOS III shared his vision of great deep seabed wealth. Much attention focused on nodules rich in manganese, nickel, copper, and cobalt that are scattered over about 15 per cent of the seabed at depths of 3,000 to 6,000 meters. Current technology allows recovery of these nodules, and companies are actively exploring for them.

Pardo referred to the seabed beyond the limits of national jurisdiction as the "common heritage of mankind," which "should be used and exploited for peaceful purposes and for the exclusive benefit of mankind as a whole." Pardo argued that developing states, "representing that part of mankind which is most in need of assistance, should receive preferential consideration" in the distribution of revenues derived from the exploitation of the seabed, an argument reflected in the following U.N. General Assembly resolution.

THE DECLARATION OF PRINCIPLES GOVERNING THE SEA-BED AND THE OCEAN FLOOR, AND THE SUBSOIL THEREOF, BEYOND THE LIMITS OF NATIONAL JURISDICTION

G.A. Res. 2749 (XXV), 25 U.N. GAOR Supp. (No. 28), at 24, U.N. Doc. A/8028 (1970)

The General Assembly, * * *

Affirming that there is an area of the sea-bed and the ocean floor, and the subsoil thereof, beyond the limits of national jurisdiction, the precise limits of which are yet to be determined,

Recognizing that the existing legal régime of the high seas does not provide substantive rules for regulating the exploration of the aforesaid area and the exploitation of its resources,

Convinced that the area shall be reserved exclusively for peaceful purposes and that the exploration of the area and the exploitation of its resources shall be carried out for the benefit of mankind as a whole,

Believing it essential that an international régime applying to the area and its resources and including appropriate international machinery should be established as soon as possible,

Bearing in mind that the development and use of the area and its resources shall be undertaken in such a manner as to foster the healthy development of the world economy and balanced growth of international trade, and to minimize any adverse economic effects caused by fluctuation of prices of raw materials resulting from such activities,

Solemnly declares that:

1. The sea-bed and ocean floor, and the subsoil thereof, beyond the limits of national jurisdiction (hereinafter referred to as the area), as well as the resources of the area, are the common heritage of mankind.

2. The area shall not be subject to appropriation by any means by States or persons, natural or juridical, and no State shall claim or exercise sovereignty or sovereign rights over any part thereof.

3. No State or person, natural or juridical, shall claim, exercise or acquire rights with respect to the area or its resources incompatible with the international régime to be established and the principles of this Declaration.

4. All activities regarding the exploration and exploitation of the resources of the area and other related activities shall be governed by the international régime to be established.

5. The area shall be open to use exclusively for peaceful purposes by all States, whether coastal or land-locked, without discrimination, in accordance with the international régime to be established.

6. States shall act in the area in accordance with the applicable principles and rules of international law, including the Charter of the United Nations and the Declaration on Principles of International Law concerning Friendly Relations and Co-operation among States in accordance with the Charter of the United Nations, adopted by the General Assembly on 24 October 1970, in the interests of maintaining international peace and security and promoting international co-operation and mutual understanding.

7. The exploration of the area and the exploitation of its resources shall be carried out for the benefit of mankind as a whole, irrespective of

the geographical location of States, whether land-locked or coastal, and taking into particular consideration the interests and needs of the developing countries.

8. The area shall be reserved exclusively for peaceful purposes, without prejudice to any measures which have been or may be agreed upon in the context of international negotiations undertaken in the field of disarmament and which may be applicable to a broader area. One or more international agreements shall be concluded as soon as possible in order to implement effectively this principle and to constitute a step towards the exclusion of the sea-bed, the ocean floor and the subsoil thereof from the arms race.

9. On the basis of the principles of this Declaration, an international régime applying to the area and its resources and including appropriate international machinery to give effect to its provisions shall be established by an international treaty of a universal character, generally agreed upon. The régime shall, *inter alia*, provide for the orderly and safe development and rational management of the area and its resources and for expanding opportunities in the use thereof, and ensure the equitable sharing by States in the benefits derived therefrom, taking into particular consideration the interests and needs of the developing countries, whether land-locked or coastal.

10. States shall promote international co-operation in scientific research exclusively for peaceful purposes:

(*a*) By participation in international programmes and by encouraging co-operation in scientific research by personnel of different countries;

(*b*) Through effective publication of research programmes and dissemination of the results of research through international channels;

(*c*) By co-operation in measures to strengthen research capabilities of developing countries, including the participation of their nationals in research programmes.

No such activity shall form the legal basis for any claims with respect to any part of the area or its resources.

11. With respect to activities in the area and acting in conformity with the international régime to be established, States shall take appropriate measures for and shall co-operate in the adoption and implementation of international rules, standards and procedures for, *inter alia*:

(*a*) The prevention of pollution and contamination, and other hazards to the marine environment, including the coastline, and of interference with the ecological balance of the marine environment;

(*b*) The protection and conservation of the natural resources of the area and prevention of damage to the flora and fauna of the marine environment.

12. In their activities in the area, including those relating to its resources, States shall pay due regard to the rights and legitimate interests of coastal States in the region of such activities, as well as of all other States which may be affected by such activities. Consultations shall be maintained with the coastal States concerned with respect to activities relating to the exploration of the area and the exploitation of its resources with a view to avoiding infringement of such rights and interests.

13. Nothing herein shall affect:

(*a*) The legal status of the waters superjacent to the area or that of the air space above those waters;

(*b*) The rights of coastal States with respect to measures to prevent, mitigate or eliminate grave and imminent danger to their coastline or related interests from pollution or threat thereof or from other hazardous occurrences resulting from or caused by any activities in the area, subject to the international régime to be established.

14. Every State shall have the responsibility to ensure that activities in the area, including those relating to its resources, whether undertaken by governmental agencies, or non-governmental entities or persons under its jurisdiction, or acting on its behalf, shall be carried out in conformity with the international régime to be established. The same responsibility applies to international organizations and their members for activities undertaken by such organizations or on their behalf. Damage caused by such activities shall entail liability.

15. The parties to any dispute relating to activities in the area and its resources shall resolve such dispute by the measures mentioned in Article 33 of the Charter of the United Nations and such procedures for settling disputes as may be agreed upon in the international régime to be established.

NOTES AND QUESTIONS

1. *The Legal Effect of U.N. General Assembly Resolutions.* The 1970 Declaration of Principles was adopted without opposition. Also important was the Moratorium Resolution, G.A. Res. 2574–D (XXIV), Dec. 15, 1969, which declared that, pending the establishment of an international regime, no state or person was to exploit the resources of the seabed beyond the limits of national jurisdiction, and that no claim to the deep seabed or its resources would be recognized. The Moratorium Resolution passed by a vote of 62 in favor, 28 opposed, and 28 abstentions; the United States and most developed states voted against the measure. What legal effect should be given to such pronouncements? Look at the reasoning of Professor Dupuy when he

addressed U.N. General Assembly resolutions in the *Texaco/Libya Case* in Chapter 3 and the discussion of soft law in Chapter 3, Part D.

2. *Differing Legal Conceptions of the Deep Seabed.* Before UNCLOS III, some argued that the seabed beyond the limits of national jurisdiction was *res nullius,* a conception that would allow unilateral claims of title or sovereignty. Others termed the deep seabed *res communis* and thus not subject to expropriation. Note that Grotius had already distinguished these concepts in the 1633 excerpt in Part A above. The General Assembly's 1970 Declaration of Principles proclaimed the deep seabed and its resources to be the "common heritage of mankind." In response to a 1974 claim by Deepsea Ventures, Inc. seeking U.S. recognition of "exclusive rights to develop, evaluate and mine" a claim in the deep seabed, the U.S. State Department declared that it did not grant or recognize exclusive mining rights in the deep seabed, but that "the mining of the seabed beyond the limits of national jurisdiction may proceed as a freedom of the high seas under existing international law." *Digest of U.S. Practice in International Law* § 5, at 342–43 (1974). Would a high seas freedoms regime for seabed minerals be similar to a common heritage regime as outlined in the Principles Resolution? Or would they differ? For discussion of the evolution and meaning of the common heritage principle, see John E. Noyes, "The Common Heritage of Mankind: Past, Present, and Future," 40 *Denver Journal of International Law and Policy* 447 (2012).

3. *International Institutions for the Deep Seabed.* Diplomats generally agreed UNCLOS III was the appropriate forum to develop a legal regime to govern the deep seabed. Much debate centered on the appropriate structure of an international seabed authority. Some favored an entity that itself would engage in exploitation; others proposed an institution that would license private claims to blocks of the seabed; and still others envisioned a supervisory and consultative body. Some states promoted an organization that would both be able to profit from mining and then redistribute wealth to developing states. The call for an international regime providing for economic assistance was not restricted to developing states. President Richard Nixon endorsed that goal in his statement on U.S. seabed policy on May 23, 1970:

> that all nations adopt as soon as possible a treaty under which they would renounce all national claims over the natural resources of the seabed beyond the point where the high seas reach a depth of 200 meters (218.8 yards) and would agree to regard these resources as the common heritage of mankind.
>
> The treaty should establish an international regime for the exploitation of seabed resources beyond this limit. The regime should include the collection of substantial mineral royalties to be used for international community purposes, particularly economic assistance to developing countries.

> [A]greed international machinery would authorize and regulate exploration and use of seabed resources beyond the continental margins.

"United States Oceans Policy: Statement by the President," 6 *Weekly Compilation of Presidential Documents* 677, 677–78 (1970).

4. *The Seabed Mining Regime of the Law of the Sea Convention.* Part XI of the 1982 Convention on the Law of the Sea contains detailed rules and procedures concerning seabed mining beyond the limits of national jurisdiction. Article 136 sets out the basic principle that the seabed beyond the limits of national jurisdiction and its resources are the "common heritage of mankind," and other articles reflect general principles articulated in the Principles Resolution. Part XI also provides for new international institutions. These include the International Seabed Authority (ISA), which is to regulate and govern seabed mining primarily through rules, regulations, and procedures adopted by an Assembly and Council. The Enterprise is the mining arm of the Authority, and a Seabed Disputes Chamber of the International Tribunal for the Law of the Sea is available for compulsory third-party adjudication. Under the "parallel system," both the Enterprise and other actors (states and commercial entities sponsored by States Parties) that pay fees to and register with the Authority would mine seabed minerals. Part XI also contains production limits, included to assuage the concerns of land-based producers of minerals that feared the economic impact of an influx of seabed minerals onto world markets. Was it wise to provide such detail in the Convention? As we see below, this seabed mining regime has been changed significantly.

5. *Equity and Seabed Minerals.* According to Article 140 of the Law of the Sea Convention, the Authority is to "provide for the equitable sharing of financial and other economic benefits derived from" seabed mining in the Area. A similar standard applies in Article 82, under which a coastal state with a continental shelf that extends beyond 200 miles from its baselines must make payments with respect to its revenues from the exploitation of the nonliving resources of the shelf beyond 200 miles. The Authority then is to distribute such payments "on the basis of equitable sharing criteria, taking into account the interests and needs of developing States, particularly the least developed and the land-locked among them." See also Article 160(2)(f)(i). Does the reference to "equitable sharing" have a definite meaning, or is it merely a grant of discretion to the Authority? Note that the use of equity here differs from treating equity as a source of international law. See Chapter 3.

6. *U.S. Objections to the Law of the Sea Convention's Seabed Mining Regime.* In 1981, near the end of the UNCLOS III negotiations, the newly elected Reagan administration announced that the United States would not accept the Law of the Sea Convention, objecting to Part XI. Articles requiring payments from miners, limits on production, and the transfer of technology to the Enterprise were deemed incompatible with the operation of market forces. The United States also sought a greater role in the decision-making

bodies of the Authority, objected to the Part XI provisions on equitable sharing of benefits (fearing that those provisions could result in payments to anti-U.S. national liberation groups), and criticized a Convention article authorizing a Review Conference, which could adopt amendments to Part XI binding on all states regardless of their concurrence. The Reagan administration expressed U.S. agreement with the non-seabed-mining portions of the Law of the Sea Convention, concluding that the administration would support U.S. accession to the Convention if the objectionable provisions of Part XI could be corrected. See "U.S. Policy and the Law of the Sea, Presidential Statement and White House Fact Sheet, Jan. 29, 1982," *Department of State Bulletin*, Mar. 1982, at 54. The United States, the Federal Republic of Germany, and the United Kingdom did not sign the Convention; other developed states signed but did not ratify. On November 16, 1993, when the Convention received its 60th acceptance—the number necessary for its entry into force a year later—virtually all ratifications were by developing states.

7. *Changing the Law of the Sea Convention's Seabed Mining Regime.* Efforts to accommodate the U.S. objections, and to provide for a workable regime to govern seabed mining, followed three different tracks outside UNCLOS III: unilateralism, implementation of the seabed mining regime by an international body, and negotiating a new multilateral regime. First, the United States and a few other developed countries enacted "interim" legislation to license deep seabed mining activities by their nationals. See, *e.g.*, Deep Seabed Hard Minerals Resource Act of 1980, 30 U.S.C. §§ 1401–1473. "Reciprocating states" treaties would respect licenses issued under national laws in order to avoid overlapping mining claims. Second, a Preparatory Commission, established at the end of UNCLOS III, drafted rules for the International Seabed Authority that would apply once the 1982 Convention entered into force. Prepcom also registered "pioneer investors" from various states, which were entitled to explore for deep seabed mineral resources in accordance with the Convention regime. Prepcom sought to avoid conflicts with mine sites licensed under the first, unilateral track, but its mandate did not extend to making fundamental changes to Part XI.

Of most interest for our purposes is the third track, involving multilateral negotiations initiated by the U.N. Secretary-General. This effort resulted in an agreement that significantly changed Part XI and accommodated the views of the United States and other developed countries. The detailed Agreement Relating to the Implementation of Part XI, July 29, 1994, 1836 U.N.T.S. 3, dispenses with annual fees for miners, production limitations, and the requirement that States Parties fund the Enterprise's mining operations. Part XI requirements concerning the transfer of private technology "shall not apply." Multinational consortia previously licensed under municipal legislation are guaranteed access to seabed mining on terms "no less favorable than" terms given to the pioneer investors registered by Prepcom. The 1994 Agreement also revises procedural aspects of Part XI; several important decisions may not be made over the objection of any state. Furthermore, provisions relating to the Review Conference "shall not apply," so no amendments to the seabed mining regime can bind any state that does not accept them. Overall, the 1994 Part XI Agreement streamlined operations of the ISA, increased the decision-making authority of industrialized countries, and changed substantive provisions of Part XI to meet the objections of the United States. See Bernard Oxman, "The 1994 Agreement and the Convention," 88 *American Journal of International Law* 687 (1994). The 1994 Part XI Agreement also contains provisions ensuring that the 1982 Convention is implemented along with the Agreement, which is to be interpreted and applied together with the Convention as a single instrument.

RESPONSIBILITIES AND OBLIGATIONS OF STATES SPONSORING PERSONS AND ENTITIES WITH RESPECT TO ACTIVITIES IN THE AREA

Seabed Disputes Chamber of the International Tribunal for the Law of the Sea, Advisory Opinion, ITLOS Case No. 17 (2011), 50 *International Legal Materials* 455 (2011)

[We excerpt only a few paragraphs from this long and complex opinion. Consider how the international regime for seabed mining operates, especially the importance of "state sponsorship" in that regime and whether special consideration is given to developing states. These passages also discuss the relevance of the *erga omnes* concept and the question of liability should contractor activities damage the marine environment in the Area.]

1. The questions on which the advisory opinion of the Seabed Disputes Chamber of the International Tribunal for the Law of the Sea (hereinafter "the Chamber") has been requested are set forth in decision ISBA/16/C/13 adopted by the Council of the International Seabed Authority (hereinafter "the Council") on 6 May 2010 at its sixteenth session. [The Council requested an advisory opinion on three questions, the first two of which were:]

> 1. What are the legal responsibilities and obligations of States Parties to the Convention with respect to the sponsorship of activities in the Area in accordance with the Convention, in particular Part XI, and the 1994 Agreement relating to the Implementation of Part XI of the United Nations Convention on the Law of the Sea of 10 December 1982?
>
> 2. What is the extent of liability of a State Party for any failure to comply with the provisions of the Convention, in particular Part XI, and the 1994 Agreement, by an entity whom it has sponsored under Article 153, paragraph 2(b), of the Convention? * * *

4. * * *

On 10 April 2008, the Authority received two applications for approval of a plan of work for exploration in the areas reserved for the conduct of activities by the Authority through the Enterprise or in association with developing States pursuant to Annex III, article 8, of the United Nations Convention on the Law of the Sea (hereinafter "the Convention"). These applications were submitted by Nauru Ocean Resources Inc. (sponsored by the Republic of Nauru) and Tonga Offshore Mining Ltd. (sponsored by the Kingdom of Tonga)[.] On 1 March 2010, the Republic of Nauru transmitted to the Secretary-General a proposal * * * to seek an advisory opinion from the Chamber on a number of specific questions regarding the responsibility and liability of sponsoring States[.]

In support of its proposal, Nauru submitted, inter alia, the following considerations:

> In 2008 the Republic of Nauru sponsored an application by Nauru Ocean Resources Inc. for a plan of work to explore for polymetallic nodules in the Area. Nauru, like many other developing States, does not yet possess the technical and financial capacity to undertake seafloor mining in international waters. To participate effectively in activities in the Area, these States must engage entities in the global private sector (in much the same way as some developing countries require foreign direct investment). Not only do some developing States lack the financial capacity to execute a seafloor mining project in international waters, but some also cannot afford exposure to the legal risks potentially associated with such a project. Recognizing this, Nauru's sponsorship of Nauru Ocean Resources Inc. was originally premised on the assumption that Nauru could effectively mitigate (with a high degree of certainty) the potential liabilities or costs arising from its sponsorship. This was important, as these liabilities or costs could, in some circumstances, far exceed the financial capacities of Nauru (as well as those of many other developing States). Unlike terrestrial mining, in which a State generally only risks losing that which it already has (for example, its natural environment), if a developing State can be held liable for activities in the Area, the State may potentially face losing more than it actually has.
>
> Ultimately, if sponsoring States are exposed to potential significant liabilities, Nauru, as well as other developing States, may be precluded from effectively participating in activities in the Area, which is one of the purposes and principles of Part XI of the Convention[.] As a result, Nauru considers it crucial that guidance be provided on the interpretation of the relevant sections of Part XI pertaining to responsibility and liability, so that developing States can assess whether it is within their capabilities to effectively mitigate such risks and in turn make

an informed decision on whether or not to participate in activities in the Area. * * *

The Council decided not to adopt the proposal as formulated by Nauru. In view of the wishes of many participants in the debate, it decided to request an advisory opinion on three more abstract but concise questions[.]

73. [Question I] concerns the obligations of sponsoring States. [T]he Chamber must [initially] determine the meaning of two of the terms used in the Question, namely: "sponsorship" and "activities in the Area." * * *

74. The notion of "sponsorship" is a key element in the system for the exploration and exploitation of the resources of the Area set out in the Convention. Article 153, paragraph 2, of the Convention describes the "parallel system" of exploration and exploitation activities indicating that such activities shall be carried out by the Enterprise, and, in association with the Authority, by States Parties or state enterprises or natural or juridical persons. It further states that, in order to be eligible to carry out such activities, natural and juridical persons must satisfy two requirements. First, they must be either nationals of a State Party or effectively controlled by it or its nationals. Second, they must be "sponsored by such States." [T]he requirement of sponsorship [applies] also to state enterprises.

75. The purpose of requiring the sponsorship of applicants for contracts for the exploration and exploitation of the resources of the Area is to achieve the result that the obligations set out in the Convention, a treaty under international law which binds only States Parties thereto, are complied with by entities that are subjects of domestic legal systems. This result is obtained through the provisions of the Authority's Regulations that apply to such entities [*i.e.*, the Regulations on Prospecting and Exploration for Polymetallic Nodules, ISBA/6/A/18 (2000) (Nodules Regulations), and the Regulations on Prospecting and Exploration for Polymetallic Sulfides, ISBA/6/A/12 (2010) (Sulfides Regulations)] and through the implementation by the sponsoring States of their obligations under the Convention and related instruments.

76. The role of the sponsoring State, as set out in the Convention, contributes to the realization of the common interest of all States in the proper application of the principle of the common heritage of mankind which requires faithful compliance with the obligations set out in Part XI.

[The Chamber explores the meaning of "activities in the Area," defined in Article 1(1)(3) of the Convention as "all activities of exploration for, and exploitation of, the resources of the Area." According to Article 133, "resources" refers to mineral resources.

Turning to the obligations of sponsoring states, the Chamber finds that each such state owes "due diligence" obligations with respect to nationals that it sponsors, including the obligations under Annex III, Article 4(4) to adopt "laws and regulations" and to take "administrative measures which are, within the framework of its legal system, reasonably appropriate for securing compliance by persons under its jurisdiction." In addition, each sponsoring state has certain direct obligations under the Convention, the 1994 Agreement, the Nodules Regulations, and the Sulfides Regulations.]

126. Principle 15 of the 1992 Rio Declaration on Environment and Development (hereinafter "the Rio Declaration") reads:

> In order to protect the environment, the precautionary approach shall be widely applied by States according to their capabilities. Where there are threats of serious or irreversible damage, lack of full scientific certainty shall not be used as a reason for postponing cost-effective measures to prevent environmental degradation.

127. The provisions of the aforementioned Regulations transform this non-binding statement of the precautionary approach in the Rio Declaration into a binding obligation. The implementation of the precautionary approach as defined in these Regulations is one of the obligations of sponsoring States. * * *

135. The Chamber observes that the precautionary approach has been incorporated into a growing number of international treaties and other instruments, many of which reflect the formulation of Principle 15 of the Rio Declaration. In the view of the Chamber, this has initiated a trend towards making this approach part of customary international law. This trend is clearly reinforced by the inclusion of the precautionary approach in the Regulations[.]

[The Chamber also discusses other direct obligations of sponsoring states, *e.g.*, obligations to apply best environmental practices, to ensure the availability of recourse for compensation for pollution damage, and to conduct environmental impact assessments.]

152. [In light of language in the Law of the Sea Convention's Preamble concerning "the realization of a just and equitable international economic order which takes into account the interests and needs of mankind as a whole and, in particular, the special interests and needs of developing countries,"] it is necessary to examine whether developing sponsoring States enjoy preferential treatment as compared with that granted to developed sponsoring States under the Convention and related instruments. * * *

158. [N]one of the general provisions of the Convention concerning the responsibilities (or the liability) of the sponsoring State "specifically provides" for according preferential treatment to sponsoring States that are developing States. [T]here is no provision requiring the consideration

of such interests and needs beyond what is specifically stated in Part XI. [T]he general provisions concerning the responsibilities and liability of the sponsoring State apply equally to all sponsoring States, whether developing or developed.

159. Equality of treatment between developing and developed sponsoring States is consistent with the need to prevent commercial enterprises based in developed States from setting up companies in developing States, acquiring their nationality and obtaining their sponsorship in the hope of being subjected to less burdensome regulations and controls. The spread of sponsoring States "of convenience" would jeopardize uniform application of the highest standards of protection of the marine environment, the safe development of activities in the Area and protection of the common heritage of mankind. * * *

161. [However,] Principle 15 of the Rio Declaration * * * provides that the precautionary approach shall be applied by States "according to their capabilities." It follows that the requirements for complying with the obligation to apply the precautionary approach may be stricter for the developed than for the developing sponsoring States. * * *

162. Furthermore, the reference to "capabilities" is only a broad and imprecise reference to the differences in developed and developing States. What counts in a specific situation is the level of scientific knowledge and technical capability available to a given State in the relevant scientific and technical fields.

[The Chamber turns to Question 2, concerning the extent of liability of a State Party should an entity it has sponsored fail to comply with requirements under Part XI of the Law of the Sea Convention and the 1994 Agreement.]

179. Neither the Convention nor the relevant Regulations * * * specifies what constitutes compensable damage, or which subjects may be entitled to claim compensation. It may be envisaged that the damage in question would include damage to the Area and its resources constituting the common heritage of mankind, and damage to the marine environment. Subjects entitled to claim compensation may include the Authority, entities engaged in deep seabed mining, other users of the sea, and coastal States.

180. No provision of the Convention can be read as explicitly entitling the Authority to make such a claim. It may, however, be argued that such entitlement is implicit in article 137, paragraph 2, of the Convention, which states that the Authority shall act "on behalf" of mankind. Each State Party may also be entitled to claim compensation in light of the *erga omnes* character of the obligations relating to preservation of the environment of the high seas and in the Area. In support of this view, reference may be made to article 48 of the

[International Law Commission (ILC)] Articles on State Responsibility, which provides:

> Any State other than an injured State is entitled to invoke the responsibility of another State . . . if: (a) the obligation breached is owed to a group of States including that State, and is established for the protection of a collective interest of the group; or (b) the obligation breached is owed to the international community as a whole. * * *

201. [T]he liability of the sponsoring State arises from its own failure to carry out its responsibilities, whereas the contractor's liability arises from its own non-compliance. Both forms of liability exist in parallel. There is only one point of connection, namely, that the liability of the sponsoring State depends upon the damage resulting from activities or omissions of the sponsored contractor. But, in the view of the Chamber, this is merely a trigger mechanism. Such damage is not, however, automatically attributable to the sponsoring State. * * *

203. [A] gap in liability may occur if, notwithstanding the fact that the sponsoring State has taken all necessary and appropriate measures, the sponsored contractor has caused damage and is unable to meet its liability in full. [A] gap in liability may also occur if the sponsoring State failed to meet its obligations but that failure is not causally linked to the damage. * * *

204. [T]he liability regime established by article 139 of the Convention and in related instruments leaves no room for residual liability [of the sponsoring State, in the event of such a gap].

[We omit discussion of Question 3, concerning the "necessary and appropriate" measures a sponsoring state must take in order to fulfill its responsibilities under the Convention and related instruments, along with the Chamber's lengthy concluding replies to all three Questions. The Chamber's replies are all given unanimously.]

NOTES AND QUESTIONS

1. *The International Seabed Authority.* The International Seabed Authority, created pursuant to the 1982 Law of the Sea Convention as modified by the 1994 Part XI Agreement, is headquartered in Kingston, Jamaica. As of April 2013 the Authority had entered into 15-year exploration contracts with 14 applicants, and contracts were pending with three others. *Report of the Secretary-General of the International Seabed Authority under Article 166, Paragraph 4 of the United Nations Convention on the Law of the Sea* ¶¶ 57–59, ISBA/19/A/2 (2013). To date, no exploitation activity has been authorized. The Seabed Disputes Chamber in the *Responsibilities and Obligations Case* noted two components of the Authority's detailed seabed mining code—the 2000 Nodules Regulations and the 2010 Sulfides Regulations—and the ISA has now also adopted regulations for cobalt-rich

ferromanganese crusts. ISBA/18/A/11 (2012). These Regulations concern both prospecting and exploration, which provides exclusive rights in the Area. The Regulations specify operating procedures and environmental responsibilities, fees, data confidentiality, and dispute settlement obligations, and contain standard clauses to be used in exploration contracts. Next to be addressed are regulations for mineral exploitation. In addition to developing the mining code and reviewing the plans and work of contracting entities, the Authority has gathered and disseminated information about the deep seabed environment, non-proprietary seabed mining technology, and the market for minerals. See http://www.isa.org.jm (last visited Dec. 10, 2013).

2. *The Seabed Disputes Chamber*. The Seabed Disputes Chamber is a separate 11-member body within the 21-member International Tribunal for the Law of the Sea, which decided the *Saiga Case* excerpted in Part B. The Chamber has jurisdiction related to seabed mining disputes; the ISA, mining entities, and states may appear as parties in contentious cases. See Convention on the Law of the Sea, arts. 186–190. As we saw in the *Responsibilities and Obligations Case*—the Seabed Disputes Chamber's first case—the Chamber also has advisory jurisdiction when requested by the ISA's "Assembly or Council on legal questions arising within the scope of their activities." *Id.* art. 191. See Duncan French, "From the Depths: Rich Pickings of Principles of Sustainable Development and General International Law on the Ocean Floor—the Seabed Disputes Chamber's 2011 Advisory Opinion," 26 *International Journal of Marine and Coastal Law* 525 (2011).

3. *Obligations* Erga Omnes. What legal mechanisms exist to promote compliance with obligations not to cause excessive harm to the environment in the Area? Do you agree with the Seabed Disputes Chamber's suggestion that provisions of the 1982 Law of the Sea Convention/1994 Part XI Agreement concerning "activities in the Area" may create obligations *erga omnes*? Who should be entitled to seek remedies for violations of those provisions? Review the materials on obligations *erga omnes* in Chapter 3.

Is the first, unilateral licensing track noted before the *Responsibilities and Obligations Case* still a legal and practical option for a deep seabed mining company from a country, such as the United States, that is not a party to the Convention on the Law of the Sea? Why might a company be reluctant to proceed with exploiting minerals in the Area even if authorized under unilateral national legislation? Does the recognition of *erga omnes* obligations make it more difficult to assert legal rights based on unilateral legislation? Could a company seeking to mine under unilateral legislation avoid the risk of its mine sites overlapping with those authorized under the Convention/1994 Implementation Agreement regime? Could the company obtain internationally recognized deep seabed property rights and title to recovered minerals? According to the Law of the Sea Convention, States Parties must refuse to recognize claims or title to minerals unless they are established in accordance with Convention procedures applicable to the Area. See Convention on the Law of the Sea, art. 137(3) and Annex III, art. 1. If a

U.S. company were to take minerals from the Area, might the company risk foreign litigation or sanctions?

Lockheed Martin, a U.S. company that as of December 2013 held the only exploration licenses under the U.S. Deep Seabed Hard Mineral Resource Act noted above, gave its "strong support for speedy [U.S.] ratification" of the Law of the Sea Convention:

> [T]he multi-billion dollar investments needed to establish an ocean-based resource development business must be predicated upon clear legal rights established and protected under the treaty-based framework of the LOS Convention, including the International Seabed Authority. [W]ithout ratifying the LOS, the United States cannot sponsor claims with, or shape the deep seabed rules of, the ISA.

The Law of the Sea Convention (Treaty Doc. 103–39): Hearing Before the Senate Committee on Foreign Relations, 112th Cong. 74–75 (2013) (Letter from Robert J. Stevens, Chairman and Chief Executive Officer, Lockheed Martin Corp., to Sen. John Kerry, Chairman, U.S. Senate Foreign Relations Committee, May 17, 2012). If the United States fails to accept the Convention/1994 Agreement, what options are realistically available to a U.S. company that wants to exploit mineral resources from the Area?

4. *Changing the Deep Seabed Mining Regime*. As noted above, the 1994 Implementation Agreement significantly modified Part XI of the Law of the Sea Convention. Going forward, what methods will most likely be used to change the Part XI/1994 Implementation Agreement regime? How viable is the second track noted above, involving changes implemented by an international organization? The third track, *i.e.*, negotiation of a new multilateral treaty? Are there alternatives? For example, if there were impetus to eliminate the gaps in liability for damage to the Area identified in the *Responsibilities and Obligations* advisory opinion, how could those gaps be filled? Does the ISA have sufficient authority to reshape the international seabed mining regime? Might formal amendments to the Convention/1994 Agreement be negotiated? The Law of the Sea Convention contains cumbersome amendment provisions that some observers suggest may never be used. See *Stability and Change in the Law of the Sea: The Role of the LOS Convention* (Alex G. Oude Elferink ed. 2005). Compare the regimes and mechanisms for change applicable to Antarctica and ozone, which we introduced in Chapter 8.

5. *New Uses of the Deep Seabed*. In recent years, much attention has focused on living resources discovered at deep-sea hydrothermal vents. The sale of marine biotechnology-related products generates over $100 billion in revenues each year, and several such products use genetic materials from living organisms found at deep-sea hydrothermal vents. See generally Salvatore Arico & Charlotte Slapin, *UNU-IAS Report: Bioprospecting the Genetic Resources in the Deep Seabed* (2005). Could the ISA regulate the harvesting of living resources at hydrothermal vents in order to protect the

fragile environment near polymetallic sulfides? See Convention on the Law of the Sea, arts. 145, 162(2)(x). Even if the Authority may not directly regulate living resources at deep-seabed vents, does the general principle, set out in Article 136 of the Convention, that the Area is the "common heritage of mankind" provide limits and direction with respect to how these living resources are to be treated? Or should the harvesting of such living resources be regarded as a high seas freedom? What rules of international law apply to this issue? Is a new international regime needed for living resources at hydrothermal vents? See Recommendations of the Open-ended Informal Ad Hoc Working Group, in Letter dated from the Co-Chairpersons of the Ad Hoc Working Group to the President of the General Assembly, Mar. 7, 2010, U.N. Doc A/65/68, ¶¶ 70–77 (2010); Craig H. Allen, "Protecting the Oceanic Gardens of Eden: International Law Issues in Deep-Sea Vent Resource Conservation and Management," 13 *Georgetown International Environmental Law Review* 563 (2001).

6. *Outer Space.* The high seas and the seabed beyond the limits of national jurisdiction are not the only common spaces subject to international law. Although every state has sovereignty over airspace above its territory, see Convention on International Civil Aviation, art. 1, Dec. 7, 1944, 61 Stat. 1180, 15 U.N.T.S. 295, sovereign airspace ends at some height (as yet imprecisely delimited). What legal regimes apply above national airspace?

The United Nations and U.N. agencies have contributed significantly to the development of the international law of outer space. In 1959—two years after the launch of Sputnik I, the first satellite to orbit Earth—the United Nations General Assembly established the Committee for Peaceful Uses of Outer Space (COPUOS). The Committee's work led to the widely accepted Treaty on Principles Governing the Activities of States in the Exploration and Use of Outer Space, Including the Moon and Other Celestial Bodies (the Outer Space Treaty), Jan. 27, 1967, 18 U.S.T. 2410, 610 U.N.T.S. 205, in force for 102 parties as of March 2013. Article I of this Treaty sets out basic principles:

> The exploration and use of outer space, including the moon and other celestial bodies, shall be carried out for the benefit and in the interests of all countries, irrespective of their degree of economic or scientific development, and shall be the province of all mankind.
>
> Outer space, including the moon and other celestial bodies, shall be free for exploration and use by all States without discrimination of any kind, on a basis of equality and in accordance with international law, and there shall be free access to all areas of celestial bodies.
>
> There shall be freedom of scientific investigation in outer space, including the moon and other celestial bodies, and States shall facilitate and encourage international co-operation in such investigation.

According to Article II, "[o]uter space, including the moon and other celestial bodies, is not subject to national appropriation." Since Article II only prohibits territorial sovereignty, might private property rights still be permitted on celestial bodies? See Thomas Gangale, *The Development of Outer Space: Sovereignty and Property Rights in International Space Law* 33–49 (2009); Richard B. Bilder, "A Legal Regime for the Mining of Helium-3 on the Moon: U.S. Policy Options," 33 *Fordham International Law Journal* 243 (2010).

Some space law issues have been regulated for decades. For example, in allocating scare geostationary orbital slots, used for satellite transmissions, countries historically relied on a "first come, first served" principle: the International Telecommunications Union, an international organization founded in 1865 and since 1947 a specialized agency of the United Nations, developed regulations to avoid interference between satellite signals and registered the first claimants who met the regulatory requirements. Should some orbital slots be reserved for developing states—a change that has in fact been implemented? Should private companies be allowed to register for orbital slots along with—or instead of—states? See Jannat C. Thompson, Comment, "Space for Rent: The International Telecommunications Union, Space Law, and Orbit/Spectrum Leasing," 62 *Journal of Air Law and Commerce* 279 (1996).

A host of other space law issues are gaining prominence, only some the subject of specific treaty regulation: registration of objects launched into outer space; liability for damage caused by space objects; remote sensing; the development of solar power; military uses of outer space; private launches and space tourism; space stations; trade in space technology; and outer space debris and environmental concerns. See I.H. Ph. Diederiks-Verschoor & V. Kopal, *An Introduction to Space Law* (3d rev. ed. 2008); Francis Lyall & Paul B. Larsen, *Space Law: A Treatise* (2009). Does the law of the sea hold useful lessons for the development of space law?

CHAPTER 11

INTERNATIONAL CONFLICT OF LAWS

■ ■ ■

The anticipation and resolution of international legal disputes is often made more complex by the fundamental contradictions that exist between the realities of international transactions and the artifices of law. A basic fact of international relations is that private, as well as public, transactions abound that overleap national boundaries. No such overleapings, however, characterize the ordinary allocation and exercise of legal authority. These remain predominately vested in sovereign states. Hence, a dispute involving a single international transaction typically triggers responses from two or more national legal systems.

The intellectual discipline concerning the international interface of municipal legal systems has no satisfactory denomination. In civil law nations the field is usually called *private international law*, even though it concerns the international relations of national courts, legislatures, and administrations, surely a matter of public concern. In the United States and some other common law countries, the subject's customary appellation is *conflict of laws*, even though the relevant laws and processes have much more to do with conflict-avoidance and international legal cooperation. What is agreed is that the substance of the discipline includes topics such as jurisdiction and the resolution of conflicts of jurisdiction. Both are examined below. In practical terms, anticipating and solving problems of international conflict of laws constitutes a large fraction of the work of most international lawyers.

A. THE PRINCIPLES OF JURISDICTION

In studying the complex world of international conflict of laws, a reasonable point of first contact is the description and analysis of the authority (sometimes called power or competence) of different states to determine and affect the legal relationships of private parties. This topic is usually denoted by the term *jurisdiction*. Legislative jurisdiction, adjudicatory jurisdiction, and executive jurisdiction are more specific terms describing the power of states to make laws, to have their courts render authoritative judgments, and to enforce laws and the decisions of courts. Almost invariably in international transactions, any one nation's exercise of any sort of jurisdiction conflicts, at least in principle and often in practice, with the jurisdictional realm of another state. The problems of jurisdiction, be they legislative, judicial, or executive, usually involve both describing and justifying permissible forms of national legal authority, the topics here, and explicating the means, municipal and international, of reconciling conflicts among such municipal assertions of legal competence, the subjects of the next part.

1. THE TERRITORIAL PRINCIPLE

AMERICAN BANANA CO. V. UNITED FRUIT CO.

213 U.S. 347 (1909)

MR. JUSTICE HOLMES delivered the opinion of the Court.

The allegations of the complaint may be summed up as follows: The plaintiff is an Alabama corporation, organized in 1904. The defendant is a New Jersey corporation, organized in 1899. Long before the plaintiff was formed, the defendant, with intent to prevent competition and to control and monopolize the banana trade, bought the property and business of several of its previous competitors, with provision against their resuming the trade, made contracts with others, including a majority of the most important, regulating the quantity to be purchased and the price to be paid, and acquired a controlling amount of stock in still others. For the same purpose it organized a selling company, of which it held the stock, that by agreement sold at fixed prices all the bananas of the bringing parties. By this and other means it did monopolize and restrain the trade and maintained unreasonable prices. The defendant being in this ominous attitude, one McConnell in 1903 started a banana plantation in Panama, then part of the United States of Colombia, and began to build a railway (which would afford his only means of export), both in accordance with the laws of the United States of Columbia. He was notified by the defendant that he must either combine or stop. Two months later, it is believed at the defendant's instigation, the governor of Panama recommended to his national government that Costa Rica be allowed to administer the territory through which the railroad was to run, and this although that territory had been awarded to Colombia under an arbitration agreed to by treaty. The defendant, and afterwards, in September, the government of Costa Rica, it is believed by the inducement of the defendant, interfered with McConnell. In November, 1903, Panama revolted and became an independent republic, declaring its boundary to be settled by the award. In June, 1904, the plaintiff bought out McConnell and went on with the work, as it had a right to do under the laws of Panama. But in July, Costa Rican soldiers and officials, instigated by the defendant, seized a part of the plantation and a cargo of supplies and have held them ever since, and stopped the construction and operation of the plantation and railway. In August one Astua, by *ex parte* proceedings, got a judgment from a Costa Rican court, declaring the plantation to be his, although, it is alleged, the proceedings were not within the jurisdiction of Costa Rica, and were contrary to its laws and void. Agents of the defendant then bought the lands from Astua. The plaintiff has tried to induce the government of Costa Rica to withdraw its soldiers and also has tried to persuade the United States to interfere, but has been thwarted in both by the defendant and has failed. The government of Costa Rica remained in possession down to the bringing of the suit.

As a result of the defendant's acts the plaintiff has been deprived of the use of the plantation, and the railway, the plantation and supplies have been injured. The defendant also, by outbidding, has driven purchasers out of the market and has compelled producers to come to its terms, and it has prevented the plaintiff from buying for export and sale. This is the substantial damage alleged. * * *

It is obvious that, however stated, the plaintiff's case depended on several rather startling propositions. In the first place the acts causing the damage were done, so far as appears, outside the jurisdiction of the United States and within that of other states. It is surprising to hear it argued that they were governed by the act of Congress.

No doubt in regions subject to no sovereign, like the high seas, or to no law that civilized countries would recognize as adequate, such countries may treat some relations between their citizens as governed by their own law, and keep to some extent the old notion of personal sovereignty alive. They go further, at times, and declare that they will punish any one, subject or not, who shall do certain things, if they can catch him, as in the case of pirates on the high seas. In cases immediately affecting national interests they may go further still and may make, and, if they get the chance, execute similar threats as to acts done within another recognized jurisdiction. An illustration from our statutes is found with regard to criminal correspondence with foreign governments. And the notion that English statutes bind British subjects everywhere has found expression in modern times and has had some startling applications. But the general and almost universal rule is that the character of an act as lawful or unlawful must be determined wholly by the law of the country where the act is done. * * * For another jurisdiction, if it should happen to lay hold of the actor, to treat him according to its own notions rather than those of the place where he did the acts, not only would be unjust, but would be an interference with the authority of another sovereign, contrary to the comity of nations, which the other state concerned justly might resent.

Law is a statement of the circumstances in which the public force will be brought to bear upon men through the courts. But the word commonly is confined to such prophecies or threats when addressed to persons living with the power of the courts. A threat that depends upon the choice of the party affected to bring himself within that power hardly would be called law in the ordinary sense. We do not speak of blockade running by neutrals as unlawful. And the usages of speech correspond to the limit of the attempts of the lawmaker, except in extraordinary cases. It is true that domestic corporations remain always with the power of the domestic law, but in the present case, at least, there is not ground for distinguishing between corporations and men.

The foregoing considerations would lead in case of doubt to a construction of any statute as intended to be confined in its operation and effect to the territorial limits over which the lawmaker has general and legitimate power. "All legislation is *prima facie* territorial." Words having universal scope, such as "Every contract in restraint of trade," "Every person who shall monopolize," etc., will be taken as a matter of course to mean only every one subject to such legislation, not all that the legislator subsequently may be able to catch. In the case of the present statute the improbability of the United States attempting to make acts done in Panama or Costa Rica criminal is obvious, yet the law begins by making criminal the acts for which it gives a right to sue. We think it entirely plain that what the defendant did in Panama or Costa Rica is not within the scope of the statute so far as the present suit is concerned. Other objections of a serious nature are urged but need not be discussed.

For again, not only were the acts of the defendant in Panama or Costa Rica not within the Sherman Act, but they were not torts by the law of the place and therefore were not torts at all, however contrary to the ethical and economic postulates of the statute. * * * Giving to this complaint every reasonable latitude of interpretation we are of opinion that it alleges no case under the act of Congress and discloses nothing that we can suppose to have been a tort where it was done. A conspiracy in this country to do acts in another jurisdiction does not draw to itself those acts and make them unlawful, if they are permitted by the local law.

NOTES AND QUESTIONS

1. *Bananas.* Bananas, one of the earliest cultivated fruits, were virtually unknown in the United States and Europe until the middle of the 19th century. "At the Philadelphia Centennial Exposition of American Independence in 1876, bananas wrapped in tinfoil were sold to intrigued buyers at 10 cents apiece." Stacy May & Galo Plaza, *The United Fruit Company in Latin America* 3–4 (1958). Aided by developments in railroads and shipping, the later decades of the 19th century witnessed an explosive growth in the banana trade. By the end of the century more than 100 companies annually imported 16 million banana stems, largely from Central America and the Caribbean, to the United States. *Id.* at 4–6. There are modern threats to banana production. See Mike Peed, "We Have No Bananas," *New Yorker*, Jan. 10, 2011, at 28.

2. *The Territorial Principle.* In *American Banana* Justice Holmes maintained that "the general and almost universal rule is that the character of an act as lawful or unlawful must be determined wholly by the law of the country where the act is done." Did he explain if this was a jurisdictional rule based on U.S. law, Panamanian or Costa Rican law, or international law? What if the Court had found that Congress indeed had intended to prohibit U.S. companies from conspiring to restrain imports to the United States? Could international law or the law of Panama or that of Costa Rica have limited the extraterritorial reach of the U.S. statute? If so, in what court(s) could those limiting laws have been applied? If acts facilitating a restraint of trade had been done in the United States, *e.g.*, by corporate officers of United Fruit, would the Supreme Court necessarily have had to construe the statute as reaching outside U.S. territory?

3. *Holmes and Legal Realism.* Holmes's reasoning in *American Banana* reflected his well-known version of American legal realism: "Law is a statement of the circumstances in which the public force will be brought to bear upon men through the courts." Holmes employed his realism to argue that it would be unusual to use the term "law" to describe one nation's prescription of rules on another nation's territory: "the word commonly is confined to such prophecies or threats when addressed to persons living within the power of the courts."

4. *Competing Principles of Jurisdiction.* Nowadays, U.S. courts often recognize forms of extraterritorial jurisdiction that severely limit *American Banana.* In the 1990 *Kirkpatrick* case, Justice Scalia, delivering the opinion of the Supreme Court, wrote that *American Banana*'s proposition "that the antitrust laws had no extraterritorial application" had been "substantially overruled," *e.g.*, by Continental Ore Co. v. Union Carbide & Carbon Corp., 370 U.S. 690, 704–05 (1962). W.S. Kirkpatrick & Co. v. Environmental Tectonics Corp., 493 U.S. 400, 407 (1990). For more on the erosion of *American Banana*, see the review of authority in Zenith Radio Corp. v. Matsushita Elec. Indus. Co., 494 F.Supp. 1161, 1181–86 (E.D.Pa. 1980). Although *American Banana* may no longer be good law respecting the exclusive potency of the territorial principle, it still can be used to support the territorial principle as one basis, albeit among several, for a state's assertion of legislative, judicial, or executive jurisdiction.

5. *The Presumption Against Extraterritoriality.* That the courts have never totally abandoned *American Banana*'s presumption against the extraterritorial application of U.S. law can be seen in EEOC v. Arabian American Oil Co., 499 U.S. 244 (1991). In that case, Chief Justice Rehnquist refused to extend U.S. anti-discrimination legislation to protect a U.S. citizen employed by a U.S. oil company (Aramco) in Saudi Arabia: "It is a longstanding principle of American law 'that legislation of Congress, unless a contrary intent appears, is meant to apply only within the territorial jurisdiction of the United States.'" *Id.* at 248, *quoting* Foley Bros. v. Filardo, 336 U.S. 281, 285. Justice Scalia agreed. In Morrison v. National Australia Bank Ltd., 130 S. Ct. 2869 (2010), he wrote: "the results of judicial-

speculation-made-law–divining what Congress would have wanted if it had thought of the situation before the court—demonstrates the wisdom of the presumption against territoriality." *Id.* at 2881. Justice Stevens concurred in the result in *Morrison* but felt that Justice Scalia's approach was overly simplistic, arguing that the presumption against extraterritoriality "does not relieve courts of their duty to give statutes the most faithful reading possible." *Id.* at 2892.

6. *Choice-of-Law Considerations. American Banana* may also be seen to reflect policy preferences justifying the act of state doctrine, a topic explored in Chapter 12. That is, instead of viewing *American Banana* as a case about adjudicatory jurisdiction, why not see it as a case about legislative jurisdiction, *i.e.,* choice of law? Holmes could be said to have chosen to respect a foreign law that permitted the company's alleged activities rather than to apply a U.S. law that prohibited them.

One reason why U.S. courts have treated cases like *American Banana* as adjudicatory jurisdiction cases rather than choice-of-law cases has been that U.S. judges have traditionally seen their role as construing a federal statute, *e.g.*, asking whether Congress "meant" to regulate the matter in controversy. Is this too artificial an inquiry? Does Congress ordinarily "mean" anything about the reach of a statute outside the United States? We see more sophisticated analyses of conflicts of jurisdiction in *Lauritzen* and *Timberlane* in Part B below.

2. THE NATIONALITY PRINCIPLE

BLACKMER V. UNITED STATES

284 U.S. 421 (1932)

MR. CHIEF JUSTICE HUGHES delivered the opinion of the Court.

The petitioner, Harry M. Blackmer, a citizen of the United States resident of Paris, France, was adjudged guilty of contempt of the Supreme Court of the District of Columbia for failure to respond to subpoenas served upon him in France and requiring him to appear as a witness on behalf of the United States at a criminal trial in that court. Two subpoenas were issued, for appearances at different times, and there was a separate proceeding with respect to each. The two cases were heard together, and a fine of $30,000 with costs was imposed in each case, to be satisfied out of the property of the petitioner which had been seized by order of the court. The decrees were affirmed by the Court of Appeals of the District, and this Court granted writs of certiorari. * * *

While it appears that the petitioner removed his residence to France in the year 1924, it is undisputed that he was, and continued to be, a citizen of the United States. He continued to owe allegiance to the United States. By virtue of the obligations of citizenship, the United States retained its authority over him, and he was bound by its laws made applicable to him in a foreign country. Thus, although resident abroad, the petitioner remained subject to the taxing power of the United States. For disobedience to its laws through conduct abroad he was subject to punishment in the courts of the United States. *United States v. Bowman*, 260 U.S. 94, 102. With respect to such an exercise of authority, there is no question of international law, but solely of the purport of the municipal law which establishes the duties of the citizen in relation to his own government. While the legislation of the Congress, unless the contrary intent appears, is construed to apply only within the territorial jurisdiction of the United States, the question of its application, so far as citizens of the United States in foreign countries are concerned, is one of construction, not of legislative power. *American Banana Co. v. United Fruit Co.*, 213 U.S. 347, 357; *United States* v. *Bowman*, *supra*. Nor can it be doubted that the United States possesses the power inherent in sovereignty to require the return to this country of a citizen, resident elsewhere, whenever the public interest requires it, and to penalize him in case of refusal. What in England was the prerogative of the sovereign in this respect, pertains under our constitutional system to the national authority which may be exercised by the Congress by virtue of the legislative power to prescribe the duties of the citizens of the United States. It is also beyond controversy that one of the duties which the citizen owes to his government is to support the administration of justice by attending its courts and giving his testimony whenever he is properly summoned. And the Congress may provide for the performance of this duty and prescribe penalties for disobedience.

In the present instance, the question concerns only the method of enforcing the obligation. The jurisdiction of the United States over its absent citizen, so far as the binding effect of its legislation is concerned, is a jurisdiction *in personam*, as he is personally bound to take notice of the laws that are applicable to him and to obey them. *United States* v. *Bowman*, supra. But, for the exercise of judicial jurisdiction *in personam*, there must be due process, which requires appropriate notice of the judicial action and an opportunity to be heard. For this notice and opportunity the statute provides. The authority to require the absent citizen to return and testify necessarily implies the authority to give him notice of the requirement. As his attendance is needed in court, it is appropriate that the Congress should authorize the court to direct the notice to be given and that it should be in the customary form of a subpoena. Obviously, the requirement would be nugatory, if provision could not be made for its communication to the witness in the foreign country. The efficacy of an attempt to provide constructive service in this country would rest upon the presumption that the notice would be given in a manner calculated to reach the witness abroad. The question of the validity of the provision for actual service of the subpoena in a foreign country is one that arises solely between the Government of the United

States and the citizen. The mere giving of such a notice to the citizen in the foreign country of the requirement of his government that he shall return is in no sense an invasion of any right of the foreign government; and the citizen has no standing to invoke any such supposed right. While consular privileges in foreign countries are the appropriate subjects of treaties, it does not follow that every act of a consul, as, *e.g.*, in communicating with citizens of his country, must be predicated upon a specific provision of a treaty. The intercourse of friendly nations, permitting travel and residence of the citizens of each in the territory of the other, presupposes and facilitates such communications. In selecting the consul for the service of the subpoena, the Congress merely prescribed a method deemed to assure the desired result but in no sense essential. The consul was not directed to perform any function involving consular privileges or depending upon any treaty relating to them, but simply to act as any designated person might act for the Government in conveying to the citizen the actual notice of the requirement of his attendance. The point raised by the petitioner with respect to the provision for the service of the subpoena abroad is without merit.

NOTES AND QUESTIONS

1. *The Nationality Principle. Blackmer* is a classic example of jurisdiction based on the principle of nationality. Did the *Blackmer* Court fail to recognize that the case raised additional jurisdictional questions, *e.g.*, about legislative and judicial jurisdiction on the one hand and executive jurisdiction on the other? Chief Justice Hughes thoroughly explained why Blackmer as a U.S. citizen was subject to the laws and courts of the United States, but how effectively did he grapple with the question whether the United States had jurisdiction to serve process on *Blackmer* in France, *i.e.,* how to reconcile U.S. executive jurisdiction with the executive jurisdiction of France?

2. *Executive Acts on Foreign Soil.* The United States employed the U.S. consul in Paris to serve process on Blackmer. Should the United States instead have used the French courts or French administrative officers? What might be the response of any country, including the United States, to the exercise of executive jurisdiction within its territorial boundaries by a foreign country? Remember the outrage in Mexico over the kidnapping of one of its citizens in Mexico by the United States in *Alvarez-Machain*, noted in Chapter 4. If France could have been offended by the exercise of U.S. jurisdiction in the case, would Blackmer himself have had standing to complain? How might the French government itself have objected?

Should U.S. courts use cases like *Blackmer* to limit assertions of U.S. governmental power in foreign countries, or would that be too politically risky? Should U.S. courts be more ready to limit their own judicial jurisdiction in cases of international conflicts than to limit extraterritorial assertions of U.S. legislative or executive power? In *Blackmer* the Supreme

Court chose not to restrain the extraterritorial reach of the U.S. executive branch.

3. *Nationality as a Form of Extraterritorial Jurisdiction.* Territoriality and nationality are the two most commonly accepted bases for jurisdiction, but, taken together, they immediately raise conflictual problems, for example, in *Blackmer* of conflicts between the territorial jurisdiction of France and the nationality jurisdiction of the United States. After territoriality, all other bases of jurisdiction are more or less extraterritorial.

In 19th- and early 20th-century China, extraterritorial nationality jurisdiction went so far as to exclude the territorial jurisdiction of China over foreign nationals of the Great Powers, who were subject only to the laws and courts of their national governments, a fact keenly resented by many Chinese. E.H. Carr, *International Relations Since the Peace Treaties* 156 (1941 rev. ed.). This so-called "consular jurisdiction" was abandoned in the course of the 20th century. Nowadays the United States "seldom relie[s] on nationality-based jurisdiction," at least for crimes committed by its citizens overseas. Geoffrey R. Watson, "Offenders Abroad: The Case for Nationality-Based Criminal Jurisdiction," 14 *Yale Journal of International Law* 41, 53 (1992).

3. THE EFFECTS PRINCIPLE

UNITED STATES V. ALUMINUM CO. OF AMERICA

148 F.2d 416 (2d Cir. 1945)

L. HAND, CIRCUIT JUDGE

[The case concerns the application of U.S. antitrust laws to "Limited," a Canadian company, spun off from "Alcoa," a U.S. company.]

"Limited" was incorporated in Canada on May 31, 1928, to take over those properties of "Alcoa" which were outside the United States. [F]ormally at any rate, the separation between the two companies was complete. At the conclusion of the transfers a majority, though only a bare majority, of the common shares of "Alcoa" was in the hands of three persons: Andrew W. Mellon, Richard B. Mellon, his brother, and Arthur V. Davis. Richard Mellon died in 1933, and Andrew in 1937, and their shares passed to their families; but in January, 1939, the Davises, the officers and directors of "Alcoa" and the Mellon families—eleven individuals in all—collectively still held 48.9 per cent of "Alcoa's" shares, and 48.5 per cent of "Limited's"; and Arthur V. Davis was then the largest shareholder in both companies.

[The court finds that "Alcoa" had not been party to the "Alliance," a foreign cartel fixing the price of aluminum world-wide.]

Whether "Limited" itself violated [Section 1 of the Sherman Act] depends upon the character of the "Alliance." It was a Swiss corporation, created in pursuance of an agreement entered into on July 3, 1931, the signatories to which were a French corporation, two German, one Swiss, a British, and "Limited." The original agreement, or "cartel," provided for the formation of a corporation in Switzerland which should issue shares, to be taken up by the signatories. This corporation was from time to time to fix a quota of production for each share, and each shareholder was to be limited to the quantity measured by the number of shares it held, but was free to sell at any price it chose. The corporation fixed a price every year at which it would take off any shareholder's hands any part of its quota which it did not sell. No shareholder was to "buy, borrow, fabricate or sell" aluminum produced by anyone not a shareholder except with the consent of the board of governors, but that must not be "unreasonably withheld." Nothing was said as to whether the arrangement extended to sales in the United States; but Article X, known as the "Conversion Clause," provided that any shareholder might exceed his quota to the extent that he converted into aluminum in the United States or Canada any ores delivered to him in either of those countries by persons situated in the United States. This was confessedly put in to allow "Limited" to receive bauxite or alumina from "Alcoa," to smelt it into aluminum and to deliver the aluminum to "Alcoa." * * *

The agreement of 1936 abandoned the system of unconditional quotas, and substituted a system of royalties. Each shareholder was to have a fixed free quota for every share it held, but as its production exceeded the sum of its quotas, it was to pay a royalty, graduated progressively in proportion to the excess; and these royalties the "Alliance" divided among the shareholders in proportion to their shares. * * * Although this agreement, like its predecessor, was silent as to imports into the United States, when that question arose during its preparation, as it did, all the shareholders agreed that such imports should be included in the quotas. * * *

Did either the agreement of 1931 or that of 1936 violate § 1 of the Act? The answer does not depend upon whether we shall recognize as a source of liability a liability imposed by another state. On the contrary we are concerned only with whether Congress chose to attach liability to the conduct outside the United States of persons not in allegiance to it. That being so, the only question open is whether Congress intended to impose the liability, and whether our own Constitution permitted it to do so: as a court of the United States, we cannot look beyond our own law. Nevertheless, it is quite true that we are not to read general words, such as those in this Act, without regard to the limitations customarily observed by nations upon the exercise of their powers; limitations which generally correspond to those fixed by the "Conflict of Laws." We should not impute to Congress an intent to punish all whom its courts can catch, for conduct which has no consequences within the United States. American Banana Co. v. United Fruit Co., 213 U.S. 347, 357; United

States v. Bowman, 260 U.S. 94, 98; Blackmer v. United States, 284 U.S. 421, 437. On the other hand, it is settled—as "Limited" itself agrees—that any state may impose liabilities, even upon persons not within its allegiance, for conduct outside its borders that has consequences within its borders which the state reprehends; and these liabilities other states will ordinarily recognize. Strassheim v. Daily, 221 U.S. 280, 284, 285; Lamar v. United States, 240 U.S. 60, 65, 66; Ford v. United States, 273 U.S. 593, 620, 621; Restatement of Conflict of Laws § 65. It may be argued that this Act extends further. Two situations are possible. There may be agreements made beyond our borders not intended to affect imports, which do affect them, or which affect exports. Almost any limitation of the supply of goods in Europe, for example, or in South America, may have repercussions in the United States if there is trade between the two. Yet when one considers the international complications likely to arise from an effort in this country to treat such agreements as unlawful, it is safe to assume that Congress certainly did not intend the Act to cover them. Such agreements may on the other hand intend to include imports into the United States, and yet it may appear that they have had no effect upon them. That situation might be thought to fall within the doctrine that intent may be a substitute for performance in the case of a contract made within the United States; or it might be thought to fall within the doctrine that a statute should not be interpreted to cover acts abroad which have no consequence here. We shall not choose between these alternatives; but for argument we shall assume that the Act does not cover agreements, even though intended to affect imports or exports, unless its performance is shown actually to have had some effect upon them.

Both agreements would clearly have been unlawful, had they been made within the United States; and it follows from what we have just said that both were unlawful, though made abroad, if they were intended to affect imports and did affect them. Since the shareholders almost at once agreed that the agreement of 1931 should not cover imports, we may ignore it and confine our discussion to that of 1936: indeed that we should have to do anyway, since it superseded the earlier agreement. The judge found that it was not the purpose of the agreement to "suppress or restrain the exportation of aluminum to the United States for sale in competition with["] "Alcoa." By that we understand that he meant that the agreement was not specifically directed to "Alcoa," because it only applied generally to the production of the shareholders. If he meant that it was not expected that the general restriction upon production would have an effect upon imports, we cannot agree, for the change made in 1936 was deliberate and was expressly made to accomplish just that. It would have been an idle gesture, unless the shareholders had supposed that it would, or at least might, have that effect. The first of the conditions which we mentioned was therefore satisfied; the intent was to set up a quota system for imports.

The judge also found that the 1936 agreement did not "materially affect the * * * foreign trade or commerce of the United States;" apparently because the imported ingot was greater in 1936 and 1937 than in earlier years. We cannot accept this finding, based as it was upon the fact that, in 1936, 1937 and the first quarter of 1938, the gross imports of ingot increased. It by no means follows from such an increase that the agreement did not restrict imports; and incidentally it so happens that in those years such inference as is possible at all, leads to the opposite conclusion. It is true that the average imports—including "Alcoa's"—for the years 1932–1935 inclusive were about 15 million pounds, and that for 1936, 1937 and one-fourth of 1938 they were about 33 million pounds; but the average domestic ingot manufacture in the first period was about 96 million and in the second about 262 million; so that the proportion of imports to domestic ingot was about 15.6 per cent for the first period and about 12.6 per cent for the second. We do not mean to infer from this that the quota system of 1936 did in fact restrain imports, as these figures might suggest; but we do mean that nothing is to be inferred from the gross increase of imports. We shall dispose of the matter therefore upon the assumption that, although the shareholders intended to restrict imports, it does not appear whether in fact they did so. Upon our hypothesis the plaintiff would therefore fail, if it carried the burden of proof upon this issue as upon others. We think, however, that, after the intent to affect imports was proved, the burden of proof shifted to "Limited." In the first place a depressant upon production which applies generally may be assumed, ceteris paribus, to distribute its effect evenly upon all markets. * * *

There remains only the question whether this assumed restriction had any influence upon prices. To that United States v. Socony-Vacuum Oil Co., 310 U.S. 150, is an entire answer. It will be remembered that, when the defendants in that case protested that the prosecution had not proved that the "distress" gasoline had affected prices, the court answered that that was not necessary, because an agreement to withdraw any substantial part of the supply from a market would, if carried out, have some effect upon prices, and was as unlawful as an agreement expressly to fix prices. The underlying doctrine was that all factors which contribute to determine prices, must be kept free to operate unhampered by agreements. For these reasons we think that the agreement of 1936 violated § 1 of the Act.

NOTES AND QUESTIONS

1. *Determining Legislative Jurisdiction*. Albeit the *Aluminum* analysis of legislative jurisdiction over an international transaction was more

sophisticated than that of *American Banana* or *Blackmer*, was it thorough enough? Learned Hand pronounced that he was "concerned only with whether Congress chose to attach liability to the conduct outside the United States of persons not in allegiance to it." This avowal to look only at the intent of Congress was remarkably narrow and probably fictitious. Interpreting congressional intent as to extraterritorial reach usually leaves courts a great deal of latitude. Happily, Hand quickly circumvented his self-imposed obstacle and paid attention to "limitations customarily observed by nations upon the exercise of their powers; limitations which generally correspond to those fixed by the 'Conflict of Laws.'" However, rather than simply elaborating how Limited's participation in the foreign cartel was justifiably within U.S. legislative jurisdiction, why did he not attempt to determine whether the United States, or Switzerland, or some other country had the better right to regulate Limited's conduct? The explicit reason given was that "as a court of the United States, we cannot look beyond our own law." How can this be true, when for centuries common law courts in England and America have routinely reviewed, incorporated, and applied rules of both foreign and international law?

2. *Origins and Implications of the Effects Doctrine*. When anyone, even Learned Hand, calls the extraterritorial assertion of jurisdiction by the United States "settled" law, the reader should be just as much on guard as when a lawyer or a judge reassuringly calls facts or law "clear" or "plain." There was then and is now no "settled" law clearly or plainly establishing what is sometimes called "effects" or "objective territorial" jurisdiction. Did the *Aluminum* court demonstrate that it understood that U.S. jurisdiction based on the effects of foreign conduct in the United States would necessarily overlap and conflict with the territorial jurisdiction of foreign countries, *e.g.*, Canada, France, Germany, Great Britain, and Switzerland? Did Learned Hand really grapple with the problem identified by Justice Holmes in *American Banana*, that U.S. antitrust law may attempt to make illegal overseas acts that are legal by the law of the foreign state in which they take place?

3. *Reconciling the Effects Doctrine and the Presumption Against Extraterritoriality*. Notwithstanding *Aluminum*, the Supreme Court, as noted above, has held that there "is a longstanding principle of American law" that the statutes of Congress are to apply only within the United States unless a contrary intent is shown. EEOC v. Arabian American Oil Co., 499 U.S. 244, 248 (1991). The so-called *Aramco Case* was re-affirmed and extended to U.S. securities laws in 2010 in a judgment by Justice Scalia in Morrison v. National Australia Bank Ltd., 130 S.Ct. 2869 (2010). The Supreme Court overturned a decision of the Second Circuit where the Court of Appeals had given a U.S. cause of action to Australian investors in unregistered Australian securities in Australia. *Inter alia,* Justice Scalia wrote, "we reject the notion that the [Securities] Exchange Act [of 1934] reaches conduct in this country affecting exchanges or transactions abroad for the same reason that *Aramco* rejected overseas application of Title VII to all domestically concluded employment contracts or all employment contracts with American

employers: The probability of incompatibility with the applicable laws of other countries is so obvious that if Congress intended such foreign application 'it would have addressed the subject of conflict with foreign laws and procedures.' " *Id.* at 2885.

How does one reconcile the effects doctrine with this presumption against extraterritoriality? Professor Stephan has suggested that the Court now requires "clear Congressional authority," Paul M. Stephan, "*Morrison v. Nat'l Australia Bank Ltd.*: The Supreme Court Rejects Extraterritoriality," 14 *ASIL Insights*, Issue 22, at 2–3 (2010), a conclusion borne out by *Kiobel*'s treatment of the Alien Tort Statute, examined in Chapter 4. Kiobel v. Royal Dutch Petroleum Co., 133 S.Ct. 1659 (2013). Professor Dodge argued that the two can be made to fit together if one accepts that Congress is presumed to intend that its laws "should be applied to conduct that affects [domestic] conditions, regardless of where that conduct occurs." William S. Dodge, "Understanding the Presumption Against Extraterritoriality," 16 *Berkeley Journal of International Law* 85, 124 (1998). Such an approach makes sense of *Aluminum* and its progeny, *e.g.*, Minn-Chem, Inc. v. Agrium, 683 F.3d 845 (7th Cir. 2012), where the Seventh Circuit en banc held, in a decision by Judge Wood, that direct and indirect purchases of potash by U.S. companies world-wide had sufficient direct, substantial, and foreseeable impacts on domestic commerce to support claims under U.S. antitrust law. Professor Bauer applauded *Minn-Chem* as "healthy," demonstrating that "antitrust laws still apply when that behavior impacts domestic commerce and harms domestic consumers." Joseph P. Bauer, "The Foreign Trade Antitrust Improvement Act: Do We Really Want to Return to *American Banana*?," 65 *Maine Law Review* 3, 20 (2012).

4. *Jurisdiction and Choice of Forum.* The variety of bases for jurisdiction leads inevitably to jurisdictional conflicts, as well as to practical questions about where to bring suit. As Professor Vagts has pointed out, in "An Introduction to International Civil Practice," 17 *Vanderbilt Journal of Transnational Law* 1, 6 (1984):

> Counsel must recommend whether to bring a suit and where it should be brought. The latter decision can be a complex one. First, the question of in personam jurisdiction must be considered. The bases for jurisdiction in the United States (from doing business, to mere presence, to long-arm statutes) vary from those recognized in Europe. Each system has some type of jurisdictional claim that others regard as "exorbitant." France allows suit by virtue of a plaintiff's nationality. Germany sustains a suit if some of the defendant's property is present; in one case, a skier's underwear provided the necessary property. Other nations may find it strange that jurisdiction can arise under United States law merely because the sheriff was able to catch the defendant in transit within United States borders.

Did Hand in *Aluminum* give us any useful guidance about how clashes between U.S. and foreign law and process ought to be settled? See the discussion in *Timberlane* and *Hartford Fire* below.

5. *Jurisdiction Over Corporations.* Note how Alcoa used the formalities of corporate law to try to avoid having its cartel activities caught up by U.S. antitrust law. Could the court have better regulated Alcoa simply by piercing the corporate veil between Alcoa and Limited? After all, Hand found as facts that "in January, 1939, the Davises, the officers and directors of 'Alcoa,' and the Mellon families—11 individuals in all—collectively still held 48.9 per cent of 'Alcoa's' shares, and 48.5 per cent of 'Limited's'; and Arthur V. Davis was then the largest shareholder in both companies."

The shareholders in *Barcelona Traction*, reproduced in Chapter 6, asked the International Court of Justice to disregard the corporate form and look at the real owners of the company, an unsuccessful argument. In *Aluminum*, the shareholders argued successfully that the corporate form should be respected. See 3 Phillip I. Blumberg, Kurt A. Strasser, Nicholas L. Georgapoulos & Eric J. Gouvin, *Blumberg on Corporate Groups* (2005). In 2011, in Goodyear Dunlop Tire Operations, S.A. v. Brown, 131 S. Ct. 2846 (2011), the Supreme Court reversed North Carolina's assertion of jurisdiction over foreign subsidiaries of a U.S. corporation in a case where Turkish-manufactured tires allegedly caused deaths of two North Carolina teenagers in France. The Supreme Court held that the foreign subsidiaries had insufficient contacts with North Carolina to satisfy the due process clause of the Constitution's 14th Amendment. *Id.* at 2850–51. Plaintiffs had failed to raise a "unitary business" claim either in the state courts or in their brief for certiorari. When a "single enterprise" theory was finally advanced in their brief to the Supreme Court, it was rejected as coming too late, having already been forfeited. *Id.* at 2857. Might an earlier assertion of a single Goodyear enterprise have succeeded?

4. OTHER PRINCIPLES OF JURISDICTION

Besides territorial, nationality, and effects jurisdiction, international lawyers traditionally refer to three other principles of jurisdiction:

—the protective principle, guarding the security or the central interests of the state;

—the universality principle, giving any state the right to extend its jurisdiction to certain sorts of offenders, *e.g.*, pirates and war criminals; and

—the passive personality principle, protecting nationals even when abroad.

See Mark Weston Janis, *International Law* 338–39 (6th ed. 2012).

NOTES AND QUESTIONS

1. *The Protective Principle.* Might the *Blackmer Case* above be viewed as an exercise of protective as well as nationality jurisdiction? Can the protective principle justify jurisdiction standing on its own? In United States v. Pizzarusso, 388 F.2d 8 (2d Cir. 1968), *cert. denied*, 392 U.S. 936 (1968), the Second Circuit held it could. Where an alien was indicted and convicted for knowingly making false statements in Canada on a U.S. visa application, the Court held that "conduct outside [U.S.] territory that threatens [U.S.] security as a state or the operation of governmental functions" validated jurisdiction "provided the conduct is generally recognized as a crime under the laws of states that have reasonably developed legal systems." *Id.* at 10. Is this then a recognition that assertions of the protective principle depend on a minimum international legal standard?

The protective principle also figured in United States v. Ayesh, 702 F.3d 162 (4th Cir. 2012), *cert. denied*, 133 S. Ct. 1619 (2013), where a Jordanian citizen working as a shipping and customs supervisor at the U.S. Embassy in Baghdad, Iraq, was charged with diverting U.S. funds to his wife's bank account in Jordan. *Id.* at 165. Upholding Ayesh's indictment, the Fourth Circuit relied on jurisdiction under *Bowman* and the protective principle. "Otherwise, government employees, contractors, or agents like Ayesh—be they United States citizens or foreign nationals—would be at liberty to pilfer public money or engage in acts of self-dealing so long as they did so abroad." *Id.* at 166.

2. *Universal Jurisdiction.* Universal jurisdiction figured prominently in three cases considered above. *Filartiga* (Chapter 1) found the Second Circuit holding that "the torturer has become—like the pirate and the slave trader before him—*hostis humani generis*, an enemy of all mankind." 630 F.2d 876, 890 (2d Cir. 1980). *Smith* (Chapter 3) acknowledged that a pirate could be criminally tried pursuant to notions of universal law, as did *Dire* (Chapter 10). Is it fair to say that universal jurisdiction protects the international community from the "evils that are regarded as enemies of all of us"? Adeno Addis, "Imagining the International Community: The Constitutive Dimension of Universal Jurisdiction," 31 *Human Rights Quarterly* 129, 160 (2009).

3. *Passive Personality Jurisdiction.* Perhaps the most famous expression of the passive personality principle is Article 14 of the French Civil Code: "L'étranger * * * pourra être traduit devant les tribunaux de France, pour les obligations par lui contractées en pays étrangers envers des Français." ("A foreigner * * * may be tried before the French courts for obligations contracted in foreign countries respecting the French.") Note how France's domestic adherence to the passive personality principle came home to roost in international law in *Lotus* (Chapter 3). The Permanent Court of International Justice recognized Turkey's right to try a French citizen for violating Turkish law while he was outside the territory of Turkey.

4. *Overlapping Bases of Jurisdiction.* The various principles of jurisdiction do not constitute hard and fast discrete categories, but are often blended together in judicial discussions about jurisdiction in specific cases. For example, in United States v. Bowman, 260 U.S. 94 (1922), a case cited in *Blackmer*, the offense was defrauding the U.S. government by claiming payment for 1,000 tons of fuel oil delivered to a U.S.-operated vessel when the ship had really taken on and paid for only 600 tons. Since three of the four malfeasors were U.S. citizens, *Bowman* could certainly be read as the *Blackmer* Court read it, *i.e.*, that a U.S. citizen "was subject to punishment in the courts of the United States" for "disobedience to its laws through conduct abroad." Yet, the actual language in *Bowman* seemed to mix nationality with protective principles. Respecting criminal statutes, at least, *Bowman* held that there is a "right of the Government to defend itself against obstruction, or fraud whenever perpetrated, especially if committed by its own citizens, officers or agents." *Id.* at 98.

B. RESOLVING CONFLICTS OF JURISDICTION

Since the time of cases such as *American Banana*, *Blackmer,* and *Aluminum*, U.S. courts have attempted to develop more sophisticated approaches for recognizing and resolving international conflicts of jurisdiction. The cases in this part of the chapter illustrate four different modern approaches to conflict resolution: party choice, the balancing test, international comity, and *forum non conveniens*. Two other somewhat older approaches, foreign sovereign immunity and act of state, are treated in Chapter 12.

1. PARTY CHOICE

An apparently simple way to resolve jurisdictional conflicts is for the parties to agree where disputes will be settled and what law will be applied. Traditionally, U.S. courts looked suspiciously on such party choice agreements, fearing that private parties were usurping judicial functions. Nowadays, judicial suspicion of party choice has been largely abandoned, especially for international transactions, thanks to the pair of Supreme Court cases examined below.

THE BREMEN V. ZAPATA OFF-SHORE CO.

407 U.S. 1 (1972)

MR. CHIEF JUSTICE BURGER delivered the opinion of the Court.

We granted certiorari to review a judgment of the United States Court of Appeals for the Fifth Circuit declining to enforce a forum-selection clause governing disputes arising under an international towage contract between petitioners and respondent. The circuits have differed in their approach to such clauses. For the reasons stated hereafter, we vacate the judgment of the Court of Appeals.

In November 1967, respondent Zapata, a Houston-based American corporation, contracted with petitioner Unterweser, a German corporation, to tow Zapata's ocean-going, self-elevating drilling rig *Chaparral* from Louisiana to a point off Ravenna, Italy, in the Adriatic Sea, where Zapata had agreed to drill certain wells.

Zapata had solicited bids for the towage, and several companies including Unterweser had responded. Unterweser was the low bidder and Zapata requested it to submit a contract, which it did. The contract submitted by Unterweser contained the following provision, which is at issue in this case:

> Any dispute arising must be treated before the London Court of Justice.

In addition the contract contained two clauses purporting to exculpate Unterweser from liability for damages to the towed barge.[2]

After reviewing the contract and making several changes, but without any alteration in the forum-selection or exculpatory clauses, a Zapata vice president executed the contract and forwarded it to Unterweser in Germany, where Unterweser accepted the changes, and the contract became effective.

On January 5, 1968, Unterweser's deep sea tug *Bremen* departed Venice, Louisiana, with the *Chaparral* in tow bound for Italy. On January 9, while the flotilla was in international waters in the middle of the Gulf of Mexico, a severe storm arose. The sharp roll of the *Chaparral* in Gulf waters caused its elevator legs, which had been raised for the voyage, to break off and fall into the sea, seriously damaging the *Chaparral*. In this emergency situation Zapata instructed the *Bremen* to tow its damaged rig to Tampa, Florida, the nearest port of refuge.

On January 12, Zapata, ignoring its contract promise to litigate "any dispute arising" in the English courts, commenced a suit in admiralty in the United States District Court at Tampa, seeking $3,500,000 damages against Unterweser *in personam* and the *Bremen in rem*, alleging negligent towage and breach of contract. Unterweser responded by invoking the forum clause of the towage contract, and moved to dismiss for lack of jurisdiction or on *forum non conveniens* grounds, or in the

---

[2] The General Towage Conditions of the contract included the following:

> 1. . . . [Unterweser and its] masters and crews are not responsible for defaults and/or errors in the navigation of the tow.
>
> 2. . . .
>
> b) Damages suffered by the towed object are in any case for account of its Owners.

In addition, the contract provided that any insurance of the *Chaparral* was to be "for account of" Zapata. Unterweser's initial telegraphic bid had also offered to "arrange insurance covering towage risk for rig if desired." As Zapata had chosen to be self-insured on all its rigs, the loss in this case was not compensated by insurance.

alternative to stay the action pending submission of the dispute to the "London Court of Justice." Shortly thereafter, in February, before the District Court had ruled on its motion to stay or dismiss the United States action, Unterweser commenced an action against Zapata seeking damages for breach of the towage contract in the High Court of Justice in London, as the contract provided. Zapata appeared in that court to contest jurisdiction, but its challenge was rejected, the English courts holding that the contractual forum provision conferred jurisdiction.

In the meantime, Unterweser was faced with a dilemma in the pending action in the United States court at Tampa. The six-month period for filing action to limit its liability to Zapata and other potential claimants was about to expire, but the United States District Court in Tampa had not yet ruled on Unterweser's motion to dismiss or stay Zapata's action. On July 2, 1968, confronted with difficult alternatives, Unterweser filed an action to limit its liability in the District Court in Tampa. That court entered the customary injunction against proceedings outside the limitation court, and Zapata refiled its initial claim in the limitation action.

It was only at this juncture, on July 29, after the six-month period for filing the limitation action had run, that the District Court denied Unterweser's January motion to dismiss or stay Zapata's initial action. In denying the motion, that court relied on the prior decision of the Court of Appeals in *Carbon Black Export, Inc. v. The Monrosa*, 254 F.2d 297 (CA5 1958), cert. dismissed, 359 U.S. 180 (1959). In that case the Court of Appeals had held a forum-selection clause unenforceable, reiterating the traditional view of many American courts that "agreements in advance of controversy whose object is to oust the jurisdiction of the courts are contrary to public policy and will not be enforced." Apparently concluding that it was bound by the *Carbon Black* case, the District Court gave the forum-selection clause little, if any, weight. Instead, the Court treated the motion to dismiss under normal *forum non conveniens* doctrine applicable in the absence of such a clause, citing *Gulf Oil Corp. v. Gilbert*, 330 U.S. 501 (1947). Under that doctrine "unless the balance is strongly in favor of the defendant, the plaintiff's choice of forum should rarely be disturbed." The District Court concluded: "The balance of conveniences here is not strongly in favor of [Unterweser] and [Zapata's] choice of forum should not be disturbed."

Thereafter, on January 21, 1969, the District Court denied another motion by Unterweser to stay the limitation action pending determination of the controversy in the High Court of Justice in London and granted Zapata's motion to restrain Unterweser from litigating further in the London court. * * *

On appeal, a divided panel of the Court of Appeals affirmed, and on rehearing *en banc* the panel opinion was adopted, with six of the 14 *en banc* judges dissenting. As had the District Court, the majority rested on the *Carbon Black* decision, concluding that " 'at the very least' " that case stood for the proposition that a forum-selection clause " 'will not be enforced unless the selected state would provide a more convenient forum than the state in which suit is brought.' " From that premise the Court of Appeals proceeded to conclude that, apart from the forum-selection clause, the District Court did not abuse its discretion in refusing to decline jurisdiction on the basis of *forum non conveniens*. It noted that (1) the flotilla never "escaped the Fifth Circuit's mare nostrum, and the casualty occurred in close proximity to the district court;" (2) a considerable number of potential witnesses, including Zapata crewmen, resided in the Gulf Coast area; (3) preparation for the voyage and inspection and repair work had been performed in the Gulf area; (4) the testimony of the *Bremen* crew was available by way of deposition; (5) England had no interest in or contact with the controversy other than the forum-selection clause. The Court of Appeals majority further noted that Zapata was a United States citizen and "[t]he discretion of the district court to remand the case to a foreign forum was consequently limited"—especially since it appeared likely that the English courts would enforce the exculpatory clauses.[8] In the Court of Appeals' view, enforcement of such clauses would be contrary to public policy in American courts under *Bisso v. Inland Waterways Corp.*, 349 U.S. 85 (1955), and *Dixilyn Drilling Corp. v. Crescent Towing & Salvage Co.*, 372 U. S. 697 (1963). Therefore, "[t]he district court was entitled to consider that remanding Zapata to a foreign forum, with no practical contact with the controversy, could raise a bar to recovery by a United States citizen which its own convenient courts would not countenance."[9]

We hold, with the six dissenting members of the Court of Appeals, that far too little weight and effect were given to the forum clause in resolving this controversy. For at least two decades we have witnessed an expansion of overseas commercial activities by business enterprises based in the United States. The barrier of distance that once tended to confine a business concern to a modest territory no longer does so. Here we see an American company with special expertise contracting with a foreign company to tow a complex machine thousands of miles across seas and oceans. The expansion of American business and industry will hardly be

---

[8] The record contains an undisputed affidavit of a British solicitor stating an opinion that the exculpatory clauses of the contract would be held "prima facie valid and enforceable" against Zapata in any action maintained in England in which Zapata alleged that defaults or errors in Unterweser's tow caused the casualty and damage to the *Chaparral*.

In addition, it is not disputed that while the limitation fund in the District Court in Tampa amounts to $1,390,000, the limitation fund in England would be only slightly in excess of $80,000 under English law.

[9] The Court of Appeals also indicated in passing that even if it took the view that choice-of-forum clauses were enforceable unless "unreasonable" it was "doubtful" that enforcement would be proper here because the exculpatory clauses would deny Zapata relief to which it was "entitled" and because England was "seriously inconvenient" for trial of the action.

encouraged if, notwithstanding solemn contracts, we insist on a parochial concept that all disputes must be resolved under our laws and in our courts. Absent a contract forum, the considerations relied on by the Court of Appeals would be persuasive reasons for holding an American forum convenient in the traditional sense, but in an era of expanding world trade and commerce, the absolute aspects of the doctrine of the *Carbon Black* case have little place and would be a heavy hand indeed on the future development of international commercial dealings by Americans. We cannot have trade and commerce in world markets and international waters exclusively on our terms, governed by our laws, and resolved in our courts.

Forum-selection clauses have historically not been favored by American courts. Many courts, federal and state, have declined to enforce such clauses on the ground that they were "contrary to public policy," or that their effect was to "oust the jurisdiction" of the court. Although this view apparently still has considerable acceptance, other courts are tending to adopt a more hospitable attitude toward forum-selection clauses. This view, advanced in the well-reasoned dissenting opinion in the instant case, is that such clauses are prima facie valid and should be enforced unless enforcement is shown by the resisting party to be "unreasonable" under the circumstances. We believe this is the correct doctrine to be followed by federal district courts sitting in admiralty. It is merely the other side of the proposition recognized by this Court in *National Equipment Rental, Ltd. v. Szukhent*, 375 U.S. 311 (1964), holding that in federal courts a party may validly consent to be sued in a jurisdiction where he cannot be found for service of process through contractual designation of an "agent" for receipt of process in that jurisdiction. In so holding, the Court stated:

> [I]t is settled . . . that parties to a contract may agree in advance to submit to the jurisdiction of a given court, to permit notice to be served by the opposing party, or even to waive notice altogether.

This approach is substantially that followed in other common-law countries including England. It is the view advanced by noted scholars and that adopted by the Restatement of the Conflict of Laws. It accords with ancient concepts of freedom of contract and reflects an appreciation of the expanding horizons of American contractors who seek business in all parts of the world. Not surprisingly, foreign businessmen prefer, as do we, to have disputes resolved in their own courts, but if that choice is not available, then in a neutral forum with expertise in the subject matter. Plainly, the courts of England meet the standards of neutrality and long experience in admiralty litigation. The choice of that forum was made in an arm's-length negotiation by experienced and sophisticated businessmen, and absent some compelling and countervailing reason it should be honored by the parties and enforced by the courts.

The argument that such clauses are improper because they tend to "oust" a court of jurisdiction is hardly more than a vestigial legal fiction. It appears to rest at core on historical judicial resistance to any attempt to reduce the power and business of a particular court and has little place in an era when all courts are overloaded and when businesses once essentially local now operate in world markets. It reflects something of a provincial attitude regarding the fairness of other tribunals. No one seriously contends in this case that the forum-selection clause "ousted" the District Court of jurisdiction over Zapata's action. The threshold question is whether that court should have exercised its jurisdiction to do more than give effect to the legitimate expectations of the parties, manifested in their freely negotiated agreement, by specifically enforcing the forum clause.

There are compelling reasons why a freely negotiated private international agreement, unaffected by fraud, undue influence, or overweening bargaining power,[14] such as that involved here, should be given full effect. In this case, for example, we are concerned with a far from routine transaction between companies of two different nations contemplating the tow of an extremely costly piece of equipment from Louisiana across the Gulf of Mexico and the Atlantic Ocean, through the Mediterranean Sea to its final destination in the Adriatic sea. In the course of its voyage, it was to traverse the waters of many jurisdictions. The *Chaparral* could have been damaged at any point along the route, and there were countless possible ports of refuge. That the accident occurred in the Gulf of Mexico and the barge was towed to Tampa in an emergency were mere fortuities. It cannot be doubted for a moment that the parties sought to provide for a neutral forum for the resolution of any disputes arising during the tow. Manifestly much uncertainty and possibly great inconvenience to both parties could arise if a suit could be maintained in any jurisdiction in which an accident might occur or if jurisdiction were left to any place where the *Bremen* or Unterweser might happen to be found. The elimination of all such uncertainties by agreeing in advance on a forum acceptable to both parties is an indispensable

---

[14] The record here refutes any notion of overweening bargaining power. Judge Wisdom, dissenting, in the Court of Appeals noted:

> Zapata has neither presented evidence of nor alleged fraud or undue bargaining power in the agreement. Unterweser was only one of several companies bidding on the project. No evidence contradicts its Managing Director's affidavit that it specified English courts 'in an effort to meet Zapata Off–Shore company half way.' Zapata's Vice President has declared by affidavit that no specific negotiations concerning the forum clause took place. But his was not simply a form contract with boilerplate language that Zapata had no power to alter. The towing of an oil rig across the Atlantic was a new business. Zapata did make alterations to the contract submitted by Unterweser. The forum clause could hardly be ignored. It is the final sentence of the agreement, immediately preceding the date and the parties' signatures. . . .

element in international trade, commerce, and contracting. There is strong evidence that the forum clause was a vital part of the agreement, and it would be unrealistic to think that the parties did not conduct their negotiations, including fixing the monetary terms, with the consequences of the forum clause figuring prominently in their calculations. Under these circumstances, as Justice Karminski reasoned in sustaining jurisdiction over Zapata in the High Court of Justice, "[t]he force of an agreement for litigation in this country, freely entered into between two competent parties seems to me to be very powerful."

Thus, in the light of present-day commercial realities and expanding international trade we conclude that the forum clause should control absent a strong showing that it should be set aside. Although their opinions are not altogether explicit, it seems reasonably clear that the District Court and the Court of Appeals placed the burden on Unterweser to show that London would be a more convenient forum than Tampa, although the contract expressly resolved that issue. The correct approach would have been to enforce the forum clause specifically unless Zapata could clearly show that enforcement would be unreasonable and unjust, or that the clause was invalid for such reasons as fraud or overreaching. Accordingly, the case must be remanded for reconsideration.

We note, however, that there is nothing in the record presently before us that would support a refusal to enforce the forum clause. * * *

This case * * * involves a freely negotiated international commercial transaction between a German and an American corporation for towage of a vessel from the Gulf of Mexico to the Adriatic Sea. As noted, selection of a London forum was clearly a reasonable effort to bring vital certainty to this international transaction and to provide a neutral forum experienced and capable in the resolution of admiralty litigation. Whatever "inconvenience" Zapata would suffer by being forced to litigate in the contractual forum as it agreed to do was clearly foreseeable at the time of contracting. In such circumstances it should be incumbent on the party seeking to escape his contract to show that trial in the contractual forum will be so gravely difficult and inconvenient that he will for all practical purposes be deprived of his day in court. Absent that, there is no basis for concluding that it would be unfair, unjust, or unreasonable to hold that party to his bargain.

NOTES AND QUESTIONS

1. *Zapata and Unterweser.* George Herbert Walker Bush, later President of the United States, joined with friends to found Zapata Petroleum in 1953 and Zapata Offshore Co. in 1954, with financial backing from Bush's father, Senator Prescott Bush of Connecticut. The company's name was inspired by the movie "Viva Zapata!" George Bush bought out his partners in Zapata Offshore in 1959 and moved the company to Houston. He sold the

company in 1966 when he won a Texas seat in the U.S. House of Representatives. Since then, Zapata has had its financial ups and downs. From off-shore oil drilling, its new owners moved the company into the fishing business and the internet. Monica Perin, "Adios, Zapata! Colorful Company Founded by Bush Relocates to N.Y.," *Houston Business Journal*, Apr. 23, 1999, *available at* http://www.bizjournals.com (last visited Dec. 9, 2013).

Unterweser, now URAG, was founded as "Schleppschiffahrtsgesellschaft Unterweser" in Bremen, Germany in 1890. It has always specialized in tugboats, operating 109 different craft from 1890, the *Meteor*, to 2006, the *Ems*. The tug in our case, the *Bremen*, was in service between 1967 and 1972, and was the 80th tug in Unterweser's history. URAG, "Tug Chronicle 1957–1970," http://www.urag.de (last visited Dec. 9, 2013).

2. Bremen*'s Rationale. Bremen* was the first in a series of important U.S. Supreme Court decisions favoring forum-selection clauses in international contracts. In *Bremen* the Court enforced a choice-of-forum clause and sent the case abroad, reasoning in part that Zapata had fairly bargained away its access to U.S. courts in the course of its international contract negotiations. Did the Supreme Court in *Bremen* rely mostly on freedom-of-contract arguments in reaching its decision? Or was it more persuaded by other policy factors? For example, did the Court attempt to protect the negotiating position of U.S. companies by enforcing forum-selection clauses? If the clause in *Bremen* had been held unenforceable, would U.S. businesses simply not be believed if in the future they promised to trade off a forum-selection clause for some other benefit in a contract because they could always find U.S. judicial support to renege on their deal?

3. *Lower Court Discretion. Bremen* did not entirely eliminate the discretion of the trial court to decide whether to respect a choice-of-forum clause in an international contract. This discretionary principle was reinforced in Lauro Lines v. Chasser, 490 U.S. 495 (1989), where the end result was that a choice-of-forum clause was not enforced. In *Lauro Lines* the Supreme Court decided that an interlocutory order of a U.S. district court denying a defendant's motion to dismiss a damages action on the basis of a contractual forum-selection clause was not immediately appealable:

> The individual respondents were, or represent the estates of persons who were, passengers aboard the cruise ship Achille Lauro when it was hijacked by terrorists in the Mediterranean in October 1985. Petitioner Lauro Lines s.r.l., an Italian company, owns the Achille Lauro. Respondents filed suits against Lauro Lines in the District Court for the Southern District of New York to recover damages for injuries sustained as a result of the hijacking, and for the wrongful death of passenger Leon Klinghoffer. Lauro Lines moved before trial to dismiss the actions, citing the forum-selection clause printed on each passenger ticket. This clause purported to obligate the passenger to institute any suit arising in connection

> with the contract in Naples, Italy, and to renounce the right to sue elsewhere.
>
> The District Court denied petitioner's motions to dismiss, holding that the ticket as a whole did not give reasonable notice to passengers that they were waiving the opportunity to sue in a domestic forum.

Id. at 496–97. Justice Scalia observed in his concurring opinion:

> While it is true * * * that the "right not to be sued elsewhere than in Naples" is not fully vindicated—indeed, to be utterly frank, is positively destroyed—by permitting the trial to occur and reversing its outcome, that is vindication enough because the right is not sufficiently important to overcome the policies militating against interlocutory appeals.

Id. at 502–03.

Has *Lauro Lines* diminished the force of *Bremen*? See also Carnival Cruise Lines v. Shute, 499 U.S. 585 (1991), in which the Supreme Court upheld a forum-selection clause in a passenger ticket that specified a U.S. forum different from the one in which the U.S. plaintiff had sued the U.S. corporate defendant. The complexity of party choice in modern U.S. law since *Bremen* is carefully explored in Robert G. Bone, "Party Rulemaking: Making Procedural Rules Through Party Choice," 90 *Texas Law Review* 1329 (2012).

4. *Choice of Law as a Factor*. What difference should choice-of-law considerations make when deciding whether to enforce a contractual choice-of-forum clause? In *Bremen*, the Supreme Court noted:

> The record contains an undisputed affidavit of a British solicitor stating an opinion that the exculpatory clauses of the contract would be held "prima facie valid and enforceable" against Zapata in any action maintained in England in which Zapata alleged that defaults or errors in Unterweser's tow caused the casualty and damage to the *Chaparral*.

407 U.S. at 8 n.8.

The Fifth Circuit Court of Appeals in *Bremen* felt that enforcement of the exculpatory clauses would be contrary to U.S. public policy and that a U.S. court presumably would have voided them. The Supreme Court, as we have seen, preferred to weigh other factors more heavily. How far must a conflicting substantive law go to trigger a U.S. public policy objection? In *Bremen* it seemed that the choice-of-law decision about the validity of the exculpatory clauses would virtually decide the case. Why did the parties not also include a choice-of-law clause in their contract?

5. *The Interests of the Chosen Forum*. The British courts accepted jurisdiction in the *Bremen* dispute, allowing Unterweser to proceed on a claim for damages there. Unterweser Reederei G.M.B.H. v. Zapata Off-shore Co., [1968] 2 Lloyd's L. Rep. 158 (Court of Appeal). All three U.K. Court of Appeal

justices affirmed a lower court's decision granting jurisdiction over Zapata. Lord Justice Willmer held that "it is the policy of the Court to hold parties to the bargain into which they have entered," finding that by "London Court" the parties meant "High Court." *Id.* at 161-62. Why should British courts hear a dispute between a U.S. and a German company about a transaction that did not touch British ports or waters? When, if ever, should a court refuse to hear a case when the parties to a dispute have freely selected that court in a forum-selection clause? See also the discussion of *forum non conveniens* below.

6. *Conflict of Laws and International Lawyering.* Although *Bremen* concerned a choice-of-forum clause, at bottom it was a battle about which set of legal rules, English or American, to apply to the substantive issues of the case. In a litigation setting, international lawyers know which legal rules will most benefit their clients. Moreover, this wisdom is part of the background that international lawyers bring to international negotiations. Cases like *Bremen* provide international lawyers with considerable flexibility and power in structuring transactions, concerning both the rules to be applied (legislative jurisdiction) and the legal processes to be made available (adjudicatory jurisdiction). Because of the variety of laws and legal processes, international transactions often give lawyers greater authority than they would have in a purely domestic context.

SCHERK V. ALBERTO-CULVER CO.

417 U.S. 506 (1974)

MR. JUSTICE STEWART delivered the opinion of the Court.

Alberto-Culver Co., the respondent, is an American company incorporated in Delaware with its principal office in Illinois. It manufactures and distributes toiletries and hair products in this country and abroad. During the 1960's Alberto-Culver decided to expand its overseas operations, and as part of this program it approached the petitioner Fritz Scherk, a German citizen residing at the time of trial in Switzerland. Scherk was the owner of three interrelated business entities, organized under the laws of Germany and Liechtenstein, that were engaged in the manufacture of toiletries and the licensing of trademarks for such toiletries. An initial contact with Scherk was made by a representative of Alberto-Culver in Germany in June 1967, and negotiations followed at further meetings in both Europe and the United States during 1967 and 1968. In February 1969 a contract was signed in Vienna, Austria, which provided for the transfer of the ownership of Scherk's enterprises to Alberto-Culver, along with all rights held by these enterprises to trademarks in cosmetic goods. The contract contained a number of express warranties whereby Scherk guaranteed the sole and unencumbered ownership of these trademarks. In addition, the contract contained an arbitration clause providing that "any controversy or claim [that] shall arise out of this agreement or the breach thereof" would be referred to arbitration before the International Chamber of Commerce in Paris, France, and that "[t]he laws of the State of Illinois, U.S.A. shall apply to and govern this agreement, its interpretation and performance."[1]

The closing of the transaction took place in Geneva, Switzerland, in June 1969. Nearly one year later Alberto-Culver allegedly discovered that the trademark rights purchased under the contract were subject to substantial encumbrances that threatened to give others superior rights to the trademarks and to restrict or preclude Alberto-Culver's use of them. Alberto-Culver thereupon tendered back to Scherk the property that had been transferred to it and offered to rescind the contract. Upon Scherk's refusal, Alberto-Culver commenced this action for damages and other relief in a Federal District Court in Illinois, contending that Scherk's fraudulent representations concerning the status of the trademark rights constituted violations of § 10(b) of the Securities Exchange Act of 1934 and Rule 10b–5 promulgated thereunder.

In response, Scherk filed a motion to dismiss the action for want of personal and subject-matter jurisdiction as well as on the basis of *forum non conveniens*, or, alternatively, to stay the action pending arbitration in Paris pursuant to the agreement of the parties. Alberto-Culver, in turn, opposed this motion and sought a preliminary injunction restraining the prosecution of arbitration proceedings.[2] On December 2, 1971, the District Court denied Scherk's motion to dismiss, and, on January 14, 1972, it granted a preliminary order enjoining Scherk from proceeding with arbitration. In taking these actions the court relied entirely on this Court's decision in *Wilko v. Swan*, 346 U.S. 427, which held that an agreement to arbitrate could not preclude a buyer of a security from seeking a judicial remedy under the Securities Act of 1933, in view of the language of § 14 of that Act, barring "[a]ny condition, stipulation, or provision binding any person acquiring any security to waive compliance with any provision of this subchapter. . . ." The Court of Appeals for the

---

[1] The arbitration clause relating to the transfer of one of Scherk's business entities, similar to the clauses covering the other two, reads in its entirety as follows:

> The parties agree that if any controversy or claim shall arise out of this agreement or the breach thereof and either party shall request that the matter shall be settled by arbitration, the matter shall be settled exclusively by arbitration in accordance with the rules then obtaining of the International Chamber of Commerce, Paris, France, by a single arbitrator, if the parties shall agree upon one, or by one arbitrator appointed by each party and a third arbitrator appointed by the other arbitrators. In case of any failure of a party to make an appointment referred to above within four weeks after notice of the controversy, such appointment shall be made by said Chamber. All arbitration proceedings shall be held in Paris, France, and each party agrees to comply in all respects with any award made in any such proceeding and to the entry of a judgment in any jurisdiction upon any award rendered in such proceeding. The laws of the State of Illinois, U.S.A. shall apply to and govern this agreement, its interpretation and performance.

[2] Scherk had taken steps to initiate arbitration in Paris in early 1971. He did not, however, file a formal request for arbitration with the International Chamber of Commerce until November 9, 1971, almost five months after the filing of Alberto–Culver's complaint in the Illinois federal court.

Seventh Circuit, with one judge dissenting, affirmed, upon what it considered the controlling authority of the *Wilko* decision. Because of the importance of the question presented we granted Scherk's petition for a writ of certiorari.

The United States Arbitration Act, now 9 U.S.C. §§ 1 *et seq.*, reversing centuries of judicial hostility to arbitration agreements,[4] was designed to allow parties to avoid "the costliness and delays of litigation," and to place arbitration agreements "upon the same footing as other contracts. . . . " Accordingly, the Act provides that an arbitration agreement such as is here involved "shall be valid, irrevocable, and enforceable, save upon such grounds as exist at law or in equity for the revocation of any contract." The Act also provides in § 3 for a stay of proceedings in a case where a court is satisfied that the issue before it is arbitrable under the agreement, and § 4 of the Act directs a federal court to order parties to proceed to arbitration if there has been a "failure, neglect, or refusal" of any party to honor an agreement to arbitrate.

In *Wilko v. Swan, supra*, this Court acknowledged that the Act reflects a legislative recognition of the "desirability of arbitration as an alternative to the complications of litigation," but nonetheless declined to apply the Act's provisions. That case involved an agreement between Anthony Wilko and Hayden, Stone & Co., a large brokerage firm, under which Wilko agreed to purchase on margin a number of shares of a corporation's common stock. Wilko alleged that his purchase of the stock was induced by false representations on the part of the defendant concerning the value of the shares, and he brought suit for damages under § 12(2) of the Securities Act of 1933. The defendant responded that Wilko had agreed to submit all controversies arising out of the purchase to arbitration, and that this agreement, contained in a written margin contract between the parties, should be given full effect under the Arbitration Act.

The Court found that "[t]wo policies, not easily reconcilable, are involved in this case." On the one hand, the Arbitration Act stressed "the need for avoiding the delay and expense of litigation," and directed that such agreements be "valid, irrevocable, and enforceable" in federal courts. On the other hand, the Securities Act of 1933 was "[d]esigned to protect investors" and to require "issuers, underwriters, and dealers to make full and fair disclosure of the character of securities sold in interstate and foreign commerce and to prevent fraud in their sale," by creating "a special right to recover for misrepresentation. . . . " In particular, the Court noted that § 14 of the Securities Act provides:

---

[4] English courts traditionally considered irrevocable arbitration agreements as "ousting" the courts of jurisdiction, and refused to enforce such agreements for this reason. This view was adopted by American courts as part of the common law up to the time of the adoption of the Arbitration Act.

> Any condition, stipulation, or provision binding any person acquiring any security to waive compliance with any provision of this subchapter or of the rules and regulations of the Commission shall be void.

The Court ruled that an agreement to arbitrate "is a 'stipulation,' and [that] the right to select the judicial forum is the kind of 'provision' that cannot be waived under § 14 of the Securities Act." Thus, Wilko's advance agreement to arbitrate any disputes subsequently arising out of his contract to purchase the securities was unenforceable under the terms of § 14 of the Securities Act of 1933.

Alberto-Culver, relying on this precedent, contends that the District Court and Court of Appeals were correct in holding that its agreement to arbitrate disputes arising under the contract with Scherk is similarly unenforceable in view of its contentions that Scherk's conduct constituted violations of the Securities Exchange Act of 1934 and rules promulgated thereunder. For the reasons that follow, we reject this contention and hold that the provisions of the Arbitration Act cannot be ignored in this case.

[W]e find crucial differences between the agreement involved in *Wilko* and the one signed by the parties here. Alberto-Culver's contract to purchase the business entities belonging to Scherk was a truly international agreement. Albeto-Culver is an American corporation with its principal place of business and the vast bulk of its activity in this country, while Scherk is a citizen of Germany whose companies were organized under the laws of Germany and Liechtenstein. The negotiations leading to the signing of the contract in Austria and to the closing in Switzerland took place in the United States, England, and Germany, and involved consultations with legal and trademark experts from each of those countries and from Liechtenstein. Finally, and most significantly, the subject matter of the contract concerned the sale of business enterprises organized under the laws of and primarily situated in European countries, whose activities were largely, if not entirely, directed to European markets.

Such a contract involves considerations and policies significantly different from those found controlling in *Wilko*. In *Wilko*, quite apart from the arbitration provision, there was no question but that the laws of the United States generally, and the federal securities laws in particular, would govern disputes arising out of the stock-purchase agreement. The parties, the negotiations, and the subject matter of the contract were all situated in this country, and no credible claim could have been entertained that any international conflict-of-laws problems would arise. In this case, by contrast, in the absence of the arbitration provision considerable uncertainty existed at the time of the agreement, and still exists, concerning the law applicable to the resolution of disputes arising out of the contract.

Such uncertainty will almost inevitably exist with respect to any contract touching two or more countries, each with its own substantive laws and conflict-of-laws rules. A contractual provision specifying in advance the forum in which disputes shall be litigated and the law to be applied is, therefore, an almost indispensable precondition to achievement of the orderliness and predictability essential to any international business transaction. Furthermore, such a provision obviates the danger that a dispute under the agreement might be submitted to a forum hostile to the interests of one of the parties or unfamiliar with the problem area involved.

A parochial refusal by the courts of one country to enforce an international arbitration agreement would not only frustrate these purposes, but would invite unseemly and mutually destructive jockeying by the parties to secure tactical litigation advantages. In the present case, for example, it is not inconceivable that if Scherk had anticipated that Alberto-Culver would be able in this country to enjoin resort to arbitration he might have sought an order in France or some other country enjoining Alberto-Culver from proceeding with its litigation in the United States. Whatever recognition the courts of this country might ultimately have granted to the order of the foreign court, the dicey atmosphere of such a legal no-man's-land would surely damage the fabric of international commerce and trade, and imperil the willingness and ability of businessmen to enter into international commercial agreements.

The exception to the clear provisions of the Arbitration Act carved out by *Wilko* is simply inapposite to a case such as the one before us. In *Wilko* the Court reasoned that "[w]hen the security buyer, prior to any violation of the Securities Act, waives his right to sue in courts, he gives up more than would a participant in other business transactions. The security buyer has a wider choice of courts and venue. He thus surrenders one of the advantages the Act gives him. . . ." In the context of an international contract, however, these advantages become chimerical since, as indicated above, an opposing party may by speedy resort to a foreign court block or hinder access to the American court of the purchaser's choice.

Two Terms ago in *The Bremen v. Zapata Off-Shore Co.*, we rejected the doctrine that a forum-selection clause of a contract, although voluntarily adopted by the parties, will not be respected in a suit brought in the United States " 'unless the selected state would provide a more convenient forum than the state in which suit is brought.' " Rather, we concluded that a "forum clause should control absent a strong showing that it should be set aside." We noted that "much uncertainty and possibly great inconvenience to both parties could arise if a suit could be maintained in any jurisdiction in which an accident might occur or if jurisdiction were left to any place [where personal or *in rem* jurisdiction might be established]. The elimination of all such uncertainties by agreeing in advance on a forum acceptable to both parties is an indispensable element in international trade, commerce, and contracting."

An agreement to arbitrate before a specified tribunal is, in effect, a specialized kind of forum-selection clause that posits not only the situs of suit but also the procedure to be used in resolving the dispute.[13] The invalidation of such an agreement in the case before us would not only allow the respondent to repudiate its solemn promise but would, as well, reflect a "parochial concept that all disputes must be resolved under our laws and in our courts. . . . We cannot have trade and commerce in world markets and international waters exclusively on our terms, governed by our laws, and resolved in our courts."[14]

For all these reasons we hold that the agreement of the parties in this case to arbitrate any dispute arising out of their international commercial transaction is to be respected and enforced by the federal courts in accord with the explicit provisions of the Arbitration Act.[15]

---

[13] Under some circumstances, the designation of arbitration in a certain place might also be viewed as implicitly selecting the law of that place to apply to that transaction. In this case, however, "[t]he laws of the State of Illinois" were explicitly made applicable by the arbitration agreement. See n. 1, *supra*.

[14] In *The Bremen* we noted that forum-selection clauses "should be given full effect" when "a freely negotiated private international agreement [is] unaffected by fraud. . . ." This qualification does not mean that any time a dispute arising out of a transaction is based upon an allegation of fraud, as in this case, the clause is unenforceable. Rather, it means that an arbitration or forum-selection clause in a contract is not enforceable if the *inclusion of that clause in the contract* was the product of fraud or coercion.

Although we do not decide the question, presumably the type of fraud alleged here could be raised, under Art. V of the Convention on the Recognition and Enforcement of Foreign Arbitral Awards, see n. 15, *infra*, in challenging the enforcement of whatever arbitral award is produced through arbitration. Article V(2)(b) of the Convention provides that a country may refuse recognition and enforcement of an award if "recognition or enforcement of the award would be contrary to the public policy of that country."

[15] Our conclusion today is confirmed by international developments and domestic legislation in the area of commercial arbitration subsequent to the *Wilko* decision. On June 10, 1958, a special conference of the United Nations Economic and Social Council adopted the Convention on the Recognition and Enforcement of Foreign Arbitral Awards. In 1970 the United States acceded to the treaty, [1970] 3 U.S.T. 2517, T.I.A.S. No. 6997, and Congress passed Chapter 2 of the United States Arbitration Act, 9 U.S.C. § 201 *et seq.*, in order to implement the Convention. Section 1 of the new chapter, 9 U.S.C. § 201, provides unequivocally that the Convention "shall be enforced in United States courts in accordance with this chapter."

The goal of the Convention, and the principal purpose underlying American adoption and implementation of it, was to encourage the recognition and enforcement of commercial arbitration agreements in international contracts and to unify the standards by which agreements to arbitrate are observed and arbitral awards are enforced in the signatory countries. Article II(1) of the convention provides:

> Each Contracting State shall recognize an agreement in writing under which the parties undertake to submit to arbitration all or any differences which have arisen or which may arise between them in respect of a defined legal relationship, whether contractual or not, concerning a subject matter capable of settlement by arbitration.

Accordingly, the judgment of the Court of Appeals is reversed and the case is remanded to that court with directions to remand to the District Court for further proceedings consistent with this opinion.

It is so ordered.

NOTES AND QUESTIONS

1. *Alberto-Culver.* The Alberto-Culver Company was founded in 1955 when Leonard Lavin bought Alberto VO5 Conditioning Hairdressing. The Company went public in 1961 and was listed on the New York Stock Exchange in 1965. It grew rapidly in the 1960s, acquiring companies like those owned by Fritz Scherk and broadening its product line to include food products and beauty salons. By 2008 Alberto-Culver had more than 13,000 employees and sales of nearly $2 billion. The sale of Alberto-Culver was announced in September 2010. Chris V. Nicholson, "Unilever Makes a $3.7 Billion Deal to Buy Alberto Culver," *New York Times*, Sept. 28, 2010, at B8.

2. *Party Choice: A Sensible Approach.* Note the number of countries connected with the transaction in *Scherk*: at least the United States, Germany, Switzerland, Liechtenstein, Austria, England, and France. Given that courts in each of these states might have jurisdiction to adjudicate a case arising out of the transaction, why did it make sense for Alberto-Culver and Scherk to settle contractually the forum for any future dispute settlement procedure? Under what circumstances might it have been in the interests of either party *not* to agree in advance as to the place and form of dispute settlement? Using the phrase of the Supreme Court, might "a legal no-man's-land" favor a party that expected to run a significant risk of breaching the contract? Should the other party be alert to a significant risk of noncompliance when there is difficulty in reaching agreement on a choice-of-forum clause?

3. *Mixing Forum and Law.* The contract in *Scherk* included an arbitration clause that selected International Chamber of Commerce arbitration in Paris as a choice of forum and Illinois law as a choice of law. Why "mix" the forum (and thus much of the procedural law) and substantive law? Was it a result of compromise? What did the two parties each gain and lose when they agreed to such an arbitration clause?

4. *The Chicago Suit.* Why did Alberto-Culver decide to sue in Chicago? Could the company offer only technical reasons justifying why it should be permitted to avoid living up to its promise to arbitrate in Paris? Could one

In their discussion of this Article, the delegates to the Convention voiced frequent concern that courts of signatory countries in which an agreement to arbitrate is sought to be enforced should not be permitted to decline enforcement of such agreements on the basis of parochial views of their desirability or in a manner that would diminish the mutually binding nature of the agreements.

Without reaching the issue of whether the Convention, apart from the considerations expressed in this opinion, would require of its own force that the agreement to arbitrate be enforced in the present case, we think that this country's adoption and ratification of the Convention and the passage of Chapter 2 of the United States Arbitration Act provide strongly persuasive evidence of congressional policy consistent with the decision we reach today.

argue that fraud voided not only the contract but also the choice-of-forum clause? Was the Chicago suit merely a means of harassing Scherk? If Alberto-Culver were to win its suit in Chicago, what obstacles might there have been in enforcing the U.S. judgment in Europe? See Note 8 below.

5. *The Rationale of the Court.* Did it make a difference to the Court that Alberto-Culver was the larger entity and that it had chosen to go to Europe to seek out acquisitions? What difference might it have made if Scherk had come to Chicago to peddle his companies? In Mitsubishi Motors Corp. v. Soler Chrysler-Plymouth, Inc., 473 U.S. 614 (1985), the Supreme Court enforced an agreement to arbitrate in Japan against the less powerful party, a Puerto Rican car dealer, to the advantage of the larger party, a Japanese auto manufacturer.

Was the Court protecting the honor of U.S. companies by making Alberto-Culver stick to its agreement to arbitrate? What would be the value of a U.S. company's promise to arbitrate abroad if such promises were *not* enforced by the U.S. legal system? Would this scenario put U.S. companies at a relative disadvantage *vis-à-vis* foreign companies, the promises of which to arbitrate might be upheld by their home courts? Compare the *Scherk Case* to *Bremen* above. Should the same rationale apply to enforcing choice-of-forum clauses selecting foreign arbitration as to enforcing choice-of-forum clauses selecting foreign municipal courts?

6. *The New York Convention.* Without the New York Convention on the Recognition and Enforcement of Foreign Arbitral Awards, discussed in footnote 15 of the *Scherk* opinion, the recognition of arbitral agreements and the enforcement of foreign arbitral awards would depend on international comity and the municipal law of each country. What are the advantages to the Convention framework? See Emmanuel Guillard & Domenico Di Pietro, *Enforcement of Arbitration Agreements and International Arbitral Awards: The New York Convention in Practice* (2008). As of December 2013, 149 states were parties to the New York Convention. See http://www.newyorkconvention.org (last visited Dec. 9, 2013). For a brief history of international agreements about foreign arbitral awards, see Jan Kleinheisterkamp, "Recognition and Enforcement of Foreign Arbitral Awards," in 8 *Max Planck Encyclopedia of Public International Law* 664 (Rüdiger Wolfrum ed. 2012).

Why did the Court in *Scherk* not rely on the New York Convention? Was it because Alberto-Culver's agreement with Scherk was made before the Convention came into force in the United States? Would the agreement to arbitrate have been enforced under the New York Convention? Article II of the Convention provides for the recognition of written agreements to arbitrate disputes "concerning a subject matter capable of settlement by arbitration." Article II(3) reads that the court of a state that has accepted the New York Convention "shall, at the request of one of the parties [to a dispute], refer the parties to arbitration, unless it finds that the said agreement is null and void, inoperative or incapable of being performed." Would this Article II(3) limitation have prevented a court from giving effect to the choice-of-forum clause in *Scherk*?

As noted in footnote 14 of *Scherk*, another provision of the New York Convention, Article V, governs judicial recognition and enforcement of awards granted by arbitral tribunals. Without the recognition and enforcement of arbitral awards by municipal courts, what would be the likelihood of such awards being respected in business practice? Would the desire to continue doing business after the dispute is arbitrated serve as something of an enforcement mechanism? Even when arbitral awards are honored without recourse to municipal legal systems, how much does the potential for municipal enforcement loom as a threat to noncompliance?

7. *International Arbitration.* The parties in *Scherk* chose to go to the International Chamber of Commerce (ICC) in Paris. The ICC was established in 1919, and its Court of Arbitration dates from 1923. It is one of the principal international arbitral centers and has administered over 17,000 arbitrations involving about 180 countries. International Court of Arbitration, *Resolving Business Disputes Worldwide* 2 (ICC Publication 810–2, Apr. 2010).

There is fierce competition among different arbitral institutes for business. How do factors of convenience, cost, efficiency, and rules governing arbitral procedures influence party choice? See Julian D.M. Lew, Loukas Mistelis & Stefan Kröll, *Comparative International Commercial Arbitration* (2003); Earl McLaren, "Effective Use of International Commercial Arbitration: A Primer for In-House Counsel," 19 *Journal of International Arbitration* 473 (2002).

Parties may also decide to resolve disputes outside the established arbitral institutes. Such *ad hoc* arbitration necessitates special agreement, *e.g.*, about the arbitrator(s), venue, language, applicable law, procedural rules, and costs. There may be advantages to *ad hoc* arbitration, *e.g.*, possibly lower costs, greater speed, acceptance by parties wary of arbitral institutes, and greater flexibility. See Harry L. Arkin, "International Ad Hoc Arbitration: A Practical Alternative," 15 *International Business Lawyer* 5 (1987). Compare the relative advantages of *ad hoc* and institutional arbitration. For more on the history of international commercial arbitration, see Sir Michael J. Mustill, "Arbitration: History and Background," 6 *Journal of International Arbitration*, No. 2, at 43 (1989).

International arbitration is becoming increasingly popular in the United States. See Christopher R. Drahozal, "New Experiences of International Arbitration in the United States," 54 *American Journal of Comparative Law* 233 (2006). Is it a problem, however, that American lawyers may be "bogg[ing international arbitration] down in long and costly legal proceedings"?, Steven Seidenberg, "International Arbitration Loses its Grip," 96 *ABA Journal*, Apr. 2010, at 50.

8. *Recognition and Enforcement of Foreign Judicial Awards.* The United States is party to no "full faith and credit" treaty for the recognition and enforcement of foreign judicial awards. Indeed, negotiation of the first multilateral Hague Convention on Choice of Court Agreements, 44

International Legal Materials 1291 (2005), which provides for the recognition and enforcement of judgments of courts chosen by parties in business-to-business agreements, only concluded in June 2005, and as of November 2013, was still not in force. See Ronald A. Brand, "The New Hague Convention on Choice of Court Agreements," 9 *ASIL Insights,* June 2005; Guy S. Lipe & Timothy J. Tyler, "The Hague Convention on Choice of Court Agreements: Creating Room for Choice in International Cases," 33 *Houston Journal of International Law* 1 (2010). Why should states have found it easier to agree on a treaty to facilitate the enforcement of awards of foreign arbitral tribunals—the New York Convention discussed in Note 6 above—than to agree on a treaty to facilitate the enforcement of judgments of foreign courts? Is it because arbitral panels are regarded as more neutral than municipal courts?

2. BALANCING

LAURITZEN V. LARSEN

345 U.S. 571 (1952)

MR. JUSTICE JACKSON delivered the opinion of the Court.

The key issue in this case is whether statutes of the United States should be applied to this claim of maritime tort. Larsen, a Danish seaman, while temporarily in New York joined the crew of the *Randa,* a ship of Danish flag and registry, owned by petitioner, a Danish citizen. Larsen signed ship's articles, written in Danish, providing that the rights of crew members would be governed by Danish law and by the employer's contract with the Danish Seamen's Union, of which Larsen was a member. He was negligently injured aboard the *Randa* in the course of employment, while in Havana harbor.

Respondent brought suit under the Jones Act[1] on the law side of the District Court for the Southern District of New York, and demanded a jury. Petitioner contended that Danish law was applicable, and that, under it, respondent had received all of the compensation to which he was entitled. He also contested the court's jurisdiction. Entertaining the cause, the court ruled that American, rather than Danish, law applied, and the jury rendered a verdict of $4,267.50. The Court of Appeals, Second Circuit, affirmed. Its decision, at least superficially, is at variance with its own earlier ones and conflicts with one by the New York Court of Appeals. We granted certiorari. * * *

Denmark has enacted a comprehensive code to govern the relations of her shipowners to her seagoing labor which by its terms and intentions

---

1 "Any seaman who shall suffer personal injury in the course of his employment may at his election, maintain an action for damages at law, with the right of trial by jury, and in such action all statutes of the United States modifying or extending the common law right or remedy in cases of personal injury to railway employees shall apply. . . . " 46 U.S.C. § 688 [now codified at 46 U.S.C. § 30104].

controls this claim. Though it is not for us to decide, it is plausibly contended that all obligations of the owner growing out of Danish law have been performed or tendered to this seaman. The shipowner, supported here by the Danish Government, asserts that the Danish law supplies the full measure of his obligation, and that maritime usage and international law as accepted by the United States exclude the application of our incompatible statute.

That allowance of an additional remedy under our Jones Act would sharply conflict with the policy and letter of Danish law is plain from a general comparison of the two systems of dealing with shipboard accidents. Both assure the ill or injured seafaring worker the conventional maintenance and cure at the shipowner's cost, regardless of fault or negligence on the part of anyone. But, while we limit this to the period within which maximum possible cure can be effected, the Danish law limits it to a fixed period of twelve weeks, and the monetary measurement is different. The two systems are in sharpest conflict as to treatment of claims for disability, partial or complete, which are permanent, or which outlast the liability for maintenance and cure, to which class this claim belongs. Such injuries Danish law relieves under a state-operated plan similar to our workmen's compensation systems. Claims for such disability are not made against the owner, but against the state's Directorate of Insurance Against the Consequences of Accidents. They may be presented directly or through any Danish Consulate. They are allowed by administrative action, not by litigation, and depend not upon fault or negligence, but only on the fact of injury and the extent of disability. Our own law, apart from indemnity for injury caused by the ship's unseaworthiness, makes no such compensation for such disability in the absence of fault or negligence. But, when such fault or negligence is established by litigation, it allows recovery for elements such as pain and suffering not compensated under Danish law, and lets the damages be fixed by jury. In this case, since negligence was found, United States law permits a larger recovery than Danish law. If the same injury were sustained but negligence was absent or not provable, the Danish law would appear to provide compensation where ours would not. * * *

Congress, in 1920, wrote these all-comprehending words [of the Jones Act], not on a clean slate, but as a postscript to a long series of enactments governing shipping. All were enacted with regard to a seasoned body of maritime law developed by the experience of American courts long accustomed to dealing with admiralty problems in reconciling our own with foreign interests and in accommodating the reach of our own laws to those of other maritime nations.

The shipping laws of the United States, set forth in Title 46 of the United States Code, comprise a patchwork of separate enactments, some tracing far back in our history and many designed for particular emergencies. While some have been specific in application to foreign shipping and others in being confined to American shipping, many give no evidence that Congress addressed itself to their foreign application and are in general terms which leave their application to be judicially determined from context and circumstance. By usage as old as the Nation, such statutes have been construed to apply only to areas and transactions in which American law would be considered operative under prevalent doctrines of international law. Thus, in *United States v. Palmer*, 3 Wheat. 610, this Court was called upon to interpret a statute of 1790 (1 Stat. 115) punishing certain acts when committed on the high seas by "any person or persons," terms which, as Mr. Chief Justice Marshall observed, are "broad enough to comprehend every human being." But the Court determined that the literal universality of the prohibition "must not only be limited to cases within the jurisdiction of the state, but also to those objects to which the legislature intended to apply them," and therefore would not reach a person performing the proscribed acts aboard the ship of a foreign state on the high seas.

This doctrine of construction is in accord with the long-heeded admonition of Mr. Chief Justice Marshall that "an Act of Congress ought never to be construed to violate the law of nations if any other possible construction remains. . . . " *The Charming Betsy*, 2 Cranch 64, 118. And it has long been accepted in maritime jurisprudence that ". . . if any construction otherwise be possible, an Act will not be construed as applying to foreigners in respect to acts done by them outside the dominions of the sovereign power enacting. That is a rule based on international law, by which one sovereign power is bound to respect the subjects and the rights of all other sovereign powers outside its own territory." Lord Russell of Killowen in *The Queen v. Jameson*, [1896] 2 Q.B. 425, 430. This is not, as sometimes is implied, any impairment of our own sovereignty, or limitation of the power of Congress. "The law of the sea," we have had occasion to observe, "is in a peculiar sense an international law, but application of its specific rules depends upon acceptance by the United States." *Farrell v. United States*, 336 U.S. 511, 517. On the contrary, we are simply dealing with a problem of statutory construction rather commonplace in a federal system by which courts often have to decide whether "any" or "every" reaches to the limits of the enacting authority's usual scope or is to be applied to foreign events or transactions. * * *

Congress could not have been unaware of the necessity of construction imposed upon courts by such generality of language and was well warned that in the absence of more definite directions than are contained in the Jones Act, it would be applied by the courts to foreign events, foreign ships and foreign seamen only in accordance with the usual doctrine and practices of maritime law.

Respondent places great stress upon the assertion that petitioner's commerce and contacts with the ports of the United States are frequent and regular, as the basis for applying our statutes to incidents aboard his ships. But the virtue and utility of sea-borne commerce lies in its frequent and important contacts with more than one country. If, to serve some immediate interest, the courts of each were to exploit every such contact to the limit of its power, it is not difficult to see that a multiplicity of conflicting and overlapping burdens would blight international carriage by sea. Hence, courts of this and other commercial nations have generally deferred to a non-national or international maritime law of impressive maturity and universality. It has the force of law, not from extraterritorial reach of national laws, nor from abdication of its sovereign powers by any nation, but from acceptance by common consent of civilized communities of rules designed to foster amicable and workable commercial relations.

International or maritime law in such matters as this does not seek uniformity and does not purport to restrict any nation from making and altering its laws to govern its own shipping and territory. However, it aims at stability and order through usages which considerations of comity, reciprocity and long-range interest have developed to define the domain which each nation will claim as its own. Maritime law, like our municipal law, has attempted to avoid or resolve conflicts between competing laws by ascertaining and valuing points of contact between the transaction and the states or governments whose competing laws are involved. The criteria, in general, appear to be arrived at from weighing of the significance of one or more connecting factors between the shipping transaction regulated and the national interest served by the assertion of authority. It would not be candid to claim that our courts have arrived at satisfactory standards or apply those that they profess with perfect consistency. But in dealing with international commerce we cannot be unmindful of the necessity for mutual forbearance if retaliations are to be avoided; nor should we forget that any contact which we hold sufficient to warrant application of our law to a foreign transaction will logically be as strong a warrant for a foreign country to apply its law to an American transaction.

In the case before us, two foreign nations can claim some connecting factor with this tort—Denmark, because, among other reasons, the ship and the seaman were Danish nationals; Cuba, because the tortious conduct occurred and caused injury in Cuban waters. The United States may also claim contacts because the seaman had been hired in and was returned to the United States, which also is the state of the forum. We therefore review the several factors which, alone or in combination, are generally conceded to influence choice of law to govern a tort claim, particularly a maritime tort claim, and the weight and significance accorded them.

1. *Place of the Wrongful Act.*—The solution most commonly accepted as to torts in our municipal and in international law is to apply the law of the place where the acts giving rise to the liability occurred, the *lex loci delicti commissi.* This rule of locality, often applied to maritime torts, would indicate application of the law of Cuba, in whose domain the actionable wrong took place.

* * * The locality test, for what it is worth, affords no support for the application of American law in this case, and probably refers us to Danish, in preference to Cuban, law, though this point we need not decide, for neither party urges Cuban law as controlling.

2. *Law of the Flag.*—Perhaps the most venerable and universal rule of maritime law relevant to our problem is that which gives cardinal importance to the law of the flag. Each state under international law may determine for itself the conditions on which it will grant its nationality to a merchant ship, thereby accepting responsibility for it and acquiring authority over it. Nationality is evidenced to the world by the ship's papers and its flag. The United States has firmly and successfully maintained that the regularity and validity of a registration can be questioned only by the registering state.

This Court has said that the law of the flag supersedes the territorial principle, even for purposes of criminal jurisdiction of personnel of a merchant ship, because it "is deemed to be a part of the territory of that sovereignty [whose flag it flies], and not to lose that character when in navigable waters within the territorial limits of another sovereignty." On this principle, we concede a territorial government involved only concurrent jurisdiction of offenses aboard our ships. *United States v. Flores*, 289 U.S. 137, 155–159, and cases cited. Some authorities reject, as a rather mischievous fiction, the doctrine that a ship is constructively a floating part of the flag state, but apply the law of the flag on the pragmatic basis that there must be some law on shipboard, that it cannot change at every change of waters, and no experience shows a better rule than that of the state that owns her.

It is significant to us here that the weight given to the ensign overbears most other connecting events in determining applicable law. As this Court held in *United States v. Flores, supra,* at 158, and iterated in *Cunard S.S. Co. v. Mellon,* [262 U.S. 100,] 123:

> And so by comity it came to be generally understood among civilized nations that all matters of discipline, and all things done on board, which affected only the vessel or those belonging to her and did not involve the peace or dignity of the country or the tranquillity of the port, should be left by the local government to be dealt with by the authorities of the nation to which the vessel belonged as the laws of that nation, or the interests of its commerce should require . . . .

This was but a repetition of settled American doctrine.

These considerations are of such weight in favor of Danish and against American law in this case that it must prevail unless some heavy counterweight appears.

3. *Allegiance or Domicile of the Injured.*—Until recent times there was little occasion for conflict between the law of the flag and the law of the state of which the seafarer was a subject, for the long-standing rule, as pronounced by this Court after exhaustive review of authority, was that the nationality of the vessel for jurisdictional purposes was attributed to all her crew. *In re Ross*, 140 U.S. 453, 472. Surely, during service under a foreign flag some duty of allegiance is due. But, also, each nation has a legitimate interest that its nationals and permanent inhabitants be not maimed or disabled from self-support. In some later American cases, courts have been prompted to apply the Jones Act by the fact that the wrongful act or omission alleged caused injury to an American citizen or domiciliary. We need not, however, weigh the seaman's nationality against that of the ship, for here the two coincide without resort to fiction. Admittedly, respondent is neither citizen nor resident of the United States. While on direct examination he answered leading questions that he was living in New York when he joined the *Randa,* the articles which he signed recited, and on cross-examination he admitted, that his home was Silkeburg, Denmark. His presence in New York was transitory, and created no such national interest in, or duty toward, him as to justify intervention of the law of one state on the shipboard of another.

4. *Allegiance of the Defendant Shipowner.*—A state "is not debarred by any rule of international law from governing the conduct of its own citizens upon the high seas or even in foreign countries when the rights of other nations or their nationals are not infringed." *Skiriotes v. Florida*, 313 U.S. 69, 73. *Steele v. Bulova Watch Co.*, 344 U.S. 280, 282. * * *

But here again the utmost liberality in disregard of formality does not support the application of American law in this case, for it appears beyond doubt that this owner is a Dane by nationality and domicile.

5. *Place of Contract.*—Place of contract, which was New York, is the factor on which respondent chiefly relies to invoke American law. It is one which often has significance in choice of law in a contract action. * * * But this action does not seek to recover anything due under the contract or damages for its breach.

The place of contracting in this instance, as is usual to such contracts, was fortuitous. A seaman takes his employment, like his fun, where he finds it; a ship takes on crew in any port where it needs them. The practical effect of making the *lex loci contractus* govern all tort claims during the service would be to subject a ship to a multitude of systems of law, to put some of the crew in a more advantageous position than others, and not unlikely in the long run to diminish hirings in ports of countries that take best care of their seamen.

But if contract law is nonetheless to be considered, we face the fact that this contract was explicit that the Danish law and the contract with the Danish union were to control. Except as forbidden by some public policy, the tendency of the law is to apply in contract matters the law which the parties intended to apply. We are aware of no public policy that would prevent the parties to this contract, which contemplates performance in a multitude of territorial jurisdictions and on the high seas, from so settling upon the law of the flag-state as their governing code. * * *

We do not think the place of contract is a substantial influence in the choice between competing laws to govern a maritime tort.

6. *Inaccessibility of Foreign Forum.*—It is argued, and particularly stressed by an *amicus* brief, that justice requires adjudication under American law to save seamen expense and loss of time in returning to a foreign forum. * * *

Confining ourselves to the case in hand, we do not find this seaman disadvantaged in obtaining his remedy under Danish law from being in New York instead of Denmark. The Danish compensation system does not necessitate delayed, prolonged, expensive and uncertain litigation. It is stipulated in this case that claims may be made through the Danish Consulate. There is not the slightest showing that to obtain any relief to which he is entitled under Danish law would require his presence in Denmark or necessitate his leaving New York. And, even if it were so, the record indicates that he was offered and declined free transportation to Denmark by petitioner.

7. *The Law of the Forum.*—It is urged that, since an American forum has perfected its jurisdiction over the parties and defendant does more or less frequent and regular business within the forum state, it should apply its own law to the controversy between them. * * * Jurisdiction of maritime cases in all countries is so wide, and the nature of its subject matter so far-flung, that there would be no justification for altering the law of a controversy just because local jurisdiction of the parties is obtainable. * * *

This review of the connecting factors which either maritime law or our municipal law of conflicts regards as significant in determining the law applicable to a claim of actionable wrong shows an overwhelming preponderance in favor of Danish law. The parties are both Danish subjects, the events took place on a Danish ship, not within our territorial waters. Against these considerations is only the fact that the defendant was served here with process and that the plaintiff signed on in New

York, where the defendant was engaged in our foreign commerce. The latter event is offset by provision of his contract that the law of Denmark should govern. We do not question the power of Congress to condition access to our ports by foreign-owned vessels upon submission to any liabilities it may consider good American policy to exact. But we can find no justification for interpreting the Jones Act to intervene between foreigners and their own law because of acts on a foreign ship not in our waters.

In apparent recognition of the weakness of the legal argument, a candid and brash appeal is made by respondent and by *amicus* briefs to extend the law to this situation as a means of benefiting seamen and enhancing the costs of foreign ship operation for the competitive advantage of our own. We are not sure that the interest of this foreign seaman, who is able to prove negligence, is the interest of all seamen, or that his interest is that of the United States. Nor do we stop to inquire which law does whom the greater or the lesser good. The argument is misaddressed. It would be within the proprieties if addressed to Congress. Counsel familiar with the traditional attitude of this Court in maritime matters could not have intended it for us.

The judgment below is reversed and the cause remanded to District Court for proceedings consistent herewith.

TIMBERLANE LUMBER CO. V. BANK OF AMERICA

549 F.2d 597 (9th Cir. 1976)

CHOY, CIRCUIT JUDGE

CAST OF CHARACTERS

There are three affiliated plaintiffs in the Timberlane action. Timberlane Lumber Company is an Oregon partnership principally involved in the purchase and distribution of lumber at wholesale in the United States and the importation of lumber into the United States for sale and use. Danli Industrial, S.A., and Maya Lumber Company, S. de R.L., are both Honduras corporations, incorporated and principally owned by the general partners of Timberlane. Danli held contracts to purchase timber in Honduras, and Maya was to conduct the milling operations to produce the lumber for export. (Timberlane, Danli, and Maya will be collectively referred to as "Timberlane.")

The primary defendants are Bank of America Corporation (Bank), a California corporation, and its wholly-owned subsidiary, Bank of America National Trust and Savings Association, which operates a branch in Tegucigalpa, Honduras. Several employees of the Bank have also been named and served as defendants. * * *

Other defendants have been named, but have not been served. * * * Also unserved are two Honduras corporations, Pedro Casanova e Hijos, S.A., and Importadore Mayorista, S. de R.L., and Michael Casanova, a citizen of Honduras (together referred to as "Casanova"), who together represent one of the two main competitors to Timberlane and its predecessor in the Honduran lumber business. * * *

The Timberlane complaint identified two co-conspirators not named as defendants. Jose Lamas, S. de R.L. (Lamas), a Honduran corporation, is the second major competitor in the lumber business. Jose Caminals Galegro (Caminals), a citizen of Spain, is described as an agent or employee of the Bank of Tegucigalpa.

FACTS AS ALLEGED

The conspiracy sketched by Timberlane actually started before the plaintiffs entered the scene. The Lima family operated a lumber mill in Honduras, competing with Lamas and Casanova, in both of which the Bank had significant financial interests. The Lima enterprise was also indebted to the Bank. By 1971, however, the Lima business was in financial trouble. Timberlane alleges that driving Lima under was the first step in the conspiracy which eventually crippled Timberlane's efforts, but the particulars do not matter for this appeal. What does matter is that various interests in the Lima assets, including its milling plant, passed to Lima's creditors: Casanova, the Bank, and the group of Lima employees who had not been paid the wages and severance pay due them. Under Honduran law, the employees' claim had priority.

Enter Timberlane, with a long history in the lumber business, in search of alternative sources of lumber for delivery to its distribution system on the East Coast of the United States. After study, it decided to try Honduras. In 1971, Danli was formed, tracts of forest land were acquired, plans for a modern log-processing plant were prepared, and equipment was purchased and assembled for shipment from the United States to Danli in Honduras. Timberlane became aware that the Lima plant might be available and began negotiating for its acquisition. Maya was formed, purchased the Lima employees' interest in the machinery and equipment in January 1972, despite opposition from the conspirators, and re-activated the Lima mill.

Realizing that they were faced with better-financed and more vigorous competition from Timberlane and its Honduran subsidiaries, the defendants and others extended the anti-Lima conspiracy to disrupt Timberlane's efforts. The primary weapons employed by the conspirators were the claim still held by the Bank in the remaining assets of the Lima enterprise under the all-inclusive mortgage Lima had been forced to sign and another claim held by Casanova. Maya made a substantial cash offer for the Bank's interest in an effort to clear its title, but the Bank refused to sell. Instead, the Bank surreptitiously conveyed the mortgage to Casanova for questionable consideration, Casanova paying nothing and agreeing only to pay the Bank a portion of what it collected. Casanova immediately assigned the Bank's claim and its own on similar terms to Caminals, who promptly set out to disrupt the Timberlane operation.

Caminals is characterized as the "front man" in the campaign to drive Timberlane out of Honduras, with the Bank and other defendants intending and carrying responsibility for his actions. Having acquired the claims of Casanova and the Bank, Caminals went to court to enforce them, ignoring throughout Timberlane's offers to purchase or settle them. Under the laws of Honduras, an "embargo" on property is a court-ordered attachment, registered with the Public Registry, which precludes the sale of that property without a court order. Honduran law provides, upon embargo, that the court appoint a judicial officer, called an "interventor" to ensure against any diminution in the value of the property. In order to paralyze the Timberlane operation, Caminals obtained embargoes against Maya and Danli. Acting through the interventor, since accused of being on the payroll of the Bank, guards and troops were used to cripple and, for a time, completely shut down Timberlane's milling operation. The harassment took other forms as well: the conspirators caused the manager of Timberlane's Honduras operations, Gordon Sloan Smith, to be falsely arrested and imprisoned and were responsible for the publication of several defamatory articles about Timberlane in the Honduran press.

As a result of the conspiracy, Timberlane's complaint claimed damages then estimated in excess of $5,000,000. Plaintiffs also allege that there has been a direct and substantial effect on United States foreign commerce, and that defendants intended the results of the conspiracy, including the impact on United States commerce.

[The court reviews and rejects the application of the act of state doctrine. The act of state doctrine is explored in Chapter 12, Part D.]

There is no doubt that American antitrust laws extend over some conduct in other nations. There was language in the first Supreme Court case in point, *American Banana Co. v. United Fruit Co.,* 213 U.S. 347 (1909), casting doubt on the extension of the Sherman Act to acts outside United States territory. But subsequent cases have limited *American Banana* to its particular facts, and the Sherman Act—and with it other antitrust laws—has been applied to extraterritorial conduct. *See, e.g., Continental Ore Co. v. Union Carbide & Carbon Corp.*, 370 U.S. 690 (1962); *United States v. Sisal Sales Corp.*, 274 U.S. 268 (1927); *United States v. Aluminum Co. of America*, 148 F.2d 416 (2d Cir. 1945) (the "*Alcoa*" case). The act may encompass the foreign activities of aliens as well as American citizens.

That American law covers some conduct beyond this nation's borders does not mean that it embraces all, however. Extraterritorial application is understandably a matter of concern for the other countries involved. Those nations have sometimes resented and protested, as excessive intrusions into their own spheres, broad assertions of authority by American courts. Our courts have recognized this concern and have, at times, responded to it, even if not always enough to satisfy all the foreign critics. In any event, it is evident that at some point the interests of the United States are too weak and the foreign harmony incentive for restraint too strong to justify an extraterritorial assertion of jurisdiction. * * *

A tripartite analysis seems to be indicated. As acknowledged above, the antitrust laws require in the first instance that there be *some* effect—actual or intended—on American foreign commerce before the federal courts may legitimately exercise subject matter jurisdiction under those statutes. Second, a greater showing of burden or restraint may be necessary to demonstrate that the effect is sufficiently large to present a cognizable injury to the plaintiffs and, therefore, a civil *violation* of the antitrust laws. Third, there is the additional question which is unique to the international setting of whether the interests of, and links to, the United States—including the magnitude of the effect on American foreign commerce—are sufficiently strong, vis-à-vis those of other nations, to justify an assertion of extraterritorial authority. * * *

What we prefer is an evaluation and balancing of the relevant considerations in each case—in the words of Kingman Brewster, a "jurisdictional rule of reason." Balancing of the foreign interests involved was the approach taken by the Supreme Court in *Continental Ore Co. v. Union Carbide & Carbon Corp.*, 370 U.S. 690 (1962), where the involvement of the Canadian government in the alleged monopolization was held not to require dismissal. The Court stressed that there was no indication that the Canadian authorities approved or would have approved of the monopolization, meaning that the Canadian interest, if any, was slight and was outweighed by the American interest in condemning the restraint. Similarly, in *Lauritzen v. Larsen*, 345 U.S. 571 (1953), the Court used a like approach in declining to apply the Jones Act to a Danish seaman, injured in Havana on a Danish ship, although he had signed on to the ship in New York.

The elements to be weighed include the degree of conflict with foreign law or policy, the nationality or allegiance of the parties and the locations or principal places of business of corporations, the extent to which enforcement by either state can be expected to achieve compliance, the relative significance of effects on the United States as compared with those elsewhere, the extent to which there is explicit purpose to harm or affect American commerce, the foreseeability of such effect, and the relative importance to the violations charged of conduct with the United States as compared with conduct abroad. A court evaluating these factors should identify the potential degree of conflict if American authority is asserted. A difference in law or policy is one likely sore spot, though one which may not always be present. Nationality is another; though foreign governments may have some concern for the treatment of American citizens and business residing there, they primarily care about their own nationals. Having assessed the conflict, the court should then determine whether in the face of it the contacts and interests of the United States are sufficient to support the exercise of extraterritorial jurisdiction. * * *

The Sherman Act is not limited to trade restraints which have both a direct and substantial effect on our foreign commerce. Timberlane has alleged that the complained of activities were intended to, and did, affect the export of lumber from Honduras to the United States—the flow of United States foreign commerce, and as such they are within the jurisdiction of the federal courts under the Sherman Act. Moreover, the magnitude of the effect alleged would appear to be sufficient to state a claim.

The comity question is more complicated. From Timberlane's complaint it is evident that there are grounds for concern as to at least a few of the defendants, for some are identified as foreign citizens: Laureano Gutierrez Falla, Michael Casanova and the Casanova firms of Honduras, and Patrick Byrne, of Canada. Moreover, it is clear that most of the activity took place in Honduras, though the conspiracy may have been directed from San Francisco, and that the most direct economic effect was probably on Honduras. However, there has been no indication of any conflict with the law or policy of the Honduran government, nor any comprehensive analysis of the relative connections and interests of Honduras and the United States. Under these circumstances, the dismissal by the district court cannot be sustained on jurisdictional grounds.

We, therefore, vacate the dismissal, and remand the Timberlane action.

NOTES AND QUESTIONS

1. Banana *Revisited.* Note how Judge Choy returned to a premise of the much-derided *American Banana* case, albeit taking extraterritorial jurisdiction doctrine into account: "That American law covers some conduct beyond this nation's borders does not mean that it embraces all, however." *American Banana* simply restricted U.S. jurisdiction to the water's edge. *Blackmer* and *Aluminum* equally simplistically looked only to the reach of U.S. law. Justice Jackson in *Lauritzen* and Judge Choy in *Timberlane*, like Justice Holmes in *American Banana*, were willing to limit U.S. jurisdiction, but refused to do so by holding that U.S. law was not meant to apply. Rather, *Timberlane* held that U.S. law sometimes ought not be employed even if it might apply. The two cases reached this result by acknowledging that, in

many international cases, laws of two or more countries govern transactions concurrently. Hence, Judge Choy's working assumption: "[I]t is evident that at some point the interests of the United States are too weak and the foreign harmony incentive for restraint too strong to justify an extraterritorial assertion of jurisdiction." Should a court therefore have discretion to weigh U.S. and foreign interests to find a balance in each individual case? If the court finds the balance tilts toward the interests of the foreign state, should the result be deemed a denial of U.S. jurisdiction or simply a choice of foreign law?

2. *Balancing Factors*. Given the recurrent problem of concurrent jurisdiction in international transactions, how should courts structure their analyses to best balance and reconcile competing national interests? Helpfully, Justice Jackson provided seven factors in *Lauritzen*: (1) place of the wrongful act, (2) law of the flag, (3) allegiance or domicile of the plaintiff, (4) allegiance of the defendant, (5) place of contract, (6) inaccessibility of the foreign forum, and (7) the law of the forum. An eighth factor was added in 1970: the defendant's base of operations. Hellenic Lines Ltd. v. Rhoditis, 398 U.S. 306 (1970). Are some factors more important than others? Do you agree, for example, with Professor Tetley that "flags of convenience [which we considered in Chapter 10] have tolled the death knell of the law of the flag as a logical solution to conflicts of law"? William Tetley, "The Law of the Flag, 'Flag Shopping,' and Choice of Law," 17 *Tulane Maritime Law Journal* 139, 183 (1993). For recent developments in the case law where judges have employed *Lauritzen* in maritime disputes, see Martin Davies, "Choice of Law and U.S. Maritime Liens," 83 *Tulane Law Review* 1435 (2009).

3. *Limits to the Balancing Test?* Professor Lea Brilmayer has identified five "considerations" U.S. courts have taken into account when deciding whether to apply U.S. law extraterritorially: the legislative intent of the Congress, the presumptive "reach" of the statute, the limits imposed by international law, judicial doctrines of discretion like comity, and the U.S. Constitution. Lea Brilmayer, "The Extraterritorial Application of American Law: A Methodological and Constitutional Approach," 50 *Law and Contemporary Problems*, Summer 1987, at 11, 14–16. In a rebuttal, Professor Friedrich Juenger argued that "the solution to the problem of extraterritoriality will remain elusive as long as the clash of regulatory policies is analyzed in terms of legislative jurisdiction," a choice-of-law analysis that he felt masked real conflicts of substantive policy. Friedrich K. Juenger, "Constitutional Control of Extraterritoriality?: A Comment on Professor Brilmayer's Appraisal," 50 *Law and Contemporary Problems*, Summer 1987, at 39, 46.

In another line of U.S. maritime cases the Supreme Court has, without explicitly adopting a balancing test, considered whether U.S. labor laws and other regulatory laws should apply on board foreign flag vessels. See Benz v. Compania Naviera Hidalgo, S.A., 353 U.S. 138 (1957); McCulloch v. Sociedad Nacional de Marineros de Honduras, 372 U.S. 10 (1963). In Spector v. Norwegian Cruise Lines Ltd., 545 U.S. 119 (2005), the U.S. Supreme Court held that Title III of the Americans with Disabilities Act of 1990, 42 U.S.C. §§ 12181 *et seq.*, applied to a foreign-flagged cruise ship in U.S. port. Would *Spector* have been an appropriate case for using a balancing approach? What foreign or international interests may compete with U.S. interests in applying this Act to foreign flag vessels?

Should a balancing test be employed at all in criminal cases where "the Executive has already done the balancing in deciding to bring the case in the first place?" A U.S. district court reserved judgment on this question after its own application of the balancing test led it to conclude it should "nevertheless" try the case. United States v. Brodie, 174 F.Supp.2d 294, 305–06 (E.D.Pa. 2001). If a balancing test is used in a criminal case, should the test employ the same factors used in a civil case? For other formulations of the balancing test, see *Restatement (Third) of the Foreign Relations Law of the United States* § 403 and Mannington Mills, Inc. v. Congoleum Corp., 595 F.2d 1287 (3d Cir. 1979).

4. *The Role of Case Law.* Granting that there may always be conflicts of substantive national policies in problems of transnational litigation, why should the courts not try to resolve such conflicts as clearly and fairly as possible? Can a consistent pattern of court decisions help bolster international comity and help develop rules of international law respecting jurisdiction? Should U.S. courts look not only to their own judgments, but also to judgments made by foreign and international courts to develop such rules? U.S. courts face similar questions when dealing with treaties, customary international law, and other sources of international law. See the discussion in Chapters 2 and 3.

3. INTERNATIONAL COMITY

HILTON V. GUYOT

159 U.S. 113 (1895)

MR. JUSTICE GRAY

International law, in its widest and most comprehensive sense—including not only questions of right between nations, governed by what has been appropriately called the law of nations, but also questions arising under what is usually called private international law, or the conflict of laws, and concerning the rights of persons within the territory and dominion of one nation, by reason of acts, private or public, done within the dominions of another nation—is part of our law, and must be ascertained and administered by the courts of justice, as often as such questions are presented in litigation between man and man, duly submitted to their determination. * * *

No law has any effect, of its own force, beyond the limits of the sovereignty from which its authority is derived. The extent to which the law of one nation, as put in force within its territory, whether by executive order, by legislative act, or by judicial decree, shall be allowed to operate within the dominion of another nation, depends upon what our greatest jurists have been content to call "the comity of nations." Although the phrase has been often criticised, no satisfactory substitute has been suggested.

"Comity," in the legal sense, is neither a matter of absolute obligation, on the one hand, nor of mere courtesy and good will, upon the other. But it is the recognition which one nation allows within its territory to the legislative, executive or judicial acts of another nation, having due regard both to international duty and convenience, and to the rights of its own citizens or of other persons who are under the protection of its laws. * * *

Chief Justice Taney, * * * speaking for this court while Mr. Justice Story was a member of it, and largely adopting his words, said: * * * "The comity thus extended to other nations is no impeachment of sovereignty. It is the voluntary act of the nation by which it is offered, and is inadmissible when contrary to its policy, or prejudicial to its interests. But it contributes so largely to promote justice between individuals, and to produce a friendly intercourse between the sovereignties to which they belong, that courts of justice have continually acted upon it, as a part of the voluntary law of nations." "It is not the comity of the courts, but the comity of the nation, which is administered and ascertained in the same way, and guided by the same reasoning, by which all other principles of municipal law are ascertained and guided." *Bank v. Earle*, (1839) 13 Pet. 519, 589; Story's Conflict of Laws, § 38.

HARTFORD FIRE INSURANCE CO. V. CALIFORNIA

509 U.S. 764 (1993)

JUSTICE SOUTER announced the judgment of the Court[.]

The Sherman Act makes every contract, combination, or conspiracy in unreasonable restraint of interstate or foreign commerce illegal. 15 U.S.C. § 1. These consolidated cases present questions about the application of that Act to the insurance industry, both here and abroad. The plaintiffs (respondents here) allege that both domestic and foreign defendants (petitioners here) violated the Sherman Act by engaging in various conspiracies to affect the American insurance market. A group of domestic defendants argues that the McCarran-Ferguson Act, 15 U.S.C. §§ 1011 *et seq.*, precludes application of the Sherman Act to the conduct alleged; a group of foreign defendants argues that the principle of international comity requires the District Court to refrain from exercising jurisdiction over certain claims against it. We hold that most of the domestic defendants' alleged conduct is not immunized from antitrust liability by the McCarran-Ferguson Act, and that, even assuming it applies, the principle of international comity does not preclude District Court jurisdiction over the foreign conduct alleged.

The two petitions before us stem from consolidated litigation comprising the complaints of 19 States and many private plaintiffs alleging that the defendants, members of the insurance industry, conspired in violation of § 1 of the Sherman Act to restrict the terms of coverage of commercial general liability (CGL) insurance available in the United States. Because the cases come to us on motions to dismiss, we take the allegations of the complaints as true.

According to the complaints, the object of the conspiracies was to force certain primary insurers (insurers who sell insurance directly to consumers) to change the terms of their standard CGL insurance policies to conform with the policies the defendant insurers wanted to sell. The defendants wanted four changes.

First, CGL insurance has traditionally been sold in the United States on an "occurrence" basis, through a policy obligating the insurer "to pay or defend claims, whenever made, resulting from an accident or 'injurious exposure to conditions' that occurred during the [specific time] period the policy was in effect." In place of this traditional "occurrence" trigger of coverage, the defendants wanted a "claims-made" trigger, obligating the insurer to pay or defend only those claims made during the policy period. Such a policy has the distinct advantage for the insurer that when the policy period ends without a claim having been made, the insurer can be certain that the policy will not expose it to any further liability. Second, the defendants wanted the "claims-made" policy to have a "retroactive date" provision, which would further restrict coverage to claims based on incidents that occurred after a certain date. Such a provision eliminates the risk that an insurer, by issuing a claims-made policy, would assume liability arising from incidents that occurred before the policy's effective date, but remained undiscovered or caused no immediate harm. Third, CGL insurance has traditionally covered "sudden and accidental" pollution; the defendants wanted to eliminate that coverage. Finally, CGL insurance has traditionally provided that the insurer would bear the legal costs of defending covered claims against the insured without regard to the policy's stated limits of coverage; the defendants wanted legal defense costs to be counted against the stated limits (providing a "legal defense cost cap").

[Justice Souter concludes that the McCarron-Ferguson Act does not protect domestic defendants from antitrust liability.]

Finally, we take up the question * * * whether certain claims against the London reinsurers should have been dismissed as improper applications of the Sherman Act to foreign conduct. The Fifth Claim for Relief of the California Complaint alleges a violation of § 1 of the Sherman Act by certain London reinsurers who conspired to coerce primary insurers in the United States to offer CGL coverage on a claims-made basis, thereby making "occurrence CGL coverage . . . unavailable in the State of California for many risks." The Sixth Claim for Relief of the California Complaint alleges that the London reinsurers violated § 1 by a conspiracy to limit coverage of pollution risks in North America, thereby rendering "pollution liability coverage . . . almost entirely unavailable for the vast majority of casualty insurance purchasers in the State of California." The Eighth Claim for Relief of the California Complaint alleges a further § 1 violation by the London reinsurers who, along with domestic retrocessional reinsurers, conspired to limit coverage of seepage, pollution, and property contamination risks in North America, thereby eliminating such coverage in the State of California.

At the outset, we note that the District Court undoubtedly had jurisdiction of these Sherman Act claims, as the London reinsurers apparently concede. ("Our position is not that the Sherman Act does not apply in the sense that a minimal basis for the exercise of jurisdiction doesn't exist here. Our position is that there are certain circumstances, and that this is one of them, in which the interests of another State are sufficient that the exercise of that jurisdiction should be restrained.") Although the proposition was perhaps not always free from doubt, see *American Banana Co. v. United Fruit Co.*, 213 U.S. 347 (1909), it is well established by now that the Sherman Act applies to foreign conduct that was meant to produce and did in fact produce some substantial effect in the United States.[22] Such is the conduct alleged here: that the London reinsurers engaged in unlawful conspiracies to affect the market for insurance in the United States and that their conduct in fact produced substantial effect.

According to the London reinsurers, the District Court should have declined to exercise such jurisdiction under the principle of international comity.[24] The Court of Appeals agreed that courts should look to that

22 JUSTICE SCALIA believes that what is at issue in this case is prescriptive, as opposed to subject-matter, jurisdiction. The parties do not question prescriptive jurisdiction, however, and for good reason: it is well established that Congress has exercised such jurisdiction under the Sherman Act. See G. Born & D. Westin, International Civil Litigation in United States Courts 542, n.5 (2d ed. 1992) (Sherman Act is a "prime exampl[e] of the simultaneous exercise of prescriptive jurisdiction and grant of subject matter jurisdiction").

24 JUSTICE SCALIA contends that comity concerns figure into the prior analysis whether jurisdiction exists under the Sherman Act. This contention is inconsistent with the general understanding that the Sherman Act covers foreign conduct producing a substantial intended effect in the United States, and that concerns of comity come into play, if at all, only after a court has determined that the acts complained of are subject to Sherman Act jurisdiction. See *United States v. Aluminum Co. of America*, 148 F.2d 416, 444 (C.A.2 1945) ("it follows from what we have . . . said that [the agreements at issue] were unlawful [under the Sherman Act], though made abroad, if they were intended to affect imports and did affect them"); *Mannington Mills, Inc. v. Congoleum Corp.*, 595 F.2d 1287, 1294 (C.A.3 1979) (once court determines that jurisdiction exists under the Sherman Act, question remains whether comity precludes its exercise); H.R. Rep. No. 97–686, p. 13 (1982). But cf. *Timberlane Lumber Co. v. Bank of America, N. T. & S. A.*, 549 F.2d 597, 613 (C.A.9 1976). In any event, the parties conceded jurisdiction at oral argument, and we see no need to address this contention here.

principle in deciding whether to exercise jurisdiction under the Sherman Act. This availed the London reinsurers nothing, however. To be sure, the Court of Appeals believed that "application of [American] antitrust laws to the London reinsurance market 'would lead to significant conflict with English law and policy,' " and that "[s]uch a conflict, unless outweighed by other factors, would by itself be reason to decline exercise of jurisdiction." But other factors, in the court's view, including the London reinsurers' express purpose to affect United States commerce and the substantial nature of the effect produced, outweighed the supposed conflict and required the exercise of jurisdiction in this case.

[E]ven assuming that in a proper case a court may decline to exercise Sherman Act jurisdiction over foreign conduct (or, as JUSTICE SCALIA would put it, may conclude by the employment of comity analysis in the first instance that there is no jurisdiction), international comity would not counsel against exercising jurisdiction in the circumstances alleged here.

The only substantial question in this case is whether "there is in fact a true conflict between domestic and foreign law." *Société Nationale Industrielle Aérospatiale v. United States District Court*, 482 U.S. 522, 555 (1987) (BLACKMUN, J., concurring in part and dissenting in part). The London reinsurers contend that applying the Act to their conduct would conflict significantly with British law, and the British Government, appearing before us as *amicus curiae,* concurs. They assert that Parliament has established a comprehensive regulatory regime over the London reinsurance market and that the conduct alleged here was perfectly consistent with British law and policy. But this is not to state a conflict. "[T]he fact that conduct is lawful in the state in which it took place will not, of itself, bar application of the United States antitrust laws," even where the foreign state has a strong policy to permit or encourage such conduct. Restatement (Third) Foreign Relations Law § 415, Comment *j*. No conflict exists, for these purposes, "where a person subject to regulation by two states can comply with the laws of both." Restatement (Third) Foreign Relations Law § 403, Comment *e*.[25] Since the London reinsurers do not argue that British law requires them to act in some fashion prohibited by the law of the United States, or claim that their compliance with the laws of both countries is otherwise impossible, we see no conflict with British law. We have no need in this case to address other considerations that might inform a decision to refrain from the exercise of jurisdiction on grounds of international comity. * * *

JUSTICE SCALIA * * * delivered a dissenting opinion with respect to [part of the judgment in which JUSTICE O'CONNOR, JUSTICE KENNEDY, and JUSTICE THOMAS join.]

[25] JUSTICE SCALIA says that we put the cart before the horse in citing this authority, for he argues it may be apposite only after a determination that jurisdiction over the foreign acts is reasonable. But whatever the order of cart and horse, conflict in this sense is the only substantial issue before the Court.

The petitioners in No. 91–1128, various British corporations and other British subjects, argue that certain of the claims against them constitute an inappropriate extraterritorial application of the Sherman Act. It is important to distinguish two distinct questions raised by this petition: whether the District Court had jurisdiction, and whether the Sherman Act reaches the extraterritorial conduct alleged here. On the first question, I believe that the District Court had subject-matter jurisdiction over the Sherman Act claims against all the defendants (personal jurisdiction is not contested). The respondents asserted nonfrivolous claims under the Sherman Act, and 28 U.S.C. § 1331 vests district courts with subject-matter jurisdiction over cases "arising under" federal statutes. As precedents such as *Lauritzen v. Larsen*, 345 U.S. 571 (1953), make clear, that is sufficient to establish the District Court's jurisdiction over these claims. *Lauritzen* involved a Jones Act claim brought by a foreign sailor against a foreign shipowner. The shipowner contested the District Court's jurisdiction, apparently on the grounds that the Jones Act did not govern the dispute between the foreign parties to the action. Though ultimately agreeing with the shipowner that the Jones Act did not apply, the Court held that the District Court had jurisdiction.

> As frequently happens, a contention that there is some barrier to granting plaintiff's claim is cast in terms of an exception to jurisdiction of subject matter. A cause of action under our law was asserted here, and the court had power to determine whether it was or was not founded in law and in fact.

The second question—the extraterritorial reach of the Sherman Act—has nothing to do with the jurisdiction of the courts. It is a question of substantive law turning on whether, in enacting the Sherman Act, Congress asserted regulatory power over the challenged conduct. See *EEOC v. Arabian American Oil Co.*, 499 U.S. 244, 248 (1991) (*Aramco*) ("It is our task to determine whether Congress intended the protections of Title VII to apply to United States citizens employed by American employers outside of the United States"). If a plaintiff fails to prevail on this issue, the court does not dismiss the claim for want of subject-matter jurisdiction—want of power to adjudicate; rather, it decides the claim, ruling on the merits that the plaintiff has failed to state a cause of action under the relevant statute. See *American Banana Co. v. United Fruit Co.*, 213 U.S. 347, 359 (1909) (holding that complaint based upon foreign conduct "alleges no case under the [Sherman Act]").

There is, however, a type of "jurisdiction" relevant to determining the extraterritorial reach of a statute; it is known as "legislative jurisdiction" or "jurisdiction to prescribe." This refers to "the authority of a state to make its law applicable to persons or activities," and is quite a separate matter from "jurisdiction to adjudicate." There is no doubt, of course, that Congress possesses legislative jurisdiction over the acts alleged in this complaint: Congress has broad power under Article I, § 8, cl. 3 "[t]o regulate Commerce with foreign Nations," and this Court has repeatedly upheld its power to make laws applicable to persons or activities beyond our territorial boundaries where United States interests are affected. But the question in this case is whether, and to what extent, Congress *has* exercised that undoubted legislative jurisdiction in enacting the Sherman Act.

Two canons of statutory construction are relevant in this inquiry. The first is the "long-standing principle of American law 'that legislation of Congress, unless a contrary intent appears, is meant to apply only within the territorial jurisdiction of the United States.'" *Aramco, supra,* at 253 (quoting *Foley Bros., Inc. v. Filardo*, 336 U.S. 281, 285 (1949)). * * * We, have, however, found the presumption to be overcome with respect to our antitrust laws; it is now well established that the Sherman Act applies extraterritorially.

But if the presumption against extraterritoriality has been overcome or is otherwise inapplicable, a second canon of statutory construction becomes relevant: "[A]n act of congress ought never to be construed to violate the law of nations if any other possible construction remains." *Murray v. The Charming Betsy*, 2 Cranch 64, 118 (1804) (Marshall, C.J.). This canon is "wholly independent" of the presumption against extraterritoriality. It is relevant to determining the substantive reach of a statute because "the law of nations," or customary international law, includes limitations on a nation's exercise of its jurisdiction to prescribe. Though it clearly has constitutional authority to do so, Congress is generally presumed not to have exceeded those customary international-law limits on jurisdiction to prescribe.

Consistent with that presumption, this and other courts have frequently recognized that, even where the presumption against extraterritoriality does not apply, statutes should not be interpreted to regulate foreign persons or conduct if that regulation would conflict with principles of international law. For example, in *Romero v. International Terminal Operating Co.*, 358 U.S. 354 (1959), the plaintiff, a Spanish sailor who had been injured while working aboard a Spanish-flag and Spanish-owned vessel, filed a Jones Act claim against his Spanish employer. The presumption against extraterritorial application of federal statutes was inapplicable to the case, as the actionable tort had occurred in American waters. The Court nonetheless stated that, "in the absence of contrary congressional direction," it would apply "principles of choice of law that are consonant with the needs of a general federal maritime law and with due recognition of our self-regarding respect for the relevant interests of foreign nations in the regulation of maritime commerce as part of the legitimate concern of the international community." "The controlling considerations" in this choice-of-law analysis were "the interacting interests of the United States and of foreign countries."

Romero referred to, and followed, the choice-of-law analysis set forth in *Lauritzen v. Larsen*, 345 U.S. 571 (1953). As previously mentioned, *Lauritzen* also involved a Jones Act claim brought by a foreign sailor against a foreign employer. The *Lauritzen* Court recognized the basic problem: "If [the Jones Act were] read literally, Congress has conferred an American right of action which requires nothing more than that plaintiff be 'any seaman who shall suffer personal injury in the course of his employment.'" The solution it adopted was to construe the statute "to apply only to areas and transactions in which *American law would be considered operative under prevalent doctrines of international law.*" To support application of international law to limit the facial breadth of the statute, the Court relied upon—of course—Chief Justice Marshall's statement in *The Charming Betsy* quoted *supra*. See also *McCulloch v. Sociedad Nacional de Marineros de Honduras*, 372 U.S. 10, 21–22 (1963) (applying *The Charming Betsy* principle to restrict application of National Labor Relations Act to foreign-flag vessels).

Lauritzen, Romero, and *McCulloch* were maritime cases, but we have recognized the principle that the scope of generally worded statutes must be construed in light of international law in other areas as well. More specifically, the principle was expressed in *United States v. Aluminum Co. of America*, 148 F.2d 416 (C.A.2 1945), the decision that established the extraterritorial reach of the Sherman Act. In his opinion for the court, Judge Learned Hand cautioned "we are not to read general words, such as those in [the Sherman] Act, without regard to the limitations customarily observed by nations upon the exercise of their powers; limitations which generally correspond to those fixed by the 'Conflict of Laws.'"

More recent lower court precedent has also tempered the extraterritorial application of the Sherman Act with considerations of "international comity." See *Timberlane Lumber Co. v. Bank of America, N.T & S.A.*, 549 F.2d 597, 608–615 (C.A.9 1976); *Mannington Mills, Inc. v. Congoleum Corp.*, 595 F.2d 1287, 1294–1298 (C.A.3 1979). The "comity" they refer to is not the comity of courts, whereby judges decline to exercise jurisdiction over matters more appropriately adjudged elsewhere, but rather what might be termed "prescriptive comity": the respect sovereign nations afford each other by limiting the reach of their laws. That comity is exercised by legislatures when they enact laws, and courts assume it has been exercised when they come to interpreting the scope of laws their legislatures have enacted. It is a traditional component of choice-of-law theory. See J. Story, Commentaries on the Conflict of Laws § 38 (1834) (distinguishing between the "comity of the courts" and the "comity of nations," and defining the latter as "the true foundation and extent of the obligation of the laws of one nation within the territories of another"). Comity in this sense includes the choice-of-law principles that, "in the absence of contrary congressional direction," are assumed to be incorporated into our substantive laws having extraterritorial reach. Considering comity in this way is just part of determining whether the Sherman Act prohibits the conduct at issue.

In sum, the practice of using international law to limit the extraterritorial reach of statutes is firmly established in our jurisprudence. In proceeding to apply that practice to the present case, I shall rely on the Restatement (Third) of Foreign Relations Law for the relevant principles of international law. Its standards appear fairly supported in the decisions of this Court construing international choice-of-law principles (*Lauritzen, Romero*, and *McCulloch)* and in the decisions of other federal courts, especially *Timberlane*. Whether the Restatement precisely reflects international law in every detail matters little here, as I believe this case would be resolved the same way under virtually any conceivable test that takes account of foreign regulatory interests.

Under the Restatement, a nation having some "basis" for jurisdiction to prescribe law should nonetheless refrain from exercising that jurisdiction "with respect to a person or activity having connections with another state when the exercise of such jurisdiction is unreasonable." Restatement (Third) § 403(*l*). The "reasonableness" inquiry turns on a number of factors including, but not limited to: "the extent to which the activity takes place within the territory [of the regulating state]," § 403(2)(a); "the connections, such as nationality, residence, or economic activity, between the regulating state and the person principally responsible for the activity to be regulated," § 403(2)(b); "the character of the activity to be regulated, the importance of regulation to the regulating state, the extent to which other states regulate such activities, and the degree to which the desirability of such regulation is generally accepted," § 403(2)(c); "the extent to which another state may have an interest in regulating the activity," § 403(2)(g); and "the likelihood of conflict with regulation by another state," § 403(2)(h). Rarely would these factors point more clearly against application of United States law. The activity relevant to the counts at issue here took place primarily in the United Kingdom, and the defendants in these counts are British corporations and British subjects having their principal place of business or residence outside the United States. Great Britain has established a comprehensive regulatory scheme governing the London reinsurance markets, and clearly has a heavy "interest in regulating the activity." Finally, § 2(b) of the McCarran-Ferguson Act allows state regulatory statutes to override the Sherman Act in the insurance field, subject only to the narrow "boycott" exception set forth in § 3(b)—suggesting that "the importance of regulation to the [United States]" is slight. Considering these factors, I think it unimaginable that an assertion of legislative jurisdiction by the

United States would be considered reasonable, and therefore it is inappropriate to assume, in the absence of statutory indication to the contrary, that Congress has made such an assertion.

It is evident from what I have said that the Court's comity analysis, which proceeds as though the issue is whether the courts should "decline to exercise . . . jurisdiction," rather than whether the Sherman Act covers this conduct, is simply misdirected. I do not at all agree, moreover, with the Court's conclusion that the issue of the substantive scope of the Sherman Act is not in the case. To be sure, the parties did not make a clear distinction between adjudicative jurisdiction and the scope of the statute. Parties often do not, as we have observed (and have declined to punish with procedural default) before. It is not realistic, and also not helpful, to pretend that the only really relevant issue in this case is not before us. In any event, if one erroneously chooses, as the Court does, to make adjudicative jurisdiction (or, more precisely, abstention) the vehicle for taking account of the needs of prescriptive comity, the Court still gets it wrong. It concludes that no "true conflict" counseling nonapplication of United States law (or rather, as it thinks, United States judicial jurisdiction) exists unless compliance with United States law would constitute a *violation* of another country's law. That breathtakingly broad proposition, which contradicts the many cases discussed earlier, will bring the Sherman Act and other laws into sharp and unnecessary conflict with the legitimate interests of other countries—particularly our closest trading partners.

In the sense in which the term "conflic[t]" was used in *Lauritzen,* and is generally understood in the field of conflicts of laws, there is clearly a conflict in this case. The petitioners here, like the defendant in *Lauritzen,* were not compelled by any foreign law to take their allegedly wrongful actions, but that no more precludes a conflict-of-laws analysis here than it did there. Where applicable foreign and domestic law provide different substantive rules of decision to govern the parties' dispute, a conflict-of-laws analysis is necessary.

Literally the *only* support that the Court adduces for its position is § 403 of the Restatement (Third) of Foreign Relations Law—or more precisely Comment *e* to that provision, which states:

> Subsection (3) [which says that a state should defer to another state if that state's interest is clearly greater] applies only when one state requires what another prohibits, or where compliance with the regulations of two states exercising jurisdiction consistently with this section is otherwise impossible. It does not apply where a person subject to regulation by two states can comply with the laws of both. . . .

The Court has completely misinterpreted this provision. Subsection (3) of § 403 (requiring one State to defer to another in the limited circumstances just described) comes into play only after subsection (1) of § 403 has been complied with—*i.e.*, after it has been determined that the exercise of jurisdiction by *both* of the two States is not "unreasonable." That prior question is answered by applying the factors (*inter alia*) set forth in subsection (2) of § 403, that is, precisely the factors that I have discussed in text and that the Court rejects.

NOTES AND QUESTIONS

1. *The Classical Definition of Comity.* In an interesting modern example of *Hilton*'s classical definition of comity, Laker Airways v. Sabena, Belgian World Airlines, 731 F.2d 909, 937 (D.C.Cir. 1984), Judge Wilkey addressed arguments that a U.S. anti-suit injunction "violates the crucial principles of comity that regulate and moderate the social and economic intercourse between independent nations":

> [C]omity serves our international system like the mortar which cements together a brick house. No one would willingly permit the mortar to crumble or be chipped away for fear of compromising the entire structure.
>
> "Comity" summarizes in a brief word a complex and elusive concept—the degree of deference that a domestic forum must pay to the act of a foreign government not otherwise binding on the forum. Since comity varies according to the factual circumstances surrounding each claim for its recognition, the absolute boundaries of the duties it imposes are inherently uncertain. However, the central precept of comity teaches that, when possible, the decisions of foreign tribunals should be given effect in domestic courts, since recognition fosters international cooperation and encourages reciprocity, thereby promoting predictability and stability through satisfaction of mutual expectations. The interests of both forums are advanced—the foreign court because its laws and policies have been vindicated; the domestic country because international cooperation and ties have been strengthened. The rule of law is also encouraged, which benefits all nations.
>
> Comity is a necessary outgrowth of our international system of politically independent, socio-economically interdependent nation states. As surely as people, products and problems move freely among adjoining countries, so national interests cross territorial borders. * * * Every nation must often rely on other countries to help it achieve its regulatory expectations. Thus, comity compels national courts to act at all times to increase the international legal ties that advance the rule of law within and among nations.
>
> However, there are limitations to the application of comity. When the foreign act is inherently inconsistent with the policies underlying comity, domestic recognition could tend either to legitimize the aberration or to encourage retaliation, undercutting

> the realization of the goals served by comity. No nation is under an unremitting obligation to enforce foreign interests which are fundamentally prejudicial to those of the domestic forum. Thus, from the earliest times, authorities have recognized that the obligation of comity expires when the strong public policies of the forum are vitiated by the foreign act.

How does a comity approach to resolving conflicts of jurisdiction differ from a balancing approach, as seen in Section 2? Does comity also involve balancing? The same sort of balancing?

2. *Comity in* Hartford Fire. Did Justice Souter's conception of comity in *Hartford Fire* differ from the more traditional notion set out in *Hilton* and *Laker Airways*? According to Justice Souter, the assertion "that Parliament has established a comprehensive regulatory regime over the London reinsurance market and that the conduct alleged here was perfectly consistent with British law and policy" did not "state a conflict" with U.S. law. Professor Dam criticized the majority opinion in *Hartford Fire* for "plung[ing] forward in applying the Sherman Act extraterritorially, whatever the foreign interests involved." Kenneth W. Dam, "Extraterritoriality in an Age of Globalization: The Hartford Fire Case," 1993 *Supreme Court Review* 289, 294. Did Justice Souter in essence make what has been called the "foreign compulsion defense" the centerpiece of his comity inquiry? Or is it more plausible that, as Professor Weintraub has concluded, "Justice Souter is saying that it would be a waste of time in such an egregious case, a conspiracy abroad solely intended to cause anticompetitive effects in the United States, to wade through the comity analysis"? Russell J. Weintraub, *Commentary on the Conflict of Laws* 761 (5th ed. 2006).

3. *Foreign Reactions to* Hartford Fire. One British commentator called the *Hartford Fire* decision a "staggeringly blinkered approach" that in effect means that the United States will respect

> only * * * the laws of those foreign States which actually legislate in favour of monopolistic, price-fixing or other anti-competitive practices. The sovereign interests of those States which actually share US free-market principles but do not regulate anti-competition with the aggression or exorbitant reach of the US can be ignored. Under this approach, greater consideration would be due to the laws of an old-style Soviet State than those of a European trading partner.

Julian Wilson, "US exports in anti-trust: the primacy of economic muscle over international law," *International Litigation News*, July 1995, at 3, 4. Might Justice Souter's narrow definition of comity encourage other states to take actions that more directly challenge the applicability of U.S. law? Might foreign governments be tempted to enact countermeasures, making it illegal under their laws to comply with U.S. laws, refusing enforcement of U.S. judgments, or providing a cause of action allowing the recovery of damages paid as a result of a U.S. court's finding of liability? For discussion of legislative responses abroad to what have been regarded as overbroad assertions of U.S. antitrust jurisdiction, see Edward T. Swaine, "The Local Law of Global Antitrust," 43 *William and Mary Law Review* 627, 643–45 (2001).

4. Hartford Fire *and the Balancing Test.* Did both Justice Souter and Justice Scalia misunderstand the balancing test of *Lauritzen* and *Timberlane*? On the one hand, Demetriou and Robertson criticized Justice Souter: "[T]he balancing test [is] meaningless. So long as the conduct concerned 'was meant to produce and did in fact produce some substantial effect in the United States,' then jurisdiction is established." Marie Demetriou & Aidan Robertson, "US Extra-territorial Jurisdiction in Anti-Trust Matters: Recent Developments," 8 *European Competition Law Review* 461, 465 (1995). On the other hand, Professor Dodge reprimanded Justice Scalia: "[E]ven if one acknowledges Britain's 'heavy' interest in regulating the conduct at issue in *Hartford*, there is no reason to think that the United States' interest was any less 'heavy.' " William S. Dodge, "Extraterritoriality and Conflict-of Laws Theory: An Argument for Judicial Unilateralism," 39 *Harvard International Law Journal* 101, 142 (1998). Are both the balancing test and comity little more than methods of exercising judicial discretion to resolve difficult cases of international conflict of laws?

5. *Construing* Hartford Fire. Should *Hartford Fire* be narrowly construed? In Sterling Drug, Inc. v. Bayer USA Inc., 14 F.3d 733 (2d Cir. 1994), the Second Circuit considered the extraterritorial application of an injunction restraining violations of the Lanham Act's trademark protection provisions. The court found that even after *Hartford Fire*, the traditional notion of international comity remained an appropriate concern: "[T]he [*Hartford Fire*] Court's approach to the comity issue . . . is not automatically transferable to the trademark context, especially where the contending parties both hold rights in the same mark under the respective laws of their countries." *Id.* at 746. In the court's view, the extraterritorial aspects of a trademark infringement injunction needed to be "carefully crafted to prohibit only those foreign uses of the mark * * * that are likely to have significant trademark-impairing effects on United States commerce." *Id.* at 747. Similarly, in a patent case, International Nutrition v. Horphag Research Ltd., 257 F.3d 1324 (Fed. Cir. 2001), a U.S. circuit court disregarded *Hartford Fire* and applied the traditional *Hilton* comity analysis. Upholding the trial court, the court of appeals deferred to French court rulings, holding that "comity is appropriate because the French courts merely determined who owned a United States patent pursuant to a French contract." *Id.* at 1329. "The French courts are courts of competent jurisdiction, and the laws and public policy of the forum state, here Connecticut, and the rights of its residents will not be violated by extending comity." *Id.* at 1330.

The Supreme Court itself, 11 years after *Hartford Fire*, invoked notions of comity in an antitrust case involving, in general, "(1) significant foreign anticompetitive conduct with (2) an adverse domestic effect and (3) an independent foreign effect giving rise to the claim" and, in particular, "vitamin sellers around the world that agreed to fix prices, leading to higher vitamin prices in the United States and independently leading to higher vitamin prices in other countries such as Ecuador." F. Hoffman-La Roche Ltd. v. Empagran S.A., 542 U.S. 155, 159 (2004). The Court overruled a D.C. Circuit interpretation of the Foreign Trade Antitrust Improvements Act (FTAIA) and dismissed an antitrust claim, concluding that U.S. antitrust law does not apply "where the plaintiff's claim rests solely on the independent foreign harm." *Id.*

> [P]rinciples of prescriptive comity counsel against the Court of Appeals' interpretation of the FTAIA. Where foreign anticompetitive conduct plays a significant role and where foreign injury is independent of domestic effects, Congress might have hoped that America's antitrust laws, so fundamental a component of our own economic system, would commend themselves to other nations as well. But, if America's antitrust policies could not win their own way in the international marketplace for such ideas, Congress, we must assume, would not have tried to impose them, in an act of legal imperialism, through legislative fiat.

Id. at 169.

6. Hartford Fire *and the Global Economy.* Does the U.S.-centric approach of *Hartford Fire* fail to respond to modern international economic needs? Professor Dam believed that the judgment sounded "a discordant note in an increasingly globalized economy in an era when the need for more outward-looking and cooperative economic policy measures has become increasingly obvious." Dam, *supra* Note 2, at 297. Professor Waller contended that though nowadays in antitrust litigation "comity is no longer important" both because the U.S. government is more restrained in attempting unilaterally to govern extraterritorial anticompetitive conduct and because U.S. courts are not required to conduct a balancing analysis, the global economy will be protected by thoughtful cooperation between U.S. and foreign regulators. Spencer Weber Waller, "The Twilight of Comity," 38 *Columbia Journal of Transnational Law* 563, 565–66 (2000).

4. FORUM NON CONVENIENS

PIPER AIRCRAFT CO. V. REYNO

454 U.S. 235 (1981)

JUSTICE MARSHALL delivered the opinion of the Court. * * *

I

A

In July 1976, a small commercial aircraft crashed in the Scottish highlands during the course of a charter flight from Blackpool to Perth. The pilot and five passengers were killed instantly. The decedents were all Scottish subjects and residents, as are their heirs and next of kin. There were no eyewitnesses to the accident. At the time of the crash the plane was subject to Scottish air traffic control.

The aircraft, a twin-engine Piper Aztec, was manufactured in Pennsylvania by petitioner Piper Aircraft Co. (Piper). The propellers were manufactured in Ohio by petitioner Hartzell Propeller, Inc. (Hartzell). At the time of the crash the aircraft was registered in Great Britain and was owned and maintained by Air Navigation and Trading Co., Ltd. (Air Navigation). It was operated by McDonald Aviation, Ltd. (McDonald), a Scottish air taxi service. Both Air Navigation and McDonald were organized in the United Kingdom. The wreckage of the plane is now in a hanger in Farnsborough, England.

The British Department of Trade investigated the accident shortly after it occurred. A preliminary report found that the plane crashed after developing a spin, and suggested that mechanical failure in the plane or the propeller was responsible. At Hartzell's request, this report was reviewed by a three-member Review Board, which held a 9-day adversary hearing attended by all interested parties. The Review Board found no evidence of defective equipment and indicated that pilot error may have contributed to the accident. The pilot, who had obtained his commercial pilot's license only three months earlier, was flying over high ground at an altitude considerably lower than the minimum height required by his company's operations manual.

In July 1977, a California probate court appointed respondent Gaynell Reyno administratrix of the estates of the five passengers. Reyno is not related to and does not know any of the decedents or their survivors; she was a legal secretary to the attorney who filed this lawsuit. Several days after her appointment, Reyno commenced separate wrongful-death actions against Piper and Hartzell in the Superior Court of California, claiming negligence and strict liability. Air Navigation, McDonald, and the estate of the pilot are not parties to this litigation. The survivors of the five passengers whose estates are represented by Reyno filed a separate action in the United Kingdom against Air Navigation, McDonald, and the pilot's estate. Reyno candidly admits that the action against Piper and Hartzell was filed in the United States because its laws regarding liability, capacity to sue, and damages are more favorable to her position than are those of Scotland. Scottish law does not recognize strict liability in tort. Moreover, it permits wrongful-death actions only when brought by a decedent's relatives. The relatives may sue only for "loss of support and society."

On petitioners' motion, the suit was removed to the United States District Court for the Central District of California. Piper then moved for transfer to the United States District Court for the Middle District of Pennsylvania, pursuant to 28 U.S.C. § 1404(a). Hartzell moved to dismiss for lack of personal jurisdiction, or in the alternative, to transfer. In December 1977, the District Court quashed service on Hartzell and transferred the case to the Middle District of Pennsylvania. Respondent then properly served process on Hartzell.

B

In May 1978, after the suit had been transferred, both Hartzell and Piper moved to dismiss the action on the ground of *forum non conveniens*. The District Court granted these motions in October 1979. It relied on the balancing test set forth by this Court in *Gulf Oil Corp. v. Gilbert*, 330 U.S. 501 (1947), and its companion case, *Koster v. Lumbermens Mut. Cas. Co.*, 330 U.S. 518 (1947). In those decisions, the Court stated that a plaintiff's choice of forum should rarely be disturbed. However, when an alternative forum has jurisdiction to hear the case, and when trial in the chosen forum would "establish . . . oppressiveness and vexation to a defendant . . . out of all proportion to plaintiff's convenience," or when the "chosen forum [is] inappropriate because of considerations affecting the court's own administrative and legal problems," the court may, in the exercise of its sound discretion, dismiss the case. To guide trial court discretion, the Court provided a list of "private interest factors" affecting the convenience of the litigants, and a list of "public interest factors" affecting the convenience of the forum.[6]

On appeal, the United States Court of Appeals for the Third Circuit reversed and remanded for trial. The decision to reverse appears to be based on two alternative grounds. First, the Court held that the District Court abused its discretion in conducting the *Gilbert* analysis. Second, the Court held that dismissal is never appropriate where the law of the alternative forum is less favorable to the plaintiff. * * *

II

The Court of Appeals erred in holding that plaintiffs may defeat a motion to dismiss on the ground of *forum non conveniens* merely by showing that the substantive law that would be applied in the alternative forum is less favorable to the plaintiffs than that of the present forum. The possibility of a change in substantive law should ordinarily not be given conclusive or even substantial weight in the *forum non conveniens* inquiry.

---

[6] The factors pertaining to the private interests of the litigants included the "relative ease of access to sources of proof; availability of compulsory process for attendance of unwilling, and the cost of obtaining attendance of willing, witnesses; possibility of view of premises, if view would be appropriate to the action; and all other practical problems that make trial of a case easy, expeditious and inexpensive." *Gilbert*, 330 U.S., at 508. The public factors bearing on the question included the administrative difficulties flowing from court congestion; the "local interest in having localized controversies decided at home"; the interest in having the trial of a diversity case in a forum that is at home with the law that must govern the action; the avoidance of unnecessary problems in conflict of laws, or in the application of foreign law; and the unfairness of burdening citizens in an unrelated forum with jury duty.

We expressly rejected the position adopted by the Court of Appeals in our decision in *Canada Malting Co. v. Paterson Steamships, Ltd.*, 285 U.S. 413 (1932). That case arose out of a collision between two vessels in American waters. The Canadian owners of cargo lost in the accident sued the Canadian owners of one of the vessels in Federal District Court. The cargo owners chose an American court in large part because the relevant American liability rules were more favorable than the Canadian rules. The District Court dismissed on grounds of *forum non conveniens*. The plaintiffs argued that dismissal was inappropriate because Canadian laws were less favorable to them. This Court nonetheless affirmed:

> We have no occasion to enquire by what law the rights of the parties are governed, as we are of the opinion that, under any view of that question, it lay within the discretion of the District Court to decline to assume jurisdiction over the controversy. . . . "[The] court will not take cognizance of the case if justice would be as well done by remitting the parties to their home forum."

The Court further stated that "[t]here was no basis for the contention that the District Court abused its discretion."

It is true that *Canada Malting* was decided before *Gilbert*, and that the doctrine of *forum non conveniens* was not fully crystallized until our decision in that case. However, *Gilbert* in no way affects the validity of *Canada Malting*. Indeed, by holding that the central focus of the *forum non conveniens* inquiry is convenience, *Gilbert* implicitly recognized that dismissal may not be barred solely because of the possibility of an unfavorable change in law. Under *Gilbert,* dismissal will ordinarily be appropriate where trial in the plaintiff's chosen forum imposes a heavy burden on the defendant or the court, and where the plaintiff is unable to offer any specific reasons of convenience supporting his choice. If substantial weight were given to the possibility of an unfavorable change in law, however, dismissal might be barred even where trial in the chosen forum was plainly inconvenient.

The Court of Appeals' decision is inconsistent with this Court's earlier *forum non conveniens* decisions in another respect. Those decisions have repeatedly emphasized the need to retain flexibility. In *Gilbert*, the Court refused to identify specific circumstances "which will justify or require either grant or denial of remedy." * * * If central emphasis were placed on any one factor, the *forum non conveniens* doctrine would lose much of the very flexibility that makes it so valuable.

In fact, if conclusive or substantial weight were given to the possibility of a change in law, the *forum non conveniens* doctrine would become virtually useless. Jurisdiction and venue requirements are often easily satisfied. As a result, many plaintiffs are able to choose from among several forums. Ordinarily, these plaintiffs will select that forum whose choice-of-law rules are most advantageous. Thus, if the possibility of an unfavorable change in substantive law is given substantial weight in the *forum non conveniens* inquiry, dismissal would rarely be proper. * * *

The Court of Appeals' approach is not only inconsistent with the purpose of the *forum non conveniens* doctrine, but also poses substantial practical problems. If the possibility of a change in law were given substantial weight, deciding motions to dismiss on the ground of *forum non conveniens* would become quite difficult. Choice-of-law analysis would become extremely important, and the courts would frequently be required to interpret the law of foreign jurisdictions. First, the trial court would have to determine what law would apply if the case were tried in the chosen forum, and what law would apply if the case were tried in the alternative forum. It would then have to compare the rights, remedies, and procedures available under the law that would be applied in each forum. Dismissal would be appropriate only if the court concluded that the law applied by the alternative forum is as favorable to the plaintiff as that of the chosen forum. The doctrine of *forum non conveniens*, however, is designed in part to help courts avoid conducting complex exercises in comparative law. As we stated in *Gilbert*, the public interest factors point towards dismissal where the court would be required to "untangle problems in conflict of laws, and in law foreign to itself."

Upholding the decision of the Court of Appeals would result in other practical problems. At least where the foreign plaintiff named an American manufacturer as defendant, a court could not dismiss the case on grounds of *forum non conveniens* where dismissal might lead to an unfavorable change in law. The American courts, which are already extremely attractive to foreign plaintiffs, would become even more attractive. The flow of litigation into the United States would increase and further congest already crowded courts.

The Court of Appeals based its decision, at least in part, on an analogy between dismissals on grounds of *forum non conveniens* and transfers between federal courts pursuant to § 1404(a). In *Van Dusen v. Barrack*, 376 U.S. 612 (1964), this Court ruled that a § 1404(a) transfer should not result in a change in the applicable law. Relying on dictum in an earlier Third Circuit opinion interpreting *Van Dusen*, the court below held that that principle is also applicable to a dismissal on *forum non conveniens* grounds. However, § 1404(a) transfers are different than dismissals on the ground of *forum non conveniens.*

Congress enacted § 1404(a) to permit change of venue between federal courts. Although the statute was drafted in accordance with the doctrine of *forum non conveniens*, it was intended to be a revision rather than a codification of the common law. District courts were given more discretion to transfer under § 1404(a) than they had to dismiss on grounds of *forum non conveniens.*

The reasoning employed in *Van Dusen v. Barrack* is simply inapplicable to dismissals on grounds of *forum non conveniens*. That case did not discuss the common-law doctrine. Rather, it focused on "the construction and application" of § 1404(a). Emphasizing the remedial purpose of the statute, *Barrack* concluded that Congress could not have intended a transfer to be accompanied by a change in law. The statute was designed as a "federal housekeeping measure," allowing easy change of venue within a unified federal system. The Court feared that if a change in venue were accompanied by a change in law, forum-shopping parties would take unfair advantage of the relaxed standards for transfer. The rule was necessary to ensure the just and efficient operation of the statute.

We do not hold that the possibility of an unfavorable change in law should *never* be a relevant consideration in a *forum non conveniens* inquiry. Of course, if the remedy provided by the alternative forum is so clearly inadequate or unsatisfactory that it is no remedy at all, the unfavorable change in law may be given substantial weight; the district court may conclude that dismissal would not be in the interest of justice.[22] In these cases, however, the remedies that would be provided by the Scottish courts do not fall within this category. Although the relatives of the decedents may not be able to rely on a strict liability theory, and although their potential damages award may be smaller, there is no danger that they will be deprived of any remedy or treated unfairly.

III

The Court of Appeals also erred in rejecting the District Court's *Gilbert* analysis. The Court of Appeals stated that more weight should have been given to the plaintiff's choice of forum, and criticized the District Court's analysis of the private and public interests. However, the District Court's decision regarding the deference due plaintiff's choice of forum was appropriate. Furthermore, we do not believe that the District Court abused its discretion in weighing the private and public interests.

A

The District Court acknowledged that there is ordinarily a strong presumption in favor of the plaintiff's choice of forum, which may be

---

[22] At the outset of any *forum non conveniens* inquiry, the court must determine whether there exists an alternative forum. Ordinarily, this requirement will be satisfied when the defendant is "amenable to process" in the other jurisdiction. *Gilbert*, 330 U.S., at 506–507. In rare circumstances, however, where the remedy offered by the other forum is clearly unsatisfactory, the other forum may not be an adequate alternative, and the initial requirement may not be satisfied. Thus, for example, dismissal would not be appropriate where the alternative forum does not permit litigation of the subject matter of the dispute. Cf. *Phoenix Canada Oil Co. Ltd. v. Texaco, Inc.*, 78 F.R.D. 445 (Del. 1978) (court refuses to dismiss, where alternative forum is Ecuador, it is unclear whether Ecuadorean tribunal will hear the case, and there is no generally codified Ecuadorean legal remedy for the unjust enrichment and tort claims asserted).

overcome only when the private and public interest factors clearly point towards trial in the alternative forum. It held, however, that the presumption applied with less force when the plaintiff or real parties in interest are foreign.

The District Court's distinction between resident or citizen plaintiffs and foreign plaintiffs is fully justified. In *Koster*, the Court indicated that a plaintiff's choice of forum is entitled to greater deference when the plaintiff has chosen the home forum. When the home forum has been chosen, it is reasonable to assume that this choice is convenient. When the plaintiff is foreign, however, this assumption is much less reasonable. Because the central purpose of any *forum non conveniens* inquiry is to ensure that the trial is convenient, a foreign plaintiff's choice deserves less deference.

B

The *forum non conveniens* determination is committed to the sound discretion of the trial court. It may be reversed only when there has been a clear abuse of discretion; where the court has considered all relevant public and private interest factors, and where its balancing of these factors is reasonable, its decision deserves substantial deference. Here, the Court of Appeals expressly acknowledged that the standard of review was one of abuse of discretion. In examining the District Court's analysis of the public and private interests, however, the Court of Appeals seems to have lost sight of this rule, and substituted its own judgment for that of the District Court.

(1)

In analyzing the private interest factors, the District Court stated that the connections with Scotland are "overwhelming." This characterization may be somewhat exaggerated. Particularly with respect to the question of relative ease of access to sources of proof, the private interests point in both directions. As respondent emphasizes, records concerning the design, manufacture, and testing of the propeller and plane are located in the United States. She would have greater access to sources of proof relevant to her strict liability and negligence theories if trial were held here. However, the District Court did not act unreasonably in concluding that fewer evidentiary problems would be posed if the trial were held in Scotland. A large proportion of the relevant evidence is located in Great Britain.

The Court of Appeals found that the problems of proof could not be given any weight because Piper and Hartzell failed to describe with specificity the evidence they would not be able to obtain if trial were held in the United States. It suggested that defendants seeking *forum non conveniens* dismissal must submit affidavits identifying the witnesses they would call and the testimony these witnesses would provide if the trial were held in the alternative forum. Such detail is not necessary. Piper and Hartzell have moved for dismissal precisely because many crucial witnesses are located beyond the reach of compulsory process, and thus are difficult to identify or interview. Requiring extensive investigation would defeat the purpose of their motion. Of course, defendants must provide enough information to enable the District Court to balance the parties' interests. Our examination of the record convinces us that sufficient information was provided here. Both Piper and Hartzell submitted affidavits describing the evidentiary problems they would face if the trial were held in the United States.

The District Court correctly concluded that the problems posed by the inability to implead potential third-party defendants clearly supported holding the trial in Scotland. Joinder of the pilot's estate, Air Navigation, and McDonald is critical to the presentation of petitioners' defense. If Piper and Hartzell can show that the accident was caused not by a design defect, but rather by the negligence of the pilot, the plane's owners, or the charter company, they will be relieved of all liability. It is true, of course, that if Hartzell and Piper were found liable after a trial in the United States, they could institute an action for indemnity or contribution against these parties in Scotland. It would be far more convenient, however, to resolve all claims in one trial. The Court of Appeals rejected this argument. Forcing petitioners to rely on actions for indemnity or contributions would be "burdensome" but not "unfair." Finding that trial in the plaintiff's chosen forum would be burdensome, however, is sufficient to support dismissal on grounds of *forum non conveniens*.

(2)

The District Court's review of the factors relating to the public interest was also reasonable. On the basis of its choice-of-law analysis, it concluded that if the case were tried in the Middle District of Pennsylvania, Pennsylvania law would apply to Piper and Scottish law to Hartzell. It stated that a trial involving two sets of laws would be confusing to the jury. It also noted its own lack of familiarity with Scottish law. Consideration of these problems was clearly appropriate under *Gilbert*; in that case we explicitly held that the need to apply foreign law pointed towards dismissal. The Court of Appeals found that the District Court's choice-of-law analysis was incorrect, and that American law would apply to both Hartzell and Piper. Thus, lack of familiarity with foreign law would not be a problem. Even if the Court of Appeals' conclusion is correct, however, all other public interest factors favored trial in Scotland.

Scotland has a very strong interest in this litigation. The accident occurred in its airspace. All of the decedents were Scottish. Apart from

Piper and Hartzell, all potential plaintiffs and defendants are either Scottish or English. As we stated in *Gilbert*, there is "a local interest in having localized controversies decided at home." Respondent argues that American citizens have an interest in ensuring that American manufacturers are deterred from producing defective products, and that additional deterrence must be obtained if Piper and Hartzell were tried in the United States, where they could be sued on the basis of both negligence and strict liability. However, the incremental deterrence that would be gained if this trial were held in an American court is likely to be insignificant. The American interest in this accident is simply not sufficient to justify the enormous commitment of judicial time and resources that would inevitably be required if the case were to be tried here.

IV

The Court of Appeals erred in holding that the possibility of an unfavorable change in law bars dismissal on the ground of *forum non conveniens*. It also erred in rejecting the District Court's *Gilbert* analysis. The District Court properly decided that the presumption in favor of the respondent's forum choice applied with less than maximum force because the real parties in interest are foreign. It did not act unreasonably in deciding that the private interests pointed towards trial in Scotland. Nor did it act unreasonably in deciding that the public interests favored trial in Scotland. Thus, the judgment of the Court of Appeals is

Reversed.

NOTES AND QUESTIONS

1. Forum Non Conveniens *and Reasonable Jurisdiction*. The *forum non conveniens* doctrine is an important tool for courts faced with problems of concurrent jurisdiction. Rather than employ the restrictive statutory analysis of *American Banana* or the jurisdictional balancing test of *Timberlane*, *Piper* used *forum non conveniens* as a factually-oriented test to evaluate the reasonableness of one jurisdiction against another. Note that there was no doubt in *Piper* that the federal court in Pennsylvania had adjudicatory jurisdiction over both Piper and Hartzell. Piper and Hartzell (though apparently not the pilot's estate, A.V. Navigation, and McDonald) could be sued in Pennsylvania. The question in the case was whether, in the trial court's opinion, it was unreasonable to try them there.

In 2007, the Supreme Court held unanimously that a trial court could dismiss a case *forum non conveniens* even before it determined if it had jurisdiction. Sinochem International Co. Ltd. v. Malaysia International Shipping Corp., 549 U.S. 422 (2007). Except for this theretofore unresolved question, Justice Ginsburg believed *Sinochem* was "a textbook case for immediate *forum non conveniens* dismissal." *Id.* at 435. Do you agree that, as with *Piper*, *Sinochem* "represents a pragmatic approach to transnational litigation"? Christopher A. Whytock, "U.S. Supreme Court Decides Forum Non Conveniens Case," 11 *ASIL Insights*, Issue 10 (2007).

2. Forum Non Conveniens *and Judicial Discretion. Piper* established how discretionary may be a trial court's power to dismiss on *forum non conveniens* grounds. In effect the Supreme Court asked a trial court to weigh public and private interests reasonably and to determine the existence of an adequate alternative forum. Under what circumstances may an appeals court review and reverse a trial court's decision which is so based on the fact-specific nature of a particular case? *In re* Disaster at Riyadh Airport, Saudi Arabia, 540 F.Supp. 1141 (D.D.C. 1982), and Nai-Chao v. Boeing Co., 555 F.Supp. 9 (N.D.Cal. 1982), show trial courts willing to dismiss cases involving foreign plaintiffs where an alternative forum was adequate and where no overwhelming U.S. forum interest outweighed the problems of federal court congestion and overrode local interests in the case at hand. However, in *In re* Air Disaster Near Bombay, India on January 1, 1978, 531 F.Supp. 1175 (W.D.Wash. 1982), the trial court denied a motion for a *forum non conveniens* dismissal, ruling there was no adequate alternative forum.

3. *The Foreign Plaintiff. Forum non conveniens* cases are sometimes ironic. In a typical case, a "far-away" foreign plaintiff chooses voluntarily to bring an action in the United States. The U.S. defendant then asserts that the U.S. court is not a "convenient" site for the action, even though it is the foreign plaintiff who chose the "inconvenient" forum otherwise apparently "home" to the defendant. Does the irony demonstrate the importance of public interest factors when a court decides a *forum non conveniens* request?

Piper held that less deference should be granted to a plaintiff's choice of a U.S. forum when the plaintiff is foreign. However, does it matter that *Piper* "did not consider the jurisdictional provisions of various FCN [friendship, commerce, and navigation] treaties which grant foreign plaintiffs equal access to American courts and apply with the force of statutory law"? Maria A. Mazzola, Note, "*Forum Non Conveniens* and Foreign Plaintiffs: Addressing the Unanswered Questions of *Reyno*," 6 *Fordham Journal of International Law* 577, 604 (1983).

4. *A Transnational Access-to-Justice Gap?* Professors Whytock and Robinson have argued that the differences between the doctrines of *forum non conveniens* and judgment enforcement create "a transnational access-to-justice gap." Christopher A. Whytock & Cassandra Burke Robertson, "Forum Non Conveniens and the Enforcement of Foreign Judgments," 111 *Columbia Law Review* 1444, 1453 (2011). Since the judgment enforcement doctrine is stricter than the *forum non conveniens* doctrine, a defendant may successfully persuade a U.S. court to dismiss a plaintiff's U.S. suit on *forum non conveniens'* grounds and then persuade another U.S. court to refuse to recognize a favorable judgment for plaintiff from the foreign court to which defendant wanted to go at the outset. *Id.* at 1446–53, 1471. Noting the leniency of U.S. courts in granting *forum non conveniens*, "almost 50% overall," should U.S. courts be stricter in granting defendant's motions to dismiss, given their record of "forum shopper's remorse"? *Id.* at 1447, 1462.

5. *International Lawyering Tactics. Piper* is a good example of lawyering in international litigation. Plaintiffs' lawyer made the first move, using his secretary to commence the action in a California state court on her home turf far away from the accident, the families of the decedents, and most, if not all, possible defendants. From then on, the tactical moves were those of defendants' lawyers. First, the case was removed to federal court in California where service on Hartzell was quashed. Second, the case was transferred to federal court in Pennsylvania, nearer Piper and Hartzell and farther from plaintiffs' attorney. Third, defendants persuaded the trial court and the Supreme Court to dismiss the case on *forum non conveniens* grounds. What likelihood was there that the California lawyer who initiated the action in California state court would follow the case all the way back to Scotland? Could the California attorney even have hoped to litigate the case in the United Kingdom? From a lawyering point of view, can the *Piper* case be viewed as the attempt of a California lawyer to use liberal U.S. jurisdictional rules to "capture" a litigation with little California connection being blocked by lawyers for Piper and Hartzell who used removal, transfer, and *forum non conveniens* rules as a way to "return" the case to Scotland where the case is most intimately connected? How much more advanced is this procedure than what went on in *American Banana* 72 years before? For more background, see Kevin M. Clermont, "The Story of *Piper*: Fracturing the Foundation of Forum Non Conveniens," in *Civil Procedure Stories* 193 (Kevin M. Clermont ed. 2004); Harold Hongju Koh, "International Business Transactions in United States Courts," 261 *Recueil des Cours* 9, 146–58 (1998).

6. *The States and* Forum Non Conveniens. The Texas Supreme Court held that the Texas legislature abolished the doctrine of *forum non conveniens* as long ago as 1913. Dow Chemical Co. v. Castro Alfaro, 786 S.W.2d 674 (Tex. 1990), *cert. denied*, 498 U.S. 1024 (1991). This curious judgment evoked four vigorous dissents, one by Justice Cook:

> Like turn-of-the century wildcatters, the plaintiffs in this case searched all across the nation for a place to make their claims. Through three courts they moved, filing their lawsuits on one coast and then on the other. By each of those courts the plaintiffs were rejected, and so they continued their search for a more willing forum. Their efforts are finally rewarded. Today they hit pay dirt in Texas.
>
> No reason exists, in law or in policy, to support their presence in this state. The legislature adopted within the statute the phrase "may be enforced" to permit plaintiffs to sue in Texas, irrespective of where they live or where the cause of action arose. The legislature did not adopt this statute, however, to remove from our courts all discretion to dismiss. To use the statute to sweep away, completely and finally, a common law doctrine painstakingly developed over the years is to infuse the statute with a power not contained in the words. Properly read, the statute is asymmetrical. Although it confers upon the plaintiffs an absolute right to bring claims in our

> courts, it does not impose upon our courts an absolute responsibility to entertain those claims.
>
> Even if the statute supported the court's interpretation, however, I would remain unwilling to join in the opinion. The decision places too great a burden on defendants who are citizens of our state because, by abolishing *forum non conveniens*, the decision exposes our citizens to the claims of any plaintiff, no matter how distant from Texas is that plaintiff's home or cause of action. The interest of Texas in these disputes is likely to be as slight as the relationship of the plaintiffs to Texas. The interest of other nations, on the other hand, is likely to be substantial. For these reasons, I fear the decision allows assertions of jurisdiction by Texas courts that are so unfair and unreasonable as to violate the due process clause of the federal constitution.

Id. at 697. The Texas legislature responded to *Dow Chemical* by enacting a limited *forum non conveniens* statute in 1993. See Louise Ellen Teitz, *Transnational Litigation* § 3–5, at 123–25 (1996).

Not only the due process clause, but also federal common law might pose a problem for the majority in *Dow Chemical*. As we see below in the *Sabbatino Case*, the federal courts are able to elaborate a federal common law in certain areas of special concern to national interests such as foreign affairs. See Gary Born, "Forum Non Conveniens Held Unavailable Under Texas Law," 18 *International Business Lawyer* 392 (1990). Moreover, in diversity cases, the federal courts will apply the federal *forum non conveniens* doctrine, even in Texas. See Villar v. Crowley Maritime Corp., 780 F.Supp. 1467, 1483–85 (S.D.Tex. 1992). However, in American Dredging Co. v. Miller, 510 U.S. 443 (1994), the Supreme Court passed by an opportunity to help nationalize the doctrine, holding that, in admiralty cases, states acting under the Jones Act and the "savings to suiters clause," which gives concurrent jurisdiction to U.S. state courts in certain admiralty actions, need not apply the federal *forum non conveniens* doctrine. Justice Scalia's majority opinion concluded that "maritime commerce in general does not require a uniform rule of *forum non conveniens*." *Id.* at 456. In dissent, Justice Kennedy for himself and Justice Thomas disapproved, believing "that *forum non conveniens* is an established feature of the general maritime law." *Id.* at 466. *American Dredging* involved only U.S. actors, however, and the Supreme Court might reach "a different result if those who raise the *forum non conveniens* objection are of foreign nationality." *Id.* at 469.

MARK W. JANIS, "THE DOCTRINE OF FORUM NON CONVENIENS AND THE BHOPAL CASE"

34 *Netherlands International Law Review* 192 (1987)

The industrial accident at the Union Carbide plant in Bhopal, India on December 3, 1984, released methyl isocyanate gas which killed more than 2,000 people and injured about 200,000. Newspaper investigations of the tragedy indicated that there were numerous violations of the operating codes established both by the company operating the plant, Union Carbide India Limited, and its parent company, Union Carbide Corporation. There may well have been negligence not only by those engaged in making the lethal chemical used in pesticides but also by the Indian governmental bodies charged with setting and enforcing safety standards. The factual pattern of the disaster and the allocation of legal responsibility for it are incredibly tangled webs.

Immediately after the accident, some American lawyers made an unseemly rush to Bhopal. As the *New York Times* reported: "Right behind the stream of scientists, executives, officials, aid givers, and others who have come to this central Indian city after the gas leak last week are American lawyers, members of a breed of legal specialists seen by some as ambulance chasers and by others as champions of the individual against the corporation and of industrial safety and consumer protection." * * *

However, not only American lawyers were interested in suing Union Carbide in American courts. On March 9, 1985, the *New York Times* reported that the Indian Government had also decided to sue on behalf of the Indian victims in United States courts in order "to secure higher compensation and also because Union Carbide has to share responsibility for the gas leak at its Indian subsidiary." On March 29, 1985, the Indian Government enacted the Bhopal Gas Leak Disaster (Processing of Claims) Act, a statute which vested in the Indian Government the exclusive right to represent the Indian plaintiffs in the Bhopal case in India and elsewhere. On April 8, 1985, pursuant to the Act, the Indian Government filed its own claims against Union Carbide in the American courts.

The Indian Government claims, along with some 144 lawsuits brought privately, were all consolidated on June 28, 1985, in a consolidated complaint filed in the federal district court for the Southern District of New York. * * *

With the filing of the Indian Government claims, the *Bhopal* case showed the peculiar circumstance of a government arguing that its own courts were less preferable than those of a foreign State for the resolution of disputes touching on both legal systems. When the defendant, Union Carbide, raised the *forum non conveniens* argument, the Indian Government was in the even more awkward posture of contending (as part of the Plaintiffs' Executive Committee) that the Indian courts were actually inadequate for handling the Bhopal claims. Although both the trial court and the appeals court recognized that their *forum non conveniens* analysis was to be conducted pursuant to the holdings in *Gilbert* and *Piper*, neither the 1947 cases nor the 1981 case faced the question of whether the arguably more convenient forum was up to the task of adequately adjudicating the dispute at hand. It had been assumed that the courts of Virginia (in *Gilbert*), Illinois (in *Koster [v. Lumbermens Mutual Casualty Co.*, another 1947 Supreme Court case]), and the United Kingdom (in *Piper*), were just as sophisticated as the courts in which the *forum non conveniens* dismissal was sought.

In *Bhopal*, both the District Court and the Court of Appeals concluded that the Indian courts could properly adjudicate the accident cases. Moreover, while the District Court imposed certain United States procedural guarantees on the Indian litigation, the Court of Appeals, even more respectful towards the foreign proceedings, modified the trial court's order and imposed none.

In reviewing the competence of the Indian courts, the District Court weighed the testimony of an American law professor, Marc Galanter, an expert on Indian law opposing the adequacy of the Indian legal system against the testimony of two senior Indian advocates, N.A. Palkhivala, formerly Ambassador of India to the United States, and J.B. Dadachanji arguing in favor of the Indian system. The court thought the conclusions of Professor Galanter "far less persuasive than those of" the two Indian lawyers. The District Court's opinion was summarized and approved by the Court of Appeal:

> The Indian judiciary was found by the court to be a developed, independent and progressive one, which has demonstrated its capability of circumventing long delays and backlogs prevalent in the Indian courts' handling of ordinary cases by devising special expediting procedures in extraordinary cases, such as by directing its High Court to hear them on a daily basis, appointing special tribunals to handle them, and assigning daily hearing duties to a single judge. [The District Court judge] found that Indian courts have competently dealt with complex technological issues. Since the Bhopal Act provides that the case may be treated speedily, effectively and to the best advantage of the claimants, and since the Union of India represents the claimants, the prosecution of the claims is expected to be adequately staffed by the Attorney General or Solicitor General of India.
>
> The tort law of India, which is derived from common law and British precedent, was found to be suitable for resolution of legal issues arising in cases involving highly complex technology. Moreover, Indian courts would be in a superior position to construe and apply applicable Indian laws and standards than would courts of the United States. Third parties may be interpleaded under Order 1, Rule 10(2) of the Indian Code of Civil Procedure, and defendants may seek contribution from third parties. The absence in India of a class action procedure comparable to that in federal courts here was found not to

> deprive the plaintiffs of a remedy, in view of existing Indian legal authorization for "representative" suits under Order 1, Rule 8 of the Indian Code of Civil Procedure, which would permit an Indian court to create representative classes. Judge Keenan further found that the absence of juries and contingent fee arrangements in India would not deprive the claimants of an adequate remedy. * * *

Having determined that Indian courts were an acceptable alternative to American courts for the adjudication of the Bhopal suits, the District and Circuit Courts turned to the weighing of private and public interest factors at the heart of any *forum non conveniens* inquiry. Both courts follow *Piper* in holding that since the plaintiffs in *Bhopal* were foreign, their choice of an American court was due less deference than had they been United States citizens seeking to sue at home. Given the factual situation surrounding the Bhopal accident, the courts had little difficulty in deciding that the claims arising from it should be decided in India, not America.

Looking first at the private interest factors, the District Court compared *Bhopal* to *Piper* where private interests pointed in two ways: "By contrast, this Court finds that the private interests point strongly one way"—India. The Circuit Court agreed:

> In short, the plant has been constructed and managed by Indians in India. No Americans were employed at the plant at the time of the accident. In the five years from 1980 to 1984, although there were more than 1,000 Indians employed at the plant, only one American was employed there and he left in 1982. No Americans visited the plant for more than one year prior to the accident, and during the 5-year period before the accident the communications between the plant and the United States were almost non-existent.
>
> The vast majority of material witnesses and documentary proof bearing on causation of and liability for the accident is located in India, not the United States, and would be more accessible to an Indian court than to a United States court. The records are almost entirely in Hindi or other Indian languages, understandable to an Indian court without translation. The witnesses for the most part do not speak English but Indian languages, understood by an Indian court but not by an American court. These witnesses could be required to appear in an Indian court but not in a court of the United States. Although witnesses in the United States could not be subpoenaed to appear in India, they are comparatively few in number and most are employed by [Union Carbide Corporation] which, as a party would produce them in India, with lower overall transportation

> costs than if the parties were to attempt to bring hundreds of Indian witnesses to the United States. Lastly, Judge Keenan properly concluded that an Indian court would be in a better position to direct and supervise a viewing of the Bhopal plant, which was sealed after the accident. Such a viewing could be of help to a court in determining liability issues.

Similarly, both courts decided that public interest factors tilted towards trying the case in India. Endorsing the findings of the District Court, the Circuit Court ruled:

> After a thorough review, the district court concluded that the public interest concerns, like the private ones, also weigh heavily in favor of India as the situs for trial and disposition of the cases. The accident and all the relevant events occurred in India. The victims, over 200,000 in number, are citizens of India and located there. The witnesses are almost entirely Indian citizens. The Union of India has a greater interest than does the United States in facilitating the trial and adjudication of the victims' claims. Despite the contentions of plaintiffs and amici that it would be in the public interest to avoid a "double standard" by requiring an American parent corporation (UCC) to submit to the jurisdiction of American courts, India has a stronger countervailing interest in adjudicating the claims in its courts according to its standards rather than having American values and standards of care imposed upon it.
>
> India's interest is increased by the fact that it has for years treated UCIL as an Indian national, subjecting it to intensive regulations and governmental supervision of the construction, development and operation of the Bhopal plant, its emissions, water and air pollution, and safety precautions. Numerous Indian government officials have regularly conducted on-site inspections of the plant and approved its machinery and equipment, including its facilities for storage of the lethal methyl isocyanate gas that escaped and caused the disaster giving rise to the claims. Thus India has considered the plant to be an Indian one and the disaster to be an Indian problem. It therefore has a deep interest in ensuring compliance with its safety standards. Moreover, plaintiffs have conceded that in view of India's strong interest and its greater contacts with the plant, its operation, its employees, and the victims of the accident, the law of India, as the place where the tort occurred, will undoubtedly govern. In contrast, the American interests are relatively minor. Indeed, a long trial of the 145 cases here would unduly burden an already overburdened court, involving both jury hardship and heavy expense. It would face the court with numerous practical

difficulties, including the most impossible task of attempting to understand extensive relevant Indian regulations published in a foreign language and the slow process of receiving testimony of scores of witnesses through interpreters.

The incongruity of finding that the public interest of India called for trying the *Bhopal* case in India even when the Indian Government sought to have it tried in America was rectified between the District Court opinion and that of the Circuit Court. The Government of India decided to support the judgment of the District Court. The private plaintiffs, however, continued in their opposition to the *forum non conveniens* dismissal. * * *

In a world increasingly filled with transactions and, sadly, accidents touching on more than one country, the need to properly allocate international judicial business becomes even more pressing. In time perhaps, public international law will help provide more answers to questions about the allocation of judicial competence between nations by the framing and application of international conventions. Until then, and, of course, in some cases even thereafter, States will have to moderate their extensions of jurisdiction to matters involving foreign countries by employing notions of comity and good sense. *Forum non conveniens* is one such useful notion, and it was rightly applied in the United States in the case of *Bhopal*.

NOTES AND QUESTIONS

1. *The Aftermath of the* Bhopal Case. Bi v. Union Carbide Chemicals & Plastics Co., 984 F.2d 582 (2d Cir. 1993), an action brought by individual Indian victims of the Bhopal tragedy who sought to supplement the relief they ultimately won in the Indian courts, recounted the aftermath of the *Bhopal Case*. In 1989, the Indian Supreme Court approved a settlement between the government of India representing all the victims and Union Carbide for $470 million. The Indian Supreme Court in a related decision that year also "upheld the constitutional validity of the Bhopal Act and confirmed the Indian Government's exclusive authority to compromise all claims arising out of the Bhopal disaster." *Id.* at 584. In 1990, Bi and another, class representatives for some of the Indian victims, filed suits against Union Carbide in Texas state court, arguing that the Indian government had a conflict of interest in trying to represent victims and that the settlement in India was too low. Union Carbide removed the suits to U.S. federal court in Texas, and the suits were then transferred to U.S. federal court in New York. The court dismissed both actions under *forum non conveniens,* and the Second Circuit affirmed: "We hold that when a recognized democracy determines that the interests of the victims of a mass tort that occurred within its borders will be best served if the foreign government exclusively represents the victims in courts around the world, we will not pass judgment on that determination[.]" *Id.* at 586.

The Bhopal saga continued. In June 2010 an Indian court convicted seven former Union Carbide executives for criminal negligence, sentencing them to two years in prison. In the same month, Indian government ministers recommended making stronger efforts to extradite Warren Anderson, the former Union Carbide Chief Executive Officer, to face criminal charges, and called for more compensation for the families of individuals who died in the 1984 disaster. "The Bhopal Disaster: The Slow Pursuit of Justice," *The Economist*, June 26, 2010, at 43.

2. *The Adequacy of the Foreign Legal System*. The U.S. Supreme Court chose not to review *Bhopal*, Executive Committee Members v. Union of India, 484 U.S. 871 (1987), letting stand the opinion of the Second Circuit. Thus, the Supreme Court did not consider the adequacy of the foreign legal system, a consideration also left unaddressed in its two key *forum non conveniens* decisions, *Gilbert* and *Piper*. Looking at the opinions of the trial court and the appellate court in *Bhopal*, we see that they at least used another balancing test to evaluate the plausibility of justice being done in a foreign court, weighing here the testimony of conflicting expert witnesses. Is this an example, once again, of the judicial discretion built into *forum non conveniens*? In Bhatnagar v. Surrendra Overseas Ltd., 52 F.3d 1220 (3d Cir. 1995), the Third Circuit held that the potential for long delay in the Indian legal system was a permissible ground for denying a motion of *forum non conveniens*.

3. Forum Non Conveniens *and* International Shoe. In the United States *forum non conveniens* may be employed even if the court has personal and subject matter jurisdiction over the defendants and the transaction. It is no coincidence that *forum non conveniens* formally entered into federal law in 1947, two years after International Shoe Co. v. State of Washington, 326 U.S. 310 (1945), extended the jurisdictional reach of courts in the United States. After *International Shoe* plaintiffs had more choice about their courts. *Forum non conveniens* and the federal transfer statute moderated the new power of plaintiffs over forum selection.

Forum non conveniens and the federal transfer statute are also used in some U.S. cases where adjudicatory jurisdiction is not based on a specific activity in the forum related to the cause of action (as in *International Shoe*), but instead is based on "systematic and continuous" activities of a corporate defendant at a place other than its headquarters or place of incorporation. Thus, in *Piper*, Reyno obtained jurisdiction in California over Piper Aircraft Co., a Pennsylvania corporation, and was able to serve process in Pennsylvania on Hartzell Propeller, Inc., an Ohio corporation.

4. *Judge-made Procedural Law*. In *Gilbert* the Supreme Court rested the doctrine of *forum non conveniens* on the foundations of a court's "inherent power." *Forum non conveniens* is an excellent example of a procedure-facilitating rule based on judge-made common law. Contrast the source of the *forum non conveniens* doctrine with the statutory source of a rule achieving similar goals: the 1948 federal transfer statute, 28 U.S.C. § 1404(a). Would anything be gained (or lost) if *forum non conveniens* were codified? Is a judge-

made rule more responsive to changing notions of comity, *e.g.*, able to respond more readily to the development of case law in other countries accommodating (or not) conflicts of jurisdiction?

5. *International Mechanisms for Resolving Jurisdictional Conflicts.* Considering the problems posed by assertions of U.S. judicial jurisdiction in the face of foreign government opposition, Professor Stephan remarked, "[t]he fundamental difficulty with all these [opposition] arguments is that no international instrument to which the United States is a party addresses these issues, and no decisionmaker has the capacity to provide authoritative and final resolution of the international law claims." Paul B. Stephan, "A Becoming Modesty—U.S. Litigation in the Mirror of International Law," 52 *DePaul Law Review* 627, 639–40 (2002. Could a treaty or even an international court or panel help reconcile conflicts of jurisdiction better than *ad hoc* national judicial decision making?

CHAPTER 12

FOREIGN LAW AND FOREIGN GOVERNMENTS

■ ■ ■

As we have seen, an important focus of international law is on legal relationships among states. We have studied the making of inter-state rules by treaty (Chapter 2) and in custom and from non-consensual sources (Chapter 3); the application of international law in municipal courts (Chapters 4 and 11) and in international tribunals (Chapter 5); and the international law protecting human rights (Chapter 6), recognizing foreign states and governments (Chapter 7), creating international organizations (Chapter 8), limiting war (Chapter 9), and regulating common spaces such as the seas (Chapter 10). Now for our final topic, we turn to the rules governing the treatment given by municipal courts, especially those in the United States, to foreign law and foreign governments. This subject is closely linked to the concerns of Chapter 4 about the incorporation of international law into municipal law and of Chapter 11 about international conflict of laws. In Chapter 12, we look first at rules relating to the proof of foreign law, second at the limits public policy sometimes puts on the application of foreign law, third, at the notion of foreign sovereign immunity, and, finally, fourth, at the act of state doctrine.

A. PROOF OF FOREIGN LAW

Traditionally, English and American common law treated foreign law as a matter of fact rather than as a matter of law. Hence, foreign law was sometimes a subject for the jury, not the judge. It often was proved, like other matters of fact, by testimony from competing experts called by opposing counsel. Moreover, as fact, it was usually settled during a "day in court" and so not ordinarily subject to review by an appellate court. The *Walton Case* is a good example both of the traditional approach and of one of its pitfalls. Following *Walton* is *Faggionato*, which explores the use of experts to prove foreign law.

WALTON V. ARABIAN AMERICAN OIL CO.

233 F.2d 541 (1956) (2d Cir.), *cert. denied*, 352 U.S. 872 (1956)

Frank, Circuit Judge

Plaintiff is a citizen and resident of Arkansas, who, while temporarily in Saudi Arabia, was seriously injured when an automobile he was driving collided with a truck owned by defendant, driven by one of defendant's employees. Defendant is a corporation incorporated in Delaware, licensed to do business in New York, and engaged in extensive business activities in Saudi Arabia. Plaintiff's complaint did not allege pertinent Saudi Arabian "law," nor at the trial did he prove or offer to prove it. Defendant did not, in its answer, allege such "law," and defendant did not prove or offer to prove it. There was evidence from which it might have been inferred, reasonably, that, under well-established New York decisions, defendant was negligent and therefore liable to plaintiff. The trial judge, saying he would not take judicial notice of "Saudi-Arabian law," directed a verdict in favor of the defendant and gave judgment against the plaintiff.

1. As jurisdiction here rests on diversity of citizenship, we must apply the New York rules of conflict of laws. It is well settled by the New York decisions that the "substantive law" applicable to an alleged tort is the "law" of the place where the alleged tort occurred. This is the federal doctrine; see, e.g., Slater v. Mexican National Railroad Co., 194 U.S. 120, Cuba R. Co. v. Crosby, 222 U.S. 473. This doctrine is often said to be based on the notion that to hold otherwise would be to interfere with the authority of the foreign sovereign.

It has been suggested that, where suit is brought in an American court by an American plaintiff against an American defendant, complaining of alleged tortious conduct by the defendant in a foreign country, and that conduct is tortious according to the rules of the forum, the court, in some circumstances, should apply the forum's tort rules. There, and in 12 Modern L. Rev. (1949) 248, Morris decries, as "mechanical jurisprudence," the invariable reference to the "law" of the place where the alleged tort happened. There may be much to Morris' suggestion; and a court—particularly with reference to torts, where conduct in reliance on precedents is ordinarily absent—should not perpetuate a doctrine which, upon re-examination, shows up as unwise and unjust. Although in a diversity case a federal court must apply the "substantive" conflicts rules of the state in which the court sits, that duty perhaps does not require acceptance of state court decisions which are clearly obsolescent. But we see no signs that the New York decisions pertinent here are obsolescent.

2. The general federal rule is that the "law" of a foreign country is a fact which must be proved. However, under Fed. Rules Civ. Proc. rule 43(a), 28 U.S.C.A., a federal court must receive evidence if it is admissible according to the rules of evidence of the state in which the court sits. At first glance, then, it may seem that the judge erred in refusing to take judicial notice of Saudi Arabian "law" in the light of New York Civil Practice Act, § 344–a. In Siegelman v. Cunard White Star, 2 Cir., 221 F.2d 189, 196–197, applying that statute, we took judicial notice of English "law" which had been neither pleaded nor proved. Our decision,

in that respect, has been criticized; but it may be justified on the ground that an American court can easily comprehend, and therefore, under the statute, take judicial notice of, English decisions, like those of any state in the United States. However, where, as here, comprehension of foreign "law" is, to say the least, not easy, then, according to the somewhat narrow interpretation of the New York statute by the New York courts, a court "abuses" its discretion under that statute perhaps if it takes judicial notice of foreign "law" when it is not pleaded, and surely does so unless the party, who would otherwise have had the burden of proving that "law," has in some way adequately assisted the court in judicially learning it.

3. Plaintiff, however, argues thus: The instant case involves such rudimentary tort principles, that the judge, absent a contrary showing, should have presumed that those principles are recognized in Saudi Arabia; therefore the burden of showing the contrary was on the defendant, which did not discharge that burden. But we do not agree that the applicable tort principles, necessary to establish plaintiff's claim, are "rudimentary": In countries where the common law does not prevail, our doctrines relative to negligence, and to a master's liability for his servant's acts, may well not exist or be vastly different. Consequently, here plaintiff had the burden of showing, to the trial court's satisfaction, Saudi Arabian "law."

4. In argument, plaintiff's counsel asserted that Saudi Arabia has "no law or legal system," and no courts open to plaintiff, but only a dictatorial monarch who decides according to his whim whether a claim like plaintiff's shall be redressed, i.e., that Saudi Arabia is, in effect, "uncivilized." According to Holmes, J.—in Slater v. Mexican National R. Co., 194 U.S. 120, 129, in American Banana Co. v. United Fruit Co., 213 U.S. 347, 355–356, and in Cuba R. Co. v. Crosby, 222 U.S. 473—the lex loci does not apply "where a tort is committed in an uncivilized country" or in one "having no law that civilized countries would recognize as adequate." If such were the case here, we think the New York courts would apply (and therefore we should) the substantive "law" of the country which is most closely connected with the parties and their conduct—in this case, American "law." But plaintiff has offered no data showing that Saudi Arabia is thus "uncivilized." We are loath to and will not believe it, absent such a showing.

5. The complaint in this action was filed on May 10, 1949. * * * At [pre-trial] hearings the question of proving Saudi-Arabian law was discussed. When the case came on for trial on November 7, 1953 Judge Bicks indicated that in his view the burden was on the plaintiff to prove the foreign "law." When the plaintiff's counsel said that he was not prepared to prove the "law" of Saudi-Arabia, Judge Bicks proposed that the case be adjourned long enough to allow the plaintiff to prepare such

proof. It was agreed that the case be put over for two days to enable the plaintiff to decide whether to request an adjournment for that purpose.

When the hearing resumed on November 9, plaintiff's counsel unequivocally took the position that he did not wish to prove the foreign "law" and wanted no adjournment. He chose to rely on the applicability of New York "law." To that end he proposed that he proceed to present his case in order to make a record for appeal. The plaintiff's evidence as to liability was presented and on a proper motion the judge dismissed the complaint. He specifically ruled that he would not take judicial notice of the "law" of Saudi-Arabia and that the plaintiff's failure to prove that "law" required dismissal.

Since the plaintiff deliberately refrained from establishing an essential element of his case, the complaint was properly dismissed.

NOTES AND QUESTIONS

1. *Foreign Law as Fact.* Treating foreign law as fact was at one time popular in the civil law as well, but the fact theory lost most of its force in continental countries during the 19th century. Arthur Nussbaum, "The Problem of Proving Foreign Law," 50 *Yale Law Journal* 1018, 1018–20 (1949); Stephen L. Sass, "Foreign Law in Civil Litigation: A Comparative Survey," 16 *American Journal of Comparative Law* 332 (1968). The foreign-law-as-fact approach, however, retained its popularity among common lawyers well into the 20th century, *Walton* being a good example. *Id.* at 335–39. Some of the consequences of the traditional doctrine were that: 1. "Foreign law must be pleaded like a fact; 2. Foreign law must be proved like a fact; 3. Foreign law questions go to the jury in appropriate cases; 4. If facts are not considered on appeal, foreign law cannot be considered on appeal; and 5. The * * * holdings of appellate courts on foreign law do not have the force of stare decisis." William B. Stern, "Foreign Law in the Courts: Judicial Notice and Proof," 45 *California Law Review* 23, 25 (1957). These outcomes were, by the time of the *Walton* judgment, already under assault by commentators. *Id.* at 47.

2. *Rule 44.1.* In 1966, acknowledging that the traditional foreign-law-as-fact approach had become archaic, the U.S. Supreme Court promulgated Rule 44.1 of the Federal Rules of Civil Procedure. Rule 44.1, as amended, now reads:

> A party who intends to raise an issue about a foreign country's law must give notice by a pleading or other writing. In determining foreign law, the court may consider any relevant material or source, including testimony, whether or not submitted by a party or admissible under the Federal Rules of Evidence. The court's determination must be treated as a ruling on a question of law.

3. *The Failure to Prove Foreign Law.* Now that proof-of-foreign-law rules have been revised to give foreign law more the character of "law" rather

than of "fact," there is less of a burden on parties to prove foreign law. So, for example, in a 1978 case about a motorcycle accident in Germany where both plaintiff and defendant were U.S. citizens, the Second Circuit held that "[w]hen there is no presumption that New York law is the same as foreign law and no evidence has been presented as to foreign law, New York courts have decided the cases in accordance with New York law." Loebig v. Larucci, 572 F.2d 81, 85 (2d Cir. 1978). In *Loebig*, the parties were deemed to have "at least acquiesced in the application of New York law by their failure to prove German law." *Id.* at 86. Is this approach sensible? If a court were convinced, under applicable choice-of-law rules, that German law should apply, might this "acquiescence" approach allow a plaintiff to win without demonstrating that he can establish all the legal elements necessary for a good cause of action? Does the *Loebig* approach in effect shift the burden of proof to the defendant to show that, under German law, the plaintiff does not have a solid case? Would the *Loebig* court's "acquiescence" approach be more plausible if the plaintiff and defendant were both New York citizens? In the actual case, the plaintiff was a resident of Pennsylvania and the defendant was from New York.

4. *The Persistence of Expert Testimony.* Regardless of the new rules, there is still much of "fact" to proving foreign law in practice. See, for example, the following case, where the testimony of conflicting foreign law experts is crucial to the outcome.

FAGGIONATO V. LERNER

500 F. Supp. 2d 237 (S.D.N.Y. 2007)

Preska, District Judge

Plaintiff Anne Faggionato ("Faggionato") brought the above-captioned action seeking specific performance, damages including lost profit and/or sales commissions and damages for loss of reputation, and costs, of a supposed agreement by Defendant Randolph D. Lerner ("Lerner") to purchase a painting. Lerner now moves to dismiss this action pursuant to Rule 12(b)(1) of the Federal Rules of Civil Procedure for lack of subject matter jurisdiction and Rule 12(b)(6) for failure to state a claim upon which relief may be granted. For the following reasons, the motion to dismiss for lack of standing is granted.

Background

Faggionato is a citizen of the United Kingdom and a dealer in paintings. Lerner is a citizen of the United States and a resident of New York City. This lawsuit alleges the breach of a contract to purchase a painting of a haystack ("meule" in French) by the painter Claude Monet[1] (the "Painting") and seeks damages in the sum of $13 million, the alleged sales price of the Painting. Faggionato alleges that Lerner entered into a

[1] The French Impressionist artist Claude Monet (1840–1926) produced a famous series of haystack paintings in the 1890's.

binding agreement to purchase the Painting, subject to receiving the customary documentation establishing its authenticity and provenance. Faggionato asserts that this documentation was supplied to Lerner on or about February 2, 2006, but that Lerner refused to consummate the purchase.

Lerner maintained a relationship with an established New York art dealer Curt Marcus ("Marcus") and informed Marcus of his desire to purchase a Monet haystack. In May, 2005, Marcus sought Faggionato's help in locating such a painting. In November, 2005, Faggionato informed Marcus that she had located an early Monet haystack, the Painting, which had not been included in the Wildenstein Institute's comprehensive catalogue of Monet's works. The Wildenstein Institute ("Wildenstein") is an expert on Monet paintings and the publisher of the comprehensive catalogue raisonné of Monet's paintings. A document issued by Wildenstein (often called an "attestation" or "certificate") attesting that a painting is or will be listed in the Wildenstein catalogue raisonné is evidence of a painting's authenticity

Between November 30, 2005, and January 10, 2006, Faggionato and Marcus exchanged a series of e-mails concerning the Painting, including Lerner's questions about the Painting. These questions concerned the authenticity of the Painting, its provenance, condition, ownership, and the reason for its absence from the Wildenstein catalogue raisonné. On September 8, 2005, the Wildenstein Institute executed an attestation letter stating that the Painting would be included in an upcoming supplement to the catalogue raisonné.

On December 22, 2005, Marcus wrote to Faggionato, stating that Lerner sought a confirmed date to view the Painting. On December 27, 2005, Marcus wrote to Faggionato, stating that Lerner "has already allocated the money for this purchase" and that "pending the viewing, confirmation of date, as well as condition, he will act fast. . . . His wife approves, his accountant completely approves, the money is sitting and waiting."

On January 4, 2006, Faggionato asked Marcus for a document from Lerner's lawyer or banker confirming Lerner's readiness to pay $13 million for the Painting. Also on January 4, 2006, Douglas C. Jacobs, an accountant for Lerner, executed a "letter of intent" stating that Lerner is, "prepared to purchase the Monet 'Meule' painting in the amount of U.S. $13 Million, subject to his viewing and approval, and the receipt of customary documentation."

On January 7, 2006, Marcus wrote to Faggionato stating that he had two questions: "1. Was the painting originally purchased from the artist or through a dealer? 2. Will my client receive a bill of sale from the owner? Will we know the original owners [sic] identity?" Faggionato responded that the first purchase would be "disclosed in 'Provenance' and can be checked in due course (through Wildenstein Institute)." However, as to the second question, Faggionato replied that Lerner would not receive a bill of sale from the owner, but would learn of his identity "in due course." Also on January 7, 2006, Marcus wrote to Faggionato expressing Lerner's concern "as to what recourse he would have, should he receive a letter one day from a collector in Paraguay stating that they are the actual owners . . . if he does not have a bill of sale from either the owners/seller or from a company that traditionally deals with this kind of transaction/money." Faggionato replied, "Fret not my friend[ ] the painting has been in the same family for the last 100 years, Art [L]oss Register ha[s] no record, I am working on the disclosure issue and the pigment analysis has already been done." * * *

On January 10, 2006, Lerner inspected the Painting at the offices of Art Transit in Paris. That day, Lerner asked Faggionato for the Painting's provenance. Faggionato replied that "she could not guarantee that she could convince the owners to reveal their identities on official documents." Faggionato claims that on January 10, 2006, at 5:00 pm, Lerner orally announced to Faggionato and Marcus, "I have made my decision. I am buying the painting." Faggionato asserts that Lerner requested no payment terms but stated that as soon as the paperwork was finished, he would pay the $13 million purchase price. Faggionato alleges that she then said to Lerner "that this was good news because it would assist her in convincing the French owners to disclose their identities on the written provenance." Faggionato claims that based on Lerner's agreement to purchase the Painting, and the terms of sale, she advised the owner's representative that the painting had been sold and she discontinued any further effort to sell the painting. * * *

On January 17, 2006, Marcus wrote to Faggionato that Lerner did not have the "comfort level" that he had requested to proceed with an immediate deposit and desired further proof. On January 21, 2006, Marcus advised Faggionato that Lerner continued to love the painting but did not like buying it without "more transparency" and was seeking more documentation and clarity.

On February 2, 2006, Faggionato wrote to Marcus stating that the Painting "finally has a full set of documents," alleging that the conditions Lerner had requested in terms of documentation had been met. Marcus replied that day to Faggionato commenting on the "terrific news" but also reminding Faggionato that there were documents that Lerner had still requested for full documentation of the Painting, including a written bill of sale. On February 4, 2006, Marcus wrote an email to Faggionato expressing Lerner's concerns, stating that part of the difficulty was that "you represent the owner and know his identity, while my client and I do not" and reiterating that there was still a pending list of required information made by Lerner and his lawyer.

On February 6, 2006, Marcus reported to Faggionato that Lerner had chosen not to purchase the Painting in part because "we were not forthcoming with his requests [for documents] and the lawyers needs." * * *

Faggionato now seeks specific performance, damages, and costs. * * *

Discussion

Jurisdiction and Venue

This Court has subject matter jurisdiction over this action under 28 U.S.C. § 1332, diversity jurisdiction, as Faggionato is a citizen of a foreign country, and Lerner is a United States citizen. Venue is proper in that Lerner resides in the Southern District of New York.

Legal Standard for Dismissal

"A case is properly dismissed for lack of subject matter jurisdiction under Rule 12(b)(1) when the district court lacks the statutory or constitutional power to adjudicate it." *Makarova v. United States*, 201 F.3d 110, 113 (2d Cir. 2000). A plaintiff bears the burden of proving by a preponderance of the evidence that subject matter jurisdiction exists. Jurisdictional allegations must be shown affirmatively and may not be inferred favorably to the party asserting them. In resolving the question of subject matter jurisdiction, the district court may refer to evidence outside the pleadings. * * *

The Supreme Court in *FW/PBS Inc. v. City of Dallas*, 493 U.S. 215, 231 (1990) has noted that "[i]t is a long-settled principle that standing cannot be inferred argumentatively from the averments in the pleadings, but rather must appear in the record." The Court of Appeals has also noted that it will "take as true uncontroverted factual allegations" and "construe jurisdictional allegations liberally" but it will "not draw 'argumentative inferences' in the plaintiff's favor." *Robinson v. Overseas Military Sales Corp.*, 21 F.3d 502, 507 (2d Cir. 1994). On this motion, the Court will follow the teaching of *FW/PBS* and *Robinson*.

Choice of Law

A federal court with diversity jurisdiction applies the choice of law rules of the forum state. *Klaxon Co. v. Stentor Elec. Mfg. Co.*, 313 U.S. 487 (1941). New York courts apply the law of the jurisdiction with the "most significant relationship with the occurrence and with the parties." *Babcock v. Jackson*, 12 N.Y.2d 473, 191 N.E.2d 279, 284 (1963). With respect to a case alleging breach of contract, New York applies a "center of gravity" or "grouping of contacts" analysis which allows a court to consider a spectrum of significant contacts.

In *In re Allstate Ins. Co.*, 613 N.E.2d 936 (1993) ("*Stolarz*"), the New York Court of Appeals listed several factors that a court should consider in a conflict of law analysis in a contract case. These factors include "the place of contracting, negotiation, and performance; the location of the subject matter of the contract; and the domicile of the contracting parties." The traditional choice of law factors, the places of contracting and performance, are given the heaviest weight in this analysis.

Here, the most significant contacts and events occurred in France. Lerner traveled to France in order to view the painting, which was located in France. At least some of the negotiations took place in France, and many of the required documents were obtained in France from either French governmental authorities or French companies. The only connection to New York is Lerner's United States citizenship and domicile.

In the choice of law analysis, New York courts also determine whether there is an actual conflict between the substantive laws of the jurisdictions involved. *Stolarz*, 613 N.E.2d at 937. As described below, the Court accepts the opinions of the French law experts and, based on their analysis of what may be used under French law to prove a contract, concludes that there is a substantive difference between applicable New York law and French law. * * *

Federal Rule of Civil Procedure 44.1 provides that "[t]he court, in determining foreign law may consider any relevant material or source, including testimony, whether or not submitted by a party or admissible under the Federal Rules of Evidence." Rule 44.1 grants the district court wide latitude in resolving issues of foreign law, and the court's determination shall be treated as a ruling on a question of law. The Court of Appeals has noted that "[f]requently, the proper determination of foreign law can be a complicated task. Rule 44.1 is intended to assist the court with its work and the court is, of course, free to enlist the parties in this effort. Ultimately, the responsibility for correctly identifying and applying foreign law rests with the court." *Rationis Enterprises Inc. of Panama v. Hyundai Mipo Dockyard Co.*, 426 F.3d 580, 586 (2d Cir. 2005). In acting under Rule 44.1, a court may reject even uncontradicted expert testimony and reach its own decisions on the basis of independent examination of foreign legal authorities. The Court of Appeals has urged district courts to "invoke the flexible provisions of Rule 44.1" to determine issues of foreign law. *Curley v. AMR Corp.*, 153 F.3d 5, 13 (2d Cir. 1998).

French Law Analysis

The Court's interpretation of French law, as set forth below, is based on the expert law declarations submitted by both parties. In the areas where the two experts, Professor Christian Larroumet and Professor Nicolas Molfessis, overlap, they do not appear to be in disagreement, and those areas of law are accepted by the Court. Ultimately, it appears that Professor Larroumet's conclusions are more persuasive and informative, and it is the "persuasive force of the opinions" expressed that is conclusive under Rule 44.1. *Itar-Tass Russian News Agency v. Russian Kurier, Inc.*,

153 F.3d 82, 92 (2d Cir. 1998). While the Court does accept most of Professor Molfessis' exposition of French law, much of the law he examines relating to a situation where Faggionato supposedly intended and had contracted to purchase the Painting from the owner or the owner's intermediary in order to resell it to Lerner is not applicable in the present action because Faggionato never pled such a relationship in her Complaint and the accompanying documents are inconsistent with such a relationship.

Professor Larroumet is a professor of civil and commercial law at the University Panthéon-Assas (Paris) and is also an attorney at law of the Paris Bar. In addition, Professor Larroumet is the director and partial author of a treatise on civil law and also has written numerous articles in French and foreign law reviews, many that specifically relate to the law of contracts. Thus, as demonstrated by his curriculum vitae, Professor Larroumet is eminently qualified to opine on the issues presented.

Professor Molfessis is a professor of, among other things, civil law and the law of obligations (contracts) at the University Panthéon-Assas (Paris). Professor Molfessis is also the member of various legal boards and committees on French law, and has published numerous books, articles, and notes including some on contract law. Thus, as demonstrated by his curriculum vitae, Professor Molfessis is eminently qualified to opine on the issues presented.

Professor Larroumet notes from the outset that under French law, "the most important requirement to admit the existence of a contract is the meeting of the minds." Professor Molfessis does not address such a requirement, but such a requirement is a widely recognized element of contract formation and the Court accepts Professor Larroumet's assessment that a meeting of the minds is necessary for a contract to be valid under French law.

Professor Larroumet proceeds to examine various relationships that might have existed between the parties involved in the action and then examines whether the facts disclosed in the Complaint and documents referred to therein would support the finding of any such relationships under French law. The first characterization of the relationships is a contract of agency (mandat), where an intermediary, the agent, enters into a legal transaction on behalf of and in the name of another person, the principal. Such a legal transaction concluded by an agent would be deemed as entered into by the principal but the agent must be in a position to "justify that it has been duly and specifically entrusted with filing such an action in the name and on behalf of the principal." However, to be duly characterized as an agent, to have such authority to enter into legal transactions for the principal, one has to justify having received powers to act in such a capacity. Professor Larroumet concludes that this relationship did not exist here for two reasons: (1) because

Faggionato has not proved, and has not even claimed, that she had been granted powers to conclude the sale of the painting with defendant in the name and on behalf of the owner of said painting; and (2) because it is necessary that the identities of both the agent and the principal and their respective capacities be known by the third party, and in this case, the name of the owner was not disclosed to Lerner at the time when the contract was allegedly entered into. Professor Molfessis does not appear to dispute this analysis of the requirements for an agent/principal relationship, and thus the Court accepts this analysis by Professor Larroumet on the lack of a proper agent/principal relationship (mandat) in this action.

Professor Larroumet then examined the possibility that the contract was concluded pursuant to a declaration de command, which is where one person (the "command") asks another person (the "commandé") to enter into a contract on behalf of the former. The commandé must tell the other party to the contract that he is not concluding the contract for himself, but at the outset, the commandé does not disclose the identity of the command. "It is only after the sale is entered into that the name of the command must be disclosed and the disclosure has to be made very quickly after the sale has been concluded." Professor Larroumet goes on to explain that this relationship could not have existed in the present action because this type of transaction is used to hide the identity of the *buyer* only, not that of a seller. In addition, Professor Larroumet notes, if a contract has been concluded by a legitimate commandé, this does not allow the commandé to sue the other party for specific performance. Professor Molfessis does not appear to dispute this legal analysis, and, pursuant to Rule 44.1, the Court accepts Professor Larroumet's analysis of this legal relationship.

[The Court examines, but rejects, other possible theories that might show that Faggionato and Lerner were parties to a contract to sell the Painting under French law.]

Faggionato Lacks Standing

In order to assert a claim in federal court, a plaintiff must be able to demonstrate that she has standing. The standing inquiry focuses on whether the plaintiff is a proper party to bring a claim and, as a result, "often turns on the nature and source of the claim asserted." *Raines v. Byrd*, 521 U.S. 811, 818 (1997). Where the claim asserted is contractual and the plaintiff is not a party to the contract or a third party beneficiary of the contract the claim must be dismissed.

In a diversity action, a plaintiff must meet both the Article III standing requirements and the standing requirements of applicable state law. Here, however, the Court has determined that French law, not New York law, applies to the action.

Under French law, as described above by Professor Larroumet and accepted by the Court, Faggionato was not a proper party to the contract and thus cannot seek relief on her claims. The Court accepts Professor Larroumet's conclusions as persuasive.

* * * Since Faggionato did not fill any of the roles necessary to be a proper party to the contract, including not being the owner of the Painting at the time of the alleged contract negotiations or properly representing the owners, she lacks standing under French law. * * *

Conclusion

Based on the Complaint as well as an examination of the documents relied on by Faggionato in her Complaint, with the aid of the declarations of the French law experts, the Court finds that Faggionato lacks standing to sue.

NOTES AND QUESTIONS

1. *The International Art Market.* We have already turned to the international art market in Chapter 7's *Autocephalous Greek-Orthodox Church of Cyprus v. Goldberg*, a case involving stolen 6th-century mosaics. There, as in *Faggionato*, large sums were at stake. Goldberg was reportedly trying to sell the Cypriot mosaics to the J. Paul Getty Museum for $20 million. Mark Rose, "From Cyprus to Munich," *Archaeology*, Apr. 20, 1998, *available at* archive.archaeology.org (last visited Dec. 9, 2013). Faggionato sought $13 million for the disputed Monet.

Both Faggionato and Lerner were sophisticated players in the international art market. Anne Faggionato's art gallery operated from 1979 to 2009 and specialized "in Modern and Contemporary paintings, sculpture and works on paper, having sold works by Matisse, Picasso, Warhol, and Damien Hirst among others." http://annefaggionato.websites.bta.com (last visited Dec. 9, 2013). Randolph Lerner was said to have inherited a fortune estimated to be worth $1.4 billion from his father, the founder of the credit card company MBNA and owner of the Cleveland Browns football team. "#562. Randolph Lerner," *Forbes*, http://www.forbes.com/lists/2006/10/Z9UN.html (last visited Dec. 9, 2013).

Both Faggionato and Lerner had reason to be concerned whether the painting in question was a genuine Monet and legally owned by the undisclosed seller. Such problems of the provenance of art are legion. Daniel Grant, "It's a Fake! Exactly how many originals of one masterpiece can there be? Art collectors are fooled more often than you think," *Christian Science Monitor,* Mar. 9, 2001, at 13. Paintings by Claude Monet are no exception: " 'Monet, Monet, Monet,' moans John Myatt, 'Sometimes I get fed up doing Monet. Bloody haystacks.' " Euan Ferguson, "Making Monet," *The Observer*, July 15, 2006. In 2009, after the decision in *Faggionato v. Lerner*, Anne Faggionato closed her art gallery to develop a project called "BlueLabel," a web-based process that "provides the global art community with unprecedented access to reliable, accurate and comprehensive art data, helping to prevent the loss of information, misrepresentation and forgery." http://annefaggionato.websites.bta.com/bluelabel.aspx; http://bluelabel.net/what_is_bluelabel (last visited Dec. 9, 2013). We cannot tell on the face of the case whether the disputed Monet in *Faggionato v. Lerner* was authentic or whether the seller was the legitimate owner. What might be other reasons why Faggionato's client would want to remain hidden from view? Could it be a question of tax avoidance or evasion? Or, simply, to keep quiet about who possessed such a valuable work of art?

2. *Proving Foreign Law Under the Modern Rule.* One of the important changes made by the modern rule is that, in the words of the Advisory Committee for new Rule 44.1, "the court is not limited by material presented by the parties; it may engage in its own research and consider any relevant material thus formed." "Rule 44.1 Advisory Committee Notes," *Federal Rules of Civil Procedure*. In *Faggionato*, how independent was the court in making a determination of the outcome under the French law of contract?

Pursuant to Rule 44.1 the judge may or may not rely on expert testimony. So, for example, in Bodum USA, Inc. v. La Cafetière, Inc., 621 F.3d 624 (7th Cir. 2010), Chief Judge Easterbrook of the Seventh Circuit did not find French law so mysterious that he wanted to rely on the testimony or beliefs of competing foreign law experts:

> Although Fed.R.Civ.P. 44.1 provides that courts may consider expert testimony when deciding questions of foreign law, it does not compel them to do so—for the Rule says that judges "may" rather than "must" receive expert testimony and adds that courts may consider "any relevant material or source." Judges should use the best of the available sources. The Committee Note in 1966, when Rule 44.1 was adopted, explains that a court "may engage in its own research and consider any relevant material thus found. The court may have at its disposal better foreign law materials than counsel have presented, or may wish to reexamine and amplify material that has been presented by counsel in partisan fashion or in insufficient detail."
>
> Sometimes federal courts must interpret foreign statutes or decisions that have not been translated into English or glossed in treatises or other sources. Then experts' declarations and testimony may be essential. But French law, and the law of most other nations that engage in extensive international commerce, is widely available in English. Judges can use not only accepted (sometimes official) translations of statutes and decisions but also ample secondary literature, such as treatises and scholarly commentary. It is no more necessary to resort to expert declarations about the law of France than about the law of Louisiana, which had its origins in the French civil code, or the law of Puerto Rico, whose origins are in the Spanish civil code. No federal judge would admit "expert"

> declarations about the meaning of Louisiana law in a commercial case.
>
> Trying to establish foreign law through experts' declarations not only is expensive (experts must be located and paid) but also adds an adversary's spin, which the court then must discount. Published sources such as treatises do not have the slant that characterizes the warring declarations presented in this case. Because objective, English-language descriptions of French law are readily available, we prefer them to the parties' declarations.

Id. at 628–29.

3. *Court-appointed Experts.* A middle ground between relying on counsel-appointed conflicting foreign law experts and using no experts at all is for the court itself to choose a neutral expert. In the words of Second Circuit Judge Roger Miner:

> It seems to me that the federal courts should make more use of court-appointed experts in all kinds of cases where an expert opinion would be helpful. I think that in close questions of foreign law, where experts engaged by the parties are in serious disagreement, the court should appoint its own expert in an effort to close the gap. * * * The issue for the expert may be clarified at a pre-trial conference and the expert's finding must be provided to the parties, who may depose or cross-examine the expert. The compensation of the court-appointed expert must [by Rule 706 of the Federal Rules of Evidence] be paid "by the parties in such proportion and at such time as the court directs, and thereafter charged in like manner as costs."
>
> The use of a court-appointed expert is a highly desirable tool for ascertaining the governing foreign law and, as one author has stated, "[p]ersuasive advice submitted to the court may prompt a stipulation that settles the foreign law question." The elaborate system provided by Rule 706 for testing the opinion of a court-appointed expert means that we are pretty sure of getting the foreign law right in a case where such an opinion is given. It does not by any means, however, divest us of our independent duty of research, for the responsibility of arriving at a correct decision is ours and ours alone. Expert opinion, whether from the parties or from a court-appointed expert is only one way for us to get there. And get there we must, without applying the law of the forum when it does not apply, without utilizing fictitious presumptions, without regarding the search for foreign law as an arcane enterprise whose mysteries we cannot fathom, and without evading the responsibility that every court in this nation has— to find the law and apply it.

Roger J. Miner, "The Reception of Foreign Law in the U.S. Federal Courts," 43 *American Journal of Comparative Law* 581, 588–89 (1995). When would it be sensible for the judge to use counsel-appointed experts? A court-appointed expert? When would it be wise for the judge to use no expert testimony at all? Will the answer vary on the expertise of the judge?

4. *Proof of International Law.* When may expert testimony be employed to explain treaties, customary international law, or other types of international law? FRCP 44.1 refers to testimony as a way to help establish the content only of "foreign law," not international law. In line with the U.S. Supreme Court's assertion in 1900 in *Paquete Habana* (Chapter 3) that "[i]nternational law is part of our law"—an assertion echoed over a century later in *Sosa* (Chapter 4)—U.S. courts have ruled that "judicial notice is taken [of] the law of nations." Brown v. Piper, 91 U.S. 37, 42 (1875). See also The Scotia, 81 U.S. (14 Wall.) 170, 188 (1871) ("[f]oreign municipal laws must indeed be proved as facts, but it is not so with the law of nations"). Still, U.S. courts may allow expert testimony concerning international law in accordance with rules of evidence. See United States v. Caribbean Cruises Ltd., 11 F. Supp. 2d 1358 (S.D. Fla. 1998); Rosman v. Trans World Airlines, Inc., 34 N.Y.2d 385, 392–93 (1974); Hans W. Baade, "Proving Foreign and International Law in Domestic Tribunals," 18 *Virginia Journal of International Law* 619 (1978). When is it appropriate to allow expert testimony on matters of international law? Other than by testifying, how may international law experts assist in municipal court cases?

B. FOREIGN LAW AND PUBLIC POLICY

The common law has long been ready to reject foreign law on public policy grounds if a foreign legal rule or legal process were in serious conflict with local standards of justice or fairness. The following two cases are good examples of American courts' consideration of challenges to foreign laws on the grounds of public policy.

SPINOZZI V. ITT SHERATON CORP.

174 F.3d 842 (7th Cir. 1999)

Posner, Chief Judge

Dr. Thomas Spinozzi, a dentist who lives and works in Illinois, and his wife Linda went to Acapulco on vacation. They stayed at a Sheraton hotel. Dr. Spinozzi fell into a maintenance pit on the hotel grounds and was seriously injured. He and his wife (the wife claiming loss of consortium) brought suit in a federal district court in Illinois, under the diversity jurisdiction, against the Mexican corporation that owns the hotel, and three affiliates of that corporation. The suit alleges negligence. It was dismissed on summary judgment. The district judge held that under Illinois conflict of laws principles, which of course bind him in this diversity suit, *Klaxon v. Stentor Electric Mfg. Co.*, 313 U.S. 487 (1941), Mexican law governs the substantive issues; and that law, he concluded, bars the plaintiff's claims, mainly because it makes contributory negligence a complete defense to negligence liability and the uncontested facts showed that Dr. Spinozzi had been contributorily negligent. The Spinozzis' appeal challenges both the conflicts ruling—they contend that Illinois rather than Mexican tort law applies—and the ruling that Dr. Spinozzi was contributorily negligent as a matter of law.

The ownership structure of the Sheraton Acapulco Resort is complex, but to simplify the opinion we shall assume, favorably to the plaintiffs, that it is owned and operated by ITT Sheraton Corporation ("Sheraton"), a Delaware corporation with its principal place of business in Massachusetts, and forget the other defendants. Sheraton advertises its hotels all over the world, including Illinois, and it was in response to an advertisement in Illinois that the Spinozzis decided to stay at the Sheraton Acapulco. In fact, because Mrs. Spinozzi is a travel agent, Sheraton granted the Spinozzis a special rate to induce them to stay at the hotel. The plaintiffs argue that by its promotional activities in Illinois directed particularly to the small group (travel agents and their spouses) to which the Spinozzis belong, Sheraton should be taken to have "caused" in Illinois the injury to Dr. Spinozzi. And this injury-causing activity in Illinois, when taken in conjunction with the fact that the plaintiffs are Illinois residents, establishes (the plaintiffs argue) that the preponderance of "contacts" between the plaintiffs and either Illinois or Mexico was with Illinois, and not, as one might suppose from the location of the accident, with Mexico.

Under the *ancien régime* of conflict of laws, this argument would have been a nonstarter. The rule was simple: the law applicable to a tort suit was the law of the place where the tort occurred, more precisely the place where the last act, namely the plaintiff's injury, necessary to make the defendant's careless or otherwise wrongful behavior actually tortious, occurred, *Restatement of Conflicts* §§ 377–378 (1934); 2 Joseph H. Beale, *A Treatise on the Conflict of Laws* § 377.2, pp. 1287–88 (1935), and here that place was Mexico. This and other simple rules of conflict of laws came to seem too rigid, mainly because of such anomalies as suits between citizens of the same state when it was not the state where the accident had occurred. See, e.g., *Babcock v. Jackson*, 12 N.Y.2d 473 (1963). But the search for flexibility led, alas, to standards that were nebulous, such as the "most significant relationship" test of the *Second Restatement* that is orthodox in Illinois, *Ingersoll v. Klein*, 46 Ill.2d 42 (1970), and a number of other states.

Often, however, the simple old rules can be glimpsed through modernity's fog, though spectrally thinned to presumptions—in the latest lingo, "default rules." For in the absence of unusual circumstances, the highest scorer on the "most significant relationship" test is—the place where the tort occurred. For that is the place that has the greatest interest in striking a reasonable balance among safety, cost, and other factors pertinent to the design and administration of a system of tort law.

Most people affected whether as victims or as injurers by accidents and other injury-causing events are residents of the jurisdiction in which the event takes place. So if law can be assumed to be generally responsive to the values and preferences of the people who live in the community that formulated the law, the law of the place of the accident can be expected to reflect the values and preferences of the people most likely to be involved in accidents—can be expected, in other words, to be responsive and responsible law, law that internalizes the costs and benefits of the people affected by it.

Only a tiny fraction of hotel guests in Mexico are from Illinois. Illinois residents may want a higher standard of care than the average hotel guest in Mexico, but to supplant Mexican by Illinois tort law would disserve the general welfare because it would mean that Mexican safety standards (insofar as they are influenced by tort suits) were being set by people having little stake in those standards.

[Chief Judge Posner concludes that Illinois conflict of laws rules point to Mexican tort law in this case.]

The plaintiffs' backup position is that a defense of contributory negligence is repugnant to the public policy of Illinois, and therefore an Illinois court would not enforce that defense even if it would apply the rest of Mexico's tort law to an accident such as this. States do refuse to enforce foreign law that is particularly obnoxious to them. E.g., *Nelson v. Hix*, 522 N.E.2d 1214, 1218 (Ill. 1988); *Maher & Associates, Inc. v. Quality Cabinets*, 267 Ill.App.3d 69 (1994); *Lyons v. Turner Construction Co.*, 551 N.E.2d 1062, 1065 (Ill. App. 1990). But obviously the mere fact that foreign and domestic law differ on some point is not enough to invoke the exception. Otherwise in every case of an actual conflict the court of the forum state would choose its own law; there would be no law of conflict of laws.

The danger of the public policy exception is provincialism: an inability to recognize that a different jurisdiction (especially a foreign country) need not be benighted to have a different approach to a particular legal problem. Recognizing this danger, the courts insist, as in the *Lyons* case, that application of foreign law yield an "evil or repugnant result" for the public policy exception to apply. In that case the Illinois legislature had declared the rule applied by another state "void as against public policy and wholly unenforceable," *id.*, and the court took this as an authoritative declaration that the rule was indeed repugnant to the public policy of Illinois. *Nelson v. Hix, supra*, states the test this way: Illinois courts will not apply foreign law that is "clearly contrary to the public morals, natural justice or the general interest of the citizens of this State." 522 N.E.2d at 1218. The foreign law in that case was Canadian law permitting spouses to sue each other in tort, which Illinois law at the time forbade; the Illinois court applied the Canadian law.

Some years ago, by decision of its highest court, Illinois joined the accelerating trend toward replacing contributory negligence by comparative negligence, that is, reducing contributory negligence from a complete defense to a partial defense. *Alvis v. Ribar*, 421 N.E.2d 886 (Ill. 1981). But it did not do so because it thought contributory negligence, like polygamous marriage, deeply offensive; it thought it outmoded and inferior to comparative negligence. It did use some strong language, calling it for example "repulsive," [*id.* at 895,] but if it had really meant this, it would not have made its decision prospective only, as it did. There is an analogy to the principle that a new rule of constitutional law will not be applied in habeas corpus proceedings arising out of convictions that became final before the new rule was announced unless it is necessary to protect the innermost core of fundamental constitutional rights. *Teague v. Lane*, 489 U.S. 288 (1989); see 28 U.S.C. § 2244(b)(2)(A). The Illinois courts have not had occasion to decide whether their preference for comparative over contributory negligence should override the different preference of the state whose law would normally govern the accident in question. Other jurisdictions have divided over the issue.

We think it unlikely that Illinois would refuse to apply Mexican law in this case. When the rule of Alvis came to be codified, 735 ILCS 5/2–1116(c), the Illinois legislature curtailed it, retaining contributory negligence as a complete bar in all cases in which the victim is found to be more than 50 percent responsible for the accident. In light of this provision it is no surprise that the legislation is notably devoid of the "void as against public policy and wholly unenforceable" language that was decisive in Lyons. * * *

It remains only to consider whether the judge was right to grant summary judgment for Sheraton on the issue of Dr. Spinozzi's contributory negligence; and this brings us at last to the facts. It was 10:30 p.m. when the Spinozzis returned to the hotel from dining out with friends only to find that because of a power outage the hotel was in darkness. Their hotel room was stifling because the air conditioning was not operating, so they went out and sat by the hotel's pool, waiting for the lights to come back on. At some distance from the pool was a maintenance pit, 12 to 14 feet deep, shielded by planters. The entrance to the pit was between two of the planters and was guarded by a low gate on the other side of which a spiral staircase led down to the bottom of the pit. Dr. Spinozzi left the garden area to see whether the lights had come back on in the room occupied by his friends. It was pitch dark, yet rather than walking on one of the paths leading from the poolside area to the hotel, Spinozzi walked into the shrubbery that surrounded that area and in a direction that would bring him to a good vantage point for seeing the window of his friends' room. The gate to the maintenance ditch had been left open. Spinozzi walked through the entrance, thinking he was on a path that would bring him near the window, and fell into the pit.

We may assume that the hotel was negligent in leaving the gate open, and perhaps in other respects, like not having emergency lighting that would show the location of the pit to any guest who happened to be wandering in the shrubbery. But the question of contributory negligence is simply whether, had Dr. Spinozzi exercised due care (negligence is an injurer's failure to use due care, contributory negligence a victim's failure to use due care), the accident would have been averted notwithstanding the hotel's negligence. The answer is yes, because Spinozzi acknowledged in his deposition that he couldn't see where he was going because of the dark. A careful person who finds himself in a strange area in a foreign country and can't see the ground in front of him will walk in a slow and gingerly manner to avoid tripping; he will feel his way. Had Dr. Spinozzi done that, he would have felt the ground drop suddenly when he reached the staircase beyond the gate and would have grabbed the rail and saved himself from falling. Having stepped off the pedestrian path into a completely darkened area of shrubbery, he had no reason to suppose the surface ahead of him smooth. He strode on regardless. He might as well have been blindfolded. His negligence came close to, if indeed it did not cross the line into, a conscious assumption of the risk of disaster, a form of aggravated negligence.

He was indeed contributorily negligent as a matter of law, and while under Illinois law that would merely have reduced his entitlement to damages unless he was adjudged more than 50 percent responsible for the accident (which, however, he very well might be), under Mexican law it bars him and his wife from all recovery. We are sorry to arrive at this conclusion because his injuries were serious and may prevent him from practicing his profession.

We have been citing American rather than Mexican cases on contributory negligence. In doing so we have been following the parties, who, whether because they don't read Spanish or because the principles of contributory negligence are the same in Mexico and the United States notwithstanding the differences between their legal systems, have treated them as the same. In effect they have stipulated to the use of American cases to determine whether Dr. Spinozzi was contributorily negligent, and this is a reasonable stipulation that we accept.

NOTES AND QUESTIONS

1. *"Pernicious and Detestable"?* Chief Judge Posner explained in *Spinozzi*, "the mere fact that foreign and domestic law differ on some point is not enough to invoke the [public policy] exception." Another commentator observed that "it is not enough that the foreign law does not seem so reasonable to the judge as his own homemade precedent, but it must appear

too 'pernicious and detestable' or, to borrow Mr. Justice Cardozo's always effective language, 'violate some fundamental principle of justice, some prevalent conception of good morals, some deep-rooted tradition of the common weal.' " Herbert F.Goodrich, "Foreign Facts and Local Fancies," 25 *Virginia Law Review* 26, 33–34 (1938). What should be the standard used to determine whether any given foreign law is "pernicious and detestable"? In practice, "one solid fact" seems to be that there are relatively few foreign laws rejected on public policy grounds: "[e]xamples are much easier to fabricate than to find in the reports." Monrad G. Paulson & Michael I. Sovern, " 'Public Policy' in the Conflict of Laws," 56 *Columbia Law Review* 969, 972 (1956).

2. *Choice of Law and the Public Policy Exception.* Modern U.S. choice-of-law approaches, such as that in the American Law Institute's *Restatement (Second) of Conflict of Laws* (1971), which Judge Posner in 1999 found "orthodox in Illinois," do not explicitly refer to a public policy exception. Section 6(2) of the *Restatement (Second)* directs a court to consider a range of factors in determining which law has the "most significant relationship" to a case and thus should apply. Among these factors are "the needs of the interstate and international systems," "the relevant policies of the forum," "the relevant policies of the interested states," "the protection of justified expectations," "ease in the determination and application of the law to be applied," and "the basic policies underlying the particular field of law." If the law of a foreign country did offend the public policy of a U.S. forum, would a judge construing those factors have sufficient flexibility simply to apply U.S. law? Might a U.S. court using a comity approach (see Chapter 11, Part B) deem it inappropriate to accord deference to a foreign country's law without explicitly invoking and applying a distinct public policy exception? Still, as the *Spinozzi Case* illustrates, modern courts sometimes do still discuss the public policy exception. What are the advantages and disadvantages to including a public policy exception as an explicit part of modern choice-of-law analysis?

Under the *First Restatement of Conflict of Laws* (1934) and the territorial approach it embodied, courts were invited to consider whether a foreign law violated the forum's public policy. The *First Restatement*'s rather rigid rules are followed only in a few U.S. states today—though one senses that Judge Posner yearned for the "good old days" of the *First Restatement.* But territorial choice-of-law rules and the public policy exception were common in 1936 when the *Holzer Case*, below, was decided.

3. *Fundamental Norms.* How close in kind are the public policy rejection of a foreign law and the "trumping" of a legal rule by a fundamental norm in international law? See the discussion of *jus cogens* in Chapter 3. Might the following case be a good example of the application of a *jus cogens* norm, as well as a public policy rejection of an obnoxious foreign law?

HOLZER V. DEUTSCHE REICHSBAHN GESELLSCHAFT

159 Misc. 830 (N.Y. S. Ct. 1936)

Collins, J.

This challenge by the plaintiff to the legal sufficiency of the separate defenses poses, *inter alia*, the vastly arresting and significant question concerning the recognition and respect by our courts of the confessed discrimination against the Jews practiced by the German government.

Though that policy be repugnant to our concept of elementary justice, does the law of comity compel us to honor it, or may we inquire into the morality of the policy, and, finding it immoral, refuse to accord it faith and credit? May the light of our public policy be shed on the law of a foreign jurisdiction, or are we forced to embrace the latter law blindly? Where the law clashes with the humanities, which shall prevail? These are a few of the salient questions which this motion propounds and which we are called upon to resolve.

The suit is by a German Jew against the corporate owners of the German forwarding, transportation, and warehousing system known as Schenker & Co., one of the defendants. The complaint alleges that this system is owned or controlled, directly or indirectly, by the other defendants, one of them Deutsche Reichsbahn Gesellschaft, hereinafter referred to as Reichsbahn, and whose separate defenses are here assailed. The Schenker system operates in approximately two hundred cities in Europe, Asia, and America. The complaint contains two causes of action. The suit is for breach of an employment contract, the plaintiff averring that prior to 1933 the defendants employed him as general executive manager of their entire system for three years beginning January 7, 1932, at a minimum salary of 72,000 marks per annum, plus a bonus graduated by the annual turnover of the enterprise. The agreement provided that: "In the event the plaintiff should die or become unable, without fault on his part, to serve during the period of the contract the defendants would pay to him or to his heirs the sum of 120,000 marks, in discharge of their obligation under the hiring." The complaint asserts that "on or about the 21st day of June, 1933, the defendants discharged the plaintiff as of October 31st, 1933, upon the sole ground that the plaintiff is a Jew." Due performance on plaintiff's part is affirmed and damages in the sum of upwards of $50,000 demanded.

The second cause contains the same preliminary allegations as the first and charges that: "In the month of April, 1933, after the coming into power of the present German Government, the plaintiff was seized by the agents of that Government and unlawfully incarcerated in prison and in a concentration camp where he was held, without indictment, and without trial, for about six months." This imprisonment, so it is claimed, stemmed from the policy of the German government banishing Jews from certain positions. Because of the enforcement of that policy, the plaintiff, and without any fault of his own, was prevented from continuing his services to the defendants, which situation, it is alleged, entitled the plaintiff to the 120,000 marks provided for in case of his inability to perform without fault on his part.

Jurisdiction of defendant Schenker was acquired by attaching its property in this forum. * * *

The answer of Reichsbahn admits the employment, and admits the discharge and internment because the plaintiff is a Jew. The answer then advances three affirmative defenses.

The first defense contends that this court "has no jurisdiction of said defendant or of any property thereof or of the plaintiff's alleged cause of action because: Said defendant and all the property thereof have the status of State property of the Government of Germany and with respect thereto said Government is entitled in this action to all the rights, privileges and immunities of sovereignty since said Government is a recognized independent sovereign power at peace with the United States of America."

This defense then asserts that such sovereign immunity is recognized by our government and by the treaty between the United States and Germany, restoring friendly relations, proclaimed November 14, 1921, which, by article II thereof, incorporated therein article 281 of part X of chapter V of the treaty of Versailles, and which treaty excepts sovereign immunity only "if the German Government engages in international trade, it shall not in respect thereof have or be deemed to have any rights, privileges or immunities of sovereignty." * * *

The second affirmative defense avers that the contract sued on "was made and was to be performed in Germany and was terminated in Germany, and was and is governed by the laws of Germany." It then undertakes to plead the law of Germany by alleging: "Said laws, decrees and orders required, among other things, the retirement of various classes of officials and employees, including certain classes of persons of non-Aryan descent, from the service of the German states, municipalities, municipal associations, bodies corporate under public law, and from institutions and enterprises and corporations of like rank, including said defendant, and prescribed the amounts that could lawfully be paid to such persons upon and after such retirement."

"The plaintiff was of non-Aryan descent and was within the classes specified and required to be retired by said laws and decrees and orders of said Government, and the plaintiff was duly retired, and the hiring of the plaintiff referred to in the complaint and the agreement therefor and the plaintiff's employment thereunder were duly and lawfully terminated and were required to be terminated as of October 31, 1933, under and pursuant to the said Law, said Second Decree and said orders, and the further performance of the plaintiff's alleged contract of employment by all parties thereto was thereby prohibited and made unlawful, excepting only that there was permitted to be paid to the plaintiff the sum of 10,000 marks per month for the fourteen months thereafter terminating on December 31, 1934."

The third and last separate defense endeavors to plead an accord and satisfaction or payment by declaring: "The plaintiff duly received and accepted the aforesaid sums in full payment and in accord and satisfaction of any and all compensation and payments and of any and all rights of the plaintiff under his aforesaid hiring and employment and of any and all rights of the plaintiff by reason of or in connection with his alleged contract, hiring, employment and discharge, and has been duly paid in full." * * *

The separate defenses will be explored in their inverse order rather than seriatim, because the troublesomeness of the questions seems to me to rate according to the inverse order.

(1) *Accord and satisfaction.* * * *

Since the answer shows that the sum paid was less than the amount due, a bona fide dispute of the debtor's liability must appear. There is no such showing. As a plea of payment the third defense is equally vulnerable; the payment of a smaller sum then the one claimed does not constitute payment.

I conclude that the third separate defense is legally insufficient and it is ordered stricken out.

(2) Must discharge of the contract, pursuant to German law, be honored here?

The plaintiff's affidavit in support of the attachment warrant reveals that the plaintiff is now a resident of Westchester county, N.Y., and has a place of business at No. 29 Broadway, city and county of New York. Concededly, however, the contract sued on was made, executed, and to be performed, partially at least, in Germany. It was terminated there by fiat of the German government. We proceed from the indubitable premise that, "The law of the place of performance generally governs the contract and its discharge." Dougherty v. Equitable Life Assurance Society, 266 N.Y. 71, 80; Restatement, Conflict of Laws, § 385; Zimmermann v. Sutherland, 274 U.S. 253. * * *

Of course, if the rule of *lex loci contractus* is inexorable, our examination has attained its terminus. But is the doctrine unyielding though its enforcement be cruel, immoral, indecent or violative of fundamental freedom? Does comity bar us from inquiring into the justice of the law we are entreated to wield? Have we no choice?

The plaintiff has applied to our courts for redress. Reichsbahn says that he is not only not entitled to that redress but that he may not even be heard because the law of Germany forbids. Is that sufficient to halt the inquiry? The answer resides in our own law, not that of Germany.

In Straus & Co. v. Canadian Pacific Railway Co. (254 N.Y. 407), where the court was considering a clause in a bill of lading which provided that it should be construed according to the laws of Great Britain, the court, rejecting the laws of Great Britain as contrary to the public policy of this state, appositely said: "As a general rule, the validity of a contract is determined by the law of the jurisdiction where made, and if legal there is generally enforcible anywhere. *There is, however, a well-established exception to the rule to the effect that a court will not enforce a contract though valid where made if its enforcement is contrary to the policy of the forum.*" (Italics mine.)

And Judge Crane, in the Dougherty Case, supra, now leaned on so heavily by Reichsbahn, makes the significant observation that: "Recognition does not compel our courts to give effect to foreign laws if they are contrary to our public policy."

Judge Crane then proceeded to examine the law of Soviet Russia, which ordered the dissolution of private insurance companies and which assumed on behalf of the Soviet: "All obligations of the defendant arising under its Russian policies of insurance, including the policy in suit." He concluded that: "It cannot be against the public policy of this State" to enforce the agreement which made it subject to Russian law.

The capital point of that holding is that the law of Russia was compared with our own public policy; inquiry was not forestalled by the mere assertion of the law of Russia.

Again, in Salimoff & Co. v. Standard Oil Co. (262 N.Y. 220) Chief Judge Pound gave recognition to the principle that our "own public policy" will be considered in applying foreign law.

And in Vladikavkazsky Ry. Co. v. N.Y. Trust Co. (263 N.Y. 369) Judge Hubbs wrote: "Where there is confliction between our public policy and comity, our own sense of justice and equity as embodied in our public policy must prevail."

Further, Judge Cardozo, in *James & Co. v. Second Russian Insurance Co.* (239 N.Y. 248) said: "The decree of the Russian Soviet government nationalizing its insurance companies has no effect in the United States unless, it may be, to such extent as justice and public policy require that effect be given. * * * We think its attempted extinguishment of liabilities is brutem fulmen, in England as well as here, and this whether the government attempting it has been recognized or not. Russia might terminate the liability of Russian corporations in Russian courts or under Russian law. Its fiat to that effect could not constrain the courts of other sovereignties, if assets of the debtor were available for seizure in the jurisdiction of the forum." * * *

An illuminating case is *Lemmon v. People* (20 N.Y. 562). In 1852 Mrs. Lemmon, of Virginia, proceeded to Texas via New York, with eight negro slaves. Slavery was lawful in Virginia but not in New York. Upon her arrival in New York a free negro, as next friend, obtained a writ of habeas corpus which was sustained.

While acknowledging the right of Virginia to maintain the system of slavery, the court, in a memorable decision, refused to recognize the system as binding on or extending to New York. Said the court:

"I do not say that she may convert any description of her free inhabitants or citizens into slaves; for slavery is repugnant to natural justice and right, has no support in any principle of international law, and is antagonistic to the genius and spirit of republican government. Besides, liberty is the natural condition of men, and is world-wide: whilst slavery is local, and beginning in physical force, can only be supported and sustained by positive law. 'Slavery * * * not only violates the laws of nature and of civil society; it also wounds the best forms of government; in a democracy where all men are equal slavery is contrary to the spirit of the Constitution.' * * *

"Instead, therefore, of recognizing or extending any law of comity towards a slave holder passing through her territory with his slaves, she [the State of New York] refuses to recognize or extend such comity, or allow the law of the sovereignty which sustains the relation of master and slave to be administered as a part of the law of the State. * * *

"The public law exacts no obligation from this State to enforce the municipal law which makes men the subject of property; but by that law the strangers stand upon our soil in their natural condition as men. Nor can it be justly pretended that by the principle which attributes to the law of the domicil the power to fix the civil *status* of persons, any obligation rests on the State to recognize and uphold within her territory the relation of slave owner and slave between strangers."

So, here, whereas it would be offensive to the German government, with which we are at peace, to presume to control or dictate or regulate the policies of the German government within the borders of Germany, we are nevertheless not obligated by the law of comity to enforce the law of Germany when its enforcement is sought here contrary to our every sense of justice and liberty and morality.

In announcing this result we are not "looking for trouble." It is Reichsbahn that is asking us to recognize and apply the German law *to an action pending here*, and we answer: "Let us see whether our public policy enables us to do what you ask."

In so doing we are in no wise seeking to interfere with the internal affairs of Germany. We are not at the moment concerned with the conscience of Germany, but with our own. We are but applying our public policy to an action pending here because the policy of Germany so shockingly conflicts with ours. It is not a gratuitous insult to resist an unsavory influence.

Let it be repeated: We do not go out of our path to manifest disrespect for a foreign government. We are not sitting in judgment on the acts of the German government; we are dispensing justice according to our own public policy. Such is the recognized exception to the rule *lex loci contractus*. "Where there is confliction between our public policy and comity, our own sense of justice and equity as embodied in our public policy must prevail." (*Vladikavkazsky Case, supra*).

I hold, therefore, that in this case we are not precluded from exploring the German policy to determine if it does violence to our own public policy.

This exploratory process need not draw us to the soapbox, the lectern, or the press. We do not have to go beyond the record—indeed, we are not permitted to go beyond the record.

Reichsbahn's answer admits "that in the month of April, 1933, after the coming into power of the present German Government, the plaintiff was seized and incarcerated by the agents of that Government." Further, Reichsbahn admits that "a policy was adopted by the German Government in respect of so-called non-Aryans which required the elimination of certain classes of persons of Jewish or partly Jewish blood from leading commercial, industrial and transportation enterprises, including said defendant, and that the plaintiff became subject to such policy by reason of the fact that he is of Jewish blood and was within said classes of persons when his aforesaid hiring and his employment thereunder were duly terminated pursuant to the laws of Germany."

More, paragraph 12 admits that "the plaintiff became unable to continue his services * * * when he was imprisoned, and thereafter."

Such, asserts Reichsbahn, is the law of Germany. A human being is discharged from his employment because of his religion and jailed. And we are called upon to sanction the act. I say that our public policy does not compel us to give the act reinforcement. To give recognition to such conduct—though it pass for law in Germany—would lacerate our conscience, traduce our Declaration of Independence, rend asunder our Constitutions, Federal and State, antagonize our traditions, mock our history, and outrage our whole philosophy of life.

Not only do we have Reichsbahn's answer, but a part of the record in this case is the "Letter of Resignation of James G. McDonald, High Commissioner for Refugees (Jewish and others) coming from Germany, and addressed to The Secretary General of the League of Nations, with an Annex, containing an analysis of the measures in Germany against 'Non-Aryans,' and of their effects in creating refuges," dated London, December 27, 1933. This is a documented, factual picture of the German scene and is one of the most incredibly shocking and severe indictments of a government in history.

The McDonald report not only boldly etches the plight of the Jews in Germany, but proves by citations that law in Germany for the Jews does not exist. He is not a citizen; he may not vote; he is barred from many businesses and the professions; he has no rights in the courts; he is an 'outcast.' The McDonald document says:

"The Courts of Germany have not only failed to safeguard the rights of equality and liberty which have become the basis of all civilized legal systems, they have even been transformed into instruments for the extension and application of the racial principle to matters unregulated by formal legislation or unreached by administrative decree.

"This development of their function has been made possible through the avowed abolition by the National Socialist regime of the three corner stones of judicial morality; equality of all men before the law; independence of judges; and the doctrine that only those acts are to come under the prohibitions of the law for which the law specifically provides (the maxim, in criminal law, nullum crimen nulla poena sine lege). These fundamental guarantees of civilized justice have been rejected as non-German, 'non-Aryan,' and as Judeo-Roman in origin.

"Therefore, in order to co-ordinate the administration of National Socialist law with the basic philosophy of the regime, equality before the law has been replaced by the doctrine of racial inequality; the independence of the judiciary has given way before the Fahrerprinzip that judges are agents of the Party and that tenure of office is dependent upon their administration of the political and moral standards of the Party, rather than upon the application of abstract justice; and the principle forbidding arbitrary judicial decisions has been abolished in favour of unlimited latitude given the Courts to adjudicate and penalize whether or not a law or a right has been violated."

And (at page 24): "These new and radical methods of administering justice have, as we shall see, profoundly affected even the minimal rights which have been left to 'non-Aryans' by the legislation of the Reich. The almost unlimited power given the National Socialist judge; the abolition of judicial safeguards for the accused; the requirement that the judiciary serve the National Socialist viewpoint which regards 'non-Aryans' as *prima facie* culpable and places their rights upon a plane inferior to those of 'Aryans'; the replacement of objective legal tests by the subjective will of the judge—all of these principles of the new German judicial administration have not only rendered useless appeals by 'non-Aryans' to the Courts for the defence of even those few rights still left to them, but have also provided the means of extending the dogma of racial inequality to spheres and cases left untouched by legislation."

Another penetrating searchlight is cast on the status of law in Germany by the absorbing article of Prof. Karl Lowenstein, of Yale, formerly lecturer on constitutional and international law at the University of Munich, and member of the Munich Bar, which appeared in the Yale Law Journal for March, 1936, under the title "Law in the Third Reich." Prof. Lowenstein writes: "National Socialism attains its political ends by destruction of the rule of law. * * * Under National Socialism, individual rights become absolute and even obnoxious." And: "Positive law is valid only so far as it corresponds with the political intentions of one man. Stripped of its metaphors, which make little sense to the unbeliever, this assertion is tantamount to a blunt denial of the separation of powers and the rule of law."

We see, therefore, that to say to this plaintiff that this court is powerless to aid him, and that he must pursue his remedy in Germany, is to tell him that he has no remedy. I am unwilling to confess that the processes of our judicial system are so sterile.

The invalidity of the second defense is further exposed by the claim that the contract was rendered impossible of performance by virtue of the law of Germany. But Reichsbahn asserts that it is Germany; hence the defendant itself created the law which it now invokes as a shield. More, Germany is the law. The defendant, curiously enough, says in effect, "I am unable to perform this contract because I have prohibited myself from performing it."

It is a cardinal rule of law that one may not take advantage of his own wrong. One who occasions a breach cannot benefit thereby. He who makes it impossible to perform a contract will not be heard to plead impossibility of performance. Yet this is precisely what Reichsbahn is essaying.

I do not view comity as a sort of chloroform which drugs our senses during the operation admitted by Reichsbahn and more fully described in the McDonald letter and the article by Prof. Lowenstein. To regard our public policy as so complaisant, so impotent, would be abdicating to futility; it would devitalize law and reduce it to nothing but verbiage. If slavery was anathema in 1852 it is anathema in 1936. The forces of civilization cannot retreat. This holding is not a departure from established doctrine; it creates no new principle. Rather, it is but the application of old law to a new situation. Nor is it intended hereby to fashion a rule to fit all cases. What was expressed by Chief Judge Crane in the *Dougherty* case is pertinent: "the language of any opinion must be confined to the facts before the court. No opinion is an authority beyond the point actually decided, and no judge can write freely if every sentence is to be taken as a rule of law separate from its association."

The second affirmative defense is declared legally insufficient and ordered stricken out.

(3) *Sovereign immunity.*

* * * Whether or not the action is really against the German government will be left to the trial. *Prima facie* the status of these corporate defendants is in doubt.

The trial will disclose the true activities of the defendants and reveal whether they are engaged in "international trade" within the meaning of the treaty granting sovereign immunity. Of course, if the suit is actually against the German government, or against a branch of that government, if the German government is the real defendant, the suit must fail. * * *

The plaintiff's motion to strike out the second and third separate defenses as legally inadequate is granted; it is denied as to the first defense.

NOTES AND QUESTIONS

1. *International Public Policy Standards.* Citing a 2002 case before the English House of Lords, Kuwait Airways v. Iraqi Airways Co., [2002] 2 A.C. 383, where a public policy rejection of foreign law was based on the U.N. Charter and on U.N. Security Council resolutions, Professor Weintraub argued that public policy objections "may be justified if the displacement is based on international standards." Russell J. Weintraub, *Commentary on the Conflict of Laws* 124 (6th ed. 2010). Is there a similar reliance on international standards in *Holzer, e.g.*, by the reference to the 1933 Letter of Resignation of the High Commissioner for Refugees to the League of Nations? Judge Collins cited the 1852 *Lemmon Case*, holding slavery as contrary to "the law of nature and of civil society." Did this holding also resemble application of an international *jus cogens* norm?

2. Holzer *Reversed.* Despite the eloquence of Judge Collins's repudiation of the German racial laws, his decision on plaintiff's first cause of action was reversed in a brief opinion by the New York's highest court, the Court of Appeals: "Within its own territory every government is supreme and our courts are not competent to review its actions." Holzer v. Deutsche Reichsbahn Gesellschaft, 227 N.Y. 474, 479 (1938). The Court of Appeals relied in part on Oetjen v. Central Leather Co., 246 U.S. 297 (1918), an act of state case (see Part D below), where the U.S. Supreme Court held that "the courts of one country will not sit in judgment on the acts of the government of another done within its own territory." *Id.* at 303. Nowadays, it is clear in both judicial opinion and executive branch pronouncement that the acts of Nazi Germany are not entitled to act of state protection. Jennifer Kreder, "State Law Holocaust-Era Art Claims and Federal Executive Power," 105 *Northwestern University Law Review: Colloquy* 315, 320, May 24, 2011,

http://colloquy.law.northwestern.edu/main/author-kreder-jennifer/ (last visited Dec. 9, 2013).

A law review note at the time of *Holzer* struggled to find legal technicalities that would justify the reversal of Judge Collins's opinion, but was forced to observe that "[i]n the instant case the New York [Court of Appeals] appears to have rejected the public policy exception despite the obvious incompatibility of discriminatory racial legislation with fundamental American legal doctrine." Recent Decision, "Conflict of Laws—Public Policy—Validity of German Non-Aryan Laws as a Defense to a Suit Begun in New York," 38 *Columbia Law Review* 1490 (1938). In 1942, Professor Nussbaum regarded the Court of Appeals's reversal of *Holzer* as "understandable only in terms of the relativity doctrine," which he argued "should not exclude instances where certain foreign rules [were] so repugnant to the policy of the forum that no recognition should be given to them." Arthur Nussbaum, "Public Policy and the Political Crisis in the Conflict of Laws," 49 *Yale Law Journal* 1027, 1032 (1940).

3. *State Statutes Rejecting Foreign and International Law.* A recent development has been the enactment of state statutes or constitutional amendments, sometimes the result of popular referenda, rejecting the use of foreign and international law in state courts. A good example is the "Save Our State Amendment" adopted by referendum in Oklahoma in November 2010:

Oklahoma Save Our State Amendment
H.R.J. Resolution 1056
52d Leg. 2d Reg. Sess. (Oklahoma) 2010

> The Courts provided for in subsection A of this section, when exercising their judicial authority, shall uphold and adhere to the law as provided in the United States Constitution, the Oklahoma Constitution, the United States Code, federal regulations promulgated pursuant thereto, established common law, the Oklahoma Statutes and rules promulgated pursuant thereto, and if necessary the law of another state of the United States provided the law of the other state does not include Sharia Law, in making judicial decisions. The courts shall not look to the legal precepts of other nations or cultures. Specifically, the courts shall not consider international law or Sharia Law. The provisions of this subsection shall apply to all cases before the respective courts including, but not limited to, cases of first impression.

U.S. federal district and appellate courts have enjoined certifying the Oklahoma referendum results, holding that the act would probably be deemed unconstitutional. *Awad v. Ziriax*, 754 F. Supp. 2d 1298 (W.D. Okla. 2010), *aff'd*, 670 F.3d 1111 (10th Cir. 2012). Professor Parry has argued that "there is at least a fair chance that portions of the amendment ultimately will go into effect." John T. Parry, "Oklahoma Save Our State Amendment and the Conflict of Laws," 65 *Oklahoma Law Review* 1, 3 (2012). He saw practical difficulties in construing the Amendment's "approved sources of law" and "the law of other states, if necessary" and raised questions about construing the Amendment's "forbidden sources of law." *Id.* at 7–22. If the Amendment did go into effect, would Oklahoma judges continue to be independent? Would the Amendment forbid an examination of other common law jurisdictions, even England?

A rather more nuanced approach was enacted in Kansas in May 2012, precluding "enforcement of contracts, foreign judgments and arbitral awards based on foreign legal codes that do not assure fundamental rights under the U.S. and Kansas Constitutions." John R. Crook, "Contemporary Practice of the United States Relating to International Law," 106 *American Journal of International Law* 843, 875–76 (2012). Similar bills have been proposed in several more states, including Alaska, Arkansas, Florida, Indiana, Iowa, Louisiana, and New Jersey. Aaron Fellmeth, "U.S. State Legislation to Limit Use of International and Foreign Law," 106 *American Journal of International Law* 107, 109 (2012). Professor Fellmeth concluded that such laws and bills "are based on several misconceptions about the roles of international law and foreign law in the U.S. legal system." *Id.* at 117. Do you agree?

4. *A Decent Respect to the Opinions of Mankind.* The critique of looking to foreign and international law in U.S. law has sparked a spirited rebuttal. Justice Ginsburg of the Supreme Court, echoing Thomas Jefferson in the Declaration of Independence, has underlined that the Court ought to continue to accord a decent respect to the Opinions of [Human] Kind "as a matter of comity and in a spirit of humility." Ruth Bader Ginsburg, "A Decent Respect to the Opinions of [Human] Kind: The Value of a Comparative Perspective in Constitutional Adjudication," International Academy of Comparative Law, American University, July 30, 2010, http://www.supremecourt.gov/publicinfo/speeches (last visited Dec. 9, 2010). Endorsing her speech, the *New York Times* attacked "[n]ativism in American politics" and argued that "[t]o the extent that the United States expects its ideals and legal system to inspire others, it should take interest in ideas from overseas." "A Respect for World Opinion," *New York Times*, Aug. 3, 2010, at A22. Do you agree?

C. FOREIGN SOVEREIGN IMMUNITY

A variety of legal rules shield foreign sovereigns and their acts from the scrutiny of national courts. Although less pervasive nowadays than before, these rules generally have been grounded on the principle or policy that to sue foreign sovereigns in local courts or to challenge the legality of foreign sovereign acts could upset friendly relations between states. It has been reckoned that questions relating to the jurisdictional immunities of foreign sovereigns figure more before national courts than do any other questions of international law. Leo J. Bouchez, "The Nature and Scope of State Immunity from Jurisdiction and Execution," 10 *Netherlands Yearbook of International Law* 3, 4 (1979). In 2010, there were over 130 published federal court opinions involving foreign sovereign immunity, including one U.S. Supreme Court case. The subject matter included both commercial disputes and politically sensitive cases involving, for example, "claims against diplomatic officials for rape and other abuse, claims by relatives of Holocaust survivors against sovereign states and state-owned museums seeking restitution for art stolen by the Nazi regime and later acquired by the defendants, and claims by victims of state sponsored terrorist attacks." Crowell & Moring LLP, "The Foreign Sovereign Immunities Act: 2010 Year in Review," 17 *Law and Business Review of the Americas* 637, 639 (2011). The number of FSIA cases has been rising dramatically. In the ten years ending in 2008, "the number of reported decisions * * * increased by nearly seventy percent." Aryeh S. Portney *et al.*, "The Foreign Sovereign Immunities Act: 2008 Year in Review," 16 *Law and Business Review of the Americas* 179, 180 (2010).

In the United States, both the doctrine of sovereign immunity and the act of state doctrine examined in Part D may be said to be rooted in the judgment in 1812 of Chief Justice John Marshall in the case of *The Schooner Exchange*. Following *Schooner Exchange* in this Part C are three more U.S. sovereign immunity cases and an excerpt from the Foreign Sovereign Immunities Act of 1976 that illustrate the development of the law governing sovereign immunity.

THE SCHOONER EXCHANGE V. MCFADDON

11 U.S. (7 Cranch) 116 (1812)

This being a cause in which the sovereign right claimed by Napoleon, the reigning Emperor of the French, and the political relations between the United States and France, were involved, it was, upon the suggestion of the Attorney General, ordered to a hearing, in preference to other causes which stood before it on the docket.

It was an appeal from the sentence of the Circuit Court of the United States, for the district of Pennsylvania, which reversed the sentence of the district court, and ordered the vessel to be restored to the libellants.

The case was this: On the 24th of August, 1811, John McFaddon & William Greetham, of the State of Maryland, filed their libel in the district court of the United States, for the district of Pennsylvania, against the Schooner Exchange, setting forth that they were her sole owners, on the 27th of October, 1809, when she sailed from Baltimore, bound to St. Sebastian, in Spain. That while lawfully and peaceably pursuing her voyage, she was, on the 30th of December 1810, violently and forcibly taken by certain persons, acting under the decrees and orders of Napoleon, Emperor of the French, out of the custody of the libellants, and of their master and agent, and was disposed of by those persons, or some of them, in violation of the rights of the libellants, and of the law of nations in that behalf. That she had been brought into the port of

Philadelphia, and was then in the jurisdiction of that court, in possession of a certain Dennis M. Begon, her reputed captain or master. That no sentence or decree of condemnation had been pronounced against her, by any court of competent jurisdiction; but that the property of the libellants in her, remained unchanged and in full force. They, therefore, prayed the usual process of the court, to attach the vessel, and that she might be restored to them. * * *

MARSHALL, Ch. J., delivered the opinion of the Court as follows:

This case involves the very delicate and important inquiry, whether an American citizen can assert, in an American court, a title to an armed national vessel, found within the waters of the United States? * * *

The jurisdiction of courts is a branch of that which is possessed by the nation as an independent sovereign power. The jurisdiction of the nation, within its own territory, is necessarily exclusive and absolute; it is susceptible of no limitation, not imposed by itself. Any restriction upon it, deriving validity from an external source, would imply a diminution of its sovereignty, to the extent of the restriction, and an investment of that sovereignty, to the same extent, in that power which could impose such restriction. All exceptions, therefore, to the full and complete power of a nation, within its own territories, must be traced up to the consent of the nation itself. They can flow from no other legitimate source.

This consent may be either express or implied. In the latter case, it is less determinate, exposed more to the uncertainties of construction; but, if understood, not less obligatory. The world being composed of distinct sovereignties, possessing equal rights and equal independence, whose mutual benefit is promoted by intercourse with each other, and by an interchange of those good offices which humanity dictates and its wants require, all sovereigns have consented to a relaxation, in practice, in cases under certain peculiar circumstances, of that absolute and complete jurisdiction within their respective territories which sovereignty confers. * * * A nation would justly be considered as violating its faith, although that faith might not be expressly plighted, which should suddenly and without previous notice, exercise its territorial powers in a manner not consonant to the usages and received obligations of the civilized world.

This full and absolute territorial jurisdiction being alike the attribute of every sovereign, and being incapable of conferring extra-territorial power, would not seem to contemplate foreign sovereigns, nor their sovereign rights, as its objects. One sovereign being in no respect amenable to another; and being bound by obligations of the highest character not to degrade the dignity of his nation, by placing himself or its sovereign rights within the jurisdiction of another, can be supposed to enter a foreign territory only under an express license, or in the confidence that the immunities belonging to his independent sovereign station, though not expressly stipulated, are reserved by implication, and will be extended to him.

This perfect equality and absolute independence of sovereigns, and this common interest impelling them to mutual intercourse, and an interchange of good offices with each other, have given rise to a class of cases in which every sovereign is understood to waive the exercise of a part of that complete exclusive territorial jurisdiction, which has been stated to be the attribute of every nation.

[Justice Marshall gives examples of such waivers, including "the exemption of the person of the sovereign from arrest or detention within a foreign territory" and "the immunity which all civilized nations allow to foreign ministers."]

When private individuals of one nation spread themselves through another, as business or caprice may direct, mingling indiscriminately with the inhabitants of that other, or when merchant vessels enter for the purposes of trade, it would be obviously inconvenient and dangerous to society, and would subject the laws to continual infraction, and the government to degradation, if such individuals or merchants did not owe temporary and local allegiance, and were not amenable to the jurisdiction of the country. Nor can the foreign sovereign have any motive for wishing such exemption. His subjects thus passing into foreign countries, are not employed by him, nor are they engaged in national pursuits. Consequently there are powerful motives for not exempting persons of this description from the jurisdiction of the country in which they are found, and no one motive for requiring it. The implied license, therefore, under which they enter, can never be construed to grant such exemption.

But in all respects different, is the situation of a public armed ship. She constitutes a part of the military force of her nation; acts under the immediate and direct command of the sovereign; is employed by him in national objects. He has many and powerful motives for preventing those objects from being defeated by the interference of a foreign state. Such interference cannot take place, without affecting his power and his dignity. The implied license, therefore, under which such vessel enters a friendly port, may reasonably be construed, and it seems to the court, ought to be construed, as containing an exemption from the jurisdiction of the sovereign, within whose territory she claims the rites of hospitality.

Upon these principles, by the unanimous consent of nations, a foreigner is amenable to the laws of the place; but certainly, in practice, nations have not yet asserted their jurisdiction over the public armed ships of a foreign sovereign entering a port open for their reception.

[T]here is a manifest distinction between the private property of the person who happens to be a prince, and that military force which supports the sovereign power, and maintains the dignity and the independence of a nation. A prince, by acquiring private property in a foreign country, may possibly be considered as subjecting that property to the territorial jurisdiction; he may be considered as so far laying down the prince, and assuming the character of a private individual; but this he cannot be presumed to do, with respect to any portion of that armed force, which upholds his crown, and the nation he is intrusted to govern. * * *

It seems, then, to the court, to be a principle of public law, that national ships of war, entering the port of a friendly power open for their reception, are to be considered as exempted by the consent of that power from its jurisdiction. * * *

If the preceding reasoning be correct, the Exchange, being a public armed ship, in the service of a foreign sovereign, with whom the government of the United States is at peace, and having entered an American port, open for her reception, on the terms on which ships of war are generally permitted to enter the ports of a friendly power, must be considered as having come into the American territory, under an implied promise, that while necessarily within it, and demeaning herself in a friendly manner, she should be exempt from the jurisdiction of the country. * * *

I am directed to deliver it, as the opinion of the court, that the sentence of the circuit court, reversing the sentence of the district court, in the case of the Exchange be reversed, and that of the district court, dismissing the libel, be affirmed.

NOTES AND QUESTIONS

1. *The Historical Context.* In 1812, how anxious would Chief Justice Marshall have been to have the U.S. legal system seize a French warship for the benefit of a private litigant? This was the very year the United States went to war with Great Britain, France's enemy in the Napoleonic Wars. France and England were blockading each other's ports, and American merchant shipping was reaping large profits (and incurring considerable risks) in blockade running. Was it the mission of Marshall both to protect the dignity of France and to bolster the sovereignty of the United States? Notice Marshall's insistence on how "distinct sovereignties" have "equal rights and equal independence." See the discussion of the equality of states in Chapter 7, Part A.

2. *Sovereigns and the Forms of Jurisdiction.* Marshall distinguished between "the jurisdiction of the courts" and the general jurisdiction "possessed by the nation as an independent sovereign power." Was this distinction an early sign of the development of what we would now call adjudicatory jurisdiction? Was the French government being protected just from the jurisdiction of the courts? Was Marshall's judgment broad enough to encompass protection from U.S. legislative and executive jurisdiction as well?

How similar was Marshall's belief in the "full and absolute territorial jurisdiction" of "every sovereign" to Holmes's belief a century later, in *American Banana* above, that "all legislation is *prima facie* territorial"? Both approaches certainly appear to limit extraterritorial jurisdiction. Why did Marshall make the territorial case so strongly when he meant to upset it with an exception for the warships of foreign sovereigns?

3. *U.S. Law or International Law?* When Marshall wrote that it seemed "to be a principle of public law, that national ships of war, entering the port of a friendly power open for their reception, are to be considered as exempted by the consent of that power from its jurisdiction," was he referring to a "principle" of U.S. law or of international law or of both? A similar confusion or conflation exists in the language of the Foreign Sovereign Immunities Act of 1976 considered below. First, though, is *Victory Transport*, a case that shows development of the foreign sovereign immunity doctrine in the United States between *Schooner Exchange* and the 1976 Act.

VICTORY TRANSPORT, INC. V. COMISARÍA GENERAL

336 F.2d 354 (2d Cir. 1964), *cert. denied*, 381 U.S. 934 (1965)

J. JOSEPH SMITH, CIRCUIT JUDGE: * * *

The appellant, a branch of the Spanish Ministry of Commerce, voyage-chartered the S.S. Hudson from its owner, the appellee, to transport a cargo of surplus wheat, purchased pursuant to the Agricultural Trade Development and Assistance Act, 7 U.S.C. § 1691 et seq., from Mobile, Alabama to one or two safe Spanish ports. * * *

Appellant's primary contention is that as an arm of the sovereign Government of Spain, it cannot be sued in the courts of the United States without its consent, which it declines to accord in this case. There is certainly a great deal of impressive precedent to support this contention, for the doctrine of the immunity of foreign sovereigns from the jurisdiction of our courts was early entrenched in our law by Chief Justice Marshall's historic decision in The Schooner Exchange v. McFaddon. The doctrine originated in an era of personal sovereignty, when kings could theoretically do no wrong and when the exercise of authority by one sovereign over another indicated hostility or superiority. With the passing of that era, sovereign immunity has been retained by the courts chiefly to avoid possible embarrassment to those responsible for the conduct of the nation's foreign relations. However, because of the dramatic changes in the nature and functioning of sovereigns, particularly in the last half century, the wisdom of retaining the doctrine has been cogently questioned. Growing concern for individual rights and public morality, coupled with the increasing entry of governments into what had previously been regarded as private pursuits, has led a substantial number of nations to abandon the absolute theory of sovereign immunity in favor of a restrictive theory.

Meeting in Brussels in 1926, representatives of twenty nations, including all the major powers except the United States and Russia, signed a convention limiting sovereign immunity in the area of maritime commerce to ships and cargoes employed exclusively for public and non-commercial purposes. After World War II the United States began to restrict immunity by negotiating treaties obligating each contracting party to waive its sovereign immunity for state-controlled enterprises engaged in business activities within the territory of the other party. Fourteen such treaties were negotiated by our State Department in the decade 1948 to 1958. And in 1952 our State Department, in a widely publicized letter from Acting Legal Adviser Jack B. Tate to the Acting Attorney General Philip B. Perlman, announced that the Department would generally adhere to the restrictive theory of sovereign immunity, recognizing immunity for a foreign state's public or sovereign acts (*jure imperii*) but denying immunity to a foreign state's private or commercial acts (*jure gestionis*). * * *

Through the "Tate letter" the State Department has made it clear that its policy is to decline immunity to friendly foreign sovereigns in suits arising from private or commercial activity. But the "Tate letter" offers no guide-lines or criteria for differentiating between a sovereign's private and public acts. Nor have the courts or commentators suggested any satisfactory test. Some have looked to the nature of the transaction, categorizing as sovereign acts only activity which could not be performed by individuals. While this criterion is relatively easy to apply, it ofttimes produces rather astonishing results, such as the holdings of some European courts that purchases of bullets or shoes for the army, the erection of fortifications for defense, or the rental of a house for an embassy, are private acts. Furthermore, this test merely postpones the difficulty, for particular contracts in some instances may be made only by states. Others have looked to the purpose of the transaction, categorizing as *jure imperii* all activities in which the object of performance is public in character. But this test is even more unsatisfactory, for conceptually the modern sovereign always acts for a public purpose. Functionally the criterion is purely arbitrary and necessarily involves the court in projecting personal notions about the proper realm of state functioning. * * *

The purpose of the restrictive theory of sovereign immunity is to try to accommodate the interest of individuals doing business with foreign governments in having their legal rights determined by the courts, with the interest of foreign governments in being free to perform certain political acts without undergoing the embarrassment or hindrance of defending the propriety of such acts before foreign courts. Sovereign immunity is a derogation from the normal exercise of jurisdiction by the courts and should be accorded only in clear cases. Since the State Department's failure or refusal to suggest immunity is significant, we are disposed to deny a claim of sovereign immunity that has not been "recognized and allowed" by the State Department unless it is plain that the activity in question falls within one of the categories of strictly political or public acts about which sovereigns have traditionally been quite sensitive. Such acts are generally limited to the following categories:

(1) internal administrative acts, such as expulsion of an alien.

(2) legislative acts, such as nationalization.

(3) acts concerning the armed forces.

(4) acts concerning diplomatic activity.

(5) public loans.

We do not think that the restrictive theory adopted by the State Department requires sacrificing the interests of private litigants to international comity in other than these limited categories. Should diplomacy require enlargement of these categories, the State Department can file a suggestion of immunity with the court. Should diplomacy require contraction of these categories, the State Department can issue a new or clarifying policy pronouncement.

The Comisaría General's chartering of the appellee's ship to transport a purchase of wheat is not a strictly public or political act. Indeed, it partakes far more of the character of a private commercial act than a public or political act.

The charter party has all the earmarks of a typical commercial transaction. It was executed for the Comisaría General by "El Jefe del Servicio Commercial," the head of its commercial division. The wheat was consigned to and shipped by a private commercial concern. And one of the most significant indicators of the private commercial nature of this charter is the inclusion of the arbitration clause. The French Court of Appeal, in dismissing a claim of sovereign immunity where the governmental charterer had agreed to arbitration, pointed out:

> A contract relating to maritime transport is a private contract where the owner merely puts his ship and the ship's crew at the disposal of the State and does not take a direct part in the performance of the public service undertaken by the State in the latter's capacity as a charterer. The charter party does not contain any clause peculiar to public law or unusual in private law. It provides for a time charter of the vessel which is put at the disposal of the State chartering it. The insertion of the arbitration clause underlines the intention of the parties to make their agreement subject to private law.

Maritime transport has been included among the commercial or business activities specifically mentioned in recent United States treaties restricting sovereign immunity. And the 1926 Brussels Convention, the first major international attempt to restrict sovereign immunity, which Spain signed but never ratified, denied immunity to all maritime governmental activities except vessels operated exclusively on non-commercial service, such as warships, patrol vessels, or hospital ships.

Even if we take a broader view of the transaction to encompass the purchase of wheat pursuant to the Surplus Agricultural Commodities Agreement to help feed the people of Spain, the activity of the Comisaría General remains more in the commercial than political realm. Appellant does not claim that the wheat will be used for the public services of Spain; presumptively the wheat will be resold to Spanish nationals. Whether the Comisaría General loses money or makes a profit on the sale, this purchasing activity has been conducted through private channels of trade. Except for United States financing, permitting payment in pesetas, the Comisaría General acted much like any private purchaser of wheat.

Our conclusion that the Comisaría General's activity is more properly labeled an act *jure gestionis* than *jure imperii* is supported by the practice of those countries which have adopted the restrictive theory of sovereign immunity. Thus the Commercial Tribunal of Alexandria declined to grant immunity to this same Spanish instrumentality in a more difficult case—a suit arising from the Comisaría's purchase of rice to help feed the people of neutral Spain during wartime.

> It is not contended in the present case that the rice in question was bought by the *Comisaría General* for the needs of the Spanish public services. On the contrary, it seems clearly established that the rice was bought for the feeding of the Spanish population during a difficult period. In negotiating this purchase herself, instead of leaving the matter to private enterprise, Spain proceeded in much the same manner as any other Spanish trader would have done who wanted to buy rice in Egypt; that is to say, she got it out of Egypt with the necessary permits and carried it to Spain in a Spanish ship in order to re-sell it on the usual commercial lines. This being so, the *Comisaría General* cannot claim immunity from jurisdiction, and the judgment entered against it must be confirmed.

Though there are a few inconsistencies, the courts in those countries which have adopted the restrictive theory have generally considered purchasing activity by a state instrumentality, particularly for resale to nationals, as commercial or private activity.

Finally, our conclusion that the Comisaría General's claim of sovereign immunity should be denied finds support in the State Department's communication to the court in New York and Cuba Mail S.S. Co. v. Republic of Korea, 132 F.Supp. 684, 685 (S.D.N.Y.1955). There the Republic of Korea was allegedly responsible for damaging a ship while assisting in the unloading of a cargo of rice for distribution without charge to its civilian and military personnel during the Korean War. Though suggesting that Korea's property was immune from attachment, the State Department refused to suggest immunity "inasmuch as the particular acts out of which the cause of action arose are not shown to be of a purely governmental character." If the wartime transportation of rice to civilian and military personnel is not an act *jure imperii, a fortiori* the peacetime transportation of wheat for presumptive resale is not an act *jure imperii.*

NOTES AND QUESTIONS

1. *The Origins of the Absolute Sovereign Immunity Doctrine. Victory Transport* dated *Schooner Exchange* by observing that Marshall's "doctrine originated in an era of personal sovereignty, when kings could theoretically do no wrong and when the exercise of authority by one sovereign over another indicated hostility or superiority." Can *Schooner Exchange* really be read so broadly? After all, Marshall carefully delineated his issue as involving only "the very delicate and important inquiry, whether an American citizen can assert, in an American court, a title to an armed national vessel, found within the waters of the United States." Presumably, the answer to this specific inquiry has remained "no" over two centuries of U.S. practice. Is the doctrine of absolute sovereign immunity properly attributable to *Schooner Exchange*? Did Marshall say anything at all about the commercial activities of states that would be helpful in deciding *Victory Transport*?

2. *The Tate Letter.* Whatever the theoretical or practical soundness of the old doctrine of absolute sovereign immunity, the Tate letter, 26 *Department of State Bulletin* 984 (1952), inaugurated the restrictive doctrine in U.S. law. What exactly was the authority of Acting Legal Adviser to the State Department Jack Tate to suggest changing U.S. common law by way of a letter to the Acting Attorney General? Did the real authority belong to the federal courts, which merely responded to the executive branch's "suggestion" and which then authoritatively reversed old and set new precedent?

3. *Sovereign Immunity and Foreign Law.* How did foreign practice, *e.g.*, the decisions of French and Egyptian courts, help the U.S. court determine what are and are not "commercial activities" of foreign governments? U.S. courts not only watch foreign courts, but they are also watched by them. Looking at judicial cross-fertilization, Professor Riesenfeld wrote that *Schooner Exchange* has been recognized as the "earliest judicial pronouncement of the doctrine of sovereign immunity by the highest court of a nation." Stefan A. Riesenfeld, "Sovereign Immunity in Perspective," 19 *Vanderbilt Journal of Transnational Law* 1, 2 (1986). *Schooner Exchange* was soon followed by lower French courts, though not confirmed by the Cour de Cassation (the highest French civil court) until 1849. *Id.* at 2–4. Riesenfeld dated other early lower court decisions on sovereign immunity to 1819 in Germany and to the early 19th century in Italy. *Id.* at 8–12. Such borrowing

of rules among municipal legal systems is an example of what might be thought of as "international common law."

4. *Codifying Sovereign Immunity*. Absolute U.S. judicial deference toward foreign governments began to be turned back in the Tate letter in 1952. *Victory Transport* in 1965 showed how exceptions to sovereign immunity were beginning to overwhelm the rule of deference. The exceptions were codified in the Foreign Sovereign Immunities Act of 1976.

THE FOREIGN SOVEREIGN IMMUNITIES ACT OF 1976

28 U.S.C. §§ 1602–1605A

§ 1602. Findings and declaration of purpose

The Congress finds that the determination by the United States courts of the claims of foreign states to immunity from the jurisdiction of such courts would serve the interests of justice and would protect the rights of both foreign states and litigants in United States courts. Under international law, states are not immune from the jurisdiction of foreign courts insofar as their commercial activities are concerned, and their commercial property may be levied upon for the satisfaction of judgments rendered against them in connection with their commercial activities. Claims of foreign states to immunity should henceforth be decided by courts of the United States and of the States in conformity with the principles set forth in this chapter.

§ 1603. Definitions

For purposes of this chapter—

(a) A "foreign state" * * * includes a political subdivision of a foreign state or an agency or instrumentality of a foreign state as defined in subsection (b).

(b) An "agency or instrumentality of a foreign state" means any entity—

(1) which is a separate legal person, corporate or otherwise, and

(2) which is an organ of a foreign state or political subdivision thereof, or a majority of whose shares or other ownership interest is owned by a foreign state or political subdivision thereof, and

(3) which is neither a citizen of a State of the United States as defined in section 1332(c) and (e) of this title, nor created under the laws of any third country.

(c) The "United States" includes all territory and waters, continental or insular, subject to the jurisdiction of the United States.

(d) A "commercial activity" means either a regular course of commercial conduct or a particular commercial transaction or act. The commercial character of an activity shall be determined by reference to the nature of the course of conduct or particular transaction or act, rather than by reference to its purpose.

(e) A "commercial activity carried on in the United States by a foreign state" means commercial activity carried on by such state and having substantial contact with the United States.

§ 1604. Immunity of a foreign state from jurisdiction

Subject to existing international agreements to which the United States is a party at the time of enactment of this Act a foreign state shall be immune from the jurisdiction of the courts of the United States and of the States except as provided in sections 1605 to 1607 of this chapter.

§ 1605. General exceptions to the jurisdictional immunity of a foreign state

(a) A foreign state shall not be immune from the jurisdiction of courts of the United States or of the States in any case—

(1) in which the foreign state has waived its immunity either explicitly or by implication, notwithstanding any withdrawal of the waiver which the foreign state may purport to effect except in accordance with the terms of the waiver;

(2) in which the action is based upon a commercial activity carried on in the United States by the foreign state; or upon an act performed in the United States in connection with a commercial activity of the foreign state elsewhere; or upon an act outside the territory of the United States in connection with a commercial activity of the foreign state elsewhere and that act causes a direct effect in the United States;

(3) in which rights in property taken in violation of international law are in issue and that property or any property exchanged for such property is present in the United States in connection with a commercial activity carried on in the United States by the foreign state; or that property or any property exchanged for such property is owned or operated by an agency or instrumentality of the foreign state and that agency or instrumentality is engaged in a commercial activity in the United States;

(4) in which rights in property in the United States acquired by succession or gift or rights in immovable property situated in the United States are in issue;

(5) not otherwise encompassed in paragraph (2) above, in which money damages are sought against a foreign state for personal injury or death, or damage to or loss of property, occurring in the United States and caused by the tortious act or omission of that foreign state or of any official or employee of that foreign state while acting within the scope of his office or employment; except this paragraph shall not apply to—

(A) any claim based upon the exercise or performance or the failure to exercise or perform a discretionary function regardless of whether the discretion be abused, or

(B) any claim arising out of malicious prosecution, abuse of process, libel, slander, misrepresentation, deceit, or interference with contract rights; or

(6) in which the action is brought, either to enforce an agreement made by the foreign state with or for the benefit of a private party to submit to arbitration all or any differences which have arisen or which may arise between the parties with respect to a defined legal relationship, whether contractual or not, concerning a subject matter capable of settlement by arbitration under the laws of the United States, or to confirm an award made pursuant to such an agreement to arbitrate, if

(A) the arbitration takes place or is intended to take place in the United States,

(B) the agreement or award is or may be governed by a treaty or other international agreement in force for the United States calling for the recognition and enforcement of arbitral awards,

(C) the underlying claim, save for the agreement to arbitrate, could have been brought in a United States court under this section or section 1607, or

(D) paragraph (1) of this subsection is otherwise applicable. * * *

§ 1605A. Terrorism exception to the jurisdictional immunity of a foreign state

(a) *In general.*

(1) A foreign state shall not be immune from the jurisdiction of courts of the United States or of the States in any case not otherwise covered by this chapter in which money damages are sought against a foreign state for personal injury or death that

was caused by an act of torture, extrajudicial killing, aircraft sabotage, hostage taking, or the provision of material support or resources for such an act if such act or provision of material support or resources is engaged in by an official, employee, or agent of such foreign state while acting within the scope of his or her office, employment, or agency.

(2) The court shall hear a claim under this section if—

(A) (i) (I) the foreign state was designated as a state sponsor of terrorism at the time the act described in paragraph (1) occurred, or was so designated as a result of such act, and, subject to subclause (II), either remains so designated when the claim is filed under this section or was so designated within the 6-month period before the claim is filed under this section; or

(II) in the case of an action that is refiled under this section by reason of section 1083(c)(2)(A) of the National Defense Authorization Act for Fiscal Year 2008 or is filed under this section by reason of section 1083(c)(3) of that Act, the foreign state was designated as a state sponsor of terrorism when the original action or the related action under section 1605(a)(7) (as in effect before the enactment of this section) or section 589 of the Foreign Operations, Export Financing, and Related Programs Appropriations Act, 1997 (as contained in section 101(c) of division A of Public Law 104–208) was filed;

(ii) the claimant or the victim was, at the time the act described in paragraph (1) occurred—

(I) a national of the United States;

(II) a member of the armed forces; or

(III) otherwise an employee of the Government of the United States, or of an individual performing a contract awarded by the United States Government, acting within the scope of the employee's employment; and

(iii) in a case in which the act occurred in the foreign state against which the claim has been brought, the claimant has afforded the foreign state a reasonable opportunity to arbitrate the claim in accordance with the accepted international rules of arbitration; or

(B) the act described in paragraph (1) is related to Case Number 1:00CV03110 (EGS) in the United States District Court for the District of Columbia.

NOTES AND QUESTIONS

1. *Case Law, International Law, and the Foreign Sovereign Immunities Act.* Note how Section 1602, "Findings and declaration of purpose," mixes possible sources of law. The first sentence seems to entrust the courts with power to decide questions of foreign sovereign immunity. The second sentence appears to incorporate rules from international law. The third instructs that the courts decide "in conformity with the principles set forth in" the statute. Deciding cases involving claims of foreign sovereign immunity has come to mean using material evidences from all three sources: case law, international law, and statute. We have, of course, studied sources of international law in Chapters 1, 2, and 3.

2. *The Presumption of Immunity.* Note that a presumption in *Victory Transport* was reversed in the FSIA. *Victory Transport* presumed to deny immunity unless the state proved it deserved to be protected. Section 1604, on the other hand, presumes to grant immunity unless a private plaintiff shows an exception. As we see in *Amerada Hess* below, this reversal can make a decisive effect in practice. If the main purpose of the FSIA was to codify the commercial activities exception, was it necessary to codify other exceptions as an exclusive list? Why not leave some flexibility for the courts to develop exceptions?

3. *The 1996 Anti-terrorism Amendment.* In 1996, the FSIA was amended by the Anti-Terrorism and Death Penalty Act, which added a seventh exception to foreign sovereign immunity in "any case * * * in which money damages are sought against a foreign state for personal injury or death that was caused by an act of torture, extrajudicial killing, aircraft sabotage, hostage taking, or the provision of material support or resources * * * for such an act[.]" Congress recodified the seventh exception as section 1605A of the FSIA in 2008. This exception applies only if the foreign state has been designated a state sponsor of terrorism by the U.S. Secretary of State and if the claimant or victim was a national of the United States when the act occurred. Unlike other exceptions, the seventh exception permits state-owned property unrelated to the claim to be executed against to satisfy a judgment based on its terms. See Monroe Leigh, "1996 Amendments to the Foreign Sovereign Immunities Act with Respect to Terrorist Activities," 91 *American Journal of International Law* 187 (1997). Even so, enforcing judgments against terrorist states has remained a problem. See Jennifer K. Elsea, "CRS Report for Congress: Lawsuits Against State Supporters of Terrorism: An Overview," Congressional Research Service, at 2, Feb. 1, 2008. In 2013, Cuba, Iran, Sudan, and Syria were designated state sponsors of terrorism. "State Sponsors of Terrorism," U.S. Department of State, www.state.gov/j/ct/list/c14151.htm (last visited Dec. 9, 2013).

Cases applying the FSIA's anti-terrorism exception include Flatow v. Islamic Republic of Iran, 999 F.Supp. 1 (D.D.C. 1998), involving a terrorist bombing in Israel killing a U.S. student, Alejandre v. Republic of Cuba, 996 F.Supp. 1239 (S.D.Fla. 1997), respecting an attack on three unarmed civilian planes over international waters killing three U.S. pilots, and Republic of Iraq v. Beaty, 556 U.S. 848 (2009), upholding a presidential waiver barring claims for state-sponsored terrorism against Iraq. See Chad G. Marzan, "The Legacy of *Rux v. Republic of Sudan* and the Future of the Judicial War on Terror," 10 *Cardozo Public Law, Policy, and Ethics Journal* 435 (2012).

The language in 28 U.S.C. § 1605A(2)(B) referring to Case 1:00CV03110 (EGS) was added to what had been 28 U.S.C. § 1605(a)(7) in 2001. It was directed at a case brought by David Roeder and other former American hostages who had been held captive in Iran following the overthrow of the Shah in the late 1970s. When the U.S. Court of Appeals for the District of Columbia Circuit decided not to permit the hostages to sue Iran under the anti-terrorism FSIA exception, it did not do so for constitutional reasons but because it reasoned that Congress had not clearly intended to reverse the U.S-Iran Algiers Accord, a 1981 executive agreement. Roeder v. Islamic Republic of Iran, 333 F.3d 228 (D.C. Cir. 2003), *cert. denied*, 542 U.S. 915 (2004). For more on the Algiers Accord, see *Dames & Moore* in Chapter 4 and the *Diplomatic and Consular Staff Case* in Chapter 5. Should the circuit court have considered the constitutionality of the exception?

TEXAS TRADING & MILLING CORP. V. FEDERAL REPUBLIC OF NIGERIA

647 F.2d 300 (2d Cir. 1981), *cert. denied*, 454 U.S. 1148 (1982)

IRVING R. KAUFMAN, CIRCUIT JUDGE:

These four appeals grow out of one of the most enormous commercial disputes in history, and present questions which strike to the very heart of the modern international economic order. An African nation, developing at breakneck speed by virtue of huge exports of high-grade oil, contracted to buy huge quantities of Portland cement, a commodity crucial to the construction of its infrastructure. It overbought, and the country's docks and harbors became clogged with ships waiting to unload. Imports of other goods ground to a halt. More vessels carrying cement arrived daily; still others were steaming toward the port. Unable to accept delivery of the cement it had bought, the nation repudiated its contracts. In response to suits brought by disgruntled suppliers, it now seeks to invoke an ancient maxim of sovereign immunity—*par in parem imperium non habet*—to insulate itself from liability. But Latin phrases speak with a hoary simplicity inappropriate to the modern financial world. For the ruling principles here, we must look instead to a new and vaguely-worded statute, the Foreign Sovereign Immunities Act of 1976 ("FSIA" or "Act")—a law described by its draftsmen as providing only "very modest guidance" on issues of preeminent importance. For answers to those most difficult questions, the authors of the law "decided to put [their] faith in the U.S. courts." Guided by reason, precedent, and equity, we have attempted to give form and substance to the legislative intent. Accordingly, we find that the defense of sovereign immunity is not available in any of these four cases.

I.

The facts of the four appeals are remarkably parallel, and can be stated in somewhat consolidated form. Early in 1975, the Federal Military Government of the Federal Republic of Nigeria ("Nigeria") embarked on an ambitious program to purchase immense amounts of cement. We have already had occasion in another case to call the program "incredible," but the statistics speak for themselves. Nigeria executed 109 contracts, with 68 suppliers. It purchased, in all, over sixteen million metric tons of cement. The price was close to one billion dollars.

Four of the 109 contracts were made with American companies that were plaintiffs below in the cases now before us: Texas Trading & Milling Corp. ("Texas Trading"), Decor by Nikkei International, Inc. ("Nikkei"), East Europe Import-Export, Inc. ("East Europe"), and Chenax Majesty, Inc. ("Chenax"). The four plaintiffs are not industrial corporations; they are, instead, "trading companies," which buy from one person and sell to another in hopes of making a profit on the differential. Each of the plaintiffs is a New York corporation.

The contracts at issue were signed early in 1975. Each is substantially similar; indeed, Nigeria seems to have mimeographed them in blank, and filled in details with individual suppliers. Overall, each contract called for the sale by the supplier to Nigeria of 240,000 metric tons of Portland cement. Specifically, the contracts required Nigeria, within a time certain after execution, to establish in the seller's favor "an Irrevocable, Transferable abroad, Divisible and Confirmed letter of credit" for the total amount due under the particular contract, slightly over $14 million in each case. The contract also named the bank through which the letter of credit was to be made payable. Nikkei and East Europe named First National City Bank in New York, and Texas Trading specified Fidelity International Bank, also in New York. Chenax denominated Schroeder, Muenchmeyer, Hengst & Co. of Hamburg, West Germany. Drafts under the letters of credit were to be "payable at sight, on presentation" of certain documents to the specified bank.

Within a time certain after establishment and receipt of the letter of credit, each seller was to start shipping cement to Nigeria. The cement was to be bagged, and was to meet certain chemical specifications. Shipments were to be from ports named in the contracts, mostly Spanish, and were to proceed at approximately 20,000 tons per month. Delivery was to the port of Lagos/Apapa, Nigeria, and the seller was obligated to insure the freight to the Nigerian quay. Each contract also provided for demurrage. The Nikkei and East Europe contracts provided they were to be governed by the laws of the United States. The Chenax contract specified the law of Switzerland, and the Texas Trading contract named the law of Nigeria. * * *

The actual financial arrangements differed from those set forth in the cement contracts. Instead of establishing "confirmed" letters of credit with the banks named, Nigeria established what it called "irrevocable" letters of credit with the Central Bank of Nigeria ("Central Bank"), an instrumentality of the Nigerian government, and advised those letters of credit through the Morgan Guaranty Trust Company ("Morgan") of New York. That is, under the letters of credit as established, each seller was to present appropriate documents not to the named bank, but to Morgan. And, since the letters were not "confirmed," Morgan did not promise to pay "on sight"; it assumed no independent liability. Each of the letters of credit provided it was to be governed by the Uniform Customs and Practice for Documentary Credits ("UCP") (1962 Revision), as set forth in Brochure No. 222 of the International Chamber of Commerce. * * *

After receiving notice that the letters of credit had been established, the suppliers set out to secure subcontracts to procure the cement, and shipping contracts to transport it. They, through their subcontractors, began to bag the cement and load it on ships, as suppliers across the globe were doing the same. Hundreds of ships arrived in Lagos/Apapa in the summer of 1975, and most were carrying cement. Nigeria's port facilities could accept only one to five million tons of cement per year; at any rate, they could not begin to unload the over sixteen million tons Nigeria had slated for delivery in eighteen short months. Based on prior experience, Nigeria had made the contracts expecting only twenty percent of the suppliers to be able to perform. By July, when the harbor held over 400 ships waiting to unload—260 of them carrying cement—Nigeria realized it had misjudged the market considerably.

With demurrage piling up at astronomical rates, and suppliers, hiring, loading, and dispatching more ships daily, Nigeria decided to act. On August 9, 1975, Nigeria caused its Ports Authority to issue Government Notice No. 1434, a regulation which stated that, effective August 18, all ships destined for Lagos/Apapa would be required to convey to the Ports Authority, two months before sailing, certain information concerning their time of arrival in the port. The regulation also stated vaguely that the Ports Authority would "co-ordinate all sailing," and that it would "refus[e] service" to vessels which did not comply with the regulation. Then, on August 18, Nigeria cabled its suppliers and asked them to stop sending cement, and to cease loading or even chartering ships. In late September, Nigeria took the crucial step: Central Bank instructed Morgan not to pay under the letters of credit unless the supplier submitted—in addition to the documents required by the letter of credit as written—a statement from Central Bank that payment ought to be made. Morgan notified each supplier of Nigeria's instructions, and Morgan commenced refusing to make payment under the letters of credit as written. Almost three months later, on December 19, 1975, Nigeria promulgated Decree No. 40, a law prohibiting entry into a Nigerian port to any ship which had not secured two months' prior approval, and imposing criminal penalties for unauthorized entry. * * *

II.

The law before us is complex and largely unconstrued, and has introduced sweeping changes in some areas of prior law. In structure, the FSIA is a marvel of compression. Within the bounds of a few tersely-worded sections, it purports to provide answers to three crucial questions in a suit against a foreign state: the availability of sovereign immunity as a defense, the presence of subject matter jurisdiction over the claim, and the propriety of personal jurisdiction over the defendant. Through a series of intricately coordinated provisions, the FSIA seems at first glance to make the answer to one of the questions, subject matter jurisdiction, dispositive of all three. * * *

Turning to the specific provisions of the law, a description of the FSIA's analytic structure is helpful. The jurisdiction-conferring provision of the Act, 28 U.S.C. § 1330(a), creates in the district courts:

> original jurisdiction without regard to amount in controversy of any nonjury civil action against a foreign state as defined in section 1603(a) of this title as to any claim for relief in personam with respect to which the foreign state is not entitled to immunity either under sections 1605–1607 of this title or any applicable international agreement.

Although § 1330(a) refers to sections 1605–1607, the section most frequently relevant, and the one applicable here, is § 1605. It provides, in part:

> (a) A foreign state shall not be immune from the jurisdiction of courts of the United States or of the States in any case—* * *
>
> (2) in which the action is based upon a commercial activity carried on in the United States by the foreign state; or upon an act performed in the United States in connection with a commercial activity of the foreign state elsewhere; or upon an act outside the territory of the United States in connection with a commercial activity of the foreign state elsewhere and that act causes a direct effect in the United States.

Crucial to each of the three clauses of § 1605(a)(2) is the phrase "commercial activity." In it is lodged centuries of Anglo-American and civil law precedent construing the term "sovereign immunity." If the activity is not "commercial," but, rather, is "governmental," then the foreign state is entitled to immunity under section 1605, and "original jurisdiction" is not present under § 1330(a).

For the definition of "commercial activity," we turn to subsection 1603(d), which provides:

> (d) A "commercial activity" means either a regular course of commercial conduct or a particular commercial transaction or act. The commercial character of an activity shall be determined by reference to the nature of the course of conduct or particular transaction or act, rather than by references to its purpose.

If "commercial activity" under § 1603(d) is present, and if it bears the relation to the United States required by § 1605(a)(2), then the foreign state is "not entitled to immunity," and the district court has statutory subject matter jurisdiction over the claim through § 1330(a). And, if the exercise of that jurisdiction falls within the judicial power set forth by Article III of the Constitution, subject matter jurisdiction over the claim exists. * * *

The determination of whether particular behavior is "commercial" is perhaps the most important decision a court faces in an FSIA suit. This problem is significant because the primary purpose of the Act is to "restrict" the immunity of a foreign state to suits involving a foreign state's public acts. If the activity is not "commercial," it satisfies none of the three clauses of § 1605(a)(2), and the foreign state is (at least under that subsection) immune from suit. Unfortunately, the definition of "commercial" is the one issue on which the Act provides almost no guidance at all. Subsection 1603(d) advances the inquiry somewhat, for it provides: "The commercial character of an activity shall be determined by reference to the nature of the course of conduct or particular transaction or act, rather than by reference to its purpose." No provision of the Act, however, defines "commercial." Congress deliberately left the meaning open and * * * "put [its] faith in the U.S. courts to work out progressively, on a case-by-case basis . . . the distinction between commercial and governmental." We are referred to no less than three separate sources of authority to resolve this fundamental definitional question.

The first source is statements contained in the legislative history itself. Perhaps the clearest of them was made by Bruno Ristau, then Chief of the Foreign Litigation Section of the Civil Division, Department of Justice. Ristau stated: "[I]f a government enters into a contract to purchase goods and services, that is considered a commercial activity. It avails itself of the ordinary contract machinery. It bargains and negotiates. It accepts an offer. It enters into a written contract and the contract is to be performed." The House Report seems to conclude that a contract or series of contracts for the purchase of goods would be *per se* a "commercial activity," and the illustrations cited by experts who testified on the bill—contracts, for example, for the sale of army boots or grain—support such a rule. Or, put another way, if the activity is one in which a private person could engage, it is not entitled to immunity.

The second source for interpreting the phrase "commercial activity" is the "very large body of case law which exist[ed]" in American law upon passage of the Act in 1976. Testifying on an earlier version of the bill, Charles N. Brower, then Legal Adviser of the Department of State, stated:

> [T]he restrictive theory of sovereign immunity from jurisdiction, which has been followed by the Department of State and the courts since it was articulated in the familiar letter of Acting Legal Adviser Jack B. Tate of May 29, 1952, would be incorporated into statutory law. This theory limits immunity to public acts, leaving so-called private acts subject to suit. The proposed legislation would make it clear that immunity cannot be claimed with respect to acts or transactions that are commercial in nature, regardless of their underlying purpose.

Finally, current standards of international law concerning sovereign immunity add content to the "commercial activity" phrase of the FSIA. Section 1602 of the Act, entitled "Findings and declaration of purpose," contains a cryptic reference to international law, but fails wholly to adopt it. The legislative history states that the Act "incorporates standards recognized under international law," and the drafters seem to have intended rather generally to bring American sovereign immunity practice into line with that of other nations. At this point, there can be little doubt that international law follows the restrictive theory of sovereign immunity.

Under each of these three standards, Nigeria's cement contracts and letters of credit qualify as "commercial activity." Lord Denning, writing in *Trendtex Trading Corp. v. Central Bank of Nigeria*, [1977] 2 W.L.R. 356, 369, 1 All E.R. 881, with his usual erudition and clarity, stated: "If a government department goes into the market places of the world and buys boots or cement—as a commercial transaction—that government department should be subject to all the rules of the marketplace." Nigeria's activity here is in the nature of a private contract for the purchase of goods. Its purpose—to build roads, army barracks, whatever—is irrelevant. Accordingly, courts in other nations have uniformly held Nigeria's 1975 cement purchase program and appurtenant letters of credit to be "commercial activity," and have denied the defense of sovereign immunity. [The Court cites decisions from the United Kingdom and Germany, as well as an International Chamber of

Commerce arbitral award.] We find defendants' activity here to constitute "commercial activity"[.]

[The Court finds there is jurisdiction over Nigeria.]

NOTES AND QUESTIONS

1. *Retroactive Application of the Foreign Sovereign Immunities Act.* Why did Judge Kaufman in *Texas Trading* apply the FSIA, a 1976 statute, to events that occurred in 1975? Was the issue of retroactivity not important because the United States had followed the restrictive theory of sovereign immunity since the 1952 Tate letter?

The question of retroactive application of the FSIA reached the U.S. Supreme Court in Republic of Austria v. Altmann, 541 U.S. 677 (2004). Altmann brought suit in U.S. court to recover some Gustav Klimt paintings, which the Austrian government had allegedly expropriated in 1948. Austria claimed that it was entitled to absolute immunity, arguing that the FSIA could not be applied retroactively and that the United States did not adopt the restrictive theory of sovereign immunity until 1952. The U.S. Departments of Justice and State, in an *amicus* brief, argued against applying the FSIA to exercise jurisdiction with respect to a pre-1952 expropriation claim. The Supreme Court found, however, that the FSIA could apply. The normal U.S. presumption against retroactive application of statutes was intended

> to avoid unnecessary *post hoc* changes to legal rules on which parties relied in shaping their primary conduct. But the principal purpose of foreign sovereign immunity has never been to permit foreign states and their instrumentalities to shape their conduct in reliance on the promise of future immunity from suit in United States courts. Rather, such immunity reflects current political realities and relationships, and aims to give foreign states and their instrumentalities some *present* "protection from the inconvenience of suit as a gesture of comity."

Id. at 696, *quoting* Dole Food Co. v. Patrickson, 538 U.S. 468, 479 (2003) (emphasis in original). The Court thought that the language of 28 U.S.C. § 1602, which provides that the FSIA applies "henceforth" to "claims" to immunity—rather than to underlying substantive actions protected by immunity—supported retroactive application of the statute. *Id.* at 697. A commentator on *Altmann* remarked that "[b]ecause principles of state immunity have an evolving character, an indeterminate content, a history of retroactive application, and a speculative role in shaping the primary conduct of foreign states, application of the FSIA to preenactment conduct appears unlikely to disturb the reliance interests of potential defendants." Charles H. Brower II, "International Decision: Republic of Austria v. Altmann," 99 *American Journal of International Law* 236, 240 (2005).

2. *Proving "Commercial Activities."* Section 1602 of the FSIA refers to the commercial activities exception as being part of international law and

also instructs courts to decide sovereign immunity cases in accordance with the statute. How well did the *Texas Trading* court employ both international law and statutory analysis to decide whether Nigeria was protected by the commercial activities exception? Did the FSIA much change the exercise of line-drawing between "public" and "private" acts as done before 1976, *e.g.*, in *Victory Transport*?

3. *Direct Effect in the United States*. Note how the *Texas Trading* court found "direct effect in the United States":

> [T]he financial loss in these cases occurred "in the United States" for two * * * simple[ ] reasons. First, the cement suppliers were to present documents and collect money in the United States, and the breaches precluded their doing so. Second, each of the plaintiffs is an American corporation. Whether a failure to pay a foreign corporation in the United States or to pay an American corporation overseas creates an effect "in the United States" under § 1605(a)(2) is not before us. Both factors are present here and the subsection is clearly satisfied.

647 F.2d at 312.

In Martin v. Republic of South Africa, 836 F.2d 91 (2d Cir. 1987), the Second Circuit ruled that an African-American could not sue the government of South Africa in U.S. courts for a delay in providing him with medical treatment following an automobile accident in South Africa. A member of a U.S. dance company performing in South Africa, Martin had to wait longer for care than did a white companion also in the car. Citing *Texas Trading*, *inter alia*, Martin argued that for the court to refuse to find "direct effect" in his case would create an "anomaly between the treatment of corporations and the treatment of individuals." How persuasive was the court's rejection of Martin's claim?:

> We do not believe that such a distinction exists, nor do we create one here. Appellant was not in the United States at the time of the accident. He was in South Africa. Indeed, he did not return to the United States until more than a year after the date of the accident. Application of the plain language of § 1605(a)(2) leads us to conclude that South Africa's conduct did not cause a direct effect in the United States.

Id. at 95.

In Republic of Argentina v. Weltover, Inc., 504 U.S. 607 (1992), Justice Scalia, writing for a unanimous Supreme Court, held that Argentina's reschedulings of debt payments had a "direct effect" in the United States since New York was the place where the debts had to be repaid. *Id.* at 617. Did *Weltover* set too low a threshold for direct effect and open the door too wide for suits against foreign sovereigns in U.S. courts?

In Voest-Alpine Trading USA Corp. v. Bank of China, 142 F.3d 887 (5th Cir.), *cert. denied*, 525 U.S. 1041 (1998), the Fifth Circuit held that the Bank of China, an instrumentality of the People's Republic of China, was open to suit in federal district court in Texas for failure to pay under a letter of credit issued to protect a U.S. seller *vis-à-vis* a Chinese buyer. The letter of credit, though telexed to the United States, did not designate a particular place of payment. Nonetheless, the Fifth Circuit ruled "that a financial loss incurred in the United States by an American plaintiff, if it is an immediate consequence of the defendant's activity, constitutes a direct effect sufficient to support jurisdiction under the third clause of the commercial activity exception to the FSIA." *Id.* at 897.

Is a U.S. court or the FSIA itself limited by jurisdictional rules of international law in determining whether an activity has "a direct effect in the United States"? Should the jurisdictional practice of other countries be taken into account? As one observer noted: "[A]ll States have a strong incentive to make reasonable rules of immunity. They know that the rules applied to other States in their national courts can be applied to them in the courts of other countries." Mark B. Feldman, "The United States Foreign Sovereign Immunities Act of 1976 in Perspective: A Founder's View," 35 *International and Comparative Law Quarterly* 302, 303 (1986).

4. *Sovereign Immunity and the Executive Branch.* What should be the role of the executive branch *vis-à-vis* the courts and the legislature in making sovereign immunity determinations? Before the Foreign Sovereign Immunities Act was enacted in 1976, the State Department recommended what position the courts should take on a case-by-case basis. An internal memo to the Legal Adviser of the State Department in 1966 commented on the "plainly unsatisfactory" state of the law of sovereign immunity:

> 1. The determination by the State Department, though generally considered conclusive by the courts, is made without clear guidelines or procedures. It is in part a "legal" determination, though it is held not to be reviewable; and in part a political determination, though made by lawyers. The determination is sometimes made after a kind of hearing, sometimes not, and there is virtually never an articulation of the reasons for the determination.
>
> 2. The courts, when asked to rule in the absence of a State Department suggestion, have no satisfactory distinctions to follow, and reach inconsistent results.
>
> 3. There is no consistency between the policy of the United States Government in defending suits abroad and in recognition by the Executive Branch of claims of immunity of foreign governments in the United States.

Quoted in Andreas F. Lowenfeld, *International Litigation and Arbitration* 627–28 (2d ed. 2002). The Foreign Sovereign Immunities Act places the burden of determining sovereign immunity with the federal courts. Was the statutory solution necessary, or could the courts have accomplished the same result simply through case law? Or would it have been wiser to leave the development of sovereign immunity to periodic executive pronouncement?

ARGENTINE REPUBLIC V. AMERADA HESS SHIPPING CORP.

488 U.S. 428 (1989)

CHIEF JUSTICE REHNQUIST delivered the opinion of the Court.

Two Liberian corporations sued the Argentine Republic in a United States District Court to recover damages for a tort allegedly committed by its armed forces on the high seas in violation of international law. We hold that the District Court correctly dismissed the action, because the Foreign Sovereign Immunities Act of 1976 (FSIA), 28 U.S.C. § 1330 *et seq.,* does not authorize jurisdiction over a foreign state in this situation.

Respondents alleged the following facts in their complaints. Respondent United Carriers, Inc., a Liberian corporation, chartered one of its oil tankers, the Hercules, to respondent Amerada Hess Shipping Corporation, also a Liberian corporation. The contract was executed in New York City. Amerada Hess used the Hercules to transport crude oil from the southern terminus of the Trans-Alaska Pipeline in Valdez, Alaska, around Cape Horn in South America, to the Hess refinery in the United States Virgin Islands. On May 25, 1982, the Hercules began a return voyage, without cargo but fully fueled, from the Virgin Islands to Alaska. At that time, Great Britain and petitioner Argentine Republic were at war over an archipelago of some 200 islands—the Falkland Islands to the British, and the Islas Malvinas to the Argentineans—in the South Atlantic off the Argentine coast. On June 3, United States officials informed the two belligerents of the location of United States vessels and Liberian tankers owned by United States interests then traversing the South Atlantic, including the Hercules, to avoid any attacks on neutral shipping.

By June 8, 1982, after a stop in Brazil, the Hercules was in international waters about 600 nautical miles from Argentina and 500 miles from the Falklands; she was outside the "war zones" designated by Britain and Argentina. At 12:15 Greenwich mean time, the ship's master made a routine report by radio to Argentina officials, providing the ship's name, international call sign, registry, position, course, speed, and voyage description. About 45 minutes later, an Argentine military aircraft began to circle the Hercules. The ship's master repeated his earlier message by radio to Argentine officials, who acknowledged receiving it. Six minutes later, without provocation, another Argentine military plane began to bomb the Hercules; the master immediately hoisted a white flag. A second bombing soon followed, and a third attack came about two hours later, when an Argentine jet struck the ship with an air-to-surface rocket. Disabled but not destroyed, the Hercules reversed course and sailed to Rio de Janeiro, the nearest safe port. At Rio de Janeiro, respondent

United Carriers determined that the ship had suffered extensive deck and hull damage, and that an undetonated bomb remained lodged in her No. 2 tank. After an investigation by the Brazilian Navy, United Carriers decided that it would be too hazardous to remove the undetonated bomb, and on July 20, 1978, the Hercules was scuttled 250 miles off the Brazilian coast.

Following unsuccessful attempts to obtain relief in Argentina, respondents commenced this action in the United States District Court for the Southern District of New York for the damage that they sustained from the attack. United Carriers sought $10 million in damages for the loss of the ship; Amerada Hess sought $1.9 million in damages for the fuel that went down with the ship. Respondents alleged that petitioner's attack on the neutral Hercules violated international law. They invoked the District Court's jurisdiction under the Alien Tort Statute, 28 U.S.C. § 1350, which provides that "[t]he district courts shall have original jurisdiction of any civil action by an alien for a tort only, committed in violation of the law of nations or a treaty of the United States." Amerada Hess also brought suit under the general admiralty and maritime jurisdiction, 28 U.S.C. § 1333, and "the principle of universal jurisdiction, recognized in customary international law." The District Court dismissed both complaints for lack of subject-matter jurisdiction, ruling that respondents' suits were barred by the FSIA.

A divided panel of the United States Court of Appeals for the Second Circuit reversed. * * *

We think that the text and structure of the FSIA demonstrate Congress' intention that the FSIA be the sole basis for obtaining jurisdiction over a foreign state in our courts. Section 1604 and § 1330(a) work in tandem; § 1604 bars federal and state courts from exercising jurisdiction when a foreign state is entitled to immunity, and § 1330(a) confers jurisdiction on district courts to hear suits brought by United States citizens and by aliens when a foreign state is *not* entitled to immunity. As we said in *Verlinden,* the FSIA "must be applied by the district courts in every action against a foreign sovereign, since subject-matter jurisdiction in any such action depends on the existence of one of the specified exceptions to foreign sovereign immunity." *Verlinden B.V. v. Central Bank of Nigeria*, 461 U.S. 480, 493 (1983).

The Court of Appeals acknowledged that the FSIA's language and legislative history support the "general rule" that the Act governs the immunity of foreign states in federal court. The Court of Appeals, however, thought that the FSIA's "focus on commercial concerns" and Congress' failure to "repeal" the Alien Tort Statute indicated Congress' intention that federal courts continue to exercise jurisdiction over foreign states in suits alleging violations of international law outside the confines of the FSIA. The Court of Appeals also believed that to construe the FSIA to bar the instant suit would "fly in the face" of Congress' intention that the FSIA be interpreted pursuant to "standards recognized under international law."

Taking the last of these points first, Congress had violations of international law by foreign states in mind when it enacted the FSIA. For example, the FSIA specifically denies foreign states immunity in suits "in which rights in property taken in violation of international law are in issue." 28 U.S.C. § 1605(a)(3). Congress also rested the FSIA in part on its power under Art. I, § 8, cl. 10, of the Constitution "[t]o define and punish Piracies and Felonies committed on the high Seas, and Offenses against the Law of Nations." From Congress' decision to deny immunity to foreign states in the class of cases just mentioned, we draw the plain implication that immunity is granted in those cases involving alleged violations of international law that do not come within one of the FSIA's exceptions.

As to the other point made by the Court of Appeals, Congress' failure to enact a *pro tanto* repealer of the Alien Tort Statute when it passed the FSIA in 1976 may be explained at least in part by the lack of certainty as to whether the Alien Tort Statute conferred jurisdiction in suits against foreign states. Enacted by the First Congress in 1789, the Alien Tort Statute provides that "[t]he district courts shall have original jurisdiction of any civil action by an alien for a tort only, committed in violation of the law of nations or a treaty of the United States." 28 U.S.C. § 1350. The Court of Appeals did not cite any decision in which a United States court exercised jurisdiction over a foreign state under the Alien Tort Statute, and only one such case has come to our attention—one which was decided after the enactment of the FSIA. * * *

We think that Congress' failure in the FSIA to enact an express *pro tanto* repealer of the Alien Tort Statute speaks only faintly, if at all, to the issue involved in this case. In light of the comprehensiveness of the statutory scheme in the FSIA, we doubt that even the most meticulous draftsman would have concluded that Congress also needed to amend *pro tanto* the Alien Tort Statute and presumably such other grants of subject-matter jurisdiction in Title 28 as § 1331 (federal question), § 1333 (admiralty), § 1335 (interpleader), § 1337 (commerce and antitrust), and § 1338 (patents, copyrights, and trademarks). Congress provided in § 1602 of the FSIA that "[c]laims of foreign states to immunity should *henceforth* be decided by courts of the United States in conformity with the principles set forth in this chapter," and very likely it thought that should be sufficient. * * *

Having determined that the FSIA provides the sole basis for obtaining jurisdiction over a foreign state in federal court, we turn to whether any of the exceptions enumerated in the Act apply here. These exceptions include cases involving the waiver of immunity, commercial activities occurring in the United States or causing a direct effect in this country, property expropriated in violation of international law, inherited, gift, or immovable property located in the United States, non-commercial torts occurring in the United States, and maritime liens. We agree with the District Court that none of the FSIA's exceptions applies on these facts.

Respondents assert that FSIA exception for noncommercial torts, § 1605(a)(5), is most in point. This provision denies immunity in a case

> in which money damages are sought against a foreign state for personal injury or death, or damage to or loss of property, occurring in the United States and caused by the tortious act or omission of that foreign state or of any official or employee of that foreign state while acting within the scope of his office or employment.

Section 1605(a)(5) is limited by its terms, however, to those cases in which the damage to or loss of property occurs *in the United States*. Congress' primary purpose in enacting § 1605(a)(5) was to eliminate a foreign state's immunity for traffic accidents and other torts committed in the United States, for which liability is imposed under domestic tort law.

In this case, the injury to respondents' ship occurred on the high seas some 5,000 miles off the nearest shores of the United States. Despite these telling facts, respondents nonetheless claim that the tortious attack on the Hercules occurred "in the United States." They point out that the FSIA defines "United States" as including all "territory and waters, continental and insular, subject to the jurisdiction of the United States," and that their injury occurred on the high seas, which is within the admiralty jurisdiction of the United States, see *The Plymouth*, 3 Wall. 20, 36 (1866). They reason, therefore, that "by statutory definition" petitioner's attack occurred in the United States.

We find this logic unpersuasive. We construe the modifying phrase "continental and insular" to restrict the definition of United States to the continental United States and those islands that are part of the United States or its possessions; any other reading would render this phrase nugatory. Likewise, the term "waters" in § 1603(c) cannot reasonably be read to cover all waters over which United States courts might exercise jurisdiction. When it desires to do so, Congress knows how to place the high seas within the jurisdiction reach of a statute. We thus apply "[t]he canon of construction which teaches that legislation of Congress, unless contrary intent appears, is meant to apply only within the territorial jurisdiction of the United States." Because respondents' injury unquestionably occurred well outside the 3-mile limit then in effect for the territorial waters of the United States, the exception for noncommercial torts cannot apply.

The result in this case is not altered by the fact that petitioner's alleged tort may have had effects in the United States. Respondents state, for example, that the Hercules was transporting oil intended for use in this country and that the loss of the ship disrupted contractual payments due in New York. Under the commercial activity exception to the FSIA, § 1605(a)(2), a foreign state may be liable for its commercial activities "outside the territory of the United States" having a "direct effect" inside the United States. But the noncommercial tort exception, § 1605(a)(5), upon which respondents rely, makes no mention of "territory outside the United States" or of "direct effects" in the United States. Congress' decision to use explicit language in § 1605(a)(2), and not to do so in § 1605(a)(5), indicates that the exception in § 1605(a)(5) covers only torts occurring within the territorial jurisdiction of the United States. Respondents do not claim that § 1605(a)(2) covers these facts.

We also disagree with respondents' claim that certain international agreements entered into by petitioner and by the United States create an exception to the FSIA here. As noted, the FSIA was adopted "[s]ubject to international agreements to which the United States [was] a party at the time of [its] enactment." This exception applies when international agreements "expressly conflic[t]" with the immunity provisions of the FSIA, hardly the circumstances in this case. Respondents point to the Geneva Convention on the High Seas, Apr. 29, 1958, [1962] 13 U.S.T. 2312, T.I.A.S. No. 5200, and the Pan-American Maritime Neutrality Convention, Feb. 20, 1928, 47 Stat. 1989, 1990–1991, T.S. No. 845. These conventions, however, only set forth substantive rules of conduct and state that compensation shall be paid for certain wrongs. They do not create private rights of action for foreign corporations to recover compensation from foreign states in United States courts. Nor do we see how a foreign state can waive its immunity under § 1605(a)(1) by signing an international agreement that contains no mention of a waiver of immunity to suit in United States courts or even the availability of a cause of action in the United States. We find similarly unpersuasive the argument of respondent and *Amicus Curiae* Republic of Liberia that the Treaty of Friendship, Commerce and Navigation, Aug. 8, 1938, United States-Liberia, 54 Stat. 1739, T.S. No. 956, carves out an exception to the FSIA. Article I of this Treaty provides, in pertinent part, that the nationals of the United States and Liberia "shall enjoy freedom of access to the courts of justice of the other on conforming to the local laws." The FSIA is clearly one of the "local laws" to which respondents must "conform" before bringing suit in United States courts.

We hold that the FSIA provides the sole basis for obtaining jurisdiction over a foreign state in the courts of this country, and that none of the enumerated exceptions to the Act applies to the facts of this case. The judgment of the Court of Appeals is therefore *Reversed.*

NOTES AND QUESTIONS

1. *The Alleged Violation of International Law.* In *Amerada Hess* the Supreme Court did not reach the issue of Argentina's alleged violation of international law. The court of appeals believed that "[t]he facts alleged by [Amerada Hess and United Carriers], if proven, would constitute a clear violation of international law." Amerada Hess Shipping Corp. v. Argentine Republic, 830 F.2d 421, 423 (2d Cir. 1987). Looking to treaties dating from the Declaration of Paris of 1856 to the Law of the Sea Convention of 1982, the Second Circuit ruled that "it is beyond controversy that attacking a neutral ship in international waters, without proper cause for suspicion or investigation, violates international law." *Id.* at 424.

Whatever the possibility of an international law violation, the Supreme Court ruled that the Liberian shipping companies could not sue the Argentine government in a U.S. court. Where could the companies then go for redress? What was the potential for other legal procedures, *e.g.*, litigation in Argentina or international arbitration? Were there political or economic avenues open to the companies, *e.g.*, diplomatic protest or economic reprisals?

2. *The Alien Tort Statute.* The Supreme Court in *Amerada Hess* was careful not to decide questions relating to the 1789 Alien Tort Statute and non-governmental defendants: "The Alien Tort Statute by its terms does not distinguish among classes of defendants, and it of course has the same effect after the passage of the FSIA as before with respect to defendants other than foreign states." With respect to government defendants, given the *Amerada Hess* decision, does the Alien Tort Statute add anything to the arsenal of a plaintiff's lawyer that is not already there courtesy of the Foreign Sovereign Immunities Act? For the Supreme Court's construction of the Alien Tort Statute, see *Sosa* and *Kiobel* in Chapter 4.

3. *Foreign Parties in U.S. Courts.* In *Amerada Hess* a foreign plaintiff sued a foreign state in U.S. federal court. In Verlinden B.V. v. Central Bank of Nigeria, 461 U.S. 480 (1983), the Supreme Court considered whether the requirements of Article III of the U.S. Constitution were met when a foreign plaintiff sued a foreign defendant in federal court on a nonfederal, breach-of-contract cause of action. The Supreme Court found that jurisdiction was constitutional:

> By reason of its authority over foreign commerce and foreign relations, Congress has the undisputed power to decide, as a matter of federal law, whether and under what circumstances foreign nations should be amenable to suit in the United States. Actions against foreign sovereigns in our courts raise sensitive issues concerning the foreign relations of the United States, and the primacy of federal concerns is evident.
>
> To promote these federal interests, Congress exercised its Art. I powers by enacting a statute comprehensively regulating the amenability of foreign nations to suit in the United States. The statute must be applied by the district court in every action against

> a foreign sovereign, since subject-matter jurisdiction in any such action depends on the existence of one of the specified exceptions to foreign sovereign immunity, 28 US.C. § 1330(a). At the threshold of every action in a district court against a foreign state, therefore, the court must satisfy itself that one of the exceptions applies—and in doing so it must apply the detailed federal law standards set forth in the [FSIA]. Accordingly, an action against a foreign sovereign arises under federal law, for purposes of Art. III jurisdiction.

Id. at 493–94.

4. *Exceptions to Immunity.* After ruling that the FSIA provided the only way to sue foreign governments, the Supreme Court in *Amerada Hess* considered whether any section 1605 exceptions to immunity existed. Justices Blackmun and Marshall dissented from this part of the judgment, arguing that the question of the FSIA's exceptions had not been fully briefed in the case. They preferred to remand. However, Justice Rehnquist and the majority rejected the possibility that there was a section 1605(a)(5) tort "occurring in the United States." Could it have been shown that Argentina had made some sort of implicit waiver in customary international law under section 1605(a)(1)? Even "explicit waivers of sovereign immunity are narrowly construed 'in favor of the sovereign' and are not enlarged 'beyond what the language requires.' " World Wide Minerals, Ltd. v. Republic of Kazakhstan, 296 F.3d 1154, 1162 (D.C. Cir. 2002). So, Kazakhstan's waiver in two of four agreements relating to the production and marketing of uranium could not by implication be extended to the two other agreements. *Id.* at 1162–64.

Justice Rehnquist also observed that the companies did not make a claim under section 1605(a)(2) for an exception based on "an act outside the territory of the United States in connection with a commercial activity of the foreign state elsewhere and that act causes a direct effect in the United States." What sort of a "commercial activities" exception claim could have been made in *Amerada Hess*? In Republic of Argentina v. Weltover, Inc., 504 U.S. 607 (1992), the Supreme Court decided that the Argentine government's issuance of bonds to protect foreign creditors did qualify as "commercial": "[T]hey are in almost all respects garden-variety debt instruments: They may be held by private parties; they are negotiable and may be traded on the international market (except in Argentina); and they promise a future stream of cash income." *Id.* at 615. In Cicippio v. Islamic Republic of Iran, 30 F.3d 164 (D.C.Cir. 1994), however, the D.C. Circuit held that kidnapping even for monetary ransom could not be characterized as "commercial" for the purpose of the FSIA. In Saudi Arabia v. Nelson, 507 U.S. 349 (1993), the Supreme Court considered whether a U.S. citizen's alleged detention and torture by the Saudi government were so intertwined with his recruitment and hiring to work in a Saudi hospital as to bring into play the "commercial activity" exception of section 1605(a)(2). The Court found the exception to immunity inapplicable.

The Supreme Court did find an exception to immunity, *i.e.*, section 1605(a)(4), in Permanent Mission of India to the United Nations v. City of

New York, 551 U.S. 193 (2007), holding 7–2 that an action seeking a declaration of a tax lien against domestic property owned by a foreign government fell within the "rights in immovable property" exception. Professor Greenawalt lamented that Justice Thomas's judgment paid so little attention either to international and foreign law or to the opinions of the executive branch. Alexander K.A. Greenawalt, "Foreign Sovereign Immunities Act: Supreme Court Upholds New York City Action for Tax Liens Against UN Mission," 11 *ASIL Insights*, Issue 22 (2007).

5. *Foreign Military Activities.* A Spanish naval treasure ship, the *Nuestra Señora de las Mercedes*, was at issue in Odyssey Marine Exploration, Inc. v. Unidentified Shipwrecked Vessel, 657 F.3d 1159 (11th Cir. 2011), *cert. denied,* 132 S. Ct. 2379 (2012). This Spanish Navy frigate carried about 594,000 coins, mostly silver and gold, from the New World, but was sunk by the British Navy off Gibraltar in 1804. The Eleventh Circuit was "persuaded that in the context of a sunken Spanish military vessel, the cargo and the shipwreck are interlinked for immunity purposes," and that there was no FSIA exception giving a U.S. court jurisdiction to decide competing claims to the treasure. *Id.* at 1179–80. *Odyssey Marine* joins *Amerada Hess* and the *Schooner Exchange*, consolidating Chief Justice Marshall's protection of military activities of foreign states against U.S. judicial jurisdiction. When might foreign military activities fall within an exception to the FSIA? See John R. Crook, "Contemporary Practice of the United States Relating to International Law," 106 *American Journal of International Law* 138, 149–53 (2012).

6. *The Presumption of Immunity.* Is the *Amerada Hess Case* a good example of the shift in presumption made, perhaps unwittingly, by the drafters of the FSIA? How might the Court's analysis in *Amerada Hess* have been changed if, as in *Victory Transport*, it was incumbent on Argentina to prove that immunity ought to be granted rather than on plaintiffs to show that an exception to immunity existed?

7. *The Definition of "Foreign State."* In *Amerada Hess* there was no question that the defendant, the Argentine Republic, was a foreign state for the purposes of the FSIA, but in other cases the definition of "foreign state" may be more perplexing. The FSIA designates that a "foreign state" includes not only the state itself but both "a political subdivision of a foreign state" and "an agency or instrumentality of a foreign state [including] a separate legal person, corporate or otherwise * * * a majority of whose shares or other ownership interest is owned by a foreign state or a political subdivision thereof." 28 U.S.C. § 1603(a), (b).

When must that majority ownership interest be owned in order for an entity to be deemed a state for purposes of the FSIA? In Dole Food Co. v. Patrickson, 538 U.S. 468 (2003), the Supreme Court decided unanimously that "the plain text" of section 1603(b)(2)—"a majority of whose shares or other ownership interest is owned by a foreign state"—"because it is expressed in the present tense, requires that instrumentality status be determined at the time suit is filed." *Id.* at 478. Is this a more straightforward statutory analysis than the Court's 7–2 holding, also in *Dole*, that "[a] corporation is an instrumentality of a foreign state under the FSIA only if the foreign state itself owns a majority of the corporation's shares"? *Id.* at 477. Is this conclusion really, as the majority believed, "supported by [both] the statutory text and elementary principles of corporate law"? *Id.* For an examination of the relevant principles of corporate law, see 3 Phillip I. Blumberg, Kurt A. Strasser, Nicholas L. Georgapoulos & Eric J. Gouvin, *Blumberg on Corporate Groups* (2005). What are the procedural ramifications of *Dole*? "Perhaps, most importantly, the FSIA affords substantial protections to the assets of foreign states and their agencies and instrumentalities from both pre- and post-judgment execution. By excluding subsidiaries of foreign state-owned corporations from the FSIA's coverage, *Dole Foods* strips these entities of the FSIA's protections." Janis H. Brennan & Andrew B. Lowenstein, "Casenote: U.S. Supreme Court Clarifies Important Foreign Sovereign Immunities Act Issues," 32 *International Law News*, No. 3, at 21, 22 (2003).

8. *The Responsibility of Foreign States for State-owned Enterprises.* A related problem concerns the responsibility of a state that is sued under the FSIA for the acts of a state-owned enterprise, especially when that owned enterprise is no longer able to pay its own debts. Here the legal issues may revolve around the control of the enterprise and raise questions similar to those touching on corporate groups in general. In Transamerica Leasing, Inc. v. La Republica de Venezuela, 200 F.3d 843 (D.C.Cir. 2000), Venezuela was held not responsible to answer for a breach of contract claim under the FSIA (commercial activities exception) for the acts of a defunct Venezuelan shipping company, Compania Anonima Venezolana de Navegacion, that had been 99.86% owned by an instrumentality of the Venezuelan government created to help restructure and privatize Venezuelan state enterprises. The D.C. Circuit held that the facts of *Transamerica Leasing* established neither actual nor apparent Venezuelan government control over the defunct company.

9. *Immunity of Foreign Officials.* Are heads of state and other foreign officials "states" within the definition of the FSIA and thus entitled to immunity from suit if their actions do not fall within one of the exceptions of the Act? The FSIA does not explicitly say, and in Samantar v. Yousuf, 560 U.S. 305 (2010), a unanimous Supreme Court held that a foreign official, in this case a former prime minister of Somalia, was not protected by the FSIA. However, the Court held open the possibility that foreign officials might still be protected by common law doctrines of immunity. See David P. Stewart, "*Samantar v. Yousuf*: Foreign Official Immunity Under the Common Law," 14 *ASIL Insights*, Issue 15 (2010). How should immunity claims of foreign officials now be evaluated? See Beth Stephens, "The Modern Common Law of Foreign Official Immunity," 79 *Fordham Law Review* 2669 (2011); Harold Hongju Koh, "Foreign Official Immunity After *Samantar*: A United States Government Perspective," 44 *Vanderbilt Journal of Transitional Law* 1411 (2011).

10. *The Customary International Law of Sovereign Immunity.* How much can U.S. courts learn from customary international law about foreign immunities? See Curtis A. Bradley & Laurence R. Helfer, "International Law and the U.S. Common Law of Foreign Official Immunity," 2010 *Supreme Court Review* 213 (2010). In 2012, the International Court of Justice decided the Jurisdictional Immunities of the State Case (Germany v. Italy), 2012 I.C.J ___. The ICJ found that Italy violated customary international law when it failed

> to respect Germany's jurisdictional immunity in three ways: first, by allowing civil claims to be brought against Germany in Italian courts for war crimes committed by German forces against Italian nationals in Italy and elsewhere during World War II; second, by taking 'measures of constraint' against *Villa Vigoni*, a building in Italy owned by the German government and used for non-commercial purposes; and third, by declaring that judgments against Germany obtained in Greece for a massacre of Greek civilians by German forces during the German occupation of Greece in 1944 were enforceable in Italian courts.

Chimène I. Keitner, "*Germany v. Italy*: The International Court of Justice Affirms Principles of State Immunity," 16 *ASIL Insights*, Issue 5, at 1 (2012). The Court ruled:

> The Court considers that the rule of State immunity occupies an important place in international law and international relations. It derives from the principle of sovereign equality of States, which, as Article 2, paragraph 1, of the Charter of the United Nations makes clear, is one of the fundamental principles of the international legal order. This principle has to be viewed together with the principle that each State possesses sovereignty over its own territory and that there flows from that sovereignty the jurisdiction of the State over events and persons within that territory. Exceptions to the immunity of the State represent a departure from the principle of sovereign equality. Immunity may represent a departure from the principle of territorial sovereignty and the jurisdiction which flows from it.

2012 I.C.J. ¶ 57. How does the ICJ judgment contribute to the customary international law of sovereign immunity? See Chapter 3.

11. *International Codification of Sovereign Immunity.* Might sovereign immunity be ripe for international codification? By now, most states "have adopted some form" of the restrictive doctrine. Generally, the adoption has been by case law in civil law countries and by statute in common law systems. Joseph W. Dellapenna, Book Review, 99 *American Journal of International Law* 730, 731 (2005) (reviewing Rachel Fox, *The Law of State Immunity* (2002)). Whatever the virtues of domestic precedent or statutes, might not international legislation better suit this field? Why should there not be a treaty providing common rules for different states? The efforts of the

International Law Commission in this regard culminated in a 2004 treaty that embraces the restrictive theory of sovereign immunity. United Nations Convention on Jurisdictional Immunities of States and Their Property, 44 *International Legal Materials* 803 (2005).

D. THE ACT OF STATE DOCTRINE

Also rooted in *The Schooner Exchange*, the act of state doctrine can be sometimes confused with the doctrine of foreign sovereign immunity. To make an easy distinction, note that act of state does not provide a jurisdictional immunity. Rather, it serves as a principle of choice of law, instructing a court to apply the law of a foreign state respecting an act made by the foreign government in its own territory. The act of state doctrine does share with the doctrine of foreign sovereign immunity (and indeed with the doctrine of *forum non conveniens*) the notion of comity; all in one way or another defer to foreign governments.

There is antique support for the act of state doctrine. In Blad v. Bamfield, 3 Swans. 605 (Chancery, 1674), Blad, a Danish subject, sued Bamfield and others, English subjects, in Chancery for an injunction to stay several actions Bamfield had commenced in the English law courts. Blad had a monopoly for certain trade in Iceland, which was Danish territory, and had seized Bamfield's goods brought to Iceland in contravention of Blad's rights. In Law, Bamfield argued that the Danish royal grants to Blad violated the free-trading terms of an English-Danish treaty. In issuing a perpetual injunction against Bamfield's legal action, Lord Nottingham ruled in Chancery:

> [C]ertainly no case [Blad's] was ever better proved; for the Plaintiff hath proved letters patent from the King of Denmark for the sole trade of Iceland; a seizure by virtue of that patent; a sentence upon that seizure; a confirmation of that sentence by the Chancellor of Denmark; an execution of that sentence after confirmation; and a payment of two thirds to the King of Denmark after that execution. Now, after all this, to send it to a trial at law, where either the Court must pretend to judge of the validity of the King's letters patent in Denmark, or of the exposition and meaning of the articles of peace; or that a common jury should try whether the English have a right to trade in Iceland, is monstrous and absurd.

Id. at 606–07.

In the United States, the act of state doctrine is usually thought to have been first separately elaborated in 1897 in *Underhill v. Hernandez* and to have reached its pinnacle in 1964 in *Banco Nacional de Cuba v. Sabbatino*. Both cases follow, along with a more recent case, *Kirkpatrick*, where the Supreme Court declined to employ the doctrine.

UNDERHILL V. HERNANDEZ

168 U.S. 250 (1897)

In the early part of 1892 a revolution was initiated in Venezuela against the administration thereof, which the revolutionists claimed had ceased to be the legitimate government. The principal parties to this conflict were those who recognized Palacio as their head and those who followed the leadership of Crespo. General Hernandez belonged to the anti-administration party, and commanded its forces in the vicinity of Ciudad Bolivar. On the 8th of August 1892, an engagement took place between the armies of the two parties at Buena Vista, some seven miles from Bolivar, in which the troops under Hernandez prevailed, and on the 13th of August, Hernandez entered Bolivar and assumed command of the city. All of the local officials had in the meantime left, and the vacant positions were filled by General Hernandez, who from that date and during the period of the transactions complained of was the civil and military chief of the city and district. In October the party in revolt had achieved success generally, taking possession of the capital of Venezuela, October 6, and on October 23, 1892, the Crespo government, so called, was formally recognized as the legitimate government of Venezuela by the United States.

George F. Underhill was a citizen of the United States, who had constructed a waterworks system for the city of Bolivar under a contract with the government, and was engaged in supplying the place with water, and he also carried on a machinery-repair business. Some time after the entry of General Hernandez, Underhill applied to him as the officer in command for a passport to leave the city. Hernandez refused this request, and requests made by others in Underhill's behalf, until October 18, when a passport was given and Underhill left the country.

This action was brought to recover damages for the detention caused by reason of the refusal to grant the passport; for the alleged confinement of Underhill to his own house; and for certain alleged assaults and affronts by the soldiers of Hernandez' army.

MR. CHIEF JUSTICE FULLER, after stating the case, delivered the opinion of the court.

Every sovereign State is bound to respect the independence of every other sovereign State, and the courts of one country will not sit in judgment on the acts of the government of another done within its own territory. Redress of grievances by reason of such acts must be obtained through the means open to be availed of by sovereign powers as between themselves.

Nor can the principle be confined to lawful or recognized governments, or to cases where redress can manifestly be had through public channels. The immunity of individuals from suits brought in foreign tribunals for acts done within their own States, in the exercise of governmental authority, whether as civil officers or as military commanders, must necessarily extend to the agents of governments ruling by paramount force as matter of fact. Where a civil war prevails, that is where the people of a country are divided into two hostile parties, who take up arms and oppose one another by military force, generally speaking foreign nations do not assume to judge of the merits of the quarrel. If the party seeking to dislodge the existing government succeeds, and the independence of the government it has set up is recognized, then the acts of such government from the commencement of its existence are regarded as those of an independent nation. If the political revolt fails of success, still if actual war has been waged, acts of legitimate warfare cannot be made the basis of individual liability. * * *

We entertain no doubt upon the evidence that Hernandez was carrying on military operations in support of the revolutionary party. It may be that adherents of the side of the controversy in the particular locality where Hernandez was the leader of the movement entertained a preference for him as the future executive head of the nation, but that is beside the question. The acts complained of were the acts of a military commander representing the authority of the revolutionary party as a government, which afterwards succeeded and was recognized by the United States. We think the Circuit Court of Appeals was justified in concluding "that the acts of the defendant were the acts of the government of Venezuela, and as such are not properly the subject of adjudication in the courts of another government."

The decisions cited on plaintiff's behalf are not in point. Cases respecting arrest by military authority in the absence of the prevalence of war; or the validity of contracts between individuals entered into in aid of insurrection; or the right of revolutionary bodies to vex the commerce of the world on its common highway without incurring the penalties denounced on piracy; and the like, do not involve the questions presented here.

We agree with Circuit Court of Appeals, that "the evidence upon the trial indicated that the purpose of the defendant in his treatment of the plaintiff was to coerce the plaintiff to operate his waterworks and his repair works for the benefit of the community and the revolutionary forces," and that "it was not sufficient to have warranted a finding by the jury that the defendant was actuated by malice or any personal or private motive"; and we concur in its disposition of the rulings below. The decree of the Circuit Court is

Affirmed.

BANCO NACIONAL DE CUBA V. SABBATINO

376 U.S. 398 (1964)

MR. JUSTICE HARLAN delivered the opinion of the Court.

The question which brought this case here, and is now found to be the dispositive issue, is whether the so-called act of state doctrine serves to sustain petitioner's claims in this litigation. Such claims are ultimately found on a decree of the Government of Cuba expropriating certain property, the right to the proceeds of which is here in controversy. The act of state doctrine in its traditional formulation precludes the courts of this country from inquiring into the validity of the public acts a recognized foreign sovereign power committed within its own territory.

I.

In February and July of 1960, respondent Farr, Whitlock & Co., an American commodity broker, contracted to purchase Cuban sugar, free alongside the streamer, from a wholly owned subsidiary of Compania Azucarera Vertientes-Camaguey de Cuba (C.A.V.), a corporation organized under Cuban law whose capital stock was owned principally by United States residents. Farr, Whitlock agreed to pay for the sugar in New York upon presentation of the shipping documents and a sight draft.

On July 6, 1960, the Congress of the United States amended the Sugar Act of 1948 to permit a presidentially directed reduction of the sugar quota for Cuba. On the same day President Eisenhower exercised the granted power. The day of the congressional enactment, the Cuban Council of Ministers adopted "Law No. 851," which characterized this reduction in the Cuban sugar quota as an act of "aggression, for political purposes" on the part of the United States, justifying the taking of countermeasures by Cuba. The law gave the Cuban President and Prime Minister discretionary power to nationalize by forced expropriation property or enterprises in which American nationals had an interest. Although a system of compensation was formally provided, the possibility of payment under it may well be deemed illusory. Our State Department has described the Cuban law as "manifestly in violation of those principles of international law which have long been accepted by the free countries of the West. It is in its essence discriminatory, arbitrary and confiscatory."

Between August 6 and August 9, 1960, the sugar covered by the contract between Farr, Whitlock and C.A.V. was loaded, destined for Morocco, onto the S.S. *Hornfels*, which was standing offshore at the Cuban port of Jucaro (Santa Maria). On the day loading commenced, the Cuban President and Prime Minister, acting pursuant to Law No. 851, issued Executive Power Resolution No. 1. It provided for the compulsory expropriation of all property and enterprises, and of rights and interests arising therefrom, of certain listed companies, including C.A.V., wholly or principally owned by American nationals. The preamble reiterated the alleged injustice of the American reduction of the Cuban sugar quota and emphasized the importance of Cuba's serving as an example for other countries to follow "in their struggle to free themselves from the brutal claws of Imperialism." In consequence of the resolution, the consent of the Cuban Government was necessary before a ship carrying sugar of a named company could leave Cuban waters. In order to obtain this consent, Farr, Whitlock, on August 11, entered into contracts, identical to those it had made with C.A.V., with the Banco Para el Comercio Exterior de Cuba, an instrumentality of the Cuban Government. The S.S. *Hornfels* sailed for Morocco on August 12.

Banco Exterior assigned the bills of lading to petitioner, also an instrumentality of the Cuban Government, which instructed its agent in New York, Société Génerale, to deliver the bills and a sight draft in the sum of $175,250.69 to Farr, Whitlock in return for payment. Société Génerale's initial tender of the documents was refused by Farr, Whitlock, which on the same day was notified of C.A.V.'s claim that as rightful owner of the sugar it was entitled to the proceeds. In return for a promise not to turn the funds over to petitioner or its agent, C.A.V. agreed to indemnify Farr, Whitlock for any loss. Farr, Whitlock subsequently accepted the shipping documents, negotiated the bills of lading to its customer, and received payment for the sugar. It refused, however, to hand over the proceeds to Société Génerale. Shortly thereafter, Farr, Whitlock was served with an order of the New York Supreme Court, which had appointed Sabbatino as Temporary Receiver of C.A.V.'s New York assets, enjoining it from taking any action in regard to the money claimed by C.A.V. that might result in its removal from the State. Following this, Farr, Whitlock, pursuant to court order, transferred the funds to Sabbatino, to abide the event of a judicial determination as to their ownership.

[The Court decides that Cuba could still sue in the United States though it was an unfriendly power, rejects the contention that the case should be decided by New York law, then turns to the act of state doctrine.]

IV.

The classic American statement of the act of state doctrine, which appears to have taken root in England as early as 1674, *Blad v. Bamfield*, 3 Swans. 604, 36 Eng.Rep. 992, and began to emerge in the jurisprudence of this country in the late eighteenth and early nineteenth centuries, see *e.g., Ware v. Hylton*, 3 Dall, 199, 230; *The Schooner Exchange v. M'Faddon*, 7 Cranch 116, 135, 136, is found in *Underhill v. Hernandez*, where Chief Justice Fuller said for a unanimous Court:

> Every sovereign State is bound to respect the independence of every other sovereign State, and the courts of one country will not sit in judgment on the acts of the government of another done within its own territory. Redress of grievances by reason of such acts must be obtained through the means open to be availed of by sovereign powers as between themselves.

Following this precept the Court in that case refused to inquire into acts of Hernandez, a revolutionary Venezuelan military commander whose government had been later recognized by the United States, which were made the basis of a damage action in this country by Underhill, an American citizen, who claimed that he had been unlawfully assaulted, coerced, and detained in Venezuela by Hernandez.

None of this Court's subsequent cases in which the act of state doctrine was directly or peripherally involved manifest any retreat from *Underhill.* * * *

V.

Preliminarily, we discuss the foundations on which we deem the act of state doctrine to rest, and more particularly the question of whether state or federal law governs its application in a federal diversity case.

We do not believe that this doctrine is compelled either by the inherent nature of sovereign authority, as some of the earlier decisions seem to imply, or by some principle of international law. If a transaction takes place in one jurisdiction and the forum is in another, the forum does not by dismissing an action or by applying its own law purport to divest the first jurisdiction of its territorial sovereignty; it merely declines to adjudicate or makes applicable its own law to parties or property before it. The refusal of one country to enforce the penal laws of another is a typical example of an instance when a court will not entertain a cause of action arising in another jurisdiction. While historic notions of sovereign authority do bear upon the wisdom of employing the act of state doctrine, they do not dictate its existence.

That international law does not require application of the doctrine is evidenced by the practice of nations. Most of the countries rendering decisions on the subject fail to follow the rule rigidly. [The Court cites authorities from France, Germany, Greece, Italy, Japan, the Netherlands, Switzerland, and the United Kingdom.] No international arbitral or judicial decision discovered suggests that international law prescribes recognition of sovereign acts of foreign governments, and apparently no claim has ever been raised before an international tribunal that failure to apply the act of state doctrine constitutes a breach of international obligation. If international law does not prescribe use of the doctrine, neither does it forbid application of the rule even if it is claimed that the act of state in question violated international law. The traditional view of international law is that it establishes substantive principles for determining whether one country has wronged another. Because of its peculiar nation-to-nation character the usual method for an individual to seek relief is to exhaust local remedies and then repair to the executive authorities of his own state to persuade them to champion his claim in diplomacy or before an international tribunal. Although it is, of course, true that United States courts apply international law as a part of our own in appropriate circumstances, the public law of nations can hardly dictate to a country which is in theory wronged how to treat that wrong within its domestic borders.

Despite the broad statement in *Oetjen* [*v. Central Leather Co.*, 246 U.S. 297 (1918),] that "The conduct of the foreign relations of our Government is committed by the Constitution to the Executive and Legislative . . . Departments," it cannot of course be thought that "every case or controversy which touches foreign relations lies beyond judicial cognizance." *Baker v. Carr*, 369 U.S. 186, 211. The text of the Constitution does not require the act of state doctrine; it does not irrevocably remove from the judiciary the capacity to review the validity of foreign acts of state.

The act of state doctrine does, however, have "constitutional" underpinnings. It arises out of the basic relationships between branches of government in a system of separation of powers. It concerns the competency of dissimilar institutions to make and implement particular kinds of decisions in the area of international relations. The doctrine as formulated in past decisions expresses the strong sense of the Judicial Branch that its engagement in the task of passing on the validity of foreign acts of state may hinder rather than further this country's pursuit of goals both for itself and for the community of nations as a whole in the international sphere. Many commentators disagree with this view; they have striven by means of distinguishing and limiting past decisions and by advancing various considerations of policy to stimulate a narrowing of the apparent scope of the rule. Whatever considerations are thought to predominate, it is plain that the problems involved are uniquely federal in nature. If federal authority, in this instance this Court, orders the field of judicial competence in this area for the federal courts, and the state courts are left free to formulate their own rules, the purposes behind the doctrine could be as effectively undermined as if there had been no federal pronouncement on the subject.

We could perhaps in this diversity action avoid the question of deciding whether federal or state law is applicable to this aspect of the litigation. New York has enunciated the act of state doctrine in terms that echo those of federal decisions decided during the reign of *Swift v. Tyson*, 16 Pet. 1. * * *

However, we are constrained to make it clear that an issue concerned with a basic choice regarding the competence and function of the Judiciary and the National Executive in ordering our relationships with other members of the international community must be treated exclusively as an aspect of federal law. It seems fair to assume that the Court did not have rules like the act of state doctrine in mind when it decided *Erie R. Co. v. Tompkins*. Soon thereafter, Professor Philip C. Jessup, now a judge of the International Court of Justice, recognized the potential dangers were *Erie* extended to legal problems affecting international relations. He cautioned that rules of international law should not be left to divergent and perhaps parochial state interpretations. His basic rationale is equally applicable to the act of state doctrine. * * *

VI.

If the act of state doctrine is a principle of decision binding on federal and state courts alike but compelled by neither international law nor the Constitution, its continuing vitality depends on its capacity to reflect the proper distribution of functions between the judicial and political branches of the Government on matters bearing upon foreign affairs. It should be apparent that the greater the degree of codification or consensus concerning a particular area of international law, the more appropriate it is for the judiciary to render decisions regarding it, since the courts can then focus on the application of an agreed principle to circumstances of fact rather than on the sensitive task of establishing a principle not inconsistent with the national interest or with international justice. It is also evident that some aspects of international law touch much more sharply on national nerves than do others; the less important the implications of an issue are for our foreign relations, the weaker the justification of exclusivity in the political branches. The balance of relevant considerations may also be shifted if the government which perpetrated the challenged act of state is no longer in existence, * * * for the political interest of this country may, as a result, be measurably altered. Therefore, rather than laying down or reaffirming an inflexible and all-encompassing rule in this case, we decide only that the Judicial Branch will not examine the validity of a taking of property within its own territory by a foreign sovereign government, extant and recognized by this country at the time of suit, in the absence of a treaty or other unambiguous agreement regarding controlling legal principles, even if the complaint alleges that the taking violates customary international law.

There are few if any issues in international law today on which opinion seems to be so divided as the limitations on a state's power to expropriate the property of aliens. There is, of course, authority, in international judicial and arbitral decisions, in the expressions of national governments, and among commentators for the view that a taking is improper under international law if it is not for a public purpose, is discriminatory, or is without provision for prompt, adequate, and effective compensation. However, Communist countries, although they have in fact provided a degree of compensation after diplomatic efforts, commonly recognize no obligation on the part of the taking country. Certain representatives of the newly independent and underdeveloped countries have questioned whether rules of state responsibility toward aliens can bind nations that have not consented to them and it is argued that the traditionally articulated standards governing expropriation of property reflect "imperialist" interests and are inappropriate to the circumstances of emergent states.

The disagreement as to relevant international law standards reflects an even more basic divergence between the national interests of capital importing and capital exporting nations and between the social ideologies of those countries that favor state control of a considerable portion of the means of production and those that adhere to a free enterprise system. It is difficult to imagine the courts of this country embarking on adjudication in an area which touches more sensitively the practical and ideological goals of the various members of the community of nations.

When we consider the prospect of the courts characterizing foreign expropriations, however justifiably, as invalid under international law and ineffective to pass title, the wisdom of the precedents is confirmed. * * *

The possible adverse consequences of a conclusion to the contrary of that implicit in these cases is highlighted by contrasting that practices of the political branch with the limitations of the judicial process in matters of this kind. Following an expropriation of any significance, the Executive engages in diplomacy aimed to assure that United States citizens who are harmed are compensated fairly. Representing all claimants of this country, it will often be able, either by bilateral or multilateral talks, by submission to the United Nations, or by the employment of economic and political sanctions, to achieve some degree of general redress. Judicial determinations of invalidity of title can, on the other hand, have only an occasional impact, since they depend on the fortuitous circumstance of the property in question being brought into this country. Such decisions would, if the acts involved were declared invalid, often be likely to give offense to the expropriating country; since the concept of territorial sovereignty is so deep seated, any state may resent the refusal of the courts of another sovereign to accord validity to acts within its territorial borders. Piecemeal dispositions of this sort involving the probability of affront to another state could seriously interfere with negotiations being carried on by the Executive Branch and might prevent or render less favorable the terms of an agreement that could otherwise be reached.

Relations with third countries which have engaged in similar expropriations would not be immune from effect.

The dangers of such adjudication are present regardless of whether the State Department has, as it did in this case, asserted that the relevant act violated international law. If the Executive Branch has undertaken negotiations with an expropriating country, but has refrained from claims of violation of the law of nations, a determination to that effect by a court might be regarded as a serious insult, while a finding of compliance with international law would greatly strengthen the bargaining hand of the other state with consequent detriment to American interests.

Even if the State Department has proclaimed the impropriety of the expropriation, the stamp of approval of its view by a judicial tribunal, however impartial, might increase any affront and the judicial decision might occur at a time, almost always well after the taking, when such an impact would be contrary to our national interest. Considerably more serious and far-reaching consequences would flow from a judicial finding that international law standards had been met if that determination flew in the face of a State Department proclamation to the contrary. When articulating principles of international law in its relations with other states, the Executive Branch speaks not only as an interpreter of generally accepted and traditional rules, as would the courts, but also as an advocate of standards it believes desirable for the community of nations and protective of national concerns. In short, whatever way the matter is cut, the possibility of conflict between the Judicial and Executive Branches could hardly be avoided. * * *

However offensive to the public policy of this country and its constituent States an expropriation of this kind may be, we conclude that both the national interest and progress toward the goal of establishing the rule of law among nations are best served by maintaining intact the act of state doctrine in this realm of its application.

NOTES AND QUESTIONS

1. *The* Underhill *Doctrine.* The famous line in *Underhill*, even reaching the *New York Times,* "Underhill's Suit Dismissed: No Judicial Remedy for His Detention in Venezuela," *New York Times*, Nov. 30, 1897, at 10, was the first one in Chief Justice Fuller's opinion: "Every sovereign State is bound to respect the independence of every other sovereign State, and the courts of one country will not sit in judgment on the acts of the government done within its own territory." Though first enunciating the act of state doctrine, could *Underhill* have also been decided simply by treating General Hernandez as an agent of the Venezuelan government and then by protecting both from the jurisdiction of U.S. courts by way of the doctrine of sovereign immunity? After all, the opinion went on to say: "The acts complained of were

the acts of a military commander representing the authority of the revolutionary party as a government, which afterwards succeeded and was recognized by the United States."

2. *The Background to* Sabbatino. The political events leading to the *Sabbatino Case* were front-page news in the United States. On June 23, 1960, "Premier Fidel Castro threatened * * * to meet 'economic aggression' by the United States with the seizure of all American-owned property and business interests in Cuba." "U.S. Holdings to Be Taken If Sugar Is Cut, Castro Says," *New York Times*, June 24, 1960, at 1. On July 6, 1960, President Eisenhower "virtually ended * * * Cuba's sugar sales to the United States for this year." Tad Szulc, "U.S. Cuts Cuba Sugar Sale By 95% for Rest of Year; President Cites Hostility," *New York Times*, July 7, 1960, at 1, 9. The next day, Castro "whipped [a] crowd of several thousand into displays of frenzied anger against the United States." R. Hart Phillips, "Castro Attacks Sugar Quota as 'Imperialism,'" *New York Times*, July 8, 1960, at 1. And on August 7, 1960, the Cuban Premier proclaimed the "forcible expropriation" of all U.S.-owned companies in his country. R. Hart Phillips, "Castro Decrees Seizure of Rest of U.S. Property; Cites Cut in Sugar Quota," *New York Times*, Aug. 7, 1960, at 1. The *Sabbatino* decision of the U.S. Supreme Court also took on a high political profile. The Court's reaffirmation of the act of state doctrine itself achieved front-page status. Anthony Lewis, "High Court Bars Judging of Cuba on Expropriation," *New York Times*, Mar. 24, 1964, at 1.

3. *The Reaction to* Sabbatino. It should be no surprise that the *Sabbatino* judgment evoked an uproar in the U.S. Congress, which promptly passed what became known as the *Sabbatino* or Second Hickenlooper Amendment to the Foreign Assistance Act of 1964. The Amendment includes the following language:

> Notwithstanding any other provision of law, no court in the United States shall decline on the ground of the federal act of state doctrine to make a determination on the merits giving effect to the principles of international law in a case in which a claim of title or other right to property is asserted by any party including a foreign state (or a party claiming through such state) based upon (or traced through) a confiscation or other taking after January 1, 1959, by an act of that state in violation of the principles of international law, including the principles of compensation and the other standards set out in this subsection: *Provided*, That this subparagraph shall not be applicable (1) in any case in which an act of a foreign state is not contrary to international law or with respect to a claim of title or other right acquired pursuant to an irrevocable letter of credit of not more than 180 days duration issued in good faith prior to the time of confiscation or other taking, or (2) in any case with respect to which the President determines the application of the act of state doctrine is required in that particular case by the foreign policy interests of the United States and a suggestion to this effect is filed on his behalf in that case with the court.

22 U.S.C. § 2370(e)(2).

On remand, the U.S. District Court for the Southern District of New York followed the dictate of the *Sabbatino* Amendment and dismissed plaintiff's complaint. The Second Circuit affirmed, while the Supreme Court denied *certiorari*, effectively permitting itself to be reversed by Congress. Banco Nacional de Cuba v. Farr, 243 F.Supp. 957 (S.D.N.Y. 1965), *aff'd*, 383 F.2d 166 (2d Cir. 1967), *cert. denied*, 390 U.S. 956 (1968). See Richard A. Falk, *The Aftermath of Sabbatino* (Lyman M. Tondel, Jr. ed. 1965). What is the authority of the *Sabbatino Case* as precedent following Congress's *Sabbatino* Amendment? Of course, a U.S. court may still decide to apply *Sabbatino* and disregard the Second Hickenlooper Amendment if it finds that a taking was *not* "in violation of the principles of international law," a condition of the Amendment. Just such a finding was made in Fogade v. ENB Revocable Trust, 263 F.3d 1274 (11th Cir. 2001), where an alleged confiscation by Venezuela of property of its own nationals was held not to "implicate principles of international law." *Id.* at 1294. Interestingly, the act of state doctrine has been employed in a number of tax cases, where "the expropriation of taxpayer property (even by a new revolutionary regime) is deemed not to constitute a 'theft' for federal income tax purposes." Bobby L. Dexter, "Shock, Awe, and Expropriation: The Act of State Doctrine and Loss Deductions Under Section 165 of the Internal Revenue Code," 82 *Tulane Law Review* 849, 852 (2008).

4. Sabbatino *and the Role of the Courts.* Was the Supreme Court too deferential in principle to the legislative and executive branches in *Sabbatino*? After all, the Court was reluctant to decide a case involving an uncertain point of international law apparently for fear of reaching a conflicting opinion with that of the President or Congress. Is not the Court the branch of the U.S. government best positioned to discover and elaborate international law? Here the international law rule could be used to trump the rule of the foreign state in U.S. litigation. When should the Court turn to the executive or legislative branches for their advice as to whether such a trumping would upset U.S. foreign relations? Compare the reasoning of the Court in *Dames & Moore, Medellín, Sosa,* and *Kiobel* in Chapter 4.

W.S. KIRKPATRICK & CO. V. ENVIRONMENTAL TECTONICS CORP. INTERNATIONAL

493 U.S. 400 (1990)

JUSTICE SCALIA delivered the opinion of the Court.

In this case we must decide whether the act of state doctrine bars a court in the United States from entertaining a cause of action that does not rest upon the asserted invalidity of an official act of a foreign sovereign, but that does require imputing to foreign officials an unlawful motivation (the obtaining of bribes) in the performance of such an official act.

I

The facts as alleged in respondent's complaint are as follows: In 1981, Harry Carpenter, who was then Chairman of the Board and Chief Executive Officer of petitioner W.S. Kirkpatrick & Co., Inc. (Kirkpatrick), learned that the Republic of Nigeria was interested in contracting for the construction and equipment of an aeromedical center at Kaduna Air Force Base in Nigeria. He made arrangements with Benson "Tunde" Akindele, a Nigerian citizen, whereby Akindele would endeavor to secure the contract for Kirkpatrick. It was agreed that, in the event the contract was awarded to Kirkpatrick, Kirkpatrick would pay to two Panamanian entities controlled by Akindele a "commission" equal to 20% of the contract price, which would in turn be given as a bribe to officials of the Nigerian Government. In accordance with this plan, the contract was awarded to petitioner W.S. Kirkpatrick & Co., International (Kirkpatrick International), a wholly owned subsidiary of Kirkpatrick; Kirkpatrick paid the promised "commission" to the appointed Panamanian entities; and those funds were disbursed as bribes. All parties agree that Nigerian law prohibits both the payment and the receipt of bribes in connection with the award of a government contract.

Respondent Environmental Tectonics Corporation, International, an unsuccessful bidder for the Kaduna contract, learned of the 20% "commission" and brought the matter to the attention of the Nigerian Air Force and the United States Embassy in Lagos. Following an investigation by the Federal Bureau of Investigation, the United States Attorney for the District of New Jersey brought charges against both Kirkpatrick and Carpenter for violations of the Foreign Corrupt Practices Act of 1977, 15 U.S.C. § 78dd–1 *et seq.*, and both pleaded guilty.

Respondent then brought this civil action in the United States District Court for District of New Jersey against Carpenter, Akindele, petitioners, and others, seeking damages under the Racketeer Influenced and Corrupt Organizations Act, 18 U.S.C. §§ 1961 *et seq.*, the Robinson-Patman Act, 15 U.S.C. §§ 13 *et seq.*, and the New Jersey Anti-Racketeering Act, N.J. Stat. Ann. §§ 2C:41–2 *et seq.* (West 1982). The defendants moved to dismiss the complaint under Rule 12(b)(6) of the Federal Rules of Civil Procedure on the ground that the action was barred by the act of state doctrine.

The District Court, having requested and received a letter expressing the views of the legal adviser to the United States Department of State as to the applicability of the act of state doctrine, treated the motion as one for summary judgment under Rule 56 of the Federal Rules of Civil Procedure and granted the motion. The District Court concluded that the act of state doctrine applies "if the inquiry presented for judicial determination includes the motivation of a sovereign act which would result in embarrassment to the sovereign or constitute interference in the conduct of foreign policy of the United States." Applying that principle to the facts at hand, the court held that respondent's suit had to be dismissed because in order to prevail respondent would have to show that "the defendants or certain of them intended to wrongfully influence the decision to award the Nigerian Contract by payment of a bribe, that the Government of Nigeria, its officials or other representatives knew of the offered consideration for awarding the Nigerian Contract to Kirkpatrick, that the bribe was actually received or anticipated and that 'but for' the payment or anticipation of the payment of the bribe, ETC would have been awarded the Nigerian Contract."

The Court of Appeals for the Third Circuit reversed. Although agreeing with the District Court that "the award of a military procurement contract can be, in certain circumstances, a sufficiently formal expression of a government's public interests to trigger application" of the act of state doctrine, it found application of the doctrine unwarranted on the facts of this case. The Court of Appeals found particularly persuasive the letter to the District Court from the legal adviser to the Department of State, which had stated that in the opinion of the Department judicial inquiry into the purpose behind the act of a foreign sovereign would not produce the "unique embarrassment, and the particular interference with the conduct of foreign affairs, that may result from the judicial determination that a foreign sovereign's acts are invalid." In light of the Department's view that the interests of the Executive Branch would not be harmed by prosecution of the action, the Court of Appeals held that Kirkpatrick had not met its burden of showing that the case should not go forward; accordingly, it reversed the judgment of the District Court and remanded the case for trial. We granted certiorari.

II

This Court's description of the jurisprudential foundation for the act of state doctrine has undergone some evolution over the years. We once viewed the doctrine as an expression of international law, resting upon "the highest considerations of international comity and expediency," *Oetjen v. Central Leather Co.*, 246 U.S. 297, 303–304 (1918). We have more recently described it, however, as a consequence of domestic separation of powers, reflecting "the strong sense of the Judicial Branch that its engagement in the task of passing on the validity of foreign acts of state may hinder" the conduct of foreign affairs, *Banco Nacional de Cuba v. Sabbatino*, 376 U.S. 398, 423 (1964). Some Justices have suggested possible exceptions to application of the doctrine, where one or both of the foregoing policies would seemingly not be served: an exception, for example, for acts of state that consist of commercial transactions, since neither modern international comity nor the current position of our Executive Branch accorded sovereign immunity to such acts; or an exception for cases in which the Executive Branch has represented that it has no objection to denying validity to the foreign sovereign act, since then the courts would be impeding no foreign policy goals.

The parties have argued at length about the applicability of these possible exceptions, and, more generally, about whether the purpose of the act of state doctrine would be furthered by its application in this case. We find it unnecessary, however, to pursue those inquiries, since the factual predicate for application of the act of state doctrine does not exist. Nothing in the present suit requires the Court to declare invalid, and thus ineffective as "a rule of decision for the courts of this country," *Ricaud v. American Metal Co.*, 246 U.S. 304, 310 (1918), the official act of a foreign sovereign.

In every case in which we have held the act of state doctrine applicable, the relief sought or the defense interposed would have required a court in the United States to declare invalid the official act of a foreign sovereign performed within its own territory. In *Underhill v. Hernandez*, 168 U.S. 250, 254 (1897), holding the defendant's detention of the plaintiff to be tortious would have required denying legal effect to "acts of a military commander representing the authority of the revolutionary party as government, which afterwards succeeded and was recognized by the United States." In *Oetjen v. Central Leather Co.* and in *Ricaud v. American Metal Co.*, denying title to the party who claimed through purchase from Mexico would have required declaring that government's prior seizure of the property, within its own territory, legally ineffective. In *Sabbatino,* upholding the defendant's claim to the funds would have required a holding that Cuba's expropriation of goods located in Havana was null and void. In the present case, by contrast, neither the claim nor any asserted defense requires a determination that Nigeria's contract with Kirkpatrick International was, or was not, effective.

Petitioners point out, however, that the facts necessary to establish respondent's claim will also establish that the contract was unlawful. Specifically, they note that in order to prevail respondent must prove that petitioner Kirkpatrick made, and Nigerian officials received, payments that violate Nigerian law, which would, they assert, support a finding that the contract is invalid under Nigerian law. Assuming that to be true, it still does not suffice. The act of state doctrine is not some vague doctrine of abstention but a "*principle of decision* binding on federal and state courts alike." *Sabbatino* (emphasis added). As we said in *Ricaud,* "the act within its own boundaries of one sovereign State . . . becomes . . . a rule of decision for the courts of this country." Act of state issues only arise when a court *must decide*—that is, when the outcome of the case turns upon—the effect of official action by a foreign sovereign. When that question is not in the case, neither is the act of state doctrine. That is the situation here. Regardless of what the court's factual findings may suggest as to the legality of the Nigerian contract, its legality is simply not a question to be decided in the present suit, and there is thus no occasion to apply the rule of decision that the act of state doctrine requires.

In support of their position that the act of state doctrine bars any factual findings that may cast doubt upon the validity of foreign sovereign acts, petitioners cite Justice Holmes' opinion for the Court in *American Banana Co. v. United Fruit Co.*, 213 U.S. 347 (1909). That was a suit under the United States antitrust laws, alleging that Costa Rica's seizure of the plaintiff's property had been induced by an unlawful conspiracy. In the course of a lengthy opinion Justice Holmes observed, citing *Underhill,* that "a seizure by a state is not a thing that can be complained of elsewhere in the courts." The statement is concededly puzzling. *Underhill* does indeed stand for the proposition that a seizure by a state cannot be complained of elsewhere—in the sense of being sought to be declared *ineffective* elsewhere. The plaintiff in *American Banana*, however, like the plaintiff here, was not trying to undo or disregard the governmental action, but only to obtain damages from private parties who had procured it. Arguably, then, the statement did imply that suit would not lie if a foreign state's actions would be, though not invalidated, impugned.

Whatever Justice Holmes may have had in mind, his statement lends inadequate support to petitioners' position here, for two reasons. First, it was a brief aside, entirely unnecessary to the decision. *American Banana* was squarely decided on the ground (later substantially overruled, see *Continental Ore Co. v. Union Carbide & Carbon Corp.*, 370 U.S. 690, 704–705 (1962)) that the antitrust laws had no extraterritorial application, so that "what the defendant did in Panama or Costa Rica is not within the scope of the statute." Second, whatever support the dictum might provide for petitioners' position is more than overcome by our later holding in *United States v. Sisal Sales Corp.*, 274 U.S. 268 (1927). There we held that, *American Banana* notwithstanding, the defendant's actions in obtaining Mexico's enactment of "discriminating legislation" could form part of the basis for suit under the United States antitrust laws. Simply put, *American Banana* was not an act of state case; and whatever it said by way of dictum that might be relevant to the present case has not survived *Sisal Sales*.

Petitioners insist, however, that the policies underlying our act of state cases—international comity, respect for the sovereignty of foreign nations on their own territory, and the avoidance of embarrassment to the Executive Branch in its conduct of foreign relations—are implicated in the present case because, as the District Court found, a determination that Nigerian officials demanded and accepted a bribe "would impugn or question the nobility of a foreign nation's motivations," and would "result in embarrassment to the sovereign or constitute interference in the conduct of foreign policy of the United States." The United States, as *amicus curiae*, favors the same approach to the act of state doctrine, though disagreeing with petitioners as to the outcome it produces in the present case. We should not, the United States urges, "attach dispositive significance to the fact that this suit involves only the 'motivation' for, rather than the 'validity' of, a foreign sovereign act," and should eschew "any rigid formula for the resolution of act of state cases generally." In some future case, perhaps, "litigation . . . based on alleged corruption in the award of contracts or other commercially oriented activities of foreign governments could sufficiently touch on 'national nerves' that the act of state doctrine or related principles of abstention would appropriately be found to bar the suit," and we should therefore resolve this case on the narrowest possible ground, viz., that the letter from the legal adviser to the District Court gives sufficient indication that, "in the setting of this case," the act of state doctrine poses no bar to adjudication.

These urgings are deceptively similar to what we said in *Sabbatino*, where we observed that sometimes, even though the validity of the act of a foreign sovereign within its own territory is called into question, the policies underlying the act of state doctrine may not justify its application. We suggested that a sort of balancing approach could be applied—the balance shifting against application of the doctrine, for example, if the government that committed the "challenged act of state" is no longer in existence. But what is appropriate in order to avoid unquestioning judicial acceptance of the acts of foreign sovereigns is not similarly appropriate for the quite opposite purpose of expanding judicial incapacities where such acts are not directly (or even indirectly) involved. It is one thing to suggest, as we have, that the policies underlying the act of state doctrine should be considered in deciding whether, despite the doctrine's technical availability, it should nonetheless not be invoked; it is something quite different to suggest that those underlying policies are a doctrine unto themselves, justifying expansion of the act of state doctrine (or, as the United States puts it, unspecified "related principles of abstention") into new and uncharted fields.

The short of the matter is this: Courts in the United States have the power, and ordinarily the obligation, to decide cases and controversies properly presented to them. The act of state doctrine does not establish an exception for cases and controversies that may embarrass foreign governments, but merely requires that, in the process of deciding, the acts of foreign sovereigns taken within their own jurisdictions shall be deemed valid. That doctrine has no application to the present case because the validity of no foreign sovereign act is at issue.

The judgment of the Court of Appeals for the Third Circuit is affirmed.

It is so ordered.

NOTES AND QUESTIONS

1. *The Act of State Doctrine as a Principle of Decision*. In *Kirkpatrick*, a unanimous opinion, Justice Scalia wrote that the act of state doctrine "is not some vague doctrine of abstention but a *principle of decision* binding on federal and state courts alike." Did this decision in effect repudiate the separation of powers rationale of *Sabbatino* and move act of state more to a choice-of-law rationale? One observer noted that *Kirkpatrick* "has sharply circumscribed the reach of the doctrine." Mark Feldman, "Supreme Court Limits the Act of State Doctrine," ABA Section of International Law and Practice, 1 *Suing Foreign States: Newsletter of the Committee on Foreign Sovereign Immunity*, No. 1, at 1 (1990). Another argued that the Supreme Court had taken a "shift away from deference to the executive branch." Nowadays, judicial "deference in foreign affairs cases properly depends on the source and nature of the law in question." Curtis A. Bradley, "*Chevron* Deference and Foreign Affairs," 86 *Virginia Law Review* 649, 720–21 (2000).

2. *Abolish the Act of State Doctrine?* Should *Sabbatino* and the act of state doctrine simply be eliminated from the common law of the United States? True, the doctrine "is being referred to repeatedly in court decisions in the United States and is used in different ways by different courts." Donald W. Hoagland, "The Act of State Doctrine: Abandon It," 14 *Denver Journal of International Law and Policy* 317 (1986). However, Hoagland, a former Assistant Administrator of the U.S. Agency for International Development, argued that there are so many exceptions to the doctrine and it has been applied so confusingly, that act of state has little "integrity" left. *Id.* at 333. As an example of an exception, consider Roxas v. Marcos, 89 Haw. 91, 969 P.2d 1209 (1998), in which the Supreme Court of Hawaii refused to apply the act of state doctrine to acts of President Marcos in the Philippines seizing buried World War II treasure, holding that the acts were "carried out for Ferdinand [Marcos]'s personal benefit and were therefore a violation of international law." *Id.* at 1251. In general, as Professor Ramsey has concluded, "[d]iscontent with the act of state doctrine is widespread." Michael D. Ramsey, "Acts of State and Foreign Sovereign Obligations," 39 *Harvard International Law Journal* 1, 99 (1998).

Would it make more sense simply to use ordinary conflict-of-laws rules to determine whether foreign law, U.S. law, or international law applies in cases where the act of state doctrine might otherwise be employed? Could *Underhill*, *Sabbatino*, and *Kirkpatrick* all have been answered in more or less the way they were with choice-of-law techniques and without employing the act of state doctrine?

Is the act of state doctrine more trouble than it is worth? Monroe Leigh, formerly Legal Adviser to the U.S. Department of State, thought not, believing the act of state doctrine should be retained, but that "the doctrine needs to be properly defined and limited," a task not accomplished, in his view, by the 1987 *Restatement (Third) of the Foreign Relations Law of the*

United States. Monroe Leigh, "*Sabbatino*'s Silver Anniversary and the Restatement: No Cause for Celebration," 24 *International Lawyer* 1, 20 (1990). Another sympathetic account of the act of state doctrine concluded that the doctrine "is in great need of reform." Daniel C.K. Chow, "Rethinking the Act of State Doctrine: An Analysis in Terms of Jurisdiction to Prescribe," 62 *Washington Law Review* 397, 475 (1987). For further discussion and more recent cases, see Gregory H. Fox, "Reexamining the Act of State Doctrine: An Integrated Conflicts Analysis," 33 *Harvard International Law Journal* 521 (1992), and Andrew D. Patterson, "The Act of State Doctrine is Alive and Well: Why Critics of the Doctrine are Wrong," 15 *University of California Davis Journal of International Law and Policy* 111 (2008).

APPENDIX

■ ■ ■

CONSTITUTION OF THE UNITED STATES OF AMERICA

ARTICLE I

SECTION 1. All legislative Powers herein granted shall be vested in a Congress of the United States, which shall consist of a Senate and House of Representatives. * * *

SECTION 8. The Congress shall have Power * * *

To regulate Commerce with foreign Nations, and among the several States, and with the Indian Tribes;

To establish an uniform Rule of Naturalization[;]

To define and punish Piracies and Felonies committed on the high Seas, and Offences against the Law of Nations;

To declare War, grant Letters of Marque and Reprisal, and make Rules concerning Captures on Land and Water;

To raise and support Armies, but no Appropriation of Money to that Use shall be for a longer Term than two Years;

To provide and maintain a Navy;

To make Rules for the Government and Regulation of the land and naval Forces;

To provide for calling forth the Militia to execute the Laws of the Union, suppress Insurrections and repel Invasions;

To provide for organizing, arming, and disciplining, the Militia, and for governing such Part of them as may be employed in the Service of the United States, reserving to the States respectively, the Appointment of the Officers, and the Authority of training the Militia according to the discipline prescribed by Congress; * * *

To make all Laws which shall be necessary and proper for carrying into Execution the foregoing Powers, and all other Powers vested by this Constitution in the Government of the United States, or in any Department or Officer thereof. * * *

SECTION 10. No State shall enter into any Treaty, Alliance, or Confederation; grant Letters of Marque and Reprisal; coin Money; emit Bills of Credit; make any Thing but gold and silver Coin a Tender in Payment of Debts; pass any Bill of Attainder, ex post facto Law, or Law impairing the Obligation of Contracts, or grant any Title of Nobility.

No State shall, without the Consent of the Congress, lay any Imposts or Duties on Imports or Exports, except what may be absolutely necessary for executing its inspection Laws; and the net Produce of all Duties and Imposts, laid by any State on Imports or Exports, shall be for the Use of the Treasury of the United States; and all such Laws shall be subject to the Revision and Controul of the Congress.

No State shall, without the Consent of Congress, lay any Duty of Tonnage, keep Troops, or Ships of War in time of Peace, enter into any Agreement or Compact with another State, or with a foreign Power, or engage in War, unless actually invaded, or in such imminent Danger as will not admit of delay.

ARTICLE II

SECTION 1. The executive Power shall be vested in a President of the United States of America. * * *

SECTION 2. The President shall be Commander in Chief of the Army and Navy of the United States, and of the Militia of the several States, when called into the actual Service of the United States[.]

He shall have Power, by and with the Advice and Consent of the Senate, to make Treaties, provided two thirds of the Senators present concur; and he shall nominate, and by and with the Advice and Consent of the Senate, shall appoint Ambassadors, other public Ministers and Consuls[.]

ARTICLE III

SECTION 1. The judicial Power of the United States, shall be vested in one supreme Court, and in such inferior Courts as the Congress may from time to time ordain and establish. * * *

SECTION 2. The judicial Power shall extend to all Cases, in Law and Equity, arising under this Constitution, the Laws of the United States, and Treaties made, or which shall be made, under their Authority;—to all Cases affecting Ambassadors, other public Ministers and Consuls;—to all Cases of admiralty and maritime Jurisdiction;—to Controversies to which the United States shall be a Party;—to Controversies between two or more States;—between a State and Citizens of another State;—between Citizens of different States;—between Citizens of the same State claiming Lands under Grants of different States, and between a State, or the Citizens thereof, and foreign States, Citizens or Subjects.

In all Cases affecting Ambassadors, other public Ministers and Consuls, and those in which a State shall be Party, the supreme Court shall have original Jurisdiction. In all the other Cases before mentioned, the supreme Court shall have appellate Jurisdiction, both as to Law and

Fact, with such Exceptions, and under such Regulations as the Congress shall make. * * *

ARTICLE IV

SECTION 1. Full Faith and Credit shall be given in each State to the public Acts, Records, and judicial Proceedings of every other State. And the Congress may by general Laws prescribe the Manner in which such Acts, Records and Proceedings shall be proved, and the Effect thereof.

SECTION 2. The Citizens of each State shall be entitled to all Privileges and Immunities of Citizens in the several States. * * *

ARTICLE VI

All Debts contracted and Engagements entered into, before the Adoption of this Constitution, shall be as valid against the United States under this Constitution, as under the Confederation.

This Constitution, and the Laws of the United States which shall be made in Pursuance thereof; and all Treaties made, or which shall be made, under the Authority of the United States, shall be the supreme Law of the Land; and the Judges in every State shall be bound thereby, any Thing in the Constitution or Laws of any State to the Contrary notwithstanding. * * *

AMENDMENT I

Congress shall make no law respecting an establishment of religion, or prohibiting the free exercise thereof; or abridging the freedom of speech, or of the press; or of the right of the people peaceably to assemble, and to petition the Government for a redress of grievances.

AMENDMENT II

A well regulated Militia, being necessary to the security of a free State, the right of the people to keep and bear Arms, shall not be infringed.

AMENDMENT III

No Soldier shall, in time of peace be quartered in any house, without the consent of the Owner, nor in time of war, but in a manner to be prescribed by law.

AMENDMENT IV

The right of the people to be secure in their persons, houses, papers, and effects, against unreasonable searches and seizures, shall not be violated, and no Warrants shall issue, but upon probable cause, supported by Oath or affirmation, and particularly describing the place to be searched, and the persons or things to be seized.

AMENDMENT V

No person shall be held to answer for a capital, or otherwise infamous crime, unless on a presentment or indictment of a Grand Jury, except in cases arising in the land or naval forces, or in the Militia, when in actual service in time of War or public danger; nor shall any person be subject for the same offence to be twice put in jeopardy of life or limb; nor shall be compelled in any criminal case to be a witness against himself, nor be deprived of life, liberty, or property, without due process of law; nor shall private property be taken for public use, without just compensation.

AMENDMENT VI

In all criminal prosecutions, the accused shall enjoy the right to a speedy and public trial, by an impartial jury of the State and district wherein the crime shall have been committed, which district shall have been previously ascertained by law, and to be informed of the nature and cause of the accusation; to be confronted with the witnesses against him; to have compulsory process for obtaining witnesses in his favor, and to have the Assistance of Counsel for his defence.

AMENDMENT VII

In suits at common law, where the value in controversy shall exceed twenty dollars, the right of trial by jury shall be preserved, and no fact tried by a jury, shall be otherwise reexamined in any Court of the United States, than according to the rules of the common law.

AMENDMENT VIII

Excessive bail shall not be required, nor excessive fines imposed, nor cruel and unusual punishments inflicted.

AMENDMENT IX

The enumeration in the Constitution, of certain rights, shall not be construed to deny or disparage others retained by the people.

AMENDMENT X

The powers not delegated to the United States by the Constitution, nor prohibited by it to the States, are reserved to the States respectively, or to the people. * * *

AMENDMENT XIV

SECTION 1. All persons born or naturalized in the United States, and subject to the jurisdiction thereof, are citizens of the United States and of the State wherein they reside. No State shall make or enforce any law which shall abridge the privileges or immunities of citizens of the United States; nor shall any State deprive any person of life, liberty, or property, without due process of law; nor deny to any person within its jurisdiction the equal protection of the laws. * * *

CHARTER OF THE UNITED NATIONS

June 26, 1945, 59 Stat. 1031, T.S. No. 993, 3 Bevans 1153

WE THE PEOPLES OF THE UNITED NATIONS DETERMINED

to save succeeding generations from the scourge of war, which twice in our lifetime has brought untold sorrow to mankind, and

to reaffirm faith in fundamental human rights, in the dignity and worth of the human person, in the equal rights of men and women and of nations large and small, and

to establish conditions under which justice and respect for the obligations arising from treaties and other sources of international law can be maintained, and

to promote social progress and better standards of life in larger freedom,

AND FOR THESE ENDS

to practice tolerance and live together in peace with one another as good neighbors, and

to unite our strength to maintain international peace and security, and

to ensure, by the acceptance of principles and the institution of methods, that armed force shall not be used, save in the common interest, and

to employ international machinery for the promotion of the economic and social advancement of all peoples,

HAVE RESOLVED TO COMBINE OUR EFFORTS TO ACCOMPLISH THESE AIMS.

Accordingly, our respective Governments, through representatives assembled in the city of San Francisco, who have exhibited their full powers found to be in good and due form, have agreed to the present Charter of the United Nations and do hereby establish an international organization to be known as the United Nations.

CHAPTER I

PURPOSES AND PRINCIPLES

Article 1

The Purposes of the United Nations are:

1. To maintain international peace and security, and to that end: to take effective collective measures for the prevention and removal of threats to the peace, and for the suppression of acts of aggression or other breaches of the peace, and to bring about by peaceful means, and in

conformity with the principles of justice and international law, adjustment or settlement of international disputes or situations which might lead to a breach of the peace;

2. To develop friendly relations among nations based on respect for the principle of equal rights and self-determination of peoples, and to take other appropriate measures to strengthen universal peace;

3. To achieve international cooperation in solving international problems of an economic, social, cultural, or humanitarian character, and in promoting and encouraging respect for human rights and for fundamental freedoms for all without distinction as to race, sex, language, or religion; and

4. To be a center for harmonizing the actions of nations in the attainment of these common ends.

Article 2

The Organization and its Members, in pursuit of the Purposes stated in Article 1, shall act in accordance with the following Principles.

1. The Organization is based on the principle of the sovereign equality of all its Members.

2. All Members, in order to ensure to all of them the rights and benefits resulting from membership, shall fulfil in good faith the obligations assumed by them in accordance with the present Charter.

3. All Members shall settle their international disputes by peaceful means in such a manner that international peace and security, and justice, are not endangered.

4. All Members shall refrain in their international relations from the threat or use of force against the territorial integrity or political independence of any state, or in any other manner inconsistent with the Purposes of the United Nations.

5. All Members shall give the United Nations every assistance in any action it takes in accordance with the present Charter, and shall refrain from giving assistance to any state against which the United Nations is taking preventive or enforcement action.

6. The Organization shall ensure that states which are not Members of the United Nations act in accordance with these Principles so far as may be necessary for the maintenance of international peace and security.

7. Nothing contained in the present Charter shall authorize the United Nations to intervene in matters which are essentially within the domestic jurisdiction of any state or shall require the Members to submit such matters to settlement under the present Charter; but this principle shall not prejudice the application of enforcement measures under Chapter VII.

CHAPTER II

MEMBERSHIP

Article 3

The original Members of the United Nations shall be the states which, having participated in the United Nations Conference on International Organization at San Francisco, or having previously signed the Declaration by United Nations of January 1, 1942, sign the present Charter and ratify it in accordance with Article 110.

Article 4

1. Membership in the United Nations is open to all other peace-loving states which accept the obligations contained in the present Charter and, in the judgment of the Organization, are able and willing to carry out these obligations.

2. The admission of any such state to membership in the United Nations will be effected by a decision of the General Assembly upon the recommendation of the Security Council.

Article 5

A Member of the United Nations against which preventive or enforcement action has been taken by the Security Council may be suspended from the exercise of the rights and privileges of membership by the General Assembly upon the recommendation of the Security Council. The exercise of these rights and privileges may be restored by the Security Council.

Article 6

A Member of the United Nations which has persistently violated the Principles contained in the present Charter may be expelled from the Organization by the General Assembly upon the recommendation of the Security Council.

CHAPTER III

ORGANS

Article 7

1. There are established as the principal organs of the United Nations: a General Assembly, a Security Council, an Economic and Social Council, a Trusteeship Council, an International Court of Justice, and a Secretariat.

2. Such subsidiary organs as may be found necessary may be established in accordance with the present Charter.

Article 8

The United Nations shall place no restrictions on the eligibility of men and women to participate in any capacity and under conditions of equality in its principal and subsidiary organs.

CHAPTER IV

THE GENERAL ASSEMBLY

Composition

Article 9

1. The General Assembly shall consist of all the Members of the United Nations.

2. Each Member shall have not more than five representatives in the General Assembly.

Functions and Powers

Article 10

The General Assembly may discuss any questions or any matters within the scope of the present Charter or relating to the powers and functions of any organs provided for in the present Charter, and, except as provided in Article 12, may make recommendations to the Members of the United Nations or to the Security Council or to both on any such questions or matters.

Article 11

1. The General Assembly may consider the general principles of cooperation in the maintenance of international peace and security, including the principles governing disarmament and the regulation of armaments, and may make recommendations with regard to such principles to the Members or to the Security Council or to both.

2. The General Assembly may discuss any questions relating to the maintenance of international peace and security brought before it by any Member of the United Nations, or by the Security Council, or by a state which is not a Member of the United Nations in accordance with Article 35, paragraph 2, and, except as provided in Article 12, may make recommendations with regard to any such questions to the state or states concerned or to the Security Council or to both. Any such question on which action is necessary shall be referred to the Security Council by the General Assembly either before or after discussion.

3. The General Assembly may call the attention of the Security Council to situations which are likely to endanger international peace and security.

4. The powers of the General Assembly set forth in this Article shall not limit the general scope of Article 10.

Article 12

1. While the Security Council is exercising in respect of any dispute or situation the functions assigned to it in the present Charter, the General Assembly shall not make any recommendation with regard to that dispute or situation unless the Security Council so requests.

2. The Secretary-General, with the consent of the Security Council, shall notify the General Assembly at each session of any matters relative to the maintenance of international peace and security which are being dealt with by the Security Council and shall similarly notify the General Assembly, or the Members of the United Nations if the General Assembly is not in session, immediately the Security Council ceases to deal with such matters.

Article 13

1. The General Assembly shall initiate studies and make recommendations for the purpose of:

a. promoting international cooperation in the political field and encouraging the progressive development of international law and its codification;

b. promoting international cooperation in the economic, social, cultural, educational, and health fields, and assisting in the realization of human rights and fundamental freedoms for all without distinction as to race, sex, language, or religion.

2. The further responsibilities, functions, and powers of the General Assembly with respect to matters mentioned in paragraph 1(b) above are set forth in Chapters IX and X.

Article 14

Subject to the provisions of Article 12, the General Assembly may recommend measures for the peaceful adjustment of any situation, regardless of origin, which it deems likely to impair the general welfare or friendly relations among nations, including situations resulting from a violation of the provisions of the present Charter setting forth the Purposes and Principles of the United Nations.

Article 15

1. The General Assembly shall receive and consider annual and special reports from the Security Council; these reports shall include an account of the measures that the Security Council has decided upon or taken to maintain international peace and security.

2. The General Assembly shall receive and consider reports from the other organs of the United Nations.

Article 16

The General Assembly shall perform such functions with respect to the international trusteeship system as are assigned to it under Chapters XII and XIII, including the approval of the trusteeship agreements for areas not designated as strategic.

Article 17

1. The General Assembly shall consider and approve the budget of the Organization.

2. The expenses of the Organization shall be borne by the Members as apportioned by the General Assembly.

3. The General Assembly shall consider and approve any financial and budgetary arrangements with specialized agencies referred to in Article 57 and shall examine the administrative budgets of such specialized agencies with a view to making recommendations to the agencies concerned.

Voting

Article 18

1. Each member of the General Assembly shall have one vote.

2. Decisions of the General Assembly on important questions shall be made by a two-thirds majority of the members present and voting. These questions shall include: recommendations with respect to the maintenance of international peace and security, the election of the non-permanent members of the Security Council, the election of the members of the Economic and Social Council, the election of the members of the Trusteeship Council in accordance with paragraph 1(c) of Article 86, the admission of new Members to the United Nations, the suspension of the rights and privileges of membership, the expulsion of Members, questions relating to the operation of the trusteeship system, and budgetary questions.

3. Decisions on other questions, including the determination of additional categories of questions to be decided by a two-thirds majority, shall be made by a majority of the members present and voting.

Article 19

A Member of the United Nations which is in arrears in the payment of its financial contributions to the Organization shall have no vote in the General Assembly if the amount of its arrears equals or exceeds the amount of the contributions due from it for the preceding two full years. The General Assembly may, nevertheless, permit such a Member to vote if it is satisfied that the failure to pay is due to conditions beyond the control of the Member.

Procedure

Article 20

The General Assembly shall meet in regular annual sessions and in such special sessions as occasion may require. Special sessions shall be convoked by the Secretary-General at the request of the Security Council or of a majority of the Members of the United Nations.

Article 21

The General Assembly shall adopt its own rules of procedure. It shall elect its President for each session.

Article 22

The General Assembly may establish such subsidiary organs as it deems necessary for the performance of its functions.

CHAPTER V

THE SECURITY COUNCIL

Composition

Article 23[a]

1. The Security Council shall consist of fifteen Members of the United Nations. The Republic of China, France, the Union of Soviet Socialist Republics, the United Kingdom of Great Britain and Northern Ireland, and the United States of America shall be permanent members of the Security Council. The General Assembly shall elect ten other Members of the United Nations to be non-permanent members of the Security Council, due regard being specially paid, in the first instance to the contribution of Members of the United Nations to the maintenance of international peace and security and to the other purposes of the Organization, and also to equitable geographical distribution.

2. The non-permanent members of the Security Council shall be elected for a term of two years. In the first election of the non-permanent members after the increase of the membership of the Security Council from eleven to fifteen, two of the four additional members shall be chosen for a term of one year. A retiring member shall not be eligible for immediate re-election.

3. Each member of the Security Council shall have one representative.

[a] Amended text of Article 23 that came into force August 31, 1965.

Functions and Powers

Article 24

1. In order to ensure prompt and effective action by the United Nations, its Members confer on the Security Council primary responsibility for the maintenance of international peace and security, and agree that in carrying out its duties under this responsibility the Security Council acts on their behalf.

2. In discharging these duties the Security Council shall act in accordance with the Purposes and Principles of the United Nations. The specific powers granted to the Security Council for the discharge of these duties are laid down in Chapters VI, VII, VIII, and XII.

3. The Security Council shall submit annual and, when necessary, special reports to the General Assembly for its consideration.

Article 25

The Members of the United Nations agree to accept and carry out the decisions of the Security Council in accordance with the present Charter.

Article 26

In order to promote the establishment and maintenance of international peace and security with the least diversion for armaments of the world's human and economic resources, the Security Council shall be responsible for formulating, with the assistance of the Military Staff Committee referred to in article 47, plans to be submitted to the Members of the United Nations for the establishment of a system for the regulation of armaments.

Voting

Article 27[b]

1. Each member of the Security Council shall have one vote.

2. Decisions of the Security Council on procedural matters shall be made by an affirmative vote of nine members.

3. Decisions of the Security Council on all other matters shall be made by an affirmative vote of nine members including the concurring votes of the permanent members; provided that, in decisions under Chapter VI, and under paragraph 3 of Article 52, a party to a dispute shall abstain from voting.

---

[b] Amended text of Article 27 that came into force August 31, 1965.

Procedure

Article 28

1. The Security Council shall be so organized as to be able to function continuously. Each member of the Security Council shall for this purpose be represented at all times at the seat of the Organization.

2. The Security Council shall hold periodic meetings at which each of its members may, if it so desires, be represented by a member of the government or by some other specially designated representative.

3. The Security Council may hold meetings at such places other than the seat of the Organization as in its judgment will best facilitate its work.

Article 29

The Security Council may establish such subsidiary organs as it deems necessary for the performance of its functions.

Article 30

The Security Council shall adopt its own rules of procedure, including the method of selecting its President.

Article 31

Any Member of the United Nations which is not a member of the Security Council may participate, without vote, in the discussion of any question brought before the Security Council whenever the latter considers that the interests of that Member are specially affected.

Article 32

Any Member of the United Nations which is not a member of the Security Council or any state which is not a Member of the United Nations, if it is a party to a dispute under consideration by the Security Council, shall be invited to participate, without vote, in the discussion relating to the dispute. The Security Council shall lay down such conditions as it deems just for the participation of a state which is not a Member of the United Nations.

CHAPTER VI

PACIFIC SETTLEMENT OF DISPUTES

Article 33

1. The parties to any dispute, the continuance of which is likely to endanger the maintenance of international peace and security, shall, first of all, seek a solution by negotiation, enquiry, mediation, conciliation, arbitration, judicial settlement, resort to regional agencies or arrangements, or other peaceful means of their own choice.

2. The Security Council shall, when it deems necessary, call upon the parties to settle their dispute by such means.

Article 34

The Security Council may investigate any dispute, or any situation which might lead to international friction or give rise to a dispute, in order to determine whether the continuance of the dispute or situation is likely to endanger the maintenance of international peace and security.

Article 35

1. Any Member of the United Nations may bring any dispute, or any situation of the nature referred to in Article 34, to the attention of the Security Council or of the General Assembly.

2. A state which is not a Member of the United Nations may bring to the attention of the Security Council or of the General Assembly any dispute to which it is a party if it accepts in advance, for the purposes of the dispute, the obligations of pacific settlement provided in the present Charter.

3. The proceedings of the General Assembly in respect of matters brought to its attention under this Article will be subject to the provisions of Articles 11 and 12.

Article 36

1. The Security Council may, at any stage of a dispute of the nature referred to in Article 33 or of a situation of like nature, recommend appropriate procedures or methods of adjustment.

2. The Security Council should take into consideration any procedures for the settlement of the dispute which have already been adopted by the parties.

3. In making recommendations under this Article the Security Council should also take into consideration that legal disputes should as a general rule be referred by the parties to the International Court of Justice in accordance with the provisions of the Statute of the Court.

Article 37

1. Should the parties to a dispute of the nature referred to in Article 33 fail to settle it by the means indicated in that Article, they shall refer it to the Security Council.

2. If the Security Council deems that the continuance of the dispute is in fact likely to endanger the maintenance of international peace and security, it shall decide whether to take action under Article 36 or to recommend such terms of settlement as it may consider appropriate.

Article 38

Without prejudice to the provisions of Articles 33 to 37, the Security Council may, if all the parties to any dispute so request, make recommendations to the parties with a view to a pacific settlement of the dispute.

CHAPTER VII

ACTION WITH RESPECT TO THREATS TO THE PEACE, BREACHES OF THE PEACE, AND ACTS OF AGGRESSION

Article 39

The Security Council shall determine the existence of any threat to the peace, breach of the peace, or act of aggression and shall make recommendations, or decide what measures shall be taken in accordance with Articles 41 and 42, to maintain or restore international peace and security.

Article 40

In order to prevent an aggravation of the situation, the Security Council may, before making the recommendations or deciding upon the measures provided for in Article 39, call upon the parties concerned to comply with such provisional measures as it deems necessary or desirable. Such provisional measures shall be without prejudice to the rights, claims, or position of the parties concerned. The Security Council shall duly take account of failure to comply with such provisional measures.

Article 41

The Security Council may decide what measures not involving the use of armed force are to be employed to give effect to its decisions, and it may call upon the Members of the United Nations to apply such measures. These may include complete or partial interruption of economic relations and of rail, sea, air, postal, telegraphic, radio, and other means of communication, and the severance of diplomatic relations.

Article 42

Should the Security Council consider that measures provided for in Article 41 would be inadequate or have proved to be inadequate, it may take such action by air, sea, or land forces as may be necessary to maintain or restore international peace and security. Such action may include demonstrations, blockade, and other operations by air, sea, or land forces of Members of the United Nations.

Article 43

1. All Members of the United Nations, in order to contribute to the maintenance of international peace and security, undertake to make

available to the Security Council, on its call and in accordance with a special agreement or agreements, armed forces, assistance, and facilities, including rights of passage, necessary for the purpose of maintaining international peace and security.

2. Such agreement or agreements shall govern the numbers and types of forces, their degree of readiness and general location, and the nature of the facilities and assistance to be provided.

3. The agreement or agreements shall be negotiated as soon as possible on the initiative of the Security Council. They shall be concluded between the Security Council and Members or between the Security Council and groups of Members and shall be subject to ratification by the signatory states in accordance with their respective constitutional processes.

Article 44

When the Security Council has decided to use force it shall, before calling upon a Member not represented on it to provide armed forces in fulfillment of the obligations assumed under Article 43, invite that Member, if the Member so desires, to participate in the decisions of the Security Council concerning the employment of contingents of that Member's armed forces.

Article 45

In order to enable the United Nations to take urgent military measures, Members shall hold immediately available national air-force contingents for combined international enforcement action. The strength and degree of readiness of these contingents and plans for their combined action shall be determined, within the limits laid down in the special agreement or agreements referred to in Article 43, by the Security Council with the assistance of the Military Staff Committee.

Article 46

Plans for the application of armed force shall be made by the Security Council with the assistance of the Military Staff Committee.

Article 47

1. There shall be established a Military Staff Committee to advise and assist the Security Council on all questions relating to the Security Council's military requirements for the maintenance of international peace and security, the employment and command of forces placed at its disposal, the regulation of armaments, and possible disarmament.

2. The Military Staff Committee shall consist of the Chiefs of Staff of the permanent members of the Security Council or their representatives. Any Member of the United Nations not permanently represented on the Committee shall be invited by the Committee to be associated with it

when the efficient discharge of the Committee's responsibilities requires the participation of that Member in its work.

3. The Military Staff Committee shall be responsible under the Security Council for the strategic direction of any armed forces placed at the disposal of the Security Council. Questions relating to the command of such forces shall be worked out subsequently.

4. The Military Staff Committee, with the authorization of the Security Council and after consultation with appropriate regional agencies, may establish regional subcommittees.

Article 48

1. The action required to carry out the decisions of the Security Council for the maintenance of international peace and security shall be taken by all the Members of the United Nations or by some of them, as the Security Council may determine.

2. Such decisions shall be carried out by the Members of the United Nations directly and through their action in the appropriate international agencies of which they are members.

Article 49

The Members of the United Nations shall join in affording mutual assistance in carrying out the measures decided upon by the Security Council.

Article 50

If preventive or enforcement measures against any state are taken by the Security Council, any other state, whether a Member of the United Nations or not, which finds itself confronted with special economic problems arising from the carrying out of those measures shall have the right to consult the Security Council with regard to a solution of those problems.

Article 51

Nothing in the present Charter shall impair the inherent right of individual or collective self-defense if an armed attack occurs against a Member of the United Nations, until the Security Council has taken measures necessary to maintain international peace and security. Measures taken by Members in the exercise of this right of self-defense shall be immediately reported to the Security Council and shall not in any way affect the authority and responsibility of the Security Council under the present Charter to take at any time such action as it deems necessary in order to maintain or restore international peace and security.

CHAPTER VIII

REGIONAL ARRANGEMENTS

Article 52

1. Nothing in the present Charter precludes the existence of regional arrangements or agencies for dealing with such matters relating to the maintenance of international peace and security as are appropriate for regional action, provided that such arrangements or agencies and their activities are consistent with the Purposes and Principles of the United Nations.

2. The Members of the United Nations entering into such arrangements or constituting such agencies shall make every effort to achieve pacific settlement of local disputes through such regional arrangements or by such regional agencies before referring them to the Security Council.

3. The Security Council shall encourage the development of pacific settlement of local disputes through such regional arrangements or by such regional agencies either on the initiative of the states concerned or by reference from the Security Council.

4. This Article in no way impairs the application of Articles 34 and 35.

Article 53

1. The Security Council shall, where appropriate, utilize such regional arrangements or agencies for enforcement action under its authority. But no enforcement action shall be taken under regional arrangements or by regional agencies without the authorization of the Security Council, with the exception of measures against any enemy state, as defined in paragraph 2 of this Article, provided for pursuant to Article 107 or in regional arrangements directed against renewal of aggressive policy on the part of any such state, until such time as the Organization may, on request of the Governments concerned, be charged with the responsibility for preventing further aggression by such a state.

2. The term enemy state as used in paragraph 1 of this Article applies to any state which during the Second World War has been an enemy of any signatory of the present Charter.

Article 54

The Security Council shall at all times be kept fully informed of activities undertaken or in contemplation under regional arrangements or by regional agencies for the maintenance of international peace and security.

CHAPTER IX

INTERNATIONAL ECONOMIC AND SOCIAL COOPERATION

Article 55

With a view to the creation of conditions of stability and well-being which are necessary for peaceful and friendly relations among nations based on respect for the principle of equal rights and self-determination of peoples, the United Nations shall promote:

a. higher standards of living, full employment, and conditions of economic and social progress and development;

b. solutions of international economic, social, health, and related problems; and international cultural and educational cooperation; and

c. universal respect for, and observance of, human rights and fundamental freedoms for all without distinction as to race, sex, language, or religion.

Article 56

All Members pledge themselves to take joint and separate action in cooperation with the Organization for the achievement of the purposes set forth in Article 55.

Article 57

1. The various specialized agencies, established by intergovernmental agreement and having wide international responsibilities, as defined in their basic instruments, in economic, social, cultural, educational, health, and related fields, shall be brought into relationship with the United Nations in accordance with the provisions of Article 63.

2. Such agencies thus brought into relationship with the United Nations are hereinafter referred to as specialized agencies.

Article 58

The Organization shall make recommendations for the coordination of the policies and activities of the specialized agencies.

Article 59

The Organization shall, where appropriate, initiate negotiations among the states concerned for the creation of any new specialized agencies required for the accomplishment of the purposes set forth in Article 55.

Article 60

Responsibility for the discharge of the functions of the Organization set forth in this Chapter shall be vested in the General Assembly and, under the authority of the General Assembly, in the Economic and Social Council, which shall have for this purpose the powers set forth in Chapter X.

CHAPTER X

THE ECONOMIC AND SOCIAL COUNCIL

Composition

Article 61

1. The Economic and Social Council shall consist of eighteen Members of the United Nations elected by the General Assembly.

2. Subject to the provisions of paragraph 3, six members of the Economic and Social Council shall be elected each year for a term of three years. A retiring member shall be eligible for immediate re-election.

3. At the first election, eighteen members of the Economic and Social Council shall be chosen. The term of office of six members so chosen shall expire at the end of one year, and of six other members at the end of two years, in accordance with arrangements made by the General Assembly.

4. Each member of the Economic and Social Council shall have one representative.

Functions and Powers

Article 62

1. The Economic and Social Council may make or initiate studies and reports with respect to international economic, social, cultural, educational, health, and related matters and may make recommendations with respect to any such matters to the General Assembly, to the Members of the United Nations, and to the specialized agencies concerned.

2. It may make recommendations for the purpose of promoting respect for, and observance of, human rights and fundamental freedoms for all.

3. It may prepare draft conventions for submission to the General Assembly, with respect to matters falling within its competence.

4. It may call, in accordance with the rules prescribed by the United Nations, international conferences on matters falling within its competence.

Article 63

1. The Economic and Social Council may enter into agreements with any of the agencies referred to in Article 57, defining the terms on which the agency concerned shall be brought into relationship with the United Nations. Such agreement shall be subject to approval by the General Assembly.

2. It may coordinate the activities of the specialized agencies through consultation with and recommendations to such agencies and through recommendations to the General Assembly and to the Members of the United Nations.

Article 64

1. The Economic and Social Council may take appropriate steps to obtain regular reports from the specialized agencies. It may make arrangements with the Members of the United Nations and with the specialized agencies to obtain reports on the steps taken to give effect to its own recommendations and to recommendations on matters falling within its competence made by the General Assembly.

2. It may communicate its observations on these reports to the General Assembly.

Article 65

The Economic and Social Council may furnish information to the Security Council and shall assist the Security Council upon its request.

Article 66

1. The Economic and Social Council shall perform such functions as fall within its competence in connection with the carrying out of the recommendations of the General Assembly.

2. It may, with the approval of the General Assembly, perform services at the request of specialized agencies.

3. It shall perform such other functions as are specified elsewhere in the present Charter or as may be assigned to it by the General Assembly.

Voting

Article 67

1. Each member of the Economic and Social Council shall have one vote.

2. Decisions of the Economic and Social Council shall be made by a majority of the members present and voting.

Procedure

Article 68

The Economic and Social Council shall set up commissions in economic and social fields and for the promotion of human rights, and such other commissions as may be required for the performance of its functions.

Article 69

The Economic and Social Council shall invite any Member of the United Nations to participate, without vote, in its deliberations on any matter of particular concern to that Member.

Article 70

The Economic and Social Council may make arrangements for representatives of the specialized agencies to participate, without vote, in its deliberations and in those of the commissions established by it, and for its representatives to participate in the deliberations of the specialized agencies.

Article 71

The Economic and Social Council may make suitable arrangements for consultation with non-governmental organizations which are concerned with matters within its competence. Such arrangements may be made with international organizations and, where appropriate, with national organizations after consultation with the Member of the United Nations concerned.

Article 72

1. The Economic and Social Council shall adopt its own rules of procedure, including the method of selecting its President.

2. The Economic and Social Council shall meet as required in accordance with its rules, which shall include provision for the convening of meetings on the request of a majority of its members.

CHAPTER XI

DECLARATION REGARDING NON-SELF-GOVERNING TERRITORIES

Article 73

Members of the United Nations which have or assume responsibilities for the administration of territories whose peoples have not yet attained a full measure of self-government recognize the principle that the interests of the inhabitants of these territories are paramount, and accept as a sacred trust the obligation to promote to the utmost, within the system of international peace and security established by the present Charter, the well-being of the inhabitants of these territories, and, to this end:

a. to ensure, with due respect for the culture of the peoples concerned, their political, economic, social, and educational advancement, their just treatment, and their protection against abuses;

b. to develop self-government, to take due account of the political aspirations of the peoples, and to assist them in the progressive development of their free political institutions, according to the particular circumstances of each territory and its peoples and their varying stages of advancement;

c. to further international peace and security;

d. to promote constructive measures of development, to encourage research, and to cooperate with one another and, when and where appropriate, with specialized international bodies with a view to the practical achievement of the social, economic, and scientific purposes set forth in this Article; and

e. to transmit regularly to the Secretary-General for information purposes, subject to such limitation as security and constitutional considerations may require, statistical and other information of a technical nature relating to economic, social, and educational conditions in the territories for which they are respectively responsible other than those territories to which Chapters XII and XIII apply.

Article 74

Members of the United Nations also agree that their policy in respect of the territories to which this Chapter applies, no less than in respect of their metropolitan areas, must be based on the general principle of good-neighborliness, due account being taken of the interests and well-being of the rest of the world, in social, economic, and commercial matters.

CHAPTER XII

INTERNATIONAL TRUSTEESHIP SYSTEM

Article 75

The United Nations shall establish under its authority an international trusteeship system for the administration and supervision of such territories as may be placed thereunder by subsequent individual agreements. These territories are hereinafter referred to as trust territories.

Article 76

The basic objectives of the trusteeship system, in accordance with the Purposes of the United Nations laid down in Article I of the present Charter, shall be:

a. to further international peace and security;

b. to promote the political, economic, social, and educational advancement of the inhabitants of the trust territories, and their progressive development towards self-government or independence as may be appropriate to the particular circumstances of each territory and its peoples and the freely expressed wishes of the peoples concerned, and as may be provided by the terms of each trusteeship agreement;

c. to encourage respect for human rights and for fundamental freedoms for all without distinction as to race, sex, language, or religion, and to encourage recognition of the interdependence of the peoples of the world; and

d. to ensure equal treatment in social, economic, and commercial matters for all Members of the United Nations and their nationals, and also equal treatment for the latter in the administration of justice, without prejudice to the attainment of the foregoing objectives and subject to the provisions of Article 80.

Article 77

1. The trusteeship system shall apply to such territories in the following categories as may be placed thereunder by means of trusteeship agreements:

a. territories now held under mandate;

b. territories which may be detached from enemy states as a result of the Second World War; and

c. territories voluntarily placed under the system by states responsible for their administration.

2. It will be a matter for subsequent agreement as to which territories in the foregoing categories will be brought under the trusteeship system and upon what terms.

Article 78

The trusteeship system shall not apply to territories which have become Members of the United Nations, relationship among which shall be based on respect for the principle of sovereign equality.

Article 79

The terms of trusteeship for each territory to be placed under the trusteeship system, including any alteration or amendment, shall he agreed upon by the states directly concerned, including the mandatory power in the case of territories held under mandate by a Member of the United Nations, and shall be approved as provided for in Articles 83 and 85.

Article 80

1. Except as may be agreed upon in individual trusteeship agreements, made under Articles 77, 79, and 81, placing each territory under the trusteeship system, and until such agreements have been concluded, nothing in this Chapter shall be construed in or of itself to alter in any manner the rights whatsoever of any states or any peoples or the terms of existing international instruments to which Members of the United Nations may respectively be parties.

2. Paragraph 1 of this Article shall not be interpreted as giving grounds for delay or postponement of the negotiation and conclusion of agreements for placing mandated and other territories under the trusteeship system as provided for in Article 77.

Article 81

The trusteeship agreement shall in each case include the terms under which the trust territory will be administered and designate the authority which will exercise the administration of the trust territory. Such authority, hereinafter called the administering authority, may be one or more states or the Organization itself.

Article 82

There may be designated, in any trusteeship agreement, a strategic area or areas which may include part or all of the trust territory to which the agreement applies, without prejudice to any special agreement or agreements made under Article 43.

Article 83

1. All functions of the United Nations relating to strategic areas, including the approval of the terms of the trusteeship agreements and of their alteration or amendment, shall be exercised by the Security Council.

2. The basic objectives set forth in Article 76 shall be applicable to the people of each strategic area.

3. The Security Council shall, subject to the provisions of the trusteeship agreements and without prejudice to security considerations, avail itself of the assistance of the Trusteeship Council to perform those

functions of the United Nations under the trusteeship system relating to political, economic, social, and educational matters in the strategic areas.

Article 84

It shall be the duty of the administering authority to ensure that the trust territory shall play its part in the maintenance of international peace and security. To this end the administering authority may make use of volunteer forces, facilities, and assistance from the trust territory in carrying the obligations towards the Security Council undertaken in this regard by the administering authority, as well as for local defense and the maintenance of law and order within the trust territory.

Article 85

1. The functions of the United Nations with regard to trusteeship agreements for all areas not designated as strategic, including the approval of the terms of the trusteeship agreements and of their alteration or amendment, shall be exercised by the General Assembly.

2. The Trusteeship Council, operating under the authority of the General Assembly, shall assist the General Assembly in carrying out these functions.

CHAPTER XIII

THE TRUSTEESHIP COUNCIL

Composition

Article 86

1. The Trusteeship Council shall consist of the following Members of the United Nations:

a. those Members administering trust territories;

b. such of those Members mentioned by name in Article 23 as are not administering trust territories; and

c. as many other Members elected for three-year terms by the General Assembly as may be necessary to ensure that the total number of members of the Trusteeship Council is equally divided between those Members of the United Nations which administer trust territories and those which do not.

2. Each member of the Trusteeship Council shall designate one specially qualified person to represent it therein.

Functions and Powers

Article 87

The General Assembly and, under its authority, the Trusteeship Council, in carrying out their functions, may:

a. consider reports submitted by the administering authority;

b. accept petitions and examine them in consultation with the administering authority;

c. provide for periodic visits to the respective trust territories at times agreed upon with the administering authority; and

d. take these and other actions in conformity with the terms of the trusteeship agreements.

Article 88

The Trusteeship Council shall formulate a questionnaire on the political, economic, social, and educational advancement of the inhabitants of each trust territory, and the administering authority for each trust territory within the competency of the General Assembly shall make an annual report to the General Assembly upon the basis of such questionnaire.

Voting

Article 89

1. Each member of the Trusteeship Council shall have one vote.

2. Decisions of the Trusteeship Council shall be made by a majority of the members present and voting.

Procedure

Article 90

1. The Trusteeship Council shall adopt its own rules of procedure, including the method of selecting its President.

2. The Trusteeship Council shall meet as required in accordance with its rules, which shall include provision for the convening of meetings on the request of a majority of its members.

Article 91

The Trusteeship Council shall, when appropriate, avail itself of the assistance of the Economic and Social Council and of the specialized agencies in regard to matters with which they are respectively concerned.

CHAPTER XIV

THE INTERNATIONAL COURT OF JUSTICE

Article 92

The International Court of Justice shall be the principal judicial organ of the United Nations. It shall function in accordance with the annexed Statute, which is based upon the Statute of the Permanent Court of International Justice and forms an integral part of the present Charter.

Article 93

1. All Members of the United Nations are *ipso facto* parties to the Statute of the International Court of Justice.

2. A state which is not a Member of the United Nations may become a party to the Statute of the International Court of Justice on conditions to be determined in each case by the General Assembly upon the recommendation of the Security Council.

Article 94

1. Each Member of the United Nations undertakes to comply with the decision of the International Court of Justice in any case to which it is a party.

2. If any party to a case fails to perform the obligations incumbent upon it under a judgment rendered by the Court, the other party may have recourse to the Security Council, which may, if it deems necessary, make recommendations or decide upon measures to be taken to give effect to the judgment.

Article 95

Nothing in the present Charter shall prevent Members of the United Nations from entrusting the solution of their differences to other tribunals by virtue of agreements already in existence or which may be concluded in the future.

Article 96

1. The General Assembly or the Security Council may request the International Court of Justice to give an advisory opinion on any legal question.

2. Other organs of the United Nations and specialized agencies, which may at any time be so authorized by the General Assembly, may also request advisory opinions of the Court on legal questions arising within the scope of their activities.

CHAPTER XV

THE SECRETARIAT

Article 97

The Secretariat shall comprise a Secretary-General and such staff as the Organization may require. The Secretary-General shall be appointed by the General Assembly upon the recommendation of the Security Council. He shall be the chief administrative officer of the Organization.

Article 98

The Secretary-General shall act in that capacity in all meetings of the General Assembly, of the Security Council, of the Economic and Social Council, and of the Trusteeship Council, and shall perform such other functions as are entrusted to him by these organs. The Secretary-General shall make an annual report to the General Assembly on the work of the Organization.

Article 99

The Secretary-General may bring to the attention of the Security Council any matter which in his opinion may threaten the maintenance of international peace and security.

Article 100

1. In the performance of their duties the Secretary-General and the staff shall not seek or receive instructions from any government or from any other authority external to the Organization. They shall refrain from any action which might reflect on their position as international officials responsible only to the Organization.

2. Each Member of the United Nations undertakes to respect the exclusively international character of the responsibilities of the Secretary-General and the staff and not to seek to influence them in the discharge of their responsibilities.

Article 101

1. The staff shall be appointed by the Secretary-General under regulations established by the General Assembly.

2. Appropriate staffs shall be permanently assigned to the Economic and Social Council, the Trusteeship Council, and, as required, to other organs of the United Nations. These staffs shall form a part of the Secretariat.

3. The paramount consideration in the employment of the staff and in the determination of the conditions of service shall be the necessity of securing the highest standards of efficiency, competence, and integrity. Due regard shall be paid to the importance of recruiting the staff on as wide a geographical basis as possible.

CHAPTER XVI

MISCELLANEOUS PROVISIONS

Article 102

1. Every treaty and every international agreement entered into by any Member of the United Nations after the present Charter comes into

force shall as soon as possible be registered with the Secretariat and published by it.

2. No party to any such treaty or international agreement which has not been registered in accordance with the provisions of paragraph 1 of this Article may invoke that treaty or agreement before any organ of the United Nations.

Article 103

In the event of a conflict between the obligations of the Members of the United Nations under the present Charter and their obligations under any other international agreement, their obligations under the present Charter shall prevail.

Article 104

The Organization shall enjoy in the territory of each of its Members such legal capacity as may be necessary for the exercise of its functions and the fulfillment of its purposes.

Article 105

1. The Organization shall enjoy in the territory of each of its Members such privileges and immunities as are necessary for the fulfillment of its purposes.

2. Representatives of the Members of the United Nations and officials of the Organization shall similarly enjoy such privileges and immunities as are necessary for the independent exercise of their functions in connection with the Organization.

3. The General Assembly may make recommendations with a view to determining the details of the application of paragraphs 1 and 2 of this Article or may propose conventions to the Members of the United Nations for this purpose.

CHAPTER XVII

TRANSITIONAL SECURITY ARRANGEMENTS

Article 106

Pending the coming into force of such special agreements referred to in Article 43 as in the opinion of the Security Council enable it to begin the exercise of its responsibilities under Article 42, the parties to the Four-Nation Declaration, signed at Moscow, October 30, 1943, and France, shall, in accordance with the provisions of paragraph 5 of that Declaration, consult with one another and as occasion requires with other Members of the United Nations with a view to such joint action on behalf of the Organization as may be necessary for the purpose of maintaining international peace and security.

Article 107

Nothing in the present Charter shall invalidate or preclude action, in relation to any state which during the Second World War has been an enemy of any signatory to the present Charter, taken or authorized as a result of that war by the Governments having responsibility for such action.

CHAPTER XVIII

AMENDMENTS

Article 108

Amendments to the present Charter shall come into force for all Members of the United Nations when they have been adopted by a vote of two thirds of the members of the General Assembly and ratified in accordance with their respective constitutional processes by two thirds of the Members of the United Nations, including all the permanent members of the Security Council.

Article 109[c]

1. A General Conference of the Members of the United Nations for the purpose of reviewing the present Charter may be held at a date and place to be fixed by a two-thirds vote of the members of the General Assembly and by a vote of any nine members of the Security Council. Each Member of the United Nations shall have one vote in the conference.

2. Any alteration of the present Charter recommended by a two-thirds vote of the conference shall take effect when ratified in accordance with their respective constitutional processes by two thirds of the Members of the United Nations including all the permanent members of the Security Council.

3. If such a conference has not been held before the tenth annual session of the General Assembly following the coming into force of the present Charter, the proposal to call such a conference shall be placed on the agenda of that session of the General Assembly, and the conference shall be held if so decided by a majority vote of the members of the General Assembly and by a vote of any seven members of the Security Council.

Article 110

1. The present Charter shall be ratified by the signatory states in accordance with their respective constitutional processes.

2. The ratifications shall be deposited with the Government of the United States of America which shall notify all the signatory states of

---

[c] Amended text of Article 109 that came into force June 12, 1968.

each deposit as well as the Secretary-General of the Organization when he has been appointed.

3. The present Charter shall come into force upon the deposit of ratifications by the Republic of China, France, the Union of Soviet Socialist Republics, the United Kingdom of Great Britain and Northern Ireland, and the united States of America, and by a majority of the other signatory states. A protocol of the ratifications deposited shall thereupon be drawn up by the Government of the United States of America, which shall communicate copies thereof to all the signatory states.

4. The states signatory to the present Charter which ratify it after it has come into force will become original Members of the United Nations on the date of the deposit of their respective ratifications.

Article 111

The present Charter, of which the Chinese, French, Russian, English, and Spanish texts are equally authentic, shall remain deposited in the archives of the Government of the United States of America. Duly certified copies thereof shall be transmitted by that Government to the Governments of the other signatory states.

IN FAITH WHEREOF the representatives of the Governments of the United Nations have signed the present Charter.

DONE at the city of San Francisco the sixth day of June, one thousand nine hundred and forty-five.

STATUTE OF THE INTERNATIONAL COURT OF JUSTICE

Article 1

THE INTERNATIONAL COURT OF JUSTICE established by the Charter of the United Nations as the principal judicial organ of the United Nations shall be constituted and shall function in accordance with the provisions of the present Statute.

CHAPTER I

ORGANIZATION OF THE COURT

Article 2

The Court shall be composed of a body of independent judges, elected regardless of their nationality from among persons of high moral character, who possess the qualifications required in their respective countries for appointment to the highest judicial offices, or are jurisconsults of recognized competence in international law.

Article 3

1. The Court shall consist of fifteen members, no two of whom may be nationals of the same state.

2. A person who for the purposes of membership in the Court could be regarded as a national of more than one state shall be deemed to be a national of the one in which he ordinarily exercises civil and political rights.

Article 4

1. The members of the Court shall be elected by the General Assembly and by the Security Council from a list of persons nominated by the national groups in the Permanent Court of Arbitration, in accordance with the following provisions.

2. In the case of Members of the United Nations not represented in the Permanent Court of Arbitration, candidates shall be nominated by national groups appointed for this purpose by their governments under the same conditions as those prescribed for members of the Permanent Court of Arbitration by Article 44 of the Convention of The Hague of 1907 for the pacific settlement of international disputes.

3. The conditions under which a state which is a party to the present Statute but is not a Member of the United Nations may participate in electing the members of the Court shall, in the absence of a special agreement, be laid down by the General Assembly upon recommendation of the Security Council.

Article 5

1. At least three months before the date of the election, the Secretary-General of the United Nations shall address a written request to the members of the Permanent Court of Arbitration belonging to the states which are parties to the present Statute, and to the members of the national groups appointed under Article 4, paragraph 2, inviting them to undertake, within a given time, by national groups, the nomination of persons in a position to accept the duties of a member of the Court.

2. No group may nominate more than four persons, not more than two of whom shall be of their own nationality. In no case may the number of candidates nominated by a group be more than double the number of seats to be filled.

Article 6

Before making these nominations, each national group is recommended to consult its highest court of justice, its legal faculties and schools of law, and its national academics and national sections of international academies devoted to the study of law.

Article 7

1. The Secretary-General shall prepare a list in alphabetical order of all the persons thus nominated. Save as provided in Article 12, Paragraph 2, these shall be the only persons eligible.

2. The Secretary-General shall submit this list to the General Assembly and to the Security Council.

Article 8

The General Assembly and the Security Council shall proceed independently of one another to elect the members of the Court.

Article 9

At every election, the electors shall bear in mind not only that the persons to be elected should individually possess the qualifications required, but also that in the body as a whole the representation of the main forms of civilization and of the principal legal systems of the world should be assured.

Article 10

1. Those candidates who obtain an absolute majority of votes in the General Assembly and in the Security Council shall be considered as elected.

2. Any vote of the Security Council, whether for the election of judges or for the appointment of members of the conference envisaged in

Article 12, shall be taken without any distinction between permanent and non-permanent members of the Security Council.

3. In the event of more than one national of the same state obtaining an absolute majority of the votes both of the General Assembly and of the Security Council, the eldest of these only shall be considered as elected.

Article 11

If, after the first meeting held for the purpose of the election, one or more seats remain to be filled, a second and, if necessary, a third meeting shall take place.

Article 12

1. If, after the third meeting, one or more seats remain unfilled, a joint conference consisting of six members, three appointed by the General Assembly and three by the Security Council, may be formed at any time at the request of either the General Assembly or the Security Council, for the purpose of choosing by the vote of an absolute majority one name for each seat still vacant, to submit to the General Assembly and the Security Council for their respective acceptance.

2. If the joint conference is unanimously agreed upon any person who fulfils the required conditions, he may be included in its list, even though he was not included in the list of nominations referred to in Article 7.

3. If the joint conference is satisfied that it will not be successful in procuring an election, those members of the Court who have already been elected shall, within a period to be fixed by the Security Council, proceed to fill the vacant seats by selection from among those candidates who have obtained votes either in the General Assembly or in the Security Council.

4. In the event of an equality of votes among the judges, the eldest judge shall have a casting vote.

Article 13

1. The members of the Court shall be elected for nine years and may be re-elected; provided, however, that of the judges elected at the first election, the terms of five judges shall expire at the end of three years and the terms of five more judges shall expire at the end of six years.

2. The judges whose terms are to expire at the end of the above-mentioned initial periods of three and six years shall be chosen by lot to be drawn by the Secretary-General immediately after the first election has been completed.

3. The members of the Court shall continue to discharge their duties until their places have been filled. Though replaced, they shall finish any cases which they may have begun.

4. In the case of the resignation of a member of the Court, the resignation shall be addressed to the President of the Court for transmission to the Secretary-General. This last notification makes the place vacant.

Article 14

Vacancies shall be filled by the same method as that laid down for the first election, subject to the following provision: the Secretary-General shall, within one month of the occurrence of the vacancy, proceed to issue the invitations provided for in Article 5, and the date of the election shall be fixed by the Security Council.

Article 15

A member of the Court elected to replace a member whose term of office has not expired shall hold office for the remainder of his predecessor's term.

Article 16

1. No member of the Court may exercise any political or administrative function, or engage in any other occupation of a professional nature.

2. Any doubt on this point shall be settled by the decision of the Court.

Article 17

1. No member of the Court may act as agent, counsel, or advocate in any case.

2. No member may participate in the decision of any case in which he has previously taken part as agent, counsel, or advocate for one of the parties, or as a member of a national or international court, or of a commission of enquiry, or in any other capacity.

3. Any doubt on this point shall be settled by the decision of the Court.

Article 18

1. No member of the Court can be dismissed unless, in the unanimous opinion of the other members, he has ceased to fulfil the required conditions.

2. Formal notification thereof shall be made to the Secretary-General by the Registrar.

3. This notification makes the place vacant.

Article 19

The members of the Court, when engaged on the business of the Court, shall enjoy diplomatic privileges and immunities.

Article 20

Every member of the Court shall, before taking up his duties, make a solemn declaration in open court that he will exercise his powers impartially and conscientiously.

Article 21

1. The Court shall elect its President and Vice President for three years; they may be re-elected.

2. The Court shall appoint its Registrar and may provide for the appointment of such others as may be necessary.

Article 22

1. The seat of the Court shall be established at The Hague. This, however, shall not prevent the Court from sitting and exercising its functions elsewhere whenever the Court considers it desirable.

2. The President and the Registrar shall reside at the seat of the Court.

Article 23

1. The Court shall remain permanently in session, except during the judicial vacations, the dates and duration of which shall be fixed by the Court.

2. Members of the Court are entitled to periodic leave, the dates and duration of which shall be fixed by the Court, having in mind the distance between The Hague and the home of each judge.

3. Members of the Court shall be bound, unless they are on leave or prevented from attending by illness or other serious reasons duly explained to the President, to hold themselves permanently at the disposal of the Court.

Article 24

1. If, for some special reason, a member of the Court considers that he should not take part in the decision of a particular case, he shall so inform the President.

2. If the President considers that for some special reason one of the members of the Court should not sit in a particular case, he shall give him notice accordingly.

3. If in any such case the member of the Court and the President disagree, the matter shall be settled by the decision of the Court.

Article 25

1. The full Court shall sit except when it is expressly provided otherwise in the present Statute.

2. Subject to the condition that the number of judges available to constitute the Court is not thereby reduced below eleven, the Rules of the Court may provide for allowing one or more judges, according to circumstances and in rotation, to be dispensed from sitting.

3. A quorum of nine judges shall suffice to constitute the Court.

Article 26

1. The Court may from time to time form one or more chambers, composed of three or more judges as the Court may determine, for dealing with particular categories of cases; for example, labor cases and cases relating to transit and communications.

2. The Court may at any time form a chamber for dealing with a particular case. The number of judges to constitute such a chamber shall be determined by the Court with the approval of the parties.

3. Cases shall be heard and determined by the chambers provided for in this Article if the parties so request.

Article 27

A judgment given by any of the chambers provided for in Articles 26 and 29 shall be considered as rendered by the Court.

Article 28

The chambers provided for in Articles 26 and 29 may, with the consent of the parties, sit and exercise their functions elsewhere than at The Hague.

Article 29

With a view to the speedy despatch of business, the Court shall form annually a chamber composed of five judges which, at the request of the parties, may hear and determine cases by summary procedure. In addition, two judges shall be selected for the purpose of replacing judges who find it impossible to sit.

Article 30

1. The Court shall frame rules for carrying out its functions. In particular, it shall lay down rules of procedure.

2. The Rules of the Court may provide for assessors to sit with the Court or with any of its chambers, without the right to vote.

Article 31

1. Judges of the nationality of each of the parties shall retain their right to sit in the case before the Court.

2. If the Court includes upon the Bench a judge of the nationality of one of the parties, any other party may choose a person to sit as judge. Such person shall be chosen preferably from among those persons who have been nominated as candidates as provided in Articles 4 and 5.

3. If the Court includes upon the Bench no judge of the nationality of the parties, each of these parties may proceed to choose a judge as provided in paragraph 2 of this Article.

4. The provisions of this Article shall apply to the case of Articles 26 and 29. In such cases, the President shall request one or, if necessary, two of the members of the Court forming the chamber to give place to the members of the Court of the nationality of the parties concerned, and, failing such, or if they are unable to be present, to the judges specially chosen by the parties.

5. Should there be several parties in the same interest, they shall, for the purpose of the preceding provisions, be reckoned as one party only. Any doubt upon this point shall be settled by the decision of the Court.

6. Judges chosen as laid down in paragraphs 2, 3, and 4 of this Article shall fulfil the conditions required by Articles 2, 17 (paragraph 2), 20, and 24 of the present Statute. They shall take part in the decision on terms of complete equality with their colleagues.

Article 32

I. Each member of the Court shall receive an annual salary.

2. The President shall receive a special annual allowance.

3. The Vice-President shall receive a special allowance for every day on which he acts as President.

4. The judges chosen under Article 31, other than members of the Court, shall receive compensation for each day on which they exercise their functions.

5. These salaries, allowances, and compensation shall be fixed by the General Assembly. They may not be decreased during the term of office.

6. The salary of the Registrar shall be fixed by the General Assembly on the proposal of the Court.

7. Regulations made by the General Assembly shall fix the conditions under which retirement pensions may be given to members of the Court and to the Registrar, and the conditions under which members

of the Court and the Registrar shall have their traveling expenses refunded.

8. The above salaries, allowances, and compensation shall be free of all taxation.

Article 33

The expenses of the Court shall be borne by the United Nations in such a manner as shall be decided by the General Assembly.

CHAPTER II

COMPETENCE OF THE COURT

Article 34

1. Only states may be parties in cases before the Court.

2. The Court, subject to and in conformity with its Rules, may request of public international organizations information relevant to cases before it, and shall receive such information presented by such organizations on their own initiative.

3. Whenever the construction of the constituent instrument of a public international organization or of an international convention adopted thereunder is in question in a case before the Court, the Registrar shall so notify the public international organization concerned and shall communicate to it copies of all the written proceedings.

Article 35

1. The Court shall be open to the states parties to the present Statute.

2. The conditions under which the Court shall be open to other states shall, subject to the special provisions contained in treaties in force, be laid down by the Security Council, but in no case shall such conditions place the parties in a position of inequality before the Court.

3. When a state which is not a Member of the United Nations is a party to a case, the Court shall fix the amount which that party is to contribute towards the expenses of the Court. This provision shall not apply if such state is bearing a share of the expenses of the Court.

Article 36

1. The jurisdiction of the Court comprises all cases which the parties refer to it and all matters specially provided for in the Charter of the United Nations or in treaties and conventions in force.

2. The states parties to the present Statute may at any time declare that they recognize as compulsory *ipso facto* and without special agreement, in relation to any other state accepting the same obligation, the jurisdiction of the Court in all legal disputes concerning:

a. the interpretation of a treaty;

b. any question of international law;

c. the existence of any fact which, if established, would constitute a breach of an international obligation;

d. the nature or extent of the reparation to be made for the breach of an international obligation.

3. The declarations referred to above may be made unconditionally or on condition of reciprocity on the part of several or certain states, or for a certain time.

4. Such declarations shall be deposited with the Secretary-General of the United Nations, who shall transmit copies thereof to the parties to the Statute and to the Registrar of the Court.

5. Declarations made under Article 36 of the Statute of the Permanent Court of International Justice and which are still in force shall be deemed, as between the parties to the present Statute, to be acceptances of the compulsory jurisdiction of the International Court of Justice for the period which they still have to run and in accordance with their terms.

6. In the event of a dispute as to whether the Court has jurisdiction, the matter shall be settled by the decision of the Court.

Article 37

Whenever a treaty or convention in force provides for reference of a matter to a tribunal to have been instituted by the League of Nations, or to the Permanent Court of International Justice, the matter shall, as between the parties to the present Statute, be referred to the International Court of Justice.

Article 38

1. The Court, whose function is to decide in accordance with international law such disputes as are submitted to it, shall apply:

a. international conventions, whether general or particular, establishing rules expressly recognized by the contesting states;

b. international custom, as evidence of a general practice accepted as law;

c. the general principles of law recognized by civilized nations;

d. subject to the provisions of Article 59, judicial decisions and the teachings of the most highly qualified publicists of the various nations, as subsidiary means for the determination of rules of law.

2. This provision shall not prejudice the power of the Court to decide a case *ex aequo et bono,* if the parties agree thereto.

CHAPTER III

PROCEDURE

Article 39

1. The official languages of the Court shall be French and English. If the parties agree that the case shall be conducted in French, the judgment shall be delivered in French. If the parties agree that the case shall be conducted in English, the judgment shall be delivered in English.

2. In the absence of an agreement as to which language shall be employed, each party may, in the pleadings, use the language which it prefers; the decision of the Court shall be given in French and English. In this case the Court shall at the same time determine which of the two texts shall be considered as authoritative.

3. The Court shall, at the request of any party, authorize a language other than French or English to be used by that party.

Article 40

1. Cases are brought before the Court, as the case may be, either by the notification of the special agreement or by a written application addressed to the Registrar. In either case the subject of the dispute and the parties shall be indicated.

2. The Registrar shall forthwith communicate the application to all concerned.

3. He shall also notify the Members of the United Nations through the Secretary-General, and also any other states entitled to appear before the Court.

Article 41

1. The Court shall have the power to indicate, if it considers that circumstances so require, any provisional measures which ought to be taken to preserve the respective rights of either party.

2. Pending the final decision, notice of the measures suggested shall forthwith be given to the parties and to the Security Council.

Article 42

1. The parties shall be represented by agents.

2. They may have the assistance of counsel or advocates before the Court.

3. The agents, counsel, and advocates of parties before the Court shall enjoy the privileges and immunities necessary to the independent exercise of their duties.

Article 43

1. The procedure shall consist of two parts: written and oral.

2. The written proceedings shall consist of the communication to the Court and to the parties of memorials, counter-memorials and, if necessary, replies; also all papers and documents in support.

3. These communications shall be made through the Registrar, in the order and within the time fixed by the Court.

4. A certified copy of every document produced by one party shall be communicated to the other party.

5. The oral proceedings shall consist of the hearing by the Court of witnesses, experts, agents, counsel, and advocates.

Article 44

1. For the service of all notices upon persons other than the agents, counsel, and advocates, the Court shall apply direct to the government of the state upon whose territory the notice has to be served.

2. The same provision shall apply whenever steps are to be taken to procure evidence on the spot.

Article 45

The hearing shall be under the control of the President or, if he is unable to preside, of the Vice President; if neither is able to preside, the senior judge present shall preside.

Article 46

The hearing in Court shall be public, unless the Court shall decide otherwise, or unless the parties demand that the public be not admitted.

Article 47

1. Minutes shall be made at each hearing and signed by the Registrar and the President.

2. These minutes alone shall be authentic.

Article 48

The Court shall make orders for the conduct of the case, shall decide the form and time in which each party must conclude its arguments, and make all arrangements connected with the taking of evidence.

Article 49

The Court may, even before the hearing begins, call upon the agents to produce any document or to supply any explanations. Formal note shall be taken of any refusal.

Article 50

The Court may, at any time, entrust any individual, body, bureau, commission, or other organization that it may select, with the task of carrying out an enquiry or giving an expert opinion.

Article 51

During the hearing any relevant questions are to be put to the witnesses and experts under the conditions laid down by the Court in the rules of procedure referred to in Article 30.

Article 52

After the Court has received the proofs and evidence within the time specified for the purpose, it may refuse to accept any further oral or written evidence that one party may desire to present unless the other side consents.

Article 53

1. Whenever one of the parties does not appear before the Court, or fails to defend its case, the other party may call upon the Court to decide in favor of its claim.

2. The Court must, before doing so, satisfy itself, not only that it has jurisdiction in accordance with Articles 36 and 37, but also that the claim is well founded in fact and law.

Article 54

1. When, subject to the control of the Court, the agents, counsel, and advocates have completed their presentation of the case, the President shall declare the hearing closed.

2. The Court shall withdraw to consider the judgment.

3. The deliberations of the Court shall take place in private and remain secret.

Article 55

1. All questions shall be decided by a majority of the judges present.

2. In the event of an equality of votes, the President or the judge who acts in his place shall have a casting vote.

Article 56

1. The judgment shall state the reasons on which it is based.

2. It shall contain the names of the judges who have taken part in the decision.

Article 57

If the judgment does not represent in whole or in part the unanimous opinion of the judges, any judge shall be entitled to deliver a separate opinion.

Article 58

The judgment shall be signed by the President and by the Registrar. It shall be read in open court, due notice having been given to the agents.

Article 59

The decision of the Court has no binding force except between the parties and in respect of that particular case.

Article 60

The judgment is final and without appeal. In the event of dispute as to the meaning or scope of the judgment, the Court shall construe it upon the request of any party.

Article 61

1. An application for revision of a judgment may be made only when it is based upon the discovery of some fact of such a nature as to be a decisive factor, which fact was, when the judgment was given, unknown to the Court and also to the party claiming revision, always provided that such ignorance was not due to negligence.

2. The proceedings for revision shall be opened by a judgment of the Court expressly recording the existence of the new fact, recognizing that it has such a character as to lay the case open to revision, and declaring the application admissible on this ground.

3. The Court may require previous compliance with the terms of the judgment before it admits proceedings in revision.

4. The application for revision must be made at latest within six months of the discovery of the new fact.

5. No application for revision may be made after the lapse of ten years from the date of the judgment.

Article 62

1. Should a state consider that it has an interest of a legal nature which may be affected by the decision in the case, it may submit a request to the Court to be permitted to intervene.

2. It shall be for the Court to decide upon this request.

Article 63

1. Whenever the construction of a convention to which states other than those concerned in the case are parties is in question, the Registrar shall notify all such states forthwith.

2. Every state so notified has the right to intervene in the proceedings; but if it uses this right, the construction given by the judgment will be equally binding upon it.

Article 64

Unless otherwise decided by the Court, each party shall bear its own costs.

CHAPTER IV

ADVISORY OPINIONS

Article 65

1. The Court may give an advisory opinion on any legal question at the request of whatever body may be authorized by or in accordance with the Charter of the United Nations to make such a request.

2. Questions upon which the advisory opinion of the Court is asked shall be laid before the Court by means of a written request containing an exact statement of the question upon which an opinion is required, and accompanied by all documents likely to throw light upon the question.

Article 66

1. The Registrar shall forthwith give notice of the request for an advisory opinion to all states entitled to appear before the Court.

2. The Registrar shall also, by means of a special and direct communication, notify any state entitled to appear before the Court or international organization considered by the Court or, should it not be sitting, by the President, as likely to be able to furnish information on the question, that the Court will be prepared to receive, within a time limit to be fixed by the President, written statements, or to hear, at a public sitting to be held for the purpose, oral statements relating to the question.

3. Should any such state entitled to appear before the Court have failed to receive the special communication referred to in paragraph 2 of this Article, such state may express a desire to submit a written statement or to be heard; and the Court will decide.

4. States and organizations having presented written or oral statements or both shall be permitted to comment on the statements made by other states or organizations in the form, to the extent, and within the time limits which the Court, or, should it not be sitting, the President, shall decide in each particular case. Accordingly, the Registrar

shall in due time communicate any such written statements to states and organizations having submitted similar statements.

Article 67

The Court shall deliver its advisory opinions in open court, notice having been given to the Secretary-General and to the representatives of Members of the United Nations, of other states and of international organizations immediately concerned.

Article 68

In the exercise of its advisory functions the Court shall further be guided by the provisions of the present Statute which apply in contentious cases to the extent to which it recognizes them to be applicable.

CHAPTER V

AMENDMENT

Article 69

Amendments to the present Statute shall be effected by the same procedure as is provided by the Charter of the United Nations for amendments to that Charter, subject however to any provisions which the General Assembly upon recommendation of the Security Council may adopt concerning the participation of states which are parties to the present Statute but are not Members of the United Nations.

Article 70

The Court shall have power to propose such amendments to the present Statute as it may deem necessary, through written communications to the Secretary-General, for consideration in conformity with the provisions of Article 69.

UNIVERSAL DECLARATION OF HUMAN RIGHTS

General Assembly Resolution 217A (III), U.N. Doc. A/810, at 71 (1948)

Article 1

All human beings are born free and equal in dignity and rights. They are endowed with reason and conscience and should act towards one another in a spirit of brotherhood.

Article 2

Everyone is entitled to all the rights and freedoms set forth in this Declaration, without distinction of any kind, such as race, colour, sex, language, religion, political or other opinion, national or social origin, property, birth or other status. Furthermore, no distinction shall be made on the basis of the political, jurisdictional or international status of the country or territory to which a person belongs, whether it be independent, trust, non-self-governing or under any other limitation of sovereignty.

Article 3

Everyone has the right to life, liberty and the security of person.

Article 4

No one shall be held in slavery or servitude; slavery and the slave trade shall be prohibited in all their forms.

Article 5

No one shall be subjected to torture or to cruel, inhuman or degrading treatment or punishment.

Article 6

Everyone has the right to recognition everywhere as a person before the law.

Article 7

All are equal before the law and are entitled without any discrimination to equal protection of the law. All are entitled to equal protection against any discrimination in violation of this Declaration and against any incitement to such discrimination.

Article 8

Everyone has the right to an effective remedy by the competent national tribunals for acts violating the fundamental rights granted him by the constitution or by law.

Article 9

No one shall be subjected to arbitrary arrest, detention or exile.

Article 10

Everyone is entitled in full equality to a fair and public hearing by an independent and impartial tribunal, in the determination of his rights and obligations and of any criminal charge against him.

Article 11

1. Everyone charged with a penal offence has the right to be presumed innocent until proved guilty according to law in a public trial at which he has had all the guarantees necessary for his defence.

2. No one shall be held guilty of any penal offence on account of any act or omission which did not constitute a penal offence, under national or international law, at the time when it was committed. Nor shall a heavier penalty be imposed than the one that was applicable at the time the penal offence was committed.

Article 12

No one shall be subjected to arbitrary interference with his privacy, family, home or correspondence, nor to attacks upon his honour and reputation. Everyone has the right to the protection of the law against such interference or attacks.

Article 13

1. Everyone has the right to freedom of movement and residence within the borders of each State.

2. Everyone has the right to leave any country, including his own, and to return to his country.

Article 14

1. Everyone has the right to seek and to enjoy in other countries asylum from persecution.

2. This right may not be invoked in the case of prosecutions genuinely arising from nonpolitical crimes or from acts contrary to the purposes and principles of the United Nations.

Article 15

1. Everyone has the right to a nationality.

2. No one shall be arbitrarily deprived of his nationality nor denied the right to change his nationality.

Article 16

1. Men and women of full age, without any limitation due to race, nationality or religion, have the right to marry and to found a family. They are entitled to equal rights as to marriage, during marriage and at its dissolution.

2. Marriage shall be entered into only with the free and full consent of the intending spouses.

3. The family is the natural and fundamental group unit of society and is entitled to protection by society and the State.

Article 17

1. Everyone has the right to own property alone as well as in association with others.

2. No one shall be arbitrarily deprived of his property.

Article 18

Everyone has the right to freedom of thought, conscience and religion; this right includes freedom to change his religion or belief, and freedom, either alone or in community with others and in public or private, to manifest his religion or belief in teaching, practice, worship and observance.

Article 19

Everyone has the right to freedom of opinion and expression; this right includes freedom to hold opinions without interference and to seek, receive and impart information and ideas through any media and regardless of frontiers.

Article 20

1. Everyone has the right to freedom of peaceful assembly and association.

2. No one may be compelled to belong to an association.

Article 21

1. Everyone has the right to take part in the government of his country, directly or through freely chosen representatives.

2. Everyone has the right of equal access to public service in his country.

3. The will of the people shall be the basis of the authority of government; this will shall be expressed in periodic and genuine elections which shall be by universal and equal suffrage and shall be held by secret vote or by equivalent free voting procedures.

Article 22

Everyone, as a member of society, has the right to social security and is entitled to realization, through national effort and international cooperation and in accordance with the organization and resources of each State, of the economic, social and cultural rights indispensable for his dignity and the free development of his personality.

Article 23

(1) Everyone has the right to work, to free choice of employment, to just and favourable conditions of work and to protection against unemployment.

(2) Everyone, without any discrimination, has the right to equal pay for equal work.

(3) Everyone who works has the right to just and favourable remuneration ensuring for himself and his family an existence worthy of human dignity, and supplemented, if necessary, by other means of social protection.

(4) Everyone has the right to form and to join trade unions for the protection of his interests.

Article 24

Everyone has the right to rest and leisure, including reasonable limitation of working hours and periodic holidays with pay.

Article 25

(1) Everyone has the right to a standard of living adequate for the health and well-being of himself and of his family, including food, clothing, housing and medical care and necessary social services, and the right to security in the event of unemployment, sickness, disability, widowhood, old age or other lack of livelihood in circumstances beyond his control.

(2) Motherhood and childhood are entitled to special care and assistance. All children, whether born in or out of wedlock, shall enjoy the same social protection.

Article 26

(1) Everyone has the right to education. Education shall be free, at least in the elementary and fundamental stages. Elementary education shall be compulsory. Technical and professional education shall be made generally available and higher education shall be equally accessible to all on the basis of merit.

(2) Education shall be directed to the full development of the human personality and to the strengthening of respect for human rights and fundamental freedoms. It shall promote understanding, tolerance and friendship among all nations, racial or religious groups, and shall further the activities of the United Nations for the maintenance of peace.

(3) Parents have a prior right to choose the kind of education that shall be given to their children.

Article 27

(1) Everyone has the right freely to participate in the cultural life of the community, to enjoy the arts and to share in scientific advancement and its benefits.

(2) Everyone has the right to the protection of the moral and material interests resulting from any scientific, literary or artistic production of which he is the author.

Article 28

Everyone is entitled to a social and international order in which the rights and freedoms set forth in this Declaration can be fully realized.

Article 29

(1) Everyone has duties to the community in which alone the free and full development of his personality is possible.

(2) In the exercise of his rights and freedoms, everyone shall be subject only to such limitations as are determined by law solely for the purpose of securing due recognition and respect for the rights and freedoms of others and of meeting the just requirements of morality, public order and the general welfare in a democratic society.

(3) These rights and freedoms may in no case be exercised contrary to the purposes and principles of the United Nations.

Article 30

Nothing in this Declaration may be interpreted as implying for any State, group or person any right to engage in any activity or to perform any act aimed at the destruction of any of the rights and freedoms set forth herein.

VIENNA CONVENTION ON THE LAW OF TREATIES

May 23, 1969, 1155 U.N.T.S. 331, 8 *International Legal Materials* 679 (1969)

PART I

INTRODUCTION

Article 1

Scope of the present Convention

The present Convention applies to treaties between States.

Article 2

Use of Terms

1. For the purposes of the present Convention:

(a) "treaty" means an international agreement concluded between States in written form and governed by international law, whether embodied in a single instrument or in two or more related instruments and whatever its particular designation;

(b) "ratification," "acceptance," "approval" and "accession" mean in each case the international act so named whereby a State establishes on the international plane its consent to be bound by a treaty;

(c) "full powers" means a document emanating from the competent authority of a State designating a person or persons to represent the State for negotiating, adopting or authenticating the text of a treaty, for expressing the consent of the State to be bound by a treaty, or for accomplishing any other act with respect to a treaty;

(d) "reservation" means a unilateral statement, however phrased or named, made by a State, when signing, ratifying, accepting, approving or acceding to a treaty, whereby it purports to exclude or to modify the legal effect of certain provisions of the treaty in their application to that State;

(e) "negotiating State" means a State which took part in the drawing up and adoption of the text of the treaty;

(f) "contracting State" means a State which has consented to be bound by the treaty, whether or not the treaty has entered into force;

(g) "party" means a State which has consented to be bound by the treaty and for which the treaty is in force;

(h) "third State" means a State not a party to the treaty;

(i) "international organization" means an intergovernmental organization.

2. The provisions of paragraph 1 regarding the use of terms in the present Convention are without prejudice to the use of those terms or to the meanings which may be given to them in the internal law of any State.

Article 3

International agreements not within the scope of the present Convention

The fact that the present Convention does not apply to international agreements concluded between States and other subjects of international law or between such other subjects of international law, or to international agreements not in written form, shall not affect:

(a) the legal force of such agreements;

(b) the application to them of any of the rules set forth in the present Convention to which they would be subject under international law independently of the Convention;

(c) the application of the Convention to the relations of States as between themselves under international agreements to which other subjects of international law are also parties.

Article 4

Non-retroactivity of the present Convention

Without prejudice to the application of any rules set forth in the present Convention to which treaties would be subject under international law independently of the Convention, the Convention applies only to treaties which are concluded by States after the entry into force of the present Convention with regard to such States.

Article 5

Treaties constituting international organizations and treaties adopted within an international organization

The present Convention applies to any treaty which is the constituent instrument of an international organization and to any treaty adopted within an international organization without prejudice to any relevant rules of the organization.

PART II

CONCLUSION AND ENTRY INTO FORCE OF TREATIES

SECTION 1: CONCLUSION OF TREATIES

Article 6

Capacity of States to conclude treaties

Every State possesses capacity to conclude treaties.

Article 7

Full powers

1. A person is considered as representing a State for the purpose of adopting or authenticating the text of a treaty or for the purpose of expressing the consent of the State to be bound by a treaty if:

(a) he produces appropriate full powers; or

(b) it appears from the practice of the States concerned or from other circumstances that their intention was to consider that person as representing the State for such purposes and to dispense with full powers.

2. In virtue of their functions and without having to produce full powers, the following are considered as representing their State:

(a) Heads of State, Heads of Government and Ministers for Foreign Affairs, for the purpose of performing all acts relating to the conclusion of a treaty;

(b) heads of diplomatic missions, for the purpose of adopting the text of a treaty between the accrediting State and the State to which they are accredited;

(c) representatives accredited by States to an international conference or to an international organization or one of its organs, for the purpose of adopting the text of a treaty in that conference, organization or organ.

Article 8

Subsequent confirmation of an act performed without authorization

An act relating to the conclusion of a treaty performed by a person who cannot be considered under article 7 as authorized to represent a State for that purpose is without legal effect unless afterwards confirmed by that State.

Article 9

Adoption of the text

1. The adoption of the text of a treaty takes place by the consent of all the States participating in its drawing up except as provided in paragraph 2.

2. The adoption of the text of a treaty at an international conference takes place by the vote of two-thirds of the States present and voting, unless by the same majority they shall decide to apply a different rule.

Article 10

Authentication of the text

The text of a treaty is established as authentic and definitive:

(a) by such procedure as may be provided for in the text or agreed upon by the States participating in its drawing up; or

(b) failing such procedure, by the signature, signature *ad referendum* or initialing by the representatives of those States of the text of the treaty or of the Final Act of a conference incorporating the text.

Article 11

Means of expressing consent to be bound by a treaty

The consent of a State to be bound by a treaty may be expressed by signature, exchange of instruments constituting a treaty, ratification, acceptance, approval or accession, or by any other means if so agreed.

Article 12

Consent to be bound by a treaty expressed by signature

1. The consent of a State to be bound by a treaty is expressed by the signature of its representative when:

(a) the treaty provides that signature shall have that effect;

(b) it is otherwise established that the negotiating States were agreed that signature should have that effect; or

(c) the intention of the State to give that effect to the signature appears from the full powers of its representative or was expressed during the negotiation.

2. For the purposes of paragraph 1:

(a) the initialing of a text constitutes a signature of the treaty when it is established that the negotiating States so agreed;

(b) the signature *ad referendum* of a treaty by a representative, if confirmed by his State, constitutes a full signature of the treaty.

Article 13

Consent to be bound by a treaty expressed by an exchange of instruments constituting a treaty

The consent of States to be bound by a treaty constituted by instruments exchanged between them is expressed by that exchange when:

(a) the instruments provide that their exchange shall have that effect; or

(b) it is otherwise established that those States were agreed that the exchange of instruments should have that effect.

Article 14

Consent to be bound by a treaty expressed by ratification, acceptance or approval

1. The consent of a State to be bound by a treaty is expressed by ratification when:

(a) the treaty provides for such consent to be expressed by means of ratification;

(b) it is otherwise established that the negotiating States were agreed that ratification should be required;

(c) the representative of the State has signed the treaty subject to ratification; or

(d) the intention of the State to sign the treaty subject to ratification appears from the full powers of its representative or was expressed during the negotiation.

2. The consent of a State to be bound by a treaty is expressed by acceptance or approval under conditions similar to those which apply to ratification.

Article 15

Consent to be bound by a treaty expressed by accession

The consent of a State to be bound by a treaty is expressed by accession when:

(a) the treaty provides that such consent may be expressed by that State by means of accession;

(b) it is otherwise established that the negotiating States were agreed that such consent may be expressed by that State by means of accession; or

(c) all the parties have subsequently agreed that such consent may be expressed by that State by means of accession.

Article 16

Exchange or deposit of instruments of ratification, acceptance, approval or accession

Unless the treaty otherwise provides, instruments of ratification, acceptance, approval or accession establish the consent of a State to be bound by a treaty upon:

(a) their exchange between the contracting States;

(b) their deposit with the depositary; or

(c) their notification to the contracting States or to the depositary, if so agreed.

Article 17

Consent to be bound by part of a treaty and choice of differing provisions

1. Without prejudice to articles 19 to 23, the consent of a State to be bound by part of a treaty is effective only if the treaty so permits or the other contracting States so agree.

2. The consent of a State to be bound by a treaty which permits a choice between differing provisions is effective only if it is made clear to which of the provisions the consent relates.

Article 18

Obligation not to defeat the object and purpose of a treaty prior to its entry into force

A State is obliged to refrain from acts which would defeat the object and purpose of a treaty when:

(a) it has signed the treaty or has exchanged instruments constituting the treaty subject to ratification, acceptance or approval, until it shall have made its intention clear not to become a party to the treaty; or

(b) it has expressed its consent to be bound by the treaty, pending the entry into force of the treaty and provided that such entry into force is not unduly delayed.

SECTION 2: RESERVATIONS

Article 19

Formulation of reservations

A State may, when signing, ratifying, accepting, approving or acceding to a treaty, formulate a reservation unless:

(a) the reservation is prohibited by the treaty;

(b) the treaty provides that only specified reservations, which do not include the reservation in question, may be made; or

(c) in cases not falling under sub-paragraphs (a) and (b), the reservation is incompatible with the object and purpose of the treaty.

Article 20

Acceptance of and objection to reservations

1. A reservation expressly authorized by a treaty does not require any subsequent acceptance by the other contracting States unless the treaty so provides.

2. When it appears from the limited number of the negotiating States and the object and purpose of a treaty that the application of the treaty in its entirety between all the parties is an essential condition of the consent of each one to be bound by the treaty, a reservation requires acceptance by all the parties.

3. When a treaty is a constituent instrument of an international organization and unless it otherwise provides, a reservation requires the acceptance of the competent organ of that organization.

4. In cases not falling under the preceding paragraphs and unless the treaty otherwise provides:

(a) acceptance by another contracting State of a reservation constitutes the reserving State a party to the treaty in relation to that other State if or when the treaty is in force for those States;

(b) an objection by another contracting State to a reservation does not preclude the entry into force of the treaty as between the objecting and reserving States unless a contrary intention is definitely expressed by the objecting State;

(c) an act expressing a State's consent to be bound by the treaty and containing a reservation is effective as soon as at least one other contracting State has accepted the reservation.

5. For the purposes of paragraphs 2 and 4 and unless the treaty otherwise provides, a reservation is considered to have been accepted by a

State if it shall have raised no objection to the reservation by the end of a period of twelve months after it was notified of the reservation or by the date on which it expressed its consent to be bound by the treaty, whichever is later.

Article 21

Legal effects of reservations and of objections to reservations

1. A reservation established with regard to another party in accordance with articles 19, 20 and 23:

(a) modifies for the reserving State in its relations with that other party the provisions of the treaty to which the reservation relates to the extent of the reservation; and

(b) modifies those provisions to the same extent for that other party in its relations with the reserving State.

2. The reservation does not modify the provisions of the treaty for the other parties to the treaty *inter se*.

3. When a State objecting to a reservation has not opposed the entry into force of the treaty between itself and the reserving State, the provisions to which the reservation relates do not apply as between the two States to the extent of the reservation.

Article 22

Withdrawal of reservations and of objections to reservations

1. Unless the treaty otherwise provides, a reservation may be withdrawn at any time and the consent of a State which has accepted the reservation is not required for its withdrawal.

2. Unless the treaty otherwise provides, an objection to a reservation may be withdrawn at any time.

3. Unless the treaty otherwise provides, or it is otherwise agreed:

(a) the withdrawal of a reservation becomes operative in relation to another contracting State only when notice of it has been received by that State;

(b) the withdrawal of an objection to a reservation becomes operative only when notice of it has been received by the State which formulated the reservation.

Article 23

Procedure regarding reservations

1. A reservation, an express acceptance of a reservation and an objection to a reservation must be formulated in writing and

communicated to the contracting States and other States entitled to become parties to the treaty.

2. If formulated when signing the treaty subject to ratification, acceptance or approval, a reservation must be formally confirmed by the reserving State when expressing its consent to be bound by the treaty. In such a case the reservation shall be considered as having been made on the date of its confirmation.

3. An express acceptance of, or an objection to, a reservation made previously to confirmation of the reservation does not itself require confirmation.

4. The withdrawal of a reservation or of an objection to a reservation must be formulated in writing.

SECTION 3: ENTRY INTO FORCE AND PROVISIONAL APPLICATION OF TREATIES

Article 24

Entry into force

1. A treaty enters into force in such manner and upon such date as it may provide or as the negotiating States may agree.

2. Failing any such provision or agreement, a treaty enters into force as soon as consent to be bound by the treaty has been established for all the negotiating States.

3. When the consent of a State to be bound by a treaty is established on a date after the treaty has come into force, the treaty enters into force for that State on that date, unless the treaty otherwise provides.

4. The provisions of a treaty regulating the authentication of its text, the establishment of the consent of States to be bound by the treaty, the manner or date of its entry into force, reservations, the functions of the depositary and other matters arising necessarily before the entry into force of the treaty apply from the time of the adoption of this text.

Article 25

Provisional application

1. A treaty or a part of a treaty is applied provisionally pending its entry into force if:

(a) the treaty itself so provides; or

(b) the negotiating States have in some other manner so agreed.

2. Unless the treaty otherwise provides or the negotiating States have otherwise agreed, the provisional application of a treaty or a part of a treaty with respect to a State shall be terminated if that State notifies

the other States between which the treaty is being applied provisionally of its intention not to become a party to the treaty.

PART III

OBSERVANCE, APPLICATION AND INTERPRETATION OF TREATIES

SECTION 1: OBSERVANCE OF TREATIES

Article 26

Pacta sunt servanda

Every treaty in force is binding upon the parties to it and must be performed by them in good faith.

Article 27

Internal law and observance of treaties

A party may not invoke the provisions of its internal law as justification for its failure to perform a treaty. This rule is without prejudice to Article 46.

SECTION 2: APPLICATION OF TREATIES

Article 28

Non-retroactivity of treaties

Unless a different intention appears from the treaty or is otherwise established, its provisions do not bind a party in relation to any act or fact which took place or any situation which ceased to exist before the date of the entry into force of the treaty with respect to that party.

Article 29

Territorial scope of treaties

Unless a different intention appears from the treaty or is otherwise established, a treaty is binding upon each party in respect of its entire territory.

Article 30

Application of successive treaties relating to the same subject-matter

1. Subject to Article 103 of the Charter of the United Nations, the rights and obligations of States parties to successive treaties relating to the same subject-matter shall be determined in accordance with the following paragraphs.

2. When a treaty specifies that it is subject to, or that is not to be considered as incompatible with, an earlier or later treaty, the provisions of that other treaty prevail.

3. When all the parties to the earlier treaty are parties also to the later treaty but the earlier treaty is not terminated or suspended in operation under article 59, the earlier treaty applies only to the extent that its provisions are compatible with those of the later treaty.

4. When the parties to the later treaty do not include all the parties to the earlier one:

(a) as between States parties to both treaties the same rule applies as in paragraph 3;

(b) as between a State party to both treaties and a State party to only one of the treaties, the treaty to which both States are parties governs their mutual rights and obligations.

5. Paragraph 4 is without prejudice to article 41, or to any question of the termination or suspension of the operation of a treaty under article 60 or to any question of responsibility which may arise for a State from the conclusion or application of a treaty the provisions of which are incompatible with its obligations towards another State under another treaty.

SECTION 3: INTERPRETATION OF TREATIES

Article 31

General rule of interpretation

1. A treaty shall be interpreted in good faith in accordance with the ordinary meaning to be given to the terms of the treaty in their context and in the light of its object and purpose.

2. The context for the purpose of the interpretation of a treaty shall comprise, in addition to the text, including its preamble and annexes:

(a) any agreement relating to the treaty which was made between all the parties in connexion with the conclusion of the treaty;

(b) any instrument which was made by one or more parties in connexion with the conclusion of the treaty and accepted by the other parties as an instrument related to the treaty.

3. There shall be taken into account, together with the context:

(a) any subsequent agreement between the parties regarding the interpretation of the treaty or the application of its provisions;

(b) any subsequent practice in the application of the treaty which establishes the agreement of the parties regarding its interpretation;

(c) any relevant rules of international law applicable in the relations between the parties.

4. A special meaning shall be given to a term if it is established that the parties so intended.

Article 32

Supplementary means of interpretation

Recourse may be had to supplementary means of interpretation, including the preparatory work of the treaty and the circumstances of its conclusion, in order to confirm the meaning resulting from the application of article 31, or to determine the meaning when the interpretation according to article 31:

(a) leaves the meaning ambiguous or obscure; or

(b) leads to a result which is manifestly absurd or unreasonable.

Article 33

Interpretation of treaties authenticated in two or more languages

1. When a treaty has been authenticated in two or more languages, the text is equally authoritative in each language, unless the treaty provides or the parties agree that, in case of divergence, a particular text shall prevail.

2. A version of the treaty in a language other than one of those in which the text was authenticated shall be considered an authentic text only if the treaty so provides or the parties so agree.

3. The terms of the treaty are presumed to have the same meaning in each authentic text.

4. Except where a particular text prevails in accordance with paragraph 1, when a comparison of the authentic texts discloses a difference of meaning which the application of articles 31 and 32 does not remove, the meaning which best reconciles the texts, having regard to the object and purpose of the treaty, shall be adopted.

SECTION 4: TREATIES AND THIRD STATES

Article 34

General rule regarding third States

A treaty does not create either obligations or rights for a third State without its consent.

Article 35

Treaties providing for obligations for third States

An obligation arises for a third State from a provision of a treaty if the parties to the treaty intend the provision to be the means of establishing the obligation and the third State expressly accepts that obligation in writing.

Article 36

Treaties providing for rights for third States

1. A right arises for a third State from a provision of a treaty if the parties to the treaty intend the provision to accord that right either to the third State, or to a group of States to which it belongs, or to all States, and the third State assents thereto. Its assent shall be presumed so long as the contrary is not indicated, unless the treaty otherwise provides.

2. A State exercising a right in accordance with paragraph 1 shall comply with the conditions for its exercise provided for in the treaty or established in conformity with the treaty.

Article 37

Revocation or modification of obligations or rights of third States

1. When an obligation has arisen for a third State in conformity with article 35, the obligation may be revoked or modified only with the consent of the parties to the treaty and of the third State, unless it is established that they had otherwise agreed.

2. When a right has arisen for a third State in conformity with article 36, the right may not be revoked or modified by the parties if it is established that the right was intended not to be revocable or subject to modification without the consent of the third State.

Article 38

Rules in a treaty becoming binding on third States through international custom

Nothing in articles 34 to 37 precludes a rule set forth in the treaty from becoming binding upon a third State as a customary rule of international law, recognized as such.

PART IV

AMENDMENT AND MODIFICATION OF TREATIES

Article 39

General rule regarding the amendment of treaties

A treaty may be amended by agreement between the parties. The rules laid down in Part II apply to such an agreement except in so far as the treaty may otherwise provide.

Article 40

Amendment of multilateral treaties

1. Unless the treaty otherwise provides, the amendment of multilateral treaties shall be governed by the following paragraphs.

2. Any proposal to amend a multilateral treaty as between all the parties must be notified to all the contracting States, each one of which shall have the right to take part in:

(a) the decision as to the action to be taken in regard to such proposal;

(b) the negotiation and conclusion of any agreement for the amendment of the treaty.

3. Every State entitled to become a party to the treaty shall also be entitled to become a party to the treaty as amended.

4. The amending agreement does not bind any State already a party to the treaty which does not become a party to the amending agreement; article 30, paragraph 4(b), applies in relation to such State.

5. Any State which becomes a party to the treaty after the entry into force of the amending agreement shall, failing an expression of a different intention by that State:

(a) be considered as a party to the treaty as amended; and

(b) be considered as a party to the unamended treaty in relation to any party to the treaty not bound by the amending agreement.

Article 41

Agreements to modify multilateral treaties between certain of the parties only

1. Two or more of the parties to a multilateral treaty may conclude an agreement to modify the treaty as between themselves alone if:

(a) the possibility of such a modification is provided for by the treaty; or

(b) the modification in question is not prohibited by the treaty and:

(i) does not affect the enjoyment by the parties of their rights under the treaty or the performance of their obligations;

(ii) does not relate to a provision, derogation from which is incompatible with the effective execution of the object and purpose of the treaty as a whole.

2. Unless in a case falling under paragraph 1(a) the treaty otherwise provides, the parties in question shall notify the other parties of their intention to conclude the agreement and of the modification to the treaty for which it provides.

PART V

INVALIDITY, TERMINATION AND SUSPENSION OF THE OPERATION OF TREATIES

SECTION 1: GENERAL PROVISIONS

Article 42

Validity and continuance in force of treaties

1. The validity of a treaty or of the consent of a State to be bound by a treaty may be impeached only through the application of the present Convention.

2. The termination of a treaty, its denunciation or the withdrawal of a party, may take place only as a result of the application of the provisions of the treaty or of the present Convention. The same rule applies to suspension of the operation of a treaty.

Article 43

Obligations imposed by international law independently of a treaty

The invalidity, termination or denunciation of a treaty, the withdrawal of a party from it, or the suspension of its operation, as a result of the application of the present Convention or of the provisions of the treaty, shall not in any way impair the duty of any State to fulfil any obligation embodied in the treaty to which it would be subject under international law independently of the treaty.

Article 44

Separability of treaty provisions

1. A right of a party, provided for in a treaty or arising under article 56, to denounce, withdraw from or suspend the operation of the treaty may be exercised only with respect to the whole treaty unless the treaty otherwise provides or the parties otherwise agree.

2. A ground for invalidating, terminating, withdrawing from or suspending the operation of a treaty recognized in the present Convention may be invoked only with respect to the whole treaty except as provided in the following paragraphs or in article 60.

3. If the ground relates solely to particular clauses, it may be invoked only with respect to those clauses where:

(a) the said clauses are separable from the remainder of the treaty with regard to their application;

(b) it appears from the treaty or is otherwise established that acceptance of those clauses was not an essential basis of the consent of the other party or parties to be bound by the treaty as a whole; and

(c) continued performance of the remainder of the treaty would not be unjust.

4. In cases falling under articles 49 and 50 the State entitled to invoke the fraud or corruption may do so with respect either to the whole treaty or, subject to paragraph 3, to the particular clauses alone.

5. In cases falling under articles 51, 52 and 53, no separation of the provisions of the treaty is permitted.

Article 45

Loss of a right to invoke a ground for invalidating, terminating, withdrawing from or suspending the operation of a treaty

A State may no longer invoke a ground for invalidating, terminating, withdrawing from or suspending the operation of a treaty under articles 46 to 50 or articles 60 and 62, if, after becoming aware of the facts:

(a) it shall have expressly agreed that the treaty is valid or remains in force or continues in operation, as the case may be; or

(b) it must by reason of its conduct be considered as having acquiesced in the validity of the treaty or in its maintenance in force or in operation, as the case may be.

SECTION 2: INVALIDITY OF TREATIES

Article 46

Provisions of internal law regarding competence to conclude treaties

1. A State may not invoke the fact that its consent to be bound by a treaty has been expressed in violation of a provision of its internal law regarding competence to conclude treaties as invalidating its consent unless that violation was manifest and concerned a rule of its internal law of fundamental importance.

2. A violation is manifest if it would be objectively evident to any State conducting itself in the matter in accordance with normal practice and in good faith.

Article 47

Specific restrictions on authority to express the consent of a State

If the authority of a representative to express the consent of a State to be bound by a particular treaty has been made subject to a specific restriction, his omission to observe that restriction may not be invoked as invalidating the consent expressed by him unless the restriction was notified to the other negotiating States prior to his expressing such consent.

Article 48

Error

1. A State may invoke an error in a treaty as invalidating its consent to be bound by the treaty if the error relates to a fact or situation which was assumed by that State to exist at the time when the treaty was concluded and formed an essential basis of its consent to be bound by the treaty.

2. Paragraph 1 shall not apply if the State in question contributed by its own conduct to the error or if the circumstances were such as to put that State on notice of a possible error.

3. An error relating only to the wording of the text of a treaty does not affect its validity; article 79 then applies.

Article 49

Fraud

If a State has been induced to conclude a treaty by the fraudulent conduct of another negotiating State, the State may invoke the fraud as invalidating its consent to be bound by the treaty.

Article 50

Corruption of a representative of a State

If the expression of a State's consent to be bound by a treaty has been procured through the corruption of its representative directly or indirectly by another negotiating State, the State may invoke such corruption as invalidating its consent to be bound by the treaty.

Article 51

Coercion of a representative of a State

The expression of a State's consent to be bound by a treaty which has been procured by the coercion of its representative through acts or threats directed against him shall be without any legal effect.

Article 52

Coercion of a State by the threat or use of force

A treaty is void if its conclusion has been procured by the threat or use of force in violation of the principles of international law embodied in the Charter of the United Nations.

Article 53

Treaties conflicting with a peremptory norm of general international law (jus cogens)

A treaty is void if, at the time of its conclusion, it conflicts with a peremptory norm of general international law. For the purposes of the present Convention, a peremptory norm of general international law is a norm accepted and recognized by the international community of States as a whole as a norm from which no derogation is permitted and which can be modified only by a subsequent norm of general international law having the same character.

SECTION 3: TERMINATION AND SUSPENSION OF THE OPERATION OF TREATIES

Article 54

Termination of or withdrawal from a treaty under its provisions or by consent of the parties

The termination of a treaty or the withdrawal of a party may take place:

(a) in conformity with the provisions of the treaty; or

(b) at any time by consent of all the parties after consultation with the other contracting States.

Article 55

Reduction of the parties to a multilateral treaty below the number necessary for its entry into force

Unless the treaty otherwise provides, a multilateral treaty does not terminate by reason only of the fact that the number of the parties falls below the number necessary for its entry into force.

Article 56

Denunciation of or withdrawal from a treaty containing no provision regarding termination, denunciation or withdrawal

1. A treaty which contains no provision regarding its termination and which does not provide for denunciation or withdrawal is not subject to denunciation or withdrawal unless:

(a) it is established that the parties intended to admit the possibility of denunciation or withdrawal; or

(b) a right of denunciation or withdrawal may be implied by the nature of the treaty.

2. A party shall give not less than twelve months' notice of its intention to denounce or withdraw from a treaty under paragraph 1.

Article 57

Suspension of the operation of a treaty under its provisions or by consent of the parties

The operation of a treaty in regard to all the parties or to a particular party may be suspended:

(a) in conformity with the provisions of the treaty; or

(b) at any time by consent of all the parties after consultation with the other contracting States.

Article 58

Suspension of the operation of a multilateral treaty by agreement between certain of the parties only

1. Two or more parties to a multilateral treaty may conclude an agreement to suspend the operation of provisions of the treaty, temporarily and as between themselves alone, if:

(a) the possibility of such a suspension is provided for by the treaty; or

(b) the suspension in question is not prohibited by the treaty and:

(i) does not affect the enjoyment by the other parties of their rights under the treaty or the performance of their obligations;

(ii) is not incompatible with the object and purpose of the treaty.

2. Unless in a case falling under paragraph 1(a) the treaty otherwise provides the parties in question shall notify the other parties of their

intention to conclude the agreement and of those provisions of the treaty the operation of which they intend to suspend.

Article 59

Termination or suspension of the operation of a treaty implied by conclusion of a later treaty

1. A treaty shall be considered as terminated if all the parties to it conclude a later treaty relating to the same subject-matter and:

(a) it appears from the later treaty or is otherwise established that the parties intended that the matter should be governed by that treaty; or

(b) the provisions of the later treaty are so far incompatible with those of the earlier one that the two treaties are not capable of being applied at the same time.

2. The earlier treaty shall be considered as only suspended in operation if it appears from the later treaty or is otherwise established that such was the intention of the parties.

Article 60

Termination or suspension of the operation of a treaty as a consequence of its breach

1. A material breach of a bilateral treaty by one of the parties entitles the other to invoke the breach as a ground for terminating the treaty or suspending its operation in whole or in part.

2. A material breach of a multilateral treaty by one of the parties entitles:

(a) the other parties by unanimous agreement to suspend the operation of the treaty in whole or in part or to terminate it either:

(i) in the relations between themselves and the defaulting State, or

(ii) as between all the parties;

(b) a party specially affected by the breach to invoke it as a ground for suspending the operation of the treaty in whole or in part in the relations between itself and the defaulting State;

(c) any party other than the defaulting State to invoke the breach as a ground for suspending the operation of the treaty in whole or in part with respect to itself if the treaty is of such a character that a material breach of its provisions by one party radically changes the position of every party with respect to the further performance of its obligations under the treaty.

3. A material breach of a treaty, for the purposes of this article, consists in:

(a) a repudiation of the treaty not sanctioned by the present Convention; or

(b) the violation of a provision essential to the accomplishment of the object or purpose of the treaty.

4. The foregoing paragraphs are without prejudice to any provision in the treaty applicable in the event of a breach.

5. Paragraphs 1 to 3 do not apply to provisions relating to the protection of the human person contained in treaties of a humanitarian character, in particular to provisions prohibiting any form of reprisals against persons protected by such treaties.

Article 61

Supervening impossibility of performance

1. A party may invoke the impossibility of performing a treaty as a ground for terminating or withdrawing from it if the impossibility results from the permanent disappearance or destruction of an object indispensable for the execution of the treaty. If the impossibility is temporary, it may be invoked only as a ground for suspending the operation of the treaty.

2. Impossibility of performance may not be invoked by a party as a ground for terminating, withdrawing from or suspending the operation of a treaty if the impossibility is the result of a breach by that party either of an obligation under the treaty or of any other international obligation owed to any other party to the treaty.

Article 62

Fundamental change of circumstances

1. A fundamental change of circumstances which has occurred with regard to those existing at the time of the conclusion of a treaty, and which was not foreseen by the parties, may not be invoked as a ground for terminating or withdrawing from the treaty unless:

(a) the existence of those circumstances constituted an essential basis of the consent of the parties to be bound by the treaty; and

(b) the effect of the change is radically to transform the extent of obligations still to be performed under the treaty.

2. A fundamental change of circumstances may not be invoked as a ground for terminating or withdrawing from a treaty:

(a) if the treaty establishes a boundary; or

(b) if the fundamental change is the result of a breach by the party invoking it either of an obligation under the treaty or of any other international obligation owed to any other party to the treaty.

3. If, under the foregoing paragraphs, a party may invoke a fundamental change of circumstances as a ground for terminating or withdrawing from a treaty it may also invoke the change as a ground for suspending the operation of the treaty.

Article 63

Severance of diplomatic or consular relations

The severance of diplomatic or consular relations between parties to a treaty does not affect the legal relations established between them by the treaty except in so far as the existence of diplomatic or consular relations is indispensable for the application of the treaty.

Article 64

Emergence of a new peremptory norm of general international la (jus cogens)

If a new peremptory norm of general international law emerges, any existing treaty which is in conflict with that norm becomes void and terminates.

SECTION 4: PROCEDURE

Article 65

Procedure to be followed with respect to invalidity, termination, withdrawal from or suspension of the operation of a treaty

1. A party which, under the provisions of the present Convention, invokes either a defect in its consent to be bound by a treaty or a ground for impeaching the validity of a treaty, terminating it, withdrawing from it or suspending its operation, must notify the other parties of its claim. The notification shall indicate the measure proposed to be taken with respect to the treaty and the reasons therefor.

2. If, after the expiry of a period which, except in cases of special urgency, shall not be less than three months after the receipt of the notification, no party has raised any objection, the party making the notification may carry out in the manner provided in article 67 the measure which it has proposed.

3. If, however, objection has been raised by any other party, the parties shall seek a solution through the means indicated in Article 33 of the Charter of the United Nations.

4. Nothing in the foregoing paragraphs shall affect the rights or obligations of the parties under any provisions in force binding the parties with regard to the settlement of disputes.

5. Without prejudice to article 45, the fact that a State has not previously made the notification prescribed in paragraph 1 shall not prevent it from making such notification in answer to another party claiming performance of the treaty or alleging its violation.

Article 66

Procedures for judicial settlement, arbitration and conciliation

If, under paragraph 3 of article 65, no solution has been reached within a period of 12 months following the date on which the objection was raised, the following procedures shall be followed:

(a) any one of the parties to a dispute concerning the application or the interpretation of article 53 or 64 may, by a written application, submit it to the International Court of Justice for a decision unless the parties by common consent agree to submit the dispute to arbitration;

(b) any one of the parties to a dispute concerning the application or the interpretation of any of the other articles in Part V of the present Convention may set in motion the procedure specified in the Annex to the Convention by submitting a request to that effect to the Secretary-General of the United Nations.

Article 67

Instruments for declaring invalid, terminating, withdrawing from or suspending the operation of a treaty

1. The notification provided for under article 65, paragraph 1 must be made in writing.

2. Any act declaring invalid, terminating, withdrawing from or suspending the operation of a treaty pursuant to the provisions of the treaty or of paragraphs 2 or 3 of article 65 shall be carried out through an instrument communicated to the other parties. If the instrument is not signed by the Head of State, Head of Government or Minister for Foreign Affairs, the representative of the State communicating it may be called upon to produce full powers.

Article 68

Revocation of notifications and instruments provided for in articles 65 and 67

A notification or instrument provided for in articles 65 or 67 may be revoked at any time before it takes effect.

SECTION 5: CONSEQUENCES OF THE INVALIDITY, TERMINATION OR SUSPENSION OF THE OPERATIONOF A TREATY

Article 69

Consequences of the invalidity of a treaty

1. A treaty the invalidity of which is established under the present Convention is void. The provisions of a void treaty have no legal force.

2. If acts have nevertheless been performed in reliance on such a treaty:

(a) each party may require any other party to establish as far as possible in their mutual relations the position that would have existed if the acts had not been performed;

(b) acts performed in good faith before the invalidity was invoked are not rendered unlawful by reason only of the invalidity of the treaty.

3. In cases falling under articles 49, 50, 51 or 52, paragraph 2 does not apply with respect to the party to which the fraud, the act of corruption or the coercion is imputable.

4. In the case of the invalidity of a particular State's consent to be bound by a multilateral treaty, the foregoing rules apply in the relations between that State and the parties to the treaty.

Article 70

Consequences of the termination of a treaty

1. Unless the treaty otherwise provides or the parties otherwise agree, the termination of a treaty under its provisions or in accordance with the present Convention:

(a) releases the parties from any obligation further to perform the treaty;

(b) does not affect any right, obligation or legal situation of the parties created through the execution of the treaty prior to its termination.

2. If a State denounces or withdraws from a multilateral treaty, paragraph 1 applies in the relations between that State and each of the other parties to the treaty from the date when such denunciation or withdrawal takes effect.

Article 71

Consequences of the invalidity of a treaty which conflicts with a peremptory norm of general international law

1. In the case of a treaty which is void under article 53 the parties shall:

(a) eliminate as far as possible the consequences of any act performed in reliance on any provision which conflicts with the peremptory norm of general international law; and

(b) bring their mutual relations into conformity with the peremptory norm of general international law.

2. In the case of a treaty which becomes void and terminates under article 64, the termination of the treaty:

(a) releases the parties from any obligation further to perform the treaty;

(b) does not affect any right, obligation or legal situation of the parties created through the execution of the treaty prior to its termination; provided that those rights, obligations or situations may thereafter be maintained only to the extent that their maintenance is not in itself in conflict with the new peremptory norm of general international law.

Article 72

Consequences of the suspension of the operation of a treaty

1. Unless the treaty otherwise provides or the parties otherwise agree, the suspension of the operation of a treaty under its provisions or in accordance with the present Convention:

(a) releases the parties between which the operation of the treaty is suspended from the obligation to perform the treaty in their mutual relations during the period of the suspension;

(b) does not otherwise affect the legal relations between the parties established by the treaty.

2. During the period of the suspension the parties shall refrain from acts tending to obstruct the resumption of the operation of the treaty.

PART VI

MISCELLANEOUS PROVISIONS

Article 73

Cases of State succession, State responsibility and outbreak of hostilities

The provisions of the present Convention shall not prejudge any question that may arise in regard to a treaty from a succession of States or from the international responsibility of a State or from the outbreak of hostilities between States.

Article 74

Diplomatic and consular relations and the conclusion of treaties

The severance or absence of diplomatic or consular relations between two or more States does not prevent the conclusion of treaties between those States. The conclusion of a treaty does not in itself affect the situation in regard to diplomatic or consular relations.

Article 75

Case of an aggressor State

The provisions of the present Convention are without prejudice to any obligation in relation to a treaty which may arise for an aggressor State in consequence of measures taken in conformity with the Charter of the United Nations with reference to that State's aggression.

PART VII

DEPOSITARIES, NOTIFICATIONS, CORRECTIONS AND REGISTRATION

Article 76

Depositaries of treaties

1. The designation of the depositary of a treaty may be made by the negotiating States, either in the treaty itself or in some other manner. The depositary may be one or more States, an international organization or the chief administrative officer of the organization.

2. The functions of the depositary of a treaty are international in character and the depositary is under an obligation to act impartially in their performance. In particular, the fact that a treaty has not entered into force between certain of the parties or that a difference has appeared between a State and a depositary with regard to the performance of the latter's functions shall not affect that obligation.

Article 77

Functions of depositaries

1. The functions of a depositary, unless otherwise provided in the treaty or agreed by the contracting States, comprise in particular:

(a) keeping custody of the original text of the treaty and of any full powers delivered to the depositary;

(b) preparing certified copies of the original text and preparing any further text of the treaty in such additional languages as may be required by the treaty and transmitting them to the parties and to the States entitled to become parties to the treaty;

(c) receiving any signatures to the treaty and receiving and keeping custody of any instruments, notifications and communications relating to it;

(d) examining whether the signature or any instrument, notification or communication relating to the treaty is in due and proper form and, if need be, bringing the matter to the attention of the State in question;

(e) informing the parties and the States entitled to become parties to the treaty of acts, notifications and communications relating to the treaty;

(f) informing the States entitled to become parties to the treaty when the number of signatures or of instruments of ratification, acceptance, approval or accession required for the entry into force of the treaty has been received or deposited;

(g) registering the treaty with the Secretariat of the United Nations;

(h) performing the functions specified in other provisions of the present Convention.

2. In the event of any difference appearing between a State and the depositary as to the performance of the latter's functions, the depositary shall bring the question to the attention of the signatory States and the contracting States or, where appropriate, of the competent organ of the international organization concerned.

Article 78

Notifications and communications

Except as the treaty or the present Convention otherwise provide, any notification or communication to be made by any State under the present Convention shall:

(a) if there is no depositary, be transmitted direct to the States for which it is intended, or if there is a depositary, to the latter;

(b) be considered as having been made by the State in question only upon its receipt by the State to which it was transmitted or, as the case may be, upon its receipt by the depositary;

(c) if transmitted to a depositary, be considered as received by the State for which it was intended only when the latter State has been informed by the depositary in accordance with article 77, paragraph l(e).

Article 79

Correction of errors in texts or in certified copies of treaties

1. Where, after the authentication of the text of a treaty, the signatory States and the contracting States are agreed that it contains an error, the error shall, unless they decide upon some other means of correction, be corrected:

(a) by having the appropriate correction made in the text and causing the correction to be initialled by duly authorized representatives;

(b) by executing or exchanging an instrument or instruments setting out the correction which it has been agreed to make; or

(c) by executing a corrected text of the whole treaty by the same procedure as in the case of the original text.

2. Where the treaty is one for which there is a depositary, the latter shall notify the signatory States and the contracting States of the error and of the proposal to correct it and shall specify an appropriate time-limit within which objection to the proposed correction may be raised. If, on the expiry of the time-limit:

(a) no objection has been raised, the depositary shall make and initial the correction in the text and shall execute a *procès-verbal* of the rectification of the text and communicate a copy of it to the parties and to the States entitled to become parties to the treaty;

(b) an objection has been raised, the depositary shall communicate the objection to the signatory States and to the contracting States.

3. The rules in paragraphs 1 and 2 apply also where the text has been authenticated in two or more languages and it appears that there is a lack of concordance which the signatory States and the contracting States agree should be corrected.

4. The corrected text replaces the defective text *ab initio*, unless the signatory States and the contracting States otherwise decide.

5. The correction of the text of a treaty that has been registered shall be notified to the Secretariat of the United Nations.

6. Where an error is discovered in a certified copy of a treaty, the depositary shall execute a *procès-verbal* specifying the rectification and communicate a copy of it to the signatory States and to the contracting States.

Article 80

Registration and publication of treaties

1. Treaties shall, after their entry into force, be transmitted to the Secretariat of the United Nations for registration or filing and recording, as the case may be, and for publication.

2. The designation of a depositary shall constitute authorization for it to perform the acts specified in the preceding paragraph.

PART VIII

FINAL PROVISIONS

Article 81

Signature

The present Convention shall be open for signature by all States Members of the United Nations or of any of the specialized agencies or of the International Atomic Energy Agency or parties to the Statute of the International Court of Justice, and by any other State invited by the General Assembly of the United Nations to become a party to the Convention, as follows: until 30 November 1969, at the Federal Ministry for Foreign Affairs of the Republic of Austria, and subsequently, until 30 April 1970, at United Nations Headquarters, New York.

Article 82

Ratification

The present Convention is subject to ratification. The instruments of ratification shall be deposited with the Secretary-General of the United Nations.

Article 83

Accession

The present Convention shall remain open for accession by any State belonging to any of the categories mentioned in article 81. The instruments of accession shall be deposited with the Secretary-General of the United Nations.

Article 84

Entry into force

1. The present Convention shall enter into force on the thirtieth day following the date of deposit of the thirty-fifth instrument of ratification or accession.

2. For each State ratifying or acceding to the Convention after the deposit of the thirty-fifth instrument of ratification or accession, the

Convention shall enter into force on the thirtieth day after deposit by such State of its instrument of ratification or accession.

Article 85

Authentic texts

The original of the present Convention, of which the Chinese, English, French, Russian and Spanish texts are equally authentic, shall be deposited with the Secretary-General of the United Nations.

IN WITNESS WHEREOF the undersigned Plenipotentiaries, being duly authorized thereto by their respective Governments, have signed the present Convention.

DONE AT VIENNA, this twenty-third day of May, one thousand nine hundred and sixty-nine.

Annex

1. A list of conciliators consisting of qualified jurists shall be drawn up and maintained by the Secretary-General of the United Nations. To this end, every State which is a Member of the United Nations or a party to the present Convention shall be invited to nominate two conciliators, and the names of the persons so nominated shall constitute the list. The term of a conciliator, including that of any conciliator nominated to fill a casual vacancy, shall be five years and may be renewed. A conciliator whose term expires shall continue to fulfil any function for which he shall have been chosen under the following paragraph.

2. When a request has been made to the Secretary-General under article 66, the Secretary-General shall bring the dispute before a conciliation commission constituted as follows:

The State or States constituting one of the parties to the dispute shall appoint:

(a) one conciliator of the nationality of that State or of one of those States, who may or may not be chosen from the list referred to in paragraph 1; and

(b) one conciliator not of the nationality of that State or of any of those States, who shall be chosen from the list.

The State or States constituting the other party to the dispute shall appoint two conciliators in the same way. The four conciliators chosen by the parties shall be appointed within sixty days following the date on which the Secretary-General receives the request.

The four conciliators shall, within sixty days following the date of the last of their own appointments, appoint a fifth conciliator chosen from the list, who shall be chairman.

If the appointment of the chairman or of any of the other conciliators has not been made within the period prescribed above for such appointment, it shall be made by the Secretary-General within sixty days following the expiry of that period. The appointment of the chairman may be made by the Secretary-General either from the list or from the membership of the International Law Commission. Any of the periods within which appointments must be made may be extended by agreement between the parties to the dispute.

Any vacancy shall be filled in the manner prescribed for the initial appointment.

3. The Conciliation Commission shall decide its own procedure. The Commission, with the consent of the parties to the dispute, may invite any party to the treaty to submit to it its views orally or in writing. Decisions and recommendations of the Commission shall be made by a majority vote of the five members.

4. The Commission may draw the attention of the parties to the dispute to any measures which might facilitate an amicable settlement.

5. The Commission shall hear the parties, examine the claims and objections, and make proposals to the parties with a view to reaching an amicable settlement of the dispute.

6. The Commission shall report within twelve months of its constitution. Its report shall be deposited with the Secretary-General and transmitted to the parties to the dispute. The report of the Commission, including any conclusions stated therein regarding the facts or questions of law, shall not be binding upon the parties and it shall have no other character than that of recommendations submitted for the consideration of the parties in order to facilitate an amicable settlement of the dispute.

7. The Secretary-General shall provide the Commission with such assistance and facilities as it may require. The expenses of the Commission shall be borne by the United Nations.

INDEX

References are to Pages